Gre

D0196674

THE ROUGH GUIDE

There are over sixty Rough Guide titles covering
destinations from Amsterdam to Zimbabwe & Botswana

Forthcoming titles include
Goa • Singapore • Hawaii • London • Moscow • Romania

Rough Guide Reference Series
Classical Music • World Music

Rough Guide Phrasebooks
Czech • French • German • Greek • Italian • Spanish

Rough Guide Credits

Edited by:	Alison Cowan, Peter Casterton, Jules Brown and Amanda Tomlin
Series Editor:	Mark Ellingham
Editorial:	Jonathan Buckley, Graham Parker, Jo Mead, Samantha Cook and Annie Shaw
Production:	Susanne Hillen, Andy Hilliard, Melissa Flack, Alan Spicer, Judy Pang, Link Hall and Nicola Williamson
Finance:	John Fisher, Celia Crowley and Simon Carloss
Marketing and Publicity:	Richard Trillo (UK); Jean-Marie Kelly (US)
Administration:	Tania Hummel

Acknowledgements

For fresh research on this edition, we're greatly indebted to Nick Edwards, Geoff Garvey, Don Grisbrook, Carol Phile, Andrew Preshous and Mick Rebane, all of whom found places that had slipped us by in the past. Many thanks, too, for the invaluable contributions of readers of the previous edition – without whom this book would be nowhere near as sharp or as comprehensive. Due to lack of space, the roll of honour appears on p.781.

For their contributions to the *Contexts* section, thanks to Pete Raine for the *Wildlife* section, Michael House and Diane Fortenberry for *250 Years of Archeology*, and Nick Edwards for updating the politics. For the advice for disabled travellers, thanks to Alison Walsh. From previous editions, continuing thanks to Tim Salmon and Stephen Lees for sharing their long and extensive knowledge of Greece.

Thanks also to Micromap and Melissa Flack for cartography, Ellen Sarowitz and Kate Chambers for proofreading, Andrew Preshous for sterling work on the Basics section, Tania Smith for vital last-minute assistance, Jonathan Buckley for updates on ancient places, and Alison, Peter, Jules and Amanda for relaxed and splendid editing.

For help on the ground, **Don** thanks Yiannis Pappas, Katerina Manou, Tony Andrews, Stephen Brown, Panayiotis and Maria Foteinakas. **Marc** thanks Yiorgos and Ivi on Kéa; Christine and Ritsa, and Thanos, Monica and Susanna in Athens; Detlef and Gisa on Lésvos for the excellent introduction; Markos Kostalas, Theodhoros Spordhilis and Stella Tsakiri on Híos; Michael and Avra Ward, and Jon Peat, on Sámos; Sotiris and Marianne Nikolis on Rhodes (again!); Katerina Tsakiri on Sími; Barry Ward on Tílos; Sam Cook, Greg Ward and David Abram for adding flavour to Hálki, Simi and Níssiros; Andrew and Tricia for indulging my choice of tavernas on Léros; and Maria Throumouli at the Ministry of Culture, for arranging a pass for admission to sites and musuems. **Mick** thanks Diana Mortimer, Nicky Hatton, Alison McDowall, Margaret Maxwell and John Stevens.

This sixth edition published in 1995 by Rough Guides Ltd, 1 Mercer St, London WC2H 9QJ.

Distributed by the Penguin Group:
Penguin Books Ltd, 27 Wrights Lane, London W8 5TZ
Penguin Books USA Inc., 375 Hudson Street, New York, NY 10014, USA
Penguin Books Australia Ltd, 487 Maroondah Highway, PO Box 257, Ringwood, Victoria 3134, Australia
Penguin Books Canada Ltd, 10 Alcorn Avenue, Toronto, Ontario, Canada M4V 1E4
Penguin Books (NZ) Ltd, 182–190 Wairau Road, Auckland 10, New Zealand.

Previous edition published in the United States and Canada as *The Real Guide Greece*.

Typeset in Linotron Univers and Century Old Style to an original design by Andrew Oliver.
Printed by Cox and Wyman Ltd (Reading).
Illustrations in Part One and Part Three by Edward Briant; illustration on p.1 by Helen Manning and p.717 by Jane Strother.

800pp, includes index

A catalogue record for this book is available from the British Library

ISBN 1–85828–131–8

Greece

THE ROUGH GUIDE

Written and researched by
**Mark Ellingham, Marc Dubin,
Natania Jansz and John Fisher**

Additional contributions by
Nick Edwards, Geoff Garvey, Don Grisbrook, Carol Phile,
Andrew Preshous and Mick Rebane

THE ROUGH GUIDES

PLACE NAMES: A WARNING!

The art of rendering Greek words in Roman letters is in a state of chaos. It's a major source of confusion with **place names**, for which seemingly each local authority, and each map-maker, uses a different system. The word for "saint", for instance, one of the most common prefixes, can be spelt Áyios, Ágios, or Ághios. And, to make matters worse, there are often two forms of a name in Greek – the popularly used *dhimotikí*, and the old "classicizing" *katharévoussa*. Thus you will see the island of Spétses written also as Spétsai, or Halkídha, capital of Évvia, as Halkís (or even Chalcís, on more traditional maps). Throw in the complexities of Greek grammar – with different case-endings for names – and the fact that there exist long-established English versions of Classical place names, which bear little relation to the Greek sounds (Mycenae for Mikínes, for example), and you have a real mare's nest.

In this book, we've used a modern and largely phonetic **system**, with *Y* rather than *G* for the Greek gamma, and *DH* rather than *D* for delta, in the spelling of all modern Greek place names. We have, however, retained the accepted "English" spellings for the **ancient sites**, and for familiar places like Athens (Athiná, in modern Greek). We have also accented (with an acute) the stressed letter of each word; getting this right in pronunciation is vital in order to be understood.

CONTENTS

MAP SYMBOLS

REGIONAL MAPS

——	Major road
——	Minor road
- - - -	Track or path
+++	Railway
▬▬▬	Chapter division boundary
▬▬▬	International boundary
✈	Airport
+	Country church
⛪	Monastery or convent
⛫	Castle
♦	Ancient site
∩	Cave
⬠	Refuge
⌁	Mountain range
▲	Peak
☀	Lighthouse

▨	Beach

TOWN MAPS

——	Railway
▬▬	Fortifications
▬	Building
✚	Church
☪	Mosque
⊹	Christian cemetery
▢	Park
Ⓜ	Metro station

GENERAL

⋈	Gorge or tunnel
– –	Ferry route

MAP LIST

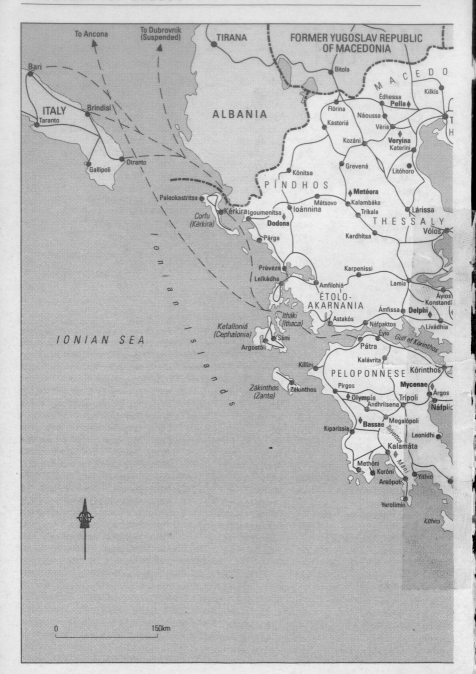

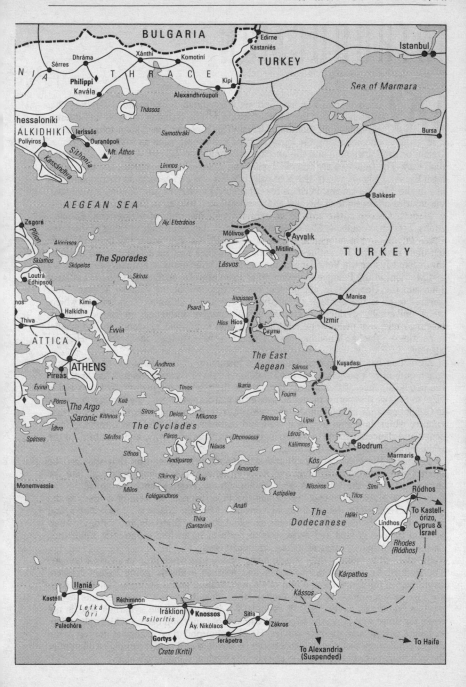

INTRODUCTION

With over one hundred and sixty inhabited islands and a territory that stretches from the Mediterranean to the Balkans, Greece has interest enough to fill months of travel. The **historic sites** span four millennia, encompassing the legendary and renowned, such as Mycenae, Olympia, Delphi or the Parthenon, and the obscure, where a visit can still seem like a personal discovery. The **beaches** are parcelled out along a convoluted coastline, and they range from those of islands where the boat calls twice a week to resorts as cosmopolitan as any in the Mediterranean. Perhaps less expected by visitors, the country's mountainous interior offers some of the best and least exploited **hiking** in Europe.

Modern Greece is the sum of an extraordinary diversity of **influences**. Romans, Arabs, French, Venetians, Slavs, Albanians, Turks, Italians, to say nothing of the great Byzantine empire, have been and gone since the time of Alexander the Great. All have left their mark: the Byzantines in countless churches and monasteries, and in ghost towns like Mystra; the Venetians in impregnable fortifications at Náfplio, Monemvassía and Methóni in the Peloponnese; and other Latin powers, such as the Knights of Saint John and the Genoese, in magnificent castles throughout the eastern Aegean. Most obvious of all is the heritage of four hundred years of Ottoman Turkish rule which, while universally derided, exercised an inestimable influence on music, cuisine, language and way of life. The contributions, and continued existence, of substantial minorities – Vlachs, Muslims, Jews, Gypsies – have helped to forge the Hellenic identity.

All of this has been instrumental in the formation of the character of the people, which embodies a powerful and hard to define strain of **Greekness** that has kept alive the people's sense of themselves throughout their turbulent history. With no ruling class to impose a superior model of taste or to patronize the arts, the last few centuries of Greek peasants, fishermen and shepherds have created a vigorous and truly popular culture, which is manifested in a thousand instinctively tasteful ways, ranging from songs and dances, costumes, embroidery, woven bags and rugs, and furniture, to the white cubist houses of popular image.

Of course there are formal cultural activites as well: **museums** that shouldn't be missed, in Athens, Thessaloníki and Iráklion; equally compelling buildings, like the **monasteries** of the Metéora and Mount Áthos; **castles** such as those in the Dodecanese, Lésvos, central Greece and the Peloponnese; as well, of course, as the great **ancient sites** dating from Mycenaean, Minoan, Classical, Macedonian and Roman times. The country hosts some excellent summer **festivals**, too, bringing international theatre groups and orchestras to perform in ancient theatres at Epidaurus, Dodona and Athens – magical settings in themselves.

But the call to cultural duty should never be too overwhelming on a Greek holiday. The **hedonistic pleasures** of languor and warmth – always going lightly dressed, swimming in the sea without a hint of a shiver, talking and drinking under the stars – are just as appealing. Be aware though, that, despite recent improvements to the tourism "product", Greece is still essentially a land for simple sybarites, and is not really for those who crave the five-star treatment of super-soft beds, faultless plumbing, exquisite cuisine and attentive service. Hotel accommodation, except at the top of the range, tends to be plain; rented rooms can be box-like and stuffy; campsites often offer the minimum of facilities; and food at its best is fresh and uncomplicated.

The Greek people

To begin to get an understanding of the Greek people, it is important to realize just how recent and profound were the events that created the **modern state** and national character. Up until the early decades of this century many parts of Greece – Crete, Macedonia, the Ionian islands and the entire eastern Aegean – were in Turkish (or in the case of the Dodecanese, Italian) hands. Meanwhile, as many ethnic Greeks lived in Asia Minor, Egypt and in the north Balkans as in the recently forged kingdom. The Balkan Wars of 1912–13 and the exchange of "Greek" and "Turkish" populations in 1922–23 changed everything in a sudden, brutal manner. Worse still was to come during World War II, and its aftermath of civil war between the Communists, who formed the core of wartime resistance against the German occupation, and the western-backed rightist, "government" forces. The viciousness of this period found a more recent echo in nearly seven years of military dictatorship under the colonels' junta between 1967 and 1974.

Such memories of brutal misrule, diaspora and catastrophe remain uncomfortably close for all Greeks, despite the last decade or so of democratic stability and integration as a member of the European Community. The resultant identity is complex, an uneasy coexistence of opposing impulses, which cannot be accounted for merely by Greece's position as a natural bridge between Europe and the Middle East. Within a generally extroverted outlook is a strong streak of pessimism, while the poverty of, and enduring paucity of opportunity in, their homeland spurs the resourcefulness of Greek entrepreneurs, many of whom choose to emigrate. Those who remain may have been lulled, until recently, by a civil-service-driven full-employment policy which resulted in the lowest jobless rate in western Europe. The downside of this is an occasionally staggering lack of initiative, but official attempts to impose a more austere economic line have usually been met by waves of popular strikes.

On the other hand, the meticulousness of Greek craftworkers is legendary, even if their values and skills took a back seat to the demands of crisis and profiteering when the evacuation of Asia Minor and the rapid depopulation of rural villages prompted the graceless urbanization of Athens and the other cities. Amid the contemporary sophistication that resulted, it's easy to forget the nearness of the agricultural past and the fact that Greece is still as much a part of the Third World as of the First. You may find that buses operate with Germanic efficiency, but ferries sail with an unpredictability little changed since the time of Odysseus.

Attitudes, too, are in a state of flux as Greece has adapted to mass tourism and the twentieth century, neither of which had made much impact up until the 1960s. The encounter has been painful and at times destructive, as a largely rural, traditional and conservative society has been lost. Though the Greeks are adaptable and the cash registers ring happily, at least in tourist areas, visitors still need to be sensitive in their behaviour towards the older generations. The mind boggles to imagine the reaction of the black-clad grandparents to nudism, or even scanty clothing, in a country where until recently the Orthodox church was all but an established faith and the guardian of national identity.

Where and when to go

There is no such thing as a typical Greek island; each has its distinctive character, appearance, history, flora, even a unique tourist clientele. And the same is true of the mainland provinces. **Landscapes** vary from the mountainous northwest and rainy, shaggy forests of the Pílion to the stony deserts of the Máni, from the soft theatricality of the Peloponnesian coastal hills to the poplar-studded plains of Macedonia, from the resin-scented ridges of Skíathos and Sámos to the wind-tormented rocks of the central Aegean. The inky plume of cypress, the silver green of olive groves, the blue outline of distant hills, an expanse of shimmering sea: these are the enduring and unfailingly pleasing motifs of the Greek landscape.

Most places and people are far more agreeable, and recognizably Greek, outside the **peak period** of late June to the end of August, when soaring temperatures and crowds can be overpowering. You won't miss out on warm weather if you come in **early June or September**, excellent times everywhere but particularly amid the Sporades and north or east Aegean islands. In **October** you might hit a stormy spell, especially in western Greece or in the mountains, but most of that month the "summer of Áyios Dhimítrios", the Greek equivalent of Indian summer, prevails. Autumn in general is beautiful; the light is softer, the sea often balmier than the air, the colours subtler.

December to March are the coldest and least reliable months, though there are many fine days of perfect crystal visibility, and the glorious lowland flowers begin to bloom very early in spring. The more northerly latitudes and high altitudes of course endure far colder and wetter conditions, with the mountains themselves snowed under from November to May. The most **dependable winter weather** is to be found in the Dodecanese, immediately around Rhodes, or in the southeastern parts of Crete. As spring slowly warms up, **April** is still uncertain, though fine for visiting the Dodecanese; by **May** the weather is more generally dependable, and Crete, the Peloponnese, the Ionian islands and the Cyclades are perhaps at their best, even if the sea's still a little cool for swimming.

Other factors that can affect the timing of your Greek travels are mainly concerned with the level of tourism. Standards of service invariably slip under the high-season pressures, and room rates are already at their highest in July and August. If you can only visit in high season, then you'll do well to plan your itinerary a little away from the beaten track. Explore the less obvious parts of the Peloponnese, or the northern mainland, for example; or island-hop with an eye for the more obscure – the places where ferries don't call more than once a day, and there's not yet an airport.

Out of season, especially between November and March, you may have to wrestle with uncertain ferry schedules to the islands, and often fairly skeletal facilities when you arrive. However, you will find reasonable service on all the main routes and at least one hotel open in the port or main town. On the mainland, out-of-season travel poses no special difficulties except, of course, in mountain villages cut off by snow.

	AVERAGE TEMPERATURES AND RAINFALL											
	Jan		March		May		July		Sept		Nov	
	°F Max Min	Rain days	°F Max Min	Rain days	°F Max Min	Rain days	°F Max Min	Rain days	°F Max Min	Rain days	°F Max Min	Rain days
Athens	54 44	13	60 46	10	76 60	9	90 72	2	84 66	4	65 52	12
Crete (Haniá)	60 46	17	64 48	11	76 56	5	86 68	0	82 64	3	70 54	10
Cyclades (Míkonos)	58 50	14	62 52	8	72 62	5	82 72	0.5	78 68	1	66 58	9
North Greece (Halkidhikí)	50 36	7	59 44	9	77 58	10	90 70	4	83 64	5	60 47	9
Ionian (Corfu)	56 44	13	62 46	10	74 58	6	88 70	2	82 64	5	66 52	12
Dodecanese (Rhodes)	58 50	15	62 48	7	74 58	2	86 70	0	82 72	1	68 60	7
Sporades (Skíathos)	55 45	12	58 47	10	71 58	3	82 71	0	75 64	8	62 53	12
East Aegean (Lésvos)	54 42	11	60 46	7	76 60	6	88 70	2	82 66	2	64 50	9

PART ONE

THE
BASICS

GETTING THERE FROM BRITAIN

It's close on 2000 miles from London to Athens, so for most visitors flying is the only viable option. There are direct flights to a variety of Greek destinations from all the major British airports. Flying time is around three and a half hours and the cost of charter flights is reasonable – sample return fares to Athens from London in midsummer start from around £160 (Manchester £180, Glasgow £200), but there are always bargains to be had. Easter is also classed as high season, but outside these periods flights can be snapped up for as little as £120 return. Costs can often be highly competitive, too, if you buy a flight as part of an all-in package: see p.5–6 for details of holiday operators.

Road or rail alternatives take a minimum of three days but are obviously worth considering if you plan to visit Greece as part of an extended trip through Europe. The most popular route is down through Italy, then across to Greece by ferry. A much longer alternative overland route is via Hungary, Romania and Bulgaria; the civil war in former Yugoslavia makes that route almost impossible.

BY PLANE

Most of the cheaper flights from Britain to Greece are **charters**, which are sold either with a package holiday or as a flight-only option. The flights have fixed and unchangeable outward and return dates, and often a maximum stay of one month.

For longer stays or more flexibility, or if you're travelling out of season (when few charters are available), you'll need a **scheduled** flight. As with charters, these are offered under a wide variety of fares, and are again often sold off at discount by agents. Useful sources for discounted flights are the classified ads in the travel sections of newspapers like the *Independent, Guardian, Observer* and *Sunday Times. Teletext* is also worth checking, while your local travel agent shouldn't be overlooked.

Although **Athens** remains the prime destination for cheap fares, there are also **direct flights** from Britain to **Thessaloníki, Kalamáta, Kavála** and **Préveza** on the Greek mainland, and to the islands of **Crete, Rhodes, Corfu, Lésvos, Páros, Zákinthos, Kefallonía, Skiáthos, Sámos** and **Kós**. And with any flight to Athens, you can buy a **domestic connecting flight** (on the national carrier, *Olympic*) to one of three dozen or so additional Greek mainland and island airports.

CHARTER FLIGHTS

Travel agents throughout Britain sell **charter flights** to Greece, which usually operate from May to October; late-night departures and early-morning arrivals are common. Even the high street chains frequently promote "flight-only" deals, or discount all-inclusive holidays, when their parent companies need to offload their seat allocations. In any case, phone around for a range of offers. Charter airlines include *GB Airways, Excalibur* and *Monarch*, but you can only book tickets on these through travel agents.

The greatest variety of **flight destinations** tends to be from London Gatwick and Manchester. In summer, if you book in advance, you should have a choice of most of the dozen Greek regional airports listed above. Flying from elsewhere in Britain (Birmingham, Cardiff, Glasgow or Newcastle), or looking for last-minute discounts, you'll find options more limited, most commonly to Athens, Corfu, Rhodes and Crete.

It's worth noting that **non-EC nationals** who buy charter tickets to Greece must buy a return ticket, of no fewer than three days and no more than four weeks, and must accompany it with an **accommodation voucher** for at least the first few nights of their stay – check that the ticket

AGENTS AND OPERATORS

Alecos Tours, 3a Camden Rd, London NW1 (☎0171/267 2092). *Regular Olympic Airways consolidator.*

Campus Travel, 52 Grosvenor Gardens, London SW1 (☎0171/730 3402); 541 Bristol Rd, Selly Oak, Birmingham (☎0121/414 1848); 39 Queen's Rd, Clifton, Bristol (☎0117/929 2494); 5 Emmanuel St, Cambridge (☎0223/324283); 53 Forest Rd, Edinburgh (☎0131/668 3303); 166 Deansgate, Manchester (☎0161/273 1721); 13 High St, Oxford (☎01865/242067). *Student/youth travel specialists, with branches also in YHA shops and on university campuses all over Britain. Campus usually has its own student/youth charter flights to Athens during the summer.*

Council Travel, 28a Poland St, London W1 (☎0171/287 3337). *Flights and student discounts.*

Flyaway Travel, Unit 4, Perronet House, St George's Rd, London SE1 (☎0171/620 3333). *Budget flights to Athens.*

South Coast Student Travel, 61 Ditchling Rd, Brighton (☎01273/570226). *Student experts but plenty to offer non-students as well.*

Springways Travel, 28 Vauxhall Bridge Rd, London SW1 (☎0171/976 5833). *Reliable discount flight agent.*

STA Travel, 74 Old Brompton Rd, London W7 (☎0171/937 9962); 25 Queen's Rd, Bristol (☎0117/294399); 38 Sidney St, Cambridge (☎01223/66966); 75 Deansgate, Manchester (☎0161/834 0668); and personal callers at 117 Euston Rd, London NW1; 28 Vicar Lane, Leeds; 36 George St, Oxford; and offices at the universities of Birmingham, London, Kent and Loughborough. *Discount fares, with particularly good deals for students and young people.*

Travel Bug, 597 Cheetham Hill Rd, Manchester (☎0161/721 4000). *Large range of discounted tickets.*

Travel Cuts, 295 Regent St, London W1 (☎0171/255 1944). *Often has discount flights.*

AIRLINES

Balkan Airlines, 322 Regent St, London W1 (☎0171/637 7637).

British Airways, 156 Regent St, London W1 (☎0181/897 4000 and ☎0345/222111).

ČSA Czechoslovak Airlines, 72 Margaret St, London W1 (☎0171/255 1898).

LOT Polish Airlines, 313 Regent St, London W1R 7PE (☎0171/580 5037).

Malev Hungarian Airlines, 10 Vigo St, London W1X 1AJ (☎0171/439 0577).

Olympic Airways, 11 Conduit St, London W1 (☎0171/409 3400).

Virgin Airways, Virgin Megastore, 14–16 Oxford St, London W1 (☎01293/747747).

satisfies these conditions or you could be refused entry. In practice, the "accommodation voucher" has become a formality; it has to name an existing hotel but you're not expected to use it (and probably won't be able to if you try).

The other important condition regards **travel to Turkey** (or any other neighbouring country). If you travel to Greece on a charter flight, you may visit another country only as a day trip; if you stay overnight, you will invalidate your ticket. This rule is justified by the Greek authorities because they subsidize charter airline landing fees, and are therefore reluctant to see tourists spending their money outside Greece. Whether you buy that excuse or not, there is no way around it, since the Turkish authorities clearly stamp all passports, and the Greeks usually check them. The package industry on the east Aegean and Dodecanese

islands bordering Turkey, however, does sometimes prevail upon customs officials to back-date re-entry stamps when bad weather strands their tour groups overnight in Anatolia.

Student/youth charters are allowed to be sold as one-way flights only. By combining two one-way charters you can, therefore, stay for over a month. Student/youth charter tickets are available to anyone under 26, and to all card-carrying full-time students under 32.

Finally, remember that **reconfirmation** of return charter flights is vital and should be done at least 72 hours before departure.

SCHEDULED FLIGHTS

The advantages of scheduled flights are that they can be pre-booked well in advance, have longer ticket validities and involve none of the above restrictions on charters. However, many of the cheaper APEX and SuperAPEX fares do have an advance-purchase and/or minimum-stay requirements, so check conditions carefully. Scheduled flights also usually operate during the day.

As with charters, discount fares on scheduled flights are available from most high-street travel **agents**, as well as from a number of specialist flight and student/youth agencies. Most discount scheduled fares have an advance-purchase requirement

The biggest choice of scheduled flights is with the Greek national carrier *Olympic Airways*, and *British Airways*, who both fly direct from London Heathrow to Athens (3 times daily) and also to Thessaloníki (daily). *Virgin Airways* also has a daily service to Athens. All these airlines offer a range of special fares and even in July and August can come up with deals as low as £200 return; more realistically, though, you'll pay around £250–325 return for a scheduled flight. You'll also be able to book onward connections to domestic Greek airports; flights from British regional airports route through Heathrow in the first instance.

East European airways like *ČSA*, *Balkan*, *Malev* and *LOT* are often cheaper – £120 one way, £240 return for much of the year – but nearly always involve delays, with connections in (respectively) Prague, Sofia, Budapest and Warsaw. It is not always possible to book discount fares direct from these airlines, and you'll often pay no more by going through an agent (see box).

PACKAGES AND TOURS

Virtually every British **tour operator** includes Greece in its programme, though with many of the larger groups you'll find choices limited to the established resorts – notably the islands of Rhodes, Kos, Crete, Skiáthos, Zákinthos and Corfu, plus Toló and the Halikidhikí on the mainland. If you buy one of these at a last-minute discount, you may find it costs little more than a flight – and you can use the accommodation offered as much or as little as you want. For a rather more low-key and genuinely "Greek" resort, however, it's better to book your holiday through one of the smaller **specialist agencies** listed below.

SPECIALIST PACKAGE OPERATORS

VILLA OR VILLAGE ACCOMMODATION

These companies are all fairly small-scale operations, offering competitively priced packages with flights and often using more traditional village accommodation. They make an effort to offer islands without over-developed tourist resorts and, increasingly, unspoiled mainland destinations.

CV Travel, 43 Cadogan St, London SW3 2PR (☎0171/581 0851). Quality villas on Corfu and Paxí.

Corfu à la Carte, The Whitehouse, Bucklebury Alley, Newbury, Berks RH16 9NN (☎01635/30671). Selected beach and rural cottages on Corfu, Paxí and Skiáthos.

Grecofile/Filoxenia, Sourdock Hill, Barkisland, Halifax, West Yorkshire HX4 0AG (☎01422/375999). Tailor-made itineraries and specialist packages to unspoiled areas.

Greek Islands Club, 66 High St, Walton-on-Thames, Kent KT12 1BU (☎01932/220477). Holidays on the Ionian islands, including Kíthira, and the Sporades.

Greek Sun Holidays, 1 Bank St, Sevenoaks, Kent TN13 1UW (☎01732/740317). Offer a variety of packages, including fly-drive, on a wide range of islands and on the Pílion peninsula.

Ilios Island Holidays, 18 Market Square, Horsham, West Sussex RH12 1EU (☎01403/259788). Features mainly Ionian and Sporades islands, plus Tínos, Páros, Náxos and the west coast of Pílion.

The Best of Greece, 23–24 Margaret St, London W1N 8LE (☎0171/677 1721). Limited number of exclusive villa and hotel arrangements from a long-established operator.

Kosmar Villa Holidays, 358 Bowes Rd, Arnos Grove, London N11 1AN (☎0181/368 6833). Self-catering apartments, including Toló, the Argo-Saronic isles and Crete.

Laskarina Holidays, St Marys Gate, Wirksworth, Derbyshire DE4 4DQ (☎01629/822203). Emphasis on a dozen of the less visited islands of the Dodecanese and Sporades.

Manos Holidays, 168–172 Old St, London EC1V 9BP (☎0171/216 8070). Operates in most of the major resorts.

Simply Crete, Chiswick Gate, 598–608 Chiswick High Rd, London W4 5RT (☎0181/994 4462); *Simply Ionian*, same address (☎0181/995 1121). High-quality apartments, villas and small hotels on Crete and Ionian islands. ***Continues over***

Skiathos Travel, 4 Holmesdale Rd, Kew Gardens, Richmond, Surrey TW9 3J2 (☎0181/940 5157). Packages to the Sporades; some flight-only deals.

Sunvil Holidays, Sunvil House, 7–8 Upper Square, Old Isleworth, Middlesex TW7 7BJ (☎0181/568 4499). Good choice of smaller resorts, including Límnos, the Peloponnese, Epirus and Pílion.

Voyages Ilena, Old Garden House, The Lanterns, Bridge Lane, London SW11 3AD (☎0171/924 4440). Peloponnese specialist, with a careful selection of accommodation in the Máni and Argolid.

HIKING TOURS

All the operators below run trekking groups, which generally consist of 10 to 15 people, plus an experienced guide. The walks tend to be day-hikes from one or more bases, or point-to-point treks staying in village accommodation en route; camping is not usually involved.

Exodus, 9 Weir Rd, London SW12 OLT (☎0181/675 5550). Treks in the Píndhos mountain range.

Explore Worldwide, 1 Frederick St, Aldershot, Hampshire GU11 1LQ (☎01252/344161). Organized hikes in central Greece, western Crete and island sailing.

Ramblers Holidays, Longcroft House, Fretherne Rd, Welwyn Garden City, Herts AL8 6PQ (☎01707/331133). Easy walking tours on Kefalloniá, Itháki and Crete.

Sherpa Expeditions, 131a Heston Rd, Hounslow, Middlesex TW5 0RD (☎0181/577 2717). Good range of tours concentrated on the mainland.

Waymark Holidays, 44 Windsor Rd, Slough SL1 2EJ (☎01753/516477). Spring and autumn walking holidays on Sámos, Náxos and Mílos; tougher hikes in the Píndhos and Peloponnese.

NATURE AND WILDLIFE

Peregrine Holidays, 40/41 South Parade, Summertown, Oxford OX2 7JP (☎01865/511642). Natural history tours around the Peloponnese, the Macedonian lakes, Crete, and select other islands; the emphasis on each tour is on wildlife – though combined with visits to archeological sites.

SAILING

Dinghy sailing, yachting and windsurfing holidays based on small flotillas of four- to six-berth yachts. Prices start at around £350 per person per week off-season; all levels of experience. Sailing holidays can be flotilla- or shore-based. If you're a confident sailor and can muster a group of people, it's possible simply to charter a yacht from a broker; the Greek National Tourist Organisation has lists of companies.

Sovereign Sailing, First Choice House, Peelcross Rd, Salford, Manchester M5 2AN (☎ 01293/599944). Independent charters and flotilla holidays. Bases on the Ionian islands and the Peloponnese.

Sunsail The Port House, Port Solent, Portsmouth, Hampshire, PO6 4TH (☎01705/210345). Tuition in dinghy sailing, yachting and windsurfing. Clubs include Paxí, Lefkás and Kos.

World Expeditions, 7 North Rd, Maidenhead, Berkshire SL6 1PE (☎01628/74174). Flotilla and bareboat sailing trips in Páros, Pátmos and Rhodes.

MIND AND BODY

Skyros Centre, 92 Prince of Wales Rd, London NW5 3NE (☎0171/267 4424). Holistic health, fitness and "personal growth" holidays on the island of Skíros, as well as writers' workshops.

BY TRAIN

Travelling by train from Britain to Greece takes around three and a half days and fares work out more expensive than flights. However, with a regular ticket stopovers are possible – in France, Switzerland and Italy – while with an *InterRail* or *Eurail* train pass you can take in Greece as part of a wider rail trip around Europe.

ROUTES

The most practical route from Britain takes in France, Switzerland and **Italy** before crossing on the ferry from Bari or Brindisi to Pátra (Patras). Because of the problems in former Yugoslavia (see below), the increased demand for tickets on the Italian route has put an extra burden on trains and ferries. Book seats on both well in advance, especially in summer (for ferry information, see "Ferries to Greece" box below).

Until the outbreak of civil war, the route through **former Yugoslavia** was the most popular. However, most services are now suspended and *British Rail* does not sell any through ticket to Greece which routes via the states of former Yugoslavia. A few trains may still operate on the

Budapest–Belgrade–Skopje–Thessaloníki
route, but reliable information on services is
almost impossible to obtain. Border crossings are
likely to be problematic and anyone willing to run
the risk would have to buy tickets locally.

A more rambling alternative from Budapest
runs via **Bucharest and Sofia to Thessaloníki**,
which is advised as your first stop since Athens is
nearly nine hours further on the train.

TICKETS AND PASSES

Regular train tickets from Britain to Greece are
not good value. London to Athens costs at least
£380 return. If you are **under 26**, you can get a
BIJ ticket, discounting these fares by around 25
percent; these are available through *Eurotrain*
and *Wasteels* (see box below for addresses).
Both regular and *BIJ* tickets have two months'
return validity, or can be purchased as one way,
and the Italy routes include the ferry crossing.
The tickets also allow for stopovers, so long as
you stick to the route prescribed.

Better value by far is to buy an **InterRail pass**,
available to anyone resident in Europe for six
months. You can buy it from *British Rail* (or any
travel agent), and the pass offers unlimited travel
on a zonal basis on up to 25 European rail
networks. The only extras you pay are supplements on certain express trains, plus half-price
fares in Britain (or the country of issue) and on the
cross-Channel ferries. The pass includes the ferry
from Brindisi in southern Italy to Pátra in Greece.
There are several types: to reach Greece from the
UK you'll need a pass valid for at least two zones
(£209 for a month), though if you're intending to
travel further in Europe you can pay up to £249;
Greece is zoned with Italy, Turkey and Slovenia.

The equivalent pass for North Americans is
the Eurail pass, for details of which, see "Getting
There from North America", below.

Finally, anyone over 60 and holding a British
Rail Senior Citizen Railcard, can buy a **Rail
Europe Senior Card** (£21 for a year). This gives
up to fifty percent reductions on rail fares throughout Europe and thirty percent off sea crossings.

BY BUS

The days of £50 Magic Bus returns to Athens are
long gone and with charter flights at such
competitive rates, it's hard to find good reasons
for wanting to spend three or four days on a bus
to Greece. However, it's still a considerably
cheaper option than taking the train.

RAIL TICKET OFFICES
Eurotrain, 52 Grosvenor Gardens, London SW1
(☎0171/730 3402).
International Rail Centre, Victoria Station,
London SW1 (☎0171/834 2345).
Wasteels, Victoria Station, London SW1
(☎0171/834 7066).

BUS TICKET OFFICES
National Express Eurolines, 52 Grosvenor
Gardens, London SW1 (☎0171/730 0202).
Olympic Bus, 70 Brunswick Centre, London
WC1 (☎0171/837 9141).

Olympic Bus offers low-cost fares (£100–120
return) but *National Express Eurolines* (bookable
through any *National Express* office; see box
above) has a more reliable reputation, better
buses, and higher prices (£200–220 return).
These days, other operators are thin on the
ground, but even so it pays to be very wary about
going for the cheapest company unless you've
heard something about them. There have been a
string of accidents in recent years with operators
flouting the terms of their licence, and horror
stories abound of drivers getting lost or their
coaches being refused entry.

The **route** is either Belgium, Germany and
Austria, or via France and Italy and then a ferry
across to Greece. Stops of about twenty minutes
are made every five or six hours, with the odd
longer break for roadside café meals.

BY CAR: LE SHUTTLE AND THE FERRIES

If you have the time and inclination, **driving to
Greece** can be a pleasant proposition.
Realistically, though, it's really only worth
considering if you have at least a month to spare,
are going to stay in Greece for an extended
period, or want to take advantage of various
stopovers en route.

It's important to plan ahead. The **Automobile
Association** (AA) provides a comprehensive
service offering general advice on all facets of
driving to Greece and the names and addresses
of useful contact organizations. Their European
Routes Service (contact AA on ☎01256/20123 or
your local branch) can arrange a detailed print-
out of a route to follow. Driving licence, vehicle
registration documents and insurance are essential; a green card is recommended.

Ferries used to operate from Dalmatian ports in **former Yugoslavia** to Greece but due to the civil war there is currently no service. Neither is driving recommended in this region. For up-to-date details about travelling through the states of former Yugoslavia, contact the Foreign Office Travel Advice Unit (☎0171/270 4129).

The most popular **route** is down through France and Italy to catch one of the Adriatic ferries. A much longer alternative through Eastern Europe (Hungary, Romania and Bulgaria) is just about feasible, but driving through former Yugoslavia is unsafe and uncertain – even before the conflicts, this was one of Europe's poorest road arteries.

CROSSING THE CHANNEL

Le Shuttle operates trains 24 hours a day, carrying cars, motorcycles, buses and their passengers, and taking 35 minutes between Folkestone and Calais. At peak times, services operate every 15 minutes, making advance bookings unnecessary; during the night, services still run hourly. Through trains connect London with Paris in just over three hours. Return fares from May to August cost around £280–310 per vehicle (passengers included), with discounts in the low season; passenger fares from London to Paris cost £95–155 return, depending on when you book.

The alternative **cross-Channel** options for most travellers are the **ferry** or **hovercraft** links between **Dover** and Calais or Boulogne (the quickest and cheapest routes), **Ramsgate** and Dunkerque, or Newhaven and Dieppe.

Ferry **prices** vary according to the time of year and, for motorists, the size of your car. The

CROSS-CHANNEL INFORMATION

Hoverspeed, Dover (☎01304/240101); London (☎0181/5547061). *To Boulogne and Calais.*

Le Shuttle, Customer Services Centre Information and ticket sales (☎01303/271100)

P&O European Ferries, Dover (☎01304/203388); Portsmouth (☎01705/772244); London (☎0181/575 8555). *To Calais*

Sally Line, Ramsgate (☎01843/595522); London (☎0181/858 1127). *To Dunkerque.*

Stena Sealink Line, Ashford (☎01233/647047). *To Calais and Dieppe.*

Dover–Calais/Boulogne runs, for example, start at about £180 return low season, £220 return high season for a car with up to five passengers. **Foot passengers** should be able to cross for about £50 return year round; taking a **motorbike** costs from £80–90 return.

VIA ITALY

Heading for western Greece, or the Ionian islands, it has always made most sense to drive **via Italy** – and whatever your final destination, taking a ferry on the final leg makes for a more relaxed journey. Initial routes down to Italy **through France and Switzerland** are very much a question of personal taste. One of the most direct is Calais–Reims–Geneva–Milan and then down the Adriatic coast to the Italian port of your choice. Even on the quickest autoroutes (with their accompanying tolls), the journey will involve two overnight stops.

Once in Italy, there's a choice of five **ports**. Regular car and passenger ferries link **Ancona**, **Bari** and **Brindisi** with **Igoumenítsa** (the port of Epirus in western Greece) and/or **Pátra** (at the northwest tip of the Peloponnese and the closest port to Athens). Most sail via the island of **Corfu**, and a few link other Ionian islands en route to Pátra; you can stop over at no extra charge if you get these stops specified on your ticket. Generally, these ferries run year round, but services are greatly reduced out of season. Ferries also sail – less frequently – from **Trieste** to Pátra, and from **Otranto** to Igoumenítsa. For more details see the box opposite.

Note that crossing to Igoumenítsa is substantially cheaper than to Pátra; the cheapest of all the crossings are from Brindisi or Otranto to Igoumenítsa. However, drivers will discover that the extra cost in Italian fuel – around double the British price – offsets the routes' savings over those from Bari or Ancona; the shipping companies are well aware of this and set their prices accordingly.

The hostilities in former Yugoslavia have led to severe strains on the Italy–Greece ferries. In summer, it is essential to **book tickets** a few days ahead, especially in the peak July–August season. During the winter you can usually just turn up at the main ports (Ancona, Bari, Brindisi, Igoumenítsa/Corfu), but it's still wise to book in advance, certainly if you are taking a car or want a cabin. A few phone calls before leaving

FERRIES TO GREECE: ROUTES AND AGENTS

THE ITALY–GREECE ROUTES

Note: all timings are approximate.

From Ancona *Marlines, Strintzis, ANEK* and *Minoan* to Igoumenítsa (24hr) and Pátra (34hr); daily or nearly so year-round. *Minoan* sails via Corfu, with separate lines for Pátra, Kefalloniá,and Cesme (Turkey) half the year; *Strintzis* and *ANEK* via Corfu; *Marlines* has a summer extension from Pátra to Iráklio (Crete). Most sailings between 8 and 10pm, but there are a number of afternoon departures.

From Bari *Ventouris* to Pátra direct (20hr), nearly daily; to Corfu, Igoumenítsa (12hr) and Pátra (20hr); daily departures year-round between 8 and 9pm. To Pátra via Corfu and/or Igoumenítsa on *Poseidon Lines*, *Arkadia Lines*.

From Brindisi *Fragline* and *Adriatica* to Corfu, Igoumenítsa (11hr) and Pátra (20hr). *Hellenic Mediterranean Lines* to Corfu and Pátra, three to seven a week depending on season; Igoumenítsa , Kefalloniá, Ithaki, Paxí and Zákinthos, served on separate sailings during summer. *European Seaways* to Corfu, Igoumenítsa and Pátra. *Marlines* to Igoumenítsa and Brindisi. Several ferries leave every day in season, most between 8 and 10.30pm; at least one daily in winter.

From Otranto *R-Lines* to Corfu and Igoumenítsa (9hr); five weekly, May–Oct only.

From Trieste *ANEK* to Igoumenítsa , Corfu and Pátra (43hr). One weekly in summer, tagged on to Ancona service.

SAMPLE FARES

Prices below are one-way high/low season fares; ***port taxes*** *(£3–5 per person in each direction) are not included. Note that substantial reductions apply on most lines for both **InterRail** or **Eurail** pass-holders, and those **under 26**. Slight discounts are usually available on **return fares**.*

Igoumenítsa from Bari or Brindisi: deck class £28–35/£15–25; car from £36–55/£20–45.

Pátra from Bari or Brindisi: deck class £31–£38/£20–30; car from £36–54/£25–45.

Igoumenítsa from Ancona: deck class £40/50; car from £65/£95.

UK AGENTS

For details of local agents in Greece, see the respective listings for Pátra and Igoumenítsa. The following are UK agents for advance bookings:

Amathis Travel, 51 Tottenham Court Rd, London W1 (☎0171/636 6158). *Agents for Hellenic Mediterranean.*

Serena Holidays, 40 Kenway Rd, London SW5 (☎0171/244 8422). *For Adriatica Lines.*

Viamare Travel Ltd, Graphic House, 2 Sumatra Rd, London NW6 (☎0171/431 4560). *For ANEK, Arkadia, Fragline, Marlines, R-Lines, Strintzis, Ventouris. Also for Salamis and Poseidon Lines, which route Pireás–Rhodes or Crete–Limassol–Haifa.*

---

are, in any case, advisable, as the range of fares and operators (from Brindisi especially) is considerable; if you do just turn up at the port, spend an hour or so shopping around the agencies.

VIA HUNGARY, ROMANIA AND BULGARIA

Avoiding former Yugoslavia involves a pretty substantial diversion through Hungary, Romania and Bulgaria. This is not a drive to contemplate unless you actively want to see some of the countries en route – it's too exhausting and too prob-

lematic. However, it's all easier than it was, with visas easier to obtain at the borders, if you haven't fixed them in advance.

From **Budapest**, the quickest route **through Romania** is via Timisoara, then to head towards Sofia in Bulgaria and on across the Rila mountains to the border at Kulata. Once at the Greek border, it's a three- to four-hour drive to Thessaloníki or Kavála. Bear in mind that road conditions are often poor and border crossings difficult. Contact the respective embassies and the AA for more advice.

GETTING THERE FROM IRELAND

Summer charters operate from Dublin and Belfast to Athens and there are additional services to Míkonos, Rhodes, Crete and

Corfu. A high-season charter from Dublin to Athens costs upwards of IR£200 return, while a week's package on one of the above islands costs from IR£440 per person for two weeks.

Year-round **scheduled services** with *Aer Lingus* and *British Airways* operate from both Dublin and Belfast via Heathrow to Athens, but you'll find them pricey compared to charters. Youth and student fares are offered by *USIT* (see below for address).

Travelling to London in the first place to pick up a cheap charter from there may save you a little money, but on the whole it's rarely worth the time and effort. For the record, budget flights to London are offered by *British Midland, Aer Lingus* and *Ryan Air,* while buying a Eurotrain boat and train ticket may also slightly undercut plane fares.

FLIGHT AGENTS IN IRELAND

Balkan Tours, 37 Ann St, Belfast BT1 4EB (☎01232/246795). Direct charter flights.

Joe Walsh Tours, 8–11 Baggot St, Dublin (☎01/676 0991). General budget fares agent.

Thomas Cook, 118 Grafton St, Dublin (☎01/677 1721). Mainstream package holiday and flight agent, with occasional discount offers.

USIT. Student and youth specialist. Branches at: Aston Quay, O'Connell Bridge, Dublin 2 (☎01/679

8833); 10–11 Market Parade, Cork (☎021/270 900); Fountain Centre, College St, Belfast (☎01232/324073).

AIRLINES

Aer Lingus, 41 Upper O'Connell St, Dublin (☎01/844 4777); 46–48 Castle St, Belfast (☎01232/245151); 2 Academy St, Cork (☎021/274331).

British Airways, 9 Fountain Centre, College St, Belfast (☎0345/222111); in Dublin, contact *Aer Lingus*.

GETTING THERE FROM NORTH AMERICA

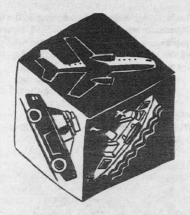

Only a few carriers fly directly to Greece from North America, so most North Americans travel to a gateway European city, and pick up a connecting flight on from there with an associated airline. If you have time, you may well discover that it's cheaper to arrange the final Greece-bound leg of the journey yourself, in which case your only criterion will be finding a suitable and good-value North America–Europe flight; for details of onward flights from the UK, see "Getting There from Britain" above.

In general there just isn't enough traffic on the US–Athens routes to make for very cheap fares. The **Greek national airline**, *Olympic Airways*, only flies out of New York (JFK), Boston, Montreal and Toronto, though the airline can offer reason-ably priced add-on flights within Greece, especially to the Greek islands, leaving from the same Athens terminal that you will fly into.

Another option to consider is picking up a flight to Europe and making your way to Greece by train, in which case a **Eurail Pass** makes a reasonable investment – all the details are covered below. For details of train routes, see "Getting There from Britain".

SHOPPING FOR TICKETS

Discount ticket outlets – advertised in the Sunday travel sections of major newspapers – come in several forms. **Consolidators** buy up blocks of tickets that airlines don't think they'll be able to sell at their published fares, and unload them at a discount. Many advertise fares on a one-way basis, enabling you to fly into one city and out from another without penalty. Consolidators normally don't impose advance purchase require-ments (although in busy times you should book ahead just to be sure of getting a ticket), but they do often charge very stiff fees for date changes. **Discount agents** also deal in blocks of tickets offloaded by the airlines, but they typically offer a range of other travel-related services like insu-rance, rail passes, youth and student ID cards, car rentals and tours. These agencies tend to be most worthwhile for students and under-26s, who can benefit from special fares and deals. **Travel clubs** are another option – most charge an annual membership fee, which may be worth it for their discounts on air tickets and car rental. Some agencies specialize in **charter flights,**

DISCOUNT TRAVEL COMPANIES

Air Brokers International, 323 Geary St, Suite 411, San Francisco, CA 94102 (☎1-800/883-3273). *Consolidator.*

Air Courier Association, 191 University Boulevard, Suite 300, Denver, CO 80206 (☎303/278-8810). *Courier flight broker.*

Airhitch, 2472 Broadway, Suite 200, New York, NY 10025 (☎212/864-2000). *Standby-seat broker. For a set price, they guarantee to get you on a flight as close to your preferred destination as possible, within a week.*

Council Travel, Head Office: 205 E 42nd St, New York, NY 10017 (☎1-800/743-1823). *Student travel organization with branches in many US cities. A sister company, Council Charter (☎1-800/223-7402), specializes in charter flights.*

Discount Travel International, Ives Bldg, 114 Forrest Ave, Suite 205, Narberth, PA 19072 (☎1-800/334-9294). *Discount travel club.*

Educational Travel Center, 438 N Frances St, Madison, WI 53703 (☎1-800/747-5551). *Student/youth discount agent.*

Encore Travel Club, 4501 Forbes Blvd, Lanham, MD 20706 (☎1-800/444-9800). *Discount travel club.*

Interworld Travel, 800 Douglass Rd, Miami, FL 33134 (☎305/443-4929). *Consolidator.*

Last Minute Travel Club, 132 Brookline Ave, Boston, MA 02215 (☎1-800/LAST MIN). *Travel club specializing in standby deals.*

Moment's Notice, 425 Madison Ave, New York, NY 10017 (☎212/486-0503). *Discount travel club.*

New Frontiers/Nouvelles Frontières, Head offices: 12 E 33rd St, New York, NY 10016 (☎1-800/366-6387); 1001 Sherbrook East, Suite 720, Montréal, Quebec H2L 1L3 (☎514/526-8444). *French discount travel firm. Other branches in LA, San Francisco and Québec City.*

Now Voyager, 74 Varick St, Suite 307, New York, NY 10013 (☎212/431-1616). *Courier flight broker.*

STA Travel, Head office: 48 East 11th St, New York, NY 10003 (☎1-800/777-0112; nationwide). *Worldwide specialist in independent travel with branches in the Los Angeles, San Francisco and Boston areas.*

TFI Tours International, Head office: 34 W 32nd St, New York, NY 10001 (☎1-800/745-8000). *Consolidator; other offices in Las Vegas, San Francisco, Los Angeles.*

Travac, Head office: 989 6th Ave, New York NY 10018 (☎1-800/872-8800). *Consolidator and charter broker; has another branch in Orlando.*

Travel Avenue, 10 S Riverside, Suite 1404, Chicago, IL 60606 (☎1-800/333-3335). *Discount travel agent.*

Travel Cuts, Head office: 187 College St, Toronto, Ontario M5T 1P7 (☎416/979-2406). *Canadian student travel organization with branches all over the country.*

Travelers Advantage, 3033 S Parker Rd, Suite 900, Aurora, CO 80014 (☎1-800/548-1116). *Discount travel club.*

UniTravel, 1177 N Warson Rd, St Louis, MO 63132 (☎1-800/325-2222). *Consolidator.*

Worldtek Travel, 111 Water St, New Haven, CT 06511 (☎1-800/243-1723). *Discount travel agency.*

Worldwide Discount Travel Club, 1674 Meridian Ave, Miami Beach, FL 33139 (☎305/534-2082). *Discount travel club.*

---

which may be even cheaper than anything available on a scheduled flight, but again there's a trade-off: departure dates are fixed, and withdrawal penalties are high (check the refund policy). Student/youth fares can sometimes save you money, though again the best deals are usually those offered by seat consolidators advertising in Sunday newspaper travel sections.

Don't automatically assume that tickets purchased through a travel specialist will be cheapest – once you get a quote, check with the airlines and you may turn up an even better deal. In addition, exercise caution and *never* deal with a company that demands cash up front or refuses to accept payment by credit card.

For destinations not handled by discounters – which applies to most regional airports – you'll have to deal with airlines' published fares. The cheapest of these is an **APEX** (Advance Purchase Excursion) ticket. This carries certain restrictions: you have to book – and pay – at least 21 days before departure and spend at least seven days abroad (maximum stay three months), and you're liable to penalties if you change your schedule. On transatlantic routes there are also winter **Super APEX** tickets, sometimes known as "Eurosavers" – slightly cheaper than ordinary Apex, but limiting your stay to between 7 and 21 days. Some airlines also issue **Special APEX** tickets to those under 24, often extending the maximum stay to a year.

SPECIALIST TOUR OPERATORS

USA

Above the Clouds Trekking, PO Box 398, Worcestor, MA 01602 (☎1-800/233-4499). *Greek trekking holidays.*

Adriatic Tours, 691 West 10th St, San Pedro, CA 90731 (☎1-800/262-1718). *City highlights tours and cruise vacations.*

Archeological Tours, 271 Madison Ave, New York, NY 10016 (☎212/986-3054). *Specialist archeological tours.*

Astro Tours, 216 Fourth Ave South, Seattle, WA 98104 (☎206/467-7777). *Cruise packages to the Greek islands.*

Brendan Tours, 15137 Califa St, Van Nuys, CA 91411 (☎1-800/421-8446). *City highlights, cruise packages and car rental.*

Caravan Tours Inc., 401 N Michigan Ave, Suite 2800, Chicago, IL 60611 (☎1-800/621-8338). *All kinds of packages covering the entire country.*

Classic Adventures, PO Box 153, Hamlin, NY 14464-0153 (☎1-800/777-8090). *Trekking, biking and walking tours in June and September, covering archeological sites and coastal trips.*

Classic Holidays, 790 Boston St, Billerica, MA 01821 (☎1-800/752-5055). *Packages from 8 to 21 days, group tours and cruises.*

Cloud Tours Inc, 645 Fifth Ave, New York, NY 10022 (☎1-800/223-7880). *Affordable escorted tours and Mediterranean cruises.*

Educational Tours and Cruises, 14 (R) Wyman St, Medford, MA 02155 (☎1-800/275-4109). *Custom-designed tours to Greece and the islands, specializing in art, history, food and wine, ancient drama, painting, birdwatching, etc.*

Epirotiki Lines, 551 Fifth Ave, New York, NY 10176 (☎212/949-7273). *Greek cruise specialist.*

Globus Gateway, 92–25 Queens Blvd, Rego Park, NY 11374 (☎1-800/221-0090). *Offers a variety of city and island packages.*

Grecian Travel Inc, 29–11 Ditmard Blvd, Astoria, NY 11105 (☎1-800/368-6262). *For years, a leader in travel to Greece.*

Guaranteed Travel, 83 South St, Box 269, Morristown, NJ 07963 (☎201/540-1770). *Specializes in "Greece-Your-Way" independent travel.*

Hellenic Adventures, 4150 Harriet Ave South, Minneapolis, MN 55409 (☎612/824-2180). *Cruises and city highlights.*

Homeric Tours, 55 E 59th St, New York, NY 10017 (☎1-800/223-5570). *All-inclusive tours from 9 to 23 days, as well as cruises and charter flights.*

Insight International Tours, 745 Atlantic Ave, Boston, MA 02111 (☎1-800/582-8380). *General Greek vacations.*

Odyssey Travel Center, 7735 Old Georgetown Rd, Bethesda, MD 20814 (☎401/657-4647). *Independent package tours, with extensions available to Egypt, Israel and Turkey.*

Topline Travel, 36-01 28 Ave, Long Island City, NY 11103 (☎1-800/221-1289). *Escorted tours of Athens and the islands.*

Triaena Travel, 850 Seventh Ave, New York, NY 10019 (☎1-800/223-1273). *Packages, cruises, apartments and villas.*

Valef Cruises, Box 391, Ambler, PA 19002 (☎215/641-1624). *Yachting trips and charters.*

CANADA

Adventures Abroad, 1027 W. Broadway, Suite 310, Vancouver, British Columbia, VGH 1E3 (☎604/732-9922). *General operator, offering group and individual tours and cruises.*

Auratours, 1470 Peel St, Suite 252, Montréal, Quebec H3A 1TL (☎1-800/363-0323). *General operator, offering group and individual tours and cruises.*

Chat Tours, 241 Bedford Rd, Toronto, Ontario M5R 2K9 (☎1-800/268-1180). *Motorcoach and sea tours, and cruises.*

Triaena Poseidon Tours International, 72 Hutchison St, Montréal, Quebec H3N 1ZL (☎1-800/361-0374). *Custom-made tours, yacht charters and cruises, and apartment and villa vacations.*

Worldwide Adventures, 920 Yonge St, Suite 747, Toronto, Ontario M4W 3C7 (☎1-800/387-1483). *General operator, offering group and individual tours and cruises.*

Note that fares are heavily dependent on **season**, and are highest from June–September; they drop either side of this, and you'll get the best deals during the low season, November–February (excluding Christmas). Note that flying on weekends ordinarily adds $50 or so to the round-trip fare; price ranges quoted in the sections below assume midweek travel.

FROM THE USA

Non-stop flights to Athens out of **New York** on *Olympic* start at around US$700 round trip in winter, rising to around $1100 in summer for a maximum thirty-day stay with seven-day advance purchase. For about the same price, *Olympic* also flies out of **Boston** once a week in winter, twice a week in summer. *Delta* and *TWA* have daily services from New York to Athens via Frankfurt and while fares cost around $300 more than with *Olympic*, a consolidator or agent might be able to get you a flight for around half the cost the airlines themselves quote; round trips run from around $600 in winter, $900 in summer. *United* flights to Athens are via Paris, and there's a good service from **Washington DC** and **Chicago** – the lowest round-trip winter fare from DC starts at around $800.

One particularly good deal is on *LOT Polish Airlines*, which flies out of New York and Chicago to Athens several times a week via Warsaw. Fares run from around $700 round trip.

Since all scheduled flights to Athens from the **West Coast** go via New York or another eastern city, you basically end up paying for a transcontinental flight on top of the transatlantic fare: round-trip APEX tickets from Seattle, San Francisco or Los Angeles on *TWA* or *Delta* start at $920 in winter, rising to over $1200 in summer. Most European airlines (including *Air France*, *British Airways*, *Iberia*, *KLM* and *Lufthansa*) also connect the West Coast with Greece via their "homeports" in Europe, but these stopovers often mean a wait of a few hours, sometimes even an overnight stop – be sure to ask your ticket agent.

EUROPEAN CONNECTIONS

There are direct flights to:

Thessaloníki from Amsterdam, Brussels, Copenhagen, Dusseldorf, Frankfurt, London, Munich, Stuttgart, Vienna, Zürich.

Corfu from Amsterdam, Dusseldorf, Frankfurt, Geneva, London, Milan, Stuttgart.

FROM CANADA

As with the US, air fares from Canada to vary tremendously depending upon whi start your journey. The best-value schedul is on *Olympic*; who fly non-stop out of M and Toronto once a week in winter for CDN round trip, twice a week in summer for $15(

KLM operates several flights a week to A via Amsterdam, from Toronto, Mon Vancouver and Edmonton – from Toronto, e to pay around $1150 in winter, $1500 in season. Travelers from Montréal can also tr European carriers *Air France*, *Alitalia*, *Br Airways*, *Iberia*, *Lufthansa*, *Sabena*, *Swissair* *TAP Air Portugal*, all of which operate sev flights a week to Athens via major Europ cities. One unlikely source for good deals *Czechoslovak Airline* (*ČSA*), which flies out Montréal to Athens via Prague for around $1100

Finally, *Air Canada* flies to Vienna with conne tions to Athens on *Olympic*; flights fro Vancouver cost $1600 in winter, $1800 in summe

RAIL PASSES

A **Eurail Pass** is not likely to pay for itself if you're planning to stick to Greece, though it's worth considering if you plan to travel to Greece across Europe from elsewhere. The pass, which must be purchased before arrival in Europe, allows unlimited free train travel in Greece and sixteen other countries. The **Eurail Youthpass** (for under-26s) costs US$398 for 15 days, $578 for one month or $768 for two months; if you're 26 or over you'll have to buy a **first-class pass**, available in 15-day ($498), 21-day ($648), one-month ($798), two-month ($1098) and three-month ($1398) increments.

You stand a better chance of getting your money's worth out of a **Eurail Flexipass**, which is good for a certain number of travel days in a

---

RAIL CONTACTS IN NORTH AMERICA

CIT Tours, 342 Madison Ave, Suite 207, New York, NY 10173 (☎1-800/223-7987).

DER Tours/GermanRail, 9501 W Divon Ave, Suite 400, Rosemont, IL 60018 (☎1-800/421-2929).

Rail Europe, 226 Westchester Ave, White Plains, NY 10604 (☎1-800/438 7245).

ScanTours, 1535 6th St, Suite 205, Santa Monica, CA 90401 (☎1-800/223-7226).

two-month period. This, too, comes in under-26/ first-class versions: 5 days cost $255/$348; 10 days, $398/$560; and 15 days, $540/$740. A further alternative is to attempt to buy an *InterRail* Pass in Europe (see "Getting There from Britain") – most agents don't check residential qualifications, but once you're in Europe it'll be too late to buy a *Eurail Pass* if you have problems. You can purchase *Eurail* passes from one of the agents listed below.

North Americans are also eligible to purchase more specific passes valid for travel in Greece only, for details of which see "Getting around", p.29.

GETTING THERE FROM AUSTRALASIA

It's fairly easy to track down flights from **Australia** to Athens, less so from **New Zealand**, but given the prices and most people's travel plans, you'll probably do better looking for some kind of Round-the-World ticket that includes Greece. If London is your first destination in Europe, and you've picked up a reasonably good deal on a flight there, it's probably best to wait until you reach the UK before arranging your onward travel to Greece; see "Getting there from Britain" for all the details.

Note that **prices** given below are in local dollars for published mid-season return fares; travel agents (see box) should be able to get at least ten percent off these. **Students** and anyone **under 26** should try *STA Travel* in the first instance which has a wide range of discounted fares on offer.

FROM AUSTRALIA

Cheapest fares to Athens **from Australia** are with *Aeroflot* ($1650), flying weekly out of

Sydney via Moscow, and *Thai* ($2242), which flies from Sydney, Melbourne, Perth or Brisbane via Bangkok. Otherwise, you can fly daily from Perth or Sydney, and several times a week from Melbourne or Brisbane, for $2399 with one of the following: *Olympic* (via Bangkok), *Alitalia* (Bangkok, Rome), *Singapore* (Singapore), *KLM* (Singapore, Amsterdam), *Lufthansa* (Frankfurt) and *United* (Los Angeles, Washington, Paris). *British Airways* and *Qantas* can get you to London via Singapore or Bangkok for the same price, but charge an extra $430 to Athens, while giving you a free return flight within Europe. You can undercut this with their *Global Explorer Pass* ($2499), a **Round-the-World** fare that allows six stopovers worldwide wherever these two airlines fly to (except South America). Also worth considering is *Garuda*'s $1685 fare from Sydney, Townsville or Cairns via Jakarta to various European cities, from where you could pick up a cheap onward flight or continue **overland** to Athens. **Departure tax** from Athens, sometimes added to the ticket at the time of purchase, is $33.

FROM NEW ZEALAND

From New Zealand, best deals to Athens are with *Thai* ($2399 via Bangkok) or *Singapore* ($2499 via Singapore), and a very versatile offer with *Lufthansa* ($2899), who can route you through anywhere that Air New Zealand or Qantas fly – including Los Angeles, Singapore, Sydney, Hong Kong or Tokyo – for a stopover. *British Airways/Qantas* can get you to Europe, but not Athens, for $2699, so again you're better off with their *Global Explorer Pass* (see above) at $3099. Surprisingly expensive at $3974 are *Alitalia* (via Rome) and *United* (Los Angeles, Washington, Paris). **Departure tax** from Athens is $42.

AGENTS AND AIRLINES IN AUSTRALASIA

Note: all Australian phone numbers are due to have extra digits added over the next two years.

TRAVEL AGENTS

Adventure World, 73 Walker St, North Sydney (☎02/956 7766); 8 Victoria Ave, Perth (☎09/221 2300).

Flight Centres, *Australia*: Circular Quay, Sydney (☎02/241 2422); Bourke St, Melbourne (☎03/650 2899); plus other branches nationwide.

New Zealand: National Bank Towers, 205–225 Queen St, Auckland (☎09/309 6171); Shop 1M, National Mutual Arcade, 152 Hereford St, Christchurch (☎09/379 7145); 50–52 Willis St, Wellington (☎04/472 8101); other branches countrywide.

Grecian Holidays, 115 Pitt St, Sydney (☎02/231 1277); 71 Grey St, Brisbane (☎07/846 4006).

Grecian Mediterranean Holidays, 49 Ventnor Ave, West Perth (☎09/321 3930).

Grecian Tours Travel, 237a Lonsdale St, Melbourne (☎03/663 3711).

Greek National Tourist Office, 51 Pitt St, Sydney (☎02/241 1663).

Greek Tours, Floor 2, 243 Edward St, Brisbane (☎07/221 9700).

House of Holidays, 298 Clayton Rd, Clayton, Victoria (☎03/543 5800).

STA Travel, *Australia*: 732 Harris St, Ultimo, Sydney (☎02/212 1255); 256 Flinders St, Melbourne (☎03/347 4711); other offices in Townsville, Cairns and state capitals.

New Zealand: Traveller's Centre, 10 High St, Auckland (☎09/309 9995); 233 Cuba St, Wellington (☎04/385 0561); 223 High St, Christchurch (☎03/379 9098); other offices in Dunedin, Palmerston North and Hamilton.

AIRLINES

☎*008 numbers are toll free, but only apply if dialled outside the city in the address.*

Aeroflot, 388 George St, Sydney (☎02/233 7148). No NZ office.

Alitalia, Orient Overseas Building, 32 Bridge St, Sydney (☎02/247 1308); Floor 6, Trust Bank Building, 229 Queen St, Auckland (☎09/379 4457).

British Airways, 64 Castlereagh St, Sydney (☎02/258 3300); Dilworth Building, cnr Queen and Customs streets, Auckland (☎09/367 7500).

Garuda, 175 Clarence St, Sydney (☎02/334 9900); 120 Albert St, Auckland (☎09/366 1855).

KLM 5 Elizabeth St, Sydney (☎02/231 6333/008 222 747). No NZ office.

Lufthansa/Air Lauda, 143 Macquarie St, Sydney (☎02/367 3800); 109 Queen St, Auckland (☎09/303 1529).

Olympic Airways, *S.A.* Floor 3, 37–49 Pitt St, Sydney (☎02/251 2044). No NZ office.

Qantas, International Square, Jamison St, Sydney (☎02/957 0111/236 3636); Qantas House, 154 Queen St, Auckland (☎09/303 2506).

Singapore Airlines, 17 Bridge St, Sydney (☎02/236 0111); Lower Ground Floor, West Plaza Building, cnr Customs and Albert streets, Auckland (☎09/379 3209).

Thai 75–77 Pitt St, Sydney (☎02/844 0999/008 221 320); Kensington Swan Building, 22 Fanshawe St, Auckland (☎09377 3886).

United 10 Barrack St, Sydney (☎02/237 8888); 7 City Road, Auckland (☎09/307 9500).

TRAVELLERS WITH DISABILITIES

It is all too easy to wax lyrical over the attractions of Greece: the stepped, narrow alleys, the ease of travel by bus and ferry, the thrill of clambering around the great archeological sites. It is almost impossible, on the other hand, for the able-bodied travel writer to see these attractions as potential hazards for anyone who has some difficulty in walking or is wheelchair-bound or suffers from some other disability.

However, don't be discouraged. It is possible to enjoy an inexpensive and trauma-free holiday in Greece if some time is devoted to gathering **information** before arrival. However, much existing or readily available information is out of date – you should always try to double-check. A number of addresses of contact organizations are published below. The Greek National Tourist Office is a good first step as long as you have specific questions to put to them; they publish a useful questionnaire which you could send to hotels or owners of apartment/villa accommodation.

PLANNING A HOLIDAY

There are **organized tours and holidays** specifically for people with disabilities – both *Thomsons* and *Horizon* in Britain will advise on the suitability of holidays advertised in their brochures. If you want to be more independent, it's perfectly possible, provided that you do not leave home with the vague hope that things will turn out all right, and that "people will help out" when you need assistance. This cannot be relied on. You must either be completely confident that you can manage alone, or travel with an able-bodied friend (or two).

It's important to become an authority on where you must be self-reliant and where you may expect help, especially regarding transport and accommodation. For example, to get between the terminals at Athens airport, you will have to fight for a taxi; it is not the duty of the airline staff to find you one, and there is no trace of an organized line.

It is also vital to **be honest** – with travel agencies, insurance companies, companions and, above all, with yourself. Know your limitations and make sure others know them. If you do not use a wheelchair all the time but your walking capabilities are limited, remember that you are likely to need to cover greater distances while travelling (often over tougher terrain and in hotter weather) than you are used to. If you use one, take a wheelchair with you, have it serviced before you go and carry a repair kit.

Read your travel **insurance** small print carefully to make sure that people with a pre-existing medical condition are not excluded. And use your travel agent to make your journey simpler: **airlines** or bus companies can cope better if they are expecting you, with a wheelchair provided at airports and staff primed to help. A **medical certificate** of your fitness to travel, provided by your doctor, is also extremely useful; some airlines or insurance companies may insist on it.

Make a **list** of all the facilities that will make your life easier while you are away. You may want a ground-floor room, or access to a large elevator; you may have special dietary requirements, or need level ground to enable you to reach shops, beaches, bars and places of interest. You should also keep track of all your other special needs, making sure, for example, that you have extra supplies of drugs – carried with you if you fly – and a prescription including the generic name in case of emergency. Carry spares of any kind of drug, clothing or equipment that might be hard to find in Greece; if there's an association representing people with your disability, contact them early in the planning process.

USEFUL CONTACTS (cont.)

Evyenia Stravropoulou, Lavinia Tours: Egnatía 101, 541 10 Thessaloníki (☎031/240 041). *Will advise disabled visitors and has tested many parts of Greece in her wheelchair. She also organizes tours within Greece.*

In the UK

Holiday Care Service, 2 Old Bank Chambers, Station Rd, Horley, Surrey RH6 9HW (☎01293/774535). *Publishes a fact sheet, and also runs a useful "Holiday Helpers" service for disabled travellers.*

Mobility International, 228 Borough High St, London SE1 1JX (☎0171/403 5688). *Issues a quarterly newsletter on developments in disabled travel.*

Opus 23, Sourdock Hill, Barkisland, Halifax, W Yorks HX4 0AG (☎01422/375999). *Part of Grecofile; will advise on and arrange independent holidays, or for those with carers.*

RADAR, 25 Mortimer St, London W1N 8AB (☎0171/250 3222). *Publish fact sheets and an annual guide to international travel for the disabled.*

Tripscope, Evelyn Rd, London W4 5JL (☎0181/994 9294). *Transport advice to most countries for all disabilities.*

North America

Directions Unlimited, 720 N Bedford Rd, Bedford Hills, NY 10507 (☎1-800/533-5343). *Tour operator specializing in custom tours for people with disabilities.*

Information Center for People with Disabilities, Fort Point Place, 27-43 Wormwood St, Boston, MA 02210 (☎617/727-5540; TDD ☎617/345-9743).

Clearing house for information, including travel, primarily in Massachusetts.

Jewish Rehabilitation Hospital, 3205 Place Alton Goldbloom, Montréal, Quebec H7V 1R2 (☎514/688-9550, ext 226).
Guidebooks and travel information.

Kéroul, 4545 Ave Pierre de Coubertin, CP 1000, Station M, Montréal, Quebec H1V 3R2 (☎514/252-3104).

Organization promoting and facilitating travel for mobility-impaired people, primarily in Quebec. Annual membership $10.

Mobility International USA, PO Box 10767, Eugene, OR 97440 (Voice & TDD: ☎503/343-1284). *Information and referral services, access guides, tours and exchange programmes. Annual membership $20 (includes quarterly newsletter).*

Society for the Advancement of Travel for the Handicapped (SATH), 347 5th Ave, New York, NY 10016 (☎212/447-7284).
Non-profit travel-industry referral service that passes queries on to its members as appropriate; allow plenty of time for a response.

Travel Information Service, Moss Rehabilitation Hospital, 1200 West Tabor Rd, Philadelphia, PA 19141 (☎215/456-9600). *Telephone information and referral service.*

Twin Peaks Press, Box 129, Vancouver, WA 98666; ☎206/694-2462 or ☎1-800/637-2256). *Publisher of the Directory of Travel Agencies for the Disabled ($19.95), listing more than 370 agencies worldwide; Travel for the Disabled ($14.95); the Directory of Accessible Van Rentals and Wheelchair Vagabond ($9.95), loaded with personal tips.*

VISAS AND RED TAPE

UK and all other EC nationals need only a valid passport for entry to Greece; you are no longer stamped in on arrival or out upon departure, and in theory at least enjoy uniform civil rights with Greek citizens. US, Australian, New Zealand, Canadian and most non-EC Europeans receive entry and exit stamps in their passports and can stay, as tourists, for ninety days.

If you are planning to **travel overland**, you should check current visa requirements for Hungary, Romania and Bulgaria, or for newly independent Slovenia and Croatia at their closest consulates; transit visas for most of these territories are at present issued at the borders, though at a higher price than if obtained in advance at a local consulate.

VISA EXTENSIONS

If you wish to stay in Greece for longer than three months, you should officially apply for an **extension**. This can be done in the larger cities like Athens, Thessaloníki, Pátra and Iráklio through the *Ipiresía Allodhapón* (Aliens' Bureau); prepare yourself for concerted bureaucracy. In remoter locations you visit the local police station, where staff are apt to be more cooperative.

Unless you are of Greek descent, visitors from **non-EC countries** are currently allowed only one six-month extension to a tourist visa, which costs 11,000dr. In theory, **EC nationals** are allowed to stay indefinitely but, at the time of writing, must still present themselves every six months or year, according to whether they have a non-employment resident visa or a work permit; the

first extension is free, but you will be charged for subsequent extensions. In all cases, the procedure should be set in motion a couple of weeks before your time runs out – and, if you don't have a work permit, you will be required to present pink, personalized bank **exchange receipts** (see "Costs, Money and Banks: Currency Regulations" below) totalling at least 45,000dr for the preceding three months, as proof that you have sufficient funds to support yourself without working.

Some individuals get around the law by leaving Greece every three months and re-entering a few days later for a new tourist stamp. However, with the recent flood of Albanian and ex-Yugoslavian refugees into the country, and a smaller influx of east Europeans looking for work, security and immigration personnel don't always look very kindly on this practice.

If you **overstay** your time and then leave under your own power – ie are not deported – you'll be given a 22,000dr spot fine upon departure, effectively a double-priced retroactive visa extension – no excuses will be entertained.

CUSTOMS REGULATIONS

For EC citizens travelling between EC countries, limits on goods which have been taxed already have been relaxed enormously. However, **duty-free allowances** are as follows: 200 cigarettes or 50 cigars, two litres of still table wine, one litre of spirits and 60ml of perfume.

Exporting **antiquities** without a permit is a serious offence; **drug smuggling**, it goes without saying, incurs severe penalties.

GREEK EMBASSIES ABROAD

Australia 9 Turrana St, Yarralumla, Canberra, ACT 2600 (☎062/273-3011).

Britain 1a Holland Park, London W11 (☎0171/221 6467).

Canada 80 Maclaren St, Ottawa, ON K2P 0K6 (☎613/238-6271).

Ireland 1 Upper Pembroke St, Dublin 2 (☎01/767254).

New Zealand Cumberland House, 237 Willis St, PO Box 27157, Wellington (☎04/847-556).

USA 2221 Massachusetts Ave NW, Washington DC 20008 (☎202/667-3168).

INSURANCE

British and other EC nationals are officially entitled to free medical care in Greece (see "Health Matters" p.23) upon presentation of an E111 form, available from most post offices. "Free", however, means admittance only to the lowest grade of state hospital (known as a *yenikó nosokomío*), and does not include nursing care or the cost of medications. In practice, hospital staff tend to greet E111s with uncomprehending looks, and you may have to request reimbursal by the NHS upon return home. If you need prolonged medical care, you'll prefer to make use of private treatment, which is expensive.

Some form of **travel insurance**, therefore, is advisable – and essential for **North Americans and Australasians**, whose countries have no formal health care agreements with Greece (other than allowing for free emergency trauma treatment). For medical claims, keep receipts, including those from pharmacies. You will have to pay for all private medical care on the spot

(insurance claims can be processed if you have hospital treatment) but it can all be (eventually) claimed back. Travel insurance usually provides cover for the loss of baggage, money and tickets, too. If you're thinking of renting a moped or motorbike in Greece, make sure the policy covers motorbike accidents.

EUROPEAN COVER

In Britain, there are a number of low-cost specialist insurance companies including *Endsleigh*, 97–107 Southampton Row, London WC1 (☎0171/436 4451), *Campus Travel*, 52 Grosvenor Gardens, London SW1 (☎0171/730 3402), and *Columbus*, 17 Devonshire Square, London EC2 (☎0171/375 0111). At all of these you can buy two weeks' basic cover in Greece for around £15, £22 for a month.

Most **banks** and **credit card** issuers also offer some sort of vacation insurance, often automatic if you pay for the holiday with a card. In these circumstances, it's vital to check what the policy actually covers.

NORTH AMERICAN COVER

Before buying an insurance policy, check that you're not already covered. **Canadians** are usually covered for medical mishaps overseas by their provincial health plans. Holders of official student/teacher/youth cards are entitled to accident coverage and hospital in-patient benefits. **Students** will often find that their student health coverage extends during the vacations and for one term beyond the date of last enrollment. Bank and credit cards (particularly *American Express*) often have certain levels of medical or other insurance included, and travel insurance may also be included if you use a major credit or

---

TRAVEL INSURANCE COMPANIES IN NORTH AMERICA

Access America, PO Box 90310, Richmond, VA 23230 (☎1-800/284-8300).

Carefree Travel Insurance, PO Box 310, 120 Mineola Blvd, Mineola, NY 11501 (☎1-800/323-3149).

International Student Insurance Service (ISIS) – sold by *STA Travel*, see "Getting There from North America" for addresses.

Travel Assistance International, 1133 15th St NW, Suite 400, Washington, DC 20005 (☎1-800/821-2828).

Travel Guard, 1145 Clark St, Stevens Point, WI 54481 (☎1-800/826-1300).

Travel Insurance Services, 2930 Camino Diablo, Suite 300, Walnut Creek, CA 94596 (☎1-800/937-1387).

charge card to pay for your trip. **Homeowners' or renters'** insurance often covers theft or loss of documents, money and valuables while overseas, though conditions and maximum amounts vary from company to company.

After exhausting the possibilities above, you might want to contact a specialist **travel insurance** company; your travel agent can usually recommend one, or see the box opposite. Policies are comprehensive (accidents, illnesses, delayed or lost luggage, cancelled flights, etc), but maximum payouts tend to be meagre. Premiums vary, so shop around. The best deals are usually to be had through student/youth travel agencies – *ISIS* policies, for example, cost $48–69 for fifteen days (depending on coverage), $80–105 for a month, $149–207 for two months, or up to $510–700 for a year.

Most North American travel policies apply only to items lost, stolen or damaged while in the custody of an identifiable, responsible third party – hotel porter, airline, luggage consignment, etc. Even in these cases you will have to contact the local police within a certain time limit to have a complete report made out so that your insurer can process the claim. Note also that very few insurers will arrange on-the-spot payments in the event of a major expense or loss; you will usually be reimbursed only after going home.

INSURANCE REPORTS

In all cases of loss or theft of goods, you will have to contact the local police to have a **report** made out so that your insurer can process the claim. This can occasionally be a tricky business in Greece, since many officials simply won't accept that anything could be stolen on their turf, or at least don't want to take responsibility for it. Be persistent and if necessary enlist the support of the local tourist police or tourist office.

COSTS, MONEY AND BANKS

The costs of living in Greece have spiralled during the years of EC membership: the days of renting a house for a few thousand drachmas a week are long gone, and food prices at corner shops now differ little from those of other member countries. However, outside the established resorts, travel in the country remains reasonably priced, with the cost of restaurant meals, accommodation and public transport as cheap as anywhere in northern or western Europe.

Prices depend on where and when you go. The cities and tourist resorts are usually more expensive and costs increase in July, August and at Easter. **Solo travellers** invariably spend more than if they were sharing food and rooms. An additional frustration is the relative lack of single rooms. **Students** with an *International Student Identity Card* (*ISIC*) can get free – or fifty percent discount off – admission fees at most archeological sites and museums. These, and other occasional discounts, tend to be more readily available to EC students. A *FIYTO* card (available to non-students) has fewer benefits. Both cards are available from student/youth travel agencies.

SOME BASIC COSTS

In most places you can get by on a **budget** of £16–20/US$24–30 a day, which will get you basic accommodation, breakfast, picnic lunch, a ferry or bus ride and a simple taverna meal. Camping would cut costs marginally. On £25–30/$38–45 a day you could be living quite well and also treating yourself to motorbike or car rental.

Domestic Aegean **ferries**, a main unavoidable expense, are quite reasonably priced, helped by government subsidies to preserve island communities. A deck-class ticket from Pireás, the port of Athens, to Crete or Sámos, both 12-to-14-hour trips, costs about £12/US$18. For half the cost, there are dozens of closer islands in reach.

Long-distance **buses** now cost nearly the same as their equivalents elsewhere in Europe, but city services are still very cheap, as are **trains** – for example Athens–Thessaloníki, the longest single journey you're likely to make, is just £10/US$15 second class.

The simplest double **room** can generally be had for £11–17/$16.50–25.50 a night, depending on the location and the plumbing arrangements. Organized **campsites** cost little more than £2.50/US$3.75 per person, with similar charges per tent and perhaps 25 percent more for a camper van. With discretion you can camp for free in the more remote, rural areas.

A basic taverna **meal** with local wine can be had for around £6/US$9 a head. Add a better bottle of wine, seafood, or more careful cooking, and it could be up to £10/US$15 a head – but you'll rarely pay more than that. Sharing seafood, Greek salads and dips is a good way to keep costs down in the better restaurants, but even in the most developed of resorts, with inflated "international" menus you'll usually be able to find a more earthy but decent taverna where the locals eat.

CURRENCY

Greek currency is the **drachma** (*dhrahmí*), and the exchange rate is currently around 360dr to the pound sterling, 235dr to the US dollar.

The most common **notes** in circulation are those of 50, 100, 500, 1000 and 5000 (a 10,000 note is due shortly) drachmas (*dhrahmés*), while **coins** come in denominations of 5, 10, 20, 50 and 100dr; you might come across 1dr and 2dr coins, too, though they're rarely used these days.

BANKS AND EXCHANGE

Greek **banks** are normally open Monday–Thursday 8.30am–2pm, Friday 8.30am–1.30pm. Certain branches in the major cities and tourist centres are open extra hours in the evenings and on Saturday mornings for exchanging money, while outside these times larger hotels and travel agencies can often change money. Always take your passport with you as proof of identity and be prepared for at least one long line – usually you have to line up once to have the transaction approved and again to pick up the cash.

The safest and easiest way to carry money is as **travellers' cheques**. These can be obtained from banks (even if you don't have an account) or from offices of *Thomas Cook* and *American Express*; you'll pay a commission of 1–2 percent. When exchanging money in Greece using travellers' cheques a **commission** of 400–800dr is charged. You can cash the cheques at most banks and post offices, and at quite a number of hotels, agencies and tourist shops – though often at poorer rates.

Alternatively, most British banks can issue current account holders with a **Eurocheque** card and chequebook, with which you can pay for things in some shops and withdraw drachmas from cash machines or Greek banks. An annual fee is payable for this service, plus 2 percent processing charge on the debit facility, but usually there's no commission on straightforward transactions. The current limit is 45,000dr per cheque.

Exchanging money at the **post office** has some considerable advantages in Greece. You miss out on the lines at banks and have access to exchange almost anywhere you go. There are a number of small islands that have no bank but they almost all have a post office. Commissions levied for both cheques and cash tend, at about 300dr per transaction, to be much lower than at banks.

Finally, there is no need to change foreign currency into drachmas **before arrival** unless you're coming in at some ungodly hour at one of the remoter land or sea frontier posts, or on a Sunday. Airport arrival lounges will always have an exchange booth operating for passengers on incoming international flights.

CREDIT CARDS AND ATMs

Major **credit cards** are accepted only by the more expensive shops, hotels and restaurants. They're useful – indeed almost essential – for renting cars, for example, but not much use in the cheaper tavernas or hotels.

If you run short of money, you can get a **cash advance on a credit card**, but be warned that the minimum amount is 15,000dr. The *Emborikí Trápeza* (Commercial Bank) handles *Visa*; the *Ethnikí Trápeza* (National Bank) services *Access/Mastercard* customers. However, there is usually a 2 percent credit card charge, often unfavourable rates and always interminable delays.

It is much easier to use the small but growing network of Greek **cashpoint machines (ATMs)**. Don't forget your PIN number. The most useful and well distributed are those of the *Trápeza Písteos* (*Credit Bank*), which will accept *Visa* and *American Express*. In the larger towns and airports the *Commercial* and *National* banks have a number of machines catering for a range of card-holders: *Plus System* and *Visa* at the *Commercial* (*Emborikí Trápeza*), *Cirrus* and *Mastercard/Access* at the *National* (*Ethnikí Trápeza*).

EMERGENCY CASH

In an emergency, you can arrange to have **money sent** from home to a bank in Greece. Receiving funds via telex takes a minimum of three days and often up to six days, so be prepared for delays. **From the UK**, a bank charge of 3 percent, or minimum £17, maximum £35, is levied. Bank drafts can also be sent, with higher commission rates.

From the US and Canada, funds can be sent via *Western Union* (☎1-800/325-6000) or *American Express MoneyGram* (☎1-800/543-4080). Both companies' fees depend on the desti-

nation and the amount being transferred, but as an example, wiring $1000 to Europe will cost around $75. The funds should be available for collection at *Amex*'s or *Western Union*'s local office within minutes of being sent.

CURRENCY REGULATIONS

You can't **import** more than 100,000dr, or export more than 20,000dr, while foreign banknotes worth more than US$1000 must be declared: it makes sense to do this to minimize the hassles if you want to take the currency out again.

If you have any reason to believe that you'll be acquiring large quantities of drachmas – from work or sale of goods – declare everything on arrival, then request (and save) pink, personalized **receipts** for each exchange transaction. Otherwise you may find that you can only re-exchange a limited sum of drachmas on departure. These pink receipts are also essential for obtaining a visa extension (see "Visas and Red Tape" p.19).

HEALTH MATTERS

There are no required inoculations for Greece, though it's wise to have a typhoid-cholera booster, and to ensure that you are up to date on tetanus and polio. Don't forget to take out travel insurance (see "Insurance" p.21), so that you're covered in case of serious illness or accidents.

The water is safe pretty much everywhere, though you will come across shortages or brackish supplies on some of the drier and more remote islands. Bottled water is widely available if you're feeling cautious.

SPECIFIC HAZARDS

The main health problems experienced by visitors have to do with over-exposure to the sun, and the odd nasty from the sea. To combat the former, wear a hat and drink plenty of fluids in the hot months to avoid any danger of **sunstroke**, and don't underestimate the power of even a hazy sun to **burn**.

For sea-wear, a pair of goggles for swimming and footwear for walking over wet rocks are useful.

HAZARDS OF THE DEEP

In the sea, you may just have the bad luck to meet an armada of **jellyfish**, especially in late summer; they come in various colours and sizes including invisible and minute. Various over-the-counter remedies are sold in resort pharmacies; baking soda or ammonia also help to lessen the sting.

Less vicious but more common are black, spiky **sea urchins**, which infest rocky shorelines year-round; if you step on or graze one, a needle (you can crudely sterilize it by heat from a cigarette lighter) and olive oil are effective for removing spines from your anatomy; they should be extracted, or they will fester.

The worst maritime danger – fortunately very rare – seems to be the **weever fish**, which buries itself in tidal zone sand with just its poisonous dorsal and gill spines protruding. If you tread on one the sudden pain is unmistakably excruciating, and the venom is exceptionally potent. Consequences can range up to permanent paralysis of the affected area, so the imperative first aid is to immerse your foot in water as hot as you can stand. This serves to degrade the toxin and relieve the swelling of joints and attendant pain.

SANDFLIES, MOSQUITOES AND SNAKES

If you are sleeping on or near a **beach**, a wise precaution is to use insect repellent, either lotion or wrist/ankle bands, and/or a tent with a screen to guard against **sandflies**. You are unlikely to be infected by these, but they are potentially dangerous, carrying visceral leishmaniasis, a rare parasitic infection characterized by chronic fever, listlessness and weight loss.

Mosquitoes (*kounóupia*) are less worrying – in Greece they don't carry anything worse than a vicious bite – but they can be infuriating. The best solution is to burn pyrethrum incense coils (*spíres* or *fidhákia* in Greek); these are widely and cheaply available, though smelly. Better if you can get them are the small electrical devices which vaporize an odourless insecticide tablet. Insect repellant is available from most general stores and kiosks.

The **adder** and **scorpion** are found in Greece, though both are shy; just take care when climbing over dry-stone walls where snakes like to sun themselves, and don't put hands/feet in places, ie shoes, where you haven't looked first.

PHARMACIES AND DRUGS

For **minor complaints** it's enough to go to the local *farmakío*. Greek pharmacists are highly trained and dispense a number of medicines which elsewhere could only be prescribed by a doctor. In the larger towns there'll usually be one who speaks good English. Pharmacies are usually closed evenings and Saturday mornings, but are supposed to have a sign on their door referring you to the nearest one open.

Homeopathic and herbal remedies are quite widely available, with homeopathic pharmacies in many of the larger towns. There is a large homeopathic centre in Athens at Nikosthénous 8, Platía Plastíra, Pangráti (☎70 98 199); the Centre of Homeopathic Medicine is at Perikleous 1, Maroussi (☎80 52 671). Others are delineated by the characteristic green cross sign.

If you regularly use any form of **prescription drug** you should bring along a copy of the prescription together with the generic name of the drug – this will help should you need to replace it and also avoid possible problems with customs officials. In this context, it's worth being aware that codeine is banned in Greece. If you import any, even the common American Empirin-Codeine compound, you just might find yourself in serious trouble, so check labels carefully.

Contraceptive pills are more readily available every year, but don't count on local availability – unfortunately abortion is still the principal form of birth control. **Condoms**, however, are inexpensive and ubiquitous – just ask for *profilaktiká* (or more slangy, *plastiká*) at any pharmacy or corner *períptero* (kiosk); the pill, too, can be obtained from a *farmakío*.

Lastly, **hay fever** sufferers should be prepared for the early Greek pollen season, at its height from April to June. If you are taken by surprise, pharmacists stock tablets and creams.

DOCTORS AND HOSPITALS

For serious **medical attention** phone ☎166 – you'll find English-speaking doctors in any of the bigger towns or resorts; the tourist police (☎171 in Athens) or your consulate should be able to come up with some names if you have any difficulty.

In **emergencies**, treatment is given free in **state hospitals** – for cuts, broken bones, etc – though you will only get the most basic level of nursing care. Greek families routinely take in food and bedding for relatives, so as a tourist you'll be at a severe disadvantage. Somewhat better are the ordinary state-run **outpatient clinics** (*yatría*) attached to most public hospitals and also found in rural locales; these operate on a first-come, first-served basis; usual hours are 8am to noon.

Don't forget to obtain receipts for the cost of all drugs and medical treatment; without them, you won't be able to claim back the money on your travel insurance.

INFORMATION AND MAPS

The National Tourist Organisation of Greece (*Ellinikós Organismós Tourismoú*, or *EOT; GNTO* abroad) publishes an impressive array of free, glossy, regional pamphlets, which are good for getting an idea of where you want to go, even if the actual text should be taken with an occasional grain of salt. Also available from the EOT are a reasonable fold-out map of Greece, a large number of brochures on special interests and festivals, and ferry timetables.

The EOT maintains **offices abroad** in most European capitals, plus major cities in Australia and North America (see box below for details).

TOURIST OFFICES

In Greece, you will find **EOT offices** in most of the larger towns and resorts. The principal Athens office is on Platía Síndagma, inside the National Bank of Greece. Here, in addition to the usual leaflets, you can pick up weekly **schedules for the inter-island ferries** – not 100 percent reliable, but useful as a guideline. The EOT staff are themselves very helpful for advice on **ferry**, **bus**, **and train departures**, and often give assistance with **accommodation**.

Where there is no EOT office, you can get information (and often a range of leaflets) from municipally run **tourist offices** or from the **Tourist Police**. The latter are basically a branch (often just a single delegate) of the local police. They can sometimes provide you with lists of rooms to let, which they regulate, and they are in general helpful and efficient.

MAPS

Maps are an endless source of confusion in Greece. Each cartographic company seems to have its own peculiar system of transcribing Greek letters into English – and these, as often as not, do not match the transliterations on the road signs.

The most reliable **road maps** of Greece are the two *Geo Center* maps "Greece and the Islands" and "Greek Islands/Aegean Sea", which together cover the country at a scale of 1:300,000. The single fold-up *Freytag-Berndt* 1:650,000 is a good alternative. The *Michelin #980* runs a poor third. All these are widely available in Britain and North America, though less easily in Greece; see the list of map outlets below. *Freytag-Berndt* also publishes a series of more detailed maps on various regions of Greece, such as the Peloponnese and the Cyclades; these are best bought overseas, from specialist outlets.

Maps of **individual islands** are more easily available on the spot, and while some are wildly inaccurate or obsolete, with strange hieroglyphic symbology, others are reliable and up-to-date. The most comprehensive, though not always the most accurate series, covering most islands of any size and available overseas, is published by *Toubi*.

The most useful map of **Athens**, easy to use and with a decent index, is the *Falkplan* – available from most specialist outlets. If you can read Greek, and plan to stay in the city some time, the *Athina-Pireas Proastia Alpha-Omega* street atlas, published by Kapranidhis and Fotis, is invaluable. It has a complete index, down to the tiniest alley – of which there are many.

HIKING/TOPOGRAPHICAL MAPS

Hiking/topographical maps, subject to uneven quality and availability, are gradually improving.

The Greek mountaineering magazine **Korfes** publishes 1:50,000 maps of select alpine areas, with Roman-alphabet lettering appearing in the last few years. More than sixty are in print and a new one is issued every other month as a centrefold in the magazine. To get back issues you may

---

MAP OUTLETS

UK

London
National Map Centre, 22–24 Caxton St, SW1 (☎0171/222 4945);

Stanfords, 12–14 Long Acre, WC2 (☎0171/836 1321);

The Travellers Bookshop, 25 Cecil Court, WC2 (☎0171/836 9132).

Edinburgh
Thomas Nelson and Sons Ltd, 51 York Place, EH1 3JD (☎0131/557 3011).

Glasgow
John Smith and Sons, 57–61 St Vincent St (☎0141/221 7472).

Maps by **mail or phone order** are available from *Stanfords* (☎0171/836 1321).

USA
Chicago
Rand McNally, 444 N Michigan Ave, IL 60611; ☎312/321-1751.

New York
British Travel Bookshop, 551 5th Ave, NY 10176; ☎1-800/448-3039 or ☎212/490-6688.

The Complete Traveler Bookstore, 199 Madison Ave, NY 10016; ☎212/685-9007.

Rand McNally, 150 E 52nd St, NY 10022; ☎212/758-7488.

Traveler's Bookstore, 22 W 52nd St, NY 10019; ☎212/664-0995.

San Francisco
The Complete Traveler Bookstore, 3207 Fillmore St, CA 92123; ☎415/923-1511.

Rand McNally, 595 Market St, CA 94105; ☎415/777-3131.

Santa Barbara
Pacific Traveler Supply, 25 E Mason St, 93101; ☎805/963-4438 (phone orders: ☎805/965-4402.

Seattle
Elliot Bay Book Company, 101 S Main St, WA 98104; ☎206/624-6600.

Washington DC
Rand McNally, 1201 Connecticut Ave NW, Washington DC 20036; ☎202/223-6751.

Note: *Rand McNally* now has more than 20 stores across the US; call ☎1-800/333-0136 (ext 2111) for the address of your nearest store, or for **direct mail** maps.

Canada
Montréal
Ulysses Travel Bookshop, 4176 St-Denis; ☎514/289-0993.

Toronto
Open Air Books and Maps, 25 Toronto St, M5R 2C1; ☎416/363-0719.

Vancouver
World Wide Books and Maps, 736A Granville St V6Z 1G3; ☎604/687-3320.

need to visit the magazine's office at Platía Kentrikí 16, Aharnés, Athens (☎24 61 528), although the more central bookstore *Iy Folia tou Vivliou* (see "Markets and Stores" in the Athens chapter) also has an extensive back catalogue.

The *Korfes* maps are, unfortunately, unreliable in the matter of trails and new roads, but extremely accurate for natural features and village position, based as they are on the older maps of the **Army Geographical Service** (*Yeografikí Ipiresía Stratoú*). If you want to obtain these for islands, and mainland areas not covered by *Korfes*, visit the *YIS* at Evelpídhon 4, north of Aréos Park in Athens, on Monday, Wednesday or Friday from 8am to noon only. All foreigners must leave their passport with the gate guard; EC citizens may proceed directly to the sales hall,

where efficient, computerized transactions take just a few minutes. Other nationals will probably have to go upstairs for an interview; if you don't speak reasonably good Greek, it's best to have a Greek friend get them for you.

As of writing, maps covering Crete, the Dodecanese, the east Aegean, Skíros, most of Corfu and much of Epirus, Macedonia and Thrace are still off-limits to all foreigners, as well as Greeks. With matters worsening across the Balkans, previous plans to lift such restrictions have been shelved indefinitely.

Recently, a German company, **Harms**, has released a series of five maps at 1:80,000 scale which cover Crete from west to east and show many hiking routes – invaluable until and unless the *YIS* declassifies this area.

GETTING AROUND

The **standard means of land transport in Greece is the bus. Train networks are usually slow and limited, though service on the northern mainland lines is improving. Buses, however, cover just about every route on the mainland – albeit infrequently on minor roads – and provide basic connections on the islands. The best way to supplement buses is to rent a moped, motorbike or car, especially on the islands, where at any substantial town or resort you can find a rental outlet.**

Inter-island travel of course means taking **ferries**. These again are extensive, and given time will get you to any of the 166 inhabited isles. Planes are expensive, at up to four times the cost of a deck-class ferry ticket and twice as much as first or cabin class, but useful for saving time at the start or finish of a visit.

BUSES

Bus services on the **major routes** – both on the mainland and islands – are highly efficient. On **secondary roads** they're less regular, with long halts, but even the most remote villages will be connected – at least on weekdays – by a school or market bus to the provincial capital. As these often leave shortly after dawn, an alarm clock can be a useful travel aid. On the **islands**, there are usually buses to connect the port and main town for ferry arrivals or departures.

The network is privately run by a syndicate of companies known as **KTEL**. However, even in medium-sized towns there can be several scattered terminals for services in different directions, so make sure you have the right station for your departure. Some **sample one-way fares** from Athens are: Thessaloníki (6300dr), Pátra (2750dr) and Delphi (2250dr).

Buses are amazingly **prompt** as a rule, so be there in plenty of time for scheduled departures. For the major, inter-city lines such as Athens–Pátra, ticketing is now computerized, with assigned seating. Buses often get fully booked. On smaller rural/island routes, it's generally first-come, first-served with some standing allowed, and tickets dispensed on the spot by a peripatetic *ispráktoros* or conductor. On some shorter routes, a day return ticket can be purchased, which is slightly cheaper than two one-way fares.

A few long-distance and international routes are also served by express buses operated by **OSE**, the State Railway Organization. These always leave from the train station and can be useful supplements to regular services.

TRAINS

The Greek railway network, run by **OSE**, is limited to the mainland, and with few exceptions trains are invariably slower than the equivalent buses. However, they're also much cheaper – nearly fifty percent less on non-express services, even more if you buy a return ticket – and some of the lines are enjoyable in themselves. The best, a real treat of a ride, is the rack-and-pinion line between **Diakoftó and Kalávrita** in the Peloponnese (see p.237).

Timetables are sporadically available during May or June, printed in Greek only; the best place to obtain one are the *OSE* offices in Athens at Sína 6, or in Thessaloníki at Aristotelous 18, or the main train stations in these cities. Always check the station placards, since with the once-yearly printing changes often crop up in the interim. Trains tend to leave promptly at the outset, though on the more circuitous lines they're invariably late by the end of the journey.

If you're starting a journey at the initial station of a run you can (at no extra cost) **reserve** a seat; a carriage and seat number will be written on the back of your ticket. At most intermediate points, it's first-come, first-served.

There are two basic **classes**: first and second. First class may be worth the extra

GREECE: TRAINS

0   100km

money, insomuch as the cars may be emptier and seats more comfortable. Of late a super-express category, the *Intercity*, has been inaugurated on certain routes between Alexandhroúpoli, Thessaloníki, Athens and Vólos – these are very sleek, with stiff supplements charged depending on distance travelled, and much faster than the bus if the timetable is to be trusted. There is also one nightly **sleeper** in each direction between Athens and Thessaloníki, again with fairly hefty surcharges. Note that any kind of ticket issued on the train carries a 50 percent surcharge.

InterRail and Eurail Pass holders (see appropriate "Getting There" sections above) can use their pass in Greece but must secure reservations like everyone else, and have to pay express supplements on a few lines. *InterRail* passes and *Eurotrain* tickets are available in Greece through the *International Student and Youth Travel Service* (*ISYTS*), Nikis 11, 2nd floor, Athens, or at *Wasteels*, Ksenofóndos 14, 6th floor, Athens.

You probably won't get sufficient value out of your *InterRail* or *Eurail* pass if you just intend to use it to travel in Greece. However, there are a couple of specific **passes** just for use in Greece, which might be worth considering. **UK citizens** can buy a *Greek Freedom Pass* (available from *British Rail International*; see "Getting There from the UK", p.7), which allows unlimited travel on the Greek network for 3 days (£44, under 26s £34), 5 days (£58/39) or 10 days (£87/58) within a one-month period. **North Americans** can buy the similar *Greek Railpass*, valid any 3 days in 15 ($80 1st class), 5 days in 15 ($130) or 10 days in one month ($223); it's available before you travel from one of the specialist agents listed on p.13.

FERRIES

Ferries are of use primarily for travel to, and between, islands, though you may also want to make use of the routes between Athens and Monemvassía in the Peloponnese. There are three different varieties of vessel: medium-sized to large **ordinary ferries** (which operate the main services), **hydrofoils** (run by the *Ceres* "*Flying Dolphins*" and *Dodecanese Hydrofoils*, among other companies), and local **kaíkia** (small boats which in season cover short island hops and excursions). Costs are very reasonable on the longer journeys, though proportionately more expensive for shorter, inter-island connections.

We've indicated most of the **ferry connections**, both on the maps (see p.396–397 for a general picture) and in the "Travel Details" at the end of each chapter. Don't take our listings as exhaustive or wholly reliable, however, as schedules are notoriously erratic, and be aware that we have given details essentially for summer departures. **Out-of-season** departure frequencies are severely reduced, with many islands connected only once or twice a week. However, in spring or autumn those ferries that do operate are often compelled by the transport ministry to call at extra islands, making possible some interesting connections.

The most reliable, up-to-date information is available from the local **port police** (*limenarhío*), which maintains offices at Pireás (☎01/42 26 000) and on virtually all fair-sized islands. They rarely speak much English, but keep complete schedules posted – and, meteorological report in hand, are the final arbiters of whether a ship will sail or not in stormy weather conditions. Another good resource is *The Thomas Cook Guide to Greek Island Hopping*, which features a comprehensive overview of past ferry patterns and what they're likely to be in the future.

REGULAR FERRIES

On most ferry routes, your only consideration will be getting a boat that leaves on the day, and for the island, that you want. However, when sailing from **Pireás**, the port of Athens, to the Cyclades or Dodecanese islands, you should have quite a range of choice and may want to bear in mind a few of the factors below.

Most importantly, bear in mind that **routes** taken and the speed of the boats vary enormously. A journey from Pireás to Thíra (Santoríni), for instance, can take anything from nine to fourteen hours. Before buying a ticket it's wise to establish how many stops there'll be before your island, and the estimated time of arrival. Many agents act only for one specific boat (they'll blithely tell you that theirs is the only available service), so you may have to ask around to uncover alternatives. Especially in high season, early arrival is critical in getting what may be a very limited stock of accommodation.

The boats themselves have improved somewhat recently, with a fair number consigned to the scrap heap or dumped overseas – just about the only ferries you might want to avoid if you have the choice are the odiferous *Ayios Rafael*, in the north Aegean, and the poorly maintained *Milena* to the Dodecanese. You will more often than not be surprised to encounter a former English

Channel or Scandinavian fjord ferry, rechristened and enjoying a new lease on life in the Aegean.

Regular ferry **tickets** are, in general, best bought on the day of departure, unless you need to reserve a cabin berth or space for a car. Buying tickets in advance will tie you down to a particular ferry at a particular time – and innumerable factors can make you regret that. Most obviously there's **bad weather**, which, particularly off-season, can play havoc with the schedules, causing some small boats to remain at anchor and others to alter their routes drastically. There are only three periods of the year – March 23–25, the week before and after Easter, and mid-August – when ferries need to be booked at least a couple of days in advance. Otherwise, you can always buy a ticket once on board with no penalty, despite what travel agents may tell you. Ticket prices for each route are currently set by the transport ministry and should not differ among ships or agencies.

The cheapest class of ticket, which you'll probably automatically be sold, is **deck class**, variously called *tríti* or *gámma*. This gives you the run of most boats except for the upper-class restaurant and bar. On the shorter, summer journeys the best place to be, in any case, is on deck – space best staked out as soon as you get on board. However, boats acquired recently seem, with their glaring overhead lights and moulded-plastic bucket seats, expressly designed to frustrate those attempting to sleep on deck. In such cases it's well worth the few thousand extra drachmas for a cabin bunk, especially if you can share with friends. Class consciousness has increased of late, so deck-class passengers will find themselves firmly locked out of second-class facilities at night to prevent them from crashing on the plush sofas. First-class cabin facilities usually cost scarcely less than a plane flight and are not terrific value – the only difference between first and second being the presence of a bathroom in the cabin. Most cabins, incidentally, are apt to be overheated, stuffy and windowless.

Motorbikes and **cars** get issued extra tickets, in the latter case up to four times the passenger fare. This obviously limits the number of islands you'll want to drag a car to – it's really only worth it for the larger ones like Crete, Rhodes, Híos, Lésvos, Sámos or Kefalloniá. Even with these, unless you're planning a stay of more than four days, you may find it cheaper to leave your car in Pireás and rent another on arrival.

Most ferries sell a limited range of **food** aboard, though it tends to be overpriced and mediocre in quality. Honourable exceptions are the decent, reasonable meals served on longer routes or overnight sailings. On the short hops in the Argo-Saronic, Cyclades and Sporades, it is well worth stocking up with your own provisions.

HYDROFOILS

Hydrofoils – more commonly known as "*Flying Dolphins*" – are roughly twice as fast (and at least twice as expensive) as ordinary ferries. They are a useful alternative to regular ferries if you are pushed for time; their network seems to be growing each year, so it's worth asking after services, even if they are not mentioned in this guide. Their drawback is that, owing to their design, they are extremely sensitive to bad weather. Most of the services don't operate – or are heavily reduced – out of season and are prone to arbitrary cancellation if not enough passengers turn up.

At present, hydrofoils operate among the **Argo-Saronic islands** close to Athens, down the **east coast of the Peloponnese** to Monemvassía and Kíthira, among the **northern Sporades** (Skiáthos, Skópelos and Alónissos), among certain of the **Cyclades** (Ándros, Tínos, Míkonos, Páros, Náxos, Amorgós, the minor islets, Íos, Thíra – and Crete), and in the **Dodecanese** among Rhodes, Kós and Pátmos, with occasional forays in the Ionian islands and up to Sámos or over to Tílos and Níssiros. The principal **mainland ports** are Zea and Flisvos marinas in Pireás and Paleó Fáliro respectively, Rafína, Vólos, Áyios Konstandínos and Thessaloníki.

Schedules and tickets for the *Ceres* company, which operates most of the "*Flying Dolphin*" lines, are available in Athens from the office, off Platía Síndagma (☎01/32 20 351), and in Pireás from *Ceres Hydrofoils*, Aktí Miaoúli 69 (☎01/42 80 001); in Vólos from *Tsoulos*, Andonopoúlou 9–11 (☎0421/39 786); and in Thessaloníki from *Strataki*, Iónis Dhragoúmi 1, (☎031/547 047). *Ilios* has offices in Pireás (☎01/42 24 772), while the head office of *Dodecanese Hydrofoils* is at Platía Kíprou 6, Ródhos (☎0241/24 000).

KAÍKIA AND OTHER SMALL FERRIES

In season *kaíkia* (caiques) and small ferries of a couple of hundred tonnes' displacement sail between adjacent islands and to a few of the more obscure ones. These can be extremely useful and often very pleasant, but are no cheaper than mainline services; indeed if they are technically tourist agency charters, and not passenger lines controlled by the transport ministry, they tend to be quite expensive, with some pressure to buy return fares.

We have tried to detail the more regular links in the text, though many, inevitably, depend on the whims of local boat-owners or fishermen. The only firm information is to be had on the quayside.

Kaíkia and small ferries, despite appearances, have a good safety record; indeed it's the larger, overloaded car-ferries that have in the past run into trouble.

MOTORBIKES, MOPEDS AND BIKES

Motorcycles, scooters, mopeds and **bicycles** are available for rent on many of the islands and in a few of the popular mainland resorts. Motorcycles and scooters cost around £10/US$15 a day up; mopeds from £6–7/$9–10.5; push-bikes as little as £3/$4.50. All rates can be reduced with bargaining outside of peak season, or if you negotiate for a longer period of rental. To rent motorcycles (usually 125cc) you will need to show a driving licence; otherwise all you need is a passport to leave as security.

MOPEDS – AND SAFETY

Mopeds are perfect for all but the hilliest islands, and you can obtain them almost everywhere. Make sure you check them thoroughly before riding off since many are only cosmetically maintained and repaired. Bad brakes and fouled spark plugs are the most common defects. If you break down it's your responsibility to return the machine, so it's worth taking down the phone number of whomever rents it to you in case it gives out in the middle of nowhere.

A warning should also be given about **mopeds and safety**. There are a stream of accidents each year involving tourists coming to grief on rutted dirt tracks or astride a mechanically dodgy machine. Very few people wear crash helmets – or much else for that matter – so it's best to take it very easy. In many cases accidents are due to attempts to cut corners, in all senses, by riding two to an underpowered scooter simply not designed to propel such a load. You won't regret getting two separate mopeds, or one powerful 125cc bike to share. Keep in mind, too,

that you're likely to be charged an exorbitant price for any repairs if you have an accident. Above all, make sure your travel insurance policy covers motorcycle accidents.

As far as **models** go, the *Honda 50* and *Suzuki 50* are the standard, easily carrying two people; the disadvantages include the small payload space and the need to learn gear-shifting (an easy pedal action). The so-called *Cub* series, either 75cc or 90cc, give extra power at nominal extra cost. A large *Vespa* scooter is more comfortable on long trips, with capacious baskets but has less stability, especially off paved surfaces. Smaller but surprisingly powerful *Piaggio Si* or *Monte Carlo* models can take one person almost everywhere, accept two baskets or bags and are automatic action.

If you intend to stay for some time in the warmer months, it's well worth considering the **purchase** of a moped or motorbike once in Greece. They are relatively inexpensive to run or repair, do not cause passport problems, can be taken on the ferries very cheaply, and can be resold easily upon departure.

CYCLING

Few people seem to **cycle** in Greece but it's not always such hard going as you might imagine. If you have a bicycle – especially a mountain bike, which is ideal for Greek terrain – you might consider taking it along by train or plane (it's free if within your twenty-kilo allowance).

Within Greece you should be able to take a bike for free on most of the **ferries**, in the guard's van on most **trains** (for a small fee – it goes on a later goods train otherwise), and with a little persuasion on the roof of **buses**. Any spare parts you might need, however, are best brought along, since the only specialist bike shops are in Athens and Thessaloníki.

Alternatively, you can **rent mountain bikes** as well as old bone-shakers on many of the larger islands.

DRIVING: CAR RENTAL

Cars have obvious advantages for getting to the more inaccessible parts of mainland Greece, but this is one of the more expensive countries in Europe to **rent a car**. If you drive **your own vehicle** to and through Greece, you'll need international third party insurance, the so-called **Green Card**, as well as an International Driving

Licence and the registration documents. Upon arrival your passport will get a **carnet stamp**; this normally allows you to keep a vehicle in Greece for up to six months, exempt from road tax. It is difficult, though not impossible, to leave the country without the vehicle; the nearest customs post will seal it for you – while you fly back home for a family emergency, for example – but you must find a Greek national to act as your guarantor. This person will assume ownership of the car should you ultimately abandon it.

CAR RENTAL

Car rental in Greece starts at £200–230/US$300–345 a week in high season for the smallest model, including unlimited mileage, tax and insurance. Outside peak season, at the smaller local outfits, you can sometimes get terms of about £27/$40 per day, all inclusive, but three days is the preferred minimum duration.

You may get a better price from one of the **foreign companies** that deal with local firms than if you negotiate for rental in Greece itself. One of the most competitive, which can arrange for cars to be picked up at most airports is *Holiday Autos* (see box for phone number). Most travel agents can also offer car rental in Greece, though their rates are generally higher than the specialist rental agents. **In Greece**, *Payless, Kenning, Thrifty, Ansa* and *Just* are reliable medium-sized companies with branches in many

---

CAR RENTAL AGENCIES

Britain

Avis (☎0181/848 8733).

Budget (☎0800/181 181).

Europcar/InterRent (☎01345/222 525)

Hertz (☎0181/679 1799).

Holiday Autos (☎0171/491 1111).

North America

Auto Europe (☎1-800/223-5555).

Avis ☎1-800/331-1084).

Budget (☎1-800/527-0700).

Dollar (☎1-800/421-6868).

Europe by Car (☎1-800/223-1516).

Hertz ☎1-800/654-3001; in Canada ☎1-800/263-0600).

Holiday Autos (☎1-800/422-7737).

Thrifty (☎1-800/367-2277).

---

towns; all are considerably cheaper than (and just as reputable) as the biggest international operators *Budget, Europcar, Hertz* and *Avis*. Specific local recommendations are given in the guide.

All agencies will want either a credit card or a large cash **deposit** up front; minimum age requirements vary from 21 to 25. In theory an **International Driving Licence** is also needed but in practice European, Australasian and North American ones are honoured.

Note that initial rental prices quoted in Greece almost never include tax, collision damage waiver fees and personal insurance. These are absolutely vital; the coverage included by law in the basic rental fee is generally inadequate, so check the fine print on your contract. Be careful of the hammering that cars get on minor roads; tyres and the underside of the vehicle are often excluded from insurance policies.

DRIVING IN GREECE

Greece has the highest **accident rate** in Europe after Portugal, and many of the roads can be quite perilous – asphalt can turn into a dirt track without warning on the smaller routes, and railway crossings are rarely guarded. Uphill drivers insist on their right of way, as do those first to approach a one-lane bridge – headlights flashed at you mean the opposite of what they mean in the UK or North America and signify that the driver is coming through. Wearing a **seatbelt** is compulsory and children under 10 are not allowed to sit in the front seats. If you are involved in any kind of accident it's illegal to drive away, and you can be held at a police station for up to 24 hours. If this happens, ring your consulate immediately, in order to get a lawyer (you have this right). Don't make a statement to anyone who doesn't speak, and write, very good English.

There are a limited number of **express highways** between Pátra, Athens, Vólos and Thessaloníki, on which tolls are levied – currently between 400dr and 700dr at each sporadically placed gate. They're nearly twice as quick as the old roads, and well worth using.

Tourists with proof of AA/RAC or similar membership are given free **road assistance** from *ELPA*, the Greek equivalent, which runs breakdown services based in Athens, Pátra, Lárissa, Vólos, Ioánnina, Corfu, Trípoli, Crete and Thessaloníki. The information number is ☎174. In an **emergency** ring their road assistance service on ☎104, anywhere in the country. Many car rental companies have an agreement with *ELPA's* competitors, *Hellas Service* and *Express Service*, but they're prohibitively expensive to summon on your own – over 25,000 drachmas to enrol you as an "instant member" in their scheme.

RUNNING A VEHICLE

Petrol/gasoline currently costs around 200dr a litre for unleaded (*amólivdhi*) or super. It is easy to run out of fuel after dark or on weekends in both rural and urban Greece. Most stations close at 7pm sharp, and nearly as many are shut all weekend. There will always be at least one pump per district open at the weekend, but it's not always apparent which station will be open. This is not so much of a problem on the major highways, but it's a factor everywhere else. So always fill, or insist on full rental vehicles at the outset, and if you've brought your own car, keep a jerrycan full at all times. Filling stations run by international companies (*BP, Mobil* and *Shell*) usually take credit cards; Greek chains like *EKO* and *Elinoil* don't.

In terms of **maintenance**, the easiest models to have serviced and buy parts for in Greece are VWs, Mercedes, Ladas, Skodas and virtually all French, Italian and Japanese makes. British models are a bit more difficult, but you should be fine as long as you haven't brought anything too esoteric.

In general, both **mechanics' workshops** and **parts retailers** are clustered at the approach and exit roads of all major towns, usually prominently signposted. For the commonest makes, emergency spares like fan belts and cables are often found at surprisingly remote service stations, so don't hesitate to ask at an unlikely looking spot. Rural mechanics are okay for quick patch-up jobs like snapped clutch cables, but for major powertrain problems it's best to limp into the nearest sizeable town for a mechanic factory-trained for your make.

HITCHING

Hitching carries the usual risks and dangers, and is obviously inadvisable for women travelling alone, but overall Greece is one of the safer countries in which to do it. It's fairly reliable, too, as a means of getting around, so long as you're not overly concerned about time; lifts are fairly frequent but tend to be short.

It's easier on islands and in rural areas than trying to hitch out of big cities, whose suburbs tend to sprawl for miles. At its best, hitching is a wonderful method of getting to know the country – there's no finer way to take in the Peloponnese than from the back of a truck that looks like it has been converted from a lawnmower – and a useful means of picking up some Greek. While you'll often get lifts from Greeks eager to display or practise their English, there will be as many where to communicate you're forced to try the language. As it can be all too easy to stay in Greece without picking up more than restaurant vocabulary, this is one way of breaking out.

TAXIS

Greek **taxis**, especially Athenian ones, are among the cheapest in western Europe and well worth making use of (though see the caveats on fares in the *Athens* chapter).

Within **city or town limits**, use of the meter is mandatory if one is present, and the flag falls at 200dr throughout the country. Double tariff applies between midnight and 5am, and outside city or town limits at any time of the day. There are also surcharges for entering a ferry harbour (currently 100dr), an airport (200dr), and per large bag (100dr), as well as the hefty Christmas and Easter bonuses. All of these may legitimately hike the fare up by as much as a third more than shown on the display.

In **rural areas**, taxis occasionally have no meters – you bargain and fix a price. A reasonable per-vehicle (*not* per-person) charge for a ten-kilometre trip will be the equivalent of about £5/US$7.50.

A special warning needs to be sounded about **unlicensed (ie pirate) taxi-drivers** who congregate outside major trains stations, particularly Athens and Lárissa. These shady characters may offer to shuttle you several hundred kilometres for the same price as the train/*KTEL* bus, or less; upon arrival you will discover that the fare quoted is per person, not per vehicle, and that along the way stops are made to cram several more passengers in – who again do not share your fare. Moreover, the condition of the vehicles usually leaves a lot to be desired. Beware.

DOMESTIC FLIGHTS

Olympic Airways and its subsidiary *Olympic Aviation* operate most **domestic flights** within Greece. They cover a fairly wide network of islands and larger towns, though most routes are to and from Athens, or the northern capital of Thessaloníki. **Schedules** can be picked up at *Olympic* offices abroad (see "Getting There" sections) or through their branch offices or representatives in Greece, which are maintained in almost every town or island of any size.

Fares usually work out around three to four times the cost of an equivalent bus or ferry journey, but on certain inter-island hauls poorly served by boat (Rhodes–Kastellórizo or Kefalloniá-Zákinthos, for example), you might consider this time well bought. For obscure reasons, flights between Athens and Mílos, Kíthira or Kalamáta are slightly better value per kilometre, so take advantage.

In addition, de-regulation of airline operations means that there are some **private companies** running internal flights from Athens to major destinations like Corfu and Crete. These generally undercut the equivalent *Olympic Airlines* flights

by quite a margin and since routes are opening up all the time, it's always worth checking on alternatives to *Olympic* with a travel agent.

Island flights are often full in peak season; if they're part of your plans, **reserve** at least a week in advance. Domestic air tickets are **non-refundable** but you can change your flight details, space permitting, as late as a day before your original intended departure without penalty.

Like ferries, **flights can be cancelled** in bad weather, since many services are on small, 20- to 50-seat turbo-prop planes that won't fly in strong winds.

Size restrictions also mean that the 15-kilo baggage **weight limit** is fairly strictly enforced; if, however, you've just arrived from overseas, or purchased your ticket outside Greèce, you are allowed the 20-kilo standard international limit. All services operated on the domestic network are **non-smoking**.

ACCOMMODATION

There are huge numbers of beds for tourists in Greece, and most of the year you can rely on turning up pretty much anywhere and finding a room – if not in a hotel, then in a private house or block of rooms (the standard island accommodation). Only in July and August, the country's high season, are you likely to experience problems. At these times, it is worth striking off the standard tourist routes, turning up at each new place early in the day, and taking whatever is available in the hope that you will be able to exchange it for something better later on.

HOTELS AND ROOMS

Hotels are categorized by the tourist police from "Luxury" down to "E-class", and all except the top category have to keep within set price limits. D- and E-class hotels are usually quite reasonable, costing around £10–15/US$15–22.50 for a double room, £7–10/$11–15 for a single. The better-value places tend to be in the less touristed areas, as ratings depend partly on location; in Athens, inevitably, you get least for your money.

If you want an inexpensive roof over your head while travelling about the mainland towns, you're generally going to have to depend on these small hotels, specific recommendations for which appear throughout the guide. In resorts, however, and throughout the islands, you can supplement them with privately let **rooms** (*dhomátia*). These are again officially controlled and are divided into three classes (A down to C). They are usually better value than hotels, and are in general spotlessly clean. These days the bulk of them are in new, purpose-built low-rise buildings, but a few are still in people's homes, where you'll occasionally be treated to disarming hospitality.

At its simplest, *dhomátia* implies a bare, concrete room, with a hook on the back of the

ROOM PRICES

All establishments listed in this book have been **price-graded** according to the scale outlined below. The rates quoted represent the **cheapest available room** in high season; all are prices for a double room, except for category ①, which are per person rates. Out of season, rates can drop by up to fifty percent, especially if you negotiate rates for a stay of three or more nights. Single rooms, where available, cost around seventy percent of the price of a double.

Rented private **rooms on the islands** usually fall into the ② or ③ categories, depending on their location and facilities, and the season; a few in the ④ category are more like plush self-catering apartments. They are not generally available from late October through to the beginning of April, when only hotels tend to remain open.

You should expect rooms in all ① and most ② range accommodation to be without private bath,

though there may a basic washbasin in the room. In the ③ category and above there are usually private facilities.

Some of the cheap places will also have more expensive rooms including en suite facilities – and vice versa, especially in the case of singles tucked in less desirable corners of the building.

Prices for rooms and hotels should by law be **displayed** on the back of the door of your room. If you feel you're being overcharged at a place which is officially registered, threatening to report it to the tourist office or police – who will generally adopt your side in such cases – should be enough to elicit compliance. Small amounts over the posted price may be legitimately explained by tax or out-of-date forms. And occasionally you may find that you have bargained so well, or arrived so far out of season, that you are actually paying less than you're supposed to.

① 1400–2000dr (£4–5.50/US$6–8.50)
② 4000–6000dr (£11–16.50/US$17–25)
③ 6000–8000dr (£16.50–22/US$25–33)

④ 8000–12000dr (£22–33/US$33–50)
⑤ 12000–16000dr (£33–44/US$50–66)
⑥ 16000dr (£44/US$66) and upwards

door and toilet facilities (cold water only) outside in the courtyard; at its fanciest it could be a modern, fully furnished place with an attached, marble-dressed bathroom. Between these two extremes you may find that there's a well-equipped kitchen on the property and a choice of rooms at various prices (they'll usually show you the most expensive first). Price and quality are not necessarily directly linked: always ask to see the room before agreeing to take it and settling on the price.

Areas to look for rooms, and some suggestions for the best, are again included in the guide. But as often as not, the rooms find you: owners descend on ferry or bus arrivals to fill any space they have, sometimes waving photos of the premises. In smaller places you'll often see rooms advertised – sometimes in German (*zimmer*); the Greek signs to look out for are *enikiazómena dhomátia* or *enikiázonteh dhomátia*, or you can just ask at the local taverna or *kafenío* (café).

Even if there are no official places around, there is very often someone prepared to earn extra money by putting you up. In island resorts, where package holidaymakers predominate, short stays of one or two nights are often unpopular with *dhomátia* owners.

If you are stranded, or arrive very late, in a **remote mountain village** with no tourist facilities whatsoever, you may very well find that you are invited to spend the night in someone's home. This should not be counted on, but things work out more often than not. The most polite course is to have a meal or drink at the taverna/ *kafenío* and then, especially if it is summer, enquire as to the possibility of sleeping either in the vacant schoolhouse or in a spare room at the *kinotikó grafío* (community records office).

In **winter**, designated to begin in November and end in early April, private rooms are closed pretty much across the board to keep the hotels in business. There's no point in traipsing about hoping to find exceptions – most rooms owners obey the system very strictly. If they don't, the owners will find you themselves and, watching out for hotel rivals, guide you back to their place.

It has become standard practice for rooms proprietors to ask to **keep your passport** – ostensibly "for the tourist police", but in reality to prevent you skipping out with an unpaid bill. Some owners may be satisfied with just taking down the details, as in hotels, and they'll almost always return the documents once you get to know them, or if you need them for another purpose (to change money, for example).

LONG-TERM RENTALS

Houses or apartments – and, out of season, **villas** – are often rented by the week or month. If you have two or three people to share costs, and want to drop roots on an island or a mainland coastal resort for a while, it's an option well worth considering. To arrange a rental, find a place you want to stay, get yourself known around the village, and ask around, particularly at the central *kafenía*; you can occasionally pick up reasonable deals in less visited spots.

If you want to rent a villa in season, see the "Getting There" sections for details of **package holiday operators** who arrange them.

YOUTH HOSTELS

Greece is not exactly packed with **youth hostels** (*ksenón neótitos*) but those that there are tend to be fairly easy-going affairs: slightly run-down and a far cry from the institutions you find in northern Europe. Competition from unofficial "student hostels" (see below) and low-budget rooms means that they are not as cost-effective as in other European countries. It's best to have a valid *IYHF* card (see box below for national organizations), but you can usually buy one on the spot, or maybe just pay a little extra for your bed. Charges for a dormitory bed are around £4–6/US$6–9 a night; most hostels have a curfew at 11pm or midnight and many places only open in spring and summer.

Hostels on the **mainland** include: Athens (1), Náfplio, Mycenae, Olympia, Pátra, Delphi, Litóhoro (Mount Olympus) and Thessaloníki. On the **islands** you'll find them only on Corfu (1), Thíra (2), and Crete (4). Not all of these are officially recognized by the IYHF. For more information, contact the **Greek national youth hostel organization** whose head office is at 4 Dragatsaniou, Athens (☎01/32 34 107).

A number of alternatives to official youth hostels exist, particularly in Athens. These inexpensive dormitory-style **"student hostels"** are open to anyone but can be rather insalubrious. Some offer **roofspace**, providing a mattress and a pleasantly cool night under the stars.

MONASTERIES

Greek **monasteries and convents** have a tradition of putting up travellers (of the appropriate sex). On the mainland, this is still a customary, if steadily decreasing, practice; on the islands, much less so. Wherever, you should always ask locally before heading out to one for the night. Also, dress modestly – shorts on either sex, and short skirts on women, are total anathema – and try to arrive early evening, not later than 8pm or sunset (whichever is earlier).

For **men**, the most exciting monastic experience is a visit to the "Monks' Republic" of **Mount Áthos**, on the Halkidhikí peninsula, near Thessaloníki. This is a far from casual travel option, involving a fair amount of advance planning and bureaucratic procedure to obtain a permit. If you are interested, see p.372 for details.

YOUTH HOSTEL ASSOCIATIONS

Australia *Australian Youth Hostels Association*, Level 3, 10 Mallett St, Camperdown, NSW (☎02/565-1325).

Canada *Hostelling International/Canadian Hostelling Association*, Room 400, 205 Catherine St, Ottawa, Ontario K2P 1C3 (☎613/237-7884 or ☎1-800/663-5777).

England and Wales *Youth Hostel Association* (*YHA*), Trevelyan House, 8 St Stephen's Hill, St Alban's, Herts AL1 (☎017278/45047). London shop and information office: 14 Southampton St, London WC2 (☎0171/836 1036).

Ireland *An Oige*, 39 Mountjoy Square, Dublin 1 (☎01/363111).

New Zealand *Youth Hostels Association of New Zealand*, PO Box 436, Christchurch 1 (☎03/799-970).

Northern Ireland *Youth Hostel Association of Northern Ireland*, 56 Bradbury Place, Belfast, BT7 (☎01232/324733).

Scotland *Scottish Youth Hostel Association*, 7 Glebe Crescent, Stirling, FK8 2JA (☎01786/51181).

USA *Hostelling International-American Youth Hostels* (*HI-AYH*), 733 15th St NW, Suite 840, PO Box 37613, Washington DC 20005 (☎202/783-6161).

CAMPING

Official campsites range from ramshackle compounds on the islands to highly organized (and rather soulless) *EOT* (Greek Tourist Organisation) – run complexes. Cheap, casual places cost from £2/US$3 a night per person, at the larger sites, though, it's not impossible for two of you and one tent (all separately charged) to add up almost to the price of a basic room. The *Greek Camping Association*, 102 Solonos, 10680 Athens (☎01/362 1560), publishes a guide covering most Greek campsites and the facilities they offer; it's available from EOT offices.

Generally, you don't have to worry about leaving tents or **baggage** unattended at campsites; the Greeks are one of the most honest races in Europe. The main risk, sadly, comes from other campers, and every year a few items disappear in that direction.

Freelance camping – outside authorized campsites – is such an established element of Greek travel that few people realize that it's officially illegal. Since 1977, however, it has indeed been forbidden by law, and increasingly the regulations are enforced.

If you do camp freelance, therefore, it is vital to exercise sensitivity and discretion. Obviously the police crack down on people camping rough (and littering) on or near popular tourist **beaches**, and they get especially concerned when a large community of campers is developing. Off the beaten track, however, and particularly in **rural inland areas**, nobody is very bothered. During high season, when everything – even campsites – is full, attitudes towards freelance camping is more relaxed, even in the most touristed places. Wherever you are, it is always best to ask permission locally – in the village taverna or café – before pitching a tent.

EATING AND DRINKING

Greeks spend a lot of time socializing outside their homes, and sharing a meal is one of the chief ways of doing it. They're not great drinkers, but what drinking they do is mainly done at the café. The atmosphere is always relaxed and informal, and pretensions (or expense-account prices) are rare outside of the more chi-chi parts of Athens or major resorts.

BREAKFAST, PICNIC FARE AND SNACKS

Greeks don't generally eat **breakfast** and the only egg-and-bacon kind of places are in resorts where foreigners congregate; they can be quite good value, especially in places with lots of competition. The alternatives are the sort of bread/jam/yoghurt compromises obtainable in some *zaharoplastia* or *galaktopolía*, or having a picnic breakfast with your own ingredients.

Picnic fare is good, cheap and easily available. Staple diet of any picnic is **bread** and the Greek version, available in different shapes and sizes, is very cheap. Try and get to the bakery (*foúrnos*) early when it's served warm from the oven – and try asking for *olikís* (wholemeal), *oktásporo* (eight-grain), or even *enneásporo* (nine-grain). When buying **olives**, go for the fat Kalamáta or Ámfissa ones; they're more expensive, but tastier and more nourishing. *Fétta* **cheese** is ubiquitous – often, ironically, imported from Holland or Denmark. It can be very dry and salty, so it's wise to ask for a piece to taste before buying. If you have access to a fridge, dunking it overnight in a plastic container with water will solve both problems. That sampling advice also goes for other cheeses, the most palatable of which are the expensive gruyère-type *graviéra*. *Kosséri* is another good option, and processed cheese and **cooked meats** are usually available, too.

Yoghurts are superlative (and good stomach settlers); honey is also wonderful, though rather costly. There's a good choice of **fruit** at reasonable prices, particularly watermelon, peaches and grapes; **salad vegetables** are cheaper and more readily available.

Useful expressions in the market are *éna tétarto* (250g) and *éna misó* (500g).

SNACKS

Traditional snacks can be one of the distinctive pleasures of Greek eating, though they are being increasingly edged out by an obsession with *tóst* (toasted sandwiches) and pizzas. However, small kebabs (*souvlákia*) are on sale at bus stations, ferry crossings and all over the place in towns.

The same goes for *tirópites* (cheese pies) and *spanokópita* (spinach pies), which can usually be found at the baker's, as can *kouloúria* (crispy baked pretzel rings sprinkled with sesame seeds) and *boutímata* (bagged biscuits heavy on the molasses, cinnamon and butter). Another city staple is *yíros* (doner kebab), in *píta* bread with garnish and often *tzatzíki*.

RESTAURANTS

Greek cuisine and **restaurants** are simple and straightforward. There's no snobbery about eating out; everyone does it some of the time, and for foreigners with strong currencies it's fairly inexpensive – around £6–8/US$9–12 for a substantial meal with a good quantity of house wine.

In choosing a restaurant, the best strategy is to go where the Greeks go. And they go late: 2pm to 3pm for **lunch**, 9pm to 11pm for **dinner**. You can eat earlier, but you're likely to get indifferent service if you frequent the purely touristic establishments. Chic appearance is not a good guide to quality; you'll mainly be paying for the linen napkins and stemmed wine glasses. Often the most basic are the best, so don't be put off by a restaurant that brings your order in a sheet of paper and plonks it directly on the table-top, as *psistariés* (see below) often do.

It's wise to keep a wary eye on the **waiters** in Athens or resort areas. They are inclined to push you into ordering more than you want and then bring things you haven't ordered. They often don't actually write anything down and may work your **bill** out by examining your empty plates. Itemized tabs, when present, may be in totally illegible Greek scribble, so the opportunities for slipping in a few extra drachmas here and there are pretty good, especially in establishments which disdain menus and published prices altogether. The **service charge** is always included, although a small tip (100–150 dr) is standard practice for the "boy" who lays the table, brings the bread and water, and so on.

If you have **children**, have no fears for them. Wherever you go they'll be welcome, and no one gives a damn if they chase the cats or play tag between the tables.

ESTIATÓRIA

There are two basic types of restaurant: the **estiatório** and the *taverna*. Distinctions between the two are slight, though the former is more commonly found in towns and it tends to have slightly more complicated dishes.

An *estiatório* will generally feature a variety of **oven-baked casserole dishes**: *moussakás*, *pastítsio*, stews like *kokinistó* and *stifádho*, *yemistá* (stuffed tomatoes or peppers), the oily vegetable casseroles called *ladherá*, and oven-baked meat and fish. Choosing these dishes is commonly done by going to the kitchen and pointing at the desired trays.

The cooking is done in the morning and then left to stand, which is why the food is often **lukewarm** or even cold. Greeks don't mind this (most actually believe that hot food is bad for you), and in fact in summertime it hardly seems to matter. Besides, dishes like *yemistá* are actually enhanced by being allowed to cool off and stand in their own juice. Similarly, you have to specify if you want your food with little or no **oil** (*horís ládhi*), but once again you will be considered a little strange since Greeks regard olive oil as essential to digestion (and indeed it is one of the least pernicious oils to ingest in large quantities).

Desserts of the pudding-and-pie variety don't exist, although fruit is always available in season and you may occasionally be able to get a yoghurt served at the end of a meal. Autumn treats worth asking after include *kidhóni* or *ahládhi sto foúrno*, baked quince or pear with some sort of syrup or nut topping.

TAVERNAS

Tavernas range from the glitzy and fashionable to rough-and-ready cabins with a bamboo awning set up by the beach. The primitive ones have a very limited menu, but the more established will offer some of the main *estiatório* dishes mentioned above as well as the standard **taverna fare**. This essentially means *mezédhes* (hors d'oeuvres) and *tis óras* (meat and fish fried or grilled to order).

Since the idea of courses is foreign to Greek cuisine, starters, main dishes and salads often arrive together. The best thing is to order a selection of *mezédhes* and salads to share among yourselves; that, after all, is what Greeks do. Waiters encourage you to take the *horiátiki* **salad** – the so-called Greek salad, with *fétta* cheese – because it is the most expensive one. If you only want tomato, or tomato and cucumber, ask for *domatosaláta* or *angourodomáta*. *Láhano* (cabbage) and *maroúli* (lettuce) are the typical winter and spring salads.

The most interesting **starters** are *tzatzíki* (yoghurt, garlic and cucumber dip), *melitzano-saláta* (aubergine/eggplant dip), *kolokithákia tiganitá* (courgette/zucchini fried in batter) or *melitzánes tiganités* (aubergine/eggplant fried in batter), *yígandes* (white haricot beans in vinaigrette or hot tomato sauce), *tiropitákia* or *spanakópittes* (small cheese and spinach pies), *saganáki* (fried cheese), *okhtapódhi* (octopus) and *mavromatiká* (black-eyed peas).

Of **meats**, *souvláki* (shish kebab) and *brizóles* (chops) are reliable choices. In both cases, pork (*hirinó*) is usually better and cheaper than veal (*moskharísio*). The best *souvláki* is lamb (*arnísio*), but it is not often available. The small lamb cutlets called *païdhákia* are very tasty, as is roast lamb (*arní psitó*) and roast kid (*katsíki*) when obtainable. *Keftédhes* (meatballs), *biftékia* (a sort of hamburger) and the spicy sausages called *loukánika* are cheap and good. *Kotópoulo* (chicken) is also usually a safe bet.

Seaside tavernas of course also offer **fish**, though the choicer varieties, such as *barboúnia* (red mullet), *tsípoura* (gilt-head bream), *fangrí* (sea bream), are expensive. The price is quoted by the kilo, and the standard procedure is to go to the glass cooler and pick your own. The cheapest widely available fish are *gópes* (bogue) and *marídhes* (tiny whitebait, eaten complete with head).

Kalamarákia (fried baby squid) and *okhtapódhi* (octopus) are a summer staple of most seaside tavernas, and occasionally, exotic **shellfish** such as *mídhia* (mussels), *kidhónia* (cherrystone clams) and *garídhes* (small prawns) will be on offer for reasonable amounts. Keep an eye out, however, to freshness and season – mussels in particular are a common cause of stomach upsets or even mild poisoning. Speaking of **seasons**, summer visitors get a relatively poor choice of fish: net trawling is prohibited from mid-May to mid-October, when only lamp-lure and multi-hook line methods are allowed. During these warmer months, such fish as are caught tend to be smaller and dry-tasting, thus requiring the butter sauce often served with fish.

As in *estiatória*, **desserts** in traditional tavernas are more or less nonexistent. Watermelons, melons and grapes are the standard summer fruit. However, desserts are increasingly common on menus in more touristed areas; by the same token, tavernas frequented by foreigners are also more inclined to serve **coffee** these days.

SPECIALIST TAVERNAS

Some tavernas specialize. *Psarotavérnes*, for example, feature fish, and *psistariés* serve spit-roasted lamb and goat or *kokorétsi* (grilled offal).

A very few other tavernas concentrate on game (*kinígi*): rabbit, quail or turtle dove in the autumn, when the migrating flocks fly over Greece on their way south. In the mountains of the north where there are rivers, trout, pike and freshwater crayfish are to be found in the local eating places.

WINES

Both *estiatória* and tavernas will usually offer you a choice of **bottled wines**, and many have their own house variety, kept in barrels and served out in metal jugs.

Among the **bottled wines**, *Cambas*, *Boutari* the Rhodian *CAIR* products, and the Cretan *Logado* are good inexpensive whites, while *Boutari Nemea* is perhaps the best mid-range red. If you want something better, *Tsantali Agioritiko* is an excellent white or red; *Boutari* do a fine *Special Reserve* red; the Macedonian *Domaine Carras* does both excellent whites and reds; and, in addition, there are various small, premium wineries whose products are currently fashionable: for example, *Hatzimihali*, *Athanasiadhi* and *Lazaridhi*.

A FOOD AND DRINK GLOSSARY

Basics

Aláti	Salt	*Neró*	Water
Avgá	Eggs	*Olikís psomí*	Wholemeal bread
(Horís) ládhi	(Without) oil	*O logariasmós*	The bill
Hortofágos	Vegetarian	*Psári(a)*	Fish
Katálogo/lísta	Menu	*Psomí*	Bread
Kréas	Meat	*Sikalísio psomí*	Rye bread
Lahaniká	Vegetables	*Tirí*	Cheese
Méli	Honey	*Yiaoúrti*	Yoghurt

Cooking terms

Ahnistó	Steamed	*Sto foúrno*	Baked
Psitó	Roasted	*Tis óras*	Grilled/fried to order
Sti soúvla	Spit roasted	*Yahní*	Stewed in oil and tomato sauce

Soups and starters

Avgolémono	Egg and lemon soup	*Mavromatiká*	Black-eyed peas
Dolmádhes	Stuffed vine leaves	*Melitzanosaláta*	Aubergine/eggplant dip
Fasoládha	Bean soup	*Skordhaliá*	Garlic dip
Florínes	Canned red Macedonian peppers	*Soúpa*	Soup
		Taramosaláta	Cod roe paté
Kápari	Pickled caper leaves	*Tzatzíki*	Yoghurt and cucumber dip
Kopanistí, Ktipití	Spicy cheese purée		

Vegetables

Angináres	Artichokes	*Koukiá*	Broad fava beans
Angoúri	Cucumber	*Maroúli*	Lettuce
Bámies	Okra, ladies' fingers	*Melitzána*	Aubergine/eggplant
Bouréki	Courgette/zucchini, potato and cheese pie	*Papoutsákia*	Stuffed aubergine/eggplant
		Patátes	Potatoes
Briám	Ratatouille	*Piperiés*	Peppers
Domátes	Tomatoes	*Radhíkia*	Wild chicory
Fakés	Lentils	*Rízi/Piláfi*	Rice (usually with *sáltsa* – sauce)
Fasolákia	French beans		
Horiátiki (saláta)	Greek salad (with olives, fetta etc)	*Saláta*	Salad
		Spanáki	Spinach
Hórta	Greens (usually wild)	*Yemistá*	Stuffed vegetables
Kolokithákia	Courgette/zucchini	*Yígandes*	White haricot beans

Fish and seafood

Astakós	Lobster	*Kalamarákia*	Baby squid	*Platís*	Skate, ray
Atherína	Sardine-like fish	*Kalamária*	Squid	*Sardhélles*	Sardines
Barbóuni	Red mullet	*Kidhónia*	Cherrystone clams	*Sinagrídha*	Dentex
Galéos	Dogfish, squale			*Skathári*	Black bream
Garídhes	Shrimp	*Ksifiás*	Swordfish	*Soupiá*	Cuttlefish
Gávros	Mild anchovy	*Marídhes*	Whitebait	*Tsipoúra*	Gilt-head bream
Glóssa	Sole	*Mídhia*	Mussels	*Vátos*	Skate, ray
Gópa	Bogue	*Okhtapódhi*	Octopus		

Meat and meat-based dishes

Arní	Lamb	*Moskhári*	Veal
Biftéki	Hamburger	*Moussaká*	Aubergine/eggplant, potato
Brizóla	Pork or beef chop		and meat pie
Hirinó	Pork	*Sikóti*	Liver
Keftédhes	Meatballs	*Païdhákia*	Lamb chops
Kleftikó	Meat, potatoes and veg cooked	*Pastítsio*	Macaroni baked with meat
	together in a pot or foil; a Cretan	*Patsás*	Tripe and trotter soup
	speciality traditionally carried to	*Soutzoukákia*	Mincemeat rissoles/beef
	bandits in hiding		patties
Kokorétsi	Liver/offal kebab	*Stifádho*	Meat stew with tomato
Kotópoulo	Chicken	*Tsalingária*	Garden snails
Kounéli	Rabbit	*Youvétsi*	Baked clay casserole of
Loukánika	Spicy sausages		meat and (pasta)

Sweets and dessert

Baklavás	Honey and nut pastry	*Loukoumádes*	Yeast doughnuts in
Bougátsa	Creamy cheese pie		honey syrup and
	served warm with		sesame seeds
	sugar and cinammon	*Pagotó*	Ice cream
Galaktobóureko	Custard pie	*Pastéli*	Sesame and honey bar
Halva	Sweetmeat	*Rizógalo*	Rice pudding
Karidhópita	Walnut cake		

Fruit and nuts

Fistíkia	Pistachio nuts	*Kidhóni*	Quince	*Portokália*	Oranges
Fráoules	Strawberries	*Lemóni*	Lemon	*Rodhákino*	Peach
Karpoúzi	Watermelon	*Míla*	Apples	*Síka*	(Dried) figs
Kerásia	Cherries	*Pepóni*	Melon	*Stafília*	Grapes

Cheese

Féta	Salty, white	*Graviéra*	Gruyère-type hard cheese
	cheese	*Kasséri*	Medium cheese

Drinks

Áspro	White	*Kafés*	Coffee	*Potíri*	Glass
Bíra	Beer	*Krasí*	Wine	*Rosé/Kokkinéli*	Rosé
Boukáli	Bottle	*Limonádha*	Lemonade	*Stinyássas!*	Cheers!
Gála	Milk	*Mávro*	Red	*Tsái*	Tea
Galakakáo	Chocolate milk	*Metalikó neró*	Mineral water		
Gazóza	Generic fizzy drink	*Portokaládh*	Orangeade		

Otherwise, go for the **local wines**. *Retsina* – pine resinated wine, a slightly acquired taste – is invariably better straight from the barrel. Not as many tavernas keep it as once did, but always ask whether they have wine *varelísio* or *híma* – both mean, in effect, "from the barrel". Non-resinated bulk wine is almost always more than decent.

CAFÉS AND BARS

The Greek eating and drinking experience encompasses a variety of other places beyond restaurants. Most importantly, there is the institution of the **kafenío**, found in every town, village and hamlet in the country. In addition, you'll come across **ouzerís**, **zaharoplastía** and **bars**.

THE KAFENÍO

The **kafenío** is the traditional Greek coffee shop or café. Although its main business is Greek coffee – prepared skéto or pikró (unsweetened), métrio (medium) or glikó (sweet) – it also serves spirits such as oúzo (aniseed-based spirit), brandy (Metaxa brand, in three grades), beer, tea (either herbal mountain tea or British-style Liptons) and soft drinks. Another refreshing drink sold in cafés is kafés frappé, a sort of iced instant coffee with or without milk and sugar – uniquely Greek despite its French-sounding name. Like Greek coffee, it is always accompanied by a welcome glass of cold water. Standard fizzy soft drinks are sold in all cafés, too.

Usually the only edibles sold in cafés are glikó koutalioú (sticky, syrupy preserves of quince, grape, fig, citrus fruit or cherry), and the old-fashioned ipovríhio, which is a piece of mastic submerged in a glass of water like a submarine, which is what the word means in Greek.

Like tavernas, kafenía range from the plastic and sophisticated to the old-fashioned, spit-on-the-floor variety, with marble or brightly painted metal tables and straw-bottomed chairs. An important institution anywhere in Greece, they are the central pivot of life in the country villages. In fact, you get the impression that many men spend most of their waking hours there. Greek **women** are rarely to be seen in the more traditional places – and foreign women may sometimes feel uneasy or unwelcome in these establishments. Even in holiday resorts, you will find there is at least one café that the local men have kept intact for themselves.

Some kafenía close at siesta time, but many remain open from early in the morning until late at night. The chief socializing time is 6–8pm, immediately after the siesta. This is the time to take your pre-dinner oúzo, as the sun begins to sink and the heat cools (see below).

OÚZO, MEZÉDHES AND OUZERÍ

Oúzo – along with the similar tsípouro (mainland) and tsikoudhiá (Crete) – are simply spirits, averaging 46 percent alcohol, distilled from grape-mash residue left over from wine-making, and then flavoured with herbs such as anise or fennel. If you order oúzo, you will be served two glasses, one with the oúzo, and one full of water, to be tipped into your oúzo until it turns a milky white. You can drink it straight, but its strong, burning taste is hardly refreshing if you do. There

are more than a dozen brands of oúzo in Greece; the best are reckoned to come from Lésvos, Tírnavos and Sámos, the best-known being the mass-produced 12 label.

Until not long ago, every oúzo you ordered was automatically accompanied by a small plate of **mezédhes**, on the house: bits of cheese, cucumber, tomato, a few olives, sometimes octopus or even a couple of small fish. Unfortunately these days you have to ask, and pay, for them.

Though they are confined to the better resorts and select neighbourhoods of the bigger cities, there is a kind of drinking establishment which specializes in oúzo and mezédhes. These are called an **ouzerí** (same in the plural) or ouzádhiko, and are well worth trying for the marvellous variety of mezédhes they serve. Several plates of these plus drinks will effectively substitute for a more involved meal at a taverna (though it usually works out more expensive if you have a healthy appetite).

ZAHAROPLASTÍO

A somewhat similar institution to the kafenío is the **zaharoplastío**. A cross between café and patisserie, it serves coffee, alcohol, yoghurt and honey, sticky cakes, etc, both to consume on the premises and to take away.

The good establishments offer an amazing variety of pastries, cream and chocolate confections, honey-soaked Greco-Turkish sweets like baklavás, kataífi (honey-drenched "shredded wheat"), loukoumádhes, puffs of batter fried in olive oil, dusted with cinnamon and dipped in syrup (if you have a sweet tooth they'll transport you); galaktoboúreko (custard pie), and so on.

If you want a stronger slant towards the dairy products and away from the pure sugar, seek out a **galaktopolío**, where you'll often find rizógalo (rice pudding), kréma (custard) and home- or at least locally made yiaoúrti (yoghurt), best if it's próvio (from sheep's milk). A sign at either establishment with the legend pagotó politikó or kaïmáki means that the shop concerned makes its own Turkish-style ice cream, and the proprietors are probably from Istanbul (Konstantinoúpoli to them, of course) – as good as or better than the usual Italian-style fare.

Both zaharoplastía and galaktopolía are more family-oriented places than the kafenío, and many also serve a basic continental-type **breakfast** of méli me voútiro (honey poured over a pat of butter) or jam (all kinds are called marmeládha in Greek; ask for *portokáli* – orange – if you want proper marmalade) with fresh bread or *friganiés* (melba-toast-type slivers). You are also more likely to find proper (*evropaïkó*) tea and different kinds of coffee. *Nescafé* has become the generic term for all instant coffee, regardless of brand.

BARS – AND BEER

Bars – *barákia* in the plural – are a recent transplant, once confined to towns, cities and holiday resorts, but now found all over Greece. They range from clones of Parisian cafés to seaside cocktail bars by way of mindless, imitation English "pubs" (*sic*), with equally mindless videos running all day. Drinks are invariably more expensive than at a café.

They are, however, most likely to stock a range of **beers**, which in Greece are all foreign labels made under licence, since the old Fix brewery closed in the 1980s. *Kronenberg* and *Kaiser* are the two most expensive brews, with the former much preferable and also offering the only dark beer in the country. *Amstel* and *Henninger* are the two ubiquitous cheapies, rather bland but inoffensive. A possible compromise is the sharper-tasting *Heineken*, universally referred to as a "*prássini*" by bar and taverna staff after its green bottle.

Incidentally, try not to be stuck with the one-third litre cans, vastly more expensive (and more of a rubbish problem) than the returnable half-litre bottles.

COMMUNICATIONS: MAIL, PHONES AND THE MEDIA

POSTAL SERVICES

Post offices are open Monday to Friday from about 7.30am to any time between 2pm and 8pm, depending on the size of the town. In the cities and important resorts, there are usually supplementary weekend opening hours, between 9am and 3pm. At such times you can have money exchanged, in addition to handling mail.

Airmail letters from the mainland take three to six days to reach the rest of Europe, five to ten days to get to North America, and a bit more for Australia and New Zealand. Allow an extra four or five days when sending from any island.

Aerograms are faster and surer. **Postcards** can be inexplicably slow: up to two weeks for

Europe, a month to North America or the Pacific. A modest (about 300dr) fee for **express** (*katapígonda*) service cuts letter delivery time by a few days to any destination. **Registered** (*sistiméno*) delivery is also available, but it is quite slow unless coupled with express service.

For a simple letter or card, **stamps** (*grammatósima*) can also be purchased at a *períptero* (corner kiosk). However, the proprietors are entitled to a ten percent commission and never seem to know the current international rates. Ordinary **post boxes** are bright yellow, express boxes dark red; if you are confronted by two slots, *esoterikó* is for domestic mail, *exoterikó* for overseas.

If you are sending large purchases home, note that **parcels** should and often can only be handled in sizeable towns, preferably a provincial capital. This way your bundle will be in Athens, and on the plane, within a few days.

RECEIVING MAIL

The **poste restante/general delivery** system is reasonably efficient, especially at the post offices of larger towns. Mail should be clearly addressed and marked *poste restante*, with your surname underlined, to the main post office of whichever town you choose. It will be held for a month and you'll need your passport to collect it.

Alternatively, you can use the *American Express* one-month mail-holding service, free of charge if you carry their cheques or hold their card, but because of new security regulations

AMERICAN EXPRESS OFFICES IN GREECE

Athens: *American Express*, Síndagma/Ermoú 2, PO Box 3325.

Iráklion (Crete): c/o *Adamis Tours*, Avgoústou 23, PO Box 1031.

Kérkira (Corfu): c/o *Greek Skies Travel*, Kapdhistríou 20A, PO Box 24.

Míkonos: c/o *Delia Travel*, at the quay, PO Box 02.

Pátra: c/o *Albatross Travel*, Amalias 48.

Rhodes Town: c/o *Rodhos Tours Ltd*, Ammohóstou 23, PO Box 252.

Skíathos: c/o *Mare Nostrum Hols Ltd*, Papadiamanti 21, PO Box 16.

they will no longer accept delivery of even small packages. *Amex* offices are open Monday to Friday, plus Saturday mornings, and are conveniently spaced (see box above).

PHONES

Local calls are relatively straightforward. In many hotel lobbies or cafés you'll find fat, **red pay-phones** which presently take a ten-drachma coin and are for local calls only — you'll be asked to give an extra 5dr to the proprietor to equal the fee at a street kiosk (see below). On street corners you will find call boxes, which work only with **phone cards** (in three sizes: 100, 500 and 1000 units), bought from kiosks, OTE offices and newsagents.

If you won't be around long enough to use up a phone card, it's probably easier to make local calls from a *períptero*, or **street kiosk**. Here the phone is connected to a meter, and you pay after you have made the call. Local calls are very cheap (15dr), but **long-distance** ones add up quickly to some of the most expensive rates in the EC — and definitely the worst connections.

For **international** (*exoterikó*) calls, it's better to use either card phones or visit the nearest *OTE* (*Organismós Tiliepikinoníon tis Elládhos*) office, where there's often a slightly better-wired booth reserved for overseas calls only. **Reverse charge (collect) calls** can also be made here, though connections are not always immediate. Be prepared to wait.

In the very largest towns there is at least one branch open 24 **hours**, or more commonly 7am to 10pm or 11pm. In smaller towns *OTE* offices can close as early as 3pm, though in a few resorts there are a few *OTE* Portakabin booths. Outgoing **faxes** can also be sent from OTE offices, post offices and some travel agencies — at a price. Receiving a fax may also incur a small charge.

Other options for calls are from a *kafenío* or bar, but make sure the phones are metered: look for a sign saying *Tiléfono meh metrití*. Avoid making long-distance calls from a hotel, as they slap a 50 percent surcharge onto the already outrageous rates.

PHONING GREECE FROM ABROAD

Dial the international access code (given below) + 30 (country code) + area code (minus initial 0, see below) + number

Australia ☎0011	New Zealand ☎00		
Canada ☎011	UK ☎00		
Ireland ☎010	USA ☎011		

PHONING ABROAD FROM GREECE

Dial the country code (given below) + area code (minus initial 0) + number

Australia ☎0061	New Zealand ☎0064
Canada ☎001	UK ☎0044
Ireland ☎00353	USA ☎001

GREEK PHONE CODES

Athens ☎01	Kós ☎0242	Pátra ☎061	Skíathos ☎0427
Corfu ☎0661	Míkonos ☎0289	Rhodes ☎0241	Thessaloníki ☎031
Iráklion ☎081	Páros ☎0284	Santoríni ☎0286	Zákinthos ☎0695

USEFUL TELEPHONE NUMBERS

Operator ☎131 (Athens)	Medical emergencies ☎166	Tourist police ☎171
Operator ☎132 (Domestic)	Police/Emergency ☎100	Fire brigade ☎199
Operator ☎161 (International)	Speaking clock ☎141	Road assistance ☎174

Calls will **cost**, very approximately, £2.75 for three minutes to all EC countries and most of the rest of Europe, or US$10 for the same time to North America or Australasia. **Cheap rates**, such as they are, apply from 3pm to 5pm and 9pm to 8am daily, plus all weekend, for calls within Greece.

For details of **phone codes and useful numbers**, see the box opposite.

British Telecom, as well as North American long-distance companies like *AT&T, MCI, Sprint* all enable their customers to make **credit-card calls** while overseas. Most provide service from Greece – contact the company for more details.

THE MEDIA

British newspapers are fairly widely available in Greece for 300–400dr, 700–800dr for Sunday editions. You'll find day-old copies of *The Independent* and *The Guardian*'s European edition in all the resorts as well as in major towns, and a few of the tabloids can be found too. **American and international** alternatives are represented by *USA Today* and the *International Herald Tribune; Time* and *Newsweek* are also widely available.

Local English-language alternatives include the daily *Athens News*, with a new colour format and improved entertainment listings, and the *Greek Weekly News*, the latter with a good summary of Athens cinema and concert offerings. The expatriate communites in Rhodes and Corfu also put out creditable information sheets.

Among **magazines**, the most enduring is *The Athenian*, an English-language monthly sold in Athens and all major resorts. It's usually worth a read for its cultural/festival listings, updates on Greek life and politics, and often excellent features.

RADIO

If you have a **radio** you may pick up something interesting. Greek music progammes are always accessible despite the language barrier, and with recent challenges to the government's former monopoly of wavelengths, regional stations have mushroomed; the airwaves are now positively cluttered, as every town of more than a few thousand sets up its own studio and transmitter.

The **BBC World Service** can be picked up on short-wave frequencies throughout Greece. For programme times and frequencies (15.07 and 12.09 Mhz are the most common), pick up a copy of "London Calling" from the library of the British Council in Athens.

GREEK TV

Greece's two centralized, government-controlled **TV stations**, ET1 and ET2, nowadays lag behind private channels – Mega-Channel, New Channel, Antenna, Star and Seven-X – in the ratings. On ET1, news summaries in English are read daily at 6pm. Programming on all stations tends to be a mix of soaps (especially Italian and Spanish ones), gameshows, westerns, B-movies and sports. All foreign films and serials are broadcast in their original language, with Greek subtitles. Except for Seven-X, which begins at 7pm, and Mega (a 24-hour channel), the main channels broadcast from breakfast time until the small hours.

Numerous **cable and satellite** channels are transmitted, including Sky, CNN, MTV, Super Channel and Italian Rai. The range available depends on the area you're in.

OPENING HOURS AND PUBLIC HOLIDAYS

It is virtually impossible to generalize about Greek opening hours, except to say that they change constantly. The traditional timetable starts at a relatively civilized hour, with shops opening between 8.30am and 9.30am, and runs through until lunchtime, when there is a long break for the hottest part of the day. Things may then reopen in the mid- to late afternoon.

Tourist areas tend to adopt a slightly more northern timetable, with shops· and offices probably staying open right through the day. Certainly the most important archeological sites and museums do so.

BUSINESS AND SHOPPING HOURS

Most **government agencies** are open to the public from 8am to 2pm. In general, however, you'd be optimistic to show up after 1pm expecting to be served the same day. **Private businesses**, or anyone providing a service – eg film processor, osteopath, electronics repair – is likely to operate on a unitary, 9am–6pm schedule. If someone is actually selling something, then they are more likely to follow a split shift.

Shopping hours during the hottest months are theoretically Monday, Wednesday and Saturday from approximately 9am–2.30pm, and Tuesday, Thursday and Friday from 8.30am–2pm and 6–9pm; during the cooler months with shorter daylight hours the morning schedule shifts slightly forward, the evening trade a half or

even a full hour back. There are so many **exceptions** to these rules, though, by virtue of holidays and professional idiosyncrasy that you can't count on getting anything done except from Monday to Friday from 9.30am to 1pm or so. It's worth noting that **delis and butchers** are not allowed to sell fresh meat during the afternoon (though some flout this rule); similarly **fishmongers** are only open in the morning.

All of the above opening hours will be regularly thrown out of sync by any of a vast range of **public holidays and festivals**. The most important, when almost everything will be closed, are listed in the box below.

ANCIENT SITES AND MONASTERIES

All the major **ancient sites** are now fenced off and, like most **museums**, charge admission. This ranges from a token 200dr to a whopping 1500dr, with an average fee of around 500dr. Anomalies are common, with some tiny one-pot museums charging the same as major attractions. At most of them there are reductions of 50–100 percent (the latter applying to EC nationals) for student card holders. In addition, entrance to all state-run sites and museums is **free** to all EC nationals on Sundays and public holidays.

Opening hours vary from site to site. As far as possible, individual times are quoted in the text, but bear in mind that these change with exasperating frequency and at smaller sites may be subject to the whim of a local keeper. The

PUBLIC HOLIDAYS

January 1
January 6
March 25
First Monday of Lent (February/March, see below)
Easter weekend (according to the Orthodox festival calendar, see below)
May 1

Whit Monday (usually in June)
August 15
October 28
December 25 & 26

There are also a large number of local holidays, which result in the closure of shops and businesses, though not government agencies.

VARIABLE RELIGIOUS FEASTS 1995–97

Lent Monday	Easter Sunday	Whit Monday
March 6	April 23	June 12
February 26	April 14	June 3
March 10	April 27	June 16

times quoted are generally summer hours, which operate from around April to the end of September. Reckon on similar days but later opening and earlier closing in winter.

Smaller sites generally close for a long lunch and **siesta** (even where they're not supposed to), as do **monasteries**. Most monasteries are fairly strict on visitors' dress, too, especially for women; they don't like shorts on either sex and often expect women to cover their arms and wear skirts, with the necessary wraps sometimes provided on the spot. They are generally open from about 9am to 1pm and 5pm to 8pm (3.30–6.30pm in winter) for limited visits.

FESTIVALS AND CULTURAL EVENTS

Many of the big Greek popular festivals have a religious base so they're observed in accordance with the Orthodox calendar. This is similar to the regular Catholic liturgical year, except for Easter, which can fall as much as three weeks to either side of the western festival. Other festivals are cultural in nature, with the highlight for most people being to catch a performance of Classical drama in one of the country's ancient theatres. There's also a full programme of cinema and modern theatre, at its best in Athens but with something on offer in even the smallest town at some point during the year.

EASTER

Easter is by far the most important festival of the Greek year – infinitely more so than Christmas – and taken much more seriously than it is anywhere in western Europe. From Wednesday of Holy Week the state radio and TV networks are given over solely to religious programmes until the following Monday.

The festival is an excellent time to be in Greece, both for the beautiful and moving religious ceremonies and for the days of feasting and celebration that follow. The mountainous island of **Ídhra** with its alleged 360 churches and monasteries is the prime Easter resort, but unless you plan well in advance you have no hope of finding accommodation at that time. Probably the best idea is to make for a medium-sized village where, in most cases, you'll be accepted into the community's celebration. Other famous Easter celebrations are held at Metsóvo, Trípoli and Livádhia.

The first great public ceremony takes place on **Good Friday** evening as the Descent from the Cross is lamented in church. At dusk the *Epitafiós*, Christ's funeral bier, lavishly decorated by the women of the parish, leaves the sanctuary and is paraded solemnly through the streets. In many places, Crete especially, this is accompanied by the burning of effigies of Judas Iscariot.

Late **Saturday** evening sees the climax in a majestic *Anástasi* mass to celebrate Christ's triumphant return. At the stroke of midnight all lights in each crowded church are extinguished and the congregation plunged into the darkness which envelops Christ as He passes through the underworld. Then there's a faint glimmer of light behind the altar screen before the priest appears, holding aloft a lighted taper and chanting "*Avtó to Fós . . .*" (This is the Light of the World). Stepping down to the level of the parishioners, he touches his flame to the unlit candle of the nearest worshipper intoning "*Dévthe, lévethe Fós*" (Come, take the Light). Those at the front of the congregation and on the aisles do the same for their neighbours until the entire church is ablaze with burning candles and the miracle re-affirmed.

Even solidly rational atheists are likely to find this moving. The traditional greeting, as fireworks explode all around you in the street, is "*Hristós*

Anésti" (Christ is risen), to which the response is *"Alithós Anésti"* (Truly He is Risen). In the week up to Easter Sunday you should wish people a Happy Easter: *"Kaló Páskha"*; after the day, you say *"Hrónia Pollá"* (Many Happy Returns).

The burning **candles** are then taken home through the streets by the worshippers, and it brings good fortune on the house if the candle arrives without having been blown out in the wind. On reaching the front door it is common practice to make the sign of the cross on the lintel with the flame, leaving a black smudge visible for the rest of the year. The Lenten fast is traditionally broken early on Sunday morning with a meal of *mayarítsa*, a soup made from lamb tripe, rice and lemon. The rest of the lamb will be roasted on spits for Sunday lunch, and festivities often take place through the rest of the day.

The Greek equivalent of **Easter eggs** are hard-boiled eggs (painted red on Holy Thursday), which are baked into twisted, sweet bread-loaves (*tsouréki*) or distributed on Easter Sunday; people rap their eggs against their friends' eggs, and the owner of the last uncracked egg is considered lucky.

THE FESTIVAL CALENDAR

Most of the other Greek festivals are celebrations of one or another of a multitude of **saints**. The most important are detailed below: wherever you are, it is worth looking out for a village, or church, bearing the saint's name, a sure sign of celebrations – sometimes across the town or island, sometimes quiet and local. Saints' days are also celebrated as **name-days**; if you learn that it's an acquaintance's name-day, you wish them *"Hrónia Pollá"* (Many Happy Returns).

Detailed below, too, is a scattering of more **secular** holidays, most enjoyable of which are the pre-Lenten carnivals.

In addition to the specific dates mentioned, there are literally scores of **local festivals**, or *paniyíria*, celebrating the patron saint of the village church. With some 330-odd possible name-saints' days you're unlikely to travel around Greece for long without stumbling on something.

It is important to remember the concept of the ***paramoní****, or eve, of the festival. Most of the events listed below are celebrated on the night before, so if you show up on the morning of the date given you will very probably have missed any music, dancing or drinking.*

January 1

New Year's Day in Greece is the feast day of **Áyios Vassílios**, their version of Santa Claus, and is celebrated with church services and the baking of a special loaf, *vassilópitta*, in which a coin is baked which brings its finder good luck throughout the year. The traditional New Year greeting is *"Kalí Hroniá"*.

January 6

The **Epiphany**, when the *kalikántzari* (hobgoblins) who run riot on earth during the twelve days of Christmas are rebanished to the nether world by various rites of the Church. The most important of these is the blessing of baptismal fonts and all outdoor bodies of water. At lakeside, river and seaside locations, the priest traditionally casts a crucifix into the deep, with local youths competing for the privilege of recovering it.

January 8

The **Gynaecocratia** in Thrace is a festival where matriarchy is celebrated by men and women reversing roles for the day. For a change, the women populate the cafés while the men do the domestic chores.

Pre-Lenten carnivals

These span three weeks, climaxing during the seventh weekend before Easter. **Pátra Carnival**, with a chariot parade and costume parties, is one of the largest and most outrageous in the Mediterranean, with events from January 17 until "Clean Monday", the last day of Lent; on the last Sunday before Lent there's a grand parade, with the city's large gay population in conspicuous participation. Interesting, too, are the *boúles* or masked revels which take place around **Macedonia** (particularly at Náoussa), and the outrageous "Goat Dance" on **Skíros** in the Sporades. The **Ionian islands**, especially Kefalloniá, are also good for carnival, while **Athenians** "celebrate" by going around hitting each other on the head with plastic hammers. In **Thebes**, a mock shepherd wedding occurs while most places celebrate with colourful pageants reflecting local traditions.

March 25

Independence Day and the **Feast of the Annunciation** (*Evangelismós* in Greek) is both a religious and a national holiday, with, on the one hand, military parades and dancing to celebrate the beginning of the revolt against Turkish rule in 1821, and, on the other, church services to honour the news being given to Mary that she was to become the Mother of Christ. There are major festivities on **Tínos**, **Ídhra (Hydra)** and many other places, particularly any monastery or church named Evangelístria or Evangelismós, whose name-day celebration it is.

April 23
The **Feast of St George (Áyios Yióryios)**, the patron of shepherds, is a big rural celebration. Good places for dancing and feasting include **Aráhova**, near Delphi. Saint George is also the patron saint of **Skíros**, so this day is celebrated in some style there, too. If April 23 falls before Easter, ie during Lent, the festivities are postponed until the Monday after Easter.

May 1
May Day, the great urban holiday when townspeople traditionally make for the countryside for picnics and to return with bunches of wild flowers. Wreaths are hung on their doorways or balconies until they are burnt on Midsummer's eve. The demise of communism in eastern Europe notwithstanding, there are still likely to be large demonstrations by the left, claiming the *Ergatikí Protomayiá* (Working-Class First of May) as their own.

May 21
The Feast of **Áyios Konstandínos** and his mother, **Ayía Eléni**, the first Orthodox Byzantine rulers. There are firewalking ceremonies in certain **Macedonian villages**, and elsewhere the day is celebrated rather more conventionally as being the name-day for two of the more popular Christian names in Greece.

June 29
The **Feast of the Holy Apostles (Ayíi Apostolí)**, **Pétros and Pávlos**. Widely celebrated name days.

July 17
The **Feast of Ayía Marína**: a big deal in rural areas, as she's an important protectress of crops.

July 18–20
The **Feast of Profítis Ilías (the Prophet Elijah)** is widely celebrated at the countless hill- or mountain-top shrines of Profítis Ilías. The most famous is on **Mount Taíyettos**, near Spárti.

July 26
Feast of **Ayiá Paraskeví**, with big village festivals, especially in **Epirus**.

August 6
The **Feast of the Metamórfosi (Transfiguration)** provides another excuse for celebrations. In fact, between mid-July and mid-September there are religious festivals every few days, especially in the rural areas, and between these and the summer heat ordinary business comes to a virtual standstill.

August 15
The **Apokímisis tis Panayías (Assumption of the Blessed Virgin Mary)**. This is the day when people traditionally return to their home village, and in many places there will be no accommodation available on any terms. Even some Greeks will resort to sleeping in the streets. There is a great pilgrimage to **Tínos**, and major festivities at **Páros**, at Ayiássos on **Lésvos**, and at Olímbos on **Kárpathos**.

September 8
The **Yénisis tis Panayías (Birth of the Virgin Mary)** sees special services in churches dedicated to the event (with major festivals 24hr beforehand), and a double cause for rejoicing on **Spétses** where they also celebrate the anniversary of the **Battle of the Straits** of Spétses, which took place on September 8, 1822. A re-enactment of the battle takes place in the harbour, followed by fireworks and feasting well into the night.

September 14
A last major summer festival, the **Ípsosi tou Stavroú (Exaltation of the Cross)**.

October 26
The **Feast of Áyios Dhimítrios**, another popular name-day, particularly celebrated in **Thessaloníki**, of which he is the patron saint. New wine is traditionally tapped on this day, a good excuse for general inebriation.

October 28
Óhki Day, the year's major patriotic shindig – a national holiday with parades, folk-dancing and feasting to commemorate Metaxas's apocryphal one-word reply to Mussolini's 1940 ultimatum: "*Okhi!*"(No!).

November 8
Another popular name-day, the **Feast of the Archangels Michael and Gabriel (Mihaíl and Gavriél)**, with rites at the numerous rural monasteries and chapels named after them.

December 6
The **Feast of Áyios Nikólaos**, the patron of seafarers, with many chapels dedicated to him.

December 25
A much less festive occasion than Greek Easter, **Christmas** is still an important religious feast celebrating the birth of Christ, and in recent years it has started to take on more of the trappings of the western Christmas, with decorations, Christmas trees and gifts. December 26 is not Boxing Day but the *Sínaksis tis Panayías*, or Meeting of the Virgin's Entourage.

December 31
New Year's Eve, when, as on the other twelve days of Christmas, children go door-to-door singing the traditional *kálanda* (carols), receiving money in return. Adults tend to sit around playing cards, often for money. The *vassilópitta* may be cut at midnight, to mark the start of another year of what sometimes seems like a non-stop round of celebrations.

CULTURAL FESTIVALS

As well as religious festivals, Greece has a full range of **cultural festivals** – highlights of which include **ancient drama** in ancient theatres, in Athens, Epidauras, Thássos, Dodona and Philippi. A leaflet entitled "Greek Festivals", available from GNTO offices abroad, includes details of smaller, **local festivals** of music, drama and dance, which take place on a more sporadic basis.

MAJOR FESTIVALS
Athens: the *Athens Festival* (mid-June to mid-Sept) encompasses a wide range of performances including modern and ancient theatre, ballet, opera, jazz and classical music, held at the open-air Herodes Atticus. *Athens International Jazz and Blues Festival* (June) puts on big-name acts at the modern open-air theatre on Likavitós hill. Details and tickets for events can be obtained from the *Athens Festival* box office (Stadiou 4, ☎32 21 459). It's worth calling in very soon after you arrive in Greece, since the more prestigious events often sell out.

Epidaurus: *Epidaurus Festival* (June–Sept) – like those at Herodes Atticus, the open-air performances of Classical drama in the ancient theatre are the main highlight.

Pátra: *International Festival* (June–Sept).

Thessaloníki: hosts the *Dhimitría Cultural Festival* and a film festival (Oct); and *Philoxenia*, a large international trade and tourism exhibition (Nov).

MINOR FESTIVALS
Itháki Music Festival (July).
Ioánnina's Cultural Summer (July/Aug).
Iráklion Festival (early Aug).
Kavala Festival (Aug).
Lefkádha Arts Jamboree (Aug).
Makrinítsa/Vólos Festival (Aug).
Réthimnon Renaissance Fair (Aug).
Santoríni Music Festival (Aug–Sept).
Rhodes Festival (Aug–Oct).

CINEMA AND THEATRE

Greek **cinemas** show a large number of American and British movies, always undubbed with Greek subtitles. They are highly affordable, currently 1000–1500dr depending on location, and in summer a number set up outside on vacant lots. An **outdoor movie** is worth catching at least once – indoor shows never quite seem the same once you've seen an open-air screening of Kirk Douglas in *The Odyssey* on Ithaca.

Theatre gets suspended during the summer months but from around September to May there's a lot of activity; Athens alone has some 45 theatres, with playbills ranging from the classics to satirical revues (both in Greek).

SPORTS AND OUTDOOR PURSUITS

The Greek seashore offers endless scope for water sports, with windsurfing-boards for rent in most resorts and, less regularly, waterskiing and parasailing facilities. On land, the greatest attraction lies in hiking, through what is one of Europe's more impressive mountain terrains. Winter also sees possibilities for skiing at one of a dozen or so underrated centres.

Spectating, the twin Greek obsessions are **football** (soccer) and **basketball**, with **volleyball** a close third in popularity.

WATER SPORTS

The last few years have seen a massive growth in the popularity of **windsurfing** in Greece. The country's bays and coves are ideal for beginners, and boards can be hired in literally hundreds of resorts. Particularly good areas include the islands of Lefkádha, Zákinthos, Náxos, Sámos, Lésvos, Corfu and Crete, and Methóni in the Peloponnese. You can almost always pay for an initial period of instruction, if you've not tried the sport previously. Rates are very reasonable – about £5/US$7.50 an hour.

Waterskiing is available at a number of larger resorts, and a fair few of the smaller ones, too. By the crippling rental standards of the ritzier parts of the Mediterranean it is a bargain, with twenty minutes' instruction often available for around £8–10/$12–15. At many resorts, **parasailing** (*parapént* in Greek) is also possible; rates start at £10/$15 a go.

From ancient times onwards, the combination of navigable waters and natural island harbours have made Greece a tremendous place for **sailing**. Holiday companies offer all sorts of packaged and tailormade cruises (see the relevant "Getting there" sections). In Greece, boats and dinghies are rented out by the day or week at many resorts. For more details, pick up the informative brochure "Sailing the Greek Sea" from GNTO offices or contact the *Hellenic Yachting Federation*, Akti Navarchou Kountouridti 7, 18534 Pireás (☎01/41 37 351).

Because of the potential for pilfering submerged antiquities, **scuba diving** is severely restricted, its legal practice confined to certain coasts around Attica, Crete, Kálimnos, Míkonos,

most of the Ionian islands and selected spots in northern Greece and the Peloponnese. For more information, contact the *Union of Greek Diving Centres* (☎01/92 29 532).

Greece also has lots of white water, especially in the Peloponnese and Epirus, so if you're into **river rafting** there is much potential. There are periodic articles and advice (in Greek) in the outdoors magazine *Korfes*.

SKIING

Skiing is a comparative newcomer to Greece, in part because snow conditions are unpredictable, and runs generally short. However, there are now a dozen **ski centres** scattered about the mountains, and what they lack in professionalism is often made up for by a very easy-going and unpretentious *après-ski* scene. Costs are an attraction, too – much lower than in northern Europe, at around £9/US$13.50 a day for rental of skis and boots, plus £6/$9 a day for a lift pass. The **season** generally lasts from the beginning of January to the end of April, with a few extra weeks possible at either end depending on snow conditions.

The most developed of the resorts is on **Parnassós**, the legendary mountain near Delphi. It's easily accessible from Athens; throughout the season Athenian operators run buses up to the resort, returning the same day. Avoid weekends (which can be chaos) and you may have the resort more or less to yourself. The leading operator is *Klaoudatos*, a big department store on Dhimarhíou street, near Platía Omónia. In winter they devote a floor to skiing, including ski rental (though this is simpler at Parnassós itself). The resort has slopes for beginners and enough to keep most experienced skiers happy, at least for a couple of days. Its main problem is that the lifts are often closed due to high winds.

Other major **ski centres** include **Veloúhi**, near Karpeníssi in central Greece; **Helmós**, near Kalávrita on the Peloponnese; **Vérmion**, near Náoussa in Macedonia; nearby **Pisodhéri** near Flórina, also in Macedonia; and **Métsovo** in Epirus, which has ample other attractions besides the skiing. **The Pílion** is another enjoyable region to ski in as part of a general holiday. Buses run to its ski centre at Haniá from Vólos.

All of these centres rent out ski equipment for casual visitors. The last two are at a lower altitude than the others, so seasons are shorter.

Further details are available from the EOT, which publishes a leaflet entitled "Ski Centres and Mountaineering Shelters".

WALKING

Greeks are just becoming used to the notion that anyone should want to walk for pleasure, yet if you have the time and stamina it is probably the single best way to see the country. This guide includes descriptions of a number of the more accessible mountain hikes, as well as suggestions for more casual walking.

In addition, you may want to acquire one or both of the specific Greek **hiking guidebooks**; – see "Books" in *Contexts*. See also p.26 for details of **hiking maps** available, and p.6, 122 and 347 for details of companies offering walking holidays in the mountains.

FOOTBALL AND BASKETBALL

Football (soccer) is far and away the most popular sport in Greece – both in terms of participating and watching. The most important (and most heavily sponsored) teams are *Panathanaïkós* and *AEK* of Athens, *Olympiakós* of Pireás, and *PAOK* of Thessaloníki. Other major teams in the provinces include *Lárissa* and the Cretan *Ofí*. If you're interested, matches (usually played on Sundays) are easy enough to catch during the winter/spring season. In mid-autumn you might even see one of the Greek teams playing European competition. The Greek national team qualified for the 1994 World Cup in some style, and then proceeded to lose all their three games heavily and returned from the USA without scoring a goal.

The nation's **basketball** team is one of the continent's strongest and won the European Championship in 1987 – cheered all the way with enormous enthusiasm. At club level, many of the football teams maintain basketball squads.

POLICE, TROUBLE AND HARASSMENT

In an **emergency**, dial ☎100 for the police, ☎171 for the tourist police; in a medical emergency, dial ☎166 for an ambulance.

persons, particularly in the cities and resorts. It's wise to lock things up and treat Greece like any other European destination. For women, **harassment** is a (relatively low-key) fact of life, given the classically Mediterranean machismo of the culture.

SPECIFIC OFFENCES

The most common causes of a brush with authority – both technically illegal – are nude bathing or sunbathing, and camping outside an authorized site.

Nude bathing is strictly legal on only a very few beaches (on Míkonos, for example), and is deeply offensive to many more traditional Greeks – exercise considerable sensitivity to local feeling and the kind of place you're in. It is, for example, very bad etiquette to swim or sunbathe nude within sight of a church. Generally, if a beach has become fairly established for nudity, or is well

Traditionally, Greece has been one of Europe's safer countries and even today the crime rate is still relatively low. If you leave a bag or wallet at a café, you'll most likely find it scrupulously looked after, pending your return. Similarly, Greeks are relaxed about leaving possessions unlocked or unattended on the beach, in rooms or on campsites.

However, in recent years, there has been a large increase in **theft and crimes** against secluded, it's highly unlikely that the police are going to come charging in. Where they do get bothered is if they feel a place is turning into a "hippie beach" or nudity is getting too overt on mainstream tourist stretches. But there are no hard and fast rules; it all depends on the local cops. Most of the time, the only action will be a warning, but you can officially be arrested straight off – facing up to three days in jail and a stiff fine.

Topless (sun)bathing for women is technically legal nationwide, but specific locales often opt out of the "liberation" by posting signs to that effect. It is best to follow their dictates.

Very similar guidelines apply to **freelance camping** – though for this you're still less likely to incur anything more than a warning to move on. The only real risk of arrest is if you are told to move on and fail to do so. In either of the above cases, even if the police do take any action against you, it's more likely to be a brief spell in their cells than any official prosecution.

Drug offences are a far more serious matter, and are treated as major crimes, particularly since there's a growing local use and addiction problem. The maximum penalty for "causing the use of drugs by someone under 18", for example, is life imprisonment and at least a 10-million-drachma fine. Theory is by no means practice, but foreigners caught in possession of small amounts of grass do get long jail sentences if there's evidence that they've been supplying others.

If you get arrested for any offence, you have a right to contact your **consulate** who will arrange a lawyer for your defence. Beyond this, there is little they can, or in most cases will, do. Details of consulates in Athens and Thessaloníki appear in their respective "Listings" sections.

SEXUAL HARASSMENT

Many women travel independently about Greece without being harassed or feeling intimidated. Greek machismo, however, is strong, if less upfront than in, for example, Spain or Italy. Most of the hassle you are likely to get is from a small minority of Greeks who migrate to the main resorts and towns in summer in pursuit of "liberated, fun-loving" tourists.

Indigenous Greeks, who are increasingly hospitable as you become more of a fixture in any one place, treat these outsiders, known as *kamákia* (harpoons), with contempt. Their obvious stake-outs are beach bars and discos. Words worth remembering for an unambiguous response include *Pávsteh* (stop it), *afístemeh* (leave me alone) and *fíyeteh* (go away).

Hitching is not advisable for lone women travellers; **camping** is generally easy and unthreatening, although away from recognized sites it is often wise to attach yourself to a local family by making arrangements to use nearby private land. In the more remote mountains and inland areas you may feel more uncomfortable travelling alone. The intensely traditional Greeks may have trouble understanding why you are unaccompanied, and might not welcome your presence in their exclusively male *kafenía* – often the only place where you can get a drink. Travelling with a man, you're more likely to be treated as a *kséni*, a word meaning both (female) stranger and guest.

FINDING WORK

The EC notwithstanding, short-term work in Greece is always on an unofficial basis and for this reason it will generally be where you can't be seen by the police or you're badly paid – or, more often, both. The recent influx of over 100,000 Albanians, Poles, Yugoslavs, Russian Greeks and assorted other refugees from the upper Balkans has resulted in a surplus of unskilled labour and severely depressed wages. There's a little more dignity to permanent employment, though as elsewhere in Europe this is largely limited to teaching English.

SHORT-TERM WORK

A few ideas to get you started – from **bars** to **harvests**. Note that **youth hostels** are a good source of information on temporary work – indeed a few may even offer you a job themselves, if you turn up at the right time.

TOURISM-RELATED WORK

Most tourists working casually in Greece find jobs in **bars or restaurants** around the main resorts. Women will generally find these jobs easier to obtain than men – who should generally count themselves lucky to get work washing up. "Trained" chefs, however, sometimes fare better.

If you're waiting or serving, most of your wages will probably have to come from tips but you may well be able to get a deal that includes free food and lodging; evening-only hours can be a good shift, leaving you a lot of free time. The main

drawback may be the machismo and/or chauvinist attitudes of your employer. (Ads in the local press for "girl bar staff" are certainly best ignored.)

Corfu, with its big British slant, is an obvious choice for bar work; Rhodes, Crete, Skíathos, Páros, Íos and Santoríni are also promising. Start looking, if you can, around April or May; you'll get better rates at this time if you're taken on for a season.

On a similar, unofficial level you might be able to get a sales job in **tourist shops** on Corfu, Rhodes or Crete, or (if you've the expertise) helping out at one of the **windsurfing** schools that have sprung up all around the coast.

Perhaps the best type of tourism-related work, though, is that of **courier/greeter/group co-ordinator** for a package holiday company. All you need is EC nationality and language proficiency compatible with the clientele, though knowledge of Greek is a big plus. English-only speakers are pretty well restricted to places with a big British package trade, namely Crete, Rhodes, Skíathos and the Ionian islands.

Many such staff are recruited through ads in newspapers issued outside Greece, but it's by no means unheard of to be hired on the spot in April or May. A big plus, however you're taken on, is that you're usually guaranteed about six months of steady work, and that if things work out you may be re-employed the following season with contract and foreign-currency wages from the home company, not from the local affiliate.

Outside the tourist season there can be **building/painting/signpainting** work preparing for the influx; ask around at Easter time. **Yacht marinas** can also prove good hunting-grounds though less for the romantic business of crewing (still a possibility if you've got the charm and arrogance) than scrubbing down and repainting. Again, the best possibilities are likely to be on Rhodes, Corfu, or Crete; the Zéa port at Pireás is actually the biggest marina, but non-Greek owners don't tend to rest up there for long.

SELLING AND BUSKING

You may do better by working for yourself. Travellers report rich pickings during the tourist season from **selling jewellery** on island beaches, or on boats – trinkets from Asia are especially popular with Greeks. Once you've

managed to get the stuff past the customs officials (who will be sceptical, for instance, that all
those trinkets are presents for friends), there
rarely seem to be problems with the local police,
though it probably pays to be discreet.

Busking can also be quite lucrative. Playing
on the Athens metro or the city's streets, it's
possible to make around 3000dr in a two-hour
session. In resorts, you might just strike luckier if
you've talent, and even back in Athens the western-style pubs occasionally hire foreign musicians
for gigs.

AGRICULTURE

Harvesting and other **agricultural jobs** are
invariably low-paid, more so now with the glutted
labour pool, but they provide a winter fallback for
a dwindling number of long-term travellers. It's
predominantly male work, however, with the
fields often quite a rough scene. In addition some
Greeks see fit to pay women a lower daily rate.

If you're still intent on doing it, the most promising course is to ask around among fellow travellers at youth hostels – at some of which you'll
find employers recruiting casual labour.

The best areas, month by month are:

November–February: Oranges, in the region
bounded by Mycenae, Árgos, Náfplio and Tólo.
Lemons at Mistrás, near Spárti, and Kiáto on the
coast by Kórinthos, after the oranges are gone.
On Crete the season may continue into April or
May, especially at Paleohóra and Falásarna in the
west.

March: Artichokes at Iría, near Tólo.

June: Peaches around Véria in Macedonia.

October–November: Olive harvest, most notably around Ámfissa, near Kalamáta, and on Crete.

TEACHING ENGLISH

Language schools (*frondistíria*) have expanded
massively through Greece over the past decade,
and English remains by far the most popularly
required tongue. To get a job in a school you
need to have a university **degree** (preferably in
English). A TEFL (Teaching of English as a Foreign
Language) **certificate** is not essential, but will
increase your chances of a better job. It isn't
necessary to speak Greek but a basic knowledge
is helpful.

The simplest way to get a teaching job is to
apply before leaving – preferably in **Britain**.
There are ads published weekly, particularly from

June to September, in the *Guardian* newspaper
(Tuesday) and in the weekly *Times Educational
Supplement* (Friday). Once accepted, you should
get one-way air fare from London paid (usually),
accommodation found for you, and a contract of
employment. The other big advantage of arranging work from abroad is that some of the red tape
will be cleared up for you before you set off. A
work permit isn't necessary for EC nationals, but
a residence permit and teacher's licence are.
You'll always be asked for a translated copy of
your degree or TEFL certificate. You may also be
obliged to present a medical certificate of good
health.

For **non-EC citizens**, it is very difficult to
obtain a work permit to teach English legally in
Greece. Indeed, numbers of American and
Australasian teachers have been refused
renewed visas recently. However, those of Greek
descent will find it easier (and in fact qualify to
operate their own schools). In practice, however,
schools don't always follow the letter of the law,
and if they like you and your qualifications, and
you're around at the right time, you're likely to
find a place.

One technique is to approach *frondistíria*
directly – dozens are listed in the phonebook for
all larger towns, and many are jointly owned and
will send you to an affiliate if they don't have a
vacancy. Try in late August/early September, or
again in January – some teachers don't last the
isolation of Greek winters. Teaching is essentially
a winter/spring exercise; most, though not all,
schools close down from the end of May until
September, operating only a few summer courses
in June and July.

The current minimum gross **salary** is about
120,000dr per month (equivalent to about £400/
US$600), or 1200–1500dr per hour. Wage
increases are indexed to approximately the rate
of inflation. Often you will be paid a net salary,
after a portion of the Greek income tax and IKA
(social security payments) have been deducted by
your employers. The average working week is
about 25 hours; contracts generally last nine
months, from September to May, with two paid
holidays and bonuses.

It's general practice to supplement your
income by giving **private lessons**, and for this
the going rate is between 2500dr and 4000dr an
hour. Many teachers finance themselves exclusively on private lessons and, although you still
officially need a teaching permit for this, few

USEFUL TEACHING ORGANIZATIONS

UK

Native English Teachers (NET). Contact Susan Lancaster at 160 Littlehampton Rd, Worthing, West Sussex BN13 1QT (☎01903/218638).

Teachers in Greece (TIG), Taxílou 79, Zográfou, 157 71 Athens (☎01/77 92 587), or 53 Talbot Rd, London W2 (☎0171/243 8260).

USA

English International, 655 Sutter St, Suite 500, San Francisco, CA 94102 (☎415/749-5633)

Transworld Teachers Training Center, 683 Sutter St, San Francisco, CA 94102 (☎415/776-8071).

Both the above offer TEFL courses, job listings and guidance for finding teaching work in Greece.

people experience any problems with it (though some schools don't like their employees to indulge, and/or may demand a cut). To obtain private students, you can advertise in the *Athens News* or *Greek Weekly News*. *Teaching English Abroad* by Susan Griffiths (Vacation Work) also provides useful information.

Examining work is another lucrative area, and the British Council recruits examiners for sessions in May–June and November–December. Both a degree and a TEFL qualification are required; if you have them, and some experience, it's worth contacting the British Council in Athens, at Filikís Etairlas, Platía Kolomaki (☎01/36 33 211 or ☎36 42 820).

AU PAIR WORK

The popularity and scale of private English teaching also means that English-speaking women are heavily in demand as **au pairs**. As ever, such positions tend to be exploitive and low-paid, but if you can use them to your own ends – living reasonably well and learning Greek – there can be mutual benefits.

It's unwise to arrange anything until you're in Greece, so you can at least meet and talk terms with your prospective family, and in Athens you should find little difficulty fixing something up. Posts are advertised in the daily *Athens News* and a couple of specialist agencies cater for women looking for employment:

Pioneer Tours, Níkis 11, Athens (☎01/32 24 321).

XEN (Greek YWCA), Amerikís 11, Athens (☎01/36 26 180).

DIRECTORY

ADMISSION FEES Admission fees to major ancient sites and most museums range from 200–1500dr, with an average fee of around 500dr. At most, there are reductions of 50–100 percent (the latter applying to EC nationals) for student card holders. In addition, entrance to all state-run sites and museums is free to all EC nationals on Sundays and public holidays – non-EC nationals will be unlucky to be detected as such on these days. It's free to take photographs, though the use of tripods or video-cameras incurs an extra charge of around 1000dr. It's also worth knowing that Classical studies students can get a free annual pass to all Greek museums and sites by presenting themselves at the office to the rear corner (Tossitsa/Bouboulinas) of the Archeological Museum in Athens – take documentation, two passport-sized photographs and be prepared to say you're a teacher.

BARGAINING isn't a regular feature of life, though you'll find it possible with private rooms and some off-season hotels. Similarly, you may be able to negotiate discounted rates for vehicle rental, especially for longer periods.

CHILDREN are worshipped and indulged in Greece, perhaps to excess, and present few problems when travelling. Baby foods and nappies/diapers are ubiquitous and reasonably priced, plus concessions are offered on most forms of transport. Private rooms establishments are more likely to offer some kind of babysitting service than the more impersonal hotels.

ELECTRICITY is 220 volt AC throughout the country. Wall outlets take double round-pin plugs as in the rest of continental Europe. North American appliances will require both a step-down transformer and a plug adapter.

DEPARTURE TAX A departure tax is levied on all international ferries – currently 1500dr per person *and* per car or motorbike. To non-EC states (Turkey, Egypt and Israel), it's 4000dr per person. There's also an airport departure tax of 2800–5600dr, depending on destination, but it's always included in the price of the ticket – there's no collection at the airport itself.

FILMS *Fuji* and *Agfa* films are reasonably priced and easy to have processed; *Kodachrome* and *Ektachrome* slide films are expensive, best bought (and processed) outside Greece.

GAY LIFE is still taboo to a certain extent and only high profile in certain areas, like Míkonos, still the most popular European gay resort after Ibiza in Spain. Lesser action occurs on Rhodes; for women, to a modest extent, at Erissós on Lésvos (appropriately). Homosexuality is legal over the age of 17, and (male) bisexuality quite widely accepted. The gay movement in Greece is represented by *Akoe Amphi*, PO Box 26022, 10022 Athens (☎01/77 19 221). See also p.116 and "Listings" in the *Athens* chapter.

GREEK LANGUAGE COURSES abound in Athens – see the city's "Listings" section for addresses.

LAUNDRIES (*plintíria*) are beginning to crop up in most of the main resort towns; sometimes an attended service wash is available for little or no extra charge over the basic cost of 1000–1200dr per wash and dry. Otherwise, ask rooms owners for a *skáfi* (laundry trough), a bucket (*kouvás*), or the special laundry area often available; they freak out if you use bathroom washbasins, Greek plumbing (and wall-mounting) being what they are.

PERÍPTERA are street-corner kiosks. They sell everything from pens to disposable razors, stationery to soap, sweets to condoms, cigarettes to plastic crucifixes . . . and are often open when nothing else is.

TIME Greek summertime begins at 4am on the last Sunday in March, when the clocks go forward one hour, and ends at 4am the last Sunday in September when they go back. Be alert to this, as scores of visitors miss planes, ferries, etc, every year; the change is not well publicized. Greek time is two hours ahead of Britain, three hours when the countries' respective changes to summertime fail to coincide. For North America, the difference is seven hours for Eastern Standard Time, ten hours for Pacific Standard Time, with again an extra hour for those weeks in April and October. A recorded time message (in Greek) is available by dialling ☎141.

TOILETS Public ones are usually in parks or squares, often subterranean; otherwise try a bus station. Except in areas frequented by tourists, public toilets tend to be pretty filthy – best to use the much cleaner ones in restaurants and bars. Note that throughout Greece, you drop paper in the adjacent wastebins, not in the bowl. Blocked toilets and dubious plumbing are common complaints among foreign visitors.

USEFUL THINGS TO BRING

An alarm clock (for early buses and ferries) and a flashlight (if you camp out); mosquito repellant, sunscreen, and ear plugs for noisy ferries and hotels.

PART TWO

THE

MAINLAND

THE NORTH:
MACEDONIA AND
THRACE

EPIRUS
AND THE
WEST

THESSALY
AND
CENTRAL
GREECE

ATHENS
AND
AROUND

THE
PELOPONNESE

0   100 km

CHAPTER ONE

ATHENS AND AROUND

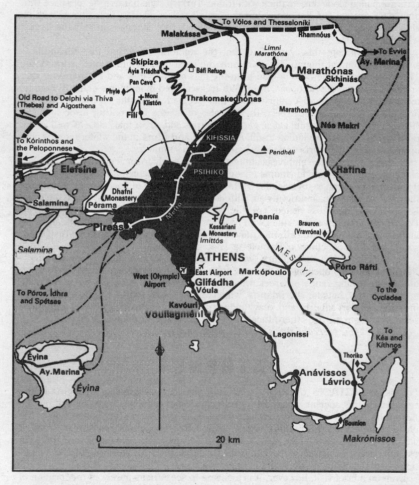

Athens is not a graceful city. It looks terrible from just about every approach; its air pollution is dire; and its traffic and postwar architecture are a disaster. For many of the four million-plus visitors who pass through each year, it can seem a dutiful stop. Their priorities usually include a visit to the Acropolis, an edifying trawl around the vast National Archeological Museum and an evening or two amid the tavernas of Pláka, the one surviving old quarter. Most tourists then get out fast, disillusioned at such sparse evidence of the past and so little apparent charm.

Such are the basic facts – yet somehow the city has the character to transcend them. An exhausting but always stimulating mix of metropolis and backwater, First and Third World, West and East, Athens has seen its population soar from 700,000 to four million – over a third of the nation's people – since World War II. The pace of this transformation is reflected in the city's chaotic mix of urban and rural: goats graze in yards, horse-carts are pulled along streets thick with traffic, Turkish-style bazaars vie for space with outlets for Armani and Benetton. And the city's hectic modernity is tempered with an air of intimacy and hominess; as any Greek will tell you, Athens is merely the largest village in the country.

Once you accept this, you'll find that the **ancient sites** and the **Acropolis** – supreme monument though it is – are only the most obvious of **Athens' attractions**. There are startling views to be had from the hills of **Likavitós** and **Filopáppou**; and, around the foot of the Acropolis, the **Pláka** has scattered monuments of the Byzantine, medieval and nineteenth-century town that seemed so exotic to Byron and the Romantics. As you might expect, the city also offers the best **eating** to be found in Greece, with some beautiful cafés, garden tavernas and street markets – as well as the most varied nightlife, including traditional **music and films** in the winter months, and open-air cinema, **concerts** and **Classical drama** in summer.

Outside Athens, the emphasis shifts more exclusively to ancient sites; the beaches along the Attic coast are functional enough escapes for Athenians, but hardly priorities if you are moving on to the islands. Of the sites, the Temple of Poseidon at **Sounion** is the most popular trip, and rightly so, with its dramatic cliff-top position above the cape. Lesser-known and less-visited are the sanctuaries at **Rhamnous** and **Brauron** (Vravróna), both rewarding ruins with beaches nearby. The committed might also take in the burial mound at **Marathon** – though this is more Classical pilgrimage than sightseeing – and the Sanctuary of Demeter at **Eleusis** (Elefsína).

For relief from all this culture, walkers may want to head for the **mountains** – **Párnitha**, most compellingly – that ring the city, where springtime hikes reveal some of the astonishing range of Greek wild flowers. Hedonists, however, will already be making escape plans for **the islands**, which are served by ferries and hydrofoils from the Athenian port-suburb (and heavy industrial centre) of **Pireás** (Piraeus) and, more selectively, from the two other Attican ferry terminals at **Ráfina** and **Lávrio**.

Coverage of the ports and sights of Attica starts on p.123.

ATHENS

For visitors, **ATHENS** (ATHINÁ in modern Greek) has stunning highlights in the vestiges of the ancient, Classical Greek city, most famously represented by the **Acropolis** and its surrounding archeological sites. These form the first section of the guide to the city's sights in this chapter – "The Acropolis and Ancient Athens" – and, if it's your first trip to the city, they're likely to occupy a fair amount of your time. An essential accompaniment is the **National Archeological Museum**: the finest collection of Greek antiquities anywhere in the world.

Even on a brief visit, however, it is a shame to see Athens purely as the location of ancient sites and museums. Although the **neighbourhoods** may lack the style and monuments of most of their European-capital counterparts, they are worth at least a casual exploration. The old nineteenth-century quarter of **Pláka**, in particular, is a delight, with its mix of Turkish and Greek-island architecture, and an array of odd little museums devoted to traditional arts, ceramics and music. Just to its north, the **bazaar** area, around Athinás and Eólou, retains an almost Middle Eastern atmosphere in its life and trade, while the **National Gardens**, elegant **Kolonáki** and the hill of **Likavitós** offer respite from the maelstrom. Further afield, but still well within the

limits of Greater Athens, are the monasteries of **Kessarianí** and **Dhafní**, the latter
with Byzantine mosaics the equal of any in Greece.

Some history

Athens has been inhabited continuously for over 7000 years. Its *acropolis*, supplied with
springwater and commanding views of all seaward approaches, and encircled by
protective mountains on its landward side, was a natural choice for prehistoric settle
ment and for the Mycenaeans, who established a palace-fortress on the rock. Its development into a city-state and artistic centre continued apace under the Dorians,
Phoenicians and various dynastic rulers, reaching its apotheosis in the fifth century
BC. This was the **Classical period**, when the Athenians, having launched themselves
into an experiment in radical democracy, celebrated their success with a flourish of art,
architecture, literature and philosophy that has pervaded Western culture ever since.
(An account of the Classical Period is given with the main sites of Ancient Athens on
p.75–77; later, Roman, history is outlined on p.91.)

The discontinuity from ancient to medieval Athens was due, essentially, to the emergence of **Christianity**. Having survived with little change through years of Roman rule,
the city lost its pivotal role in the Roman-Greek world after the division of the Roman
empire into eastern and western halves, and the establishment of Byzantium
(Constantinople) as capital of the eastern – **Byzantine** – empire. There, a new
Christian sensibility soon outshone the prevailing ethic of Athens, where schools of
philosophy continued to teach a pagan Neoplatonism. In 529 these schools were finally
closed by Justinian I and the city's temples, including the Parthenon, were reconsecrated as churches.

Athens featured rarely in the chronicles of the time, enjoying a brief revival under
the foreign powers of the Middle Ages: in the aftermath of the piratical Fourth
Crusade, Athens – together with the Peloponnese and much of Central Greece –
passed into the hands of the **Franks**. At the Acropolis they established a ducal court
(of some magnificence, according to contemporary accounts) and for a century Athens
was back in the mainstream of Europe. Frankish control, however, was based on little
more than a provincial aristocracy. In 1311 their forces battled **Catalan** mercenaries,
who had a stronghold in Thebes, and were driven to oblivion in a swamp. The Catalans,
having set up their own duchy, in turn gave way to **Florentines** and, briefly,
Venetians, before the arrival in 1456 of **Sultan Mehmet II**, the Turkish conqueror of
Constantinople.

Turkish Athens was never much more than a garrison town. The links with the
West, which had preserved a sense of continuity with the Classical and Roman city,
were severed, and the flood of visitors was reduced to a trickle of French and Italian
ambassadors to the Sublime Porte and the occasional traveller or painter. The town
does not seem to have been oppressed by Ottoman rule, however: the Greeks enjoyed
some autonomy, and both Jesuit and Capuchin monasteries continued to thrive.
Although the Acropolis became the home of the Turkish governor and the Parthenon
was used as a mosque, life in the village-like quarters around the Acropolis drifted back
to a semi-rural existence. Similarly, the great port of **Pireás**, still partially enclosed
within its ancient walls, was left to serve just a few dozen fishing boats.

After four centuries of Ottoman occupation, **Independence** was just two decades
away. In 1821, in common with the inhabitants of a score of other towns across the
country, the Greeks of Athens rose in rebellion. They occupied the Turkish quarters of
the lower town – the current **Pláka** – and laid siege to the Acropolis. The Turks withdrew, but five years later were back to reoccupy the Acropolis fortifications, while the
Greeks evacuated to the countryside. When the Ottoman garrison finally left in 1834,
and the Bavarian architects of the new German-born monarchy moved in, Athens was
arguably at its nadir.

For all the claims of its ancient past, and despite the city's natural advantages, Athens was not the first-choice capital of modern Greece. That honour went instead to Náfplio in the Peloponnese, where the War of Independence was masterminded by Capodistrias and where the first Greek National Assembly met in 1828. Had Capodistrias not been assassinated, in 1831, the capital would most likely have remained in the Peloponnese – if not at Náfplio, then at Trípoli, Kórinthos (Corinth) or Pátra, all much more established and sizeable towns. But following Capodistrias's death, the "Great Powers" of Western Europe intervened, inflicting on the Greeks a king of their own choosing – **Otho**, son of Ludwig I of Bavaria – and, in 1834, transferring the capital and court to Athens. The reasoning was almost purely symbolic and sentimental: Athens was not only insignificant in terms of population and physical extent but was then at the edge of the territories of the new Greek state, which was yet to include Northern Thessaly, Epirus and Macedonia, or any of the islands beyond the Cyclades.

The **nineteenth-century development** of Athens was a gradual and fairly controlled process. While the archeologists stripped away all the Turkish and Frankish embellishments from the Acropolis, a modest city took shape along the lines of the Bavarians' Neoclassical grid. **Pireás**, meanwhile, grew into a port again, though until this century its activities continued to be dwarfed by the main Greek shipping centres on the islands of Síros and Ídhra (Hydra).

The first mass expansion of both municipalities came suddenly, in 1923, as the result of the tragic Greek–Turkish war in **Asia Minor**. The peace treaty that resolved the war entailed the exchange of Greek and Turkish ethnic populations, their identity being determined solely on the basis of religion. A million and a half Greeks, mostly from the age-old settlements along the Asia Minor coast, but also many Turkish-speaking peoples from the communities of inland Anatolia, arrived in Greece as refugees. Over half of them settled in Athens, Pireás and the neighbouring villages, changing at a stroke the whole make-up of the capital. Their integration, and survival, is one of the great events of the city's history, and has left its mark on the Athens of today. The web of suburbs that straddle the metro line from Athens to Pireás, and sprawl out into the hills, bear nostalgic names of their refugees' origins – *Néa Smírni* (New Smyrna), *Néa Iónia*, *Néa Filadhélfia* – as do many streets. Originally, these neighbourhoods were exactly that: refugee villages with populations primarily from one or another Anatolian town, built in ramshackle fashion, often with a single water source for two dozen families.

The merging of these shanty-suburbs and their populations with the established communities of Athens and Pireás dominated the years leading up to **World War II**. With the war, however, new concerns emerged. Athens was hit hard by German occupation: during the winter of 1942 there were an estimated 2000 deaths from starvation each day. In late 1944, when the Germans had finally left (Allied policy was to tie them down in the Balkans), the capital saw the first skirmishes of **civil war**, with British forces being ordered to fight against their former Greek allies in the Communist-dominated resistance army, ELAS. Physical evidence of the ensuing month-long battle, the *Dhekemvrianá*, can still be seen in a handful of bullet-pocked walls. From 1946 to 1949 Athens was a virtual island in the civil war, with road approaches to the Peloponnese and the north only tenuously kept open.

During the 1950s, however, after the civil war, the city started to expand rapidly. A massive **industrial investment** programme – financed largely by the Americans, who had won Greece for their sphere of influence – took place, and, concurrently, the capital saw huge **immigration** from the war-torn, impoverished countryside. The open spaces between the old refugee suburbs began to fill and, by the late 1960s, Greater Athens covered a continuous area from the slopes of mounts Pendéli and Párnitha down to Pireás and Elefsína.

On a visual level, much of the modern city is unremittingly ugly, since old buildings were demolished wholesale in the name of quick-buck development, particularly during the colonels' junta of 1967–74. Only now are planning and preservation measures being enforced – in a last-ditch attempt to rescue the city from its engulfing **pollution** (see box below). The PASOK administration of the late 1980s endowed the city with thousands of trees, shrubs, patches of garden and an ever-growing number of pedestrian-only streets – though Athens still lags far behind Paris or London in terms of open space. There is also increasing awareness of the nineteenth-century architectural heritage – what's left of it – with many old houses being restored and repainted.

Long-term solutions are proving more elusive: priorities include decanting industry and services into the provinces to ease the stresses on the city's environment (see box below) and its ailing infrastructure, and creating a mass transport network capable of meeting the needs of a modern capital city. While progress is being made, it all came too late – and was far too little – to impress the International Olympic Committee, which favoured Atlanta's bid for the 1996 Olympics over that of Athens, to Greece's great chagrin and disappointment.

ATHENS AND ITS ENVIRONMENT

The enormous and rapid population increase and attendant industrial development that characterized the postwar period had a disastrous effect on the **environment of Athens**. With a third of the Greek population, half the country's industry and over two-thirds of its cars crammed into Greater Athens, the capital has found itself with one of the world's worst **pollution** problems. A noxious cloud, the *néfos*, trapped by the circle of mountains and aerial inversion layers, can frequently be seen hovering over the city. Despite what your burning eyes and throat may tell you, some improvement in the situation has been registered in recent decades, though not in the critical pollutant nitrogen dioxide. Moreover, the level of pollution still aggravates acute respiratory diseases and arguably contributed to the high death toll in the freak heatwaves or *kávsones* during the summers of 1987 and 1988. Alarmingly, the *néfos* is also gnawing away at the very fabric of the ancient city, including the Parthenon Marbles. As sulphur dioxide settles on the columns and statuary, it becomes a friable coating of calcium sulphate, which is washed off by the winter rains, taking a thin layer of stone with it.

Despite the severity of the situation, the main anti-pollution measure of recent years has been restrictions on the use of **private cars**. Successive governments have toyed with limitations on weekday use of vehicles in a central restricted zone, stipulating alternate days for odd- and even-numbered licence plates, but their efforts are undermined by the fact that most shops, offices and businesses persist in closing for a three-hour summer siesta – making for four rush hours a day and double the amount of pollution and traffic problems. Additionally, short-sighted government taxation and duty policies mean that Athenians keep their beloved autos until they die of metal fatigue, rarely maintaining or tuning them to optimum, low-exhaust running conditions.

More far-reaching measures are at last being taken to help the city's public transport system rise to the challenge: the extra airport at Spata creeps slowly towards realization and, back in the heart of the city, virtually every landmark square is currently being excavated for the expansion of the metro system – nominally scheduled for completion in 1997, although a more realistic finish-date might be early in the next millennium. The three-line metro will be complemented by a circular tram system downtown and the operation of passenger ferries between the coastal suburbs and metro stations at Pireás and Fáliro.

Furthermore, all electricity, most heating and some cooking may soon be fuelled by copious supplies of Russian natural gas, which are supposed to arrive (along with their pipeline) in 1996 or 1997. With air inversion layers prompting pollution alerts in both summer and winter, there is still a long way to go, but these policies do at least offer a ray of hope.

LOCAL BUSES
- ▽A Dháfni, Eléfsina
- ▽B Ráfina, Soúnion, Lávrio, Marathón, Rhámnous
- ▽C Glifádha, Voúla and the beaches
- ▽D Sounion extra stop and # 40 stop
- ▽E # 051 terminal
- ▽F # 090 & # 091 stops
- Ⓜ Metro stations

500 m

0

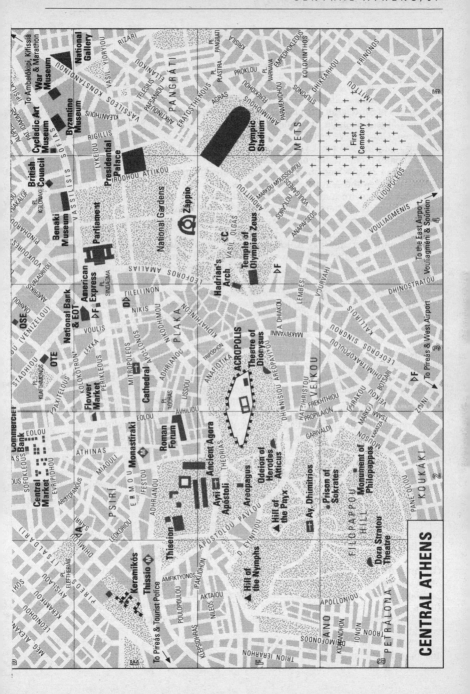

CENTRAL ATHENS

Orientation, arrival and information

As a visitor, you're likely to spend most time in the central grid of Athens, a compact, walkable area. Only on arrival at, or departure from, the various far-flung stations and terminals (see below), do you have to confront the confused urban sprawl. Once in the centre, it's a simple matter to **orient** yourself. There are four strategic reference points: the squares of **Síndagma** ("Syntagma" on many English-language maps) and **Omónia**, the hills of the **Acropolis** (unmistakable with its temple crown) and (to the northeast) **Likavitós**. Once you've established these as a mental compass you shouldn't get lost for long – anyone will point you back in the direction of Síndagma or Omónia at the (approximate) pronunciation of their names.

Síndagma (Platía Sindágmatos, "Constitution Square", to give it its full title) lies midway between the Acropolis and Likavitós. With the Greek Parliament building – plus mammoth metro tunnelling and traffic diversions – on its uphill side, and banks and airline offices clustered around, it is to all intents and purposes the centre of the capital. Almost everything of daytime interest is within twenty to thirty minutes' walk of the square.

To the northeast, the ritzy **Kolonáki** quarter curls around the slopes of **Likavitós**, with a funicular up the hillside to save you the final climb. To the east, behind the Parliament, the jungly **National Gardens** function as the city's chief lung and meeting place; beyond them are the 1896 Olympic stadium and the attractive neighbourhoods of **Pangráti** and **Méts**, both thronged with restaurants and bars.

To the southwest, lapping up to the base of the **Acropolis**, spread the ramshackle but much-commercialized lanes of **Pláka**, the lone surviving area of the nineteenth-century, pre-independence village. Beyond the Acropolis itself huddles **Filopáppou hill**, an area of parkland ringed by the neighbourhoods of **Veïkoú, Koukáki** and **Áno Petrálona**, also good choices for accommodation and meals. (Filopáppou Hill itself should be avoided at night, when it has a reputation for rapes and muggings.)

Northwest of Síndagma, two broad thoroughfares, **Stadhíou** and **Panepistimíou** (officially but ineffectually renamed Venizélou), run in just under a kilometre to **Omónia** (fully, Platía Omonías, "Concord Square"). This is an approximate Athenian equivalent of Piccadilly Circus or Times Square: more than a bit seedy, with fast-food cafés, gypsies, pickpockets and a scattering of porno shows in the backstreets around. To the northeast, beyond Panepistimíou, is the student neighbourhood of **Exárhia**, a slightly "alternative" district, with a concentration of lively tavernas and bars there and in its extension **Neápoli**. South of Omónia, stretching down to **Ermoú** street and the **Monastiráki** bazaar district on the borders of Pláka, lies the main commercial centre, crammed with offices and shops offering everything from insurance to machine tools.

Points of arrival

Athens airport – **Ellinikón** – is 9km out of the city, southeast along the coast towards Glifádha. It has two distinct sections – **west** (*dhitikó*) and **east** (*anatolikó*) – whose separate entrances are five minutes' drive apart on either side of the perimeter fence. **Olympic Airways** flights, domestic and foreign, operate from the western terminal; all **other airlines** use the eastern. Both terminals have **money exchange** facilities, open 24 hours at the eastern terminal, but only from 7am to 11pm at the western one (though there are two automatic teller machines that accept Visa, Mastercard, Cirrus and Plus); insist on some small-denomination notes for paying for your bus ticket or taxi ride.

To get into the city, the quickest and simplest way is to get a **taxi**, which, at 1000–1500dr – depending on traffic and number of bags – to central Athens or Pireás, is a modest cost split two or more ways. Make sure before setting out that the meter is switched on, and visible. Overcharging of tourists can be brutal. You may find (see comments on taxis overleaf) that you'll have fellow passengers in the cab; each drop-off will pay the full fare.

If you're willing to wait a bit, and carry your bags around, a blue-and-yellow **express bus** (see box below) calls at both terminals on a variable schedule around the clock, dropping you at selected points in the city centre. You should note that the wait can be up to an hour at night, and 30–40 minutes during the day. Service from the west terminal tends to be less consistent; the schedule is further cut back between October and April. The fare is currently 160dr (200dr between midnight and 5.30am); tickets can usually be bought on the bus if you're forearmed with small change.

EXPRESS AIRPORT BUSES

Owing to the metro uproar and funding problems, express bus services linking the airport terminals, the centre of the city and the port of Pireás can often be disrupted, particularly between October and April.

In summer at least, there are **two Athens lines**, the **#90** single-decker from Omónia via Síndagma to the west airport, and the double-decker **#91** from the same in-town terminals, which calls at the east airport, before ending up at the west airport. The most obvious stops for the centre of town are Stadhíou, near Omónia, and Síndagma; the Singroú 96 and Stilés stops are useful if you plan to stay in the Veïkoú/Koukáki area. Heading out to the airport, it's safest to flag the buses down at the corner of Othónos and Amalías at Síndagma, where they make a short halt. In theory, both services operate every half-hour 6am–9pm, with the #91 service continuing to run every 40 minutes from 9pm to 12.20am. In practice, the #90 in particular can be so unreliable – especially in winter – that it's easier on your nerves to take a taxi when leaving to catch a flight.

The **Pireás route**, #19, is as follows: Platía Karaïskáki/Aktí Tselépi–Telonío–Mégaro–Fálirou–Airport (west terminal)–Airport (east terminal).The frequency is just 12 times daily 5am–8.20pm from Pireás, 6am–9.20pm from the airport. For hydrofoils from the Zéa port, the best stop is Telonío, although trolley #20 (labelled Fáliro) from the Pireás subway station passes much closer to Zéa. The Mégaro stop is by the international ferry dock; Aktí Tselépi and the landscaped Platía Karaïskáki front the main harbour, where most island ferries depart and ticket agents are concentrated.

Each service has a 160dr flat fare (200dr from midnight to 5.30am).

Train stations

There are two train stations, almost adjacent, a couple of hundred metres northwest of Omónia, off Dheliyáni street. The **Stathmós Laríssis** handles the main lines coming from the north (Lárissa, Thessaloníki, the Balkans, Western Europe and Turkey). The **Stathmós Peloponníssou** three blocks south, is the terminal for the narrow-gauge line circling the Peloponnese, including the stretch to Pátra (the main port for the ferries from Italy and Corfu).

From either station, you are five to fifteen minutes' walk away from the concentration of hotels around Platía Viktorías and Exárhia, both handy for the National Archeological Museum and excellent restaurants. For hotels elsewhere, the yellow trolley **bus #1** southbound passes along Sámou, one block east of the Laríssis station (to get to it from the Peloponníssou terminal, use the giant metal overpass, then detour around the metro works) and makes a strategic loop down through Omónia, along Stadhíou to Síndagma, then down Filellínon to Hadrian's Arch (for Méts), and finally along Veïkoú to Koukáki (on the southeast side of Fílopáppou hill).

Be wary of **taxis** (both official and unlicensed) at the train stations – some thrive on newly arrived tourists, shuttling them a couple of blocks for highly inflated fares.

Bus stations

Again, there are two principal terminals. Coming into Athens **from Northern Greece or the Peloponnese**, you'll find yourself at **Kifissoú 100**, a ten-minute bus ride from the centre. The least expensive way into town is to take city bus #051 to the corner of Zinónos/ Menándhrou, just off Omónia and only a block or two from a yellow trolley-bus stop. **Routes from central Greece** (see p.135 for specific destinations) arrive at **Liossíon 260**, north of the train stations; to get into the centre, take the blue city bus #024 to Síndagma.

In addition, there are international **OSE buses**, run by the railway company, which arrive at the Stathmós Peloponnísou. Private **international bus companies** arrive at, and leave from, a variety of locations. Most will take you to the train station or to Kifissoú 100; a few drop passengers right in the city centre.

Pireás: the ferries

If you arrive by boat at **Pireás**, the simplest access to Athens is by **metro** to the stations at Monastiráki, Omónia or Viktorías. Trains run from 6am to midnight, with fares varying from 75 to 100dr according to a zone system. For the airport, take express bus **#19** (see box on p.000). **Taxis** between Pireás and central Athens should cost around 1000dr, including baggage, although rates double at night – again, see the comments below.

There's a full **account of Pireás**, together with a **map of the central area**, showing the metro station and harbours, on p.123–27.

Information

The city's main **EOT tourist office** is located inside the National Bank of Greece on the Stadhíou corner of Síndagma, and is an invaluable source of information, dispensing ferry timetable sheets (use these as guidelines only), along with maps and pamphlets for all parts of the country. The office is useful, too, for enquiries about the **Athens Festival** (see p.117).

To complement our plans and the free EOT map, the street-indexed **Falk-Plan** is a good, **large-scale map** of the city (hard to obtain in Athens, but see the bookshop listings on p.119). If you're planning a long stay, the **Athína-Pireás Proastia** A–Ω atlas, co-published by Kapranidhis and Fotis, is available from kiosks and bookshops, but is in Greek only and is quite pricey at around 5000dr.

FINDING AN ADDRESS

The Greek for street is **odhós** but – both when addressing letters and in speech – people usually refer only to the name of the street: Ermoú, Márkou Moussoúrou, etc. The practice is different with **platía** (square) and **leofóros** (avenue), which always appear before the name. In written addresses, the house number is written after the street name, thus: Ermoú 13. We have adopted the same practice. **Grid keys**, given in italics throughout this chapter, refer to the main Athens map on pp.66–67; for more detail on the Pláka area, see the map on p.88.

City transport

Athens is served by slow but wide-ranging buses, and a fast but very limited metro system; taxis are generally ready to fill in the gaps. Public transport networks operate from around **5am to midnight**, with a skeleton service on some of the buses in the small hours. In addition, a few of the yellow trolleys, including the useful #1 route, run all night on Saturdays.

Buses

The **bus network** is extensive and cheap, with a flat fare (currently 75dr, soon to rise to 100dr). Tickets must be bought in advance from kiosks, certain shops and newsagents, or from the limited number of booths run by bus personnel near major stops – look for the brown, red and white logo proclaiming *"Isitiria edho"* (tickets here). They're sold individually or in bundles of ten, and must be cancelled in a special machine when boarding. Fare-dodgers risk an on-the-spot fine equivalent to twenty times the current fare. Cancelled tickets apply only to a particular journey and vehicle; there are no transfers. If you're staying long enough, there's a monthly pass for 3750dr – a saving of two-thirds if you ride four times daily.

Buses are very crowded at peak times, unbearably hot in summer traffic jams, and chronically plagued by strikes and slow-downs; where you can walk instead, you probably will. Express services run to and from the airport – see box on p.69. Other **routes**, where relevant, are detailed in the text. The most straightforward are the **yellow trolley buses** #1–19: **#1** connects the Laríssis train station with Omónia, Síndagma and Veïkoú/Koukáki; **#2**, **#3**, **#4**, **#5** and **#12** all link Síndagma with Omónia and the National Archeological Museum on Patissíon. In addition, there are scores of **blue city buses**, all with three-digit numbers and serving an infinity of routes out into the straggling suburbs and beyond.

The metro

The single-line **metro** (75dr single-zone fare, 25dr supplement for passing Omónia in either direction) runs from Pireás in the south to Kifissiá in the north; in the centre, there are stops at Thissío, Monastiráki, Omónia and Platía Viktorías. Long-awaited work on lateral extensions to the system has finally begun, but don't expect much before the new millennium; archeological finds are hindering progress. Metro and bus tickets are not interchangeable.

Taxis

Athenian **taxis** are the cheapest of any EU capital – fares around the city centre will rarely run above 700dr, with the airport and Pireás only 1000–1700dr – the exact amount determined by traffic and amount of luggage. All officially licensed cars are painted yellow and have a special red-on-white number plate. You can wave them down on the street, pick them up at ranks at the train station, airport or the National Gardens corner of Síndagma, or get your hotel to phone one for you. They are most elusive during the rush hours of 1.30–2.30pm and 7.30–8.30pm.

Make sure the **meter** is switched on when you get in, with its display visible and properly zeroed; theoretically, it's illegal to quote a flat fare for a ride within city limits – the meter must be used. If it's "not working", find another taxi. Attempts at **overcharging** tourists are particularly common with small-hours arrivals at the airport; a threat to have hotel staff or the police adjudicate usually elicits cooperation, as they will very likely take your side and the police have the power to revoke a driver's operating permit.

Legitimate surcharges – in force since 1990 and likely to increase before too long – can considerably bump up the final bill from the total shown on the meter. Currently the flag falls at 200dr, there's an automatic 200dr supplement for entering the confines of the airport, and a 100dr surcharge for journeys involving train or ferry terminals; luggage is about 40dr extra per piece; double tariff applies between midnight and 5am; and there are Easter and Christmas bonuses which seem to extend for a week or two either side of the actual date. Every taxi must have a plastic dash-mounted placard listing extra charges in English and Greek.

Every taxi also has mounted on its roof either an "M" (for *monó* or odd-numbered) or "Z" (for *zigó* or even-numbered), corresponding to the last digit of the registration number. On odd-numbered days of each month, vehicles classified as "Z" or even-numbered are banned from entering a large central grid, and vice-versa on even-numbered dates; this may account for reluctance on the part of a driver to take you to your destination. The restrictions do not apply to cars with foreign registration plates.

To try and make ends meet on government-regulated fare limits, taxi drivers will often pick up a whole **string of passengers** along the way. This is technically illegal but universally practised. There is no fare-sharing: each passenger (or group of passengers) pays the full fare for their journey. So if you're picked up by an already-occupied taxi, memorize the meter reading at once; you'll pay from that point on, plus the 200dr minimum. When hailing an occupied taxi, yell out your destination, so the kerb-crawling driver can decide whether you suit him or not.

Accommodation

Hotels and **hostels** can be packed to the gills in midsummer – August especially – but for most of the year there are enough beds in the city to go around, and to suit most wallets and tastes. It makes sense to **phone** before turning up: if you just set out and do the rounds, you'll find somewhere, but in summer, unless you're early in the day, it's likely to be at the fourth or fifth attempt. If you have the money for a hotel officially categorized by tourist authorities as C-class (④ or above – see box below; for more on the official designations, see *Basics*), you can book through the **hotel reservations desk** inside the National Bank of Greece on Síndagma.

For cheaper places, you're on your own. Find a street kiosk (there are hundreds in Athens) and ask to use their phone; you pay 15dr per unit after you've finished making all the calls – there's no need to find coins. Virtually every hotel and hostel in the city will have an English-speaking receptionist. Once you locate a vacancy, ask to see the room before booking in – standards vary greatly even within the same building, and you can avoid occasional overcharging by checking the government-regulated room prices displayed by law on the back of the door in each room.

Our listings are grouped into four main areas. The quarters of **Pláka and Síndagma**, despite their commercialization, are highly atmospheric – and within easy walking distance of all the main sites and the Monastiráki metro station (a useful gateway for the port of Pireás). Occasionally gritty and sleazy, the **bazaar area** is the city at its most authentic. The downside of some of the hotels in these areas is that they are subject to round-the-clock noise; if you want uninterrupted sleep, you're better off heading for one of the quieter neighbourhoods a little further out.

Veïkoú, Koukáki and Pangráti are attractive parts of the city, and though slightly out of the way – twenty minutes' walk from Síndagma or the heart of Pláka – compensate with excellent neighbourhood tavernas and cafés. Veïkoú and Koukáki are easiest reached from Pireás via the #9 trolley bus, whose terminus is just outside the Petrálona metro station, while Pangráti is on the #4 or #12 trolleys from Záppio. Around **Exárhia and Platía Viktorías** (officially Platía Kiriákou), to the north of Omónia, you are again out of the tourist mainstream, but benefit from good-value local restaurants and the proximity of cinemas, clubs and bars. These areas now have clusters of very good-value, mid-range hotels, just a short walk away from the train stations (and metros Omónia or Viktorías).

The city's **campsites** are out in the suburbs, not especially cheap, and only worth using if you have a camper-van to park; phone ahead to book space in season. **Camping out rough** in Athens is not a good idea. Police patrol many of the parks, especially those by the train stations, and muggings are commonplace. Even the train stations are no real refuge, closing up when services stop and cleared of any stragglers.

Grid references (in italics) refer to the map on pp.66–67.

The **telephone code** for Greater Athens and Pireás is ☎01; calling from overseas, omit the zero.

Pláka and Síndagma

Acropolis House, Kódhrou 6, *E3* (☎32 22 344). A very clean, well-sited pension; all rooms with baths, though some are across the hall. Rates include breakfast. ④–⑤.

Adonis, Kodhroú 3, *E3* (☎32 49 737). A modern but unobjectionable low-rise pension across the street from *Acropolis House*, with some suites. ④–⑤.

Byron, Víronos 19, *F3* (☎32 53 554). Smallish, pleasant pension that should definitely be booked in advance. The front rooms with balconies justify the rather stiff prices. ④.

Dioskouri, Pittákou 6, *F3* (☎32 48 165). Under new and energetic management; renovated, this pension benefits from a breakfast garden and a good locale (one block in from Leofóros Amalías). No singles per se. ③.

George's Guest House, Níkis 46, *E3* (☎32 36 474). One of the cheapest and most enduring of the hostel-type places, located just a block west of Síndagma. Various-sized dorms and some doubles, but cramped bathrooms are consistently grubby. ②.

John's Place Patróoü 5, *E3* (☎32 29 719). Basic (no en suite baths) but acceptable pension. ②–③.

Kouros, Kódhrou 11, *E3* (☎32 27 431). Slightly faded pension, but with reasonable facilities; shared baths, sinks in rooms. Located on a pedestrianized street (the continuation of Voulís – two blocks southwest of Síndagma). ③.

Myrto, Níkis 40, *E3* (☎32 27 237). A bit over-priced, but has baths in all rooms and a small bar. Just off Síndagma. ⑤.

Nefeli, Iperídhou 16, *E3* (☎32 28 044). Another mid-range hotel, mercifully not usually block-booked by tour groups. ④–⑤.

Phaedra, Herefóndos 16 at the Adhrianoú junction, *F3* (☎32 27 795). Very plain and ripe for an overhaul, but clean and quiet at night – thanks to its location at the junction of two pedestrian malls. Prices fluctuate wildly with season. ③–④.

Solonion, Spírou Tsángari 11, *F3* (☎32 20 008). Eccentric and (usually) friendly staff in a rather run-down 1950s building; no single rooms. ②.

Student Inn, Kidhathinéon 18, *E3* (☎32 44 808). A hostel that's recently become a bona fide hotel; singles, doubles and triples with shared baths. Prone to nocturnal noise from outside, but otherwise OK; 1.30am curfew. ③.

Thisseus Inn, Thisséos 10, *E3* (☎32 45 960). You don't get much more central than this – three blocks west of Síndagma – nor much cheaper. No frills, but clean enough, and with a kitchen for guests' use. Some 3- and 4-bed rooms. ①.

XEN (YWCA), Amerikís 11, *D3* (☎36 24 291). **Women-only** hostel just north of Síndagma – *not* in Pláka – that provides clean, relatively quiet rooms, a self-service restaurant, a small library and Greek classes. Well worth considering. The YMCA (**men-only**) equivalent nearby, the **XAN** (Omírou 28, *D3*; ☎36 26 970), is less inspiring. ①–②.

ROOM PRICE CODES

All establishments listed in this book have been price-graded according to the scale below. The rates quoted represent the cheapest available room in high season; all are prices for a double room, except for category ①, which are per person rates. Out of season, rates can drop by up to fifty percent, especially if you negotiate rates for a stay of three or more nights. Single rooms, where available, cost around seventy percent of the price of a double.

① 1400–2000dr (£4–5.50/US$6–8.50)   ④ 8000–12000dr (£22–33/US$33–50)

② 4000–6000dr (£11–16.50/US$17–25)   ⑤ 12000–16000dr (£33–44/US$50–66)

③ 6000–8000dr (£16.50–22/US$25–33)   ⑥ 16000dr (£44/US$66) and upwards

For more accommodation details, see pp.34–35.

The Bazaar area

Note that most of the hotels on Sofokléous (F2), and on adjacent Athinás, up towards Omónia, are worked by prostitutes. The area is tame enough, even at night, but you wouldn't want to actually stay in these places unless you're a compulsive slummer.

Anatoli, Ermoú 69, *E2*. Basic rooms with shared baths, but the price is right. ②.

Carolina, Kolokotróni 55, *E3* (☎32 28 148). A quieter and and more savoury location; some rooms with bath. ④.

Hermion, Ermoú 66c, *E2* (☎32 12 753). Not the most salubrious part of the bazaar, but the hotel itself is okay, if a little overpriced. ③.

Pella Inn, Ermoú 104, *E2* (☎32 50 598). Despite hints of use by prostitutes, fair enough value and helpful proprietor. ②.

Tembi, Eólou 29, *E2* (☎32 13 175). Used to foreigners: book exchange, drinks, fridge, etc plus handy, affiliated travel agency. Rooms with and without bath. ③.

Veïkoú, Koukáki and Pangráti

Acropolis View, Webster 10, Veïkoú, *F2* (☎92 17 303). Stone-clad, smallish hotel whose front rooms and roof café live up to its name. ⑤–⑥.

Art Gallery, Erekhthíou 5, Veïkoú, *G3* (☎92 38 376). Original paintings on the walls lend this good-value pension its name. A relative bargain; all rooms have private baths. ③.

Austria, Moussón 7, Veïkoú, *G2* (☎92 35 151). Owned and staffed by Greek-Austrians, hence the name; real filter coffee, at last. ⑤ – bargainable to ⑤, without breakfast.

Marble House, in a quiet cul-de-sac off A. Zinni 35, Koukáki, *F2* (☎92 34 058). Probably the best value in Koukáki, with a very helpful French/Greek management. Often full, so call ahead. Most rooms with bath; also two self-catering studios. ③–④.

Tony's, Zaharítsa 26, Koukáki, *G2* (☎92 36 370). A quiet and clean pension favoured, for some reason, by visiting models; all rooms en suite. ③–④.

Youth Hostel #5, Damaréos 75, Pangráti, off map beyond *G5* (☎75 19 530). A bit out of the way but friendly, no curfew and in a decent, quiet neighbourhood; trolleys #2, #11 or #12 from downtown will get you most of the way there. ①.

Exárhia and Platía Viktorías

Athenian Inn, Háritos 22, Kolonáki, *D5* (☎72 38 097). Not actually in Exárhia but listed here as it's virtually the only place in this posh neighbourhood. Small, elegant and dead convenient for most of the museums around the National Gardens. ⑥.

Brazil, Fílis 62, Platía Viktorías, *B2* (☎88 14 944). Small, modernized, quiet hotel with garden. Bargain rates, depending on seasonal fluctuations. ②–④.

Dryades, Dhriadhón 4, off Anexartisías, Exárhia, *C3* (☎36 20 191). A small, quiet hotel, co-managed with the *Orion*, behind the National Archeological Museum. ④.

Elli, Heïdhen 29, Platía Viktorías, *B2* (☎88 15 876). Characterful, B-class pension in refurbished Neoclassical building on quiet tree-lined street. ③–④.

Exarhion, Themistokléous 55, Platía Exárhia, *C3* (☎36 01 256). Big 1960s high-rise hotel that's surprisingly inexpensive and well placed, if a bit noisy. ③.

Feron, Férron 43, near Aharnón, Platía Viktorías, *B2* (☎82 32 083). Actually a hostel, although it calls itself a hotel, with two eight-bedded rooms and a few doubles. ②–③.

Museum, Bouboulínas 16, corner Tossítsa, Exárhia, *C3* (☎36 05 611). Nicely placed, good-value hotel, right behind the National Archeological Museum and parkland. ③.

Orion, Anexartisías 5, corner Benáki, Exárhia, *C3* (☎36 27 362). Very quiet, well-run hotel across from the Lófos Stréfi park – a steep uphill walk. Self-service kitchen and common area on the roof with amazing view of central Athens. ③.

Youth Hostel #1, Kipsélis 57, Kipséli, just north of *A3* (☎82 25 860). A second choice to the other hostels – due to its remote location out in Kipséli, a 15-min ride from the centre on yellow trolley #2, #4 or #9. Phone first as it's often full in season. ①.

Campsites

Camping Acropolis (☎80 75 253) and **Camping Nea Kifissia** (☎80 71 494) are a kilometre or so apart in the cool, leafy suburb of Kifissiá. Both have swimming pools. To reach either, take bus #528 from just north of Omónia to the final stop, from where the sites are just a short walk. Alternatively, you can take the metro all the way to its end in Kifissiá, flagging down the #528 from behind the station for the final stretch.

Dhafní Camping, on the main road towards Kórinthos, near the Dhafní monastery (☎58 11 563). Accessible by any Dhafní bus (prefixed #8) from Platía Eleftherías, halfway between Omónia and Keramikós. Driving, head down towards Keramikós and take Ierá Odhós, which later becomes the main highway to Dhafní and Elefsína. Poor and often crowded facilities, but convenient if you want an early start heading west.

The Acropolis and Ancient Athens

This section covers the **Acropolis** and the assorted Classical and Roman sites on its **slopes**; the hills of the **Pnyx** and **Philoppapus (Filopáppou)** over to the southwest; and the neighbouring **Ancient Agora** (marketplace) and **Keramikos** (cemetery) to the northwest. This is essentially the core of the ancient, Classical Greek city, though a few further pockets and Roman extensions are covered in the Pláka section, beginning on p.87.

THE SITES: A WARNING ON OPENING HOURS

Summer opening hours for the **sites and museums** in Athens are included with some trepidation. They are notorious for changing: without notice, from one season to another, or from one week to the next, due to staff shortages.

To be sure of admission, it's best to visit between 9am and noon, and to be wary of Monday – when most museums and sites commonly close for the whole day. Last tickets are sold at the time given for closure, although the site may be open 15 minutes more. For (generally) reliable and up-to-the-minute details, ask at the tourist office in Síndagma for their printed list of opening hours.

Classical Athens: some history

Perhaps the most startling aspect of ancient, Classical Athens is how suddenly it emerged to the power and glory for which we remember it – and how short its heyday proved to be. In the middle of the **fifth century BC**, Athens was little more than a country town in its street layout and buildings. These comprised a scattered jumble of single-storey houses or wattled huts, intersected by narrow lanes. Sanitary conditions were notoriously lax: human waste and rubbish were dumped outside the town with an almost suicidal disregard for plague and disease. And on the rock of the Acropolis, a site reserved for the city's most sacred monuments, stood blackened ruins – temples and sanctuaries burnt to the ground during the Persian invasion of 480 BC.

There was little to suggest that the city was entering a unique phase of its history in terms of power, prestige and creativity. But following the victories over the Persians at Marathon (470 BC) and Salamis (460 BC), Athens stood unchallenged for a generation. It grew rich on the export of olive oil and of silver from the mines of Attica, but above all it benefitted from its control of the Delian League, an alliance of Greek city-states formed as insurance against Persian resurgence. The Athenians relocated the League's treasury from the island of Delos to their own acropolis, ostensibly on the grounds of safety, and with its revenues their leader **Pericles** was able to create the so-

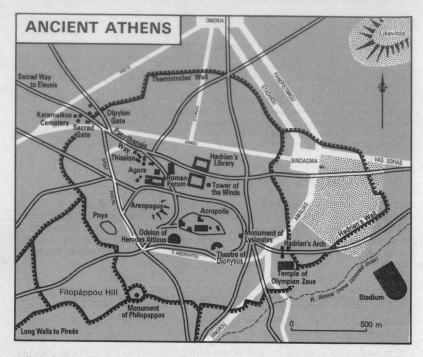

ANCIENT ATHENS

called **Golden Age** of the city. Great endowments were made for monumental construction; arts in all spheres were promoted; and – most significantly – a form of **democracy** emerged.

This democracy had its beginnings in the sixth-century BC reforms of Solon, in which the political rights of the old land-owning class had been claimed by farmer- and craftsmen-soldiers. With the emergence of Pericles the political process was radically overhauled, aided in large part by the Delian League's wealth – which enabled office-holders to be paid, thereby making it possible for the poor to play a part in government. Pericles's constitution ensured that all policies of the state were to be decided by a general assembly of Athenian male citizens – six thousand constituted a quorum. The assembly, which met outside at either the **Agora** or the **Pnyx**, elected a council of five hundred members to carry out the everyday administration of the city and a board of ten *strategoi* or generals to guide it. Pericles, one of the best known and most influential of the *strategoi*, was as vulnerable as any other to the electoral process: if sufficient numbers had cast their lot (*ostra*) against him, his citizenship would be forfeited (he would be literally ostracized); as it was, he managed to stave off such a fate and died with his popularity intact.

In line with this system of democratic participation, a new and exalted notion of the Athenian citizen emerged. This was a man who could shoulder political responsibility, take public office, and play a part in the **cultural and religious events** of the time. The latter assumed ever-increasing importance. The city's Panathenaic festival, honouring its protectress deity Athena, was upgraded along the lines of the Olympic Games to include drama, music and athletic contests. Athenians rose easily to the challenge. The next five decades were to witness the great dramatic works of **Aeschylus, Sophocles** and **Euripides**, and the comedies of **Aristophanes**. Foreigners such as **Herodotus**, considered the inventor of history, and **Anaxagoras**, the philosopher, were drawn to live in the city. And they, in turn, were surpassed by native Athenians. **Thucydides** wrote *The Peloponnesian War*, a pioneering work of documentation and analysis, while **Socrates** posed the problems of philosophy that were to exercise his follower **Plato** and to shape the discipline to the present day.

But it was the great civic **building programme** that became the most visible and powerful symbol of the age. Under the patronage of Pericles and with vast public funds made available from the Delian treasury, the architects **Iktinos**, **Mnesikles** and **Callicrates**, and the sculptor **Pheidias**, transformed the city. Their buildings, justified in part as a comprehensive job-creation scheme, included the Parthenon and Erechtheion on the Acropolis; the Thiseion (or Hephaisteion) and several *stoas* (arcades) in the Agora; a new Odeion (theatre) on the south slope of the Acropolis hill; and, outside the city, the temples at Sounion and Rhamnous.

Athenian culture flourished under democracy, but the system was not without its contradictions and failures. Only one in seven inhabitants of the city were actual citizens; the political status and civil rights that they enjoyed were denied to the many thousands of women, *metics* (foreigners) and slaves. While the lives of men became increasingly public and sociable, with meetings at the Agora or Pnyx and visits to the gymnasiums and theatres, **women** remained secluded in small and insanitary homes. Their subordination was in fact reinforced by a decree in 451 BC, which restricted their property rights, placing them under the control of fathers, husbands or guardians. At any one time, only forty women could be appointed priestesses – one of the few positions of female power. Aeschylus summed up the prevailing attitude when he declared that the mother does no more than foster the father's seed.

The city's democracy was also sullied by its **imperialist** designs and actions, which could be brutal and exploitative, although acts of mercy against rebellious allies were also documented. Atrocities included the wholesale massacre of the male population of Melos – and the building programme of Pericles itself relied on easy pickings from weaker neighbours and allies. In the *polis* of Athens the achievements of democracy could be overshadowed, too, with attacks on the very talents it had nurtured and celebrated: Aristophanes was impeached, Pheidias and Thucydides were exiled, Socrates was tried and executed.

But, historically, the fatal mistake of the Athenian democracy was allowing itself to be drawn into the **Peloponnesian war** against Sparta, its persistent rival, in 431 BC. Pericles, having roused the assembly to a pitch of patriotic fervour, died of the plague two years after war began, leaving Athens at the mercy of a series of far less capable leaders. In 415 BC a disastrous campaign in Sicily saw a third of the navy lost; in 405 BC defeat was finally accepted after the rest of the fleet was destroyed by Sparta in the Dardanelles. Demoralized, Athens succumbed to a brief period of oligarchy.

Through succeeding decades Athens was overshadowed by Thebes, though it recovered sufficiently to enter a new phase of democracy, the **age of Plato**. However, in 338 BC, nearly one and a half centuries after the original defeat of the Persians, Athens was again called to defend the Greek city-states, this time against the incursions of **Philip of Macedon**. Demosthenes, said to be as powerful an orator as Pericles, spurred the Athenians to fight, in alliance with the Thebans, at Chaironeia. There they were routed, in large part by the cavalry commanded by Philip's son, Alexander, and Athens fell under the control of the Macedonian empire.

The city continued to be favoured, particularly by **Alexander the Great**, a former pupil of Aristotle, who respected both Athenian culture and its democratic institutions. Following his death, however, came a more uncertain era, which saw periods of independence and Macedonian rule, until 146 BC when the **Romans** swept through southern Greece, subjugating it as an imperial province (see p.91).

The Acropolis

Summer Mon–Fri 8am–6.45pm, Sat & Sun 8.30am–2.45pm; winter Mon–Fri 8am–4.45pm, Sat & Sun 8.30am–2.45pm; museum Mon 11am–6.45pm, Tues–Fri 8am–6.45pm, Sat & Sun 8.30am–2.30pm. Site and museum entrance 1500dr, students 800dr, free to EU citizens on Sun.

The **rock of the Acropolis**, with the ruins of the Parthenon rising above it, is one of the archetypal images of western culture. A first glimpse of it above the traffic is a revelation, and yet feels utterly familiar. Pericles had intended the temple to be a spectacular landmark, a "School for Hellas" and a symbol of the city's imperial confidence – and, as such, it was famous throughout the ancient world. Even Pericles, however, could not have anticipated that his ruined temple would come to symbolize the emergence of Western civilization – nor that, two millennia on, it would attract some three million tourists a year.

As Donald Horne points out in *The Great Museum*, it would be hard to imagine the ruins having such a wide appeal if they had retained more of their former glory: if, for example, the Parthenon "still had a roof, and no longer appealed to the modern stereotype for outline emerging from rough stone", or if "we repainted it in its original red, blue and gold and if we reinstalled the huge, gaudy cult-figure of Athena festooned in bracelets, rings and necklaces". Yet it's hard not to feel a sense of wonderment as you catch glimpses of the ancient ruins from the city below. The best of these street-level **views** are along Eólou, where the Parthenon forms the focal point of the horizon. Calmer and quieter vantage points higher up include the nearby hills of **Likavitós**, **Ardhittós** and **Filopáppou**, where you can look on, undisturbed, from among the pine groves; a walk to one of these is highly recommended.

The main **approach** to the ruins is the path that extends above Odhós Dhioskoúron, where it joins Theorías at the northwest corner of Pláka. Two alternatives – though both perhaps better as ways down from the rock – are to make your way through the ancient Agora (entrance on Adhrianoú, *E2*; see p.85) or, from the south side of the slope, around the footpath beside the Odeion of Herodes Atticus (*F2*).

The Propylaia and Athena Nike temple

Today, as throughout its history, the Acropolis offers but one entrance – from a terrace above the Agora. Here in Classical times the Panathenaic Way extended along a steep ramp to a massive monumental double-gatehouse, the **Propylaia**; the modern path makes a more gradual, zigzagging ascent through an arched Roman entrance, the **Beule Gate**, added in the third century AD.

THE PROPYLAIA

The **Propylaia** were constructed by Mnesikles upon completion of the Parthenon, in 437 BC, and their axis and proportions aligned to balance the temple. They were built from the same Pentelic marble (from Mount Pendéli, northeast of the city), and in grandeur and architectural achievement are no mean rival to the Parthenon temple. In order to offset the difficulties of a sloping site, Mnesikles combined for the first time standard Doric columns with the taller and more delicate Ionic order. The ancient Athenians, awed by the fact that such wealth and craftsmanship should be used for a purely secular building, ranked this as their most prestigious monument.

The halls had a variety of uses, even in Classical times. To the left of the central hall (which before Venetian bombardment supported a great coffered roof, painted blue and gilded with stars), the Pinakotheke – currently in scaffolding – exhibited paintings of Homeric subjects by Polygnotus. Executed in the mid-fifth century BC, these were described 600 years later by Pausanias in his Roman-era *Guide to Greece*. There was to have been a similar wing-room to the right, but Mnesikles's design trespassed on ground sacred to the Goddess of Victory and the premises had to be adapted as a waiting room for her shrine – the Temple of Athena Nike.

TEMPLE OF ATHENA NIKE

Simple and elegant, the **Temple of Athena Nike** was begun late in the rebuilding scheme (probably due to conflict over the extent of the Propylaia's south wing) and stands on a precipitous platform overlooking the port of Pireás and the Saronic Gulf. Pausanias recounts that it was from this bastion that King Aegeus maintained a vigil for the tell-tale white sails that would indicate the safe return of his son Theseus from his mission to slay the Minotaur on Crete. Theseus, flushed with success, forgot his promise to swap the boat's black sails for white. On seeing the black sails, Aegeus assumed his son had perished and, racked with grief, plunged to his death. The temple's frieze, with more attention to realism than triumph, depicts the Athenians' victory over the Persians at Plateia.

Amazingly, the whole temple was reconstructed, from its original blocks, in the nineteenth century; the Turks had demolished the building two hundred years previously, using it as material for a gun emplacement. Recovered in this same feat of jigsaw-puzzle archeology were the reliefs from its parapet – among them *Victory Adjusting her Sandal*, the most beautiful exhibit in the Acropolis Museum.

In front of this small temple are the scant remains of a **Sanctuary of Brauronian Artemis**. Although its function remains obscure, it is known that the precinct once housed a colossal bronze representation of the Wooden Horse of Troy. More noticeable is a nearby stretch of **Mycenaean wall** (running parallel to the Propylaia) that was incorporated into the Classical design.

The Parthenon

Seen from the Propylaia, the Acropolis is today dominated by the Parthenon, set on the rock's highest ground. In Classical times, however, only the temple's pediment could be viewed through the intervening mass of statues and buildings. The ancient focus was a ten-metre-high bronze statue of *Athena Promachos* (Athena the Champion), moved to Constantinople in Byzantine times and there destroyed by a mob who believed that its beckoning hand had directed the Crusaders to the city in 1204. The statue was created by Pheidias as a symbol of the Athenians' defiance of Persia; its spear and helmet were visible to sailors approaching from Sounion.

To the right of the statue passed the Panathenaic Way, the route of the quadrennial festival in honour of the city's patroness, the goddess Athena. Following this route up today, you can make out grooves cut for footholds in the rock and, to either side, niches for innumerable statues and offerings.

The **Parthenon** was the first great building in Pericles's scheme. Designed by Iktinos, it utilizes all the refinements available to the Doric order of architecture to achieve an extraordinary and unequalled harmony. Its proportions maintain a universal 9:4 ratio, not only in the calculations of length:width, or width:height, but in such relationships as the distances between the columns and their diameter. Additionally, any possible appearance of disproportion is corrected by meticulous mathematics and craftsmanship. All seemingly straight lines are in fact slightly curved, an optical illusion known as *entasis* (intensification). The columns (their profile bowed slightly to avoid seeming concave) are slanted inwards by 6cm, while each of the steps along the sides of the temple was made to incline just 12cm over a length of 70 metres.

Built on the site of earlier archaic temples, the Parthenon was intended as a new sanctuary for Athena and a home for her cult image – a colossal wooden statue of *Athena Polias* (Athena of the City) decked in ivory and gold plate, with precious gems as eyes and sporting an ivory gorgon death's-head on her breast. Designed by Pheidias, the statue was installed in the semi-darkness of the *cella* (cult chamber), where it remained an object of prestige and wealth, if not veneration, until at least the fifth century AD. The sculpture has been lost since ancient times but its characteristics are known through numerous later copies (including a fine Roman one in the National Archeological Museum).

THE ACROPOLIS: PERICLES TO ELGIN – AND BEYOND

The Acropolis's natural setting, a craggy mass of limestone plateau, watered by springs and rising an abrupt hundred metres out of the plain of Attica, has made it a focus and nucleus during every phase of the city's development.

The site was one of the earliest settlements in Greece, its slopes inhabited by a **Neolithic** community around 5000 BC. In **Mycenaean** times it was fortified with Cyclopean walls (parts of which can still be seen), enclosing a royal palace and temples which fostered the cult of Athena. City and goddess were integrated by the **Dorians** and, with the union of Attic towns and villages in the ninth century BC, the Acropolis became the heart of the first Greek city-state, sheltering its principal public buildings. So it was to remain, save for an interval under the **Peisistratid tyrants** of the seventh and sixth centuries BC, who re-established a fortified residence on the rock. But when the last tyrant was overthrown in 510 BC, the Delphic Oracle ordered that the Acropolis should remain forever the **province of the gods**, unoccupied by humans.

It was in this context that the monuments visible today were built. Most of the substantial remains date from the **fifth century BC** or later; there are outlines of earlier temples and sanctuaries but these are hardly impressive, for they were burnt to the ground when the Persians sacked Athens in 480 BC. For some decades, until Pericles promoted his grand plan, the temples were left in their ruined state as a reminder of the Persian action. But with that threat removed, in the wake of Athenian military supremacy and a peace treaty with the Persians in 449 BC, the walls were rebuilt and architects drew up plans for a reconstruction worthy of the city's cultural and political position.

Pericles's rebuilding plan was both magnificent and enormously expensive but it won the backing of the democracy, for many of whose citizens it must have created both wealth and work – paid for from the unfortunate Delian League's coffers. The work was under the general direction of the architect and sculptor **Pheidias** and it was completed in an incredibly short time. The Parthenon itself took only ten years to finish: "every architect", wrote Plutarch, "striving to surpass the magnificence of the design with the elegance of the execution".

Their monuments survived unaltered – save for some modest Roman tinkering – for close to a thousand years, until in the reign of the Emperor Justinian the temples were converted to **Christian** worship. In subsequent years the uses became secular as well as religious, and embellishments increased, gradually obscuring the Classical designs. Fifteenth-century Italian princes held court in the Propylaia, the entrance hall to the complex, and the same quarters were later used by the **Turks** as their commander's headquarters and as a powder magazine. The Parthenon underwent similar changes from Greek to Roman temple, from Byzantine church to Frankish cathedral, before several centuries of use as a Turkish mosque. The Erechtheion, with its graceful female figures, saw service as a harem. A Venetian diplomat, Hugo Favoli, described the Acropolis in 1563 as "looming beneath a swarm of glittering golden crescents", with a minaret rising from the Parthenon. For all their changes in use, however, the buildings would have resembled – very much more than today's bare ruins – the bustling and ornate ancient Acropolis, covered in sculpture and painted in bright colours.

Sadly, such images remain only in the prints and sketches of that period: the Acropolis buildings finally fell victim to the demands of war, blown up during the successive attempts by the Venetians to oust the Turks. In 1684 the Turks demolished the temple of

The name "Parthenon" means "virgins' chamber", and initially referred only to a room at the west end of the temple occupied by the priestesses of Athena. However, the temple never rivalled the Erechtheion in sanctity and its role tended to remain that of treasury and artistic showcase, devoted rather more to the new god of the *polis* than to Athena herself. Originally its columns were painted and it was decorated with the finest frieze and pedimental sculpture of the Classsical age, depicting the Panathenaic

Athena Nike to gain a brief tactical advantage. Three years later the Venetians, laying siege to the garrison, ignited a Turkish gunpowder magazine in the Parthenon, and in the process blasted off its roof and set a **fire** that raged within its precincts for two days and nights. The apricot-tinged glow of the Parthenon marbles so admired by the Neoclassicists of the eighteenth century was one of the more aesthetic results.

Arguably surpassing this destruction, at least in the minds of modern Greeks, were the activities of Western looters at the start of the nineteenth century: the French ambassador Fauvel gathering antiquities for the Louvre, and **Lord Elgin** levering away sculptures from the Parthenon in 1801. As British Ambassador to the Porte, Elgin obtained permission from the Turks to erect scaffolding, excavate and remove stones with inscriptions. He interpreted this concession as a licence to make off with almost all of the bas-reliefs from the Parthenon's frieze, most of its pedimental structures and a caryatid from the Erechtheion – which he later sold to the British Museum. There were perhaps justifications for Elgin's action at the time – not least the Turks' tendency to use Parthenon stones in their lime kilns, and possible further ravages of war – though it was controversial even then. Byron, a more sympathetic character who roundly disparaged all this activity, visited in 1810–11, just in time to see the last of Elgin's ships loaded with the marbles. Today, however, the British Museum's continued retention of the "Elgin Marbles" (a phrase that Greek guides on the Acropolis, who portray Elgin unequivocally as a vandal, do not use) rests on legal rather than moral claims. Hopefully the British Museum will soon find a graceful pretext to back down; the long-awaited completion of the new Acropolis Museum, slated to occupy land around the Makriyánni barracks just south of the bluffs, would be a perfect opportunity.

As for the Acropolis **buildings**, their fate since the Greeks regained the Acropolis after the war of independence has not been entirely happy. Almost immediately, Greek archeologists began clearing the Turkish village that had developed around the Parthenon–mosque; a Greek regent lamented in vain that they "would destroy all the picturesque additions of the Middle Ages in their zeal to lay bare the ancient monuments". Much of this early work was indeed destructive: the iron clamps and supports used to reinforce the marble structures were, contrary to ancient example, not sheathed in lead, so they have since rusted and warped, causing the stones to crack. Meanwhile, earthquakes have dislodged the foundations; generations of feet have slowly worn down surfaces; and, more recently, sulphur dioxide deposits, caused by vehicle and industrial pollution, have been turning the marble to dust.

Since a 1975 report predicted the collapse of the Parthenon, visitors have been barred from its actual precinct, and a major, long-term restoration scheme embarked upon. Inevitably this has its frustrations, with many of the buildings scaffolded and the whole Acropolis at times taking on the appearance of a building site. However, attempts have been made to keep this as discreet as possible: a giant crane was designed that could be folded and concealed behind the temple columns at night. Of late, progress has been delayed by a bitter dispute between purists opposed to the introduction of any new, bright marble to the structure, and those who favour a complete reconstruction – to give the monument's five million non-specialist annual visitors a clearer idea of the building in its heyday. The purists have demanded the installation of plaster casts of the proposed new work to evaluate its visual effect, much to the irritation of such pragmatists as Manolis Korres, architect in charge. The Minister of Culture is currently reviewing this strategy, and there is as yet no sign of any plaster mock-ups on high.

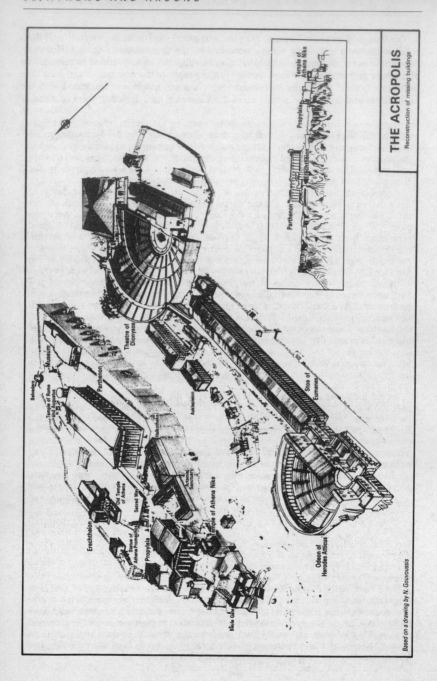

THE ACROPOLIS
Reconstruction of missing buildings

Based on a drawing by N. Gouvoussis

procession, the birth of Athena, and the struggles of Greeks to overcome giants, Amazons and centaurs. Of these, the best surviving examples are in the British Museum, but the greater part of the pediments, along with the central columns and the *cella*, were destroyed by the Venetian bombardment in 1687.

The Erechtheion

To the north of the Parthenon, beyond the foundations of the Old Temple of Athena, stands the **Erechtheion**, the last of the great works of Pericles to be completed. It was built over ancient sanctuaries, which in turn were predated by a Mycenaean palace. Here, in a symbolic reconciliation, both Athena and the city's old patron of Poseidon-Erechtheus were worshipped; the site, according to myth, was that on which they had contested possession of the Acropolis. The myth (which probably recalls the integration of the Mycenaeans with earlier pre-Hellenic settlers) tells how an olive tree sprang from the ground at the touch of Athena's spear, while Poseidon summoned forth a seawater spring. The Olympian gods voted Athena the victor.

Pausanias wrote of seeing both olive tree and seawater in the temple, adding that "the extraordinary thing about this well is that when the wind blows south a sound of waves comes from it".

Today, in common with all buildings on the Acropolis, entrance is no longer permitted, but its series of elegant Ionic porticoes are worth close attention, particularly the north one with its fine decorated doorway and frieze of blue Eleusinian marble. On the south side is the famous **Porch of the Caryatids**, whose columns are transformed into the tunics of six tall maidens holding the entablature on their heads. The statues were long supposed to have been modelled on the widows of Karyai, a small city in the Peloponnese that was punished for its alliance with the Persians by the slaughter of its menfolk and the enslavement of the women. There is, though, little suggestion of grieving or humbled captives in the serene poses of the Caryatid women. Some authorities believe that they instead represent the Arrephoroi, young, high-born girls in the service of Athena. The ones in situ are now, sadly, replacements. Five of the originals are in the Acropolis Museum, a sixth was looted by Elgin, who also removed a column and other purely architectural features – pieces that become completely meaningless out of context in the British Museum and which are replaced here by casts in a different colour marble. The stunted olive tree growing in the precinct was planted by an American archeologist in 1917.

The Acropolis Museum

Placed discreetly on a level below that of the main monuments, the **Acropolis Museum** contains all of the portable objects removed from the site since 1834 (with the exception of a few bronzes displayed in the National Archeological Museum). Over recent years, as increasing amounts of stone and sculptures have been removed from the ravages of environmental pollution, the collection has grown considerably. Labelling is rudimentary at best; a supplementary guide is useful.

In the first rooms to the left of the vestibule are fragments of pedimental sculptures from the **old Temple of Athena** (seventh to sixth century BC), whose traces of paint give a good impression of the vivid colours that were used in temple decoration. Further on is the **Moschophoros**, a painted marble statue of a young man carrying a sacrificial calf, dated 570 BC and one of the earliest examples of Greek art in marble. Room 4 displays one of the chief treasures of the building, a unique collection of **Korai**, or maidens, dedicated as votive offerings to Athena at some point in the sixth century BC. Between them they represent a shift in art and fashion, from the simply contoured Doric clothing to the more elegant and voluminous Ionic designs; the figures' smiles also change subtly, becoming increasingly loose and natural.

The pieces of the **Parthenon frieze** in Room 8 were sundered from the temple by the Venetian explosion and subsequently buried, thereby escaping the clutches of Lord Elgin. They portray scenes of Athenian citizens in the Panathenaic procession; the fact that mortals featured so prominently in the decoration of the temple indicates the immense collective self-pride of the Athenians at the height of their Golden Age. This room also contains a graceful and fluid sculpture, known as **Iy Sandalízoussa**, which depicts **Athena Nike** adjusting her sandal. Finally, in the last room are four authentic and semi-eroded **caryatids** from the Erectheion, displayed behind a glass screen in a carefully rarified atmosphere.

West and south of the Acropolis

Most visitors to the Acropolis leave by the same route they arrived – north through Pláka. For a calmer and increasingly panoramic view of the rock, it's worth taking the time to explore something of the area to the **west of the Acropolis**, punctuated by the hills of the Areopagus, Pnyx and Filopáppou, each of which had a distinct function in the life of the ancient city.

The **south slope** is rewarding, too, with its Greek and Roman theatres and the remains of *stoas* and sanctuaries. It can be approached from the Acropolis, with an entrance just above the Herodes Atticus theatre, though its main entrance is some way to the south along Leofóros Dhionissíou Areopayítou.

No less important, these sites all give access to the neighbourhoods of **Veïkoú**, **Koukáki** and **Áno Petrálona**, three of the least spoilt quarters in Athens, and with some of the city's best tavernas (see pp.110–11).

The Areopagus, Pnyx and Filopáppou Hill

Rock-hewn stairs ascend the low hill of the **Areopagus** immediately below the entrance to the Acropolis. The "Hill of Mars" was the site of the Council of Nobles and the Judicial Court under the aristocratic rule of ancient Athens. During the Classical period the court lost its powers of government to the Assembly (held on the Pnyx) but it remained the court of criminal justice, dealing primarily with cases of homicide. Aeschylus used this setting in *The Eumenides* for the trial of Orestes, who, pursued by the Furies' demand of "a life for a life", stood accused of murdering his mother Clytemnestra.

The hill was used as a campsite by the Persians during their siege of the Acropolis in 480 BC, and in the Roman era by Saint Paul, who preached the *Sermon on an Unknown God* here, winning amongst his converts Dionysius "the Areopagite", who became the city's patron saint. Today, there are various foundation cuttings on the site, and the ruins of a church of Áyios Dhioníssios (possibly built over the court), though nothing is actually left standing. The Areopagus's historic associations apart, it is notable mainly for the views, not only of the Acropolis, but down over the Agora and towards Kerameikos – the ancient cemetery (see p.86).

Following the road or path over the flank of the Acropolis, you come out onto Leofóros Dhionissíou Areopayítou, by the Herodes Atticus theatre. Turning right, 100m or so down (and across) the avenue, a network of paths leads up **Filopáppou Hill**, also known as the "Hill of the Muses" (*Lófos Moussón*). This strategic height has played an important, if generally sorry, role in the city's history. It was from here that the shell which destroyed the roof of the Parthenon was lobbed; more recently, the colonels placed tanks on the slopes during their coup of 1967. (Avoid the area at night, when it has a reputation for rapes and muggings.)

The hill's summit is capped by a somewhat grandiose monument to a Roman senator and consul, Filopappus, who is depicted driving his chariot on its frieze. Again, it is a place above all for views. To the west is the Dora Stratou Theatre (or Filopáppou Theatre) where Greek music and dance performances (see p.117) are held. Northwest, along the main path, and following a line of truncated ancient walls, is the church of **Áyios Dhimítrios**, an unsung gingerbread gem, which has kept its original Byzantine frescoes. In the cliff face across from this to the south you can make out a kind of cave dwelling, known (more from imagination than evidence) as the **prison of Socrates**.

Further to the north, above the church, rises the **Hill of the Pnyx**, an area used in Classical Athens as the meeting place for the democratic assembly, which gathered more than forty times a year. All except the most serious political issues, such as ostracism, were aired here, the hill on the north side providing a convenient semicircular terrace from which to address the crowd. All male citizens could vote and, at least in theory, all could voice their opinions, though the assembly was harsh on inarticulate or foolish speakers. There are remains of the original walls, used to form the theatre-like court, and of *stoas* for the assembly's refreshment. The arena is today used for the *son-et-lumière* (not greatly recommended) of the Acropolis, which takes place on most summer evenings.

Beyond the Pnyx, still another hill, **Lófos Nimfón** (Hill of the Nymphs), is dominated by a nineteenth-century observatory and gardens, occasionally open to visitors.

The south slope of the Acropolis

Entrances above the Herodes Atticus theatre and on Leofóros Dhionissíou Areopayítou. Mon–Sat 9am–2.45pm, Sun 9am–1.45pm; entrance 400dr.

The second-century Roman **Odeion of Herodes Atticus**, restored for performances of music and Classical drama during the summer festival (see p.117), dominates the south slope of the Acropolis hill. It is open only for shows, though; the main reason to come here otherwise is the earlier Greek sites to the east.

Pre-eminent among these is the **Theatre of Dionysos**, beside the main site entrance. One of the most evocative locations in the city, it was here that the masterpieces of Aeschylus, Sophocles, Euripides and Aristophanes were first performed. It was also the venue for the annual festival of tragic drama, where each Greek citizen would take his turn as member of the chorus. The ruins are impressive. Rebuilt in the fourth century BC, the theatre could hold some 17,000 spectators – considerably more than the Herodes Atticus's 5000–6000 seats; twenty of the theatre's sixty-four tiers of seats survive. Most notable are the great marble thrones in the front row, each inscribed with the name of an official of the festival or of an important priest; in the middle sat the Priest of Dionysos and on his right the representative of the Delphic Oracle. At the rear of the stage along the Roman *bema* (rostrum) are reliefs of episodes in the life of Dionysos flanked by two squatting Silcni, devotees of the satyrs. Sadly, all this is roped off to protect the stage-floor **mosaic** – itself a magnificent diamond of multicoloured marble best seen from above.

Above the theatre – reached by steps, then a path to the right – looms a vast grotto, converted perhaps a millennium ago into the chapel of **Panayía Hrissospiliótissa**; it's worth a look for the setting rather than its kitsch iconography. To the west of the theatre extend the ruins of the **Asclepion**, a sanctuary devoted to the healing god Asclepius (see p.160) and built around a sacred spring. The curative centre was probably incorporated into the Byzantine church of the doctor-saints Kosmas and Damian, of which there are prominent remains. Nearer to the road lie the foundations of the Roman **Stoa of Eumencs**, a colonnade of stalls that stretched to the Herodes Atticus Odeion.

The Ancient Agora

South entrance by the Areopagus; north entrance on Adhrianoú (*E2*); Tues–Sun 8.30am–2.45pm; entrance 800dr.

The **Agora** (market) was the nexus of ancient Athenian city life. Competing for space were the various claims of administration, commerce, market and public assembly.

The result was ordered chaos. Eubolus, a fourth-century poet, observed that "you will find everything sold together in the same place at Athens: figs, witnesses to summonses, bunches of grapes, turnips, pears, apples, givers of evidence, roses, medlars . . . water clocks, laws, indictments". Women, however, were not in evidence; secluded by custom, they would delegate any business in the Agora to slaves. Before shifting location to the Pnyx, the assembly also met here, and continued to do so when discussing cases of ostracism for most of the fifth and fourth centuries BC.

Originally the Agora was a rectangle, divided diagonally by the Panathenaic Way and enclosed by temples, administrative buildings, and long porticoed *stoas* (arcades of shops) where idlers and philosophers gathered to exchange views and listen to the orators. In the centre was an open space, defined by boundary stones at the beginning of the fifth century BC; considered sacred and essential to the life of the community, those accused of homicide or other serious crimes were excluded from it by law.

The site today is a confused, if extensive, jumble of ruins, dating from various stages of building between the sixth century BC and the fifth century AD. The best overview is from the Areopagus, by the north entrance. For some idea of what you are surveying, however, the place to head for is the **Museum**, housed in the reconstructed **Stoa of Attalos**. The stoa itself was a US$1.5 million project of the American School of Archeology in Athens. It is, in every respect bar one, an entirely faithful reconstruction of the original. What is missing is colour: in Classical times the exterior would have been painted in bright red and blue (like the Minoan palaces of Crete). Of the displays – mostly pottery from the sixth to fourth century BC, plus some early Geometric grave offerings – highlights are the red-figure dishes depicting athletes, musicians and minor deities, together with the adjacent oil flask in the form of a kneeling boy (both exhibits are in the centre of the hall).

Around the site, the most prominent ruins are of various other stoas, including the recently excavated "Painted Stoa" where Zeno expounded his Stoic philosophy, and those of the city's gymnasiums and council hall (*bouleuterion*). Somewhat above the general elevation, to the west, is the **Thiseion**, or Temple of Hephaistos. The best preserved, though perhaps least admired, of all Doric temples, it lacks the curvature and "lightness" of the Parthenon's design. Dedicated to the patron of blacksmiths and metalworkers – hence its popular name – it was the first building of Pericles's programme, though not the first completed. Its remaining *metopes* depict the labours of Hercules and the exploits of Theseus, while the barrel-vaulted roof dates from the Byzantine conversion of the temple into a church of Saint George. The other bona fide church on the site – that of **Áyii Apóstoli** (the Holy Apostles), by the south entrance – is worth a glance inside for its fresco fragments, exposed during a 1950s restoration of the eleventh-century shrine.

Kerameikos (Keramikós)

Entrance at Ermoú 148, (*E1*); Tues–Sun 8.30am–2.45pm; entrance 400dr.

The Kerameikos site, encompassing the principal cemetery of ancient Athens, provides a fascinating and quiet retreat from the Acropolis. It is little visited and in addition has something of an oasis feel about it, with the lush Iridhanós channel, speckled with water lilies, flowing across it from east to west.

From the entrance can be seen the double line of the **Long Walls**, which ran to the port at Pireás; the inner wall was hastily cobbled together by the men, women and children of Athens while Themistocles was pretending to negotiate a mutual disarmament treaty with Sparta in 479 BC. The barriers are interrupted by the great **Dipylon Gate**, where travellers from Pireás, Eleusis and Boeotia entered the ancient city, and the **Sacred Gate**, used for the Eleusinian and Panathenaic processions. These followed the Sacred Way, once lined by colonnades and bronze statues, into the Agora. Between the two gates are the foundations of the **Pompeion**, where preparations for the processions were made and where the main vehicles were stored.

Branching off from the Sacred Way is the **Street of the Tombs**, begun in 394 BC and now excavated along a hundred or so metres. Both sides were reserved for the plots of wealthy Athenians. Some twenty, each containing numerous commemorative monuments, have been excavated, and their original stones, or replicas, reinstated. The flat vertical *stelai* were the main funerary monuments of the Classical world; the sarcophagus belonged to Hellenistic and Roman times. The sculpted crescent with the massive conglomerate base to the left of the path is the *Memorial of Dexileos*, the twenty-year-old son of Lysanias of Thorikos, who was killed in action at Corinth in 394 BC. The adjacent plot contains the *Monument of Dionysios of Kollytos*, in the shape of a pillar *stele* supporting a bull carved from Pentelic marble. As with any cemetery, however, it is the more humble monuments, such as the statue of a girl with a dog on the north side of the street, that connect past and present in the shared experience of loss. From the terrace overlooking the tombs, Pericles delivered his famous funeral oration dedicated to those who died in the first years of the Peloponnesian War. His propaganda coup inspired thousands more to enlist in a campaign during which one-third of the Athenian force was wiped out.

The **Oberlaender Museum**, named after the German-American manufacturer who financed it, contains an extensive collection of *stelai*, terracotta figures, vases and sculptures from the site. Among them, Room 1's *Ampharete Holding her Infant Grandchild*, and *The Boxer*, with a cauliflower ear and the thongs of a glove tied around his wrist, are remarkable in their detailed execution. The terracotta figures and vases of Room 2 include some of the earliest art objects yet found in Greece.

Pláka and Monastiráki

Pláka, with its alleys and stairs built on the Turkish plan, is the most rewarding Athenian area for daytime wanderings – not least because of its pedestrianization, with cars banished from all but a few main streets. In addition to a scattering of Roman sites and various offbeat and enjoyable museums, it offers glimpses of an exotic past, refreshingly at odds with the concrete blocks of the metropolis. If you can, time your visit to coincide with the Sunday morning **flea market** around Monastiráki square.

Roughly delineated by Síndagma, Odhós Ermoú and the Acropolis, the district was basically the extent of nineteenth-century, pre-independence Athens, and provided the core of the city for the next few decades. Once away from Síndagma, the narrow winding streets are lined with nineteenth-century Neoclassical houses, some grand, some humble, with gateways opening onto verdant courtyards overlooked by wooden verandas. Tiled roofs are edged with terracotta medusa-heads, goddesses and foliage designs, ornaments known collectively as *akrokerámata*; the grander facades are decorated with pilasters and capitals and wrought-iron balconies. Poor and working class for most of this century, the district has lately been extensively gentrified and renovated.

From Síndagma to Adhrianoú

An attractive approach to Pláka is to follow **Odhós Kidhathinéon**, a pedestrian walkway that starts near the **English and Russian churches** on Odhós Filellínon, south of Síndagma. It leads gently downhill, past the Popular Arts Museum, on a leafy square with one of the few remaining old-time cafés on the corner, on through café-crowded Platía Pláka to Hadrian's street, **Odhós Adhrianoú**, which runs nearly the whole length of Pláka from Hadrian's Arch to the Thiseion.

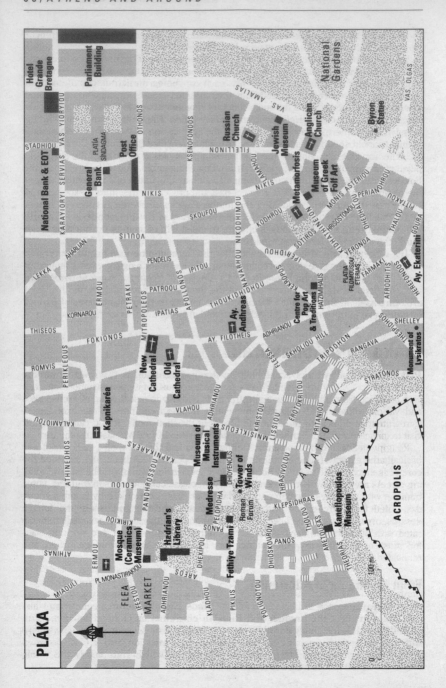

PLÁKA

The **Museum of Greek Folk Art** (Tues–Sun 10am–2pm; 400dr), at Kidhathinéon 17, is one of the most enjoyable in the city. A surprisingly extensive museum, its five floors are mostly devoted to collections of weaving, pottery, regional costumes and embroidery, which reveal both the sophistication and the strong Middle Eastern influence of Greek popular arts. On the second floor, the carnival tradition of northern Greece, and the all-but-vanished shadow-puppet theatre, are featured. The fourth floor dazzles with its exhibits of gold and silver jewellery and weaponry. Most compelling of all, on the third floor, is the reconstructed village room with a series of murals by the primitive artist Theophilos (1873–1934). Theophilos was one of the characters of turn-of-the-century Greece, dressing in War of Independence outfits and painting tavernas and cafés for a meal or a small fee. Several examples of his work – usually scenes from peasant life or of battles from the War of Independence – survive in situ in the Peloponnese and on Mount Pílion, though they have only in the last few decades been recognized as worth preserving.

Two other museums, close by, provide interesting supplements. A couple of blocks to the northwest, at Angelikís Hatzimiháli 6, the **Centre for Popular Arts and Traditions** (temporarily closed; usual hours Tues & Thurs 9am–9pm, Wed, Fri & Sat 9am–1pm & 5–9pm, Sun 9am–1pm, depending on availability of staff; free) features costumes, cloth, musical instruments, and so forth, in another grand Pláka mansion.

A similar distance to the southeast, above the French Chamber of Commerce at Amaliás 36, is the **Jewish Museum of Greece** (daily except Sat 9am–1pm; free, but donations welcome). Displaying art and religious artefacts from the very ancient Jewish communities scattered throughout Greece, the centrepiece is the reconstructed synagogue of Pátra, dating from the 1920s, whose furnishings have been moved here en bloc and remounted.

The Monument of Lysikrates and around

At the eastern end of Pláka, Odhós Lissikrátous gives onto a small, fenced-off archeological park at one end of Odhós Tripódhon, the **Street of the Tripods**, where winners of the ancient dramatic contests dedicated their tripod-trophies to Dionysos. The park can't be entered, but you can walk around the outside to admire the **Monument of Lysikrates**, a tall and graceful stone and marble structure from 335 BC, which stands as a surprisingly complete example of these ancient exhibits. A four-metre-high stone base supports six Corinthian columns rising up to a marble dome on which, in a flourish of acanthus leaf carvings, a winning tripod was placed. The inscription on its architrave tells us that "Lysikrates of Kikyna, son of Lysitheides was *choregos* (sponsor); the tribe of Akamantis won the victory with a chorus of boys; Theon played the flute; Lysiades of Athens trained the chorus; Evainetos was archon". The monument was incorporated into a French Capuchin convent in 1667, and tradition asserts that Byron used it as a study, writing part of *Childe Harold* here; at the time Athens had no inn and the convent was a regular lodging for European travellers.

The street beyond, **Víronos**, is named after the poet (*O Lórdhos Víronos* to Greeks). At its far end, facing you across the road, is the old Makriyánni police barracks, revered by Greek rightists for its stout resistance to Communist attack during December 1944. Part of it has been transformed into the so-called **Acropolis Study Centre** (Mon–Fri 9am–2pm, Mon, Wed & Fri also 6–8pm, Sat & Sun 10am–2pm; free), so far containing little beyond plaster casts of the Elgin Marbles and models of the new, Italian-planned, **Acropolis Museum**. Originally scheduled for completion in 1996, to coincide with the centenary of the modern Olympic Games (for which Greece made an unsuccessful bid), immediate plans for construction seem to have been shelved. The metro station under construction here has taken priority and, with the death of Melina Mercouri in early 1994, the project lost considerable impetus.

Hadrian's Arch and the Temple of Olympian Zeus

Had you taken the other street at the Lysikrates monument crossroads, Ódhos Lissikratoús, you would emerge at the edge of Pláka near one of the most hazardous road junctions in Athens, the meeting of Dhionissíou Areopayítou, Amalías and Singroú. Across the way, facing Leofóros Amalias, stands **Hadrian's Arch**, erected by that emperor to mark the edge of the Classical city and the beginning of his own. On the near side its frieze is inscribed "This is Athens, the ancient city of Theseus", and on the other "This is the City of Hadrian and not of Theseus".

Directly behind the arch, the colossal pillars of the **Temple of Olympian Zeus** (Tues–Sun 8.30am–2.45pm; 400dr; entrance on Leofóros Amalías) dominate their surroundings, and go some way towards justifying this show of arrogance. The largest temple in Greece, and according to Livy, "the only temple on earth to do justice to the god", it was dedicated by Hadrian in 131 AD, some 700 years after the tyrant Peisistratos had laid its foundations. Hadrian marked the occasion by contributing a statue of Zeus and a suitably monumental one of himself, although both have since been lost. Just fifteen of the temple's original 104 Pentelic marble pillars remain erect, though the column drums of another, which fell in 1852, litter the ground, giving a startling idea of the project's size. Almost equally impressive is the fact that in the Byzantine era a stylite made his hermitage on the temple architrave.

From the Olympian Zeus temple, you could, if you wanted, take a shady route up to Síndagma or Kolonáki through the **National Gardens** (see p.99).

Anafiótika and the Kanellópoulos Museum

Were you to continue straight ahead from the Kidhathinéon–Adhrianoú intersection, up **Odhós Thespídhos**, you would reach the edge of the Acropolis precinct. Up to the right, the whitewashed cubist houses of **Anafiótika** cheerfully proclaim an architect-free zone amid the highest crags of the Acropolis rock. The pleasingly haphazard buildings here were erected by workers from the island of Anáfi in the southern Aegean, who were employed in the mid-nineteenth-century construction of Athens. Unable to afford land, they took advantage of a customary law to the effect that if a roof and four walls could be thrown up overnight, the premises were yours at sunrise. The houses, and the two churches that serve them, are the image of those the Cycladic islanders had left behind. Today, many stand empty on their mule-width lanes and steps.

Follow Rangáva or Stratoús anticlockwise around the Acropolis rock and you will eventually emerge on Theoriás, outside the eclectic **Kanellópoulos Museum** (Tues–Sun 8.30am–2.45pm; 400dr). Though there is nothing here that you won't see examples of in the bigger museums, this collection of treasures, exhibited in the topmost house under the Acropolis, has a calm appeal of its own. The bulk of the ground-floor exhibits are icons but there is also Byzantine jewellery, bronze oil-lamps and crosses, and Roman funerary ornaments from Fayum. The top floor is given over entirely to Geometric, Classical and Hellenistic art, primarily pottery and votive figurines, generally of a high standard and distinguished by whimsical execution. The middle floor and the stairwells are devoted to Near Eastern and Cypriot art of various periods from the Bronze Age on, including some exquisite Persian goldwork and flamboyantly painted "Phoenician" vials.

A block east of the museum, straddling Klepsídhras and Alimbérti, is a building thought to be the oldest of post-Independence Athens – the **Panepistímiou**. Once housing the first university in modern Greece, it is now a minor museum, used for special exhibitions (Mon & Wed 2.30–7pm, Tues, Thurs & Fri 8am–2.30pm).

The Roman Forum and Tower of the Winds

The western reaches of Adhrianoú, past the newly restored Neoclassical Demotic School, is largely commercial – souvenir shops and sandals – as far as the **Roman Forum** (entrance corner Pelopídha/Eólou; Tues–Sun 8.30am–2.45pm; 400dr), a large irregularly shaped excavation site bounded by railings.

The forum was built by Julius Caesar and Augustus (Octavian) as an extension of the older ancient Greek *agora* to its west. It has undergone substantial excavation in recent years, but the majority of it is now open to visitors. Its main entrance, on the west side, was through the relatively intact **Gate of Athena Archegetis**, which consisted of a Doric portico and four columns supporting an entablature and pediment. On the pilaster facing the Acropolis is engraved an edict of Hadrian announcing the rules and taxes on the sale of oil.

The Tower of the Winds

The best-preserved and easily the most intriguing of the forum ruins is the graceful octagonal structure known as the **Tower of the Winds** (*Aéridhes* in Greek). Designed in the first century BC by Andronikos of Kyrrhos, a Syrian astronomer, it served as a compass, sundial, weather vane and water clock – the latter powered by a stream from one of the Acropolis springs.

Each face of the tower is adorned with a relief of a figure floating through the air, personifying the eight winds. On the **north** side (facing Eólou) is Boreas blowing into a conch shell; **northwest**, Skiron holding a vessel of charcoal; **west**, Zephyros tossing flowers from his lap; **southwest**, Lips speeding the voyage of a ship; **south**, Notos upturning an urn to make a shower; **southeast**, Euros with his arm hidden in his mantle summoning a hurricane; **east**, Apiliotis carrying fruits and wheat; and **north-**

ROMAN ATHENS

When the **Romans** ousted Athens' Macedonian rulers and incorporated the city into the vast new province of Achaia in 146 BC, Athens continued to enjoy rare political privileges. Its status as a respected seat of learning and great artistic centre had already been firmly established throughout the ancient world: Cicero and Horace were educated here and Athenian sculptors and architects were supported by Roman commissions. Unlike Corinth, though, which became the administrative capital of the province, the city was endowed with relatively few imperial Roman **monuments**, Hadrian's Arch being perhaps the most obvious. Athenian magistrates, exercising a fair amount of local autonomy, tended to employ architects who would reflect the public taste for the simpler *propylaion*, gymnasium and old-fashioned theatre, albeit with a few Roman amendments.

The city's Roman **history** was shaped pre-eminently by its alliances, which often proved unfortunate. The first major onslaught occurred in 86 BC, when Sulla punished Athens for its allegiance to his rival Mithridates by burning its fortifications and looting its treasures. His successors were more lenient. Julius Caesar preferred a free pardon after Athens had sided with Pompey; and Octavian, who extended the old *agora* by building a forum, showed similar clemency when Athens harboured Brutus following the Ides of March. The most frequent visitor was the **Emperor Hadrian**, who used the occasions to bestow grandiose monuments, including his eponymous arch, a magnificent and immense library and (though it had been begun centuries before) the Temple of Olympian Zeus. A generation later **Herodes Atticus**, a Roman senator born in Marathon, became the city's last major benefactor of ancient times. His great wealth came purely and simply from a lucky find: his father had stumbled upon a vast treasure buried in an old house and, with permission from the emperor, kept it all.

east, Kaikias emptying a shield full of hailstones. Beneath each of these, it is still possible to make out the markings of eight sundials.

The semicircular tower attached to the south face was the reservoir from which water was channelled in a steady flow into a cylinder in the main tower; the time was read by the water level viewed through the open northwest door. On the top of the building a bronze Triton revolved with the winds. In Ottoman times dervishes used the tower as a *tekke* or ceremonial hall, terrifying their superstitious Orthodox neighbours with their chanting, music and exercises.

Other forum ruins – and Hadrian's library

The other forum ruins open to view are somewhat obscure. Among the more prominent Roman bits and pieces are a large public latrine, a number of shops and a stepped *propylaion* or entrance gate just below the Tower of the Winds. To the northwest, an old Ottoman mosque, the **Fethiye Tzami**, serves as an archeological warehouse.

Bordering the north end of the forum site, stretching between Áreos and Eólou, stand the surviving walls of **Hadrian's Library**, an enormous building which once enclosed a cloistered court of a hundred columns. **Odhós Aréos**, alongside, signals the beginning of the Monastiráki flea market area (see below). At its end, round behind the forum, are some of the quietest, prettiest and least spoiled streets in the whole of Pláka – many of them ending in steps up to the Anafiótika quarter (see p.90).

Across the street from the Tower of the Winds stands another Turkish relic – a gateway and single dome from a **Medresse**, an Islamic college or "seminary". Here in 1821 the Ottoman judge, Hatzi Halil, successfully dissuaded a Turkish mob from indiscriminate massacre of the entire male population of Attica; the Greek rebels were not so scrupulous, and Hatzi Halil's clemency was repaid by the destruction of the *medresse* during or shortly after the War of Independence.

The Museum of Musical Instruments

Just beside the *medresse*, at Dhioyénous 1–3, is a **Museum of Musical Instruments** (Tues & Thurs–Sun 10am–2pm, Wed noon–8pm; free). Superbly accommodated in the rooms of a Neoclassical building, this wonderful display traces the history and distribution of virtually everything that has ever been played in Greece, including (in the basement) some not-so-obvious festival and liturgical instruments such as triangles, strikers, livestock bells and coin garlands worn by Carnival masquers. Reproductions of frescoes show the Byzantine antecedents of many instruments, and headphone sets are provided for sampling the music made by the various exhibits.

After all this plenty, it's difficult to resist the stock of the museum shop, which includes virtually the entire backlist of the Society for the Dissemination of Greek Music's excellent "Songs of . . . " series (see "Music" in *Contexts* for more).

Monastiráki: the Flea Market area

The northwest districts of Pláka, along Ermoú and Mitropóleos, are noisier, busier and more geared to the Greek life of the city. Neither street lays any claim to beauty, though the bottom (west) half of **Ermoú**, with its metalworkers and other craftsmen, has an attractive workaday character; the top half has unhappily transformed the pretty Byzantine church of the **Kapnikaréa** into a traffic island.

Churches are also the chief feature of **Odhós Mitropóleos** (Cathedral Street). The dusty, tiny chapel of **Ayía Dhinamí** crouches surreally below the concrete piers of the Ministry of Education and Religion; the **Mitrópolis** itself, an undistinguished nineteenth-century cannibal of dozens of older buildings, carves out a square midway along; and the **old cathedral** stands alongside it, a beautiful little twelfth-century church cobbled together from plain and carved blocks as ancient as Christendom itself.

Pandhróssou, Platía Monastirakioú and the Mosque of Tzistarákis

From the bottom corner of the pedestrianized cathedral square, **Odhós Pandhróssou** leads the way into the **Monastiráki Flea Market** – not that its name is really justified by the rich and conventional jewellery and fur shops that pack the first section. In fact, not many genuine market shops remain at all this side of Platía Monastirakíou. With the exception of a couple of specialist icon dealers, everything is geared to the tourist. The most quirky among them is the shop of *Stavros Melissinos*, the "poet sandalmaker of Athens", at Pandhróssou 89. Melissinos enjoyed a sort of fame in the 1960s, hammering out sandals for The Beatles, Jackie Onassis and the like; it is said that John Lennon sought him out specifically for his poetic musings on wine and the sea, which Melissinos continues to sell alongside the footwear.

Platía Monastirakioú, full of nut sellers, lottery sellers, fruit stalls, kiosks – and currently metro-digging paraphernalia – gets it name from the little monastery church (*monastiráki*) at its centre, tenth century in origin and recently restored. The area around has been a marketplace since Turkish times, and maintains a number of Ottoman features. On the south side of the square, rising from the walls of Hadrian's Library and the shacks of Pandhróssou, is the eighteenth-century **Mosque of Tzistarákis**, nowadays secularized, minus minaret and home to the **Kyriazopoulos Ceramic Collection of the Museum of Greek Folk Art** (daily except Tues; 9am–2.30pm; 400dr). Donated by a Thessaloníki professor, the collection is devoted to folk sculpture and pottery, mostly by refugee artists from Asia Minor, together with some decorated household items from various points in the Hellenic world.

The mosque itself, especially its striped *mihrab* (the niche indicating the direction of Mecca) is equally interesting. Outside, by the entrance gate, are calligraphic inscriptions proclaiming the mosque's founder and date, and a series of niches used as extra *mihrabs* for occasions when worshippers could not fit into the main hall.

West of Platía Monastirakioú: the flea market proper

West of Monastiráki square, the **flea market** caters more and more for local needs, with clothes, iron- and copperware, tools and records in **Odhós Iféstou**; old furniture, bric-a-brac and camping gear in **Platía Avissinías**; chairs, office equipment, wood-burning stoves, mirrors, canaries and sundry other goods in **Astíngos**, **Ermoú** and nearby. Beside the church of **Ayíou Filípou**, there's a market in hopeless jumble-sale rejects, touted by a cast of eccentrics (especially on Sundays); of late this extends around the corner, along Adhrianoú, as far as Platía Thisíou.

The north entrance to the **Agora** (see p.85) is just south of Platía Avissinías on Adhrianoú, across the cutting where the metro line for Pireás re-emerges into open air after tunnelling under the city centre. Odhós Adhrianoú is here at its most appealing, with a couple of interesting antique shops, a shady *kafenío* above the metro tunnel, and the best views of the Acropolis. Following the Agora fence around to the southwest, you'll come to another good café vantage-point on busy **Apostólou Pávlou**, which shares the same view. On the hill above is the old **Observatory**, surrounded by a last enclave of streets untroubled by tourism or redevelopment: no special features, just a pleasant wander through the very north end of Áno Petrálona.

North from Pláka: the Bazaar, Omónia square and the National Archeological Museum

When the German Neoclassicists descended on Athens in the 1830s, the land between Pláka and present-day **Omónia square** was envisaged as a spacious and European expansion of the Classical and medieval town. Time and the realities of Athens's status as a commercial capital have made a mockery of that grandiose vision: the main **bazaar area** is no less crowded and oriental than Monastiráki, while Omónia itself stubbornly retains a mix of gritty Balkan and Greek-American bad taste. For visitors, the focus of interest is the **National Archeological Museum**, which, with its neighbour, the **Politehnío**, fronts the student/alternative quarter of **Exárhia**, currently the city's liveliest option for nights out.

The Bazaar: Athinás to Omónia

A broad triangle of streets, delineated by Piréos (officially Tsaldhári) in the west and Stadhíou in the east, reaches north to its apex at Omónia square. Through the middle run **Athinás** and **Eólou streets** – the modern **bazaar**, whose stores, though stocked mainly with imported manufactured goods, still reflect their origins in their unaffected decor, unsophisticated packaging and, most strikingly, their specialization. Each street has a concentration of particular stores and wares, flouting modern marketing theory. Hence the Monastiráki end of Athinás is dedicated to tools; food stores are gathered around the central market in the middle, especially along Evripídhou; there's glass to the west; paint and brasswork to the east; and clothes in Eólou and Ayíou Márkou. Praxitélous is full of lettering merchants; Platía Klafthmónos and Aristídhou of electrical goods; and department stores cluster around Omónia. Always raucous and teeming with shoppers, *kouloúri* (bread-ring) sellers, gypsies and other vendors, the whole area is great free entertainment.

The best bit is the **central meat and seafood market**, on the corner of Athinás and Evripídhou. The building itself is a grand nineteenth-century relic, with fretted iron awnings sheltering forests of carcasses and mounds of hearts, livers and ears – no place for the squeamish. In the middle section of the hall is the fish market, with all manner of bounty from the sea squirming and glistening on the marble slabs. A little to the west is the temporary **fruit and vegetable bazaar**, open-air stalls arrayed around a suspended archeological dig. On the surrounding streets are rows of grocers, their stalls piled high with sacks of pulses, salt cod, barrels of olives and wheels of cheese.

To the north is the **flower market**, gathered around the church of Ayía Iríni on Eólou. This has stalls through the week but really comes alive with the crowds on a Sunday morning. An additional feature of **Eólou** is its views: walk it north to south, coming from Omónia, and your approach takes you towards the rock of the Acropolis, with the Erechtheion's slender columns and pediment peeking over the edge of the crag.

Around Omónia square

Omónia itself has little to offer. A continuous turmoil of people and cars, it is Athens at its sleaziest and most urban. There are sporadically functioning escalators (the only public ones in Greece) down to the **metro**, and, at the top, every kind of junk food imaginable – the pride of returned Greek-Americans. The centre has become another metro building site, and the young palms around the perimeter are mournful replacements for their predecessors, which were cut down in the 1950s lest foreigners think Greece "too Asiatic". Destitute Albanian refugees congregate around the square, which has recently developed a reputation for hustle and petty crime, while after dark the area is also frequented by prostitutes and their customers (the main red-light district is on nearby Sofokléous).

To the north, just beside the National Archeological Museum on Patissíon, is the **Politehnío**, a Neoclassical building housing the university's school of engineering and science. It was here in late 1973 that students launched their protests against the repressive regime of the colonels' junta, occupying the building and courtyards, and broadcasting calls for mass resistance from a pirate radio transmitter. Large numbers defied the military cordons to demonstrate support and to smuggle in food and medicines. The colonels' answer came on the night of November 16. Snipers were positioned in neighbouring houses and ordered to fire indiscriminately into the courtyards while tanks broke down the gates – with students still clinging on. Nobody knows how many of the unarmed students were killed, since their bodies were secretly buried in mass graves – figures range from twenty to three hundred. Although the junta's leader, Papodopoulos, was able publicly to congratulate the officers involved before being sacked in favour of secret police chief Ioannidhes, a new, more urgent sense of outrage was spreading; within a year the dictatorship was toppled.

Evidence of the incident can still be seen today, in the bullet-marked pillars and staircases, though these may be patched up during ongoing restoration works. The anniversary of the massacre is invariably commemorated by a march on the US Embassy, outpost of the the colonels' greatest ally; it's a bit apathetic nowadays, but still a day out for the Left. The date is also a significant one for the shadowy terrorist group *Dhekaeftá Noemvríou* (17 November), who have operated since the early 1980s, with just two or three low-ranking members caught or arrested to date; rumour has it that the group enjoys semi-official protection from rogue elements of the powers-that-be.

The National Archeological Museum

Patissíon 28 (*C2/3*); Mon 12.30–6.45pm, Tues–Fri 8am–6.45pm, Sat & Sun 8.30am–2.45pm; pottery section Mon 12.30–5.15pm, Tues–Sun 8.30am–2.45pm; entrance1500dr, students 750dr, free on Sun & public holidays.

The National Archeological Museum is an unrivalled treasure house of Cycladic, Minoan, Mycenaean and Classical Greek art – and an essential Athens experience. Despite haphazard labelling and generally unimaginative displays, it elbows its way into the list of the world's top ten museums. To avoid disappointment, make sure you check the latest opening times and give yourself a clear morning or afternoon for a visit; better still, take in the collection – which can be overwhelming if you delve beyond the obvious highlights – in two or more separate trips.

The museum's main divisions are **prehistoric**, with Mycenae predominating; **sculpture** from the Archaic (eighth century BC) to Hellenistic (third to second century BC) periods; and **pottery** from Geometric (ninth century BC) to the end of the fourth century AD. Smaller self-contained collections include **bronzes** in Rooms 36 to 40; immensely covetable **jewellery** in Room 32; and the brilliant Minoan-style **frescoes from Thira (Santorini)** upstairs in Room 48.

Mycenaean and Cycladic art

The biggest crowd-puller is the **Mycenaean hall**, usually in Room 4, opposite the main entrance, but currently housed in the temporary exhibition hall while Room 4 gets an overhaul. During these temporary arrangements, the locations of specific exhibits, as keyed on the floor plan and noted in the text below, may not apply.

Schliemann's gold finds from the grave circle at Mycenae are the main attraction: as hard to get a look at on a summer's day as the Louvre's *Mona Lisa*, is the so-called funerary *Mask of Agamemnon* [a] in Case 3. Despite the proof offered by modern dating techniques, which indicate that it belonged to some more ancient Achaian king, crowds are still drawn by its correspondence with the Homeric myth.

The Mycenaeans' consummate art was small-scale decoration of rings, cups, seals and inlaid daggers – requiring eye-tiring scrutiny of the packed showcases to appreciate. Don't be entirely mesmerized by the death masks, or the superb golden-horned *Bull's Head* [b] in Case 27. In Case 5 there's a lovely duck-shaped vase of rock crystal; in Case 3, with the "Agamemnon" mask, a magnificent inlaid dagger. Case 8 has

NATIONAL ARCHAEOLOGICAL MUSEUM

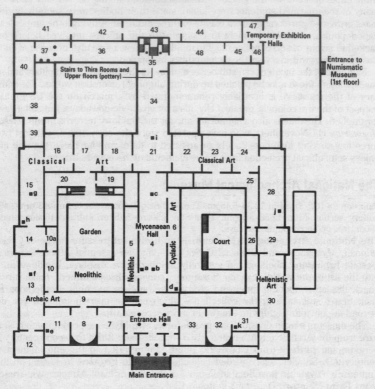

jewellery, daggers and a miniature golden owl and frog from Nestor's palace at Pylos; alongside, in Case 9, are baked tablets of Linear B, the earliest Greek writing.

On the wall in this section are Cretan-style frescoes from Tiryns which depict chariot-borne women watching spotted hounds in pursuit of boar, and bull-vaulting reminiscent of Knossos. More finds from Tiryns, in Case 15, include a huge ring depicting four demons presenting gifts to a goddess. In Case 32 **[c]** are the superb *Vafio cups*, with their scenes of wild bulls and long-tressed, narrow-waisted men, while in Case 33 an equally eye-catching cup is decorated with twining octopuses and dolphins. Further references to Homer abound: in Case 18 there's a magnificent *Boar's Tusk Helmet* and an ivory lyre with sphinxes adorning the soundboard; on the frescoes in the corner of the room you can pick out Achilles-style figure-of-eight shields.

To the right of the Mycenaean hall, Room 6 houses a large collection of **Cycladic art** – pre-Mycenaean pieces from the Aegean islands. Many of these suggest the abstract forms of modern Cubist art – most strikingly in the much-reproduced *Man Playing a Lyre* [d]. Another unusual piece, at the opposite end of the room, is a sixteenth-century BC cylindrical vase depicting a ring of fishermen carrying fish by their tails. Room 5, to the left of the Mycenaean hall, contains **Neolithic** finds, primarily from excavations in Thessaly.

Sculpture

Most of the rest of the ground floor is occupied by **sculpture**. Beginning in Room 7, on the left of the museum's main entrance, the exhibition proceeds chronologically (and this is the best way to see it) from the Archaic through the Classical and Hellenistic periods (Rooms 7–31) to the Roman- and Egyptian-influenced (Rooms 41–43). The gradual development from the stiff, stylized representations of the seventh century BC towards ever freer and looser naturalism is excitingly evident as you go through these cold and rather shabby rooms.

Early highlights include the Aristion *Stele of a Young Warrior* [e], with delicately carved beard, hair and tunic-folds in Room 11, and the Croesus *kouros* (statue of an idealized youth) in Room 13 [f]; both are from the late sixth century BC. You need sharp eyes not to miss some of the less obvious delights. Behind the Croesus *kouros*, for instance, and quite untrumpeted, a statueless plinth is carved with reliefs showing, on one side, young men exercising in the gymnasium, on the other a group of amused friends setting a dog and cat to fight each other – a common enough sight in contemporary Greece.

Room 15, which heralds the **Classical art** collection, leaves you in rather less doubt as to its central focus. Right in the middle stands a mid-fifth-century BC *Statue of Poseidon* [g], dredged from the sea off Évvia in the 1920s. The god stands poised to throw his trident – weight on the front foot, athlete's body perfectly balanced, the model of idealized male beauty. A less dramatic, though no less important, piece in the same room is the *Eleusinian Relief* [h]. Highly deliberate in its composition, the relief shows the goddess of fertility, accompanied by her daughter Persephone, giving to mankind an ear of corn – symbol of the knowledge of agriculture.

Other major Classical sculptures include the virtuoso *Little Jockey* (Room 21; [i]) urging on his galloping horse, found in the same shipwreck as the *Poseidon*; the fourth-century BC bronze *Ephebe of Antikithira* [j] in Room 28; and the three portrait heads in Room 30: a *Boxer*, burly and battered; the furrowed brow and intellectual's unkempt hairdo of the third-century BC *Philosopher;* and the expressive, sorrowful first-century face of the *Man from Delos*. The most reproduced of all the sculptures is in Room 31: a first-century AD statue of a naked and indulgent *Aphrodite* [k] about to rap Pan's knuckles for getting too fresh – a far cry (a long fall, some would say) from the reverent, idealizing portrayals of the gods in Classical times.

Too numerous to list, but offering fascinating glimpses of everyday life and changing styles of craftsmanship and perception of the human form, are the many **stelai** or carved gravestones found in several of the Classical rooms. Also worth a mention is Room 20, where various Roman copies of the lost Pheidias *Athena*, the original centrepiece sculpture of the Parthenon, are displayed. And in Room 32 is the **Hélène Stathatos Collection of gold jewellery** – amazing pieces all – from the ancient and Byzantine worlds.

Upstairs: the Thíra rooms, pottery and coins

Keep a reserve of energy for the **Thíra rooms** upstairs. A visual knockout, these have been reconstructed in situ, with their frescoes of monkeys, antelopes and flowers, and furnishings of painted wooden chairs and beds. Discovered at Akrotiri on the island of Thíra (Santoríni), they date from around 1450 BC, contemporary with the flourishing Minoan civilization on Crete.

The other upper rooms are occupied by a dizzying array of **pottery**. Rooms 49 and 50 are devoted to the Geometric Period (1000–700 BC); 52 and 53 to sixth-century black-figured pottery; 54 to black- and red-figured pots; and 55 and 56 to funerary white urns and fourth-century pottery. Beautiful though many of the items are, there is absolutely nothing in the way of explanation, and this is probably the section to omit if you are running short of time or stamina.

In the south wing of the museum, entered from the first floor, is the extensive **Numismatic Collection**. This takes in over 400,000 coins, from Mycenaean times (with the Homeric double-axe motif) to Macedonian, though only a fraction are on display – and again with little imagination.

Exárhia and back towards Síndagma

Exárhia, fifty-odd blocks squeezed between the National Archeological Museum and Stréfi hill, is perhaps the city's liveliest and most enjoyable night-time location. Since the early 1980s it has become home to a concentration of *ouzerí*, nightclubs and genuine music tavernas, many relocated from the Pláka; student budgets confronting bistro prices results in the nursing of a single drink all evening.

In the early 1990s, the area was linked – in the press at least – with Athens' disaffected youth, and became synonymous with the so-called anarchists who frightened the sedate and respectable by staving in car windscreens, splattering walls with black graffiti and drug-dealing. Since then, Exárhia has been resolutely cleaned up and gentrified, and the reality is not so extreme as Athenians – who like their city pretty savoury – would lead you to believe.

Back towards Síndagma

Between the counter-culturality of Exárhia and the occasional frowsiness of the bazaar, the broad busy avenues of Stadhíou, Panepistimíou and Akadhimías are lined with mainstream retailers, usually tucked into cavernous, occasionally opulent arcades that would have gained the approval of the original Bavarian planners.

Except for the blue city buses peeling off behind on Akadhimías and the metro works along Panepistimíou, the grounds of the Neoclassical **National Library** and **University** buildings, bang in the middle of all this, are an oasis of calm. The scattered buildings, designed by the Dane Christian Hansen, deserve a look, since their garish decoration gives an alarming impression of what the Classical monuments might have looked like when their paintwork was intact. Also worth a stop if you've time are two minor but quite enjoyable museums, devoted to the city's and nation's history.

The first of these, housed in the original Parliament building, in use from the 1860s until 1935, on Platía Kolokotróni, is the **National Historical Museum** (Tues–Fri 9am–1.30pm, Sat & Sun 9am–12.30pm; 500dr; *D3*). Its exhibits are predominantly Byzantine and medieval, though there is also a strong section on the War of Independence that includes Byron's sword and helmet.

The other, the **City of Athens Museum** (Mon, Wed, Fri & Sat 9am–1.30pm; 200dr; *D3*) occupies the original Royal Palace at Paparigopoúlou 7, on Platía Klafthmónos. This was the residence of the German-born King Otho in the 1830s before the new palace (now the Parliament, on Síndagma) was completed in 1842. Exhibits – mainly prints, and still somewhat sparse – feature an interesting model of the city as it was in 1842, with just 300 houses.

Síndagma, the National Gardens and south

All roads lead to Platía Sindágmatos – **Síndagma** (Syntagma) square – so you'll find yourself there sooner or later. Catering to tourism, with the main EOT information posts (in the National Bank), post office (extended hours), American Express, airline and travel offices grouped around – not to mention *McDonalds* and *Wendy's* – it has convenience but not much else to recommend it. The cafés, patrolled through the summer by Greek males on the lookout for foreign affairs, are overpriced and dangerously exposed to exhaust fumes, but make a handy rendezvous spot.

The square

Most of the square's buildings are modern and characterless, though earlier times prevail on the uphill (east) side where the **Voulí**, the Greek National Parliament, presides. This was built as the royal palace for Greece's first monarch, the Bavarian King Otho, in the 1830s. In front of it, goose-stepping **Evzónes** in tasselled caps, kilt and woolly leggings – a prettified version of traditional mountain costume – change their guard at intervals in front of the **Tomb of the Unknown Soldier,** to the rhythm of camera shutters. Hemingway, among others, impugned their masculinity but they are in fact a highly trained elite corps with rigorous height and weight requirements; formerly they were recruited almost exclusively from mountain villages.

Other flanking buildings to have survived postwar development include the vast **Hotel Grande Bretagne** – Athens' grandest. In the course of one of the more nefarious episodes of British meddling in Greek affairs, it nearly became the tomb of Winston Churchill. He had arrived on Christmas Day 1944 to sort out the *Dhekemvrianá*, the "events of December": a month of serious street-fighting between British forces and the Communist-led ELAS resistance movement, whom the British were trying to disarm. ELAS saboteurs had placed an enormous explosive charge in the drains, intending to blow up various Greek and Allied VIPs; according to whom you believe, it was either discovered in time by a kitchen employee, or removed by ELAS themselves when they realised they might get Churchill as well.

"Síndagma" means "constitution" and the name derives from the fact that Greece's first one was proclaimed by a reluctant King Otho from a palace balcony in 1843. The square is still the principal venue for mass **demonstrations**, whether trade-union protests against government austerity programmes or "drive-in" sabotage by taxi drivers outraged at proposals to curtail their movements in the interest of cleaner air. In the run-up to elections, the major political parties stage their final campaign rallies here – a pretty intimidating sight, with around 100,000 singing, flag-waving Greeks packed into the square. At such times, overground city transport comes to a halt, with the metro the only way around the bottleneck – although ironically, the expanding metro is creating considerable bottlenecks of its own, with a one-way system currently in effect on the east side, and the south edge (Othónos) completely closed off.

The National Gardens

At the back of the Voulí, the **National Gardens** (sunrise to sunset; free) are the most refreshing acres in the whole city – not so much a flower garden as a luxuriant tangle of trees, shrubs and creepers, whose shade, duck ponds, and murmuring irrigation channels provide palpable relief from the heat and smog of summer. They were originally the private palace gardens – a pet project of Queen Amalia in the 1840s; purportedly the main duty of the minuscule Greek navy in its early days was the fetching of rare plants, often the gifts of other royal houses, from remote corners of the globe.

Of late, however, the gardens have fallen on hard times: pond-cleaning and pruning are done only when funding permits, a botanical museum is closed more often than not, and a sorry excuse for a mini-zoo has become the target of criticism by environmental and animal-welfare groups. To add insult to injury, the metro project has requisitioned a large area of the gardens for air vents and site bungalows. The general air of dereliction is further fuelled by the packs of half-wild cats, abandoned in such numbers here that the city has seen fit to post a sign forbidding the practice. Despite all this, there are few better places in the city to read or wait for an evening ferry or plane.

The southern extension of the gardens, open 24 hours, consists of the graceful crescent-shaped grounds of the **Záppio**. This grand Neoclassical exhibition hall, another creation of the Danish architect Hansen (he of the University), was for a period the Greek State Radio headquarters but is now used mainly for press conferences and commercial exhibitions. The café–*ouzerí Aigli*, adjacent to the Záppio, offers outdoor seating in summer and a fitfully operating cinema, both favoured haunts of rich young things. There's a more basic but shaded **café**, the *Oasis*, up at the east (uphill) exit of the park on to Iródhou Attikoú (see "Eating and drinking", p.112, for more on these).

Iródhou Attikoú also fronts the **Presidential Palace**, the royal residence until Constantine's exit from the scene in 1967, where more *evzónes* stand sentry duty. The surrounding streets, with a full complement of foreign embassies and hardly a store or taverna, are very posh and heavily policed. The centre-right party, *Néa Dhimokratía*, has its headquarters in Odhós Rigílis nearby, as does the army's Officers' Club, scene of much anti-democratic intriguing in the past.

The Olympic Stadium

A walk to the base of Iródhou Attikoú and across busy Leofóros Ardhittoú will bring you to the **Olympic Stadium**, a nineteenth-century reconstruction on Roman foundations, slotting tightly between the pine-covered spurs of Ardhittós hill.

This site was originally marked out in the fourth century BC for the Panathenaic athletic contests, but in Roman times, as a grand gesture to mark the reign of the Emperor Hadrian, it was adapted for an orgy of blood sports, with thousands of wild beasts baited and slaughtered in the arena. Herodes Atticus (see p.85) later undertook to refurbish the 60,000 seats of the entire stadium; his white marble gift was to provide the city with a convenient quarry through the ensuing seventeen centuries.

The stadium's reconstruction dates from the modern revival of the Olympic Games in 1896 and to the efforts of another wealthy benefactor, the Alexandrian Greek Yiorgos Averoff. Its appearance – pristine whiteness and meticulous symmetry – must be very much as it was when first restored and reopened under the Roman senator, and indeed it's still used by local athletes despite the tight curves. Above the stadium to the south, on the secluded **Hill of Ardhittós**, are a few scant remnants of a Temple of Fortune, again constructed by Herodes Atticus. There is no public access, since the entire hill, with its pine groves, is an arsonist's paradise – the upper concourse, reached by a gate on Arhimídhous, is for the use of athletes in training only.

Méts and Pangráti

South and east of Ardhittós are the only two central neighbourhoods outside Pláka to have retained something of their traditional flavour – **Méts** and **Pangráti**. Particularly in Méts, a steep hillside quarter on the southwest side of the stadium, there are still nearly intact streets of pre-World War II houses, with tiled roofs, shuttered windows, and courtyards with spiral metal staircases and potted plants. They're a sad reminder of how beautiful this out-of-control city once was, even quite recently.

Méts and the Próto Nekrotafío

More specific attractions in **Méts** are the concentration of tavernas and bars around Márkou Moussoúrou and Arhimídhous (see p.110), and the Próto Nekrotafío (First Cemetery), at the top end of Anapáfseos (Eternal Rest) street, itself lined with shops catering to the funerary trade.

The **Próto Nekrotafío** shelters just about everybody who was anybody in twentieth-century Greek public life: the humbler tombs of singers, artists and writers are interspersed with ornate mausolea of soldiers, statesmen and "good" families, whose descendants come to picnic, stroll and tend the graves. One of the "unregarded wonders of Athenian life", Peter Levi called it; "the neoclassical marbles run riot, they reflower as rococo, they burst into sunblasts of baroque". The graveside statuary occasionally attains the status of high art, most notably in the works of Ianoulis Halepas, a Belle Epoque sculptor from Tínos generally acknowledged to be the greatest of a school of fellow-islanders. Halepas battled with mental illness for most of his life and died in extreme poverty in 1943; his masterpiece is the idealized **Kimiméni** (Sleeping Girl), on the right about 300 metres in.

Pangráti

Pangráti is the unremarkable but pleasant quarter to the north and east of the Stadium. Platía Plastíra, Platía Varnáva and Platía Pangratíou are the focal points, the first with a vast old-fashioned *kafenío* where you can sit for hours on a leafy terrace for the price of a coffee. Pangratíou, fringed by the local *álsos* or grove-park, is the rallying place for the neighbourhood's youthful posers. Several good tavernas are tucked away between (and on) Varnáva and nearby Odhós Arhimídhous, and the latter has an impressive *laikí agorá* – **street market** – every Friday.

More Pangráti eating places are down towards Leofóros Konstandínou, among the rather claustrophobic alleys opposite the **statue of Harry Truman** – repeatedly restored to his pedestal after being blown off it by leftists in reprisal for his notorious doctrine promulgated in 1947 to justify US intervention in the Greek civil war. The Nobel-laureate poet **George Seferis** lived not far away in Odhós Ágras, an attractive stair-street flanking the northeast wall of the Olympic Stadium.

North of Síndagma: Kolonáki, Likavitós and the Benáki and Cycladic Art museums

Athens is at its trendiest north of Síndagma, and if you have money to spend, **Kolonáki** is the place to do it, catering to every western taste from jazz bars to high fashion. The quarter is not especially interesting for visitors to the city – though it's a fond haunt of expatriates – but it does give access to **Likavitós hill**, where a funicular hauls you up for some of the best views of the city. Also close by are two fine museums: one devoted to **Cycladic Art**, the other, the **Benáki**, an assembly of just about all things Greek, from Mycenaean artefacts to twentieth-century memorabilia.

Kolonáki

Kolonáki is the city's most chic central address and shopping area. Although no great shakes architecturally, it enjoys a superb site on the southwest-facing slopes of Likavitós (Lycabettus), looking out over the Acropolis and National Gardens. From its summit, on one of those increasingly rare clear days, you can just about make out the mountains of the Peloponnese. The lower limits of Kolonáki are defined by Akadhimías and Vassilísis Sofías streets, where in grand Neoclassical palaces Egypt, France and

Italy have their embassies. The middle stretches of the quarter are for shopping, while the highest are purely residential.

The heart of the district is **Kolonáki square**, officially called Platía Filikís Eterías after the ancient "little column" that hides in the trees on the southwest side. The square's location should be committed to memory, for beneath the central garden, where kids, pensioners, nannies and pigeons compete for limited bench space, glistens the city's cleanest public toilet. Other diversions include the kiosks with their stocks of foreign papers and magazines, the **British Council library** on the downhill side, where you can read the paper for free and browse upcoming programme flybills, and numerous cafés on Patriárhou Ioakím to the east – the principal display ground for Kolonáki's well-heeled natives. Assorted cafés and pubs nearby on pedestrianized Tsakálof, Milióni and Valaoritou are better and slightly cheaper options for snacks and drinks.

Kolonáki's streets also contain an amazing density of small, classy **shops**, with the accent firmly on **fashion and design**. In a half-hour walk around the neighbourhood you can view the whole gamut of consumer style. Patriárhou Ioakím and Skoufá, with its cross-streets to the northwest, comprise the most promising area, along with the pedestrianized Voukourestíou-Valaorítou-Kriezótou block, just below Akadhimías.

For more random strolling, the highest tiers of Kolonáki are pleasant, with steep streets ending in long flights of steps, planted with oleander, jasmine and other flowering shrubs. The one **café** spot up here is at **Platía Dhexamenís**, a small and attractive square close to the Likavitós loop road, where in summertime tables are set under the trees around the **Dhexamení**, a covered reservoir begun by the Emperor Hadrian.

Likavitós

Not far away from Kolonáki square, at the top of Ploutárhou, a **funicular** (8am–10pm, every 20min in summer, less frequent the rest of the year; 400dr) begins its ascent to the summit of **Likavitós Hill**. For the more energetic, the principal path up the hill begins here, too, rambling through woods that are a favourite spot with amorous couples. On the summit, the chapel of **Áyios Yióryios** dominates – a spectacular place to celebrate the saint's name-day if you're around on April 23. There's a **café** on the adjacent terrace, and another, less plastic, halfway down; both have morning and sunset views – you're eyeball-to-eyeball with the Acropolis – glorious enough to excuse the inflated prices and unenthusiastic service.

Most paths and driveways up the hill converge at the open-air **Likavitós Theatre**, used primarily as a music venue during the Athens Summer Festival (see p.117). If you come down by the southeast slopes, you emerge in the very lovely but privileged little enclave that the British and American archeological schools have managed to retain for themselves on Odhós Souidhías. Here, too, is the **Yennádhion Library**, with large collections of books on Greece and an unpublicized drawerfull of Edward Lear's watercolour sketches; good-quality and reasonably priced reproductions are on sale.

The Benáki Museum

Koumbári 1/corner Vassilísis Sofías, *D4*; currently closed for the building of an extension, but gift shop open daily except Sun 9am–3pm.

Once it re-opens (scheduled for 1996), this museum – overlooked by about ninety percent of visitors to Athens – should not be missed. Housing a private collection given to the state by **Emmanuel Benáki**, an Egyptian-Greek collector who had grown wealthy on the Nile cotton trade, it is constantly surprising and fascinating, with exhibits ranging from Ottoman ceramics, Mycenaean jewellery, Coptic textiles, Greek costumes and folk artefacts, Byronia, and memorabilia of the Greek War of

Independence – even a reconstructed Egyptian palace reception hall. These, together with displays of jewellery and other items from the Hélène Stathatos collection (of National Archeological Museum fame) are worth an hour or two of anyone's time.

Among the more unusual exhibits are collections of early Greek Gospels, liturgical vestments and church ornaments rescued by Greek refugees from Asia Minor in 1922 (Rooms 4 and 10); some dazzling embroideries and body ornaments (in the basement); and some unique historical material – on the Cretan statesman Eleftherios Venizelos, Asia Minor, and the Cretan Revolution (Room 9); and material on the 1821 rising against the Turks upstairs. Don't miss the museum's two very early **El Greco** panels, dating from the time when he painted in the Byzantine style on his native Crete.

An additional attraction, especially if you've been dodging traffic all day, is the **rooftop café**, with good snacks and views over the nearby National Gardens. A **shop**, by the entrance, stocks a fine selection of books on Greek folk art, records of regional music and some of the best posters and postcards in the city.

Museum of Cycladic and Ancient Greek Art

Neofítou Dhouká 4 – second left off Vassilísis Sofías after the Benáki museum, *D4*; Mon & Wed–Fri 10am–4pm, Sat 10am–3pm; 250dr.

For display, labelling, explanation and comfort, this small private museum is way ahead of anything else in Athens. Though the collections are restricted – to the Cycladic civilization (third millennium BC), pre-Minoan Bronze Age (second millennium BC) and the period from the fall of Mycenae to the beginning of historic times around 700 BC, plus a selection of Classical pottery – you learn far more about these periods than from the corresponding sections of the National Archeological Museum.

If Cycladic art seems an esoteric field, don't be put off. The distinctive marble bowls and folded-arm figurines with their sloping wedge heads are displayed in a way that highlights their supreme purity and simplicity, and elucidates their appeal to twentieth-century artists like Moore, Picasso and Brancusi. You can also see in the figurines the remote ancestry of the Archaic style that evolved into the great sculptures of the Classical period. The exact purpose of the mostly female effigies is unknown but, given their frequent discovery in grave-barrows, it has been variously surmised that they were spirit-world guides for the deceased, substitutes for the sacrifice of servants and attendants, or representations of the Earth Goddess in her role of reclaiming yet another of her children.

Much of the top floor is devoted to a collection of painted Classical bowls, often showing two unrelated scenes on opposite sides. The curators consider the one with a depiction of revellers on one face and three men in cloaks conversing on the other to be the star exhibit, but there is not one dud. Most of the more exquisite items date from the fifth century BC – not for nothing was it referred to as a "Golden Age".

To round off the experience, there's a **shop**, **snack bar** and shaded courtyard.

Other nearby museums

A number of other museums – of somewhat more specialist interest – are grouped conveniently close together near the angled intersection of Vassilísis Sofías and Vassiléos Konstandínou, close by the Benáki and Cycladic Art museums.

Byzantine Museum

Vassilísis Sofías 22, 400m from the Benáki, *D5*; daily except Mon 8.30am–2.45pm; 500dr.

The Byzantine Museum's setting is perhaps its best feature: a peaceful, courtyarded villa that once belonged to the Duchesse de Plaisance, an extravagantly eccentric French philhellene and widow of a Napoleonic general who helped to fund the War of

Independence. To enjoy the exhibits — almost exclusively icons, housed in two restored side galleries – requires some prior interest, best developed by a trip to the churches at Mystra, Dhafní or Óssios Loukás. Labelling is generally Greek-only and you are told little of the development of styles, which towards the sixteenth century show an increasing post-Renaissance Italian influence, due to the presence of the Venetians in Greece. The rear hall contains marble artefacts, plus a reconstructed basilica. An annexe is currently under construction, which will hopefully mean better exposure for artefacts previously held in storage.

War Museum

Vassilísis Sofías 24, just beyond the Byzantine museum, *D5*; daily except Mon 9am–2pm; free.

The only "cultural" endowment of the 1967–74 junta, this museum becomes predictably militaristic and right-wing as it approaches modern events: the Asia Minor campaign, the civil war, Greek forces in Korea, etc. Earlier times, however, are covered with a more scholarly concern and this gives an interesting insight into changes in warfare from Mycenae through to the Byzantines and Turks. Among an array of models is a fascinating series on the acropolises and castles of Greece, both Classical and medieval.

National Gallery of Art

Vassiléos Konstandínou 50, past the War Museum by the Hilton, *E5*; Tues–Sat 9am–3pm, Sun 10am–2pm; 500dr.

The National Gallery has a rather disappointing core collection of Greek art from the sixteenth century to the present. One of the few modern painters to stand out is Nikos Hatzikyriakos-Ghikas (Ghika), who is well represented on the ground floor. On the mezzanine is a small group of canvases by the primitive painter Theophilos (more of whose work can be seen at the Museum of Greek Folk Art in Pláka – see p.89). Temporary exhibitions can be worth catching; keep an eye out for posters or check the listings in *The Athenian* magazine.

The outskirts: Dhafní, Kessarianí and Kifissiá

Athens pushes its suburbs higher and wider with each year and the **monasteries of Dhafní and Kessarianí**, once well outside the city limits, are now approached through more or less continuous cityscape. However, each retains a definite country-side setting and makes for a good respite from the central sights.

The monasteries are easily reached by taxi or by local **city transport**. For Dhafní (9km west of the centre), take more or less any bus prefixed #8 (#853, #862, #880 are most frequent) from Platía Elefthérias (*D1*); the monastery is signposted on the right of the road, about twenty minutes' ride. For Kessarianí, take blue bus #224 from Akadhimías (*D3/4*) to the last stop, from where the church is a thirty- to forty-minute climb up the lower slopes of Mount Imittós.

The northern suburb of **Kifissiá** is included in this section as an insight into wealthy Athenian life – it has long been where the rich have their villas – and for natural history enthusiasts, who may want to check out the Goulandhrís Museum. Kifissiá is the most northerly stop on the metro.

Classical enthusiasts may want to continue from Dhafní to the site of **Eleusis** (see p.133), a further twenty-minute ride on the #853 or #862 bus routes.

Dhafní

Dhafní Monastery (daily 8.30am–2.45pm; 500dr) is one of the great buildings of Byzantine architecture. Its classic Greek-cross-octagon design is a refinement of a plan first used at Óssios Loukás, on the road to Delphi (see p.250), and its mosaics are considered among the great masterpieces of the Middle Ages.

The monastic church replaced a fortified fifth-century basilica, which in turn had been adapted from the ruins of a sanctuary of Apollo – the name is derived from the *daphnai* (laurels) sacred to the god. Both the church and the fortifications which enclose it incorporate blocks from the ancient sanctuary; a porch featuring Classical columns was present up until two centuries ago, when it was hauled off among Lord Elgin's swag.

The Byzantines, ironically, occupied the building for little over a century. When the monastery was established, in 1070, the Greek Church was undergoing an intellectual revival, but the state was in terminal collapse. The following year the Normans took Bari, the last Byzantine possession in southern Italy, and the Seljuk Turks defeated the Byzantine army in Armenia – a prelude to the loss of Asia Minor and, before long, Greece itself. The fortifications and remains of a Gothic cloister show evidence of later building under the Cistercians, who replaced Dhafní's Orthodox monks after the Frankish conquest of Athens in 1204. The monastery today is unoccupied; the Cistercians were banished by the Turks, and Orthodox monks, allowed to return in the sixteenth century, were duly expelled for harbouring rebels during the War of Independence.

Inside the church, the **mosaic cycle** is remarkable for its completeness: there are scenes from the life of Christ and the Virgin, saints (a predominance of Eastern figures from Syria and elsewhere in the Levant), archangels and prophets. The greatest triumph is the *Pandokrátor* (Christ in Majesty) on the dome: lit by the sixteen windows of the drum, and set against a background of gold, this stern image directs a tremendous and piercing gaze, his finger poised on the Book of Judgement. A perfect encapsulation of the strict orthodoxy of Byzantine belief, the scene is rendered poignant by the troubled circumstances in which it was created.

Kessarianí

What it loses in a strict architectural comparison with Dhafní, **Kessarianí monastery** makes up for in its location. Although just five kilometres from the centre of the city, it is high enough up the slopes of Mount Imittós to escape the *néfos* and the noise. The sources of the river Ilissos provide for extensive gardens hereabouts, as they have since ancient times (Ovid mentions them), and Athenians still come to collect water from the local fountains.

The monastery buildings date from the eleventh century, though the frescoes in the chapel are much later – executed during the sixteenth and seventeenth centuries. In contrast to Dhafní's clerics, Kessarianí's abbot agreed to submit to Roman authority when the Franks took Athens, so the monastery remained in continuous Greek (if not quite Orthodox) occupation through the Middle Ages. Today the monastery maintains a small group of monks, who allow **visits** (daily except Mon, 8.30am–2.45pm; 500dr). Outside these hours you can while away the time in the well-maintained grounds, full of picnickers in summertime.

On the **way up to the monastery**, which is fairly obvious from the bus terminal, don't overlook the refugee neighbourhood of Kessarianí. With an attractively casual, ramshackle aspect, its streets were used as a 1920s location for the Greek movie *Rembetiko*.

Kifissiá

Kifissiá, Athens' most desirable suburb, edges up the leafy slopes of Mount Pendéli, about eight kilometres north of the city centre. A surprising 300m above sea level and a good 5°F cooler than central Athens, it appealed to the nineteenth-century bourgeoisie as a suitable site for summer residence. Their villas – Neoclassical, Swiss, Alsatian and fantasy-melange – still hold their own amid the newer concrete models. Indeed, despite the encroachments of speculators' apartment buildings and trendy boutiques, the suburb's village-like character prevails.

The centre of the old "village" is the crossroads called Plátanos – though the mighty plane tree that gave it its name has long since fallen under the axe of the traffic planners – just at the uphill end of the gardens opposite the Kifissiá metro station. The hub is the two or three streets around Plátanos: *Varsos*, opposite the metro station, an old-fashioned patisserie specializing in home-made yoghurts, jams and sticky cakes, acts as a meeting place for the whole neighbourhood, while a good lunchtime stop is the *Estiatorio O Platanos* by the above-mentioned crossroads.

If you want some direction to your wanderings around trees and gardens, head for the **Goulandhrís Natural History Museum** (daily except Fri 9am–2pm; 400dr) at Levídhou 13, ten minutes' walk from the metro. The modest but well-displayed collection has especially good coverage of Greek birds and butterflies and endangered species like the monk seal (*Monachus monachus*) and sea turtle (*Caretta caretta*). Housed in a grand marble mansion, with a 250,000-specimen herbarium attached, the museum also boasts a café and a shop selling superb illustrated books, postcards, posters and prints.

Eating and drinking

As you'd expect in a city that houses almost half the Greek population, Athens has the best and the most varied **restaurants and tavernas** in the country – and most places are sources not just of good food but of a good night out.

Starting with **breakfast**, most Athenians survive on a thimbleful of coffee, but if you need a bit more to set you up for the day, it's little problem finding a bakery, yoghurt shop or fruit stall. Veïkoú and Koukáki are particularly good for this, with the *Nestoras Tzatsos* **bakery** at Veïkoú 45, another at no. 75 and still another on pedestrianized Olimbíou, just off Platía Koukáki, offering excellent wholegrain bread and milk products. Alternatively, you could try one of the places listed under "Tea houses and patisseries" on p.112. For a regular **bacon/egg/juice breakfast**, there are several options in and around Pláka. The cheapest and friendliest place is at Níkis 26 (*E3*); a second choice is nearby at Apollonós 11; and a third is at Kidathinéon 10, near the corner of Moní Asteríou (*E3*).

Later in the day, a host of **snack** stalls and outlets get going. If your budget is low you can fill up at them exclusively, forgetting sit-down restaurants altogether. If it's not, you'll still probably want to indulge. The standard **snacks** are *souvláki me píta* (kebab in pitta bread), *tirópites* (cheese pies) and *spanakópites* (spinach pies), along with *bougátses* (cream pies) and a host of other speciality pastries. The best downtown **souvláki stand** is widely acknowledged to be *Kostas'*, at Adhrianoú 116 (*E3*), which always has a line, despite its unpredictable opening hours.

For **main meals**, Pláka's hills and lanes are full of character, and provide a pleasant evening setting, despite the aggressive touts and general tourist hype. But for good value and good quality, only a few of the quarter's restaurants and tavernas are these days worth a second glance. For quality Greek cooking, if you're staying any length of time in the city, it's better to strike out into the ring of **neighbourhoods** around: to Méts, Pangráti, Exárhia/Neápoli, Veïkoú/Koukáki, Áno Petrálona, or the more upmarket Kolonáki. None of these is more than a half hour's walk, or a quicker trolley bus or taxi ride, from the centre – effort well repaid in increased menu choice and a more authentic and often livelier atmosphere.

Restaurants

The listings below are devoted mainly to **restaurant meals**, grouped according to district and divided into cheap (under 3000dr per person) and less so (over 3000dr). Note that several of our recommendations are closed in summer (usually June to August), and for five days or so around Easter; this is usually due to hot, un-air-conditioned locales, or the exodus of their regular business trade. All grid listings refer to the map on pp.66–67.

Pláka

Selections here represent just about all of note that **Pláka** has to offer; most, sadly, are on the periphery of the quarter, rather than on the more picturesque squares and stairways. At the latter, don't be bamboozled by the touts, positioned at crucial locations to lure you over to their tavernas' tables – invariably a bad sign.

UNDER 3000DR

Damingos, Kidhathinéon 41, *F3*. Tucked away in the basement, this place has dour service, but is good value, with barrelled wine and excellent *bakaliáro skordhaliá* (cod with garlic sauce). Evenings only; closed midsummer.

Kouklis (Yeranis Skolarhío), Tripódhon 14, corner Epihármou, *F3*. Attractive split-level taverna with two aliases which serves a good selection of *mezédhes* and good house red wines; it has a perennially popular summer terrace.

O Platanos, Dhioyénous 4, *E3*. One of the oldest tavernas in the district, with outdoor summer seating under the namesake tree. Lunch & supper; closed Sun.

Toh Ipoyio, Kidathinéon 30 (in the basement), *E3*. Wide range of grills, vegetable *mezédhes*, bulk wine. Evenings only; closed late May–late Sept.

OVER 3000DR

Eden, Lissíou 12, off Mnesikléous, *E3*. The city's oldest vegetarian restaurant offers dishes you'll pine for on travels around Greece; the setting is pleasant as well, on the ground floor of an old house 300m from *Eden*'s original site. Portions not huge but very tasty.

Iy Klimataria, Klepsídhras 5, *E3*. Decent food, with live, unamplified, passably authentic music in the bargain – rare in the Pláka. Open winter and summer (when the roof comes off); there's a good combination bar and sweetshop adjacent.

Monastiráki and the Bazaar

The shift from Pláka to the more genuinely commercial quarter of Monastiráki is refreshing, since the area attracts serious eaters. There is a definite character about the streets, too, at its best around the flea market.

UNDER 3000DR

Bretannia, corner of Athinás, Omónia, *D2*. Wonderful old caféteria serving superb *rizógalo* (rice pudding with cinnamon) and yoghurt.

Ipiros, Platía Ayíou Filíppou, *E2*. An old restaurant in a great location, right at the heart of the flea market. If the food – casserole dishes – is occasionally a bit listless, the prices and quantity are fair enough.

O Savvas, Mitropóleos 92, *E2*. Souvlaki and kebab joint with a wide menu, outdoor seating and a rather touristy feel.

O Thanasis, Mitropóleos 69, *E2*. Reckoned to be the best souvlaki and kebab place in this part of Athens. Always packed with locals at lunchtime.

Sigalas, Platía Monastirakioú 2, *E2*. Huge old restaurant whose walls are lined with retsina barrels. Straightforward menu. Closes 11pm.

Toh Monastiri, in the central meat market (entrances at Eolóu 80 and off Evripídhou or Sofokléous), *D2*. The last surviving – and luckily the best – restaurant here; the raw ingredients are certainly fresh, and there's *patsás* (tripe and trotter soup) if you're in need of a hangover cure. Open 6am–3am.

Exárhia/Platía Viktorías

Exárhia is still surprisingly untrodden by tourists, considering its proximity to the centre. Its eating and drinking establishments are conveniently close to the National Archeological Museum and several recommended hotels, and exploring them gives some insight into how the student/youth/alternative crowd carries on.

UNDER 3000DR

Barba Yannis, Emmanuíl Benáki 94, Exárhia, *C3*. Varied menu (changes daily) and good cooking in a relaxed atmosphere, aided and abetted by barrel wine. Tables outside in summer.

Mainas, Kallidhromíou 27, Exárhia, *C3*. Fine pizza and other main courses to eat in or take away.

Ouzeri, Elpídhos 16, Platía Viktorías. Mostly seafood – a midtown rarity – and a few *mezédhes* with ouzo or barrel wine. Ungreasy, moderately pricey dishes for lunch and supper; closed Sun.

Vangelis, Sahíni, off Liossíon (200m up from Platía Váthis), *C2*. Simply one of the friendliest and most traditional tavernas in the city; oven casseroles are complemented by 1950s decor.

OVER 3000DR

Greenery, Kodringtónos 14, Exárhia, *C2*. Vegetarian snack bar open for lunch and dinner; closed Sun.

Kostoyiannis, Zaími 37 (behind the National Archeological Museum, off Ioulianoú), *C3*. One of the city's best restaurants – much frequented by crowds from the theatres and cinemas around. Quality *mezédhes* and delicacies like rabbit stew. Evenings only; closed Sun.

Rozalia, Valtetsíou 58, Exárhia, *C3*. The best *mezédhes*-plus-grills-type taverna immediately around the *platía*, with the bonus of highly palatable sparkling red wine – and the accompaniment of corny serenading musicians. You order from the proffered tray as the waiters thread their way through the throng. Suppers only; garden in summer.

Strefis Taverna tis Xanthis, Irínis Athinéas 5, in Neápoli behind Lófos Stréfi, *B4*. House specialities include rabbit stew and schnitzel. A pleasant old mansion with a roof garden that offers fine view across northern Athens. Closed Sun.

Neápoli

This district is a long walk or short bus ride up Hariláou Trikoúpi from Exárhia, with a concentration of calmer clubs, bars and cinemas that make it a favourite dining-out area for savvy locals. The food here is good, teetering to either side of the 3000dr divider. Mavromiháli is one street over from Hariláou Trikoúpi.

O Fondas, Arianítou 6, just off Mavromiháli, *C4*. Probably the most expensive of the four along this street, but high-quality food.

Iy Lefka, Mavromiháli 121, *C4*. Standard taverna fare, with barrelled retsina. Summer seating in a huge garden enclosed by barrels.

O Pinaleo, Mavromiháli 152, *B4*. Rich *mezédhes* and meaty entrées, washed down with unresinated bulk wine and served up by a young couple from Híos. Oct to mid-May only.

O Vlasis, Armatólon Kléfton 20, Neápoli/Ambelókipi border, *B5*. Elegant and filling traditional Greek cooking; not cheap but always packed – the most telling recommendation. Evenings only; closed mid-summer.

Ta Bakiria, Mavromiháli 117, *C4*. Similar to *Iy Lefka* but marginally less expensive and with a more imaginative menu. Atmospheric interior for wintertime and a summer garden. Closed Sun.

Ta Tria Adhelfia, Leofóros Alexándhras 116, *B5*. Good, straightforward taverna food.

Kolonáki

Kolonáki has a ritzy, upmarket reputation that puts off a lot of tourists. Nonetheless, among the boutiques are some surprising finds.

FOREIGN CUISINE RESTAURANTS

Healthy as it may be, it's not difficult to get tired of Greek food, especially during an extended visit, and you may find your thoughts turning to other cuisines. Unlike the rest of the country, Athens offers a fair selection, from highly chi-chi French places, through Armenian and Arabic, Spanish and Balkan, to Japanese and Korean. Listed below are some of the more central places, which don't require a large outlay in taxi fares to reach – others are to be found at the beach suburbs to the south. Economy ends there, however, since they are all comparatively expensive: budget for 4000–6000dr per person, depending on what you order.

Unless otherwise indicated, the places listed below are closed in summer and on Sunday, but stay open until 1.30am. Reservations are advisable.

ARMENIAN-TURKISH
Tria Asteria, Mélitos 7/corner Plastíra, Néa Smírni (☎93 58 134; off map below *G3*, at end of #10 trolley line). Specialities include *tandir kebab* and *kionefe*, a special stuffed-filo dessert. Open in summer.

CHINESE
Dragon Palace, Andínoros 3, Pangráti, behind several museums (☎72 42 795; *D5*). Cantonese dishes such as Peking duck. Open in summer.
Golden Dragon, Olimbíou 27–29/Singroú 122, Koukáki (☎92 32 315; off map, below *G2/3*). A cut above average: ginger chicken, stuffed chicken wings, etc. Open in summer.
Golden Flower, Níkis 30, Síndagma (☎32 30 113; *E3*). Open daily and in summer.

CZECH
Bohemia, Dhímou Tséliou, Ambelókipi (☎64 26 341; *A5*). Czech beers (of course); open in summer.
Svejk, Roúmbesi 8a, Néos Kósmos, 15min walk from Koukáki (☎90 18 389; off map, below *G3*). Rich stew-like main courses, also duck and carp according to season. Closed Mon & Tues.

FRENCH
Prunier, Ipsilándou 63, Kolonáki (☎72 27 379; *D5*). Central and unpretentious bistro.
Calvados, Alkmános 5, Ilísia (☎72 26 291; off map, just past *D5*). Normandy cuisine.

GERMAN
Ritterburg, Formíonos 11, Pangráti (☎72 38 421; off map, past *E/F5*). Schnitzels, sausages and the like.

ITALIAN
Al Convento, Anapíron Polémou 4–6, Kolonáki. (☎72 39 163; *D5*). Claims to be the oldest Italian restaurant in Athens. Speciality pasta and scallopine. Open in summer; closed Sun.
Mona Lisa, Loukianoú, Kolonáki (☎72 47 283; *F4*). Some more interesting main courses – not just the usual pasta variations. Closed Mon.

JAPANESE
Kyoto, Garivaldi 5, Veïkoú (☎92 32 047; *F2*). A quite reasonable, long-established place; unusual specials as well as the expected *tempura* and *sushi*. Open in summer, evenings only. **Michiko**, Kidathinéon 27, Pláka (☎32 20 980; *E3*). Touristy and expensive – but very central and surprisingly authentic. Open in summer.

KOREAN
Seoul, Evritanías 8, off Panórmou in Ambelókipi (☎69 24 669; off map beyond *A/B5*). Speciality Korean barbecue. Garden seating in summer.
Orient, Lékka 26, Síndagma (☎32 21 192; *E3*). Also Chinese and Japanese dishes. Open in summer.

MEXICAN
Blue Velvet, Ermoú 116, Thisió (☎32 39 047; *E2*). Jazz and blues with your chilli on Fri and Sun; closed Mon.

SPANISH
Ispaniki Gonia, Theayénous 22, Pangráti (☎72 31 393; off map, past *E5*). Housed in an old mansion near the *Caravel Hotel*. Occasional live music. Open in summer.

UNDER 3000DR

Toh Kioupí, Platía Kolonáki, near corner of Skoufá, *D4*. Subterranean lunchtime taverna; standard Greek casseroles in all their salty glory.

OVER 3000DR

Rodhia, Aristípou 44, near the base of the téléférique, *D5*. Elegant main courses; open year round; but closed Sun.

Taverna Dhimokritos, Dhimokrítou 23/corner Tsakálof, *D4*. A bit snooty, but a beautiful building and wel- prepared food from a vast menu. Open lunchtime and evenings, but closed in late summer and Sun.

Toh Grafio, Spevsípou 1, Platía Dhexamení, *D4*. Cool, modern *ouzerí* with a wide selection of Greek and non-Greek snacks and dishes; nice location, too. Closed Sun.

Pangráti and Méts

These two neighbourhoods feature many of the city's best eating places. All the places below are a short (if generally uphill) walk across busy Ardhitoú and past the Olympic stadium, or accessible via a #4 trolley ride to Platía Plastíra. **Goúva** is an extension of Méts, just south of the First Cemetery.

UNDER 3000DR

O Ilias, corner Stasínou/Telesílis (near Leofóros Konstandínou), *E5*. A very good and very popular taverna. Tables outside in summer.

O Megaritis, Ferekídhou 2, corner Arátou, Pangráti, *F5*. Casserole food, barrel wine, indoor/pavement seating. Open all year.

Prasino, Kenedy 23, Pangráti/Kaisariani border, off map beyond *F5*. Caters to refugee clientele with Anatolian-style food, including brains. Tables out on pavement in summer. Closed Mon.

To Kalivi, Empedhokléous 26/corner Proklóu, above Platía Varnáva, Pangráti, *F5*. Excellent, traditional *mezédhes*-type fare; rustic decor. Closed late May–late Sept.

Vellis, Platía Varnáva/corner Stilpónos (between Pangráti and Méts), *F5*. Limited choice, but very characterful little place at the west end of the square. One of the last of a dying breed of tradesmen's wine-with-food shops. Evenings only; indoor and outdoor seating.

OVER 3000DR

Karavitis, Arktínou 35, off Leofóros Konstandínou, *F5*. Old-style taverna with bulk wine, *mezédhes*, clay-cooked main courses. Indoor and outdoor seating.

Manesis, Márkou Moussoúrou 3, *F4*. Egyptian co-management reflected in such *mezédhes* as humous, tabouli and falafel; the red house wine is excellent. Long list of daily specials; pricey but worth it. Tables in walled garden in summer. Evenings only; closed Sun.

O Virinis, Arhimídhous 11 (off Platía Plastíra), *F5*. Good-quality, regular-priced taverna, with its own house wine and a wide variety of *mezédhes*. Tables in garden in summer.

Ta Pergoulia, Márkou Moussoúrou 16, *F4*. Delicious, unusual *mezédhes* – order seven or eight and you'll have a fair-sized bill but a big meal. Closed May–Oct.

Toh Paragoni, Platía Plíta 3, Goúva, off map below *G5*. A good, slightly upmarket *psistaria*; outdoor seating facing the park in summer.

Toh Spiti Mas, Dhafnopáti, just off Platía Plíta, just below *G5*. Features an expensive but imaginative menu and garden dining in summer.

Veïkoú/Koukáki

This is one of the most pleasant parts of the city in which to while away the middle of a day or round off an evening, having wandered down from the south slope of the Acropolis or Fílopáppou hill. It's very much middle-class, residential Athens – uneventful and a bit early-to-bed. The districts straddle the #1, #5 and #9 trolley lines.

UNDER 3000DR

Iy Gardhinia, Zínni 29, Koukáki, *G3*. Extremely basic, occasionally oily, but inexpensive casserole food and barrel wine in a cool, cavernous setting. Lunchtime only in summer.

Ouzeri Evvia, G. Olimbíou 8, Koukáki, off map below *G2*. Hearty food as well as drink served on the pedestrian way; very reasonable and informal.

Ouzedhiko Toh Meltemi, Zínni 26, Koukáki, *G2/G3*. A modest-priced *ouzerí* that shields its customers from street traffic with banks of greenery. Offers a wide range of *mezédhes* dishes, but the emphasis is on seafood. Closed Sun.

O Yeros tou Morea, Arváli 4, Koukáki, *G2*. Best for lunch when the oven food and *mezédhes* are fresh. Full of Koukáki bachelors of all ages, who can eat here more cheaply than at home, and indulge in the bulk wine from the barrels that form the main decor. Closed Sun.

Psitopolio O Kalyvas, G. Olimbíou 10, Koukáki, off map below *G3*. Good grills and *mezédhes*, washed down with barrel wine and beer on tap, served outdoors on a pedestrianized street.

Toh Ikositeserooro, Singroú 42/44, Veïkoú, *F3*. The name means "(Open) round-the-clock", and that's it's main virtue. Fair, if rather overpriced, portions of anti-hangover food such as lamb tongues and *patsás*. At its liveliest after midnight in summer.

Toh Triandookto (O Periklís), Veïkoú 38, Veïkoú, *G3*. Recently expanded sideways into an old barbershop, this unmarked taverna offers one of the best deals in town. Large portions of simple, well-prepared food; wonderful Nemea red and Attica white wine from the barrel. Evenings only; closed June–Sept.

OVER 3000DR

Baladha, Yennéou Koloktrón 66, Filopáppou, off map just below *G1*. Recently opened *mezedhofolío*, offering more unusual dishes like mushroom casseroles; summer garden.

Panathinea, Makriyánni 29, Veïkoú, *F3*. Looks like a tourist trap, but isn't; very good Greek and international food, reasonably priced for the location. Full breakfast available.

Toh Dhikti, G. Olimbíou 2, off map past *G2*. Much fancier than its neighbour, the *Evvia*, with such delicacies as mussels, crab croquettes, snails – and animal unmentionables. Closed Mon.

Toh Sokaki, Aryiríou 6 (an alley – *sokáki* in Greek – off Veïkoú, near Zínni), *G2*. Slightly more upmarket *psistariá*; the house specialities are grilled chicken and *mezédhes*. A quiet place with outdoor seating in summer.

Áno Petrálona

This old refugee neighbourhood, on the west flank of Filopáppou Hill, is the least touristed district of central Athens. Just why is a mystery: the range of tavernas is excellent, the #9 trolley bus appears regularly, and it's a natural choice for eating after an evening at the Dora Stratou folk-dance theatre. There's a trolley stop on the Platía Amalías Merkoúri, from where the main artery of Dhimifóndos is a short stroll northwest. All of the places listed below are off our map beyond *G1*.

UNDER 3000DR

Iy Avli tou Pikiliou, Dhimifóndos 116. Despite the name (which means "Variety Courtyard"), this is a standard limited-menu, but very inexpensive, taverna with a garden.

Ikonomou (no sign displayed), corner Tróön/Kidhandídhon. Basic home cooking served to packed pavement tables in summer.

Toh Monastiri, Dhimifóndos 46. Very popular, moderately priced neighbourhood place; occasional guitar music on an informal basis after 11.30pm.

OVER 3000DR

O Haris, corner Tróön/Kidhandídhon. Newer and smarter rival to *Ikonómou* across the way, but with indoor seating only; long and interesting menu.

T'Askimopapo, Iónon 61. For many years, this was known as the PASOK (a reference to the political party) house taverna. It's still quite popular – and does unusual dishes. Closed Sun.

Tea houses and patisseries

With a couple of honourable exceptions, **tea houses** and continental-style **patisseries** are a recent phenomenon in Athens. Quiet, rather consciously sophisticated places, they're essentially a reaction against the traditional and basic *kafenía*. Most are concentrated around the Pláka and in Kolonáki and the more upmarket suburbs: the pedestrianized streets of Milióni and Valaorítou in Kolonaki, D4, in particular, seem to be one uninterrupted pavement café.

Aigli, just east of Záppio exhibition hall, *E4*. The terrace, with its views over Zeus temple and the Acropolis, is *the* place to be seen lingering over an expensive coffee.

De Profundis, Angelikís Hatzimihális 1, Pláka, *E3*. A trendy-looking tea house but reasonably priced; herb teas, quiches, small main courses, pastries. Open Mon–Fri 5pm–2am; Sat & Sun noon–2am. Closed Aug.

Floca, in the Stóa Athinás between Panepistimíou and Koráï, *D3*. The longest-established Athenian café-patisserie – and still the best. Their *chocalatina* (cream chocolate cake) is unrivalled. City-centre branches at Leofóros Kifisías 118, Ambelókipi (off map), corner Panepistimíou/Voukourestíou (in the arcade), *D3*, and just south of junction Veïkoú/Dhimitrakopoúlou, Veïkoú, *F3*.

Gelateria Firenze, Dhimitrakopoúlou 42, corner Dhrákou, Veïkoú, *G3*. Athens' most extensive range of rich and wonderful Italian *gelati* – not exorbitant for the quality. Seating indoors and out.

Galaktopolio Iy Amalthea, Trípodhou 16, Pláka, *F3*. Recent, pricey arrival, serving mostly crepes as well as non-alcoholic drinks.

Koperti, Skoufá 60a, *F3*. Popular, youthful *salon de thé* in a handsome old shop close to the French Institute. Also serves salads, cheese and hot entrées.

La Chocolatiere, Skoufá/corner Dhimokrítou, Kolonáki, *D4*. Exquisite chocolates and cakes; also light snacks, shakes and drinks, served under trees on the Platía opposite. A good place to come for a present if you're invited to a Greek's nameday.

Milioni, Milioni 3, Kolonáki, *D4*. One of the most popular of the many café-patisseries on this pedestrianized lane, just north of Kolonaki square.

Oasis (no sign), at the east gate of the National Gardens, just south of the corner of Iródhou Attikoú and V. Sofías, *E4*. Overpriced ice cream, hot and cold drinks in a shaded locale.

Strofes, Hamilton 7, Platía Viktorías, *B2*. Claims to serve sixty varieties of tea.

Toh Tristrato, corner Dedhálou/Angélou Yerónda, Pláka, *F3*. Coffee, fruit juices, and salads, eggs, desserts, cakes; comfortable but expensive. Evenings only.

Zonar's, Panepistimíou 9, *D3*. *Floca's* equally traditional rival – still much as it was described, as a haunt of Harriet and Guy Pringle, and Yakimov, in Olivia Manning's *Fortunes of War*.

Ouzerí and bars

Ouzerí – also called *ouzédhika* or *mezedhopolía* – are essentially bars selling *oúzo*, beer and wine (occasionally just *oúzo*), along with *mezédhes* (hors d'oeuvres) to reduce the impact. A special treat is a *pikilía* (usually about 1500–2000dr), a selection of all the *mezédhes* available; this will probably include fried shrimp, pieces of squid, cheese, olives, tongue, cheese pies, sausage and other delicacies. Ordinarily, you should allow about 6000dr for two with drinks. The food, while good, is on an equal footing with the drink – as in a Spanish *tapas* bar – and you never need reservations.

The listings in this section also include more western-style – and more expensive – **bars**, which serve cocktails and suchlike. All the places included here put their drinks on at least equal footing with their snacks; certain *ouzédhika* that put more emphasis on the food side of things are listed in the main restaurant section above.

Apotsos, Panepistimíou 10 (at the end of the arcade), *D3*. Lunchtime-only bar (Mon–Sat 11am–4pm) with a wide range of *mezédhes*. A landmark through most of this century, frequented by journalists, politicians, writers and the rest. Highly recommended.

Balthazar, Vournázou 14/Tsóha 27, Ambelókipi, off map past *B5*. An "in" brasserie (the bar part's more fun) installed amid the palm-tree gardens and on the ground floor of a palatial old mansion. A long list of cocktails, plus snacks and main courses.

Dhexameni, Platía Dhexamenís, Kolonáki, *D4*. Unnamed café-*ouzerí* that serves drinks and snacks in summer under the trees. Shaded and moderately expensive.

Epistrofi Stin Ithaki, corner Kolléti and Benáki, Exárhia, *C3*. Featuring Santorini wine, this is just one of more than a dozen along Emmanuíl Benáki and its cross streets. Closed Sun.

Ileana Tounda Centre of Contemporary Art, Armatólon Kléfton 48, Néapoli/Ambelókipi border, *B5*. Combination bar/art gallery serving drinks only; fairly expensive.

Neon, Mitropóleos 3, *E3*. Glitzy bistro on two levels that's worth a drink (alcoholic or otherwise) just for the setting. With moderately pricey food, this is a new branch of the famous original *Neon* at Omónia. Open long hours.

Rue de la Presse, Valtetsíou 44, Exárhia, *C3*. Magnificently shady garden bar (summer only). Open 11am–2pm.

Solonos Keh Massalias, corner of Sólonos and Massalías, opposite the law school, *D3*. Mostly coffees and juices, tables inside and out.

Salamandra, Mantzárou 3, Kolonáki, *D4*. Moderately expensive *mezédhes* bar, with a wide-ranging menu, in a restored Neoclassical house. Open lunchtimes and evenings; closed Sun.

Toh Athinaikon, Themistokléous 2, corner Panepistimíou, *D3*. An old *ouzerí* in a new location, but retaining its style – marble tables, old posters, etc. Variety of good-sized *mezédhes*, such as shrimp croquettes and mussels in cheese sauce. Closed Sun.

Music and nightlife

Traditional **Greek music** – *rembétika* and *dhimotiká* – can, at its best, provide the city's most compelling night-time entertainment. To partake, however, you really need to visit during the winter months; from around May to October most clubs and *boîtes* close their doors, while the musicians head off to tour the countryside and islands. Most of the places that remain open are a tourist travesty of over-amplified and over-priced *bouzouki* noise – at their nadir, not surprisingly, in the Pláka.

As for other forms of live music, there are small, indigenous **jazz** and **rock** scenes, perennially strapped for funds and venues but worth checking out. **Classical** music performances tend to form the core of the summer Athens Festival, but with the completion in 1991 of the city's concert hall out on Vassilísis Sofías there's now a long-running winter season as well. **Discos** and **music bars** are very much in the European mould. The clubs in the city tend to close during the summer, unless they have roof terraces; Athenian youth, meanwhile, move out to a series of huge hangar-like disco-palaces in the coastal suburbs.

For **information** and knowledgeable advice on all kinds of Athens music – traditional, rock and jazz – look in at the **record shops** *Philodisc* Emmanuel Benáki 9, Exárhia, *C3*; *Melody House*, Mitropóleos 88, Monastiráki, *E2*; *Music Corner*,

Panepistimíou 36, *D3*; or *Pop 11*, Pindhárou 38/corner Tsakálof, Kolonáki, *D4*. All of these generally display posters for the more interesting events and have tickets on sale for rock, jazz or festival concerts.

Traditional music

An introduction to Greek **traditional and folk music** is included in *Contexts*. In Athens, the various styles can coexist or be heard on alternate evenings at a number of music clubs or *boîtes*. There are purely traditional music venues (such as *Toh Armenaki*, especially for island music from the Cyclades and Crete), where people go to dance, or to celebrate weddings and other occasions. Most gigs start pretty late – there's little point in arriving much before 10.30pm – and continue until 3 or 4am. After midnight (and a few drinks) people tend to loosen up and start dancing; at around 1am there's generally an interval, when patrons may move to other clubs down the street or across town. Prices tend to be pretty stiff, with expensive drinks (and sometimes food), plus an admission fee or a minimum consumption per set.

Rembétika

For anyone with an interest in folk sounds, *rembétika*, the old drugs-and-outcast music brought over by Asia Minor Greeks, is worth catching live. The form was revived in the late 1970s and, though the fad has waned, there are still good sounds to be heard. If possible, phone to make a reservation and check who's playing.

EXÁRHIA/PLÁKA/BAZAAR

Boemissa, Solomoú 19, Exárhia, *C3* (☎36 43 836). *Rembétika*, old folk songs, and music from the Cyclades – the most popular with Greeks, irrespective of their place of origin. Drinks 1000dr. Closed Mon.

Iy Palia Markiza, Próklou 41, Pangráti, *F5*. (☎75 25 074). Claims to offer *rembétika* "as you would have heard it in Smyrna and Pireás". Housed in a fine old turn-of-the-century building above Platía Varnáva. Open Wed–Sun 11pm–5am, and occasionally 3.30–8pm; afternoon sessions are cheaper, otherwise count on 3000dr per person.

Nihtes Mayikes, Vouliagaménis 85, Glifádha, off map (☎94 47 600). Plays host to some of the big names. Drinks at the bar 2000dr; menu 7000dr; whisky 22,000dr per bottle.

Reportaz, corner of Athanasíou Dhiákou and Singroú, Veïkoú, *F3* (☎92 32 114). Owned by the chief editor of a Sunday newspaper, this joint is popular with journalists. Good singing and fine folk atmosphere. Drinks 1000dr.

Stoa Athanoton, Sofokléous 19 (in the old meat market), *D2* (☎32 14 362). A new club fronted by veterans Hondronakos and Koulis Skarpelis (*bouzouki*/song). Good taverna food; 2000dr minimum. Open 3–6pm and midnight–6am. Closed Sun.

Taksimi, Isávron 29, off Hariláou Trikoúpi, Exárhia, *C3* (☎36 39 919). Crowded salon on third floor of a Neoclassical building; no food, no cover, but reckon on 3000dr for drinks. Closed Sun and throughout July & Aug.

FURTHER AFIELD

Kendro Daskalakis, Leofóros Marathónos (☎66 77 255). Out-of-town taverna run by veteran *bouzouki* star Michalis Daskalakis. Open Wed–Sat.

Marabou, Panórmou 113, near Leofóros Alexándhras in Ambelókipi (look for a sign with a toucan), off map past *B5*. One of the first *rembétika* revival clubs, and still one of the most popular – mobbed at weekends. For four nights of the week the music is taped, but on Fri and Sat they feature *laterna* (hurdy-gurdy) by an old man in his early 80s. Expensive food and drink, at around 3000–4000dr a head; no reservations. Open year-round.

Toh Palio Mas Spiti, Odhemissíou 9, Kessarianí (☎72 14 934), off map past *F5*. Arguably the best and most genuine of all the surviving clubs – a real neighbourhood place with decent food, reasonable drinks, no minimum charge and no amplification. The part-owner, Girogos Tzortzis, plays *baglama*, alongside a *bouzouki*-ist, guitarist and singer; excellent house band album on sale. Closed Sun and in summer.

Dhimotiká (folk) music

There's a real mix of styles at these clubs – everything from Zorba-like Cretan *santoúri* music to wailing clarinet from the mountains of Epirus, from ballroom dancing to lyrical ballads from Asia Minor. Venues are scattered throughout the city and are rather pricier than their *rembétika* equivalents; reservations are advisable.

Elatos, Trítis Septemvríou 16 at Platía Lavríou, *C2* (☎52 34 262). An eclectic assortment of *dhimotiká*. Closed Wed.

Kriti, Ayíou Thomá 8, Ambelókipi, off map past *D5* (☎77 58 258). Specializes in Cretan music. Closed Mon.

Toh Armenaki, Patriárhou Ioakím 1/corner Piréos, a long walk or short taxi ride from the Venizélou/Távros metro station, off map past *G1* (☎34 74 716). Island music, with the classic singer Iríni Konitopoulou-Legaki often putting in an appearance. Closed Mon & Tues.

Tsai sti Sahara, Laodhikías 18, Ilíssia, off map past *E5* (☎77 80 669). Quality venue for traditional and ethnic music from Greece and elswehere; limited seating. Owned by Greek popular singer Arletta, who may put in a rare guest appearance; arrive by 10.30 pm to secure yourself a space. 3000dr minimum.

Jazz and Latin

Jazz has a rather small following in Greece, and the main club, *Half-Note,* has moved several times in recent years. The main events take place as part of the **Bic Jazz and Blues Festival** at the end of June; information and tickets are available from the Athens Festival box office (see p.117) and select record stores.

Semi-permanent venues include:

The French Quarter, Mavromiháli 78, Exárhia, *C4*. Recorded jazz and blues only. Closed in summer.

Half-Note, Fthiótidhos 68, Ambelókipi, off map beyond *A/B5* (☎64 49 236). Live jazz most nights but closed Tues and for much of the summer.

La Joya, Tsóha 43, near American Embassy, Ambelókipi, off map past *D5* (☎64 40 030). Great atmosphere. The live or taped rock, jazz and Latin accounts for some of its considerable success – as does beautiful decor, adventurous food and its popularity as a venue for celebrity parties. Open until 2.30am.

Latin, Kallidhromíou 69, Exárhia, *C3* (☎36 45 978). A ground-breaking venue that mixes salsa, Andean folk and occasionally traditional Greek sounds, according to the night of the week.

Take Five, Patriárhou Ioakím 37, Kolonáki, *D5* (☎72 40 736). Supper club with live bands; reservations suggested. Closed Mon & Thurs.

Rock: live venues and music bars

The tiny indigenous Greek rock scene is beset by difficulties. Instruments are the most expensive in Europe, audiences the smallest, and the whole activity is still looked upon with some official disfavour. Clubs pop up and disappear like mushrooms, though there are a number of semi-permanent music bars, especially in Exárhia (*C3*). Many of these host the occasional gig and generally have a dance floor of sorts.

Allothi, Themistokléous 66, Exárhia, *C3*. Up-to-date programme of mainly indie/garage/punk sounds. Reasonable prices.

Decadence, at the junction of Poulherías/Voulgaroktónou, around the corner from *Strefis Taverna tis Xanthis*, *B4*. Features indie/alternative sounds; fairly expensive drinks.

Green Door Cafe, Kallidhromíou 52, Exárhia, *C3*. One of the longest-established local bars, with classic 1970s and 1980s rock sounds.

Kittaro Retro Club, Ipírou 48, between the train stations and Archeological Museum, *C2*. Open Thurs–Sun only, with live bands most nights.

Rodhon, Márni 24, Platía Váthis, *C2* (☎52 37 418 or 52 47 427). The city's most important venue for foreign and Greek rock, soul and reggae groups. Good atmosphere in a converted cinema. Closed in summer.

Stadhio, corner Márkou Moussoúrou/Ardhittoú, Méts, *F4*. A high-tech, fashionable bar – extremely pricey, attracting rich, well-dressed young Greeks. However, there's good music, enjoyably exorbitant cocktails and a terrace open to the stars and to views of the Acropolis.

Trito Mati, Zozimádhon 10, Exárhia, *C3*. Pleasant small bar with an eclectic choice of music; drinks cheaper than at other bars in the same area. Closed in summer.

Wild Rose, Panepistimíou 10, *D3*. House soundtrack for fashion-model types and wealthier students from the northern suburbs.

Discos and clubs

The music bars detailed above are probably the most enjoyable of downtown Athens's disco options. **Rave parties** do happen, with local and foreign DJs, but, as elsewhere, the business operates underground, so look out for posters or ask compulsive clubbers. Expect the unexpected at these clubs: most play recent hits, but don't be surprised if the music turns to Greek or belly-dancing music towards the end of the night; 1994 legislation compelled all clubs within Athens to shut at 2am, but it's hard to predict how long this will last. Although most Athenian clubs close during the summer, you can still find life in the fashionable clubs of Glifádha (16km from Athens) and Kalamáki (18km), out past the aiport along the east coast of Attica, where Athens youth congregate at weekends. If you join them, bear in mind that the taxi fare will be the first of several hefty bills, although admission prices usually include a free drink.

Amazon, opposite the eastern Ellenikó airport, off map (☎98 20 300). The summer face of the live *bouzouki* restaurant *Fantasia*. Drinks 1700dr. Open summer only.

Black Hole, Astéria, Glifádha, off map (☎89 46 898). The place to be seen. Drinks 2000dr.

Bouzios, Vassiléos Yeoryíou 2, Kalamáki, off map (☎98 12 004). Heavyweight clubbing spot. Spacious, glamorous and very popular with celebrities. Open year-round.

Mercedes Rex, Panepistimíou 48, *D3* (☎36 14 591).Very popular club in recently refurbished premises, with multifarious attractions – film premieres 10pm–midnight, live music, laser show, celebrities, the works… Open year-round.

Gay venues

The gay scene is fairly discreet but Athens has a handful of clubs, especially in the Makriyánni district to either side of Singroú, with an established reputation. For further ideas, check the (brief and not entirely reliable) gay sections in the listings magazines *Athinorama* or *Athenscope*.

Alekos Island, Tsakálof 42, Kolonáki, *D4*. Easy-going atmosphere, with rock/pop music. Owned by Alekos, who claims to be known around Europe.

Alexandher's, Anagnostopoúlou 44, *D4*. Relaxed, slightly middle-of-the-road gay bar in the Kolonáki district.

City, Korizí 4, Makriyánni, *F3/G3* border (☎92 40 740). Glamorous marble decor and quality drag show. Drinks 1500dr. Closed Mon & Tues.

Granazi, Lembési 20, near Singroú, *F3/4*. Gay bar close by the transvestite cruising area.

Arts and culture

Unless your Greek is fluent, the contemporary **Greek theatre** scene is likely to be inaccessible. As with Greek music, it is essentially a winter pursuit; in summer, the only theatre tends to be satirical and (to outsiders) totally incomprehensible revues. **Dance**, however, is more accessible and includes a fine traditional Greek show, while **cinema** is un-dubbed – and out of doors in summer.

In addition, in winter months, you might catch **ballet** (and **world music** concerts) at the convenient but acoustically awful *Pallas Theatre*, at Voukourestíou 1; **opera** from the Greek National Opera, *Lyrikí Skiní*, in the *Olympia Theatre* at Akadhimías 59, corner of Mavromiháli; and **classical events** in the *Hall of the Friends of Music*, out on Leofóros Vassilísis Sofías, next to the US embassy or at the *Filippos Nakas Concert Hall*, at Ippokrátous 41. Also worth looking out for are events at the various **foreign cultural institutes**. Among these are the *Hellenic American Union*, Massalías 22 (*D3*), *British Council*, Platía Kolonáki 17 (*D4*), *French Institute*, Sína 29/Massalías 18 (*D3*), and *Goethe Institute*, Omírou 14–16 (*D3*).

Athens Festival

The summer **Athens Festival** has, over the years, come to encompass a broad spectrum of cultural events: most famously **ancient Greek theatre** (performed, in modern Greek, at the Herodes Atticus theatre on the south slope of the Acropolis), but also traditional and contemporary dance, classical music, jazz, traditional Greek music, and even a smattering of rock shows. The **Herodes Atticus theatre**, known popularly as the *Iródhio*, is memorable in itself on a warm summer's evening – although you should avoid the cheapest seats, or you won't see a thing. Other festival venues include the open-air Lycabettus Theatre on **Likavitós Hill**, the **mansion of the Duchess of Plakentia** in Pendéli and (with special but expensive bus excursions) to the great ancient **theatre at Epidaurus** (for further details of which, see p.160).

Events are scheduled from early June until September, although the exact dates may vary each year. Programmes of performances are best picked up as soon as you arrive in the city, and for theatre, especially, you'll need to move fast to get tickets. The **festival box office** is in the arcade at Stadhíou 4 (*D4*; ☎32 21 459 or 32 23 111, ext 240; Mon–Sat 8.30am–2pm and 5–7pm, Sun 10.30am–1pm); most events are held in the *Herodes Atticus Theatre*, where the box office is open 5–9pm on the day of performance. Schedules of the main drama and music events are available in advance from EOT offices abroad (though they don't handle tickets). For student discounts, you must buy tickets in advance.

Dance

On the **dance** front, one worthwhile "permanent" performance is that of the **Dora Stratou Ethnic Dance Company** in their own theatre on Filopáppou hill (*G1*). Gathered on a single stage are traditional music, choreography and costumes you'd be hard put to encounter in many years' travelling around Greece. Performances are held nightly at 10.15pm (with an extra show at 8.15pm on Wed and Sun) from June to September. To reach the theatre, walk up the busy Areopayítou street, along the south flank of the Acropolis, until you see the signs. Tickets (900–1300dr) can almost always be picked up at the door; take your own refreshments, or rely on the somewhat pricey snacks on offer.

Cinema

Athens is – surprisingly perhaps – a great place to catch up on movies. There are literally dozens of indoor cinemas in the city, many of them moody relics of the 1920s and 1930s, whilst in summer outdoor screens spring up all over the place – in parks, abandoned lots, anywhere there's space. Unless they have air conditioning or a roll-back roof, the indoor venues tend to be closed between mid-May and October; all-year cinemas include the *Philip*, *Amalia* and *Alfaville* (see below).

Admission, whether at indoor or outdoor venues, is reasonable: count on 1000–1200dr for outdoor screenings, 1200–1600dr for first-run fare at a midtown theatre. Films are always shown in the original language with Greek **subtitles** (a good way to increase your vocabulary). For **listings**, the weekly magazine *Athinorama* (every

Thurs; 300dr), is the most reliable source of programme information if you can decipher Greek script. Films are divided according to category and geographical location of the cinema. English-language cinema listings – less complete – can be found in the *Athens News* or *Athenscope* magazine.

Among **indoor cinemas**, a cluster showing regular English-language films can be found in three main central areas: Patission/Kipséli; downtown, on the three main thoroughfares connecting Omónia and Síndagma; and Ambelókipi. **Oldies** and **art films** tend to be shown at the *Asti* on Koraï downtown (*D3*); the *Orfeus*, Artémonos 57, (off map below *G5*, a fifteen-minute walk from Pangráti or Koukáki); the *Alfaville*, Mavromiháli 168, (*B4*); the *Aavora*, Ippokrátous 180 (*B4*); and the *Studio*, Stavropoúlou 33, Platía Amerikís, Kipséli (off map above *A2*). Catch **horror/cult films** at the *Pti-Paleh* (corner Vasilíou Yioryíou Víta/Rizári (*E5*); the *Plaza*, Kifissiás 118, Ambelókipi (off map); the *Philip*, Platía Amerikís/Thássou 11 (off map above *A2*); the *Amalia*, Dhrossopoúlou 197 (off map above *A2*); the *Nirvana*, Leofóros Alexándhras 192 (*B5*); and the *Rialto*, Kipsélis 54, Kipséli (off map above *A2*). The *Hadjikyriakos-Ghika Cinema Museum*, at Kriezotóu 3, has screenings of classic art-house films each Saturday at 6pm.

The summer **outdoor screens** are less imaginative in their selections – second-run offerings abound – though to attend simply for the film is to miss much of the point. You may in any case never hear the soundtrack above the din of Greeks cracking *passatémpo* (pumpkin seeds), drinking and conversing; while at late screenings (11pm), the sound is turned right down anyway, so as not to disturb local residents. The most central and reliable outdoor venues are *Sine Pari*, Kidathinéon 22, Pláka (*F3*); *Thissio*, Apostólou Pávlou 7, under the Acropolis (*F1*); *Nea Panathinea*, Mavromiháli 165, Neápoli (*B4*); *Zefiros*, Tróön 36, Áno Petrálona, (*G1*) and the *Riviera* in Exárhia, at Valtetsíou 46 (*C3*).

Markets and shops

You can buy just about anything in Athens and even on a purely visual level the city's **markets** and **bazaar** areas are worth an hour or two's wandering. Among the markets, don't miss the Athinás food halls, nor, if you're into bargain-sifting through junk, the Sunday morning **flea markets** in Monastiráki, Thissíon and Pireás. The **Athens flea market** spreads over a half-dozen or so blocks around Monastiráki square each Sunday from around 6am until 2.30pm. In parts it is an extension of the tourist trade – the shops in this area are promoted as a "flea market" every day of the week – but there is authentic Greek (and nowadays Soviet refugee-Greek) junk, too, notably along (and off) Iféstou and Pandhróssou streets (*E2/3*). The real McCoy, most noticeable at the Thissío metro station end of Adhrianoú and the *platía* off Kinéttou near the church of Áyios Fílippos, is just a bag of odds and ends strewn on the ground or on a low table: dive in.

For the more seriously inclined, **Pireás flea market** – at similar times on Sunday mornings – has fewer tourists and more goods. The market is concentrated in a couple of streets just behind the Aktí Possidhónios seafront (see the map on p.124), and is a venue for serious antique trading, as well as the more simple commerce of ordinary people offloading ordinary (sometimes extraordinarily ordinary) everyday items.

In addition, many Athenian **neighbourhoods** have a *laikí agorá* – **street market** – on a set day of the week. Usually running from 7am to 2pm, these are inexpensive and enjoyable, selling household items and dry goods, as well as fruit and vegetables. The most centrally located ones are: Hánsen in Patissíon (*A20*) on **Monday**; Lésvou in Kipséli (off map) and Láskou in Pangráti (off map), both on **Tuesday**; Xenokrátous in Kolonáki (*D5*), Tsámi Karatássou in Veïkoú (*B4*), and Arhimídhous in Méts (*F5*), all on **Friday**; and Plakendías in Ambelókipi (one of the largest; off map) and Kallidhromíou in

Exárhia (*C3*), both on **Saturday**. Finally, if you're after live Greek **plants or herbs**, there's a Sunday-morning gathering of stalls on Vikéla street in Patissíon (off map) and plants and flowers on sale daily at the Platía Ayía Iríni near Ermoú (*E2*).

The selections below include some of the most enjoyable shops for souvenir-hunting, plus a few more functional places for those in search of books and outdoor gear.

Books

Compendium, Níkis 28 (upstairs), off Síndagma, *E3*. Friendliest and best value of the English-language bookstores, featuring Penguins, Picadors, *Rough Guides* and other paperbacks, plus a small secondhand section.

Eleftheroudhakis, Níkis 4, *E3*. Probably the best source of books about Greece – in English and Greek – and an extensive general English-language stock, too.

Estia-Kollarou, Sólonos 60, *D3*. Big Greek-language bookshop, strong on modern history, politics, folk traditions, fiction, etc.

Iy Folia tou Vivliou, Panepistimíou 25, *D4*, in the arcade and upstairs. The city's biggest selection of English-language fiction; also stocks back issues of the *Korfes* hiking magazine.

Reymondos, Voukourestíou 18, *E4*. Good for foreign periodicals in particular.

Crafts and antiques

Greek handicrafts are not particularly cheap but the workmanship is usually very high. In addition to the stores listed below, consider those at the **National Archeological Museum**, **Benáki Museum** and **Cycladic Art Museum**, which sell excellent, original designs as well as reproductions; and the cluster of antique shops at the base of **Adhrianoú**, near the corner of Kinnéttou, which are good for Ottoman and rural Greek items like backgammon boards, hubble-bubbles, kilims, etc – the best is at Adhrianoú 25.

Athens Design Centre, Valaorítou 4, *D4*. A highly original modern potter has her base here. Prices aren't exorbitant considering the quality.

Gravoures, Kolokotróni 15, Síndagma, *D3/E3*. Engravings and prints.

Karamichos, Voulís 31–33, *E3*. A central outlet for *flokátes*, those hairy-pile wool rugs that are still the best thing to warm up a cold stone floor.

Lalaounis, Panepistimíou 6, *D3*. Home-base outlet of the world-renowned family of goldsmiths, whose designs are superbly imaginative.

Les Amis de Livres, Valaorítou 9, in a cul-de-sac, *D4*. Prints and engravings.

National Welfare Organisation, Ipatías 6, corner Apóllonos, Pláka, *E3*. Rugs, embroideries, copperware – traditional craft products made in remote country districts.

Stavros Melissinos, Pandhróssou 89, off Monastiráki, *E3*. The "poet-sandalmaker" of Athens – see p.93. The sandals perhaps translate better than the poems but nevertheless an inspiring (and not especially inflated) place to be cobbled.

Skyros, corner Makriyánni/Hadzihrístou, Veïkoú, *F3*. Traditional, if not very portable, Greek village furniture (particularly from Skíros), and more practical cushions, lamps, etc.

Toh Kati ti Sas, Iperídhou 23, Pláka, *E3*. Eclectic stock of craft items.

Health and speciality food

Herbs and herb teas are sold dry and fresh at most street markets and at the Athinás bazaar. Otherwise, the following central outlets are useful.

AB Vassilopoulos Leofóros Kifissías, Psihikó, and also out by east airport (off map). A gigantic supermarket stocking esoteric ingredients for just about every cuisine or diet – at a price.

Aralus, Sofokléous 17, Central Bazaar, *D2*. Fruits, nuts, wholegrain bread, pasta, etc, lightly wrapped in a manner suitable for trekking; also supplements and vitamins.

Kendro Fizikis Zois keh Iyias, Panepistimíou 57, *D3*. Headquarters of the Greek Green Party, but also a tremendously well-stocked store and vegetarian snack bar with a pleasant loft where afternoon snacks are served.

Toh Stakhi, Mikrás Asías 61–63, Ambelókipi (off map). Well-stocked store.

Outdoor supplies

Aegean Dive Shop, Pandhóras 31, Glifádha, off map, on the coast to the southeast (☎89 45 409). Very good-value one-day dive trips to a reef near Vouil_lagméni.

Alpamayo, Panepistimíou 44, *D3*. Well-balanced, small hiking store which also stocks some *Korfes* back issues (see also "Books", above).

Army & Navy, Kinéttou 4, on Ayíou Filíppou square, *E2*. Good for ponchos, stoves, mess kits, boots, knives and survival gear in general.

Kataskinotis, Ayías Triádhos 18, Néa Filadhélfia (off map; take a #18 trolley or the metro to Veríssou station). Big barn of a place claiming to be Athens's biggest outdoor activity store.

Kazos, in the arcade between Panepistimíou and Koraï, *D3*. A bit pricey due to its central location, but handy for small items like socks, knives, water bottles, etc.

Marabout, Sólonos 74, behind the university, *C3*. Soft goods only – parkas, packs, sleeping bags, etc.

No-Name Bike Shop, Trítis Septemvríou 40/corner Stournári, *C2*; **Alberto's**, Patissíon 37 (in the arcade, *B2*); plus many others on same s treet heading towards Omónia. This is in effect the "bike bazaar", for repairs, parts and sales. For mountain bikes, try **Gatsoúlis** at Thessaloníkis 8 in Néa Filadhélfia (off map; #18 trolley bus).

Pindhos, Patissíon 52, *B2*. State-of-the-art hiking/climbing gear: Lowe packs, ice axes, stoves, water containers, parkas, foam pads, etc.

Records and tapes

If you hear music you like, or want to explore Greek sounds of bygone days (or today), refer to the discography in *Contexts* (p.754) and then try the outlets below. When shopping, beware of records warped by poor stacking in the racks. The big advantage of shopping here is that the vinyl industry is still alive and well, having survived the CD onslaught; thus you may find pressings discontinued elsewhere.

Jazz Rock, Akadhimías 45, *D3*. Specializes in just that, and also a good source of information and tickets for upcoming concerts.

Music Corner, basement of Panepistimíou 36, near Ippokrátous, *D3*. The Athenian equivalent of *Tower Records*, with a good range of traditional Greek music, plus rock and jazz. Often has discounted items.

Metropolis, Panepistimíou 54, *D3*. Well-stocked with Greek CDs upstairs, foreign down in the stone-wall basement.

Philodisc, Gambétta 1, corner of Benáki, *C2/C3*. Good for R & B, classical, jazz, CDs, plus lots of moderately priced sounds on Greek vinyl.

Pop 11, Pindhárou 38/corner Tsakálof, Kolonáki, *D4*. Limited stocks, but an excellent source for lyra recordings and Falirea Bros releases on their own label, *Adherfí Falirea*, since Grigoris Falireas owns the shop (for more, see "Music" in *Contexts*).

Tzina, Panepistimíou 57, *D3*. If *Xilouris* or *Music Corner* doesn't have it, then this shop will – best choice for Greek pop or folk music.

Xilouris, Panepistimíou 39, in the arcade, *D3*. Run by the widow of the late, great Cretan singer Nikos Xilouris, this is currently one of the best places for Greek popular, folk and (of course) Cretan music. On the expensive side.

Listings

Airlines Almost all the following – Singroú and Eólou addresses apart – are within 100m or so of Síndagma: *Olympic,* ticket office at Óthonos 6, on Síndagma, *E4*; ☎92 67 555, international; ☎92 67 444, domestic; main office at Singroú 96, *G3*; ☎92 67 333; *Air Canada,* Óthonos 10, *E4*; ☎32 23 206; *Alitalia,* Níkis 10, *E3*; ☎32 29 414; *Balkan,* Voukourestíou 16, *D4*; ☎36 35 070; *Britannia,* Hariláou Trikoúpi 6–10, *C3*; ☎36 05 920; *British Airways,* Óthonos 10, *E4*; ☎32 50 601; *Canadian Airlines,* Karayióryi Servías 4, *E3*; ☎32 30 344; *ČSA,* Panepistimíou 15, *D3*; ☎32 32 303; *Cyprus Airways,* Filellínon 10, *E3*; ☎32 47 801; *Delta,* Óthonos 4, *E4*; ☎32 35 242; *Egyptair,* Óthonos 10, *E4*; ☎32 33 575; *El Al,* Óthonos 8, *E4*; ☎32 30 116; *Kenya Airways,* Hariláou Trikoúpi 6–10, *C3*; ☎36 07 502; *KLM,* corner Vouliagménis & Lóndou, Glifádha, off map; ☎93 80 177; *Malev,* Panepistimíou 15, *D3*;

☎32 41 116; *Qantas*, Eólou 104, *D2*; ☎32 39 063; *Sabena*, Óhonos 8, *E4*; ☎32 36 821; *SAS*, Sína 6, *D3*; ☎36 34 444; *Singapore Airlines*, Xenofóndos 8, *E4*; ☎32 39 111; *South African Airways*, Vassilísis Sofías 11, *D/E4*; ☎36 16 305; *Turkish Airlines*, Filellínon 19, *E4*; ☎32 46 024; *TWA*, Xenofóndos 8, *E4*; ☎32 26 451; *United*, Singroú 5, *F3*; 92 42 645; *Virgin Atlantic*, Voulís 7, *E3*; 32 50 117.

Airport enquiries ☎93 63 363 for *Olympic* flight enquiries; ☎96 99 466 for all other carriers.

American Express Poste restante and money changing at the main branch at Ermoú 2 (1st floor), on the corner of Síndagma (*E3*). Mail pick-up desk open in summer Mon–Fri 8.30am–7.30pm, Sat 8.30am–1.30pm; shorter weekday hours in winter. Banking facilities open Mon–Thurs 8.30am–2pm, Fri 8.30am–1.30pm, Sat 8.30am–12.30pm.

Banks The *National Bank of Greece* at Síndagma (*E3*) stays open for **exchange** Mon–Fri 8 am–2pm & 3.30–6.30pm, Sat 9am–3pm & Sun 9am–1pm. The nearby, less crowded *Yeniki Trapeza/ General Bank* on the corner of Ermoú and Síndagma, has longer hours: Mon–Thurs 8am–6.30pm, Fri 8am–6pm, Sat 8am–2pm, closed Sun. **Foreign banks**, keeping normal hours of Mon–Thurs 8am–2pm, Fri 8am–1.30pm, include *Barclays*, Voukourestíou 15, off Panepistimíou, *D4* (☎36 44 311); *Citibank*, Óthonos 8, *E4* (☎32 27 471); *Midland Bank*, Sekéri 1a, Kolonáki, *D5* (☎36 47 410); and *National Westminster*, Korãï 5, *D3* (☎32 11 562). *Royal Bank of Scotland* have a branch in Pireás at Aktí Miaoúli 61 (☎42 93 210). Most of these branches have ATMs which should accept standard European and US banking cards. Outside of normal banking hours, you can use automatic foreign note changing machines – most are located around Síndagma. Along Leofóros Amalías, and on Síndagma itself, there are also a number of staffed kiosks that stay open until around 9pm.

Buses For information on buses out of Athens (and the respective terminals), see "Travel Details" at the end of this chapter.

Camera repair Most central at *Pikopoulos*, Lékka 26, off Ermoú, 3rd floor, *E3*, and *Kriton Kremnitsios*, Karayióryi Servías 7, 5th floor, *E3*. All makes; remove easily lost accessories and get an estimate.

Car rental A number of companies are to be found along Leofóros Singroú, *F3*, including *InterRent/EuropCar*, at no. 4 (*F3*), *Holiday Autos* (no. 8, *F3*), *Thrifty* (no. 24, *F3*), *Eurodollar* (no. 29, *F3*), *Just* (no. 43, *G3*), *Avanti* (no. 50, *G3*), *Antena* (no. 52, *G3*) and *Autorent* (no. 118; *G3*); the latter three give student discounts. *Ansa* at no. 33 (*G3*) also gets good reports from users, while *Payless* is just off Singroú at Hatzihristou 20 (*F3*).

Car repairs, tyres, and assistance VW vans are well looked after at *Grigoris Steryiadhis*, Melandhías 56, Goúva (between Pangráti and Néos Kósmos; off map just below *G4*). Mechanics for virtually any make are scattered around Néos Kósmos district, while spares stores congregate along and between Kallirόïs and Vouliagménis. If they don't have the part, or the know-how, they'll refer you to someone who does. Tyre stores are grouped between Tritis Septemvríou 60–80 (north of Omónia, *B2*). **ELPA** – the Greek automobile association – gives free **help and information** to foreign motorists at Leof. Mesoyíon 2 (northeast of Likavitós, off map) and at the Athens Tower in Ambelókipi. For **Emergency Assistance** ☎104 (free, though you'll pay for any parts).

Dentists Free treatment at the Evangelismos Hospital, Ipsilándou 45, Kolonáki, *D5* and at the Pireás Dentistry School (*Odhondoiatrikó Skolío*), corner Thívon/Livadhías, well north of the metro and public buses. For private treatment, check the ads in the *Athens News* or ask your embassy for addresses.

Embassies/Consulates include: *Australia*, Dhimitríou Soútsou 37, *B5* (☎64 47 303); *Britain*, Ploutárhou 1, Kolonáki, *D5* (☎72 36 211); *Bulgaria*, Stratigoú Kallári 33a, Paleó Psihikó, off map (Mon–Fri 10am–noon); *Canada*, Ioánnou Yennadhíou 4, *D5* (☎72 54 011); *Denmark*, Vassilísis Sofías 11, *D5* (☎36 08 315); *Egypt*, Zalakósta 1, *D4* (Mon–Fri 9am–noon); *Hungary*, Kálvou 16, Paleó Psihikó, off map (Mon–Fri 9am–noon); *Ireland*, Vassiléos Konstandínou 7, *E5* (☎72 32 771); *Netherlands*, Vassiléos Konstandínou 5–7, *E5* (☎72 39 701); *Norway*, Vassiléos Konstandínou 7, *E5* (☎72 46 173); *Romania*, Emmanuel Benáki 7, Paleó Psihikó, off map (Mon–Fri 10am–noon); *South Africa*, Kifissías 124, Ambelókipi, off map (☎69 22 125); *Sweden*, Vassiléos Konstandínou 7, *E5* (☎72 90 421); *USA*, Vassilísis Sofías 91, off map (☎72 12 951). The *New Zealand* embassy has closed and citizens should apply to the British embassy for assistance.

Emergencies Dial the tourist police (☎171; 24hr) for medical or other assistance. In a **medical emergency**, don't wait for an ambulance if you can travel safely – get a taxi straight to the hospital address that the Tourist Police give you. If your Greek is up to it, ☎166 summons an ambulance. ☎105 gets you a rota of night-duty doctors, and ☎106 ascertains the best hospital for you to head for. Otherwise, *KAT*, way out in Kifissiá at Níkis 2, is excellent for trauma and acute complaints if you can hold out that long – it's the designated casualty ward for Greater Athens.

Environment *Greenpeace* recently opened an Athens office at Kallidhromíou 44, Exárhia, *C3* (☎36 40 774). Stop by if you want information, or are staying long-term in Greece and would like to participate in volunteer work and campaigns.

Ferries Most central offices for major lines like *ANEK, Strintzis, Hellenic Mediterranean, G&A* and *Ventouris* flank Leofóros Amalías between Síndagma and Hadrian's Gate; a prominent exception is *Minoan Lines*, on Vassiléos Konstandínou, next to the Olympic Stadium. Phone ☎143 for an information hotline (in Greek).

Football The Athens team *Panathinaïkós*, owned by the shipping magnate Yiorgos Vardinoyannis, is Greece's wealthiest and as a rule most successful club. Catch them at the 25,000-capacity stadium on Leof. Alexándhras (*B5*). Their traditional rival, *Olympiakós* of Pireás plays at the Karaïskáki stadium (by the Néo Fáliro metro stop; see the Pireás map on p.124). Also worth looking out for are *AEK*, which has had some recent European success. Football being an obsession in Greece (there are daily sports papers), matches are not hard to discover: just ask at a kiosk or bar.

Gay groups The *Autonomous Group of Gay Women* meet weekly at *The Women's House* (see "Women's movement", below). *Akoe Amphi*, the (predominantly male) *Greek Gay Liberation Movement*, have an office at Zalóngou 6 (Mon–Fri 6–11pm).

Greek language courses *Athens Centre*, Arhimídhous 48, Pangráti (*F5*); ☎70 12 268, fax 70 18 603, is considered the best for foreigners. The *Hellenic American Union*, Massalías 22 (*D4*), is more geared to the needs of Greeks learning English, while the *Ionic Centre*, Lissíou 4, Pláka (*D4*), has a few summer courses on Hios island.

Hiking *Trekking Hellas*, Filellínon 7, 3rd floor (*E3*), arrange hiking tours throughout Greece.

Hospital clinics For minor injuries the *Hellenic Red Cross*, Trítis Septemvríou/Kapodhistríou (*C2*), is fairly good; *The Women's House* (see below) has addresses of English-speaking gynecologists. For **inoculations**, try the *Vaccination Centre*, Leof. Alexándhras 196/corner Vassilísis Sofías, Ambelókipi (off map; Mon–Fri 8.30am–12.30pm), where most jabs are free; phone ☎64 60 493 for details.

Laundry Numerous dry/wet cleaners will do your laundry for you, or there are coin-ops at Angélou Yerónda 10, off Platía Filomoussoú Eterías (aka Platía Plákas, *F3*), at Dhidhótou 46, Exárhia (*C3*), and at Ioulianoú 72–78 (*B2*).

Lost property The transport police have a lost property office (*Grafío Haménon Andikiménon*) at Ayíou Konstandínou 33 (*D2*),☎64 21 616.

Luggage storage Best arranged with your hotel; many places will keep the bulk of your luggage for free or a nominal amount while you head off to the islands. *Pacific Ltd*, Níkis 24 (*E3*), stores luggage for 1800dr per item per month, 600dr per week.

Motorbike rental Available from **Motorent**, whose head office is at 5 Fálirou, corner of Makriyánni, Veïkoú (*F3*), ☎92 34 939, fax 92 34 885.

Mount Áthos permits See p.372 for details if you're planning a trip to Athos. In Athens, the Ministry of Foreign Affairs, Akadhimías 3, in the arcade, 5th floor (*E4*), is the first stop in securing a permit; office hours are Mon, Wed & Fri 11am–1pm.

Opticians Quick repairs at *Paraskevopoulos* in the arcade between Voukourestíou and Kriezótou, by the parcel post office (*D3*). **Contact lens solutions** available at *Katsimandis*, at Amerikís 11.

Pharmacies (*farmakía*) The *Marinopoulos* branches (in Patission and Panepistimíou streets, *C2/D3*) are particularly good and also sell homeopathic remedies, as does (supposedly) any establishment with a green cross outside. *Bakakos*, on Omónia square (*D2*), is the largest general pharmacy in Athens and will have just about anything – for a price. ☎107 for after-hours pharmacies, or consult daily listings in *Athens News*.

Phones You can phone locally from a *períptero* (kiosk), where you pay afterwards. Phone boxes require phone cards – an irritating investment (minimum 1000dr) if you won't be around very long. International calls are best made at the central OTE offices at Stadhíou 15 (*D3*) and Patissíon 25, Oktovríou 85 (*B2*); the latter is open 24hr.

Police Dialling ☎100 gets the flying squad; for thefts, problems with hotel overcharging, etc, contact the **Tourist Police** at Piréos 158, corner Pétrou Rallí, near Thisío metro (*E1*); ☎171.

Post offices (*Tahidhromío*) For ordinary letters and parcels up to 2kg, the branch on Síndagma (corner Mitropóleos, *E3*) is open Mon–Fri 7.30am–8pm, Sat 8am–3pm, Sun 9am–1.30pm. To send home parcels of personal effects, use the post office in the arcade between Voukourestíou and Kriezótou, *D3* (Mon–Fri 7.30am–2pm) – or, closer to Omónia at Koumoundoúrou 29. Paper and string are supplied – *you* bring box and tape. "Surface/air lift" will get parcels home to North

America or Europe in two weeks. For souvenirs, a branch at Níkis 37 (*E3*) expedites shipments and minimizes duty/declaration problems.

Poste restante Main post office for Athens is at Eólou 100, just off Omónia, *D2* (Mon–Fri 7.30am–8pm, Sat 7.30am–2pm).

Swimming pools There are no public pools at all, though the *Hilton* permits non-guests to use their pool for a stiff (around 1500dr) fee.

Train information, reservations and tickets Most central OSE offices are at Filellínon 17 (*E3*) and Sína 6 (*D3*). In theory, both offices handle domestic and international journeys; in practice, Filellínon 17 is primarily an information outlet – the only tickets available are for international OSE coaches.

Travel agencies Most budget and youth/student agencies are to be found just off Síndagma, on and around Filellínon and Níkis streets. The cheapest ferry tickets to Italy are usually sold through *USIT*, Filellínon 1 (☎32 41 884), or *Transalpino* (Níkis 28), still trading despite the demise of its namesake. Among other agencies, *Highway Express*, Níkis 42, *Periscope*, Filellínon 22, *Himalaya*, Filellínon 7 and *Arcturus*, Apóllonos 20 are worth scanning for air travel deals. For the hardy, the widest range of north-bound buses is still available at *Magic Bus*, Filellínon 20. All these addresses are *E3/F3*.

Women's movement Most accessible of the women's groups is the *Multinational Liberation Group of Athens* (☎86 70 523); like most other women's organizations, they meet at *The Women's House*, Románou Melódhou 4, Likavitós, *C3* (☎28 14 823).

Work/residence permits/visa extensions at the Aliens' Bureau (*Ipiresía Allodhapón*), Leof. Alexándhras 173, off map past *B5*; open Mon–Fri 8am–1pm, but go early or you won't get seen. Also, come armed with small notes for revenue stamps, large notes for the extension fee(s), wads of passport photos, pink personalized bank receipts, and plenty of patience.

AROUND ATHENS: ATTICA

Attica (*Attikí*), the region encompassing the capital, is not much explored by tourists. Only the great romantic ruin of the **Temple of Apollo at Sounion** is on the excursion circuit. The rest, if seen at all, tends to be en route to the islands – from the ports of **Pireás**, **Rafína** (a fast and cheap route to many of the Cyclades) or **Lávrio** (which serves Kéa).

The neglect is not surprising. The mountains of **Imittós**, **Pendéli** and **Párnitha**, which surround Athens on three sides, are progressively less successful in confining the urban sprawl, and the routes out of the city to the south and west are unenticing to say the least. But if you're planning on an extended stay in the capital, a day trip or two, or a brief circuit by car, can make a rewarding break, with much of Greece in microcosm to be seen within an hour or two's ride: mountainside at **Párnitha**, minor archeological sites in **Brauron** and **Rhamnous**, and the odd unspoilt beach, too.

Pireás (Piraeus)

PIREÁS has been the port of Athens since Classical times. Today it is a substantial metropolis in its own right, containing much of Greater Athens' industry, as well as the various commercial activities associated with a port: banking, import–export, freight and so on. For most visitors, though, it is Pireás's inter-island ferries that provide the reason for coming (see "The Ferries" below for details).

The port at Pireás was founded at the beginning of the fifth century BC by **Themistocles**, who realized the potential of its three natural harbours. His work was consolidated by Pericles with the building of the **"Long Walls"** to protect the corridor to Athens, and it remained active under Roman and Macedonian rulers. Subsequently, under Turkish rule, the place declined to the extent that there was just one building there, a monastery, by the end of the War of Independence. From the 1830s on, though, Pireás grew by leaps and bounds. The original influx into the port was a group of immigrants from Híos, whose island had been devastated by the Turks; later came populations from Ídhra, Crete and the Peloponnese. By World War I, Pireás had outstripped the island of Síros as the nation's first port, its strategic position enhanced by the opening of the Suez and Corinth canals in 1862 and 1893 respectively. Like Athens, the city's great period of expansion began in 1923, with the exchange of populations with Turkey. Over 100,000 Asia Minor Greeks decided to settle in Pireás, doubling the population almost overnight – and giving a boost to a pre-existing semi-underworld culture, whose enduring legacy was *rembétika*, outcasts' music played in hashish dens along the waterside.

The city these days is almost indistinguishable from Athens, with its scruffy web of suburbs merging into those of the capital. Economically, it is at present on a mild upswing, boosted by two successive go-ahead mayors and the prominence of its late

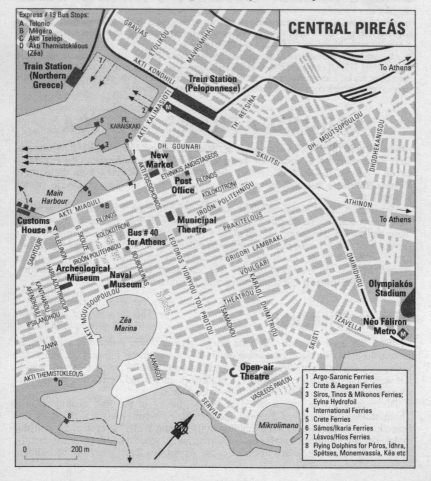

CENTRAL PIREÁS

Express # 19 Bus Stops:
A Telonío
B Mégaro
C Aktí Tselépi
D Aktí Themistokléous
   (Zéa)

Train Station (Northern Greece)

To Athens

Train Station (Peloponnese)

PL. KARAISKAKI

New Market

Post Office

Main Harbour

Customs House

Municipal Theatre

Bus # 40 for Athens

Archeological Museum

Naval Museum

Zéa Marina

Olympiakós Stadium

Néo Fáliron Metro

Open-air Theatre

Mikrolimano

0   200 m

1 Argo-Saronic Ferries
2 Crete & Aegean Ferries
3 Síros, Tinos & Míkonos Ferries;
   Eyína Hydrofoil
4 International Ferries
5 Crete Ferries
6 Sámos/Ikaría Ferries
7 Lésvos/Híos Ferries
8 Flying Dolphins for Póros, Ídhra,
   Spétses, Monemvassía, Kéa etc

MP, former actress and Minister of Culture, Melina Mercouri. An unashamedly functional place, with its port despatching up to sixty ships a day in season – both to the islands and to a range of international destinations – there are few sights beyond the numbers and diversity of the sailors in the harbour. The ancient walls are long gone, and the junta years saw misguided demolition of many buildings of character. On the plus side, there's a nice enough **park** (three blocks back from the main harbour, intersected by Vassiléos Konstandínou); a scattering of genuine antique/junk shops, full of peasant copper and wood, plus a big **Sunday morning flea market**, near Platía Ipodhamías, at the top end of Goúnari (behind the train station); and a couple of more than respectable museums.

The Archeological and Maritime museums

The **Archeological Museum** (Hariláou Trikoúpi 31, Mon 12.30–6.45: Tues–Fri 8–6.45; Sat & Sun 8.30–2.45; 400dr) is the best time-filler in Pireás, and enthusiasts will certainly want to make a special trip out here. Upper-floor exhibits include a *kouros* (idealized male statue) dedicated to Apollo, which was dragged out of the sea in 1959. Dating from 520 BC, this is the earliest known life-size bronze, and is displayed with two other fifth-century bronzes of Artemis and Athena found in the same manner at about the same time.

On the ground floor are more submarine finds, this time second-century AD stone reliefs of battles between Greeks and Amazons, apparently made for export to Rome. The sea's effect on them was far more corrosive than in the case of the bronzes, but you can still tell that some scenes are duplicated – showing that the ancients weren't above a bit of mass artistic production.

A few blocks away, on Aktí Theonistokléous, near Zéa, the **Maritime Museum** (Tues–Sat 8.30am–1.30pm; 300dr) is more specialist, tracing developments with models and the odd ancient piece.

The Ferries

If you're staying in Athens prior to heading out to the islands, it's worth calling in at the EOT office in Síndagma to pick up a **schedule of departures** from Pireás. These can't be relied upon implicitly, but they do give a reasonable indication of what boats are leaving when and for where; note that the Argo-Saronic sailings and ships based on Síros or Páros are omitted.

The majority of the boats – for the Argo-Saronic, Ikaría or Sámos, and the popular Cyclades – leave between 8 and 9am. There is then another burst of activity between noon and 3pm towards the Cyclades and Dodecanese, and a final battery of sailings from 4 to 10pm (sometimes later), bound for a wide variety of ports, but especially Crete, the northeast Aegean and the western Cyclades. The frequency of sailings is such that, in high season at least, you need never spend the night in Athens or Pireás.

There's no need to **buy tickets** for conventional ferries before you get here, unless you want a cabin berth or are taking a car on board (in which case, consult agents in Athens or Pireás); *Flying Dolphin* reservations are a good idea during July and August. In general, the best plan is to get to Pireás early, say at 7am, and check with the various **shipping agents** around the metro station and along the quayside Platía Karaïskáki. Keep in mind that many of these act only for particular lines, so for a full picture of the various boats sailing you will need to ask at three or four outlets. Prices for all domestic boat journeys are standard, but the quality of the craft and circuitousness of routes vary greatly. If you are heading for Thíra (Santorini) or Rhodes, for example, try to get a boat that stops at only three or four islands en route; for Crete settle for direct ferries only.

FERRY DEPARTURE POINTS

Aegean islands (Cyclades/Dodecanese)
These leave from either Aktí Kalimasióti, the quay right in front of the metro station (#2 on the map), or from Aktí Kondhíli (#7, perpendicular to Possidhónios). The big boats going to the major Dodecanese only usually share point (#5) with some of the Cretan ferries.

Crete
Some ferries dock at Aktí Kalimasióti (#2), but most use the promontory by Aktí Miaoúli (#5), or (#7) on Aktí Kondhíli.

Síros, Tínos, Míkonos
The morning departures tend to go from (#3), next to the Éyina hydrofoils.

Sámos/Ikaría
Boats ending up at these islands, whether morning or evening services, use the far end of the dock beyond Platía Karaïskáki (#6).

Híos/Lésvos
Most Híos and Mitilíni (Lésvos) boats leave from (#6), with a very few going from #7.

Argo-Saronic
Ordinary ferries leave from the junction of Aktí Possidhónios and Aktí Miaoúli, and also west along Possidhónios (#1), a ten-minute walk from the metro.

International destinations (Limassol, Haifa, Izmir, etc)
These leave further around the main harbour (#4), towards the Customs House (where you should check passports before boarding).

Hydrofoils
Except for departures direct to Éyina, which leave from Aktí Tselépi (#3), hydrofoils for **Argo-Saronic and Peloponnesian** destinations leave from the **Zéa marina** (#8), a twenty-minute uphill walk from the metro.

Tickets are on sale from the *Flying Dolphins* office at the quay from about an hour before departure. To be sure of a particular sailing in high season, it is wise to book ahead in Athens. Equally, if your schedule is tight, book your seat back to Pireás when you arrive.

Boats for different destinations leave from a variety of points along the main harbour, usually following the pattern in the box above, though it's wise to leave time for wayward ships and look for the signs (indicating name of boat and a clockface with departure time) hung in front of the relevant boats on the waterside railings or on the stern of the boats themselves. The ticket agent should know the whereabouts of the boat on the particular day.

Practicalities

The easiest way to get to Pireás from Athens is on the **metro**. There are central stops in Athens at Platía Viktorías, Omónia and Monastiráki squares, plus Thissío for those in Veΐkou, and Petrálona for those in Koukáki; the journey takes about 25 minutes from Omónia to the Pireás train station stop (the end of the line). Metro trains run from 6am, early enough to catch the first ferries, until midnight, long after the arrival of all but the most delayed boats. Tickets cost 75dr a journey, 100dr if you start your journey north of Omónia square.

Alternatively, you could take a bus or a taxi. **Green bus #40** (about every 20min during the day; hourly from 1am to 5am) will deposit you on Vassiléos Konstandínou, half a dozen blocks from the docks, but it's very slow – allow nearly an hour from Síndagma, the most obvious boarding point. The **express buses** (see p.69) are quicker and provide a particularly useful link with the airport. **Taxis** cost about 1000dr at day tariff from the centre of Athens or the airport – worth considering, especially if you're taking one of the hydrofoils from the Zéa marina, which is a fair walk from the metro.

Accommodation

Few visitors stay in Pireás, and most of the port's **hotels** are geared to a steady clientele of seamen, resting between ships. For this reason, picking somewhere at random is not always a good idea. A trio of places close by the main harbour, and used to tourists, are the *Hotel Aenos*, Ethnikís Andistáseos 14 (☎41 74 879; ②), the *Hotel Santorini*, Trikoúpi 6 (☎45 521 47; ③), and the *Hotel Acropole*, Goúnari 7 (☎41 73 313; ③), the last of which has a sporadically functioning bar and sunroof. If you have a bit more money to spend, consider the *Hotel Park* (☎45 24 611; ④), a couple of blocks back from the port at Kolokotróni 103, or the very pleasant and luxurious *Cavo d'Oro* (☎41 13 742; ⑥), overlooking the Mikrolímano yacht harbour.

Sleeping rough in Platía Karaïskáki, as some exhausted travellers attempt to do, is unwise. If thieves or the police don't rouse you, street-cleaners armed with hoses certainly will – at 5am.

Eating and drinking

If you're simply looking for **food to take on board**, or breakfast, you'll find numerous places (as well as several budget restaurants) around the market area, back from the waterside Aktí Miaoúli/Ethnikís Andistáseos, open from 6.30am.

For more substantial **meals**, there are a string of *ouzerí* and seafood tavernas along Aktí Themistokléous, west of the Zéa marina, most of them pretty good and reasonably priced, or try the Indian restaurant *Maharajah Navarhou* at Notará 122. Alternatively, for a real blowout, the *Vassilenas* at Etolikoú 72 (the street running inland from Aktí Kondhíli) is a fine choice. Housed in an old grocery store, its set menu provides *mezédhes* enough to defy all appetites; at 2900dr a head, drinks extra, it's not especially cheap, but enough Athenians consider it worth the drive that most evenings you need to book a table (☎46 12 457). Otherwise, a good bet for seafood is *Kefalonitis*, on the corner of Rethímnis and Tsakálof, up by the open-air theatre. As the name implies, this place is run by a Kefallonian family, and is far superior to the tourist-traps on **Mikrolímano**.

Entertainment, restaurants and nightlife

Culturally, there's not a great deal going on at Pireás, though a **summer festival**, run alongside that of Athens, features events in the open-air theatre set back from the yacht harbour of Mikrolímano (or Tourkolímano, as it has been called for centuries). In winter there's always **football**: *Olympiakós* are the port's big team, rivals to the capital's *AEK* and *Panathenaikós*.

Finally, a word for the port's best **rembétika venue** (see "Music" in *Contexts*), the *Ondas tis Konstandinas* at Koundouriótou 109 on the corner of Károli Dhimitríou (☎42 20 459; closed Sun & Mon, and in summer). This is a very friendly taverna, with *rembétika* music each night and a special *Smirneïka* show every Tuesday. On Friday and Saturday nights there's a minimum charge of 4000dr per person.

The "Apollo Coast", Cape Sounion and Lávrio

The seventy kilometres of coast south of Athens – the tourist-board-dubbed **"Apollo Coast"** – has some good but highly developed beaches. At weekends, when Athenians flee the city, the sands fill fast, as do the innumerable bars, restaurants and discos at night. If this is what you're after, then resorts like **Glifádha** and **Vouliagméni** are functional enough. But for most foreign visitors, the coast's lure is at the end of the road, in the form of the Temple of Poseidon at **Cape Sounion**.

Access to Sounion (Soúnio in the modern spelling) is straightforward. There are buses on the hour and half-hour from the *KTEL* terminal ("B" on the Athens map; *B2*) on Mavromatéon at the southwest corner of Áreos Park; there's also a more central (but in summer, very full) stop ten minutes later at point "D" on Filellínon street, south of Síndagma (corner of Xenofóndos, in front of the *Middle East Airways* office). There are both coastal (*paraliakó*) and inland (*mesoyiakó*) services, the latter slightly longer and more expensive. The coast route normally takes around two hours; last departures back to Athens are posted at the Sounion stop.

For **Glifádha/Voúla** and **Vouliagméni/Várkiza** – the main resorts – there are additional, more regular, city buses from the Záppion gardens (stop "C" on the Athens map; *F4*). Most frequent are #128/129 for Glifádha; #122 for Voúla; and #116/117 for Vouliagméni/Várkiza.

The resorts: Glifádha to Anávissos

Although some Greeks swim at Pireás itself, few would recommend the sea much before **GLIFÁDHA**, half an hour's drive southeast from the city centre. The major resort along the "Apollo Coast", merged almost indistinguishably with its neighbour **VOÚLA**, this is lined with seafood restaurants, ice-cream bars and discos, as well as a couple of marinas and a golf course. Its popularity, though, is hard to fathom, built as it is in the shadow of the airport. The only possible appeal is in the beaches, the best of which is the Astir, privately owned and with a stiff admission charge; others are gritty. Hotels are all on the expensive side, and in any case are permanently full of package tours; there is a **campsite** at Voúla (☎01/89 52 712).

VOULIAGMÉNI, which in turn has swallowed up **Kavoúri**, is a little quieter than Glifádha, and a little ritzier. Set back from a small natural saltwater lake, it boasts a waterski school, some extremely chi-chi restaurants, and an EOT pay-beach. Again, budget accommodation is hard to come by, though there is a **campsite** (☎01/89 73 613) – and another EOT pay-beach – just to the south at **Várkiza** (☎01/89 73 613).

South from Várkiza, there are further beaches en route to Sounion, though unless you've a car to pick your spot they're not really worth the effort. The resorts of **Lagoníssi** and **Anávissos** are in the Glifádha mould, and only slightly less crowded, despite the extra distance from Athens.

Cape Sounion

Cape Sounion – Akrí Soúnio – is one of the most imposing spots in Greece, for centuries a landmark for boats sailing between Pireás and the islands, and an equally dramatic vantage point in itself to look out over the Aegean. On its tip stands the fifth-century BC **Temple of Poseidon**, built in the time of Pericles as part of a major sanctuary to the sea god.

The Temple of Poseidon

The temple (Daily 10am–sunset, Sun from 10am; 600dr) owes its fame above all to **Byron**, who visited in 1810, carved his name on the nearest pillar (an unfortunate precedent), and commemorated the event in the finale of his hymn to Greek independence, the "Isles of Greece" segment of *Don Juan*:

> *Place me on Sunium's marbled steep,*
> *Where nothing, save the waves and I,*
> *May hear our mutual murmurs sweep;*
> *There, swan like, let me sing and die:*
> *A land of slaves shall ne'er be mine –*
> *Dash down yon cup of Samian wine!*

In summer, at least, there is faint hope of solitude, unless you slip into the site before the tour groups arrive. But the temple is as evocative a ruin as any in Greece. Doric in style, it was probably built by the architect of the Thiseion in the Athens *agora*. That it is so admired and visited is in part due to its site, but also perhaps to its picturesque state of ruin – preserving, as if by design, sixteen of its thirty-four columns. On a clear day, the view from the temple takes in the islands of Kéa, Kíthnos and Sérifos to the southeast, Éyina and the Peloponnese to the west.

The rest of the site is of more academic interest. There are remains of a fortification wall around the sanctuary; a **Propylaion** (entrance hall) and **Stoa**; and, to the north, the foundations of a small **Temple of Athena**.

Beaches – and staying at Sounion

Below the promontory are several **coves** – the most sheltered a five-minute walk east from the car park and site entrance. The main Sounion beach is more crowded, but has a group of tavernas at the far end – pretty reasonably priced, considering the location.

If you want to stay, there are a couple of **campsites** just around the coast: *Camping Bacchus* (the nearest; ☎0292/39 262) and *Sounion Beach Camping* (5km; ☎0292/39 358). Alternatively, for the more affluent, there's the 1960s-style *Hotel Aegeon* (☎0292/39 262; ⑤), right on the Sounion beach.

Lávrio

Ten kilometres north of Sounion, around the cape, is the port of **LÁVRIO**. This has daily ferry connections with Kéa and a single weekly boat to Kíthnos. It can be reached by **bus** from the Mavromatéon terminal in Athens, or from Sounion.

The port's ancient predecessor, Laurion, was famous for its silver mines – a mainstay of the Classical Athenian economy – which were worked almost exclusively by slaves. The port today remains an industrial and mining town, though nowadays for less precious minerals – cadmium and manganese – and also hosts the country's principal transit camp for political refugees: mostly Kurds from Iraq and Turkey at present, with a scattering of Eastern Europeans, awaiting resettlement in North America, Australia or Europe. The island offshore, **Makrónissos**, now uninhabited, has an even more sinister past, for it was here that hundreds of ELAS members and other leftists were imprisoned in "re-education" labour camps during and after the civil war.

As you might imagine, this is not really a place to linger between buses and ferries. However, if you have time to kill, the site of **ancient Thoriko** is of some interest. It lies down a zigzag track from the village of Pláka, 5km north of Lávrio. A defensive outpost of the mining area in Classical times, its most prominent ruins are of a theatre, crudely engineered into an irregular slope in the hill.

East of Athens: the Mesóyia and Brauron

The area east of Athens is one of the least visited parts of Attica. The mountain of **Imittós** (Hymettus) forms an initial barrier, with Kessarianí monastery (see p.105) on its cityside flank. Beyond extends the plateau of the **Mesóyia** (Midland), a gentle landscape whose villages have a quiet renown for their *retsina* and for their churches, many of which date to Byzantine times. On towards the coast, there is the remote and beautiful site of **ancient Brauron**, and the developing resort of **Pórto Ráfti**.

The Mesóyia

The best-known attraction of the Mesóyia is at the village of **PEANÍA**, on the east slope of Imittós: the **Koutoúki cave** (daily 9.30am–4.30pm; 500dr), endowed with spectacularly illuminated stalactites and stalagmites and multicoloured curtains of rock. It is fairly easily reached by taking the Athens–Markópoulo bus, stopping at Peanía and then walking up. Close by the village – just to the east on the Spáta road – is the chapel of **Áyios Athanásios**, built with old Roman blocks and fragments.

MARKÓPOULO, the main Mesóyia village, shelters a further clutch of chapels. Within the village, in a walled garden, stand the twin chapels of **Áyia Paraskeví** and **Áyia Thékla**; ring for admission and a nun will open them up to show you the seventeenth-century frescoes. Over to the west, on the road to Koropí, is one of the oldest churches in Attica, tenth-century **Metamórfosi** – the keys to which can be obtained from the Análipsi church in Koropí.

Heading east from Markópoulo, the road runs past the unusual double-naved **Áyia Triádha** (2500m out) and on to the coast at **PÓRTO RÁFTI**, whose bay, protected by islets, forms an almost perfect natural harbour. It's been comprehensively developed, with an EOT pay-beach and a fair number of tavernas, but remains a good place to stay if you can find a room. On the islet of Rafti, facing the harbour, is a huge, curious Roman statue of a woman tailor, probably intended as a beacon.

From here, if you've your own vehicle, you can make your way along the coast road to the village of Vravróna and the site of **Ancient Brauron**.

Brauron

Brauron (site daily except Mon 8.30am–2.45pm; museum Mon 12.30–6.45pm,Tues–Fri 8am–6.45pm, Sat & Sun 8.30am–2.45pm; 400dr) is one of the most enjoyable minor Greek sites. It lies just outside the modern village of Vravróna (40km from Athens), in a marshy valley at the base of a low, chapel-topped hill. The marsh and surrounding fields are alive with birdsong, only partly drowned out by traffic noise from the nearby busy road.

The remains are of a **Sanctuary of Artemis**, centred on a vast *stoa*. This was the chief site of the Artemis cult, legendarily founded by Iphigeneia, whose "tomb" has also been identified here. It was she who, with Orestes, stole the image of Artemis from Tauris (as commemorated in Euripides's *Iphigeneia at Tauris*) and introduced worship of the goddess to Greece. The main event of the cult was a quadrennial festival, now shrouded in mystery, in which young girls dressed as bears to enact a ritual connected with the goddess and childbirth.

The **"Stoa of the Bears"**, where these initiates would have stayed, has been substantially reconstructed, along with a stone **bridge**; both are fifth century BC and provide a graceful focus to the semi-waterlogged site. Somewhat scantier are the ruins of the temple itself, whose stepped foundations can be made out; immediately adjacent, the sacred spring still wells up, today squirming with tadpoles. Nearby, steps lead up to the chapel, which contains some damaged frescoes. At the site **museum**, a short walk from the ruins, various finds from the sanctuary are displayed.

Practicalities

Getting to Brauron from Athens will involve a walk if you're dependent on public transport. Buses #304 or #305 from the Thissío metro (*E1*) terminates at "Artémi", from where you must continue along the main road for two kilometres until you see the *stoa* marked by a clump of trees in the middle of the marsh on your left; the museum building, just before it, is actually more conspicuous. More frequent are certain identically numbered buses from the same terminal to the beach-village of Loútsa, but this is 6km northwest of Brauron.

At the site, there's just a single **taverna**, *Iy Artemis*, located midway between the "Artémi" stop and the ruins, from where you've a fine view of the bay.

Rafína, Marathon and Rhamnous

The port of **RAFÍNA** has **ferries**, the **"Catamaran"** (in fact a sort of jet-boat) and **hydrofoils** to a wide assortment of the Cyclades, the Dodecanese, and the northeast Aegean, as well as to nearby Évvia. It is connected regularly by bus with Athens: a forty-minute trip (from Mavromatéon) through the "gap" in Mount Pendéli.

Boats aside, the appeal of the place is mainly gastronomic. Though much of the town has been spoilt by tacky seaside development, the little fishing harbour with its line of **roof-terrace seafood restaurants** remains one of the most attractive spots on the Attic coast. A lunchtime outing is an easy operation, given the frequency of the bus service. Evenings, when it's more fun, you need to arrange your own transport back, or make for the beachside **campsite** at nearby Kókkino Limanáki. The town's half-dozen **hotels** are often full, so you need to phone ahead to be sure of a room; the best value are the *Rafina* (☎0294/23 460; ②), *Corali* (☎0294/22 477; ③) and *Kymata* (☎0294/23 406; ③), all of which are located in the central Platía Nikifórou Plastíra.

Marathon

The village of **MARATHÓNAS**, 42km from Athens, is on the same bus route as Rafína. Four kilometres before you arrive, the **Tímfos Marathóna** stands to the side of the road: the ancient burial mound raised over 192 Athenians who died in the city's famous victory over the Persians in 490 BC. Although ten metres high, it is a strangely uninspiring monument. A kilometre to the west of the burial mound is a small **archeological museum** (open, as is the mound precinct, June–Aug only daily except Mon 8.30am–2.45pm; 400dr), with a sparse collection of artefacts mainly from the local Cave of Pan, a deity felt to have aided the victory. Closer to the town is another burial mound, the **Tímvos Platéon**, built for the Athenians' only allies in the battle.

Marathóna village itself is a dull place, with just a couple of cafés and restaurants for the passing trade. Nearby, though, to the west, and quite an impressive site, is **Límni Marathóna** – Marathon Lake – with its huge marble dam. This provided Athens's entire water supply until the 1950s and it is still used as a storage facility for water from the giant Mórnos project in central Greece.

The coast around ancient Marathon takes in some good stretches of sand, walkable from the tomb if you want to cool off. The best and most popular **beach** is to the north at **SKHINIÁS**, a long, pine-backed strand full of windsurfers at the weekends. There is a **campsite**, *Camping Marathon*, midway along the road from Marathónas.

Rhamnous

Further to the north, the ruins of **RHAMNOUS** (Tues–Sun 8.30am–2.45pm; 400dr) occupy a beautiful and totally isolated site above the sea. Among the scattered and overgrown remains is a Doric **Temple of Nemesis**, goddess of retribution. Pausanias records that the Persians who landed nearby before their defeat incurred her wrath by carrying off a marble block – upon which they intended to commemorate their conquest of Athens. There are also the remains of a smaller temple dedicated to Themis, goddess of justice. Rhamnous can be reached just five times daily by bus from the Mavromatéon terminal; the village name to look for is Káfo Soúli.

Mount Párnitha and Phyle

Scarcely an hour's bus ride north from the city centre, **Mount Párnitha** is an unexpectedly vast and – where it has escaped fire damage – virgin tract of forest, rock and ravine. If you've no time for expeditions further afield, it will give you a taste of what Greek mountains are all about, including a good selection of mountain flowers. If you're here in March or April, it merits a visit in its own right. Snow lies surprisingly late on the north side and, in its wake, carpets of crocus, alpine squills and mountain windflower spring from the mossy ground, while lower down you'll find aubretia, tulips, dwarf iris, and a whole range of orchids.

There are numerous **waymarked paths** on the mountain (look for red discs and multicoloured paint splodges on the trees). The principal and most representative ones are the approach **to the Báfi refuge up the Hoúni ravine**, and the walk **to the Skípiza** spring. These, along with a couple of lesser excursions, to the **ancient fort at Phyle** and one of the many legendary **Caves of Pan**, are detailed below.

The hike to the Báfi refuge

To get to the start of this walk, take bus #714 at 6.30am from the corner of Aharnón and Stournári (north side of Platía Váthi; *C2* on the main Athens map) to the suburb of Thrakomakedhónes, whose topmost houses are beginning to steal up the flanks of the mountain beside the mouth of the Hoúni ravine. Get off at the highest stop and keep on, bearing left, up Odhós Thrákis to where the road ends at the foot of a cliff beside two new blocks of flats. Keep straight ahead along the foot of the cliff and in a few metres you come to the start of the path, turning down left into a dry streambed, before crossing and continuing on the opposite bank.

The refuge is about two hours' walk away. The track curves slowly leftward up the craggy, well-defined ravine, at first through thick scrub, then through more open forest of Greek fir, crossing the stream two or three times. At a junction reached after about 45 minutes, signposted "Katára–Mesanó Neró–Móla", keep straight ahead. At the next fork, some ten minutes later, keep right. After a further five minutes, at the top of a sparsely vegetated slope, you get your first glimpse of the pink-roofed refuge high on a rocky spur in front of you. Another twenty minutes brings you to the confluence of two small streams, where a sign on a tree points left to Ayía Triádha (see below), and a second path branches right to Móla and Koromiliá. Take the third, middle, path, up a scrubby spur. At the top a broad path goes off left to meet the ring road leading to Ayía Triádha.

From here, turn right, down into the head of a gully, where the path doubles back and climbs up to the refuge. Normally the refuge warden provides **board and lodging**, particularly on weekends, but it would be wise to check opening times and accommodation policy with the Athens EOS on Platía Kapnikaréas (weekday evenings only) in advance, as the schedule changes periodically. Water is usually available at the back of the building, except in winter.

To the Skípiza spring

For the walk to the Skípiza spring, you need to get off at the chapel of Ayía Triádha in the heart of the mountains. There are two #714 connections a day: at 6.30am, returning at 8am; and at 2pm, returning at 4pm. If you get stuck, you can continue to the *Hotel Mount Parnes* and take the *téléférique* down if it's operating – otherwise there's a rough trail down a gully near the *Xenia Hotel*, spilling out near the Metóhi picnic grounds.

The **Skípiza spring** is an hour and a half to two hours' walk away. From the bus stop by the chapel, walk west past the *Hotel-Chalet Kiklamina*, continuing straight on to the ring road. After the first ascent and descent, you come after fifteen minutes to the Paliohóri spring on the right of the road in the middle of a left-hand bend, opposite a piece of flat ground marked with pointed-hat pipes. A beautiful and well-defined path is clearly marked by discs on trees, beginning by the spring and following the course of a small stream up through the fir woods.

From Skípiza you can continue right around the summit to **Móla** (about 90min) and from there, in another hour, back to the Báfi refuge. Alternatively, by setting your back to the Skípiza spring and taking the path that charges up the ridge almost directly behind, you can get to **Báfi** in around forty minutes. Turn left when you hit the paved road after about half an hour; follow it ten minutes more down to the ring road and turn left again. In a few paces you are in the refuge car park. To get back to Ayía Triádha by the road it's about 6km (an hour's walk).

The Cave of Pan

Another highly evocative spot for lovers of Classical ghosts is the **Cave of Pan**, which Menander used as the setting for one of his plays. The best approach is by track and trail from the chapel of Ayía Triádha: a map showing local landmarks (labelled in Greek), superimposed on a topographical map, is posted just behind the church.

Phyle

Over to the west of the main Párnitha trails, another route up the mountain will take you to the nearly complete fourth-century BC Athenian fort of **Phyle**, about an hour and three quarters on foot beyond the village of Filí (known locally as Hasiá). Buses to Filí leave near the Aharnón/Stournára stop on Odhós Sourméli (*C2*).

On the way up to the fort you pass the unattractively restored fourteenth-century **monastery of Klistón** in the mouth of the Goúra ravine that splits through the middle of the Párnitha range. The walking, unfortunately, is all on asphalt, but the fort, built to defend the road from Athens to Thebes, is impressive.

Eleusis and west to the Peloponnese

The main **highway to Kórinthos** (Corinth) is about as unattractive a road as any in Greece. For the first thirty or so kilometres you have little sense of leaving Athens, whose western suburbs merge into the industrial wastelands of first Elefsína and then Mégara. Offshore, almost closing off the bay, is **Salamína** (ancient Salamis), not a dream island in anyone's book but a nicer escape than it looks, and accessible by ferries from the mainland here at Lákki Kaloírou (and at Pérama, near Pireás).

A train or bus direct to Kórinthos or beyond, though, is perhaps the wisest option. Only the site of **ancient Eleusis** is in any way a temptation to stop, and even this is strictly for Classical enthusiasts. **Drivers** should note that the Athens–Kórinthos non-toll road is one of the most dangerous in the country, switching from four-lane highway to a rutted two-laner without warning and full of trucks careening along; it is best driven in daytime – or preserve your sanity and pay the toll.

Eleusis

The **Sanctuary of Demeter** at **ELEUSIS** was one of the most important in the Greek world. Here, for two millennia, at the beginning of the Sacred Way to Athens, were performed ritual ceremonies – the Mysteries – that had an effect on their ancient initiates the equal of any modern cult. According to Pindar, who experienced the rites in Classical times and, like all others, was bound by pain of death not to reveal their content, anyone who had "seen the holy things [at Eleusis] and goes in death beneath the earth is happy, for he knows life's end and he knows the new divine beginning".

Established in Mycenaean times, perhaps as early as 1500 BC, the cult centred around the figure of Demeter (Ceres to the Romans), the goddess of corn, and the myth of her daughter Persephone's annual descent into and resurrection from the underworld, which came to symbolize the rebirth of the crops (and the gods responsible for them) in the miracle of fertility. By the fifth century BC the cult had developed into a sophisticated annual festival, attracting up to 30,000 from all over the Greek world. Participants gathered in Athens, outside the Propylaia on the Acropolis, and, after various rituals, including mass bathing and purification in Phaleron Bay, followed the Sacred Way to the sanctuary here at Eleusis. It has been speculated by some, such as the late ethnomycologist R. Gordon Wasson, that one of the rituals entailed the ingestion of a potion containing grain-ergot fungus, the effects of which would be almost identical to those of modern psychedelic drugs.

The site

The **ruins** (daily except Mon 8.30am–3pm; 400dr) are obscure in the extreme, dating from several different ages of rebuilding and largely reduced to foundations; any imaginings of mystic goings-on are further hampered by the spectacularly unromantic setting. The best plan is to head straight for the **museum**, which features models of the site at various stages in its history. This will at least point you in the direction of the **Telesterion**, the windowless Hall of Initiation, where the priests of Demeter would exhibit the "Holy Things" – presumably sheaves of fungus-infected grain, or vessels containing the magic potion – and speak "the Unutterable Words".

To reach the site from Athens, take **bus** #853 or #862 (signposted Elefsína, Skaramangás or Asprópirgos) from Platía Eleftherías ("A" on the main Athens map; *E2*). Ask to be dropped at the *Heroon* (Sanctuary), to the left of the main road, a short way into Elefsína. The trip can easily be combined with a visit to the monastery at Dhafní (see p.104), on the same road and bus routes.

On from Elefsína

Northwest from Elefsína, the **old road to Thebes and Delphi** heads into the hills. This route is described in the *Thessaly and Central Greece* chapter, and is highly worthwhile, with its detours to **ancient Aegosthena** and the tiny resort of **Pórto Yermenó**. At Mégara another, more minor road heads north to reach the sea at the village of Alepohóri, where it deteriorates to a track to loop around to Pórto Yermenó.

Heading directly west, **on towards the Peloponnese**, there are shingle beaches – more or less clear of pollution – along the old, parallel coastal road at Kinéta and Áyii Theódhori. This highway, with the Yeránia mountains to the north and those of the Peloponnese across the water, has a small place in pre-Homeric myth, as the route where Theseus slew the bandit Sciron and threw him off the cliffs to be eaten by a giant sea turtle. Thus, Sciron met the same fate as the generations of travellers he had preyed upon.

You leave Attica at Isthmía, a village beside the **Corinth Canal** (see p.146), where most of the buses break the journey for a drink at the café by the bridge. To the north of the canal, Loutráki and Perahóra are technically part of Attica but, as they are more easily reached from Kórinthos, are covered in *The Peloponnese* chapter following – on p.147.

travel details

Buses

Attica Buses for most destinations in **Attica** (ie within this chapter) leave from the **Mavromatéon terminal** (250m north of the National Archeological Museum, at the junction with Leof. Alexándhras, "B" on the Athens map, *B2*). Exceptions are specified in the text.

Destinations include: Lávrio (every 30min until 6pm, then hourly until 9pm; 1hr); Marathon Tomb (every 30min until 2pm, hourly thereafter; 1hr); Rafína (every 30min; 1hr); Sounion by the coast (hourly on the half-hour; 1hr); Sounion by the inland route (hourly on the hour; 1hr 15min).

Peloponnese and western/northern Greece Most buses leave from the terminal at **Kifissoú 100**, a good 4km northeast of the city centre, in the industrial district of Peristéri; the easiest way to get there is on the **#051 bus** from the corner of Vilára and Menándhrou (near Omónia; "E" on the map, *D2*).

Destinations include: Árgos (hourly; 2hr 45min; Árta (8 daily; 6hr); Corfu (3 daily; 11hr); Igoumenítsa (3 daily; 8hr 30min); Ioánnina (8 daily; 7hr 30min); Kefalloniá (4 daily; 8hr); Kórinthos (every 30min; 1hr 30min); Lefkádha (4 daily; 6hr); Mycenae/Náfplio (hourly; 2hr 30min); Olympia (4 daily; 6hr); Pátra (every 45min; 3hr); Pílos (2 daily; 6hr); Spárti (9 daily; 4hr 30min); Thessaloníki (10 daily; 7hr); Trípoli (12 daily; 4hr); Zákinthos (3 daily; 7hr).

Central Greece Buses for most other destinations in central Greece leave from the **Liossíon 260** terminal, easiest reached by **taxi**. Alternatively, take either **bus #024** at the Amalías entrance of the National Gardens (by Síndagma, *E4*), almost to the end of its route (about 25min; the stop is 200m south of the terminal); or the **metro** from Omónia/Monastiráki to the Áyios Nikólaos station (800m southeast of the terminal; coming out, go under the rail line, turn left and look out for the buses).

Destinations include: Áyios Konstandínos (hourly at quarter past the hour; 2hr 30min); Delphi (5 daily; 3hr); Halkídha (every 30min; 1hr); Karpeníssi (2 daily; 6hr); Kími, for Skíros ferries (6 daily; 3hr 30min); Óssios Loukás (2 daily; 4hr); Thíva/Thebes (hourly; 1hr); Tríkala (7daily; 5hr 30min); Vólos (9 daily; 5hr).

Trains

Trains for **Kórinthos and the Peloponnese** leave from the **Stathmós Peloponíssou**, those for **northern Greece** from **Stathmós Laríssis**. The stations adjoin each other, just west of Deliyánni (*B/C1*), on the #1 trolley bus route. To reach the Peloponnese station, use the metal overpass next to the Laríssis station. "OSE" signs direct you through the maze of metro-works.

Island ferries and hydrofoils

Pireás Ferries and hydrofoils to the Argo-Saronic, Monemvassía, Crete, the Cyclades, Dodecanese and northeast Aegean islands. See p.126 for details of how to get to Pireás.

Lávrio Ferries daily to Kéa; one weekly to Kíthnos. Bus from Mavromatéon ("B", *B2*).

Rafína Ferries daily to Mármari, Káristos and Stíra on Évia; most days to Ándhros, Tínos, Síros, Míkonos, Páros and Náxos, plus less frequently to Amorgós; and two or three weekly to Híos, Lésvos and Límnos. Hydrofoils to Évvia (Stíra, Mármari and Karístos), Ándhros, Tínos, Míkonos, Páros, Náxos and beyond. Most ferries from Rafína to the Cyclades leave in the **late afternoon** – a boon if you've missed the morning Pireás boats. Bus from Mavromatéon ("B", *B2*).

Information For details of ferries from **Rafína or Lávrio** call their respective port police offices (Rafína: ☎0294/232 888; Lávrio: ☎0292/25 249). For **hydrofoils** call *Ilios Lines* in Pireás (☎01/41 37 725) or Rafína (☎0294/22 888).

International ferries

From Pireás Destinations include: İzmir or Çeşme, Turkey (once weekly); Kuşadası, Turkey (once weekly May–Oct); Ancona, Italy (2 weekly); Limassol, Cyprus and Haifa, Israel (at least weekly, via Rhodes or Crete); Venice, Italy (3–4 monthly). Services to Alexandria, Egypt are currently suspended

Domestic flights

Olympic Airways operate regular flights from the **west airport** to the following destinations:

Alexandhroúpoli, Astipálea, Haniá (Crete), Híos, Iráklion (Crete), Ioánnina, Kalamáta, Kárpathos,

Kastoriá, Kavála, Kefalloniá, Kérkira (Corfu), Kíthira, Kós, Kozáni, Léros, Límnos, Mílos, Míkonos, Mitilíni (Lésvos), Náxos, Páros, Préveza, Ródhos (Rhodes), Sámos, Sitía (Crete), Skiáthos, Síros, Sitía, Skíros, Thessaloníki, Thíra (Santoríni) and Zákinthos.

All services are heavily reduced out of season.

CHAPTER TWO

THE PELOPONNESE

The appeal of the **Peloponnese** (*Pelopónnisos* in Greek) is hard to overstate. This southern peninsula, technically an island since the cutting of the Corinth Canal, seems to have the best of almost everything Greek. Its ancient sites include the Homeric palaces of Agamemnon at **Mycenae** and of Nestor at **Pílos**, the best preserved of all Greek theatres at **Epidaurus**, and the lush sanctuary of **Olympia**, host for a millennium to the Olympic Games. The medieval remains are scarcely less rich, with the fabulous Venetian, Frankish and Turkish castles of **Náfplio**, **Methóni** and **Kórinthos**; the strange tower-houses and frescoed churches of the **Máni**; and the extraordinarily well-preserved Byzantine shells of **Mystra** and **Monemvassía**.

Beyond this incredible profusion of cultural monuments, the Peloponnese is also a superb place to relax and wander. Its **beaches**, especially along the west coast, are among the finest and least developed in the country, and the **landscape** itself is superb – dominated by range after range of forested mountains, and cut by some of the lushest valleys and gorges to be imagined. Not for nothing did its heartland province of Arcadia lend its name to the concept of a classical rural idyll.

The Peloponnese is at its most enjoyable and intriguing when you venture off the beaten track: to the old hill towns of Arcadia like **Karítena** and **Dhimitsána**; the bizarre semi-desert of the **Máni** or the castles and beaches of **Messínia** in the south; or the trip along the astonishing **rack-and-pinion railway** leading inland from **Dhiakoftó** on the north coast.

The province will amply repay any amount of time that you devote to it. The Argolid, the area richest in ancient history, is just a couple of hours from Athens, and if pushed you could complete a circuit of the main sights here – Corinth, Mycenae and Epidaurus – in a couple of days, making your base by the sea in Náfplio. Given a week, you could take in the two sites of Mystra and Olympia at a more leisurely pace. To get to grips with all this, however, plus the wonderful southern peninsulas of the Máni and Messínia, and the hill towns of Arcadia, you'll need at least a couple of weeks.

If you were planning on a combination of **Peloponnese-plus-islands**, the Argo-Saronic or Ionian islands are the most convenient, although you might well be better off limiting yourself to the mainland on a short trip. The **Argo-Saronic** islands (see pp.399–414) are linked by hydrofoil with the Argolid and Pireás. Of the **Ionian** islands, **Kíthira** is covered in this chapter since it's easiest reached from the southern Peloponnese ports, but **Zákinthos** (see p.710) can also be reached from the western port of Killíni, and Greece's second port city of **Pátra** serves as a gateway to the other islands of the Ionian group – and to southern Italy.

Travelling about the peninsula by **public transport**, you'll be dependent mostly on the **buses**, which are fast and regular on the main routes, and get to most other places at least once a day. The Peloponnese **train line**, now a century old, is in a poor state, especially on its highly scenic southern loop, with trains risking mishaps on defective sleepers if they exceed the leisurely timetable. Renting a **car** is worthwhile if you can afford it, even for just a few days – exploring the south from Kalamáta or Sparta, or Arcadia from Náfplio or Trípoli.

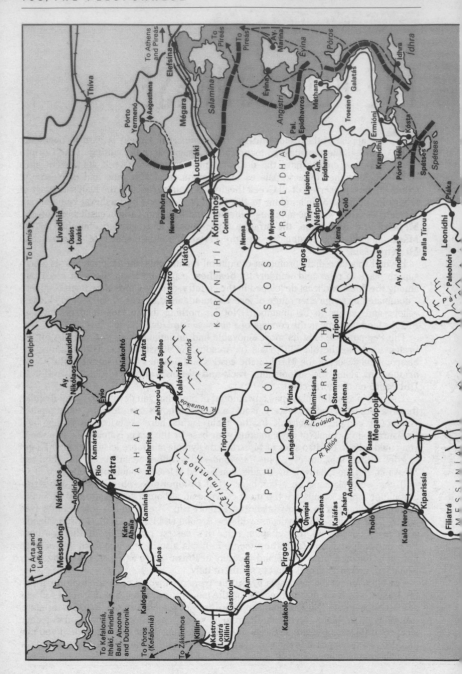

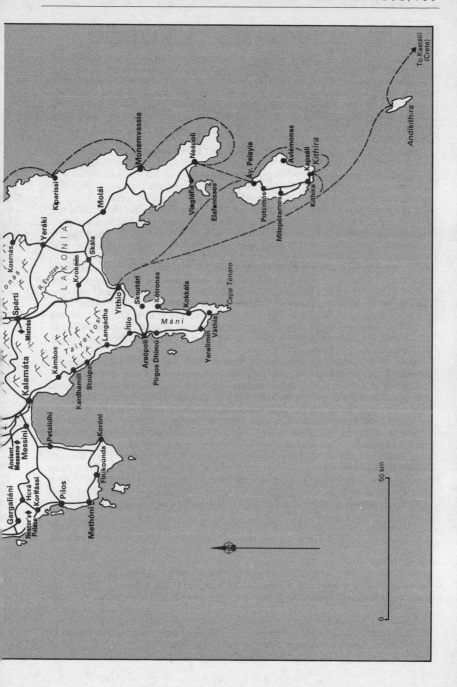

PELOPÓNISSOS – MOREÁ: SOME HISTORY

The **ancient history** of the Peloponnese is very much that of the Greek mainstream. During the **Mycenaean period** (around 2000–1100 BC), the peninsula hosted the semi-legendary kingdoms of Agamemnon at Mycenae, Nestor at Pylos and Menelaus at Sparta. In the **Dorian and Classical eras**, the region's principal city-state was Sparta, which, with its allies, brought down Athens in the ruinous Peloponnesian wars. Under **Roman** rule, Corinth was the capital of the southern Greek province. For more on all these periods, see the "Historical framework" (in *Contexts*) and the individual accounts in this chapter.

From the decline of the Romans, through to the Turkish conquest, the Peloponnese – or the **Moreá**, as it became known, from the resemblance of the peninsula's map-outline to the leaf of a mulberry tree (*moreá*) – pursued a more complex and individual course. A succession of occupations and conquests, with attendant outposts and castles, has left an extraordinary legacy of castles and medieval remains throughout the region.

The Peloponnese retained a nominally Roman civilization well after the colonial rule had dissipated, with Corinth at the fore, until the city was destroyed by two major earthquakes in the sixth century. Around this time, too, came attacks from barbarian tribes of Avars and Slavs, who were to pose sporadic problems for the new rulers – the **Byzantines**, the eastern emperors of the now-divided Roman Empire.

The Byzantines established their courts, castles and towns from the ninth century on; their control, however, was only partial, as large swathes of the Moreá fell under the control of the Franks and Venetians. The **Venetians** settled along the coast, founding trading ports at Monemvassía, Pílos and Koróni, which endured, for the most part, into the fifteenth century. The **Franks**, led by the Champlitte and Villehardouin clans, arrived in 1204, bloodied and eager from the sacking of Constantinople in the piratical Fourth Crusade. They swiftly conquered large tracts of the peninsula, and divided it into feudal baronies under a Prince of the Moreá.

Towards the middle of the thirteenth century, there was a remarkable **Byzantine revival**, which spread from the court at Mystra to reassert control over the peninsula. A last flicker of "Greek" rule, it was eventually extinguished by the **Turkish conquest**, between 1458 and 1460, and was to lie dormant, save for sporadic rebellions in the Máni, until the nineteenth-century **War of Greek Independence**.

In this, the Peloponnese played a major part. The banner of rebellion was raised near **Kalávrita**, in Arcadia, by Yermanos, Archbishop of Pátra, and the Greek forces' two most successful leaders – **Mavromihalis** and **Kolokotronis** – were natives of, and carried out most of their actions in, the Peloponnese. The battle that accidently decided the war, **Navarino Bay**, was fought off the west coast at Pílos; and the first Greek parliament convened here, too, at **Náfplio**. After independence, however, power passed swiftly away from the Peloponnese to Athens, where it was to stay. The peninsula's contribution to the early Greek state was a disaffected one, highlighted by the assassination of Capodistrias, the first Greek president, by Maniots.

Throughout the **nineteenth and early twentieth centuries**, the region developed important ports at Pátra, Kórinthos and Kalamáta, but its interior reverted to backwater status. It was little disturbed until **World War II**, during which the area saw some of the worst German atrocities; there was much brave resistance in the mountains, but also some of the most shameful collaboration. The **civil war** which followed left many of the towns polarized and physically in ruins. In its wake there was substantial **emigration** from both towns and countryside, to the US in particular, as well as to Athens and other Greek cities.

Today, the Peloponnese has a reputation for being one of the most traditional and politically conservative regions of Greece. The people are held in rather poor regard by other Greeks, though to outsiders they seem unfailingly hospitable.

CORINTH AND THE ARGOLID

The usual approach from Athens to the Peloponnese is along the highway through Elefsína and across the Corinth Canal to modern-day **Kórinthos** (Corinth); buses and trains come this way at least every hour, the former halting at the canal (see p.146). Another, more attractive approach to the peninsula is by ferry or *Flying Dolphin* hydrofoil, via the islands of the **Argo-Saronic** (see p.333–414); routes run from Pireás through those islands, with brief hops over to the Argolid ports of Ermióni, Pórto Héli and Náfplio.

The region that you enter, to the south and southeast of Kórinthos, is known as the **Argolid** (*Argolídha* in modern Greek), after the city of Argos which held sway in Classical times. The greatest concentration of ancient sites in Greece is found in this compact little peninsula – its western boundary delineated by the main road south from Kórinthos. Within an hour or so's journey of each other are Agamemnon's fortress at **Mycenae**, the great theatre of **Epidaurus**, and lesser sites at **Tiryns**, **Árgos** and **Lerna**. Inevitably these, along with the great Roman site at **Ancient Corinth**, draw the crowds, and in peak season you may want to see the sites early or late in the day to realize their magic.

When ruin-hopping palls, there are the small-town pleasures of elegant **Náfplio**, and a handful of pleasant **coastal resorts**. The best beaches in these parts, however, are to be found along the coast road south from Árgos – at the Astrós and Tirós beaches, where there are some good campsites. Technically outside the Argolid, both of these are easiest reached by bus from Árgos or by *Flying Dolphin* hydrofoil from Náfplio (summer only), Pórto Héli or the island of Spétses. The southern continuation of these hydrofoil routes takes you on down the coast to the Byzantine remains of Monemvassía.

Kórinthos – modern Corinth

Like its ancient predecessor, the modern city of **KÓRINTHOS** has been levelled on several occasions by earthquakes – most recently in 1981, when a serious quake left thousands in tented homes for most of the following year. Repaired and reconstructed, with buildings of prudent but characterless concrete, the modern city has little of intrinsic interest: it is largely an industrial-agriculture centre, its economy bolstered by the drying and shipping of currants, for centuries one of Greece's few successful exports (the word currant itself derives from Corinth).

Nevertheless, you could do worse than base yourself here for a night or two, for the setting, with the sea on two sides and the mountains across the gulf, is magnificent, and there are some pleasant quarters along the shore, plus a nice provincial main square centred around a park. In addition, of course, there are the remains of ancient and medieval Corinth – **Arhéa Kórinthos** – 7km to the southwest, as well as access to Perahóra and a couple of other minor sites (see below).

The only specific sight in the modern city itself is the **Folklore Museum** (daily 8am–1pm; free), located in a tasteful modern building near the harbour. This contains the usual array of peasant costumes, old engravings and dioramas of traditional crafts.

Arrival and information

The **bus station for Athens** and most local destinations (including Arhéa Kórinthos, Isthmía, Loutráki and Neméa) is on the Ermoú side of the park, at the corner with Koliátsou. **Long-distance buses** (to Spárti, Kalamáta, Trípoli, Mycenae, Árgos and Náfplio) use a terminal on the other side of the park, at the corner of Ethnikís Andístasis and Arátou. The **train station** is a couple of blocks to the east.

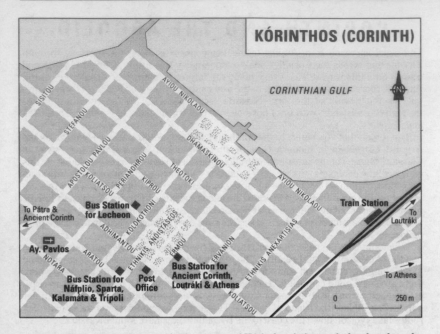

Orientation is straightforward. The centre of Kórinthos is its **park**, bordered on the longer sides by Ermoú and Ethnikís Andístasis (formerly Konstantinou) streets. You'll find the *National* and *Commercial* **banks** along the latter, and the main **post office** on Adimantoú street, on the south side of the park. There's a **tourist police** post at Ermoú 5 (☎0741/23 282), near the Athens bus station, and a **taxi rank** on the Ethnikís Andístassis side of the park. If you want to rent your own transport, for **mopeds and bikes** check out *Liberopoulos*, at Ethnikís Andístasis 27 (☎0741/72 937); for **cars,** try *Grigoris Lagos* (☎0741/22 617) at Ethnikís Andístasis 42 or *Vasilopoulis* at Adímantou 30 (☎0741/28 437).

Accommodation

At most times of year, **hotels** are reasonably easy to find, with two or three on the road into town from the train station and a couple of less expensive ones on or near the waterside. A selection is given below.

Alternatively, there are a couple of **campsites** along the gulf to the west: *Korinth Beach* is 3km out at Dhiavakíta (☎0741/27 967; April–Oct) – to reach the beach, such as it is, you must cross the coastal road and the railway line. *Blue Dolphin* is a bit further away at Léheo (☎0741/25 766; mid-May to mid-Oct), but it is on the seaward side of the tracks and for that alone is preferable. For both sites, take the bus to Léheo (a part of Ancient Corinth) from alongside the park in modern Kórinthos.

Acropolis, Vassiléos Yeoryiou 25 (☎0741/22 430). On the way into town from the train station. Good value. ④.

Belle-Vue, Dhamaskinou 41 (☎0741/22 088). Central, if a little shabby. Can be noisy, so ask for a back room if you prefer sound sleep to a sea view. Used by groups, so book early. ②.

Ephira, Ethnikís Andístasis 52 (☎0741/22 434). One block from the park and near the long-distance bus station. A modern hotel and a good mid-priced choice. ③–④.

Konstantatos, Dhamaskinou 3 (☎0741/22 120). Upmarket with private bathrooms and elegant
decor; at the bottom end of its price category. ⑤.
Korinthos, Dhamaskinou 26 (☎0741/22 631). Near the *Konstantatos* and slightly cheaper, but
otherwise little to choose between them. ⑤.

Eating and drinking

Kórinthos has a few tavernas, and rather more fast-food places along the waterfront, all
modestly priced.

Anaxagoras, Áyiou Nikólaou 31. Good range of *mézedhes* and grilled meats.
Kanata, Dhamiskinóu 41. One of the best restaurants in the centre of town. Open all day.
Arhontiko (☎0741/27 968). A favourite with the locals. As this place is out near the campsites, you
might want to phone first.

Ancient Corinth

Buses to Ancient Corinth, **ARHÉA KÓRINTHOS**, leave modern Kórinthos every hour
from 8am to 9pm and return on the half-hour, a taxi is also a possibility, since fares are
not exorbitant at around 2000dr return, and drivers will wait. The ruins of the **ancient
city**, which displaced Athens as capital of the Greek province in Roman times, occupy a
rambling sequence of sites, the main enclosure of which is given a sense of scale by the
majestic ruin of a Temple of Apollo. Most compelling, though, are the ruins of the medieval city, which occupy the stunning acropolis site of **Acrocorinth**, towering 565m above.

The Ancient City

The ruins of Ancient Corinth spread over a vast area, and include sections of ancient
walls (the Roman city had a fifteen-kilometre circuit), outlying stadiums, gymnasiums
and necropolises. Only the central area, around the Roman forum and the Classical
Temple of Apollo, is preserved in an excavated state; the rest, odd patches of semi-
enclosed and often overgrown ruin, you come across unexpectedly while walking
about the village and up to Acrocorinth.

The overall effect is impressive, but it only begins to suggest the majesty of this
once supremely wealthy city. Ancient Corinth was a key centre of the Greek and
Roman worlds, whose possession meant the control of trade between northern Greece
and the Peloponnese. In addition, the twin ports of **Lechaion**, on the gulf of Corinth,
and **Kenchreai,** on the Saronic Gulf, provided a trade link between the Ionian and
Aegean seas – the western and eastern Mediterranean. Not surprisingly, this meant

that the city's ancient (and medieval) history was one of invasions and power struggles which, in Classical times, was dominated by Corinth's rivalry with Athens – against whom it sided with Sparta in the Peloponnesian War.

Despite this, Corinth suffered only one major setback, in 146 BC, when the Romans, having defeated the Greek city states of the Achaean League, razed the site to the ground. For a century the city lay in ruins before being rebuilt, on a majestic scale, by Julius Caesar in 44 BC: initially intended as a colony for veterans, it was later made the provincial capital. Once again Corinth grew rich on trade – with Rome to the west, Syria and Egypt to the east. Its population increased to 300,000, but never attained the extraordinary peak of 750,000 it had enjoyed in Classical times.

Roman Corinth's reputation for wealth, fuelled by its trading access to luxury goods, was soon equalled by its appetite for earthly pleasures – including sex. Corinthian women were renowned for their beauty and much sought after as *hetairai* (courtesans); a temple to Aphrodite/Venus, on the acropolis of Acrocorinth, was served by over a thousand sacred prostitutes. **Saint Paul** stayed in Corinth for eighteen months in 54 AD, though his attempts to reform the citizens' ways were met only by rioting – tribulations recorded in his two "letters to the Corinthians". The city endured until rocked by two major earthquakes, in 522 and 551, which brought down the Roman buildings, and again depopulated the site until a brief Byzantine revival in the eleventh century.

The excavations

Site Mon–Fri 8.30am–7pm (5pm in winter), Sat & Sun 8.30am–3pm; museum same hours except Mon 12.30pm–7pm (5pm in winter); 1000dr fee covers admission to both.

Inevitably, given successive waves of earthquakes and destruction, the **main excavated site** is dominated by the remains of the Roman city. Entering from the north side, just behind the road where the buses pull in, you find yourself in the **Roman agora**, an enormous marketplace flanked by the substantial foundations of a huge *stoa*, once a structure of several storeys, with 33 shops on the ground floor. Opposite the *stoa* is a *bema*, a marble platform used for public announcements. At the far end are remains of a **basilica,** while the area behind the *bema* is strewn with the remnants of numerous Roman administrative buildings. Back across the *agora*, almost hidden in a swirl of broken marble and shattered architecture, there's a fascinating trace of the Greek city – a **sacred spring**, covered over by a grille at the base of a narrow flight of steps.

More substantial is the elaborate Roman **Fountain of Peirene**, which stands below the level of the *agora*, to the side of a wide excavated stretch of what was the main approach to the city, the marble-paved **Lechaion Way.** Taking the form of a colonnaded and frescoed recess, the fountain occupies the site of one of two natural springs in Corinth – the other is up on the acropolis – and its cool water was channelled into a magnificent fountain and pool in the courtyard. The fountain house was, like many of Athens's Roman public buildings, the gift of the wealthy Athenian and friend of the Emperor Hadrian, Herodes Atticus. The waters still flow through the underground cisterns and supply the modern village.

The real focus of the ancient site, though, is a rare survival from the Classical Greek era, the fifth-century BC **Temple of Apollo**, whose seven austere Doric columns stand slightly above the level of the forum and are flanked by foundations of another market-place and baths. Over to the west is the site **museum**, housing a large collection of domestic pieces, some good Roman mosaics and a frieze depicting some of the labours of Heracles (Hercules), several of which were performed nearby – at Nemea, Stymphalia and Lerna. The city's other claim to mythic fame, incidentally, is as the home of the infant Oedipus and his step-parents, prior to his travels of discovery to Thebes.

A number of miscellaneous smaller excavations surround the main site. To the west, just across the road from the enclosing wire, there are outlines of two **theatres**: a Roman **odeion** (once again endowed by Herodes Atticus) and a larger Greek amphi-theatre, adapted by the Romans for gladiatorial sea battles. To the north are the inac-cessible but visible remains of an **Asclepion** (dedicated to the healing god).

Acrocorinth

Daily except Mon 8.30am–3pm free

Rising almost sheer above the lower town, **Acrocorinth** is sited on an amazing mass of rock, still largely encircled by two kilometres of wall. The ancient acropolis of Corinth, it became during the Middle Ages one of Greece's most powerful fortresses, besieged by successive waves of invaders, who considered it the key to the Morea.

Despite the long, four-kilometre climb – or a taxi ride from ancient Corinth, reason-able if shared – a visit to the summit is unreservedly recommended. Looking down over the Saronic and Corinthian gulfs, you really get a sense the strategic importance of the fortress's position. Amid the sixty-acre site, you wander through a jumble of chapels, mosques, houses and battlements, erected in turn by Greeks, Romans, Byzantines, Frankish Crusaders, Venetians and Turks.

The Turkish remains are unusually substantial. Elsewhere in Greece evidence of the Ottoman occupation has been physically removed or defaced, but here, halfway up the hill, you can see a midway point in the process: the still functioning **Fountain of Hatzi Mustafa**, which has been Christianized by the addition of great carved crosses. The outer of the citadel's **triple gates**, too, is largely Turkish; the middle is a combination of Venetian and Frankish; the inner, Byzantine, incorporating fourth-century BC towers. Within the citadel, the first summit (to the right) is enclosed by a **Frankish keep** – as striking as they come – which last saw action in 1828 during the War of Independence. Keeping along the track to the left, you pass some interesting (if peri-lous) cisterns, remains of a Turkish bath house and crumbling Byzantine chapels.

In the southeast corner of the citadel, hidden away in the lower ground, is the **upper Peirene spring**. This is not easy to find: look out for a narrow, overgrown entrance, from which a flight of iron stairs leads down some three metres to a metal screen. Here, broad stone steps descend into the dark depths, where a fourth-century BC arch stands guard over a pool of water that has never been known to dry up. To the north of the fountain, on the second and higher summit, is the site of the **Temple of Aphrodite** mentioned above; after its days as a brothel, it saw use as a church, mosque and belvedere.

Practicalities

To explore both ancient and medieval Corinth you need a full day, or better still, to stay here overnight. A modern **village** spreads around the edge of the main ancient site and there are a scattering of **rooms** to rent in its backstreets – follow the signs or ask at the cafés. Two upmarket, but good-value, options are the *Hotel Shadow* (☎0741/31 481; ③) and the *Marinos Rooms* (☎0741/31 209; ④).

A rather wonderful alternative, for those with transport or energy for the walk, would be to stay at the solitary modern building up in **Acrocorinth**: the *Acrocorinthos* café (☎0741/31 099 or 31 285; ②); phone ahead, as it only has a few rooms. The café also serves drinks and snacks, and sells souvenirs.

Around Corinth

As well as the **Corinth Canal**, which you can't help but pass en route between Kórinthos and Athens, a number of minor sites are accessible by bus (at least most of the way) from Kórinthos, both on the Peloponnese and Attic peninsulas. Just south of the canal is ancient **Isthmia**, site of the Panhellenic Isthmian Games. To the northwest are the spa of Loutráki and the classical **sanctuary of Hera** at Perahóra on Cape Melangávi. If you have a car, there's a grand and rather wild route **east from the cape**, around the Alkionid Gulf to Pórto Yermenó (see p.246). There are beaches along the way, though little settlement or development, and the final stretch of road beyond Káto Alepohóri is scarcely better than a jeep track.

Back in the Peloponnese proper, **Neméa** – as in the lion of Hercules's labour – is a brief detour southwest of Kórinthos, off the road to Árgos or Mycenae. **Sikyon** is a bit more remote, 25km up the coast towards Pátra, but again accessible by bus.

The Corinth Canal

The idea for a **Corinth Canal**, providing a short cut and safe passage between the Aegean and Ionian seas, dates back at least to Roman times, when the Emperor Nero performed initial excavations with a silver shovel and Jewish slave labour. It was only in the 1890s, however, that the technology became available to cut across the six-kilometre isthmus. Opened in July 1893, the canal, along with its near-contemporary Suez, helped establish Pireás as a major Mediterranean port and shipping centre, although the projected toll revenues were never realized. Today, supertankers have made it something of an anachronism and the canal has fallen into disrepair, but remains a memorable sight nonetheless.

Approaching on the main Athens road, you cross the canal near its eastern end. At the **bridge** there's a line of **cafés**, where buses from Athens usually stop if they're going beyond Kórinthos. Peering over from the bridge, the canal appears a tiny strip of water until some huge freighter assumes toy-like dimensions as it passes hundreds of metres below. If you were to take one of the few remaining ferries from Pireás to the Ionian, you would actually sail through the canal – a trip almost worthwhile for its own sake. At the western end of the canal, by the old Kórinthos–Loutráki ferry dock, there are remains of the **diolkos**, a paved way along which a wheeled platform used to carry boats across the isthmus. In use from Roman times until the twelfth century, the boats were strapped onto the platform after being relieved temporarily of their cargo.

Ancient Isthmia

Modern Isthmía lies either side of the Saronic Gulf entrance to the canal, and is served by regular buses from Kórinthos. To the south of the modern settlement, on a hillock alongside the present-day village of Kryravryssi, is the site of ancient **ISTHMIA**.

There is nothing very notable to see at the site, though the ancient settlement was an important one, due to its **Sanctuary of Poseidon** – of which just the foundations remain – and Panhellenic Isthmian games. The latter ranked with those of Delphi, Nemea and Olympia, though they have left scant evidence in the form of a **stadium**

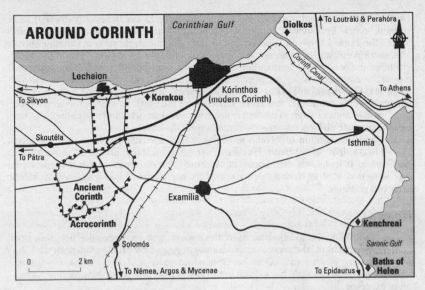

and **theatre**, together with a few curiosities, including starting blocks used for foot races, in the small adjacent **museum** which also houses some of the finds from Cenchreai. The opening hours of the museum are currently uncertain, but you can roam the site at will.

Loutráki

Six kilometres north of the canal is the spa resort of **LOUTRÁKI**. The epicentre of the 1901 Corinth earthquake, it may once have had its charms but today the concrete line of buildings casts a leaden air over the town. The resort is nonetheless immensely popular, with a larger concentration of hotels than anywhere else in the Peloponnese. The visitors are virtually all Greek, coming here for the "cure" at the hot springs, and to sample Loutráki mineral water – the country's leading bottled brand. A sign of the times is the new Pepsi-Cola bottling plant on the outskirts of Loutráki.

With your own transport, you'd be better off using the town simply as a staging post en route to the site of **Ancient Perahora** and making Lake Vouliagméni your base (see below). Otherwise, Loutráki is connected by bus and special summer trains with Athens, and by half-hourly bus with Kórinthos. If you end up staying, *Hotel Brettagne*, at Yior Lekka 28 (☎0744/02 349; ②), makes a refreshing change from the many expensive spa-resort hotels; *Hotel Pappas* (☎0744/23 026; ④), to the left of the Perahóra road, has better facilities and fine views across the gulf.

Perahóra

The **road to Cape Melangávi** is enjoyable in itself, looping above the sea in the shadow of the Yeránia mountains, whose pine forests are slowly recovering from fire devastation in 1986. En route the road offers a loop through the modern village of **PERAHÓRA** (10km) before heading out to the cape along the shore of **Lake Vouliagméni**, a beautiful lagoon with sheltered swimming, a new hotel, the *Philoxenia*

(☎0741/91 294; open all year; ③), and a small campsite, *Limni Heraiou* (☎0741/91 230; summer only). Perahóra is connected by hourly bus with Loutráki; one daily bus makes the journey between Loutráki and Lake Vouliagméni, but runs in summer only.

Ancient Perahóra – also known as the Heraion Melangavi – stands right on the western tip of the peninsula, commanding a marvellous, sweeping view of the coastline and mountains along both sides of the gulf. The site's position is its chief attraction, though there are the identifiable ruins of two sanctuaries, the **Hera Akraia** (*akron* is the extremity of the peninsula) and **Hera Limenia** (of the port), as well as the submerged **stoa** of the ancient port. The latter provides great snorkelling opportunities, but beware the potentially dangerous currents beyond the cove.

The initial excavation of Perahóra, between 1930 and 1933, is described by Dilys Powell in *An Affair of the Heart*. Humfrey Payne, her husband, directed the work until his death in 1936; he was then buried at Mycenae. The site also features in myth, for it was here that Medea, having been spurned by her husband Jason at Corinth, killed their two children.

Neméa

Ancient **NEMÉA**, the location for Hercules's slaying of its namesake lion (his first labour), lies 10km off the road from Kórinthos to Árgos. By public transport, take the bus to modern Neméa and ask to be dropped en route at *Arhéa Neméa*; moving on from the site, you can walk back down to the Árgos road and possibly wave down a bus on to Mycenae.

Like Olympia and Isthmia, Neméa held athletic games – supposedly inaugurated by Hercules – for the Greek world. A sanctuary rather than a town, the principal remains at the **site** (Tues–Sun 8.30am–3pm; 500dr) are of a **Temple of Nemean Zeus**, currently three slender Doric columns surrounded by other fallen and broken drums, but slowly being reassembled by a team of University of California archeologists. Nearby are a **palaestra** with **baths** and a Christian basilica, built with blocks from the temple. Outside the site, half a kilometre east, is a **stadium** whose starting line has been unearthed. There is also a **museum** (same hours; entrance included in site ticket), with excellent contextual models and displays relating to the biennial games.

The Stymphalean Lake

If you have transport, it's possible to cut across the hills from Neméa into Arcadia, via another Herculean locale, the **Stymphalean Lake** (around 35km from Neméa). In myth, this was the nesting-ground of man-eating birds who preyed upon travellers, suffocating them with their wings, and also poisoned local crops with their excrement. Hercules roused them from the water with a rattle, then shot them down – one of the more straightforward of his labours.

The lake is known in modern Greek as **Límni Stimfalías**, though it is really more marsh: an enormous depression with seasonal waters, ringed by woods and the dark peaks of Mount Killíni. There are no buildings for miles around, save for the ruins of the thirteenth-century Frankish Cistercian **Abbey of Zaráka** (east of the road), one of the few Gothic buildings in Greece – and a rather appropriate backdrop to the myths.

If you don't have your own transport, the most promising approach to the lake is from Kiáto on the Gulf of Corinth, where there are several hotels and rooms to rent; the road, much better than that from Neméa, has the occasional bus. The nearest places to stay are the *Hotel Stymfalia* (☎0742/22 072; ②) at **Stimfália** village, just before the abbey, or the *Xenia* (☎0747/31 283; ④) at **Kastaniá**, a mountain village famed for its butterflies, 20km to the west.

Ancient Sikyon (Sikyóna)

Six kilometres inland from Kiáto (see above), ancient **SIKYON** (Sikyóna) is a fairly accessible if little-known site, which deserves more than the few dozen visitors it attracts each year. Six buses a day run from Kiáto (on the bus and train routes from Kórinthos) to the village of Vasilikó, on the edge of a broad escarpment running parallel to the sea, from where it's a kilometre's walk to the site.

In ancient history, Sikyon's principal claim to fame came early in the sixth century BC, when the tyrant Kleisthenes kept a court of sufficient wealth and influence to purportedly entertain suitors for his daughter's hand for a full year. After his death the place was rarely heard from politically except as a consistent ally of the Spartans, but a mild renaissance ensued at the end of the fourth century when Demetrios Poliorketes moved Sikyon to its present location from the plain below. The town became renowned for sculptors, painters and artisans, and flourished well into Roman times; it was the birthplace of Alexander the Great's chief sculptor, Lysippus and, allegedly, of the art of sculptural relief.

The road from Vasilikó cuts through the site, which is fenced off into a number of enclosures. To the right is the **Roman baths museum** (closed at time of going to press, due to reopen in 1996), which shelters mosaics of griffons from the second to third century AD. To the left are the majority of the public buildings, with a theatre and stadium on the hillside above. As you enter the **main site** (unrestricted access), opposite the Roman baths, the foundations of a **Temple of Artemis** are visible to your left. Beyond it are traces of a **bouleuterion** (senate house) dating from the first half of the third century BC. The most important remains in this section are of the **Gymnasium of Kleinias** in the far right-hand corner, at the base of the hill; this is on two levels, the lower dating from around 300 BC, the other from Roman times.

Although only the first few rows of seats have been excavated, the outline of the **Theatre** – larger than that of Epidaurus – is impressive and obvious. Pine trees have taken root in the upper half, from where you've a marvellous view encompassing the rest of the site, the village of Vasilikó, the lemon and olive groves around Kiáto, plus gulf and mountains in the distance.

Mycenae (Mikínes)

Tucked into a fold of the hills just east of the road from Kórinthos to Árgos, Agamemnon's citadel at **MYCENAE** fits the legend better than any other place in Greece. It was uncovered in 1874 by the German archeologist Heinrich Schliemann (who also excavated the site of Troy), impelled by his single-minded belief that there was a factual basis to Homer's epics. Schliemann's finds of brilliantly crafted gold and sophisticated tomb-architecture bore out the accuracy of Homer's epithets of "well-built Mycenae, rich in gold".

Mycenaean history and legend

The Mycenae–Árgos region is one of the longest occupied in Greece, with evidence of Neolithic settlements from around 3000 BC. But it is to a period of three centuries at the end of the second millennium BC – from around 1550 to 1200 BC – that the citadel of Mycenae and its associated drama belong. This period is known as Mycenaean, a term which covers not just the Mycenae region but a whole civilization that flourished in southern Greece at the time.

According to the **legend** related in Homer's *Iliad* and *Odyssey* and Aeschylus's *Oresteia*, the city of Mycenae was founded by Perseus, the slayer of Medusa the

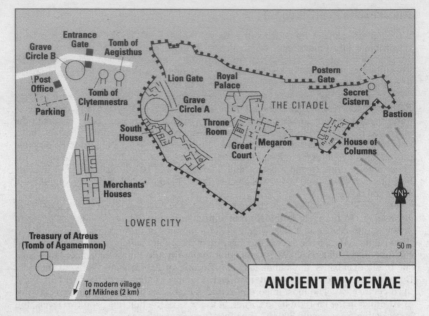

Grave Circle B
Entrance Gate
Tomb of Aegisthus
Post Office
Tomb of Clytemnestra
Parking
Lion Gate
Royal Palace
Postern Gate
Secret Cistern
Bastion
Grave Circle A
THE CITADEL
South House
Throne Room
Great Court
Megaron
House of Columns
Merchants' Houses
LOWER CITY
Treasury of Atreus (Tomb of Agamemnon)
0   50 m
N
To modern village of Mikines (2 km)

ANCIENT MYCENAE

gorgon, before it fell into the bloodied hands of the **House of Atreus**. In an act of vengeance for his brother Thyestes's seduction of his wife, Atreus murdered Thyestes's children, and fed them to their own father. Not surprisingly, this incurred the wrath of the gods. Thyestes's own daughter, Pelopia, subsequently bore him a son, Aegisthus, who promptly murdered Atreus and restored his father to the throne.

The next generation saw the gods' curse fall upon Atreus's son Agamemnon. On his return to Mycenae after commanding the Greek forces in the Trojan War – a role in which he had earlier consented to the sacrifice of his own daughter, Iphigeneia – he was killed in his bath by his wife Clytemnestra and her lover, the very same Aegisthus who had killed his father. The tragic cycle was completed by Agamemnon's son, Orestes, who took revenge by murdering his mother, Clytemnestra, and was pursued by the Furies until Athena finally lifted the curse on the house.

The **archeological remains** of Mycenae fit remarkably easily with the tale, at least if it is taken as a poetic rendering of dynastic struggles, or, as most scholars now believe it to be, a merging of stories from various periods. The buildings unearthed by Schliemann show signs of occupation from around 1950 BC, as well as two periods of intense disruption, around 1200 BC and again in 1100 BC – at which stage the town, though still prosperous, was abandoned.

No coherent explanation has been put forward for these events, since the traditional "Dorian invasions" theory (see "The Historical Framework" in *Contexts* for more) has fallen from favour, but it seems that war among the rival kingdoms was a major factor in the Mycenaean decline. These struggles appear to have escalated as the civilization developed in the thirteenth century BC, and excavations at Troy have revealed the sacking of that city, quite possibly by forces led by a king from Mycenae, in 1240 BC. The citadel of Mycenae seems to have been replanned, and heavily fortified, during this period.

The Citadel

Summer Mon–Fri 8am–6pm, Sat & Sun 8am–3pm, winter Mon–Fri 8am–3pm, Sat & Sun 8.30am–3pm; 1000dr.

The **Citadel of Mycenae** is entered through the famous **Lion Gate**, whose huge sloping gateposts bolster walls termed "Cyclopean" by later Greeks in bewildered explanation of their construction. Above them a graceful carved relief stands out in confident assertion: Mycenae at its height led a confederation of Argolid towns (Tiryns, Árgos, Asine, Hermione – the present-day Ermióni), dominated the Peloponnese and exerted influence throughout the Aegean. The motif of a pillar supported by two muscular lions was probably the symbol of the Mycenaean royal house, for a seal found on the site bears a similar device. Inside the walls to the right is **Grave Circle A**, the royal cemetery excavated by Schliemann and believed by him to contain the bodies of Agamemnon and his followers, murdered on their triumphant return from Troy. Opening one of the graves, he found a tightly fitting and magnificent gold mask that had somehow preserved the flesh of a Mycenaean noble; "I have gazed upon the face of Agamemnon," he exclaimed in an excited cable to the king of Greece. For a time it seemed that this provided irrefutable evidence of the truth of Homer's tale. In fact, the burials date from about three centuries before the Trojan war, though, given Homer's possible accumulation of different and earlier sagas, there's no reason why they should not have been connected with a Mycenaean king Agamemnon. They were certainly royal graves, for the finds (now in the National Archeological Museum in Athens) are among the richest archeology has yet unearthed.

Schliemann took the extensive **South House**, beyond the grave circle, to be the Palace of Agamemnon. However, a building much grander and more likely to be the **Royal Palace**, was later discovered near the summit of the acropolis. Rebuilt in the thirteenth century BC, this is an impressively elaborate and evocative building complex; although the ruins are only at ground level, the different rooms are easily discernible. Like all Mycenaean palaces, it is centred around a **Great Court** on the south side, a staircase would have led via an anteroom to the big rectangular **Throne Room**; on the east, a double porch gave access to the **Megaron**, the grand reception hall with its traditional circular hearth. The small rooms to the north are believed to have been royal apartments, and in one of them the remains of a red stuccoed bath have led to its fanciful identification as the scene of Agamemnon's murder.

With the accompaniment of the sound of bells drifting down from goats scratching about the mountainside, a stroll round the ramparts is evocative. A more salutary reminder of the nature of life in Mycenaean times is the **secret cistern** at the western end of the ramparts, created in the twelfth century BC. Whether it was designed to enable the citadel's occupants to withstand siege from outsiders, rival Mycenaeans, or even an increasingly alienated peasantry, is not known. Steps lead down to a deep underground spring; it's still possible to descend the whole way, though you'll need to have a torch and be sure-footed, since there's a seventy-metre drop to the water (depth unknown) at the final turn of the twisting passageways. Nearby is the **House of Columns**, a large and stately building with the base of a stairway that once led to an upper storey.

Only the ruling Mycenaean elite could live within the citadel itself. Hence the main part of town lay outside the walls and, in fact, extensive remains of **merchants' houses** have been uncovered near the road. Their contents included Linear B tablets recording the spices used to scent oils, along with large amounts of pottery, the quantity suggesting that the early Mycenaeans may have dabbled in the perfume trade. The discovery of the tablets has also prompted a reassessment of the sophistication of Mycenaean civilization for they show that, here at least, writing was not limited to government scribes working in the royal palaces as had previously been thought, and that around the citadel may have been a commercial city of some size and wealth.

Alongside the merchants' houses are the remains of another Grave Circle (B), dating from around 1650 BC and possibly representing an earlier, rival dynasty to the kings buried in Grave Circle A, and two **tholos** (circular chamber-type) tombs, speculatively identified by Schliemann as the **Tombs of Aegisthus and Clytemnestra**. The former, closer to the Lion Gate, dates from around 1500 BC and has now collapsed, so is roped off; the latter dates from some two centuries later – thus corresponding with the Trojan timescale – and can still be entered.

The Treasury of Atreus

Same hours as the Citadel; admission included in Citadel entrance fee.

Four hundred metres down the road from the Citadel site is another, infinitely more startling *tholos*, known as the **Treasury of Atreus** or "Tomb of Agamemnon". This was certainly a royal burial vault at a late stage in Mycenae's history, contemporary with the "Clytemnestra Tomb", so the attribution to Agamemnon or his father is as good as any – if the king was indeed the historic leader of the Trojan expedition. In any case, it is an impressive monument to Mycenaean building skills, a beehive-like structure built without the use of mortar. Entering the tomb through a majestic fifteen-metre corridor, you come face to face with the chamber doorway, above which is a great lintel formed by two immense slabs of stone – one of which, a staggering nine metres long, is estimated to weigh 118 tonnes.

Practicalities: Mikínes

The modern village of **MIKÍNES** is 2km from the Kórinthos–Árgos road and the train station, but not all trains on the Kórinthos–Árgos–Trípoli line stop here. Buses from Athens to Árgos or Náfplio usually drop passengers at the turning rather than in the village; local buses from Nápflio serve the village itself. The walk in from the main road is along a beautiful straight road lined with eucalyptus trees, through which glimpses of the Citadel appear, flanked by the twin mountains of Zára and Ilías. The site is a further 2km, uphill walk from the village.

Accommodation and eating

Unless you have your own transport, you'll probably want to stay at Mikínes, which is heavily touristed by day but quiet once the site has closed and the tour buses depart. Along the village's single street, there is quite an array of hotels – most of their names taken from characters in the House of Atreus saga – as well as a number of signs for rooms. Mycenae's two **campsites** are both centrally located, on the way into the village. There's not a great deal to choose between them, though *Camping Mykines* (☎0751/66 247; open all year) is smaller and a little closer to the site than *Camping Atreus* (☎0751/66 221; March–Oct).

All the hotels listed below have **restaurants** catering for the lunchtime tour-group trade; don't raise your expectations too high, though. Other eating places worth trying are the *Electra* (☎ 0751/76 447), the *King Menelaos* (☎0751/76 300) and the *Menelaos* (☎0751/76 311), all along the main street.

Agamemnon (☎0751/76 222). Small hotel whose modern facade belies the older comfortable rooms inside. ③.

Belle Hélène (☎0751/76 225). The village's most characterful hotel, converted from the house used by Schliemann during his excavations. Signatures in its visitors' book include Virginia Woolf, Henry Moore, Sartre and Debussy. Very friendly, good restaurant, a definite first choice. ②.

Rooms Dassis (☎0751/76 123). A pleasant, well-organized set-up, run, along with a useful travel agency, by Canadian Marion Dassis, who married into the local Dassis dynasty. ⑤.

Klitemnestra, up the hill (☎0751/76 451). Pleasant, modern hotel – the nearest to the site. ③.

Petite Planète (☎0751/76 240). An ugly but comfortable hotel at the top end of the village, with great views and a swimming pool. Owned by another of the Dassis dynasty. ⑤.

Youth Hostel, above the *Restaurant Iphigeneia* (☎0751/76 285). Easy-going hostel with rather cramped dorm-rooms on the roof. IYHF card required. ①.

The Argive Heraion

The little-visited **Argive Heraion** (daily 8.30am–3pm; free) is an important sanctuary from Mycenaean and Classical times and the site where Agamemnon is said to have been chosen as leader of the Greek expedition to Troy. It lies 7km south of Mycenae, off the minor road which runs east of Argos through Hónikas, and on to Náfplio. The lonely site is above the village of Hónikas; before you reach the village, look out for signs to 'Ancient Ireo'. There are various Mycenaean tombs near the site, but the principal remains of a temple complex, baths and a *palaestra* (wrestling/athletics gym), built over three interconnnecting terraces, all date from the fifth century BC.

The Heraion makes a pleasant diversion for anyone driving between Mycenae and Náfplio, or an enjoyable afternoon's walk from Mikínes – it takes a little over an hour on foot if you follow the old track southeast from the village, parallelling the minor road to Ayía Triádha and Náfplio. Hónikas has the occasional bus to Árgos; Ayía Triádha, 4km on, has more frequent connections to Náfplio.

Árgos

ÁRGOS, 12km south of the Mikínes junction, is said to be the oldest inhabited town in Greece, although you wouldn't know it from first impressions. However, this turn-of-the-century trading centre has some pleasant squares and Neoclassical buildings, and a brief stop is worthwhile for the excellent museum and mainly Roman ruins. Try to time your visit to coincide with the regular **Wednesday market**, which draws locals from all the surrounding hill villages.

The modern **Archeological Museum** (daily except Mon 8.30am–3pm; 400dr) is just off the main market square, Platía Áyios Pétrou, and makes an interesting detour after Mycenae, with a good collection of Mycenaean tomb objects and armour as well as extensive pottery finds. The region's Roman occupation is well represented here, in sculpture and mosaics, and there are also some lesser finds from Lerna on display.

Before you leave Árgos, ask to be pointed in the direction of the town's ancient remains – a few minutes' walk down the Trípoli road, struggling to hold their own next to a tyre yard. The **site** (open all hours; free), once located, turns out to be surprisingly extensive. The **theatre**, built by Classical Greeks and adapted by the Romans, looks oddly narrow from the road, but climb up there and it feels immense. Estimated to have held 20,000 spectators – six thousand more than Epidaurus, it is matched on the Greek mainland only by the theatres at Megalopolis and Dodona. Alongside are the remains of an **odeion** and **Roman baths**.

Above the site looms the ancient **acropolis**, capped by the largely Frankish **medieval castle** of Lárissa, built on ancient foundations and later augmented by the Venetians and Turks. Massively cisterned and guttered, the sprawling ruins offer the views you'd expect – the reward for a long, steep haul up, either on indistinct trails beyond the theatre, or a very roundabout road.

Practicalities

You may well need to change **buses** in Árgos: its connections are considerably better than those of Náfplio. There are two *KTEL* kiosks, a block apart from each other and the central square; the one to the south, on Vassiléos Yioryíou tou Dheftérou, is for buses back towards Athens and various points in the Argolid; the other, at Plíthonos 24, beyond the museum, is for Trípoli, Spárti and down the coast towards Leonídhi.

For a good meal between buses, try the *Retro Restaurant* on the central square or, for a quick snack, *Miku*, 50m from the square on Papafléssa. Staying overnight shouldn't prove necessary, unless you find Náfplio full – a possibility in high season. Good, modest **hotels** on, or just off, the central square, include *Mycenae Hotel* (☎0751/68 754; ③), *Hotel Palladin* (☎0751/66 248; ③) and *Hotel Telesilla* (☎0751/68 317; ③).

Tiryns (Tírinthos)

In Mycenaean times **TIRYNS** stood by the sea, commanding the coastal approaches to Árgos and Mycenae. Today the Aegean has receded, leaving the fortress stranded on a low hillock in the plains, surrounded by citrus groves – alongside the Argolid's principal modern prison. It's not the most enchanting of settings, which in part explains why this accessible, substantial site is relatively empty of visitors. After the crowds at Mycenae, however, the opportunity to wander about Homer's "wall-girt Tiryns" in near-solitude is worth taking.

The site lies just to the east of the Árgos–Náfplio road, and buses will drop off and pick up passengers, on request, at the café opposite.

The Citadel

Daily 8am–7pm (closes at 5pm in winter); 400dr.

As at Mycenae, Homer's epigrams correspond remarkably well to what you can see on the ground at Tiryns. The fortress, now over 3000 years old, is undeniably impressive. The walls, formed of huge Cyclopean stones, dominate the site; the Roman guidebook writer Pausanias, happening on the site in the second century AD, found them "more amazing than the Pyramids" – a claim that seems a little exaggerated, even considering that the walls then stood twice their present height.

The entrance is on the far side of the fortress from the road, and visitors are restricted to exploring certain passages, staircases and the palace. Despite this, the sophistication and defensive function of the citadel's layout are evident as soon as you climb up the **entrance ramp**. Wide enough to allow access to chariots, the ramp is angled so as to leave the right-hand, unshielded side of any invading force exposed for the entire ascent, before forcing a sharp turn at the top – surveyed by defenders from within. The **gateways**, too, constitute a formidable barrier; the outer one would have been similar in design to Mycenae's Lion Gate, though unfortunately its lintel is missing, so there is no heraldic motif that might confirm a dynastic link between the sites.

Of the **palace** itself only the limestone foundations survive, but the fact that they occupy a level site makes them generally more legible than the ruins of hilly and boulder-strewn Mycenae and you can gain a clearer idea of its structure. The walls themselves would have been of sun-dried brick, covered in stucco and decorated with frescoes. Fragments of the latter were found on the site: one depicting a boar hunt, the other a life-sized frieze of courtly women, both now in Náfplio's museum. From the forecourt, you enter a spacious **colonnaded court** with a round sacrificial altar in the middle. A typically Mycenaean double porch leads directly ahead to the **megaron** (great hall), where the base of a throne was found – it's now in the Archeological Museum in Athens, with miscellaneous finds and frescoes from the site. The massive round clay hearth that's characteristic of these Mycenean halls – there's a perfect example at Nestor's Palace (see p.212) – is no longer to be seen at Tiryns, because some time in the sixth century BC this part of the palace became the site of a Temple to Hera, a structure whose column bases now pepper the ground. **Royal apartments** lead off on either side; the women's quarters are thought to have been to the right, while to the left is the bathroom, its floor – a huge, single flat stone – intact. The **lower acropolis**, north of the *megaron*, is currently out of bounds due to the excavation of two underground cisterns recently discovered at its far end.

A tower further off to the left of the *megaron* gives access to a **secret staircase**, as at Mycenae, which winds down to an inconspicuous **postern gate**. The site beyond the *megaron* is separated by an enormous inner wall and can only be viewed from a distance.

Náfplio

NÁFPLIO (which you may also see as *Nauplia* or *Navplion*), is a rarity amongst Greek towns. A lively, beautifully sited place, it exudes a rather grand, fading elegance, inherited from the days when it was the fledgling capital of modern Greece. The seat of government was here from 1829 to 1834 and it was in Náfplio that the first prime minister, Capodistrias, was assassinated by vengeful Maniot clansmen. It was here, too, that the Bavarian Prince Otho, put forward by the European powers to be the first King of Greece, had his initial royal residence. Today the town is becoming increasingly popular, with the result that hotel rooms and meals have crept up to Athens rates and above, but it remains by far the most attractive base for exploring the Argolid and resting up for a while by the sea.

Arrival and accommodation

Wedged between the sea and a fortress-topped headland, Náfplio is an easy town to find your way around. Arriving by **bus**, you are set down at one of two adjacent terminals just south of the interlocking squares, **Platía Tríon Navárhon** and **Platía Kapodhistría**, on Singroú. The **train** will deposit you at the junction of Polizoídhou and Irakleous, where a new station has been built, with two old red carriages serving as ticket office and waiting room.

Accommodation

Accommodation in Náfplio is generally overpriced for what you get, though out of season most hotels drop their prices significantly. There are a number of private rooms advertised – and sometimes touted to new arrivals; most cluster on the slope south above the main squares. A few other hotels and rooms, generally the last to fill, are located out on the road to Árgos. There is nowhere to **camp** in Náfplio itself, but southeast on the stretch of coast from Toló (11km from Náfplio) to Iría (26km away), there are a dozen or so campsites (see p.160).

Agamemnon, Aktí Miaoúli 3 (☎0752/28 021). On the waterfront, with an upmarket restaurant and roof garden giving great views. Rates are inclusive of obligatory half-board. ⑥.

Argolis, Árgos 32 (☎0752/27 721). On the left coming from Árgos, just before the turning to the *Youth Hostel*, this modern, comfortable hotel can be noisy at the front. ③.

Discouri, junction of Zygomála and Vyronos (☎0752/28 550). A pleasant hotel, reached via a steep flight of steps. Rooms at the front overlook the old town and the port. ⑤.

Economou, Argonafton 22 (☎0752/23 955). Opposite the *Youth Hostel* and worth the walk from the centre. Recently refurbished; some rooms with private facilities. ②.

Epidauros, Kokkinou 2 (☎0752/27 541). Well-maintained building in the old town. Opposite is a pension owned by the same people, with slightly cheaper rooms. ②–③.

King Othon, Farmakopoúlou 2 (☎0752/27 585). Popular, well-placed hotel, close to the waterfront and Platía Síndagma. In good weather, breakfast is served in the garden. ③.

Leto, Zigomála 28 (☎0752/28 093). Located at the base of the Íts Kalé fortress, but worth the climb, this is a more expensive sister hotel to the *King Othon*. ⑤.

Mariana, Potamianon 9 (☎0752/24 256). From the bus station, walk up Syngroú away from the sea, turn right into Papanikolaou, then take the steps on the left towards the Catholic church. This pension offers a warm welcome and is in a quiet quarter. ②.

Park, Dhervenakion 1, off Platía Khapodhístrias (☎0752/28 093). Large, well-run 1960s hotel which may well have space when the smaller old-town places are full. ④.

Youth Hostel, Argonafton 15 (☎0752/27 754). Situated in the new-town area, this friendly and well-managed hostel is open March–Oct (8–10am & 5–10pm); IYHF card required. ①.

The Town

There's ample pleasure in just wandering about Náfplio: looking around the harbour-front, walking over to the rocky town beach and, when you're feeling energetic, exploring the great twin fortresses of Palamídhi and Íts Kalé on the headland. Náfplio also offers the best restaurants and shops in the eastern Peloponnese, plus a range of useful facilities including car rental and, in summer, hydrofoils down the coast to Monemvassía and to the Argo-Saronic islands.

Palamídhi

The **Palamídhi**, Náfplio's principal fort, was one of the key military flashpoints of the War of Independence. The Greek commander Kolokotronis – of whom there's a majestically bewhiskered statue down in the Platía Kapodhistría – laid siege to the castle for over a year before finally gaining control. After independence, ironically, he was imprisoned in the fortress by the new Greek government; wary of their attempts to curtail his powers, he had kidnapped four members of the parliament.

The most direct approach to the **fortress** (Mon–Fri 8am–4.45pm, Sat & Sun 8.30am–2.45pm, later closing in summer; 400dr) is by a stairway from the end of Polizídhou street, beside a Venetian bastion, though there is also a circuitous road up from the town. On foot, it's a pretty killing climb up 899 stone-hewn steps and, when you reach the summit, you're confronted with a bewilderingly vast complex. Within the outer walls are three self-contained castles, all of them built by the Venetians between 1711 and 1714, which accounts for the appearance of that city's symbol, the Lion of Saint Mark, above the various gateways. The middle fort, San Niccolo, was the one where Kolokotronis was imprisoned; it later became a notorious prison during the civil war.

The fortress takes its name, incidentally, from Náfplio's most famous and most brilliant legendary son, **Palamedes** – the inventor of dice, lighthouses and measuring scales. He was killed by the Greeks at Troy, on charges of treachery trumped up by Odysseus, who regarded himself as the cleverest of the Greeks.

Íts Kalé and Boúrtzi

The **Íts Kalé** ("Inner Castle" in Turkish), to the west of the Palamídhi, occupies the ancient acropolis, whose walls were adapted by three successive medieval restorers – hence the name. The fortifications are today far less complete than those of the Palamídhi, and the most intact section, the lower Torrione castle, has been adapted to house a *Xenia Hotel*. There's little of interest, but the hotel has meant a road has been carved out over the headland, and this brings you down to a small **beach**, overcrowded in season but nevertheless an enjoyable spot to cool off in the shadow of the forts. In the early evening, it is the province of just a few swimmers, though the refreshment kiosks operate only at peak hours and in season.

The town's third fort, the **Boúrtzi**, occupies the islet offshore from the harbour. Built in the fifteenth century, the castle has seen various uses in modern times: from the nineteenth-century home of the town's public executioner to a luxury hotel earlier this century. The late actress and politician, Melina Mercouri, claimed in her autobiography (*I Was Born Greek*) to have consummated her first marriage there.

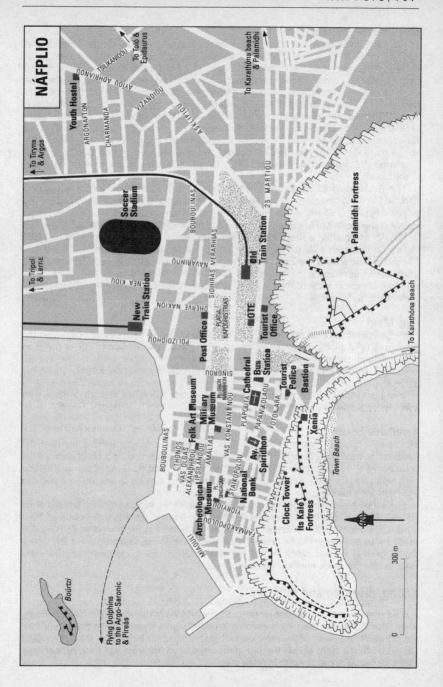

NÁFPLIO

To Tólo &
Epidaurus

To Karathóna beach
& Palamídhi

TSILIKANDOU

AVION ADHRIANOU

Youth Hostel

VIZANDIOU

ARGONAFTON

CHARMANDA

ASKLIPIOU

To Tiryns
& Argos

25 MARTIOU

Soccer
Stadium

BOUBOULINAS

Palamídhi Fortress

To Tripol
& Lárne

NEA KIOU

SIDHRAS VERARHAS

NAVARINOU

DHERVE NAXION

Old
Train Station

New
Train Station

OTE

PLATIA
KAPODHISTRIAS

Tourist
Office

POLIZOIDHOU

To Karathóna beach

Post Office

SINGROU

Bus
Station

Cathedral

PAPANIKOLAOU

Tourist
Police

PL. TRION
NAVARHON

PLAPOUTA

Bastion

Folk Art Museum

FOTOLARA

Military
Museum

VAS KONSTANTINOU

Xenia

AMALIAS

Ay.
Spiridhon

Town Beach

Archaeological Museum

National
Bank

BOUBOULINAS

CTHONOS

VAS OLGAS

ALEXANDHROU IPSILANDOU

PL.
SINDAGMA

STAIKOPOLOU

VDHRAIOU

FARMAKOPOULOU

Clock Tower

Íts Kalé
Fortress

MIAOULI

N

300 m

0

Boúrtzi

Flying Dolphins
to the Argo-Saronic
& Pireás

Mosques and museums

In the town itself, there are a few minor sights, mainly from the town's Turkish past, and two excellent museums. **Platía Síndagma**, the main square of the old town, is the focus of most interest. In the vicinity, three converted **Ottoman mosques** survive: one, in the southeast corner of the square, is an occasional theatre and cinema; another, just off the southwest corner, was the modern Greek state's original **Vouli** (parliament building). A third, fronting nearby Staikopoúlou, has been reconsecrated as the cathedral of **Áyios Yióryios**, having actually started life as a Venetian Catholic church. In the same area are a pair of handsome **Turkish fountains** – one abutting the south wall of the theatre-mosque, the other on Kapodhistría, opposite the church of Áyios Spíridhon. On the steps of the latter, Ioannis Capodistrias was assassinated by two members of the Mavromihalis clan from the Máni in 1831; you can still see a scar left in the stone by one of the bullets.

The **Archeological Museum** (daily except Mon 8.30am–3pm; 400dr) occupies a dignified Venetian mansion on the west side of Síndagma. It has some good collections, as you'd expect in a town at the heart of the Argolid sites, including a unique and more or less complete suit of Mycenaean armour and reconstructed frescoes from Tiryns.

Equally worthwhile is the **Folk Art Museum** (daily except Tues 9am–2.30pm, later closing in summer; closed Feb; 300dr) on Ipsilándhou, just off Sofróni. This won a European "Museum of the Year" award when it was opened in 1981, and features some gorgeous embroideries, costumes and traditional household tools and goods – all presented in the context of their use and production. An adjoining shop sells unusually high-quality handicrafts.

Ayía Moní

More handicrafts are on sale at the convent of **Ayía Moní**, 2km east of Náfplio on the Epidaurus road, just south of the village of Ária. The monastic church, one of the most accomplished Byzantine buildings in the Peloponnese, dates back to the twelfth century. From the outer wall bubbles a nineteenth-century fountain, identified with the ancient spring of Kanthanos, in whose waters the goddess Hera bathed each year to restore her virginity. Modern Greeks similarly esteem the water, though perhaps with less specific miracles in mind.

Karathóna beach

The closest "proper" beach to Náfplio is at Karathóna, a fishing hamlet just over the headland beyond the Palamídhi fortress, which can be reached by a short spur off the drive going up to the ramparts. A more direct road around the base of the intervening cliffs was recently opened, and there's a morning bus service in season – or you can walk it in forty minutes.

The sandy beach stretches for a couple of kilometres, with a summer taverna at its far end. There were plans to develop it during the junta years, when the old road here was built, along with the concrete foundations of a hotel, but the project was suspended in the 1970s and has yet to be revived. At present Karathóna attracts quite a few Greek day-trippers in season, along with a handful of foreigners in camper-vans; there are cafés in summer, plus windsurf boards for rent.

Eating, drinking and nightlife

A good place to start restaurant menu-gazing in Náfplio is the waterside **Bouboulínas**, where the locals take their early evening *volta*, or take a wander down **Staïkopoúlou**, too, off which are many of the most enjoyable tavernas. For **breakfast**, it's hard to beat the *zaharoplastío* right beside the bus station; assorted bakeries and juice bars around Platía Síndagma are also worth investigating.

Nightlife is low key, with a few late-night bars and the occasional seasonal disco on and around Bouboulínas and Singróu. *Sirena*, on the corner of Bouboulínas and Sofróni, has Greek dancing (in summer from 9.30pm). A quieter drink can be had at the **cafés** on Platía Síndagma, which stay open late, too.

Restaurants

Arapakos, Bouboulínas 81. Best value on the waterfront; recently moved from Vassilísis Ólgas. Friendly with excellent cooking and a varied menu. Open until late.

Champagne Restaurant, Papanikólou 32. Authentic French meals served on the terrace in summer. Expensive but worthwhile.

Ellas, Platía Síndagma. One of the best on the square. Service can be slow, but the food (largely traditional dishes) is worth waiting for.

Kakanarakis, Vassilísis Ólgas 18 (☎0752/25 371). In the former *Arapakos* building, a lively place serving a variety of Greek dishes. Open evenings only; arrive early or book ahead.

Noufara, Platía Síndagma. Pizzas go for around 1000dr at this Italian restaurant which also serves Greek dishes.

Zorba, Staikopoúlou 30. Traditional Greek cuisine, with a devoted clientele.

Listings

Banks are concentrated around Platía Síndagma and along Amalías.

Bookshops *Odyssey*, on Platía Síndagma (April–Oct 8am–10pm, Nov–March 8am–2pm), has a good stock of English-language books, newspapers, casettes, CDs and videos.

Car rental Pick from: *Safeway* (☎0752/22 155; including convertibles), Eyíou 2; *Champ* (☎0752/24 930) on Staikopoúlou, just off Platía Síndagma; or *Ikaros* (☎0752/23 594).

Hydrofoils Náfplio is a stop for *Flying Dolphin* hydrofoils from April to September only. Services connect the town with Spétses and the other Argo-Saronic islands, plus Pireás and Monemvassía; some involve a change at Pórto Héli. The ticket office is at Bouboulínas 2.

Moped/motorbike/bicycle rental From *Nikopoulos*, Bouboulínas 49; *Moto Sakis*, Sidhirás Merarhías 15; *Hi-Fly*, 25 Martiou; or *Bourtzi Tours*, next door to the bus station.

Phones The OTE is on 25 Martíou. An easier place to make international phone calls, however, is the souvenir shop on Farmakopoúlou opposite the *Hotel King Othon*.

Post office The main branch (Mon–Fri 7.30am–2pm) is on the northwest corner of Platía Kapodhistría.

Taxis There's a rank on Singroú, opposite the bus station.

Tourist office 25 Martiou 2, opposite OTE; open daily, but unpredictable hours.

Tourist police (☎0752/28 131). On the right at top of Syngróu. Helpful, open daily 7.30am–9pm.

Beaches around Náfplio: Tólo, Kastráki and beyond

Southeast from Náfplio are the fast-growing resorts of **Tólo** and **Kastráki** – popular and established enough to feature in many British holiday brochures. Inevitably, this means that they get packed at the height of the season, although they're still more tranquil than the main island resorts; you can always seek refuge at the more low-key places further along the coast.

Tólo (Tolon)

TÓLO, 11km from Náfplio (hourly buses in season; last back at 8.30pm), is beginning to get rather overdeveloped, with a line of thirty or more hotels and campsites swamping its limited sands. Out of season it can still be quite a pleasant resort, but in summer it is about as un-Greek an experience as you'll find in the Peloponnese. Redeeming features include views of the islets of Platía and Romví on the horizon, and in summer a good range of watersports (windsurfing, waterskiing, paragliding).

Hotels in Tólo tend to be block-booked through the summer but you could try some of the smaller **hotels**, like the *Hotel Artemis* (☎0752/59 458; ④) and *Hotel Tolo* (☎0752/59 248; ⑤). If they're full or beyond your budget, it's usually possible to find **rooms** by asking around or following the signs, but be prepared for inflated prices during the summer. The three **campsites** charge similar rates: try *Sunset* (☎0752/59 556; March–Oct) first; failing that, there's *Lido II* and *Tolo Beach*.

In July and August, there are **hydrofoils** to the Argo-Saronic islands of Ídhra (Hydra) and Spétses.

Kastráki and Ancient Assine

A pleasant alternative to Tólo, especially if you're looking for a campsite, is the longer beach at **KASTRÁKI**, 2km to the east; coming from Náfplio by bus, ask to be let off where the road reaches the sea – it forks right to Tólo and left (500m) to Kastráki, marked on some maps as Paralía Asínis. Here, too, development is underway, but it's a fair bit behind that of Tólo, limited to a scattering of small-scale hotels and campsites. *Camping Kastraki* (☎0752/59 386; April–late Oct) is on the beach, and has windsurfing equipment, pedaloes and canoes for hire.

If you get tired of the water, wander along the beach to the scrub-covered rock by the Náfplio road junction. This is, or was, ancient Assine, an important Mycenaean and Classical city destroyed by the jealous and more powerful Argos in retribution for their having sided with the Spartans against them. There's little to see, other than a 200-metre length of ancient wall, but it's an oddly atmospheric spot.

East to Íria

Further around the coast, to the east of Kastráki, the road runs on to **DHRÉPANO**, a sizeable village with four **campsites**, and a very expensive **hotel**. The best campsite is *Triton* (☎0752/92 228; March–Nov); it's 1200m from the main square of Dhrépano – follow signs to the beach. Beyond Dhrépano, the **Vivári lagoon** has a couple of good fish tavernas on its shore. If you continue this way for another 13km, you reach a turning and poor track down to the beach and the *Poseidon* campsite (☎0752/913 41; May to mid-Oct) at **ÍRIA**.

For the coast south of here, towards Pórto Héli, Ermióni, Galatás and Méthana – each a local port for the Argo-Saronic islands – see p.399–414.

Epidaurus (Epídhavros)

EPIDAURUS is a major Greek site, visited for its stunning **ancient theatre**, built by Polykleitos in the fourth century BC. With its extraordinary acoustics, this has become a very popular venue for the annual Athens Festival productions of **Classical drama** which are staged on Friday and Saturday nights from June through until the last weekend in August. The works are principally those of Sophocles, Euripides and Aeschylus and, given the spectacular setting, they are worth arranging your plans around whether or not you understand the modern Greek in which they're performed.

The theatre, however, is just a component of what was one of the most important sanctuaries in the ancient world, dedicated to the healing god, Asclepius, and a site of pilgrimage for half a millennium, from the sixth century BC into Roman times.

The Ancient Theatre and Asclepion

Daily 8am–7pm (5pm in winter); 1000dr. For festival performances you are admitted to the theatre after 7pm, but not to the rest of the site.

The dedication of the sanctuary at Epidaurus to **Asclepius**, the legendary son of Apollo, probably owes its origin to an early healer from northern Greece who settled in

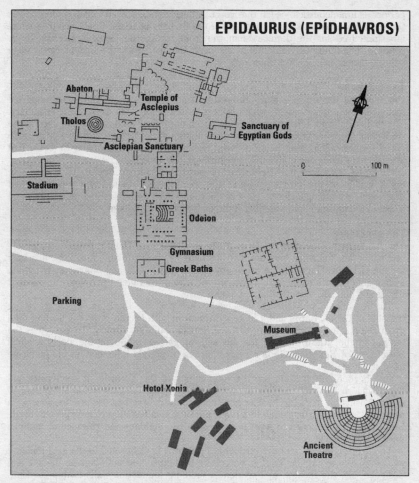

EPIDAURUS (EPÍDHAVROS)

Abaton

Temple of Asclepius

Tholos

Asclepian Sanctuary

Sanctuary of Egyptian Gods

0   100 m

Stadium

Odeion

Gymnasium

Greek Baths

Parking

Museum

Hotel Xenia

Ancient Theatre

the area. There were Asclepian sanctuaries throughout Greece (Athens has ruins of one on the south slope of its Acropolis) and they were sited, rationally enough, along-side natural springs. Epidaurus, along with the island of Kos, was the most famous and inspirational of them all, and probably the richest. The sanctuary was much endowed by wealthy visitors and hosted a quadrennial festival, including drama in the ancient theatre, which followed the Isthmian games. Its heyday was in the fourth and third centuries BC; Rome, when ravaged by an epidemic in 293 BC, sent for the serpent that was kept in the sanctuary.

This aspect of the site, however, along with most of the associated Asclepian ruins, is incidental for most visitors. Epidaurus's **Ancient Theatre** is a sight – not a ruin or anecdote – par excellence. With its backdrop of rolling hills, this 14,000-seat arena merges perfectly into the landscape, so well in fact that it was rediscovered and unearthed only last century. Constructed with mathematical precision, it has an extraordinary equilibrium and, as guides on the stage are forever demonstrating, near-perfect natural acoustics – such that you can hear coins, or even matches, dropped in the circular *orchestra* from the highest of the 54 tiers of seats. Constructed in white limestone (red for the dignitaries in the front rows), the tiered seats have been repaired, but otherwise restoration has been minimal, with the beaten earth stage being retained, as in ancient times.

The museum

Close by the theatre is a small **museum** (8am–7pm, 5pm in winter; entrance fee included in site ticket price), which is best visited before you explore the sanctuary. The finds displayed here show the progression of medical skills and cures used at the Asclepion; there are tablets recording miraculous and outrageous cures – like the man cured from paralysis after being ordered to heave the biggest boulder he could find into the sea – alongside quite advanced surgical instruments.

In 86 BC, by which time Epidaurus's reputation was in decline, the Roman consul Sulla, leader of the forces invading the Peloponnese, looted the sanctuary and destroyed its buildings. Hence, most of the ruins visible today are just foundations and a visit to the museum helps identify some of the former buildings.

The sanctuary

The **Asclepian Sanctuary**, as large a site as Olympia or Delphi, holds considerable fascination, for the ruins here are all of buildings with identifiable functions: hospitals for the sick, dwellings for the priest-physicians, and hotels and amusements for the fashionable visitors to the spa. Their setting, a wooded valley thick with the scent of thyme and pine, is evidently that of a health farm.

The reasonably well-labelled **site** begins just past the museum, where there are remains of **Greek baths** and a huge **gymnasium** with scores of rooms leading off a great colonnaded court; in its centre the Romans built an **odeion**. To the left is the outline of the **stadium** used for the ancient games, while to the right, a small **Sanctuary of Egyptian Gods** reveals a strong presumed influence on the medicine used at the site.

Just beyond the stadium are the foundations of the **Temple of Asclepius** and beside it a rectangular building known as the **Abaton**. Patients would sleep here to await a visitation from the healing god, commonly believed to assume the form of a serpent. He probably appeared in a more physical manifestation than expected; harmless snakes are believed to have been kept in the building and released at night to bestow a curative lick.

The deep significance of the serpent at Epidaurus is elaborated in the next building you come to: the circular **Tholos**, one of the best-preserved buildings on the site and designed, like the theatre, by Polykleitos. Its inner foundation walls form a labyrinth which is thought to have been used as a snakepit and, according to one theory, to administer a primitive form of shock therapy to the mentally ill. The afflicted would crawl in darkness through the outer circuit of the maze, guided by a crack of light towards the middle, where they would find themselves surrounded by writhing snakes. Presumably, on occasions, it worked. Another theory is that the labyrinth was used as an initiation chamber for the priests of Asclepius, who underwent a symbolic death and rebirth in it.

Practicalities

Most people take in Epidaurus as a day trip, though there's a **hotel** at the site, the unattractive and expensive *Xenia* (☎0753/22 003; June–Sept; ⑤). There are better and more modestly priced hotels on the way to and in nearby **LIGOÚRIO** village, 5km northwest of the site. Possibilities here include the *Hotel Alkion* (☎0753/22 552; ②) at the

Tickets for the plays are available at the site on the day of performance, or in advance in Athens (at the festival box office) or Náfplio (from *Bourtzi Tours* or *Olympic Airways* at Boubouĺinas 2). In Athens you can buy all-inclusive tickets for performances and return bus travel. There are also special evening buses from the site to Náfplio after the show. English translations of the plays are available at the site and at the *Odyssey* bookshop in Náfplio. Normally there are six buses **daily** from Náfplio to the site; they are marked "Theatre", "Asklipion" or "Epidhavros" and shouldn't be confused with those to the modern villages of Néa or Paleá Epídhavros (see below).

turning off the main road to the village, or *Hotel Koronis* (☎0753/22 267; ②) in the village itself; both are open all year. Alternatively, it's possible to **camp** in the grass car park on days of performances, though you must wait until an hour after the play's end before setting up a tent. Beachside accommodation is available at Paléa Epídhavros, 15km northeast (see below).

For meals, the nearest **restaurant** to the site is the *Oasis* on the Ligoúrio road. Much better is *Taverna Leonides* (☎0752/22 115), in the village proper, a friendly spot with a garden out the back; you'd be wise to book ahead if your visit coincides with a performance at the ancient theatre. Actors eat here after shows, and photos on the wall testify to the patronage of the likes of Melina Mercouri, the Papandreous, François Mitterrand and Peter Hall.

Paleá Epídhavros

The closest beach resort to Epidaurus is **Paleá Epídhavros**, which has mushroomed since the recent improvement of the direct coast road from Kórinthos. Facing the beach, there are at least a dozen **hotels**, as many purpose-built **rooms**, and four **campsites**, all very popular with festival patrons in season. If you want to book ahead, three hotels to try are the *Christina* (☎0753/41 451; ④), *Epidavria* (☎0753/41 222; ②) and *Paola Beach* (☎0753/41 397; ④); all these close over winter. Three of the four campsites are on the beach to the south of the village in the district known as Yialassi: they are *Verdelis* (☎0753/41 425; March–late Oct), *Bekas* (☎0753/41 714; late March to mid-Oct) and *Nicholas II* (☎0753/41 445; April to mid-Oct).

The Saronic ports: Méthana to Porto Héli

The roads across and around the southern tip of the Argolid are sensational scenic rides, but the handful of resorts here are lacking in character and generally overdeveloped. With a car, you can pick your beaches and take a leisurely route back to Náfplio, perhaps exploring the site of **Ancient Troezen** and the **Limonódhassos** lemon groves. Otherwise, you'll probably travel this way only if heading for one of the **Argo-Saronic islands**: **Méthana** has local connections to Éyina (Aegina); **Galatás** to Póros; **Ermióni** to Ídhra (Hydra) and Spétses; **Kósta** and **Pórto Héli** to Spétses.

Méthana and Ancient Troezen

It's a sixty-kilometre drive from Epidaurus to **MÉTHANA**, the last section along a cliff-hugging corniche road. Set on its own peninsula, Méthana is a disappointing spa-town, whose devotees are apparently attracted by foul-smelling sulphur springs. Of its half-dozen hotels, the most pleasant is the seafront *Avra* (☎0298/92 382; ④).

Close by the village of Trizína, just south and inland of the turning to the Méthana peninsula, are the ruins of ancient **TROEZEN**, the legendary birthplace of Theseus and location of his domestic dramas. The root of his problems was Aphrodite, who, having been rejected by Theseus's virgin son Hippolytus, contrived to make Phaedra – Theseus's then wife – fall in love with the boy (her stepson). She, too, was rejected and responded by accusing Hippolytus of attempted rape. He promptly fled. After he was killed when his horses took fright at a sea monster, Phaedra confessed her guilt and committed suicide. Originally told by Euripides (and later reworked by Racine), a full account of the tragedy, together with a map of the remains, is on sale for 300dr in the modern village. For the romantic, there's always Theseus's autobiography in Mary Renault's *The King Must Die*, which starts, "The Citadel of Troizen, where the palace stands, was built by giants before anyone remembers. But the Palace was built by my great-grandfather. At sunrise…the columns glow fire-red and the walls are golden. It shines bright against the dark woods on the mountainside."

Such **remains** as exist of the ancient town are spread over a wide site. Most conspicuous are three ruined Byzantine chapels, constructed of ancient blocks, and a structure known as the **Tower of Theseus**, whose lower half is third century BC and top half is medieval. This stands at the lower end of a gorge, the course of an ancient **aqueduct**, which you can follow in a half an hour's walk up a bulldozer track to the **Yéfira tou Dhiavólou** (Devil's Bridge), a natural rock formation spanning a chasm; a rare black butterfly is said to be endemic to the ravine.

Galatás and Limonódhassos

GALATÁS lies only 350m across the water from the island of Póros, with which it is connected by skiffs, sailing more or less continuously in the summer months. The town has a cluster of **hotels**, of which the best value is the *Saronis* (☎0298/22 356; ④), and **rooms** for rent, plus a handy **bike rental** place, *Fotis Bikes*. The village is connected by a daily bus with Epidaurus and Náfplio.

On the coast road to the south, there are the beaches of **Pláka** (2km) and **Alíki** (4km); just back from the latter, a path, signposted "Restaurant Cardassi", leads into the **Limonódhassos** – a vast, irrigated lemon grove. Though one travel brochure says there are 300,000 lemon trees here, the consensus tallies about 30,000, not that it matters much as you pick your way along the various paths that meander through them, all heading upwards to an inspiringly positioned **taverna**, where a charming old man serves fresh lemonade as you sit on the terrace. Henry Miller recounts a visit here in *Colossus of Maroussi*, hyperbolizing that "in the spring young and old go mad from the fragrance of sap and blossom".

Ermióni, Kósta and Pórto Héli

Continuing clockwise around the coast from Galatás, you follow a narrow, modern road, cut from the mountainside to open up additional resorts close to Athens. Plépi (or Hydra Beach) is a villa-urbanization, visited by boats from beachless Ídhra opposite. **ERMIÓNI** (ancient Hermione) is better: a real village, enclosed by a rocky bay and saved from development perhaps by lack of a sandy beach. It has three modest **hotels**: the *Akti* (☎0754/31 241; ②), the *Olympion* (☎0754/31 214; ②) and the *Nadia* (☎0754/31 706; ③); the owner of the *Nadia* also runs the *Ganossis* apartments (☎0754/31 218; ④–⑤). *Aris Skouris*, on the seafront south of the harbour, has bikes and mopeds for rent.

Further round, **KÓSTA** and **PÓRTO HÉLI**, on either side of a bay, are purpose-built resorts that have swallowed up their original hamlets and are slowly merging into each other. Both feature a rather soulless mix of package-tour hotels and facilities for yachters exploring the Argo-Saronic islands.

The circuitous **route back to Náfplio** from Pórto Héli runs inland, via attractive Kranídhi, scrambling its way up through the mountains. It is covered four times daily by a bus, which usually dovetails in Pórto Héli with ferries and hydrofoils to and from Spétses and elsewhere; in low season, however, you may have to change buses in Kranídhi.

The east coast: Náfplio to Leonídhi

The **coastline between Náfplio and Leonídhi** is mountainous terrain, increasingly so as you move south towards Monemvassía where the few villages seem carved out from their dramatic backdrop. Considering its proximity to Náfplio – and Athens – the whole stretch is remarkably unexploited, remaining more popular with Greek holiday-makers than with foreign tourists, and enjoyably low key.

Getting to the beaches – **Parália Ástros**, **Áyios Andréas**, **Parália Tiroú** and **Pláka** – is perhaps best done by car, though there are also **buses** twice daily from Árgos to Leonídhi, while **Pláka** (the port/beach of Leonídhi) is served by the *Flying Dolphin* **hydrofoils** en route from Spétses/Pórto Héli to Monemvassía. However you travel, change money in advance, as there are few banks between Náfplio and Leonídhi.

Right at the beginning of the route, around the coast from Náfplio, the minor site of **Ancient Lerna** makes an interesting halt. If you are travelling by train from Árgos to Trípoli, you could stop off at the station of Míli, only 500m from the site; alternatively, a trip there makes a nice ride around the coast if you rent a bike in Náfplio.

Ancient Lerna

The site of ancient **LERNA** (daily except Mon 8.30am–3pm; 400dr) lies 10km south of Árgos and 12km from Náfplio by the minor road around the coast via Néa Kíos. The nearest village is Míli, at the foot of Mount Pontinus, where buses between Trípoli and Kórinthos break their journey at a group of *souvláki* stands, open virtually 24 hours. Just beyond the straggle of the village a narrow, poorly signposted lane leads to the prehistoric site, which now lies between the main road and the railway; surrounded by an orange grove and close to the sea, it makes a fine picnic spot. The warden, unused to visitors, may volunteer to show you around this important Bronze Age settlement. Excavations carried out in the 1950s unearthed ruins of an early **Neolithic house**, and a well-preserved **fortification wall**, revealing it as one of the most ancient of Greek sites, inhabited from as early as 4000 BC.

Another large house at the north end of the site is thought to have been an early palace, but was superseded, in about 2200 BC, by a much larger and more important structure known as the **House of the Tiles**. Measuring approximately 24m by 9m, this dwelling, labelled as another palace, takes its name from the numerous terracotta roof tiles found inside, where they are thought to have fallen when either lightning or enemy raiders set the building ablaze in approximately 2100 BC. The house represents the earliest known instance of the use of terracotta as a building material, and is the most impressive pre-Helladic structure to have been unearthed on the Greek mainland. A symmetrical ground plan of small rooms surrounding larger interior ones is today protected by a huge canopy, with stairs mounting to a now-vanished second storey. The substantial walls, made of sun-dried brick on stone foundations, were originally covered with plaster. Even after its destruction, this palace may have retained some ritual significance, since two Mycenaean **shaft graves** were sunk into the ruins in around 1600 BC, and the site was not completely abandoned until the end of the Mycenaean period.

As implied by the chronology, the founders and early inhabitants of Lerna were not Greeks. Certain similarities in sculpture and architecture with contemporary Anatolia suggest an Asiatic origin but this has yet to be proved conclusively. Excavated finds, however, demonstrate that the Lerneans traded across the Aegean and well up into the Balkan peninsula, cultivated all the staple crops still found in the Argolid, and raised livestock, as much for wool and hides as for food. Elegant terracotta sauce tureens and "teaspoons", which may be seen in the Árgos archeological museum (see p.153), hint at a sophisticated cuisine.

According to myth, Hercules performed the second of his labours, the slaying of the nine-headed Hydra, at Lerna. And, as if in corroboration of the legend, the nearby swamps are still swarming with eels.

Along the coast to Ástros and Paralía Tiróu

The initial section of coast from Lerna to Ástros and Áyios Andhréas is low-lying: less spectacular than the sections further south, but pleasant enough. The first village of any size is **PARALÍA ÁSTROS**, whose houses are tiered against a headland shared by a medieval fort and the ruins of an ancient acropolis. Back from the sand and gravel beach, which extends for 6km south of the fishing harbour, there are half a dozen tavernas, some **rooms** to let, a couple of **hotels** – the *Chrissi Akti* (☎0755/51 294; ③) and the *Hotel Crystal* (☎0755/51 313; ④) – and the lively *Thirea* **campsite** (☎0755/51 002; mid-March to mid-Nov).

Just to the south, a trio of surprisingly neat and compact villages, Ástros, Korakavóuni and Áyios Andhréas, perch on the foothills of **Mount Párnon** as it drops to meet the lush, olive-green plain. A little beyond Áyios Andhréas (10km from Ástros), the road curls down to the coast and the first in a series of fine-pebbled swimming coves, crammed between the massive spurs of Párnon. There are seasonal **rooms** at several of the coves, plus the *Arcadia* **campsite** (☎ 0755/31 190; May–Oct) on the main road, 6km beyond Áyios Andréas; popular with middle-aged Greeks, the site has a friendly but noisy atmosphere, particularly at weekends. Few concessions are made to tourists along this stretch of coast, apart from the occasional makeshift taverna; out of season, you'll definitely need your own supplies.

PARALÍA TIROÚ is a fair-sized town and a reasonably popular resort, mostly with older Greeks; the younger Greeks tend to go further south along the coast, to Pláka. The place feels quite sedate, with comfortable, mid-range hotels and cafés spread back from its long pebble beach. **Accommodation** options include the *Hotel Apollon* (☎0757/41 268; ③), the *Hotel Kamuyssis* (☎0757/41 424; ④), the *Hotel Galazia Thelassa* (also known as the *Blue Sea*; ☎0757/41 369; ④), and the well-equipped campsite, *Zaritsi* (☎0757/41 429; April to mid-Oct), on the coast north of Paralía Tiroú.

Leonídhi, Pláka and south towards Monemvassía

Gigantic red cliffs that wouldn't look out of place in deserts of the American Southwest confine **LEONÍDHI**, the terminus of the Árgos bus route. Set inland, with good agricultural land stretching down to the sea, this prosperous and traditional market town sees little need to pander to tourists. Most in any case end up down by the sea at Leonídhi's diminutive port, Pláka. If you prefer to stay here, you might find space in the town's one modest **hotel**, the *Alexaki* (also known as the *Neon*; ☎0757/22 383; ②), or the few advertised **rooms for rent** (☎0757/22 505 or 22 872; ②). There are some enjoyable, small town tavernas.

Pláka to Yérakas

PLÁKA, 4km away, is a tiny place consisting of a harbour, a couple of **hotels** and **eating places**. It also has a fine pebble beach, which in recent years has become pretty popular with Greek and European tourists, plus a sporadic influx of yachties. In summer, it would be wise to phone ahead to reserve a balconied room with sea view in the first-choice *Hotel Dionysos* (☎0757/22 379; ③), run by the Bekeros family, who also own the taverna opposite. There are excellent meals to be had on the beach, too, at the taverna twenty minutes' walk to the north along the bay, across the river bed (dry in summer).

The hamlet of **POÚLITHRES**, 3km south of Pláka around the bay, marks the end of the coast road – which deteriorates to a track as it heads inland. There is a taverna, with a terrace, close by the narrow strip of beach, a **hotel**, the *Kentauros* (☎0757/51 214; ④), favoured by groups, and a large rooms place by the waterfront.

South of Leonídhi the coastline is wilder and sparsely inhabited, with just a couple of coastal settlements cut into the cliffs. To reach the two little settlements – **KIPARÍSSI** and **YÉRAKAS** – you are better off taking the *Flying Dolphin* hydrofoil, which stops at both on the way to Monemvassía. By road, it's a very roundabout route (though in better shape than it looks on the map) from Molái, on the Spárti–Monemvassía road.

Inland from Leonídhi

The route **inland from Leonídhi** is worth taking for its own sake, climbing over a spur of **Mount Párnon**, past the **monastery of Elónis** and the high mountain village of **Kosmás** – quite a temperature shock in the height of summer. It is a decent road for cars, and brings you out at the minor Byzantine site of **Yeráki** (aka Pírgos Yerakíou; see p.180); from there, you have a choice of roads – to Spárti and Yíthio (Githion) via Skála and Monemvassía, via Molái.

Without a car, you'll have to plan very carefully: a daily **bus** runs from Leonídhi to Yeráki, and goes on to Spárti twice a week – currently on Tuesday afternoons and Saturday mornings, but check first.

Moní Elónis

Visible from Leonídhi, the **Moní Elónis** stands out as a white slash in the mountainside – though as you twist around Mount Párnon, and up a ravine, it drops away from view. The turn-off to the monastery (visitors permitted from sunrise to sunset) in fact comes 13km from Leonídhi, via an approach road which ends at a seemingly impregnable gateway; if all looks closed, pull the wire, which passes along the cliff to a large bell. Once admitted, you can wander down to a small chapel crammed with icons and lanterns and to a spring, whose icy-cold water has supposedly curative powers. Most of the monastery, originally founded in medieval times following the appearance of a miraculous and inaccessible icon, was rebuilt following the War of Independence. Today, it is maintained by four nuns, who sell a classic little history (in Greek only) of the monastery's legends and vicissitudes.

Kosmás

Continuing south, past the Elónis turning, you reach **KOSMÁS**, a handsome village set about a grand *platía*, with rooms and a couple of tavernas. Straddling the most important pass of Párnon, at nearly 1200m, it can be a chilly place during the spring or winter, but beautiful, too, with its streams, cherry and walnut trees, and fir forests all around.

Beyond the village the road runs through an uninhabited valley, then lurches slowly down to the village and Byzantine ruins of Yeráki (see p.180).

Trípoli: the crossroads

Trípoli is a major crossroads of the Peloponnese, from where most travellers either head **north** through Arcadia towards Olympia, or **south** to Spárti and Mystra or Kalamáta (see below). To the **east**, a recently improved road, looping around Mount Ktenías, connects Trípoli with Árgos and Náfplio, via Lerna. To the **west**, you can reach the coast on a reasonably fast road to Kiparissía, via the evocative, scattered ruins of Ancient Megalopolis. To the **northeast**, a new fast highway links Trípoli with Kórinthos and Athens.

The Peloponnese **railway** also passes through Trípoli, continuing its meandering course from Kórinthos and Árgos to Kiparissía and Kalamáta. Those with passes might be tempted to use the train to Trípoli and then take a bus to Spárti, but it's not a good idea, as Árgos–Spárti buses are not sheduled to meet trains in Trípoli and furthermore they often pass through full; better to take a direct bus (seven daily from Athens to Spárti, via Árgos and Trípoli), or approach Spárti more enjoyably via the hydrofoil to Monemvassía.

The Town

The Arcadian capital doesn't live up to expectations: **TRÍPOLI** is a large, modern town, and home to one of the country's biggest army barracks. It doesn't exactly bombard you with its charm and has few obvious attractions, although the **Archeological Museum** (daily except Mon 8.30am–3pm; 400dr), signposted off Vassiléos Yioryíou and housed in a Neoclassical building with a beautiful rose garden, makes a pleasant diversion. Medieval *Tripolitsa* was destroyed by retreating Turkish forces during the War of Independence, the Greek forces, led by Kolokotronis, having earlier massacred the town's population. Trípoli's ancient predecessors, the rival towns of Mantinea to the north and Tegea to the south, are the only local points of interest.

Getting in and out of the town can be fairly complicated. The major **bus terminal**, serving all destinations in Arcadia and the northern Peloponnese, is on Platía Kolokotróni, one of the three main squares. Services to Pátra, Messinía, Kalamáta, the outer Máni, Pílos and Spárti leave from the "milk" shop directly opposite the train station, at the southeastern edge of town.

If you need to spend a night here, there are four reliable **hotels**: the *Arcadia* (☎071/ 225 551; ⑤), on Platía Koloktróni; the *Alex*, Vassiléos Yioryíou 26 (☎071/223 465; ③); the *Menalon* (☎ 071/222 450; ④), on Platía Áreos; and the *Artemis* (☎071/225 221; ④), Dimitrakopoulóu 1. Cheaper **rooms** are advertised on Lambráki on the way into town from the train station.

Ancient Mantinea

Ancient **MANTINEA**, known to Homer as "pleasant Mantinea", was throughout its history a bitter rival of nearby Tegea, invariably forming an alliance with Athens when Tegea stood with Sparta, then switching allegiance to Sparta when Tegea allied with Thebes. Its site stands 15km north of Trípoli and is served by hourly buses from Platía Kolokotróni in Trípoli, between the road to Dhimitsána/Pátra and the new Kórinthos–Trípoli highway. It is unenclosed, the principal remains being a circuit of fourth-century BC **walls**, still more or less intact, though much reduced in height, and a few tiers of its theatre.

Alongside the site, however, is one of the most bizarre sights in Greece: a modern **church** constructed in an eccentric pastiche of Byzantine and Egyptian styles. Put together in the 1970s by a Greek-American architect, it is dedicated to "The Virgin, the Muses and Beethoven".

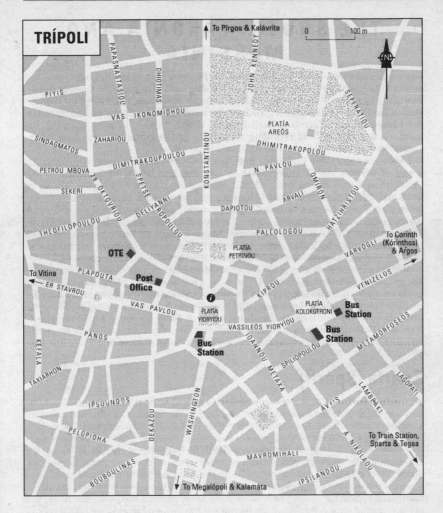

Ancient Tegea

Ancient **TEGEA**, 8km south of Trípoli, was the main city of the central Peloponnese in Classical and Roman times, and, refounded in the tenth century, was an important town again under the Byzantines. The diffuse and partially excavated site lies just outside the village of Aléa (modern Tegea), on the Spárti road. Local buses from Trípoli stop in the village beside a small **museum** (daily except Mon 8.30am–3pm; 400dr), well stocked with sculptures from the site. Take the road to the left as you leave, which leads in 100m to the main remains, the **Temple of Athena Alea**, in whose sanctuary two kings of Sparta once took refuge. Keeping on the road past the site, it's a twenty-minute walk to the village of Paleá Episkopí, whose church – a huge modern pilgrim shrine – incorporates part of ancient Tegea's theatre and a number of Byzantine mosaics.

THE SOUTH: LAKONÍA AND MESSINÍA

Draw a line on a map from Kalamáta over the Taíyettos mountains, through Spárti and across to Leonídhi. Broadly, everything below this line is **Lakonía**, the ancient territories of the Spartans. It's a dramatic country of harsh mountains and, except for the lush strip of the Evrótas valley, of poor, rocky soil – terrain that has kept it isolated throughout history. **Mount Taíyettos** itself is a formidable barrier, looming ahead if you approach from Trípoli, and providing an exciting exit or entrance in the form of the Langádha Pass between Spárti and Kalamáta.

Landscapes apart, the highlights here are the extraordinarily preserved Byzantine towns of **Mystra** and **Monemvassía** – both essential visits for any tour of the Peloponnese – and the remote and arid **Máni** peninsula, with its bizarre history of feuds and unique tower houses and churches with barrel roofs. Monemvassía is a regular stop for *Flying Dolphin* hydrofoils (plus a weekly boat) from Pireás and the Argo-Saronic islands and would make a superb entry point to the peninsula. In summer, the Maniot port of **Yíthio** (Gythion) and tiny **Neápoli**, south of Monemvassía, are additional stops on the hydrofoil and provide the easiest links to **Kíthira**, technically an Ionian island but covered – due to its Peloponnesian access – in this section.

Moving west across the region, you enter **Messinía**, with its mellower countryside and gorgeous, little-developed coast. There are good beaches at Messinía's own duo of medieval sites – the twin fortresses of **Koróni** and **Methóni** – but if you are looking for sands to yourself in the Peloponnese, and you're unperturbed by a lack of facilities, you could do no better than explore the **shore north of Pílos**. En route are the remains of **Nestor's Palace**, foundations only, but the most important ancient site in the south and, like Mycenae, keying remarkably well with the Homeric legend.

Sparta (Spárti)

Thucydides predicted that if the city of Sparta were deserted, "distant ages would be very unwilling to believe its power at all equal to its fame". The city had no great temples or public buildings and throughout its period of greatness remained unfortified: Lycurgus, architect of the Spartan constitution, declared that "it is men not walls that make a city". Consequently, modern **SPÁRTI**, laid out grid-style in 1834, has few ancient ruins to speak of, and is today a rather gritty market and agricultural town. Spárti's appeal is in its ordinariness – in its pedestrianized side streets, its café-lined squares, orange trees and evening *volta* – but it isn't the most rewarding of Greek towns. The reason for coming here is basically to see **Mystra**, the Byzantine town 5km to the east, that once controlled great swathes of the medieval world (see p.173).

Ancient Sparta

Descending from the mountains that ring Spárti on all side, you get a sense of how strategic was the location of the ancient city-state of **SPARTA**. The ancient "capital" occupied more or less the site of today's town, though it was in fact less a city than a grouping of villages, commanding the Laconian plain and fertile Evrótas valley from a series of low hills to the east of the river.

The Greek city was at the height of its powers from the eighth to the fourth century BC, the period when Sparta structured its society according to the laws of **Lycurgus**, defeated Athens in the Peloponnesian War, established colonies around the Greek world, and eventually lost hegemony through defeat to Thebes. A second period of

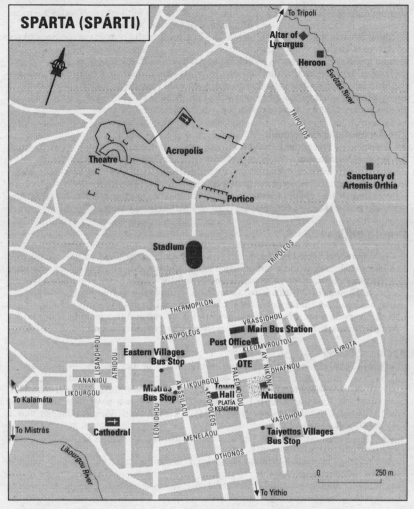

SPARTA (SPÁRTI)

To Tripoli

Altar of Lycurgus

Heroon

Evrótas River

Acropolis

Theatre

TRIPOLEOS

Portico

Sanctuary of Artemis Orthia

Stadium

TRIPOLEOS

THERMOPILON

VRASSIDHOU

AKROPOLEUS

Main Bus Station

Post Office

KLEOMVROUTOU

OTE

AY. NIKONE

EVROTA

LISANDHROU

ATRIDOU

Eastern Villages Bus Stop

DHAFNOU

ANANIOU

LIKOURGOU

Town Hall

Museum

To Kalamáta

Mistrás Bus Stop

ASSILAOU

PALEOLOGOU

AKROPOLEOS

VASIDHOU

PLATÍA KENDRIKI

LEON DHOU

To Mistrás

Cathedral

MENELÁOU

Taiyettos Villages Bus Stop

OTHONOS

Likourgou River

0   250 m

To Yíthio

prosperity came under the Romans – for whom this was an outpost in the south of Greece, with the Máni never properly subdued – though from the third century AD Sparta declined as nearby Mystra became the focus of Byzantine interest.

The sites

Traces of ancient Spartan glory are in short supply, but there are some ruins to be seen to the north of the city: follow the track behind the football stadium towards the old **Acropolis**, tallest of the Spartan hills. An immense **Theatre** here, built into the side of the hill, can be quite clearly traced, even though today most of its masonry has gone – hurriedly adapted for fortification when the Spartans' power declined and, later still, used in the building of the Byzantine city of Mystra. Above the theatre, to the left, are the foundations of a **Temple to Athena**, while at the top of the acropolis sits the more substantial Byzantine church and **Monastery of Óssios Nikónas**.

About 500m along the Trípoli road, a path descends to the remains of the **Sanctuary of Artemis Orthia**, where Spartan boys underwent endurance tests by flogging. The Roman geographer and travel writer Pausanias records that young men often expired under the lash, adding that the altar had to be splashed with blood before the goddess was satisfied. Perhaps it was the promise of such a gory spectacle that led the Romans to revive the custom: the main ruins here are of the grandstand they built. Neither of these sites is enclosed, and you can explore them along pleasant walkways.

The Archeological Museum

All movable artifacts and mosaics have been transferred to the town's small **Archeological Museum** (daily except Mon 8.30am–2.30pm; 400dr). Among its more interesting exhibits are a number of votive offerings found on the sanctuary site – knives set in stone that were presented as prizes to the Spartan youths and solemnly rededicated to the goddess – and a marble bust of a Spartan hoplite, found on the acropolis and said to be Leonidas, the hero of Thermopylae (see p.263).

Practicalities

If it is Mystra that brings you here, and you arrive early in the day, you may well decide to move straight on. Getting out of Spárti is straightforward. The **main bus terminal** (for Trípoli, Athens, Monemvassía, Kalamáta and the Máni) is on Vrassídhou, just off Stadhíou. **Buses for Mystra** leave (hourly on weekdays; less frequently at lunchtime and at weekends) from the corner of the main streets Likoúrgou and Ayissiláou; schedules are posted on the window of the café there. To reach Áyios Ioánnis, trailhead for hikes up **Mount Taíyettos**, you'll need to take a bus from Meneláou, east of Stadhíou.

Accommodation

There are usually enough **hotels** to go around, many of them on the main avenue of Paleológou. **Camping** is available at two sites out along the Mystra road; both can be reached via the Mystra bus, which will stop by the sites on request. The nearest, 2.5km from Spárti, is *Camping Mystra* (☎0731/22 724) which has a swimming pool and is open year-round. Two kilometres closer to Mystra is the *Castle View* (☎0731/93 303), a very clean, well-managed site.

Apollo, Thermopílon 84, corner of Tripoléos (☎0731/22 491). A graceless but functional hotel; breakfast costs extra. ③.

Cecil, Paleológou 125, corner of Thermopílon (☎0731/24 980). Small and old, but cosy – and good value. Private bathrooms available. ②.

Lida, corner of AtridoU and Ananíou (☎0731/23 601). The most expensive place in town, with all mod cons, including a restaurants and parking. ⑥.

ROOM PRICE SCALES

All the accommodation prices in this book have been coded using the symbols below below. The rates quoted represent the cheapest available room in high season; all are prices for a double room, except for category ①, which are per person rates.

① 1400–2000dr (£4–5.50/US$6–8.50)	④ 8000–12000dr (£22–33/US$33–50)
② 4000–6000dr (£11–16.50/US$17–25)	⑤ 12000–16000dr (£33–44/US$50–66)
③ 6000–8000dr (£16.50–22/US$25–33)	⑥ 16000dr (£44/US$66) and upwards

For more accommodation details, see pp.34–35.

Maniatis, Paleológou 72, corner of Likoúrgou (☎0731/22 665). Modern and ugly, but with good facilities at a reasonable price. ④.

Menelaion, Paleológou 91 (☎0731/22 161). A modernized turn-of-the-century hotel, functional but charmless. Rooms at the front are best avoided due to their proximity to the all-night taxi rank outside. ⑤.

Sparta Inn, Thermopílon 105, corner of Akropoleos (0731/25 021). Modern and better-looking than average; first choice if you want a roof-garden and two swimming pools. ④.

Eating and drinking

There is a wide choice for meals, with most restaurants and tavernas concentrated on the main street of Paleológou – including a nameless *psistaria* at no.124.

Averof, Paleológou 77. A long-established and reasonably priced taverna with tasty Greek home-cooking; outdoor tables in summer.

Diethnou, Paleológou 105. Self-service restaurant with an international flavour. Interior lacks atmosphere, but a delightful garden with orange and lemon trees compensates.

Dionysos, Meneláou 79 (☎0731/25 050). Out on the road towards Mystra, this restaurant offers more expensive dishes, but they're served with style – outdoors on a summer's evening.

Elysse, Paleológou 113. Run by French-Canadians, this place has a continental look and menu; good char-grilled meat dishes.

Lambrou, Paleológou 82. On the corner of Kleomvroutou, this is another traditional Greek place; open lunchtimes only.

Semiramis, Paleológou 58. Taverna, tucked away in the basement, with a traditional Greek menu; the house speciality is roast pork with eggplant.

Mystra (Mistrás)

A glorious, airy place, hugging a steep flank of Taíyettos, **Mystra** is arguably the most exciting and dramatic site that the Peloponnese can offer. Winding up the hillside is an astonishingly complete Byzantine city that once sheltered a population of some 42,000, and through which you can now wander. Winding alleys lead through monumental gates, past medieval houses and palaces and above all into a sequence of churches, several of which yield superb and radiant frescoes. The effect is of straying into a massive museum of architecture, painting and sculpture – and into a different age.

There are few facilities at the site itself, so you'll need to base yourself at either Spartí (see above) or the modern settlement of Néos Mistrás (see p.178).

Some history

Mystra was basically a Frankish creation. In 1249, Guillaume II de Villehardouin, fourth Frankish Prince of the Morea, built a castle here – one of a trio of fortresses (the others were at Monemvassía and in the Máni) designed to garrison his domain. The Franks, however, were driven out of Mystra by the Byzantines in 1271, and this isolated triangle of land in the southeastern Peloponnese, encompassing the old Spartan territories, became the **Despotate of Mystra**. This was the last province of the Greek Byzantine Empire and for years, with Constantinople in terminal decay, was its virtual capital.

During the next two centuries, Mystra was the focus of a defiant rebirth of Byzantine power. The Despotate's rulers – usually the son or brother of the eastern emperor, often the heir-apparent – recaptured and controlled much of the Peloponnese, which became the largest of the ever-shrinking Byzantine provinces. They and their province were to endure for two centuries before eventual subjugation by the Turks. The end came in 1460, seven years after the fall of Constantinople, when the despot Demetrius, feuding with his brothers, handed the city over to the Sultan Mehmet II.

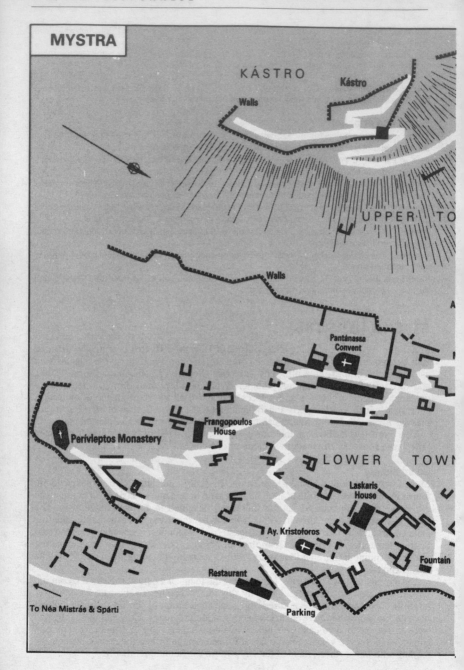

MYSTRA

KÁSTRO

Kástro

Walls

UPPER TO

Walls

Pantánassa
Convent

A

Frangopoulos
House

Perívleptos Monastery

LOWER TOWN

Laskaris
House

Ay. Kristoforos

Fountain

Restaurant

To Néa Mistrás & Spárti

Parking

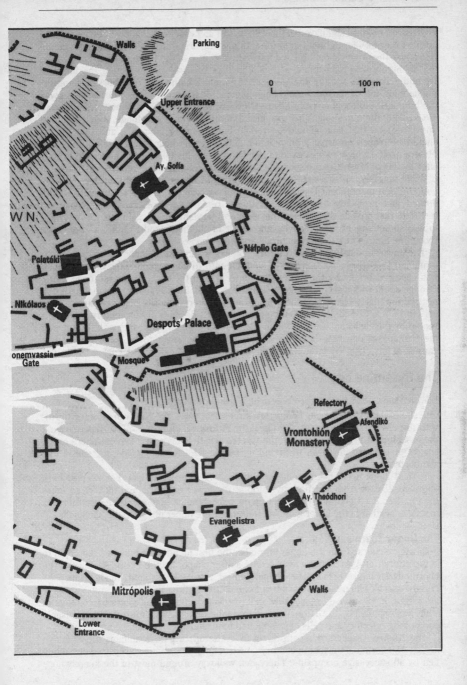

Walls
Parking
Upper Entrance
Ay. Sofía
N
Náfplio Gate
Palatáki
. Nikólaos
Despots' Palace
onemvassía Gate
Mosque
Refectory
Afendikó
Vrontohión Monastery
Ay. Theódhori
Evangelistra
Mitrópolis
Walls
Lower Entrance

0   100 m

Mystra's political significance, though, was in any case overshadowed by its **artistic achievements**. Throughout the fourteenth and the first decades of the fifteenth centuries it was the principal cultural and intellectual centre of the Byzantine world, sponsoring, in highly uncertain times, a renaissance in the arts and attracting the finest of Byzantine scholars and theologians – among them a number of members of the imperial families, the Cantacuzenes and Paleologues. Most notable of the court scholars was the humanist philosopher **Gemisthus Plethon**, who revived and reinterpreted Plato's ideas, using them to support his own brand of revolutionary teachings, which included the assertions that land should be redistributed among labourers and that reason should be placed on a par with religion. Although his beliefs had limited impact in Mystra itself – whose monks excommunicated him – his followers, who taught in Italy after the fall of Mystra, exercised wide influence in Renaissance Florence and Rome.

More tangibly, Mystra also saw a last flourish of **Byzantine architecture**, with the building of a magnificent Despots' Palace and a perfect sequence of churches, multi-domed and brilliantly frescoed. It is these, remarkably preserved and sensitively restored, that provide the focus of this extraordinary site. In the painting, it is not hard to see something of the creativity and spirit of Plethon's court circle, as the stock Byzantine figures turn to more naturalistic forms and settings.

The town's **post-Byzantine history** follows a familiar Peloponnesian pattern. It remained in Turkish hands from the mid-fifteenth to late seventeenth centuries, then was captured briefly by the Venetians, under whom the town prospered once more. Decline set in with a second stage of Turkish control, from 1715 on, culminating in the destruction that accompanied the War of Independence, the site being evacuated after fires in 1770 and 1825. Restoration began in the first decades of this century, was interrupted by the civil war – during which it was, for a while, a battle site, with the ruins of the Pantánassa convent sheltering children from the lower town – and renewed in earnest in the 1950s when the last inhabitants were relocated.

The Byzantine city

Daily 8.30am–3pm, may stay open later in high season; 1000dr.

The site of the Byzantine city comprises three main parts: the **Katohóra** (lower town), with the city's most important churches; the **Anohóra** (upper town), grouped around the vast shell of a royal palace; and the **Kástro** (castle). There are two entrances to the site: at the base of the lower town and up by the Kástro; once inside, the site is well signposted.

A road loops up from the modern village of Néos Mistrás (see below) past both entrances. Buses from Spárti always stop at the lower entrance, and usually go up to the top, too. It's a good idea to stock up on refreshments before setting out; there's a mobile snack bar at the lower gate, but nothing at the upper one or in the site itself.

The Upper Town and Kástro

Following a course from the upper entrance, the first identifiable building you come to is the church of **Ayía Sofía**, which served as the chapel for the Despots' Palace – the enormous structure below. The chapel's finest feature is its floor, made from polychrome marble. Its frescoes, notably a *Pandokrator* (Christ in Majesty) and *Nativity of the Virgin*, have survived reasonably well, protected until recent years by coatings of whitewash applied by the Turks, who adapted the building as a mosque. Recognisable parts of the refectory and cells of its attached monastery also remain.

The **Kástro**, reached by a path direct from the upper gate, maintains the Frankish design of its original thirteenth-century construction, though it was repaired and modified by all successive occupants. There is a walkway around most of the keep, whose views allow an intricate panorama of the town below. The castle itself was the court of Guillaume II de Villehardouin but was used primarily as a citadel in later years.

Heading down from Ayía Sofía, there is a choice of routes. The right fork winds past ruins of a Byzantine mansion, the **Palatáki** (Small Palace), and **Áyios Nikólaos**, a large seventeenth-century building decorated with crude paintings. The left fork is more interesting, passing the massively fortified **Náfplio Gate**, which was the principal entrance to the upper town, and the vast, multi-storeyed, gothic-looking complex of the **Despots' Palace**.

Parts of the palace (currently closed for extensive restoration) probably date back to the Franks. Most prominent among its numerous rooms is a great vaulted audience hall, built at right angles to the line of the building, with ostentatious windows regally dominating the skyline; this was once heated by eight great chimneys and sported a painted facade. Behind it are the ruins of various official public buildings, while to the right of the lower wing, flanking one side of a square used by the Turks as a marketplace, are the remains of a **mosque**.

The Lower Town

At the **Monemvassía Gate**, which links the upper and lower towns, there is a further choice of routes: right to the Pantánassa and Perívleptos monasteries; left to the Vrontohión monastery and cathedral. If time is running out, it is easier to head right first, then double back down to the Vrontohión.

When excavations were resumed in 1952, the last thirty or so families who still lived in the lower town were moved out to Néos Mistrás. Only the nuns of the **Pantánassa** (Queen of the World) **convent** have remained; currently, there are six in residence. The convent's church is perhaps the finest surviving in Mystra, perfectly proportioned in its blend of Byzantine and Gothic. The **frescoes** date from various centuries, with some superb fifteenth-century work, including one in the gallery (entered by an external staircase) which depicts scenes from the life of Christ. David Talbot Rice, in his classic study *Byzantine Art*, wrote of these frescoes that "Only El Greco in the west, and later Gauguin, would have used their colours in just this way". Other of the frescoes were painted between 1687 and 1715, when Mystra was held by the Venetians.

Further down on this side of the lower town is a balconied Byzantine mansion, the **House of Frangopoulos**, once the home of the Despotate's chief minister – who was, incidentally, the founder of the Pantánassa.

Beyond it is the diminutive **Perívleptos monastery**, whose single-domed church, partially carved out of the rock, contains Mystra's most complete cycle of frescoes, almost all of which date from the fourteenth century. They are in some ways finer than those of the Pantánassa, blending an easy humanism with the spirituality of the Byzantine icon traditions, and demonstrating the structured iconography of a Byzantine church. The position of each figure depended upon its sanctity and so here upon the dome, the image of heaven, is the *Pandokrator* (the all-powerful Christ in glory after the Ascension); on the apse is the Virgin, and the higher expanses of wall portray scenes from the life of Christ. Prophets and saints could only appear on the lower walls, decreasing in importance according to their distance from the sanctuary.

Along the path leading from Perívleptos to the lower gate are a couple of minor, much-restored churches, and, just above them, the **Laskaris House**, a mansion thought to have belonged to relatives of the emperors. Like the Frangopoulos House, it is balconied; its ground floor probably served as stables. Close by, beside the path, is an old Turkish fountain.

The **Mitrópolis** or cathedral, immediately beyond the gateway, is the oldest of Mystra's churches, built in 1309 under the first Paleologue ruler. A marble slab set in its floor is carved with the double-headed eagle of Byzantium, commemorating the spot where Constantine XI Paleologus, the last Eastern emperor, was crowned in 1448; he was soon to perish, with his empire, in the Turkish sacking of Constantinople in 1453. Of the church's frescoes, the earliest, in the north aisle, depict the torture and burial of Áyios Dhimítrios, the saint to whom the church is dedicated. The comparative stiffness of their figures contrasts with the later works opposite. These, illustrating the miracles of Christ and the life of the Virgin, are more intimate and lighter of touch; they date from the last great years before Mystra's fall. A small **museum** (included in main admission charge), adjacent to the cathedral, contains various fragments of sculpture and pottery and a few icons from the churches.

Finally, a short way uphill, is the **Vrontohión monastery**. This was the centre of cultural and intellectual life in the fifteenth-century town – the cells of the monastery can still be discerned – and was also the burial place of the despots. Of the two attached churches, the further one, **Afendikó** has been beautifully restored, revealing late frescoes similar to those of Perívleptos, with startlingly bold juxtapositions of colour.

Practicalities: Néos Mistrás

Buses run regularly through the day from Spárti to the lower Mystra site entrance, stopping en route at the modern village of **NÉOS MISTRÁS**. This is quite attractive in its own right: a small roadside community whose half-dozen tavernas, crowded with tour buses by day, revert to a low-key life at night.

In general, staying in Néos Mistrás is worth the bit extra over Spárti, for the setting and early access to the site, though you will need to book ahead, or arrive early in the day, to find a place. **Accommodation** is limited to a single hotel, the *Byzantion* (☎0731/93 309; ④), which is pleasant but oversubscribed for most of the year, and a small number of private rooms – those run by *Dimitrios Vahaviolos* (☎0731/93 432; ②) are especially recommended. There are campsites along the Mystra–Spárti road: all the details are on p.172.

The Vahaviolos family also has a decent taverna, while the **restaurant** opposite the hotel, *Toh Kastro*, is excellent, if a bit on the expensive side. Between the village and the site, *Taverna Marmara* and the *Paleológos* are both good – and quieter in the evenings after the tour buses have gone.

West from Spartí: Mount Taíyettos and the Langádha pass

Moving **on from Spárti** there is a tough choice of routes: west over Mount Taíyettos, either on foot or by road through the dramatic **Langádha pass to Kalamáta**; east to the Byzantine towns of **Yeráki and Monemvassía**; or south, skirting the mountain's foothills, to **Yíthio and the Máni.**

For anyone wanting to get to grips with the Greek mountains, there is **Mount Taíyettos** itself. Although the range is one of the most dramatic and hazardous in Greece, with vast grey boulders and scree along much of its length, it has one reasonably straightforward path to the highest peak, Profítis Ilías.

Mount Taíyettos (Taygettus)

Gazing up at the crags above the castle at Mystra, Mount Taíyettos looks daunting and inviting in pretty equal measure. If all you want is a different perspective on the mountain, then the simplest course is to take a bus from Spárti to **ÁYIOS IOÁNNIS**, a little way to the south of Mystra and closer to the peaks. From there a spectacular *kalderími*

HIKING IN THE TAIYETTOS RANGE

Most **hikes beyond Anavrití** need experience and proper equipment, including the relevant *Korfes* or *YIS* maps, and should definitely not be undertaken alone – a sprained ankle could be fatal up here. The area is prone to flash floods, so seek advice locally. If you are confident, however, there are various routes to the Profítis Ilías summit and beyond:

The only straightforward route is to **follow the E4** long-distance footpath, here a forest road marked variously by yellow diamonds or red-and-white stripes, for five hours south to the **alpine refuge at Ayía Varvára** (see below).

The classic approach to the **Profítis Ilías summit** used to entail a dusty, eleven-kilometre road-walk up from the village of Paleopanayía, a short bus ride south of Spárti off the Yíthio road, to the spring and ex-trailhead at Bóliana, where there's a single ramshackle hut owned by the Dousmanis family that serves drinks and sometimes meals in summer. You now have to proceed past Bóliana towards Anavrití on the E4 track for about half an hour, then bear left near a picnic ground and spring (the last reliable water on the mountain). Another half-hour above this, following E4 blazes, what's left of the old trail appears on the right, signposted *EOS Spárti Katafíyio*. This short-cuts the new road except for the very last 50 m to the Ayía Varvára refuge.

A more challenging option, requiring mountaineering skills and camping equipment, is to adopt the red-dotted trail veering off the E4 early on, and follow it to a point just below the 1700-metre saddle described by Patrick Leigh Fermor in *Mani*, where you must choose between dropping over the pass to the far side of the range or precarious ridge-walking to the Profítis Ilías summit (2404m). **Crossing the pass** would land you at the head of the **Ríndomo gorge**, where you can camp at the chapel-monastery of Panayía Kavsodhematúsa before descending the next day to either Gaïtses or Pigádhia, near the Messinian coast. Keeping to the watershed it is seven tough hours to the peak even in optimum conditions and with a light load, involving exposed rock pinnacles, sheer drops and rotten surfaces. This is not a hike to be lightly undertaken.

AYÍA VARVÁRA TO THE SUMMIT

The **Ayía Varvára refuge** (unstaffed, but open sporadically – more likely at weekends), above Bolianá, sits on a beautiful grassy knoll shaded by tremendous storm-blasted black pines. The conical peak of Profítis Ilías rises directly above; if you can get your climb to coincide with a full moon you won't regret it. There is plenty of room for camping, and the hut has a porch to provide shelter in bad weather.

The **path to the summit** starts at the rear left corner of the refuge and swings right on a long reach. Level and stony at first, it leaves the treeline and loops up a steep bank to a sloping meadow, where it is ineffectually marked by twisted, rusting signs with their lettering long obliterated. Keep heading right across the slope towards a distinct secondary peak until, once around a steep bend, the path begins to veer left in the direction of the summit. It slants steadily upward following a natural ledge until, at a very clear nick in the ridge above you, it turns right and crosses to the far side, from where you look down on the Gulf of Messinía. Turn left and you climb steeply to the summit in around 25 minutes.

There is a squat stone chapel and outbuildings on the **summit**, used during the celebrations of the Feast of the Prophet Elijah (Profítis Ilías) on July 18–20. The views, as you would expect, are breathtaking, encompassing the sea to east and west.

SUMMIT TO THE COAST

The terrain **beyond the peak** is beyond the ambitions of casual hikers. The easiest and safest way off the mountain **towards the Messinian coast** is to follow the E4 from Ayía Varvára to the gushing springs at Pendávli, and then over a low saddle to the summer hamlet of Áyios Dhimítrios. This takes just a couple of hours and you can camp in the beautiful surroundings. In the morning you're well poised, at the head of the **Víros gorge**, to handle the all-day descent to Kardhamíli through the other great Taiyettan canyon. At one point you negotiate stretches of the **Kakí Skála**, one of the oldest paths in Greece, built to link ancient Sparta and Messene.

(cobbled way) leads up from the gravel-crushing mill behind the village to **ANAVRITÍ**, which boasts superb vistas, a single friendly **hotel** (☎0731/21 788 or 91 288; ②) and one very basic taverna aside from the one in the hotel. An alternative, more popular approach involves following the marked E4 overland route, partly on track, partly on trail, up from Néos Mistrás via the **monastery of Faneroméni**. Neither the E4 nor the *kalderími* take more than two hours uphill, and they can be combined as follows for a wonderful day's outing: bus to Áyios Ioánnis, taxi to rock-crushing mill (2.5km), hike up to Anavrití, have a look around and a meal, then descend via Faneroméni to Néos Mistrás. Note that this route is best tackled from Áyios Ioánnis; from Mistrás, the start of the *kalderími* just east of Anavrití isn't marked, and can be difficult to locate.

Spárti to Kalamáta: the Langádha pass

The **Langádha pass**, the sixty-kilometre route across the Taíyettos from **Spárti to Kalamáta**, was the former alternative to the Kakí Skála and is still the only paved road across the mountain. Remote and barren, with no habitation at all for the central 25km section, it unveils a constant drama of peaks, magnificent at all times but startling at sunrise. This was, incidentally, the route that Telemachus took in *The Odyssey* on his way from Nestor's palace at Pylos to that of Menelaus at Sparta. It took him a day's journey by chariot – good going by any standards, since today's buses take three hours.

Heading from Spárti, the last settlement is **TRÍPI**, 14km out, where there is a small **hotel**, the *Keadas* (☎0731/98 222; ③), with a restaurant. Just beyond the village, the road climbs steeply into the mountains and enters the **gorge of Langádha**, a wild sequence of hairpins through the pines. To the north of the gorge, so it is said, the Spartans used to leave their sick or puny babies to die from exposure. Beyond the gorge, close to the summit of the pass, and 22km from Spartí, the *Canadas* hotel (☎0721/76 821; ②–③) is built in the style of an alpine chalet, with a restaurant that serves *bacalhau* (Portuguese-style dried codfish); both are open year-round.

The first actual village on the Kalamáta side is Artemisía, where you often have to change buses, before entering another gorge for the final zigzagging descent to Kalamáta.

East from Spárti: Yeráki

A kilometre or two north of Spárti, a roadside sign suggests a detour to "visit the Byzantine antiquities" at **YERÁKI**. Too often in Greece, such signs make mountains out of archeological molehills, but in this case the advice is sound. With its Frankish castle and fifteen chapels spread over a spur of Mount Párnon, Yeráki stands a creditable third to the sites of Mystra and Monemvassía.

Medieval Yeráki

Yeráki was one of the original twelve Frankish baronies set up in the wake of the Fourth Crusade, and remained through the fourteenth century an important Byzantine town, straddling the road between Mystra and its port at Monemvássia. The site is spectacular, with sweeping vistas over the olive-covered Evrótas plain and across to Taíyettos. It stands four kilometres outside the current village of Yeráki (see below), on the first outcrop of the Párnon mountains.

Although the site itself is unenclosed, all the main churches are kept locked, and to visit them you should first make enquiries at the café on the village square for the caretaker; he can usually be found here, unless he's already up at the site. You'll be given a tour by him, clambering around the rocks to the best-preserved chapels.

The most substantial remains of the medieval town are of its fortress, the **Kástro**, built in 1256 by the local Frankish baron, Jean de Nivelet, who had inherited Yeráki, with six other lordships, from his father. Its heavily fortified design is based on that of the Villehardouin fortress at Mystra, for this was one of the most vulnerable Frankish castles of the Morea, intended to control the wild and only partially conquered territories of Taíyettos and the Máni. In the event, Jean retained his castle for less than a decade, surrendering to the Byzantines in 1262 and buying an estate near Kórinthos on the proceeds. Within the fortress are huge **cisterns** for withstanding siege, and the largest of Yeráki's churches: the thirteenth-century **Mitrópolis**, also known as **Áyios Yióryios**, which features blackened Byzantine frescoes, a Frankish iconostasis and the Villehardouin arms.

The churches on the slope below also mix Frankish and Byzantine features, and many incorporate ancient blocks from Yeráki's ancient predecessor, Geronthrai. The caretaker is usually prepared to unlock two or three, including **Áyios Dhimítrios**, **Zoödóhos Píyi**, and **Ayía Paraskeví** (at the base of the hill), each of which has restored frescoes.

Practicalities

The "modern" village of Yeráki has no regular accommodation, though rooms may be negotiable through the café or taverna in the square. If you're dependent on public transport, you'll need to take in Yeráki as day-trip from Spárti: **buses** run several times daily, but not along the splendid route over Mount Párnon to Leonídhi (see p.167).

Monemvassía

After Mystra you half-expect Byzantine sites to be disappointing – or at least low-key like Yeráki. **MONEMVASSÍA** is emphatically neither. Set impregnably on a great island-like irruption of rock, the medieval seaport and commercial centre of the Byzantine Peloponnese is equally as exciting as its spiritual counterpart of Mystra: a place of grand, haunting atmosphere, whose houses and churches are all the more evocative for being populated, albeit on a largely weekend and touristic basis.

The town's name, an elision of *Moni Emvasis* or "single entrance", is a reference to its approach from the mainland, across a kilometre-long causeway and a small bridge built this century to replace a sequence of wooden bridges. Such a defensible and strategic position gave it control of the sea-lines from Italy and the West to Constantinople and the Levant. Fortified on all approaches, it was invariably the last outpost of the Peloponnese to fall to invaders, and was only ever taken through siege.

Some history

Founded by the **Byzantines** in the sixth century, Monemvassía soon became an important port. It remained in Byzantine possession for almost seven hundred years, passing only very briefly to the Franks – who took it in 1249 after a three-year siege but had to ransom it back for the captured Guillaume de Villehardouin. Subsequently, it served as the chief commercial port of the Despotate of the Morea and was to all effects the Greek Byzantine capital. Mystra, despite the presence of the court, was never much more than a large village; Monemvassía at its peak had a population of almost 60,000.

Like Mystra, Monemvassía had something of a golden age in the thirteenth century: during this period, it was populated by a number of noble Byzantine families, and reaped considerable wealth from estates inland, from the export of wine (the famed *Malmsey*, mentioned by Shakespeare) and from roving corsairs who preyed on Latin shipping heading for the East. When the rest of the Morea fell to the Turks in 1460, Monemvassía was able to seal itself off, placing itself first under the control of the

Papacy, later under the **Venetians**. Only in 1540 did the **Turks** gain control, the Venetians having abandoned their garrison after the defeat of their navy at Préveza.

Turkish occupation precipitated a steady decline, both in prestige and population, though the town experienced something of a revival during the period of Venetian control of the Peloponnese. Monemvassía was again thrust to the fore in the **War of Independence**, being the first of the major Turkish fortresses to fall, after a terrible siege and wholesale massacre of the Turkish inhabitants, in April 1821.

After the war, there was no longer the need for such strongholds, and, at the end of the nineteenth century, shipping routes changed, too, with the opening of the Corinth Canal. The population plummeted and the town drifted into a village existence, its buildings for the most part allowed to fall into ruin. By the time of World War II – during which 4000 New Zealand troops were dramatically evacuated from the rock – only eighty families remained. Today there are just ten in permanent residence.

The rock: medieval Monemvassía

From the mainland village of **Yéfira** – where the causeway to **Monemvassía** (or **Kástro**, as locals call it) begins – nothing can be seen of the medieval town, which is built purely on the seaward face of the rock. Little more is revealed as you walk across the causeway, past a spectral-looking garage with a Mobil sign. Then suddenly the road is barred by huge castellated walls. Once through the fortified entrance gate, wide enough only for a single person or a donkey, everything looms into view: piled upon one another amid narrow stone streets and alleyways are houses with tiled roofs and walled gardens, distinctively Byzantine churches, and high above, the improbably long castle walls protecting the upper town on the summit.

The Lower Town

Standing at the **gateway** to the rock there is the same sense of luxury and excitement as at Mystra: the prospect of being able to walk each street, explore every possible turn of this extraordinary place. The **Lower Town** here once numbered forty churches and over eight hundred homes, an incredible mass of building, which explains the intricate network of alleys. A single main street – up and slightly to the left from the gateway – shelters most of the restored houses, as well as a scattering of cafés, tavernas and souvenir shops. One of the tavernas is owned by the Ritsos family, relatives of the late Yannis Ritsos, one of Greece's leading poets and a lifelong communist, who was born on the rock; a plaque on a house near the main gate commemorates his birthplace.

At the end of this street is the lower town's main square, a beautiful public space, with a cannon and a well in its centre, a *kafenío* along one side, and, on the other, the great, vaulted **cathedral** built by the Byzantine Emperor Andronicus II Comnenus when he made Monemvassía a see in 1293. The largest medieval church in southern Greece, it is dedicated to Christ in Chains, and is thus known as *Hristós Elkómenos*. Across the square is the domed church of **Áyios Petros**, which was transformed by the Turks into a mosque and now houses a small museum of local finds (open, but keeps unpredictable hours). Unusually for Ottoman Greece, the Christian cathedral was allowed to function during the occupation, and must have done so beside this mosque – hence the name of this square, *Platía Dzamíou*, the square of the mosque.

Down towards the sea is a third notable church, the **Hrissafítissa**, whose bell hangs from a bent-over old cypress tree in the courtyard. It was restored and adapted by the Venetians in their second, eighteenth-century, occupation. The **Portello** is a small gate in the sea wall, due south of Platía Dzamíou; you can **swim** safely off the rocks here.

In peaceful times, the town was supplied from the tiny harbour, **Kourkoula**, outside the town and below the road as you approach the entrance gateway. There are two minor churches just off the main street. **Panayía Mirtidhiótissa**, to the north of the

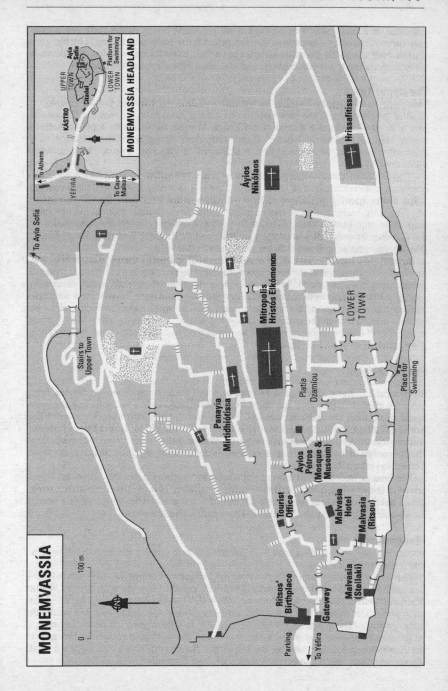

MONEMVASSÍA

0   100 m

MONEMVASSÍA HEADLAND

KÁSTRO

UPPER TOWN

Ayia Sofia

LOWER TOWN

Platform for Swimming

Citadel

To Athens

YÉFIRA

To Cape Maléas

To Ayía Sofía

Stairs to Upper Town

Áyios Nikólaos

Hrissafítissa

Mitrópolis Hristós Elkómenos

LOWER TOWN

Place for Swimming

Platía Dzamíou

Panayía Mirtidhiótissa

Áyios Pétros (Mosque & Museum)

Tourist Office

Malvasía Hotel

Malvasía (Ritsou)

Rítsos' Birthplace

Gateway

Malvasía (Stellaki)

Parking

To Yéfira

cathedral, in a small, single-aisled basilica with a single dome; inside there is a beautifully carved *iconostási* – ask around for the priest if the basilica is locked. The big grey church built alongside the main street, above the Hrissafítissa, is **Áyios Nikólaos**; it dates from the early seventh century, and was used for many years as a school.

The Upper Town

The climb to the **Upper Town** is highly worthwhile – not least for the solitude, since most of the day-trippers stay down below. To get the most from the vast site, it's a good idea to bring some food and drink (from Yéfira: Monemvássia has no supermarket), to enable you to explore at leisure. There are sheer drops from the rockface, and unguarded cisterns, so descend before dusk and if you have young children, keep them close by.

The fortifications, like those of the lower town, are substantially intact; indeed the **entrance gate** retains its iron slats. Within, the site is a ruin, unrestored and deserted – the last resident moved down in 1911 – though many structures are still recognizable. The only building that is relatively complete, even though its outbuildings have long since crumbled to foundations, is the beautiful thirteenth-century **Ayía Sofía**, by the gateway. Founded as a monastery by Andronikos II, along a plan similar to that of Dhafní, the chapel candles still flicker perilously in the wind.

Beyond the church extend acres of ruins: in medieval times the population here was much greater than that of the lower town. Among the remains are the stumpy bases of Byzantine houses and public buildings, and, perhaps most striking, a vast **cistern** to ensure a water supply in time of siege. Monemvassía must have been more or less self-sufficient in this respect, but its weak point was its food supply, which had to be entirely imported from the mainland. In the last siege, by Mavromihalis's Maniot army in the War of Independence, the Turks were reduced to eating rats – and, so the propagandists claimed, Greek children.

Practicalities

Monemvassía can be approached by road or sea. There are twice-weekly **ferries** from Pireás, and Kastélli on Crete, and more frequent **hydrofoils** in season, linking the town to the north with Leonídhi, Spétses and Pireás, and to the south with Neápoli and the island of Kíthira; currently there is no hydrofoil link with Yíthio. Direct **buses** connect with Spárti three times daily and twice (in season only) with Yíthio; occasionally a change at Mólai is necessary. Out of season it's best to alight at Skála, 17km from Yíthio, and take a local bus or taxi.

The boat or hydrofoil will drop you at a mooring midway down the causeway; buses arrive in the modern village of Yéfira on the mainland. This is little more than a straggle of hotels, rooms and restaurants for the rock's tourist trade, with a pebble beach; for a **beach** day-trip, it's best to head 3–4km north along the coast.

Monemvassía

Rooms on the rock are expensive – in season and out – and from June to September, you'll need to book ahead.

The choice is between three very attractive and upmarket **hotels**, each of which has beautifully restored and traditionally furnished rooms. The most renowned is the *Malvasia* (☎0732/61 323; ⑤), which occupies three separate mansions between the main street and the sea; call first at the hotel reception, well signposted just inside the main gateway. The *Byzantio* (☎0732/61 351; ⑤) is similarly characterful, but marginally more expensive; it's on the main street near the *Malvasia* reception. Down near the Hrissafítissa, looking out over the sea, is the *Kellia* (☎0732/61 520; ④); it's a small place and rather remote, so advance booking is recommended.

Several other **furnished apartments** on the rock are available for long-term rental. If you ask around at the shops and taverna on the main street, it's just possible that you might get one of these on a more temporary basis, out of season. Or you could seek the help of *Malvasia Travel* (see below).

Eating out in the old village is enjoyable, though as much for location as food. Establishments run the gamut from *Toh Kanoni* – a very pricey fish and seafood restaurant – to pizzas at *Toh Kastro*, down towards the sea.

Yéfira

There's more accommodation in **YÉFIRA**, along with various other useful tourist services: **bank, post office, OTE** and a **travel agent**, *Malvasia Travel* (☎0732/61 432), which can help with rooms, sells ferry tickets and rents out **mopeds**; the Mobil garage (☎0732 /61 219) handles the **hydrofoils**.

There are several **hotels** near the causeway. The cheapest are the refurbished *Akroyiali* (☎0732/61 360; ③) and the *Aktaion* (☎0732/61 234; ③); the latter's enterprising owner has also recently opened the *Filoxenia* (☎0732/61 716; ④–⑤), with balconies and wonderful sea views. The *Monemvassia* (☎0732/61 381; ③) is also newish, with colourful decor inspired by the Aegean scenery. If these are full, there are plenty of others to choose from, plus dozens of **rooms** for rent, advertised along the waterfront. The nearest **campsite** is 3km to the south, along the coast road; *Kapsis Paradise* (☎0732/61 123) is open year-round, and has water skis and mopeds for rent.

Back in the village, the best **taverna** is undoubtedly the *Nikolaos* (around 1500dr per person); if you have transport, you could also try the *Pipinelis* (☎0732/61 044; May–Oct), about 2km out on the road south to the campsite, but ring first to be sure it's open and to make a reservation if the weather's cool, as indoor seating is limited.

South to Neápoli and Elafónissos

The isolated southeasternmost "finger" of the Peloponnese below Monemvassía is a bit disappointing, with little of interest in either its villages or its landscape. However, the tiny port of Neápoli, the southernmost town in mainland Greece, offers access to the islet of Elafónissos, just offshore, and to the larger Ionian islands of Kíthira and Andíkithira, midway to Crete.

Neápoli

NEÁPOLI is a mix of old buildings and modern Greek concrete behind a grey sand beach – hardly compelling, aside from its ferry and hydrofoil connections. For such an out of the way (and not especially attractive) place, it is surprisingly developed, catering mainly to Greek holidaymakers. Besides **rooms**, there are two modest hotels: the *Aivali* (☎0734/22 287; ②) and the *Arsenakos* (☎0734/22 991; ③), both small and worth booking ahead in summer. The huge new *Hotel Limara Mare* (☎0734/22 236; ⑥) is a fall-back, if an expensive one. If you are waiting for the ferry or hydrofoil, you can eat well at the *Restaurant Metaxia Manalitsi*, by the bridge on the seafront; *Captain D Alexandrakis* (☎0734/22 940), also on the seafront, acts as an agent for ferries, hydrofoils and rooms.

Neápoli **beach** extends north to the village of Vingláfia, where you can negotiate for a fishing boat across the 400-metre channel to the islet of Elafónissos. Alternatively, you can get a small ferry to Elafónissos from Neápoli.

Elafónissos island

Like Neápoli, **Elafónissos** is relatively busy in summer, and again is frequented mainly by Greek visitors. The island's lone village is largely modern and functional, but has plenty of rooms and some good fish tavernas. The two **pensions**, the *Asteri* (☎0734/61 271; ③) and *Elafonissos* (☎0734/61 210; ③), are worth booking.

Although scenically barren, the island has one of the best **beaches** in this part of Greece at Káto Nísso, a large double bay of fine white sand; it's 5km southeast of the village, from where a caique leaves every morning in summer. There's one basic sandwich-and-drinks stand at the beach, and usually a small community of people camping here. Another beach to the southwest of the village is quieter but less spectacular.

Kíthira island

Isolated at the foot of the Peloponnese, the island of **Kíthira** traditionally belongs to the Ionian islands, and shares their history of Venetian, and later, British rule; under the former it was known as Cerigo. For the most part, the similarities end there. The island architecture, whitewashed and flat-roofed, looks more like that of the Cyclades, albeit with a strong Venetian influence. The landscape is different, too: wild scrub- and gorse-covered hills or moorland sliced by deep valleys and ravines.

Depopulation has left the land underfarmed and the abandoned fields overgrown, for, since the war, most of the islanders have left for Athens or Australia, giving Kíthira the reputation of being a classic emigrant island; it is known locally as "Australian Colony" or "Kangaroo Island", and Australia is referred to as "Big Kíthira". Many of the villages are deserted, their *platías* empty and the schools and *kafenía* closed. Kíthira was never a rich island, but, along with Monemvassía, it did once have a military and economic significance – which it likewise lost with Greek independence and the opening of the Corinth Canal. These days, tourism has brought a little prosperity (and a few luxury hotels), but most summer visitors are Greeks and especially Greek-Australians. For the few foreigners who reach Kíthira, it remains something of a refuge, with its fine and remarkably undeveloped beaches the principal attraction. A word of warning, though: out of season, very little stays open outside of Potámos.

Arriving – and getting around

If you arrive by **boat or hydrofoil** from Pireás or Neápoli in the Peloponnese, you'll normally disembark at Ayía Pelayía in the north of the island. In bad weather, for example when the *meltémi* is blowing from the north (common during July and August), boats – particularly hydrofoils – may use Kapsáli, below Kíthira's capital, Hóra, in the south. The **airport** is deep in the interior, 8km southeast of Potámos; taxis meet arrivals.

You can generally find a **taxi** at either harbour, but don't hope for public transport – in summer, the island **bus** runs just once a day between Ayía Pelayía, Potámos, Hóra and Kapsáli, and out of season reverts to its role as the school bus – although you can generally flag it down if you don't mind joining the kids. In fact, most places on Kíthira, beaches in particular, are difficult to reach without your own transport, so you're well advised to rent a **car** or **moped**, bearing in mind that there is no reliable service station south of Potámos.

Ayía Pelayía and northern Kíthira

There's a reasonable choice of **tavernas** and **rooms** in Ayía Pelayía; the *Faros Taverna* (☎0735/33 282; ③) offers both, from its waterfront location. The clean and comfortable *Hotel Kytheria* (☎0735/33 3221; ④) is more luxurious, as are the more recent *Filoxenia Apartments* (☎0735/33 100; ⑥), with striking blue shutters and an imaginative layout around small courtyards. Ferry and hydrofoil **tickets** are available from *Conomos Travel* (☎0735/33490), on the ground floor of the *Kytheria*.

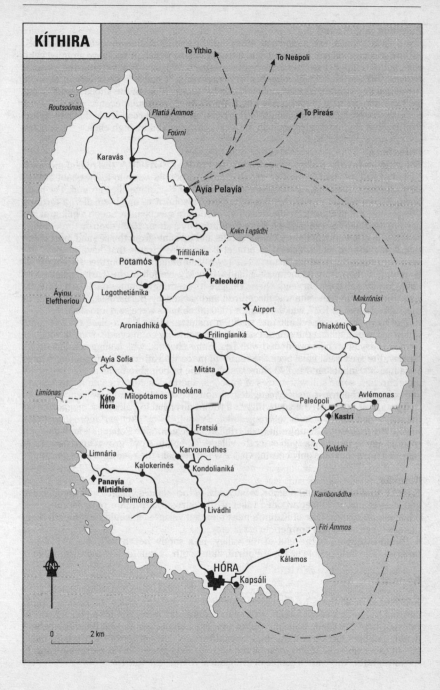

KÍTHIRA

To Yíthio

To Neápoli

To Pireás

Routsoúnas

Platiá Ámmos

Foúrni

Karavás

Ayía Pelayía

Kako Iagádhi

Trifiliánika

Potamós

Paleohóra

Áyiou Eleftheríou

Logothetiánika

Makrónisi

✈ Airport

Aroniadhiká

Frilingianiká

Dhiakófti

Ayía Sofía

Mitáta

Limiónas

Dhokána

Paleópoli

Avlémonas

Káto Hora

Milopótamos

Kastrí

Fratsiá

Keládhi

Limnária

Karvounádhes

Kalokerinés

Kondolianiká

Kambonádha

◆**Panayía Mirtidhíon**

Dhrimónas

Livádhi

Fíri Ámmos

Kálamos

HÓRA

Kapsáli

0   2 km

Potamós and around

From Ayía Pelayía, the main road winds up the mountainside towards **POTAMÓS**, Kíthira's largest village. A pleasant and unspoilt village which, if you have a rented vehicle, makes a good base for exploring the island. It has a few **rooms**, the *Pension Porfyra* (☎0735/33 329; ④), together with **tavernas**, a **bank**, a **post office**, *Olympic Airways* office (☎0735/33 688) and two petrol stations. Most of the shops on the island are here, too, as is the **Sunday market**, Kíthira's liveliest regular event.

From Logothetiánika, just south of Potamós, an unpaved road leads down to **Áyiou Eleftheríou**, a good sandy beach on the west coast, backed by high cliffs.

Paleohóra

The main reason for visiting Potamós is to get to **PALEOHÓRA**, the ruined medieval capital of Kíthira, 3km to the east of the town. Few people seem to know about or visit these remains, though they constitute one of the best Byzantine sites around. The most obvious comparison is with Mystra: although Paleohóra is much smaller, a fortified village rather than a town, its natural setting is equally spectacular. Set on a hilltop at the head of the Káko Langádhi gorge, it is surrounded by a sheer 100m drop on three sides.

The site is lower than the surrounding hills and invisible from the sea and most of the island, something which served to protect it from the pirates that have plagued the island through much of its history. The town was built in the fourteenth century by Byzantine nobles from Monemvassía, and when Mystra fell to the Turks, many of its noble families also sought refuge here. Despite its seemingly impregnable and perfectly concealed position, the site was discovered and sacked by Barbarossa, commander of the Turkish fleet, in 1537, and the island's 7000 inhabitants were sold into slavery.

The town was never rebuilt, and tradition maintains that it is a place of ill fortune, which perhaps explains the emptiness of the surrounding countryside, none of which is farmed today. The hills are dotted with Byzantine chapels, which suggests that, in its heyday, the area must have been the centre of medieval Kíthira; it is rumoured to have once had 800 inhabitants and 72 churches. Now the principal remains are of the surviving churches, some still with traces of frescoes, and the castle. The site is unenclosed and has never been seriously investigated, although excavations are now planned.

If you have your own transport, there's a rough dirt road to Paleohóra, signposted off the main road from Potamós to Aroniadhiká. By foot, it's quicker and more interesting to take the path from the tiny village of Trifiliánika, just outside Potamós – look out for a rusting sign to the right as you enter the village. The path is overgrown in parts and not easy to follow; the ruins only become visible when you join the road above the gorge.

Karavás

KARAVÁS, 6km north of Potamós, is untypical of the island's villages – its architecture and the setting, in a deep wooded valley with a stream, are more reminiscent of the other Ionian islands. One of Kíthira's most pleasant villages, it would be a superb base, though there is (as yet) nowhere to eat or stay.

Platiá Ámmos, at the end of the valley, is a sandy beach with a seasonal fish **taverna**. The little pebble beach at **Foúrni**, 2km south, is quieter and more attractive.

Kapsáli

KAPSÁLI, in addition to its harbour function, is the one place on Kíthira largely devoted to tourism. Most foreign visitors to Kíthira stay here, and it's a popular port of call for yachts heading from the Aegean to the Ionian islands and Italy. Set behind double pebble-sand bays, it is certainly picturesque. The larger of its two bays has a line of **tavernas**; the *Magus*, nearest the harbour, has good food at reasonable prices. As for nightlife, there are a couple of lively **bars**: *Bikini Red* and *Yacht Inn*.

The best **accommodation** is usually booked up in summer by a British holiday company; rooms for more casual visitors can be hard to find, and expensive when you do. Phoning ahead, you might try for a stay at the apartments owned by Kalokerines Katikies (☎0735/31 265; ④), Byron Duponte (☎0735/31 245; ④) or the Megalondis (☎0735/31 340; ④); more luxury is to be had at the sophisticated *Hotel Raikos* (☎0735/31 629; ⑤). A fairly basic **campsite** (June–Sept) nestles in the pine trees behind the village.

There's a mobile **post office** in summer, and a couple of travel agents near the harbour: *Kythoros International* (☎0735/31 925) deals with travel, accommodation and vehicle rental, while *Roma Travel* (☎0735/31 561) deals with accommodation only. *Panayiotis* (☎0735/31 600) and *Nikos* (☎0735/31 5700) both rent **cars, motorbikes and mopeds**. Some of these operate in summer only; if closed, you could try their Hóra branches – see below.

Hóra

HÓRA (or Kíthira town), a steep 2km haul above Kapsáli, has an equally dramatic site, its Cycladic-style houses tiered about the walls of a Venetian castle. Within the **castle**, most of the buildings are ruined, but there are spectacular views of Kapsáli and, out to sea, to the islet of Avgó (Egg), legendary birthplace of Aphrodite. Below the castle are the remains of older Byzantine walls, and 21 Byzantine churches in various states of dereliction. A small **museum** (Tues–Fri 8.45am–3pm; Sun 9.30am–2.30pm) houses modest remnants of the island's numerous occupiers, in particular Minoan finds from excavations at Paleópoli.

Compared to Kapsáli, Hóra stays quiet and many places are closed out of season. A few **tavernas** open in summer, of which *Zorba* is by far the best, but the climb from Kapsáli discourages the crowds. Out of season, only one café/fast-food place stays open, near the square. **Accommodation** is slightly easier to find than in Kapsáli. Two good possibilities are the *Hotel Kathy* (☎0735/31 318; ②) or the *Pension Kythira*, at Manitohóri, 2km further inland (☎0735/31 563; ③). Back in Hóra, are the *Castello Studios* (☎0735/31 068; ④; year-round) and the old-style *Hotel Margarita* (☎0735/31 711; ⑤). Other facilities include a couple of **banks**, an **OTE**, **post office**, and branches of *Panayiotis* (☎0735/31 004) and *Nikos* (☎0735/31 767) vehicle rental.

The southeast coast

The beach at Kapsáli is decent but gets very crowded in July and August. For quieter, undeveloped beaches, it's better to head out to the east coast, towards Avlémonas. Be warned, however, that the roads are unpaved and can be hazardous on moped.

Fíri Ámmos and Kambonádha
Fíri Ámmos, the nearest good sand beach to Kapsáli, is popular but not overcrowded, even in summer. To get there, you can follow a paved road as far as the sleepy village of Kálamos (take the northerly side road between Kapsáli and Hóra); the beach is signposted down a dirt track on the far side of the village. Fíri Ámmos can also be reached from the inland village of Livádhi, on the Hóra–Arodhiánika road – as can **Kambonádha**, the next beach north.

Paleópoli and Avlémonas
PALEÓPOLI, a hamlet of a few scattered houses, is accessible by a paved road from Aroniádhika. The area is the site of the ancient city of **Skandia**, and excavations on the headland of **Kastrí** have revealed remains of an important Minoan colony. There's little visible evidence, apart from shards of pottery in the low crumbling cliffs, but happily,

tourist development in the area has been barred because of its archeological significance. Consequently, there's just one solitary **taverna**, the *Skandia* (June–Sept), on the excellent two-kilometre, sand-and-pebble **beach** that stretches to either side of the headland.

The surrounding countryside, a broad, cultivated valley surrounded by wild hills, is equally attractive. **Paleokástro**, the mountain to the west, is the site of ancient Kíthira and a sanctuary of Aphrodite, but again, there's little to be seen today. Heading across the valley and turning right, an unpaved road leads up to a tiny, whitewashed church above the cliffs. From there, a track leads down to **Keládhi**, a beautiful pebble beach with caves and rocks jutting out to sea.

AVLÉMONAS, 2km east of Paleópoli, is a tiny fishing port with two tavernas, a few rooms and a rather unimpressive Venetian fortress. The coast is rocky, the scenery bleak and exposed, and the village has something of an end-of-the-world feel.

Dhiakófti

DHIAKÓFTI, over the mountain to the north of Avlémonas, is equally bleak and remote, but surprisingly has developed into something of a resort for Greek families. The main attraction is a tiny white sand beach, which is picturesque, but crowded in summer; backed by a few fishermen's cottages, it has fine views across to the islet of **Makrónisi**. The village is well supplied with plenty of **rooms**, a few **tavernas** – and prominent "No Camping" signs.

North and west of Hóra

LIVÁDHI, 4km north of Hóra, has **rooms** and, on the main road, the newish *Hotel Aposperides* (☎0735/31656; ⑤) which, together with the Toxotis retaurant opposite, would make a good base if you had transport. At Katouni (2km out), there is an incongruous arched bridge; a legacy of the nineteenth century when all the Ionian islands were a British protectorate, it was built by a Scottish engineer. From the village, a fork heads west to Kalokerinés, and continues 3km further to the island's principal monastery, **Panayía Mirtidhíon**, set among cypress trees above the wild and windswept west coast. Beyond the monastery, a track leads down to a small anchorage at Limnária; there are few beaches along this rocky, forbidding shore.

Milopótamos, Káto Hóra and the Áyia Sofía cave

North of Livádhi, the main road crosses a bleak plateau whose few settlements are near-deserted. At Dhokána it's worth making a detour off the main road for **MILOPÓTAMOS**, a lovely traditional village and a virtual oasis, set in a wooded valley occupied by a small stream. Nearby is a waterfall, hidden from view by lush vegetation – follow the sign for "Neraidha" past an abandoned restaurant. The valley below the falls is overgrown but contains the remains of the watermill that gave the village its name.

Káto Hóra, 500m down the road, was Milopótamos's predecessor. Now derelict, it remains half-enclosed within the walls of a Venetian fortress. The fortress is small and has a rather domestic appearance: unlike the castle at Hóra, it was built as a place of refuge for the villagers in case of attack, rather than as a base for a Venetian garrison. All the houses within the walls, and many outside, are abandoned. Beyond here, an unpaved and precipitous road continues 5km through spectacular scenery to **Limiónas**, a rocky bay with a small beach of fine white sand.

The reason most visitors come to Milopótamos is to see the cave of **Áyia Sofía**, the largest and most impressive of a number of caverns on the island. A half-hour signposted walk from the village, the cave is open regularly (but not necessarily every day) from mid-June to mid-September (4–8pm). When the cave is closed, you can probably find a guide in Milopótamos; ask at the village, giving a day's notice, if possible.

The cave is worth the effort to see: the whitewashed entrance has been used as a church and has a painted iconostasis. Once inside, the cave system comprises a series of chambers with stalactites and stalagmites, down to a depth of 250m; inevitably in Kíthira, the highlights include the Apartment of Aphrodite – with her bedroom and boudoir on show.

Andikíthira island

The tiny island of **Andikíthira** has twice-weekly connections in summer only on the Kíthira–Kastélli run. Rocky and poor, it only received electricity in 1984. Attractions include a good birdlife and flora, but it's not the place if you want company. With only fifty or so inhabitants divided between two settlements – **Potamós**, the harbour, and **Sohória**, the village – people are rather thin on the ground. A resident doctor and a teacher serve the dwindling community (there are three children at the village school, as compared with nearly forty in the 1960s).

Both places offer a few rather primitive **rooms** (no toilet/running water) in summer; out of season, they may need a bit of persuasion to open up. Those in Sohória are by the island shop, which is also basic in the extreme: no wine, produce or eggs, and bread baked once a week (on Mondays).

Yíthio (Gythion)

YÍTHIO, Sparta's ancient port, is the gateway to the dramatic Máni peninsula, and one of the south's most attractive seaside towns in its own right. Its somewhat low key harbour, with intermittent ferries to Pireás, Kíthira and Crete, gives on to a graceful nineteenth-century waterside of tiled-roof houses – some of them now showing their age. There's a beach within walking distance and rooms are relatively easy to find. In addition, the town has a site as exotic and alluring as any in Greece. In the bay, tethered by a long narrow mole, is the **islet of Marathónissi**, ancient Kranae, where Paris of Troy, having abducted Helen from Menelaus's palace at Sparta, dropped anchor, and where the lovers spent their first night.

The Town

Marathónissi is the town's main sight, a pleasant place to while away an hour or so in the early evening, with swimming off the rocks towards the lighthouse (beware sea urchins). Amid the island's trees and scrub stands a recently restored tower-fortress built in the 1780s by the Turkish-appointed Bey of the Máni to guard the harbour against his lawless countrymen. It now houses the **Museum of the Máni** (9am–5pm; 300dr), which deals with the exploration of the Máni from Ciriaco de Pizzikoli (1447) to Henri Belle (1861), with captions in Greek and English.

For an aerial view of the islet and town, climb up through Yíthio's stepped streets on to the hill behind – the town's ancient acropolis. The settlement around it, known as **Laryssion**, was quite substantial in Roman times, enjoying a wealth from the export of murex, the purple-pigmented mollusc used to dye imperial togas.

Much of the ancient site now lies submerged but there are some impressive remains of a **Roman theatre** to be seen at the northeast end of the town. Follow the road past the post office for about 300m, until you reach an army barracks, where a sign in the road says "stop" and the theatre stands before you. A modest 80m in diameter but with most of its stone seats intact, it illustrates perfectly how buildings in Greece take on different guises through the ages: built into the side is a Byzantine church (now ruined) which, in turn, has been pressed into service as the outer wall of the barracks.

Beaches near Yíthio

For swimming, there are a number of coves within reach of Yíthio, on both sides of which rise an intermittent sequence of cliffs. The **beach** at Mavrovoúni, by the camp-sites detailed below, is one of the best; a smaller one, north of the town, has a nominal admission charge. Many of the buses serving Yíthio from Spárti routinely continue to Mavrovoúni – ask on board. Alternatively, if you've got transport, there are the superb beaches in Váthi Bay, further along, off the Areópoli road (see p.196).

Practicalities

Buses drop you close to the centre of town, with the main waterfront street, **Vassiléos Pávlou**, right ahead of you.

The *Ladopoulou* and *Andreikos* **bookstores** are worth scouring for books on the Máni. At least three days is worth considering for an exploration of the Máni and, if you're heading that way, **banks** should also be visited; there are three near the bus station. *Moto Mani* (by the causeway, on the Areópoli road; ☎0733/22 853) has mopeds for rent, and *Supercycle* (on the main square; ☎0733/24 407), rents out **motorcycles** by the day and, by negotiation, for longer periods. If you are headed for Kíthira, Pireás, Monemvassía or Crete, you can check **ferry** sailings at the *Rozakis Shipping and Travel Agency* on the waterfront; the latter will also change travellers' cheques and money.

Accommodation

Finding **accommodation** shouldn't be hard, with a fair selection of hotels and rooms – most along the waterfront, signposted up the steps behind, or facing the Marathónissi islet. There are three **campsites** along Mavrovoúni beach, which begins 3km south of the town off the Areópoli road. The nearest and best of these is the *Meltími* (☎0733/23 260; April–Oct); a couple of kilometres further on are the *Gythion Beach* (☎0733/22 522; year-round) and *Mani Beach* (☎0733/23 450; mid-April to mid-Oct).

Githion, Vassiléos Pávlou (☎0733/23 452). A fine old hotel on the waterfront; good value for money. ④.

Kondoyannis, Vassileos Pávlou 19 (☎0733/22 518). A small, friendly pension with a family feel. Up steep steps alongside – and above – the management's jewellery shop. ②.

Koutsouris, junction of Larysiou and Moretti (☎0733/22 321). Excellent-value pension, friendly and comfortable, with a lovely garden, a dog and five tortoises. Can be tricky to find: it's off Platía Mavromichali; look out for a church with a clock. ②.

Kranae, Vassiléos Pávlou 15 (☎0733/22 011). On the waterfront, next to the police station; try for a room at the front with a balcony. ③.

Milton (☎0733/22 091). Open year-round, this hotel is out at the Mavrovoúni beach. ③.

Saga, Dzanetaki (☎733/23 220). Pension run by a French family, with a popular restaurant on the ground floor. Overlooks the Marathonissi islet; recommended. ④.

Eating and drinking

For **meals**, the waterside is the obvious location – though choose carefully from among the tavernas since most have inflated prices for fish and seafood. A much more genuine local taverna serving traditional casseroles, *Petakos* is to be found tucked away in the sports stadium at the northern end of town. *Kostas*, by the bus station and facing the shore, is also a no-nonsense place. Besides these, and the restaurant in the *Pension Saga* (see above), look out for the *Taverna Poulikakos*, by the taxi rank, which offers good home cooking at reasonable prices.

The Máni

The southernmost peninsula of Greece, **the Máni**, stretches from Yíthio in the east, Kardhamíli in the west and down to Cape Ténaro, mythical entrance to the underworld. Its spine, negotiated by road at just a few points, is the vast grey mass of Mount Taíyettos and its southern extension, Sangiás. It is a wild landscape, an arid Mediterranean counterpart to Cornwall, say, or the Scottish highlands, and with an idiosyncratic culture and history to match. Nowhere in Greece does a region seem so close to its medieval past – which continued largely unchanged until the end of the last century.

The peninsula has two distinct regions: the Éxo (Outer) Máni and the Mésa (Inner) Máni. The **Mésa Máni** – that part of the peninsula south of a line drawn east from Areópoli – is the classic Máni territory, its jagged coast relieved only by the occasional cove, and its land a mass of rocks. It has one major sight, the remarkable caves at **Pírgos Dhiroú**, which are now very much on the tourist circuit. Beyond this point, though, tourists thin out fast. The attractions are in small part the coastal villages, like **Yerolimín** on the west coast, or **Kótronas** on the east, but the pleasure is mainly in the walking, and in exploring the **tower houses** and **churches**. A fair number of the tower houses survive, their groupings most dramatic at **Kítta**, **Váthia** and **Flomohóri**. The churches are harder to find, often hidden away from actual villages, but worth the effort. Many were built during the tenth and twelfth centuries, when the Maniots enthusiastically embraced Christianity; almost all retain primitive-looking frescoes.

The **Éxo Máni** – the coast up from Areópoli to Kalamáta – sees the emphasis shift much more to beaches. **Stoúpa** and **Kardhamíli** are both beautiful resorts, developing now but far from spoilt. And the road itself is an experience, threading precipitously up into the foothills of Taíyettos before looping down to the sea.

MANIOT BLOOD FEUDS

These were the result of an intricate feudal society that seems to have developed across the peninsula in the fourteenth century. After the arrival of refugee Byzantine families, an aristocracy known as Nyklians arose and the various clans gradually developed strongholds in the tightly clustered villages. The poor, rocky soil was totally inadequate for the population and over the next five centuries the clans clashed frequently and bloodily for land, power and prestige.

The feuds became ever more complex and gave rise to the building of strongholds: marble-roofed **tower houses** which, in the elaborate rule-system of the peninsula, could be raised only by those of Nyklian descent. From these local forts the clans – often based in the same village – conducted their vendettas according to strict rules and aims. The object was to annihilate both the tower house and the male members of the opposing clan. The favourite method of attack was to smash the prestigious tower roofs; the forts consequently rose to four and five storeys.

Feuds would customarily be signalled by the ringing of church bells and from this moment the adversaries would confine themselves to their towers, firing at each other with all available weaponry. The battles could last for years, even decades, with women (who were safe from attack) shuttling in food, ammunition and supplies. With the really prolonged feuds, temporary truces were declared at harvest times, then with business completed the battle would recommence. Ordinary villagers – the non-Nyklian peasantry – would, meanwhile, evacuate for the duration of the conflict. The feuds would end in one of two ways: destruction of a family in battle, or total surrender of a whole clan in a gesture of *psihikó* (a thing of the soul), when they would file out to kiss the hands of enemy parents who had lost "guns" (the Maniot term for male children) in the feud; the victors would then dictate strict terms by which the vanquished could remain in the village.

The last full-scale feud took place as late as 1870, in the village of Kítta, and required a full detachment of the regular army to put down.

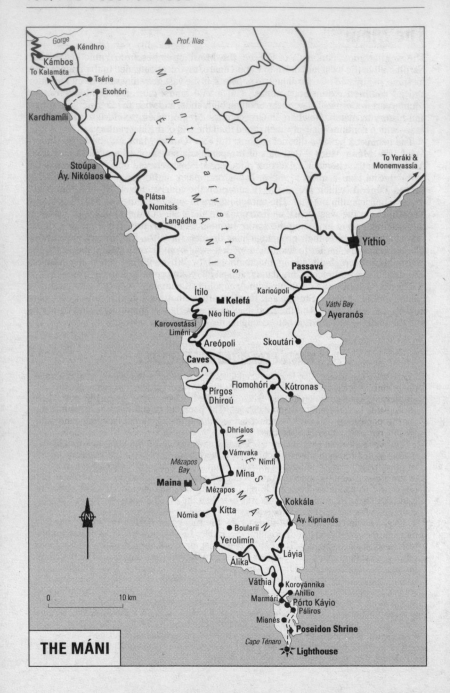

THE MÁNI

0   10 km

Some Maniot history

The mountains offer the key to Maniot history. Formidable natural barriers, they provided a refuge from, and bastion of resistance to, every occupying force of the last two millennia. The Dorians never reached this far south in the wake of the Mycenaeans, Roman occupation was perfunctory and Christianity did not take root in the interior until the ninth century (some 500 years after the establishment of Byzantium). Throughout the years of Venetian and Turkish control of the Peloponnese there were constant rebellions, climaxing in the Maniot uprising on March 17, 1821, a week before Archbishop Yermanos raised the Greek flag at Kalávrita to launch the War of Independence.

Alongside this national assertiveness was an equally intense and violent internal tribalism, seen at its most extreme in the Maniots' bizarrely elaborate tradition of **blood feuds** (see box on p.193), probably prolonged, and certainly exploited, by the **Turks**. The first Maniot uprising against them had taken place in 1571, a year after the Ottoman occupation. There were to be renewed attempts through the succeeding centuries, involving plots with Venetians, French and Russians. But the Turks, wisely, opted to control the Máni by granting a level of local autonomy, investing power in one or other clan whose leader they designated "Bey" of the region. The position provided a focus for the obsession with arms and war and worked well until the nineteenth-century appointment of **Petrobey Mavromihalis**. With a power base at Liméni he managed to unite the clans in revolution, and his Maniot army was to prove vital in the success of the War of Independence.

Perhaps unsurprisingly, the end of the war and the formation of an **independent Greece** was not quite the end of Maniot rebellion. Mavromihalis swiftly fell out with the first president of the nation, Capodistrias and, with other members of the clan, was imprisoned by him at Náfplio – an act which led to the president's assassination at the hands of Petrobey's brothers. The monarchy fared little better until one of the king's German officers was sent to the Máni to enlist soldiers in a special Maniot militia. The idea was adopted with enthusiasm, and was the start of an enduring tradition of Maniot service in the modern Greek military.

In this century, sadly, all has been decline, with persistent **depopulation** of the villages. In places like Váthia and Kítta, which once held populations in the hundreds, the numbers are now down to single figures, predominantly the old. Socially and politically the region is notorious as the most conservative in Greece. The Maniots reputedly enjoyed an influence during the colonels' junta, when the region first acquired roads, mains electricity and running water. They voted almost unanimously for the monarchy in the 1974 plebiscite, and this is one of the very few parts of Greece where you may still see visible support for the far-right National Party.

PRACTICALITIES IN THE MÁNI

Getting around can be time-consuming unless you have your own transport, and you may want to consider renting a **moped** or **motorbike** from Yíthio or Kalamáta, or a **car** from Kalamáta. Without a vehicle, you will need to walk or hitch to supplement the buses. In Mésa Máni, there are just two services: Areópoli–Yerolimín–Váthia (daily in summer; 3 weekly out of season); Areópoli–Kótronas–Láyia (daily).

An alternative is to make use of the handful of **taxis**, generally negotiable at Areópoli, Yerolimín and Kótronas, as well as at Yíthio. Currently, for example, a taxi from Areópoli to Váthia would cost 3500dr, and then you could return by bus.

The Mésa Máni has no regular **bank**. You can change travellers' cheques at the **post offices** (Mon–Fri 7.30am–2pm) in Yerolimín or Areópoli, but it's wise to collect as much as you think you'll need for a visit in advance at either Yíthio or Kalamáta.

Into the Máni: Yíthio to Areópoli

The road from Yíthio into the Máni begins amid a fertile and gentle landscape, running slightly inland of the coast and the Yíthio/Mavrovoúni beaches, through tracts of orange and olive groves. About 12km beyond Yíthio, the Máni suddenly asserts itself as the road enters a gorge below the Turkish **Castle of Passavá**.

The castle is one of a pair (with Kelefá to the west) guarding the Máni, or perhaps more accurately guarding against the Máni. It's quite a scramble up, with no regular path, but the site is ample reward, with views out across two bays and for some miles along the defile from Areópoli. There has been a fortress on Passavá since Mycenaean times; the present version is an eighteenth-century Turkish rebuilding of a Frankish fort that the Venetians had destroyed on their flight from the Peloponnese in 1684. It was abandoned by the Turks in 1780 following the massacre of its garrison by the Maniot Grigorakis clan – their vengeance for the arrest and execution by the Turks of the clan chief.

Shortly after Passavá a turning to the left, signposted "Belle Hélène", leads down to a long sandy beach at **Váthi Bay**, which is dominated by German tourists. Before you reach the beach, there is the *Pension Tassia* (☎0733/93 433; ④), with four comfortable rooms, each with a kitchen. At the southern end of the beach is the grand *Hotel Belle Hélène* (☎0733/93 001; ⑤), which is often block booked by German groups, and the *Kronos* campsite (☎0733/93 320; mid-April–Oct), which is well suited to families; once past the camper vans, there is plenty to explore, turtles and tortoises to find and horse riding nearby.

The road beyond the beach deteriorates rapidly, though it is possible to continue through woods to the village of Ayeranós, with a couple of tower houses, and thence, if you can find your way among the numerous rough tracks, to Skoutári, below which is another good beach with some Roman remains. A better road to Skoutári leaves the main Yíthio–Areópoli road at Karioúpoli, itself dominated by an imposing tower house.

Continuing towards Areópoli from Passavá, the landscape remains fertile until the wild, scrubby mass of Mount Kouskoúni signals the final approach to Mésa Máni. You enter another pass, with **Kelefá Castle** (see p.201) above to the north, and beyond it several southerly peaks of Mount Taíyettos. Areópoli, as you curl down from the hills, radiates a real sense of arrival.

Areópoli and around

An austere-looking town, **AREÓPOLI** sets an immediate mood for the region. It was, until the last century, secondary to Ítilo, 6km north, as the gateway to Mésa Máni, but the modern road (and the provincial border, placing Ítilo in Messinía) has made it, to all intents, the region's centre. Its name, meaning the Town of Ares (the god of war), was bestowed for its efforts during the War of Independence. It was here that Mavromihalis (commemorated by a statue in the main *platía*) declared the uprising.

The town's sights are archetypically Maniot in their apparent confusion of ages. The **Taxiárhis** cathedral, for example, has primitive reliefs above its doors which look twelfth century until you notice their date of 1798. Similarly, its tower houses could readily be described as medieval, though most of them were built in the early 1800s. On its own, in a little *platía*, is the church of **Áyios Ioannis**, the Mavromihalis family church; the interior has strip-cartoon frescoes.

Buses leave Areópoli from the main *platía*; if you are heading north, towards Kalamáta, you may need to change at Ítilo. On or just off the *platía* is a **bank** (Tues & Thurs 9am–noon), a **post office**, OTE and a useful **supermarket**.

There are several **rooms** around the cathedral and two **hotels**: the *Kounis* (☎0733/51 340; ④) near the main *platía*, and the *Mani* (☎0733/51 269; ④) ten minutes from the main *platía* and 50m beyond the bank. One of the towers, the *Pirgos Kapetanakou* (☎0733/51 233; ⑤), has been restored by the EOT as a "traditional guesthouse"; the rooms are beautiful but expensive. Nearby is the *Pension Londas* (☎0733/51 360; ⑤), another converted tower house, and the much cheaper *Pirgos Tsimova* (☎0733/51 301; ③), which has more of a lived-in feel to it.

There are a number of **café-restaurants** around the main *platía*; the most popular (and the bus agent) is *Nikola's Corner*, which does good *mézedhes*; try the general assortment.

North to Liméni

Areópoli stands back a kilometre or so from the sea – an enjoyable walk. The best local beach is at **LIMÉNI**, the town's tiny, traditional port, 3km to the north, whose scattering of houses are dominated by the restored tower house of Petrobey Mavromihalis, which looks like nothing so much as an English country parish church. On one of the hairpin bends on the road from Areópoli to Liméni is the newly completed *Limeni Village* (☎0733/51 111;⑤–⑥), a recreation, in unusually good taste, of Maniot towers, high above the rocky shore, but with its own swimming pool. Further round the bay, on the waterside, there are a few tavernas and *Toh Limeni* (☎0733/51 458; ③), a restaurant with rooms.

South to the Pírgos Dhiroú caves

Eight kilometres south from Areópoli, at the village of **PÍRGOS DHIROÚ**, the road forks off to the underground caves – the Máni's major tourist attraction. The village itself has an isolated 21-metre-tower house, but is otherwise geared to the cave trade, with numerous tavernas and cafés, and dozens of **rooms** for rent. The closest to the caves – and the sea – are at the *Panorama* restaurant (☎0733/52 280; ③); the rooms are better than the meals, which are only marginally offset by the view.

The **Pírgos Dhiroú caves** (June–Sept 8am–6pm; Oct–May 8am–3pm; 1800dr) are 4km beyond the main village, set beside the sea and a small beach. They are very much a packaged attraction, with long queues for admission in season. However, unless caves leave you cold, they are worth a visit, especially on weekday afternoons when the wait is shorter. Visits consist of a half-hour punt around the underground waterways of the **Glifádha caves**, well-lit and crammed with stalactites, whose reflections are a remarkable sight in the two- to twenty-metre-deep water. You are then allowed a brief tour on foot of the **Alepótripa caves** – huge chambers (one of them 100m by 60m) in which excavation has unearthed evidence of prehistoric occupation. One disappointment is the absence of any foreign-language commentary.

You should buy a ticket as soon as you arrive at the caves: this gives you a priority number for the tours. On a mid-season weekend you can wait for an hour or more, so it's best to arrive as early as possible in the day with gear to make the most of the adjacent beach. If time is short, taxis from Areópoli will take you to the caves, then wait and take you back; prices, especially split four ways, are reasonable.

The adjoining **museum** (daily except Mon 8.30am–3pm; 400dr) of neolithic finds from the caves is interesting, but again the few captions are in Greek only; a small guide in several languages is promised.

South to Yerolimín

The narrow plain between Pírgos Dhiroú and Yerolimín is one of the more fertile parts of Mésa Máni. This seventeen-kilometre stretch of the so-called "shadow coast" supported, until this century, an extraordinary number of villages. It retains a major concentration of **churches**, many of them Byzantine, dating from the eleventh to the fourteenth centuries. These are especially hard to find, though well detailed in Peter

Greenhalgh's *Deep Into Mani*. The main feature to look for is a barrel roof. Almost all are kept unlocked or a key can be found.

Among Greenhalgh's favourites on the seaward side are the eleventh-century **church of the Taxiárkhis** at Haroúdha (3km south of Pírgos Dhiroú), **Trissákia church** by a reservoir near Tsópokas (5km south of Pírgos Dhiroú) and **Ayía Varvára** at Éremos (8km south of Pírgos Dhiroú). Equally rewarding is a walk along the **old road** east of, and parallel to, the main road. This begins near the village of Dhríalos and rejoins the main road beyond the tower houses at Mína. Midway is Vámvaka and its eleventh-century church of **Áyios Theódhoros**, with superb carved marbles and decorative brickwork; unfortunately, most of the frescoes have been whitewashed over.

Mézapos and the Castle of the Maina

An easier excursion from the main road is to the village of **MÉZAPOS**, whose deep-water harbour made it one of the chief settlements of Máni, until the road was built this century. From the main road, take the side road to Áyios Yioryios and then to Mézapos, where there are a few rooms. The best of some fine coastal walks leads to the castle at **Tigáni** (Frying Pan) **rock**, 4km around the cliffs, past the twelfth-century **church of Vlacherna**, which has a few fresco fragments, including a memorable John the Baptist.

The fortress, by general consensus, seems to have been the **Castle of the Maina**, constructed like those of Mystra and Monemvassía by the Frankish baron, Guillaume de Villehardouin, and ceded with them by the Byzantines in 1261. Tigáni is as arid a site as any in Greece – a dry Monemvassía in effect – whose fortress seems scarcely man-made, blending as it does into the terrain. It's a jagged walk out to the castle across rocks fashioned into pans for salt-gathering; within the walls are ruins of a Byzantine church and numerous cisterns. If you ask at one of the cafés in Mézapos it's sometimes possible to negotiate a boat trip out to Tigáni, or even around the cape to Yerolimín.

The nearby village of **STAVRÍ** offers traditional **tower-house accommodation** in the converted *Tsitsiris Castle* (☎0733/56 297; ⑤), much the same price as the other tower hotels in Areópoli and Váthia, but in a more exciting setting. To the north of Stavrí, but within walking distance, is the twelfth-century **church of Episkopí**; the roof has been restored, while inside there are some fine, but faded, frescoes and columns crowned by Ionic capitals, with a surprising marble arch at the entry to the *ikonostasí*.

Kítta and Boularíí

Continuing along the main road, **KÍTTA**, once the largest and most powerful village in the region, boasts the crumbling remains of more than twenty tower houses. It was here in 1870 that the last feudal war took place, eventually being suppressed by a full battalion of 400 regular soldiers. Over to the west, visible from the village, is another eruption of tower houses at Kítta's traditional rival, Nómia.

Two kilometres south of Kítta and east of the main road, **BOULARÍÍ** is one of the most interesting and accessible villages in Mésa Máni. It is clearly divided into "upper" and "lower" quarters, both of which retain well-preserved tower houses and, in varying states of decay, some twenty churches. The two most impressive are tenth-century **Áyios Pandelímon** (roofless and unlocked, with several frescoes) and eleventh-century **Áyios Stratigós**, which is just over the brow of the hill at the top of the village. This second church is locked and the keys with the priest at Eliá village, but it is usually possible to gain peaceable entry without them since the doorframe itself is barely secured by a piece of twisted wire; many seem to have squeezed in this way, as the pile of donated money inside confirms. The effort is well rewarded for the church possesses a spectacular series of frescoes from the twelfth to the eighteenth centuries.

Yerolimín and south to the Mátapan

After the journey from Areópoli, **YEROLIMÍN** (YEROLIMÉNAS) has an end-of-the-world air, and it makes a good base for exploring the southern extremities of the Máni. Despite appearances, the village was only developed in the 1870s – around a jetty and warehouses built by a local (a non-Nyklian migrant) who had made good on the island of Síros. There are a few shops, a **post office**, a couple of **cafés** and two **hotels**, run by cousins. Of these, the *Akroyali* (☎0733/54 204; ③) is the more comfortable, with some air-conditioned rooms; the *Akrotenaritis* (☎0733/54 205; ②) is slightly cheaper and now has four new rooms that rival those at the *Akroyali*. There are several **places to eat** between the two hotels, but the baked fish in lemon juice and olive oil served at the *Akroyali* takes some beating.

At the dock, occasional boat trips are offered – when the local owners feel like it – around Cape Ténaro (see below).

Álika to Pórto Káyio

South from Yerolimín, a good road (and the bus) continues to Álika, where it divides. One fork leads east through the mountains to Láyia (see below), and the other continues to Váthia and across the Marmári isthmus to Páliros. Between Álika and Váthia there are good coves for swimming. One of the best is a place known as **Kipárissos**, reached by following a riverbed (dry in summer) about midway to Váthia. On the headland above are scattered Roman remains of ancient Kaenipolis, including (amid the walled fields) the excavated ruins of a sixth-century basilica.

VÁTHIA, a group of tower houses set uncompromisingly on a scorching mass of rocks, is one of the most dramatic villages in Mésa Máni. It features in Colonel Leake's account of his travels, one of the best sources on Greece in the early nineteenth century. He was warned to avoid going through the village as a feud had been running between two families for the previous forty years. Today it is a blend of ghost town and building site as the EOT is restoring the tower houses to accommodate guests; eight houses (☎0733/55 244; ⑤) have already been restored and work is underway on the remaining four. As word spreads, it is likely that advance booking will be advisable, certainly in the high season; rooms are marginally cheaper if you are prepared to share bathroom facilities.

From Váthia the road south to the cape starts out uphill, edging around the mountain in what appears to be quite the wrong direction. It slowly descends, however, bringing you out at the beach and hamlet of **PÓRTO KÁYIO** (7km from Váthia). There are comfortable rooms at the *Akroteri Domatia* (③), and two or three tavernas, the best of which is the *Hippocampos*. Above the village, a road branches west (past a rusting, bullet-ridden sign for Páliros) around the headland, capped by ruins of a Turkish **castle** contemporary with Kelefá, to sandy **beaches** at the double bay of Marmári.

On to Cape Ténaro

At the bullet-ridden sign, just out of Pórto Káyio, a track forks to the left and heads towards the Máni's last, barren peninsula. The track leads up to the hilltop church visible from the village below. A track from here forks to the left for a few hundred metres to the deserted hamlet of Páliros. Ignore the right-hand fork at the church (a dead end) and bear left for Páliros. After a few metres, a second right-hand fork heads for the cape, towards Mianés, another hamlet with a single-figure population. Beyond here the road descends towards the sea, ending by a knoll crowned with the squat **chapel of Asómati**, constructed largely of materials from an ancient Temple of Poseidon.

To the left (east) as you face the chapel is the little pebbly **bay of Asómati**, often with a fishing boat at anchor; on the shore is a small **cave**, another addition to the list of sites said to be the mythical entrance to the underworld. Patrick Leigh Fermor, in *Mani*, writes of another "Gates of Hades" cave, which he swam into on the western shore of Mátapan, just below Marmári. To the right (west) of the Asómati hill, the main path, marked by red dots, continues along the shore of another cove and through the metre-high foundations of a **Roman town** that grew up around the Poseidon shrine; there is even a good mosaic in one structure. From here the old trail, which existed before the road was bulldozed, reappears as a walled path, allowing 180° views of the sea on its 25-minute course to the lighthouse on **Cape Ténaro**.

The east coast

The east coast of Mésa Máni is most easily approached from Areópoli, whence there's a daily **bus** through Kótronas to Láyia. However, if you have transport, or you're prepared to walk and hitch, there's satisfaction in doing a full loop of the peninsula, crossing over to Láyia from Yerolimín or Pórto Káyio. The east-coast landscape is almost remorselessly barren, little more than scrub and prickly pears. This is the Mésa Máni's "sunward coast", far harsher than the "shadow coast" of the west side. There are few beaches, with most of the scattered villages hanging on the cliffs.

Láyia to Kokkála

From the fork at Álika (see above), it is about an hour and a half's walk by road to **LÁYIA**. Coming from Pórto Káyio it takes around three hours, though the route, at times on narrow tracks, is more dramatic, passing the virtually deserted hilltop village of Korogoniánika. Láyia itself is a multi-towered village that perfectly exemplifies the feudal setup of the old Máni. Four Nyklian families lived here, and their four independently sited settlements, each with its own church, survive. One of the taller towers, so the locals claim, was built overnight by the four hundred men of one clan, hoping to gain an advantage at sunrise. During the eighteenth century the village was home to the Mésa Máni doctor – a strategic base from which to attend the war-wounded across the peninsula. Today there is a single taverna, with a limited menu and a few rather overpriced **rooms** for rent.

The first village beyond Láyia, over on the east coast, is **ÁYIOS KIPRIANÓS**. Inexplicably towerless, it, too, has a few rooms, though the proprietor may prove elusive in the off-season.

Five kilometres on is **KOKKÁLA**, a larger village and enclosed by a rare patch of greenery. It has a harbour, a very pretty cove, a longer beach to the north and walking possibilities. Three kilometres to the northwest, up on the mountainside, is a spot known as Kiónia (columns), with the foundations of two Roman temples. The village boasts several café-restaurants, the *Pension Kokkala* (☎0733/58 307; ③) and several rooms for rent above the *Taverna Marathos* (summer only; ②) on the beach. Looking over the village is the newly opened *Kastro* (☎0733/58 290; ④), expensive but value for money.

Kótronas and Flomohóri

KÓTRONAS is still a fishing village, and its pebble beach (there are sandy strips further around the bay) and causeway-islet make it a good last stop in the region. The village is frequented by a fair number of tourists (mainly Germans) each summer, and has a trio of pensions. The most pleasant is the *Kalikardia* (☎0733/53 246; ②–③), on the seafront; rooms with private facilities are significantly dearer. The *Adelfia* (☎0733/53 209; ②) is cheaper, and, with its multi-coloured exterior, brighter.

The land hereabouts is relatively fertile, and **FLOMOHÓRI**, half an hour's walk in the hills behind, has maintained a reasonable population as well as a last imposing group of tower houses.

The Éxo Máni: Areópoli to Kalamáta

The forty kilometres of road between Areópoli and Kalamáta is as dramatic and beautiful as any in Greece, a virtual corniche route between **Mount Taíyettos** and the **Gulf of Messinía**. The first few settlements en route are classic Maniot villages, their towers packed against the hillside. As you move north, with the road dropping to near sea level, there are three or four small resorts, which are becoming increasingly popular but are as yet relatively unspoilt. For walkers, there is a reasonably well-preserved *kalderími* paralleling (or short-cutting) much of the paved route, and a **superb gorge hike** just north of Kardhamíli.

Ítilo and around

ÍTILO, 11km from Areópoli, is the transport hub for the region. If you are heading towards Kalamáta, either from Yíthio or Areópoli, you'll need to change here. It looks tremendous from a distance, though close up it is a little depressing; its population is in decline, and many of the tower houses are collapsing into decay. In better days, Ítilo was the capital of the Máni, and from the sixteenth to the eighteenth century it was the region's most notorious base for piracy and slave trading. The Maniots traded amorally and efficiently in slaves, selling Turks to Venetians, Venetians to Turks, and, at times of feud, the women of each others' clans. Irritated by their piracy and hoping to control the important pass to the north, the Turks built the **Castle of Kelefá**. This is just a kilometre's walk from Ítilo across a gorge and its walls and bastions, built for a garrison of five hundred, are substantially intact.

Also worth exploring is the monastery of **Dhekoúlou**, down towards the coast; its setting is beautiful and there are some fine eighteenth-century frescoes in the chapel.

If you were obliged to spend some time in Ítilo, there are a few **rooms** to rent, but you would be better advised to stay at the *Pension Galarie* (☎0733/59 390; ③) on the road down to the beach. Better still would be to look for accommodation by the beach in **NÉO ÍTILO**, which is just round the bay from Ítilo's ancient seaport, Karavostássi. Néo Ítilo is a tiny hamlet, but as well as rooms for rent it boasts the luxury *Hotel Itilo* (☎0733/59 222; ⑥); half board is obligatory, a la carte at 3000dr a day. The hotel has a guesthouse, the *Alevras*, across the road. It's marginally cheaper and half board is optional, but the luxury is spread more thinly and the view is less stunning.

Langádha, Nomitsís and Thalamés

If you want to walk for a stretch of the onward route, you can pick up the *kalderími* just below the main road out of Ítilo. As it continues north, the track occasionally crosses the modern road, but it is distinct at least as far as Ríglia, and probably (we've not tried) beyond to Kardhamíli. The most interesting of the villages along this mountainous leg of the way are **LANGÁDHA**, for its setting that bristles with towers, and **NOMITSÍS**, for its trio of frescoed Byzantine churches strung out along the main street. A couple more churches are to be found off the road just to the north; in one of these, the **Metamórfosi**, there are delightful sculpted animal capitals.

Just before Nomitsís, you pass the hamlet of **THALAMÉS**, where a local enthusiast has set up a widely advertised **Museum of Maniot Folklore and History** (May–Sept daily 8am–8pm). The tag "museum" is perhaps a bit inflated for what is really a collection of junkshop items, but it's a nice stop nonetheless and sells superb local honey.

Áyios Nikólaos and Stoupa

The beaches of Éxo Máni begin at **ÁYIOS NIKÓLAOS**, whose quiet little harbour, flanked by old stone houses, seems fated for higher things. At present it's a delightful place, with four tavernas and a scattering of **rooms** and apartments. A good choice, for both rooms and food, is the *Lofos*, a little below the village.

Just to the north, **STOÚPA** is much more developed, and justifiably so. It has possibly the best sands along this coast with two glorious **beaches** (Stoúpa and the smaller Kalogría) separated by a headland, each sloping into the sea and superb for children. Submarine freshwater springs gush into the bay, keeping it unusually clean – if also a bit cold – while banana trees lend an exotic air. Ten minutes to the north of Kalogría beach is a delightful rocky and deserted cove. The resort was home for a while to Nikos Kazantzakis, who is said to have based his novel *Zorba the Greek* on a worker at the coal mine in nearby Pastrova.

Out of peak season, Stoúpa is certainly recommended. In July and August, you may find the crowds a bit overwhelming, and space at a premium. There are plenty of tavernas and a **bank** (Mon–Fri 9am–3pm), but the local supermarket will change money and travellers' cheques during opening hours. Accommodation includes numerous **rooms** and apartments for rent, and several **hotels**. The cheapest are the *Lefktron* (☎0721/77 322; ③–④), the *Stoupa* (☎0721/77 485; ④) and the new *Halikoura Bay* (☎0721/77 303; ④). Halfway to Kardhamíli is a **campsite**, *Ta Delfinia* (☎0721/54 318; April–Oct), which tends to attract a youngish crowd.

Kardhamíli

KARDHAMÍLI, 10km north of Stoúpa, is also a major resort, by Peloponnese standards at least, with ranks of self-catering apartments and pensions, block-booked by the package trade in season. But once again the **beach** is superb – a long pebble strip north of the the village and fronted by acres of olive trees.

Back from the road, it's a nice walk up to "Old Kardhamíli", the medieval quarter on the hillside. Here a group of abandoned tower houses are gathered about the eighteenth-century church of **Áyios Spíridhon** with its unusual multi-storey bell tower. Further back is a pair of ancient tombs and the old acropolis, where the Maniot chieftains Kolokotronis and Mavromihalis played human chess with their troops during the War of Independence.

On the main road and *platía*, you'll find a branch of the *Agricultural Bank* (Mon & Thurs), a **post office** (Mon–Fri), which will change money and travellers' cheques, and *Morgan Holiday* (☎0721/73 220), which is open all hours and will help you with everything from accommodation to **moped rental**. Bookable **hotels** include the *Patriarxea* (☎0721/73 366; ④), by the main road but attractive, and the imaginatively named *Kardamyli Beach* (☎0721/73 180; ⑤) on the beach. Also on the beach is *Lela's* (☎0721/73 541; ③), a good taverna with fine sea-view **rooms**, which should be booked well ahead in summer. There's also a good beachside **campsite**, *Melitsina* (May–Sept; ☎0721/73 461). Among Kardhamíli's **tavernas**, try *Kiki's* as well as *Lela's*, whose eponymous owner was once housekeeper to Patrick Leigh Fermor, who lives locally. Otherwise, around the *platía*, there are a few low-key bars and a superb ice-cream place.

Inland to the Víros gorge

North of Kardhamíli the road leaves the coast, which rises to cliffs around a cape, before dropping back to the sea in the bay around Kalamáta. But before moving on, a day or two spent exploring Kardhamíli's immediate environs on foot is time well spent.

The giant **Víros gorge** plunges down from the very summit of Taíyettos to meet the sea just north of the resort, and tracks penetrate the gorge from various directions. From Kardhamíli, a path at the acropolis continues to the village and church of Ayía Sofía, and then proceeds on a mixture of tracks and lanes either across a plateau to the hamlet of Exohóri or down into the gorge, where two **monasteries** nestle at the base of sheer walls. An hour or so inland along the canyon, more cobbled ways lead up to either Tséria on the north bank (taverna but no accommodation) or back towards Exohóri on the south flank. Linking any or all of these points is an easy day's hiking at most; forays further upstream require full hiking gear and detailed local maps.

Kalamáta and beyond

KALAMÁTA is by far the largest city of the southern Peloponnese, spreading for some four kilometres back from the sea, and into the hills. It's quite a metropolitan shock after the small-town life of the rest of the region.

The city has a long-established export trade in olives and figs from the Messinian plain, and, until recently, it had a prospering industrial base. In 1986, however, Kalamáta was near the epicentre of a severe **earthquake** that killed twenty people and left 12,000 families homeless. But for the fact that the quake struck in the early evening, when many people were outside, the death toll would have been much higher. As it was, large numbers of buildings were levelled throughout the town. The intensity of the damage was in part due to the city's position over several subterranean streams, but mostly, it seems, the legacy of poor 1960s construction. The result has been an economic depression across the whole area, and a startling fifty percent drop in the city's former 60,000 population.

The City

The physical effects of the earthquake are still evident in temporary housing around the suburbs of the city, and few visitors will want to linger here. However, if you are travelling for a while, it is a good place to get things done, and there are other simple pleasures such as eating at untouristed tavernas on the waterfront or around the centre, which is taken to be the wide avenue formed by Platía Yioryíou and the larger Platía Konstandínos Dhiadhóknou.

With a little time to fill, a twenty-minute walk north of the centre will bring you to the most pleasing area of the city, around the **Kástro**. Built by the Franks and destroyed and adapted in turn by the Turks and Venetians, the *kástro* survived the quake with little damage. An **amphitheatre** at its base hosts summer concerts.

Kalamáta's **beach**, a ten-minute bus ride (#1) south of the centre, is always crowded along the central section. The gritty sands are functional but the harbour itself has a welcome touch of life and activity.

If you prefer to walk to the harbour from the centre, it's a thirty-minute walk down Aristoménous, and you can loiter in the park alongside and admire the old steam engines and rolling stock from the three-foot gauge Peloponnese railway.

Practicalities

If you're looking to get transport straight through, arrive early to make connections. The **bus station** is about 600m north of the centre; follow the river along Nedhóndos and look out for the **market** nearby. The most regular buses run north to Megalópoli/ Trípoli and southwest to Koróni; the magnificent route over the Taíyettos to Spárti is covered twice daily, and the one to Kardhamíli and Ítilo (connection to Areópoli) four times daily.

The **train station** is 300m to the west of Platía Konstandínou Dhiadhóknou. Kalamáta is the railhead for trains chugging along the slow but enjoyable route to Kiparissía (and ultimately to Pátra, with a possible detour to Olympia) or inland to Trípoli and Árgos. There are daily **flights** to and from Athens; tickets are sold at the *Olympic Airways* office across from the train station. **Taxis** usually meet trains; otherwise there is a taxi rank on Platía Konstandínou Dhiadhóknou and another at the junction with Navarínou. Three rival agencies offer **car rental**: *Maniatis*, Iatropoúlou 1 (☎0721/27 694), *Theodorakopoulos*, Kessári 2 (☎0721/20 352), and *Stavrianos*, Nedhóndos 89 (☎0721/23 041). There are two reliable **moped rental** outlets: *Bastakos*, Fáron 190 (☎0721/26 638), and *Alpha*, Virónos 156 (☎0721/93 423).

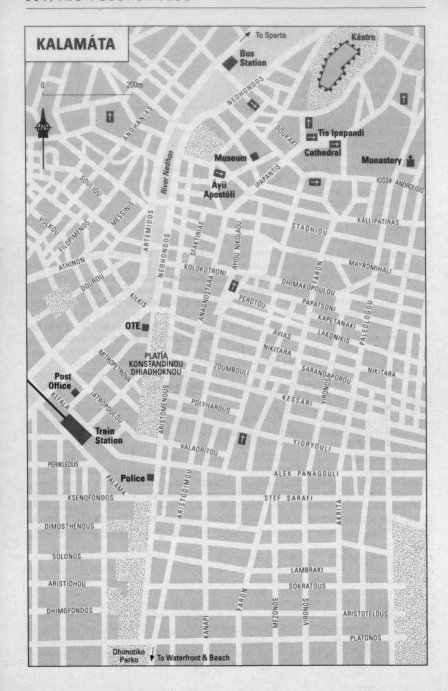

KALAMÁTA

To Sparta

Kástro

Bus Station

0   200m

N

ANOHANIAS

NEDHONDOS

DOUKAKI

Tis Ipapandi

Cathedral

Monastery

Museum

River Nedhon

Áyii Apostóli

IPAPANTIS

IOSSIF ANDROUSIS

SOULIOU

KALLIPATIRAS

VOLKOU

MESSINIS

ARTEMIDOS

SFAKTIRIAS

AYIOU NIKOLAOU

STADHIOÚ

FILOPIMENOS

NEDHONDOS

KOLOKOTRONI

DHIMAKOPOULOU

FARON

MAVROMIHALI

ATHINON

DOUROU

KILKIS

ANAGNOSTARA

PEROTOU

PAPATSONI

KAPETANAKI

PALEOLOGOU

AVIAS

LAKONIKIS

OTÉ

MITROPETROVA

NIKITARA

ZOUMBOULI

SARANDAPOROU

NIKITARA

PLATÍA KONSTANDÍNOU DHIADHÓKHNOU

VIRONOS

Post Office

KEFALA

IATROPOULOU

ARISTOMENOUS

POLYHAROUS

KESSARI

Train Station

VALAORITOU

YIORYOULI

PERIKLEOUS

PALAMA

Police

ALEX PANAGOULI

KSENOFONDOS

ARISTODIMOU

STEF SARAFI

AKRITA

DIMOSTHENOUS

SOLONOS

LAMBRAKI

ARISTIDHOU

SOKRATOUS

FARON

VIRONOS

ARISTOTELOUS

DHIMOFONDOS

KANAPI

MEZONOS

PLATONOS

Dhimotiko Parko   To Waterfront & Beach

Most facilities, including the **banks**, **post office** and **OTE**, are in the streets around Platía Konstandínou Dhiadhóknou, though there is a second **post office** near the customs house at the seaward end of Aristoménous. In the summer, *Hobby* at Fáron 237 sells English-language newspapers and books.

Accommodation

In the city centre, there are very few mid-range **hotels** left. One of the best in terms of value for money is the *George*, Frantzi 5 (☎0721/27 225; ②). In general you'll do better down by the waterfront, where there are many more hotels. Some of these are expensive, though they seem to have spent more on the reception areas than the bedrooms. Even so, they are often full by mid-afternoon and if you have not booked ahead you may have to shop around. Most serve breakfast, for which you may have to pay more.

Choices include the *Flisvos*, Navarínou 135 (☎0721/82 177; ④), which has quiet, comfortable rooms on the waterfront next to the church of Ayía Anastasis. Nearby and next to the *platía*, the *Haikos*, Navarínou 115 (☎0721/88 902; ④), is a modern hotel with pleasant rooms and helpful staff. The *Nevada*, Santaroza 9 (☎0721/82 429; ②), is carefully tended by a Greek matriarch, and though there are a number of house rules (in Greek and interpreted by her son), the rooms are cosy; there is no breakfast, but you can eat very cheaply on the waterfront close by.

The nearest **campsites** are to be found along the stretch of beach to the east of the city. The first, about 5km from the waterfront, is the *Elite* (☎0721/80 365; April to mid-Oct). It is behind the *Hotel Elite* (☎0721/27 368; ⑤), where campers can eat, and swim in the pool. If you want to swim off the pebble beach you will have to cross the Areópoli–Kalamáta highway, or stay at the *Maria*, also known as the *Sea and Sun*, (☎0721/41 060), a popular and friendly campsite 500m down the road, which fronts onto the sea. However, unless stuck, you'd do better heading west towards Petalídhi (see below).

ROOM PRICE SCALES

All the accommodation prices in this book have been coded using the symbols below below. The rates quoted represent the cheapest available room in high season; all are prices for a double room, except for category ①, which are per person rates.

① 1400–2000dr (£4–5.50/US$6–8.50)   ④ 8000–12000dr (£22–33/US$33–50)
② 4000–6000dr (£11–16.50/US$17–25)   ⑤ 12000–16000dr (£33–44/US$50–66)
③ 6000–8000dr (£16.50–22/US$25–33)   ⑥ 16000dr (£44/US$66) and upwards

For more accommodation details, see pp.34–35.

Eating and drinking

The best **restaurants** in the summer months are down by the **harbour**, which has been set up as a yacht marina. Moving from west to east, you have quite a selection: *Krini* at Evangelistrías 40, a neighbourhood fish-and-wine taverna open most of the year; *Katofli* on Salamínos near the marina, with outdoor summer seating and a huge menu; *Meltemi*, near the corner of Navarínou and Fáron, a very basic *psistariá* with tasty food; *Tabaki*, Navarínou 91, with a wide menu and cheerful service; almost opposite, the *Akroyiali* has a better sea view and good but pricey fish, though the service can be surly.

Only in winter does the **centre** get into its culinary stride. At this time, pick from: *Koutivas*, 100m north of the bus station, with spicy food and bulk wine; *Kannas*, Lakonikís 18, an atmospheric place with occasional live music, which featured in

Sheelagh Kanelli's novel, *Earth and Water*, or *Kioupi*, Alexíki 52 (off the Areópoli road), idiosyncratically decorated and with clay-pot cooking (as the name implies).

If you're not after a full meal, Kalamáta has plenty of *mezedhopolía*, the better among them serving the traditional local snack – roast pork and potatoes. Down at the harbour, the *ouzerí* west of the post office does a nice fish *meze*; and there's another good one at the bottom of Fáron, near a *souvlaki* stand and video-games arcade, which does an excellent *pikilía* (grand selection of *mezédhes*).

Northwest to ancient Messene

The ruins of ancient **MESSENE** (ITHOMI) lie 25km northwest of Kalamáta and 20km northwest of modern Messini. The ancient city was the fortified capital of the Messenians, and achieved some fame in the ancient world as a showcase of military architecture. The highlights of the widely dispersed site are the outcrops of its giant walls, towers and gates.

The the ruins share the lower slopes of Mount Ithómi (800m) with the pretty village of **MAVROMÁTI**. A climb to the summit is rewarded with spectacular views of the region of Messinía and the southern Peloponnese. If you wished to stay and see the sunset from the site of the Temple of Zeus which crowns this peak, there are **rooms** at the *Zeus* (☎0724/51 025; ②), a pension in the village.

The site is a tricky place to get to, unless you're driving. Buses run only twice a day from Kalamáta (one departure is at 6am). With a car it's a fairly easy detour en route to either Kiparissía, Pílos or Petalídhi/Koróni.

The site

Messene's fortifications were designed as the southernmost link in a defensive chain of walled cities (others included Megalopolis and Argos) masterminded by the Theban leader Epaminondas to keep the Spartans at bay. Having managed to halt them at the battle of Leuctra in 371 BC, he set about building a nine-kilometre circuit of walls and restoring the Messenians to their native acropolis. The Messenians, who had resisted Spartan oppression from the eighth century BC onwards, wasted no time in re-establishing their capital; the city, so chronicles say, was built in 85 days.

The most interesting of the remains is the **Arcadia gate** at the north end of the site, through which the side road to Meligalá still runs. It consisted of an outer and inner portal separated by a circular courtyard made up of massive chunks of stone precisely cut to fit together without mortar. The outer gate, the foundations of which are fairly evident, was flanked by two square towers from where volleys of javelins and arrows would rain down on attackers. The inner gate, a similarly impregnable barrier, comprised a huge monolithic doorpost, half of which still stands. You can still trace the ruts of chariot wheels in paved stretches of ancient road within the gateway.

Further south, and signposted "Ithomi: Archeological site" on the road running northwest from Mavrómati, is a newly excavated **Sanctuary of Asclepius**. This site, which was first mistakenly marked out as the *agora*, consisted of a temple surrounded by a porticoed courtyard. The bases of some of the colonnades have been unearthed along with traces of benches. Next to it you can make out the site of a theatre or meeting place. Excavations continue in the summer with archeologists digging in the shade of semi-permanent canopies.

Other remains are to be seen up Mount Ithómi, an hour's hike along a steep path forking north from the track at the Laconia gate, which is to the southeast of the site. Along the way you pass remains of an Ionic **Temple of Artemis**. At the top, on the site of a Temple of Zeus, are the ruins of the small **Monastery of Vourkanó**, founded in the eighth century but dating in its present form from the sixteenth. Spread below are the lush and fertile valleys of Messinía.

Around the coast to Koróni

Beaches stretch for virtually the entire distance southwest from Kalamáta to Koróni, along what is steadily developing as a major resort coast. At present, however, it is more popular with Greeks than foreigners, and the resorts, tucked away in the pines, consist primarily of campsites, interspersed with the odd room for rent.

The beach at Boúka, 5km south of modern Messini, is a fine stretch of sand with views of the Máni. It is popular with the locals, especially as a place to go for Sunday lunch. The best of the beaches are around **PETALÍDHI**, 25km west around the coast from Kalamáta. The village itself is not unattractive and there are a couple of good **campsites**: *Petalidi Beach* (☎0722/31 154; April–Sept), 3km north of the village, is well established and reasonably priced; *Sun Beach* (☎0722/31 200; May–Oct), 500m south of the village, is not on the beach, which is reached by a subway under the road.

Koróni and Methóni

The twin **fortresses** at Koróni and Methóni were the Venetians' oldest and longest-held possessions in the Peloponnese: strategic outposts on the route to Crete and known through the Middle Ages as "the eyes of the Serene Republic". Today they shelter two of the most attractive small resorts in the south.

If you have transport, the duo form an obvious route from Kalamáta to Pílos. Once you are in Methóni, you can hire a **moped**, but if you have to rely on **buses**, the 47-kilometre road across the peninsula can be a problem; Koróni is well connected with Kalamáta (30km), and Methóni with Pílos (12km), but there is only the occasional bus in summer between the two.

Koróni

KORÓNI has one of the most picturesque sites in Greece, stacked against a fortified bluff and commanding grand views across the Messenian gulf to the Taíyettos peaks. Alas, the town is not undiscovered. The Germans arrived in the early 1080s and in recent years have been buying up houses in the town and surrounding countryside. However, the process is decidedly low-key and the German tide has ebbed now they can no longer drive through the former Yugoslavia. Consequently, outside high season Koróni still feels quite unspoilt.

The town and beach

The town is beautiful in itself, with tiled and pastel-washed houses arrayed in a maze of stair-and-ramp streets that can have changed little since the medieval Venetian occupation. Koróni's **Citadel** is one of the least militaristic-looking in Greece, crowning rather than dwarfing the town. Much of it is given over to private houses and garden plots, but the greater part is occupied by the flower-strewn nunnery of **Timíou Prodhrómou**, whose chapels, outbuildings and gardens occupy nearly every bastion.

From the southwest gate of the fortress, stairs descend to the park-like grounds of **Panayía Elestrías**, a church erected at the end of the last century to house a miraculous icon – unearthed with the assistance of the vision of one Maria Stathaki (buried close by). The whole arrangement, with fountains, shrubbery and benches for watching the sunset, is more like the Adriatic than the Aegean.

Continuing downhill, you reach the amazing **Zánga beach**, a two-kilometre stretch of sand and preternaturally clear water that sets the seal on Koróni's superiority as a place to relax, drink wine and amble about a countryside lush with vineyards, olives and banana trees.

Practicalities

To be sure of a room in summer, it's worth trying to phone ahead. In the town there are just two **hotels**, the *Flisvos* (☎0725/22 238; ②), and the *Auberge de la Plage* (☎0725/22 401; ④). Looking for **private rooms** on arrival, try the places to the right of the fishing port as you face the water, and don't leave it too late in the day. Several of the tavernas rent rooms on a regular basis, including the *Parthenon* (☎0725/22 146; ②) near the port and the *Pension Koroni* (☎0725/22 385; ②) above the *Symposium* restaurant on the main street. There are two **campsites**: *Memi Beach* (☎0725/22 130; May–Oct) is 2km before Koróni as you approach from Petalídhi or Methóni; and *Koroni* (☎0725/22 119; May–Sept) is on the road into town; both have sandy beaches, though from *Memi Beach* you have to cross the road.

There is a reasonable selection of **restaurants** on the waterfront, and some authentic **tavernas** (barrel-wine and oven-food places) along the main shopping street. The *Parthenon* has good food and efficient service, and the *Symposium* serves moussaka and fish dishes. The *Flisvos* hotel also has a good restaurant.

Many people make wine or raki in their basement and the heady local tipple figures prominently in the nightlife. There are two or three tavernas on the beach and by night a solitary disco, though all of these close down by mid-September. Otherwise, there is a surprisingly fancy *zaharoplastío* for such a small place, plus two **banks** and a **post office** for money matters.

Finikoúnda

FINIKOÚNDA, 20km west of Koróni, is a small fishing village with a superb cove-beach. Over recent years it has gained a reputation as a backpackers' – and especially windsurfers' – resort, with half the summer intake at a pair of campsites on either side of the village, the others housed in a variety of rooms. It can be a fun, laid-back place.

To book **rooms** in advance, try the **hotels** *Finikounda* (☎0723/71 208; ④) and *Finissia* (☎0723/71 358; ③; summer only), or the restaurant *Moudakis* (☎0273/71 224; ②). The local **campsites** are the *Ammos* (☎0723/71 262; May–Oct), 2km to the east of the village, and the *Loutsa* (☎0723/71 445; June–Sept), 3km to the west.

Methóni

In contrast to the almost domesticated citadel at Koróni, the fortress at **METHÓNI** is as imposing as they come – massively bastioned, washed on three sides by the sea, and cut off altogether from the land by a great moat. It was maintained by the Venetians in part for its military function, in part as a staging post for pilgrims en route, via Crete and Cyprus, to the Holy Land, and from the thirteenth to the nineteenth centuries it sheltered a substantial town.

Within the **fortress** (Mon–Sat 8.30am–7pm, Sun 9am–7pm; closes 3pm in winter), entered across the moat along a stone bridge, are the remains of a Venetian cathedral (the Venetians' Lion of Saint Mark emblem is ubiquitous), along with a Turkish bath, dozens of houses and some awesome underground passages, the last unfortunately cordoned off. Walking around the walls, a sea gate midway along leads out across a causeway to the **Boúrtzi**, a small fortified island. The octagonal tower was built by the Turks in the sixteenth century to replace an earlier Venetian fortification.

Practicalities

The modern village, on the landward side of the moat, has a **bank**, **OTE** and **post office**, all easily located in the three-street-wide grid.

Methóni is geared more conspicuously to tourism than Koróni and can get very crowded in season when accommodation can be expensive and often oversubscribed.

Out of season, the **hotels** are cheaper and a number stay open all year. The *Amalia* (☎0723/31 129; ⑥) is the height of luxury, with a fine view over the town, but only open from May to October. The *Castello* (☎0723/31 300; ④) is a new hotel near the entrance to the fortress, with beautiful gardens, balconies and a stunning view. The *Aris* (☎0723/31 336; ④) on a small *platía* in the town centre is friendly and good value. The *Dionysos* (☎0723/31 317; ②) is a small, welcoming hotel in town, which is worth booking in advance; the owner's son speaks English. In addition, there is the usual collection of cheaper **rooms**, including some above the *Rex* (☎0723/31 239; ②; Jan–Oct). At the east end of the beach is a municipal **campsite**, the *Methoni* (☎0723/31 228; mid-May to mid-Oct). It's popular and gets crowded, but the facilities are good and the beach pleasant.

Methóni has one of the best **restaurants** you'll come upon anywhere in the Peloponnese, the *Klimataria* (☎0723/31 544; May–Oct), which serves a mouthwatering selection of dishes (including good veggie choices) in a courtyard garden. At the *Rex*, which is open all day, you can eat in the shade of pine trees.

Pílos and around

PÍLOS (PYLOS) is a little like a small-scale, less sophisticated Náfplio – quite a stylish town for rural Messinía, and the more so after Kalamáta. It is fronted by a pair of medieval castles and occupies a superb position on one of the finest natural harbours in Greece, the landlocked **Navarino Bay** (see box below). Given the town's romantic associations with the Battle of Navarino, and, more anciently, with Homer's "sandy Pylos", the domain of "wise King Nestor" whose palace (see p.212) has been identified 16km to the north, a better base for exploring this part of the Peloponnese is hard to imagine – particularly if equipped with a car or moped (both for rent here). Relying on public transport, however, you'll find the long afternoon gaps in services make day trips difficult.

THE BATTLES OF NAVARINO BAY

Arriving at Pílos your gaze is inevitably drawn to the bay, virtually landlocked by the offshore island of Sfaktiría (Sphacteria). Its name, Ormós Navarínou – **Navarino Bay** – commemorates the battle that effectively sealed Greek independence from the Turks on the night of October 20, 1827. The battle itself seems to have been accidental. The Great Powers of Britain, France and Russia, having established diplomatic relations with the Greek insurgent leaders, were attempting to force an armistice on the Turks. To this end they sent a fleet of 27 warships to Navarino, where Ibrahim Pasha had gathered his forces – 16,000 men in 89 ships. The declared intention was to coerce Ibrahim into leaving Messinía, which he had been raiding.

In the confusion of the night an Egyptian frigate, part of the Turks' supporting force, fired its cannons and full-scale battle broke out. Without intending to take up arms for the Greeks, the "allies" found themselves responding to attack and, extraordinarily, sank and destroyed 53 of the Turkish fleet without a single loss. There was considerable international embarrassment when news filtered through to the "victors" but the action had nevertheless ended effective Turkish control of Greek waters and within a year Greek independence was secured and recognized.

Navarino Bay also features in one of the most famous battles of Classical times, described in great detail by Thucydides. In 425 BC, during the Peloponnesian War, an Athenian force encamped in Paleó Kástro (the old castle of Pílos) laid siege to a group of Spartans on the island of **Sfaktiría**, just across the straits. In a complete break with tradition, which decreed fighting to the death, the Spartans surrendered. "Nothing that happened in the war surprised the Hellenes as much as this," commented Thucydides.

The Town

The main pleasures of Pílos are exploring the hillside alleys, waterside streets and fortress. Getting your bearings is easy as it's not a large town, and buses drop you close by the central Platía Tríon Navárhon and the port.

Shaded by a vast plane tree and scented by limes, **Platía Tríon Navárhon** is a beautiful public *platía*, completely encircled by cafés and very much the heart of the town. At its centre is a **war memorial** commemorating admirals Codrington, de Rigny and von Heyden, who commanded the British, French and Russian forces in the Battle of Navarino (see box on p.209). Nearby, just off the main waterside *platía* on Filellínon, a little **museum** (daily except Mon 8.30am–3pm; 400dr) also boasts remains from the battle, along with archeological finds from the region.

Further memories of the Navarino battles can be evoked by a visit to the **island of Sfaktiría**, across the bay, where there are various tombs of Philhellenes, a chapel, and a memorial to the Russian sailors. In summer, some of the fishing boats offer trips. If you're interested, enquire at the cafés by the port.

The principal sight in town, however, is the **Néo Kástro** (daily except Mon 8.30am–3pm; free), close by the port on the south side of the bay (off the Methóni road). The "new castle" was built by the Turks in 1572, and allows a 1500-metre walk right around the arcaded battlements. For much of the last two centuries, it served as a prison and its inner courtyard was divided into a warren of narrow yards separated by high walls, a design completely at odds with most Greek prisons, which were fairly open on the inside. This peculiar feature is explained by the garrison's proximity to the Máni. So frequently was it filled with Maniots imprisoned for vendettas, and so great was the crop of internal murders, that these pens had to be built to keep the imprisoned clansmen apart. The pens and walls have recently been pulled down as part of an ongoing programme to restore and convert the castle into a **museum** for underwater archeology (daily except Mon 8.30am–3pm; free). So far, the only attraction is a collection of René Puaux pictures of the 1821 revolution.

Practicalities

The *National Bank* is to be found on the central *platía* and the **post office** just back from there on Niléos. **Mopeds, motorbikes** and **cars**, ideal for taking in both Methóni and Nestor's Palace, are available at *Venus Rent* (☎0723/22 312) on the road north out of town. Mopeds and motorbikes can also be rented from *Sapienza Travel* (☎0723/23 207) near the *Miramare* (see below), and cars from the *Miramare* itself. You can hire a **boat** from the port to visit Sfaktiría island, where you can snorkle and see the remains of the Turkish fleet lying on the sea bed; ask at the Harbourmaster's Office.

Pílos has somewhat limited accommodation and in the summer months you should definitely try to phone ahead. Among the **hotels**, the *Arvaniti* (☎0723/23 050; ④), beyond the post office on Niléos, is the best of the mid-priced options, but is closed between October and March. The *Galaxy*, Platía Tríon Navárhon (☎0723/22 780; ④), is a fall-back choice if the *Arvaniti* is closed or full. The *Karalis*, Kalamatas 26 (☎0723/22 960; ⑤), is an attractive, if pricey, hotel with a good restaurant, and may offer discounts outside the summer season. The *Miramare*, Myrtidiotissis 35 (☎0723/22 751; ⑤), has a restaurant and bar, and fine views by the port, but it is also closed between October and March.

For **drinks**, the Platía Tríon Navárhon cafés are the obvious choice. Among **tavernas**, try *Grigori's*, signposted from the *platía*. Nightlife is pretty much nonexistent, with just a single **music-bar/disco**, *MusicContacts*, by the beach, and a summer **outdoor cinema**.

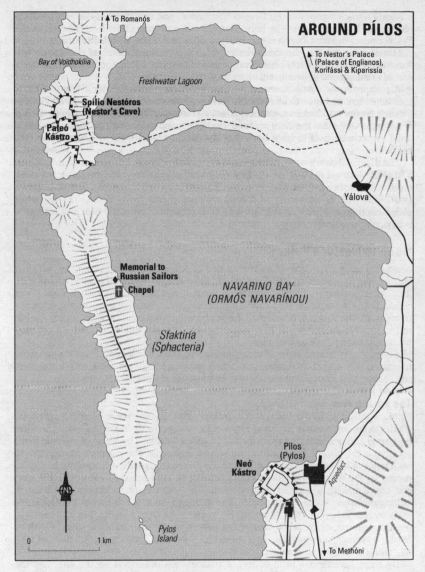

AROUND PÍLOS

To Romanós

Bay of Voidhokília

Freshwater Lagoon

To Nestor's Palace
(Palace of Englianos),
Korifássi & Kiparissía

Spílio Nestóros
(Nestor's Cave)

Paleó
Kástro

Yálova

Memorial to
Russian Sailors

Chapel

NAVARINO BAY
(ORMÓS NAVARÍNOU)

Sfaktiría
(Sphacteria)

Pílos
(Pylos)

Neó
Kástro

Aqueduct

N

0   1 km

Pylos
Island

To Methóni

The northern rim of Navarino Bay

Pílos's northern castle, and ancient acropolis, **Paleó Kástro**, stands on a hill almost touching the island of Sfaktiría, at the end of the bay. It's a seven-kilometre trip from the town, for which you'll need transport. To get there, follow the main road north towards Korifássi and then take a side road southwest to the hamlet of Romános; turn off along a track signposted (in Greek) "Navarino", and cross a bridge over a freshwater lagoon. If you find your way here, you will end up at one of the best beaches in the Peloponnese – a lovely sweep of sand curling around the **Bay of Voïdhokília**.

Overlooking the bay, the Paleó Kástro, known in medieval times as Port Jonch, has substantial walls, and identifiable courtyards and cisterns within; the fortifications are a mix of Frankish and Venetian, set upon ancient foundations.

A path from the castle descends to the **Spílio Nestóros** (Nestor's Cave). This is fancifully identified (due to its stalactite forms) as the grotto in which, according to the *Odyssey*, Nestor and Neleus kept their cows, and in which Hermes hid Apollo's cattle. It is not impossible that the cave sparked Homer's imagination, for this location is reckoned by archeologists to have been the Mycenaean-era harbour of King Nestor (see below).

The Bay of Navarino encompasses a couple of additional **beaches** and hamlets. **YÁLOVA**, 4km out of Pílos and the first resort around the bay, has tamarisk trees shading the sands, two **hotels**, the delightful *Zoe* (☎0723/22 025; ⑤) and *Helonaki House* (☎0723/23 080; ③), a variety of rooms and apartments for rent, and the *Navarino Beach* **campsite** (☎0723/22 761; April–Oct). Just north of here, the beach of **Maistrós** is a popular windsurfing strip.

North to Nestor's Palace

Nestor's Palace (also known as the Palace of Englianos, after the hill on which it stands) was discovered in 1939, but left virtually undisturbed until after World War II; thus its excavation – unlike Mycenae, or most of the other major Greek sites – was conducted in accordance with modern archeological techniques. In consequence, its remains are the best preserved of all the Mycenaean royal palaces, though they shelter rather prosaically beneath a giant plastic roof. The site guide by Carl Blegen and Marion Rawson is an excellent buy.

The palace is located some 16km from modern Pílos, a half-hour drive. Using public transport, take any of the **buses** from Pílos towards Kiparissía; these follow the main road inland past Korifássi to the site and its museum at Hóra (3km to the east).

The palace site

Flanked by deep, fertile valleys, the **palace site** (daily except Mon 8.30am–3pm; 400dr) looks out towards Navarino Bay – a location perfectly in keeping with the wise, measured and peaceful king described in Homer's *Odyssey*. The scene of the epic that's set here is the visit of Telemachus, the son of Odysseus, who journeys from Ithaca to seek news of his father from King Nestor. As Telemachus arrives at the beach, accompanied by the disguised goddess Pallas Athena, he comes upon Nestor with his sons and court making a sacrifice to Poseidon. The visitors are welcomed and feasted, "sitting on downy fleeces on the sand", and although the king has no news of Odysseus he promises Telemachus a chariot so he can enquire from Menelaus at Sparta. First, however, the guests are taken back to the palace, where Telemachus is given a bath by Nestor's "youngest grown daughter, beautiful Polycaste", and emerges, anointed with oil, "with the body of an immortal".

By some harmonious twist of fate, a bathtub was unearthed on the site, and the palace ruins as a whole are potent ground for Homeric imaginings. The walls stand a metre high, enabling you to make out a very full plan. They were originally half-timbered (like Tudor houses), with upper sections of sun-baked brick held together by vertical and horizontal beams, and brilliant frescoes within. Even in their diminished state they suggest a building of considerable prestige. No less should be expected, for Nestor sent the second largest contingent to Troy – a fleet of "ninety black ships". The remains of the massive complex are in three principal groups: the **main palace** in the middle; on the left an earlier and **smaller palace**; and on the right either **guard-houses** or **workshops**.

The basic design will be familiar if you've been to Mycenae or Tiryns: an internal court, guarded by a sentry box, gives access to the main sections of the principal palace. This contained some 45 rooms and halls. The **Megaron** (throne room), with its characteristic open hearth, lies directly ahead of the entrance, through a double porch. Discovered here was the finest of the frescoes, depicting a griffin (perhaps the royal emblem) standing guard over the throne; this is now in the museum at Hóra. Arranged around are domestic quarters and **storerooms**, which yielded literally thousands of pots and cups during excavations; the rooms may have served as a distribution centre for the produce of the palace workshops. Further back, the famous **bathroom**, its terracotta tub in situ, adjoins a smaller complex of rooms, centred on another, smaller *megaron*, identified as the **queen's quarters**.

Archeologically, the most important find at the site was a group of several hundred tablets inscribed in **Linear B**. These were discovered on the first day of digging, in the two small rooms to the left of the entrance courtyard. They were the first such inscriptions to be discovered on the Greek mainland and proved conclusively a link between the Mycenaean and Minoan civilizations; like those found by Sir Arthur Evans at Knossos on Crete, the language was unmistakably Greek. The tablets were baked hard in the fire which destroyed the palace around 1200 BC, perhaps as little as one generation after the fall of Troy.

The museum at Hóra

At Hóra, the **museum** (daily except Mon 8.30am–3pm; 400dr) adds significantly to a visit to the site. If you've no transport, it might be better to take a bus here first, and then walk the 45 minutes to the site after viewing the exhibits. In spring or autumn this is a pleasure; shy golden orioles have been seen in trees alongside the road. In hot weather, or if pressed for time, you can hitch fairly easily or get a taxi.

Pride of place in the display goes to the **palace frescoes**, one of which, bearing out Homer's descriptions, shows a warrior in a boar-tusk helmet. Lesser finds include much pottery, some beautiful gold cups and other objects gathered both from the site and from various Mycenaean tombs in the region.

The coast north of Pílos

The stretch of coast between Pílos and Pírgos is defined by its **beaches**, which are on a different scale to those elsewhere in the Peloponnese, or indeed anywhere else in Greece – fine sands, long enough (and undeveloped enough) to satisfy the most jaded Australian or Californian. Their relative anonymity is something of a mystery, though one accounted for in part by the poor communications. For those without transport this entails slow and patient progress along the main "coast" road, which for much of the way runs two or three kilometres inland, and a walk from road junction to beach.

Heading north from the Bay of Voïdhokília, near the turning inland to Korifássi and Nestor's Palace, you can take a very rough and beautiful track, flanked by orange and olive orchards. This keeps close to the sea for most of the way to Kiparissía, allowing access to isolated beaches and villages.

If you're travelling to Olympia by **train** from this coast, you can save the detour to Pírgos (not really an exhilarating town – see p.229) by getting a connection at Alfiós, a tiny station at the junction of the Olympia line and as bucolic a halt as any on the network.

Marathópoli and Filiatrá

If you are looking for the rudiments of accommodation and a little more than a village café then Marathópoli and Filiatrá hold most promise. **MARATHÓPOLI** has a long beach, rockier than most along this coast and facing the little islet of Próti. It has two **hotels**: on the beach, the *Artina* (☎0723/61 400; ④) has en suite facilities and should be booked in advance; in the village, the *Rania* (☎0723/61 404; ④) is a new hotel and the rooms have small kitchenettes. There are some **rooms** for rent; a **campsite**, *Proti* (☎0723/61 211; May–Oct), with a swimming pool on account of the rocky beach; and two or three summer tavernas by the sea.

The track rejoins the paved road at **FILIATRÁ**, which is linked by bus with Pílos and Kiparissía. There are two **hotels**: in the village itself, the recently renovated *Trifylia* (☎0761/32 233; ④) is more like a pension, though the rooms have en suite facilities including a small kitchenette; the run-of-the-mill *Limenari* (☎0761/32 935; ③) is down by the sea.

Fournier's Castle

By a curious pattern of emigration, just as Kíthira is home to Greek-Australians, the villages along the Kiparissía coast have a concentration of returned Greek-Americans, virtually all of them having done a stint of work in New York or New Jersey. Disgraced ex-Vice President Spiro Agnew (1968–1973) was perhaps the most infamous local boy.

However, the Greek-American who has left most mark on his home domain is one Haris Fournaki, also known as **Harry Fournier**, a doctor from Chicago who came back in the 1960s and started building his fantasies. At the entrance to Filiatrá, Fournier constructed a garden-furniture version of the **Eiffel Tower** (illuminated at night by fairy lights) and a mini-replica of the globe from the 1964 New York Expo.

His most ambitious project, however, was his **Kastro Ton Paramithia** (Castle of the Fairytales), a truly loopy folly with white concrete battlements and outcrops of towers, plus thirty- to forty-foot-high statues of Poseidon's horse (flanked by vases of flowers) and the goddess Athena. The castle is located right on the sea, near Filiatrá beach, and can reached from Filiatrá by following the road for 6km north, through the hamlet of Agríli.

Kiparissía

KIPARISSÍA is a small, congenial market town, positioned hard against the Eyaléo mountains. On the first outcrop of the range is a Byzantine-Frankish **castle**, around which is spread the **old town**. Its ochre-hued mansions stand abandoned, having suffered heavy damage in the civil war, though a couple of tavernas still function here, lovely old places and very welcoming.

Below the hill, the modern town goes about its business, with a small harbour and real shops. A few tourist boutiques and a night club or two have sprung up recently, but it's still a pleasant place to rest up, and certainly preferable to a night in Kalamáta if you're on your way to Olympia by bus or train (Kiparissía is the junction of the Kalamáta and Pírgos lines). Within walking distance of the town are long, near-deserted sands and rocky cliff paths.

Practicalities

The centre of the modern town, a couple of blocks inland from the train station, is Platía Kalantzákou, where you'll find a **bank, OTE** and **post office**.

Accommodation consists of a half-dozen **hotels**, divided between the modern town and the beach. The cheapest place to stay in town is the *Trifolia*, 25 Martíon (☎0761/22 066; ②), a down-to-earth and welcoming pension. Other town hotels are the *Vasilikon*,

Alexopoúlou 7 (☎0761/22 655; ④), which is well kept, though without any particular charm, and the comfortable *Ionion* (☎0761/22 511; ④), an older hotel facing the train station. By the beach, the best value is the *Apollon* (☎0761/24 411; ⑤); there is also a campsite, *Kyparissia* (☎0761/23 491).

There are a handful of no-nonsense **restaurants** and pizzerias in Platía Kalantzákou and in the adjacent streets; one of the best is *Nynio*, at 25 Martíon 52. For atmosphere it's better to eat down at the beach, or up at the old town, where the liveliest place to eat is the *Psisteria Arcadia*.

Beaches north from Kiparissía

Between Kiparissía and Kaïáfas, the road and rail lines continue a kilometre or so back from the coast, with the occasional **campsite** advertising its particular stretch of beach. These include the *Apollo Village* (☎0625/61 200) at Yiannitsohóri (18km along) and the *Tholó Beach* (☎0625/61 345; March–Oct), a better one at Tholó (8km further on). Néo Hóri, just past Tholó, has a few rooms to rent, as does Yiannitsohóri.

All of these hamlets have superb stretches of sandy beach, edged with olive groves, in the light of which their lack of development seems almost miraculous. One of the nicest of all the beaches is at **KAKOVÁTOS** (5km beyond Tholó), which combines breakers with incredibly shallow, slowly shelving waters. There is a beach café here and a few summer rooms – nothing more.

At **ZAHÁRO**, the largest village between Kiparissía and Pírgos, and a train stop, there are a few shops and four **hotels**. The *Rex* (☎0625/31 221; ④) has en suite facilities and some rooms have kitchenettes; the *Nestor* (☎0625/31 206; ③) has clean if spartan rooms; the *Sugar Town* (☎0625/31 985; ②) is a new and slightly inelegant hotel by the train station; and the *Diethnes* (☎0625/31 221; ③), which also has en suite facilities, is near the church at the top end of the village. Midway to the excellent beach is the *Banana Place* (☎0625/32 997;②), set in a banana plantation. It offers chalet-type accommodation with cooking facilities, and is open between mid-April and mid-October; booking is advisable.

Another enormous strand, backed by sand dunes and pine groves, is to be found just before the roads loop inland at **Kaïáfas**. At the beach there's just a single, rather uninspired taverna and the train station. A couple of kilometres inland, however, the village of **LOUTRÁ KAÏÁFAS** assumes the atmosphere of a spa. Strung out alongside a lagoon are a dozen or so hotels and pensions, frequented mainly by Greeks seeking hydrotherapy cures. Each morning a small shuttle-boat takes the patients from their hotels to the hot springs across the lagoon.

ARCADIA AND THE NORTH

Arcadia (*Arkadhía* in modern Greek), the heartland province of the Peloponnese, lives up to its name. It contains some of the most beautiful landscapes in Greece: rich rolling hills crowned by a string of medieval towns, and the occasional Classical antiquity. The best area of all is around **Andhrítsena** and **Karítena**, where walkers are rewarded with the luxuriant (and rarely visited) **Lousíos gorge**, and archeology buffs by the remote, though currently scaffolded, **Temple of Bassae**. En route, if approaching from Trípoli, you may also be tempted by the ancient theatre at **Megalópoli**. The one site everyone heads for is, of course, **Olympia**, whose remains, if at times obscure, are again enhanced by the scenery.

Beaches are not a highlight in this northwest corner, nor along the north coast between Pátra and Kórinthos – technically the province of Akhaïa. However, if you are travelling this way, or are arriving in or leaving Greece at the (modern) port of Pátra, a detour along the rack-and-pinion **Kalávrita railway** should on no account be missed. This takes off through a gorge into the mountains at Dhiakoftó.

If heading for Delphi, or central or western Greece, car-drivers and pedestrians alike can save backtracking to Athens by using the **ferry links** across the Gulf of Kórinthos at either Río–Andírio (the most routine) or Éyio–Áyios Nikólaos.

Megalópoli (Megalopolis)

Modern **MEGALÓPOLI** is an important road and bus junction, and your first thoughts on arrival are likely to be directed towards getting out. Like Trípoli, it's a dusty, characterless place, with a military presence and two vast power stations; there's little in the way of hotels or food. The adoption of its ancient name, "Great City", was an altogether empty joke.

However, the impulse to leave should be resisted, at least for an hour or two, because just outside the city to the northwest is one of the most extensive and least touristed sites in the Peloponnese: **ancient Megalopolis**.

Practicalities

Megalópoli has good **bus connections** with Trípoli (and on to Árgos and Athens) and Kalamáta. Arrive at a reasonable hour and you should be able to make either of these connections. Moving north or west into Arcadia is slightly more problematic, with just two buses daily to Karítena/Andhrítsena (currently at noon and 7pm). However, hitching is a viable proposition along this route, as local drivers are aware of the paucity of transport, and it's also possible to negotiate a **taxi** to Karítena. For **train connections** west to Kiparissía or east to Trípoli/Árgos, the *OSE* operates special shuttle buses to Lefktró, since the branch rail line from Megalópoli has been closed down.

Should you need to stay in Megalópoli, there are four or five **hotels**, most of them catering to local business travellers rather than tourists. The cheapest are all in the vicinity of the central Platía Gortinías and include the *Pan*, Papanastassíou 7 (☎0791/22 270; ②–③), which is rather old, but acceptable with private facilities in the more expensive rooms; the better presented *Paris*, Ayíou Nikólaou 5 (☎0791/22 410; ③); and the *Achillion*, Papaionánnou 67 (☎0791/22 311; ③), which has clean, comfortable rooms with en suite showers.

Other facilities, such as **banks**, **post office** and **OTE** are also to be found around the central *platía*.

Ancient Megalopolis

Ancient Megalopolis (daily except Mon 8.30am–3pm; free) was one of the most ambitious building projects of the Classical age, a city intended by the Theban leader Epaminondas, who oversaw construction from 371 to 368 BC, to be the finest of a chain of Arcadian settlements designed to hold back the Spartans. However, although no expense was spared on its construction, nor on its extent – nine kilometres of walls alone – the city never took root. It suffered from sporadic Spartan aggression and the citizens, transplanted from forty local villages, preferred, and returned to, their old homes. Within two centuries it had been broken up, abandoned and ruined.

As you approach the site, along a tree-lined track off the Andhrítsena road (signposted "Ancient Theatre"), the countryside is beautiful enough; a fertile valley whose steaming cooling towers seem to give it added grandeur; beyond the riverbed is just a low hill, and no sign of any ruins. Suddenly, you round the corner of the rise and its function is revealed: carved into its side is the largest **theatre** built in ancient Greece.

Only the first few rows are excavated, but the earthen mounds and ridges of the rest are clearly visible as stepped tiers to the summit where, from the back rows, trees look on like immense spectators.

The theatre was built to a scale similar to those at Árgos and Dodóna, and could seat 20,000; the **Thersileion** (Assembly Hall) at its base could hold 16,000. Today you're likely to be alone at the site, save perhaps for the custodian (who has plans of the ruins). Out beyond the enclosed part of the site you can wander over a vast area, and with a little imagination make out the foundations of walls and towers, temples, gymnasiums and markets. "The Great City", wrote Kazantzakis in *Journey to the Morea*, "has become a great wasteland". But it's the richest of wastelands, gently and resolutely reclaimed by nature.

Megalópoli to Dhimitsána

North of Megalópoli the best of Arcadia lies before you: minor roads that curl through a series of lush valleys and below the province's most exquisite medieval hill towns. The obvious first stop and most enjoyable base for exploring the region is **Karítena**. From here you can visit the dramatic and remote site of **ancient Gortys** and explore the **Lousíos gorge**, above which, outrageously sited on 300-metre-high cliffs, is the eleventh-century **monastery of Ayíou Ioánni Prodhrómou** (commonly abbreviated to Prodhrómou).

Moving on from Karítena, there is a choice of roads. The "main" route loops west through **Andhrítsena** to Créstena, from where irregular buses run to Olympia. An alternative route to the northwest winds around the edge of the Ménalo mountains to the delightful towns of **Stemnítsa** and **Dhimitsána**, meeting the main Tripoli–Pírgos road at Karkaloú. If you have time on your hands, perhaps the most attractive option is to explore the region north as far as Dhimitsána, then backtrack to Karíténa to proceed on to Olympia via Andhrítsena.

Karítena

Set high above the Megalópoli–Andhrítsena road, **KARÍTENA** may look familiar; with its medieval bridge over the River Alfíos (Alpheus), it graces the 5000-drachma note. Like many of the Arcadian hill-towns hereabouts, its history is a mix of Frankish, Byzantine and Turkish contributions, the Venetians having passed over much of the northern interior. It was founded by the Byzantines in the seventh century and had attained a population of some 20,000 when the Franks took it in 1209. Under their century-long rule, Karítena was the capital of a large barony under Geoffroy de Bruyères, the paragon of chivalry in the medieval ballad *The Chronicle of the Morea* and virtually the only well-liked Frankish overlord.

The village these days has a population of just a couple of hundred, though there were at least ten times that figure until the beginning of this century. Approaching, you can stop on the modern bridge over the Alfíos and peer down at the **medieval bridge**, which is immediately adjacent. It is missing the central section, but is an intriguing structure nonetheless, with a small Byzantine chapel built into one of the central pillars.

From the main road, there's a winding three-kilometre road up to the village, in the upper part of which is a small central *platía* with a *kafenío*. Off the *platía* are signposted the Byzantine churches of **Zoödhóhos Piyí** (with a Romanesque belfry) and **Áyios Nikólaos** (with crumbling frescoes) to the west, down towards the river; ask at the *kafenío* for the keys. Also off the *platía* is the **Frourio**, the castle built by the Franks and with added Turkish towers. It was here that Theodoros Kolokotronis held out against

Ibrahim Pasha in 1826 and turned the tide of the War of Independence; hence the view of Karítena on the 5000-drachma note and a portrait of Kolokotrónis on the reverse.

There are two places to rent **rooms**: one signposted opposite the post office, run by Stamata Kondopoúlou (☎0791/31 262; ②); the other, a very comfortable apartment 200m beyond the *platía*, run by Hristos and Athalassia Papodopoulos (☎0791/31 203; ②), who, given notice, will provide fine evening meals and wine.

North through the Lousíos River valley

The site of **ancient Gortys** can be approached either from Karítena or from Stemnítsa (8km northwest of the site). From Karítena the most direct route to the valley runs up and through the town to Astílohos (11km), a village 2km southwest of the site; a taxi should cost in the region of 3000dr return. This route is no more than a jeep track, and twenty minutes from the site it becomes a trail. If you don't have a car, it is easier to follow the road north towards Stemnítsa and Dhimitsána for 6km to the hamlet of Ellinikó. From the edge of Ellinikó, a dirt track signposted "Gortys" descends west; after a rough six kilometres (ignore the right-hand fork at the five-kilometre point – this heads north to Prodhrómou before winding east towards Stemnítsa) it ends at the bank of the Lousíos River. Here is an old bridge, which you cross to reach the site of ancient Gortys. It is possible to camp overnight at Gortys, or to stay at the nearby monastery of Prodhrómou.

The town of Stemnítsa probably makes a better base for exploring the area, and walkers may want to do so by following the Stemnítsa–Prodhrómou–Gortys–Ellinikó–Stemnítsa circuit (see below).

Ancient Gortys

Ancient Gortys is one of the most stirring of all Greek sites, set beside the rushing river known in ancient times as the Gortynios. The relics are widely strewn amongst the vegetation on the west (true right) bank of the stream, but the main attraction, below contemporary ground level and not at all obvious until well to the west of the little chapel of Áyios Andhréas (by the old bridge), is the huge excavation containing the remains of a **Temple to Asclepius** (the god of healing) and an adjoining **bath**, both dating from the fourth century BC.

The most curious feature of the site is a circular **portico** enclosing round-backed seats which most certainly would have been part of the therapeutic centre. It's an extraordinary place, especially if you camp with the roar of the Lousíos to lull you to sleep. The only drawback is the climate: temperatures up here plummet at night, no matter what the season, and heavy mists, wet as a soaking rain, envelop the mountains from midnight to mid-morning.

The Lousíos gorge and monastery of Prodhrómou

The farmland surrounding ancient Gortys belongs to the monks of the nearby **Monastery of Prodhrómou**, who have carved a donkey path along the **gorge of the Lousíos** between Áyios Andhréas and the monastery. It's about forty minutes' walk upstream, with an initially gradual and later steady ascent up a well-graded, switch-backed trail. A set of park benches by a formal gate heralds arrival at the cloister, and the whole area is well stamped about by the monks' mules. If you look up through the trees above the path, the monastery, stuck on to the cliff like a swallow's nest, is plainly visible a couple of hundred metres above.

The interior of the monastery does not disappoint this promise; the local villagers accurately describe it as *politisméno* (cultured) as opposed to *ágrio* (wild). Once inside it is surprisingly small; there were never more than about fifteen tenants, and currently there are twelve monks, four of them very young and committed. Visitors are received in the *arhondarikí* (guest lounge and adjoining quarters), and then shown the tiny frescoed *katholikón*, and possibly invited to evening services there. The strictest rules of dress apply, but the monks welcome visitors who wish to stay the night. The only problem, especially on weekends, is that there are only a dozen or so beds, and people from Trípoli and even Athens make pilgrimages and retreats here, arriving by the carload along a circuitous dirt track from Stemnítsa. Be prepared for this possibility, and arrive in time to get back to level ground to camp.

Prodhrómou to Stemnítsa

Beyond Prodhrómou the path continues clearly to the outlying monasteries of **Paleá** and **Néa Filosófou**. The older dates from the tenth century but, virtually ruined, is easy to miss since it blends into the cliff on which it's built. The newer (seventeenth-century) monastery has been restored, but has fine frescoes inside; ask the monks at Prodhrómou for the key, or content yourself with a peek in through the door grille. North from here the trail becomes almost impassable, though there is a jeep track from near Néa Filosófou upstream to Dhimitsána.

At Prodhrómou you can pick up the dirt track (described above as the fork off the Ellinikó–Gortys track) and head for Stemnítsa. If you are walking it is more pleasant, and quicker, to follow instead the old *kalderími* from Prodhrómou to Stemnítsa – a climb, but not a killing one, of about ninety minutes through scrub oak with fine views over the valley. Usually one of the monks or lay workers will be free to point out the start of the path; once clear of the roadhead confusion by the modern little chapel at the edge of the canyon, there's little possiblity of getting lost.

If Stemnítsa is your base rather than your destination, you can take this route in reverse by heading out of town on the paved road to Dhimitsána and (just after the town-limits sign) bear down and left onto the obvious beginning of the upper end of the *kalderími*. The loop can be completed by following the walk all the way back to Ellinikó, where a proper trail leads north back to Stemnítsa.

Stemnítsa

Fifteen kilometres north of Karítena, **STEMNÍTSA** (or Ipsoúnda in its official Hellenized form, or Ipsoús on many maps) was for centuries one of the premier metalsmithing centres of the Balkans. Although much depopulated, it remains a fascinating town, with a small folklore museum, a revived artisan school (and workshop near the bus stop) and a handful of quietly magnificent medieval churches.

The town is divided by ravines into three distinct quarters: the Kástro (the ancient acropolis hill), Ayía Paraskeví (east of the stream) and Áyios Ioánnis (west of it). The **Folklore Museum** (summer Mon–Fri 6–8pm, Sat & Sun 11am–1pm; winter Mon–Fri 5–7pm, Sat & Sun 11am–1pm; free) is just off the main road in the Áyios Ioánnis quarter, and repays the trip out in itself. The ground floor is devoted to mock-ups of the workshops of indigenous crafts such as candle-making, bell-casting, shoe-making and jewellery. The next floor up features re-creations of the salon of a well-to-do family and a humbler cottage. The top storey is taken up by the rather random collections of the Savopoulos family: plates by Avramides (a refugee from Asia Minor and ceramics master), textiles and costumes from all over Greece, weapons, copperware, and eighteenth- and nineteenth-century icons. Across the way you can visit the **Artisan School** (Mon–Fri 8am–2pm & some Mon evenings), staffed by the remaining local silver-, gold- and coppersmiths. Next door to the school is the seventeenth-century **basilica of Tríon Ierarhón**, most accessible of the town's Byzantine churches; its caretaker lives in the low white house west of the main door.

To visit the other churches, all of which are frescoed and locked, requires more determined enquiries to find a key. The *katholikón* of the seventeenth-century **monas-**

tery of **Zoödhóhos Piyí** has perhaps the finest setting, on the hillside above Ayía Paraskeví, but the tiny windows do not permit much of an interior view. The little adjoining monastery hosted the first *yerousía* (convention) of guerrilla captains in the War of Independence, giving rise to the local claim that Stemnítsa was Greece's first capital.

Near the summit of the Kástro hill are two adjacent chapels: the tenth-century **Profitis Ilías** (with a convenient window for fresco-viewing) and the twelfth-century **Panayía Vaferón** (with an unusual colonnade). The last of the town's five churches, **Áyios Pandelímon**, is located at the western edge of the town, to the left of the paved road to Dhimitsána.

Accommodation is limited to the pleasant *Hotel Trikolonion* (☎0795/81 297; ③), which has regular rooms and some luxurious suites in a fine traditional building in the centre of town; the inclusive breakfasts are substantial and, with adequate notice, you can dine here. Failing that, you can eat well in town at the *Café Psigoporio*. There are two **buses** a day linking Stemnítsa with Trípoli via Dhimitsána.

Dhimitsána

Like Stemnítsa, **DHIMITSÁNA** has an immediately seductive appearance, its cobbled streets and tottering houses straddling a twin hillside overlooking the Lousíos River. Views from the village are stunning. It stands at the head of the gorge, and looking downriver you can just see the cooling towers of the Megalópoli power plant and the bluff that supports Karítena. To the east are the lower folds of the Ménalo mountains, most visible if you climb up to the local **Kástro**, whose stretch of Cyclopean walls attests to its ancient use.

In the town, a half-dozen churches with tall, squarish belfries recall the extended Frankish, and especially Norman, tenure in this part of the Morea during the thirteenth century. Yet none should dispute the deep-dyed Greekness of Dhimitsána. It was the birthplace of Archbishop Yermanos, who first raised the flag of rebellion at Kalávrita in 1821, and of the hapless patriarch, Grigoris V, hanged in Constantinople upon the Sultan's receiving news of the insurrection mounted by his co-religionist. During the hostilities the ubiquitous Kolokotronis maintained a lair and a powder mill in this then well-nigh inaccessible town. Even before the War of Independence, the nunnery of **Emyalón** (daylight hours, except 2–5pm), 3km south towards Stemnítsa, was used by the Kolokotronis clan as a hideout.

Accommodation is limited to the modern *Dimitsana* (☎0795/31 518; ④), 1km out on the road to Stemnítsa; though well appointed it is popular with rambling groups. The *Taverna Kallithea*, just across the road from the hotel, is Dhimitsána's best and not too expensive; other than that there's a lone *souvláki* stall in town, and the eminently avoidable *Vlahos*, a stygian basement dive.

Moving on to Olympia

Keep in mind that through buses from Dhimitsána are scarce, and you may well need to hitch (or take a taxi) to Karkaloú or Vitína, on the main Trípoli–Pírgos road, where you can pick up buses more easily. Once on the road, the most enjoyable halt is **LANGÁDHIA** (18km from Dhimitsána), whose tiers of houses and bubbling sluices both tumble downhill to the river far below the road. Often you can stop on a late-morning bus, eat lunch and pick up the next through service with little lost time. If you decide to stay the night, there's a couple of **hotels** on the main road: the rather ritzy *Kentrikon* (☎0795/43 221; ③) and the municipal motel *Langadia* (☎0795/43 202; ②).

You may well find that you have fewer changes and stops if you backtrack south to join the **Karítena–Andhrítsena route** and moving on to Olympia from there.

Andhrítsena and the Temple of Bassae

Moving west from Karítena towards Andhrítsena, the Alfíos River falls away to the north and the hills become mountains – Líkeo to the south and Mínthi to the west. The route, only slightly less remote than the twists of road around Dhimitsána, is a superb one for its own sake, with the added attractions of **Andhrítsena**, a traditional mountain town, and the **Temple of Apollo at Bassae** up in the flanks of Mount Líkeo.

Andhrítsena

ANDHRÍTSENA, 28km west of Karítena, is a beautiful stop and the traditional base from which to visit the Temple of Apollo at Bassae up in the mountains to the south. Though very much a roadside settlement today, it too was a major hill town through the years of Turkish occupation and the first century of independent Greece. It is remarkably untouched, with wooden houses spilling down to a stream, whose clear, ice-cold headwaters are channelled into a fountain that's set within a plane tree in the central *platía*.

Hotel accommodation is available at the *Pan* (☎0626/22 213; ②; summer only), at the far-west end of town by the *Shell* station, with clean, comfortable rooms, and the fancier, somewhat overrated, overpriced *Theoxenia* (☎0626/22 219; ④), on the Karítena side of town. For **meals**, try any of the restaurants on the main *platía*, and especially the one up the steps beside the old (and closed) *Vassae* hotel.

The Temple of Apollo at Bassae

Fourteen kilometres into the mountains south from Andhrítsena, the **Temple of Apollo** at **BASSAE** (Vassés, in the modern idiom) is the most remote and arguably the most spectacular site in Greece. In addition, it is, after the Thiseion in Athens, the best-preserved Classical monument in the country, and for many years was considered to have been designed by Iktinos, architect of the Parthenon – though this theory has recently fallen from favour.

There the superlatives must cease. Romantic though the temple was in the past, for the forseeable future it is swathed in a gigantic grey marquee supported on metal girders and set in concrete with wire stays; its entablature and frieze lie dissected in neat rows on the ground to one side. No doubt the restoration is badly needed for its preservation – and the marquee is quite a sight in itself – but it has to be said that visitors are likely to be a bit disappointed. If you are not put off, take the Kréstena road out of town and then, almost immediately, turn off to the left and you begin the climb to the temple. The simplest approach is to share a taxi, which should charge 2500–3000dr for the round trip, waiting an hour at the site. On foot it's a pretty agonizing ascent, with little likelihood of a lift. The site is not enclosed, but has a full-time guardian who lives alongside. It's a lonely place, and must have felt even more isolated in ancient times.

The temple was erected in dedication to **Apollo Epikourios** ("the Succourer") by the Phigalians. It's known that they built it in gratitude for being spared from plague, but beyond this it is something of a puzzle. It is oddly aligned on a north–south axis and, being way up in the mountains, is only visible when you are comparatively near. There are oddities, too, in the architecture: the columns on its north side are strangely thicker than in the rest of the building, and incorporated into its *cella* was a single Corinthian column, the first known in Greece (though now vanished save for its base). Unusually again, the cult statue, probably a four-metre-high bronze, would have stood in front of this pillar.

Moving on from Bassae or Andhrítsena

Leaving the Bassae/Andhrítsena area, you've a number of choices. From Andhrítsena there are two daily **buses** back up towards Karítena/Megalópoli and two down to Pírgos. If you are headed for **Olympia**, take the Pírgos bus and get off in Kréstena, from where you can hitch or take a taxi along the 12km side road up to the site. You'll certainly save time and maybe some money.

For the adventurous, an unsurfaced track winds through the mountains from Bassae down to the coast at **Tholó** (see p.215). According to the signpost, it's a mere 46km, but don't be misled. It's a dusty, very bumpy ride, but for the unhurried there's an opportunity to stop at Perivólia (10km). This mountain hamlet has a two-kilometre dirt road connecting it with the similarly diminutive Figalía, close by the ruins of the enormous Classical walls of **ancient Phigalia**.

Olympia (Olimbía)

The historic associations and resonance of **OLYMPIA**, which for over a millennium hosted the most important **Panhellenic games**, are rivalled only by Delphi or Mycenae. It is one of the largest and most beautiful sites in Greece, and the setting is as perfect as could be imagined: a luxuriant valley of wild olive and plane trees, spread beside twin rivers of Alfíos (Alpheus) and Kládhios, and overlooked by the pine-covered hill of Krónos. Sadly, the actual ruins of the sanctuary are jumbled and confusing, and seem to cry out for reconstruction, even on a modest scale. The great temple columns lie half-buried amid the trees and undergrowth: picturesque and shaded, perfect ground for picnics, but offering little real impression of their ancient grandeur or function. Their fame, however, prevails over circumstance and walking through the arch from the sanctuary to the stadium it is hard not to feel in awe of the Olympian history. Despite the crowds, the tour buses, the souvenir shops and other trappings of mass tourism, it demands and deserves a lengthy visit.

The modern village of Olimbía acts as a service centre for the site, and has little in the way of distractions, save a somewhat dutiful **Museum of the Olympic Games** (Tues–Sat 8am–3.30pm, Sun & Mon 9am–4.30pm; 500dr), with commemorative postage stamps and the odd memento from the modern games, including the box that conveyed the heart of Pierre de Coubertin (reviver of the modern games) from Paris to Olympia, where it was buried.

The site

May to mid-Oct Mon–Fri 8am–7pm, Sat & Sun 8.30am–3pm; mid-Oct to April Mon–Fri 8am–5pm, Sat & Sun 8.30am–3pm; 1000dr

From its beginnings, the site was a sanctuary, with a permanent population limited to the temple priests. At first the games took place within the sacred precinct, the walled, rectangular **Altis**, but as events became more sophisticated a new **stadium** was built to adjoin it. The whole sanctuary was throughout its history a treasure-trove of public and religious statuary. Victors were allowed to erect a statue in the *Altis* (in their likeness if they won three events) and numerous city-states installed treasuries. Pausanias, writing in the fourth century AD, after the Romans had already looted the sanctuary several times, fills almost a whole book of his *Guide to Greece* with descriptions.

The entrance to the site leads along the west side of the **Altis wall**, past a group of public and official buildings. On the left, beyond some Roman baths, is the **Prytaneion**, the administrators' residence where athletes were lodged and feasted at official expense. On the right are the ruins of a **Gymnasium** and a **Palaestra** (wrestling school), used by the competitors during their obligatory month of pre-games training.

Beyond these stood the Priests' House, the **Theokoleion**, a substantial colonnaded building in the southeast corner of which is a structure adapted as a Byzantine church. This was originally the **studio of Pheidias**, the fifth-century BC sculptor responsible for the great cult statue in Olympia's Temple of Zeus. It was identified by following a description by Pausanias, and through the discovery of tools, moulds for the statue and a cup engraved with the sculptor's name. The studio's dimensions are exactly those of the *cella* in which the statue was to be placed.

To the south of the studio lie further administrative buildings, including the **Leonidaion**, a large and doubtless luxurious hostel endowed for the most important of the festival guests. It was the first building visitors would reach along the original approach road to the site.

The Altis

Admission to the **Altis** was in the earlier centuries of the games limited to free-born Greeks – whether spectators or competitors. Throughout its history it was a male-only preserve, save for the sanctuary's priestess. An Olympian anecdote records how a woman from Rhodes disguised herself as her son's trainer to gain admission, but revealed her identity in the joy of his victory. She was spared the legislated death penalty, though subsequently all trainers had to appear naked.

The main focus of the precinct, today as in ancient times, is provided by the great Doric **Temple of Zeus**. Built between 470 and 456 BC, it was as large as the (virtually contemporary) Parthenon, a fact quietly substantiated by the vast column drums littering the ground. The temple's decoration, too, rivalled the finest in Athens; partially recovered, its sculptures of Pelops in a chariot race, of Lapiths and Centaurs, and the Labours of Herakles, are now in the museum. In the *cella* was exhibited the (lost) gold-and-ivory cult statue by Pheidias, one of the seven wonders of the ancient world. Here, too, the Olympian flame was kept alight, from the time of the games until the following spring – a tradition continued at an altar for the modern games.

The smaller **Temple of Hera**, behind, was the first built in the *Altis*; prior to its completion in the seventh century BC, the sanctuary had only open-air altars, dedicated to Zeus and a variety of other cult gods. The temple, rebuilt in the Doric style in the sixth century BC, is the most complete building on the site, with some thirty of its columns surviving in part, along with a section of the inner wall. The levels above this wall were composed only of sun-baked brick, and the lightness of this building material must have helped to preserve the sculptures – most notably the *Hermes of Praxiteles* – found amid the earthquake ruins.

Between the temples of Hera and Zeus is a grove described by Pausanias, and identified as the **Pelopeion**. In addition to a cult altar to the Olympian hero, this enclosed a small mound formed by sacrificial ashes, among which excavations unearthed many of the terracotta finds in the museum. The sanctuary's principal altar, dedicated to Zeus, probably stood just to the east.

West of the Temple of Hera, and bordering the wall of the *Altis*, are remains of the circular **Philippeion**, the first monument in the sanctuary to be built to secular glory. It was begun by Philip II after the Battle of Chaeronea gave him control over the Greek mainland, and may have been completed by Alexander the Great. To the east of the Hera temple is a small, second-century AD **fountain house**, the gift of the ubiquitous Herodes Atticus. Beyond, lining a terrace at the base of the Hill of Kronos, are the **state treasuries**. All except two of these were constructed by cities outside of Greece proper, as they functioned principally as storage chambers for sacrificial items and sporting equipment used in the games. They are built in the form of temples, as at Delphi; the oldest and grandest, at the east end, belonged to Gela in Sicily. In front of the treasuries are the foundations of a the **Metroön**, a fourth-century BC Doric temple dedicated to the mother of the gods.

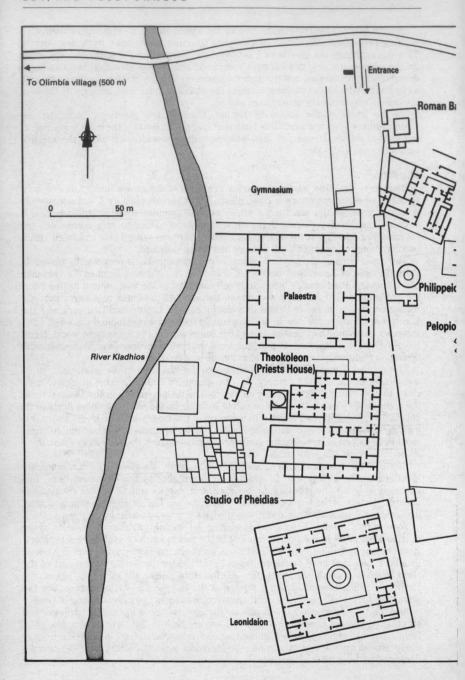

To Olimbía village (500 m)

Entrance

Roman Ba

Gymnasium

0   50 m

Palaestra

Philippei

River Kladhios

Pelopio

Theokoleon
(Priests House)

Studio of Pheidias

Leonidaion

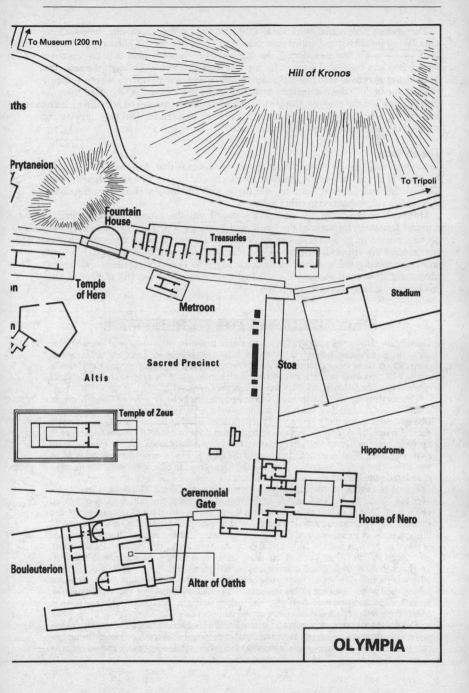

To Museum (200 m)

Hill of Kronos

ths

Prytaneion

To Trípoli

Fountain House

Treasuries

Temple of Hera

Stadium

Metroon

Sacred Precinct

Stoa

Altis

Temple of Zeus

Hippodrome

Ceremonial Gate

House of Nero

Bouleuterion

Altar of Oaths

OLYMPIA

The ancient ceremonial entrance to the *Altis* was on the south side, below a long **stoa** taking up almost the entire east side of the precinct. At the corner was a house built by Nero for his stay during the games. The emperor also had the entrance remodelled as a triumphal arch, fit for his anticipated victories. Through the arch, just outside the precinct, stood the **Bouleuterion** or council chamber, where before a great statue of Zeus the competitors took their oaths to observe the Olympian rules. As they approached the stadium, the gravity of this would be impressed upon them: lining the way were bronze statues paid for with the fines exacted for foul play, bearing the name of the disgraced athlete, his father and city.

The stadium

In the final analysis, it's neither foundations nor columns that make sense of Olympia, but the 200-metre track of the **Stadium** itself, entered by way of a long arched tunnel. The starting and finishing lines are still there, with the judges' thrones in the middle and seating ridges banked to either side.

Originally unstructured, the stadium developed with the games' popularity, forming a model for others throughout the Greek and Roman world. The tiers here eventually accommodated up to 20,000 spectators, with a smaller number on the southern slope overlooking the **Hippodrome** where the chariot races were held. Even so, the seats were reserved for the wealthier strata of society. The ordinary populace – along with slaves and all women spectators – watched the events from the Hill of Krónos, then treeless and a natural grandstand to the north.

THE OLYMPIC GAMES: SOME HISTORY

The origins of the games at Olympia are rooted in **legends** – the most predominant relating to the god **Pelops**, revered in the region before his eclipse by Zeus, and to **Herakles**, one of the earliest victors. Historically, the contests probably began around the eleventh century BC, growing over the next two centuries from a local festival to the quadrennial celebration attended by states from throughout the Greek world.

The impetus for this change seems to have come from the **Oracle of Delphi**, which, with the local ruler of Elis, **Iphitos**, and the Spartan ruler **Lycurgus**, helped to codify the Olympic rules in the ninth century BC. Among their most important introductions was a **sacred truce**, the *Ekeheiria*, announced by heralds prior to the celebrations and enforced for their duration. It was virtually unbroken throughout the games' history (Sparta, ironically, was fined at one point) and as host of the games, Elis, a comparatively weak state, was able to keep itself away from political disputes, growing rich meanwhile on the associated trade and kudos.

From the beginning, the main Olympic **events** were athletic. The earliest was a race over the course of the stadium – roughly 200m. Later came the introduction of two-lap (400m) and 24-lap (5000m) races, along with the most revered of the Olympiad events, the **Pentathlon**. This encompassed running, jumping, discus and javelin events, the competitors gradually reduced to a final pair for a wrestling-and-boxing combat. It was, like much of these early Olympiads, a fairly brutal contest. More brutal still was the **Pancratium**, introduced in 680 BC and one of the most prestigious events. *Pancratium* contestants fought each other, naked and unarmed, using any means except biting or gouging each others' eyes; the olive wreath had on one occasion to be awarded posthumously, the victor having died at the moment of his opponent's submission. Similarly, the **chariot races**, introduced in the same year, were extreme tests of strength and control, only one team in twenty completing the seven-kilometre course without mishap.

The great gathering of people and nations at the festival extended the games' importance and purpose well beyond the winning of olive wreaths; assembled under the temporary truce, nobles and ambassadors negotiated treaties, while merchants chased contacts

The stadium was unearthed only in the World War II, during a second phase of German excavations between 1941 and 1944, allegedly on the direct orders of Hitler. It's a sobering thought to see this ancient site in the context of the 1936 Berlin Olympics.

The Archeological Museum

May to mid-Oct Mon 12.30–7pm, Tues–Fri 8am–7pm, Sat & Sun 8.30am–3pm; mid-Oct to April Mon 12.30–5pm, Tues–Fri 8am–5pm, Sat & Sun 8.30am–3pm; 1000dr

Olympia's site museum lies a couple of hundred metres north of the sanctuary; some of the signposts still refer to it as the "New Museum". It contains some of the finest Classical and Roman sculptures in the country, all superbly displayed, and amply justifies the rather high admission fee.

The most famous of the individual sculptures are the **Head of Hera** and the **Hermes of Praxiteles**, both dating from the fourth century BC and discovered in the Temple of Hera. The Hermes is one of the best preserved of all Classical sculptures, and remarkable in the easy informality of its pose; it retains traces of its original paint. On a grander scale is the **Nike of Paionios**, which was originally ten metres high. Though no longer complete (and currently sequestered for restoration), it hints at how the sanctuary must once have appeared, crowded with statuary.

The best of the smaller objects are housed in Room 4. They include several fine bronze items, among them a **Persian Helmet**, captured by the Athenians at the Battle of Marathon, and (displayed alongside) the **Helmet of Miltiades**, the victorious

and foreign markets. Sculptors and poets, too, would seek commissions for their work. Herodotus read aloud the first books of his history at an Olympian festival to an audience that included Thucydides – who was to date events in his own work by reference to the winners of the *Pancratium*.

In the early Olympiads, the **rules of competition** were strict. Only free-born – and male – Greeks could take part, and the rewards of victory were entirely honorary: a palm, given to the victor immediately after the contest, and an olive branch, presented in a ceremony closing the games. As the games developed, however, the rules were loosened to allow participation by athletes from all parts of the Greek and Roman world, and nationalism and professionalism gradually crept in. By the fourth century BC, when the games were at their peak, the athletes were virtually all professionals, heavily sponsored by their home states and, if they won at Olympia, commanding huge appearance money at games elsewhere. Bribery became an all too common feature, despite the solemn religious oaths sworn in front of the sanctuary priests prior to the contests.

Under the **Romans**, predictably, the process was accelerated. The palms and olive branches were replaced by rich monetary prizes, and a sequence of new events was introduced. The nadir was reached in 69 AD when the Emperor Nero delayed the games for two years so that he could compete in (and win) special singing and lyre-playing events – in addition to the chariot race in which he was tactfully declared victor despite falling twice and failing to finish.

Notwithstanding all this abuse the Olympian tradition was popular enough to be maintained for another three centuries, and the games' eventual **closure** happened as a result of religious dogma rather than lack of support. In 393 AD the Emperor Theodosius, newly converted to Christianity, suspended the games as part of a general crackdown on public pagan festivities. This suspension proved final, for Theodosius's successor ordered the destruction of the temples, a process completed by barbarian invasion, earthquakes and, lastly, by the Alfios River changing its course to cover the sanctuary site. There it remained, covered by seven metres of silt and sand, until the first excavation by German archeologists in the 1870s.

Athenian general; both were found with votive objects dedicated in the stadium. There is also a superb terracotta group of **Zeus abducting Ganymede** and a group of finds from the workshop of **Pheidias**, including the cup with his name inscribed.

In the main hall of the museum is the centrepiece of the Olympia finds – statuary and scupture reassembled from the **Temple of Zeus**. This includes three groups, all of which were once painted. From the *cella* is a frieze of the **Twelve Labours of Herakles**, delicately moulded and for the most part identifiably preserved.

The other groups are from the east and west pediments. The east, reflecting Olympian pursuits, depicts Zeus presiding over a **Chariot race between Pelops and Oinamaos**. The story has several versions. King Oinamaos, warned that he would be killed by his son-in-law, challenged each of his daughter Hippomadeia's suitors to a chariot race. After allowing them a start he would catch up and kill them from behind. The king (depicted on the left of the frieze) was eventually defeated by Pelops (on the right with Hippomadeia), after – depending on the version – assistance from Zeus (depicted at the centre), magic steeds from Poseidon or, most un-Olympian, bribing Oinamaos's charioteer to tamper with the wheels.

The west pediment, less controversially mythological, illustrates the **Battle of Lapiths and Centaurs** at the wedding of the Lapith king, Peirithous. This time, Apollo presides over the scene while Theseus helps the Lapiths defeat the drunken centaurs, depicted, with fairly brutal realism, attacking the women and boy guests. Many of the metope fragments are today in the Louvre Museum, Paris, and some of what you see here are plaster-cast copies.

In the last rooms of the museum are a collection of **objects relating to the games** – including *halteres* (jumping weights), discuses, weightlifters' stones, and so on. Also displayed are a number of funerary inscriptions, including that of a boxer, Camelos of Alexandria, who died in the stadium after praying to Zeus for victory or death.

Practicalities: Olimbía

Modern **OLIMBÍA** is a village that has grown up simply to serve the excavations and tourist trade. It's essentially one long main avenue, **Praxiteles Kondhíli**, with a few side streets. Nevertheless, Olimbía is quite a pleasant place to stay, and certainly preferable to Pírgos (see below), with the prospect of good countryside walks along the Alfíos River and around the hill of Krónos.

Most people arrive at Olympia **via Pírgos**, which is on the main Peloponnese rail line and has frequent bus connections with Pátra and a couple daily with Kalamáta/Kiparissía. The last of five daily **trains** from Pírgos to Olympia leaves at 6.50pm; if you have time to kill between buses or trains, the city square, two blocks north, is pleasant.

Buses leave 16 times daily on weekdays (10 on weekends) between Pírgos and Olympia, though with a break between 12.30pm and 3.30pm and a last service at 9pm. The only other direct buses to Olympia are **from Trípoli**, via Langádhia. These run twice daily in either direction. If you are approaching **from Andhrítsena**, either take the bus to Pírgos and change, or stop at Kréstena and hitch or take a taxi the final 12km on from there.

There is a most helpful **tourist office** (May–Oct daily 9am–10pm; Nov–April Mon–Sat 11am–5pm; ☎0624/23 100), on the right of Praxiteles Kondhíl as you head towards the site. Olimbía has two **banks** and an **OTE** on the main avenue, a **post office** (just uphill) with Saturday and Sunday morning hours. **English-language books** are to be found at the back of the *Galerie d'Orphée* crafts shop on Praxiteles Kondhíli.

Accommodation

Accommodation is fairly easy to come by, with a swift turnaround of clientele and a range of hotels and private rooms whose prices are kept modest by competition. Most

rooms are signposted on Stefanopoúlou or on the road parallel to and above Praxiteles Kondhíli, though you may well be offered one on arrival. As elsewhere, rates can drop substantially out of season, though many of the smaller and cheaper places close during the off season (never precisely defined), and it's best to check in advance.

The **youth hostel** at Praxiteles Kondhíli 18 (☎0624/22 580; ①), which is open all day and has no curfew, is probably the cheapest option for lone travellers. There are three **campsites**, closest of which is *Diana* (☎0624/22 314), 1km back from the main street, with a pool and good facilities. The others are *Alphios* (☎0624/22 950; April–Sept), 1km out on the Kréstena road, and *Olympía* (☎0624/22 745; April–Oct), 2km out on the Pírgos road.

Achilles, Stefanopoúlou 4 (☎0624/22 562). A pension on a side street behind the *National Bank*; large and comfortable rooms above a snack bar. ②.

Antonios (☎0624/22 348). A hotel in the woods on the Kréstena road; expensive and not particularly well furnished, but it is peaceful, and has a swimming pool and a stunning view; open April–Oct. ⑥.

Europa (☎0624/22 650). A modern hotel on the hill overlooking the village; it's a good, reasonably priced hotel, which also has a swiming pool. ④–⑤.

Heracles (☎0624/22 696). A welcoming hotel on a side street off Praxiteles Kondhíli; big breakfasts and small balconies. ③.

Hermes (☎0624/22 577). A comfortable hotel 400m out on the Pírgos road, rooms have private facilities and there is a good restaurant. ②.

Pelops, Barelas 2 (☎0624/22 543). A hotel run by a Greek/Australian couple and strongly recommended by those who stay there often; open March–Oct. ④.

Praxiteles, Spiliopoúlou (☎0624/22 592). Quiet hotel next to the police station; good restaurant, and both meals and rooms are competitively priced. ②.

Eating and drinking

Many of the hotels have excellent **restaurants**, where non-residents can eat. The main avenue is lined with **tavernas**, which offer standard tourist meals at mildly inflated prices in high season, and there is a growing number of fast-food kerbside cafés. The **Taverna Kladhios**, out of the village and not surprisingly on the bank of the Kládhios River, serves good food in a pleasant setting. In Mirálta village (1km out on the Trípoli road), the family-run **Taverna Drosia** offers a friendly service and fresh, home-made food; the excellent "house" wine is made by the owner's father. For picnics, bread from the bakery on the road to Kréstena is very good.

The northwest coast to Pátra

Despite the proximity of Olympia and Pátra, the northwest corner of the Peloponnese is not much explored by foreign visitors. Admittedly, it's not the most glamorous of coasts, but for a day or two's beach stop, either the old port of **Katákolo** or one of the campsites near **Loutrá Killínis** is functional and pleasant.

Ferry connections may add further purpose: from Killíni there are regular crossings to Zákinthos, and in summer to Kefalloniá, while Katákolo has (summer-only) *kaíkia* to Zákinthos.

Pírgos

PÍRGOS has a grim recent history. When the Germans withdrew at the end of World War II, it remained under the control of Greek Nazi collaborators. These negotiated surrender with the resistance, who were met by gunfire as they entered the town. Full-scale battle erupted and for five days the town burned. Today, it's a drab, 1950s-looking place, which earns few plaudits from casual visitors. If you can avoid an enforced over-night stay, do so. The hotels are overpriced, the food uninspiring and diversions nonexistent.

The main escape routes are by **train** or **bus** to Pátra, Kiparissía or Olympia; there is a daily bus to Itéa, usually in the morning and this should put you within striking distance of Delphi on the same day. Closer to hand, there are frequent buses to Katákolo by local bus #4. The bus station is at the top of the hill and the train station 400m away at the bottom, so allow a little time for interchange.

If you have to stay the night, the cheapest hotels are the *Marily*, Deliyiánni 48 (☎0621/28 133; ④), and the *Pantheon*, Themistokleous 7 (☎0621/29 748; ④).

Katákolo

Thirteen kilometres west of Pírgos, **KATÁKOLO** is somewhat more enticing: a decayed, ramshackle old port with good beaches close by. Until the last few decades, when new roads improved connections with Pátra, it controlled the trade for Ilía province. Today only a few tramp steamers rust at anchor, though the navy calls occasionally and, oddly, the port remains a stop for Italian summer-cruise ships, including the *Orient Express*. What the cruise passengers make of the caved-in warehouses and the little two-street town, before they board their air-conditioned buses to Olympia, is hard to say. But arriving from Pírgos it feels an easy place to settle into, and to the south there's a pleasant twenty-minute walk out to the **lighthouse**, set on a plateau among arbutus and pine.

There are three reasonable **hotels**, best value of which is the *Delfini* (☎0621/41 592; ③), which is popular with the locals, who play cards and backgammon on green-baize tables in the snack bar on Sundays. At the top of steps leading from the road are several **room** establishments with cabins fronted by peach and apricot trees. Try to avoid staying on the main drag, which proves to be incredibly noisy at night, belying the town's torpid daytime appearance. For **meals**, there are a handful of excellent tavernas on the quay.

Beaches

Katákolo's beach, the **Spiátza**, stretches away for miles to the north, a popular spot with Greeks, many of whom own shuttered little cottages set just back from the sea. It is sandy, though hard-packed: more of a spot for football or jogging, with the sea too shallow for real swimming.

However, a thirty-minute walk north, past the overgrown Byzantine-Frankish **Castle of Beauvoir**, will take you to much better swimming at **Áyios Andhréas** beach – two hundred metres of sloping, outcrop-studded sand, with views over a few attendant islets and out to Zákinthos. There are summer tavernas here and a few rooms to let.

An even better beach is to be found at **Skafídhia**, 3km north of Katákolo and accessible by road via Korakohóri.

The cape north of Pírgos

North from Pírgos, road and rail meander through a series of uneventful market towns, but there are two forks west to a sandy cape and the coast. The first is at Gastoúni and heads for the spa of **Loutrá Killínis** (occasional buses from Pírgos and Pátra); the second is at Kavássilas, where a side road (buses from Pátra) heads down to **Killíni** proper. Take care not to confuse the two.

LOUTRÁ KILLÍNIS has a long beach, and at its north end you'll find a crop of upmarket **hotels** catering for the resort's spa-trade, including the over-priced and under-resourced *Kyllini Spa Xenia Tourist Complex* run by the EOT. Better to walk south where the development soon gives way to sand dunes. There are two campsites further to the southeast and best approached from Lygía on the road from Gastoúni. The *Aginara Beach* (☎0623/96 411) and the *Ionian Beach* (☎0623/96 395) are both bordered by trees and beaches of fine shingle and sand.

Cheerless little **KILLÍNI** (which can be reached by taxi from Loutrá Killínis) has little more to offer than its **ferry connections**. It is the principal port for **Zákinthos** (3–7 departures daily) and in season has boats to Póros or Argostóli on **Kefalloniá** (4 departures daily). Be warned, however, that there are only two daily bus arrivals/departures so you are often forced into a two- or three-hour stopover at the harbour. If you're stuck the night in Killíni, **places to stay** are limited: the choice is between sleeping on the beach, rooms on the main street, or the *Hotel Ionian* (☎0623/92 318; ④), also on the main street, where some rooms have private facilities. The *Taverna Anna*, beyond the harbour, serves a wide range of traditional dishes and is particularly popular with locals at Sunday lunchtimes.

Using Loutrá Killínis or Killíni as a base, it's worth taking time to hitch or walk to the village of **KÁSTRO**, 6km from either town, at the centre of the cape. Looming above the village is the Frankish **Castle of Hlemoútsi** (also known as Chlemoutsi or Khlemoutsi), a vast hexagonal structure built in 1220 by Guillaume de Villchardouin, the founder of Mystra. Its function was principally to control the province of Akhaïa, though it served also as a strategic fortress on the Adriatic. Haze permitting, there are sweeping views across the straits to Zákinthos, and even to Kefalloniá and Itháki, from the well-preserved and restored ramparts. Kástro has a hotel, the *Chryssi Avgi* at Loutropoleos 9 (☎0623/95 224; ③), which is open from May to mid-October; Chrístos Lepídas and Catherine, his French wife, are excellent hosts. You can eat here by arrangement, or dine equally well at the nearby *Taverna Apollon*.

Kalógria

Midway between Killíni and Pátra, **KALÓGRIA** is an eight-kilometre strand of beach, bordered by a swathe of pine forests. A fair proportion of Pátra descends here at the weekend as it's the nearest good beach to the city, but it's also a respected place (the beach for its sands and the forest for its birdlife) and permanent development remains low key. It is not actually a village – the nearest bona fide town is Metóhi – but rather a cluster of tavernas and stores. At the far north end of the beach there's both the *Kalogria Beach* (☎0693/31 276; ④–⑤), a large hotel, and the *Barracuda Club* complex. A novelty for wildlife aficionados are the estuaries nearby in which you may find yourself swimming alongside harmless metre-long watersnakes.

Pátra (Patras)

PÁTRA is the largest town in the Peloponnese and, after Pireás, the major port of Greece. From here you can go to Italy and Turkey as well as to certain Ionian islands and Crete; services to the coast of the former Yugoslavia are suspended. The city is also the hub of the Greek-mainland transport network, with connections throughout the Peloponnese and, via the ferry at Río, across the straits to Delphi or western Greece.

Unless you arrive late in the day from Italy, you shouldn't need to spend more than a few hours in the city. A conurbation of close to half a million souls, it's not the ideal holiday retreat: there are no beaches, no particular sights, and traffic noise well into the night and earlier than you'd want to get up. Nor has there been much effort to make the place attractive to visitors, save for a **summer festival** which sponsors events in August and September. These include classical plays and the occasional rock concert in the Roman **Odeion**, and art and photographic exhibitions that bring a bit of life to the warehouses by the harbour (details from the EOT, Tourist Police or the theatre on Platía Yioryíou). The three-week **carnival** (ending on Ash Wednesday) is one of the biggest in the country, with a grand parade through the city centre on the last Sunday.

The Town

At other times, if you've an afternoon to fill, the best places to make for are the café-table-studded **Platía Psilá Alónia** or the **Kástro** (daily except Mon 8am–5pm; free), a mainly Venetian citadel. This is not particularly exciting, but it is away from the city bustle, surrounded by a park and only a ten-minute walk up from the water. At the southwest end of the waterfront itself is the neo-Byzantine **church of Áyios Andhréas**, which opened in 1979 and houses relics of St Andrew, said to have been martyred on this spot. The church is a massive confection of yellow and cream walls, red-tiled domes and marmoreal excess that takes in the pillars and arches.

Swimming near Pátra isn't really advisable, with the sea polluted for some kilometres to the southwest. Locals go to the **beaches** around Río (7km northeast; bus #6 from the stop on Kanakári) or to Kalógria (32km southwest – see above; bus from *KTEL* station).

The Akhaïa Clauss factory

Daily tours April–Aug 9am–7.30pm; Sept–March 9am–5pm; free. Telephone first for group tours, and ask for Dora Tsafalopoulou; ☎061/325 051.

The **Akhaïa Clauss** factory is an out-of-town time-filler, 9km southeast of Pátra; take the #7 bus from the stop on Kanakári (see map opposite). Tours show you around its wine- and *ouzo*-making process, and feature some treasured, century-old barrels of *Mavrodhafni* – a dark dessert wine named after the woman Clauss wanted to marry. You're given a glass of this to sample (and a postcard, which they post) on reaching the factory's rather Teutonic bar, an echo of its founder's nationality. Along the walls are signed letters from celebrity recipients of *Mavrodhafni* (first prize for arrogance to the British judge who sent a signed photo). A shop sells all the factory's products, if you want a bottle for yourself.

Practicalities

If you are driving in or through Pátra, you will find the traffic and one-way system no less frustrating than Athens. An EOT map showing the direction of traffic, if not vital, will at least save time and probably maintain sanity.

For **tourist information**, try the useful *Europa Centre* (☎061/434 801), at the corner of Óthonos Amalías and Karólou (which also has a café-restaurant, a ticket agency and a currency exchange), the **EOT** office, Iróön Politehníou 115 (Mon–Fri 7am–9.30pm, Sat & Sun 2–9.30pm; ☎061/653 358), and the helpful **Tourist Police** (7am–10pm; ☎061/220 902) at Patreos 53.

For **money exchange**, there is an automatic machine near the EOT office, and *Thomas Cook*, 200m towards the waterfront, will change currency or travellers' cheques. The *National Bank of Greece*, on the waterside Platía Tríon Simáhon, also keeps special daily evening hours (5.30–8pm).

There is an **OTE** (7.30am–10pm) on the *platía* and the main **post office** on the corner of Mesonós and Záïmi is open in summer until 8pm.

Departures

The **ferry agents**, **train station** and main **KTEL bus terminal** could hardly be easier to find, grouped on the harbour road, Óthonos Amalías. Full details of **ferry routes** are shown in the box below.

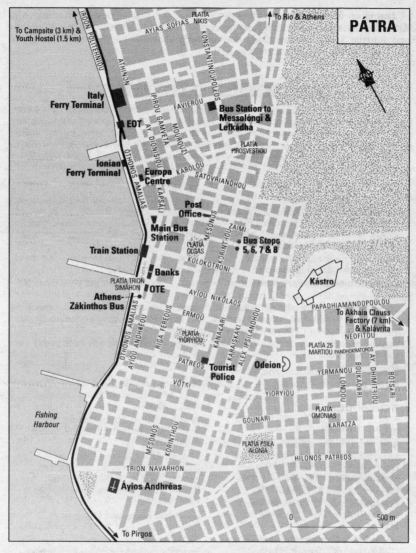

Buses go almost everywhere from Pátra. From the main **KTEL** station, there are departures to Athens, Killíni, Pírgos and other towns in the Peloponnese, as well as to Ioánnina. From the **KTEL station** on Faviérou, the Étolo-Akarnanía service will take you to Lefkádha (change at Agrínio) and Messolóngi. You can pick up the Athens–Zákinthos bus on Óthonos Amalías, an alternative to the regular Killíni port departure. Heading for Delphi, take the local bus #6 from the **Kanakári stop**, which will take you to Río and the ferry to Andírio, where you can pick up a local bus to Náfpaktos and from there a regular bus to Delphi.

Trains go from Pátra down the west coast of the Peloponnese, with changes at Alfiós for Olympia, and at Kaló Neró for routes inland to Kalamáta, Trípoli, Kórinthos and Athens. Trains go east along the southern shore of the Gulf of Kórinthos to Dhiakoftó, Kórinthos, Athens and Pireás.

FERRY ROUTES AND COMPANIES

Innumerable ticket agents along the waterfront each sell different permutations of ferry crossings to Italy on one or more of the lines detailed below. It is worth spending an hour or so researching these, especially if you're taking a car, since costs, journey times and routes all differ from one company to another. En route to Italy, it is possible to make stopovers on Kefalloniá and, most commonly, Igoumenítsa and Corfu (Kérkira). Domestic tickets to these **Greek island stops** (plus Itháki) are also available from Pátra.

General points

High season All frequencies of ferry crossings detailed below are for the high season, the definition of which varies slightly from company to company. Broadly, for crossings from Italy to Greece, high season is between early July and mid-August; from Greece to Italy, it is between early August and early September. Check with company agents for exact dates. Out of season, all services are reduced.

Fares All companies offer a variety of fares for cabin, airline-type seats, and deck passage, less reductions according to age, student or rail-card status.

Embarkation tax All international departures carry a levy of 1500dr per person and per car.

Checking in If you have bought tickets in advance, or from a travel agent other than the official agent listed below, you must check in (to the appropriate agent's office, or at their booth in the departure hall) at least three hours before departure.

Stopovers Free if you specify them when booking, though you will have to pay re-embarkation taxes.

Companies, destinations and agents

ANEK Ancona (29hr) via Igoumenítsa and Corfu; Mon, Tues, Thurs, Fri. Continues to Trieste (58hr total) on Thurs. *United Ferries,* Óthonos Amalías 25; ☎061/226 053.

Adriatica Brindisi (19hr) via Igoumenítsa and Corfu; daily. Also direct to Iráklion (20hr), Bari (21hr), Venice (23hr) and Alexandria (23hr). *Charilaos Cacouris,* Óthonos Amalías 8; ☎061/421 995.

Fragline Brindisi (18hr 30min) direct; 3 weekly. *Inglessis Bros,* Óthonos Amalías 12; ☎061/275 445.

Hellenic Mediterranean Lines Brindisi (17hr) direct or (19hr 30min) via Igoumenítsa and Corfu; daily. *Hellenic Mediterranean Lines,* corner of Sarandapórou and Athinón; ☎061/429 520.

Horizon Sea Lines Ancona (29hr) direct. Also Çeşme (22hr) direct. *N. Petropoulis Shipping and Tourism,* Óthonos Amalías 32; ☎061/274 554.

Marlines Brindisi (18hr) via Igoumenítsa and Corfu. *Marlines,* Óthonos Amalías 56; ☎061/226 666.

Mediterranean Lines Brindisi (18hr) direct; daily. *Yannatos,* Óthonos Amalías 47; ☎061/623 011.

Minoan Lines Ancona (34hr) via Igoumenítsa and Corfu. Also direct to Kefellonía (3hr), Çeşme (37hr) and Iráklion (19hr). *Minoan Lines,* Athínon 2; ☎061/421 500.

Poseidon Lines Bari (19hr) via Igoumenítsa. *Cargo Sea,* Óthonos Amalías 85; ☎061/224 847.

Strintzis Ancona (34hr) via Igoumenítsa and Corfu. Also Itháki direct or via Kefellonía. *Tsimaras,* Óthonos Amalías 14; ☎061/622 602.

Ventouris Bari (17hr 30min) direct or (19hr 30min) via Igoumenítsa and Corfu; daily. *Express Shipping Agencies Co.,* Óthonos Amalías 81; ☎061/222 958.

Accommodation

If you need to stay, you will find most of the **hotels** on Ayíou Andhréou, one block back from Óthonos Amalías, or on Ayíou Nikólaos, which runs back from the sea, near the train station and Platía Tríon Simáhon. Don't expect too much in the way of standards or value for money; most of the places cater for a very passing trade and don't make great efforts. The best budget option is the **youth hostel** at Iróön Politehníou 68 (☎061/222 707; ①), a kilometre-plus walk northeast of the train station along the water-front; it's clean, cheap, very popular, has no curfew and is housed in a nineteenth-century mansion within a small courtyard.

There are two **campsites** to choose from: the *Kavouri* (☎061/422 145), along the coast road 2km northeast of the city centre, near the public swimming pool; and *Patra EOT* (☎061/424 131), a further kilometre towards Río; take bus #1 from the waterfront for both.

Most of the older hotels nearer the waterfront have closed, or indeed collapsed. Of those still standing, choices include:

Adonis, Záïmi 9 (☎061/224 213). On the junction with Kapsáli opposite the bus station; well furnished and maintained and includes a buffet-style breakfast; good value. ⑤.

Astir, Ayíou Andhréou 16 (☎061/277 502). Modern hotel with a swimming pool, sauna, roof garden and car parking, which still don't justify the price. ⑥.

El Greco, Ayíou Andhréou 145 (☎061/272 931). A good bargain hotel and top of its class; the manager, George Vlachoyiánnis is attentive and speaks English. ③.

Esperia, Záïmi 10 (☎061/276 476). Central hotel, but still quiet and good value; out of season you should get a competitive price. ②.

Galaxy, Ayíou Andhréou 9 (☎061/275 981). A well-placed hotel, if a touch pretentious, and serves a good breakfast. ⑥.

Mediterranée, Ayíou Nikólaous 18 (☎061/279 602). Modern and adequate hotel, if undistin-guished, with a helpful staff. ④.

Nicos, Ayíou Andhréou 121 (☎061/623 757). Clean, cheerfully run pension with character; good terrace and bar; cheaper if you share facilities; 1am curfew. ②.

Rannia, Riga Feréou 53 (☎061/220 114). Clean, faultless and well placed, with a café and snack bar. ③.

ROOM PRICE CODES

All the accommodation prices in this book have been coded using the symbols below below. The rates quoted represent the cheapest available room in high season; all are prices for a double room, except for category ①, which are per person rates.

① 1400–2000dr (£4–5.50/US$6–8.50)	④ 8000–12000dr (£22–33/US$33–50)
② 4000–6000dr (£11–16.50/US$17–25)	⑤ 12000–16000dr (£33–44/US$50–66)
③ 6000–8000dr (£16.50–22/US$25–33)	⑥ 16000dr (£44/US$66) and upwards

For more accommodation details, see pp.34–35.

Eating and drinking

Pátra's **restaurants** seem to constitute a fairly wretched bunch, with countless fast-food places around Platía Tríon Simáhon, and along Ayíou Andhréou and Ayíou Nikólaou. But even here there are, if you search, some reliable restaurants with charac-ter, and there is a mouth-watering patisserie-bakery at Ayíou Nikólaou 82. For fish, the best places are a couple of tavernas down by the fishing harbour, home to a somewhat half-hearted fleet, while for spit-roast specialities, several *psistariés* are grouped around Platía Omonías and Platía Pirosvestíou.

If you're stuck for the night and feel the urge to escape to a quieter stretch of sea, hop on any #5 blue bus labelled "Tsoukaleíka" and alight at either Monodhéndhri or Vrahneíka, 4km south of the city. There are five tavernas or *psistariés* in a row at Monodhéndhri, plus a few more at Vrahneíka – none are utterly superlative, but they have reasonable prices and wonderful outdoor tables facing the sunset. Choices in Pátra include:

7 Thalassa, Ayíou Andhréou 128. A smart restaurant with a wide range of dishes.

Hartofilacas, corner of Riga Feréou/Karolou. A good-value *estiatório*, serving traditional food.

Krini, Pandokrátoros 57. An endearing place at the top of the old town, by the *kástro*. It has a limited but exemplary menu, and is a favourite with locals; it's possible to eat in the little garden at the back.

Majestic, Ayíou Nikólaos 2/4. Old-style *estiatório*, where you can choose from the day's hot dishes, which are tasty and cheap.

Nikolaous, Ayíou Nikólaos 50. Another old-style *estiatório*, serving good, traditional food.

Peking, corner of Iröön Politéhniou and Terpsithéas. A rare Chinese restaurant; modestly priced and none too bad.

Listings

American Express Handled by *Albatros Travel*, Óthonos Amalías 48 (☎061/220 993).

Books and newspapers *Book's Corner*, Ayíou Nikólaou 32, stocks useful maps and English-language newspapers. *Kyklos*, Riga Feréou 33, has guide books, second-hand books and a large selection of paperbacks, some in English. *Lexis*, Mesonos 38, stocks maps and a selection of *Penguins*. *Romios* on Kapsáli, behind the bus station, sells English-language books, and English-language papers are available from kiosks on the waterfront.

Car rental Major operators include: *Ansa*, Vótsi 2 (☎061/277 329); *Delta*, Óthonos Amalías 32 (☎061/272 764); *Eurodollar*, *Albatros Travel*, Óthonos Amalías 48 (☎061/220 993); *Hertz*, Karolóu 2 (☎061/220 990); *InterRent-EuropCar*, Ayíou Andhréou 106 (☎061/221 511); *Just*, Óthonos Amalías 37 (☎061/275 495); *Thrifty*, Óthonos Amalías 14 (☎061/623 200).

Consulates *Britain*, Vótsi 2 (☎061/277 329); *Finland*, Riga Feréou 46 (☎061/277 707); *Germany*, Mesonós 98 (☎061/221 943); *Netherlands*, Philopimónos 39 (☎061/271 846); *Norway*, Karolóu 85c (☎061/435 090); *Sweden*, Óthonos Amalías 62 (☎061/271 702).

Laundry *Laundromat Self Service*, corner of Záïmi and Korinthóu (Mon–Sat 9am–9pm); *Plintirios*, Tríon Navarhón 74 (Mon–Fri 9am–9pm, Sat 9am–1pm).

Poste restante Contact the main post office on the corner of Mesonós and Záïmi.

Travel agents These can help with information and reservations, and all line Óthonos Amalías: *Albatros Travel* (☎061/220 993); *Marine Tours* (☎061/621 166); *Olympias Shipping and Travel Enterprises* (☎061/275 495); *Thomas Cook* (☎061/226 053).

The north coast and the Kalávrita railway

From Pátra you can reach Kórinthos in two hours by by **train** or **bus** along the national highway; the onward journey to Athens takes another hour and a half. The resorts and villages lining the Gulf of Kórinthos are nothing very special, though none are too developed either. At most of them you find little more than a campsite, a few rooms for rent and a couple of seasonal tavernas. At both **Río** and **Éyio**, you can cross the gulf by ferry. Beyond **Dhiakoftó**, if you're unhurried, it's worth taking the old **coast road** along the Gulf of Kórinthos; this runs below the national highway, often right by the sea.

However, to travel from Pátra to Kórinthos without taking the time to detour along the **Kalávrita railway** from Dhiakoftó would be to miss one of the best treats the Peloponnese has to offer – and certainly the finest train journey in Greece. Even if you have a car, this trip should still be part of your plans.

Río and Éyio

RÍO, connected by local bus #6 to Pátra (30min journey), signals the beginning of swimmable water, though most travellers stop here only to make use of the **ferry** across the gulf to Andírio. This runs every fifteen minutes through the day and early evening (hourly or half-hourly thereafter), shuttling cars (1000dr including driver) and passengers (90dr) across to the central mainland. It is a long-established crossing, testimony to which are a pair of diminutive Turkish **forts** on either side of the gulf.

If you are crossing into the Peloponnese from Andírio, you might be tempted to stop by the sea here, rather than at Pátra. There are a couple of **hotels**, the *Georgios* (☎061/ 992 627; ④) and *Rio Beach* (☎061/991 421; ④), and two **campsites**: the *Rio Mare* (☎061/992 263; May–Oct), just before the jetty and 120m from the beach, and the *Rion* (☎061/993 388; April–Oct); beyond the jetty but closer to the beach, which is poor.

Moving east, there are better beaches, and a further **campsite**, the *Tsolis* (☎0691/31 469), at **ÉYIO**. The best sands are at the village of **RHODHODHÁFNI**, 2km northwest of Éyio, the *Corali Beach* (☎0691/71 546; May–Sept) and the *Acoli Beach* (☎0691/ 71 317; April–Oct), **campsites** are close to the beach. At Éyio, a **ferry** crosses the gulf three times daily (7.30am, 1.30pm & 5pm; car and driver 2500dr, passengers 400dr) to Áyios Nikólaos, well placed for Delphi.

Dhiakoftó and beyond

It is at **DHIAKOFTÓ** that the rack-and-pinion railway heads south into the Vouraïkós gorge for Kalávrita (see below). If you arrive late in the day, it's worth spending the night here and making the train journey in daylight; the town can, in any case, be an attractive alternative to staying overnight in Pátra. There are four **hotels**: the pleasant, upmarket *Chris-Paul* (☎0691/41 715; ④); the beautiful but basic *Helmos* (☎0691/41 236; ②; closed in winter); the *Lemonies* (☎0691/41 821; ②; April–Oct), set in a lemon grove by the road to the beach; and the *Panorama* (☎0691/41 614; ④), by the beach itself. There are adequate **restaurants** at the *Lemonies* and the *Panorama*, though the *Taverna Spiros*, on the beach, is a better if slightly expensive option, with excellent fish.

Beyond Dhiakoftó there are minor resorts at Akráta and Xilókastro. **AKRÁTA**, a small town with a beach hamlet, is a little crowded with three hotels and three campsites set along a rather drab, exposed stretch of beach. **DHERVÉNI**, another 8km east, is more attractive, though there is no hotel or campsite; there are **rooms** for rent, and those offered by *Konstantinos Stathakopoulou* (☎0743/31 223; ②) are comfortable. **XILÓKASTRO**, a popular weekend escape from Kórinthos, has both good beaches and accommodation, and a pleasant setting below Mount Zíria. Cheapest of its dozen **hotels** are the *Hermes*, Ioánou 81 (☎0743/22 250; ②), and *Kyani Akti*, Tsaldhári 68 (☎0743/22 225; ③).

Dhiakoftó to Kalávrita: the rack-and-pinion railway

Even if you have no interest in trains, the **rack-and-pinion railway** from Dhiakoftó to Kalávrita is a must. It's a crazy feat of engineering, rising at gradients of up to one in seven as it cuts through the course of the **Vouraïkós gorge**. En route is a toy-train fantasy of tunnels, bridges and precipitous overhangs.

The railway was built by an Italian company between 1885 and 1895 to bring minerals from the mountains to the sea. Its steam locomotives were replaced some years ago – one remains by the line at Dhiakoftó and another at Kalávrita – but the track itself retains all the charm of its period. The tunnels, for example, have delicately carved windows, and the narrow bridges zigzagging across the Vouraïkós seem engineered for sheer virtuosity.

It takes up to an hour to get from Dhiakoftó to Zahloroú (confusingly listed on time-tables as Méga Spílio), and about another twenty minutes from there to Kalávrita. The best part of the trip is **the stretch to Zahloroú**, along which the gorge narrows to a few feet at points, only to open out into brilliant, open shafts of light beside the Vouraïkós, clear and fast-running even in midsummer. In peak season the ride is very popular, so you'll probably need to buy tickets some hours before your preferred departure (including the return journey).

Zahloroú and Méga Spílio

ZAHLOROÚ is as perfect a train stop as could be imagined: a tiny hamlet echoing with the sound of the Vouraïkós River, which splits it into two neighbourhoods. It's a lovely, peaceful place with a gorgeous old wooden hotel, the very friendly and very reasonably priced *Romantzo* (☎0692/22 758; ③).

The **Monastery of Méga Spílio** (Great Cave) is a 45-minute walk from the village, up a rough donkey track along the cliff; this joins an access drive along the final stretch, which is often chock-a-block with tour buses. The monastery is reputedly the oldest in Greece, but it has burnt down and been rebuilt so many times that you'd hardly guess its erstwhile antiquity. The last major fire took place in the 1930s, after a keg of gunpowder left behind from the War of Independence exploded. Dress conduct for visitors is strict: skirts for women and long sleeves and trousers for men. Only men are allowed to stay overnight, and the monks like visitors to arrive before 8pm, serving up a rough repast before closing the gates.

The view of the gorge from the monastery is for many the principal attraction. However, the cloister was once among the richest in the Greek world, owning properties throughout the Peloponnese, in Macedonia, Constantinople and Asia Minor. In consequence, its treasury, arranged as a small **museum**, is outstanding. In the church, among its icons, is a curiously moving charred black image of the Virgin, one of three in Greece said to be by the hand of Saint Luke. The monastery was founded by saints Theodhoros and Simeon, after a vision by the shepherdess Euphrosyne in 362 AD led to the discovery of the icon in the large cave behind the site of the later church.

Kalávrita and around

From Méga Spílio a new road has been hacked down to **KALÁVRITA**. The train line is more in harmony with the surroundings, though coming from Zahloroú the drama of the route is diminished as the gorge opens out. Kalávrita itself is beautifully positioned, with Mount Helmós as a backdrop, though it wears a sad edge. During World War II the Germans carried out one of their most brutal reprisal massacres, killing the entire male population – 1436 men and boys – and leaving the town in flames. Rebuilt, it is both depressing and poignant. The first and last sight is a mural, opposite the station, that reads: "Kalavrita, founder member of the Union of Martyred Towns, appeals to all to fight for world peace." The left clocktower on the central church stands fixed at 2.34pm – the hour of the massacre. Out in the countryside behind the town is a shrine to those massacred, its way gratified with the single word "Peace" (*Iríni*).

The Nazis also burnt the **monastery of Ayía Lávra**, 6km out of Kalávrita. As the site where Yermanos, Archbishop of Pátra, raised the flag to signal the War of Independence, the monastery is one of the great Greek national shrines. It, too, has been rebuilt, along with a small historical museum.

Staying at Kalávrita has a sense of pilgrimage about it for Greeks, and it's crowded with school parties during the week and with families at weekends. It probably will not have the same appeal for the casual visitor, but if you miss the last train back to Zahloroú (currently at 5.35pm, but check on the day) there are several pleasant **hotels**. Among them are the *Megas Alexandhros*, Lohagon Vassileos Kapota 1 (☎0692/22 221; ③), with small rooms but value for money; the *Paradissos*, Lohagon Vassileos Kapota 10 (☎0692/22 303; ③), a clean and agreeable hotel; and the *Villa Kalavrita* (☎0692/22 712; ③), across the rail track from the station, which has comfortable, modern rooms, some with a small kitchen.

A half-hour's drive southeast of Kalávrita is the **Spílio Límnon** or Cave of the Lakes (Mon–Fri 9am–4.30pm, Sat & Sun 9am–6pm; 700dr; ☎0692/31 588). Mineral-saturated water trickling through a two-kilometre cavern system has precipitated natural dams, trapping a series of small underground lakes. Only the first 300m or so are as yet open to the public but the chambers are still well worth the trip.

The cave is on the same **bus** line from Kalávrita as the villages of Káto Loussí, Kastriá and Planitéro, and is 2km north of Kastriá. Buses also run from Kalávrita to Pátra four times daily.

Mount Helmós

The highest peaks of the imposing Helmós range rear up a dozen or so kilometres to the southeast of Kalávrita. **Mount Helmós** itself, at 2341m, is only 60m short of the summit of Taíyettos to the south. However, the walk from Kalávrita is not an interesting approach, the trail having vanished under a paved road and the new ski centre approached by it. To get the most from hiking on the mountain you need to climb up from the village of **Sólos**, on the west side – a five-hour-plus walk which takes you to the **Mavronéri waterfall**, source of the legendary Styx, which the souls of the dead had to cross in order to enter Hades.

The hike from Sólos

To reach the path opening at Sólos, start at **Akráta** on the Pátra–Kórinthos road. From here it's a slow but beautiful haul up a winding dirt road. Buses run only three times a week, but hitching isn't too difficult in high summer.

SÓLOS is a tiny place, a cluster of stone cottages on a steep hillside just below the fir trees, and inhabited only in summer. Facing it across the valley is the larger but more scattered village of Peristéra, past which runs the easiest of the routes to Mavronéri.

Follow the **track through Sólos**, past the inn (all of ten beds), and the *magazí* (café-store), where you can get a simple meal. Beyond the last houses the track curves around the head of a gully. On the right, going down its wooded flank, is a good path which leads to a bridge over the river at the bottom. Just beyond (15min; this and all subsequent times are from Sólos), you reach another track. There is a **chapel** on the left, and, on the wall of a house on the right, a sign saying "Pros Gounariánika" that points up a path to the left. Follow it past a **church** on a prominent knoll and on to the jeep track again, where, at 75 minutes out, you turn left to the half-ruined hamlet of **Gounariánika**. From there continue steadily upward along the west (right) flank of the valley through abandoned fields until you come to a stream gully running down off the ridge above you on your right. On the far side of the stream the fir forest begins. It's an ideal camping place (2hr 30min; 1hr 30min going back down).

Once into the **woods**, the path is very clear. After about an hour (3hr 30min) you descend to a boulder-strewn **stream bed** with a rocky ravine to the right leading up to the foot of a huge bare crag, the east side of the Neraïdhórahi peak visible from Kalávrita. Cross the stream and continue leftward up the opposite bank. In June there are the most incredible wild flowers, including at least half a dozen different orchids, all the way up from here.

After fifteen minutes' climb above the bank, you come out on top of a **grassy knoll** (3hr 30min), then dip back into the trees again. At the four-hour mark, you turn a corner into the mouth of the **Styx ravine**. Another five minutes' walk brings you to a **deep gully** where enormous banks of snow lie late into the spring. A few paces across a dividing rib of rock there is a second gully, where the path has been eroded and you have to cross some slippery scree.

Here you come to a wooded spur running down from the crag on the right. The trail winds up to a shoulder (4hr 20min), descends into another gully, and then winds up to a second shoulder of level rocky ground by some large black pines (4hr 30min), known as *Toh Dhiásselo tou Kinigoú* (the Hunter's Saddle). From there you can look into the Styx ravine. Continue down the path towards the right until it dwindles at the foot of a vast crag (4hr 45min). You can now see the **Mavronéri waterfall**, a 200-metre-long, wavering plume of water pouring off the red cliffs up ahead.

To get to it, angle across the scree bank without losing altitude – for the track is obliterated soon after the saddle – until you reach the base of the falls (5hr). There's a small **cave** under the fall, where a rare columbine grows. It is possible to continue up the valley, past some turf next to a seasonal pond where people camp, but the summit area proper is a bit of a let-down after the majesty of the Styx valley. Fairly clear and easy trails lead down from the south side of the watershed to the villages of Káto Loussí or Planitéro; the appropriate *Korfes* or *YIS* maps have more details on these routes.

travel details

Trains

There are two main Peloponnesian lines:

Athens–Kórinthos–Dhiakoftó–Pátra–Pírgos–Kiparissía–Kalamáta 1 train daily makes the full run in each direction. Another 8 daily run between Athens and Pátra, 6 continuing to Pírgos, the other as far as Kiparissía. Another 1 train daily covers the route between Pátra and Kiparissía.

Approximate journey times are:

Athens–Kórinthos (2hr)

Kórinthos–Dhiakoftó (1–1hr 30min)

Dhiakoftó–Pátra (1hr)

Pátra–Pírgos (2 hr 15min)

Pírgos–Kiparissiá (1hr–1hr 20min)

Kiparissía–Kalamáta (1hr 40min).

Athens (starts in Pireás)–Kórinthos–Mikínes (Mycenae)–Árgos–Trípoli–Kalamáta 3 trains daily cover the full route, in each direction.

Approximate journey times are:

Athens–Kórinthos (2hr)

Kórinthos–Mikínes (50min)

Mikínes–Árgos (10min)

Árgos–Trípoli (1hr 30min)

Trípoli–Kalamáta (2hr 40min).

In addition, there are the following branch lines:

Pírgos–Olympia 5 trains daily (40min).

Pírgos–Katákolo 5 daily at 1.54pm (25min).

Kavássila–Killíni 5 daily (35min).

Dhiakoftó–Zahloroú–Kalávrita 6 daily; Dhiakoftó–Zakhloroú (50min); Zahlaroú–Kalávrita (20min).

Lefktró-Megalópoli Service replaced by *OSE* buses, connecting with services to Lefktró (between Árgos and Kalamáta).

Buses

Buses detailed have similar frequency in each direction, so entries are given just once; for reference check under both starting-point and destination.

Connections with Athens: Kórinthos (hourly; 1hr); Mikínes (Mycenae)/Árgos/Tíryns/Náfplio (hourly to 8.30pm; 2hr/2hr 15min/2hr 45min/3hr); Spárti (7 daily; 4hr 30min); Olympia (4 daily; 5hr 30min).

Areópoli to: Yerolimín (daily in season only; 1 hr); Kalamáta (4 daily changing at Ítilo; 2hr 30min) Láyia (daily; 1hr).

Árgos to: Náfplio (half hourly; 30min; Mikínes (Mycenae; 6 daily; 30min); Neméa (3 daily; 1hr); Ástros/Leonídhi (3 daily; 1 hr/3 hr); Trípoli (9 daily; 1hr 20min); Spárti (8 daily; 3hr); Andhrítsena (daily at 10am; 3hr); Olympia (3 daily on weekdays; 4hr 30min).

Kalamáta to: Koróni (7 daily; 1hr 30min); Ítilo/ Areópoli (4 daily; 1hr 30min); Pátra (2 daily; 4hr); Pílos (8 daily; 1 hr 20 min); Megalópoli/Trípoli (10 daily; 1 hr/1hr 45min).

Kórinthos to: Mikínes (Mycenae)/Árgos/Tíryns/ Náfplio (hourly; 30min/1hr/1hr 15min/1hr 30min); Loutráki (half-hourly; 20min); Neméa (5 daily; 45 min); Trípoli (9 daily; 1hr 30min); Spárti (8 daily; 4hr); Kalamáta (7 daily; 4 hr).

Megalópoli to: Andhrítsena/Pírgos (2 daily; 3hr/ 4hr); Trípoli (8 daily; 40min).

Náfplio to: Epidaurus (5 daily; 45min); Tólo (half-hourly; 25min); Trípoli (6 daily; 50min).

Pílos to: Methóni (5 daily; 15min); Kalamáta (9 daily; 1hr 20min); Kiparissía (6 daily, but none 3– 7pm; 2hr).

Pátra to: Kalávrita (4 daily; 2hr 30min); Zákinthos (3 daily; 2hr 30min including ferry from Killíni); Ioánnina (2 daily; 5hr); Kalamáta (2 daily; 4hr); Vólos (daily; 6hr).

Pírgos to: Olympia (hourly, but none 12.30– 3.30pm; 45min); Andhrítsena (2 daily; 2hr); Pátra (10 daily; 2hr); Kiparissía/Kalamáta (2 daily; 1hr/ 2hr).

Spárti to: Místras (12 daily, 6 on Sun; 15 min); Monemvassía (2 or 3 daily; 3 hr); Kalamáta (2 daily; 2hr 30min); Yíthio (6 daily; 1hr); Neápoli (3 daily; 4hr).

Trípoli to: Megalópoli (8 daily; 40min); Spárti (2 daily; 1hr 20min); Olympia (3 daily, in stages; 5 hr); Pátra (via Lámbia; 2 daily; 4hr); Pírgos (3 daily; 3 hr); Andhrítsena (2 daily; 1hr 30min); Dhimitsána (2 daily; 1hr 30min); Kalamáta (6 daily; 2 hr); Pílos (3 daily; 3hr); Kiparissía (2 daily; 2hr); Megalópoli (8 daily; 35min).

Yíthio to: Areópoli (4 daily; 50min); Láyia (daily; 1hr); Monemvassía (2 daily; 2hr 30min).

Ferries

Across the Gulf of Kórinthos Andírio–Río (every 15 min, much less often between 11pm and dawn; 20min); Éyio–Áyios Nikólaos (3–5 daily; 35min).

Galatás to: Póros (every 15min from dawn till past midnight; 5min).

Killíni to: Zákinthos (3–7 daily; 2hr); Kefalloniá (1-3 daily; 1hr).

Kíthira to: Kastélli, Crete (twice weekly in season; 4hr).

Pátra to: Igoumenítsa and Corfu (2 or 3 daily; 7– 9hr/9–11hr); Kefalloniá and Itháki (most days; 4– 5hr); Paxí (2 or 3 weekly; 6hr); Iráklion (Crete) and Rhodes (weekly on stop-over basis only; 18hr/ 28hr), also to Brindisi, Ancona, Bari, Trieste (Italy), Limassol (Cyprus); unreliably to Split, Croatia; and Kuşadası (Turkey) as politics, war and shipowner whim permit. See under "Pátra"for details.

Pireás–Kiparíssi–Monemvassía–Neápoli– Elafónissos–Kíthira–Andíkithira–Kastélli (Crete). At least once weekly – currently Sunday – a boat departs Kastélli for Pireás via all of the ports listed, returning on the same route on Monday; the complete trip takes about 16 hours. For current schedules, phone *Miras Ferries* (☎01/ 41 27 225) or *Ventouris Ferries* (☎01/41 14 011).

Yíthio to: Kíthira (almost daily service; 2hr 30min); contact *Haloulakos* (☎0733/24 501) or *Rozakis* (☎0733/22 207) for current information.

Hydrofoils

"Flying Dolphin" hydrofoils run between the following ports:

Kiparíssi/Monemvassía/Leonídhi to Spétses, Póros and Pireás.

Neápoli/Kíthira to Pireás.

Méthana to Éyina and Póros.

Ermióni to Ídhra (Hydra) and Spétses.

Náfplio (midsummer only) to Monemvassía, Toló, Spétses, Póros and Pireás.

For details and frequencies of services, which vary drastically with season, contact local agents or the Ceres Hydrofoils' *main office in Pireás (Aktí Themistokléous 8; ☎01/412 8001).*

Summer-only excursion boats
From Katákolo Zákinthos (3 weekly; 2hr 30min).
From Portohéli Water-taxis to Spétses according to demand (20min).

Flights
To/from Athens Kalamáta (1 daily; 50min); Kíthira (1–2 daily; 50min).

CHAPTER THREE

THESSALY AND CENTRAL GREECE

U nlike the Peloponnese, Central Greece is a region of scattered highlights –
above all the site of the ancient oracle at **Delphi**, and, further, to the north, the
unworldly rock-monasteries of the **Metéora**. The area as a whole, dominated by
the vast agricultural plain of Thessaly, is less exciting, with rather drab market
and industrial towns. For scenic drama – and most of the historic sights – you have to
head for the edge.

The southern part of this region, before you enter Thessaly proper, is known as the
Stereá Elládhos – literally "Greek Continent", a name that reflects its nineteenth-
century past as the only Greek mainland territory, along with Attica and the quasi-
island of the Peloponnese. It corresponds to the ancient divisions of Boeotia and
Phocis, the domains respectively of Thebes and Delphi. Most visitors head straight
through these territories to Delphi but, if you have time, there are rewarding if minor
detours in the monastery of **Óssios Loukás** – with the finest Byzantine frescoes in the
country – and **Gla**, the largest and most obscure of the Mycenaean sites. For hikers
there is also the opportunity of climbing **Mount Parnassós**, the Muses' mountain.

The central plains of **Thessaly** (*Thessalía*), beyond, formed the bed of an ancient
inland sea – rich agricultural land that was ceded reluctantly to the modern nation by
the Turks in 1878. The province's attractions lie on the periphery, chained in by the
mountain ranges of Ólimbos (Olympus), Píndhos (Pindus), Ossa and Pílion (Pelion).
Picking a route is a hard choice. East from the major city and port of Vólos extends the
slender peninsula of **Mount Pílion**, whose luxuriant woods and beaches are easily
combined with island-hopping to the Sporades. To the west, **Kalambáka** gives access
to the Metéora (not to be missed) and across the dramatic **Katára Pass** over the
Píndhos to Epirus. North, the horizon is increasingly filled with the silhouette of
Mount Olympus (covered in *The North: Macedonia and Thrace*), home of the gods.

ROOM PRICE SCALES

All establishments listed in this book have been price-graded according to the scale
outlined below. The rates quoted represent the cheapest available room in high season;
all are prices for a double room, except for category ①, which are per person rates. Out
of season, rates can drop by up to fifty percent, especially if you negotiate rates for a stay
of three or more nights. Single rooms, where available, cost around seventy percent of
the price of a double.

① 1400–2000dr (£4–5.50/US$6–8.50)   ④ 8000–12000dr (£22–33/US$33–50)

② 4000–6000dr (£11–16.50/US$17–25)   ⑤ 12000–16000dr (£33–44/US$50–66)

③ 6000–8000dr (£16.50–22/US$25–33)   ⑥ 16000dr (£44/US$66) and upwards

For more accommodation details see p.34–35.

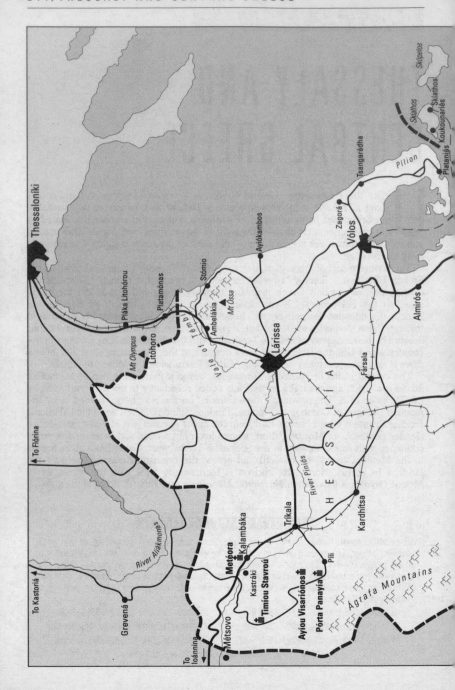

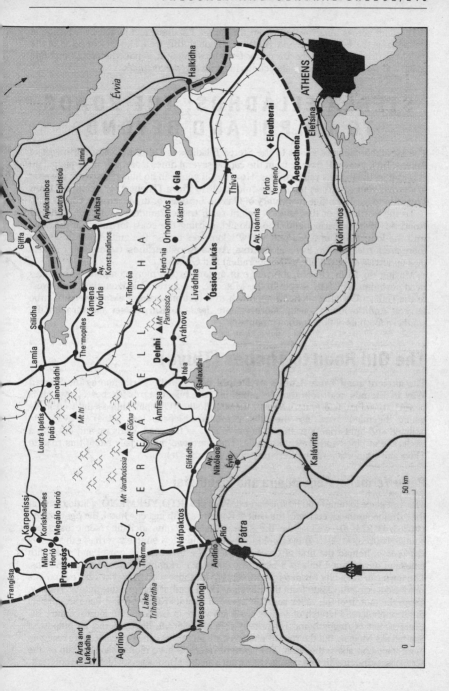

Looming across a narrow gulf from the Stereá Elládhos, and joined by a bridge at Halkídha, is the **island of Évvia** (Euboea). Though this feels like an extension of the mainland (from where there are many ferry crossings), it is nonetheless a bona fide island and we have detailed its attractions in *Evvia and the Sporades*.

STEREÁ ELLÁDHOS: THE ROADS TO DELPHI AND BEYOND

The inevitable focus of a visit to the Stereá Elládhos is **Delphi**, 150km northwest of Athens. Buses cover the route from the capital several times a day, or can be picked up at Livádhia, the nearest rail terminus. However, if you're in no hurry, there are rewards in slowing your progress: taking the "old road" to Thíva (Thebes), or detouring from Livádhia to the Byzantine monastery of **Óssios Loukás**, or to Mycenaean **Glá**.

To the northeast of the Athens–Delphi road, traffic thunders along the **National Road #1** towards Lárissa and Thessaloníki, skirting the coast for much of the way, with the long island of Évvia only a few kilometres across the gulf. Along this route there are ferries over to Évvia at **Arkítsa**, **Áyios Konstandínos** (where you can also pick up ferries or hydrofoils to the Sporades) and **Glífa**.

Moving **on from Delphi**, the range of options grows more complex. Two routes head north into Thessaly – west to the Metéora, east to the Pílion; another, southwest to the Gulf of Corinth, offers an approach to – or from – **the Peloponnese**, via the ferry at Andírio–Río; a fourth, more remote, leads to **Karpeníssi** and through the southern foothills of the Píndhos mountains.

The Old Road to Thebes (Thíva)

The **ancient road from Athens to Delphi** began at the Parthenon as the **Sacred Way to Eleusis**, and from there climbed into the hills towards Thebes (Thíva). It is possible to follow this route, almost unchanged since Oedipus supposedly trod it, by taking the minor road into the hills at modern Elefsína (see p.134). Leaving the polluted and industrial port, things improve fast, as the road winds up and out into a landscape of pines and grey stony hills. There are two buses daily along this road to Thíva and connections from there on to Livádhia and Delphi.

Pórto Yermenó, Aegosthena and Eleutherai

The first place to tempt you off the Sacred Way is **PÓRTO YERMENÓ**, a little resort at the extreme northeast corner of the Gulf of Kórinthos, with just one **hotel**, the *Egosthenion* (☎0263/41 226; ④) well above the shore, several rooms including some nameless studios (☎0263/41 394; ③) overlooking the bay, and a few simple tavernas – the best is *Psaropoula*, behind the first of three beaches. The beaches are gravel and sand with pine- and olive-draped hills as a backdrop, and are certainly the cleanest near Athens. The town can get a bit crowded in summer, but for those with transport (there is no bus service covering the 23km from the Elefsína–Thíva road) it makes a fine detour. Nearby, above the mouth of the valley running between mounts Kithairon and Pateras, sprawls the best-preserved stretch of ancient walls anywhere in Greece – the fourth-century BC Classical fort of **Aegosthena**. Historically it is insignificant, being merely an outpost of Spartan ally Megara, but the ruins themselves are impressive, the two end towers rising up more than 12m above the walls. The seaward ramparts have mostly vanished; up on the acropolis, a church with frescoes survives from a medieval monastery which took root here.

Back on the Thebes road, a kilometre north of the Pórto Yermenó turning, you pass another Classical fortress, fourth-century BC **Eleutherai**. Signposted from the road, 400m to the east, the fort is again well preserved, with its northeast side almost intact and six of its circuit of towers surviving to varying degrees. The scant ruins of Eleutherai town itself lie down by the Aegosthena junction, while the fort defends a critical pass above; both sites have unlimited access.

Thíva (Thebes)

The modern town of **THÍVA** (Thebes) lies 20km north of Eleutherai, built right on the site of its mighty, ancient predecessor. For this very reason, however, it boasts scant remains of the past: archeologists have had little success in excavating the crucial central areas, and the most interesting visit is to the excellent town **museum** (daily except Mon 8.30am–3pm; 400dr). This is to be found at the far (downhill) end of Pindhárou, the main street; look out for the Frankish tower in its forecourt. Among many fine exhibits is a unique collection of painted *larnakes* (Mycenaean sarcophagi) depicting, in bold expressionistic strokes, women lamenting their dead.

There are no direct **buses** from Thíva to Delphi but services run frequently to Livádhia (where there are better connections) and a couple of times a day to Halkídha, gateway to Evvia. If you get stranded between buses, the *Niobe* **hotel** at Epaminónda 63 (☎0262/27 949; ③) makes a pleasant enough stop.

Livádhia and around

Livádhia lies at the edge of a great agricultural plain, much of it reclaimed lakebed, speckled with a few minor but enjoyable sites. It's a part of Greece that sees few tourists, most of whom are in a hurry to reach the glories of the Parnassós country just to the west.

Livádhia

LIVÁDHIA is a pleasant town on the banks of the Herkína, a river of ancient fame which emerges from a dark gorge at the base of a fortress. It is an attractive place for a brief halt, with a unique duo of ancient and medieval sights.

The ancient curiosity is the site of the **Oracle of Trophonios**, a ten-minute walk from the main square, beside an old Turkish bridge. Here the waters of the Herkína rise from a series of springs, now channelled beside the (signposted) *Xenia* restaurant and hotel. Above the springs, cut into the rock, are niches for votive offerings – in one of which, a large chamber with a bench, the Turkish governor would sit for a quiet smoke. In antiquity they marked the Springs of Memory and Forgetfulness, where all who sought to consult the Oracle of Trophonios had first to bathe. The oracle, a circular structure which gave entrance to caves deep in the gorge, has been tentatively identified at the top of the hill, near the remains of an unfinished Temple of Zeus. It was visited by the Roman traveller–scholar Pausanias, who wrote that it left him "possessed with terror and hardly knowing himself or anything around him".

The **Froúrio**, or castle, again a short walk from the centre (along Odhós Froúrio), provides the medieval interest. An impressive, well-bastioned square structure, it was built in the fourteenth century and was a key early conquest in the War of Independence. But it's the history that's most interesting. The castle was the stronghold of a small group of Catalan mercenaries, the Grand Company, who took control of central Greece in 1311 and, appointing a Sicilian prince as their ruler, held it for sixty years. They were a tiny, brutal band who had arrived in Greece from Spain in the wake of the Fourth Crusade. They wrested control from the Franks, who were then established in Athens and Thebes, in a cunning deviation from traditional rules of engagement. As the Frankish nobility approached Livádhia, the vastly outnumbered Catalans diverted the river to flood the surrounding fields. The Frankish cavalry advanced into the unexpected marsh and were cut down to a man.

Practicalities

The town is today a minor provincial capital with a trade in milling cotton from the area. It is completely off the tourist route and so an enjoyable daytime pause before, or after, Delphi, though in season buses on towards Delphi often arrive and leave full. Arriving by **bus**, you'll be dropped near the central square, **Platía Dhiákou**; the **train station** is 3km out but arrivals may be met by a shuttle bus (or more likely taxis) into town.

Staying overnight is highly problematic since the closure of several central hotels. If your budget won't run to the fancy *Livadhia* on Platia Kutsoni (☎0261/23 611;④–⑤), you'd be well advised to press on towards Delphi. **Eating** options are limited to a few *souvlaki* stands and an *ouzerí* at the top end of Eleftheríou Venizélou.

Orhomenós

Just 10km east of Livádhia (10min by hourly local bus) is the site of ancient **ORHOMENÓS**, inhabited from Neolithic to Classical times. As the capital of the Minyans, a native Thessalian dynasty, it was one of the wealthiest Mycenaean cities.

Near the middle of the rather drab modern village, along the road signposted Diónisos village, is the **Treasury of Minyas** (Tues–Sat 9am–3pm, Sun 10am–2pm), a stone *tholos* similar to the tomb of Atreus at Mycenae. The roof has collapsed but it is otherwise complete, and its inner chamber, hewn from the rock, has an intricately carved marble ceiling. Much closer to the road are the remains of a fourth-century BC **theatre**, and behind, on the rocky hilltop, a tiny fortified acropolis from the same period.

Across the road from the theatre is the ninth-century Byzantine **Church of the Dormition**, built entirely of blocks from the theatre and column drums from a Classical temple – as is the minute Byzantine church in the main village square. The larger triple-apsed church has some fine reliefs including a sundial, with the remains of a monastery just to the south.

The Citadel of Gla

Continuing east, in a highly worthwhile diversion, it's a further twenty minutes by bus (5 daily, but they stop early) to the village of Kástro, right next to the National Road towards Lárissa. If you walk through the village, cross the highway and then walk for about 100m south along it (towards Athens) you come to an unsignposted road behind a *Shell* garage and tyre store. This leads in around 200m to the Mycenaean Citadel of Gla.

An enormous and extraordinary site, **GLA** (unrestricted entrance) stands within a three-kilometre circuit of Cyclopean walls – a far larger citadel than either Tiryns or Mycenae. Almost nothing, however, is known about the site, save that it was once an island in Lake Copais (which was drained in the last century) and that it may have been an outpost of the Minyans. The **walls** and **city gates** still stand to five metres in places, and are almost three kilometres in length, despite being damaged when the city fell. Inside, on the higher ground, what is thought to have been a huge Mycenaean **palace** has been revealed; it appears to include a *megaron* (throne room) and various store-rooms, though archeologists are puzzled by differences from the standard Mycenean palace form. Further down, and currently being excavated, is a vast walled area believed to have been the **marketplace**.

Almost anywhere you walk in this rarely visited site, you come across evocative traces of its former buildings. One **word of warning** about the site: there are said to be snakes among the ruins, so tread with care.

Chaironeia

Directly north of Livádhia, on the main road to Lamía, is **CHAIRONEIA**, once the home of the writer Plutarch but more famous as the site of one of the most decisive battles of ancient Greece. Here, in 338 BC, Philip of Macedon won a resounding victory over an alliance of Athenians, Thebans and Peloponnesians put together by Demosthenes. This defeat marked the death of the old city-states, from whom control passed forever into foreign hands: first Macedonian, later Roman.

Set beside the road, at modern Herónia, is a remarkable six-metre-high **stone lion**, originally part of the funerary monument to the Thebans (or, some say, to the Macedonians) killed in the battle. Adjacent is a small museum of local finds, and there are remains of ancient **acropolis** fortifications, with a theatre at their base, above the village.

The Oedipus crossroads and Óssios Loukás

West from Livádhia, the scenery becomes ever more dramatic as Mount Parnassós and its attendant peaks loom high above the road. At 24km, about halfway to Delphi, you reach the so-called **Schist** (split) or **Triodos** (triple way) **Crossroads** – also known as the **Oedipus crossroads** – junction of the ancient roads from Delphi, Daulis (today Dávlia), Thebes (Thíva) and Ambrossos (Dhístomo). The old road actually lay in the gorge, below the modern one.

It is this spot that Pausanias identified as the site of **Oedipus's murder of his father**, King Laertes of Thebes, and his two attendants. According to the myth, Oedipus was returning on foot from Delphi while Laertes was speeding towards him from the opposite direction on a chariot. Neither would give way, and in the altercation that followed Oedipus killed the trio, ignorant of who they were. It was to be, as Pausanias put it mildly, "the beginning of his troubles". Continuing to Thebes, Oedipus solved the riddle of the Sphinx, which had been ravaging the area, and was given the hand of widowed Queen Jocasta in marriage – unaware that he was marrying his own mother.

Getting to Óssios Loukás: Dhístomo

If you have transport, you can turn left at the crossroads and follow the minor road to Dhístomo, and thence to the Monastery of Óssios Loukás (see below). Travelling by bus, you may need to take a more roundabout route: first from Livádhia to Dhístomo, then another bus on from there towards Kiriakí – getting off at the fork to Óssios Loukás (leaving just a 2500m walk). Alternatively, it's possible to charter a taxi in **DHÍSTOMO**, which also has a couple of hotels, on the town square facing the church: the *America* (☎0267/22 079; ③) and *Koutriaris* (☎0267/22 268; ③).

It is a drab place, though, with a tragic wartime history: the Germans shot over 200 of the townsfolk on June 10, 1944, in reprisal for a guerrilla attack. The event is immortalized in a bleak grey and white memorial on a nearby hilltop – follow the signs to the "mausoleum".

Óssios Loukás Monastery

Daily summer 8am–2pm & 4–7pm; winter 8am–6pm; 400dr.

The **Monastery of Óssios Loukás** was a precursor of that last defiant flourish of Byzantine art that produced the great churches at Mystra in the Peloponnese. It is modest in scale, but from an architectural or decorative point of view, ranks as one of the great buildings of medieval Greece. The setting, too, is exquisite – as beautiful as it is remote. Hidden by trees along the approach from Dhístomo, the monastery's shady terrace suddenly appears, and opens out on to a spectacular sweep of the Elikónas peaks and countryside.

The main structure comprises two domed churches, the larger **Katholikón** of Óssios Loukás and the attendant chapel of the **Theotókos**. They are joined by a common foundation wall but otherwise share few architectural features. Ten monks still live in the monastic buildings around the courtyard, but the monastery is essentially maintained as a museum, with an occasionally operating café in the grounds. Skirts or long trousers (no shorts) must be worn.

The Katholikón

The **Katholikón**, built in the early eleventh century, is dedicated to a local beatified hermit, Saint Luke of Stiri (not the Evangelist). Its design formed the basis of Byzantine octagonal-style churches, and was later copied at Dhafní and at Mystra. Externally it is modest, with rough brick and stone walls surmounted by a well-proportioned dome. The inside, however, is startling. A conventional cross-in-square plan, its atmosphere switches from austere to exultant as the eye moves along walls lined in red and green marble to the gold-backed mosaics on the high ceiling. Light filtering through marble-encrusted windows reflects across the curved surfaces of the mosaics in the narthex and the nave and bounces onto the marble walls, bringing out the subtlety of their shades.

The original **mosaics** were damaged by an earthquake in 1659, and in the dome and elsewhere have been replaced by unmemorable frescoes. But other surviving examples testify to their effect. The mosaic of *The Washing of the Apostles' Feet* in the narthex is one of the finest; its theme is an especially human one and the expressions of the apostles, seen varying between diffidence and surprise, do it justice. This dynamic and richly humanized approach is again illustrated by the *Baptism*, high up on one of the curved squinches that support the dome. Here the naked Jesus reaches for the cross amid a swirling mass of water, an illusion of depth created by the angle and curvature of the wall. The church's original **frescoes** are confined to the vaulted chambers at the corners of the cross plan and, though less imposing than the mosaics, are far more sympathetic in colour and shade to their subjects, particularly that of *Christ Walking towards the Baptism*.

The Theotókos and Crypt

The church of the **Theotókos** (literally "God-Bearing", ie the Virgin Mary) is a century older than the *katholikón*. From the outside it overshadows the main church with its elaborate brick decoration culminating in a highly Eastern-influenced, marble-panelled drum. The interior, though, seems gloomy and cramped by comparison, highlighted only by a couple of fine Corinthian capitals and an original floor mosaic, now dimmed by the passage of time.

Finally, do not miss the vivid frescoes in the **crypt** of the *katholikón*, entered on the lower right-hand side of the building. It's a good idea to bring a torch, if possible, since there is limited lighting and the same darkness that has preserved the colours also hides them.

Aráhova

Arriving at **ARÁHOVA**, the last town east of Delphi (just 11km further on), you are properly in Parnassós country. The peaks stand tiered above, sullied somewhat by the wide asphalt road cut to a ski-resort – the winter-weekend haunt of BMW-driving Athenians. If you want to ski, it's possible to hire equipment on a daily basis at the resort and even to get an all-in day package from Athens (see p.51). The resort's main problem is high winds, which often lead to the closure of its ski lifts, so check the forecast before you set off.

Skiing aside, the town is a delight, despite being split in two by the Livádhia–Delphi road. If you're not making for any other mountain areas, Aráhova is well worth an afternoon's pause before continuing to Delphi, and if you've got your own transport you might consider staying here as a base for visiting the site. Houses in Aráhova are predominantly traditional in style, twisting up narrow lanes into the hills and poised to the south on the edge of the olive-tree-choked Pleistos gorge. The area is renowned for its strong wines, honey, *flokáti* (sheepskin) rugs and woollen weavings; all are much in evidence in the roadside shops, though some of the goods are nowadays imported from Albania and northern Greece. Also of note is the local **Festival of Áyios Yióryios** (23 April, or the Tuesday after Easter if this date falls within Lent), which is centred on the church at the top of the hill, and is one of the best opportunities to catch genuine folk-dancing during almost 48 hours of continuous partying.

For details of hiking on Parnassós from Aráhova, see p.258.

Practicalities

Five **buses** daily go to Athens and more to Delphi and Itéa, two of which go on to Náfpaktos; bus timetables are displayed in the window of the *Celena Cafeteria Bar* (see below).

In the summer most people stop long enough for a meal and to shop only, so finding **accommodation** is easy. In winter, particularly at weekends, rooms are at a premium. At the cheaper end of the scale, there are two pleasant and modest **hotels**, side by side at the Livádhia end of town; *Apollon Hotel* (✆0267/31 427; ③) and *Hotel Parnassos* (✆0267/31 307; ③). At the Delphi end of town, the *Pension Nostos* (✆0267/31 385; ③), *Xenia Hotel* (✆0267/31 230; ⑤, but in winter up to ⑥) and the new *Apollon Inn* (✆0267/31 057; ④), an offshoot of the *Apollon Hotel*, are all worth a try.

There is also an excellent **taverna**, the *Karathanasi* (open evenings only), while the *Celena Cafeteria Bar*, also on the main street opposite the small square which doubles as a bus station, is open all day; its helpful Danish owner offers information on rooms and buses.

Delphi (Dhelfí)

With its site raised on the slopes of a high mountain terrace and dwarfed to either side by the great and ominous crags of Parnassós, it's easy to see why the ancients believed **DELPHI** to be the centre of the earth. But more than the natural setting or even the occasional earthquake and avalanche were needed to confirm a divine presence. This, according to Plutarch, was achieved through the discovery of a rock chasm that exuded strange vapours and reduced all comers to frenzied, incoherent and undoubtedly prophetic mutterings.

The Oracle: some history

The first **oracle** established on this spot was dedicated to **Gea** ("Mother Earth") and to **Poseidon** ("the Earth Shaker"). The serpent **Python**, son of Gea, was installed in a nearby cave and communication made through the Pythian priestess. Python was subsequently slain by **Apollo**, whose cult had been imported from Crete (legend has it that he arrived in the form of a dolphin – hence the name *Delphoi*). The **Pythian Games** were established on an eight-year cycle to commemorate the feat, and perhaps also to placate the ancient deities.

The place was known to the **Mycenaeans**, whose votive offerings (tiny striped statues of goddesses and worshipping women) have been discovered near the site of Apollo's temple. Following the arrival of the **Dorians** in Greece at the beginning of the twelfth century BC, the sanctuary became the centre of the loose-knit association of Greek city-states known as the **Amphyctionic League**. The territory still belonged, however, to the city of Krissa, which as the oracle gained in popularity began to extort heavy dues from the pilgrims arriving at the port of Kirrha. In the sixth century BC the league was called on to intervene, and the first of a series of **Sacred Wars** broke out. The league wrested Delphi from the Krissaeans and made it an autonomous state. From then on Delphi experienced a rapid ascent to fame and respect, becoming within a few decades one of the major sanctuaries of Greece, with its tried-and-tested oracle generally thought to be the arbiter of truth.

For over a thousand years thereafter, a steady stream of **pilgrims** worked their way up the dangerous mountain paths to seek divine direction in matters of war, worship, love or business. On arrival they would sacrifice a sheep or a goat and, depending on the omens, wait to submit questions inscribed on leaden tablets. The Pythian priestess, a simple and devout village woman of fifty or more years, would chant her prophecies from a tripod positioned over the oracular chasm. Crucially, an attendant priest would then "interpret" her utterings and relay them to the enquirer in hexameter verse.

Many of the **oracular answers** were equivocal: Croesus, for example, was told that if he embarked on war against neighbouring Cyrus he would destroy a mighty empire – he did, and destroyed his own. But it's hard to imagine that the oracle would have retained its popularity and influence for so long without offering predominantly sound advice. Indeed, Strabo wrote that "of all oracles in the world, it had the reputation of being the most truthful". One explanation is that the Delphic priests were simply better informed than any other corporate body around at the time. Positioned at the centre of the Amphyctionic League, which became a kind of "United Nations" of the Greek city-states, they were in a position to amass a wealth of political, economic and social information – and from the seventh century BC on, Delphi had its own network of informants throughout the Greek world.

The **influence** of the oracle spread abroad with the age of Classical colonization and its patronage grew, reaching a peak in the sixth century BC, with powerful benefactors such as Amasis, King of Egypt, and the unfortunate King Croesus of Lydia; many of the Greek city-states also dedicated treasuries at this time. Privileged position and enormous wealth, however, made Delphi vulnerable to Greek rivalries: the first Sacred Wars left it autonomous, but in the fifth century BC the oracle began to be too closely identified with individual states. Worse, it maintained a defeatist, almost treacherous attitude towards the Persian invasions – only partially mitigated when a Persian force, sent by Xerxes to raid Delphi, was crushed at the entrance to the Sanctuary by a well-timed earthquake.

It never quite regained the same level of trust – and consequently of power – after these instances of bias and corruption. However, real **decline** did not set in until the fourth century BC, with the resumption of the Sacred Wars and the emergence of Macedonian control. Following prolonged squabbling among the Greek city-states, the Sanctuary was seized by the Phocians in 356 BC, leading to Philip of Macedon's intervention to restore the Amphyctionic League to power. Seven years later, when the league again invited

Philip to settle a dispute, this time provoked by the Amphissans, he responded by invading southern Greece. The independence of the city-states was brought to an end at the Battle of Chaironeia (see p249); Delphi's political intriguing was effectively over.

Under **Macedonian** and later **Roman** control, the oracle's role became increasingly domestic and insignificant, dispensing advice on marriages, loans, voyages and the like. The Romans thought little of its utterances and of its treasure: Sulla plundered the sanctuary in 86 BC and Nero, outraged when the oracle pronounced judgement on the murder of his mother, carted away some 500 bronze statues. Finally, with the demise of paganism under Constantine and Theodosius in the fourth century AD, the oracle became defunct.

In modern times, the sanctuary site was rediscovered towards the end of the seventeenth century and explored, haphazardly, from the 1840s onwards. Real **excavation** of the site came only in 1892 when the French School of Archeology leased the land, in exchange for a French government agreement to buy the Greek currant crop. There was little to be seen other than the outline of a stadium and theatre but the villagers who lived there were persuaded (with the help of an army detachment) to move to a new town 1km west, and digging commenced. Over the next decade or so most of the excavations and reconstruction visible today were completed.

The most interesting development in Delphi's recent history came through the efforts of the poet Angelos Sikelianos and his wife Eva Palmer to set up a "University of the World" in the 1920s. The project eventually failed, though it inspired an annual **Delphic Festival**, held now in June of each year with performances of Classical drama in the ancient theatre.

The Sites

Split by the road from Aráhova, the ancient site divides essentially into three parts: the **Sacred Precinct**, the **Marmaria** and the **Castalian spring**. In addition there is a worthwhile, though poorly presented, **museum**. All in all it's a large and complex ruin, best taken in two stages, with the sanctuary ideally at the beginning or end of the day, or at lunchtime, to escape the crowds.

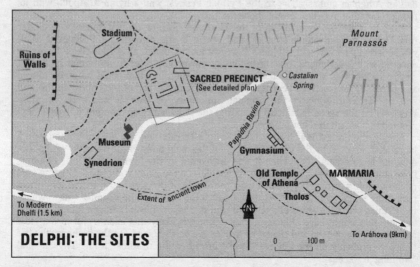

DELPHI: THE SITES

Make sure you have sturdy footwear as there's a lot of clambering up rough stone steps and paths, and take food and drink if you're planning a full day's visit; good picnicking spots are the amphitheatre with its seats and panorama of the sanctuary, or try the stadium for fewer interruptions.

The Sacred Precinct

Mon–Fri 8am–7pm, Sat & Sun 8.30am–3pm; 1000dr.

The **Sacred Precinct**, or Temenos (Sanctuary) of Apollo, is entered, as in ancient times, by way of a small **Agora** enclosed by ruins of Roman porticoes and shops for the sale of votive offerings. The paved **Sacred Way** begins after a few stairs and zigzags uphill between the foundations of memorials and treasuries to the Temple of Apollo. Along each edge is a litter of statue bases where gold, bronze and painted marble figures once stood; Pliny counted more than three thousand on his visit, and that was after Nero's infamous raid.

The choice and position of these **memorials** were dictated by more than religious zeal; many were used as a deliberate show of strength or often as a direct insult against a rival Greek state. For instance, the **Offering of the Arcadians** on the right of the entrance (a line of bases that supported nine bronzes) was erected to commemorate their invasion of Laconia in 369 BC, and pointedly placed in front of the Lacedaemonians' own monument. Beside this, and following the same logic, the Spartans celebrated their victory over Athens by erecting their **Monument of the Admirals** – a large recessed structure, which once held 37 bronze statues of gods and generals – directly opposite the Athenians' **Offering of Marathon**.

Further up the path, past the Doric remains of the **Sikyonian Treasury** on the left, stretch the expansive foundations of the **Siphnian Treasury**, a grandiose Ionic temple erected in 525 BC. Siphnos had rich gold mines and intended the building to be an unrivalled show of opulence. Fragments of the caryatids that supported its west entrance, and the fine Parian marble frieze that covered all four sides, are now in the museum. Above this is the **Treasury of the Athenians**, built, like the city's "Offering", after Marathon (490 BC). It was reconstructed in 1904–6 by matching the inscriptions that completely cover its blocks. These include honorific decrees in favour of Athens, lists of Athenian ambassadors to the Pythian Festival, and a hymn to Apollo with its musical notation in Greek letters above the text.

Next to it are the foundations of the **Bouleuterion**, or council house, a reminder that Delphi needed administrators, and above is the remarkable **Polygonal Wall** whose irregular interlocking blocks have withstood, intact, all earthquakes. It, too, is covered with inscriptions, but these almost universally refer to the emancipation of slaves; Delphi was one of the few places where such freedom could be made official and public by an inscribed register. An incongruous outcrop of rock between the wall and the Treasuries marks the original **Sanctuary of Gea**. It was here, or more precisely on the recently built-up rock, that the Sibyl, an early itinerant priestess, was reputed to have uttered her prophecies.

Finally, the Sacred Way leads to the Temple Terrace and you are confronted with a large altar, erected by the island of Híos. Of the main body of the **Temple of Apollo**, only the foundations stood when it was uncovered by the French. Six Doric columns have since been re-erected, giving a vertical line to the ruins and providing some idea of the temple's former dominance over the whole of the sanctuary. In the innermost part of the temple was the *adyton*, a dark cell at the mouth of the oracular chasm where the Pythian priestess would officiate. No sign of cave or chasm has been found, nor any vapours that might have induced a trance, but it is likely that such a chasm did exist and was simply opened and closed by successive earthquakes. On the architrave of the temple – probably on the interior – were inscribed the maxims "Know Thyself" and "Nothing in Excess".

DELPHI: THE SACRED PRECINCT

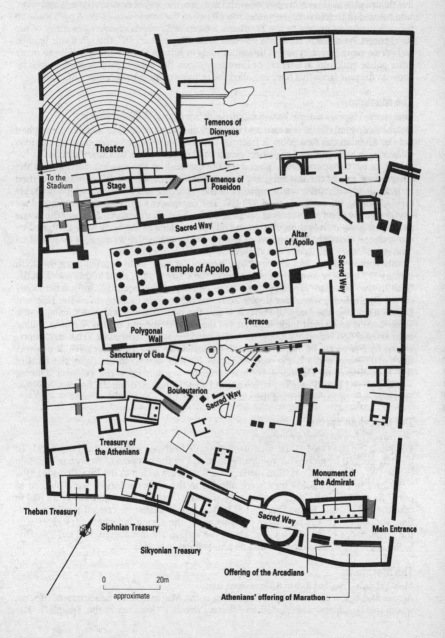

Temenos of Dionysus

Theater

To the Stadium

Stage

Temenos of Poseidon

Sacred Way

Altar of Apollo

Sacred Way

Temple of Apollo

Terrace

Polygonal Wall

Sanctuary of Gea

Bouleuterion

Sacred Way

Treasury of the Athenians

Monument of the Admirals

Theban Treasury

Siphnian Treasury

Sacred Way

Main Entrance

Sikyonian Treasury

Offering of the Arcadians

0   20m
approximate

Athenians' offering of Marathon

The theatre and stadium used for the main events of the Pythian Festival are on terraces above the temple. The **Theatre**, built in the fourth century BC with a capacity of five thousand, was closely connected with Dionysos, the god of ecstasy, the arts and wine, who reigned in Delphi over the winter months when the oracle was silent. A path leads up through cool pine groves to the **Stadium**, a steep walk which discourages many of the tour groups. Its site was artificially levelled in the fifth century BC, though it was banked with stone seats (capacity seven thousand) only in Roman times – the gift (like so many other public buildings in Greece) of Herodes Atticus. For even greater solitude, climb up above to the pine trees that have engulfed the remains of the fourth-century BC walls.

The Museum

Mon noon–6.45pm, Tues–Fri 8am–6.45pm, Sat & Sun 8.30am–2.45pm; 1000dr.

Delphi's museum contains a rare and exquisite collection of archaic sculpture, matched only by finds on the Acropolis. It features pottery, figures and friezes from the various treasuries, which, grouped together, give a good picture of the sanctuary's riches.

The most famous exhibit, placed at the far end of the central corridor, is the **Charioteer**, one of the few surviving bronzes of the fifth century BC. It was unearthed in 1896 along with other scant remains of the "Offering of Polyzalos", which probably toppled during the earthquake of 373 BC. The charioteer's eyes, made of onyx and set slightly askew, lend it a startling realism, while the demure expression sets the scene as a lap of honour. It is thought that the odd proportions of the body were designed by the sculptor (possibly Pythagoras of Samos) with perspective in mind; they would be "corrected" when the figure was viewed, as intended, from below.

Other major pieces include two huge **Kouroi** (archaic male figures) from the sixth century BC in the second room at the top of the stairs. To the right of this room, in the "Hall of the Siphnian Treasury", are large chunks of the beautiful and meticulously carved **Syphnian frieze**; they depict Zeus and other gods looking on as the Homeric heroes fight over the body of Patroclus, and the gods battling with the giants. In the same room is an elegant Ionic sculpture of the winged **Sphynx of the Naxians**, dating from around 560 BC. Back along the main corridor is the **Athenian Treasury**, represented by fragments of the metopes, which depict the labours of Herakles, the adventures of Theseus and a battle with Amazons. Further on and to the right, the **Hall of the Monument of Daochos** is dominated by a group of three colossal dancing women, carved from Pentelic marble around an acanthus column; the figures, celebrating Dionysus, probably formed the stand for a tripod.

The Castalian spring

Site partially fenced in; free admission.

Following the road east of the sanctuary, towards Aráhova, you reach a sharp bend. To the left, marked by niches for votive offerings and by the remains of an archaic fountain house, the celebrated **Castalian spring** still flows from a cleft in the Phaedriades cliffs.

Visitors to Delphi (only men were allowed in the early centuries) were obliged to purify themselves in its waters, usually by washing their hair, though murderers had to take the full plunge. Byron, impressed by the legend that it succoured poetic inspiration, jumped in. This is no longer possible, since the spring is fenced off; sadder still, the Phaedriades cliffs, which tower above the spring, are threatened with collapse due to the impact of traffic vibration, and so are swathed in scaffolding.

The Marmaria

Mon–Fri 8am–7pm, Sat & Sun 8.30am–3pm; free.

Across and below the road from the spring is the **Marmaria**, or Sanctuary of Athena, whom the Delphians worshipped as Athena Pronoia ("Guardian of the Temple"). The name Marmaria means "marble quarry" and derives from the medieval practice of filching the ancient blocks for private use.

The most conspicuous building in the precinct, and the first visible from the road, is the **Tholos**, a fourth-century BC rotunda. Three of its dome-columns and their entablature have been set up, but while these amply demonstrate the original beauty of the building (which is *the* postcard image of Delphi), its purpose remains a mystery.

At the entrance to the sanctuary stood the **Old Temple of Athena**, destroyed by the Persians and rebuilt in the Doric order in the fourth century BC; foundations of both can be traced. Outside the precinct on the northwest side (above the Marmaria) is a **Gymnasium**, again built in the fourth century BC, but later enlarged by the Romans who added a running track on the now collapsed terrace; prominent among the ruins is a circular plunge bath which, filled with cold water, served to refresh the athletes after their exertions.

Practicalities: Modern Dhelfí

Modern Dhelfí is as inconsequential as its ancient namesake, 1500m to the east, is impressive. Entirely geared to tourism, its attraction lies in its mountain setting, proximity to the ruins, and access to Mount Parnassós (see the following section).

There is a single **bus terminal**, located at the Itéa (west) end of town. Westbound buses go to Ámfissa (whence you can pick up connections north), Itéa and (usually with a change) Náfpaktos, while eastbound services go only to Livádhia or Athens. The main difficulty, since all coaches originate elsewhere, is that seats allocated for the Dhelfí ticket booth are limited and they sell out some hours in advance. If you're going to be stuck standing all the way to Athens, it's better to get off at Livádhia and continue by train – there are four morning departures and five later departures. Bus timetables are available from the **Tourist Information Office**, Vassiléos Pávlou keh Frideríkis 44 (☎0265/82 000), or, if closed, are displayed in its window. Other amenities include **banks**, a **post office** and an **OTE**, all along the main street.

Accommodation

Accommodation is plentiful: like most Greek site villages, Dhelfí has a quick turn around of visitors and, with close on twenty hotels and pensions, finding a place to stay should present few problems. There are three **campsites** in the area: the closest is *Camping Apollon* (☎0265/82 762; open all year), alongside the road to Ámfissa/Itéa and less than 1km west of Dhelfí. *Camping Delphi* (☎0265/82 363; open all year) is 3km further along the same road, just after Chrysso, and *Camping Chrysso* (☎0265/82 050; April–Oct) is another 3km on, along the same road.

Athena, Vassiléos Pávlou 55 (☎0265/82 239) Near the bus station at the Itéa (west) end of town, this comfortable hotel has views of the gulf from back rooms. ②.

Loula Sotiríou, Apollonos 84 (☎0265/82 349) Inexpensive *dhomátia* rooms. ②.

Odysseus, Isaía 1 (☎0265/82 235). On a street below and parallel to the main street; descend the steps by the *Sibylla*. Quiet pension, with flowered terrace and fine views. ②.

Olympic Hotel, Vassiléos Pávlou keh Frederíkis 57 (☎0265/82 793). Tasteful, pricey, but value-for-money, hotel with the same owner as the cheaper *Hermes Hotel* at no. 29. ⑤.

Pan, Vassiléos Pávlou and Frederíkis 53 (☎0265/82 294). The same owner (currently the mayor) as the *Pythia*. Adequate and comfortable with fine views of the gulf. ①.

Pythia, (☎0265/82 328). Vassiléos Pávlou 68. Close to the site and museum. ④.

Sybilla, Vassiléos Pávlou keh Frederíkis 9 (☎0265/82 353). Older, conventional hotel with reductions for groups of four or more. Try for rooms at the back. ③.

Varanos, Vassiléos Pávlou keh Frederíkis 27 (☎0265/82 345). Welcoming hotel, with private facilities in all rooms. Copious breakfasts are extra. ④.

Youth hostel, Apollónos 29 (☎0265/82 268). This hostel used to have a good reputation, but recent reports have been mixed – for two people sharing, it's as cheap to opt for rooms; 11pm curfew. ①.

Eating and drinking

Meals are best at the incredibly cheap *Taverna Vakhos*, next to the youth hostel, and at the nearby *Taverna Lefkaria*, which is dearer, but no less popular; both have views down to the gulf from their terraces. Nearer to the museum and site is the *Apollonio Restaurant*, which is ideal for a quick lunch or snack. Back in town, try the *Psistaria Arahova*, opposite the *Hotel Pan* at the west end of town, for excellent *kokorétsi* and wine, or the *Stammatis*, 200m beyond the *Arahova*.

Mount Parnassós

For a quick sniff of the Greek alpine scene, **Parnassós** is probably the most convenient peak in the land, though it is no longer a wilderness, having been disfigured by the ski-station above Aráhova and its accompanying paraphernalia of lifts, snack bars and access roads. The best routes for walkers are those up from Delphi to the **Corycian Cave** (practicable from April to November), or to the **Liákoura summit ascent** (May to September only). Those with their own transport can take advantage of metalled **roads** up the mountain from Aráhova and Graviá or the jeep track from Amfíklia; these could easily be combined with a walk.

Delphi to the Corycian Cave

To reach the **trailhead** for this walk – and the initial path up the mountain – take the right-hand (approaching from Athens), uphill road through Dhelfí village. At the top of the slope turn right onto a road that doubles back to the **museum-house** (Tues–Fri 8am–8pm, Mon, Sat & Sun 9am–3pm) where the poet **Angelos Sikelianos** – he of the briefly revived ancient festival – once lived. There is a bust of him outside.

Continue climbing from here, on a gravel surface, and you reach the highest point of the fence enclosing the sanctuary ruins. Where it ends at a locked gate, adopt a trail on your left, well marked by black-on-yellow metal diamonds since it's part of the E4 European long-distance trail. Initially steep, the way soon flattens out on a grassy knoll overlooking the stadium, and continues along a ridge next to a line of burnt cypresses.

Soon after, you join up with an ancient cobbled trail coming from inside the fenced precinct, the "**Kakí Skála**", which zigzags up the slope above you in broad reaches. The view from here is fantastic, stretching back over the Gulf of Kórinthos to the mountains of the Peloponnese. The cobbles come to an end by a large concrete inspection cover in the Delphi water supply, an hour above the village, at the top of the Phaedriades cliffs. Nearby stand a pair of rock pinnacles, from one of which those guilty of sacrilege in ancient times were thrown to their deaths – a custom perhaps giving rise to the name *Kakí Skála* or "Evil Stairway".

E4 markers remain visible in the valley which opens out ahead of you. You can get simultaneous views south, and northeast towards the Parnassan summits, by detouring a little to the right to a wooden hut and a barn, then to a slight rise perhaps 150m further. The principal route becomes a gravel route bearing northeast; beyond, you take the right fork near a spring and watering troughs, with some shepherds' huts scattered under the trees. The track passes a picnic grounds and a chapel within the next fifteen minutes, and acquires intermittent paved surface before skirting a sheepfold and another hut on the left. Some two hours above Dhelfí, you emerge from the fir woods with a view ahead of the rounded mass of the Yerondóvrahos peak (2367m) of the Parnassós massif.

Another fifteen minutes brings you to a spring, followed by another chapel and lean-to on the left, with a patch of grass that would do for camping. Just beyond is a muddy tarn backed by a low ridge. To the left rises a much steeper ridge, on whose flank lies the ancient **Corycian cave**. Scramble up the slope, meeting a dirt road about three-quarters of the way up; turn left and follow it to the end, about 10m below the conspicuous cave mouth.

This was sacred to Pan and the nymphs in ancient times, the presiding deities of Delphi during the winter months when Apollo was said to desert the oracle. Orgiastic rites were celebrated in November at the cave by women acting as the nymphs, who made the long hike up from Delphi on the Kakí Skála by torchlight. The cavern itself is chilly and forbidding, but if you look carefully with a torch you can find ancient inscriptions near the entrance; without artificial light you can't see more than a hundred metres inside. By the entrance you'll notice a rock with a man-made circular indentation – possibly an ancient altar to hold libations.

Descending to Dhelfí takes rather less than the roughly three-hour ascent. The marked E4 route, on the other hand, continues almost due north over a mixture of trails and tracks to the village of **EPTÁLOFOS**, on the Aráhova–Graviá paved road, where simple **rooms** and meals are available.

The Liákoura summit

Liákoura is Parnassós's highest and finest peak (2457m) and can be approached either from the Delphi side or from around the mountain to the north. The latter is the best walk, starting **from Áno Tithoréa**, but it involves taking a bus or train and then local taxi to the trailhead – plus camping out on the mountain. If you want a more casual look at Parnassós, it's probably better to walk up **from the Delphi side**. This is very enjoyable as far as the *EOS* (Hellenic Alpine Club) refuge – about six hours' walk – and you could either turn back here or a couple of hours lower down on the Livádhi plateau if you don't fancy a night on the mountain and the final, rather dull, four hours' slog up to Liákoura.

For the energetic, it's possible to **traverse the whole massif** in around fifteen hours' walking, starting from Dhelfí and descending at Áno Tithoréa, or vice versa.

Áno Tithoréa to Liákoura via the Velítsa Ravine

This last surviving wilderness route up Parnassós to Liákoura involves starting with a trip by train or bus as far as Káto Tithoréa, which is on the Livádhia–Amfíklia road and the Athens–Thessaloníki railway. You then need to get to the higher, twin village of **ÁNO TITHORÉA**, a four-kilometre haul easiest accomplished by taxi (usually available, but bargain for the price beforehand). You should allow at least six hours for the ascent, and around four and a half hours for the descent, so it's best to arrive early in the day; come equipped for camping out on the mountain as lodging can be difficult to find.

From the *platía* in Áno Tithoréa, head southwest out of town until you reach some park benches overlooking the giant **Velítsa ravine**. Adjacent is a "waterfall", in reality a leak in an aqueduct, which crosses the path beginning here a few minutes above the benches. A hundred metres further, bear left away from what seems to be the main track and descend towards the bed of the canyon. Once you're on the far side you can see the aqueduct again, now uncovered. Follow it until you reach the isolated chapel of Áyios Ioánnis (1hr from Áno Tithoréa).

Past the chapel, bulldozer scrapings cease and a fine alpine path heads off through the firs before you. The way is obvious for the next ninety minutes, with tremendous views of the crags filing up to the Liákoura summit, on your right across the valley. You emerge on a narrow neck of land, with a brief glimpse over the Ayía Marína valley and its namesake monastery to the east (left). The path, faint for an interval, heads slightly downhill and to the right to meet the floor of the Velítsa at the Tsáres spring (3hr 30min) – the last reliable water supply, so best fill up.

On the far bank of the river, head up a steep, scree-laden slope through the last of the trees to some sheep pens (4hr), then climb up to another pastoral hut (4hr 30min) at the base of the defile leading down from the main summit ridge. Beyond this point the going is gentler for much of the final ascent to the northwest (top right-hand) corner of this valley. A brief scramble up a rockfall to a gap in the ridge and you are at the base of Liákoura (5hr 30min). Orange paint-splashes – primarily oriented for those descending – stake out most of the approach from the Tsáres spring.

The **final ascent** is an easy twenty-minute scramble more or less up to the ridge line. On a clear morning, especially after rain, you're supposed to be able to see Mount Olympus in the north, the Aegean to the east, the Ionian to the west and way down into the Peloponnese to the south. The best viewing is said to be in midsummer; all too often you can see only cloud.

Down to the gulf: Delphi to Náfpaktos

The train-less, almost beach-less **north shore of the Gulf of Kórinthos** is even less frequented than the south coast. The arid landscape, with harsh mountains inland, can be initially off-putting, but there are attractive and low-key resorts in **Galaxídhi** and **Náfpaktos** – both reasonably well connected by bus, and offering connections on south to the Peloponnese, via the ferries at Áyios Nikólaos–Éyio or Andírio–Río. From both Éyio and Río, you can reach Pátra by rail or road. Alternatively, heading in the opposite direction, it is easy to reach Dhiakoftó and the Kalávrita rack-and-pinion railway (see p.237).

All buses heading southwest of Delphi towards the Gulf of Kórinthos stop first at Itéa, a gritty little town (literally, owing to the bauxite-ore dust everywhere) where you may have to change buses for the next leg of the journey. (For the continuation of the route west from Andírio to Messolóngi and Agrínio, see p.324.)

Galaxídhi

GALAXÍDHI, 17km southwest of Itéa, is a quiet port, rearing mirage-like out of an otherwise lifeless shore. The old town stands on a raised headland, crowned by the photogenic church of Áyios Nikólaos, patron saint of sailors. Wooden *kaíkia* were built alongside the old harbour to the north of the headland until the beginning of this century. Still standing is the superb waterfront of nineteenth-century shipowners' houses. These have lately become the haunt of Athenian second-homers, plus a smattering of French and Italians. Despite the restorations and a bit of a marina ethos down at the "new" southern harbour, the town still remains just the right side of tweeness, with an animated market high street and a variety of watering-holes. Above the new harbour, a small **archeological museum** (Sat–Tues 9.30am–1pm, Wed–Fri 9.30am–2pm; free) traces the history of the town.

There is no real beach – something that's no doubt acted as a healthy brake on development – but if you stroll around the pine-covered headland to the north, you'll find some pebbly **coves**, with chapel-crowned islets offshore. Another good walk is to the thirteenth-century **Moní Metamórfosis**, an archetypal rural monastery looking out over the bay towards Parnassós. It's an hour on foot to the west, through terraced fields and olive and almond groves; take the track under the flyover at the western edge of the village and look out for a footpath to the right after about twenty minutes.

Practicalities
Accommodation is on the pricey side and hard to find in summer. The central *Hotel Poseidon* (☎0265/41 426; ③) is the cheapest option but a bit sleazy; better are the

Rooms Scorpios (☎0265/41 198; ⑤), over the supermarket next to the post office, and near the bus station. Not so central, but with fine views, are the *Hotel Galaxidi* (☎0265/41 850; ⑤), inland from the old harbour, the *Hotel Galaxa* (☎0265/41 620; ⑤), beyond the new harbour, and the nearby Italian-run *Ganimede Hotel* (☎0265/41 328; ⑤), with a beautiful garden and homemade jams at breakfast.

Eating out, far and away the best of the tavernas is *O Dervenis* (May–Sept), near the *Ganimede*, with fair prices and impeccable food. For budget eating, a string of restaurants on the waterfront serve inexpensive traditional food: try *O Alekos* or *Steki*, before wandering across to *Toh Konaki*, on the market street, for a lethal dessert.

The Áyios Nikólaos–Éyio ferry

West of Galaxídhi is some of the sparsest scenery of the Greek shoreline; there are few villages and none which seems to warrant a stop, scrappy beaches notwithstanding. At ÁYIOS NIKÓLAOS, however, there's a year-round **ferry across the gulf** to the Peloponnese – an alternative to the crossing at Andírio–Río, 60km further west (see below). The boats leave Áyios Nikólaos for Éyio three times daily, at 8.30am, 3.30pm and 6.30pm, with an additional crossing in high season at noon; the journey takes 40 minutes and costs 400dr for passengers, 2500dr for a car and driver.

If you miss the last sailing, **accommodation** possibilities include the nearby *Hotel Ayios Nikolaos* (☎0266/31 176; ③), with a restaurant, and Theodore Kafarkis's rooms (☎0266/31 177; ③), by the café. On a bluff, high above the coastal road and bay, is the well-maintained campsite, the *Doric Village* (☎0266/31 195), with bungalows (③).

Náfpaktos

The one place that stands out to the west of Galaxídhi is **NÁFPAKTOS**, a lively resort sprawling along the seafront below a rambling Venetian castle. Two hours by bus from Dhelfí, and an hour by bus and ferry from Pátra, it makes a convenient stopover – though, surprisingly, most of its visitors are Greek.

The **Kástro** provides a picturesque backdrop to the town, and enjoyable rambling to the top of its fortifications. The walls run down to the sea, enclosing the old harbour and the **beach**, which are entered through one of the original gates. The castle was long a formidable part of the Venetian defences, and the **Battle of Lepanto** was fought offshore from here in 1571. Under the command of John of Austria, an allied Christian armada devastated an Ottoman fleet – the first European naval victory over the Turks since the death of the dreaded pirate-admiral Barbarossa; Cervantes, author of *Don Quixote*, lost his left arm to a cannonball in the conflict.

Practicalities

Buses run northwest to Agrínio (where you can pick up services to Ioánnina or Lefkádha), and east to Itéa and Ámfissa (for connections north into Thessaly). Local city buses go to the ferry at Andírio, or you can sometimes get a seat on a long-distance bus heading to Pátra.

Despite the dozen or so hotels and assorted rooms places, **accommodation** can be in short supply in summer. The *Hotel Amaryllis* (☎0634/27 237; ③), on Platía Liménos, facing the port, is recommended; in the same price range, *Hotel Aegli* (☎0634/27 271; ③), at Ilárhou Tzavéla 75, is central and open all year. For a more tranquil setting, there's a cluster of hotels on the beach: try the *Nafpakatos* (☎0634/23 788; ④), a modern place which promises an "American-style" breakfast, or the *Akki* (☎0634/28 464; ④–⑤). There's a good **campsite**, *Platanitis Beach* (☎0634/31 555; mid-May to Sept), 5km west of the town towards Andírio; to get there, catch a blue city bus from the main square – the last one leaves at 10pm.

There are a number of waterfront **restaurants** and, by the old port, the new and lively *Cafe Aroma*; on the outskirts of town to the west there are a few other tavernas along a stretch of beach.

The Andírio–Río Ferry

The ferry at **ANDÍRIO** runs across the Gulf of Kórinthos to Río (see p.237) every fifteen minutes from 6.45am to 10.45pm and less frequently during the night. The trip takes just fifteen minutes, and fares are 90dr per passenger, 1000dr per car and driver. Once across, you can generally pick up a city bus immediately for Pátra but as through bus services between the Dhelfí area and Pátra have improved in recent years, it might be worth hanging on for one. Drivers should count on waiting for 30 minutes or so for the ferry in summer. There's a moderately priced restaurant and the *Hotel Andirrion* (☎0634/31 450; ③) or the *Dounis Beach* campsite (☎0634/31 565; May–Sept) on the Náfpaktos/Andírio road, 1km from the ferry.

North to Lamía

Lamía is a half-day's journey north from Dhelfí, with a connection at Ámfissa: a slow but pleasant route skirting mounts Parnassós, Gióna and (to the northwest) Íti. At the historic pass of **Thermopylae** the road joins the **coastal highway** from Athens.

Inland via Ámfissa

The inland road west from Dhelfí climbs slowly through a sea of olive groves to **ÁMFISSA**, a small town in the foothills of Mount Gióna. Like Livádhia, this strategic military location was a base for the Catalan Grand Company, who have left their mark on the **castle**. If you have time to kill between buses, its ruins, which include remnants of an ancient acropolis, make for a pleasant walk, if only to enjoy the shade of the pine trees and examine a few stretches of Classical polygonal masonry. The **market** quarter of town is also good for a stroll. Ámfissa was once one of the major bell-making centres in the Balkans, and copper-alloy sheep bells are still produced and sold here. The local olives – green and salty – are also acclaimed.

Serious **walkers** may want to use Ámfissa as a jumping-off point for the mountains west and north towards Karpeníssi: **Gióna**, **Vardhoússia** and **Oxía**. There are routes through from Ámfissa (and from Lidhoríki, west of Ámfissa) **to Karpeníssi**. Most travellers, however, roll north on the dramatic **Lamía road**, dividing mounts Parnassós and Gióna, or along the **rail line** from Livadhiá to Lamía. This railway is one of the most dramatic stretches of line in Europe and has a history to match: it runs through the foothills of Mount Íti and over the precipitous **defile of the Gorgopótamos** River, where in 1942 the Greek resistance – all factions united for the first and last time, under the command of the British intelligence officer C M Woodhouse – blew up a railway viaduct, cutting one of the Germans' vital supply lines to their army in North Africa.

The coastal highway

The **Athens–Lamía** coastal highway is fast, efficient and generally dull. For the first 90km or so it runs a little inland, though skirting various pockets of lake, like Límni Ilíki, north of Thíva. The most interesting stop, along with Thíva (see p.247) is the Mycenaean citadel of **Glá** (see p.248), by the village of Kástro.

There are various **links with the island of Évvia**: first at Halkídha, where there's a causeway; then by ferry at **Arkítsa** to Loutrá Edhipsoú (about every hour in season, every two hours out of season, last at 9pm; 50min; passengers 400dr, cars 1800dr). Arkítsa itself is a rather upmarket resort, popular mainly with Greeks. A short way to the north of here is the more general port of Áyios Konstandínos, which has ferry connections with the Sporades.

Áyios Konstandínos and Kámena Voúrla

ÁYIOS KONSTANDÍNOS is the closest port to Athens if you're heading for the islands of the Sporades. There are daily car **ferries**, usually just after midday, to Skiáthos and Skópelos, with an additional evening departure in season which sometimes continues to Alónissos. In summer there are also at least three daily *Flying Dolphin* **hydrofoils** (passengers only) to Skiáthos, Skópelos and Alónissos; these are about twice as fast and twice as expensive as the ferry. For ferry information contact *Alkion Travel* (☎0235/31 920); for hydrofoil information call *Bilalis Travel* (☎0235/ 318 74).

There should be no reason to stay in Áyios Konstandínos, but if you're stranded it has eight or so **hotels** – try the *Pension O Tassos* (☎0235/31 610; ②) or *Hotel Poulia* (☎0235/31 663; ③) – and a **campsite**, *Camping Blue Bay* (☎0235/314 25). *O Pharos Taverna* serves up a variety of fishy delights.

A better beach, if you find yourself with time on your hands, is at KÁMENA VOÚRLA, 9km north; this is, however, very much a resort, used mainly by Greeks attracted by the spas here and at neighbouring Loutrá Thermopilíon (see below). Seafood aficionados are well looked after at the long line of decent fish tavernas along the promenade here, and Mr Kolofoti has **rooms** (☎0235/22 601; ②) at Kanyás 7, a leafy backstreet.

Thermopylae and its spa

Just before joining the inland road, the highway enters the **Pass of Thermopylae**, where Leonidas and three hundred Spartans made a last stand against Xerxes's 30,000-strong Persian army in 480 BC. The pass was in ancient times much more defined, a narrow defile with Mount Kalídhromo on its south and the sea – which has silted and retreated nearly 4km – to the north.

The tale of Spartan bravery is described at length by Herodotus. Leonidas, King of Sparta, stood guard over the pass with a mixed force of 7000 Greeks, confident that it was the only approach an army could take to enter Greece from Thessaly. At night, however, Xerxes sent an advance part of his forces along a mountain trail and broke through the pass to attack the Greeks from the rear. Leonidas ordered a retreat of the main army, but remained in the pass himself, with his Spartan guard, to delay the Persians' progress. He and all but two of the guard fought to their deaths.

LOUTRÁ THERMOPILÍON, midway through the pass, is named for the hot springs present since antiquity. The grave mound of the fallen Spartans lies 500m away, opposite a gloriously heroic statue of Leonidas. The spa and restaurant facilities are intimidatingly built up, but there are a few cascades and drainage sluices where you can bathe undisturbed in the open air, if you can stomach the sulphurous stench.

Lamía and onward routes

LAMÍA is a busy provincial capital and an important transport junction for travellers. It sees few overnight visitors, but abounds in excellent *ouzerí* and *kafenía*. Looking down on the city is the Catalan castle, which boasts superb views – and will soon house a new archeological museum exhibiting Hellenic and Classical finds.

Heading **north from Lamía** there's a choice of three routes: to Tríkala and Kalambáka, to Lárissa, or around the coast to Vólos. None is especially memorable.

Fársala and Kardhítsa, on the routes to Lárissa and Tríkala respectively, are small, very ordinary country towns. The **Vólos road**, however, **east** along the coast, has a little more to delay your progress.

Lamía

The town is arranged around three main squares: Platía Párhou, Platía Eleftherías and Platía Laoú, all good venues for sipping a *frappé* and watching Greek life go by. **Platía Eleftherías** is the town's social hub, full of outdoor cafés and restaurants, and the scene of the evening *volta*. The cathedral and town hall occupy two sides of the square, the latter pockmarked by bullets dating from riots during the colonels' junta; every Sunday, the flag that flies above the square is lowered in solemn ceremony, to the wayward accompaniment of the local band.

Just to the south of Eleftherías is the atmospheric **Platía Laoú**, shaded by plane trees which in autumn are crowded with migratory birds. Here you'll find the town's main taxi rank and an all-night kiosk. Leading off to the right is Karaiskáki – a vegetarian's nightmare of a street, with meat roasting on spits and the smell of *patsás* (tripe-and-trotter soup) hanging in the air. For a look at **bread-making** by the oldest of methods, leave Platía Laoú on Isáia and follow it for 200m into the old part of town: the bakery is on the left, recognizable by the quarter-glazed windows and stable door. Another noteworthy bakery, supplying perhaps the best *tirópites* in Greece, is *Kalouzani* on the corner of Platía Laoú.

The third square, **Platía Párhou** is the main shopping area, with **banks** also grouped around it. On Saturdays, the streets below Párhou turn into a lively **market**, with everything from goats to plastic combs on sale.

Other diversions in Lamía include live **bouzouki music**, untainted by the sophisticated tastes of Athenians, nor pandering to tourists, on the Stilídha road, opposite the high school; a **theatre** on Ipsilándou, used for art exhibitions and in winter as an art-film cinema; and *The Velvet Underground*, behind the cathedral on Androutsóu, the best of the winter-only clubs. Finally, every Sunday there is a **puppet show** in the small theatre 200m up the road past the OTE; it's designed for children, telling classic Greek stories that are understandable even with a very hazy knowledge of the language.

Practicalities

The **buses**, including a local service from the train station (6km out), arrive at terminals scattered throughout the town, though none is much further than ten minutes' walk away from Platía Párhou. Ámfissa and Karpeníssi services use a terminal on Márkou Bótsari; those for Lárissa, Tríkala and the north, one on Thermopilón; those for Vólos, one at the corner of Levadhítou and Rozáki-Ángeli; while buses for Athens and Thessaloníki go from the corner of Papakiriazi and Satovriándou.

Accommodation is not expensive in Lamia; there are a couple of moderate hotels on Ódhos Rozáki-Ángeli: *Thermopylae* (☎0231/21 366; ③) at no. 36 and *Athina* (☎0231/20 700; ④) at no. 41. A couple of budget places, sleazy but nicely situated, are on Platía Laoú: the *Emborikon* (☎0231/22 654; ②) and *Neon Astron* (☎0231/26 245; ②), but note that both these places are used by prostitutes.

For **food and drink**, good *ouzerís* exist on Androutsóu, between *platías* Laoú and Eleftherías. *Aman Aman* is the best, with palatable barrelled wine, closely followed by *Asterias*, one of three fine places to eat in a small courtyard below Eleftherías. *Psilidhas*, on the road out towards Vólos has a glowing reputation and is more upmarket. The trendiest cafés in Platía Eleftherías are the *Viva* and the *Remezzo*, diagonally opposite the *Galaxy Cinema*. From a smaller square above Platía Párhou, steps lead up to a peaceful but more pricey hilltop café-restaurant, *Ayios Loukas*, with great views from the terrace.

Lamía to Vólos

First temptation on the coast road to Vólos is **AYÍA MARÍNA**, 12km east of Lamía, where the seafood tavernas – a popular weekend jaunt for Lamian families – are much better than the rather pathetic beach.

A couple of kilometres further, **STILÍDHA** was once one of the major ports of the Aegean – it was at the opera house here that Maria Callas's grandfather outsang a visiting Italian star and started a dynasty. Today the unsightly town is chiefly concerned with olive-oil bottling and cement: not an inspiring prospect. Probably the only reason to stop is to catch the seasonal hydrofoil to the Sporades; tickets can be bought from *Zontanos Bros*, Falaróu 2 (✆0238/22 820). If you get stuck, the accommodation options are the *Hotel Skyland* (✆0238/22 798; ③) and *Parras Camping* (✆0238/22 221). There are passable beaches at Karavómilos and Ahládhi, 8km and 19km east of Stilídha respectively; both are suitable for a dip and a fish-taverna lunch, though you'll need your own transport. Look out for nesting herons on the road back to Lamía.

The best beaches along this route are near **GLÍFA**, 30km further north, though it is 11km off the highway and served only by one afternoon bus from Lamía. It has the mainland's northernmost **ferry crossing to Évvia**: eight times daily in July and August to Áyiokambos (last at 8.15pm; 30min journey; passengers 300dr, cars 2000dr), with a reduced service the rest of the year. **Rooms** are on offer in private houses and at half a dozen hotels, cheapest of which is the *Oassis* (✆0238/61 201; ③). Akhílio, 7km north, is less attractive, though it has a **campsite**.

Finally, rounding the Pagasitic Gulf towards Vólos, car-drivers might want to stop at **NÉA ANHIÁLOS**, where five early Christian basilicas have been uncovered. Their mosaics and the small site museum are interesting, though perhaps not enough to make it worth risking a three-hour wait between buses.

West to Karpeníssi – and beyond

The road **west from Lamía** climbs out of the Sperhiós valley, with glimpses on the way of mounts Íti, Gióna and Vardhoússia, 10km to the south. If you want to do some **hiking**, there are spectacular routes on Mount Íti (the Classical Oita), easiest approached from the village of Ipáti. The **Karpeníssi valley**, too, lends itself to walking trips amid a countryside of dark fir forest and snow-fringed mountains, which the EOT promotes (with some justice) as "the Greek Switzerland". Neither area sees more than a few dozen summer tourists, most of these on rafting trips arranged by *Trekking Hellas* (see p.347).

Ipáti and paths on Mount Íti

Mount Íti is an unusually accessible mountain. There are buses almost hourly from Lamía to Ipáti, its main trailhead; if you arrive by train, these can be picked up en route at Lamía's "local" station, Lianokládhi, 6km from the town. Be sure not to be get off the bus at the sulphurous spa of Loutrá Ipátis, 5km south of Ipáti proper.

IPÁTI is a small village, clustered below a castle, with two good-value **hotels**, catering mainly for Greek families: the *Panorama* (✆0231/59 222; ②) and *Panhellinion* (✆0231/59 640; ②). There are also a couple of reasonable tavernas.

Trail-finding on Mount Íti can be an ambitious undertaking and requires detailed maps and/or a hiking guidebook. A limited trek, however, should be feasible if you've reasonable orientation skills. From the village, a path loosely marked by red splashes of paint leads in around four hours to an *EOS* refuge known as **Trápeza** (usually locked, but with a spring and camping space nearby). This is a steep but rewarding walk, giving a good idea of Íti's sheer rock ramparts and high lush meadows.

Karpeníssi

The main road west from Ipáti, after scaling a spur of Mount Timvristós, and passing the turnoff to a tiny **ski centre** (uncrowded and with equipment to rent), drops down to the town of **KARPENÍSSI**. Its site is spectacular – huddled at the base of the peak and head of the Karpenissiótis valley, which extends south all the way to the wall-like Mount Panetolikó – though the town itself is entirely nondescript, having been destroyed in World War II by the Germans and again during the civil war. During the latter, it was captured and held for a week by Communist guerrillas in January 1949. In the course of the fighting, an American pilot was shot down – thereby gaining, as CM Woodhouse observes in *Modern Greece*, "probably the unenviable distinction of being the first American serviceman to be killed in action by Communist arms".

Except on weekends in summer or skiing season, **accommodation** is easily found, if not that appealing; most of the eight hotels are noisy and expensive. The cheapest and quietest is the *Panhellinion* at Tsitsára 9 (☎0237/22 330; ②); there's little to distinguish the three other hotels within sight of the central square and its adjacent bus terminal: *Elvetia* at Zinopoúlou 33 (☎0237/22 465); *Anesis* (☎0237/22 840), 660m towards Lamia; and the calmer *Galini* (☎0237/22 914), near the *Penhellinion*. All these are in the ④ price category at weekends, but midweek rates drop to ②.

Eating options are similarly limited; two exceptions to the bland array of fast food snack bars are the *Psistaria Poniras*, opposite the bus station, or *Adherfi Triandafilli*, opposite the OTE, just southwest of the square.

Around Karpeníssi

A pleasant four-kilometre walk from Karpeníssi is the traditional mountain village of **KORISKHÁDHES**, whose stone houses display the ornate wooden balconies typical of the region. It has a single *kafenío* where you can order *mezédhes* and gaze over the trees at Mount Helidhóna. To reach the village, follow the road south out of town (towards Proussós) and look for the turning to the right after about 1km.

If your appetite is whetted for more of this countryside, a twice-daily bus trundles 15km downriver, again along the Proussós road, to **MEGÁLO HORIÓ** and **MIKRÓ HORIÓ** ("Big Village" and "Little Village"). Both have **inns** and the possibility of day hikes up the respective peaks presiding over them.

Beyond these villages, the valley narrows to a gorge, the road loses its paved surface, and only occasional buses brave the hair-raising drive to the monastery and village of **PROUSSÓS** (33km out of Karpeníssi). The **monastery** is large and much rebuilt after a succession of fires (always a hazard with candles), and presently inhabited by just five monks. Visitors are welcomed and are shown curiosities in the ninth-century *katholikón*, such as paper made from the skin of goat-kid embryo and an icon of the Panayía with its eyes gouged out. (According to the monks, the Communist rebels of the 1940s were responsible for this, though the Turks were wont to perform the same sacrilege, and credulous villagers attributed magical powers to the dust thus obtained.)

In summer the monastery will host men for a one-night stay; otherwise there are a couple of tavernas in the **village** (1km further on) and probably a bed or two – useful, since the bus only appears three times a week.

The road to Agrínio

The roads west from Karpeníssi climb high into the mountains of **Ágrafa**, the southernmost extension of the Píndhos. In winter critical passes are generally closed, but through the summer they're serviceable, if lightly travelled.

The most remote and dramatic route, with no bus service, is on **south from Proussós** (see above): 33km of dirt track which eventually brings you out at

THÉRMO, on the shores of Lake Trihonídha. There you are within striking distance (and a daily bus ride) of Agrínio, with its connections to Patrá and Ioánnina (see p.231 and p.294 respectively).

The direct **Karpeníssi–Agrínio** road is paved, but extremely sinuous, so it still takes the one morning bus a good three and a half hours to cover the 115km. The beauty of the first half of the journey cannot be overemphasized; it's largely empty country, with the only place of any size (having a filling station and a taverna) being the village of **FRANGÍSTA**, which straddles a valley, 41km from Karpeníssi. Beyond Frangísta, the bus lumbers past the giant **Kremastón dam** on the Tavropós, Trikeriótis and Ahelóös rivers, skirts Panetolikó, then winds down through tobacco-planted hills to Agrínio. If you wish to explore the Ágrafa wilderness to the north, leave the bus at the turnoff for Kerasohóri, 27km out of Karpeníssi.

THESSALY

The highlights of travelling through **Thessaly** are easily summarized. Over to the east, curling down from the industrial port-city of Vólos, is the **Pílion** (Pelion) mountain peninsula. The villages on its lush, orchard-covered slopes are among the most beautiful in the country: an established resort area for Greeks and numerous camper-van tourists, though still surprisingly unspoilt. To the west – a sight not to be missed in any mainland exploration – are the extraordinary "monasteries in the air" of the **Metéora**.

The **central plains** are to be passed through, rather than visited. **Lárissa**, the region's capital, is nothing much in itself, though it provides efficient connections by bus, and rather slower ones by train, to Vólos and to Kalambáka (via Tríkala).

Heading north or west from Lárissa, you will find yourself in one mountain range or another. The dramatic route over the Píndhos, from Kalambáka to Ioánnina, is covered in the following chapter. North from Kalambáka there are reasonable roads, though few buses, into western Macedonia, with the lakeside town of Kastoriá an obvious focus. Most travellers, however, head north from Lárissa towards Thessaloníki, a very beautiful route in the shadow of Mount Olympus (see *The North: Macedonia and Thrace*).

Vólos

Arriving at the city of **VÓLOS** gives little hint of the Pílion's promise. This is Greece's fastest-growing industrial centre and a major depot for long-distance truck drivers. It's hard to imagine the mythological past of this busy modern port, but it is the site of ancient Iolkos, from where Jason and the Argonauts set off on their quest for the Golden Fleece. Except for isolated nooks and crannies, it is not a pretty sight – or smell when the homegrown *néfos* (pollution cloud) hovers. Physically, it's mainly modern concrete sprawl, rebuilt after a devastating 1955 earthquake, and now edging to its natural limits against the Pílion foothills behind. That said, you may well find yourself spending a night or at least a few hours here, for in addition to serving as a gateway to the Pílion, Vólos is the **main port for the northern Sporades**: Skiáthos, Skópelos and Alónissos.

The most attractive place to linger is along the eastern waterfront esplanade, between the landscaped **Platía Yioryíou** and the archeological museum, which is itself a highly recommended diversion. Imaginatively laid out and clearly labelled in English, the **Archeological Museum** (daily except Mon 8.30am–3pm; 400dr, students 200dr) features a unique collection of painted grave *stelai* depicting, in now-faded colours, the everyday scenarios of fifth-century BC life, as well as a variety of graves

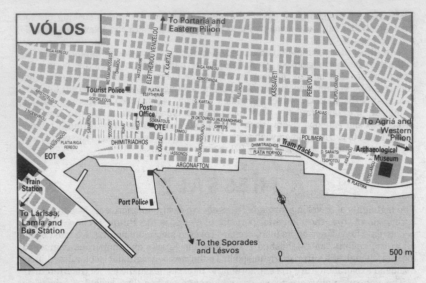

complete with skeletons. It also hosts one of the best European collections of Neolithic pottery, tools and figurines, from the local sites of Sesklo and Dimini (both of which – respectively 15km and 3km from Vólos – can be visited, though they are of essentially specialist interest).

Practicalities

Ferries and hydrofoils arrive and depart from the central **port**, and most other services are found within a couple of blocks. An exception is the **bus station**, off our map on Grigoríou Lambráki and ten minutes' walk southwest of the main square, **Platía Ríga Feréou**. Arrayed around the latter are the **train station** and the helpful **EOT** office (☎0421/24 915), which provides information on bus and ferry services as well as accommodation. Like Áyios Konstandínos, Vólos has regular ferries and in summer (for nearly double the price) the quicker *Flying Dolphin* hydrofoils to the Sporades.

The **ferries** leave two to four times daily for Skiáthos and Skópelos, with at least one continuing to Alónissos; the last departure is generally 7pm (Sun 1pm); for information phone the port police on ☎0421/38 888 or 31 059.

Hydrofoils (☎0421/39 786) run two or three times daily to Skiáthos, Skópelos and Alónissos, continuing two or three times a week to Skíros. In midsummer there are also hydrofoils to the islands from **Plataniás** at the foot of the Pílion (see p.275).

If you want to **rent a car** to explore the Pílion, try *European Cars* (☎0421/36 238) at Iassónos 83, one block inland and parallel to the waterfront.

Accommodation

Hotels are fairly plentiful, with a concentration of acceptable ones in the grid of streets behind the port. Budget options include the spotless and friendly *Acropole* at Korai 17, the *Avra* at Sólonos 3, or the *Iasson*, near the port at Pavlóu Méla 1. For a splurge, try the *Aigli*, at Argonáfton 24, an Art Deco hotel on the quayside.

Further out at Tzánou 1, but handy for the museums, the *Roussas* is handy for the museum and *ouzerís*, and has helpful staff.

Restaurants and nightlife

Vólos specializes in one of Greece's most endearing institutions – the authentic **ouzerí**. *Nauftilia* at Argonáfton 1 is one of the best, where you can wash your *mézedhes* down with *tsíporo*, the local and lethal spirit. Continuing along the seafront, *Ouzerí Argonaftes* is also good. More pricey, but excellent, **tavernas** are on Nikifórou Plastíra: these include *Ta Palia Kalamakia*, *Sarri* and *Akti Tselepi*, all specializing in seafood. For more conventional and cheap casserole dishes, try *Athnaiki* taverna at Venizélou 11.

As for **nightlife**, there's a rash of swish cafés on the waterfront with comfortable chairs and uncomfortable prices. *Minerva* is one of the oldest established, and is popular with the youth of Vólos. There's a good summer cinema, *Exoraistiki*, at one corner of Platía Yioryíou. *Archetypo*, the local disco, is located 5km east of the city, on the beach at Paralía Agriás.

Mount Pílion (Pelion)

There is something decidedly un-Greek about the **Mount Pílion peninsula**, with its lush orchards of apple, pear and nut trees and dense forests of beech and oak. Scarcely a rock is visible along the slopes, and the sound of water comes gurgling up from crevices beside every track; summer temperatures here are a good 15°F cooler than the rest of Thessaly. Pílion is reputed to be the land of the mythical centaurs, and the site of ancient gods' revelries.

Pílion **villages** are idiosyncratic, spread out along the slopes – due to easy availability of water – and with their various quarters linked by winding cobbled paths. They formed a semi-autonomous district during the Turkish occupation, and during the eighteenth century became something of a nursery for Greek culture, fostered by an Othodox education (imparted through semi-underground schooling) and a revival of **folk art** and **traditional architecture**. There is also, by Greek standards, a strong regional **cuisine**, with specialities such as *spédzofai* (sausage and pepper casserole), *kounéli kokkinistó* (rabbit stew) and *gída vrastí* (goat pot-au-feu). Apart from a wide range of fruit, herbs, spices and honey are important local products.

Many of the villages have changed little in appearance over the centuries, and offer rich rewards with their mansions, churches and sprawling *platías* – invariably shaded by a vast plane tree, sheltering the local café. The **churches** are highly distinctive, built in a low, wide style, often with a detached belltower and always ornamented with carved wood. Two communities, **Makrinítsa** and **Vizítsa**, have been designated by the EOT as protected showpieces of the region, but almost every hamlet boasts its own unique attractions.

Add to the above the delights of a half-dozen or so excellent **beaches**, and you have a recipe for an instant holiday idyll – or disaster, if your timing is wrong. Lying roughly midway between Athens and Thessaloníki, the Pílion is all too convenient for Greek vacationers, and you'd be pushing your luck more than usual to show up in August without a reservation; prices are also comparatively high for the mainland.

Getting around Pílion

The peninsula is divided into three regions, with the best concentration of traditional villages **north** of Vólos and along the **east coast**. The **west** coast is less scenically interesting, with much more beach development. The **south**, low-lying and sparsely populated, has just one major resort, Plataniás, and a few small inland hamlets.

Travelling between the villages can be tricky without your own transport. **Buses** to the east cover two main routes: Vólos–Haniá–Zagorá (3–5 daily) and Vólos–Tsangarádha–Áyios Ioánnis via Míles (2 daily), with just one daily service linking Zagorá and

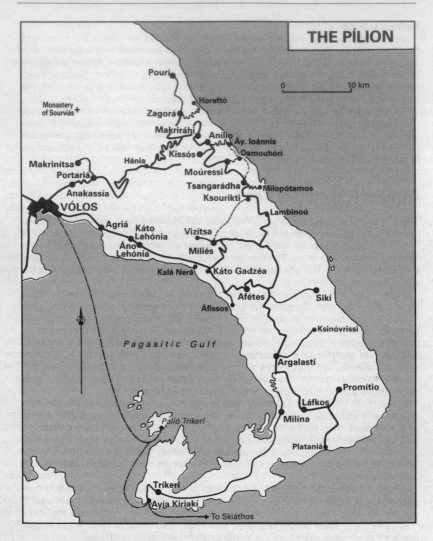

THE PÍLION

Pourí
Horeftó
Monastery
of Sourviás
Zagorá
Makriráhi
Anílio · Áy. Ioánnis
Hánia
Kissós
Damouhóri
Makrinítsa
Moúressi
Portariá
Tsangarádha · Milopótamos
Anakassía
Ksourikti
VÓLOS
Lambinoú
Agriá
Káto
Lehónia
Vizítsa
Áno
Lehónia
Miliés
Kalá Nerá
Káto Gadzéa
Afétes
Sikí
Áfissos
Ksinóvrissi
Pagasitic Gulf
Argalastí
Promítio
Láfkos
Palió Tríkeri
Milína
Plataniá
Tríkeri
Ayía Kiriakí
→ To Skiáthos

0   10 km

Tsangarádha to complete the loop. The far south is equally sparsely served, with just two or three departures a day to Plataniás and Tríkeri, though the respective northern and western highlights of Makrinítsa and Vizítsa both have excellent connections.

Alternatives are to **rent a car** in Vólos (especially advisable if you're pushed for time), some very uncertain hitching, or **walking**. The latter means slow progress, since roads snake around ravine contours, seeming never to get closer to villages just across the way, though a limited number of old cobbled **paths** (*kalderími*) provide short cuts.

Leaving the Pílion, you needn't necessarily return to Vólos but can take advantage of a daily summer **hydrofoil from Plataniás** to islands of the Sporades; this seems to have replaced the former *kaíkia* service from Plataniás to Koukounariés on Skiáthos.

The north

Before crossing over to the east coast on the main Vólos–Zagorá axis, consider pausing en route: both **Portariá** and **Makrinítsa** villages have intrinsic attractions and make good first or last stops out of Vólos.

Anakassía and Portariá

The first of the Pílion villages, **ANAKASSÍA** is just 4km out of Vólos, and few casual visitors give it more than a passing glance. What they miss is a small but very beautiful museum dedicated to the "naive" painter **Theophilos** (1873–1934). A grand eccentric, originally from Lésvos, Theophilos lived for long periods in both Athens and Vólos, where he wandered around, often dressed in traditional costumes, painting frescoes for anyone prepared either to pay or feed him. In the Pílion you find his work in the most unlikely places, mostly unheralded, including a number of village tavernas and *kafenía*. Here, the **museum** (daily 9am–1pm) occupies the **Arhondikó Kondós**, an eighteenth-century mansion whose first floor he entirely frescoed with scenes from the Greek War of Independence – one of his favourite themes.

PORTARIÁ, 10km on, has a more mountainous feel with a startling soundtrack of running streams. Of late, regrettably, it has become tackily commercialized – the areas closest to the busy road at least. Its chief glory, as so often in the Pílion, is its main square, shaded by a tremendous plane tree. If you decide to stay, you can pick from almost a dozen pensions, traditional inns and **hotels**, cheapest among which are the *Filoxenia* (☎0421/99 160; ④) and *Theoxenia* (☎0421/99 527; ④), or **rooms** (☎0421/99 437; ③) next to the filling station.

Makrinítsa

From Portariá many buses detour northwest to **MAKRINÍTSA**, 17km from Volos, where the stone houses are picturesquely scattered on the mountainside. If your time in the Pílion is severely limited, this is perhaps the best single target. Founded in 1204 by refugees from the first sacking of Constantinople, it boasts six outstanding churches and a monastery, and a group of **traditional mansions** – three of which have been restored as lodges by the EOT. Up against stiff competition, Makrinítsa, with its splendid views, ranks as one of Greece's prettiest villages. Inevitably, there are souvenir shops and plenty of day-trippers, but these are easy to escape – and exploration can be rewarding.

There's a 200-metre altitude difference between the upper and lower quarters of Makrinítsa, so to get a full sense of the village takes a full day's rambling. Most impressive of the churches are **Áyios Ioánnis**, next to the fountain on the shady main *platía*, and the beautiful **monastery of Theotókos**, right under the clock tower. Many of the sanctuaries and frescoes here are only a few centuries old, but the marble relief work on some of the apses (the curvature behind the altar) is the best of its type in Greece. A few metres on from the Áyios Ioánnis square there are **Theophilos frescoes** in a café. If you are looking for a more challenging walk in Pílion, the village is also the starting point for a long **trail** over to the deserted monastery of Sourviás. A half-hour walk from the car park (at the end of the road next to the entrance to the village) leads to Ayiós Ycrásimos.

Accommodation in Makrinítsa is not cheap. The EOT lodges are very pleasant but pricey; the best ones are *Arhondiko Mousli* (☎0421/99 228; ⑤) and *Pension Xiradaki* (☎0521/99 250; ⑤). Cheaper private operations – again in traditional mansions – are *Pilioritiko Spiti* (☎0421/99 194; ④), *Arhondiko Dhiomidis* (☎0421/99 430; ④) and *Dhomatia Makropoulo* (☎0421/99 016; ③). The *Kafe-Bar Pantheon*, by the square, is the best place to **eat**, specializing in the local *spédzofai* – an oven-baked dish of sausages and peppers.

Hánia

Travelling on over the mountain, beyond Portariá, the road hairpins up to the **Hánia pass**, and the village of the same name, a stark cluster of modern houses and a **youth hostel** (☎0421/24 290; ①), open only at weekends. To the south a road leads in 4km to a small, winter **ski resort** (open Jan–March). Once over the Hánia pass, the view suddenly opens to take in the whole east coast, as you spiral down to a fork: the left turning leads to Zagorá, the right towards Tsangarádha.

The east coast

The Pílion's best (and most popular) beaches and lushest scenery are to be found on the Aegean-facing **east coast**. Transport hub for the region and major producer and packer of fruit is Zagorá.

Zagorá and Pourí

The largest Pílion village, **ZAGORÁ**, has a life more independent of tourism than its neighbours, and is a lot more interesting than first impressions of its concrete main street suggest. In addition to this modern section of the village, there are three well-preserved and architecturally more varied areas, based around the squares of **Ayía Paraskeví**, **Ayía Kiriakí** and **Ayía Yiórgis**. Coming from Vólos, turn left at the filling station to find Ayía Paraskeví; Ayía Kiriakí is in the centre of the village. A left turn as the road swings away from Horeftó will bring you to the majestic Ayía Yiórgos, which languishes in the shadow of a lovely plane tree and the beautiful eighteenth-century church. Close to the second bend of the road to Horeftó beach, is the **Riga Fereou** "secret school", now an art gallery/folk museum (daily 9.30am–1.30pm & 5.30–8.30pm).

Accommodation in Zagorá is more reasonably priced than elsewhere in the region. There are several rooms places, such as *Manika Vlahou* (☎0426/22 153; ③) and a spruce little hotel, the *Haravghi* (☎0426/22 550; ④), near Ayía Kiriakí. All three squares host grill-tavernas: *O Takis* in Ayía Kiriakí is reasonable, but the best food in Zagorá is at *O Petros*, just up from Ayía Yiórgos. There's also an **OTE**, a **post office** and bank agent – the main official services between here and Tsangarádha, though the nearby coastal resorts provide similar amenities.

The road from Zagorá to **POURÍ**, one of the northernmost communities on Pílion, is a spectacular approach to a regally situated and appealing village. Sadly, there is no accommodation here, and the path that once led into the hills towards Makrinítsa, via the deserted monastery of Sourviás, is now hopelessly jumbled and overgrown.

Horeftó

A great coastal base is eight twisting kilometres down the mountain at **HOREFTÓ** (3 buses daily). There is a choice of beaches on offer here: an excellent one in front of the former fishing village, and another smaller bay (used by nude bathers) around the headland at the north end, where the road stops. Determined explorers can follow a coastal path for twenty minutes more to the coves of **Análipsi** – the southerly one a little paradise with a spring, popular with freelance campers, the further road-accessible and rockier.

Horeftó supports half a dozen **hotels** and lots of rooms for rent. The best-value and best-located hotels are the *Hayiati* (☎0426/22 405; ④) and *Erato* (☎0426/22 445; ③), both at the quiet, southern end of the coast road. The *Cleopatra* (☎0426/22 606; ④), small, central and noisier, or the *Aegeus* (☎0426/22 778; ④), uphill above the road in from Zagorá, would be second choices, though in high season you'll be lucky to find space at any. The village also has a **campsite** (☎0426/22 180), with decent amenities but a rather remote location at the extreme south end of the main beach.

Among **restaurants**, the oddly named *Ahilleio OK* on the esplanade is filling if unimaginative. Near the pavilion is *Milo tis Eridhos*, which has the best food in the village. Two or three bar-pubs provide evening distraction.

Áyios Ioánnis and around

Bearing east at the junction below Haniá, the road winds down from Mount Pílion past Makriráhi and Aníllo (meaning "without sun"), both spoilt by concrete development, towards KISSÓS. This is a much more traditional slice of Pílion – and an enjoyable stop. Set just off the main road, it is virtually buried in foliage, with sleepy residential quarters ascending in terraces and, in eighteenth-century Ayía Marína, one of the finest churches on the peninsula. **Rooms and meals** are available at the *Ksenonas Kissos* (☎0426/31 214; ③); the friendly family there serve homemade delicacies such as *ktipití*, a piquant cheese dip, and their own yoghurt, nuts and honey. Half-overgrown tracks meander tentatively from the village up towards the ski-lift ridge.

Heading for the coast, it's six kilometres of twisting paved road down to **ÁYIOS IOÁNNIS**, eastern Pílion's major resort. Despite the many hotels and private rooms, finding a bed here is as problematic as anywhere on the peninsula in summer; a small **tourist office** can advise on where there are vacancies or, if necessary on times of buses out. Budget **accommodation** doesn't really exist, so the best options are the hotels *Kohyli* (☎0426/31 229; ④), *Armonia* (☎0426/31 242; ④), with a decent taverna, and *Avra* (☎0426/31 224; ③). There is also a **campsite**, ten minutes' walk south of the village, and *Disco Kirki*, nearby. For a splurge meal, try the elegant *Ostria* taverna, which features traditional Pílion dishes.

The **beach** at Áyios Ioánnis is popular and commercialized, with windsurfing boards and waterskis for rent. For a quieter time, walk either ten minutes north to **Pláka** beach, with its mostly young, Greek clientele, or fifteen minutes south (past the campsite) to **Papaneró** beach, the best bronzing spot in the vicinity, fronted by a few rooms for rent and two tavernas. South from Papaneró, past *Katerina's Hostel*, a secluded building with balconied apartments (☎0426/31 624; ④) overlooks the Aegean, and a fairly well-marked mix of tracks and paths leads to **DAMOÚHORI**, a hamlet set amid olive trees and fringing a secluded fishing harbour.

The construction of a road down from Mouréssi has put an end to its seclusion. However, there is a large pebble beach, two pleasant tavernas and the ruins of a Venetian castle; attractive footpaths thread through the tiny settlement and a sense of peace still pervades in the evenings.

From Damoúhori, it's possible to **walk to Tsangarádha** in a little over an hour. At the mouth of the ravine leading down to the larger bay, a spectacular *kalderími* or stairway begins its ascent, allowing glimpses of up to six villages simultaneously, and even the Sporades on a clear day, from points along the way. The path emerges in the Ayía Paraskeví quarter of Tsangarádha (see below).

Tsangarádha and Mouréssi

TSANGARÁDHA is the largest northeastern village after Zagorá, though it may not seem so at first since it's divided into four distinct quarters, spread out along several kilometres of road. Each of these is grouped around a namesake church and *platía*, the finest of which is **Ayía Paraskeví**, shaded by reputedly the largest plane tree in Greece – a thousand years old and with an eighteen-metre trunk.

Most **accommodation** around the village is on the noisy main highway. Exceptions include the modern, friendly *Villa ton Rodhon* (☎0426/49 340; ③), on the cobbled path to Damoúhori, and the traditional *Hostel Edem* (☎0426/49 377; ④), ten minutes further down the same way. In Ayíou Stefánou, the easternmost district, there are panoramic views from the *Hotel San Stefano* (☎0426/49 213; ⑤), plus an average taverna by the church. There are also some rooms for rent in the southern parish of **Taxiárhes** (linked by a *kalderími* with Ayía Paraskeví), and an acceptable **taverna**, *Toh Kaliví*. Below the massive tree in Ayía Paraskeví is a *kafenío* and another, rather uninspiring taverna, *Iy Anatolí*, open only in the evening.

In general, better cooking is to be had at **MOÚRESSI**, a few kilometres northwest on the road. At either *Iy Dhrosia* or *Toh Tavernáki* here, you can get specialities like *fasólies hándres* (delicately flavoured white pinto beans) and assorted offal-on-a-spit.

Milopótamos and the coast to Lambinoú

From Tsangarádha a hairpin road (with a daily bus) snakes seven kilometres down to **MILOPÓTAMOS**, a pair of attractive pebble coves separated by a naturally tunnelled rock wall. At the larger bay, there are a couple of tavernas; on the smaller, some interesting rock formations to dive off. They attract an international summer crowd, who are catered for by a series of rooms for rent on the approach road; the nearest is *Diakoumis* (☎0423/49 203; ③), with decent views from precarious wooden terraces.

If you want to swim in more solitude, try **Fakístra beach**, a cliff-girt, white-gravel bay, just to the north; the new road from Tsangarádha may soon bring the crowds, though. Other beaches on the south side of Milopótamos include **Lambinoú** and **Kalamáki**, both well signposted, along with their inland villages. They have a more open feel, since the dramatic terrain begins to subside here.

En route from Tsangarádha to Lambinoú, the village of Ksoríhti is the eastern trailhead for an enjoyable three-hour **trail to Miliés**. The path, which wends its way through a mix of open hillside and shady dell, has been marked throughout by a distinctive three-serial-dot tracing. Before the road around the hill via Lambinoú and Kalamáki was built in 1938, this was the principal thoroughfare between the railhead at Miliés and the Tsangarádha area.

Miliés, Vizítsa and the western coast

Lying in the "rain shadow" of the mountain, the western Pílion villages and coast have a drier, more Mediterranean climate, with olives and arbutus shrubs. The beaches, at least until you get past Kalá Nerá, are a bit overdeveloped and in any case lack the character of those on the east side. Inland it is a different story, with pleasant foothill villages and, for a change, a decent bus service. Miliés and Vizítsa both make good bases for exploring local traditions and taking short walks in the Pílion interior.

Miliés

Like Tsangarádha, **MILIÉS** (variously spelled Miléës, Mileaí) is a sizeable village that was an important centre of culture during the eighteenth century. It retains a number of imposing mansions and an interesting church, the **Taxiárhis**, whose narthex (usually kept open) is decorated with brilliant frescoes. There is also a small **Folk Museum** (daily except Mon 10am–2pm; free), which displays local artefacts. Another attraction is the old terminus of the *trenáki* – miniature railway – line between Vólos and Miliés. The line, in service until 1972, was laid out early this century by an Italian company. Every year, there is talk of reintroducing a summer steam locomotive service, but in the meantime a lovely two- to three-hour walk follows the line to Áno Lehónia.

Accommodation is a choice between a handful of inexpensive rooms overlooking the church and *platía*, run by Mihalis Pappas (☎0423/86 207; ②), and *O Paleos Stathmos* (☎0423/86 425; ⑤), a luxury inn and restaurant converted from the old 1920s train station below the town. Other food choices are a couple of café-restaurants on the village square; a simple grill, *Panorama*; and *Toh Aloni*, a fancy, overpriced restaurant on the Vizítsa road. But the most distinctive food in town emanates from a superb **bakery** down on the road by the bus stop, which cranks out every kind of Pílion bread, pie, turnover and cake imaginable.

Vizítsa

VIZÍTSA, 3km further up the mountain and full of babbling brooks, is preserved as a "traditional settlement" by the EOT. It has a more open and less pickled feel than Makrinítsa, though it draws surprisingly large crowds of day-trippers in summer. The best way to enjoy the place is to stay at one of the **EOT guesthouses**, converted from the finest of the mansions – try *Kondos* (☎0423/86 793; ⑤) and *Karayianopoulos* (☎0423/86 373; ⑤); cheaper **rooms** establishments include that of *Kalliroi Dhimou* (☎0423/86 484; ④). *O Yiorgaras* is by far the best of three tavernas on the *platía*.

Agriá, Káto Gatzéa and inland

As noted, most of the coast between Vólos and Korópi (below Miliés) is unenticing. At **AGRIÁ**, for example, a cement plant casts its shadow over rashes of hotels and neongarish tavernas. Heading southeast, things improve temporarily around **KÁTO GATZÉA**, with olive groves lining the road, which now runs well inland; of the two **campsites** here, *Hellas* has the edge over the *Marína*.

A better inland route, if you have your own transport, is through the larger settlements of **Dhrakiá** and **Áyios Lavréndis**. Dhrakiá boasts the Triandafillou mansion and an August 23 festival; Áyios Lavréndis is more homogenous and has the *Pension Kentavros* (☎0421/96 224; ①), if you want to stay in a typical, quieter Pílion village.

The south

Once **south of the loop road** around the mountain, the Pílion becomes more arid and less dramatic, its villages lacking the historic interest and character of their northern counterparts. There are, though, some interesting pockets and, save for a French-run **riding stables** near Promíri, a distinct lack of tourism.

The area can be reached a little tortuously by bus, but much more easily by sea. In summer, **hydrofoils** from Vólos call at least daily at the port of **Ayía Kiriakí** (Tríkeri), and pause first at the little island of **Paleó Tríkeri**.

Argalastí and around

To get a better idea of the low-lying olive-grove countryside of the western Pílion, press on south from Kalá Nerá to the junction of **ARGALASTÍ**, the "county town", with its obligatory square, and a fine taverna, *Apothiki*, nearby. From here you can get several daily buses to **Áffisos**, a crowded, swish resort, but nicer are **Hórto** (7km) and **Milína** (10km), small beach villages with seasonal **campsites** and rooms for rent. Just south of Milína, there's a picturesque bay, where fishing boats moor and the restaurant *Favios*, with its alluring smells, serves barrelled retsina.

Plataniás

Argalastí or Kalá Nerá are also the pick-up points for Vólos-based buses passing three times daily on their way to **PLATANIÁS**, a small resort, cheaper and less commercialized than Áyios Ioánnis, near the end of the Pílion peninsula. The beach is excellent though the resort is often a bit crowded with Greek holidaymakers: walk to the second beach, **Mikró**, for more seclusion. From the quayside, hydrofoils ply the short distance over to the Sporades islands, and also back to Vólos (see "Travel Details").

Among the half-dozen **hotels**, try the *Des Roses* (☎0423/71 230; ③), *Kyma* (☎0423/71 269; ③) or *Platania* (☎0423/71 250; ③). Most of the waterside **restaurants** serve tasty seafood, but none really stand out.

Tríkeri peninsula

Stranded at the far end of the Pílion, the semi-peninsula of **Tríkeri** feels very remote. It was used after the 1946–49 civil war as a place of exile for political prisoners (along with the island of Paleó Tríkeri), and until a few years ago there was no real road connecting it with the rest of the Pílion. There's now an unpaved (but decent enough), scenic road from Milína and a daily bus from Vólos, but the area can be reached more conveniently by hydrofoil from Vólos or the Sporades (daily from April to October, going up to twice daily between June and September).

The port of **AYÍA KIRIAKÍ** is still strictly a working fishing village, something of a rarity in modern Greece. A few sweaty **rooms** are to be had behind *Ouzerí Korai* (☎0423/91 341; ②), but otherwise there are few concessions to tourism, perhaps because there's no good beach. However, orange fishing boats, paths adorned with bougainvillea and excellent seafood combine to make it a captivating, unspoilt little port. In the local boatyard, large caiques, and occasionally yachts, are built in much the same way they must have been for the last hundred years.

From Ayia Kiriakí, it's a 25-minute walk up to the village of **TRÍKERI**, either by an old *kalderími* or a series of steps that starts behind the port police building or by road. This is a pleasant hilltop village with a scattering of mansions and a useful post office and money exchange; the most common mode of transport for villagers appears to be by horse or donkey. The tree-shaded *platía* has a *kafenío* and an excellent traditional *ouzerí*; there's also a taverna, with some **rooms** above, by the road down to the harbour.

Paleó Tríkeri

Paleó Tríkeri (or Nisí Tríkeri – Tríkeri island) has a village, two hotels, a couple of tavernas and sand – which perhaps makes it the smallest Greek island with everything you really need. Little more than a kilometre end to end, it consists of a few olive-covered hills and a fringe of small, rocky beaches; it is friendly and uncrowded, and has its own charm.

The port and village, **AÏ YÁNNI**, is tiny, with a single shop and a good taverna by the harbour. Around the island from here, there are just donkey tracks. Following the track up from the village, for around ten minutes, you reach the nineteenth-century **Evangelistrías monastery** (daily 8am–3pm & 6–8pm) and the centre of the island. Past here, you reach a large bay and the island **hotel** – the *Paleo Trikeri* (☎0423/91 432; ③), with a restaurant overlooking the beach. The *Galatia* also offers a few **rooms** (☎0423/91 031; ③), and there's generally no problem camping under the olive trees nearby.

The island is connected with Ayía Kiriakí by *Flying Dolphin* **hydrofoil**: these run daily in July and August (but sporadically at other times of year), and take just ten minutes. Standard **ferries** to and from the Sporades (usually the first departure of the day) also stop here daily. Information on ferry connections to the island can be hard to come by, since they aren't always mentioned in the published *Nomicos Line* timetables, and coming from the Sporades you may find that everyone denies the existence of a stop. If all else fails, try calling the port police in Vólos (☎0421/38 888).

Lárissa

LÁRISSA stands at the heart of the Thessalian plain: a large market centre approached across a prosperous but dull landscape of wheat and corn fields. It is for the most part modern and unremarkable, but retains a few old streets (Venizélou, most notably) that hint at its recent past as a Turkish provincial capital. The highest point of the town is dominated by the remains of a medieval fortress, which is closed to the public. Down below, the centre is marked by **Platía Kendrikí**, a kilometre from the train station, while the most pleasant place to while away a few hours is the **Alcazar** park, beside the Piniós, Thessaly's major river.

As a major **road and rail junction**, the town has efficient connections with most places you'd want to reach: Vólos to the east; Tríkala and Kalambáka to the west; Lamía to the south; the Vale of Témbi (see below), Mount Olympus and Thessaloníki along the national highway to the northeast.

You probably won't choose to stay in Lárissa, but if you need to, there are numerous **hotels**. The cheapest are a trio of places in the square by the train station: the *Diethnes* (☎041/234 210; ②), *Neon* (☎041/236 268; ②) and *Pantheon* (☎041/236 726; ②); more savoury options include the *Acropole* at Venizélou 142 (☎041/227 843; ④) and the *Atlantic* at Panagoúli 1 (☎041/287 711; ④). *Éllas,* at Roosevelt 28, serves inexpensive **meals** and is always packed with locals.

North towards Mount Olympus: the Vale of Témbi and the coast

Travelling north from Lárisssa, the National Highway heads towards Thessaloníki, a highly scenic route through the **Vale of Témbi**, between mounts Olympus and Óssa, before emerging on the coast. The valley and the best of the **beaches**, east of Mount Óssa, follow; for details on Mount Olympus, see *The North: Macedonia and Thrace*.

Ambelákia

If you have time, or a vehicle, a worthwhile first stop in the Témbi region is **AMBELÁKIA**, a small town in the foothills of Mount Óssa. In the eighteenth century this community supported the world's first **industrial cooperative**, producing, dyeing and exporting textiles, and maintaining its own branch offices as far afield as London. With the cooperative came a rare and enlightened prosperity. At a time when most of Greece lay stagnant under Turkish rule, Ambelákia was largely autonomous; it held democratic assemblies, offered free education and medical care, and even subsidized weekly performances of ancient drama. The brave experiment lasted over a century, eventually succumbing to the triple ravages of war, economics and the industrial revolution. In 1811 Ali Pasha raided the town and a decade later any chance of recovery was lost with the collapse of the Viennese bank in which the town's wealth was deposited.

Until World War II, however, over six hundred mansions survived in the town. Today there are just thirty-six, most in poor condition. You can still get some idea of the former prosperity by visiting the restored **Mansion of George Schwartz**. The home of the cooperative's last president, this *arhondikó* (daily except Mon 9.30am–3.30pm) is built in grand, old-Constantinople style. Schwartz, incidentally, was a Greek, despite the German-sounding name, which was merely the Austrian bank's translation of his real surname, Mavros (Black).

The town is connected by bus with Lárissa (3 daily); or you can walk up a cobbled way in about an hour from the Témbi train station. There is a single **inn**, the *Ennea Mousses* (☎0495/93 405; ④), and a couple of tavernas.

The Vale of Témbi

Two kilometres beyond the Ambelákia turn-off, you enter the **Vale of Témbi**, a valley cut over the eons by the Piniósa, which runs for nearly ten kilometres, between the steep cliffs of the Olympus (Ólimbos) and Óssa ranges. In antiquity it was sacred to Apollo and constituted one of the few possible approaches into Greece – being the path taken by both Xerxes and Alexander the Great – and it remained an important passage during the Middle Ages. Walkers might consider a hike along the valley, which can also be traversed by canoe on the Piniós. However, both the National Road #1 and the railway forge through Témbi, impinging somewhat on its beauties. One of the most popular stops is the **Spring of Venus**. Halfway through the vale (on the right, coming from Lárissa) are the ruins of the **Kástro tis Oreás** (Castle of the Beautiful Maiden), one of four Frankish guardposts here, while marking the northern end of the pass is a second medieval **fortress** at Platamónas, this time built by the Crusaders.

Platamónas marks the beginning of **Macedonia** and heralds a rather grim succession of resorts fronting the narrow, pebbly beaches of the Thermaíkos gulf. The coast south of the castles is a better bet (see below). Inland, the mountain spectacle continues, with **Mount Olympus** (Óros Ólimbos) casting ever-longer shadows; the trailhead for climbing it is Litóhoro, 7km to the north (see p.351).

Stómio and the Óssa Coast

A side road, close by the Kástro tis Oreás, takes you the 13km to **STÓMIO**, an attractive seaside town at the mouth of the river Piniós. The dense beech trees of Óssa march down almost to the shore, giving Stómio almost the appearance of a mountain rather than coastal village. It's a fine spot for birdwatchers and swimmers can bathe in clear waters, while gazing at Mount Olympus, visible to the north.

Outside July and August – when Stómio draws big crowds – you shouldn't have any trouble finding **accommodation**. Choose from private rooms with *Vounda* (☎0495/91 256; ②), near the start of the seafront, next to a bakery; *Pension Anatoli* (☎0495/91 350; ③); and *Hotel Argithea* (☎0495/91 323; ④). The free municipal **campsite** behind the beach is popular with camper-vans, but a bit squalid, offering cold-water sinks and toilets only, though there are showers on the beach. The high street (closed to traffic in the evenings) has two reliable grill-cafés, facing each other, dishing up chicken and lamb kebab – a Thessalian speciality – by weight. Five minutes' walk along the seafront, a clutch of fish tavernas and bars are the focus of Stómio's low-key nightlife.

Down the coast towards the Pílion, Kókkino Neró and Koutsópia have smaller beaches and are both rather scruffy resorts for Larissans and Trikalans. Ayiókambos, southeast of the attractive Óssa hill villages of Ayiá and Melívia, gets a more international crowd. All three beaches are served by bus from Lárissa, and Ayiókambos boasts a beach, a campsite and several pensions.

West from Lárissa: Tríkala and Píli

West from Lárissa, the road trails the river Piniós to **Tríkala**, a quiet provincial town with a scattering of Byzantine monuments nearby. For most travellers, it is simply a staging post en route to Kalambáka and the Metéora; five buses daily connect it with Lárissa and there are connections north and west also. The railway loops around between Vólos, Lárissa, Tríkala and Kalambáka, via the uninteresting market town of Kardhítsa.

Tríkala

TRÍKALA is quite a lively metropolis after the agricultural towns of central Thessaly, spread along the banks of the Lethéos, a tributary of the Piniós, and backed by the mountains of the Koziakas range. It was the main town of the nineteenth-century Turkish province and retains numerous houses from that era, stacked around the clock tower at the north end of town. Downriver from the bus station, a minaret-less and very neglected Turkish mosque, the **Koursoum Tzami**, survives, too, a graceful accompaniment to the town's numerous stone-built churches.

The town's **fortress**, a Turkish adaptation of a Byzantine structure, is closed to the public, but around it are attractive gardens, a pleasantly shaded café and the meagre remains of a **sanctuary of Asclepius**; according to some accounts, the cult of the healing god originated here (see p.160). The liveliest part of town, encompassing the **bazaar**, is in the streets around the central Platía Iróön Politehníou on the riverside.

Practicalities

The **post office** and **OTE** are situated off Platía Iróön Politehníou. The **bus station** is on the west bank of the river, 300m southeast of the square; the **train station** is found at the southwestern edge of town, at the end of Odhós Asklipíou. Accommodation should pose few problems, with two decent and inexpensive **hotels** across the river from the main square in the lively area around Platía Ríga Feréou: the rock-bottom *Panhellinion*, Vassilísis Olgas 2 (☎0431/27 644; ②), and the rather more comfortable *Palladion*, Víronos 4 (☎0431/28 091; ③). Other mid-range alternatives include the *Lithaeon*, Óthonos 18 (☎0431/20 690; ④), and the slightly cushier *Hotel Dina*, on the corner of Asklipíou and Karanasíou, near the square (☎0431/74 777; ④).

Aside from a rash of *ouzerí*-bars in the old bazaar, **restaurants** are scarce. The best lunch to be had is at *O Elatos*, at the junction of Asklipíou and Víronos in the pedestrian zone behind the hotels, while *Taverna O Babis*, next to *Hotel Dina*, is good for a classier, pricier meal. There is no shortage of cafés and bars as well as some good *zaharoplastía* along Asklipíou; if you have time to spare, take a look at the traditional Thessalian cheese shop *Galaktos Batayanni*, on parallel Adhám 10 – recognizable from its range of goatbells hanging up.

Píli

It takes some effort of will to delay immediate progress to Kalambáka and the Metéora. Byzantine aficionados, however, may be tempted by a detour to **PÍLI**, 20km southwest of Tríkala, for the thirteenth-century church of **Pórta Panayía**, one of the unsung beauties of Thessaly, in a superb setting at the beginning of a gorge. Nearby, there is an outstanding cycle of frescoe at the monastery of **Ayíou Visariónos Dousíkou** (men only admitted), which would be a major tourist attraction were it not overshadowed by its spectacular neighbour, Metéora.

Regular **buses** run to the village from Tríkala. Near Pórta Panayía and beside a fountain-fed oasis there are two **tavernas** – a far nicer lunch stop than Tríkala; in the village there is a single **hotel**, the *Babanara* (☎0431/22 325; ③).

The Pórta Panayía

The **Pórta Panayía** (summer 8am–noon & 4–8pm; winter 9am–1pm & 3–5pm; 100dr) is a ten-minute walk uphill from the bus-stop in Píli village. Cross the Portaikós River on the foot bridge, then bear left on the far bank until you see its dome in a clump of trees below the rough road; a slightly longer route is via the roadbridge. The caretaker lives in a white house below the nearby tavernas.

Much of the church was completed in 1283 by one Ioannis Doukas, a prince of the Despotate of Epirus. Its architecture is somewhat bizarre, in that the current narthex is probably a fourteenth-century Serbian remodelling of the original dome and transept. The original nave on its west side collapsed in an earthquake, and its replacement to the east gives the whole a "backwards" orientation. In the Doukas section, perpendicular barrel vaults over a narrow transept and more generous nave lend antiseismic properties, with further support from six columns. The highlights of the interior are a pair of **mosaic icons** depicting Joseph and Mary with the Child, both showing extensive westernizing influences, and a marble iconostasis, which unusually (for Orthodox iconography) shows Christ on the left of the Virgin. The **frescoes** have fared less well and many of the figures are peppered with holes, probably from bullets. The most interesting image is next to the tiny font, over Ioannis Doukas's tomb, where a lunette shows the Archangel Michael leading a realistically portrayed Doukas by the hand to the enthroned Virgin with Child.

A kilometre upstream, best reached along the Píli bank of the river (there are savage dogs beyond the church), a graceful **medieval bridge** spans the Portaïkós at the point where it exits a narrow mountain gorge. A couple of cafés and snack bars take advantage of the setting, and you can cross the bridge to follow paths some distance along the gorge on the opposite side, although the tranquil beauty is set to be shattered by the construction of a couple of hotels.

Ayíou Visariónos Dousíkou

The monastery of **Ayíou Visariónos Dousíkou** – known locally as Aï Vissáris – has a stunning setting, 500m up a flank of Mount Kóziakas, looking out over most of Thessaly. The small community of monks is keen to maintain its isolation, excluding women from visits, and admitting men only with suspicion; in theory, visits are allowed from 8am to noon and 3.30pm to 7.30pm, with preference given to Orthodox and/or Greek speakers. To reach the monastery, cross the road bridge over the Portaïkós as for Pórta Panayía, but turn right instead, then left almost instantly onto a signed dirt track which leads up for 4km.

The monastery was founded in 1530 by Visarionos (Bessarion), a native of Píli, and contains a perfect **cycle of frescoes** by Tzortzis – one of the major painters on Mount Athos – executed between 1550 and 1558 and recently restored to brilliance. These, and the cloister as a whole, miraculously escaped damage in 1940, when two Italian bombs fell in the court but failed to explode.

Originally, the monastery perched on a cliff as steep as any at Metéora, but in 1962 the abyss was largely filled in with kitchen gardens and a new road and gate opened. This rendered ornamental the pulleys and ladder on the east, which, like much of the place, had survived intact since its foundation. In its heyday, nearly three hundred monks lived at the monastery; currently there are around ten.

The Monasteries of the Metéora

The **Monasteries of the Metéora** are one of the great sights of mainland Greece. These extraordinary buildings, perched on seemingly inaccessible pinnacles of rock, occupy a valley just to the north of **Kalambáka**; the name *metéora* means literally "rocks in the air". Arriving at the town, your eye is drawn in an unremitting vertical ascent to the first weird grey cylinders. Overhead to the right you can make out the closest of the monasteries, Ayíou Stefánou, firmly entrenched on a massive pedestal; beyond stretch a chaotic confusion of spikes, cones and cliffs – beaten into bizarre and otherworldly shapes by the action of the prehistoric sea that covered the plain of Thessaly around thirty million years ago.

Some history

The Meteorite monasteries are as enigmatic as they are spectacular. Legend has it that **Saint Athanasios**, who founded Megálou Meteórou (the Great Meteoron), the earliest of the buildings, flew up to the rocks on the back of an eagle. More rational interpretations of their history suggest that the villagers of Stáyi, the medieval precursor of Kalambáka, may have become adept at climbing, and helped the original monks up. Whatever, the difficulties of access and building are hard to overstate; a German guide published for rock climbers grades almost all the Metéora routes as "advanced", even with modern high-tech climbing gear.

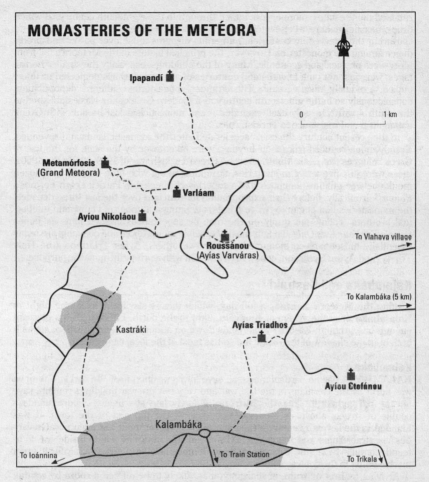

MONASTERIES OF THE METÉORA

Ipapandí

Metamórfosis
(Grand Meteora)

Varláam

Ayíou Nikoláou

Roussánou
(Ayías Varváras)

To Vlahava village

To Kalambáka (5 km)

Kastráki

Ayías Triadhos

Ayíou Ctefánou

Kalambáka

To Ioánnina

To Train Station

To Tríkala

0   1 km

The earliest religious communities here appeared in the late tenth century, when groups of **hermits** made their homes in the caves that score many of the rocks. In 1336 they were joined by two monks from Mount Athos, **Gregorios**, Abbot of Magoula, and his companion, **Athanasios**. Gregorios returned shortly to Athos but he left Athanasios behind, ordering him to establish a monastery. This Athanasios did, whether supernaturally aided or not, and despite imposing a particularly austere and ascetic rule he was quickly joined by many brothers, including, in 1371, **John Paleologos**, who refused the throne of Serbia to become the monk Ioasaph.

Such a royal presence was an important aid to the **endowment** of the monasteries, which followed swiftly on all the accessible and many of the inaccessible rocks. They reached their zenith during the Ottoman reign of Süleyman the Magnificent (1520–66), by which time 24 of the rocks had been surmounted by monasteries and hermitages. The major establishments accumulated great wealth, flourishing on revenues of estates granted them in distant Wallachia and Moldavia, as well as in Thessaly itself. They retained these estates, more or less intact, through to the eighteenth century, at which time monasticism here, as elsewhere in Greece, was in decline.

During the intervening centuries, numerous disputes arose over power and precedence among the monasteries. However, the principal factors in the Metéora's fall from glory were physical and economic. Many of the buildings, especially the smaller hermitages, were just not built to withstand centuries of use and, perhaps neglected or unoccupied, gradually disintegrated. The grander monasteries suffered depopulation, conspicuously so in the nineteenth century as a modern Greek state was established to the south – with Thessaly itself excluded – and monasticism lost its link with Greek nationalism and resistance to Turkish rule.

In the present century the crisis accelerated after the monastic lands and revenues, already much reduced from their heyday, were taken over by the state for the use of Greek refugees from Asia Minor, after the Greco-Turkish war of 1919–22. By the 1950s, there were just five active monasteries, struggling along with little more than a dozen monks between them – an epoch that's superbly chronicled in Patrick Leigh Fermor's *Roumeli*. Ironically, before their expropriation for **tourism** over the last three decades, the monasteries had begun to revive a little, attracting a number of young and intellectual brothers. Today, put firmly on the map by appearances in such films as James Bond's *For Your Eyes Only*, the four most accessible monasteries and convents are today essentially museum-piece monuments. Only two others, **Ayías Triádhos** (the Holy Trinity) and **Ayíou Stefánou**, continue to function with a primarily monastic purpose.

Kalambáka and Kastráki

Visiting the Metéora demands a full day, which means staying at least one night in **Kalambáka** or at the village of **Kastráki**, 2km to the north. Either makes a pleasant enough base, though Kastráki wins hands down on atmosphere and situation, set as it is right in the shadow of the rocks. It also has most of the local campsites.

Kalambáka

KALAMBÁKA has no particular appeal, save for its position near the rocks. The town was burnt by the Germans in the last war and very few pre-war buildings remain, save for the old cathedral. This, the **Mitrópolis** (daily late afternoons; 200dr) stands a couple of streets above its modern successor, at the top end of the town. It was founded in the seventh century on the site of a temple to Apollo and incorporates various classical drums and fragments in its erratically designed walls. Inside are fourteenth-century Byzantine frescoes and, most unusually in a Greek church, a great marble pulpit in the central aisle.

Arriving by **bus or train**, in season, you are likely to be offered a **room** by waiting householders – often the Totis family, who have three separate premises (☎0432/22 251 or 23 588; ③). If not, there are numerous signs on the road into town from the bus station. The dozen or so **hotels** have little to distinguish them – they all have a tendency to noise, with minimal views and character and above-average rates, reflecting the tourist status of the Metéora. Least expensive, and fairly quiet, is the *Astoria*, Kondhíli 93 (☎0432/22 213; ②), in sight of the train station; mid-budget options include the *Odyssion* (☎0432/22 320; ④) and the *Helvetia* (☎0432/23 041; ④), both bunker-like establishments on the road to Kastráki, with only views to redeem them.

Kastráki

KASTRÁKI is twenty minutes' walk out of Kalambáka; there's a short cut if you follow a footpath out of the northwest corner of the town. In season there are occasional buses.

Along the way to the village you pass the first of two **campsites** here, *Camping Vrahos* (☎0432/22 293), with an English-speaking **rock-climbing** school, *Climb a Rock* (fax 0432/23134), on the premises. The other, *Camping Boufidhis/The Cave*, is a bit more cramped but incomparably set on the far side of the village, with the monasteries of Ayíou Nikoláou and Roussánou rearing above. Both have swimming pools, as do the other two more distant sites out on the Tríkala and Ioánnina roads.

The village has literally hundreds of **rooms** for rent (all around ③), and nearly as many **places to eat**. Arrayed around the central church and *platía*, are four reasonable tavernas, of which *Gardhenia* is probably the best.

Visiting the monasteries

There are six Metéora monasteries, each open to visits at slightly different hours (see below). To see them all in a day, start early to take in Ayíou Nikoláou, Varlaám and Megálou Meteórou before 1pm, leaving the rest of the day for Roussánou, Ayías Triádhos and Ayíou Stefánou.

The road route from **Kastráki to Ayíou Stefánou** is just under 10km. Walking, you can veer off the tarmac occasionally onto a few short-cut paths; at Ayíou Stefánou the "circuit" stops (the road signposted Kalambáka just before Ayías Triádhos is a highly indirect 5km), though there is a walkers' path from here back to Kalambáka. In season there are a couple of daily buses from Kalambáka up the road as far as Megálou Meteórou/Varlaám; even taken just part of the way they will give you the necessary head start to make a hiking day manageable. Hitching is also pretty straightforward.

Before setting out it is worth buying **food and drink** to last the day; there are only a couple of drinks/fruit stands on the circuit, by Varlaám and Megálou Meteórou. And finally, don't forget to carry money with you: each monastery levies an admission charge – currently 300–400dr depending on the monastery, with students half price except at Ayías Triádhos.

For visits to all the monasteries, **dress code** is strict. For women this means wearing a skirt – not trousers; for men, long trousers. Both sexes must cover their shoulders. Skirts are often lent to female visitors, but it's best not to count on this.

Doupianí and Ayíou Nikoláou Anapavsás

North from Kastráki the road loops around between huge outcrops of rock, passing below the chapel-hermitage of **Doupianí**, the first communal church of the early monastic settlements. This stretch takes around twenty minutes to walk from the centre of Kastráki. A further ten minutes and you reach a stepped path to the left, which winds around and up a low rock, on which is sited **Ayíou Nikoláou Anapavsás** (daily summer 9am–6pm; winter 9am–1pm & 3–5pm). A small, recently restored monastery, this has some superb sixteenth-century frescoes in its *katholikón* (main chapel) by the Cretan painter Theophanes. Oddly, the *katholikón* faces almost due north rather than east because of the rock's shape. As well as the Theophanes paintings there are later, naive-style images that show Adam naming the animals, including a basilisk – the legendary lizard-like beast that could kill by a breath or glance. Ayíou Nikoláou is also accessible, more directly, by dirt track and path, directly from the *platía* of Kastráki in fifteen minutes.

Next to Ayíou Nikoláou, on a needle-thin shaft, sits **Ayía Moní**, inaccessible now, ruined and empty since an earthquake in 1858.

Roussánou

Bearing off to the right, fifteen minutes or so further on from Ayíou Nikoláou, a well-signed and cobbled path ascends to the tiny and compact convent of **Roussánou** (daily, summer 9am–6pm; winter 9am–1pm & 3.30–6pm), also known as Ayías Varváras; from another descending trail off a higher loop of road, the final approach is across a dizzying bridge from an adjacent rock. Roussánou has perhaps the most extraordinary site of all the monasteries, its walls built right on a knife edge. Inside, the narthex of its main chapel, or *katholikón*, has particularly gruesome seventeenth-century frescoes of martyrdom and judgement, the only respite from sundry beheadings, spearings and mutilations being the lions licking Daniel's feet in his imprisonment, near the window.

A short way beyond Roussánou the road divides, the left fork heading towards Varlaám and the Megálou Meteórou. Both monasteries are also more directly accessible on foot via a partly cobbled and shaded path leading off the road, 250m past Ayíou Nikoláou; twenty minutes up this path bear right at a T-junction to reach Varlaám in ten minutes, or left for Megálou Meteórou within twenty steeper minutes.

Varlaám (Balaam)

Varlaám (daily except Fri, 9am–1pm & 3.20–6pm) is one of the earliest-established monasteries, standing on the site of a hermitage established by Saint Varlaam – a key figure in Meteorite history – shortly after Athanasios's arrival. The present building was founded by two brothers from Ioánnina in 1517 and is one of the most beautiful in the valley.

The monastery's *katholikón*, dedicated to Ayíon Pándon (All Saints), is small but glorious, supported by painted beams and with walls and pillars totally covered in frescoes. A dominant theme, well suited to the Metéora, are the desert ascetics; more conventionally, there are martyrdoms, a highly vivid *Last Judgement*, with a gaping Leviathan swallowing the Damned, and, dominating the hierarchy of paintings, a great *Pandokrátor* (Christ in Majesty) in the inner of two domes; they were painted in 1548 and 1566. In the refectory is a small museum of icons, inlaid furniture and textiles; elsewhere the monks' original water barrel is displayed.

Varlaám also retains intact its old **Ascent Tower**, with a precipitous reception platform and dubious windlass mechanism. Until the 1920s the only way of reaching most of the Meteorite monasteries was by being hauled up in a net drawn by rope and windlass, or by the equally perilous retractable ladders. Patrick Leigh Fermor, who stayed at Varlaám in the 1950s, reported the anecdote of a former abbot; asked how often the rope was changed, he gave the macabre, if logical, reply: "When it breaks."

Steps were eventually cut to all of the monasteries on the orders of the Bishop of Tríkala, doubtless unnerved by the vulnerability of his authority on visits. Today the ropes are used only for carrying up supplies and building materials.

Megálou Meteórou (Great Meteoron)

The **Megálou Meteórou** (daily except Tues, 9am–1pm & 3.20–6pm) is the grandest and highest of the monasteries, built on the "Broad Rock" some 600m above sea level. It had extensive privileges and held sway over the area for several centuries; in an eighteenth-century engraving (displayed in the museum) it is depicted literally towering above the others. How Athanasios got onto this rock is a wonder.

The monastery's **katholikón**, dedicated to the *Metamórfosis* (Transfiguration), is the most magnificent in Metéora, a beautiful cross-in-square church, its columns and beams supporting a lofty dome with another *Pandokrátor*. It was rebuilt in the sixteenth century, with the original chapel, constructed by Athanasios and Ioasaph, forming just the *ierón*, the sanctuary behind the intricately carved *témblon*, or altar screen. Frescoes, however, are much later than those of the preceding monasteries and not as significant artistically; those in the narthex concentrate almost exclusively on grisly martyrdoms. The other monastery rooms comprise a vast, arcaded cluster of buildings. The *Kellari* or storage cellar holds an exhibit of rural impedimenta, including a stuffed wolf; in the domed and vaulted refectory is a **museum**, featuring a number of exquisite carved-wood crosses, rare icons and an incense-burner, made from a conch shell, as well as a calendar of saints in wood. The ancient domed and smoke-blackened kitchen can also be visited.

Ipapandí, Ayías Triádhos and Ayíou Stefánou

If you are visiting the valley in midsummer, you may by this point be impressed by the buildings but depressed by the crowds, which blur much of the wild, spiritual romance of the valley. The remaining monasteries on the "east loop" are less visited, or for a real escape, you can take a path leading north from just past the Varlaám/Great Meteora fork which will bring you out, in around half an hour's walk, at the abandoned four-teenth-century monastery of **Ipapandí**, a church huddled inside a small cave.

Following the main road, it's about thirty minutes' walk from the Varlaám/Great Meteora fork to **Ayías Triádhos** (daily 9am–6pm), whose final approach consists of 130 steps carved into a tunnel in the rock. You emerge into a light and airy cloister, recently renovated, though a new winch and water system are still needed. There's a small folk museum of weavings and kitchen/farm implements, but in general less to be seen than elsewhere – many of the frescoes in the *katholikón* are black with soot and damp, a project to clean and restore them having stalled at an early stage. Most tour buses, mercifully, do not stop here, and the life of the place remains essentially monastic – even if there are only three brothers to maintain it.

Ayíou Stefánou (daily except Mon, 9am–1pm and 3.20–6pm), the last and easternmost of the monasteries, is twenty minutes' walk beyond here, appearing suddenly at a bend in the road. Again it is active, occupied this time by nuns, but the buildings are a little disap-pointing. The *katholikón* is whitewashed and simple, while the rock on which it stands is spanned by a bridge from the road. Its view, of course, is amazing – like every turn and twist of this valley – but if you're pushed for time it's the obvious one to leave out.

Although Ayías Triádhos teeters above a deep ravine and the little garden ends in a precipitous drop, there is an obvious, well-signposted **path** at the bottom of the monastery's steps that leads **back to Kalambáka**. This is about three kilometres in length, saving a long trudge back around the circuit; it's a partly cobbled, all-weather surface in decent shape.

On from Kalambáka

West from Kalambáka runs one of the most dramatic roads in Greece, negotiating the **Katára Pass** across the Píndhos mountains to Métsovo and Ioánnina. This route, taking you into northern Epirus, is covered at the beginning of the next chapter.

North from Kalambáka a road leads into Macedonia, through Grevená and then forks: north to Kastoriá, or east to Siátista, Kozáni, Véria and Thessaloníki (see *The North: Macedonia and Thrace*). The **Grevená road**, despite its uncertain appearance on most maps, is quite reasonable; its only drawback is that there are just two daily buses to dull Grevená itself, and not a lot of other transport. Finally, there's a possible side trip into the mountains west of Metéora to visit one of Greece's most peculiar churches.

The church of Timíou Stavroú

If you have your own transport, the flamboyant medieval **church of Timíou Stavroú**, 42km northwest from Kalambáka, between the villages of Kranía (Kranéa on some maps) and Dholianá, is well worth a visit. The church itself, eighteenth century but seeming far older, is a masterpiece of whimsy, matched in concept only by two specimens in Romania and Russia. It sports no less than twelve turret-like cupolas, higher than they are wide; three are over the nave, one over each of the three apses, and six over the ends of the triple transept. The church is in perfect repair, despite some ill-advised restoration and bull dozing, and a terrace below with a fountain makes an ideal picnic spot.

To reach it, head 10km north of Kalambáka and instead of taking the Métsovo/Ioánnina-bound highway, bear left into a narrower road with multiple signposts for high villages. Climb steadily over a pass on the shoulder of Mount Tringía and then drop sharply into the densely forested valley of the River Aspropótamos, one of the loveliest in the Píndhos. From the *Psistaria Aspropotamos* grill-taverna, continue 1500m further south to a tiny bridge and a signposted track on the left which leads after 500m to the church, at a height of 1150m. There's an afternoon bus from Tríkala to Kranía most days in the summer, but you'll have to overnight at the *Hotel Monastiri* (③).

travel details

Trains

Athens–Thíva–Livádhia–Lianokládhi (Lamía)–Lárissa

14 trains daily, in each direction: some expresses (marked *IC* on schedules) don't stop at Thíva or Livádhia.

Approximate journey times:

Athens–Thíva (1hr 15min)

Thíva–Livádhia (30min)

Livádhia–Lianokládhi (1hr–2hr)

Lianokládhi–Lárissa (1hr 30min–2hr 30min).

Lárissa–Kateríni–Thessaloníki 10 daily in each direction.

Approximate journey times:

Lárissa–Kateríni (1hr 10min)

Kateríni–Thessaloníki (1hr 10min).

Vólos–Lárissa–Platamónas–Litóhoro– Kateríni–Thessaloníki 3 daily in each direction; all involve a change of trains in Lárissa.

Approximate journey times:

Vólos–Lárissa (1hr 10min)

Lárissa–Platamónas (45min)

Platamónas–Litóhoro (25min)

Litóhoro–Kateríni (15–30min)

Kateríni–Thessaloníki (1hr 30min).

Lárissa–Vólos 15 daily in each direction (1hr 10min).

Vólos–Fársala–Kardhítsa–Tríkala– Kalambáka 5 daily in each direction.

Approximate journey times:

Vólos–Farsála (1hr 30min)

Farsála–Kardhítsa (1 hr)

Kardhítsa–Tríkala (30min)

Tríkala–Kalambáka (20min).

Buses

Buses detailed have similar frequency in each direction, so entries are given just once; for reference check under both starting-point and destination.

Connections with Athens Thíva/Livádhia (hourly; 1hr 30min/2hr 10min); Dhelfí (4–6 daily; 3hr 30min); Lamía (hourly; 3hr 15min); Karpeníssi (2 daily; 6hr); Vólos (9 daily; 4hr 30min); Lárissa (6 daily; 5hr); Tríkala (7 daily; 5hr 30min).

Ámfissa to: Lamía (3–4 daily; 2hr 30min).

Andírio to: Messolóngi/Agrínio (12 daily; 1hr 30min).

Dhelfí to: Itéa (5 to 9 daily; 30min); Ámfissa (4 daily; 40min); Náfpaktos (4 daily – not direct; 2hr).

Elefsína to: Thíva [Thebes] (2 daily; 1hr 30min).

Itéa to: Galaxídhi/Náfpaktos (4 daily; 30min/1hr 30min).

Kalambáka to: Métsovo/Ioánnina (3 daily; 1hr 30min/3hr 30min); Grevená (2 daily; 1hr 30min); Vólos (4 daily; 2hr 30 min).

Karpeníssi to: Agrínio (1 or 2 daily; 3hr 30min).

Lamía to: Karpeníssi (4 daily; 2hr); Vólos (2 daily; 3hr); Lárissa (4 daily; 3hr 30min); Tríkala, via Kardhítsa (4 daily; 3hr); Thessaloníki (2 daily; 4hr 30min).

Lárissa to: Stómio (3 daily; 1hr 25min); Litóhoro junction (almost hourly; 1hr 45min); Tríkala (every half-hour; 1hr); Kalambáka (hourly; 2hr).

Livádhia to: Aráhova/Delphi (6 daily; 40min/1hr); Dhístomo, for Óssios Loukás (10 daily; 45min); Óssios Loukás, direct (daily at 1pm; 1hr).

Náfpaktos: City bus to Andírio for most connections.

Thíva to: Livádhia (hourly; 1hr); Halkídha (2 daily; 1hr 20min).

Tríkala to: Kalambáka (hourly; 30min); Kalambáka–Métsovo–Ioánnina (3 daily; 30min/ 2hr/4hr); Kalambáka–Grevená (2 daily; 30min/2hr).

Vólos to: Lárissa (hourly; 1hr 30min); Tríkala (4 daily; 2hr 30min); Thessaloníki (4 daily; 3hr 20min); Portaría/Makrinítsa (9 daily; 40min/50min); Zagorá (4 daily; 2hr); Tsangarádha/Áyios Ioánnis (2 daily; 2hr/2hr 30min); Miliés/Vizítsa (6 daily; 1hr/1hr 10min); Plataniás (3 daily; 2hr); Tríkeri (2 daily; 2hr).

Ferries

Áyios Konstandínos to: Skiáthos (daily; 2hr 30min), Skópelos (daily; 3hr 30min) and Alónissos (daily; 4hr 40min); ☎0235/31 920 for information.

Vólos to: Skiáthos (2–4 daily; 2hr 30min–3hr) and Skópelos (2–4 daily; 4–5hr), at least one continuing to Alónissos (5–6hr); at least one daily to Tríkeri and Tríkeri island (☎0421/31 059 for information). Also twice weekly to Thessaloníki.

To Évvia Arkítsa–Loutrá Edhípsou (hourly, half as often in winter, last at 11pm/8pm; 50min); Glífa-Ayiókambos (8 daily, 4 in winter; last at 8.15pm/5pm; 30min).

Across the Gulf of Kórinthos Andírio–Río (every 15min, much less often after midnight; 20min); Áyios Nikólaos–Éyio (3 times daily, 5 in summer; 35–40min).

Hydrofoils

Flying Dolphins run from the following ports:

Áyios Konstandínos At least 3 daily in season to Skiáthos, Skópelos and Alónissos, some stopping at Tríkeri, Paleó Tríkeri and Plataniás on the South Pílion.

Plataniás At least 2 daily in season to Skiáthos, Skópelos and Alónissos.

Stilídha 4 weekly in season to Skiáthos, Skópelos and Alónissos. Also to Plataniás on Pílion and Vólos.

Tríkeri and Paleó Tríkeri At least 2 daily in season to Skiáthos, Skópelos and Alónissos.

Vólos 2–4 daily in season to Skiáthos, Skópelos and Alónissos, with three weekly continuing to Skíros; last reliable departure to Skiáthos usually mid-afternoon; at least one daily stops at Plataniás, Tríkeri and Paleó Tríkeri.

For details of services, which vary drastically with the seasons, your best bet is to contact local agents (in Áyios Konstandínos ☎0235/31 614; in Vólos ☎0241/39 786; in Plataniás ☎0423/71 231; in Tríkeri ☎0423/91 556).

CHAPTER FOUR

EPIRUS AND THE WEST

E pirus (*Ípiros* in modern Greek) has the strongest regional identity in mainland Greece. It owes this character to its mountains: the rugged peaks and passes, forested ravines and turbulent rivers of the **Píndhos** (Pindus) **range**. They have protected and isolated Epirus from outside interference, securing it a large measure of autonomy even under Turkish rule.

Because of this isolation, the region's role in Greek affairs was peripheral in ancient times. There are just two archeological sites of importance, both of them oracles chosen for their end-of-the-world isolation. At **Dodona**, the sanctuary includes a spectacular Classical theatre; at **Ephyra**, the weird remains of a Necromanteion (Oracle of the Dead) was touted by the ancients as the gateway to Hades.

In more recent times, **Lord Byron** has been the region's greatest publicist. Byron visited in 1809 when the tyrannical ruler Ali Pasha was at the height of his power, and the poet's tales of passionate intrigue, fierce-eyed brigandage and colourful braggadocio came just at the right moment to send a frisson of horror down romantic western spines. The poet went on to distinguished himself in the southern province of **Étolo-Akarnanía** by supplying and training troops for the Greek War of Independence, and of course dying at **Messolóngi**.

Despite eventual Greek victory in the War of Independence, the Turks remained in Epirus, and were not finally ousted until 1913. A disputed frontier territory throughout the nineteenth century, the region never recovered its medieval prosperity. When the Italians invaded in 1940, followed by the Germans in 1941, its mountains became first the stronghold of the Resistance, then a battleground for rival political factions, and finally, after 1946, the chief bastion of the Communist Democratic Army in the **civil war**. The events of this period (see the box overleaf) are among the saddest of modern Greek history, and continue to reverberate today.

However, the **mountains** are still the place to head for in Epirus. The people are the friendliest and most hospitable you could find, and many aspects of their traditional way of life are still in force. Latinate-speaking Vlach and Doric-speaking Sarakatsan shepherds (see "Greek Minorities" in *Contexts*) still bring their flocks to the high mountain pastures in summer. Bears leave footprints on riverbanks or raid beehives, risking an (illegal) bullet in the head, while wolves keep a hungry eye out for stray ewes.

The best single area to visit is around **mounts Gamíla** and **Smólikas**, with the **Aóös** and **Víkos gorges** to walk through and the splendid **villages of the Zagóri** to stay in. You have to explore on foot to get a full flavour of the place, and not surprisingly the Píndhos is now a popular hiking ground.

Some of the road routes offer less strenuous travelling highlights – above all the Kalambáka–Ioánnina highway as it negotiates the **Katára pass**. En route is **Métsovo**, perhaps the easiest location for a taste of mountain life, though increasingly commercialized of late. **Ioánnina**, Ali Pasha's capital, is a town of some character, with its island and lake, and the main transport hub for trips into the Zagóri. Other than **Árta**, prettily set and with some fine Byzantine churches, there are few other urban attractions.

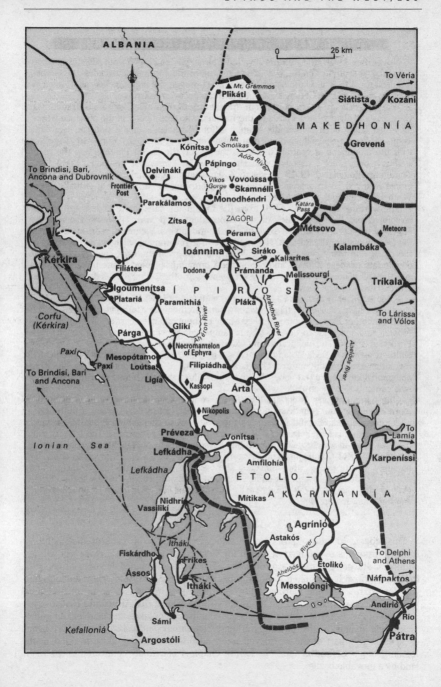

WORLD WAR II AND THE CIVIL WAR IN EPIRUS

In **November 1940**, the **Italians** invaded Epirus, pushing down from Albania as far as Kalpáki, just south of Kónitsa. United as a nation for the first time in decades, the Greeks repulsed the attack and humiliated Mussolini. However, the euphoria was short-lived as the following April the Germans attacked and rapidly overran Greece.

When parcelling out key portions of the country to their allies for administration, the Germans initially assigned Epirus to the Italians, who trod lightly in the province where they had lately been so soundly beaten. After Mussolini's capitulation the Germans assumed direct responsibility for Epirus, and conditions markedly worsened. Together with the mountains of central Greece to the south, the Epirot Píndhos was the main staging point for various **guerrilla bands**, foremost among them the Communist-dominated **ELAS**. Resistance harassment and ambush of the occupying forces incurred harsh reprisals, including the burning in early 1944 of virtually every Vlach village along the Aóös River.

The wartime flight to the cities from the mountains dates more or less from these atrocities, and the vicissitudes of the subsequent **civil war** (1946–49) dashed any lingering hope of a reasonable existence in the mountains. Victims of reprisals by either the Communists or the Royalist/Nationalist central government, villagers fled to safety in the cities, and many never returned. Wherever you go in the back country you'll hear people talk of these times. Some blame the Communists, some blame the Nationalists and they all blame the British: "They set us at each other's throats," they say, and with much justice.

Since 1975, many men (and a few women) who fought in ELAS, either as volunteers or conscripts, have returned to their villages – some of them after thirty years of exile in the USSR and other Eastern Bloc countries. Many of them had been carried off as children to Albania, and and made to work in labour camps before being distributed to various East European states. The political Right claim that this *pedhomázema* – the roundup of children – was a cynical and merciless ploy to train up an army of dedicated revolutionaries for the future. The Left retort that it was a prudent evacuation of noncombatants from a war zone. Which merely illustrates the futility of arguments over who committed more atrocities.

One thing, however, is certain. The Right won, with the backing of the British and, more especially, the Americans, and they used that victory to maintain a thoroughly undemocratic and vengeful regime for the best part of the following quarter-century. Many Epirot villagers, regardless of political conviction, believe that the poverty and backwardness in which their communities have remained was a deliberate punishment for being part of Communist-held territory during the civil war. They were constantly harassed by the police, who controlled the issue of all sorts of licences and permits needed to find work, travel, put children in better schools, run a business and so forth. Only during the 1980s did things really change, and the past begin to be treated as another, and separate, age.

The coast, in both Epirus and Étolo-Akarnanía, is in general disappointing. **Igoumenítsa** is a useful ferry terminal for Corfu and Italy, but otherwise will win few admirers. **Párga**, the major Epirot resort, has been developed beyond its capacity, though **Préveza** has retained some character against the odds and is now a major gateway for charter-package patrons. Between these two towns is a string of functional beaches and, just inland, a scenic highlight – the **gorge of the Aherónda River**.

South of Préveza, you enter a low, marshy landscape of lakes and land-locked gulfs – of interest mainly to the birdwatcher and fish-dinner enthusiast. For better beach escapes in this part of the world you need islands, fortunately close at hand in the Ionian group – **Lefkádha** (see *The Ionian* chapter) is actually connected to the mainland by a movable bridge.

THE PÍNDHOS MOUNTAINS

Even if you have no plans to go hiking, the **Píndhos range** deserves a few days' detour. The remoteness and traditional architecture, the air, the peaks – all constitute a very different Greece to the popular tourist image and, despite increasing popularity as a trekking destination, the range is relatively unspoilt.

If you are coming from central Greece, the best of the main routes is **Kalambáka–Métsovo–Ioánnina**, which divides the **north Píndhos** from the **south Píndhos**. If you are arriving by ferry at Igoumenítsa, getting up to **Ioánnina** enables you to reverse this itinerary, which is quite the most attractive route into the mainland. **Walkers** will want to make directly for the **Zagóri**, north of Ioánnina, where trekking excitements beckon.

A number of **hiking routes** are detailed in the text; others can be found in the specialist guides (see "Books" in *Contexts*). Most of the routes are arduous and lonesome, rather than dangerous. But all the same, this is high-mountain country, with rather unpredictable microclimates, and it's inadvisable to set off on the longer, more ambitious itineraries unless you are already familiar with basic trekking routines.

Kalambáka to Ioánnina

West of Kalambáka (see p.282), the 1694-metre **Katára pass** cuts across the central range of the Píndhos to link Thessaly and Epirus. This route, the only motor road across these mountains that is kept open in winter (except during blizzards), is one of the most spectacular in the country and worth taking for the sake of the journey alone. It is the shortest east–west crossing in Greece, though distances here are deceptive. The road switchbacks and zigzags through folds in the enormous peaks, which rise to more than 2300m around Métsovo, and from November to April the snowline must be crossed. All this, however, will soon be a bygone thing, as an enormous tunnel is being bored through the ridge here to spare drivers the dangerously curvy present highway.

Just three **buses** daily cover the entire route, running between Tríkala and Ioánnina, with stops at Kalambáka and Métsovo. If you're **driving**, allow half a day for the journey from Kalambáka to Ioánnina (114km), and in winter check on conditions before setting out. Anyone planning on **hitching** from Kalambáka should take a lift only if it's going through to Ioánnina or Métsovo, for there's little but mountain forest in between.

Métsovo

MÉTSOVO spreads just west of the Katára pass, and just off the Kalambáka–Ioánnina highway – a small, often rainy alpine town built on two sides of a ravine and guarded by a forbidding range of peaks to the south and east. This startling site is matched, albeit in a slightly showcase way, by a traditional architecture and way of life. Immediately below the highway begin tiers of eighteenth- and nineteenth-century stone houses with wooden balconies. The dwellings spill down the slope to and past the main *platía*, where a dwindling number of old men still loiter, especially after Sunday mass, magnificent in full traditional dress, from flat black caps to pompommed shoes; the women, enveloped in rich blue weave and a kerchief over a pair of braids, have a more subdued appearance.

If you arrive outside of the main summer season, stay overnight and take the time to walk in the valley below, the place can seem magical. During the summer, however, your experience may not be so positive. Métsovo has become a favourite target for bus tours, and its beauty veers perilously close to the artificially quaint. Souvenir shops selling "traditional" handcrafts (the weavings often imported from Albania these days) have proliferated, while the stone roofs of the mansions have been completely replaced by ugly pantiles.

Nonetheless, it would be a shame to pass through Métsovo too speedily, for its history and status as the Vlach "capital" (see "Greek Minorities" in *Contexts*) are unique. Positioned on the only commercially and militarily viable route across the Píndhos, it won a measure of independence, both political and economic, in the earliest days of Turkish rule. These privileges were greatly extended in 1659 by a grateful Turkish vizier who, restored to the sultan's favour, wanted to say a proper "thank you" to the Metsovite shepherd who had protected him during his disgrace.

Métsovo's continued prosperity, and the preservation of some of its traditions, are largely due to Baron Tosítsas, banker scion of a Metsovite family living in Switzerland, who left his colossal fortune to an endowment that benefits industries and crafts in and around the town.

The town and around

The Métsovo **museum** occupies the eighteenth-century **Arhondikó Tosítsa** (daily except Thurs 8.30am–1pm & 4–6pm; group tours every half-hour; 250dr), the old Tosítsa mansion just off the main thoroughfare. This has been restored to its full glory, and with its panelled rooms, rugs and fine collection of Epirot crafts and costumes, gives a real sense of the town's wealth and grandeur in that era.

The **Ídhrima Tosítsa** (Tosítsa Foundation) building down in the *platía* serves as an outlet for contemporary handicrafts, stocking some of the more tasteful and finely woven cloth, rugs and blankets to be found in Greece – no relation to most of the schlock in the souvenir stalls. They are expensive, but not outrageously so, considering the quality of the hand-weaving.

The other major Métsovo attraction is the relatively remote monastery of **Áyios Nikólaos**, signposted from the main *platía* but in fact twenty minutes' walk below town, just off the half-cemented-over *kalderími* headed for Anílio, the village across the ravine. The *katholikón* was built in the fourteenth century to a bizarre plan. It is topped by a simple barrel vault, and what might once have been the narthex became over time a *yinaikonítis* or women's gallery, something seen rarely elsewhere in Greece, except Kastoriá. The brilliant **frescoes**, mostly scenes from Christ's life and assorted martyrdoms, exhibit a highly unusual style dating from the eighteenth century, and were recently cleaned and illuminated courtesy of the Tosítsa Foundation. Since there is no dome, the Four Evangelists are painted on four partly recessed columns rather than on pendentives, as is the norm. The barrel vault features three medallions – the Virgin and Child, an Archangel and a Christ *Pandokrátor* (in Majesty) – an unusual series of iconographies. A warden couple live on the premises and receive visitors until 7.30pm. You'll be shown the monks' former cells, with insulating walls of mud and straw, and the abbot's more sumptuous quarters; a donation or purchase of post-cards is expected.

The village of **ANÍLIO** (Sunless) is a further half-hour down, then up, and you'll have to make the gruelling trek back the same way. Like Métsovo, its population is Vlach-speaking, and its life more genuinely traditional. There are no pretensions to tourist appeal, and its architecture is executed in dull cement. You can, however, get an excellent, reasonably priced lunch at the *platía* before starting back.

Practicalities

The **bus stop** is in the town centre, and though most departures are from here, a few, particularly the Tríkala–Ioánnina through service, merely pass by on the upper high-way. The **post office** is on the main street.

Métsovo has a wide range of **accommodation** with twelve hotels plus quite a few rooms and apartments for rent. Outside of the ski season, the town's festival (July 26) or late August, you should have little trouble in getting a bed or bargaining posted rates down a category. **Hotels** include the *Acropolis* (☎0656/41 672; ③), towards the upper highway, and the *Bitounis* (☎0656/41 545; ④), at the top of the main street. The *Athens*, just off the main *platía* (☎0656/41 217; ③), is an inexpensive and friendly hotel, with clean rooms and en-suite showers; it has a slightly fancier annexe called the *Filokseni* (☎0656/41 021; ③). The *Kassaros* (☎0656/41 346; ④) is comfortable, compact and quiet; some rooms have views over to Anílio.

Meals are overwhelmingly meat-oriented, as befits a pastoral centre. Two of the simpler grills are *Krifi Folia* on the main *platía*, and *Toh Arhondiko* directly behind the post office; both function only in the evening. At lunchtime especially, the *Athens* does good, reasonably priced casserole food, accompanied by decent house wine. *Toh Spitiko*, just downhill from the *Bitounis*, serves Metsovite specialities (including several vegetarian plates) at a fair price, washed down by excellent rosé from the barrel. Wine buffs may want to try the fabled *Katoyi*, available in some of these restaurants and in local shops – an expensive limited bottling from tiny vineyards down on the Árakhthos River.

Nightlife takes the form of a half-dozen conspicuously noisy pubs, cafés and a few discos uphill from the post office on the main street.

Villages of the upper Aóös valley

For a taste of wilder, remoter scenery, and a truer, grittier picture of contemporary mountain life, follow the road up into the Píndhos from the Baldhoúma junction on the Métsovo–Ioánnina highway. It is a precipitous road which snakes its way north along the valley of the Várdhas River, through a lush landscape of broad-leafed trees and scrub. At **GREVENÍTI**, the first of a series of predominantly Vlach villages, a black pine forest takes over and continues virtually all the way to Albania.

Greveníti and the neighbouring villages of **FLAMBOURÁRI** and **ELATOHÓRI** have basic *ksenónes* (inns) or rooms and places to eat, though the villages are badly depopulated, having failed to recover from wartime destruction inflicted by Germans in pursuit of Resistance fighters. What remains is very attractive: stone-roofed churches, vine-shaded terraces and courtyards full of flowers and logs stacked for winter. Best of all is the beautiful village of **MAKRINÓ** and its fine monastery, an hour's glorious walk across the ravine from Elatohóri.

The road continues, winding northeast to **VOVOÚSSA**, which lies right on the Aóös River, its milky green waters spanned here by a high-arched eighteenth-century bridge. On either side, wooded ridges rise steeply to the skyline. The village has a couple of *psistariés*, and a single (poorly stocked) shop, all of which are open more or less year-round. The large riverside **hotel**, the *Perivoli* (③), is worth a look for its layout alone. If you prefer to camp, turn left off the road onto the old path just past the Vovoússa roadsign, and walk for about fifteen minutes downstream to where a stretch of riverbank meadow makes an idyllic site, so long as the thought of bears in the vicinity doesn't alarm you. Fresh prints are often seen in the riverside mud here, but the locals swear they are timid creatures and avoid contact with humans.

There is a sporadic **bus** services to Vovoússa from Ioánnina at 2pm on Monday, Tuesday and Friday, returning to Ioánnina the next morning at 6am; Sunday out from Ioánnina at 7.30am, returning at 2pm. Alternatively, you could hike along the "E6", a marked long-distance trail through the Aóös River valley to Dhístrato on Smólikas, where there's an inn and early morning bus four days a week to Kónitsa (see p.307). The trail keeps to the east bank of the Aóös and takes a full day to accomplish.

Ioánnina and around

Descending from Métsovo, you approach **IOÁNNINA** through more spectacular folds of the Píndhos, emerging high above the great lake of **Pamvótis** (Pamvotídha). The town stands on a rocky promontory jutting out into the water, its fortifications punctuated by towers and minarets as if to declare its history. From this base, Ali Pasha carved from the Turks a fiefdom that encompassed much of western Greece – an act of contemptuous rebellion that portended wider defiance in the Greeks' own War of Independence.

Disappointingly, most of the city is modern and undistinguished – a testimony not so much to Ali Pasha, although he did burn much of it to the ground when under siege in 1820, as to developers in the 1950s. However, there are crumbling **mosques**, their minarets capped by storks' nests, to evoke the old Turkish atmosphere, and the fortifications of Ali Pasha's citadel, the Froúrio, survive more or less intact.

Ioánnina is also the jump-off point for visits to the **caves of Pérama**, some of Greece's largest, on the west shore of the lake, and the longer excursion to the mysterious and remote Oracle of Zeus at **Dodoni**.

ALI PASHA

Ali Pasha, a highly ambivalent "heroic rebel", was the major figure in Ioanninan and Epirot history. The so-called Lion of Ioánnina pursued a policy that was consistent only in its ambition and self-interest. His attacks on the Ottoman imperial government were matched by acts of appalling and vindictive savagery against his Greek subjects.

He was born in 1741 in Tepelene, Albania and rose to power under Turkish patronage, being made pasha of Tríkala in reward for his efforts in the sultan's war against Austria. His ambitions, however, were of a grander order and that same year, 1788, he seized Ioánnina, an important town since the thirteenth century, with a population of 30,000 – probably the largest in Greece at the time. Paying sporadic and usually token tribute to the sultan, he operated from this power-base for the next 33 years, allying in turn, and as the moment suited him, with the British, French and Turks.

In 1809, when his dependence upon the sultan was nominal, Ali was visited by the young **Lord Byron**, whom he overwhelmed with hospitality and attention. (The tyrant's sexual tastes were famously omnivorous, and it is recorded that he was particularly taken with the poet's "small ears", a purported mark of good breeding.) Byron, impressed for his part with the rebel's daring and stature, and the lively revival of Greek culture in Ioánnina (which, he wrote, was "superior in wealth, refinement and learning" to any town in Greece), commemorated the meeting in *Childe Harold*. The portrait that he draws, however, is an ambiguous one, well aware that beneath the Pasha's splendid court and deceptively mild countenance there were "deeds that lurk" and "stain him with disgrace".

In a letter to his mother Byron was more explicit, concluding that "His highness is a remorseless tyrant, guilty of the most horrible cruelties, very brave, so good a general that they call him the Mahometan Buonaparte . . . but as barbarous as he is successful, roasting rebels, etc, etc". Of the rebels, the most illustrious was Katsandonis the Klepht, who wracked by smallpox was captured by Ali in a cave in the Ágrafa mountains. He imprisoned the unfortunate wretch in a waterlogged lakeside dungeon, and finally executed him in public by breaking his bones with a sledgehammer.

Arrival and information

Ioánnina **airport** is on the road out to the Pérama caves; it's connected to town by city bus #8; all such buses leave Ioánnina from a stop below the central **Platía Pírrou**.

Arriving by **bus**, you'll find yourself at one of two terminals. The main station is at **Zozimádhou 4**, north of Platía Pírrou; this serves most points north and west, including

Métsovo, Kalambáka, Igoumenítsa, Kónitsa and the villages of the Zagóri. A smaller terminal at **Vizaníou 19** connects Árta, Préveza, Dodona and all villages in the south or east parts of Epirus. It is advisable, especially at weekends, to buy tickets for both coast and mountains the day before.

The axis of the town centre is the confusing, oddly angled jumble of streeets between Platía Pirroú and the **Froúrio**, Ali Pasha's old citadel. Near the latter is the old bazaar area – still in part an artesans' marketplace. Within sight of Platía Pírrou are most essential services: the **OTE, EOT** (Sept–June Mon–Fri 7.30am–2.30pm; additional hours July–Aug Mon–Fri 5.30–8.30pm & Sat 9am–2pm), **post office** (Oct–May Mon–Fri 7.30am–8pm; additional hours June–Sept Sat 9am–2pm) and **banks**.

Information on accommodation and bus timetables and departure points can be obtained at the friendly EOT office or at the **tourist police** both on 28 Oktovriou.

Accommodation

If you arrive early enough in the day, or book ahead, it is worth heading straight out to Nissí island (see below), where two adjoining **inns**, the *Sotiris Dellas* and the *Varvara Varaka*, offer the cheapest, most attractive accommodation available, otherwise there are plenty of **hotels** in town; choices are listed below. You will also find dozens of **rooms** as you walk to the caves from Pérama village.

Camping, unusually for a town, is an attractive alternative and *Camping Limnopoula*, 2km out of town on the Pérama road (city bus #2 or a 15–20min walk from Platía Mavíli), is a pleasant, mosquito-free site. Amenities are reasonable, but in summer it fills early in the day and is a bit cramped at the best of times.

Egnatia, Danglí 2 on corner of Aravandínou (☎0651/25 667). A decent hotel near Zozimádhou bus station, though favoured by trekking groups and often block booked. ④.

King Pyrros, Gounári 1, just off Platía Akadhimías (☎0651/27 652). Mid-range option with en-suite facilities; okay if you can get a room facing the pedestrianized side-street Goúnari, otherwise it's noisy. ④.

Metropolis, Kristálli 2 on corner of Avéroff (☎0651/26 207). Pretty basic, but clean enough budget hotel. ②.

Palladion, Botsári 1 (☎0651/25 856). The city's best hotel, and one of the quietest. ⑤.

Sotiris Dellas (☎0651/81 494). A good, cheap pension on Nissí; you'll find the owner at the house next to the school. ②.

Tourist, Kolétti 18 (☎0651/26 443). Around the corner from the *Metropolis*, but quieter and more comfortable; has a range of rooms with and without a bath. ②–③.

Varvara Varaka (☎0651/81 596). A good, cheap pension next to the *Sotiris Dellas* on Nissí; you'll find the owner at the house next to shut-down taverna *Saraï*. ②.

The Town

The **Froúrio** is an obvious point to direct your explorations. In its heyday the walls dropped abruptly to the lake, and were moated on their (southwest) landward side. The moat has been filled in, and a quay-esplanade now extends below the lakeside ramparts, but there is still the feel of a citadel.

Signs inside direct you to the **Popular Art Museum** (summer Mon–Sat 8am–8pm, Sun 9am–8pm; winter daily 8am–3pm; 550dr), an elegantly arranged collection of Epirot costumes, guns and jewellery. More poignant is a section devoted to synagogue rugs and tapestries recently donated by the dwindling Jewish community; the so-called Muslim wing features a mother-of-pearl suite, with the pipe of Esat Pasha, last Ottoman governor here. The museum is housed in the well-preserved **Aslan Pasha Tzami**, allowing a rare glimpse of the interior of a mosque; it retains the decoration on its dome and the recesses in the vestibule for the shoes of worshippers. In the adjacent quarters, tradition places Ali's rape and subsequent

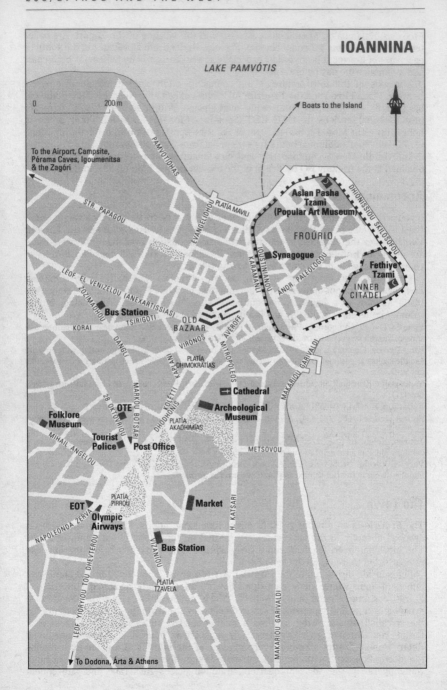

IOÁNNINA

LAKE PAMVÓTIS

0   200 m

➤ Boats to the Island

To the Airport, Campsite,
Pérama Caves, Igoumenitsa
& the Zagóri

PAMVOTIDHAS

STR. PAPAGOU

EVANGELIDHOU

PLATÍA MAVÍLI

Aslan Pasha
Tzami
(Popular Art Museum)

DHIONISSIOU SKILOSOFOU

FROÚRIO

IOUSTINIANOU

KARAMANLI

Synagogue

ANDR. PALEOLOGOU

Fethiye
Tzami

INNER
CITADEL

LEOF. EL VENIZELOU (ANEXARTISSIAS)

ZOZIMADHOU

Bus Station

KORAI

TSIRIGOTI

DANGLI

OLD
BAZAAR

VIRONOS

AVEROFF

MITROPOLEOS

PLATÍA
DHIMOKRATÍAS

MAKARIOU GARIVALDI

MARKOU BOTSARI

KOLETTI

KAPLANI

DHODHONIS

OTE

28 OKTOVRIOU

PLATÍA
AKADHIMIAS

Cathedral

Archeological
Museum

METSOVOU

Folklore
Museum

MIHAIL ANGELOU

Tourist
Police

Post Office

EOT

PLATÍA
PIRROU

Olympic
Airways

NAPOLEONDA ZERVA

Market

H. KATSARI

VLTANIOU

Bus Station

PLATÍA
TZAVELA

LEOF. YIORYIOU TOU DHEVTEROU

MAKARIOU GARIVALDI

➤ To Dodona, Árta & Athens

murder in 1801 of Kyra Phrosyne, the mistress of his eldest son. Her "provocation" had been to refuse the 62-year-old tyrant's sexual advances; together with seventeen of her companions, she was bound, weighted and thrown alive into Lake Pamvótis. The incident gave rise to several folk songs, and her ghost is still said to walk on the water on moonlit nights.

To the east of the Aslan Pasha Tzami is the **inner citadel** of the fortress. This was used for some years by the Greek military and most of its buildings – including Ali's palace where Byron was entertained – have unfortunately been adapted or restored to a point where they can no longer be recognized as eighteenth-century structures. A circular tower remains, however, along with the old **Fethiye Tzami** (Victory Mosque); Ali Pasha's tomb is purported to be close by.

Apart from the Froúrio, the town's most enjoyable quarter is that of the old **bazaar**, a roughly semicircular area focused on the citadel's gate. This has a cluster of Turkish-era buildings, as well as a scattering of copper- and tin-smiths, and the silver-smiths that were for centuries a mainstay of the town's economy.

Just off the central Platía Dhimokratías, set beside a small park behind the *National Bank*, is the well-lit and well-labelled **archeological museum** (Mon 12.30–7pm, Tues–Fri 8am–7pm, Sat & Sun 8.30am–3pm; 400dr). It's certainly a must if you're planning a visit to the theatre and oracle of Dodona, for on display here – along with some exceptional crafted bronze seals – is a fascinating collection of lead tablets inscribed with questions to the Oracle. Other standouts include ornate relief-carved Roman sarcophagi from Paramithía and Igoumenítsa, and among numerous bronze statuettes, two Hellenistic children respectively throwing a ball and holding a dove. The ancient collection is rounded off by burial finds and pottery from Ambracia (Árta), Acheron (the Necromanteion of Ephyra) and Vítsa; an incongruous modern-art collection at the rear is of minimal interest.

Nissí and Lake Pamvótis

The island of **Nissí** on Lake Pamvótis is connected by motor-launches (half-hourly in summer, hourly otherwise, 6.30am–11pm; 150dr) from the quay northwest of the Froúrio on Platía Mavíli. The beautiful island village, founded in the sixteenth century by refugees from the Máni in the Peloponnese, is flanked by a group of five **monasteries**, providing a perfect focus for an afternoon's visit. By day the street leading up from the boat dock is crammed with stalls selling jewellery and kitsch souvenirs. Commercialization diminishes as evening approaches, and you can watch the sun setting superbly over the reedbeds that surround the island. Quiet descends with the sun, except at the string of restaurants on the waterfront and another cluster by Pandelímonos.

The **Monastery of Pandelímonos**, just to the east of the village, is perhaps the most dramatic of Ioánnina's Ali Pasha sites, though it is in fact a complete reconstruction, as the original building was smashed some years ago by a falling tree. In January 1822 Ali was assassinated here, his hiding place having been revealed to the Turks, who had finally lost patience with the wayward ruler. Trapped in his rooms on the upper storey, he was shot from the floor below. The fateful bullet holes in the floorboards form the centrepiece of a small **museum** (summer daily; 100dr) to the tyrant, along with numerous wonderful period prints and knick-knacks like Ali's splendid hubble-bubble on the fireplace.

Three other **monasteries** – **Ayíou Nikoláou Filanthropinón, Stratigopoúlou Dilíou**, and **Eleoússas** (permanently locked) – are over to the south of the village. They are quite clearly signposted and stand within a few hundred yards of one another along a lovely treelined lane; the first two are maintained by a resident family, which allows brief visits (knock for admission). Both monasteries are attractively situated, with pleasant courtyards, though visits essentially consist of being shown the main chapel, or *katholikón*. These feature Byzantine **frescoes**, in various stages of decay or preservation. The finest are those of Filanthropinón, portraying some extraordinarily bloody and graphic seventeenth-century scenes of early Christian martyrdoms. Additionally, there are complete life cycles of the Virgin and Christ, and (by the south door) rare depictions of ancient-Greek sages, indicating that this was a secret school for Hellenic culture during the Turkish period. Beyond the monasteries the track loops around the island to bring you out by a fourth monastery, **Ioánnou Prodhrómou**, right behind Pandelímonos, which holds the keys.

Lake Pamvótis

Murkily green and visibly dirty, **Lake Pamvótis** is not simply polluted but also slowly shrinking. The springs along its north shore, which historically fed it, suddenly dried up in the early 1980s, and the lake stopped draining towards the Adriatic. Contaminated runoff from Ioánnina and surrounding farmland began to accumulate, a problem exacerbated by four dry years between 1989 and 1992, which lowered the water level almost 2m in a lake that's at best 15m deep. Swimming is forbidden, though few would want to under present circumstances.

In the face of all this, the inhabitants of the island struggle to continue **fishing**. The lake was stocked with three species from Hungary in 1986, though all but one of these have been fished out as they failed to reproduce. Not even the normally hardy carp can tolerate the lake water. Ioánnina inhabitants refuse to eat anything out of the lake, so the islanders are forced to sell their catch at a pittance for shipment to Thessaloníki, where it retails for ten times the price. The deal is so bad, fishing continues as much to pass the time and supplement local diets. The only lake item on Nissí restaurant menus are the legs of frogs caught in the surrounding reed beds.

Eating, nightlife and entertainment

For **meals**, the island is the best location with its four, slightly expensive tavernas featuring lake specialities like eel (*héli*), crayfish (*karavídhes*) and frogs' legs. If you'd rather not sample anything fished from those murky waters, the farmed trout (*péstrofa*) is cheaper and possibly safer. In winter the tavernas provide lunch only.

In town, *Ouzerí Toh Sinonimo*, at Gounári 3, serves salt-water seafood as well as meat dishes, evenings only. More standard fare can be found around the bazaar near the Froúrio gate; try the basic, oven-food *Pantheon* restaurant, or, for grills, the excellent *Toh Kourmanio*, exactly opposite the gate and inexpensive with good portions. Note that Ioánnina is also the original home of the *bougátsa* (custard-tart), fresh at breakfast time from *Select* at Platía Dhimokratías 3. Alternatively, there's an English-style breakfast salon at Avéroff 39, which also does good puddings and yoghurts as well.

Nightlife oscillates between the calmer **cafés** on and around Platía Pírrou (where *Old Post*, the former mail office, is of interest to Rococo fans) and the **bars** and (generally mediocre) **tavernas** on Platía Mavíli. The bars, especially the *Gallery*, are more fun, in conjunction with the prevailing, gas-lantern carnival atmosphere outside, enlivened by sellers of *halva* (sweetmeat) and roast corn. The waterfront to the north is being prettified, with more *ouzerís* springing up along Odhós Pamvotídhas. Back up on Platía Pírrou, there are also three **cinemas**, at which – thanks to the university students – there is usually quite a decent programme of films.

In summer, the biggest events are part of the *Politístiko Kalokéri* (Cultural Summer) **festival**, which runs from mid-July to mid-August, made up of music and theatre performances, plus the odd cultural exhibition. Most of the events take place in a hillside theatre, known as the **Fróntzos** or **EHM theatre**, just outside the town (there is also a pleasant summer restaurant here, with fine views down to the town and lake). Tickets are available from the Folklore Museum (rarely open) at Miháil Angélou 42 or the EOT office. Some years there are one or two performances of classical drama and contemporary music at the ancient **theatre of Dodona** (see below).

North to the Pérama caves

Five kilometres north of Ioánnina, the village of **PÉRAMA** boasts what are reputed to be Greece's largest system of **caves** (daily summer 8am–8pm; winter 8am–4pm; 800dr, students half-price), which extend and echo for kilometres beneath a low hill. They were discovered during the last war by a guerrilla in hiding from the Germans. The half-hour tours of the complex are a little perfunctory (consisting in the main of a student reeling off the names of various suggestively shaped formations), but not enough to spoil the experience.

To reach the caves, take a #8 blue city bus (buy your ticket in advance from a kiosk) from the terminal below Platía Pírrou to Pérama village; the caves are a ten-minute walk inland from the bus stop, past tacky souvenir shops. If you are driving, you can make a circuit of it. The road splits shortly after Pérama: one fork leading up towards Métsovo, with superb views down over Ioánnina and the lake; the other running around the lake, with a beachside café midway.

South to Dodona: the Oracle of Zeus

There is a certain romantic egocentricity in being a tourist which demands that a site should not only be beautiful beyond one's expectations but should also be a personal and private discovery. If you've ever felt like this, go to **DODONA**, 22km southwest of Ioánnina. Here, in a wildly mountainous and once-isolated region lie the ruins of the **Oracle of Zeus** – the oldest in Greece – dominated by a vast and elegant theatre.

The oracle is a very ancient site indeed. "Wintry Dodona" is mentioned in Homer and the worship here of Zeus and of the sacred oak tree seems to have been connected with the first Hellenic tribes who arrived in Epirus around 1900 BC.

The origins of the site are shadowy: Herodotus gives an enigmatic story about the arrival of a *peleiae* or dove from Egyptian Thebes which settled in an oak tree and ordered a place of divination to be made. The word *peleiae* in fact meant both dove and old woman, so it's possible that the legend he heard refers to an original priestess – perhaps captured from the East and having some knowledge of divination. The **oak tree**, stamped on the ancient coins of the area, was central to the cult. Herodotus recorded that the oracle spoke through the rustling of the oak's leaves in sounds amplified by copper vessels suspended from its branches. These would then be interpreted by frenzied priestesses and strange priests who slept on the ground and never washed their feet.

The site

Mon–Fri 8am–7pm (winter 8am–5pm), Sat & Sun 8am–3pm; 500dr.

Entering the site past a few seat-tiers of a third-century BC **Stadium**, you are immediately confronted by the massive western retaining wall of the **Theatre**. Built during the time of Pyrrhus (297–272 BC), this was one of the largest on the Greek mainland, rivalled only by those at Argos and Megalopolis. Later, the Romans made adaptations necessary for their blood sports, adding a protective wall over the lower seating and also a drainage channel, cut in a horseshoe shape around the orchestra. What you see today is a meticulous late-nineteenth-century reconstruction, since until then the amphitheatre had been an almost incomprehensible jumble of stones.

The theatre is used occasionally for weekend ancient drama and music performances during Ioánnina's summer cultural festival (see p298), which must be terrific, for this is one of the most glorious settings in Greece. The seats face out across a green, silent valley to the slopes of Mount Tómaros, as though one peak is challenging the other. At the top of the *cavea*, or seating curve, a grand entrance gate leads into the **Acropolis**, an overgrown and largely unexcavated area. The foundations of its walls, mostly Hellenistic, are a remarkable 4–5m wide.

Beside the theatre, and tiered uncharacteristically against the same slope, are the foundations of a *bouleuterion*, beyond which lie the complex ruins of the **Sanctuary of Zeus**, site of the oracle itself. There was no temple as such until the end of the fifth century BC. Until then, worship had centred upon the sacred oak, which stood alone within a circle of votive tripods and cauldrons. Building began modestly with a small stone temple-precinct, and in the time of Pyrrhus the precinct was enclosed with Ionic colonnades. In 219 BC the sacred house was sacked by the Aetolians and a larger temple was built with a monumental *propylaion*. This survived until the fourth century AD, when the oak tree was hacked down by Christian reformists. It is remains of the later precinct that can be seen today. They are distinguishable by an oak planted at the centre by a helpfully reverent archeologist.

Many **oracular inscriptions** were found scattered around the site when it was excavated in 1952. Now displayed in Ioánnina's archeological museum, they give you a good idea of the personal realm of the oracle's influence in the years after it had been eclipsed by Delphi. More interestingly, they also offer a glimpse of the fears and inadequacies that motivated the pilgrims of the age to journey here, asking such domestic questions as: "Am I her children's father?" and, memorably, "Has Pleistos stolen the wool from my mattress?".

Ruins of an early Christian **Basilica**, constructed on a Sanctuary of Herakles, are also prominent nearby – distinguished by rounded column stumps.

Practicalities

Few people make the detour to Dodona, so the site and **DHODHÓNI** – the little village to the west of it – are completely unspoilt. **Transport** is accordingly sparse, with only two buses a day from Ioánnina (Mon–Wed, Fri & Sat 6.30am & 4.30, Sun 7.30am & 6pm). Hitching to the site from the junction 7km south of Ioánnina should be feasible in summer, or a round trip by taxi from Ioánnina with an hour at the site can be negotiated for a reasonable amount – say 5000dr per carload.

Alternatively, you could always stay the night here. There are some lovely spots to **camp**, a friendly if basic **taverna** in the village, and a tiny, reasonably priced **pension/taverna** at the site, the *Xenia Andromachi* (☎0651/82 296; ②), which fills only at festival time.

The Zagóri

Few parts of Greece are more surprising, or more beguiling, than the **Zagóri**. A wild, infertile region, it lies to the north of Ioánnina, bounded by the roads to Kónitsa and Métsovo on the west and south and the Aóös River valley to the northeast. The beauty of its landscapes is unquestionable: miles of forest, barren limestone wastes, rugged mountains deeply furrowed by foaming rivers and partly subterranean streams. But there is hardly a cultivatable inch anywhere, and scarcely a job for any of its few remaining inhabitants. The last place, in fact, that one would expect to find some of the most imposing architecture in Greece.

Yet the **Zagorohória**, as the 46 villages of Zagóri are called, are full of grand stone *arhondiká* (mansions), enclosed by semi-fortified walls and with deep-eaved porches

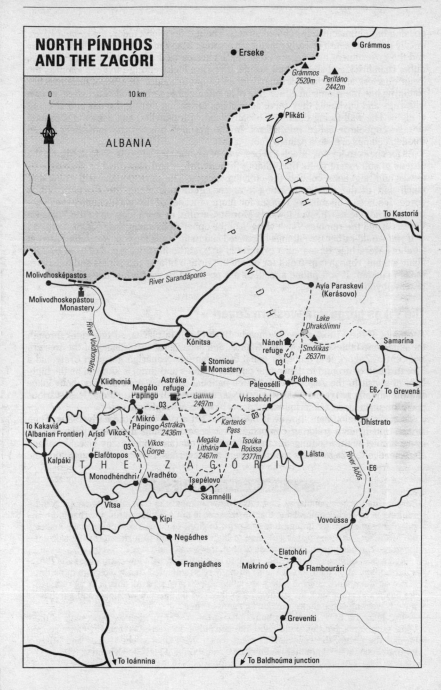

NORTH PÍNDHOS AND THE ZAGÓRI

0   10 km

ALBANIA

Erseke

Grámmos

Grámmos 2520m

Perífáno 2442m

Plikáti

To Kastoriá

Molivdhosképastos

River Sarandáporos

Ayía Paraskeví (Kerásovo)

Molivodhoskepástou Monastery

River Voïdhomátis

Kónitsa

Lake Dhrakólimni

Náneh refuge

Smólikas 2637m

Samarína

Stomíou Monastery

Astráka refuge

Paleosélli

Pádhes

Klidhoniá

Megálo Pápingo

03

Gamíla 2497m

Vrissohóri

03

E6

To Grevená

Mikró Pápingo

Astráka 2436m

Karterós Pass

Dhístrato

To Kakaviá (Albanian Frontier)

Arísti   Víkos

03

V*íkos Gorge*

Megála Lithária 2467m

Tsoúka Roússa 2377m

Láïsta

Kalpáki

T H E   Z A G Ó R I

Elafótopos

River Aóös

E6

Monodhéndhri

Vradhéto

Tsepélovo

Vítsa

Skamnélli

Kípi

Vovoússa

Negádhes

Elatohóri

Frangádhes

Makrinó

Flambourári

Grevéníti

To Ioánnina

To Baldhoúma junction

opening onto immaculately cobbled streets. Though they look older, the *arhondiká* are mostly late eighteenth or early nineteenth century. Many have long fallen into disrepair and the government now ensures that repairs are carried out in the proper materials, rather than brick and sheet metal. Inside, if you are lucky enough to get a glimpse, the living quarters are upstairs, arranged on an Ottoman model. Instead of furniture, low platforms line the rooms on either side of an often elaborately hooded fireplace; strewn with rugs and cushions, they serve as couches for sitting during the day and sleeping at night. The wall facing the fire is usually lined with panelled and sometimes painted storage cupboards called *misándhres*. In the grander houses the intricately fretted wooden ceilings are often painted, too.

As for the countryside, much the best way of savouring its joys is on foot, **hiking** the dozens of still extant paths that, gliding through forest and sheepfold or slipping over passes and hogbacks, connect the outlying villages. The most popular trip – now very much part of the holiday trekking-company circuit – is along the awesome **Víkos gorge**. It's not to be missed, though for more of a feel of the back country, you may want to continue north, over towards **Mount Gamíla**, or even loop up to the Víkos via Vovoússa and the remoter Vlach villages of the upper Aöös valley (see p.308).

If you would rather have things organized and made easy for you, *Robinson Travel* at Ogdhóïs Merarhías 10, Ioánnina (☎0651/29 402), at the northwest end of town by a *BP* filling station, runs **group treks** for one of the British hiking companies and welcomes walk-in custom. If you phone ahead, or are prepared to wait a few days, it will do its best to fit you in.

The Víkos gorge and western Zagóri

The walls of the **Víkos gorge** are nearly 1000m high in places, cutting right through the limestone tablelands of Mount Gamíla, and separating the villages of the western and central Zagóri. It is quite the equal of the famous Samarian gorge in Crete and a hike through or around it, depending on your abilities and time, is likely to be the highlight of a visit to the Zagóri. Since 1975 a national park has encompassed both Víkos and the equally gorgeous Aöös River canyon to the north and, to date at least, various plans for ski centres, téléfériques and dams have been fought off.

Touristic development, however, has proceeded apace since the early 1980s, when British and French trekking companies first began coming here, and today almost every hamlet within spitting distance of the canyon (and indeed any sizeable village elsewhere in the Zagóri) has rooms for rent and tavernas. Be warned, though, that the

---

HIKING WARNINGS

Despite the gorge's popularity, and recent improvements in trail surface, mapping and marking, it is worth emphasizing that the traverse is not a Sunday stroll and that there is still plenty of scope for getting lost or worse. In April or May, snowmelt usually makes the Monodhéndhri end impassable due to high run-off, and in a rainstorm the sides of the gorge can become an oozing mass of mud, tree-trunks and scree.

At the best of times it's not really a hike to be attempted with low-cut trainers and PVC water bottles, as so many do. It is also strongly recommended that walkers go in parties of two or more, since isolated hikers are vulnerable to attack by Albanians living rough in the bushes. A stout stick for warding off snakes and belligerent livestock, and purchase when traversing scree-slopes, wouldn't go amiss either.

The Ioánnina EOT hand out photocopies of the *Korfes* magazine's **topo map** of the Víkos gorge area, but this is old (1984–85) and full of dangerous errors. If you are going beyond the gorge, the collection of maps which the EOS reps in Megálo and Mikró Pápingo keep on hand are more authoritative and should at least be glanced at.

area's popularity is such that you won't get a room to save your life in July or August, when a tent can provide a useful fallback.

Monondhéndhri is the most popular start point for a traverse of the gorge; explorations in the area generally lend themselves to linear or loop trips of some days, rather than basing yourself somewhere for a week.

Monodhéndhri

Near the south end of the gorge, perched right on the rim, is the handsome village of **MONODHÉNDHRI**. It is one of the best preserved of the western Zagóri communities, all of which escaped the wartime devastation suffered by their eastern cousins. The lane leading off from the far end of the *platía*, signposted "Vicos Canyon M/ry Snt Paraskevi" (*sic*), leads to the eagle's nest monastery of **Áyia Paraskeví**, teetering on the very brink of the gorge. If you have a good head for heights, continue on around the adjacent cliff face and the path eventually comes to a dead end near a well-hidden **cave** where the villagers used to barricade themselves in times of danger. In all, count on an hour for visiting these sites.

On weekdays there are two daily **buses** here from Ioánnina, at 6am and 4.15pm. If you take the later one, you can stay the night at the luxury *Ksenonas Vikos* (☎0653/61 232; ⑤) or at four or five more modest inns near the well-marked upper *platía*, such as the *Monodendri* (☎0653/61 233; ③). For **meals** you have a choice of a *psistariá* by the bus stop in the upper quarter or a taverna in the lower *platía*, but there is no shop, so come supplied for your gorge trek.

At nearby **VÍTSA**, a fifteen-minute walk below by a footpath, additional en-suite accommodation is available at *Dhanou* (☎0653/61 271; ③), a renovated *arhondikó* in the upper quarter, and at *Ksenonas Karayiannis* (☎0653/61 350; ③) in the lower of the two ridgeline neighbourhoods. To some tastes it's a less claustrophobic, more attractive village than Monodhéndhri, with a few **tavernas** and alternative access to the gorge, a half-hour walk away down a stair-path to a double-humpback bridge.

Monodhéndhri to the Pápingo villages: through the gorge

Much the clearest **path down to the gorge** begins beside the church in the lower *platía*, where a sign reading "Víkos Arísti Pápingo" shows a schematic pedestrian figure and the misleading estimate of "10km" (it's more like 13km by the time you reach the Pápingo villages).

The path is paved for most of the way down to the riverbed, whose stony course you can quite easily parallel for the first hour or so of the walk. The walk along the gorge is not difficult to follow, since the entire route is waymarked, in parts a bit faintly, by red-paint dots and white-on-red stencilled metal diamonds with the legend "O3". This refers to a recently staked-out long-distance path, which begins in Monodhéndhri and as of writing can be followed across Mount Gamíla all the way to Mount Smólikas. In reality all you need to do is keep straight, occasionally crossing from one to the other side of the riverbed or climbing for a while through the wooded banks.

About two and a half hours out of Monodhéndhri you draw even with the mouth of the **Mégas Lákkos ravine**, the only major breach in the eastern wall of the gorge; its water is drinkable, and the sole reliable source en route. Another forty minutes' level tramping brings you past the small, white shrine of **Ayía Triádha** with a recessed well opposite. A further hour yet (around 4hr 30min from Monodhéndhri) sees the gorge begin to open out and the sheer walls recede.

As the gorge widens you are faced with a choice. Continuing straight, on the best-defined path, takes you close to a beautifully set eighteenth-century chapel of the Panayía, past which the route becomes a well-paved *kalderími*, climbing up and left to the hamlet of **VÍKOS** (VITSIKÓ). This route has been kept in good repair by the locals and takes half an hour to walk. The hamlet has a single small **inn** (☎0653/41 176; ③), run by Kostas Karpouzis.

Most walkers, however, prefer to follow the marked "O3" route to the two **Pápingo villages**, crossing the gorge bed at the **Voïdhomátis springs**, some five hours from Monodhéndhri. This trail was regraded and rerouted in 1985 and is fairly straightforward to follow. It's about two hours' walk to Mikró Pápingo, slightly less to Megálo, with the divide in the trail nearly ninety minutes above the riverbed crossing. Midway, after an initial steep climb, there's a fine view down into the north end of the gorge in the vicinity of some weathered, tooth-like pinnacles, before the trail traverses a stable rock slide to the fork. Should you be taking the same route, but in reverse, the start of the path in each Pápingo village is currently signposted in Greek.

The Pápingo villages

MEGÁLO PÁPINGO is, as its name suggests, the larger of the two villages: a sprawl of fifty or so houses along a tributary of the Voïdhomátis River. Despite a blanket preservation order, an enormous cement hotel is creeping towards completion and Megálo has been discovered with a vengeance by wealthy Greeks of late, making it a poor choice of base in high season. Behind the central café is a refurbished seventeen-bed **inn** (☎0653/41 138 or 41 115; ④) with en-suite rooms, run by the Hristodhoulos family, who are also the local EOS representatives. As such, they can advise on space in the Astráka hut and walks towards Mount Gamíla (see below), and the eldest son, Nikos, speaks English. On the south side of the village, a second and newly revamped inn (☎0653/41 081; ④), run by Kalliopi Ranga, offers good home-style meals, and there are a number of *dhomátia* on the way. There is also a former EOT-run (and now privately operated) scheme of luxury inns in converted *arhondiká* (☎0653/41 615; ⑥), a memorable stay if you have the money. Across from the Hristodhoulos inn and store is the most active of three **tavernas**, a surprisingly trendy place with *calzone*, pizza and wine.

MIKRÓ PÁPINGO, around half the size of its neighbour, crouches below an outcrop of grey limestone rocks known as the *Pírgi* (Towers). The village has one main **inn**, *O Dhias* (☎0653/41 257; ④), which is on a par with those in Megálo and whose proprietor Kostas Tsoumanis is sympathetic to trekkers; for instance, he can arrange shuttles back to cars left in Monodhéndhri. Less pricey are various rented **rooms** (③) around the inn, and self-catering studios. If you are still stuck for accommodation, there are almost always less expensive vacancies in **ARÍSTI**, 13km across the Voïdhomátis River and untouched by tourism.

If you finish your trek at Pápingo, and wish to get back to Ioánnina, the return trip by **bus** can be a rather haphazard affair, since the service is erratic. Scheduled departures from Ioánnina are on Monday, Wednesday and Friday at 5am and 2.30pm, turning around for the return trip immediately upon arrival at Megálo Pápingo, an hour or so later; in the summer there is also a service on Sunday, leaving Ioánnina at 9.30am and getting back to town in the late afternoon. If you strike unlucky, the best course is to walk to the village of Klidhoniá on the Kónitsa–Ioánnina highway, which has regular buses. It's around a two-and-a-half-hour walk west from Megálo Pápingo, via the nearly abandoned hamlet of Áno Klidhoniá, on a better-than-average, marked path, and certainly quicker than the dreary nineteen-kilometre haul to the highway along the paved road which passes through Arísti.

The lower Voïdhomátis River valley

Roughly halfway between the Kónitsa–Ioánnina highway and Megálo Pápingo, the paved side road descends to cross the Voïdhomátis as it flows out of the Víkos gorge. The immediate environs of the bridge is a popular picnic area in summer (no camping allowed), but river-bank trails allow you to hike to more peaceful, tree-shaded spots upstream before the gorge blocks further progress. Swimming in the Voïdhomátis is a privilege enjoyed only by the trout, though anyone ignoring the ban would probably perish anyway in the icy waters. Downstream lies the restored, cliff-clinging monastery of **Spiliotíssas**; a track leads to it through a plane grove, west of the road, about 400m before the bridge. It must be said, though, that the best views of the monastery are from the road as it ascends to Pápingo.

Hikes across the Gamíla range

For walkers keen on further, fairly arduous hiking, there are a number of routes on from the Pápingo villages, up and across the **Gamíla** range into the central Zagóri. These are linked by the newly marked "O3" long-distance trail.

Mikró Pápingo to the Astráka refuge

All onward hikes east into Gamíla begin with the steep but straightforward ascent to the **refuge** on **Astráka col**. Though the refuge is clearly visible from Megálo Pápingo, you have to start at Mikró Pápingo. The two villages are linked by a three-kilometre asphalt road, which takes 45 minutes to walk; it's better to take the marked short cut off the road, via an old historic bridge, which reduces the journey time to half an hour.

At the top of Mikró Pápingo, the well-signed, regularly maintained "O3" trail resumes. Ten minutes out, you pass a chapel (Áyios Pandelímon), then head through forest to the Antálki spring (about 40min from Mikró Pápingo). From here the forest thins as you climb towards the Tráfos spring (1hr 40min from Mikró). Twenty minutes beyond Tráfos, a signposted trail branches right towards the **Astráka summit** (2436m), which is a three-hour round-trip from this point. If you ignore this trail, and keep straight with the "O3" markers, in around 35 minutes you will reach the **EOS refuge**, perched on the saddle joining Astráka with Mount Lápatos (2hr 45min from Mikró Pápingo).

Astráka refuge and its day hikes

The hut is open and permanently staffed from mid-May to mid-October, but space is at a premium and bunks are the refuge standard ①, and the meals are relatively expensive. If you want to squeeze in amongst the Greek and foreign trekking/climbing groups, phone the Hristodhoulos inn at Megálo Pápingo; they're in radio contact with the hut, who can confirm space.

Northeast of the refuge, on the far side of the boggy Lákka Tsoumáni valley below, the gleaming **lake of Dhrakólimni** is tucked on the very edge of the Gamíla range. This is about an hour from the refuge, along a well-grooved-in and marked path.

East of the refuge, the "O3" route takes you on a strenuous nine-hour hike to the village of Vrissohóri via the **Karterós pass**. Despite the waymarking, the casual walker may find this an intimidating hike; it's best attempted only if you're an experienced trekker and equipped with the appropriate maps. At first, the trail heads for **Mount Gamíla** (2497m), itself a good two-and-a-half-hour climb from the refuge, but then veers off south from the final summit approach to negotiate the pass between the Karterós and Gamíla peaks, with a nasty scree slide on the far side. Near the usually empty sheepfold of Kátsanos, this route eventually joins an easier, unmarked trail coming over from the village of Skamnélli in the south, before the final descent to the village of Vrissohóri.

South to Tsepélovo

A more obvious, less demanding onward trek from Astráka col is the five-hour route, on an often faint trail, south across the Gamíla uplands, via the Mirioúli sheepfold and the head of the Mégas Lákkos gorge, to the village of **TSEPÉLOVO**. Besides spring water at Mirioúli, there is only one other tiny spring en route, and for the most part the

PACKHORSE BRIDGES

A perennial pleasure as you stumble down boulder-strewn ravine beds that are bone-dry an hour after a thunderstorm is coming upon one of the many fine high-arched "packhorse" bridges that abound in the Zagóri. One-, two- or three-arched, these bridges, and the old cobbled paths serving them, were the only link with the outside world for these remote communities until motor roads were opened up in the 1950s. They were erected mainly in the nineteenth century by gangs of itinerant craftsmen and financed by local worthies.

Like the semi-nomadic Vlach and Sarakatsan shepherds of Epirus, these wandering construction gangs or *bouloúkia* left home between the feasts of Áyios Yióryios (St George's Day) in April and Áyios Dhimítrios in October. As in other mountainous regions of Europe – the Alps, for example – they came from remote and poor communities, Pirsóyianni and Voúrbiani in particular in the Kónitsa area, and Ágnanda, Prámanda and Houliarádhes southeast of Ioánnina. Closely guarding the secrets of their trade with their own invented private language, they travelled the length and breadth of Greece and the Balkans, right up to World War II.

While you're in the Zagóri region, a good side trip, easiest done from Vítsa, Kípi or Tsepélovo, would be to take a look at the half-dozen fantastic bridges in the vicinity. One is below Vítsa; one right beside the main road; one between Kípi and Koukoúli; and the remainder upstream of the main road, just below and past Kípi. The bridges span the upper reaches of the Víkos gorge and its tributaries, and constitute the most representative and accessible examples of the vanished craft of packhorse-bridge building.

scenery consists of forbidding limestone-dell-scape; but the destination is one of the finest of the Zagorohória. Tsepélovo seems to have **pensions** and **hotels** opening all the time, making it the biggest tourist centre in the Zagóri after the Pápingo villages. English-speaking Alekos Gouris runs a store and keeps a taverna and rooms (☎0653/ 81 214 and 81 288; ③) on the *platía*. There is a good-value pension, the *Fanis* (☎0653/ 81 271; ③), higher in the village, as well as independent tavernas on the *platía* and out on the road by the school. A recent entry on the scene is *Toh Palio Arhondiko* (☎0653/ 81 216; ③), which provides rooms with or without a bath in a restored mansion. Two **buses** daily (Mon–Fri) connect the village with Ioánnina; they leave Ioánnina at 7am (6am in summer) and at 3.15pm, returning from Tsepélovo an hour or so later.

This side of Mount Gamíla is treeless and rather dull, though there are good day excursions. The adjacent village of **SKAMNÉLLI** (which has another **pension**, the *Pindos*; ③) is an easy road-walk east, with a medieval monastery en route. Descending 12km by road from Tsepélovo towards Ioánnina, brings you to the celebrated cluster of **old bridges** (see the box above) around Kípi, plus the amazing coiled-spring *kalderími* linking Kepésovo and Vradhéto. The bridges span the very upper reaches of the Víkos gorge, which can be reached just as easily from here as it can from Monodhéndhri or Vítsa. **KÍPI** is an attractive village with **accommodation** at *Artemis* (☎0653/51 262; ③) and a friendly *ouzerí* called *Fagadhiko*. A twice-daily **bus** (Mon–Fri) leaves for Ioánnina at 7am and 5pm.

Roads and trails north towards the Aóös valley

Beyond Skamnélli forest appears, extending north to the **Aóös valley**. Fourteen kilometres or so out of the village, the now-dirt road branches north towards Vrissohóri, and east towards Láista. The daily **bus** linking Ioánnina with Tsepélovo and Skamnélli continues to both on Monday, Wednesday and Friday only. **LÁISTA** has a fine, though damaged church, and an incongruously large **hotel**, the *Robolo* (☎0653/81 286; ③), which is the only bone fide place to stay in this area.

Rather than follow this relatively dull road to Vrissohóri, you can get there in seven hours by walking over a pass between the peaks of **Megála Lithária** (2467m) and **Tsoúka Roússa** (2377m). This is a rather easier walk than that through the Karterós pass previously described, and covered by many of the organized trekking groups. An added bonus of this choice is the unrivalled display of mountain wildflowers in the **Goúra valley**, directly below Tsoúka Roússa.

After the approach, **VRISSOHÓRI** is a little anticlimactic, being almost swallowed by the dense woods at the base of Tsoúka Roússa peak. Tiny and ramshackle (this was one of the settlements burnt by the Germans in the war) the village has rumours of **rooms**, but no proper taverna or even a store. You can camp at the edge of town by one of two springs on either side of the "O3" coming down from Karterós.

Moving on to north Píndhos

The "O3" trail used to continue across the Aóös from Vrissohóri to **Paleosélli** in the north Píndhos but the path was bulldozed in 1989, extending the road up from Skamnélli. If you are purist about cross-country hiking, you will have to follow a slightly longer, pretty, but as yet unmarked trail from Vrissohóri via **Áyios Minás** chapel down to the Aóös. Ford the river (at low water only), and bushwhack a bit on the other side up to Paleosélli. You would need to allow about three and a half hours. The attraction of trail or road is access to the villages of Paleosélli and Pádhes on the southern slopes of Mount Smólikas (see p.308).

The north Píndhos

The region **north of the Aóös River** is far less visited than the Zagóri. Its landscape is just as scenic but its villages are very poor relatives – virtually all those within sight of the river were burnt in the war, accounting for their present haphazard appearance. The villagers claim that before 1943 their houses exceeded in splendour those of the Zagóri, since they had ample timber to span huge widths and for carved interiors.

The region is dominated by mounts **Smólikas** and **Grámmos**, two of the highest peaks in Greece. It can be approached on foot from **Mount Gamíla** (see p.305) or by vehicle from **Kónitsa**, the largest settlement in these parts, just off the Ioánnina–Kastoriá highway.

Kónitsa and around

KÓNITSA is a sleepy little town. Its most memorable features are a famous bridge and a view. The **bridge**, over the Aóös, is a giant, built around 1870 but looking far older. The **view** comes from the town's amphitheatrical setting on the slopes of Mount Trapezítsa, above a broad flood plain where the Aóös and Voïdhomátis rivers mingle with the Sarandáporos before flowing through Albania to the sea.

The town was besieged by the Communist Democratic Army over the New Year in 1948, in a last and unsuccessful bid to establish a provisional capital. Much was destroyed in the fighting, though parts of the old bazaar and a tiny Turkish neighbourhood near the river survive.

The **bus terminal** (7 buses daily to Ioánnina and connections to most villages in this section) is on the central *platía*; the **OTE**, the **bank** and the **post office** are just to the south. Kónitsa has recently acquired some importance as a kayakers' and walkers' centre. Accordingly, *dhomátia* have sprung up like mushrooms on the serpentine approach road up from the main highway and the historic bridge. Longest established, and one of the best, is *Toh Dhendro* (☎0655/22 055; ③), with congenial English-speaking owners and also a source of good meals and local info. The *Tymfí* (☎0655/22

035; ③), next to the bus station, and the *Aoos* (☎0655/22 079; ④), down on the bypass road next to the *Shell* station, are the only hotels in town and less inspiring choices. The *O Makedhonas* on the central *platía* is a good, inexpensive taverna offering oven food.

The Aóös gorge

Kónitsa can serve as a base for a fine afternoon's walking. Beginning at the old bridge over the Aóös, either of two interweaving paths on the south bank lead within an hour and a half to the eighteenth-century **monastery of Stomíou**, perched on a bluff overlooking the narrowest part of the Aóös gorge. The *katholikón* here is of minimal interest, and the premises have been rather brutally restored, but the setting is sublime. There are two springs to drink from, and many visitors camp in the surroundings, after bathing in the river below.

Beyond Stomíou the slopes are shaggy with vegetation constituting one of the last pristine habitats for lynx, roe deer and birds of prey. A minimally waymarked path climbs from the monastery gate up to the **Astráka area** (see p.305). This is a five-hour walk, rather less coming back down, and a very useful trekkers' link between the Gamíla and the Smólikas regions, provided you have a good map. It is less arduous than the Astráka–Vrissohóri route and allows all sorts of loops through both Gamíla and the north Píndhos.

Molivdhosképastos: village and monastery

The tiny hillside village of **MOLIVDHOSKÉPASTOS** hugs the Albanian border 23km west of Kónista. Strange as it seems today, the village was once a haunt of the seventh-century emperor, Constantine IV Pogonatos, though only a few of his monuments survive intact. One of these is the tiny chapel of **Ayía Triádha**, on a crag below; another is the present parish church of **Áyii Apóstoli**, right on the frontier. If you can get in, the church has fine frescoes, and the view from its terrace – into Albania, over the Aóös valley, and east to Smólikas and Gamíla – is among the finest in Epirus. Unfortunately, photography is forbidden and you'll need to present ID at a military checkpoint back at the Aóös bridge.

A daily **bus** comes out to Molivdhosképastos at 2.45pm from Kónitsa, but it might not return until the next morning, in which case the only **place to stay** is at the *Hotel Bourazani* (☎0655/61 283; ④), by the river bridge. On June 29, the village itself comes to life for the **festival** of its patron saints, Peter and Paul, with music and feasting until dawn.

Five kilometres below the village is the **monastery of Molivdhoskepástou**, the most important of the emperor's surviving monuments. Recently repopulated and attractively restored by its half-dozen monks, the monastery enjoys a bucolic setting on the bank of the Aóös. The curiously long and narrow church, with a precariously high Serbian-type dome, is thirteenth century. The nave ceiling is supported by arches and vaults; the airier exonarthex was a later addition. Frescoes throughout are in a poor state. This is a working monastery, so don't visit between 3pm and 5pm; the monks are quite zealous, which is not uncommon in cases of monastic revival, and if you admit to Christian sentiments, you'll be whipped off to a confessional chapel to account for your sins.

East of Kónitsa: Mount Smólikas

Mount Smólikas (2637m) is the second highest peak in Greece. It dominates a beautiful and very extensive range, covering a hundred square kilometres of mountain territory, all of it above 1700m, and including a lovely mountain lake, **Dhrakólimni**. The region is also one of the last heartlands of traditional shepherd life, which is best witnessed in summer at the Vlach village of **Samarína**.

Kónitsa–Dhístrato **buses** (Sat 6am & Tues, Thurs, Sat & Sun 2.45pm) roll through the mountains, stopping en route at **PALEOSÉLLI** and **PÁDHES**, the two best trail-heads on the mountain's southern flank. Paleosélli has two simple stores and an **inn-taverna**, run by Sotiris Rouvalis (☎0655/71 216). Evening meals can be arranged here and in Pádhes, at the inn-taverna run by Olga Sugarou.

Hiking routes from Paleosélli

There is a fine trail from Paleosélli up to **Dhrakólimni** (a little over 4hr), and from there you can make an ascent of **Mount Smólikas** (another 1hr 30min). There is also a marked path to the lake from Pádhes, though a new road cuts across it at several points.

The Paleosélli–Dhrakólimni trail has been waymarked as part of the "O3" and a **refuge** established midway, at a spring and sheepfold known as Náneh, an idyllic little spot 1600m up with camping space, an external water supply and a toilet. Keys for this shelter are available from the Paleosélli inn. Beyond the refuge, the trail becomes less distinct but waymarks lead you up onto a ridge aiming for the summit of Mount Smólikas, though the path markings disappear at the treeline. At a little over two walk-ing hours from the refuge you should emerge into the little depression containing the **lake**. You can camp here, but level space is at a premium and you'll need a tent to protect against the cold and damp.

Moving along the ridge above the lake, you can reach the **summit of Smólikas** in about an hour and a quarter, tackling a rather steep, pathless slope with grass and stone underfoot. It is not unusual to see chamoix near the top.

The easiest way down from Smólikas is a scenic and well-trodden two-and-a-half-hour path to the hamlet of **AYÍA PARASKEVÍ** (also known as KERÁSOVO). The path leads off at a sheepfold in the vale between the lake and the summit. There are a couple of **tavernas** in the village (one a popular, outdoor pizzeria), a grossly overpriced **inn** (open July & Aug) and a **bus** (daily 7am, Tues & Thurs also at 2.30pm) to Kónitsa. Camping near the village is tolerated.

Hiking from Dhrakólimni to Samarína

If you have a good head for heights, and you're not carrying too heavy a pack, the best of possible hiking routes from **Dhrakólimni to Samarína** involves tracing the ridge east from the summit, the start of a seven-hour walking day. After a generous hour of cross-country progress, you'll reach a small, bleak pass in the watershed, where you link up with a real path coming up from the village of Pádhes, hereabouts marked by faint yellow paint splodges on the rocks. Once through this gap, you descend into the rather lunar, northwest-facing cirque which eventually drains down to the hamlet of Ayía Paraskeví.

Next you traverse the base of one of Smólikas's secondary peaks as a prelude to creeping up a scree-laden rock "stair". From the top of this waymarks change from yellow to red, and a line of cairns guides you across a broad, flat-topped ridge. The path soon levels out on another neck of land. To the left yawns a dry gully (to be avoided) and way off to the right (south) can be glimpsed the other of Smólikas's lakes, as large as Dhrakólimni but difficult of access. Try not to stray in either direction in poor visibil-ity, as there are steep drops to either side.

Beyond, you encounter the leading edge of the black pine forest, at the foot of a peak, which is capped by a wooden altimeter. The trail threads between this knoll and another at the foot of which lies Samarína. Twenty minutes or so beyond this pass, a spring oozes from serpentine strata, some six hours from Smólikas summit. There follows a sharper descent through thick forest, with a second spring gurgling into a log-trough set in a beautiful mountain clearing, to which there is now a direct road. Below this, the woods end abruptly and you'll emerge on a bare slope directly above Samarína.

Samarína

At 1450m, **SAMARÍNA** is claimed to be the highest village in Greece. It's only inhabited in the summer when it fills up with Vlachs from the plains of Thessaly – and their sheep, some 50,000 of them. The village was burnt during both World War II and the civil war, and not surprisingly looks a bit of a mess. Even so, it's a thriving and friendly place and very proud of its Vlach traditions. The high point of the year is the **Feast of the Assumption** on August 15, when there is much music and merry-making and the place is swamped by nostalgic Vlachs from Athens and all over the country.

The interior of the main church, the **Panayía**, is superb, with frescoes and painted ceilings and an intricately carved *témblon*, where the angels, soldiers and biblical figures are dressed in mustachios and *fustanélles* (the Greek kilt). Though it looks a lot older, like many other churches in the region it dates from around 1800. Its special hallmark is an adult black pine growing out of the roof of the apse, and no one can remember a time without it. The keys are with the priest, who lives opposite the main gate.

The improbably large, stone building that confronts you at the top of the village is a **hotel** and there is another basic **inn** by the *platía*, but both of these may well be full during the summer. There may be a better chance of a vacancy at the *Hotel Kiparissi*, out on the east edge of the village, though no one will mind if you camp beyond the village itself. There is an **OTE** office and numerous *psistariés* on the *platía*.

Moving on

Leaving Samarína, you have two choices. There is a bus to **Grevená** from June to September, but not every day, though a lift is not too hard to get if you ask around. If you are committed to staying in Epirus, follow the E6 trail via the monastery of Ayía Paraskeví and Goúrna ridge to Dhístrato, where you can pick up the early morning bus back to **Kónitsa** (see p.307), or keep going to Vovoússa on the east bank of the Aóös, also with several weekly buses to Ioánnina.

North of Kónitsa into the Grámmos range

It was on **Mount Grámmos** that the Democratic Communist Army made its last stand in the civil war. Its eventual retreat into Albania followed a bitter campaign which saw tens of thousands of deaths and the world's first use of napalm (supplied by the United States). The upper slopes of the mountain remain totally bare, and as you walk in the range you still see rusting cartridges and trenches from the fighting.

If you want to visit the range, and peer down into the wilds of Albania, the most useful base is **Plikáti**. The simplest way here is from Kónitsa by **bus** (daily 6.30am, Mon, Wed & Fri 2pm). Coming from the Smólikas area, you're best off walking out to **Ayía Paraskeví**, where there are daily **buses** to Kónitsa (see p.307); if you time it right you could get off at the junction with the main highway and flag down the Kónitsa–Plikáti bus.

Plikáti and a hike up Mount Grámmos

There's a singularly end-of-the-world feel to **PLIKÁTI** – as indeed there should be, for this is the closest Greek village to the Albanian frontier, and trailhead for Greece's remotest, least frequented mountain, Grámmos. It's a traditional-looking place, with stone houses, a tiny permanent population, a couple of exceedingly basic **inns** and a combination taverna/general store.

Mount Grámmos (2520m) is the fourth loftiest Greek peak, and in making the ascent you should plan on a round trip of eight hours from Plikáti. The easiest strategy is to angle northeast up the gentler slopes leading to Perífano (2442m), second highest point in the range, rather than tackling head-on the badly eroded and steep incline immediately below the main peak. The trail in the indicated direction is clear for the first two hours out of the village, crossing the river and switchbacking up through bushes and then beech trees before it peters out at a sheepfold. Just above this are the last water sources on this side of the ridge – various trickles feeding a pond. Bearing west along a plain trail, you can thread along the crest for roughly an hour to the **summit**, its cairn covered in a babel of initials and multilingual graffiti. Below, to the west, a cultivated Albanian valley stretches to the barns of Erseke, 5km distant.

In the opposite direction from the summit, you can follow the watershed to the lower **Aréna massif**, which is garnished with a trio of small lakes and clumps of beech trees. The summer-only village of Grámmos is visible from the summit ridge, and though a clear trail leads to the village, there is no onward means of transport.

The south Píndhos

Most hikers arriving at Ioánnina have their sights firmly set to the north, especially on the Víkos gorge and the Zagóri villages. If you're feeling adventurous, however, and are not too particular about where you sleep or what you eat, the **remote villages** of the south Píndhos provide an interesting alternative. They perch on the beetling flanks of **mounts Tzoumérka** and **Kakardhítsa**, two overlapping ridges of bare mountains linked by a high plateau, plainly visible from Ioánnina. There are few special sights, but you'll get a solid, undiluted experience of Epirot life.

On weekdays **buses** leave from Ioánnina's southern station at 5am and 3.15pm for Ágnanda and Prámanda. Many of the villages can also be approached from Árta. Buses run a couple of times daily in either direction along the secondary road between Árta and Ioánnina, stopping at **Pláka**, which has an eighteenth-century bridge over the Arakhthós amid stunning scenery. Here you can flag down another of the twice daily Árta-based buses continuing along the side road east as far as Melissourgí.

Áganda to Melissourgí

The first village of any size is 12km above Pláka at **ÁGNANDA**, which was heavily damaged in the last war and is not particularly attractive, though it does have one **inn** (☎0685/31 332; ②). It's better to continue on to **PRÁMANDA**, which is no more distinguished architecturally than Ágnanda, but enjoys a wonderful setting strewn across several ridges. The village is dominated by Mount Kakardhítsa behind and commands fine views of the Kallaritikós valley. Nearby there is a huge cave, inhabited in Neolithic times, to which any villager will give you directions if you ask for the *Spíliá*. The enormous church of **Ayía Paraskeví** almost uniquely escaped wartime devastation, and as an example of nineteenth-century kitsch it is hard to beat. The village has a **post office**, a rather primitive *ksenónas* (inn), plus a handful of **tavernas** and *psistariés*, though there is a more comfortable **hotel**, the *Tzoumérka* (☎0659/61 336; ③), in the tiny hamlet of **TSÓPELAS**, 2km out on the road to Melissourgí.

MELISSOURGÍ, 5km to the southeast of Prámanda, is more rewarding. The village escaped destruction during the war, though since 1985 most buildings – including the historic church – have lost their slate roofs in favour of ugly pantiles. There is a **taverna** and one large **inn** (☎0659/61 357; ②), run by a Mr Karadhimas, though it is not to be counted on in midsummer, when all accommodation is likely to be booked by holidaying relatives from the cities. There are two daily weekday **buses** to Árta from Melissourgí, at 6am and 5pm.

Hikes from Melissourgí

Melissourgí is a good jump-off point for rambles on the **Kostelláta plateau** to the south. This upland separates Mount Kakardhítsa (2429m), which looms sheer above the village, from the more pyramidal Mount Tzoumérka (2399m). You can cross these high pastures, heading south, in a day and a half. The initial stretch of path from Melissourgí is very faintly waymarked with red-paint arrows, and there are intermittent *stánes* (summer sheepfolds) if you need water or directions. You can descend to the villages of **THEODHÓRIANA** or **DHROSSOPIYÍ**, at the edge of the Ahelóös river basin; both have daily early-morning buses **buses** to Árta, as well as modest **inns** and **tavernas**.

Prámanda to Siráko

Some days the **bus** from Ioánnina continues to **MATSOÚKI**, the last village on the provincial route, beautifully set near the head of a partly forested valley and offering easy access to Mount Kakardhítsa, as well as a few beds. On days when the bus doesn't serve Matsoúki, it runs instead as far as the hamlet of **KIPÍNA**. A famous namesake **monastery**, founded in 1381 but uninhabited today, hangs like a martin's nest from the cliff face a half hour's walk beyond the hamlet.

Kallarítes

Beyond this point, you can follow the road upstream for around half an hour through a tunnel and past a road bridge to join the remnant of a wonderful *kalderími* climbing up to the village of **KALLARÍTES**, perched superbly above the upper reaches of the Kallaritikós river. This depleted village, one of the southernmost Vlach settlements in the Píndhos, was a veritable eldorado until the close of the last century. Fame and fortune were based on its specialization in gold- and silver-smithing, and even today the craftsmen of Ioánnina are mostly of Kallaritiot descent – as in fact is Vulgari, one of the world's most celebrated contemporary jewellers. Though the village is all but deserted except during summer holidays, the grand houses of the departed rich are kept in excellent repair by their descendants. The flagstoned *platía* has probably remained unchanged for a century, with its old-fashioned stores and *stele* commemorating local emigré Kallaritiots, who helped finance the Greek revolution. There are two **café-grills** on the *platía*, but the municipal **inn** (☎0659/61 251) is not operating at the time of writing, so you should plan on camping out.

Hroússias gorge and Siráko

Just beyond Kallarítes, the awesome **Hroússias gorge** separates the village from its neighbour Siráko, visible high up on the west bank but a good hour's walk away. The trail is spectacular, including a near-vertical "ladder" hewn out of the rockface. Down on the bridge over the river you can peer upstream at a pair of abandoned watermills. The canyon walls are steep and the sun shines down here for only a few hours a day even in summer.

SIRÁKO, with a cliffside locale, is even more strikingly set than Kallarítes. Its well-preserved *arhondiká*, archways and churches are more reminiscent of those in the Zagóri. Not to be upstaged by Kallarítes, the village has also erected a number of monuments to various national figures (including the poet Krystallis) that hailed from here. There is a **taverna** (summer only) and a *kafenío*, but no formal inn; you can beg a mattress on the floor in the school during the summer.

There is an alternative route back to Ioánnina from Siráko, **via Petrovoúni**, though it is covered by just two **buses** a week (Fri & Sun), leaving from Ioánnina at 2pm and returning from Siráko at 4.30pm.

THE COAST AND THE SOUTH

The **Epirot coast** is nothing special, with **Igoumenítsa** a purely functional ferry port and **Párga**, the most attractive resort, overdeveloped and best left for out-of-season travel. Head a little inland, however, and things look up. Close by Párga, the **Necromanteion of Ephyra** (the legendary gate of Hades) is an intriguing ancient detour; the **gorge of the Aherónda** offers fine hiking; and the imposing Roman ruins of **Nikópolis** break the journey to Préveza. Best of all is **Árta**, an interesting little provincial town, approached either around the Amvrakikós gulf, or more impressively along the plane-shaded Loúros river gorge from Ioánnina.

Moving south into **Étolo-Akarnanía**, the landscape becomes increasingly desolate with little to delay your progress to the island of Lefkádha (see *The Ionian* chapter) or to Andírio, for the ferry to the Peloponnese. For committed isolates, there's **Kálamos** islet, south of Vónitsa. For diehard romantics, **Messolóngi**, though unglamorous, retains its name, its situation and Byron's buried heart.

Igoumenítsa and around

IGOUMENÍTSA is Greece's third passenger port, after Pireás and Pátra, with almost hourly ferries to Corfu and several daily to Italy. In 1992, summer hydrofoils were introduced to Páxi, Corfu and Brindisi. Though these did not operate in subsequent years, they may re-emerge. In the past, there were regular connections north along the coast of the former Yugoslavia. As travelling in that area is no longer a viable option, the sea traffic between Greece and Italy has increased significantly.

These ferry functions and a lively waterfront apart, the town is pretty unappealing; it was levelled during the last war and rebuilt in a sprawling, functional style. If you can arrange it, try to get a ferry out on the day you arrive. Heading for Italy, you may find this tricky, as most departures are early morning, forcing an overnight stay in or near the port; to get a berth, or take a vehicle on the few afternoon or evening sailings (see box overleaf), it's best to make reservations in advance. If you find yourself stuck for the day, you are better off taking one of the limited **excursions** from Igoumenítsa than hanging around town.

Practicalities

Arriving at Igoumenítsa by sea is straightforward. Ships dock in the central part of the **quay**, conveniently close to the town and the **EOT office** (Mon–Fri 7am–2pm; ☎0665/

IGOUMENÍTSA FERRY COMPANIES

If you arrive late and stay overnight in Igoumenítsa, you can at least shop around for tickets; travel and ticket agencies' offices tend to stay open until around 9pm. Most **ferries** leave for Italy between 7am and 10am, with usually at least one afternoon or evening departure in season.

General points

High season All frequencies of ferry crossings detailed below are for the high season, the definition of which varies slightly from company to campany. Broadly, for crossings from Italy to Greece, high season is between early July and mid-August; from Greece to Italy, it is between early August and early September. Check with company agents for exact dates. Out of season, all services are reduced.

Currency exchange Arriving in Igoumenítsa from Italy, a word of warning. If you miss the banks (which all close at 2pm) you're dependent on travel agents for changing money and rates are not good. It's best to buy a few drachmas on board before you arrive.

Tickets Travel and ticket agencies for international ferries are found on Ethnikís Andistásis, which lines the waterfront. Ticket for domestic services are purchased at an office on the domestic ferry quay, west of the main dock.

Fares All companies offer a variety of fares for cabin, "airline" seats and deck passage, as well as reductions according to age, student or rail-card status. High-season fares to Italy range from 12,500dr for the cheapest deck seats to 60,000dr for an expensive two-berth cabin. Cars are carried on all ferries.

Embarkation tax All international departures carry a levy of 1500dr per person and per car.

Checking in If you have bought tickets in advance, or from a travel agent other than the official agent listed below, you must check in (to the appropriate official agent, or at their booth in the port) at least two hours before departure.

22 227), which is on the dock, next to Customs House. The **bus station** is five minutes away at Kíprou 47 (☎0665/22 309).

The town is not large·but **hotels** are plentiful if uninspiring. Most are to be found either along or just back from the waterfront. The nearest budget hotel to the port is the *Lux*, Saldari 19 (☎0665/22 223; ③), which has a gloomy, run-down feel. Otherwise, the *Rhodos*, Kíprou 19 (☎0665/22 248; ③), has cheap rooms in town, near the main *platía*; similarly positioned is the slightly overpriced *Egnatia*, at Elefthérias 1 (☎0665/23 648; ④). Better than all these, though, are the *Stavrodhromi*, Soulíou 14 (☎0665/22 343; ④), a good choice, with a pleasant atmosphere and a restaurant that makes its own wine; and *Xenia*, Vassiléos Pavloú 2 (☎0665/22 282; ⑤), a comfortable place nicely sited near the north entrance to the town. The closest **campsite** is at Kalami Beach (☎0665/71 211), next to Platariá, a 10-kilometre bus ride away.

There are plenty of **restaurants** and **cafés** lining the waterfront along Ethnikís Andistásis, but none really stand out. The main shopping hub centres around Platía Dhimarhíou.

Excursions from Igoumenítsa

The best escapes are probably to the **beach**. The closest strands are to the south alongside the campsites at Kalámi (10km) and Platariá (12km) and at **SÍVOTA** (23km). Sívota, by far the most attractive option, is a sleepy resort in the initial stages of development, surrounded by olive groves, and draped over some evocative coastal topography. It's the sort of place Greeks favour for *their* holidays and, accordingly, summer apartments predominate. Best value among the half-dozen **hotels** are the *Acropolis*

Stopovers Unlike sailings from Pátra, ferries from Igoumenítsa to Italy are not allowed to sell tickets with stopover on Corfu. You can, however, take the regular Corfu ferry over and then pick up most ferry routes on from there.

International ferry companies, destinations and agents

ANEK Ancona (21hr 30min), direct Thurs, Sat & Sun 10.30am; Trieste (24hr), direct Tues & Fri 9.30am. *Revis Brothers*, Ethnikís Andístasis 34; ☎0665/22 104.

Adriatica Brindisi (10hr) via Corfu, daily 7am. Ethnikís Andístasis 58; ☎0665/22 952.

Arkadia Bari (11hr), direct daily 9am. *Alfa Travel*, Ayíion Apostólon 13; ☎0665/22 797.

European Seaways Brindisi (9hr) via Corfu, daily 6am. *Katsios Shipping*, 44A Ethnikís Andístasis; ☎0665/22 409.

Fragline Brindisi (10–11hr) via Corfu, Mon, Wed & Fri 6.30am & 9.30pm, Sat 6.30am & 10pm. *Revis Brothers*, Ethnikís Andístassis 34; ☎0665/22 158.

Hellenic Mediterranean Lines Brindisi (10hr) via Corfu, daily 9am & 10am. *Hellenic Mediterranean Lines*, Ethnikís Andístasis 30; ☎0665/22 180.

Marlines Ancona (24hr), direct Tues 8am & Fri 10am. Also a service to Cesme (Turkey). *Marlines*, Ethnikís Andístasis 42; ☎0665/23 301.

Minoan Ancona (21hr), direct, daily 11am. Ethnikís Andístasis 58A; ☎0665/22 952.

Strintzis Ancona (22hr), direct daily except Mon 10.30am; Brindisi (8hr) via Corfu, daily 11.30pm. *G. Pitoulis*, Ethnikís Andístasis 14; ☎0665/24 252.

Ventouris Bari (10hr–12hr 30min), via Corfu; daily 8.30pm. *Milano Travel*, Ayíion Apostólon 11B; ☎0665/24 237.

Domestic ferries

Corfu Hourly ferries in season from 5.30am to 10pm (1–2hr).

Kefalloniá, Itháki Sporadic ferry services operate in July and August.

Paxí Ferry operates daily in the high season, and five times a week otherwise.

(☎0665/93 263; ④) and *Hellas* (☎0665/93 227; ④). Down at Sívota's small harbour, there's a seasonal ferry to Paxí; contact *Sivota Travel* (☎0665/93 264) for schedules.

Inland, few destinations reward the effort expended to get to them, despite earnest promotion in the EOT brochures. There is a regular bus to the "traditional village" of **FILIÁTES**, 19km to the northwest, but it is a drab place, with a paltry number of old Epirot houses and nothing much else, not even a taverna, to redeem it.

The old hill town of **PARAMITHÍA**, 38km to the southeast (2 buses daily), is another disappointment. A castle and Byzantine church are scarcely in evidence, and despite touting as a centre for copper-working, just two mediocre metal shops remain in a tiny bazaar much encroached on by 1960s architecture – nothing comparable to what you'd more easily and conveniently see in Ioánnina.

For an inland excursion, your time would be much better spent at the remarkable **Necromanteion of Ephyra** or the **Aherónda gorge** (see below).

Párga and around

PÁRGA is a charming and popular coastal town, approximately 50km south of Igoumenítsa on the Epirot shoreline. Its crescent of tiered houses, set below a Norman-Venetian **Kástro**, and its superb **beach**, with a trail of rocky islets offshore, constitute as enticing a resort as any in western Greece. However, the last few years have seen all of this swamped by concrete apartment buildings, and the accompanying crowds. The Corfu model, presumably, was just too close. These days, in season, it's hard to recommend more than a brief stopover (if you can find a room) before taking the local ferry to **Paxí**. And in July and August even the ferry may need to be reserved a day ahead.

Párga's fate is sadder still given its highly evocative and idiosyncratic **history**. From the fourteenth to eighteenth centuries Párga was a lone Venetian toehold in Epirus, complementing the Serene Republic's offshore possessions in the Ionian islands. The Lion of Saint Mark – symbol of Venice – is still present on the *kástro* keep. Later, the Napoleonic French took the town for a brief period, leaving additional fortifications on the largest **islet**, a 200-metre swim from the harbour beach.

At the start of the nineteenth century, the town enjoyed a stint of independence, self-sufficient through the export of olives, still a mainstay of the region's agriculture. After that, the British acquired Párga and subsequently sold it to Ali Pasha. The townspeople, knowing his reputation, decamped to the Ionian islands, the area being resettled by Muslims who remained until the exchange of populations in 1924, when they were replaced by Orthodox Greeks from the area around Constantinople.

The town and its beaches

The town is dominated by the bluff-top **Kástro** (open all day). It is worth walking up the steps to its ruined ramparts, which offer excellent views of the town, its waterfront and a mountainous backdrop. Nestling among cypresses, the *kástro* is a haven from Párga's bustle.

Párga's fine **beaches** line three consecutive bays, split by the headland of the fortress hill, and often get very crowded in midsummer. Immediately beyond the *kástro* (and on foot easiest reached by the long stairway from the *kástro* gate) is **Váltos beach**, more than a kilometre in length as it sprawls around to the hamlet of the same name. **Lihnós**, 3km in the opposite (southeast) direction, is a similarly huge beach.

Practicalities

Buses link Párga with Igoumenítsa and Préveza four times daily, more in season; the stop is to the right of a crossroads on Alexandrou Varga, next to a small café that doubles as a ticket office. *West Travel* (☎0684/31 223), just inland from the dock, rents **mopeds** – worth considering for the trip to the Necromanteion of Ephyra (see below). *Ephira Travel* (☎0684/31 439), near the bus station, does **car rental**. Most tour agents sell tickets for the daily (in season) passenger **ferry** to Paxí. *West Travel* also runs **boat tours** up the Aherónda River to the Necromanteion of Ephyra, allowing good views of the delta birdlife en route.

Rooms are plentiful if a little pricey: someone will probably approach you on arrival at the bus station or ferry quay. Coastal **hotels** in particular are often block-booked in season, but in the town itself try the good-value *Tourist* (☎0684/31 239; ③), or the plusher *Acropol* (☎0684/31 239; ④). Under the same management, both hotels are next to the central Platía Vasilá, a two-minute walk from the harbour. The *Ayios Nektarios* (☎0684/31 150; ④) is worth trying, and there are a few *dhomátia* up near the *kástro*. There are **campsites** at both beaches and at *Parga Camping* (☎0684/31 130), among olive groves 600m inland to the north.

For **meals**, the taverna *Toh Kandouni*, at the rear of the market on Platía Vasilá, serves good cheap meals, and *Triadas*, in Platía Dhimarhíou next to the dock, is a friendly, good-value restaurant with local wine from a barrel. On the waterside, the family-run *Toh Souli* is the best of the bunch, offering wholesome local dishes.

Southeast to the Necromanteion of Ephyra

The **Necromanteion of Ephyra** (or Sanctuary of Persephone and Hades) stands just above the village of Mesopótamo, 22km southeast of Párga. Compared with Greece's other ancient remains, the site has few visitors, and this, coupled with its obscure location, make it a worthwhile and slightly unusual excursion. The sanctuary is sited on a low, rocky hill, above what in ancient times was the mouth of the Aherónda, the mythical Styx, river of the underworld. According to mythology, this was the spot where Charon rowed the dead across the Styx to Hades, and from Mycenacan to Roman times it maintained an elaborate Oracle of the Dead. The oracle never achieved the stature of Delphi or Dodona but its fame was sufficient for Homer, writing (it is assumed) in the ninth century BC, to use it as the setting for Odysseus's visit to Hades. This he does explicitly, with Circe advising Odysseus:

> You will come to a wild coast and to Persephone's grove, where the hill poplars grow and the willows that so quickly lose their seeds. Beach your boat there by Ocean's swirling stream and march on into Hades' Kingdom of Decay. There the River of Flaming Fire and the River of Lamentation, which is a branch of the Waters of the Styx, unite around a pinnacle of rock to pour their thundering streams into Acheron. This is the spot, my lord, that I bid you seek out . . . then the souls of the dead and departed will come up in their multitudes.

The sanctuary

Open summer daily 8am–5pm; rest of year daily 8am–3pm; 400dr, students 200dr.

The trees of Homer's account still mark the sanctuary's site, though the lake, which once enclosed the island-oracle, has receded to the vague line of the Aherónda skirting the plain: from the sanctuary you can pick out its course from the vegetation. As for the sanctuary itself, its **ruins**, flanked by an early Christian basilica, offer a fascinating exposé of the confidence tricks pulled by its priestly initiates.

According to contemporary accounts, pilgrims arriving on the oracle-island were accommodated for a night in windowless rooms. Impressed by the atmosphere, and by their mission to consult with the souls of the dead, they would then be relieved of their votive offerings, while awaiting their consultation with the dead. When their turn came, they would be sent groping along labyrinthine corridors into the heart of the sanctuary, where, further disoriented by hallucinogenic vapours, they would be lowered into the antechamber of "Hades" itself to witness whatever spiritual visitation the priests might have devised.

The remains of the sanctuary allow each of these function room to be identified, and there is a plan at the entrance. At the centre is a long room with high walls, flanked by chambers used for votive offerings. And from here metal steps lead to the underground chamber where the necromantic audiences took place. Originally this descent was by means of a precarious windlass mechanism – which was found on the site.

Practicalities

The Necromanteion is most easily reached by **tour** (or rented moped) from Párga. There are also daily **buses** from Párga and Préveza to **KANALÁKI**, where mopeds can be rented in summer. Buses from Párga stop at Kastrí (2km before Kanaláki), 5km from the site.

There are two basic **hotels** in Kanaláki, the *Ephyra* (☎0684/22 128; ③) and *Aheron* (☎0684/22 241; ③). The village could make a useful base for leisurely exploration of both the Necromanteion and the Soúli area (see below).

East into Souliot country

The highland region east of Párga was the traditional heartland of the **Souliots**, an independent-spirited tribe of Orthodox Christians and great mountain-warriors. During the last decades of the eighteenth century and the first of the nineteenth, the Souliots conducted a perennial rebellion against Ali Pasha and the Turks from their village strongholds above the **Aherónda gorge** and the mountains to the south.

Although it seems hard today to think of the placid Aherónda, near the Necromanteion of Ephyra, as the pathway to hell, only a few kilometres to the east its waters cut deep into rock strata and swirl in unnavigable eddies as the river saws a course through the gorge. While not in quite the same league as the Víkos, it is certainly a respectable wilderness, and if you're looking for an adventure inland from Párga you won't find better.

The hike up the gorge starts at **GLIKÍ**, a twelve-kilometre bus ride from Kanaláki on a side road between Préveza and Paramithía (one daily bus from the former). The river here, still relatively calm, is flanked on one bank by a reasonable **café-grill** ideal for a lunch before or after the trek, and on the other (the south or true-left bank) by a sign reading "Skála Tzavélainas", pointing up a dirt road. Following this, bear left after about one kilometre, towards a chapel, and within ten minutes you'll reach a laboriously wrought tunnel, where the wider track ends and the *skála* (a well-constructed path) begins. Below, the canyon walls have suddenly squeezed together, and upstream a carpet of greenery covers a wilderness, rolling up to the plainly visible castle of Kiáfa.

The main trail, waymarked by a Swiss tour company, descends to the Aherónda and crosses a relatively recent bridge. It then immediately takes a much older bridge over a tributary, the outflow of the Tsangariótiko River, known locally as the **Piyés Soulíou** (Souliot Springs). Beyond here the marked route climbs up through the oaks out of the Aherónda valley. After paralleling the Tsangariótiko, the trail turns up yet another side ravine to reach the tiny, poor hamlet of **SAMONÍDHA** – around two hours from Glikí – where there's a well behind the community office; the nearest *kafenío*/taverna is in the village of **SOÚLI**, 3km to the north.

From Samonídha a bulldozed track leads up to within another half-hour to **Kiáfa castle**, one of several the local Souliots erected in their many and protracted wars with the Turks.

South to Préveza

Approaches to Préveza (see below) from the Necromanteion and Aherónda area feature a few more minor sites and resorts before edging out onto the landlocked **Amvrakikós (Ambracian) Gulf**, where in 31 BC Octavian defeated Antony and Cleopatra at the Battle of Actium. Suitably enough, the most substantial of the ruins is Octavian's "Victory City" of **Nikopolis,** a bit south of the point where the Igoumenítsa–Préveza and the Árta–Préveza highways meet.

Two local **buses** cover the coastal route to Préveza from **AMMOUDHIÁ**, a surprisingly unspoilt little resort with an excellent beach, 4km due west of the Necromanteion. Most of the resorts down the coast attract mainly Germans and Italians equipped with campervans. The best place to break your journey, if you take this route, is at **LIYIÁ**, unmarked on many maps. There are **rooms** to rent, an impromptu campsite, several tavernas and an enormous, boulder-strewn beach, all overlooked by a crumbling castle in the distance. The long-distance buses to and from Párga or Igoumenítsa don't pass this way, but head inland at Mesopótamo, before joining the coastal road near Nikopolis.

Inland: Zalóngo and ancient Kassopi

Some 28km on the inland route from Messopótamo, you pass a turning east to the village of **KAMARÍNA**, which is overlooked by the monastery and monument of Zalóngo and the ruins of ancient Kassopi. These are a steep four-kilometre climb from the village, though a daily **bus** from Préveza goes direct to the site each morning at 6am. Such an early start does have its reward however; both places are glorious vantage points from which to watch the sunrise.

The **Monastery of Zalóngo** is a staple of Greek schoolbook history, its fame immortalized by the defiant mass suicide of a group of Souliot women. In 1806, Albanian troops cornered a large band of Souliots in the monastery. As this refuge was overrun, about sixty Souliot women and children fled to the top of the cliff above and, to the amazement of the approaching Muslim troops, the mothers danced one by one, with their children in their arms, over the edge of the precipice. This act is commemorated by a modern cement-and-stone **sculpture**, one of whose figures is currently headless after a lightning strike. Along with the monastery nearby, it draws regular groups of Greek schoolchildren.

Slightly to the northwest of the monastery, on a similar bluff, are the remains of **Ancient Kassopi** (daily 8am–3pm), a minor Thesprotian city-state. The ruins, dating mainly from the fourth century BC, are at present under excavation, though an excellent site plan helps to locate highlights, most of which are visible from the publicly accessible areas. You can view the walls and column bases of the central *agora*, *stoas*, a tiny theatre and a *katagoyeion* or guest hostelry. Principally, though, Kassopi is memorable for its superb location – some 600m above sea level, with the coast and Ionian islands laid out below.

Nikopolis

The "Victory City" of **NIKOPOLIS** was founded by Octavian on the site where his army had camped prior to the Battle of Actium. An arrogant and ill-considered gesture, it made little geographical sense. The settlement was on unfirm ground, water had to be transported by aqueduct from the distant springs of the Loúros mountains, and a population had to be forcibly imported from towns as far afield as Náfpaktos. However, such delusionary posturing was perhaps understandable. At Actium, Octavian had first blockaded and then largely annihilated the combined fleets of Antony and Cleopatra, gathered there for the invasion of Italy. The rewards were sweet, subsequently transforming Octavian from military commander to emperor of Rome, with the adopted title, Augustus.

The history of Nikopolis is undistinguished, with much of its original population drifting back to their homes. As the Roman Empire declined, the city suffered sacking by Vandals and Goths. Later, in the sixth century AD, it was restored by Justininan and flourished for a while as a Byzantine city, but within four centuries it had sunk again into the earth, devastated by the combined effect of earthquakes and Bulgar raids.

The site and museum

Open daily except Mon 8.30am–3pm; 400dr, students 200dr.

The far-flung and overgrown ruins stand 7km north of Préveza, on either side of the main road. Travelling by **bus**, you could just ask to be set down here, though it's a long walk back to town. If you can afford it, it would be better to engage a taxi in Préveza for a couple of hours.

The site looks impressive from the road. A great **theatre** stands to the east and as you approach the site museum, past remnants of the **baths**, there is a formidable stretch of **fortified walls**. Walking around, however, the promise of this enormous site is unfulfilled; few other remains reward close inspection, though they contribute to the once-grand feel. The ruins are also a home to snakes, butterflies and the odd tortoise. In spring, the spot is adorned with wild flowers.

From the scant foundations of the sixth-century **basilica of Bishop Alkyon**, it's a two-kilometre walk to the main **theatre**, whose arches stand amidst dangerously crumbling masonry. To the left of this you can just make out the sunken outline of the **stadium**, below the modern village of Smirtoúna. Octavian's own tent was pitched upon the hill above the village, and a massive **podium** remains from the commemorative monument that he erected. On a terrace alongside, recent excavations have revealed the remains of "beaks" (ramming protruberances) of some of the captured warships, which he dedicated to the gods.

The **museum** (sporadically open) houses a rather miscellaneous array of Roman sculpture. Its caretaker's main function used to be the wardership of the Roman and Byzantine mosaics unearthed amidst the foundations of the sixth-century **basilica of Doumetios** nearby, but these have recently been recovered by a protective layer of sand and polythene. If available, the caretaker will escort you to the Roman **Odeion**, for which he has the keys. This dates from the original construction of the city and has been well restored for use in a summer music festival (see "Préveza" below).

Préveza

Modern **PRÉVEZA**, at the tip of the Amvrakikós Gulf, is a relatively insignificant successor to Nikopolis, but not without its charm. Numerous **cafés** and **tavernas** line the waterfront, facing Actium where the forces of Antony and Cleopatra were defeated. With the advent of charter traffic to nearby Áktio airport in recent years, the town has had a facelift of sorts, and more character remains in the old market than, say, at Párga. Préveza merits a brief stopover, not only for Nikopolis, but also for its lively evenings and particularly the deliciously fresh fish on offer at the *psarotavérnes*. In the summer months, the town also has useful **hydrofoils** to Páxi, Itháki, Kefalloniá and Zákinthos, though services are rather sporadic.

Charter flights arriving at the **airport** generally have transport laid on to Lefkádha or Párga; otherwise there are taxis. The **bus station** in Préveza is on Leofóros Irínis, a kilometre north of the ferry dock. **Ferries** across the gulf ply across to Áktio jetty, where you can pick up buses (four or five daily) to Vónitsa and Lefkádha (times are displayed on the quayside ticket office).

Sharing a building on the quay are a **post office** and **tourist office**. The **OTE** is in a pedestrian grid, near the *Minos* hotel.

Accommodation

The half-dozen **hotels** are neither especially inviting nor geared to budget travellers. The cheapest and most basic is the *Urania* (☎0682/27 123; ③), near the bus terminal at Irínis 17. Next comes the *Minos*, a clean but characterless hotel on 21 Oktovriou (☎0682/28 424; ④). Reasonable mid-range options include the comfortable *Dioni* at Kaloú 4 (☎0682/27 432; ④) and the more businesslike *Préveza City*, also on Irínis (☎0682/27 365; ④). Good value but out of town at Áyios Thomas is the *Savvas* (☎0682/27 432; ③).

The nearest **campsites** are *Camping Indian Village* (☎0682/27 185) and *Camping Kalamitsi* (☎0682/22 368), around 4km from town on the promontory south of the ferry dock out towards Kalamítsi. In the opposite direction, any bus running through Kanáli (not to be confused with Kanaláki) will pass the summer-only sites of *Monolíthi* (☎0682/51 755) and *Kanali* (☎0682/22 741), on either side of the road at Monolíthi beach, a fine stretch of sand 11km from Préveza.

Eating, drinking and nightlife

There are at least a dozen **tavernas** scattered around the centre of Préveza, many dotted around the *platía* by the waterfront. Some good choices include *Psatha*, Dhardhanellíou 2 (up from the main shopping thoroughfare), for fresh fish; the *Ouzerí Kaiksis* at Parthenagoyíou 9 for seafood *mezédhes*; and *Amvrosios*, specializing in grilled sardines and barrel wine at budget prices, virtually under the Venetian clock tower. *G. Peponis* offers reasonable waterfront eating on Venizélou, the quay. *Patsás* fans might try *Treis Adherfes* at Tsaldári 51, just up from the bus station. If you can afford it, *Toh Dhelfinaki*, behind the *Credit Bank*, specializes in fish.

At **night**, the alleys in the bazaar, especially around the fish-market building, come alive with an assortment of bars, cafés and shops, producing a vibrant, yet relaxed atmosphere.

As for culture, July and August see a range of musical and theatrical events as part of the **Nikopolia festival**, held at Nikopolis. On Platía Androútsou by the port is the only **shadow puppet** (*karaghiosis*) theatre left in the country .

Árta and around

Fifty kilometres northeast of Préveza is **ÁRTA**, finely situated in a loop of the broad Árakhthos River as it meanders towards **Amvrakikós Gulf**, 20km to the south. It is one of the more pleasant Greek towns: a quiet place, very much the provincial capital, with an old centre that retains much of its Turkish bazaar aspect, and some celebrated medieval monuments.

From the west, you enter town by the recently restored packhorse **bridge**, which is the subject of song and poetry throughout the mainland. Legend maintains that the bridge builder, continually thwarted by the current washing his foundations away, took the advice of a bird and sealed up his wife in the central pier; the bridge finally held but the woman's voice haunted the place thereafter.

The Town

Árta was known anciently as Ambracia and had a brief period of fame as the capital of Pyrrhus, king of Epirus; it was the base for the king's hard-won campaigns ("Another such victory and I am lost") in Italy – the original Pyrrhic victories. The foundations of a **Temple of Apollo** and an **Odeion** lie on either side of Udhós Pírrou, otherwise there are very few remains from this period. At the northeast end of the street is the **Froúrio**, the ancient acropolis and the citadel in every subsequent era. Its keep is now occupied by a hotel, an open-air theatre and fragrant citrus trees; the walls are almost entirely Byzantine, and you can pace their circuit.

More substantial monuments date from Árta's second burst of glory, following the 1204 fall of Constantinople, when the town became aggrandized as the **Despotate of Epirus**, an autonomous Byzantine state. The despotate, which stretched from Corfu to Thessaloníki, was governed by the Angelos dynasty (the imperial family expelled from Constantinople) and survived until 1449, when the garrison surrendered to the Turks.

Most striking and certainly the most bizarre of the Byzantine monuments is the **Panayía Paragorítissa** (sometimes rendered Paragorítria; Tues–Sat 8.30am–3pm; 500dr), a grandiose, five-domed cube that rears above Platía Skoufá, at the west end of that street. The interior is almost Gothic in appearance, the main dome being supported by an extraordinary cantilever system that looks unwieldy and unsafe. Up top, this inse-curity is accentuated by a looming *Pandokrátor* (Christ in Majesty) mosaic in excellent condition, overshadowing the sixteenth-century frescoes. The church, flanked by two side chapels, was built in 1283–96 by Despot Nikiforos I as part of a monastic complex.

Two smaller Byzantine churches from the same period also survive in the town. Both have a more conventional structure but are enlivened by highly elaborate brick and tile decorations on the outside walls. They're usually locked but this is no tragedy since the exteriors are the main interest. **Ayía Theódhora**, containing the fine marble tomb of the wife of the Epirot ruler Michael II, stands in its own courtyard halfway

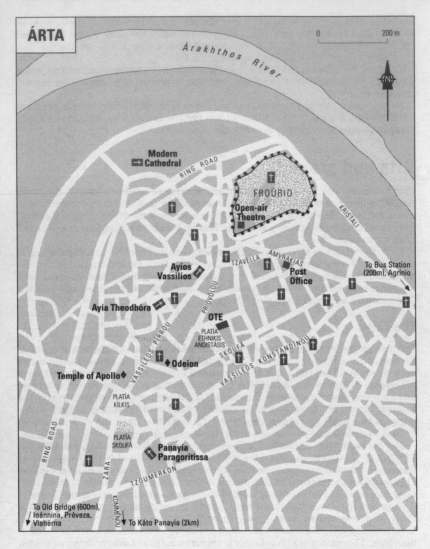

down Pírrou. A little further north, opposite the produce market, is thirteenth-century **Áyios Vassílios**, a gem ornamented with glazed polychrome tiles and bas-reliefs.

Nearby monasteries

Amid the orange groves surrounding Árta, a number of **monasteries** were built during the despotate, many of them by members of the imperial Angelos dynasty.

Within easy walking distance (2km along Odhós Komméno) stands **Káto Panayía**, erected by Michael II between 1231 and 1271. The gabled roof of the triple-aisled nave is supported by six columns; one of the two cross-vaults serves as a narthex. Many of the frescoes are badly smudged, but the highlight is an undamaged version of Christ as Emmanuel in the front vault. The west outer wall sports a graphic *Last Judgement*, but this is definitely a case where the interior is more compelling than the exterior. The *katholikón* in a shaded courtyard (May–Sept 7am–1pm & 4.30–7.30pm; Oct–Apr 8am–1pm & 3–6pm), has extravagant exterior decoration, and frescoes inside showing Christ in three guises. This is a working convent occupied by a dozen nuns, and in one corner of the garden, several caged peacocks.

Further out of Árta, 6km north by a circuitous route (11–12 buses daily from the ring-road stop), the monastic church of **Panayía Vlahernón** in Vlahérna village is engaging inside and out. To the basic three-aisled twelfth-century plan, Michael II added the trio of domes in the following century, as well as the narthex; one of the two tombs inside is thought to his. Having found the key custodian at the nearby *kafenío*, you enter the south narthex door under a fine **relief** of the Archangel Michael. Dissimilar columns support the added cupolas, but the church is more remarkable for what is hidden from view. The warden will lift a trap door to reveal a magnificent **mosaic**, just one portion of a vast marble floor punctuated with such tesselations. Only a few of numerous **frescoes** thought to be under plaster are exposed. This is the most beautiful of Árta's churches, worth contemplating at length from the *kafenío*.

Practicalities

Arriving by **bus**, you'll be dropped at a terminus on the riverbank, on the northern outskirts of town, though there is a discretional stop on the ring road east of both the modern and the Byzantine bridges. From the main station it's a ten-minute walk along **Odhós Skoufá**, the main thoroughfare, to the central **Platía Ethnikís Andistásis**. Skoufá, which is the town's main commercial street and partly pedestrianized, and its parallel streets, Pírrou and Konstandínou, wind through the oldest part of town.

There are just four **hotels**, normally enough for the trickle of tourists and business visitors. Most are close by the Platía Ethnikís Andistásis. The *Amvrakia*, Priovólou 13 (☎0681/28 311; ④), is a comfortable hotel with a good position on a pedestrian way, just off Platía Ethnikís. The *Chronos* (☎0681/22 211; ④) is in Platía Kílkis; it's noisy and grossly overpriced. The *Rex*, Skoufá 9 (☎0681/27 563; ②), is cheap, grimy and a desperation option. The *Xenia*, Froúrio (☎0681/27 413; ④), is brilliantly sited in the castle, and good value if a little soulless.

The town's **restaurants** are excellent value, catering for locals rather than tourists. Best of the cheapies is *Averoff*, at the corner of Skoufá and Grimbóvou, or the *Ellinikon* at Skoufá 5. For more formal meals of grilled or *ouzerí*-type fare, try the *Skaraveos* at Priovólou 11, by the *Amvrakia*, or two tavernas, the *Iy Oasi* and the *Protomastoras*, both well sited by the old bridge.

On Pírrou, you can find the covered fruit and vegetable **market** and the *Pallas* **cinema** (often showing films in English). In the evenings, people tend to perform their *voltas* around Platía Ethnikís Andistásis, or congregate in its cafés.

The Amvrakikós Gulf

Árta is a bright spot close to the **Amvrakikós Gulf**. Further around, and in fact all the way south to the open sea, there is little to prompt a stop. Locals from Árta head at weekends for seafood meals at the fishing villages of **MENÍDHI** (21km) or **KORONÍSIA** (25km), the latter also a low-key windsurfing resort. The best extended escape is to **Lefkádha** (see *The Ionian* chapter), which can be reached either via Amfilohía–Vónitsa, or on one of the few direct buses daily from Ioánnina running through Filipiádha and Préveza. If you're approaching from Árta you might try flagging down a Ioánnina–Lefkádha bus at the Filipiádha junction.

AMFILOHÍA is promisingly situated at the head of the gulf, but in reality is a very dull small town. The chance for a swim would seem on the map a redeeming feature, but the water here is at its most stagnant.

If you needed to stay the night, **VÓNITSA**, 38km west of Amfilóhia, would be a convenient choice. Again it's not an exciting place, and frustratingly distant from real sea. But there's a quiet waterside, squares lined with plane trees, and a substantial **castle** above. There are four **hotels**, including the modestly priced but basic *Leto* (☎0643/22 246; ③) on Platía Anaktorioú, and the slightly more comfortable *Bel Mare* (☎0643/22 394; ④) on the *paralia*. Infrequent local **buses** cover the 14km to **ÁKTIO**, the south ferry terminal across the gulf from Préveza, passing Áktio airport.

The coast south to Messolóngi

Heading south for Messolóngi and the gulf of Kórinthos, there is not much more of interest, at least on the direct gulf and **inland route**. From Amfilohía, you pass a few swampy patches of lake pumped for irrigating the local tobacco. Midway down the Amfilohía–Messolóngi road, **AGRÍNIO** is little more than a transport link for this area, with buses to Árta/Ioánnina, Karpeníssi and south to Andírio, where there are local buses to Náfpaktos, as well as the ferry across the Gulf of Kórinthos to the Peloponnese.

The **coast south from Vónitsa** is bleakly impressive, with a quiet stretch of road that skirts the shoreline with nothing but an arid wilderness inland. However, if you have transport there are great opportunities for finding tiny deserted beaches. There is just one sleepy but pleasant settlement, **MÍTIKAS**, whose rows of rickety houses strung along a pebbly shore look out onto the island of Kálamos. As yet development is minimal, confined to a couple of **hotels**, including *Simos* (☎0646/81 380; ③), and some **tavernas** pitched at locals; it's a pleasant place to break a journey or wait for a boat across to either **Kálamos** or (less reliable and summer-only) **Lefkádha**. A kilometre of uncommercialized beach leads from the village, and behind lies a sheer wall of amphitheatric mountainside.

South from here, the coast road runs through **ASTAKÓS**, a village whose name means "lobster". Patrick Leigh Fermor, in *Roumeli*, fantasizes about arriving at this gastronomic-sounding place; it turned out to be a crashing non-event, and it hasn't changed much since. Like Amfilohía, the location of the village is its most attractive attribute. The *Stratos* (☎0646/41 096; ④) is the sole option for accommodation; it's a mid-range, respectable **hotel**, and the price includes breakfast. You may want to make use of this if you are taking the ferry across to **Itháki**, which generally leaves in the early afternoon.

Hardly more enticing is **ETOLIKÓ**, perched on a causeway across the Messolóngi gulf. The lagoon is sumpy, the buildings neglected, poverty palpable. Its main virtues are two low-grade **hotels** that are cheaper than any options in Messolóngi: the *Alexandra* (☎0632/22 243; ③) and *Liberty Inn* (☎0632/22 206; ②). There is a sporadic **bus** service to Messolóngi, which is just 10km south, past the salt factories that are today the area's mainstay.

Kálamos

The island of **Kálamos** is essentially a bare mountain that rises abruptly from the sea. In summer there are usually a few yachts moored in the small fishing harbour below the main port and village, Hóra, but otherwise the island sees few visitors. The only regular connection is a daily *kaíki* from Mítikas, which leaves the mainland at noon and returns from the island at 7am the next day. The few **rooms** in Hóra are usually booked through the summer, so come prepared to camp.

HÓRA, on the south coast, is spread out among gardens and olive groves, and largely survived the 1953 earthquake, which devastated so much of the Ionian. There's a basic *kafenío*/taverna and a "supermarket" by the harbour, and two more **cafés** higher up, next to a **post office** where you can change money. The village **beach**, to the southwest, has a couple of tavernas behind a long stretch of shingle; in summer a few people camp beyond the windmills at the end. There's a much better, but less accessible pebble beach fifteen minutes to the east of the harbour.

KÁSTRO, the old fortified main village, is a ninety-minute walk from Hóra. Its walls are surrounded by roofless and abandoned houses and its *platía* is overgrown, used by villagers to keep their hens and sheep. Down towards its harbour, more of the houses are still inhabited, though there's no shop or café.

There are more good beaches between Hóra and Episkopí, on the north coast facing Mítikas. The island's strip of road runs this way but the beaches can be reached more easily by boat than by scrambling down the forested slopes from the road. To the southeast of Hóra, a mule track leads to the village of Pórto Leóne, deserted since the 1953 earthquake. It's a two-hour walk across scrub-covered mountainside, with views across to the neighbouring island of Kástos.

Kástos and Átokos

The island of **Kástos** has one village with a harbour and taverna. Only a few families still live here permanently and there's no regular *kaíki*. If you want to get across, you could ask around in Mítikas or Kálamos to see if anybody is planning a trip, but you'll probably have to hire a *kaíki* to take you. Normally the only visitors are from the occasional yachts calling in at the harbour.

The islet of **Átokos**, to the southwest, has a few ruined houses, but is now completely uninhabited, as are the other islets scattered off the coast to the south.

Messolóngi

MESSOLÓNGI (MISSOLONGI), for most visitors, is irrevocably bound with the name of **Lord Byron**, who died in the town, to dramatic world effect, while organizer of the local Greek forces during the War of Independence (see box overleaf). The town has an obvious interest in this literary past, though be aware that, as in Byron's time, it's a pretty miserable and desperately unromantic place: wet through autumn and spring, and comprised of drab, modern buildings. If you come here on a pilgrimage, it's best to plan on moving ahead within the day.

The Town

You enter the town by the **Gate of the Exodus**, whose name recalls an attempt by 9000 men, women and children to break out during the Turks' year-long siege in 1826. In one wild dash they managed to get free of the town, leaving a group of defenders to destroy it in their wake. But they were betrayed and in the supposed safety of nearby Mount Zígos were ambushed and massacred by a large Albanian mercenary force.

Just inside this gate, on the right, is the **Heroón**, or **Garden of Heroes** (summer 9am–8pm; earlier closing at other times of year) – though it is signposted in English as "Heroes' Tombs" – where a tumulus covers the bodies of the town's unnamed defenders. Beside the tomb of the Greek Souliot commander, Markos Botsaris, is a **statue of Byron**, erected in 1881, under which is buried the poet's heart. The rest of Byron's remains were taken back to his family home, Newstead Abbey, despite his dying request: "here let my bones moulder; lay me in the first corner without pomp or

O LÓRDHOS VÍRONOS: BYRON IN MESSOLONG

Byron arrived at Messolóngi, a squalid and inhospitable town surrounded by marshland, in January 1824. The town, with its small port allowing access to the Ionian islands, was the western centre of resistance against the Turks. The poet, who had contributed much of his personal fortune to the war effort, as well as his own fame, was enthusiastically greeted with a 21-gun salute.

On landing, he was made commander-in-chief of the five thousand soldiers gathered at the garrison: a role that was as much political as military. The Greek forces, led by Klephtic brigand-generals, were divided among themselves and each faction separately and persistently petitioned him for money. He had already wasted months on the island of Kefalloniá, trying to assess their claims and quarrels before finalizing his own military plan – to march full force on Náfpaktos and from there take control of the Gulf of Corinth – but in Messolóngi he was again forced to delay.

Occasionally Byron despaired: "Here we sit in this realm of mud and discord", he wrote in his journal. But while other Philhellenes were returning home, disillusioned by the squabbles and larceny of the Greeks, or appalled by the conditions in this damp, stagnant town, he stayed, campaigning eloquently and profitably for the cause. Outside his house, he drilled soldiers; in the lagoon he rowed, and shot, and caught a fever. It was, bathetically, the most important contribution he could have made to the struggle. On April 19, 1824, Byron died, pronouncing a few days earlier, in a moment of resignation, "My wealth, my abilities, I devoted to the cause of Greece – well, here is my life to her!"

The news of the poet's death reverberated across northern Europe, swelled to heroic proportions by his admirers. Arguably it changed the course of the war in Greece. When Messolóngi fell again to the Turks, in 1826, there was outcry in the European press, and the French and English forces were finally galvanized into action, sending a joint naval force for protection. It was this force that accidentally engaged the Turks at Navarino Bay (see p.209), casting a fatal blow against the Turkish navy.

Byron, ever since independence, has been a Greek national hero. Almost every town in the country has a street – Víronos – named after him; there was once a brand of cigarettes (perhaps the ultimate Greek tribute); and, perhaps more important, the respect he inspired was for many years generalized to his fellow countrymen – before being dissipated in this century by British interference in the civil war and bungling in Cyprus.

nonsense." Perhaps he knew this would be disregarded. There is certainly a touch of pomp in the carving of Byron's coat of arms with a royal crown above; there had been speculation that Byron would be offered the crown of an independent Greece. Among the palm trees and rusty cannons there are also monuments to American, German and French Philhellenes.

Elsewhere in the town, traces of Byron are sparse. The **house** in which he lived and died was destroyed during World War II and its site is marked by a clumsy memorial garden. It's on Odhós Levídhou, reached from the central *platía* by walking down to the end of Trikoúpi and turning left.

Back in the central Platía Bótsari, the town hall houses a small **museum** devoted to the revolution (8am–1.30pm & 4–6pm), with some emotive paintings of the independence struggle (including a reproduction of Delacroix's *Gate of the Sortie*) and a rather desperate collection of Byronia, padded out with postcards from Newstead Abbey and the branch of an elm from his old school, Harrow. The credibility of the museum is further overreached by a central display of ephemera from the Nottinghamshire town of Gedling, which is twinned with Messolóngi.

Perhaps more interesting and enjoyable than any of this is a walk across the **lagoon**, past the **forts** of Vassiládhi and Kleissoúra, which were vital defences against the

Turkish navy. The lagoon, with its salt-pans and fish farms, attracts coastal birds. Migrant waders pass through and, in spring, avocets and black-winged stilts nest here. A causeway extends for about 5km and reaches the open sea at Tourlídha, where there are a number of *psarotavérnes*.

Practicalities

Long-distance **buses** arrive at Mavro Kordhato 5 (☎0631/ 22 371), next to Platía Bótsari, and the local ones just a block away. You can **rent bicycles** from the *Theoxenia* should you wish to explore the lagoon.

Hotels in Messolóngi are a bit cheerless, expensive and often block-booked by tour groups. Etolikó (see p.324), 10km to the west, would be a cheaper alternative for the night. If you need or want to stay in the town, a good option is the *Avra,* Hariláou Trikoúpi 5 (☎0631/22 284; ③); it's adjacent to the central *platía* and close to an inexpensive taverna, *Toh Elleniko,* which offers reasonable cuisine. More upmarket and impersonal choices include the *Liberty,* Iróön Politehníou 41 (☎0631/28 089; ④), one block from the Heroón, or the *Theoxenia* (☎0631/22 493; ④), which is on the landward side of the lagoon. Both hotels have decent if unmemorable **restaurants**, otherwise apart from the usual grills around the central Platía Bótsari, there is a dearth of places to eat in town.

travel details

Buses

Buses detailed have similar frequency in each direction, so entries are given just once; for reference check under both starting-point and destination.

Agrínio to: Karpeníssi (1–2 daily; 3hr 30min); Corfu (bus/ferry, 2 daily in season; 4hr); Lefkádha (5 daily; 2hr); Messolóngi–Andírio (12 daily; 1hr/ 1hr 30min).

Áktio to: Lefkádha (5 daily; 45 min).

Árta to: Ioánnina (11 daily; 2hr 30min); Prámanda and Melissourgí (2 daily Mon–Fri 5am/2pm; 1hr 30min); Préveza (5 daily; 1hr); Theodhóriana (daily Mon–Fri at 1.30pm; 1hr 15min).

Igoumenítsa to: Athens (4 daily; 8hr); Párga (5 daily; 1hr 30min); Préveza (2 daily; 3hr); Thessaloníki (1 daily; 8hr 30min).

Ioánnina to: Árta (11 daily; 2hr 30min); Athens (11 daily; 7hr 30min); Dodona (Mon–Sat except Thurs 6.30am & 4.30pm; Sun 6pm only; 40min); Igoumenítsa (9 daily; 2hr 30min); Kastoriá, via Kónitsa (2 daily, change at Neápoli; 6hr); Kónitsa (7 daily; 1hr 30min); Métsovo (6 daily; 1hr 30min); Monodhéndhri (2 daily Mon–Fri 6am/ 4.15pm; 45min); Pápingo (Mon, Wed & Fri 5am/

2.30pm; 1hr); Paramithiá/Párga (1 daily; 2hr/3hr); Patra (5 daily; 4hr 30min); Prámanda (2 daily Mon–Fri 5am/3.15pm; 2hr); Préveza (10 daily; 2hr 30min); Sirákö (2 weekly Fri & Sun, 2hr 30min); Thessaloníki (5 daily; 8hr); Tríkala, via Métsovo and Kalambáka (3 daily; 1hr 30min/3hr); Tsepélovo (2 daily Mon–Fri; 1hr); Vovoússa (Mon, Tues & Fri 2pm, Sun 7.30am; 1hr 30min).

Messolóngi to: Astakós (2 daily; 1hr 15min); Athens (5 daily; 4hr).

Préveza to: Glikí (1 daily; 1hr); Párga (5 daily; 1hr 30min).

Vónitsa to: Áktio (3 daily; 30 min); Lefkádha (5 daily; 30min).

Ferries

Astakós to: Itháki (daily early afternoon, almost year-round).

Igoumenítsa to: Corfu (hourly, last at 10pm; 1–2hr). Also to Ancona, Bari, Trieste and Brindisi (Italy). See "Igoumenítsa and around" for details.

Párga to: Paxí (2 daily June–Sept; 2hr).

Préveza to: Áktio (every 20min 9am–9pm, every half hour 6am–9am & 9pm–midnight, every hour midnight–6am; 10min).

Sívota to: Paxí (2 weekly, in season; 2hr).

Hydrofoils and catamarans (summer only)
Routes and services change annually, and some years don't operate at all. Check at the Igoumenítsa Port Authority (☎0665/22 240) for details of future services.
Igoumenítsa In the past, services to Corfu, Páxi and other Ionian islands, and Brindisi (Italy). No service at all in 1994. There are plans for catamaran services to Corfu and Brindisi.

Préveza Infrequent services to Páxi, Itháki and Kefalloniá in season.

Flights
Ioánnina to: Athens (2 daily); Thessaloníki (3–5 weekly).
Préveza to: Athens (5–7 weekly).
Also occasional international charters between Préveza (Áktion) and Britain.

CHAPTER FIVE

THE NORTH: MACEDONIA AND THRACE

The two northern provinces – **Macedonia** and **Thrace** – have been part of the Greek state for little more than two generations. Macedonia (*Makedhonía*) was surrendered by the Turks after the Balkan wars in 1913; Thrace (*Thráki*) only in 1923. As such, the region stands slightly apart from the rest of the nation – an impression reinforced for visitors by scenery and climate that are essentially Balkan. Macedonia is characterized by lake-sprinkled vistas to the west and – to the east, towards Thrace – by heavily cultivated flood plains and the deltas of rivers finishing courses begun in former Yugoslavia or Bulgaria. The climate can be harsh, with steamy summers and bitterly cold winters, especially up in the Rhodópi mountains that form a natural frontier with Bulgaria.

These factors, along with a dearth of beaches, may explain why the north is so little-known to outsiders, even those who have travelled widely throughout the rest of the mainland and the islands. The only areas to draw more than a scattering of visitors, even at the height of the summer, are Halkidhíkí and Mount Olympus, **Halkidhíkí**, the three-pronged peninsula that trails below Thessaloníki, provides the city's beach-playground in rapidly expanding resort areas, such as Kassándhra and Sithonía. More hard-won pleasures – and stunning views – are on offer amid the slopes of **Mount Olympus**, the mythical abode of the gods and a mecca for walkers in the south of the region. For the rest, few travellers look beyond the dull farmland trunk routes to Turkey and Bulgaria.

With a more prolonged acquaintance, the north may well grow on you. Part of its appeal lies in its vigorous day-to-day life, independent of tourism, at its most evident in the relaxed Macedonian capital of **Thessaloníki** (Salonica) and the north's chief port **Kavála**. Another lies, as in Epirus, in the mountain areas of the west, around **Flórina** and the lakeside city of **Kastoriá**. Monuments are on the whole modest, with the exception of Philip II of Macedon's tomb, discovered at **Veryína** and now open to visitors. There are lesser Macedonian and Roman sites at **Pella** and at **Philippi**, Saint Paul's first stop in Greece.

If you are male, over 21, and interested enough in monasticism – or Byzantine art and architecture – to pursue the applications procedure, **Mount Áthos** may prove to be a highlight of a Greek stay. This "Monks' Republic" occupies the mountainous easternmost prong of Halkidhíkí, maintaining control over twenty monasteries and numerous dependencies and hermitages. **Women** (and female animals) have been excluded from the peninsula since a decree of 1060, although it is possible for both sexes to view the monasteries from the sea by taking a boat tour from the resorts of Ierissós and Ouranoúpoli in the "secular" part of Athos.

THESSALONÍKI AND WESTERN MACEDONIA

Thessaloníki is the fulcrum, and focus, to Macedonian travel. If you are heading for the west of the province – to **Kastoriá**, **Édhessa** or **Flórina** – you will usually do best to go by bus or train. The train ride between Édhessa and Flórina, edging around Lake Vegoritídha, is one of the most scenic in the country, and Kastoriá, for those who like their towns remote and speckled with Byzantine monuments, is also highly worthwhile. Beyond Flórina, the secluded **Préspa lakes**, straddling the frontiers of three countries, constitute one of the finest wildlife refuges in the Balkans. The biggest attraction in this part of Macedonia, however, has to be **Mount Olympus** (Óros

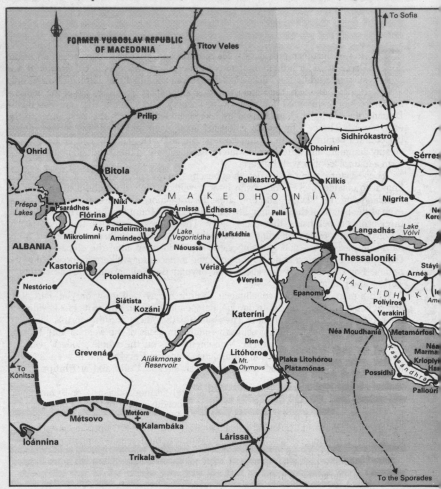

Ólimbos). The fabled home of the gods soars high above the town of Litóhoro, easily approached from the highway or rail line between Lárissa and Thessaloníki.

Thessaloníki (Salonica)

The second city of Greece and administrative centre for the north, **THESSALONÍKI** – or Salonica, as the city was known in western Europe until this century – has a very different feel to Athens: more Balkan-European and modern, less Middle Eastern. Situated at the head of the Thermaikós gulf, it also seems more open; you're never far from the sea, and the air actually circulates, though this is a bit of mixed blessing since the bay, anywhere near town, is pretty much a sump.

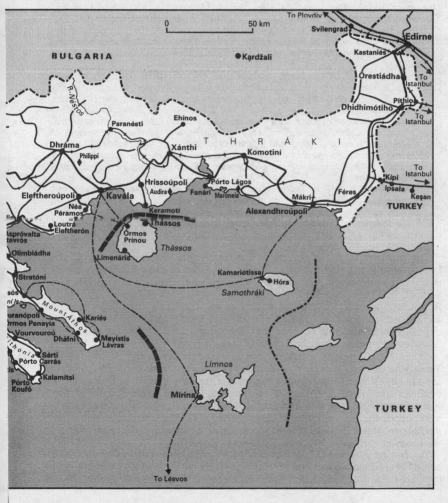

A NOTE ON MACEDONIA

The name "Macedonia" is a geographical term of long standing, applied to an area that has always been populated by a variety of races and cultures.

The original Kingdom of Macedonia, which gained pre-eminence under Philip II and Alexander the Great, was a Greek affair – governed by Greek kings and inhabited by a predominantly Greek population. Its early borders spread south to Mount Olympus, west to present-day Kastoriá, east to Kavála, and north into parts of what was Yugoslavia. It lasted, however, for little more than two centuries. In subsequent years the region fell under the successive control of Romans, Slavs, Byzantines, Saracens and Bulgars, before eventual subjugation, with southern Greece, under Ottoman Turkish rule.

In the late nineteenth century, when the disintegration of the Ottoman Empire began to throw into question future national territories, the name Macedonia denoted simply the region. Its population included Greeks, Slavs and Bulgarians – who referred to themselves and their language as "Macedonian" – as well as large numbers of Jews, Serbs, Vlachs, Albanians and Turks. The first nationalist struggles for the territory began in the 1870s, when small armies of Greek *andartes*, Serbian *chetniks* and Bulgarian *comitadjis* took root in the mountain areas, coming together against the Ottomans in the first Balkan War.

Following Turkish defeat, things swiftly became more complex. The Bulgarians laid sole claim to Macedonia in the second Balkan War, but were defeated, and a 1912 Greco-Serbian agreement divided the bulk of Macedonian territory between the two states along linguistic/ethnic lines. During World War I, however, the Bulgarians occupied much of Macedonia and Thrace, until their capitulation in 1917. After Versailles, a small part of Slavic-speaking Macedonia remained in Bulgaria, and there were exchanges of Greek-speakers living in Bulgaria, and Bulgarians in Greece. This was followed, in 1924, by the arrival and settlement of hundreds of thousands of Greek refugees from Asia Minor, who – settling throughout Greek Macedonia – effectively swamped any remaining Slavophone population.

During World War II the Bulgarians again occupied all of eastern Macedonia and Thrace (beyond the River Strímon), as allies of Nazi Germany. Their defeat by the Allies led to withdrawal and seems to have vanquished ambitions. Recent Bulgarian leaders, both Communist and post-Communist, have renounced all territorial claims and

The "modern" quality of the city is due largely to a disastrous 1917 fire, which levelled most of the old labyrinth of Turkish lanes; the city was rebuilt over the next eight years on a French grid plan, with long central avenues running parallel to the seafront. The result is a more liveable, though arguably less interesting, city than Athens, with a more cosmopolitan, wealthy aspect, stimulated by its major university and international trade fair. Thessaloníki will have soon outgrown its self-deprecating nicknames of *I Protévoussa ton Prosfigón* ("The Refugee Capital", after the ring of 1920s Anatolian settlements, all prefixed by "Nea", around it) and *Ftohómana* (Poor-Mother).

Before 1923, the city's population was as mixed as any in the Balkans. Besides Turks, who had been occupiers for close to five centuries, there were Slavs, Albanians and the largest European **Jewish** community of the age: 100,000, or over half of the inhabitants, before the first waves of emigration to Palestine began after World War I. Numbers remained at around 70,000 up until World War II, when all but a tiny fraction were deported to the concentration camps, in one of the worst atrocities committed in the Balkans. It was this operation in which former Austrian president Kurt Waldheim was involved – or, rather, which he claims not to have noticed.

You can get glimpses of "Old Salonica" today in the walled **Kástra** quarter, on the hillside beyond the modern grid of streets. Even amidst the post-1917 flatlands below, there are pockets of Turkish, and Greek Art Deco, buildings – mostly uncared for, and "minority rights" for "Greek-Bulgarians". The position of Yugoslavia, though, which under Tito established the Socialist Republic of Macedonia in its share of the historical territory, was more ambiguous. During the decades of its unity there were Yugoslav propaganda attempts to suggest Slav affinities with the ancient Macedonian kingdom, and, by extension, with the present Greek population.

When the Yugoslav federation fell apart violently in mid-1991, the issue resurfaced at the top of the Greeks' political agenda, after the population of Yugoslav Macedonia voted overwhelmingly for an independent nation of Macedonia. Greek reaction was vitriolic, and all the more so when the fledgeling nation adopted the star of Veryina (the symbol of Alexander the Great) as their national symbol and flag. Had the new state opted for a new name and symbol, the Greeks, doubtless, would have had no quarrel: an impoverished nation of two million, after all, posed little strategic threat. But their adoption of the Macedonian name and symbol was too much: Greeks claimed a cultural and historical copyright over both, and felt their "expropriation" as an act of aggression. The Right even called for invasion.

The Mitsotakis government, ensnared in this nightmare, managed to resist military action, but spared no effort to thwart the Yugoslav-Macedonian aspirations, spurred along by huge popular demonstrations in Thessaloníki and Athens. Ministers were sent on interminable rounds of EC capitals, imploring their allies not to recognize any state assuming the name of "Macedonia", and, increasingly isolated by the international community, the Greeks instigated an economic boycott of the fledgeling state.

These moves severely destablized the new country but did nothing to halt its recognition by the UN and EC – albeit under a convoluted (and presumably interim) title, The Former Yugoslav Republic of Macedonia. Greeks have had to accept this de facto situation, but they still refuse to use the name, referring to the territory as *Ta Skópia*, after the capital. References in the press tend to use the phrase the "rump Skopje republic" in terms scarcely less disparaging than those reserved for the "Turkish pseudo-state of Northern Cyprus"; indeed it is prohibited to refer in print to Yugoslav "Macedonia" except in inverted commas, and official posters throughout Greece proclaim that "Macedonia was, is and always will be Greek and only Greek". This war of words is probably louder than any likely deeds but it is bad news for the beleaguered rump population, and for those Slavs remaining in Greek Macedonia and Thrace, whose existence Greece refuses to admit.

doubtless earmarked for redevelopment. For most visitors, however, it is Thessaloníki's excellent **Archeological Museum**, with its spectacular exhibits from the tombs of Philip of Macedon and others of his dynasty, that stands out. Additionally, if you have developed a taste for Byzantine monuments, a unique array of **churches** dating from Roman times to the fifteenth century constitutes a showcase of the changing styles of Orthodox religious architecture.

The downside, for visitors as well as residents, is a complex of **problems** all too reminiscent of Athens. Industries and residences alike discharge their waste, untreated, into the gulf, and traffic on the main avenues, despite a comprehensive one-way system, is often at a standstill. The former *Néa Dhimokratía* mayor, Sotiris Kouvelas, elected on the promise of a clean-up, had ambitious plans for a metro line and a widening of the waterfront boulevard – never acted on. Indeed his only claim to fame was to defy the central government by being the first official to oversee the introduction of satellite television, officially forbidden in Greece until the late 1980s but now commonplace.

The Thessaloníki phone code is ☎031

Arrival, orientation and information

Arriving in Thessaloníki is fairly straightforward. The **train station** on the west side of town is just a short walk from the central grid of streets and the harbour. The previously scattered provincial KTELs are being gradually gathered into one giant **bus terminal** at the bottom of 28 Oktovríou, in the Sfayiá district, accessible on local bus #31. Coming from the **airport**, city bus #78 (115dr) shuttles back and forth hourly between 7am and midnight; the most convenient town stops are the train station and Platía Aristotélous. All **ferries and hydrofoils** call at the passenger port, within walking distance of the train station, at the western end of the seafront. For all departure and booking details, see the relevant sections of "Listings", p.346.

Once within the grid, **orientation** is made relatively straightforward by the presence of several main avenues: Ayíou Dhimitríou, Egnatías, Tsimiskí and Mitropóleos. All run parallel to the quay, but confusingly change their names repeatedly as they head east into the city's modern annexe. The divide between the older and newer parts of town is marked by the exhibition grounds and the start of the seaside park strip, known locally as Zoo Park and dominated by the **Lefkós Pírgos** or White Tower, the city's symbol.

THESSALONÍKI'S FESTIVALS

The city's festival season begins in September with the International Trade Fair, the major event of the year. This is followed almost immediately by a Festival of Greek Song, and finally, for the last week of October, by the Dhimitría celebrations for the city's patron saint; these coincide with the parades and parties held for Óhi Day on October 28. The Film Festival was moved in 1992 from September to November, merely prolonging the hoteliers' high season. The period of the Trade Fair, particularly, is not a good time to visit. Hotels are full, with across-the-board price increases of up to 80 percent.

City transport

There are two types of **local buses**: the orange "caterpillar" models which operate within the city, and the blue-and-orange buses which travel further afield. The fare within the city is 75dr; it's 100dr to the suburbs and 115dr out to nearby villages. In most cases, there's an automatic ticket machine on the bus, but there are still some city buses where you pay the conductor at the rear entrance. Useful lines include #10 and #11, which both ply the length of Egnatías. From Platía Eleftherías (just behind the sea front), buses initially run east along Mitropóleos; line #5 takes you to the archeological and folklore museums, and #22/23 heads north through Kástra to the highest quarter, known as Eptapirgíou, the most pleasant part of town.

If you bring your own **car**, it's best to use the free parking area near the exhibition grounds, or the fee parking area that occupies all of Platía Eleftherías. Staff will sell you strip tickets for ninety minutes each, which you cancel yourself; buy as many as you need in advance for display in the windscreen. Tokens for the rare kerbside meters are more expensive. Both the parking area and meters are attended 8am to 8pm Monday to Friday, 8am to 3pm on Saturday. If you intend to drive around the city, arm yourself with a map showing the one-way system (the one provided by the EOT is good enough), which, otherwise, can be infuriating.

Information

The main **EOT** office is at Platía Aristotélous 8 (Mon–Fri 8am–8pm, Sat 8.30am–2pm); ☎271 888). There are also booths in the train station and at the airport. When these are closed, try the **tourist police** post (daily 8am–2pm, and Tues, Thurs & Fri 5–9pm;

☎254 871) at Dhodhekanísson 4, near the harbour. A useful **book**, with a large-scale folding map, is *Monuments of Thessaloníki* by Apostolos Papagiannopoulos (1500dr), usually available in English-language bookshops, or in the major churches.

Accommodation

Outside of the festival season, reasonably priced hotel rooms are fairly easy to find – if not always very attractively situated. Modest to comfortable hotels tend to cluster in two areas: around the beginning of Egnatías, although many of the establishments here are plagued by street noise, or in the more agreeable zone between Eleftherías and Aristotélous squares. There are also some good bets between Egnatías and Platía Dhikitiríou, and to the east, at the far end of Egnatías and beyond.

The closest **campsites** are at the small resorts of Ayía Triádha and Órmos Epanomís, 24km and 33km away respectively; see p.347 for more information. Both are EOT sites and, of the two, the further is the better – as is the beach there. Take bus #72 from Platía Dhikastiríon for Ayía Triádha; bus #69 for Órmos Epanomís.

Lower Egnatías

Acropol, Egnatías 10, corner of Tantalou (☎536 170). Quiet and clean, this is a good option (at the bottom of its price range), with toilet and shower down the corridor. No breakfast. ③.

Aegean, Egnatías 19 (☎522 921). Functional, comfortable and central. Breakfast extra. ④.

Alexandria, Egnatías 18 (☎536 185). Opposite the *Aegean*, and half the price. Rooms have private toilet and shower – a bargain. ③.

Argo, Egnatías 11 (☎519 770). An old building with basic, but but acceptable, rooms, some of which have private facilities. ②.

Atlantis Egnatías 14 (☎540 131). Another, similarly run-of-the-mill hotel, with the better rooms facing a side street. ②.

Atlas, Egnatías 40 (☎537 046). Choose a room with private facilities, or for 2000dr less, you can share. Rooms at the front are noisy. Note that it's furthest from the train station of the places in this list. ③.

Avgoustos, Svorónou 4 (☎522 550). A block north of Egnatías, so quieter. Rooms come with and without private facilities. ②–③.

Averof, Sofou (☎538 498). A bit pricey for rooms with shared shower and toilet, but this is offset by the warm welcome and pleasant furnishings. ④.

Emborikon, Sigrou 14 (☎525 560). Good value, despite the shared bathrooms, and with helpful staff. ③.

Ilisia, Egnatías 24 (☎528 492). Considered one of the best bargains in town, this has good facilities and a courteous, cheerful welcome. ④.

Kastoria, Egnatías 24, corner with Sofou (☎536 250). Not the most relaxing place in town – and very noisy – but well placed and reasonable value for money. ②.

Mandrino, Antigonidhou 2 (☎526 321). Now nearly twenty years old, but well maintained and comfortable. ④.

ROOM PRICE SCALES

All establishments listed in this book have been price-graded according to the scale outlined below. The rates quoted represent the cheapest available room in high season; all are prices for a double room, except for category ①, which are per person rates. Out of season, rates can drop by up to fifty percent, especially if you negotiate rates for a stay of three or more nights. Single rooms, where available, cost around seventy percent of the price of a double.

① 1400–2000dr (£4–5.50/US$6–8.50)	④ 8000–12000dr (£22–33/US$33–50)
② 4000–6000dr (£11–16.50/US$17–25)	⑤ 12000–16000dr (£33–44/US$50–66)
③ 6000–8000dr (£16.50–22/US$25–33)	⑥ 16000dr (£44/US$66) and upwards

For more accommodation details, see p.34–35.

Eleftherías/Aristotélous

Bristol, Ilía Oplopíou 2 (☎ 530 351). Creaky but clean, right near Eleftherías and the port. ②.

Continental, Komnínon 5 (☎277 553). A decent, central hotel, with rooms with and without bath and all the usual facilities. ⑥.

Electra Palace, Platía Aristotélous (☎232 221). The most expensive hotel in town (around 33,000dr a room) and in the most prestigious position. ⑥.

Louxembourg, Komnínon 6 (☎278 449). A small hotel in a quieter than usual corner; worth a try. ④.

Palace, Tsimiskí 12 (☎270 855). Fairly fancy but good value with discounts for longer stays. ⑤.

Tourist, Mitropóleos 21 (☎276 335). Older than most in this area, but not without charm (a quality that doesn't always extend to the staff). ④.

Between Egnatías and Platía Dhikastiríon

Brill, Sigou 29, corner of Amvrossiou (☎531 666). In a quiet, tree-lined side street, this is a real bargain – an extra 2000dr gets you private shower and toilet. ②–③.

Esperia, Olímbou 58 (☎269 321). An old hotel, recently renovated, in a quiet part of the city. Better value than most in this range, and worth the money. ⑥.

Orestias Kastorias, Agnóstou Stratiótou 14, corner of Olímbou (☎276 517). Quiet and excellent value; you'll share toilet and shower. ②.

Youth hostel

Youth Hostel, Svólou 44 (☎225 946). The official *IYHF* hostel; take bus #10 from the train station and ask for the Kamana stop. The office is closed from 11am to 7pm and there's an 11pm curfew, though it's not rigorously applied. You'll need an IYHF card, though it's not always essential. The hostel is close to the White Tower and Archeological Museum, and there are several good eating places nearby. ①.

Central Thessaloníki

Although scholarly opinion now holds that the main Via Egnatia skirted the ancient city walls, there is no doubt that the modern **Odhós Egnatías** follows the course of an important Roman street or processional way. At some point during your time in town you are likely to ride or walk down it, catching glimpses of various monuments that line it.

Near the eastern corner of Platía Dhikastiríon, stands the disused fifteenth-century **Hamam Bey** or Turkish **bath**, its doorway surmounted by elaborate stalactite ornamentation. The eleventh-century **Panayía Halkéon**, close to the western corner of the *platía*, is a classic though rather unimaginative example of the cross-in-square form (see feature on Roman and Byzantine Salonica below). Until its restoration is complete there is limited entry, but you should be able to make out the founder's dedicatory inscription over one door. As the name indicates, it served during the Ottoman occupation as the copperworkers' guild mosque, and in continuation of that tradition several copperware shops, among the last remaining in Thessaloníki, still operate just across the street.

Across the way from Panayía Halkéon, take time to explore the **bazaar** area, bounded roughly by Egnatías on the northwest, Dhragoúmi on the southwest, Aristotélous on the northeast, and Tsimiskí to the southeast. At the very heart of this quad sprawls the **Modiáno**, or the central meat, fish and produce market; jewellery and watches hold forth around the corner of Venizélou and Ermoú, humbler household items are found along the latter street. It is said that until the last war, Ladino (Judaeo-Spanish) was the principal language of commerce here. Down towards the sea at Singroú 35, the old **main synagogue** is now used only at the time of major festivals, but can be visited by prior arrangement with the director of the Jewish Community Centre, in the shopping arcade at Tsimiskí 24 (☎272 840).

Remains of Salonica's formative years in the early eastern empire are thin on the ground; those that survive are concentrated, appropriately enough, just to either side of Egnatías. Ruins of the **Roman agora** were unearthed in the 1970s in the vast Platía Dhikastiríon, behind Panayía Halkéon; they have yielded little in the way of structures, though they're still being excavated. Rather more prominent is an **odeion** in the north corner of the square.

Tucked just out of sight north of the boulevard, the church of **Panayía Ahiropíitos** is the oldest in the city, featuring arcades, monolithic columns and often highly elaborate capitals – a popular development under Theodosius. Only the mosaics beneath the arches survive, depicting birds, fruits and flowers in a rich Alexandrian style. Further along on the same side of Egnatías, the **Rotunda**, later converted rather strangely to the church of **Áyios Yióryios**, is the most striking single Roman monument – designed, but never used, as an imperial mausoleum (possibly for Galerius) and consecrated for Christian use in the late fourth century by adding a sanctuary, a narthex and rich mosaics. Later it became one of the city's major mosques, from which the minaret remains. Sadly the church's interior has been closed since the 1978 earthquake, and the minaret caged in scaffolding. If it is open – as happens sometimes for special exhibitions – the superb mosaics of peacocks, elaborate temples and martyred saints are definitely worth time.

The Rotunda originally formed part of a larger complex linking the **Arch of Galerius** with a palace and hippodrome. Now also swathed in scaffolding to prevent its collapse from pollution damage, the arch is the surviving span of a dome-surmounted arcade leading to a group of Roman palaces. Built to commemorate the emperor's victories over the Persians in 297 AD, its piers contain reliefs of the battle scenes interspersed with symbolic poses of Galerius himself. The scant remains of **Galerius's palace** can be viewed, below the modern street level, along pedestrianized Dhimitríou Goúnari and its extension, Platía Navarínou.

Ayía Sofía

Between Egnatías and Navarínou, and not to be confused with the city's undistinguished modern cathedral on Mitropolis, the eighth-century church of **Ayía Sofía** was consciously modelled on its more illustrious namesake in Constantinople. Its dome, ten metres in diameter, bears a splendid mosaic of the *Ascension*: Christ, borne up to the heavens by two angels, sits resplendent on a rainbow throne; below a wry inscription reads "Ye Men of Galilee, Why stand ye Gazing up into Heaven?" The dome has been recently restored; the rest of the interior decoration was plastered over after the 1917 fire. Another fine mosaic of the *Virgin Enthroned*, in the apse, may be easier to study; it apparently replaced a cross, of which traces are visible, dating from the Iconoclast period.

The White Tower

The most prominent central post-Byzantine monument is a short walk southeast of here on the seafront: the **White Tower**, which formed the southeast corner of the city's Byzantine and Turkish defences before most of the walls were demolished late in the nineteenth century. Prior to this, it was the "Bloody Tower", a place of imprisonment and (in 1826) excecution of the Janissaries, until the Ottomans whitewashed both the building and its image. Today it looks a little stagey in its isolation, but is a graceful symbol nonetheless, which for years appeared as the background logo on the evening TV news. It was restored in 1985 for Salonica's 2300th birthday celebrations and now houses a small museum of early Christian art and several displays on the history of Thessaloníki (summer Mon 12.30–7pm, Tues–Fri 8am–7pm, Sat & Sun 8.30am–3pm; winter Mon–Fri same opening hours but closes at 5pm; 500dr). You can climb to the top for the views and a pleasant café.

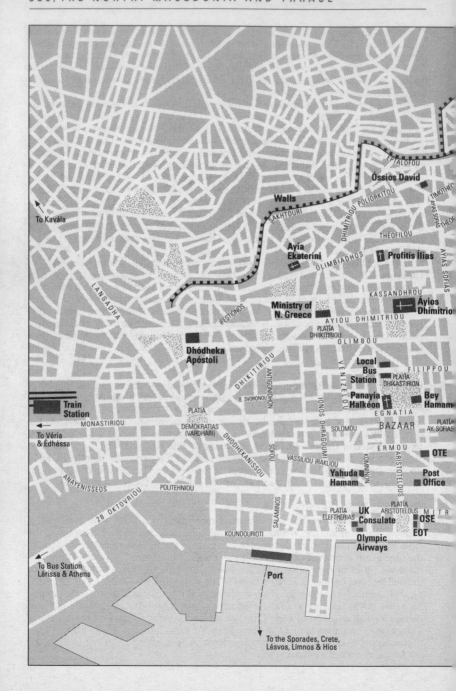

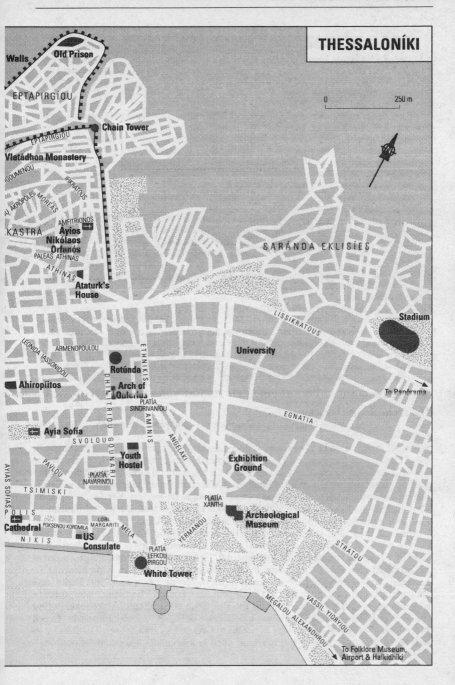

THESSALONÍKI

Walls
Old Prison
EPTAPIRGIOU
Chain Tower
EPTAPIRGIOU
Vlatádhon Monastery
IGOUMENOU
IKRATOUS
AL AKRÓPOLIS MOREAS
KASTRA
AMFITRIONOS
Áyios
Nikólaos
Orfanós
PALEAS ATHINAS
ATHINAS
Ataturk's
House
LEONIDA IASSONIDOU
ARMENOPOULOU
ETHNIKIS
Rotúnda
Ahiropíitos
DHIMITRIOU
Arch of
Galerius
AMINIS
PLATÍA
SINDRIVANÍOU
Ayía Sofía
SVOLOU
GOUNARI
ANGELAKI
Youth
Hostel
PAVLOU
PLATÍA
NAVARÍNOU
AVÍAS SOFÍAS
TSIMISKI
POLIS
PLATÍA
XANTHI
Cathedral
POKSENOU KOROMILA
LORI
MARGARITI MELA
US
Consulate
NIKIS
YERMANOU
PLATÍA
LEFKOU
PIRGOU
White Tower

SARÁNDA EKLISÍES

LISSIKRATOUS
Stadium
University
To Panórama
EGNATIA
Exhibition
Ground
Archeological
Museum
STRATOU
MEGALOU ALEXANDHROU
VASSIL YIORYIOU

To Folklore Museum,
Airport & Halkidhíki

0   250 m

ROMAN AND BYZANTINE SALONIKA AND ITS CHURCHES

Macedonia became a Roman province in 146 BC, and Salonica, with its strategic position for both land and sea access, was the natural and immediate choice of capital. Its fortunes and significance were boosted by the building of the Via Egnatia, the great road linking Rome (via Brindisi) with Byzantium and the East, along whose course Amphipolis, Philippi and Kavála were also to develop.

Christianity had slow beginnings in the city. Saint Paul visited twice, being driven out on the first occasion after provoking the Jewish community. On the second, in 56, he stayed long enough to found a church, later writing the two Epistles to the Thessalonians, his congregation. It was another three centuries, however, before the new religion took full root. Galerius, who acceded as eastern emperor upon Byzantium's break with Rome, provided the city with virtually all its surviving late Roman monuments – and its patron saint, Dhimitrios, whom he martyred. The first resident Christian emperor was Theodosius (375–395), who after his conversion issued here the Edict of Salonica, officially ending paganism.

Under Justinian's rule (527–565) Salonica became the second city of Byzantium after Constantinople, which it remained – under constant pressure from Goths and Slavs – until its sacking by Saracens in 904. The storming and sacking continued under the Normans of Sicily (1185) and with the Fourth Crusade (1204), when the city became for a time capital of the Latin Kingdom of Salonica. It was, however, restored to the Byzantine Empire of Nicea in 1246, reaching a cultural "Golden Age" amid the theological conflict and political rebellion of the next two centuries, until Turkish conquest and occupation in 1430.

The most prevalent of Roman public buildings had been the basilica: a large wooden-roofed hall, with aisles split by rows of columns. It was ideally suited for conversion to Christian congregational worship, a process achieved simply by placing a canopied altar at what became the apse, and dividing it from the main body of the church (the nave) by a screen (a forerunner to the temblon). The baptistry, a small distinct building, was then added to one side. The upper reaches of wall were adorned with mosaics illustrating Christ's transfiguration and man's redemption, while at eye level stood a blank lining of

The archeological museum

Mon 12.30–7pm (winter 11am–5pm), Tues–Fri 8am–7pm (winter 8am–5pm), Sat & Sun 8.30am–3pm; 1000dr.

Whatever else you do in Thessaloníki, find time for the superb **Veryína exhibition** at the archeological museum, on Platía Xanthi, just a few minutes' walk from the White Tower. Displayed – and clearly labelled in both English and Greek – are almost all of the finds from the Royal Tombs of Philip II of Macedon (father of Alexander the Great) and others at the ancient Macedonian capital of Aigai (at modern Veryína, see p.355). They include startling amounts of gold – masks, crowns, wreaths, pins and figurines – all of extraordinary craftsmanship and often astounding richness.

Through these and other local finds, the history of the Macedonian dynasty and empire is traced: a surprisingly political act, for the discoveries at Veryína have been used by Greece to emphasize the fundamental "Greekness" of the modern provinces of Makhedonía and Thráki. Although to an outsider these territories might seem an accepted and inviolable part of Greece, their recent occupation by Turks and Bulgarians is still very much part of Greek political memory. The ancient sites, too, are a significant part of the debate; during the Bulgarian occupation of Macedonia during World War II, for example, there was a deliberate policy of vandalism towards "Greek Macedonian" remains. Archeology in northern Greece has always been a nationalist as well as an academic issue – the museum itself is a brilliantly executed "educational" endeavour.

marble. (Frescoes, a far more economical medium, did not become fashionable until much later – during the thirteenth and fourteenth centuries – when their scope for expression and movement was realized.)

By the sixth century architects had succumbed to eastern influence and set about improving their basilicas with the addition of a dome. For inspiration they turned to the highly effective Ayía Sofía in Constantinople – the most striking of all Justinian's churches. Aesthetic effect, however, was not the only accomplishment, for the structure lent itself perfectly to the prevailing representational art. The mosaics and frescoes adorning its surfaces became physically interrelated or counterposed, creating a powerful spiritual aid. The eye would be uplifted at once to meet the gaze of the *Pandokrátor* (Christ in Majesty) illuminated by the windows of the drum. Between these windows the prophets and apostles would be depicted, and as the lower levels were scanned the liturgy would unfold amid a hierarchy of saints.

The most successful shape to emerge during later experiments with the dome was the "Greek cross-in-square" – four equal arms that efficiently absorb the weight of the dome, passing it from high barrel vaults to lower vaulted chambers fitted inside its angles. Architecturally it was a perfect solution; a square ground plan was produced inside the church with an aesthetically pleasing cruciform shape evident in the superstructure. Best of all, it was entirely self-supporting.

By the mid-tenth century it had become the conventional form. Architects, no longer interested in new designs, exploited the old, which proved remarkably flexible; subsidiary drums were introduced above corners of the square, proportions were stretched ever taller, and the outer walls became refashioned with elaborate brick and stone patterning.

Almost all the main Byzantine churches can be found in central Thessaloníki. Under the Turks most of the buildings were converted for use as mosques, a process that obscured many of their original features and destroyed (by whitewashing) the majority of their frescoes and mosaics. Further damage came with the 1917 fire and more recently with the earthquake of 1978. Restoration seems a glacially slow process, guaranteeing that many of the sanctuaries are locked, or shrouded in scaffolding, or both, at any given moment. But these disappointments acknowledged, the churches of Thessaloníki remain an impressive and illuminating group.

"Folklife" (Ethnological) Museum of Macedonia

Vassilísis Ólgas 68. Daily except Thurs 9.30am–2pm; 200dr.

This is the best museum of its kind in Greece, with well-written commentaries (in English and Greek) accompanying displays on housing, costumes, day-to-day work and crafts. The exhibits, on weaving and spinning especially, are beautiful. And there is a sharp, highly un-folkloric emphasis on context: on the role of women in the community, the clash between tradition and progress, and the yearly cycle of agricultural and religious festivals. Even the traditional costumes are presented in a manner that goes beyond the mere picturesque.

The collection is housed in an elegant turn-of-the-century mansion, just a twenty-minute walk (or short bus ride) from the archeological museum; catch the #5 bus as it runs east along Mitropóli.

Museum of Macedonian Struggle

Proksénou Koromilá 23. Mon–Fri 9am–2pm, also Wed 6–8pm, Sun 11am–2pm; closed Sat; free.

If the archeological museum helps the visitor better understand the present-day importance to Greeks of the Royal Tombs at Veryína, the **Museum of Macedonian Struggle** helps to explain their ongoing concern about Bulgarian claims to "Greek" Macedonia. The museum illustrates the struggle to liberate greater Greece, from the 1870s onwards, by means of photographs, posters, pamphlets and dioramas. It's (understandably) all in Greek, but you can borrow an English-language commentary and appreciate the significance of the building in which the museum is housed – the former Greek consulate, from which the struggle was masterminded. To find the museum, walk down Ayías Sofías towards the waterfront and it's on your left, on the corner with Koromilá.

Kástra and Eptapirgíou

Above Odhós Ayíou Dhimitríou, hillside Kástra is the main surviving quarter of Ottoman Thessaloníki. Although they are gradually becoming swamped by new apartment buildings, the streets here remain ramshackle and atmospheric, a labyrinth of timber-framed houses and winding steps. In the past few years the stigma of the district's "Turkishness" has been overcome as the older houses are bought up and restored, and it is justifiably one of the city's favourite after-dark destinations.

Áyios Dhimítrios and other churches

At the very foot of the slope is a massive yet simple church, **Áyios Dhimítrios** (Sun–Fri 9.30am–2.30pm & 5.30–9.30pm, Sat 9.30am–3pm), conceived in the fifth century though heavily restored since; indeed it was almost entirely rebuilt after the 1917 fire, which destroyed all but the apse. The church is dedicated to the city's patron saint and stands on the site of his martyrdom, and even if you know that it is the largest church in Greece, its immense interior comes as a surprise. Tall facades supported on red, green and white columns run alongside the nave. However, amid so much space and white plaster, the few small surviving mosaics make an easy focal point; five are grouped to either side of the temblon and of these three date back to the church's second building in the late seventh century. The mosaic of *Áyios Dhimítrios with the Church's Founders* was described by Osbert Lancaster as "the greatest remaining masterpiece of pictorial art of the pre-Iconoclastic era in Greece"; it contrasts well with its contemporary neighbour, a warm and humane mosaic of the saint with two young children. The **crypt** (daily except Mon 8.30am–3pm; free), unearthed after the great fire, contains the *martyrion* of the saint – probably an adaption of the Roman baths in which he was imprisoned – and a beautiful column-capital carved with birds.

Around Áyios Dhimítrios are several more churches, utterly different in feel. West along Ayíou Dhimitríou, is the somewhat remote church of **Dhódheka Apóstoli**, built with three more centuries of experience and the bold Renaissance influence of Mystra (see *The Peloponnese* chapter). Its five domes rise in perfect symmetry above walls of fine brickwork, though its interior no longer does it justice. To the west, **Ayía Ekateríni**, contemporary with Dhódheka Apóstoli, has fine brickwork, exploiting all the natural colours of the stones. Fourteenth-century **Áyios Nikólaos Orfanós** (daily except Mon 8.45am–3pm; entrance from Irodotou) is a diminutive basilica to the north of Áyios Dhimítrios, maintaining its original imaginative and well-preserved frescoes. **Profítis Ilías**, between Ayía Ekateríni and Áyios Dhimítrios, is in the same vein as Dhódheka Apóstoli, though less imposing, with negligible surviving interior decoration.

The ramparts and Eptapirgíou

Sections of the fourteenth-century **Byzantine ramparts**, constructed with brick and rubble on top of old Roman foundations, crop up all around the northern part of town. The best-preserved portion begins at a large circular keep, known as the "Chain Tower" (after its encircling ornamental moulding), in the northeast angle. It then rambles north around the district of **Eptapirgíou**, enclosing the old acropolis at the top end. For centuries it served as the city's prison, described in a number of plaintive old songs as "Yediküle" (Turkish for "Eptapirgíou" or "Seven Towers") until abandoned as too inhumane in 1988. On its south side, the wall is followed by Odhós

Eptapirgíou and edged by a small strip of park – a good place to sit and scan the town. Nearby, various *psistariés* and *kafenía* come alive in the late afternoon and evening; see "Eating" below.

Although, strictly speaking, the following two monuments lie within Kástra, they are easier to find walking downhill from the Eptapirgíou area. **Óssios David** (officially daily 8.30am–3pm, though often open later), a tiny fifth-century church on Odhós Timothéou, does not really fit into any architectural progression, since the Turks, over-zealous in their conversion, hacked most of it apart. However, it has arguably the finest mosaic in the city, depicting a clean-shaven Christ Emmanuel appearing in a vision, to the amazement of the prophets Ezekiel and Habakkuk. Ask the curator to switch on the floodlights for a better view. Nearby, the **monastery of Vlatádhon** is noteworthy for its peaceful, tree-shaded courtyard, a perfect place to complete a tour; if you can gain entrance to the much-restored *katholikón*, there are fourteenth-century frescoes inside.

Ataturk's house

If you approach or leave Kástra on its east side, it's worth casting an eye at the Turkish Consulate at the bottom of Apostólou Pávlou. In the pink building beside it **Kemal Ataturk**, first president and creator of the modern state of Turkey, was born. The consulate maintains the house as a small museum, with its original fixtures. To visit you must apply for admission at the main building, with your passport (Mon–Fri 9am–1pm & 2–6pm). Security is tight, and for good reason – Ataturk has been held largely responsible for the traumatic exchange of Greek and Turkish populations in 1923. In 1981 a Turkish celebration of the centenary of his birth had to be called off after a Greek stunt pilot threatened a kamikaze-dive at the house.

Eating

In recent years there has been an explosion of interesting places to eat and drink in Thessaloníki, paralleling the increasing prosperity of the city; and there's little excuse for frequenting the fast-food outlets that, at first glance, seem to dominate the centre. Most of the listings below, categorized both by district and price per person, are within walking distance of Platía Aristotélous, and for those that aren't we've given the appropriate transport connections. Thessalonians take their summer holidays a bit earlier than Athenians, so a notation of "closed in midsummer" tends to mean mid-July to mid-August.

Downtown: between the sea and Odhós Ayíou Dhimitríou
UNDER 2000DR

Adelfia, Platía Navarínou 9. Lunch and supper rendezvouz for the city's yuppies, with stylish kebab meals for around 1100dr. It's often packed, so go early.

Babel, Komninón 18. A snack bar, open all day, useful for breakfast.

Bekris, Goúnari 74. On the pedestrian walkway, north of the Rotunda. Speciality sausage and *kopanistí* (spicy cheese mash). Closed Thurs.

Cookies, Egnatías 144. A cookies-by-weight shop that is one of the best in Greece, with imaginative varieties. There's another branch at Venizélou 10.

Corner, Ethnikis Amínis 6, near the White Tower. Not just great desserts, but pizza, sandwiches, draught beer and a full bar, with indoor and outside seating. Very fair priced for what it is: a multi-disciplinary, California-bistro-meets-London-pub hybrid.

Intermezo, Svólou 46. Open for lunch and dinner year round, serving 18 types of pizza and a range of grills. It's close to the youth hostel.

Irida, Olímbou 83. An excellent and inexpensive grill near the hotel *Orestias Kastorias*. The speciaity *soudzoukákia* bear little relation to the usual Greek version, being more like Turkish *inegól köfte*. Outside seating; open all year.

Koumbarakia, Egnatías 140. Tucked behind the little chapel of the Transfiguration, the outdoor tables of this *ouzerí* are always packed with those dining on Macedonian-style grills, seafood and salads (including *túrsi*, pickled vegetables). Closed Sun and midsummer.

Loutros, Komninón 15. Partly housed in the old Turkish bath, which also accommodates the flower market, spilling onto the adjacent pavement. This taverna has good fried fish and excellent retsina, compensating somewhat for the abruptness of the staff and the rough-and-ready surroundings. Closed in summer.

Nea Ilisia, Sofou 17. Opposite the *Averof* hotel, this popular neighbourhood restaurant is open all hours (8.30am–2am) and serves traditional food. Good value all round.

Pazar Hamam, Komninón 15a. A new restaurant alongside the Loutros, quieter and more polished than its neighbour and rapidly gaining a good reputation.

Rafaelo, corner Mitropóleos and Komnínon. With coffees, juices and croissants, this is the fanciest of several *bougátsa* and other filled-pastry establishments along Komnínon, as you walk seaward from the Modiáno. There's no sign outside – look for the busy tables.

Stenaki, Svólou 22, at the rear of alley opposite cinema *Esperos*. An *ouzerí* with outdoor seating in the cul-de-sac. Near the youth hostel and open during summer..

Tottis, Platía Aristotélous 2–3. Café, bistro and (pricey) restaurant, that's as much a meeting place as a dining spot. There's another *Tottis* in the arcade at Tsimiski 24, this a pleasant self-service restaurant with a wide choice and helpful staff.

OVER 2000DR

Aproöpto, Lóri. Margaríti 11. A hearty-eating *ouzerí* in an area known more for bars and clubs. Open all year round, but closed Sun.

Aristotelous, Aristotélous 8. On a courtyard off Aristotélous, just above the *platía*, this upmarket *ouzerí* gets very crowded. Open noon–6pm and, except Sun, 8pm–midnight; closed Aug.

Bextsinar, Katoúni 11. There's no sign outside, but persevere to find this newish *ouzerí*-housed in one of the bazaar's older remaining buildings. Open 1–5pm & 9pm–1.30am; closed midsummer.

Olymbos Naoussa, Níkis 5. White tablecloths, 1920s atmosphere and service, sea views and excellent, deceptively unadorned food make this a perennial favourite with locals. Open weekdays for lunch only, but open throughout summer when you can eat outside.

Rongotis, Venizélou 8, corner of Kalapotháki. Varied menu, but famous for its *tsoudzoukákia*; consumed daily by a business clientele. Note that the restaurant's real name is the *Souzoukákia*. Closed midsummer.

Tsarouhas, Olímbou 78, near Platía Dhikastiríon. Reputedly the best, and certainly the most famous, of the city's *patsatzídhika* – kitchens devoted to tripe-and-trotter soup. Closed midsummer.

Kástra and Eptapirgíou

Most of the places listed below cling to either side of the walls encircling Eptapirgíou district; bus #22 or #23 from Platía Eleftherías spares you the walk.

UNDER 2000DR

Hiotis, Graviás 2. Just inside the second (eastern) castle gate, near the Chain Tower. Goat, kebabs and *kokorétsi* served on the pavement under the ramparts, or inside in colder weather. This is probably the best of the six similar establishments arranged here cheek-by-jowl. Dinner only in summer, lunch and dinner rest of the year.

Kastroperpatimatia, Steryíou Polidhórou 15. Inside the main gate of the Kástra. Smallish portions of good Greek/Turkish Cypriot food, served alongside the park strip inside the walls. Open July–Sept daily except Tues for dinner; Oct–June Sun lunch only.

Vangos, Kaíri 15, above Platía Pávlou Melá in the hillside area of Saránda Eklisíes. Tiny hole-in-the-wall joint, popular with students, tucked away in an alley; ask in the square for directions (bus #15 runs to the square). Closed mid-July to mid-Aug.

The eastern suburbs

The establishments below cater primarily to the well-heeled residents of the "better" part of town, so food is consequently more elegant – and routinely more than 2000dr per person.

Archipelagos, Kanári 1, Néa Kríni. A fancy seafood place and one of the best in the area. Take bus #5 or a taxi. Open daily 1pm–midnight.

Batis, Platía Eleftherías 22, Néa Kríni. Sea view with your grilled octopus; other fish dishes as well. Bus #5.

Dheka Vimata, Fléming 16, near the ethnological museum. One of the better indoor *bouzoúki* tavernas. Closed Mon and all summer.

Krikelas, Ethnikís Andistásis 32, in Byzándio district, on the way to the airport. A bit touristy, but the chef here is one of the best in Greece, drawing on almost half a century of experience. Closed in summer.

Pringiponissia, Krítis 60, near 25 Martíou, 600m beyond the ethnological museum. Delicious Constantinople-Greek food served in a pleasant two-level modern building; you select from proferred trays of hot and cold *mezé.dhes* Open all year; closed Sun.

Drinking, nightlife and entertainment

In winter, after-dark activities tend to focus in the warren of streets behind the quay-side boulevard Níkis, and at certain theatres and concert halls near the White Tower. Proksénou Koromilá and Lóri Margaríti, two narrow alleys, essentially continuations of each other, just a block back from the water, are home to a huge number of bars and clubs. During the warmer months, action shifts to various glitzy establishments lining the coast road out to Kalamariá, and to the nightly *vólta* (promenade) that takes place between the Arch of Galerius and the seafront along pedestrianized Dhimitríou Goúnari, which bulges out halfway down to include Platía Navarínou.

Bars and clubs

Avantage, Ayiou Dhimitríou 158, opposite the Turkish consulate. Greek folk and *bouzoúki*.

Chic, Lóri Margaríti 5. Women-only piano bar; shut in summer.

Mandragoras, Mitropóleos 98. A large and elegant upstairs wine-and-*mezédhes* bar, run by a man who twice won the state lottery. Closed in summer.

Pirgos OTE, International Fair Grounds. Not the trendiest place in town, but reasonably priced drinks and snacks up in the tower salon (open until 2am).

Zythos, Katoúni 5, near the ferry terminal. A pub-like wine bar and *ouzeri*, though you can get plenty of quality beer, as the Greek name ("beer") suggests.

Events

Winter **dance**, **concert** and **theatre** events tend to take place in the *Kratikó Théatro* (State Theatre) and the *Vassilikó Théatro* (Royal Theatre), within sight of each other behind the White Tower. In summer things move to either the *Théatro Kípou* (Garden Theatre), near the archeological museum, or well up the hill into the *Théatro Dhássous* (Forest Theatre), in the pines beyond the upper town. *Milos*, at Andhréou Yioryíon 56, is a new multi-functional cultural centre housed in an old warehouse, southeast of the centre. Here you'll find a couple of bars, a live jazz café, popular taverna, summer cinema, concert hall and theatre. Cultural events should thrive in the run-up to 1997, when Thessaloníki will become European Cultural Capital.

Indoor cinemas tend to cluster between the White Tower and the Galerius arch; those known to concentrate on first-run material, rather than porno or kung fu flicks, include *Alexandhros*, Ethnikís Amínis 1; *Aristotelion*, Ethnikís Amínis 2; *Esperos*, Svólou 22; *Makedhonikon*, between Ethnikís Amínis and Fílikis Eterías; *Navarinon*, on the namesake plaza; and *Olympian*, on Platía Aristotélous. **Summer cinemas** have all but vanished from downtown Thessaloníki, owing to spiralling property values; the only one left is the *Alex*, at Olímbou 106. The *Natali*, on the landward side at the start of Megalou Alexandhrou, is the only other outdoor cinema operating in summer. There is no comprehensive listings magazine on a par with Athens' *Athinorama*, so you'll have to stroll by to see what's playing unless you can read the daily Greek papers.

Listings

Airlines *American Airlines*, Mitropóleos 51 (☎286 750); *British Airways*, Ionos Dragoumi 4 (☎242 005); *Olympic*, Kommínon 1 (☎281 880). Most other airlines are represented by general sales agents (see below).

Airport At Mikrá, 16km out and served by bus #78; ☎411 977 for flight information.

Banks and exchange Outside usual banking hours, try the *Ethniki Trapeza* at Tsimiskí 11, which has evening and Saturday morning opening. There are also the post offices (see below), or, as a last resort, the booth in the train station. For changing notes, use the 24h automatic exchange machine at the *Ktimatiki* bank on Platía Aristotélous.

Books and papers *Molho*, Tsimiskí 10, has an excellent stock of English-language books, magazines and newspapers. Next door, *Saliveros* has a better range of local guides. *Promithevs*, at Ermoú 75, is also good for books, while there are a number of bookshops on Ethnikís Amínis. For English-language newspapers, visit the *International Press* kiosk on the corner of Angeláki and Svólou.

Bus terminal Bottom of 28 Oktovríou, in the Sfayiá district; ☎513 734 for departure information.

Camping gear *Petridhis*, Vassilíou Iraklíou 43; and *World Jamboree*, at Iónnos Deliou 6, off Ethnikís Amínis.

Car rental *Ansa/Holiday Autos*, Laskaráta 19 (☎471 040); *Avis*, Níkis 3 (☎227 126); *Europcar/Inter Rent*, Papandhréou 5 (☎826 333); *European*, Níkis 21 (☎265 400); *Hertz*, Venizelou 4 (☎224 906) and airport (☎473 952); *Payless*, Angeláki 3 (☎286 327); *Salonica*, Tsimiskí 114 (☎228 751); *Thrifty*, Angeláki 15 (☎241 241); the leading agencies have kiosks at the airport, too.

Consulates Important for getting letters of introduction for Mount Áthos (see "Ministry of Macedonia and Thrace", below): *Denmark*, Kommínon 26 (☎284 065); *Germany*, Karólou Díehil 4 (☎236 315); *UK/Commonwealth*: honorary consul is at Venizélou 8, 8th floor, by appointment only (Mon–Fri 8am–1pm; ☎278 006); *USA*, Níkis 59 (Tues & Thurs 9am–noon; ☎266 121);

Cultural institutes *British Council*, Ethnikís Amínis 9; free library and reading room, plus various events in the winter months. *USIS Library*, Mitropóleos 34 (closed summer).

Ferry tickets For the large *Nomikos* and *NEL* ferries to the northeast Aegean, the Sporades, Cyclades and Crete, buy tickets at *Karaharissis*, Koundourióti 8 (☎513 005), on the corner of Vótsi, by the harbour. Hydrofoils to the Sporades are handled by *Egnatia Tours*, Kamvouníon 9 (☎223 811; near the Arch of Galerius). For routes and frequencies, see "Travel details" at the end of each chapter.

Football Thessaloníki's main team is PAOK, whose stadium is in the east of the city – off our map, though visible in square A5 of the EOT "Thessaloniki/Halkidhiki" handout.

Hospitals For minor trauma, use the *Érithros Stavrós* (Red Cross) post down at the harbour; otherwise, head for the *Ippokration* at Konstandinopóleos 49, in the eastern part of town.

Laundries There are several coin-ops where you can leave your clothes to be washed, and collect them later, including *Bianca*, Antoniádhou 3, near the Arch of Galerius, and *Bubbles*, Menikou 15, behind *Bianca* and towards the Rotunda.

Ministry of Macedonia and Thrace This is on Platía Dhikitiríou and you'll have to visit to obtain a Mount Áthos permit. Go first to your consulate for a letter of recommendation (free to US citizens, 5700dr to UK and Commonwealth citizens; take your passport). At the ministry, make your way to Room 218 (Mon–Fri 11am–1.45pm).

Post office Main branch (for poste restante and after-hours exchange) is at Tsimiskí 47 (Mon–Fri 7.30am–8pm, Sat 7.30am–2.15pm, Sun 9am–1.30pm). There are other post offices around the city: two useful ones are at Tsimiskí 5 and Ethnikís Amínis 9a.

Shopping Chic boutiques line Tsimiskí and its side streets. For shoes, try *Sevastakis* at no. 33, *Papadhakis* at no. 38 or *Tsakiris Mallas* at no. 43. You won't undercut North American or British prices but you may find something unique. Humbler styles can be found in the central bazaar and along Svólou or Egnatías. For copper goods, there are eight stores across the street from the Panayía Halkéon; *Makis Sismandis*, Halkéon 13, has a wide selection. Three good record stores are *Stereodisc*, Aristotélous 4, *Studio 52*, Goúnari 46, basement, and *Patsis Music*, Tsimiskí 29.

Telephone office Ermoú 40, at junction with Karólou Díehil. Open daily 24hr.

Train tickets All services depart from the giant station down on Monastiríou, the southwestern continuation of Egnatías, well served by buses. If you want to buy tickets or make reservations in advance, the *OSE* office at Aristotélous 18 (Tues–Fri 8am–9pm, Mon & Sat 8am–3pm) is more central and helpful than the station ticket-windows.

Travel agents Flights out of Thessaloníki are not cheap, but for what they're worth air ticket shops cluster around Platía Eleftherías, especially on Kalapotháki, Komnínon and Mitropóleos. More specifically, *Kinissi Tours*, Tsimiskí 17 (☎237 000), and *Oceanic World*, Níkis 21 (☎265 400), handle the major airlines. Students and youth travellers should try *USIT*, Ipodhromíou 15 (☎263 814). Specialist hiking and other expeditions throughout Greece are offered by *Trekking Hellas*, Aristotélous 11 (☎242 190).

Out from the city

The big weekend escape from Thessaloníki is to the three-pronged Halkidhikí peninsula. To get to its better beaches, however, requires more than a day trip. If you just want a respite from the city, or a walk in the hills, think instead in terms of Thessaloníki's own local villages and suburbs. Further out, drivers en route to Néa Moudhanía can take in the extraordinary cave near Petrálona – though half-day trips with a local tour operator make this a possibility for those without their own transport, too.

Panórama and Hortiátis

On the hillside overlooking the city, 11km east, **PANÓRAMA**, the closest escape from the city, is exactly what its name suggests: a high, hillside viewpoint looking down over Thessaloníki and the gulf. The original village was razed to the ground by the Germans in retaliation for partisan sabotage during World War II, and Panorama has been rebuilt with smart villas, coffee shops and a large, modern shopping mall. Of more appeal are a number of cafés, tavernas and *zakoroplastía*. The best-known of these is *Elenidhi-To Ariston*, which serves up the premier local speciality, *trígona* (custard-filled triangular confections), wonderful *dondurma* (Turkish-style ice-cream) and *salépi* (a beverage made from the ground-up root of *Orchis mascula*). The village can be reached by #57 or #58 bus from Platía Dhikastiríon, or by taxi (around 1000dr).

Still more of a retreat is **HORTIÁTIS**, 11km further on (or 16km direct from Thessaloníki), set in an area known as *Hília Dhéndhra* (Thousand Trees). This is accessible on the #61 city bus from Egnatias. Again, it offers sweeping views over the city, good walking among the pines and some popular places to eat; the *Sakis* taverna (☎349 874) has a well-deserved reputation and you can eat there for around 1700dr a head. In summer, phone to avoid disappointment.

Beaches

To swim near Thessaloníki you need to get well clear of the gulf, where the pollution is all too visible – and odorous. This means heading southwest towards Kateríni and the beaches below Mount Olympus (along the fast National Road), or southeast towards Halkidhikí.

If all you want is a meal by the sea, then you can take local buses around the gulf. Buses #72 or #69 run to **PERÉA**, 20km from Thessaloníki, a small resort with good seafront tavernas but a rather unpleasant beach; try the inexpensive evening grill, *O Fotis*; you could even stay at the friendly *Hotel Lena* (☎0392/22 755; ④). Bus #72 continues to **AYÍA TRIÁDHA**, where there is an EOT **campsite**, the *Akti Thermaikou* (☎0392/51 352; open all year), rooms to rent and three reasonable **hotels**, all with swimming pools: cheapest is the *Xenia Helos* (☎0392/25 551; ⑤), but better value for money is the recently renovated *Galaxias* (☎0392/22 291; ⑥), 1km before Ayía Triádha.

Bus #69 sweeps north, via Epanomís, to the better strand of **ÓRMOS EPANOMÍS**, 33km from Thessaloníki, although some people prefer to travel on to Néa Kallikkrátia before taking to the water. There is a second EOT **campsite** at Órmos Epanomís (☎0392/41 378; April–Oct), more attractive and with more shade than the one at Ayía Triádha.

Petrálona

Fifty kilometres southeast of Thessaloníki is the **cave of Kókkines Pétres** (Red Stones), discovered in 1959 by villagers from nearby **PETRÁLONA** looking for water. Besides an impressive display of stalagmites and stalactites, the villagers – and, later, the academics – found the fossilized remains of prehistoric animals and, most dramatic of all, a Neanderthal skull.

The cave, well worth a visit, makes an interesting diversion on the way to or from the Kassándhra peninsula; you'll find the village of Petrálona itself roughly 4km north of Eleohória, on the old road running from Thessaloníki to Néa Moudhanía at the neck of the peninsula. It's open every day (9am–7pm; closes 5pm in winter; 700dr) and there's a small café on site, though the museum there is closed indefinitely. *Doucas Tours* in Thessaloníki (Venizélou 8, under the UK consulate) operates a half-day trip.

ANASTENARIÁ: THE FIRE WALKERS OF LANGADHÁS

On May 21, the feast day of Saints Constantine and Helen, villagers at **LANGADHÁS**, 20km north of Thessaloníki, used to (and may still) perform a ritual barefoot dance across a bed of burning coals. The festival rites are of unknown and strongly disputed origin. It has been suggested that they are remnants of a Dionysiac cult, though devotees assert a purely Christian tradition. This seems to relate to a fire, around 1250, in the Thracian village of Kósti: holy icons were heard groaning from the flames and were rescued by villagers, who emerged miraculously unburnt from the blazing church. The icons, passed down by their families, are believed to ensure protection. Equally important is piety and purity of heart: it is said that no one with any harboured grudges or unconfessed sins can pass through the coals unscathed. The Greek church authorities, meanwhile, refuse to sanction any service on the day of the ritual; it has even been accused of planting glass among the coals to try and discredit this "devil's gift".

Whatever the origin, the rite was until recently still performed each year – lately as something of a tourist attraction, with an admission charge and repeat performances over the next two days. It was nevertheless strange and impressive, beginning around 7pm with the lighting of a cone of hardwood logs. A couple of hours later their embers were raked into a circle and, just before complete darkness, a traditional Macedonian *daoúli* drummer and two lyra players preceded about sixteen women and men into the arena. These *anastenarídhes* (literally "groaners"), in partial trance, then shuffled across the coals for about a quarter of an hour.

Recently the cult members were subjected to various scientific tests. The only established clues were that the dancers' brain waves indicate some altered state – when brain activity returns to normal they instinctively left the embers – and that their rhythmical steps maintain minimum skin contact with the fires. There was no suggestion of fraud, however. In 1981 an Englishman jumped into the arena, was badly burnt, and had to be rescued by the police from irate devotees and dancers. In 1991, however, the rites failed to take place, owing to continued pressure from the Church and the *anastenarídhes'* own ire at being viewed merely as freak-show attractions. The ceremony's future seems uncertain, with the likelihood of it taking place, if at all, in private at an undisclosed location.

If the *anastenariá* are taking place in public this year, and you decide to go, arrive early at Langadhás – by 5.30pm at the latest – in order to get a good seat. Be prepared, too, for the circus-like commercialism, though this in itself can be quite fun.

Other *anastenarídhes* used to "perform" at **MELÍKI**, near Véria, and at the villages of **AYÍA ELÉNI** and **ÁYIOS PÉTROS** near Sérres. Crowds, though, were reputed to be just as large and fire-walkers fewer. If you're in Greece, anywhere, and moderately interested, you can catch the show (if it happens) on the ET TV news at 9pm. Their cameramen are at Langadhás, too.

Pella

PELLA was the capital of Macedonia throughout its greatest period and the first real capital of Greece, after Philip II forcibly unified the country around 338 BC. It was founded some sixty years earlier by King Archelaus, who transferred the royal Macedonian court here from Aigai (see "Veryína", p.355), and from its beginnings it was a major centre of culture. The royal palace was decorated by Zeuxis and said to be the greatest artistic showplace since the time of Classical Athens. Euripides wrote and produced his last plays at the court, and here, too, Aristotle was to tutor the young Alexander the Great – born, like his father Philip II, in the city.

The site today, split by the road to Édhessa, is an easy and rewarding day trip from Thessaloníki. Its main treasures are a series of pebble mosaics, some in the museum, a couple in situ. For an understanding of the context, it is best to visit after looking around the archeological museum at Thessaloníki.

The site

Mon–Sat 8am–7pm (5pm in winter), Sun 8.30am–3pm; 400dr.

When Archelaus founded Pella, it lay at the head of a broad lake, connected to the Thermaíkos gulf by a navigable river. By the second century BC the river had begun to silt up and the city fell into decline. It was destroyed by the Romans in 146 BC and never rebuilt. Today its **ruins** stand in the middle of a broad expanse of plain, 40km from Thessaloníki and the sea.

The city was located by chance finds in 1957; preliminary excavations have revealed a vast site covering over 485 hectares. As yet, only a few blocks of the city have been fully excavated but they have proved exciting. To the right of the road is a grand official building, probably a government office; it is divided into three large open courts, each enclosed by a *peristyle*, or portico (the columns of the central one have been re-erected), and bordered by wide streets with a sophisticated drainage system.

The three main rooms of the first court have patterned geometric floors, in the centre of which were found superb, intricate **pebble mosaics** depicting scenes of a lion hunt, a griffin attacking a deer, and Dionysus riding a panther. These are now in the **museum** across the road (Mon 12.30–7pm, Tues–Sat 8am–7pm, winter closes at 5pm, Sun 8.30am–3pm; separate 400dr admission). But in the third court three mosaics have been left in situ; one, a stag hunt, is complete, and astounding in its dynamism and use of perspective. Others represent the rape of Helen and a fight between a Greek and an Amazon.

It is the inherently graceful and fluid quality of these compositions that sets them apart from later Roman and Byzantine mosaics and that more than justifies a visit. The uncut pebbles, carefully chosen for their soft shades, blend so naturally that the shapes and movements of the subjects seem gradated rather than fixed, especially in the action of the hunting scenes and the sloping movement of the leopard with Dionysus. Strips of lead or clay are used to outline special features; the eyes, all now missing, were probably semiprecious stones.

The **acropolis** at Pella is a low hill to the west of the modern village. Excavation is in progress on a sizeable building, probably a palace, but at present it's illuminating mainly for the idea it gives you of the size and scope of the site.

Getting there

Pella is easiest reached from Thessaloníki. Just take any of the Édhessa **buses**, which run more or less half-hourly through the day and stop by the Pella museum. If you arrive late and want to stay, the nearest **hotel** is at Halkidhóna, 8km east on the road back to Thessaloniki: the *Fillipos* (☎0391/22 125; ③–④).

Continuing to **Aigai/Veryína** by public transport, you'll need to get a bus, or walk, back down the Thessaloníki road to the junction at Halkidhóna. From here you can pick up the Thessaloníki–Véria buses.

Dion

Ancient DION, in the foothills of Mount Olympus, was the Macedonians' sacred city. At this site – a harbour before the river mouth silted up – the kingdom maintained its principal sanctuaries: to Zeus (from which the name *Dion*, or *Dios*, is derived) above all, but also to Demeter, Artemis, Asclepius and, later, to foreign gods such as the Egyptians Isis and Serapis. Philip II and Alexander both came to sacrifice to Zeus here before their expeditions. Inscriptions found at the sanctuaries referring to boundary disputes, treaties and other affairs of state suggest that the political and social importance of the city's festivals exceeded a purely Macedonian domain.

Most exciting for visitors, however, are the finds of mosaics, temples and baths that have been excavated over the last five years – work that remains in progress whenever funds allow. These are not quite on a par with the Veryína tombs, but still rank among the major discoveries of Macedonian history and culture. If you are heading for Mount Olympus, they are certainly worth a half-day detour. At the village of **DHIÓN** (old Malathiriá), just north of Litóhoro beach, take a side road inland, to the east, past the remains of a theatre. The main **site** lies ahead (daily 8am–7pm; winter closes at 3pm; 500dr). The integrity of the site and its finds is due to the nature of the city's demise. At some point in the fifth century a series of earthquakes prompted an evacuation of the city, which was then swallowed up by mud from the mountain. The main visible excavations are of the vast **public baths** complex and, outside the city **walls**, the **sanctuaries** of Demeter and Aphrodite-Isis. In the latter a small temple has been unearthed, along with its cult statue – which remains in situ. The finest mosaics so far discovered (and which may be on view) are in a former banquet room; they depict the god Dionysus on a chariot. Christian **basilicas** attest to the town's later years as a Roman bishopric in the fourth and fifth centuries AD. An observation platform allows you to view the layout of the site more clearly.

Back in the village, a small **museum** (Mon 12.30–7pm; Tues–Fri 8am–7pm; winter Mon–Fri closes at 5pm; 400dr) houses most of the finds. The sculpture, perfectly preserved by the mud, is impressive, and accompanied by various tombstones and altars. Below the stairs there is a fine mosaic of Medusa. Upstairs, along with extensive displays of pottery and coinage, is a collection of everyday items, including surgical and dental tools perhaps connected with the sanctuary of Asclepius, the healing god. Pride of place, however, goes to the remains of a first-century BC pipe organ, discovered in 1992.

Note that the village cannot be approached directly from Mount Olympus, since an army firing range bars the way. If you want to **stay overnight**, the *Hotel Dion* stands at the crossroads by the bus stop (☎0351/53 682; ③). The nearest campsites are on the beach at Variko, 5km away: *Stani* (☎0352/61 277) and *Niteas* (☎0352/61 290), both open year round.

Mount Olympus (Óros Ólimbos)

The highest, most magical and most dramatic of all Greek mountains, **Mount Olympus** – *Ólimbos* in Greek – rears nigh on 3000 metres straight from the shores of the Thermaíkos gulf. Dense forests cover its slopes and its wild flowers are without parallel even by Greek standards. To make the most of it, you need to allow two to three days' hiking.

Equipped with decent boots and warm clothing, no special expertise is necessary to get to the top in summer (mid-June to October), though it's a long hard pull requiring a good deal of stamina; winter climbs, of course, are another matter. At any time of year Olympus is a mountain to be treated with respect: its weather is notoriously fickle and it does claim lives.

Litóhoro and Olympus practicalities

The best base for a walk up the mountain is the village of **LITÓHORO** on the eastern side. Unexciting in itself, in good weather it affords intoxicating eve-of-climb views into the heart of the range. To reach Litóhoro is fairly easy. There's a train station 9km distant on the coast, from where there are frequent taxis and the occasional connecting bus; or you can get the same bus direct from Thessaloníki or the market town of Kateríni (where there's the inexpensive *Hotel Olympion*, at Eirinis 15).

The cheapest lodgings in Litóhoro are at the **youth hostel** (☎0352/81 311; ①), near the main square, whose enterprising manager can arrange bike and mountain gear rental. Otherwise, of the **hotels**, try the *Mirto* on Áyios Nikólaos, also near the main square (☎0352/81 398; ③), open all year and considered to be the best hotel in the village; the relatively new *Enipeas* (☎0352/81 328; ③), near the *National Bank* and above the post office; or the *Aphrodite*, on the main square near the post office (☎0352/81 415; ④). The cheaper *Hotel Park*, at Áyios Nikólaos 23 (☎0352/81 252; ②), is the least exciting hotel choice, but can't be beaten for price. As for **eating**, there's a rash of fast-food places in the square but if you explore the side streets, there are more attractive possibilities, like the *Dhamaskinia*, on Vassileas Konstantinos, which has excellent food.

Accommodation on Olympus itself is better organized than on any other mountain in Greece. There are two staffed **refuges**: the EOS-run *Spílios Agapitós* at 2100m (open May 15–Oct 15; ☎0352/81 800, reservations recommended in summer), and the SEO-managed *Yiósos Apostolídhis* hut at 2700m (open only July–Sept, though its glassed-in porch is always available for climbers in need). There is no longer a set phone number for this refuge, since the wardership is in a state of flux. Both currently charge around 1500dr for a bunk, with lights out and outer door locked at 10pm. Meals at either shelter are relatively expensive, and mandatory since no cooking is allowed inside; bring more money than you think you'll need, as bad weather can ground you a day or two longer than planned.

For sustenance while walking, you'll need to buy food in Litóhoro, though water can wait until you're at the vicinity of either of two trailheads (see below). The free leaflet handed out at the EOS kiosk in Litóhoro is quite useless; buy a proper **map**, co-produced by *Korfes* magazine and EOS Aharnés, from the youth hostel.

The mountain

To reach alpine Olympus, you've a choice of road or foot routes. With your own vehicle, you can **drive** deep into the mountain along a fairly decent road, the first 6km of which is now paved. There is a control/education post at Km2, where your nationality is recorded and you're given some literature advising you of the park rules, but so far there's no admission charge, though this will certainly change in the future. Conservationists are agitating for a total ban on private vehicles within the park, and all and all it is much better to **walk** in from Litóhoro, as far as the ruined monastery of Ayíou Dhionisíou, and beyond to the two trailheads following.

As for the final **ascent routes**, there are two main paths: one beginning at Priónia, just under 18km up the mountain at the road's end, where a primitive taverna operates by the spring in summer; the other at a spot called Dhiakládhosi or Gortsiá (14km up), marked by a signboard displaying a map of the range. The Prióniia path is more frequented and more convenient, the Dhiakládhosi trail longer but more beautiful. A 1800m driveway, appearing on the main road about halfway between the two trailheads, leads down to Ayíou Dhionisíou.

The Mavrólongos canyon and Ayíou Dhionisíou monastery

Some years ago the Greek overland-trail committee rehabilitated old paths in the superlatively beautiful Mavrólongos (Enipévs) river canyon to make a fine section of the **E4 overland trail**, thus sparing hikers the drudgery of walking up the road or the expense of a taxi. Black-on-yellow diamond markers begin near the youth hostel and lead you along a roller-coaster course by the river for three and a half hours to Ayíou Dhionisíou. It's a delightful route, but you'll need basic hiking skills as there are some ladder-assisted scrambles and water crossings.

The **monastery** itself was burned by the Germans in 1943 for allegedly harbouring guerrillas, and the surviving monks, rather than rebuilding, relocated to new premises near Litóhoro. On summer weekends the half-ruined structure is a bit of a zoo, with the still-intact cells long since looted of their beds and blankets; a caretaker monk seems rather jaded by those hoping to sleep for free, and in season at least the only advantage of an overnight here are the running water taps. Many people prefer to camp along the riverbanks below the perimeter wall (tolerated despite falling within national park territory).

From Ayíou Dhionisíou it's about an hour more along the riverside E4 to Prióniia, or slightly less up the driveway and then east to the Dhiakládhosi trailhead.

The ascent from Prióniia

The E4 carries on just uphill from the taverna by an EOS signpost giving the time to the refuge as two hours thirty minutes (allow 3hr). You cross a stream (last water before the *Spílios Agapitós* refuge, purification advisable) and start to climb steeply up through woods of beech and black pine. The path, the continuation of the E4, is well trodden and marked, so there is no danger of getting lost. As you gain height there are superb views across the Mavrólongos ravine to your left and to the peaks towering above you.

The *Spílios Agapitós* **refuge** perches on the edge of an abrupt spur, surrounded by huge storm-beaten trees. You need to let the warden know in good time if you want a meal and a bed. It's best to stay overnight here, as you should make an early start for the three-hour ascent to Mítikas, the highest peak at 2917m. The peaks frequently cloud up towards midday and you lose the view, to say nothing of the danger of catching one of Zeus's thunderbolts, for this was the mythical seat of the gods. Besides, nights at the refuge are fantastic: a log fire blazes; you watch the sun set on the peaks, and dawn come up over the Aegean; there are billions of stars.

The summit area

The E4 path continues behind the refuge (the last water source on the mountain), climbing to the left up a steep spur among the last of the trees. In an hour you reach a signposted **fork** above the treeline. Straight on takes you across the range to Kokkinopilós village with the E4 waymarks, or with a slight deviation right to Mítikas, via the ridge known as Kakí Skála (1hr 30min). An immediate right turn leads to the Yiósos Apostolídhis hut in one hour, with the option after forty minutes of taking the very steep Loúki couloir left up to Mítikas; if you do this, be wary of rockfalls.

For the safer **Kakí Skála route**, continue up the right flank of the stony featureless valley in front of you, with the Áyios Andónios peak up to your left. An hour's dull climb brings you to the summit ridge between the peaks of Skolió on the left and Skála on the right. You know you're there when one more step would tip you over a 500-metre sheer drop into the Kazánia chasm; take great care. The Kakí Skála (Evil Stairway) begins in a narrow cleft on the right just short of the ridge; paint splashes mark the way. The route keeps just below the ridge, so you are protected from the drop into Kázania. Even so, those who don't like heights will feel pretty uncomfortable.

You start with a slightly descending rightward traverse to a narrow nick in the ridge revealing the drop to Kazánia – easily negotiated. Continue traversing right, skirting the base of the Skála peak, then climb leftwards up a steepish gully made a little awkward by loose rock on sloping footholds. Bear right at the top over steep but reassuringly solid rock, and across a narrow neck. Step left around an awkward corner and there in front of you, scarcely 100 metres away, is **Mítikas summit**, an airy, boulder-strewn platform with a trigonometric point, tin Greek flag and visitors' book. In reasonable conditions it's about forty minutes to the summit from the start of Káki Skála; three hours from the refuge; five and a half hours from Priónia.

A stone's throw to the north of Mítikas is the **Stefáni peak**, also known as the Throne of Zeus, a bristling hog's back of rock with a couple of nastily exposed moves to scale the last few feet.

Descending from Mítikas, you can either go back the way you came, with the option of turning left at the signpost (see above) for the Apostolídhis hut (2hr 30min from Mítikas by this route), or you can step out, apparently into space, in the direction of Stefáni and turn immediately down to the right into the mouth of the Loúki couloir. It takes about forty minutes of downward scrambling to reach the main path where you turn left for the hut, skirting the impressive northeast face of Stefáni (1hr), or go right, back to the familiar signpost and down the E4 to Spílios Agapitós (2hr altogether).

The ascent from Dhiakládhosi (Gortsiá)
Starting from the small parking area beyond the information placard, it's critically important to take the narrow path going up and left, not the forest track heading down and right. An hour along, you reach the meadow of **Bárba**, and two hours out you'll arrive at a messy junction with a new water tank and various placards – take left forks en route when given the choice. The signs point hard left to the spring at Stáángo, right for the direct path to Petróstrounga; and straight on the old, more scenic way to **Petróstrounga**, passed some two and a half hours along.

Beyond this summer pastoral colony, there's a signed right, then the trail wanders up to the base of **Skoúrta** knoll (4hr 15min), above the treeline. After crossing the Lemós (Neck) ridge dividing the Papá Réma and Mavrólongos ravines, with spectacular views into both, five and a quarter hours should see you up on the Oropédhio Musón (Plateau of the Muses), five and a half hours to the Apostolídhis refuge, visible the last fifteen minutes. But you should count on seven hours, including rests, for this route; going down takes about four and a half hours, a highly recommended descent if you've come up from Priónia.

It takes about an hour, losing altitude, to traverse the onward path linking Apostolídhis and the E4, skimming the base of the peaks – about the same as coming the other way as described above.

The southern ridge route
To experience complete solitude on Olympus, continue past Áyios Andónios, the peak just south of Skála and the E4 trail, and begin to ridge-walk the line of peaks that bounds the Mavrólongos to the south. Much of this trek past Metamórfosi, Kalóyeros, and Págos summits is cross-country, but with the recommended map, route-finding is easy on a clear day. It's six and a half walking hours from the Apostolídhis hut to the dilapidated but serviceable, unstaffed shelter at **Livadháki**, with unreliable cistern

water only – you'll need to carry at least a couple litres in with you. From Livadháki a good trail descends via the ridges of Pelekoudhiá and Tsouknídha, coming out three and a quarter hours on at the meadow of **Déli**, where you're just above a forest road which leads 7km down to Litóhoro.

Alternatively, a faint but followable trail at Déli dips down into a ravine and up onto **Gólna** knoll, intersecting another, sporadically marked path up from Litóhoro that leads over into the Mavrólongos watershed to join up with the E4. Just above the junction woodcutters have hopelessly messed up the path, but persevere, and you'll suddenly drop down on to the E4 about halfway along its course, some ninety minutes out of Déli. This last section makes a beautiful, if challenging walk. For full details, consult one of the specialist hiking guides (see " Books" in *Contexts*).

Véria and Veryína

The broad agricultural plain extending west from Thessaloníki eventually collides with an abrupt, wooded escarpment, at the panoramic edge of which several towns have grown up. The largest of these, **Véria**, has no particular sites or monuments, but it is one of the more interesting northern Greek communities and is within twenty minutes' drive of the excavations of ancient Aigai at **Veryína**

Véria

The **train station** is hopelessly inconvenient, 3km east of the centre; most arrivals will hike up Odhós Venizélou from the **bus terminal** to Odhós Elías, the short but fashionable street leading in turn to the Belvedere, the escarpment view-park. Odhós Anixéos snakes north along the cliff edge to intersect Venizélou, passing the **archeological museum** (daily except Mon 8.30am–3pm; 400dr). It has no finds from Veryína (see below), but contains mostly Roman oddments from the area.

For the most part, however, Véria is more of a place to wander about, stumbling across some of the fifty or so seventeenth- and eighteenth-century churches. Certain central streets preserve much of their old Ottoman atmosphere, including a largely untouched nineteenth-century bazaar, which see few tourists from one year to the next. The **churches** were were once disguised as barns or warehouses, but today, often surrounded by cleared spaces, are not hard to find. There is, for example, one on Megálou Alexándhrou, within sight of the Belvedere, and two more just beyond – though they are generally locked. One that's not is that of **Hristós** (daily except Mon 8.30am–3pm), with recently restored fourteenth-century frescoes, near the junction of Elías and Mitropóleos.

Mitropóleos bisects the town, running southwest towards the actual centre, past the new cathedral. The old one, opposite a gnarled plane tree from which the Turks hung the town's archbishop in 1436, is just off Odhós Vassiléos Konstandínou, which links Venizélou and the main square at the far end of Mitropóleos. Near the tree, the old **bazaar** straddles Vassiléos Konstandínou, and a small number of crumbling old houses overlook the river, five minutes' walk west from either the central square or the bazaar.

Practicalities

OTE, the **post office** and most **banks** are on or around Mitropóleos, near the new cathedral. **Hotels** are scattered throughout town: the best of the cheaper ones is the *Veroi* on the central square (☎0331/22 866; ③), which is adequate and clean. Nearer to the bus station there's also a good-value but noisy budget hotel, the *Vasilissa Veryina* at Venizélou 31 (☎0331/22 301; ③). More upmarket are the *Vila Elia*, Elías 16 (☎0331/26 800; ⑤), and the *Macedonia*, Kondoyiorgáki 15 (☎0331/66 902; ⑤).

Eating out, most authentic option is *Toh Hriso Pagoni*, a little *ouzerí* with tables in the courtyard of Ayía Ánna church, at Tsoúpeli 1, just southwest of Venizélou. Alternatively, try *Pitsaria Porto Fino*, at the corner of Merkouríou Karakostí and Anixéos. Nocturnal **bar** life is mostly confined to the Belvedere park strip, culminating in the expensive but pleasant tourist pavilion; this district, which takes its name from nearby Odhós Elías, is Véria's wealthiest. Finally, you can get home-made yoghurt and ice-cream nearby from *O Stergios* at Elías 11.

Veryína: ancient Aigai

Excavations at **VERYÍNA**, twenty minutes' drive southwest of Véria, have revolutionized Macedonian archeology since the 1970s. A series of chamber tombs, unearthed here by Professor Manolis Andronikos (1919–1992), are now unequivocally accepted as those of Philip II and other members of the Macedonian royal family. This means that the site itself must be that of **Aigai**, the original Macedonian royal capital before the shift to Pella, and later its necropolis. Finds from the site and tombs, the richest Greek trove since the discovery of Mycenae, are exhibited at Thessaloníki's archeological museum.

The main tombs can now be seen in situ; visitors walk down a narrow stone passage into an air-conditioned bunker which allows them to see the ornamental facades and the empty chambers beyond. Overhead, the earth of the tumulus has been put back. Until recently, the modern village of Veryína had limited resources, but as tourism picks up, locals plan to improve on the few tavernas and rooms to let. The first **pension**, as yet nameless, is now in business, on the road into the village (☎0331/92 510; ④).

The sites

Ancient Aigai is documented as the sanctuary and royal burial place of the Macedonian kings. It was here that Philip II was assassinated and buried – and tradition maintained that the dynasty would be destroyed if any king were buried elsewhere, as indeed happened after the death of Alexander the Great in Asia. Until Andronikos's finds in November 1977 – the culmination of years working on the site – Aigai had long been assumed to be lost beneath modern Édhessa, a theory now completely discarded.

What Andronikos discovered, under a tumulus just outside Veryína, were two large and indisputably Macedonian **chamber tombs**. The first had been looted in antiquity but retained a mural of the rape of Persephone by Pluto, the only complete example of an ancient Greek painting that has yet been found. The second, a grander vaulted tomb with a Doric facade adorned by a superb painted frieze of a lion hunt, was – incredibly – intact, having been deliberately disguised with rubble from later tomb pillagings. Among the treasures to emerge were a marble sarcophagus containing a gold casket of bones bearing the exploding-star symbol of the royal line on its lid, and, still more significantly, five small ivory heads, among them representations of both Philip II and Alexander. It was this clue, as well as the fact that the skull bore marks of a disfiguring facial wound Philip was known to have sustained, that led to the identification of the tomb as his.

It is these **Royal Tombs** (known as Tomb 1: Persephone and Tomb 2: Phillip II), together with two more adjacent tombs (Tomb 3: Prince's and Tomb 4: unnamed), which can now be seen underground (daily except Mon 8.30am–3pm; 400dr). The so-called "**Macedonian Tomb**", actually three adjacent tombs, can also be visited after a fashion (same times above; free). They are about 500m uphill and south of the village and, like the Royal Tombs, lie well below the modern ground level, protected by a vast tin roof. When he's around, the guard will let you into the dig, though not into the tombs themselves. Excavated by the French in 1861, the most prominent one has the form of a temple, with an Ionic facade of half-columns breached by two marble doors. Inside you can just make out an imposing marble throne with sphinxes carved on the sides, armrests and footstool. The neighbouring pair of tombs, still under excavation, are said to be similar in design.

A few hundred metres further on, at the end of the same road, the ruins of the **Palace of Palatitsa** (same times as above; 400dr) occupy a low hill. This complex was probably built during the third century BC as a summer residence for the last great Macedonian king, Antigonus Gonatus. It is now little more than foundations, but amidst the confusing litter of column drums and capitals you can make out a triple *propylaion* (entrance gate) opening onto a central courtyard. This is framed by broad porticoes and colonnades which, on the south side, preserve a well-executed if rather unexciting mosaic. Despite its lack of substance it is an attractive site, dominated by a grand old oak tree looking out across the plains, scattered with Iron-Age (tenth- to seventh-century BC) tumuli and who knows what else. The only substantial items dug up to date are the first two tiers of the **theatre** just below, where Philip II was assassinated, some say at the wedding of his daughter.

Édhessa, Lefkádhia and Náoussa

With your own vehicle, the other two escarpment towns can be easily and enjoyably toured in a day or less, with an unspoilt archeological site – Lefkádhia – in between. Travelling by public transport, however, especially by train, stopping off is time-consuming and probably more trouble than it's worth, in which case Édhessa, astride the main route between Thessaloníki and the far west of Macedonia, is the place you're most likely to halt.

Édhessa

ÉDHESSA, like Véria, is a pleasant stopover, its modest fame attributed to the waters that flow through the town. Coming down from the mountains to the north, they flow swiftly through the middle of town and then, just to the east, cascade down a dramatic ravine, luxuriant with vegetation, to the plain below. From the train station, walk straight for 400m until you see the walled-in river, paralleled by Tsimiskí street. Turn left and you will come to the **waterfalls**, the focus of a park with a couple of cafés. For the **Byzantine bridge** turn right from here and follow the river for about 600 metres. Paths also lead down the ravine, providing access to caves below.

The town itself is a little ordinary, but the various riverside parks and wide pedestrian pavements are a rare pleasure in a country where the car is tyrant, and the train and bus stations are both well placed for breaking a journey. For **accommodation**, choose between the comfortable but noisy *Pella*, Egnatia 30 (☎0381/23 541, ④), or the *Alfa*, next door (☎0381/22 221; ④), which is adequate if a little cheerlesss; both are near the bus station. Simple but good and inexpensive **food** is served at the *Egnatia* restaurant, Egnatía 23, almost opposite the hotels, and the *Taverna Roloi*, Áyios Dhimitriou 5, near the clock tower and OTE.

Lefkádhia

Thirty kilometres south of Édhessa on the road to Véria, Lefkádhia has not been positively identified with any Macedonian city, but it is thought possibly to have been Mieza, where Aristotle taught. The modern village of **LEFKÁDHIA** lies just west of the main road, but you should turn off east at a sign reading "To the Macedonian

Tombs". There are, in fact, four Macedonian tombs in all – today quite subterranean like the Veryína group – though only one has a guard, who keeps the keys to the other three.

The staffed one, the so-called **Great Tomb** or **Tomb of Judgement** (daily except Mon 8.30am–3pm), east of the main road just past the train tracks, is the largest Macedonian temple-tomb yet discovered. Despite extensive cement protection, it has been so badly damaged by creeping damp from the very high local water table that there's progressively less to see; plans are afoot to dismantle, consolidate and reassemble the whole thing stone by stone. It dates from the third century BC, and was probably built for a general, depicted on the left, in one of the barely surviving frescoes, being led by Hermes (the Conductor of Souls). Other faded frescoes on the right represent the Judges of Hades – hence the tomb's alias. A once-elaborate double-storeyed facade, half Doric and half Ionic, has almost completely crumbled away; on the entablature frieze you can barely make out a battle between Persians and Macedonians.

The **Anthimíon Tomb**, 150m further along the same country road, is more impressive, with its four Ionic facade columns, two marble interior sarcophagi with inscribed lids, and well-preserved frescoes. The typanum bears portraits of a couple, presumably the tomb occupants, though the man's face has been rubbed out. Ornamental designs and three giant *akrokerámata* complete the pediment decoration. Between the double set of portals, the ceiling frescoes are sensually vegetal – or perhaps stylized representations of octopi. Frogs, in fact, live through the summer in the bilge of the pump protecting the site.

The other two local tombs are of essentially specialist interest. The one signposted "Kinch's Macedonian Tomb", after its Danish discoverer, is on the east side of the main road, on the way back towards the village. That of **Lyson-Kallikles** is signed west of the main road, before the turning to the village, at the end of a 1km dirt track through peach orchards; to visit you have lower yourself through a usually locked grating in the ceiling, the original entrance having been long since buried.

Náoussa

Four kilometres south of the tombs is a turning west, off the main road, to **NÁOUSSA**, a small country town whose vintners, the **Boutari** company, produce some of Greece's best wines. Along with Véria, the town is also at the heart of the country's main peach-growing region – excuse enough for at least a stop in July – and hosts one of Macedonia's most elaborate pre-Lenten carnivals. That said, Náoussa is generally the sleepiest and least distinguished of the three escarpment towns – a pleasant enough place to live but not necessarily to holiday at. In winter, however, Náoussa is very busy with Greeks enjoying the two superb ski centres overhead on Mount Vermion.

If you do drop in, the big attraction is the parkland of **Áyios Nikólaos**, 4km beyond town (6km west of the main road), an oasis of giant plane trees nourished by the streams that bubble from the earth here. The riverbanks are lined with several more or less identically priced tavernas featuring farm-raised trout (the *Nisaki* is the most pleasantly set). Just upstream, the *Hotel Vermion* (☎0332/29 311; ⑤) is open year-round and has a fine restaurant. The torrents eventually cut through the town below, lending it some definition and a green vegetation belt, but it's a distinct miniature of Édhessa. South of the large belfried church, which you pass as you wind up from the main road, there's a small park strip, lined with the bulk of Náoussa's restaurants and bars. If you need to stay here, there is only the *Hellas* at Megálou Alexándhrou 16 (☎0332/22 006; ④). Leaving, you'll almost certainly be doing so by **bus** or under your own power, since the **train station** is a good 7km distant.

West from Édhessa: Flórina and the lakes

West of Édhessa lies **Límni Vegoritídha**, the first of a series of lakes that punctuate the landscape towards Kastoriá and up to and across the border with the former Yugoslav republic of Macedonia (FYROM). The rail line between Édhessa and Flórina traces the lake's west shore: a fine journey which could be broken at either of the two village train stops, Árnissa and Áyios Pandelímonas.

ÁRNISSA has perhaps the better setting, opposite an islet and amidst apple orchards. The one-street village itself is a little drab, though it does have the convenience of the attractive *Megali Hellas* (☎0381/31 232; ③). The village comes alive on Tuesdays when the weekly market attracts families from miles around, using their tractors as taxis. To the north of the village rises **Mount Kaimaktsalán**, scene of one of the bloodiest and more important battles of World War I, which raged intermittently from 1916 to 1918 until a Yugoslav force managed to break through the German–Bulgarian lines. The 2524-metre summit marks the Greek–"Yugoslav" frontier and bears a small memorial chapel to the fallen. If you can get a lift to the end of the road at Kalívia, it's a beautiful walk beyond.

The more attractive of the villages, however, is **ÁYIOS PANDELÍMONAS**, with its red-roofed houses crowned by a windmill, and a small beach if you're prepared to swim in the slightly algae-ridden waters. The lakeside *Epiheirisi* **restaurant** has no rooms available, but keeps watch over the basic **campsite** alongside. Rail and road then pass through Amíndeo (no accommodation) before turning north towards Flórina. Three kilometres north of Amíndeo, a short diversion to the right brings you to the smaller lake of **Petro** and the hillside ruins of the Hellenistic Petres, recently excavated and the subject of an interesting display on the first floor of the museum at Flórina (see below).

Flórina

FLÓRINA, surrounded by wooded hills, is the last town before the FYROM border 13km to the north and as such, is quite a lively market centre. Cars can cross the border but at present there are no through-trains. There is little of intrinsic interest in the town itself and the main reason for a visit is to see the Préspa lakes, 40km west (see below), or to get onward transport to Kastoriá. The local economy has been hard hit by the collapse of Yugoslavia, mainly because Germans and Austrians no longer pass through on their way to the Peloponnese beaches. Consequently, if you do stay, there are **hotel** bargains to be had: try *Ellinis*, Pávlou Méla 61 (☎0385/22 671; ③–④), near the train station and the cheapest in town; or the *Lingos*, very near the market and easy to find (☎0385/28 322; ⑤), a comfortable and roomy choice. For Macedonian **food** at its best, follow the locals to *Taverna Orea Elladha* on the main square, or try the *Restaurant Olympos* nearby on Megálou Alexándhrou.

Transport to the Former Yugoslav Republic of Macedonia or Kastoriá

At the moment, no trains run from **Flórina to Bitola** in the Former Yugoslav Republic of Macedonia (FYROM). There are four daily buses (morning and mid-day) to the frontier post at Níki. However, it's still 18km to Bitola from the frontier post and you have to hitch the first 6km to Medzitlija, where bus services resume.

There's one daily bus direct **to Kastoriá**, along the recently paved road that climbs west out of Flórina through dense beech forests to the 1600-metre Pisodhéri saddle, site of a ski lift. Since its resurfacing, the road is kept snow-ploughed in winter; it follows the headwaters of the Aliákmonas River, the longest in Greece, most of the way to Kastoriá.

The Préspa lakes

Rising out of the Aliákmonas valley on the recently paved side road towards Préspa, you have little hint of what's ahead until suddenly you top a pass, and a shimmering expanse of water riven by islets and ridges appears. It is not, at first glance, postcard-pretty, but the basin has an eerie, back-of-beyond quality that grows on you with further acquaintance – and a turbulent recent history that belies its current role as one of the Balkans' most important wildlife sanctuaries.

During the Byzantine era, Préspa became a prominent place of exile for troublesome noblemen, thus accounting for the surprising number of ecclesiastical monuments in this backwater. In the tenth century it briefly hosted the court of the Bulgarian Tsar Samuel before his defeat by Byzantine Emperor Basil II. Under the Ottomans the area again lapsed into obscurity, only to regain the dubious benefits of strategic importance in just about every European war of this century, culminating in vicious local battles during the 1947–49 Greek civil war. In 1988 a forest fire on the eastern ridge treated observers to a dangerous fireworks display, as dozens of unexploded artillery shells were touched off by the heat. After World War II Préspa lay desolate and largely depopulated, as the locals fled abroad to Eastern Europe, North America and Australia, in response to a punitive government policy of forced assimilation against Macedonian-speakers – as all the lake-dwellers are. It is only in the last decade or so that the villages, still relatively primitive and neglected, have begun to refill during the summer, when beans and hay are grown as close to the two lakes as the national park authorities allow.

Mikrí Préspa, the southerly lake, is mostly shallow and reedy, with a narrow fjord curling west just penetrating Albania. The borders of Greece, Albania and FYROM meet in the middle of deeper **Megáli Préspa**, dividing its waters unequally, making the area doomed to play some role in whatever Balkan uproars lie in the future. During the past few years a steady stream of Albanian refugees used the basin as an exit corridor. Current policy is for those fleeing to be returned, and almost every day some are caught, taken to an army guard post for a meal, and then sent back the way they came. Considering that for years you needed an official permit to visit Préspa, and the uncertain future, the Greek military presence is surprisingly unobtrusive and sovereignty lightly exercised; it's almost as if they couldn't be bothered investing resources on an indigenously Slavic area of suspect political sympathies.

The core of the **national park**, established in 1971, barely encompasses Mikrí Préspa and its shores, but the peripheral zone extends well into the surrounding mountains, affording protection of sorts to a variety of land mammals. You'll almost certainly see foxes crossing the road, though the wolves and bears up on the ridges are considerably shyer, although it is the **bird life** for which the Préspa basin, particularly the smaller lake, is most famous. There are few birds of prey, but you should see a fair number of egrets, cormorants, crested grebes and pelicans, which nest in the spring, with the chicks out and about by summer. They feed partly on the large numbers of snakes, which include vipers, whip snakes and harmless water snakes which you may encounter while swimming. Observation towers, for example at the site Opáyia, are still marked on the occasional orientation placards, but they are virtually all rotten and unclimbable. Don't despair, however, since any dawn spent at the edge of the reedbeds with a pair of binoculars will be immensely rewarding (though bear in mind that you are not allowed to boat or wade into the reeds). There's a **park information centre** in the village of Áyios Yermanós (see below).

While you may arrive from Flórina by bus, the service is unreliably infrequent and you really can't hope to tour the area without some **means of transport** – either a mountain bike or a car. Similarly, in view of the area's past under-development, don't expect much in the way of **facilities**: food is adequate and inexpensive, but exceedingly simple; the same might be said of some places to sleep, although recently, better accommodation has become available.

The way in: Mikrolímni

MIKROLÍMNI, 5km up a side track off the main road into the valley, would be a first conceivable stop. The small shop and fish taverna, on the shore square, has three **rooms** to let (☎0385/61 221; ②). In the evening, you can look towards sunsets over reedbeds and the snake-infested Vitrinítsi islet, though swimming isn't good here. At the far end of the hamlet is a sporadically used biological observation station, literally the last house in Greece, and beyond that the lake narrows between sheer hillsides on its way to Albania. A prominent trail, much used by fleeing Albanians, leads there, paralleling the long inlet, but it would be unwise to walk its full length.

Regaining the main road, it reaches a T-junction, 16km from the main Flórina–Kastoriá highway, on the spit which separates the larger and smaller lakes. It's probable that at one time there was just one lake here, but now there's a five-metre elevation difference. Bearing right at trhe junction leads within 4km to Áyios Yermanós; the left option splits again at the west end of the spit, bearing south toward the islet of Áyios Ahillíos or northwest toward the hamlet of Psarádhes – for all of which, see below.

Áyios Yermanós

ÁYIOS YERMANÓS proves to be a surprisingly large village of tile-roofed houses, very much the district "town", overlooking a patch of Megáli Préspa in the distance. It's worth making the trip up just to see two tiny late Byzantine churches, whose frescoes date from the time when the place belonged to the bishopric of Ohrid and thus display a marked Macedonian influence. The lower church, **Áyios Athanásios**, has been recently renovated but if it's open you can glimpse a dog-faced *Saint Christopher* among a line of saints opposite the door.

The main thing to see, however, is the tiny, eleventh-century parish church of **Áyios Yermanós** up on the square, hidden behind a new monster awkwardly tacked onto it in 1882. The Byzantine structure has its own unlocked door, and the frescoes, skilfully retouched in 1743, can be lit (switch hidden in narthex). There are more hagiographies and martyrdoms than space allows to list here, but if you read Greek there's a complete catalogue of them by the door. Among the best are the dome's *Pandokrátor*, a *Nativity* and *Baptism* right of the dome; a *Crucifixion* and *Resurrection* to the left; plus the saints *Peter and Paul, Kosmas and Damian, Triphon and Pandelimon* by the door. Less conventional scenes include the *Entry into Jerusalem* and *Simon Helping Christ with the Cross*, opposite the door, and the *Apocalypse*, with the *Succouring of Mary the Beatified by Zozimas*, in the narthex. Mary was an Alexandrine courtesan who, repenting of her ways, retired to the desert for forty years. She was found, a withered crone on the point of death, by Zozimas, abbot of a desert monastery, and is traditionally shown being spoon-fed like an infant.

The village has the excellent **Préspa information centre** (mid-March to mid-Sept daily 9.30am–1.30pm & 4.30–7.30pm; mid-Sept to mid-March daily 10am–2pm), focusing on the wildlife of the national park – given sufficient warning the centre can arrange guides for trips into the park. In addition to a **post office** – the only one in the Préspa basin – the village has two places to **stay**: *Les Pelicans* (☎0385/51 442; ③), across from Áyios Athanásios and with a bit of lake view from its terrace, or several renovated old houses at the very top of the village, run by a local women's cooperative. Reservations (☎0385/51 320; ③) are strongly advised, especially in August when a folk-dance seminar takes place here. In the evenings an unlikely-looking taverna across from the main church dishes up good **meals**.

Across the spit and beyond

At the far end of the causeway dividing the two lakes, 4km from the T-junction, is a cluster of what passes for touristic development hereabouts: a patch of beach from where you can swim in Megáli Préspa, a free but basic camping area, and a clutch of tavernas. Tents and vans sprout by the "sailing club", actually a sporadically operating taverna of sorts, but *Iy Koula*, up by the army guard-post, offers the best value. Just below it you can see where Mikrí Préspa drains into Mégali Préspa.

If you don't intend to camp, it's best to bear right just above the army post, reaching after 6km the picturesque village of **PSARÁDHES**, whose alleys – and a plaza *kafenío* just inland where the elders gabble away in mixed Macedonian and Greek – make for an hour's stroll. Across the rather stagnant inlet here, the EOT is building a smart new hotel, from which tracks and paths lead to a white-pebble beach, near which are two cave-churches with rock paintings. In the village there are **rooms** to rent, a new six-roomed **hotel**, the *Sindrofía* (☎0385/51 327; ②–③), and three of the four **tavernas** run by people surnamed Papadopoulos; *Paradhosi* seems the best of the bunch. You won't see the fish fried here anywhere else in Greece; similarly, the cows ambling the lanes of Psarádhes are a locally adapted dwarf variety.

The leftward option at the end of the causeway takes you, after 2km or so, to the jetty for the islet of **Áyios Ahillíos**, with a hamlet of the same name. Five families still live there and with luck you might coincide with a resident's boat across, but even then you could easily be stranded on the other side. Once on the island, you can see the ruins of a monastery, a medieval church and the ruins of a Byzantine basilica, the latter with an egret mosaic in the floor. The hill above the jetty is also an excellent vantage point for spotting live birds in the reedbeds below.

Kastoriá and around

Set on a peninsula extending deep into a chill-blue lake, **KASTORIÁ** is one of the most interesting and attractive towns of mainland Greece. It is a wealthy place and has been so for centuries as the centre of the Greek (and Balkan) fur trade; Kastoriá is not a trapping centre, and never really was, but instead boasts a considerable industry of furriers who make up coats, gloves and other items from fur scraps imported from Canada and Scandinavia. For visitors, the main appeal lies in the town's traces of former prosperity. From the seventeenth to nineteenth centuries, when the town was perhaps at its peak, survive half a dozen splendid *arhondiká* – **mansions** of the old fur families. Dotted about as well are some fifty Byzantine and medieval churches.

The Town

The best part of town, for a sense of what Kastoriá must once have been, is the lakeside quarter and former Christian ghetto of **Kariádhi**, around Platía Immanouíl. In nearby Kapitán Lázou (at no. 10) the seventeenth-century Aïvazís family mansion has been turned into a **Folklore Museum** (daily 8.30am–6pm; 200dr). The house was inhabited until 1972 and its furnishings and ceilings are in excellent repair. The caretaker, on request, will show you some of the other surviving *arhondiká*. The most notable – the nearby **Basára Natzí**, and **Immanouíl** – are marked on the map and though all are a bit decrepit, they are currently undergoing restoration.

Kastoriá's **churches** are harder to visit. Although hours of admission are posted on some of the doors, they are irregularly kept. To be sure of entry, it's best to enquire of the two *fílakes* (caretakers) at one of the *kafenía* in Platía Omonías. One has keys for Taxiárhes, Áyios Nikólaos and Koumbelidhikí; the other for Áyii Anáryiri and Áyios Stéfanos. **Áyii Anáryiri** dates from the eleventh century, with three layers of frescoes spanning the following two hundred years. Only one of the frescoes, *Áyios Yióryios and Áyios Dhimítrios*, has been cleared of grime. **Áyios Stéfanos** is of the tenth century and has been little changed over the years. Its frescoes are insignificant but it

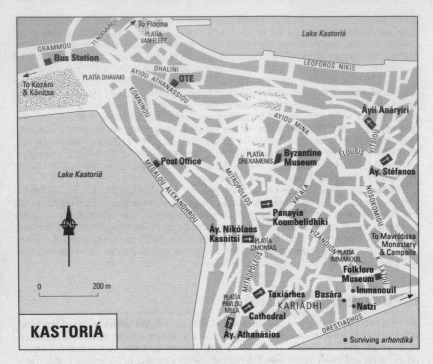

KASTORIÁ

does have an unusual women's gallery, or *yinaikonítis*. The excellent frescoes of twelfth-century **Áyios Nikólaos Kasnítsi** have recently been returned to their former glory. **Taxiárhes**, the oldest (ninth-century) church, hides various treasures beneath layers of soot and damp; some of its more visible frescoes, such as that of the *Virgin and Archangels*, are fourteenth century. Lastly, the **Panayía Koumbelidhikí**, so named because of its unusual dome (*kübe* in Turkish), has the best-preserved and illuminated frescoes, including a highly unusual portrayal of God the Father in a ceiling mural of the *Holy Trinity*. The building was done in stages, with the apse completed in the tenth century and the narthex in the fifteenth. The dome was meticulously restored after being destroyed by Italian bombing in World War II.

Kastoriá also suffered heavily during the civil war. Platía Van Fleet, by the lakeside at the neck of the promontory, commemorates the US general – Van Fleet – who supervised the Greek Nationalist Army's operations against the Communist Democratic Army in the final campaigns of 1948–49. The town was nearly captured by the communists in 1948, and Vítsi, the conical peak dominating the north shore of the lake, was, together with Mount Grámmos, the scene of their last stand in August 1949. However, most of the destruction of Kastoriá's architectural heritage is not due so much to munitions as to 1950s neglect and 1960s development.

If tracking down buildings seems too frustrating a pursuit, perhaps the nicest thing to do in Kastoriá is to follow the paved track which runs all around the **lake shore** to the east of town. Although the lake itself is heavily polluted, the path has been deliberately created by one of Greece's few environmentalists. It has almost a country-park atmosphere, and wildlife abounds – frogs, tortoises and water snakes especially. At the southern end of the peninsula, about twenty minutes' walk, are the **Mavrótissa**

monastery, with more fine frescoes in its eleventh-century church, a restaurant and a small **campsite** (April–Sept; free).

Finally, back in town and for aficionados, there's a **Byzantine museum** on Platía Dhexamenis (daily except Mon 8.30am–3pm; free), containing an ever-expanding collection of restored Byzantine icons.

Practicalities

Arriving at the **bus station**, you'll find yourself at the edge of the peninsula. There are a number of hotels within walking distance of the bus station, but if you don't arrive early enough, finding a **hotel** can be a struggle, as the town's business means places are full pretty much year-round. They are also expensive, so if you plan on staying try to phone ahead. Choices by the bus station on Grámmou include the *Anessis* at no. 10 (☎0467/33 908; ③) and *Acropolis* at no. 16 (☎0467/83 737; ②), the latter with rooms with and without private facilities. Another, *Keletron*, is on the street's extension, Éndheka Noemvríou, at no. 52 (☎0467/22 676; ③), a little shabby but with an affable owner. The *Kastoria*, Nikís 122 (☎0467/29 453; ③), faces the lake at the far end of the northern waterfront, and has fine views from its front rooms, all of which have balconies.

The best area for **restaurants** is around Platía Omonías, where the *Omonoia* and the *Mantziaris* are both good. The *Stakhi* bakery, below the square, is good for *bougátzes* (custard tarts), *tirópites* and pizzas.

Around Kastoriá

If you have transport, you might make a trip 14km west to OMORFOKLISSIÁ, an eerie village of mud houses inherited from Turkish peasants. It has a Byzantine church with a high cupola, attached belfry and, inside, a huge, primitive wooden **statue-icon of Saint George** thought to date from the eleventh century.

SIÁTISTA, draped along a single ridge in a forbiddingly bare landscape 70km south of Kastoriá, is also a worthy destination. Located just above the point where the road splits for Kozáni or Kastoriá, it was, like the latter, an important fur centre, and boasts a handful of eighteenth-century mansions or *arhondiká*, which can be visited. The eighteenth-century house of **Hatzimihaíl Kanatsoúli** at Mitropóleos 1, near the police station, is still lived in but you can ring to be shown around. The first two floors are occupied; upstairs, a corner room has naive murals of mythological scenes (including Kronos's castration of Ouranos). The dilapidated **Nerantzópoulos mansion** (Mon–Sat 8.30am–3pm, Sun 9.30am–2.30pm) is on the upper square, by the *Ethniki Trapeza*; the warden here has the keys for several other houses, of which the largest and most elaborate is the **Manoúsi mansion**, dating from 1763, in a vale below the Kanatsoúli along with various other surviving *arhondiká*. Ceiling medallions often sport a carved cluster of fruit or a melon with a slice missing, where you'd expect a chandelier attachment point; there are more three-dimensional floral and fruit carvings up at the tops of the walls, which are adorned with stylized murals of pastoral and fictitious urban scenes. The church of **Áyia Paraskeví**, on the lowest *platía*, has soot-blackened seventeenth-century frescoes inside; until the scheduled cleaning occurs, you're better off glancing at the exterior ones.

Almost everything you need in Siátista – banks, OTE, post office – is along the single main street, including the impressive *Archondiko* **hotel** (☎0465/21 298; ④), which has a reasonable restaurant and café on the ground floor. Other options for **eating** out are limited; the *Psistaria Ouzerí O Platanos*, just below Áyia Paraskeví, has acceptable food but a rather boozy male environment – the hotel is more genteel. The easiest bus connections are with Kozáni.

HALKIDHIKÍ AND EASTERN MACEDONIA

Halkidhikí, easily reached by bus from Thessaloníki, is the clear highlight of Macedonia's eastern half. Its first two peninsulas, **Kassándhra** and **Sithonía**, shelter the north's main concentration of beaches; the third, **Áthos**, the country's finest, though most secretive, monasteries.

Moving east, there are a few more good beaches en route to **Kavála**, but little of interest inland, with a scattering of small market towns serving a population that – as in neighbouring Thrace – produces the main Greek tobacco crop.

Kassándhra, Sithonía and secular Áthos

The squid-shaped peninsula of **Halkidhikí** begins at a perforated edge of lakes east of Thessaloníki and extends into three prongs of land – Kassándhra, Sithonía, and Áthos – trailing like tentacles into the Aegean sea.

Mount Áthos, the easternmost peninsula, is in all ways separate, a "Holy Mountain", whose monastic population, semi-autonomous within the Greek state, excludes all women – even as visitors. For men who wish to experience Athonite life, a visit involves suitably Byzantine procedures which are detailed, with the monastic sights, in the section that follows. The most that women can do is to glimpse the buildings from offshore. It is possible to take *kaíki* rides from the two small resorts on the periphery of the peninsula – Ierissós and Ouranoúpoli, the "secular" part of Áthos covered in this section.

Kassándhra and **Sithonía**, by contrast, host some of the fastest-growing holiday resorts in Greece. Up until the late 1980s these were popular mainly with Greeks, but they're now in the process of a staggering development, with most European package-tour companies maintaining a presence. On Kassándhra, especially, almost any reasonable beach is accompanied by a crop of villas or a hotel development, while huge billboards advertise campsite complexes miles in advance. A still larger billboard at the entrance to the Kassándhra peninsula reminds you that camping outside the authorized grounds is strictly prohibited, although you may have no other choice if you're so bold as to show up in high season without a reservation. One consolation is that most beaches here are equipped with free freshwater showers.

Both Kassándhra and Sithonía are connected to Thessaloníki by a network of fast new roads which extend around their coastlines; buses run frequently to all the larger resorts. In spite of this, neither peninsula is that easy to travel around if you are dependent on public **transport**. You really have to pick a place and stay there, perhaps renting a moped for local excursions.

Kassándhra

Kassándhra, the nearest prong to Thessaloníki, is also by far the most developed. Unless you're very pushed for time and want a couple of days' escape from Thessaloníki, it's best to keep on to Sithonía, or, better still, the top end of Áthos. Apart from resorts, there is very little to Kassándhra. Its population took part in the independence uprising of 1821, but was defeated and massacred; as a result, there were only a few small fishing hamlets here until after 1923, when the peninsula was resettled by refugees from around the Sea of Marmara.

On the peninsula's west coast, the first resort you come to, **NÉA MOUDHANIÁ**, has a campsite on the sandy beach – the *Ouzouni Beach* (☎0373/23 394; May–Sept) – and a reasonable hotel, the *Thalia* (☎0373/23 106; ④). Hydrofoils sail from here to

Skiáthos, Skópelos and Alónissos, but only in summer, and even then only twice a week. The second resort, **NÉA POTÍDHEA**, at the neck of the peninsula, is a tiny place, overlooked by a medieval watchtower. It has a laidback feel, which attracts Greek families and a fairly young crowd. The *Golden Beach* **apartments** (☎0373/41 657; ④) are new and friendly, while on the promenade are a number of good **tavernas** – look for the *Philippos* or the *Marina*.

Just before Néa Fokea, a turning to the right takes you to the west corner of the peninsula, where at **SANÍ** there is the *Blue Dream* campsite (☎0374/31 435; May–Sept); it's operated by the village and is more relaxed than most. The nearby *Sani Beach Complex* (hotel, campsite and club) is more frenetic – and expensive. Continuing south from Néa Fokea, the next east coast resort is **KALLITHÉA**, a large and busy place and a slightly better option if you want a straightforward holiday spot. There are a large number of **rooms** to let – not just package hotels – and you can rent bikes and mopeds on the main street, or windsurfers on the beach. Don't expect much character, though.

HANIÓTIS, further south still, is an old-fashioned resort with a good long beach and numerous hotels and tavernas. If you want to stay, you'll have to arrive early in the day and shop around – the *Hermes* (☎0374/51 245; ③) lacks charm but is good value. Finally, at **PALIOÚRI**, close to the southern tip of the peninsula, there's an expensive hotel and campsite.

Sithonía

Things improve considerably as you move east across the Halkidhikí and away from the frontline of tourism; the landscape also becomes increasingly green and hilly, culminating in the isolated and spectacular scenery of the Holy Mountain, looming across the gulf lapping Sithonía's east coast. As for the peninsula itself, **Sithonía** is more rugged but better vegetated than Kassándhra, though once again there are few true villages, and those that do exist date from the 1920s resettlement era. Pine forests cover many of the slopes, particularly in the south, giving way to olive groves on the coast. Small sandy inlets with relatively discreet pockets of campsites and tavernas make a welcome change from sprawling mega-resorts.

Metamórfosi

Suitably enough, **METAMÓRFOSI** ("Transfiguration"), at the western base of Sithonía, signals the transformation. Its beach is only adequate but there's good swimming to be had, and the village, while relentlessly modern, has an easy-going air. In addition to the friendly *Hotel Golden Beach* (☎0375/22 063; ③), with its cool courtyard and café on the village square, there's a **campsite** a couple of kilometres beyond. This, the *Sithon* (☎0375/22 414; May–Sept), is not on the beach but you only have to cross the coast road to reach the sand. In high season, the campsite and village can be a little crowded, but there's a fair number of **tavernas** clustered in and around the village square which seem to soak up business.

Moving on to Sithonía proper, it's best to follow the loop road clockwise around the east coast, so that Áthos is always before you. **Bus services** are sparse, however: there are up to five buses daily around the west coast to Sárti, and up to three a day to Vourvouroú, but there's no KTEL connection between these two endpoints. A complete circuit is only really possible with your own transport.

Órmos Panayía to Vourvouroú

ÓRMOS PANAYÍA, first of the east coast resorts, is nowadays well developed; ranks of villas dwarf the picturesque hamlet and tiny harbour, and the nearest decent beaches are 4km north at **ÁYIOS NIKÓLAOS**, which is marginally more attractive.

The only conceivable reason to stop at Órmos would be to catch the excursion boats that sail around Áthos from here, but these are expensive and often pre-reserved for tourists bused in from the big Halkidhikí resorts.

VOURVOUROÚ, 8km downcoast, is not a typical resort, since it's essentially a 35-year-old vacation-villa project for Thessaloníki professors, built on land expropriated from Vatopedhíou monastery on Áthos. There is relatively little short-term **accommodation** – the hotels *Dhiaporos* (☎0375/91 313; ⑥; half-board obligatory), with its cool rooftop restaurant, and the faded *Vourvourou* (☎0375/91 261; ③), are about the size of it. The strange feel is accentuated by those plot owners who haven't bothered to build villas (so far very scattered) and merely tent down, making it hard to tell which are the real campsites. The setting, with islets astride the mouth of the bay, is very fine, but the beach, while sandy, is extremely narrow, and Vourvouroú is really more of a yachters' haven. **Tavernas** are relatively inexpensive because they're banking on a return clientele (which includes lots of Germans); the *Itamos*, inland from the road, is the best; the *Gorgona*, while the nicest positioned, is rather surly; *Dionisos* is intermediate in position and quality, but has a simple though adequate **campsite** (☎0375/91 214; April–Oct), one half of which is on the beach.

Some of Sithonía's best **beaches** line the thirty kilometres of road between Vourvouroú and Sárti: five signposted sandy coves, each with a **campsite** and little else. The names of the bays reflect the fact that most of the land here belonged to various Athonite monasteries until confiscated by the civil government to resettle Anatolian refugees.

Sárti

Concrete-grid **SÁRTI** itself is set well back from its broad, two-kilometre-long beach, with only the scale of the bay protecting it from being utterly overrun in summer by Germans. There are hundreds of **rooms** (though often not enough to go around), and the cheaper of the **tavernas** lining the landscaped, gravel shore esplanade include *Neraida* and *O Stavros*. Inland you'll find a short-hours **bank** and a rather tacky square with forgettable tavernas – although it does boast a **moped rental** place. One kilometre to the south, at the end of the beach, there are the *Sarti Beach Apartments* (☎0375/94 250; ⑤) and the shady *Camping Sarti Beach* (☎0375/94 629; May–Sept), the campsite laid out between the road and the hotel grounds.

Paralía Sikiás and Kalamítsi

If you want reasonably priced facilities, **PARALÍA SIKIÁS**, 8km further along, has a beach the equal of Sárti's but is so far undeveloped except for a basic **campsite** and a few **tavernas**. **KALAMÍTSI**, as many kilometres again to the south, consists of a beautiful double bay sheltered by islets, but the two **campsites** monopolize both coves, and the handful of **rooms** and **tavernas** just behind the sandy beach combines with the habitual crowds to cramp matters. You can easily swim out to the islets for less company, or (taking things to extremes) arrange an excursion with the scuba-diving centre *Nireas*, which you can contact at *Camping Kalamitsi* (☎0375/41 410; May–Sept) or *Porto Camping* (☎0375/41 346; May–Oct; in winter contact ☎031/812 698).

Pórto Koufó and Toróni

Sithonía's forest cover has been diminishing since Sárti, and as you round the tip of the peninsula it vanishes completely, with bare hills spilling into the sea to create a handful of deep bays. **PÓRTO KOUFÓ**, just northwest of the cape, is the most dramatic of these, almost completely cut off from the open sea by high cliffs. There's a decent beach near where the road drops down from the east. The north end of the inlet, a kilometre from the beach area, is a yacht harbour with a string of somewhat expensive seafood **tavernas**; *O Pefkos* is a cheaper, though not very inspired alternative.

TORÓNI, 2km north, is the antithesis of this, an exposed, two-kilometre-long crescent of sand, still at the developmental stage where each of the half-dozen **tavernas** also rents out **rooms**. There's a new **campsite**, too, *Camping Isa* (☎0375/51 235; May–Sept). It's probably your best Sithonian bet as a base if you just want to flop on a beach for a few days; for more stimulation there is a minimal **archeological site** on the southern cape, sporting the remains of an ancient fortress and early Christian basilica. Just to the north are more coves especially popular with car-campers, accessible on a dirt coastal track as far as **Aretes**, where most vehicles and people give up.

Pórto Carrás to Parthenónas

Beyond here, you edge back into high-tech resort territory, epitomized by Greece's largest planned holiday complex, **PÓRTO CARRÁS**. Established by the Carras wine and shipping dynasty, it takes Spanish Marbella as its model, featuring its own shopping centre, golf course and vineyards. From the beach in front of the complex, you can indulge in every imaginable watersport. The nearest town to all this is **NÉOS MARMARÁS**, a once-attractive fishing port and small beach. Nowadays, it's popular with Greeks who stay at family hotels like the *Platamos* (☎0375/71 234; ④). Failing that, the last **campsite** in Sithonía is 3km to the north – *Castello* (☎0375/71 094; May–Sept) – at which point the beach is sandy, and there's tennis, volleyball and a restaurant.

If you're curious as to what Sithonía looked like before all this happened, a dirt road leads 5km from Néos Marmarás to **PARTHENÓNAS**, the lone "traditional" village on Sithonía, crouched at the base of 808-metre Mount Ítamos. The place was abandoned in the 1960s in favour of the shore, and never even provided with mains electricity; its dilapidated but appealing houses are now slowly being sold off to wealthy Greeks and Germans.

East to secular Áthos

From Órmos Panayía a partly paved road winds around the coast to Ierissós at the head of the Áthos peninsula. No buses cover this stretch, however, and if you're dependent on public transport you'll have to backtrack as far as Yerakiní and then inland to Halkidhikí's capital, **POLÍYIROS**, a drab market town with an unexciting archeological museum. Here, or from Áyios Pródhromos, 20km north, you can pick up buses heading for Áthos via **ARNÉA**, which has some fine old quarters and a reputation for (somewhat touristy) carpets and other colourful handwoven goods; it could be worth a brief stopover, though there's no longer any hotel here. The nearest **accommodation** is at **PALEOHÓRI**, 5km further east, towards Stáyira, where the *Hotel Park Tasos* (☎0372/41 722; ④), on the outskirts, is a delightful place with well-furnished rooms and a county-style restaurant.

After Stáyira, the road continues on to Ierissós, and the only place you'd think to stop is **PIRGADHÍKIA**, a hill-set former fishing village now taken over by German holidaymakers.

Ierissós

IERISSÓS, with a good, long beach and a vast, promontory-flanked gulf, is probably the best "secular Athos" resort, although the town itself, set well back from the shore and with room to expand, is a sterile concrete grid dating from after a devastating 1932 earthquake. The only hint of pre-touristic life is the vast caique-building dry dock to the south.

There are numerous **rooms**, two inexpensive **hotels** – the *Akanthos* (☎0377/22 359; ③) and slightly classier *Marcos* (☎0377/22 518; ④) – and two basic **campsites** (one at the north edge of town, the other on the way to Néa Ródha). The beach is surprisingly uncluttered, with just a handful of shore **tavernas** and **bars**. Rounding off the list of amenities, there's a **post office**, two **banks** and a summer **cinema** by the campsite. Ierissós is also the main port for the northeast shore of Áthos; summer sailings take place daily in the morning, with only three or four weekly in winter as weather – which can turn very stormy on this side – allows.

Néa Ródha and Amoulianí

The road beyond Ierissós passes through the resort of **NÉA RÓDHA**, with a small beach and no more claim to architectural distinction than its neighbour, but worth knowing about as an alternative point for picking up the morning boat. Just beyond here your route veers inland to follow a boggy depression that's the remaining stretch of **Xerxes's canal**, cut by the Persian invader in 48 BC to spare his fleet the shipwreck at the tip of Áthos that had befallen the previous expedition eleven years before.

You emerge on the southwest facing coast at **Tripití**, not a settlement but merely the ferry jetty for the small island of **AMOULIANÍ** (regular crossings in summer, especially at weekends). On the island's further, southwest side is a beautiful beach, **Alikés**, with a namesake campsite and small taverna. The island's town itself, after decades of eking out an existence as a refugee fishing community from the Sea of Marmara, is having to adjust to the relatively sudden arrival of well-heeled Greek and foreign visitors – you can even arrange scuba expeditions here.

Ouranópoli

Fifteen kilometres beyond Ierissós, **OURANÓPOLI** is the last community before the restricted monastic domains, with a centre that's downright tatty, showing the effects of too much Greek-weekender and German-package tourism, and sandy **beaches**, (though stretching intermittently for several kilometres to the north) which can be cramped. The pebbly coves in the opposite direction, up to the Athonite frontier, are less used. If you're compelled to stay the night while waiting for passage to Áthos, the best temporary escape would be either to take a cruise, or to rent a **motor boat**, to the mini-archipelago of **Dhrénia** just opposite, with almost tropical sands and tavernas on the larger islets.

The only other conceivable diversion in Ouranópoli is the Byzantine **Phosphori tower** by the bus stop, where for nearly thirty years lived Sydney Loch, author of *Athos: the Holy Mountain*, published posthumously in 1957 but still an excellent guide to the monasteries. Sydney Loch and his wife Joyce, who died in the tower in 1982, were a Scots-Australian missionary couple who devoted most of their lives to the refugees of Halkidhikí. The cottage industry of carpet-weaving, which they taught the local villagers, is unfortunately increasingly less in evidence.

Three **ferries** – the *Ayios Nikolaos*, the *Poseidon* and the *Axion Esti* – take turns calling along the southwest shore of Áthos, and they're probably the main reason you're here. Much of the year there's just one daily departure, at around 9.45am, though in summer there may be two: one earlier, one around 11.30am. If you need to stay, there are a fair number of **rooms**, like the *Athos* and *Niki* on the main thoroughfare, and a few cheaper hotels such as the *Galini* (☎0377/71 217; ③), the *Ouranopolis* (☎0377/71 205; ③) or the seafront *Akrogiali* (☎0377/71 201; ③). A **campsite**, better appointed than those in Ierissós, is 2km north of the village, amidst a crop of luxury hotel complexes that have sprung up where there's more space to spread out. Ouranópoli has a **post office** and an **OTE** but no bank. The four or five waterfront **tavernas** all tout identical rip-off menus, though you're unlikely to care much about value for money before (or especially after) several lean days on Áthos. If budgeting is an issue, there are a few marginally less expensive places in the inland alleys.

Mount Áthos: the monks' republic

The population of the **Mount Áthos** peninsula has been exclusively male – farm animals included – since an edict, the *Ávaton*, banning females permanent or transient, was issued by the Byzantine emperor Constantine Monomachos in 1060. Known in Greek as the **Áyiou Óros** ("Holy Mount"), it is an administratively autonomous part of the country – a "monks' republic" – on whose slopes are gathered twenty monasteries, plus a number of smaller dependencies and hermitages.

Most of the **monasteries** were founded in the tenth and eleventh centuries. Today, all survive in a state of comparative decline but they remain unsurpassed in their general and architectural interest, and for the art treasures they contain. If you are male, over 21 years old, and have a genuine interest in monasticism or Greek Orthodoxy, or simply in Byzantine and medieval architecture, a visit is strongly recommended. It takes a couple of hours to arrange, either in Thessaloníki or Athens (see below for details), but the rewards more than justify your efforts. In addition to the religious and architectural aspects of Áthos, it should be added that the peninsula, despite some horrific fires and heavy logging in recent years, is still one of the most beautiful parts of Greece. With only the occasional service vehicle, two buses and sporadic coastal boats, a visit necessarily involves walking between settlements – preferably on paths through dense woods, up the main peak, or above what is perhaps the Mediterranean's last undeveloped coastline. For many visitors, this – as much as the experience of monasticism – is the highlight of time spent on the Holy Mountain.

The Theocratic Republic: some history

By a legislative decree of 1926, Áthos has the status of **Theocratic Republic**. It is governed from the small town and capital of Karlés by the *Ayía Epistasía* (Holy Superintendency), a council of twenty representatives elected for one-year terms by each of the monasteries. At the same time Áthos remains a part of Greece. All foreign monks must adopt Greek citizenship and the Greek civil government is represented by an appointed governor and a small police force.

Each monastery has a distinct place in the **Athonite hierarchy**: Meyístis Lávras holds the prestigious first place, Kastamonítou ranks twentieth. All other settlements are attached to one or other of the twenty "ruling" monasteries; the dependencies range from a *skíti* (either a group of houses, or a cloister-like structure scarcely distinguishable from a monastery) through a *kellí* (a sort of farmhouse) to an *isikhastírio* (a solitary hermitage, often a cave). As many laymen as monks live on Áthos, mostly employed as agricultural or manual labourers by the monasteries.

The **development of monasticism** on Áthos is a matter of some controversy, and foundation legends abound. The most popular asserts that the Virgin Mary was blown ashore here on her way to Cyprus, and while overcome by the great beauty of the mountain, a mysterious voice consecrated the place in her name. Another tradition relates that Constantine the Great founded the first monastery in the fourth century, but this is certainly far too early. The earliest historical reference to Athonite monks is to their attendance at a council of the Empress Theodora in 843; probably there were some monks here by the end of the seventh century. Áthos was particularly appropriate for early Christian monasticism, its deserted and isolated slopes providing a natural refuge from the outside world – especially from the Arab conquests in the east, and the iconoclastic phase of the Byzantine Empire (eighth to ninth centuries). Moreover its awesome beauty, which had so impressed the Virgin, facilitated communion with God.

The most famous of the **early monks** were Peter the Athonite and Saint Euthimios of Salonica, both of whom lived in cave-hermitages on the slopes during the mid-ninth century. In 885 an edict of Emperor Basil I recognized Áthos as the sole preserve of

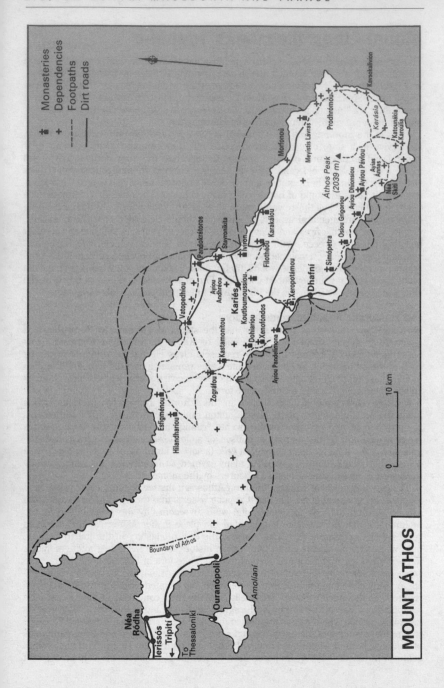

MOUNT ÁTHOS

monks, and gradually hermits came together to form communities known as *cenobia* (literally "common living"). The year 963 is the traditional date for the **foundation of the first monastery**, Meyístis Lávras, by Athanasios the Athonite; the Emperor Nikephoros Phocas provided considerable financial assistance. Over the next two centuries, with the protection of other Byzantine emperors, foundations were frequent, the monasteries reaching forty in number (reputedly with a thousand monks in each), alongside many smaller communities.

Troubles for Áthos began at the end of the eleventh century. The monasteries suffered sporadically from pirate raids and from the settlement of 300 Vlach shepherd families on the mountain. After a reputedly scandalous time between the monks and the shepherdesses, the Vlachs were ejected and a new imperial *chryssobul* (edict) was issued, confirming that no female, human or animal, be allowed to set foot on Áthos. This edict, called the *ávaton*, remains in force today.

During the twelfth century, the monasteries gained an international – or at least, a **pan-Orthodox** – aspect, as Romanian, Russian and Serbian monks flocked to the mountain in retreat from the turbulence of the age. Athos itself was subjected to Frankish raids during the Latin occupation of Constantinople (1204–61) and, even after this, faced great pressure from the Unionists of Latin Salonica to unite with western Catholics; in the courtyard of Zográfou there is still a monument to the monks who were martyred at this time while attempting to preserve the independence of Orthodox Christianity. In the early fourteenth century the monasteries suffered two disastrous years of pillage by Catalan mercenaries but they recovered, primarily through Serbian benefactors, to enjoy a period of great prosperity in the fifteenth and sixteenth centuries.

After the fall of the Byzantine Empire to the Ottomans, the fathers wisely declined to resist, maintaining good relations with the early sultans, one of whom paid a state visit. The later Middle Ages brought **economic problems**, with heavy taxes and confiscations, and as a defence many of the monasteries dissolved their common holdings and reverted to an idiorrhythmic system, a self-regulating form of monasticism where monks live and worship in a loosely bound community but work and eat individually.

ATHONITE TERMS

Arhondáris Guestmaster of a monastery or *skíti*, responsible for all visitors; similarly, *arhondaríki*, the guest quarters themselves.

Arsanás Harbour annexe of each monastery or *skíti*, where the *kaíkia* anchor; they can be a considerable distance from the institution in question.

Cenobitic/Idiorrythmic This is (increasingly, was) the major distinction between religious foundations on the Mountain. At cenobitic establishments the monks eat all meals together, hold all property in common and have rigidly scheduled days. Those that are idiorrhythmic are more individualistic: the monks eat in their own quarters and study or worship when and as they wish. Over the past decade all of the remaining idiorrhythmic monasteries have reverted to cenobitic status, with Pandokrátoros the last hold-out until 1992. Currently monks wishing to follow a more independent path must take up residence in an idiorrhythmic *skíti* (most of them are) or a *kellí*.

Dhíkeos The "righteous one" – head of an idiorrhythmic foundation.

Dhókimos A novice monk.

Fiáli The covered font for holy water in some monastery courtyards; often very ornate.

Igoúmenos Abbot, the head of a cenobitic house.

Katholikón Main church of a monastery.

Kiriakón Central chapel of a *skíti*, where the residents worship together once weekly.

Trapezaría Refectory, or dining room.

However, Athos remained the spiritual centre of Orthodoxy, and during the seventeenth and eighteenth centuries even built and maintained its own schools.

The mountain's real decline came after the **War of Independence**, in which many of the monks fought alongside the Greek *klephts*. In Macedonia the insurrectionists were easily subdued, the region remaining under Ottoman control, and the monks paid the price. A permanent Turkish garrison was established on the mountain and monastery populations fell sharply as, in the wake of independence for southern Greece, monasticism became less of a focus for Greek Orthodox Christianity.

At the end of the last century and the beginning of this one **foreign Orthodox** monks, particularly Russian ones, tried to step in and fill the vacuum. But the Athonite fathers have always resisted any move that might dilute the Greek quality of the Holy Mount, even – until recently – at the expense of its material prosperity. During the early 1960s, numbers were at their lowest ever, barely a thousand, compared to 20,000 in Áthos's heyday. Today, however, the monastic population has climbed to about 1700, and its average age has dropped significantly.

This modest revival is due partly to the increasingly appeal of the contemplative life in a blatantly materialistic age, but more importantly to a wave of rather militant sectarian sentiment, which has swept both the Holy Mountain and world Orthodoxy at large. Active recruitment and evangelizing has produced a large crop of novices from every continent, particularly visible in such monasteries as Simópetra, Filothéou and Vatopedhíou.

On the negative side, critics assert that the zealots have transformed Áthos with little tact, compelling many supposedly lax idiorryhythmic houses to become cenobitic as the price of their revitalization. In an echo of the conflicts earlier this century, there has also allegedly been interference with the efforts of the non-Greek foundations to recruit brothers and receive pilgrims from the home country, and in general a confusion of the aims of Orthodoxy and Hellenism. If these tensions appear unseemly in a commonwealth devoted to spiritual perfection, it's worth remembering that doctrinal strife has always been part of Athonite history; that most of the monks still are Greek; and that donning the habit doesn't quell their inborn love of politicking. Also, in a perverse way, the ongoing controversies demonstrate a renewed vitality, inasmuch as Mount Athos, and who controls it, are seen once again as having some global importance.

Permits and entry

Until a few decades ago foreigners could visit Áthos quite easily, but in the early 1970s the number of tourists grew so great that the monasteries could no longer cope. Since then a permit system has been instituted, and only Greeks – and to a lesser extent foreign Orthodox – are exempt from it.

The first step in **acquiring a permit** to visit and stay on Áthos is to obtain a **letter of recommendation** from your embassy or consulate in Athens or Thessaloníki; see those respective cities' "Listings" for addresses. The letter should be purely a formality; the US consulate issues it free, UK ones make a charge – though as a courtesy, before charging you, they suggest you contact the relevant Greek ministries first to see if space is available when you want to go. It is best to have yourself described in the text as a university-level scholar or graduate in art, religion or architecture – or as a "man of letters", which description covers just about any published (or hopeful) writer.

Take the consular letter either to the **Ministry of Foreign Affairs in Athens** (Akadhimías 3, 5th floor; Mon, Wed & Fri 11am–1pm) or to the **Ministry of Macedonia and Thrace in Thessaloníki** (Platía Dhikitiríou, Room 218; Mon–Fri 11am–1.45pm). In exchange for the letter you will be issued a permit valid for four days' residence on Áthos, which must be used "within a reasonable amount of time" and which will have a date specified for the beginning of the visit. This may not be the date of your choice in high summer, when it's all but mandatory to apply for permission at least two months in advance. Each of the ministries described above is alotted ten slots for foreigners of all nationalities on each day of the year, for a total of twenty new arrivals on Áthos per day. Therefore if your day, or week, of choice is full up in one city, there is some chance that there may be space in the other, though this can't be relied on.

To get to Áthos, take a Halkidhikí KTEL bus (either from the new joint station or the old terminal at Karakássi 68) to Ouranópoli or Ierissós (see "East to secular Áthos", p.367). From Ouranópoli at least one **boat** daily sails as far as **Dháfni**, the main port on the southwestern coast of Áthos, where there's a connecting service onward to the *skíti* of Ayías Ánnas. If you're setting out on the day your permit starts, you'll have to take the earliest (6am) KTEL departure to connect with the boat. At Ierissós, the boat usually leaves earlier in the morning than the first bus will pass through, entailing an overnight stop here – and a chance to see if bad weather will force a cancellation. Service along the northeast shore always goes as far as the monastery of **Ivíron**, usually up to Meyístis Lávras, and turns around more or less immediately. Ouranópoli–Dháfni takes about ninety minutes; Ierissós–Ivíron more than two hours.

At the first port of call – the *arsanás* (harbour annexe) of Zográfou on the southwest side, the *arsanás* of Hilandharíou on the northeast – all passengers will be ushered off the boat to the police post, where your ministry permit and a fee of 2000dr will be exchanged for a document called the **dhiamonitírion**, which entitles you to stay at any of the main monasteries. You are now free to leave the boat or continue with it to any destination you wish – they stop at the dock for every monastery on their respective coasts.

Many visitors wish to arrange for an **extension** of the basic four-day period. There is little point in asking for one, either at your first landfall or later in Kariés, for the simple reason that it will be routinely denied. In actual fact, however, nobody is terribly bothered if you stay five days or even a week, except in high summer when monastic accommodation can get quite crowded. It is rare that guestmasters ask to see your *dhiamonitírion*, much less scrutinize it carefully, and the four-day limit was originally enforced to discourage gawkers and others with frivolous motives for visiting. If you are regarded as a sincere pilgrim, and move on to a different monastery each day as the regulations require you to, there are no problems with a do-it-yourself extension. Conversely, if you strike the monks as behaving presumptuously or inappropriately, no amount of time remaining on your permit will persuade them to grant you hospitality. As signs on walls repeatedly remind you, "Hospitality is not obligatory".

The way of life

With *dhiamonitírion* in hand, you will be admitted to stay and eat in the main monasteries – and certain *skítes* – free of charge. If you offer money it will be refused, though Orthodox pilgrims are encourgaged to buy candles, incense, icon reproductions and the like at those *skítes* which specialize in their production. **Accommodation** is usually in dormitories, and fairly spartan, but you're always given sheets and blankets; you don't need to lug a sleeping bag around. Áthos grows much of its own **food**, and the monastic diet is based on tomatoes, beans, cheese and pasta, with occasional treats like *halva* and fruit included. After Sunday morning service, wine often accompanies fish in the heartiest meal of the week. Normally only two meals a day are served, the first at mid-morning, the latter about an hour and a half to two hours before sunset. You will need to be partly self-sufficient in provisions – especially dried fruits, nuts, sweets – both for the times when you fail to coincide with meals and for the long walks between monasteries. (If you arrive after the evening meal you will generally be served leftovers set aside for latecomers.) There are a few shops in Kariés, but for better selection and to save valuable time you should stock up before coming to Áthos.

If you're planning to **walk between monasteries**, you should get hold of one of two **maps**: the first simply entitled "Athos", produced in Austria at a scale of 1:50,000 by Reinhold Zwerger and Klaus Schöpfleuthner (Wohlmutstr 8, A 1020 Wien) but usually available in Ouranópoli; the other, a simple sketch map of all the roads and trails on the Mount, by Theodhoros Tsiropoulos of Thessaloníki (☎031/430 196). The *Korfes* magazine map is now obsolete and contains potentially dangerous errors, but it's still more useful than any of the touristic productions sold in Ouranópoli. Even equipped with these, you'll still need to be pointed to the start of trails at each monastery, and confirm walking times and path conditions. New roads are constantly being built, and trails accordingly abandoned, and in the jungly local climate they become completely overgrown within two years if not used.

If need be, you can supplement walking with the regular **kaíki services** that ply between the main establishments on each coast. The return time out of Ayías Ánnas to Dháfni is about 8am in summer, with onward connections towards the "border" just after noon. On the other side, the single craft leaves Meyístis Lávras at about 2pm, bound for Ierissós. On alternate days in summer there is also a useful *kaíki* linking Meyístis Lávras and Ayías Ánnas, stopping at the *skíti* of Kavsokalivíon on its way around the south tip of the peninsula.

However you move around, you must reach your destination **before dark**, since all monasteries and many *skítes* lock their front gates at sunset – leaving you out with the wild boars and (it is claimed) a handful of wolves. Upon arrival you should ask for the *arhondáris* (**guestmaster**), who will proffer the traditional welcome of a *tsípouro* (distilled spirits) and *loukoúmi* (Turkish delight) before showing you to your bed. These days guestmasters tend to speak at least some English, a reflection of the increasing numbers of Cypriot, Australian or educated Greek novices on Áthos.

You will find the monastic **daily schedule** somewhat disorienting, and adapted according to the seasonal time of sunrise and sunset. On the northeast side of the peninsula 12 o'clock is reckoned from the hour of sunrise, and on the opposite side clocktowers may show both hands up at sunset. Yet Vatopedhíou keeps "worldly" time, as do most monks' wristwatches. However the Julian calendar, thirteen days behind the outside world, is universally observed, and will be the date appearing on your *dhiamonitírion*. More and more monasteries are getting electric power but this has affected the round of life very little; both you and the monks will go to bed early, shortly after sunset. Sometimes in the small hours your hosts will awake for solitary meditation and study, followed by *órthros* or matins. Around sunrise there is another quiet period, just before the *akolouthía* or main liturgy. Next comes the morning meal, anywhere from 9.30am to 11.30am depending on the time of year. The afternoon is devoted to manual labour until the *esperinós* or vespers, actually almost three hours before sunset in summer (much less in winter). This is followed immediately by the evening meal and the short *apódhipno* or compline service.

A few words about **attitudes and behaviour** towards your hosts (and vice versa), as many misunderstandings arise from mutual perceptions of disrespect, real or imagined. For your part, you should be fully clad at all times, even when going from dormitory to bathroom; this in effect means no shorts, no hats inside monasteries, and sleeves that come down to the middle of the biceps. If you swim, do so where nobody can see you, and don't do it naked. Smoking in most foundations is forbidden, though a few allow you to indulge out on the balconies. It would be criminal to do so on the trail, given the chronic fire danger; you might just want to give it up as a penance for the duration of your stay. Singing, whistling and raised voices are taboo; so is standing with your hands behind your back or crossing your legs when seated, both considered overbearing stances. If you want to photograph monks you should always ask permission, though photography is forbidden altogether in several monasteries. It's best not to go poking your nose into corners of the buildings where you're not specifically invited, even if they seem open to the public.

Monasteries, and their tenants, tend to vary a good deal in their handling of visitors, and their reputations, deserved or otherwise, tend to precede them as a favourite subject of trail gossip among foreigners. You will find that as a non-Orthodox you may be politely ignored, or worse, with signs at some institutions specifically forbidding you from attending services or sharing meals with the monks. Other monasteries are by contrast very engaging, putting themselves at the disposal of visitors of whatever creed. It is not uncommon to be treated to extreme bigotry and disarming gentility at the same place within the space of ten minutes, making it very difficult to draw conclusions about Áthos in general and monasteries in particular. If you are not even a Christian as well as non-Orthodox, and seem to understand enough Greek to get the message, you'll probably be told at some point during your visit that you'll burn in Hell unless you convert to the True Faith forthwith. While this may seem offensive, considering your probable motivation for being here, it pays to remember that the monks are expecting religious pilgrims, not tourists, and that their role is to be committed, not tolerant. On average, expect those monks with some level of education or smattering of foreign languages to be benignly interested in you, and a very soft-sell in the form of a reading library of pamphlets and books left at your disposal. Incidentally, idiorrhythmic *skítes* (see below) and *kelliá* are not bound by the monastic rule of hospitality, and you really need to know someone at one of these to be asked to stay the night.

The monasteries

Obviously you can't hope to visit all twenty monasteries during a short stay, though if you're able to extend the basic four-day period for a few days you can fairly easily see the peninsula's most prominent foundations. The dirt road linking the southwestern port of Dháfni with the northeastern coastal monastery of Ivíron by way of Kariés, the capital, not only cuts the peninsula roughly in two but also separates the monasteries into equal southeastern and northwestern groups; the division is not so arbitrary as it seems, since the remaining path system seems to reflect it and the feel of the two halves is very different.

The southeastern group

IVÍRON
The vast **IVÍRON** monastery is not a bad introduction to Áthos, and is well poised for walks or rides in various directions. Although founded late in the tenth century by Iberian (Georgian) monks, the last Georgian died in the 1950s and today it is a cenobitic house of 35 Greek monks, some of whom moved here from nearby Stavronikíta. The focus of pilgrimage is the miraculous **icon** of the *Portaítissa*, the Virgin Guarding the Gate, housed in a special chapel to the left of the entrance. It is believed that if this protecting image ever leaves Áthos, then great misfortune will befall the monks. The **katholikón** is among the largest on the mountain, with an elaborate mosaic floor dating from 1030. The frescoes are recent and of limited interest, but not so various pagan touches such as the Persian-influenced gold crown around the chandelier, and two Hellenistic columns from a temple of Poseidon with rams-head capitals which once stood here. There's also a silver-leaf lemon tree crafted in Moscow; because of the Georgian connection, Russians were lavish donors to this monastery. There is also an immensely rich library and treasury, but you are unlikely to be able to see these.

KARIÉS AND AROUND: SOME MINOR MONASTERIES
A look around **KARIÉS** is rewarding: the main church of the Protáton, dating from 965, contains exceptional fourteenth-century **frescoes** of the Macedonian school. Kariés also has a few **restaurants** where you may be able to get heartier fare than is

typical in the monasteries, and a simple inn – though there seems little reason to patronize it. At the northern edge of "town" sprawls the enormous cloister-like *skíti* of **Ayíou Andhréou**, a Russian dependency of the great Vatopedhíou monastery, erected in a hurry last century but today virtually deserted.

A signposted trail leads up within an hour to **KOUTLOUMOUSÍOU**, at the very edge of Kariés. Much the most interesting thing about it is its name, which appears to be that of a Selçuk chieftain converted to Christianity.

From Ivíron a path stumbles uphill, tangling with roads, to reach **FILOTHÉOU**, which was at the forefront of the monastic revival in the early 1980s and hence one of the more vital monasteries. It is not, however, one of the more impressive foundations from an architectural or artistic point of view – though the lawn surfacing the entire courtyard is an interesting touch – and it's one of those houses where the non-Orthodox are forbidden from attending church or eating with the monks.

The same is true at **KARAKÁLOU**, 45 minutes' walk (mostly on paths) below Filothéou, also accessible via a short trail up from its *arsanás*. The lofty keep is typical of the fortress-monasteries built close enough to the shore to be victimized by pirates; note that there's limited space in the guest wing.

Between here and Meyístis Lávras the trail system has been destroyed, replaced by a road (no bus) that makes for dreary tramping, so it's advisable to continue southeast on the boat, or by arranging a lift with a service vehicle.

MEYÍSTIS LÁVRAS AND THE ATHONITE WILDERNESS

MEYÍSTIS LÁVRAS (the Great Lavra) is the oldest and foremost of the ruling monasteries, and physically the most imposing establishment on Áthos, with no fewer than fifteen chapels within its walls. Although there are a fair number of additions from the last century and, more recently, electric current, it has (uniquely among the twenty) never suffered from fire. The treasury and library are both predictably rich, the latter containing over 2000 precious manuscripts, though the ordinary traveller is unlikely to view them; as is usual, several monks (out of the 25 here) have complementary keys which must be operated together to gain entrance. What you will see at mealtime are the superior **frescoes** in the **trapezaría**, executed by Theophanes the Cretan in 1535. Hagiographies and grisly martyrdoms line the apse, while there's a *Tree of Jesse* in the south transept, the *Death of Athanasios* (the founder) opposite, and an *Apocalypse* to the left of the main entry. In the western apse is a *Last Supper*, not surprisingly a popular theme in refectories. Just outside the door stands a huge **fiáli**, largest on the mountain, with pagan columns supporting the canopy. The **katholikón**, near the rear of the large but cluttered courtyard, contains more frescoes by Theophanes.

Beyond Meyístis Lávras lies some of the most beautiful, and deserted country on the peninsula, traced by a lovely path unlikely to ever be bulldozed. One of Meyístis Lávras's many dependencies, **Skíti Prodhrómou**, is just over an hour's walk to the south, but its formerly Romanian inmates seem to have departed. Nonetheless, it is a fairly hospitable house, little visited, and only ten minutes away by marked path there's the **hermitage-cave of Saint Athanasios**, watched over by five skulls.

Most first-time visitors will, however, proceed without delay on what ends up being a five-hour traverse across the tip of Áthos. You might consider dropping down off the main trail to see the *skíti* of **Ayías Triádhas (Kavsokalivíon)**, its *kiriákon* surrounded by many cottages, but the commonest strategy involves heading straight for **Skíti Ayías Ánnas**, whose buildings tumble downslope to a perennial-summer patch of coast capable of ripening lemons. This is the usual "base camp" for the climb of **Áthos peak** itself (2030m) – best left for the next morning, and the months from May to September.

With a (pre-)dawn start, you gain the necessary mercy of a little shade and can expect to be up top just over four walking hours from Ayías Ánnas, with the combination refuge-church of **Panayía** passed a little over an hour before reaching the summit. Some hikers plan an overnight stop at this shelter, to watch the sunrise from the peak, but for this you must be self-sufficent in **food** – as you may well be at the *skíti*, which being idiorrhythmic does not set a particularly sumptuous table, even allowing for monastic austerities. There's no spring **water** en route – you drink from cisterns at Panayía or at **Metamórfosi**, the tiny chapel atop the peak.

Returning from the peak before noon, you'll still have time to reach one of the monasteries north of Ayías Ánnas; the path continues to be delightful, and affords a sudden, breathtaking view of **AYÍOU PÁVLOU** as you round a bend. Except for the ugly scar of the new access road off to the left, little can have changed in the perspective since Edward Lear painted it in the 1850s. The monastery, just over an hour from Ayías Ánnas, is irregularly shaped owing to the constraints of the inland site at the base of Áthos peak, and is currently home to 36 monks, many of them from the island of Kefalloniá.

THE "HANGING" MONASTERIES

From Ayíou Pávlou it's another hour to **DHIONISÍOU**, a fortified structure perched spectacularly on a coastal cliff, which has overcome a former grim reputation and is now both one of the better houses to stay at, and among the most richly endowed monasteries, with neat and airy *arhondaríki* that come as a relief after so many claustrophobic facilities. Sadly, it is difficult to make out the sixteenth-century **frescoes** by the Cretan Tzortzis in the hopelessly dim *katholikón*, likewise an icon attributed to the Evangelist Luke; however, those of Theophanes on the inside and out of the **trapezaría** are another story. The interior features *The Entry of the Saints into Paradise* and *The Ladder to Heaven*; the exterior wall bears a version of the *Apocalypse*, complete with what looks suspiciously like a nuclear mushroom cloud. Unusually, you may be offered a tour of the **library** with its illuminated gospels on silk-fortified paper, wooden carved miniature of the Passion week, and ivory crucifixes. You've little chance, however, of seeing Dhionisíou's great treasure, the three-metre-long **chrysobull** of the Trapezuntine emperor Alexios III Comnene. Extensive modernization has been carried out here, with mixed results: clean electric power is supplied by a water turbine up-canyon, but the old half-timbered facade has been replaced with a rather brutal concrete-stucco one.

The onward path to **OSÍOU GRIGORÍOU** is a bit neglected but still usable, depositing you at the front door within an hour and a quarter. Of all the monasteries and *skítes* it has the most intimate relation with the sea, though every building dates from after a devastating 1761 fire. Some of the guest rooms overlook the water, and the monks are exceptionally hospitable.

The southwest coastal trail system ends just over an hour later at **SÍMONOS PÉTRA** (abbreviated **Simópetra**) or "The Rock of Simon", after the foundation legend asserting that the hermit Simon was directed to build a monastery here by a mysterious light hovering over the sheer pinnacle. Though entirely rebuilt in the wake of a fire a century ago, Simópetra is perhaps the most visually striking monastery on Áthos. With its multiple storeys, ringed by wooden balconies overhanging sheer 300-metre drops, it resembles nothing so much as a Tibetan lamasery. As at Dhionisíou, of which it seems an exaggerated rendition, the courtyard is quite narrow. Thanks to the fire there are no material treasures worth mentioning, though the monastery rivals Filothéou in vigour, with sixty monks from a dozen countries around the world. Unfortunately, because of the spectacle it presents, and its role as an easy first stop in the days when everyone started out from Kariés, Simópetra is always crowded with foreigners and might be better admired from a distance, at least in season.

Further walking is inadvisable and it's best to arrange a lift further up the peninsula, or catch the morning boat in the same direction.

The northwestern group

DHÁFNI PORT AND THE RUSSIAN MONASTERY

Though you may not ever pass through Kariés, at some point you're likely to make the acquaintance of **DHÁFNI**, if only to change boats, since the service on this coast is not continuous. There's a **post office**, some rather tacky souvenir shops, and a **customs** post – much more vigilant when you leave than upon entry; all passengers' baggage is inspected to check traffic in smuggled-out treasures. A number of eagle-brooch-capped Athonite police skulk about as well. There's a **taverna** where you can get a beer and bean soup, but no shops adequate for restocking on food and drink.

The *kaíki* usually has an hour's layover here before heading back towards Ayías Ánnas, during which time the captain can often be persuaded (for a reasonable fee) to take groups as far as the Russian monastery of **AYÍOU PANDELÍMONA** (Roussikó), a dull forty-minute walk from the port, allowing a look at the premises before the scheduled departure to Ouranópoli appears. Most of the monks are Russian, an ethnic predominance strongly reflected in onion-shaped **domes** and the softer faces of the frescoes. The majority of the buildings were erected in a hurry just after the mid-1800s, as part of Tsarist Russia's campaign for eminence on the Mountain, and have a utilitarian, barracks-like quality. The sole unique features are the corrosion-green lead roofs and the enormous **bell** over the refectory, the second largest in the world, which always prompts speculation as to how it got there. Otherwise, the small population fairly rattles around the echoing halls, the effect of desolation increased by ranks of outer dormitories gutted by a fire in 1968. If you're an architecture buff, Roussikó can probably be omitted without a twinge of conscience; students of turn-of-the-century kitsch will be delighted, however, with mass-produced saints' calendars, gaudy reliquaries, and a torrent of gold (or at least gilt) fixtures in the seldom-used *katholikón*. If you are permitted to attend service in the top-storey chapel north of the belfry, do so for the sake of the Slavonic chanting, though it must be said that the residents don't exactly put themselves out for non-Slavs. However, with the collapse of the Soviet Union, Ayíou Panentelímona can now look forward to a material and spiritual renaissance of sorts.

Actually closer to Dháfni is the square compound of **XEROPOTÁMOU**, with most of its construction and church frescoes dating from the eighteenth century, except for two wings that were fire-damaged in 1952.

GREEK COASTAL MONASTERIES

From the vicinity of Dháfni or Roussikó, most pilgrims continue along the coast, reaching **XENOFÓNDOS** along a mix of trail and tractor track an hour after quitting the Russian monastery. Approached from this direction, Xenofóndos's busy sawmill gives it a vaguely industrial air, accentuated by ongoing, extensive renovations. The enormous, sloping, irregularly shaped court, expanded upward last century, is unique in possessing two *katholiká*. The small, older one – with exterior frescoes of the Cretan school – was outgrown and replaced during the 1830s by the huge upper one, currently shut for repairs. Among its many icons are two fine **mosaic** ones of saints Yióryios and Dhimítrios. The guest quarters occupy a modern wing overlooking the sea at the extreme south end of the perimeter.

A half-hour's walk separates Xenofóndos from **DOHIARÍOU**, one of the more picturesque monasteries on this coast but not conspicuously friendly, and currently in the throes of renovation; this hasn't yet extended to the primitive but clean *arhondaríki*, which see few foreigners. An exceptionally lofty, large **katholikón** nearly fills the court, though its Cretan-school frescoes, possibly by Tzortzis, were clumsily retouched in 1855. Much better are the late seventeenth-century ones in the long, narrow **refectory**, with its sea views some of the nicest on Áthos. Even Orthodox pilgrims have trouble getting to see the wonder-working icon of *Gorgoipikóöu* (She Who is Quick to Hear), housed in a chapel between church and *trapezaría*.

THE FAR NORTHERN MONASTERIES

The direct trail inland and up to Konstamonítou has been reclaimed by the forest, so to get there you have to go in a roundabout fashion 45 minutes along the coast to its *arsanás*, and then as much time again sharply up on tracks and cobbled way. **KONSTAMONÍTOU**, hidden up in a thickly wooded valley, seems as humble, bare and poor as you'd expect from the last-ranking monastery; the *katholikón* nearly fills the quadrangular court where the grass is literally growing up through the cracks. Non-Orthodox and believers are segregated, not that many foreigners make it this far; as a consolation a carillon "concert" of some musicality announces vespers.

From here you can continue on foot ninety minutes to **ZOGRÁFOU**, the furthest inland of the monasteries, today populated by a handful of Bulgarian monks. More than at most large, understaffed houses, you gain an appreciation of the enormous workload that falls on so few shoulders; a walk down the empty, rambling corridors past the seventeenth- and eighteenth-century cells, now unmaintained, is a sobering experience. "Zográfou" means "of the Painter", in reference to a tenth-century legend: the Slavs who founded the monastery couldn't decide on a patron saint, so they put a wooden panel by the altar, and after lengthy prayer a painting of Áyios Yióryios – henceforth the institution's protector – appeared.

Near Zográfou the trail splits, presenting you with a three-fold choice. In two and a half hours along the leftmost option, you arrive at the large, irregularly shaped monastery of **HILANDHARÍOU**, which was in the past patronized by the thirteenth-century Serbian kings and has to this day remained a Serbian house (and lately hotbed of Serbian nationalism). The **katholikón** dates in its present form from the fourteenth century, but its frescoes, similar in style to those in the Protáton at Kariés, have been retouched. As you'd expect for a beacon of medieval Serbian culture, the library and treasury are well endowed.

The central, down-valley route out of Zográfou leads in three hours to **ESFIGMÉNOU**, built directly on the water and reputedly the strictest foundation on the mountain – a banner hung out of the top-storey window reading "Orthodoxy or Death" would seem to confirm this and does not encourage a casual visit. In any case the path veers down the coast for three hours to **VATOPEDHÍOU**, a similar distance away if setting out directly from Zográfou. Exceeding Meyístis Lávras in size, it also vies with it in importance and wealth, and makes a good beginning or farewell to Áthos. The cobbled, slanting court with its freestanding belfry (which can be climbed) seems more like a town plaza, ringed by stairways and stacks of cells for more than 300. The **katholikón**, one of the oldest on the mountain, has the usual array of frescoes painted over for better or worse, but more uniquely two **mosaics** of the *Annunciation* and the *Deisis* flanking the door of the inner narthex. The population of forty monks, mostly young and two-thirds Cypriot (as is the abbot), includes a handful of French novices and a brotherhood of nine Australians who have had to change residence four times (a common drama for non-Greek monks on the peninsula) and hope that this is their last home.

With the proper maps it is just possible to short-cut the dusty track above Vatopedhíou en route to **PANDOKRÁTOROS**, two and a half hours away, the last half of the journey on scenic coastal paths. Other than the setting on a hill overlooking its own picturesque fishing harbour, and the courtyard with its eight Valencia orange trees, there is little of note. But most of the 35 monks are welcoming, perhaps the more so since the community succumbed to pressure from its peersand converted to the cenobitic mode. The guest wing overlooks the sea and there is a (cold) **shower** – a boon after days of trekking. In a valley above looms the *skíti* of **Profítis Ilías**, a relic of the Russian expansion drive and today home to just nine monks from several different countries.

Continuing on the coastal trail, it's under an hour door-to-door to tiny **STAVRONIKÍTA**, the best example of the Athonite coastal fortress-monastery and distinctly vertical in orientation. Long one of the poorest houses, it has recently been completely redone, and, surrounded by aqueduct-fed kitchen gardens, is pin-neat. Several Australians, including the abbot, number among the fifteen monks, but they're ill-equipped to cope with the relatively large numbers of guests and it no longer rates as one of the more outgoing monasteries. The modernized guest quarters, despite the showers, are similarly meagre, and fill early in the day in summer. There's little chance of a seaside room, though by virtue of its rock-top position Stavronikíta has some of the best views of Áthos peak on the peninsula. The narrow **katholikón** occupies virtually all of the gloomy courtyard, and the **refectory**, normally opposite, had to be shifted upstairs to the south wing, where it's a spartan room with a single window on the water, and fresco fragments by Theophanes of the *Death of Áyios Nikólaos* (the patron) and the *Last Supper*. From here an hour's walk separates you from Iviron.

The coast to Kavála

Heading towards Kavála from Sithonía or Áthos is surprisingly tricky, since buses from either peninsula run only back to Thessaloníki. However, the gap between the Thessaloníki–Halkidhikí and Thessaloníki–Kavála services is only 16km wide at one point, with a couple of places you wouldn't mind getting stuck at along the way, so if you don't have your own transport, you could always walk.

To begin, you should get off the Ouranópoli–Thessaloníki bus at the small coastal village of **STRATÓNI**. The bay here is dominated by the local mine workings, and there is little incentive to stay, though there are several tavernas on the grey-black beach and even one hotel, the *Angelika* (☎0376/22 075; ②). From Stratóni, the scenic road glides over the ridge north 15km to the beach resort of Olimbiádha and regular buses to the Thessaloníki–Kavála highway.

OLIMBIÁDHA itself is still very low-key, with **rooms,** three hotels – two of which, the *Germany* and *Liotopi* (both ☎0376/51 255; ②–③), have the same owner – and a campsite 3km north that's 500 metres from the beach but has its own pool. There are three **tavernas** on the southern bay, cheapest and most characterful being the *Kapetan Manolis/Platanos* by the concrete jetty. All along this shore the local speciality is **mussels** (*mídhia*), farmed in floating nursery beds and typically served in a spicy cheese sauce. The small town beaches are fine, but there are far better ones 2–3km back towards Stratóni, behind the promontory with a few cursory walls of **ancient Stayira**, birthplace of Aristotle.

STAVRÓS, 10km north of Olimbiádha – the interval again dotted with semi-accessible coves – is a lively place with a beautiful seafront of plane trees. The cheapest of five inexpensive **hotels** is the *Avra Strymonikou* (☎0397/61 278; ②), though you'd be more likely to end up in **rooms**.

From here you're just 4km from the main E90 highway, where the first coastal place of any size – **ASPRÓVALTA** – will come as a jolt after the relative calmness of Halkidhikí. However, despite recent speculative development, it's still attractive and is essentially a summer suburb of Thessaloníki, an impression reinforced by the frequent urban bus service from Platía Dhikastiríon.

Ten kilometres from Aspróvalta, the road to Kavála crosses the River Strimónas, beyond which long-distance buses tend to veer inland to hug the base of Mount Pangéo. With your own transport it's worth following the coast road to Kavála. If you keep to the old road, rather than the flyover, you'll cross the river by a long bridge, before which – approaching from Thessaloníki – you'll see on your left the colossal marble **Lion of Amphipolis**. This was reconstructed in 1937 from fragments found when excavating the ancient city of Amphipolis nearby, and is thought to date from the end of the fourth century BC.

Twenty-eight kilometres beyond Amphipolis, **LOUTRÁ ELEFTHERÓN**, just 2km inland of the coast road to Kavála, is an old-fashioned spa set in a riverside oasis, though the thermal springs themselves are a bit difficult to bathe in, and the old Turkish domed bath has been closed down, leaving only the rather clinical indoor plunge-pools (open in the morning and evening).

Approaching Néa Péramos, a narrow frontage road seaward from the main highway threads past very impromptu **campsites** among vineyards and fine, duned **beaches**, the best in eastern Macedonia. **NÉA PÉRAMOS** itself, 14km before Kavála, sports an unheralded **castle** at one corner of its sandy, sheltered bay, and isn't a bad place to spend a couple of hours. *Camping Anatoli* (☎0594/21 590; May–Sept) can be recommended if you want to spend the night; it has its own salt-water swimming pool. The only other **campsites** between here and Kavála are the *Estella*, 5km east, or the expensive EOT site, *Batis*, 10km along and already hedged by Kavála's sprawl.

Kavála

KAVÁLA, backing on to the lower slopes of Mount Simbólon, is the second largest city of Macedonia and the principal port for northern Greece. Coming in through the suburbs, there seems little to commend a stay. But the centre, at least, is pleasant and characterful, grouped about the old nineteenth-century harbour area and its old tobacco warehouses. A citadel looks down from a rocky promontory to the east, and an elegant Turkish aqueduct leaps over modern buildings into the old quarter on the bluff.

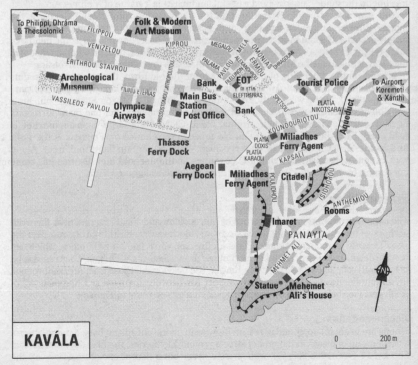

The town was known anciently as Neapolis and as such served for two centuries or more as a terminus of the Via Egnatía and the first European port of call for merchants and travellers from the Middle East. It was here that Saint Paul landed on his way to Philippi (see below), on his initial mission to Europe. In later years, the port and citadel took on considerable military significance, being occupied in turn by Byzantines, Normans, Franks, Venetians, Turks and (during both world wars) Bulgarians.

The Town

Although the remnants of Kavála's Turkish past are neglected, the **Panayía** quarter above the port preserves a scattering of eighteenth- and nineteenth-century buildings, and considerable atmosphere. It is by far the most attractive part of town to explore, wandering amid the twisting wedge of lanes and up towards the citadel.

The most conspicuous and interesting of its buildings is the **Imaret**, overlooking the harbour on Poulidhoú. An elongated, multi-domed structure covered in Islamic inscriptions, it was originally an almshouse housing three hundred *softas*, or theological students. After many decades of neglect, it has recently been partially refurbished, appropriately enough, as a restaurant. Said to be the largest Muslim building in Europe, it was endowed by **Mehmet Ali**, the Pasha of Egypt and founder of the dynasty which ended with King Farouk. Born in Kavála in 1769, his birthplace, near the corner of Pavlídhou and Méhmet Alí, is maintained as a monument. It provides an opportunity, rare in Greece, to look over a prestigious Turkish house, with its wood-panelled reception rooms, ground-floor stables and first-floor harem (daily except Mon 10am–2pm; free but tip the guide); nearby (and a useful landmark) is a statue of Mehmet Ali.

You can also visit the Byzantine **citadel** (daily 10am–7pm; free) to explore the ramparts, towers, dungeon and cistern; in season it hosts a few festival performances, mainly drama and some music, in its main court. From here, down towards the middle of town, north of Panayía's narrow maze of streets, the **aqueduct**, built on a Roman model in the reign of Suleiman the Magnificent (1520–66), spans the traffic in Platía Nikotsára.

Finally, on the other side of the harbour from the old town, there are two museums of moderate interest. The **Archeological Museum** (Sat 8.30am–3pm, Sun 9.30am–2.30pm; 500dr), at the west end of the waterfront, just off Erithroú Stavroú, contains a fine dolphin mosaic, a reconstructed Macedonian funeral chamber and many terracotta figurines still decorated in their original paint. Close by, a large open-air **market** is held every Saturday, while next to an old tobacco warehouse on Filíppou, is the **Folk and Modern Art Museum** (Mon–Fri 8.30am–2pm, Sat & Sun 9am–1pm; free). Along with various collections of traditional costumes and household utensils, this has some interesting rooms devoted to the locally born sculptor Polignotos Vigis.

Practicalities

The main **bus station** is on the corner of Mitropolítou and Filikís Eterías, near the main anchorage; buses for Alexandhroúpoli stop some blocks away on Erithroú Stavroú, near the *Hotel Oceanis*. In the main square, Platía Eleftherías, you'll find an **EOT** office, which can provide details (and sell tickets) for the summer drama festivals at Philippi. They can also be of help with schedules for ferries from Kavála (see below), and those from Alexandhroúpoli to Samothráki. Kavála's "international" **airport** lies between the town and Keramotí, 46km southwest (see below), used by package holidaymakers en route to Thássos.

Accommodation

Hotels are in short supply and in season it's wise to phone ahead and book a room. There's a small group of places in the grid of streets around Eleftherías, the best the *Parthenon*, at Spétson 14 (☎051/223 205; ②), with strange decor but a decent enough place; or try the nearby *Attikon*, Megálou Alexándhrou 8 (☎051/222 257; ②). Moving up a grade, the *Akropolis* (☎051/223 543; ③) at Eleftheríou Venizélou 29, west of Platía Eleftherías, is an old establishment whose reception is on the first floor, while *Panorama* (☎051/224 205; ③-④), Eleftheríou Venizélou 26, is clean, convenient and cheerful, with a choice of rooms. Also on the same street is the *Galaxy* (☎051/224 812; ⑤), at no. 27 facing the harbour, with large, superior rooms. The only private **rooms** in the centre are those of *Yiorgos Alvanos* at Anthemíou 35 (☎051/228 412; ②), in the heart of the old Panayía quarter – worth trying if you arrive early in the day. An alternative place to stay, frequented by many Greeek tourists, is the beach-suburb of Kalamítsa, to the west of town. The closest **campsite** is *Irini* (☎051/ 229 785; open all year), on the shore 3km east of the port; city bus #2 goes there.

Eating

For **meals**, ignore the tourist traps along the waterfront and walk instead up into the Panayía district, where rows of tavernas with outdoor seating on Poulídhou tempt you with good and reasonably priced seafood; this is where the locals eat.

Ferry services

Ferries sail from Kavála to **Thássos** almost hourly in season; most run to the port of Órmos Prínou, though a few continue to the capital, called Thássos (or Liménas), an hour-long journey in total. Out of season, when services drop to just two boats daily, you may be better off taking the bus or driving to **KERAMOTÍ**, 46km southwest and then car ferry on from there to Thássos. Keramotí itself provides an alternative, though unexciting, stopover. It's a small, rather drab village, with a functional beach, a few rooms and three hotels: *Evropa* (☎0591/51 277; ③), *Holiday* (☎0591/51 151; ②) and the older and larger *Xastero* (☎0591/51 230; ④).

Other ferry services from Kavála are less predictable. In season, there are generally five weekly departures to **Samothráki** (Mon, Tues, Wed, Fri & Sat; 4hr; foot passenger 2600dr, car and driver 10,500dr), and six to **Límnos** (Tues, Wed, Thurs, Fri, Sat & Sun). Two or three of these continue to various islands, among them Áyios Efstrátios, Lésvos, Híos and Rafína/Pireás. Details are available from *Nikos Miliadhes*, Platía Karaóli Dhimitríou 36 (☎051/226 147), or Koundourioti 4 (☎051/230 576)

Philippi

As you might expect, **PHILIPPI** was named after Philip II of Macedon, who wrested the town from the Thracians in 356 BC. However, it owed its later importance and prosperity to the Roman building of the Via Egnatia, which ran from the Adriatic to Byzantium. With Kavála/Neápolis as its port, Philippi was essentially the easternmost town of Roman-occupied Europe.

Here also, as at Actium, the fate of the Roman Empire was decided on Greek soil, at the **Battle of Philippi** in 42 BC. After assassinating Julius Caesar, Brutus and Cassius had fled east of the Adriatic and, against their better judgement, were forced into confrontation on the Philippi plains with the pursuing armies of Antony and Octavian. The "honourable conspirators", who could have successfully exhausted the enemy by avoiding action, were decimated by Octavian in two successive battles, and, as defeat became imminent, first Cassius, then Brutus killed himself – the latter running on his comrade's sword with the Shakespearian sentiment, "Caesar now be still, I killed thee not with half so good a will".

Saint Paul landed at Kavála and visited Philippi in 49 AD and so began his mission in Europe. Despite being cast into prison he retained a special affection for the Philippians, his first converts, and the congregation that he established was one of the earliest to flourish in Greece. It furnished the principal remains of the site: several impressive, although ruined, basilican churches.

The Site

Daily except Mon 8.30am–3pm; 400dr.

Philippi is easily reached from Kavála, just 14km distant; buses (which continue to Dhráma) leave at least every half-hour, and drop you by the road that now splits the site.

The most conspicuous of the churches is the **Direkler**, to the south of the modern road which here follows the line of the Via Egnatia. This was an unsuccessful attempt by its sixth-century architect to improve the basilica design by adding a dome. In this instance the entire east wall collapsed under the weight, leaving only the narthex convertible for worship. The central arch of its west wall and a few pillars of reused antique drums stand amid remains of the Roman **forum**. A line of second-century porticoes spreads outwards in front of the church, and on their east side are the foundations of a colonnaded octagonal church which was approached from the Via Egnatia by a great gate. Behind the Direkler, and perversely the most interesting and best-preserved building of the site, is a huge monumental **public latrine** with nearly fifty of its original marble seats still intact.

Across the road on the northern side, stone steps climb up to a terrace passing on the right a Roman crypt, reputed to have been the **prison of Saint Paul** and appropriately frescoed. The terrace flattens out onto a huge paved atrium that extends to the foundations of another extremely large basilica. Continuing in the same direction around the base of a hill you emerge above a **theatre** cut into its side. Though dating from the original town it was heavily remodelled as an amphitheatre by the Romans – the bas-reliefs of Nemesis, Mars and Victory (on the left of the stage) all belong to this period. It is used for the annual drama festival, held every weekend from mid-July to early August. The **museum** (daily except Mon 8.30am–3pm; separate 400dr admission), above the road at the far end of the site, is rather dreary.

The best general impression of the site – which is very extensive despite a lack of obviously notable buildings – and of the battlefield behind it can be gained from the **acropolis**, a steep climp along a path from the museum. Its own remains are predominantly medieval.

THRACE (THRÁKI)

Separated from Macedonia to the west by the Néstos River and from (Turkish) Eastern Thrace by the Évros river delta, **Western Thrace** is the Greek state's most recent addition. Under effective Greek control from 1920, the Treaty of Lausanne (1923) confirmed Greek sovereignty over the area, and also sanctioned the exchange of 390,000 Muslims, principally from Macedonia, for more than a million ethnic Greeks from Eastern Thrace and Asia Minor. But the Muslims of Western Thrace, acknowledged as a community of long standing, were exempt from the exchanges and continue to live in the region.

Thrace was originally inhabited by a people with their own, non-Hellenic, language and religion. From the seventh century BC on it was colonized by Greeks, and after Alexander the area took on a strategic significance as the land route between Greece and Byzantium. It was later controlled by the Roman and Byzantine empires, and after 1361 the Ottoman Turks.

Nowadays, out of a total population of 360,000, there are around 120,000 Muslims, made up of 60,000 **Turkish-speakers**, 40,000 **Pomaks** and 20,000 **Gypsies**. These figures are disputed by Turkish Muslims who put their numbers alone at something between 100,000 and 120,000. The Greek government lumps all three groups together as "a Muslim minority" principally of Turkish descent, and provides Turkish-language education for all the Muslim minorities (despite the fact that the Pomaks speak a language very similar to Bulgarian). Greek authorities also point to the 336 mosques, the Turkish-language newspapers and a Turkish language radio station in Komotiní as evidence of their goodwill. However, since 1968 only graduates from a special Academy in Thessaloníki have been allowed to teach in the Turkish-language schools here, thus isolating Thracian Turks from mainstream Turkish culture, and on various occasions, the Greek authorities have interfered with Muslim religious appointments. In 1985, when the Mufti of Komotiní died, he was replaced by a government appointee. When he resigned, another Mufti was appointed by the authorities. In August 1991, the Greeks appointed a new Muslim leader in Xánthi, again without consulting the Muslim community.

There is no doubt in the minds of local Turks and Pomaks that in secular matters, too, they are the victims of **discrimination**. Muslim villages, they say, receive less help from the state than Greek villages: some are without electricity; many lack proper roads. Muslim schools are underfunded; Muslims are unable to join the police force; and it is extremely difficult for them to buy property or get bank loans – although most ethnic Turks do also acknowledge that they are better off than their counterparts in Turkey.

There have been occasional explosions of inter-communal violence and matters have only worsened since the re-incorporation, in neighbouring Bulgaria, of the Turkish minority into the commercial and political life of that country, with the Greeks becoming increasingly aware of the potential for unrest. In July 1991 the Greek government put forward a plan to demilitarize the whole of Thrace, including Bulgarian and Turkish sectors. The plan received a positive reply from the Bulgarian government, but ominously Turkey reserved its position, and Greece remains fearful of Turkish agitation in Western Thrace that might lead to a Cyprus-type military operation where Turkish forces "come to the assistance" of an oppressed minority.

As an outsider you will probably not notice the intercommunal tensions, but you will not be able to avoid the many military installations in the province; some Muslim areas near the Bulgarian border north of Komotiní and Xánthi are subject to police and army restrictions. However, there are mixed villages where Muslims and Greeks appear to coexist quite amicably, and Thracians, both Muslim and Orthodox, have a deserved reputation for hospitality.

There is little tangible to see, and most travellers take a bus straight through to **Alexandhroúpoli**, for the ferry to Samothráki, or head straight on to **Istanbul**. But Thrace's many rulers left some mark on the area, and there are a few well-preserved monuments, most significant the remains of the coastal cities of Avdira, south of Xánthi, and Maroneia, southeast of Komotiní – Greek colonies in the seventh century BC that were abandoned in Byzantine times when the inhabitants moved inland to escape pirate raids. Otherwise, it's the landscape itself that is of most appeal, the train line forging a circuitous but scenic route below the foothills of the Rodhópi mountains that's at its best in the **Néstos valley** between Paranésti and Xánthi. Indeed if you make time to explore the backstreets of the towns, or venture up the myriad tracks to tiny, isolated villages in the Rhodópi mountains, you'll find an atmosphere quite unlike any other part of Greece.

Xánthi and around

Coming from Kavála, after the turning to the airport and shortly after the turning to Keramotí you cross the Néstos River, which with the **Rhodópi mountains** forms the border of Thrace. The Greek/Turkish, Christian/Muslim make-up is almost immediately apparent in the villages: the Turkish ones, long established, with their tiled, whitewashed houses and pencil-thin minarets; the Greek settlements, often adjacent, built in drab modern style for the refugees of the 1920s.

Xánthi

XÁNTHI (Ksánthi; Iskeçe to the Turks), the first town of any size, is perhaps the most interesting point to break a journey. There is a busy market area, good Turko-Greek food, and, up the hill to the north of the main café-lined square, a very attractive old quarter. The town also has a recently established university, which lends a lively air to the place, particularly in the area between the bazaar and the campus, where bars, cinemas and bistros are busy in term time. Try if you can to visit on Saturday, the day of Xánthi's **market** – a huge affair, attended equally by Greeks, Pomaks and Turks, held in a large open space near the fire station on the eastern side of the town.

The narrow, cobbled streets of the Old Town are home to a number of very fine mansions, some restored, some derelict, with painted exteriors, bow windows and wrought-iron balconies; most date from the mid-nineteenth century when Xánthi's tobacco merchants made their fortunes. One of them has been turned into a **Folk Museum** (Mon & Wed–Sat 6–8pm, Oct–April 5–7pm, Sun 11am–1pm; 100dr), found at at Antika 7. Originally the home of two tobacco magnate brothers, it has been lovingly restored with painted wooden panels and decorated plaster and floral designs on the walls and ceilings, as well as displays of Thracian clothes and jewellery, a postcard collection and cakes of tobacco.

Further up, the roads become increasingly narrow and steep, and the Turkish presence is more noticeable: most of the women have their heads covered; the stricter ones wear full-length cloaks. Churches and mosques hide behind whitewashed houses with red-tiled roofs; orange-brown tobacco leaves are strung along drying frames.

To the north, overlooking the town from on high, is the **Panayía Convent** which is being restored, though it's still open to the public in the meantime. Beyond, the **Áyios Nikólaos Monastery** is also being restored, and from here there are fine views north into the forested Rhodópi mountains.

Accommodation

There are several **hotels** in town, the best value a straight choice between the *Paris* at Dhimokrítou 12 (☎0541/20 531; ②), by the crossroads with the traffic lights on the way out of town towards Komotiní, and the *Demokritos*, Octavíou 41 (☎0541/25 111; ③), near the central square. The *Lux* at Stavroú 18 (☎0541/22 341; ②) is clean, cheap and friendly, while for not a lot more, try the *Sissy*, Lefkípou 14 (☎0541/22 996; ②), opposite the *Paris*, which has a noisy café where breakfast is served.

North of Xánthi

Much of the countryside north of Xánthi, towards the Bulgarian border, is a military "controlled area", and dotted with signs denoting the fact. Greeks will tell you that access to areas like this is restricted because of the sensitivity of the border with Bulgaria: ethnic Turks and Pomaks claim the army uses the border as an excuse to keep tabs on them. It is possible to enter the controlled areas, but you need a pass from the police and army in Míki.

If you do venture up into the mountains here, the reward is some magnificent scenery, the road twisting up through forests and tobacco terraces into the highest and wildest part of the Rhodópi range. There are a number of Muslim villages: SMÍNTHI, a large and dispersed Pomak settlement with a mosque and tall minaret, and, further on and much more isolated, MÍKI, with long single-storey stone houses and a large mosque. The road north of here, towards Ehínos, leads into a restricted area, and you will need a pass to get through. If you do have one, EHÍNOS is a fine-looking town that is the main market for the surrounding Pomak community – Bogomil-Christian Slavs forcibly converted to Islam in the sixteenth century. They still speak a corrupt dialect of Bulgarian with generous mixtures of Greek and Turkish.

Otherwise, the most northerly place you can get to without a pass is **ORÉA**, to the west of Ehínos, another Pomak village, set on a steep hillside with cloud-covered peaks behind and terraces falling away to the riverbed – a dramatic setting in the extreme. It has a mosque and Turkish-language school, but it is grindingly poor: the ground floors of the houses are used for corralling animals or storing farm produce, and it has no bar or taverna, at least not for visitors. If you pass through, don't expect much of a welcome.

South of Xánthi: along the coast

Travelling south from Xánthi is less problematic. The coastal plain, bright with cotton, tobacco and cereals, stretches to the sea. Heading towards Ávdira, you might stop briefly in **YENISSÉA**, an unspectacular farming village with a mixed Greek-Turkish population, and, behind its nondescript centre, one of the oldest mosques in Thrace, more than four hundred years old. Now derelict, it's a low whitewashed building, with a tiled roof: a wooden portico running round its four sides is dangerously rotten and its minaret has been truncated. Across the road, behind a service station, is a second mosque, door locked and windows boarded, though its minaret still stands.

Ávdira and along the coast

A few kilometres further on, regular buses go to the village of **ÁVDIRA**, and, in summer, to the beach of the same name, 7km beyond and passing through the ancient site of **Avdira** (daily 9am–3pm; free). The walls of the ancient acropolis are visible on a low headland above the sea, and there are traces of Roman baths, a theatre and an ancient acropolis. However, the best finds have been taken off to museums in Kavála and Komotiní, the remains are unspectacular, and the setting not particularly attractive. If you have time only for one site, you're better off going to Marónia (see below).

For the most part, the coast between Ávdira and Marónia is flat and dull. At the southern end of Lake Vistonís is **PORTO LÁGOS**, a semi-derelict harbour redeemed by the low white monastery of **Áyios Nikólaos** built on a reef in the lagoon. The surrounding marshland is an important site for birdlife, and is more accessible than the Evros delta. Nearby, the small resort of **FANARI** has a long sandy beach with two hotels: the all-white, modern *Fanari Hotel* (☎0535/31 300; ④) and the smaller *Pension Theodora* (☎0535/31 242; ④), both good value for money. The *Fanari* has a restaurant and there are a number of other fish **restaurants**, too. There's also an EOT campsite, the Fanari (☎0535/31 270; May–Oct), alongside the public beach. Fanári itself is popular with Komotiniots in the evenings and at weekends, and its beach gets busy in the high summer, but there are less crowded spots east along the coast.

Marónia and further east

Further along the coast, **ancient Maroneia** has little more to see than Ávdira, but the site is altogether more attractive. Most of it is still unexcavated, and the visible remains are scattered among the olive trees and undergrowth at the foot of Mount Ísmaros, now anachronistically crowned with large, white radar station golf balls. The founder of the city is reckoned to be Maron, the son of the god of wine, Dionysus (Ísmaros is known locally as the Mountain of Dionysus) and the city became one of the most powerful in all of ancient Thrace. The site, which can be explored at will, is badly signposted, but you should be able to track down traces of a theatre, a sanctuary of Dionysus, and various buildings including a house with a well-preserved mosaic floor. The land walls of the city are preserved to a height of two metres, together with a Roman tower above the harbour. Over time, the sea has done its own excavation, eroding the crumbling cliffs, revealing shards of pottery and ancient walls. There can be fewer more magical places to watch the sun set over the Thracian Sea.

The harbour of **ÁYIOS HARÁLAMBOS**, at the edge of the site, has been enlarged recently; there are a couple of cafés and tavernas, plus a few **rooms** and one **hotel**, the imposing Hotel King Maron Beach (☎0533/61 345; ⑤), which stands alone on the clifftop overlooking the sea. A number of Roman and Byzantine buildings, including baths and a church, have been excavated between the modern houses. There are reasonable beaches in both directions, and in summer the area is popular with Greeks from Komotiní.

The pleasant, modern village of **MARÓNIA**, 4km inland, has some fine old Thracian mansions with jutting balconies and some **rooms** (☎0533/41 158). It's connected with Komotiní by six daily buses.

Towards Alexandhroúpoli, there are good beaches at **MESIMVRÍA** and **MÁKRI**, though with few facilities except for Mákri's Hotel Kleio (☎0551/71 311; ③), which has a good restaurant. If you have your own transport, you can continue east to the **Évros delta**, one of Europe's most important wetland areas for birds – and one of Greece's most sensitive military areas.

Komotiní

KOMOTINÍ, 48km east of Xánthi, the road skirting the Rodhópi foothills, is larger and less attractive, with ranks of apartment buildings and gridded suburbs to the south and west, and dusty, noisy streets, clogged with traffic. It is more markedly Turkish with its fourteen functioning mosques, and social mixing between the different ethnic groups is less common, although Orthodox and Muslim continue to live in the same neighbourhoods.

During the thirteenth century, the city gained importance and wealth due to its position on the Via Egnatia. When the Ottomans took the city in 1361, they changed its name to Gümülçine, which is what it was called during the long centuries of the tourkokratía, the period of Turkish rule. In 1912, at the outbreak of the First Balkan War, Komotiní was taken by the Bulgarians; it was liberated by Greek forces in the following year, only to be taken once more by the Bulgarians. It was finally and definitively liberated on the May 14, 1920.

The old **bazaar**, to the north of Platía Eirínis, the central square, is very pleasant, caught between mosques and a fine Turkish clock tower: shady cafés and tiny shops sell everything from carpets to iron buckets, and it's especially busy on Tuesdays when the villagers from the surrounding area come into town to sell their wares. Behind this old quarter, you can see the modern **Cathedral** and the remains of Komotiní's **Byzantine walls.**

Traditionally a city with Greek and Turkish inhabitants, Greek influence began to dominate in the waning years of the Ottoman Empire, with rich Greeks funding schools and colleges in the city to develop Greek culture and ideals. Some of these educational foundations still survive: one, the **Hellenic Civic School of Nestor Tanakali**, a Neoclassical structure on Dhimokritoú, behind the Central Park, is now the official residence of the Dean of the University of Thrace; another, at Áyios Yióryos 13, on the other side of the park, has become Komotiní's **Folk Museum** (daily except Sun 10am–1pm; free), displaying examples of Thracian embroidery, traditional Thracian dress, silverware, copperware and a collection of religious seals. The **Archeological Museum** at Simeonídhi 4 (daily 9am–5pm; 400dr), just off to the right of the main road from Xánthi and well signposted, is also worth a visit, giving a lucid overview of Thracian history, by means of plans and finds from local sites, from its beginnings up to the Byzantine era. On display are a number of statues, busts, bas reliefs, jewellery and artefacts from the archeological sites around Komotiní.

If you need to **stay**, choose between the Astoria on the main Platía Eirínis (☎0531/35 054; ④), recently given a facelift, or the slightly more reasonable Democritus at Platía Viziníou 8 (☎0531/22 044; ④), an old hotel near the Central Park. Cheapest in town is the Hellas at Dhimokrítou 31 (☎0531/22 055; ②), with shared showers and toilets; if you want a balcony and a built-in restaurant, then it has to be the pricey Hotel Rodopi, Makariou 3

(☎0531/35 988; ⑥), on the main road from Xánthi and 750m from the town centre.

North of Komotiní

If you want to escape the heat and noise, to the north of the city is the forest of **Nymphaia**, well used by the locals for jogging and walking, and home to a number of cafés. Further up the road, you come to the ruins of the Byzantine fortress of **Nymphias**, with a wonderful view over Komotiní down to the sea. It is said that on a clear day, you can see Mount Áthos, more than 100km away over the Thracian Sea.

Alexandhroúpoli

A modern city, designed by Russian military architects during the Russian-Turkish war of 1878, **ALEXANDHROÚPOLI** – Dedeağaç to the Turks and Bulgars – does not, on first acquaintance, have much to recommend it: a border town and military garrison, with overland travellers and Greek holidaymakers in transit competing for limited space in the few hotels and the campsite.

The town became Greek in 1920, when it was renamed Alexandhroúpoli after a visit from the Greek King Alexander. There are no obvious sights and the heavy military presence can be oppressive – especially for single women. The Turkish quarter, literally on the wrong side of the tracks, may whet the appetite for the genuine article across the border. Otherwise it's the seafront that best characterises the town. Dominated by a huge **lighthouse** built in 1880 (and adopted as the town's symbol), the area comes alive at dusk when the Alexandriots begin their evening volta. Traffic is diverted and the cafés spill out onto the road and around the lighthouse; makeshift stalls along the pavements sell salted seeds, pirated cassettes and grilled sweetcorn. There is also a little funfair on waste ground between the lighthouse and the harbour. On summer evenings, there are concerts and shows in the makeshift amphitheatre in the municipal gardens beyond the western end of the seafront.

Practicalities

Heading for the island of **Samothráki** (see the East and North Aegean chapter), there is at least one daily ferry year-round and, in July and August, two a day – three on Fridays and Sundays. Tickets can be bought from Vatsis Shipping Agency, Kyprou 5 (☎0551/26 721). Flying Dolphin sailings to Samothráki are in the pipeline, though there's no timetable yet. The **bus station** is at the junction of Venizelou and 14 Maiou. There's a **tourist office** at the town hall in Venizelou, which hands out a map; if you're intent upon visiting the Évros delta (see below), you can glean useful advice from Stella Kladara, Moschonision 1 (☎0551/22 124).

The hotels nearest the port and train station cater for those just passing through, whether by ferry to and from Samothráki or by train into Turkey or back to Thessaloníki. There is a better choice of hotels on Dhimokratía, the main street which runs parallel to the seafront, one block inland. The best place near the train station is the imaculate Metropolis, Athanasíou Dhiákou 11 (☎0551/26 443; ④), with en suite rooms, while also very central is the Majestic, Platía Eleftherias 7 (☎0551/26 444; ②), where there's a warm welcome from the couple who own it. Other good choices include the Ira at Dhimokratía179 (☎0551/23 941; ⑤); and the adjacent Lido, Paleologou 15 (☎0551/28 808; ②), and Hotel Okeanis at no. 20 (☎0551/28 830; ④), where another 1000dr gets you air-conditioning. You'll probably need to book in advance to stay at the Okeanis.

Food is a bright spot. There are at least three excellent places in a small square which is no more than a widening in Kyprou, including the popular Ouzerí Paradhosiako and the Restaurant Klimataria, which has a large menu. You can also have a fine meal at Neraidha, a couple of blocks from the train station and across from the town hall.

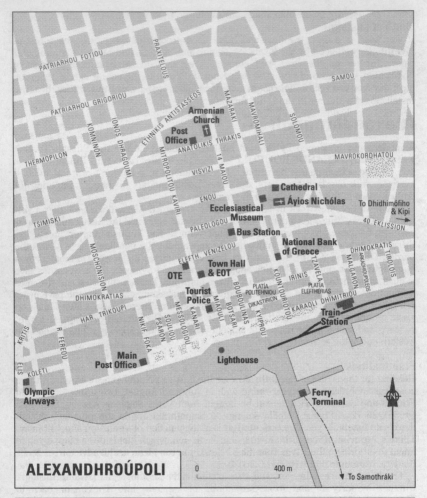

ALEXANDHROÚPOLI

0   400 m

To Samothráki

The Évros Valley and northeastern Thrace

The **Évros Valley**, northeast of Alexandhroúpoli, is a prosperous but dull agricultural area. The towns are in general ugly, modern concrete affairs full of bored soldiers, with little to delay you. If you have time, however, there are a number of possible attractions.

The Évros Delta

To the southeast, the **Évros Delta** is one of Europe's most important wetlands, and home to more than 250 different species of birds, including sea-eagles. The easiest way to get there (if you have a car) is to leave Alexandhroúpoli on the main road (E90/E85) towards Turkey and Bulgaria and, after passing the airport on the right, drive to **Loutra Traianopolis**, 13km away, the site of an ancient Roman spa. There are three hotels (all ②–③) in present-day Loutra, any of which would make a good base for exploring the delta, best approached by turning right off the main road and taking the dirt track that runs alongside the *Hotel Isidora*. The delta is crisscrossed with tracks along the dykes that are mainly used by farmers taking advantage of the plentiful water supply for growing sweetcorn and cotton. The south is the most inspiring part, well away from the army installations to the north, and, the further into the wetlands you go, the landscapes becomes utterly desolate, with decrepit clusters of fishing huts among the sandbars and inlets. At the mouth of the delta is a huge saltwater lake called **Límni Dhrakónda**. Obviously what you see depends on the time of year, but even if the birdlife is a bit thin on the ground, the atmosphere of the place is worth experiencing.

Féres to Dhidhimótiho

Further up the valley, at **FÉRES**, close by the frontier, the exquisite twelfth-century Byzantine church of **Theotokós Kosmosotíra** is also worth a look, originally part of a monastery and founded by a member of the Comnene dynasty. Its interior frescoes are in mediocre condition but the five-domed design is rare in Greece outside of Thessaloníki. If you have to change buses en route to the border post at Kípi, as sometimes happens, and have some time to wait, it's well worth seeking out. With your own car, there's no excuse for missing it. There's a hotel in Féres, the *Anthi* (☎0555/24 201; ④), on the way into town as you approach from the south.

Continuing north, the next attraction is the **Dhadhiá Forest Reserve**, reached by a road off to the left 1km after passing through Likófos. After a five-kilometre drive through the rolling, forested hills, you reach the reserve **information centre** (☎0554/32 397), at the heart of 35,000 hectares of protected oak and pine forest. The diversity of landscape and vegetation, the proximity of important migration routes and the outstanding wetland of the nearby Évros delta make for an extremely diverse flora and fauna: black and white vultures hold pride of place. If you want to stay, the information centre can point you towards the purpose-built visitors' **accommodation** (☎0554/32 263; ②).

DHIDHIMÓTIHO, further north by the border, is the only other stop of any interest. The old part of town is still partially enclosed by the remains of double Byzantine fortifications (hence the name, which means "double wall"), and some old houses and churches survive, but the area has a feeling of decay despite continuing efforts at restoration. Finally pulled down in 1985 was the **synagogue** which the townspeople ransacked during World War II at the instigation of the Nazis – who had spread about the (false) rumour that treasure was secreted in its walls. Outside the old quarter, the most important monument is the fourteenth-century **mosque**, the oldest and second largest in Greece, an unelaborate square stone building with a pyramid-shaped roof. Unfortunately, the interior is closed indefinitely for restoration. Excavations just outside the town have revealed the site of the Roman city of **Plotinoupolis**, but there's really nothing to see. The *Hotel Plotini* (☎0553/23 400; ④) is a substantial building, on your left as you enter the town from the south.

Metaxádhes and Orestiádha

Further north still, smaller roads take you through isolated villages and beautiful countryside. **METAXÁDHES** is one of the most handsome villages in the area, sited on a steep hill, its large houses built traditionally of stone and wood with red tiled roofs and lush gardens. Fought over by Bulgars and Turks, Metaxádhes used to support a Turkish community but now its population is exclusively Greek, although older residents still speak some Turkish. Beyond Metaxádhes, you descend to the vast, fertile **Árdha plain** that dominates the northerneastern tip of Greek Thrace: rich farmland –

the main crops are sunflowers, sweetcorn and (increasingly) sugar beet – that supports a large number of modern villages, many of them populated by settlers from Asia Minor. Hemmed in on three sides by Bulgaria and Turkey, it has been a Greek priority to establish a Greek population in this extremely sensitive corner of Thrace, and, apart from its agricultural importance, the area has great strategic significance. Barracks are liberally scatted through the hinterland and along the eastern border with Turkey; there are numerous surveillance posts, all flying Greek flags, and looking over to the minarets of Turkey across the Évros river valley.

The main town in this northeastern corner is **ORESTIÁDHA**, a busy market town with restaurants, bars and lots of cake shops in its main square. It also has a branch of the *National Bank of Greece*, something worth bearing in mind when returning from Bulgaria or Turkey. You could do worse than spend a night here before/after crossing the border. Hotels include the new *Alexandros* (☎0552/27 000; ④), the older *Elektra* (☎0552/23 174; ④), with the *Iridanos* restaurant alongside, and the now very old *Vienni* (☎0552/22 578; ⑤).

On to Turkey or Bulgaria

Crossing into Turkey from Alexandhroúpoli, you are presented with a bewildering choice of routes; currently there's only one daily rail link to Bulgaria.

British passport holders now need a **Turkish visa**, which costs £5 at the border; if you don't have the exact amount in sterling, you'll have to change more. **Bulgarian visas** are required for all nationals and are expensive; prices fluctuate, but count on £20 for a transit pass at the border, somewhat less if you obtain it at a consulate beforehand.

By bus to Turkey

The simplest way to travel from northern Greece to Turkey, if you can get a ticket, is to go by **bus** direct to Istanbul. There are several departures daily, one run by OSE (tickets from the train station), the others by private companies (ask at travel agents). The problem is that most of the buses start in Thessaloníki, and by this stage most are full. In addition to buses to Istanbul, there are private buses three or four times a week to Edirne, just across the border; ask for details at travel agents in Xánthi, Komotiní or Alexandhroúpoli.

An alternative is to take a local bus to the border at **KÍPI** (6 daily). You are not allowed to cross the frontier here on foot, but it is generally no problem to get a driver to shuttle you the 500m across to the Turkish post, and perhaps even to give you a lift beyond. The nearest town is Ipsala (5km further on), but if possible get as far as Keşan, (30km), from where buses to Istanbul are much more frequent.

By train to Turkey

Travelling by **train** to Istanbul should in theory be simpler. However, the only through connection leaves Alexandhroúpoli at 9.17pm, crossing the border at Píthio and taking about eleven hours in total (including a long halt at the frontier) to reach Istanbul. This is nominally an important express, with seat reservations applicable, so try not to leave tickets to the last minute.

You might prefer to go by day, taking a train through Píthio and on to **KASTANIÉS**, opposite Turkish Edirne. The most useful departure is currently at 6.58am; later ones arrive after the border post (daily 9am–1pm) has closed. There's no accommodation in Kastaniés, but unlike Kípi you are allowed to walk across the border (under army escort). Once on the Turkish side, there's bus service to the first Turkish village, 2km beyond the frontier; it's 7km from the border to Edirne (Adrianoúpoli to the Greeks) – an attractive and historic city with some important Ottoman monuments and frequent buses making the three-hour trip to Istanbul. For more information, there's no better source than *The Rough Guide to Turkey*.

Into Bulgaria

To Bulgaria, from Alexandhroúpoli, there is one just train daily, leaving at 6.58am and reaching Greek Dhikéa just under three hours later, where you then have a 75-minute wait before the special twenty-minute connection to Svilengrad inside Bulgaria. (Curiously, this turns around to provide a through service to Alexandhroúpoli in the early afternoon.) From Svilengrad (which has just one, five-star, hotel), it is best to plan on moving on the same day towards Plovdiv.

travel details

Note: *services into the states of the former Yugoslavia are currently suspended, and it is impossible to obtain reliable information on future schedules; these routes are, in any case, inadvisable for independent travellers.*

Trains

Alexandhroúpoli–Istanbul (Turkey) Semi-direct (change cars at Píthio) night train (9.17pm), arriving Istanbul around 8am, after an hour or longer wait at the border.

Alexandhroúpoli–Dhidhimótiho–Orestiádha–Kastaniés (for Edirne) 7 daily, but only 1 departure (6.58am) reaches frontier post while open; 2hr/2hr 30min/3hr.

Alexandhroúpoli–Svilengrad (Bulgaria) 1 daily (6.58am); 5hr 20min, including 75min stopover at Dhikéa.

Thessaloníki–Kateríni/Lárissa/Athens 4 express, 6 slower trains daily in each direction (1hr 30min/2hr 20min/6– 8hr).

Thessaloníki–Kateríni/Litóhoro/Platamónas/Lárissa/Vólos 3 daily in each direction (2hr/2hr 25min/4hr 30min/5 hr).

Thessaloníki–Véria/Édhessa/Amíndeo/Flórina 5 daily in each direction; connections between Amíndeo and Kozáni 4 times daily; 2 daily only to Édhessa.

Thessaloníki–Sérres–Dhráma–Xánthi–Komotiní–Alexandhroúpoli 1 afternoon express, 4 slower trains daily (Thessaloníki–Dhráma 2hr 45min–3hr 30min; Dhráma–Xánthi Komotíni 1hr/ 15min/2hr 30min; Xánthi–Alexandhropoúli 1hr 30min–2hr).

Thessaloníki–Sofia, via Promahón (1 daily; 8hr 30min).

N.B. *OSE* also operate **long-distance buses** from Thessaloníki to Istanbul, Sofia, Milan, Paris, London, Vienna and towns in Germany.

Buses

Alexandhroúpoli to Dhidhimótiho (8–9 daily; 2hr); Kípi (6 daily; 45min); Istanbul (daily *OSE* and other private buses; 8hr).

Édhessa to Flórina (5–6 daily; 2hr); Kastoriá (4 daily; 2hr 30min).

Kastoriá to Flórina (1 direct, daily; 2hr; other indirect services via Amíndeo).

Kateríni to Litóhoro, for Mount Olympus (4 daily; 45min).

Kavála to Keramotí (every 30min; 1hr); Philippi (every 20min; 20min); Xánthi/Komotiní (every 30min; 1hr/2hr); Alexandhroúpoli (5 daily; 3hr).

Kozáni to Grevená (8 daily; 1hr); Siátista (4 daily; 30min).

Thessaloníki to Alexandhroúpoli (7 daily; 6hr); Arnéa-Ierissós/Ouranópoli (5–7 daily; 2hr/3hr 30min); Athens (hourly; 7hr 30min); Flórina (5 daily; 3hr 30min); Istanbul (daily *OSE*, others privately operated; 14hr); Kalambáka/Ioánnina (4–5 daily; 4hr 30min/7hr 30min); Kastoriá (5 daily; 4hr 30min); Kateríni, for Mount Olympus (hourly; 1hr 30min); Kavála (hourly; 3hr); Pélla/Édhessa (hourly; 1hr/1hr 15min); Sárti, via Políyiros (4 daily; 4hr 30min); Sofia (Thurs & Fri; 7hr 30min); Véria (hourly; 1hr 15min); Vólos (4 daily; 4hr); Vourvouroú, via Políyiros (3 daily; 3hr).

Véria to Édhessa, via Náoussa (6 daily; 1hr 15min); Kozáni (8 daily; 1hr).

Ferries

Thessaloníki to: Límnos, Lésvos and Híos (2–4 weekly); to Iraklion (Crete) via a selection among Skíathos, Skíros, Tínos, Míkonos, Páros, Íos and Thíra (2–3 weekly, always Mon & Fri year-round); to Skíros, Skópelos, Alónissos (3 weekly in summer).

Kavála to: Thássos (Órmos Prínou; 7–11 daily, depending on season); to Samothráki (2 weekly in season); to Límnos and Áyios Efstrátios (3–5 weekly); to Lésvos and Híos (2–3 weekly); to Límnos / Lésvos / Híos / Sámos / Kálimnos / Kos / Rhodes (1 weekly in summer). In winter this long-haul service sails out of Thessaloníki.

Keramotí to: Thássos (Thássos Town/Liménas) (7–12 daily, year-round).

Alexandhroúpoli to: Samothráki (1–2 daily in season, 4 weekly out of season).

Hydrofoils

Thessaloníki to: Skíathos, Skópelos and Alónissos, via Néa Moudhaniá (Halkidhikí) (May–June & Sept 5 weekly, July & Aug daily).

For details, contact *Egnatia Tours*, Kamvouníon 9, Thessaloníki (☎031/223 811).

Flights

Alexandhroúpoli to: Athens (1–3 daily).

Kastoriá to: Athens (3–7 weekly).

Kozáni to: Athens (3–6 weekly).

Thessaloníki to: Athens (5 daily); Ioánnina (3–5 weekly); Iráklion, Crete (3 weekly); Haniá, Crete (1 weekly); Lésvos (3–6 weekly); Límnos (4–7 weekly); Rhodes (2 weekly).

PART THREE

THE

ISLANDS

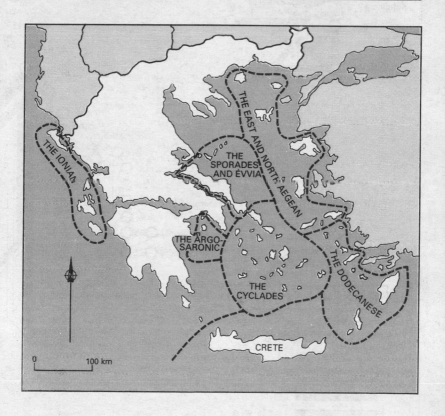

THE IONIAN

THE EAST AND NORTH AEGEAN

THE SPORADES AND ÉVVIA

THE ARGO-SARONIC

THE CYCLADES

THE DODECANESE

CRETE

0   100 km

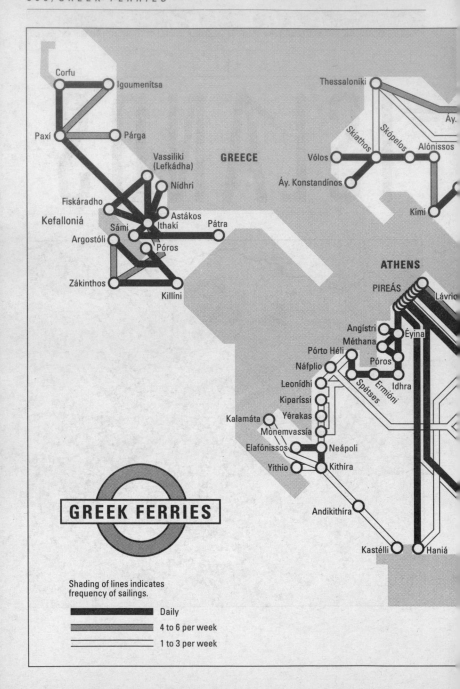

Corfu

Igoumenítsa

Thessaloníki

Áy.

Paxí

Párga

Skíathos Skópelos Alónissos

GREECE

Vólos

Vassilikí
(Lefkádha)

Áy. Konstandínos

Nídhri

Fiskáradho

Kími

Kefaloniá

Astákos

Sámi Itháki Pátra

Argostóli

Póros

ATHENS

Zákinthos

PIREÁS

Lávrio

Killíni

Angístri Éyina

Méthana

Pórto Héli

Póros

Náfplio

Leonídhi

Spétses Ermióni Idhra

Kiparíssi

Kalamáta Yérakas

Monemvassía

Elafónissos Neápoli

Yíthio Kithíra

Andikithíra

Kastélli Haniá

GREEK FERRIES

Shading of lines indicates
frequency of sailings.

Daily

4 to 6 per week

1 to 3 per week

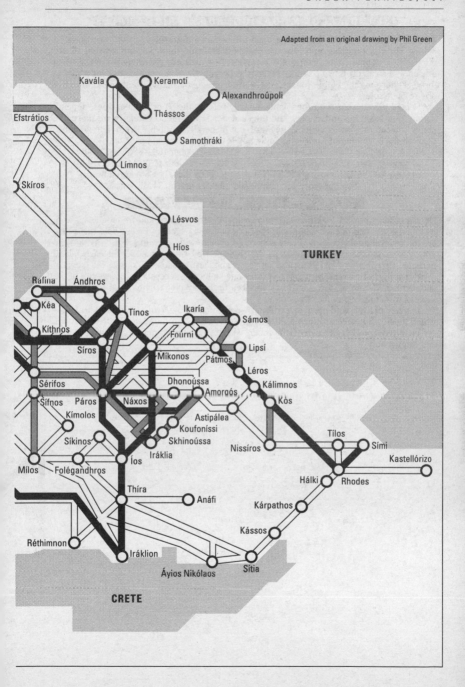

Adapted from an original drawing by Phil Green

ISLAND ACCOMMODATION: ROOM PRICE SCALES

All establishments in this book have been price-graded according to the scale outlined below. The rates quoted represent the cheapest available room in high season; all are prices for a double room, except for category ①, which are per person rates. Out of season, rates can drop by up to fifty percent, especially if you negotiate rates for a stay of three or more nights. Single rooms, where available, cost around seventy percent of the price of a double.

Rented private rooms on the islands usually fall into the ② or ③ categories, depending on their location and facilities, and the season; a few in the ④ category are more like plush self-catering apartments. They are not generally available from late October through the beginning of April, when only hotels tend to remain open.

① 1400–2000dr (£4–5.50/US$6–8.50) ④ 8000–12000dr (£22–33/US$33–50)
② 4000–6000dr (£11–16.50/US$17–25) ⑤ 12000–16000dr (£33–44/US$50–66)
③ 6000–8000dr (£16.50–22/US$25–33) ⑥ 16000dr (£44/US$66) and upwards

For more accommodation details, see pp.34–35.

FERRY ROUTES AND SCHEDULES

Details of ferry routes, together with approximate journey times and frequencies, are to be found at the end of each chapter in the "Travel details" section. Please note that these are for general guidance only. Ferry schedules change with alarming regularity and the only information to be relied upon is that provided by the port police in each island harbour. Ferry agents in Pireás and on the islands are helpful, of course, but keep in mind that they often represent just one ferry line and won't necessarily inform you of the competition. Be aware, too, that ferry services to the smaller islands tend to be pretty skeletal from mid-September through to May.

In many of the island groups, ferries are supplemented by *Flying Dolphin* hydrofoils – which tend to be twice as quick and twice the price. Most of the major hydrofoil routes are operated from May to early September, with lesser ones sometimes running in July and August only.

CHAPTER SIX

THE ARGO-SARONIC

The rocky, volcanic chain of **Argo-Saronic** islands, most of them barely an olive's throw from the Argolid, differ to a surprising extent not just from the mainland but from one another. Less surprising is their massive popularity, with Éyina (Aegina) especially becoming something of an Athenian suburb at weekends.

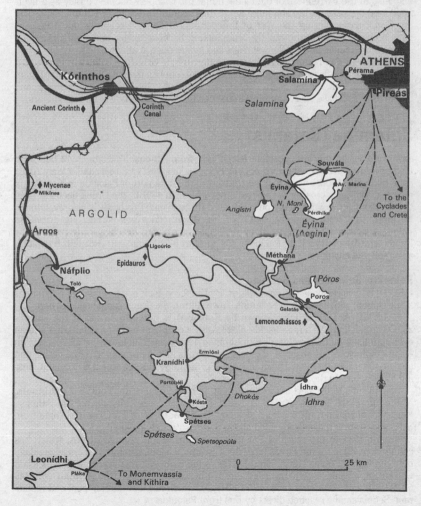

Ídhra (Hydra), Póros and Spétses are not far behind in summer, though their visitors tend to be predominantly cruise- and package-tourists. More than any other group, these islands are at their best out of season, when populations fall dramatically and the port towns return to quiet, provincial-backwater life.

Éyina, important in antiquity and more or less continually inhabited since then, is the most fertile of the group, famous for its pistachio nuts, as well as for one of the finest ancient temples in Greece. Its main problem – the crowds – can be escaped by avoiding weekends, or taking the time to explore its satellite isles, **Angístri** and **Moní**.

The three southerly islands, **Spétses**, **Ídhra** and **Póros**, are pine-cloaked and relatively infertile. They were not really settled until medieval times, when refugees from the mainland – principally Albanian Christians – established themselves here. In response to the barrenness of their new home the islanders adopted piracy as a livelihood, and the seamanship and huge fleets thus acquired were placed at the disposal of the Greek nation during the War of Independence. Today foreigners and Athenians have replaced locals in the rapidly depopulating harbour towns, and windsurfers and sailboats are faint echoes of the warships and *kaíkia* once at anchor.

The closest island of the Argo-Saronic, **Salamína**, is virtually a suburb of Pireás, just over a kilometre offshore to its east, and it almost touches the industrial city of Mégara to the west as well. As you might expect, it is frequented by Athenian weekenders, and is also used as a base for commuting to the capital, but sees very few foreign visitors.

Salamína (Salamis)

Salamína is the quickest possible island hop from Athens. Take the #842 bus from Platía Eleftherias to the shipyard port of Pérama, just west of Pireás, and a ferry (daily 5am–midnight; 100dr) will whisk you across to the little port of Paloukía in a matter of minutes. The ferry crosses the narrow strait where, in 480BC, the Greek fleet trounced the Persian fleet, despite being outnumbered three to one; this battle is said by some to be more significant than the battle of Marathon, ten years earlier. On arrival in Paloukía, you won't be rewarded by desirable or isolated beaches – the pollution of Pireás and Athens is a little too close for comfort – but you soon escape the capital's *néfos* and and city pace.

Paloukía, Salamína and Selínia

PALOUKÍA is really just a transit point. By the ferry dock is a taverna and opposite is a bus station, with services to Salamína Town (3km), the island capital and beyond.

SALAMÍNA TOWN (also known as Kouloúri) is home to 18,000 of the island's 23,000 population. It's a ramshackle place, with a couple of banks, a fishmarket and an over-optimistic (and long-closed) tourist office. Pretty much uniquely for an island town – and emphasizing its absence of tourists – there is no bike or moped rental outlet, and also no hotel (not that you'd want to stay). Fortunately, bus services are excellent, linking most points on the island.

Bus #8 runs to the port at the northwest tip of the island, the **Voudoro peninsula**, where there are ferries across to Lákki Kalomírou, near Mégara on the Athens–Kórinthos road. En route it passes close by the **Monastery of Faneroméni** (6km from Salamína), rather majestically sited above the frustratingly polluted gulf.

Around 6km to the south of Paloukía is a third island port, SELÍNIA, which has connections direct to the Pireás ferry dock (winter 9.30am, summer five crossings daily between 8am–2.30pm; 210dr; 30min). This is the main summer resort, with a pleasant waterfront, a bank, several tavernas and two inexpensive hotels, the *Akroyali* (☎01/46 53 341; ②) and *Votsalakia* (☎01/46 71 334; ②), which has a swimming pool and restaurant. Selínia can be reached direct by bus from Paloukía.

Eándio and the south

South from Salamína Town, the road edges the coast towards Eándio (6km; regular buses). There are a few tavernas along the way, but the sea vistas are not inspiring. **EÁNDIO**, however, is quite a pleasant village, with a little pebble beach and the island's best **hotel**, the *Gabriel* (☎01/46 62 275; ③), owned by poet and journalist, Giorgos Tzimas, who is usually only too keen to recite a poem or two. The hotel overlooks the bay, whose waters are again unenticing (probably a health risk) for swimming, but it could be an enjoyable off-season stay.

Two roads continue from Eándio. The one to the southeast runs to the unassuming village resorts of Peráni and Paralía (both around 4km from Eándio). The more interesting route is southeast to Kanákia (8km from Eándio; no buses), over the island's pine-covered mountain, and passing (at around 5km) a monastery – dedicated, like almost all Salamína churches, to Áyios Nikólaos. At the monastery you could turn off the road (left) along a track to the harbour and small-scale resort of Peristéria (5km). This is a much more attractive settlement than the littered beach and scruffy huts of Kanákia itself.

Éyina (Aegina)

Given its current population of a little over 10,000, it seems incredible that **Éyina** (Aegina) was a major power in Classical times – and a rival to Athens. It carried on trade to the limits of the known world, maintained a sophisticated silver coinage system (the first in Greece) and had prominent athletes and craftsmen. However, during the fifth century BC the islanders made the political mistake of siding with their

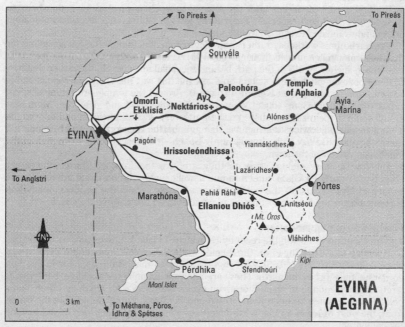

fellow Dorians, the Spartans, which Athens seized on as an excuse to act on a long-standing jealousy; her fleets defeated those of the islanders in two separate sea battles and, after the second, the population was expelled and replaced by more tractable colonists.

Subsequent history was less distinguished, with the familiar central Greece pattern of occupation, by Romans, Franks, Venetians, Catalans and Turks, before the War of Independence brought a brief period as seat of government for the fledgling Greek nation. These days, the island is most famous for its **pistachio orchards**, whose thirsty trees lower the water table several feet annually; hence the notices warning you of the perennial water crisis.

Athenians regard Éyina as a beach annexe for their city, being the closest place to the capital most of them would swim at, though for tourists it has a monument as fine as any in the Aegean in its beautiful fifth-century BC **Temple of Aphaia**. This is located on the east coast, close to the port of **Ayía Marína**, and if it is your primary goal, you'd do best to take one of the ferries that in season run directly to that port. If you plan to stay, then make sure your boat will dock at **Éyina Town**, the island capital. Ferries also occasionally stop at **Souvála**, a Greek weekend retreat between the two ports devoid of interest to outsiders. Hydrofoils, incidentally, are far more frequent, run from the same quay in Pireás as the conventional boats, and cost hardly any more for this particular destination.

Éyina Town

A solitary column of a Temple of Apollo beckons as your ferry or hydrofoil steams around the point into the harbour at **ÉYINA TOWN**. The island's capital, it makes an attractive base, with some grand old buildings from the time (1826–28) when it served as the first capital of Greece after the War of Independence. And for somewhere so close to Athens, it isn't especially overrun by foreign tourists, nor are accommodation prices unduly inflated except on weekends.

The **harbour** is workaday rather than picturesque, but is nonetheless appealing for that: fishermen talk and tend their nets, and *kaíkia* loaded with produce from the mainland bob at anchor. North of the port, behind the small town beach, the rather weatherbeaten Apollo-temple column stands on a low hill that was the ancient acropolis and is known, logically enough, as **Kolóna** (Column). Around the temple are rather obscure **ruins** (daily 8.30am–3pm; 400dr), only worth it for the sweeping view from Moní islet on the south to the mainland shore on the northwest. A small museum on the grounds is shut indefinitely owing to structural damage, but on the north flank of Kolóna hill there's an attractive bay with a small, sandy **beach** – the best spot for swimming in the immediate vicinity of the town.

The town's other sights, such as they are, are the frescoed thirteenth-century church of **Ómorfi Ekklisía**, fifteen minutes' walk east of the port, and a house in the suburb of Livádhi, just to the north, where a plaque recalls the residence of **Nikos Kazantzakis**, when he was writing his most celebrated book, *Zorba the Greek*.

Arrival and accommodation

The **bus station** is also on the recently refurbished Platía Ethneyersías, with an excellent service to most villages on the island, while the largest moped and cycle rental place – *Stratos* (☎0297/24 865), with slightly above normal island rates – is in the pink corner building just to the north. There are a few mountain bikes available, but Éyina is large and hilly enough to make motorized cycles worthwhile for anything other than a pedal to the beaches between Éyina Town and Pérdhika. Three **banks** line the waterfront; the **post office** is on Platía Ethneyersías; while the **OTE** lies well inland beyond the cathedral.

Rooms can be hard to come by in Éyina Town, with many of the more comfortable hotels block-booked in the summer months. You would be well advised to phone ahead, or to take whatever you're offered on arrival, at least for the first night. Hard bargaining can be productive, especially out of season and midweek, when rates tend to be two-thirds or less what they are on Friday or Saturday nights. Try the streets inland from Platía Ethneyersías, a couple of hundred metres to the left of the jetty as you disembark; if you really get stuck, there's a **tourist police** post in the same building as the regular police, but reached from a narrow alley just off Ethneyersías, and the unofficial but helpful "Aegina Tourist Board" above a *gelateria* on the corner of Leonárdhou Ladhá and the waterfront.

Best inexpensive accommodation option are rooms, either those inland by the OTE (☎0297/22 334; ②), or those of *Andonis Marmarinos* at Leonárdhou Ladhá 30 (☎0297/ 22 954; ②), spotless, fairly quiet though not en suite. For more comfort try the *Hotel Marmarinos* nearby at no. 24, run by a branch of the same family (☎0297/23 510; ②–③ midweek, ③–④ weekend). Across the street, *Hotel Artemis* (☎0297/25 195; ④) is appealingly set in a pistachio orchard. Slightly fancier is the *Hotel Areti* on the seafront between Platía Ethneyersías and Kolóna (☎0297/23 593; ②–③ midweek, ③–④ weekend), where ocean views offset a certain amount of traffic noise.

Food and entertainment

When searching for a **meal out**, forego the obvious and touristy glitz outfits on the front in favour of more obscure nooks and crannies. The pistachio nuts for which Éyina is famed make a good snack: they are best unsalted, but are not very cheap.

Directly behind the fish market is a particularly good and inexpensive seafood taverna, the *Psarotaverna Agora*, with outdoor seating on the cobbles in summer. Similar in concept, though not quite as good value, is *Ta Vrehamena*, a little hole-in-the-wall on Leonárdhou Ladhá just seaward from the police station, offering a very limited menu of bulk wine, ouzo and grilled octopus. Just around the corner, the bakery *O Bogris* has good whole grain bread suitable for breakfast or picnics. Next to the *Hotel Areti*, the *Psitopolio Lekkus* is excellent for no-nonsense meat grills by the waterside. At the opposite (south) end of the quay, by the *Trapeza Pisteos* (Credit Bank), *Maridhaki* is a less carniverous traditional place, dishing up the usual Greek oven standards. Finally, for a mild blowout, *Taverna Votsitsanos*, two blocks straight inland from the centre of the front, has a particularly full menu of fish and oven specialities, with seating in its own garden, the alley or (in winter) indoors.

In terms of **nightlife**, Éyina Town can boast no less than two summer **cinemas**, the *Olympia* and the *Anesis*, and a winter one, the *Titina*, by the park with the medieval tower-house, near OTE. On the cormer of Aiándos and Piléos, the *Belle Epoque* bar is worth a visit for its ornate turn-of-the-century architecture.

The Temple of Aphaia

The Doric **Temple of Aphaia** (Mon–Fri 8.30am–7pm, Sat & Sun 8.30am–3pm; 600dr) lies 12km east of Éyina Town, standing among pines that are tapped to flavour the local retsina, beside a less aesthetic radio mast. It is one of the most complete and visually complex ancient buildings in Greece, with superimposed arrays of columns and lintels evocative of an Escher drawing. Built early in the fifth century BC, or possibly at the end of the sixth century, it predates the Parthenon by around sixty years. The dedication is unusual: Aphaia was a Cretan nymph who had fled from the lust of King Minos, and seems to have been worshipped almost exclusively on Éyina. As recently as two centuries ago the temple's pediments were intact and virtually perfect, depicting two battles at Troy. However, like the Elgin marbles they were "bought" from the Turks: this time by Ludwig of Bavaria, which explains their current residence in the Munich Glyptothek museum.

There are buses to the temple from Éyina Town, or you could walk from Ayía Marina along the path that takes up where Kolokotroni leaves off, but the best approach is by rented motorbike, which allows you to stop at the monastery of Áyios Nektários, and the island's former capital of Paleohóra.

Áyios Nektários and Paleohóra

Áyios Nektários, a garishly modern monastery situated around halfway to the Temple of Aphaia, was named in honour of a controversial and high-living worthy who died in 1920 and was canonized in 1961, in a highly irregular fashion.

Paleohóra, a kilometre or so further east, was built in the ninth century as protection against piracy, but it failed singularly in this capacity during Barbarossa's 1537 raid. Abandoned in 1826, following Greek independence, Paleohóra is now utterly deserted, but possesses the romantic appeal of a ghost village. You can drive right up to the site: take the turning signposted for Áyios Nektários and keep going about 400m. Some 20 of Paleohóra's reputed 365 churches and monasteries – one for every saint's day – remain in recognizable state, and can be visited, but only those of Episkopí (locked), Áyios Yióryios and Metamórfosis (on the lower of the two trails) retain frescoes of any merit or in any state of preservation. Nothing remains of the town itself; when the islanders left, they simply dismantled their houses and moved them to Éyina Town.

The East: Ayía Marína and Pórtes

The island's major package resort of **AYÍA MARÍNA**, 15km from Éyina Town, lies on the east coast of the island, south of the Aphaia Temple ridge. The concentrated tackiness of its jam-packed high street is something rarely seen this side of Corfu: signs for Guinness, burger bars and salaciously named ice creams and cocktails. The mediocre beach is packed, overlooked by constantly sprouting, half-built hotels, and the water is frankly filthy. In short, it's only worth coming here for the ferries to Pireás (some five a day in season, with departures in the morning and late in the afternoon).

Beyond the resort, the paved road continues south 8km to **PÓRTES**, a pokey, low-key shore hamlet, dramatically set with a cliff on the north and wooded valleys behind. Among the uneasy mix of new summer villas-in-progress (no short-term accommodation) and old basalt cottages are scattered two or three tiny fish **tavernas** and snack bars, with a functional beach between the two fishing anchorages. Soon the road deteriorates to a steep, rough dirt track climbing to the village of Anitséou, just below an important saddle on the flank of Mount Óros. The road surface improves slightly as it forges west towards the scenic hamlet of **Pahiá Ráhi**, where there's a seasonal taverna. From here, a sharp, paved descent leads to the main west-coast road at Marathóna (for which see below), or a longer, gentler route back to Éyina Town. Just past Pahía Ráhi on the latter option is the signposted side-turning for the **nunnery of Hrissoleóndissa**, which can also be reached from the settlements of Yiannákidhes and Lazáridhes to the east.

Mount Óros

Just south of the saddle between Pahiá Ráhi and Anitséou, mentioned above, are the massive foundations of the shrine of **Ellaníou Dhiós**, with the monastery of Taxiárhes squatting amid the massive masonry. The 532m summit of **Mount Óros**, an hour's walk from the highest point of the road, is capped by a chapel and promises views across the entire island and over much of the Argo-Saronic Gulf.

A few **other paths** cross the largely roadless, volcanic flanks of Óros. From **Anitséou** a one-lane tractor track goes southeast, ending after 15 minutes' walk at the six-house hamlet of **Vláhidhes**, below which stretches the small, shingle beach of **Kípi**, most often visited by boats but also accessible by trail from Vláhidhes. Amazingly

FLATTERY WILL GET YOU ROUND THE WORLD!

"The excellence of the TV series is only surpassed by the books. All who have had any involvement in Rough Guides deserve accolades heaped upon them and free beer for life."
Diane Evans, Ontario, Canada

"I've yet to find a presentation style that can match the Rough Guide's. I was very impressed with the amount of detail, ease of reference and the smooth way it swapped from giving sound advice to being entertaining."
Ruth Higginbotham, Bedford, UK

"What an excellent book the Rough Guide was, like having a local showing us round for our first few days."
Andy Leadham, Stoke, UK

"Thank you for putting together such an excellent guidebook. In terms of accuracy and historical/cultural information, it is head and shoulders above the other books."
John Speyer, Yorba Linda, California

"We were absolutely amazed at the mass of detail which the Rough Guide contains. I imagine the word Rough is a deliberate misnomer!"
Rev. Peter McEachran, Aylesbury, UK

"I have rarely, if ever, come across a travel guide quite so informative, practical and accurate! Bravo!"
Alan Dempster, Dublin, Ireland

"The Rough Guide proved to be a very popular and useful book and was often scanned by other travellers whose own guides were not quite so thorough."
Helen Jones, Avon, UK

"My husband and I enjoyed the Rough Guide very much. Not only was it informative, but very helpful and great fun!"
Felice Pomeranz, Massachusetts, USA

"I found the Rough Guide the most valuable thing I took with me – it was fun to read and completely honest about everywhere we visited."
Matthew Rodda, Oxford, UK

"Congratulations on your bible – well worth the money!"
Jenny Angel, New South Wales, Australia

"Our Rough Guide has been as indispensable as the other Rough Guides we have used on our previous journeys."
Enric Torres, Barcelona, Spain

We don't promise the earth, but if your letter is really useful (criticism is welcome as well as praise!), we'll certainly send you a free copy of a Rough Guide. Legibility is a big help and, if you're writing about more than one country, please keep the updates on separate pages. All letters are acknowledged and forwarded to the authors.

Please write, indicating which book you're updating, to:

Rough Guides, 1 Mercer St, London WC2H 9QJ, England
or
Rough Guides, 375 Hudson St, New York, NY 10014-3657, USA

Travel the world
HIV *Safe*

Travel *Safe*

HIV, the virus that causes AIDS, is worldwide.

You're probably aware of the dangers of getting it from unprotected sex, but there are many other risks when travelling.

Wherever you're visiting it makes sense to take precautions. Try to avoid any medical or dental treatment, but if it's necessary, make sure the equipment is sterilised. Likewise, if you really need to have a blood transfusion, always ask for screened blood.

Make sure your travelling companions are aware of the risks and the necessary precautions. In fact, you should take your own sterile medical pack, available from larger high street pharmacies.

Remember, ear and body piercing, acupuncture and even tattoos could be risky, because they all involve puncturing the skin. And although you might not normally consider any of these things now, after a few drinks - you never know.

Of course, the things that are dangerous at home are just as dangerous when you travel. So don't inject drugs or share works.

Avoid casual sex and always use a good quality condom when having sex with a new partner (and each time you have sex with them).

And it's not just a 'gay disease' either. In fact, worldwide, it's most commonly transmitted through sex between men and women.

For information in the UK:

Ring for the TravelSafe leaflet on the Health Literature Line freephone 0800 555 777, or pick one up at a doctor's surgery or pharmacy.

Further advice on HIV and AIDS: National AIDS Helpline: 0800 567 123. (Cannot be reached from abroad).

The Terrence Higgins Trust Helpline (12 noon–1Opm) provides advice and counselling on HIV/AIDS issues: 0171 242 1010.

MASTA Travellers Health Line: 0891 224 100.

Travel *Safe*

Travel the world HIV *Safe*

in this bulldozer-mad country, another path, initially marked by white paint dots to **Sfendhoúri** hamlet southwest of the peak, still survives. Sfendhoúri itself has a road link with Pérdhika (see below); there is also another direct path from near the Zeus temple to Pérdhika, though this is cut across by a new jeep track.

The West: Marathóna, Pérdhika and Moní islet

The road due south of Éyina Town running along the west coast of the island is served by regular buses (8–10 daily). **MARATHÓNA**, 5km from Éyina, constitutes the only sandy-beach resort on the west coast, though tolerable enough, with its clutch of rooms and tavernas along the shore.

PÉRDHIKA, 9km along and the end of the line, is more scenically set on its little bay and certainly has the best range of non-packaged accommodation on the island, besides the main town. There are **rooms**, and the *Hotel Hippocampus* (0297/61 363; ③). On the pedestrianized esplanade overlooking the water are a dozen **tavernas**, the best being *Toh Proreo*, one of the first encountered, and affiliated with an unusual general store, which boasts log-cabin-like decor.

The only other diversion at Pérdhika is a day-trip to **Moní islet** just offshore (250dr one way; 10min; several departures daily). There was once an EOT-run campsite on Móni, but this is now abandoned and derelict. There are no facilities on the islet and most of it is fenced off as a nature conservation area. It's really only worth the trip for a swim in relatively clear water, as Pérdhika bay itself is of dubious cleanliness and has but the smallest of beaches.

Angístri

Angístri, a half-hour by boat from Éyina, is small enough to be overlooked by most island-hoppers, though it's now in many foreign holiday brochures. Thus the island fosters an uneasy coexistence between Athenian and German old-timers, who bought property here years ago, and British newcomers on package trips. Beaches, however, remain better and less crowded than on Éyina, and out of season the pine-covered island succumbs to a leisurely village pace, with many islanders still making a living from fishing and farming. Headscarves worn by the old women indicate the islanders' Albanian ancestry, and among themselves they still speak *Arvanítika*, a dialect of medieval Albanian with Greek accretions – as do the elders of Póros and Méthana (see below).

The Angístri dock in Éyina Town, separate from the main harbour, is directly opposite the *Ethniki Trapeza* (National Bank). **Boats** from Éyina and Pireás call at both the main villages, Skála and Mílos. **From Pireás**, a direct ferry runs at least twice daily in season, once a day out of season: the journey takes two hours. From Éyina (departures from the fish-market harbour), there are boats four or five times a day in season, twice a day out of season.

Skála and Mílos

The essentially modern resort of **SKÁLA** is dominated by dreary modern apartment buildings and hotels with little to distinguish or commend them; they tend to face either inland or the windswept north side of the peninsula over which Skála is rapidly spreading. The popular town beach, the island's only sandy one, nestles against the protected south shore of this headland, below an enormous church that is the local landmark. Between the beach and the ferry dock are two **hotels** with a bit more going for them position-wise: the *Aktaion* (☎0297/91 222; ②–③) and the *Anayennisis* (☎0297/91 332; ②–③); on summer weekends you would be well advised to reserve ahead at one of these. No tavernas demand special recognition. Both **mopeds** and **mountain**

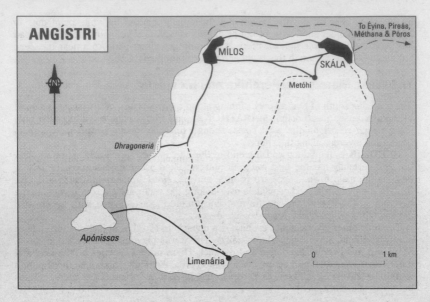

bikes are available for rent at slightly inflated rates (even compared to Éyina); Limenária, the end of the trans-island road, is only 8km distant, so in cooler weather you can comfortably cross Angístri on foot or by pedalling in a couple of hours. A road to the left of the harbour leads within fifteen minutes to the *Angistri Club*, with a disco-bar on the rocks above the sea. From there, it's another ten minutes' walk to a secluded **pebble beach** backed by crumbling cliffs and pine-covered hills; along with Dhragoneriá (see below), this is the best the island has to offer, and is clothing-optional.

Metóhi, the hillside hamlet just above Skála, was once the main village, and in recent years has been completely bought up and restored by foreigners and Athenians; there are no facilities.

Utterly overbuilt Skála threatens in the near future to merge with **MÍLOS**, just 1500m west along the north coast. Once you penetrate a husk of new construction, you find an attractive village centre built in the traditional Argo-Saronic style. Although there's no decent beach nearby, it makes a preferable base to Skála, with plenty of rented **rooms** and some **hotels**. The *Milos Hotel* (☎0297/91 241; ③) is a good, well-positioned choice, and *Ta Tria Adherfia*, in the centre of the village, is the island's best taverna.

The rest of the island

A regular bus service, designed to dovetail with the ferry schedule, connects Skála and Mílos with Limenária on the far side of the island – or you could hike from Metóhi along a winding track through the pine forest, with views across to Éyina and the Peloponnese. The paved west-coast road takes you past the turning for **Dhragoneriá**, an appealing pebble beach with a dramatic backdrop.

LIMENÁRIA is a small farming community, still largely unaffected by tourism. There are two tavernas, a few rooms and a sign pointing to a misleadingly named "beach", which is really just a spot, often monopolized by male naturists, where you can swim off the rocks. A half-hour walk northwest of here, through olive and pine trees, and past a shallow lake, will bring you to a causeway linking Angístri with the tiny islet of **Apónissos**, where there's a seasonal taverna.

Póros

Separated from the mainland by a 350-metre strait, **Póros** ("the ford") only just counts as an island. But qualify it does, making it fair game for the package tours, while its proximity to Pireás also means a weekend invasion by Athenians. Unspoilt it isn't, and the beaches are few and poor, especially compared to neighbouring Ídhra and Spétses. The island town, however, has a bit of character, and the topography is interesting. Póros is in fact two islands, **Sferiá** (which shelters Póros Town) and the more extensive **Kalávria**, separated from each other by a shallow engineered canal. According to one local guide book "the canal reminds you of Venice" – a phrase which must have gained much in the translation.

In addition to its regular ferry and hydrofoil connections with Pireás and the other Argo-Saronics, Póros has frequent boats shuttling across from the mainland port of **Galatás** in the Peloponnese: there's a car ferry every 20 minutes. This allows for some interesting excursions – locally to the lemon groves of **Limonódhassos**, **Ancient Troezen**, near Trizini, and the nearby **Devil's Bridge** (see p.164). Further afield, day-trips to Nápflio or to performances of ancient drama at the great theatre of Epidaurus (see p.160) are possible by car, or by taking an excursion, available from travel agents in Poros Town (see below).

Póros Town

Ferries from the Argo-Saronics or from Galatás drop you at **PÓROS**, the only town on the island, which rises steeply on all sides of the tiny volcanic peninsula of Sferiá. The harbour and town are picturesque from the sea and the cafés and the waterfront have quite an animation about them. There are no special sights, save for a little **archeological museum** (Mon–Sat 9am–3pm; free) with a display on the mainland site of Troezen.

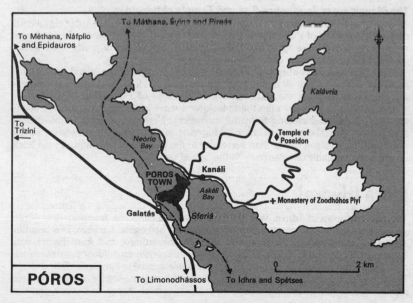

Just back from the waterfront are three **travel agents**: *Marinos Tours* (☎0298/23 423), sole agents for the *Flying Dolphin* hydrofoils, *Family Tours* (☎0298/23 743) and *Saronic Gulf Travel* (☎0298/24 555) all exchange money, sell island maps and arrange accommodation in **rented rooms**. If you want to look around on your own, the quieter and preferable places are in the streets back – and up – from the clocktower, although prices are generally on the high side. Here you'll find two reasonable hotels; *Dimitra* (☎0298/22 697; ④) and *Latsi* (☎0298/22 392; ③). Most of the other hotels are across the canal on Kalávria. Camping is not encouraged anywhere on the island and there is no official campsite.

Down on the quayside, good-value **restaurants** include *Grill Oasis* and *Mouragio*, at the far end away from the ferry dock, while up in the town the *Three Brothers* taverna (open June–Sept) is pricier but recommended.

Additional facilities around the waterfront include a couple of **moped and bicycle rental** outlets (you can take either across on boats to the mainland), a **bank**, **post office**, **tourist police** (☎0298/22 256; mid-May to end Sept) and a **bookstore**, *Anita's* (by the filling station), which trades secondhand paperbacks.

Kalávria

Most of Póros's **hotels** are to be found on Kalávria, the main body of the island, just across the canal beyond the Naval Cadets' Training School. They stretch for two kilometres or so on either side of the bridge, with some of those to the west ideally situated to catch the dawn chorus – the Navy's marching band. If you'd rather sleep on, head beyond the first bay where the fishing boats tie up. Here, on **Neório Bay** 2km from the bridge, is the pleasant *Hotel Pavlou* (☎0298/22 734; ③).

Alternatively, turn right around **Askéli Bay**, where there is a group of hotels and villas facing good clear water, if not much in the way of beaches. The best island beach is **Kanáli**, near the beginning of the bridge, which usually charges admission – a reflection both of Póros's commercialism and the premium on sand.

The Monastery of Zoodhóhos Piyí and Temple of Poseidon
At the end of the four-kilometre stretch of road around Askéli is the simple eighteenth-century **Monastery of Zoodhóhos Piyí**, whose monks have fled the tourists and been replaced by a caretaker to collect the admission charges. It's a pretty spot, with a couple of summer tavernas under the nearby plane trees.

From here you can either walk up across to the far side of the island through the pines and olives, or bike along the road. Either route will lead you to the few columns and ruins that make up the sixth-century BC **Temple of Poseidon** – though keep your eyes open or you may miss them; look for a small white sign on a green fence to the right of the road coming from the monastery. Here, supposedly, Demosthenes, fleeing from the Macedonians after taking part in the last-ditch resistance of the Athenians, took poison rather than surrender to the posse sent after him. A road leads on and back down in a circular route to the "grand canal".

Ídhra (Hydra)

The port and town of **Ídhra**, with its tiers of substantial stone mansions and white-walled, red-tiled houses climbing up from a perfect horseshoe harbour, is a beautiful spectacle. Unfortunately, thousands of others think so, too, and from Easter until September it's packed to the gills. The front becomes one long outdoor café, the hotels are full and the discos flourish. Once a fashionable artists' colony, established in the 1960s as people restored the grand old houses, it has experienced a predictable metamorphosis into one of the more popular (and expensive) resorts in Greece. But this

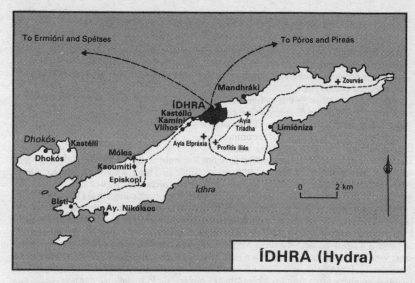

ÍDHRA (Hydra)

acknowledged, a visit is still to be recommended, especially if you can get here some time other than peak season.

Ídhra Town

The waterfront of **ÍDHRA TOWN** is lined with mansions, most of them built during the eighteenth century, on the accumulated wealth of a remarkable merchant fleet of 160 ships which traded as far afield as America and, during the Napoleonic Wars, broke the British blockade to sell grain to France. Fortunes were made and the island also enjoyed a special relationship with the Turkish Porte, governing itself, paying no tax, but providing sailors for the Sultan's navy. These conditions naturally attracted Greek immigrants from the less-privileged mainland, and by the 1820s the town's population stood at nearly 20,000, an incredible figure when you reflect that today it is under 3000. During the War of Independence, Hydriot merchants provided many of the ships for the Greek forces and inevitably many of the commanders.

The **mansions** of these merchant families, designed by architects from Venice and Genoa, are still the great monuments of the town. If you are interested in seeking them out, a town map is available locally – or ask the tourist police (see below) for help in locating them. On the western waterfront, and the hill behind, are the **Voulgaris** mansion, with its interesting interior, and the **Tombazis** mansion, used as a holiday hostel for arts students. Higher up, the **Koundouriotis** mansion was once the proud home of George Koundouriotis, a wealthy shipowner who fought in the War of Independence and whose great grandson, Pavlos Koundouriotis, was president of Greece in the 1920s. On the eastern waterfront are the **Kriezis** mansion, the **Tsamados** mansion, now the national merchant navy college which you can visit between lectures, and the **Spiliopoulous** mansion.

Ídhra is also reputedly hallowed by no less than 365 churches – a total claimed by many a Greek island, but here with some justice. The most important is the cathedral of **Panayía Mitropóleos**, built around a courtyard down by the port, and with a distinctive clocktower.

> ### THE MIAOULIA FESTIVAL
>
> On the second or third weekend in June, Ídhra Town celebrates the Miaoulia, in honour of Admiral Andreas Miaoulis whose "fire boats", packed with explosives, were set adrift upwind of the Turkish fleet during the War of Independence. The highlight of the celebrations is the burning of a boat at sea as a tribute to the sailors who risked their lives in this dangerous enterprise.
>
> On an altogether more peaceful note, the International Puppet Theatre Festival takes place here at the end of July, and appeals to children of all ages.

Practicalities

The town is small and compact, but away from the waterfront the streets and alleyways are steep and finding your way around can be difficult. There are several **banks** along the waterfront, the *National Bank* is close to Miaouli; the **tourist police** (☎0298/52 205; mid-May to mid-October, daily 9am–10pm) are on Votsi, oppposite the OTE.

Staying on Ídhra means finding a room in the town or, if you're lucky, at Vlihós (see below). There are a number of **pensions and hotels** along, or just behind, the waterfront, often charging up to a third more than usual island rates. Some of the restaurants along the waterfront act as agents for the outlying pensions and hotels, which could save you time and footwork; better still, phone ahead and book. *Hotel Amarylis* at Tombazi 15 (☎0298/53 611; ③) is a small hotel with comfortable rooms and private facilities, or there are a couple of beautifully converted old mansions, *Pension Angelika*, Miaouli 42 (☎0298/52 202; ④) and *Hotel Hydra*, at Voulgari 8 (☎0298/52 102; ④). On the waterfront, but entered from Miaouli, is the slightly rundown but very welcoming *Hotel Sofia* (☎0298/52 313; ②).

There's no shortage of **restaurants** around the waterfront. *Ta Tria Adhelfia* is a good, inexpensive, friendly taverna next to the cathedral. The *Ambrosia Café*, back from the front, serves vegetarian meals and excellent breakfasts, and the new *Veranda Restaurant* (below the *Hotel Hydra*) has stunning views of the sunset. For nightlife, try the **discos** *Heaven*, with impressive views from its hillside site, or the long-established *Kavos*, above the harbour, with a garden for dance breaks.

Beaches around Ídhra Town

The island's only sandy beach is at **MANDHRÁKI**, 2km east of Ídhra Town along a concrete track; it's the private domain of the *Miramare Hotel* (☎0298/52 300; ⑥), although the windsurfing centre is open to all.

On the opposite side of the harbour a coastal path leads around to a pebbly but popular stretch, just before **KAMÍNI**, where there's a good year-round taverna, *George and Anna's*. Continuing along the water on an unsurfaced mule track you'll come to **KASTÉLLO**, another small, rocky beach with the ruins of a tiny fort.

Thirty minutes' walk beyond Kamíni (or a boat ride from the port) will bring you to **VLIHÓS**, a small hamlet with three tavernas, **rooms** and a historic nineteenth-century bridge. **Camping** is tolerated here (though nowhere else closer to town) and the swimming in the lee of an offshore islet is good. Further out is the islet of **Dhokós**, only seasonally inhabited by goatherds and people tending their olives.

The interior and south coast

There are no motor vehicles of any kind on Ídhra, except for two lorries to pick up the rubbish, and no metalled roads away from the port, for the island is mountainous and its interior accessible only by foot or donkey. The net result of this is that most tourists don't venture beyond the town, so with a little walking you can find yourself in a quite different kind of island. A dampener on this is that the pines that formerly covered the island were devastated by forest fires in 1985 and are still recovering.

Following the streets of the town upwards and inland you reach a path which winds up the mountain, in about an hour's walk, to the **Monastery of Profítis Ilías** and the **Convent of Ayía Efpraxía**. Both are beautifully situated; the nuns at the convent (the lower of the two) offer hand-woven fabrics for sale. Further on, to the left if you face away from the town, is the **Monastery of Ayía Triádha**, occupied by a few monks (no women admitted). From here a path continues east for two more hours to the cloister of **Zourvás** in the extreme east of the island.

The donkey path continues west of Vlíhos to **Episkopí**, a high plateau planted with olives and vineyards and dotted by perhaps a dozen summer homes (no facilities). An inconspicuous turning roughly half an hour below leads to Mólos Bay, dirty and sea-urchin-infested, and to the more pleasant farming hamlet of **KAOUMÍTI**. From Episkopí itself faint tracks lead to the western extreme of the island, on either side of which the bays of **BÍSTI** and **ÁYIOS NIKÓLAOS** offer solitude and good swimming.

The south coast, too, if you're energetic and armed with a map, is scattered with coves, the best of which, **LIMIÓNIZA** (beyond Ayía Triádha), is also served by **boat excursions** in season from Ídhra Town.

Spétses (Spetsai)

Spétses was the island where John Fowles once lived and which he used, thinly disguised as Phraxos, as the setting for *The Magus*. It is today very popular, with signs for fast food and English breakfasts lining rather too many of the old town lanes. However, as a whole, the island clings onto its charms quite tenaciously. The architecture of Spétses Town is characterful and distinguished, if less dramatic than that of Ídhra. And, despite a bout of forest fire devastation in 1990, the landscape described by Fowles is still to be seen: "away from its inhabited corner [it is] truly haunted . . . its pine forests uncanny". Remarkably, too, at Spétses's best beach (and arguably the best in the Argo-Saronic), Áyii Anáryiri, development has been limited to a scattering of holiday villas.

Spétses Town

SPÉTSES TOWN (also known as Kastélli) is the island's port – and its only town. It shares with Ídhra the same history of late eighteenth-century mercantile adventure and prosperity, and the same leading role in the War of Independence, which made its foremost citizens the aristocrats of the newly independent Greek state. Pebble-mosaic courtyards and streets sprawl between 200-year-old mansions, whose architecture is quite distinct from the Peloponnesian styles across the straits. As on Ídhra, there are no private cars; horse-drawn cabs connect the various quarters of town, which are strung out along the waterfront.

The sights are principally the majestic old houses and gardens, the finest of which is the magnificent Mexis family mansion, built in 1795 and now used as the **local museum** (daily except Mon 8.30am–2.30pm; 400dr), housing a display of relics from the War of Independence that includes the bones of the Spetsiot admiral-heroine Lascarina Bouboulina.

Just outside the town, Fowles aficionados will notice **Anáryiros College**, a curious Greek recreation of an English public school where the author was employed and set part of his tale; it is now vacant, save for the occasional conference or kids' holiday programme. Like the massive Edwardian **Hotel Possidonion**, another *Magus* setting, on the waterside, it was endowed by Sotirios Anáryiros, the island's great nineteenth-

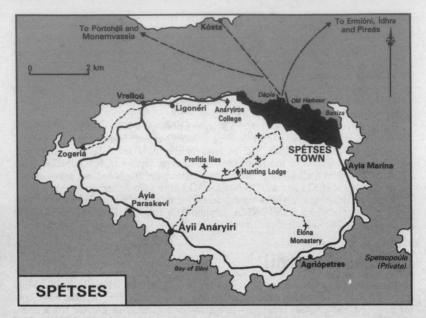

SPÉTSES

century benefactor. An enormously rich self-made man he was also responsible for planting the pine forest that now covers the island. His former house, behind the *Hotel Roumani*, is a monument to bad taste, decked out like a pharaoh's tomb.

Perhaps more interesting than chasing *Magus* settings, though, is a walk east from the **Dápia**, the cannon-studded main harbour. En route, you pass the smaller "old harbour", where the Athenian rich moor their yachts, and the church of **Áyios Nikólaos** with its graceful belfry and some giant pebble mosaics. At the end of the road you reach the **Baltíza** inlet, where half a dozen boatyards continue to build *kaíkia* in the traditional manner; it was one of these that recreated the *Argo* for Tim Severin's re-enactment of the "Jason Voyage".

Practicalities

A good way to get around the island is by bike and, despite the poor roads, you can reach most points or make a circuit without too much exertion. The most reliable of the **bike and moped rental outlets** is on the road to the old harbour, past the *Rendez-vous* bar.

All kinds of **accommodation** are available in Spétses Town, from the unmissable and unforgettable *Hotel Possidonion* (☎0298/72 208; ⑥; slightly cheaper rooms at the back), where kings and presidents have slept, to more modest **rooms**. Prices are inflated in high season, but the town is smaller and less steep than Ídhra, so hunting around for a good deal is not such hard work. If you don't fancy pounding the streets yourself, try *Pine Island Travel* (☎0298/72 314) or *Meldon Tourist and Travel Agency* (☎0298/74 497), both within 50m of the jetty. Two simple but comfortable places are *Faros* (☎0298/72 613; ④) and *Stelios* (☎0298/72 971; ③). Few places stay open all year – exceptions include the central *Pension Alexandris* (☎0298/72 211; ④) and the *Klimis Hotel* (☎0298/74 497; ④), a quiet and pleasant place run by a formidable matriarch.

In Spétses Town, **food and drink** tend to be a bit on the pricey side. Best options along the waterfront are *Roussos* (formerly *Ta Tzakia*), 300m to the left of the Dápia, and *Taverna Haralambos,* on Baltíza inlet, by the smaller harbour. The only traditional taverna is *Lazaros'* (400m inland and uphill from Dápia: ask for directions), though it can't cope with large parties. For a splurge, try *Trehandiri,* next to the church of Áyios Nikólaos on the way to the old harbour; it's the best of an expensive group of restaurants there. Vegetarian meals are available at *Lirakis,* a rooftop restaurant on the waterfront.

By day, Stambolis's *kafenío,* by the *Flying Dolphin* quay at Dápia, remains steadfastly traditional. By night, clubbers divide between the **discos** *Coconuts* and *Figaro* – the latter being the summer base of DJs from the trendy Athenian club *Papagayo.*

Spétses has a couple of good **crafts shops,** *Pityousa* (behind the *Hotel Soleil*) and *Gorgona,* opposite; both are upmarket establishments and offer some attractive original work, as well as genuine pieces from the Pireás antique markets.

Around the island

For **swimming** you need to get clear of the town. Beaches within walking distance are at **Ayía Marína** (twenty minutes east, with a taverna), at various spots beyond the **old harbour,** and several other spots half an hour away in either direction. The tempting islet of **Spetsopoúla,** just offshore from Ayía Marína, is, unfortunately, off-limits. It's the private property of shipping magnate Stavros Niarchos, of dubious repute, who maintains it as a pleasure park for his associates; his yacht (the largest in Greece) can sometimes be seen moored offshore.

For heading further afield, you'll need to hire a **bike or moped,** or use the **kaíkia** rides from the Dápia, which run to beaches around the island in summer. A very expensive alternative are the **waterboat taxis,** though they can take up to ten people. **Walkers** might want to go over the top of the island to Áyii Anáryiri, though this is not so fine a walk since the forest fire, which destroyed most of the pines between Ayía Marína and Áyii Anáryiri. The route out of town starts from behind *Lazaros' Taverna.*

West from Spétses Town

Heading west from the Dápia around the coast, the road is paved until the houses run out after a kilometre or so; thereafter it is a dirt track which winds through pine trees and around inlets. The forest stretches from the central hills right down to the shore and it makes for a beautiful coastline with little coves and rocky promontories, all shaded by trees.

VRELLOÚ is one of the first places you come to, at the mouth of a wooded valley known locally as "Paradise", which would be a fairly apt description, except that, like so many of the beaches, it becomes polluted every year by tourists' rubbish. However, the entire shore is dotted with coves and in a few places there are small tavernas – a good one at **ZOGERIÁ,** for instance, where the scenery and rocks more than make up for the inadequate little beach.

Working your way anti-clockwise around the coast towards Áyii Anáryiri you reach **ÁYIA PARASKEVÍ** with its small church and beach – one of the most beautiful coves on Spétses and an alternate stop on some of the *kaíki* runs. There's a basic beach café here in summer. On the hill above is the house John Fowles used as the setting for *The Magus,* the **Villa Yasemia.** It was once owned by the late Alkis Botassis, who claimed to be the model for the *Magus* character – though Fowles denies "appropriating" anything more than his "outward appearance" and the "superb site" of his house.

Áyii Anáryiri

Áyii Anáryiri, on the south side of the island, is the best, if also the most popular, beach: a beautiful, long, sheltered bay of fine sand. Gorgeous first thing in the morning, it fills up later in the day, with bathers, windsurfers and rather manic speedboat-driving waterski instructors. On the right-hand side of the bay, looking out to sea, there's a sea cave, which you can swim out to and explore within. There's a self-service taverna on the beach and, just behind, *Tassos'*, Spétses' finest (and a well-priced) eating establishment: a meal here, prepared with real care and enthusiasm, is not to be missed.

The road and coves continue **east of Áyii Anáryiri**, though often at some distance from each other until you loop back to Ayía Marína.

travel details

Ferries

From the central harbour at **Pireás** at least 4 boats daily run to Ayía Marína (1hr) and 11 to Éyina (1hr 30min); 1–2 daily to Skála and Mílos (2hr); 4 daily to Póros (3hr 30min); 1–2 daily to Ídhra (4hr 30min) and Spétses (5hr 30min). About 4 connections daily between Éyina and Póros; 4–5 daily between Éyina and Angístri; from Angístri about 4 weekly to Paleá Epídhavros, far less frequently to Póros and Méthana.

Most of the ferries stop on the mainland at Méthana (between Éyina and Póros) and Ermióni (between Ídhra and Spétses); it is possible to board them here from the Peloponnese. Some continue from Spétses to Portohéli. There are also constant boats between Póros and Galatás (10min) from dawn until late at night, and boat-taxis between Spétses and Portohéli.

NB There are more ferries at weekends and fewer out of season (although the service remains good); for Éyina and Póros they leave Pireás most frequently between 7.30am and 9am, and 2pm and 4pm. Do not buy a return ticket as it saves no money and limits you to one specific boat. The general information number for the Argo-Saronic ferries is ☎01/41 75 382 or 42 94 533.

Flying Dolphin hydrofoils

Approximately hourly services from the central harbour at Pireás to **Éyina** only 6am–8pm in season, 7am–5pm out (40min).

All hydrofoils going beyond Éyina leave from the **Zea Marina**: 4–15 times daily to Póros (1hr), Ídhra (1hr 40min), and Spétses (2–2hr 30min). All these times depend upon the stops en route, and frequencies vary with the season.

Éyina is connected with the other three islands twice a day; Póros, Ídhra and Spétses with each other 3–5 times daily. Some hydrofoils also stop at Méthana and Ermióni and all of those to Spétses continue to Portohéli (15min more). This is a junction of the hydrofoil route – there is usually one a day onwards to Toló and Náfplio (and vice versa; 30 and 45min) in season and another (almost year-round) to Monemvassía (2hr). The Monemvassía hydrofoil continues 2–4 times a week to the island of Kíthira.

NB Once again services are heavily reduced out of season, though all the routes between Portohéli and Pireás still run. Hydrofoils are usually twice as fast and twice as expensive as ordinary boats, though to Éyina the price is little different. You can now buy round-trip tickets, so if you need to return on a certain day buy your ticket back when purchasing your outbound leg. In season, it's not unusual for departures to be fully booked for a day or so at a time.

Details and tickets available from the Pireás ticket office at Ákti Themistokléous 8 (☎01/42 80 001, perennially engaged; if you can, try the fax ☎42 83 526). Tickets can also be bought at the departure quays on Aktí Tsélepi in Pireás and at Zéa.

CHAPTER SEVEN

THE CYCLADES

Named for the circle they form around the sacred island of Delos, the **Cyclades** (*Kikládhes*) is the most satisfying Greek archipelago for island-hopping. On no other group do you get quite such a strong feeling of each island as a microcosm, each with its own distinct traditions, customs and path of modern development. Most of these self-contained realms are compact enough to walk around in a few days, giving you a sense of completeness and identity impossible on, say, Crete or most of the Ionian islands.

There is some unity. The majority of the islands – Ándhros, Náxos, Sérifos and Kéa notably excepted – are both arid and rocky, and most share the "Cycladic" style of brilliant-white, cubist architecture. The extent and impact of tourism, however, is markedly haphazard, so that although some English is spoken on most islands, a slight detour from the beaten track – from Íos to Síkinos, for example – can have you groping for your Greek phrasebook.

But whatever the level of tourist development, there are only two islands where it has come completely to dominate their character: **Íos**, the original hippie-island and still a paradise for hard-drinking backpackers, and **Míkonos**, by far the most popular of the group, with its teeming old town, selection of nude beaches and sophisticated clubs and gay bars. After these two, **Páros**, **Sífnos**, **Náxos**, and **Thíra** (Santoríni) are currently the most popular, with their beaches and main towns drastically overcrowded at the height of the season. To avoid the hordes altogether – except in August, when nearly everywhere is overrun and escape is impossible – the most promising islands are Síkinos, Kímolos or Anáfi, or even (going to extremes) the minor islets around Náxos. For a different view of the Cyclades, visit **Tínos** and its imposing pilgrimage church, a major spiritual centre of Greek Orthodoxy, or **Síros** with its elegant townscape, and (like Tínos), large Catholic minority. Due to their closeness to Athens, adjacent **Kíthnos** and **Kéa** are predictably popular – and relatively expensive – weekend havens for Greeks. The one major ancient site is **Delos** (Dhílos), certainly worth making time for: the commercial and religious centre of the Classical Greek world, it's visited most easily on a day trip, by *kaíki* or jet boat from Míkonos.

When it comes to **moving on**, many of the islands – in particular Mílos, Páros, Náxos and Thíra – are handily connected with Crete (easier in season), while from Tínos, Míkonos, Síros, Páros, Náxos, Thíra or Amorgós you can reach many of the Dodecanese by direct boat. Similarly, you can regularly get from Míkonos, Náxos, Síros and Páros to Ikaría and Sámos (in the eastern Aegean – see pp.597 and 609), and there is even a weekly connection from several of the most central Cyclades to Náfplio on the Peloponnese.

Another consideration for the timing of your visit is that the Cyclades often get frustratingly **stormy**, particularly in early spring or late autumn, and it's also the group worst affected by the *meltémi*, which blows sand and tables about with equal ease throughout much of July and August. Delayed or cancelled ferries are not uncommon, so if you're heading back to Athens to catch a flight leave yourself a day or two's leeway.

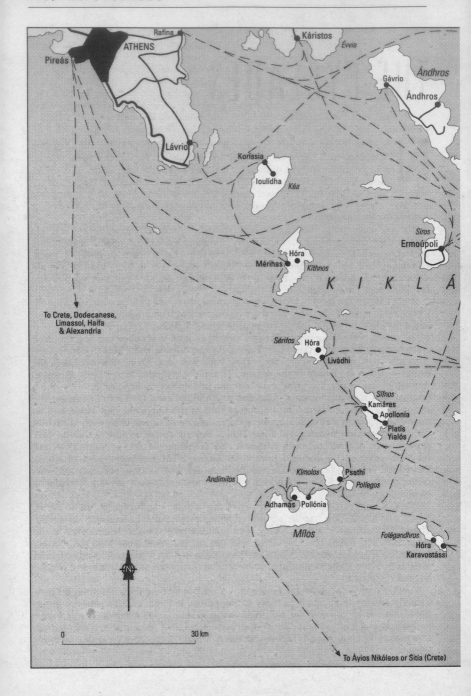

Rafina

Káristos

Évvia

ATHENS

Pireás

Gávrio

Ándhros

Ándhros

Lávrio

Korissia

Ioulídha *Kéa*

Síros

Ermoúpoli

Hóra

Mérihas *Kíthnos*

K I K L Á

To Crete, Dodecanese,
Limassol, Haifa
& Alexandria

Sérifos Hóra

Livádhi

Sífnos
Kamáres
Apollonia

Platís
Yialós

Kímolos Psathí

Andímilos *Políegos*

Adhamás Pollónia

Mílos

Folégandhros
Hóra
Karavostássi

0   30 km

To Áyios Nikólaos or Sitía (Crete)

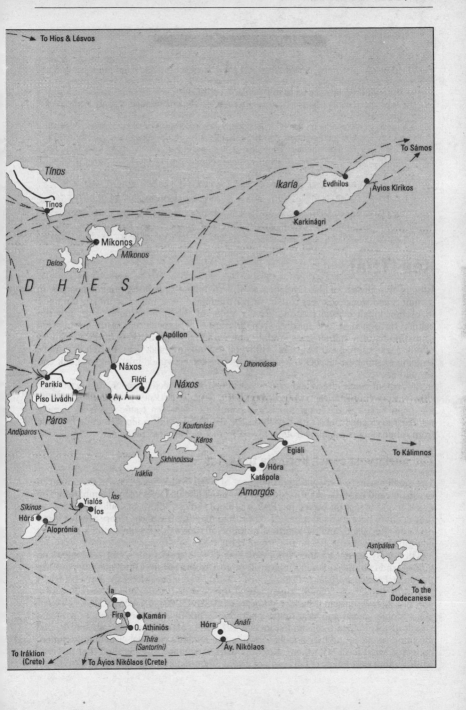

Kéa (Tziá)

Kéa is the closest of the Cyclades to the mainland and is extremely popular in summer, and weekends year-round, with Athenians. Their impact is mostly confined to certain small coastal resorts, leaving most of the interior quiet, although the vistors' presence is felt in the preponderance of expensive apartment or villa accommodation – and a corresponding abundance of supermarkets to the detriment of any remarkably good tavernas. Midweek, or outside peak season, Kéa is a more enticing destination, its rocky, forbidding perimeter enlivened inland by vast oak and almond groves.

As ancient Keos, the island and its strategic well-placed harbour supported four cities – a pre-eminence that continued until the nineteenth century when Síros became the main Greek port. Today tourists account for what sea traffic there is, namely regular ferry connections with Lávrio on the mainland – only a ninety-minute bus ride from Athens – plus useful hydrofoils to and from Zéa, Kíthnos and Rafína.

The northwest coast: Korissía to Otziás

The small northern ferry and hydrofoil port of **KORISSÍA** has fallen victim to uneven expansion and has little beauty to lose; if you don't like its looks upon disembarking, be quick to get a seat on **buses** for Písses (16km), Otziás (6km) or Ioulídha (6km), as they seem to have no fixed schedule other than meeting the boats. There are just three **taxis** on the island, and an identical number of **motorbike-rental** outfits, the latter charging nearly double the normal island rates.

The kindly agents for the *Flying Dolphins* (*Toh Stegadhi* gift shop) sell maps and guides, and can phone around in search of **accommodation**. Three good options are the quiet *Pension Korissia* (☎0288/21 484; ③–④), well inland along the stream bed; *Iy Tzia Mas* (☎0288/21 305; ④), right behind the best end of the otherwise uninspiring port beach; and the somewhat noisy *Karthea* (☎0288/21 204; ③), which does, however, boast single rooms and year-round operation – and a cameo appearance in recent Greek history. When the junta fell in July 1974, the colonels were initially imprisoned for some weeks in the then-new hotel while the recently restored civilian government pondered what to do with them; Kéa was then so remote and unvisited that the erstwhile tyrants were safely out of reach of a vengeful populace.

VOURKÁRI, a couple of kilometres north, is more compact and arguably more attractive than Korissía, serving as the favourite hangout of the well-heeled yachting set. There's no beach to speak of, and little accommodation, merely three fairly expensive and indistinguishable **tavernas** that are better for a seafood treat than ordinary dishes, and the *Vinylio* **bar**, popular with an older crowd. Swimming is better at **Yialiskári**, a small, eucalyptus-fringed beach about halfway back towards Korissía. Across the bay from Vourkári, on a promontory, the Minoan site of **Ayía Iríni** was excavated during the 1960s to reveal the remains of a small settlement, temple and road. There is currently no admission to the public, but you can glimpse the essentials through the perimeter fence.

Another 3km along, **OTZIÁS** has a small beach that's a bit better than that at Korissía, though more exposed to prevailing winds; facilities are limited to a pair of tavernas and a fair number of *garsoniéres* (self-catering units) for rent. Kéa's only functioning monastery, the eighteenth-century **Panayía Kastrianí**, can be reached along a dirt road from Otziás in an hour's walk, or ten minutes by bike. Although more remarkable for its fine setting on a high bluff than for any intrinsic interest, from here you can easily and pleasantly walk on to the island capital, Ioulídha, in another two hours.

Ioulídha

IOULÍDHA, the ancient Ioulis and birthplace of the renowned early fifth-century BC poets Simonides and Bacchylides, is more usually reached directly from Korissía. With its numerous red-tiled roofs Ioulídha is by no means a typical Cycladic village, but it is beautifully situated in an amphitheatric fold in the hills, and architecturally the most interesting spot on the island. Accordingly it has "arrived" in recent years, with numerous, increasingly trendy bars and bistros well patronized on weekends. The lower reaches stretch across a spur to the **Kástro**, a tumbledown Venetian fortress incorporating stones from an ancient temple of Apollo. Fifteen minutes' walk northeast of town, on the path toward Panayía Kastrianí, you pass the **Lion of Kea**, a sixth-centuryBC sculpture carved out of the living rock. Six metres long and two high (at the head), it's an imposing beast, with crudely powerful haunches and a bizarre facial expression. There are steps right down to it, but the effect is most striking from a distance. Back in town, the **Archeological Museum** (daily except Mon 8.30am–3pm; free) displays finds from the four ancient city-states of Kéa, though sadly, the best items were long ago spirited away to Athens.

Practicalities

There are two rather dissimilar **hotels** in Ioulídha, either of them quieter than anything down in Korissía, and both much in demand: the somewhat pokey *Filoxenia* (☎0288/22 057; ③), engagingly perched above the shoeshop, but with no en-suite plumbing and saggy beds; or the more comfortable *Ioulis* (☎0288/22 177; ④) up in the *kástro*, with superb views from its terrace and west-facing rooms.

You're spoilt for choice in the matter of **eating and drinking**, with quality generally higher here than near Korissía. The old standby tavernas *Iy Piatsa* and *Iy Ioulídha* – the latter, on the main *platía*, with exceptionally palatable and potent local wine – have recently been joined by *Toh Steki tis Tzias*, serving no-nonsense oven food on a terrace, and an as-yet-unnamed but highly regarded *ouzerí* uphill from (and owned by) the pharmacy; to find it, follow the steps you come to before the arcade that leads into the village centre. The aptly named *Panorama* is the place to linger over a sunset pastry and coffee, while after-dark action seems to oscillate between such bars as *Kamini*, *Leon* and *Kouiz*. Finally, an **OTE**, **post office** and **bank agent** round out the list of amenities.

The south

About 8km southwest of Ioulídha, reached via a mix of tracks and paths, or by mostly paved road, the crumbling Hellenistic watchtower of **Ayía Marína** sprouts dramatically from the grounds of a small nineteenth-century monastery. Beyond, the paved main road twists around the dramatically scenic head of the lovely agricultural valley at **PÍSSES**, emerging at a large and little-developed beach, albeit of middling cleanliness and with little shade. There are three tavernas behind, plus a pleasant **campsite** (☎0288/31 335) with turfy ground for tents. More substantial development inland consists of studios (☎0288/31 302; ④) lining the access road.

Beyond Písses, road paving – and bus service – fizzles out along the 5km south to **KOÚNDOUROS**, a sheltered, convoluted bay popular with yachters; there's a single taverna behind the largest of several sandy coves, none cleaner or bigger than the beach at Písses. The luxury *Kea Beach* hotel sits out on its own promontory with tennis courts and pool, but the latest curiosity hereabouts is the hamlet of dummy windmills; built as holiday homes, they are "authentic" right down to the masts, thatching and stone cladding.

Besides the very scant ruins of ancient Poiessa near Písses, the only remains of any real significance from Kéa's past are at **ancient Karthaia**, tucked away on the southeastern edge of the island above Póles Bay, and easiest reached by boat. Otherwise, it's a good three hours' round-trip walk from the hamlet of Stavroudháki, some way off the lower road linking Koúndouros, Hávouna and Káto Meriá. Travelling by motorbike, the upper road, which more directly plies between Písses and Káto Meriá, is worth following as an alternative return along the island's summit to Ioulídha; it's paved once you get to Elliniká, and the entire way affords fine views, not least over the thousands of magnificent oaks which constitute Kéa's most distinctive feature.

Kíthnos (Thermiá)

Though perhaps the dullest and certainly the most barren of the Cyclades, a short stay on **Kíthnos** is a good antidote to the exploitation likely to be encountered elsewhere. Few foreigners bother to visit; the island is quieter than Kéa, even in midsummer; while the inhabitants (except in more commercialized Mérihas) are overtly friendly – all factors that compensate for the paucity of specific diversions. Like Kéa, it's a place where Athenians

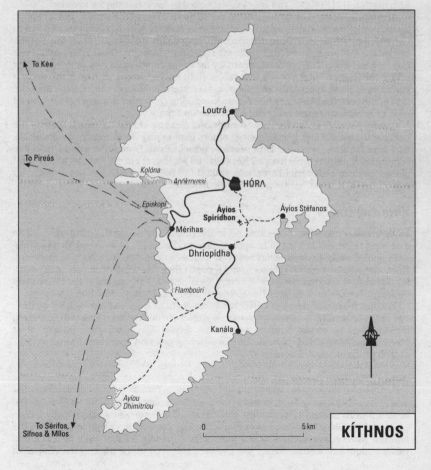

come to buy land for villas, go spear-fishing and sprawl on generally mediocre beaches without having to jostle mass-tourism clients for space. You could use it as a first or, better, last island stop: there are weekly ferry connections with Kéa, more frequent services to and from Sérifos, Sífnos and Mílos, as well as seasonal hydrofoils to Kéa, Zéa and Rafína.

Mérihas and around

In good weather boats dock on the west coast at **MÉRIHAS**, a rather functional ferry and fishing port with most of the island's facilities. This fact almost obliges you to stay here, and makes Mérihas something of a tourist ghetto, but it's redeemed by proximity to the island's best beaches. The closest beach of any repute is **Episkopí**, a stretch of 500m of averagely clean grey sand, with a single taverna, forty minutes' walk north of the town; you can shorten this considerably by sticking to coast-hugging trails and tracks below the road. Far better are the adjacent beaches of **Apókroussi** and **Kolóna**, the latter essentially a sandspit joining the islet of Áyios Loukás to Kíthnos. They lie more than an hour's walk northwest of Episkopí, and are easiest reached by boat-trip from the harbour.

Accommodation proprietors tend to come down to meet the ferries, and a relative abundance of rooms makes for lower prices than on Kéa. Aim to bargain them down to the mid-③ range for something in a garden setting south of the small, gritty town beach behind the (not recommended) *Posidhonio Hotel*; few places have sea views. Studios can also be good value. The best **restaurant** by far is *Toh Kandouni*, a reasonable and tasty grill at the west end of the beach with tables right on the water – or even in the water if you're so inclined; specialities include *sfougáto* fritters and island wine. On the opposite side of the port, the blue-and-white *Kafezaharoplastio O Merihas* is a strategically placed spot for breakfast or some cake, and has rooms upstairs.

Among purveyors of a very modest **nightlife**, *Remezzo* behind the beach is about the best bar in terms of location and music; others tend to play Frank Sinatra covers of *The Girl from Ipanema*, or worse. **Bus service**, principally to Loutrá, Hóra and Driopídha, is marginally more reliable than on Kéa, but still elusive; there are just two **bike-rental** places, one run by Katerini Larentzaki (☎0281/32 248), who also has some rooms. In season, an **OTE** booth functions behind the *Remezzo*.

Hóra and Loutrá

HÓRA is 6km northeast of Mérihas, set in the middle of the island. Tilting south off an east–west ridge, and laid out to an approximate grid plan, it's an awkward blend of Kéa-style gabled roofs, Cycladic churches with dunce-cap cupolas, and concrete monsters. Hóra supports the main **OTE** branch, and a **post office** (the latter open only until noon), but the closest accommodation is at Loutrá (see below). You can **eat** at the taverna run by *Marya Tzoyiou*, or at the grill *Toh Steki*, and there's a single outdoor **bar**, *Apokalypsi*.

The much-vaunted resort of **LOUTRÁ** (3km north of Hóra and named after its thermal baths) is scruffy, its nineteenth-century spa long since replaced by a sterile modern construction. In certain weather conditions, ferries may dock here instead of at Mérihas; facilities include tavernas on the beach, a **pension** (the *Porto Klaras*; ☎0281/ 31 276; ③) and a few rooms to let.

Driopídha and the south

You're handily placed in Hóra to tackle the most interesting thing to do on Kíthnos: the beautiful **walk south** to Dhriopídha. It takes about an hour and a half, initially following the old cobbled way that leaves Hóra heading due south; critical junctions in the first few minutes are marked by red paint dots. The only reliable water is a well in a valley bottom half an hour along, just before a side trail to the triple-naved **chapel of**

Áyios Sprídhon with recycled Byzantine columns. Just beyond this, you collide with a bulldozed track between Dhriopídha and Áyios Stéfanos, but purists can avoid this by bearing west toward some ruined ridgetop windmills, and picking up secondary paths for the final forty minutes of the hike.

More appealing than Hóra by virtue of spanning a ravine, **DHRIOPÍDHA**'s pleasing tiled roofs are reminiscent of Spain or Tuscany. A surprisingly large place, it was once the island's capital, built around a famous cave, the Katafíki, at the head of a well-watered valley. Behind the main cathedral, there is a single **taverna**, *Iy Pelegra*, serving cheap grills, salad and beer only. For the closest **accommodation**, you must head 6km south to **KANÁLA**, basically some twenty non-descript houses and a church on a sea-washed headland, with tavernas and rooms to rent in season.

From Kanála, a succession of small coves extends up the east coast as far as **ÁYIOS STÉFANOS**, a small coastal hamlet with no facilities opposite a chapel-crowned islet tied by causeway to the body of the island. Southwest of Driopídha, reached by a turning off the road to Kanála, **Flamboúri** is the most presentable beach on the west coast; the double bay of **Ayíou Dhimitríou**, at the extreme southern tip of the island, and reached over a rough road, is not worth the effort.

Sérifos

Sérifos has languished outside the mainstream of history and modern tourism. Little has happened here since the legendary Perseus returned with the Gorgon's head in time to save his mother Danaë from being ravished by the local king Polydectes. Many would-be visitors are deterred by the apparently barren, hilly interior which, with the stark, rocky coastline, makes Sérifos appear uninhabited until your ferry turns into Livádhi bay. The island is recommended for serious walkers, who can head for several small villages and isolated coves in the little-explored interior. Modern Serifots love seclusion, and here, more than anywhere else in the Cyclades, you will find farmsteads miles from anywhere, with only a donkey path to their door. Everyone here seems to keep livestock, and to produce their own wines, and many also cultivate the wild narcissus for the export market.

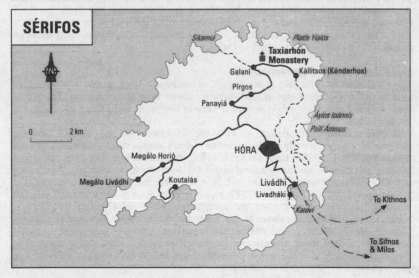

Few islanders speak much English, and many have a deserved reputation of being slow to warm to outsiders. One suspects that the locals still don't quite know what to make of the hordes of trendy northern Europeans who descend on the place for a brief but intense July and August season. American yachties drop anchor here in some numbers as well, to take on fresh water which, despite appearances, Sérifos has in abundance.

Livádhi and the main beaches

Most visitors stay in the port, **LIVÁDHI**, set in a wide greenery-fringed bay and handy for most of the island's beaches. The usually calm bay here is a magnet for island-hopping yachts, whose crews chug to and fro 'n dinghies all day and night. It's not the most attractive place on Sérifos – and to stay here exclusively would be to miss some fine walks – but Livádhi and the neighbouring cove of Livadháki are certainly the easiest place to find rooms and any other amenities you might need, all of which are very scarce elsewhere.

Unfortunately, the **beach** at Livádhi is nothing to write home about: long, but of hard-packed, muddy sand, the water weedy and prone to intermittent jellyfish flotillas; only the far northeastern end is at all usable. Walk uphill along the street from the *Galanos* bakery, or over the southerly headland from the cemetery, to reach the neighbouring, far superior **Livadháki**. This golden-sand beach, shaded by tamarisk trees, offers snorkelling and other watersports, one rather average taverna and some furtive nudism. If you prefer more seclusion, five minutes' stroll across the headland to the south brings you to the smaller **Karávi** beach, which is cleaner and almost totally naturist, but has no shade or facilities.

A slightly longer 45-minute walk north of the port along a bumpy track leads to **Psilí Ámmos**, a sheltered, white-sand beach considered the best on the island. Accordingly, it's popular, with two rival tavernas, both of which tend to be full in high season. Naturists are pointed – via a ten-minute walk across the headland – towards the beach beyond, the larger and often deserted **Áyios Ioánnis**, but this is rather exposed to weather, has no facilities at all, and only the far south end is inviting. Both beaches are theoretically visited by *kaíkia* from Livádhi, as are two nearby sea-caves, but don't count on it. Additionally, and plainly visible from arriving ferries, two more sandy coves hide at the far southeastern flank of the island, opposite an islet; they are accessible on foot only, by a variation of the track to Psilí Ámmos.

Livádhi and Livadháki practicalities
The **OTE** office is at the foot of the quay. You can **rent a bike or car** from *Blue Bird* next to the single filling station, and there are three **boat-ticket agents**. The public **bus stop** and posted schedule are at the base of the yacht and fishing boat jetty, *not* the ferry dock.

Accommodation proprietors – with the exception of the *Coralli Camping Bungalows*, which regularly sends a minibus – don't always meet ferries, and in high season you'll have to step lively off the boat to get a decent bed. The most rewarding hunting grounds are on the headland above the ferry dock, or Livadháki beach (see below); anything without a sea view will be a notch cheaper. Up on the headland, the *Pansion Cristi* (☎0281/51 214 or 51 775; ④, lower rates June & Sept) has an excellent, quiet position overlooking the bay; the nearby *Areti* (☎0281/51 479; ④) is snootier and a bit pricier. Alternatively, down in the flatlands, the relatively inexpensive seafront *Kyklades Hotel* (☎0281/51 553; ②) has the important virtues of year-round operation and kindly management, though the bay-view rooms get some traffic noise. The *Galanos* (☎0281/51 277; ②), above the eponymous bakery, is useful as a fall back in peak season.

Livadháki, ten to fifteen minutes' walk south, offers more nocturnal peace, choice and quality, though it has a more touristy feel, and the mosquitoes are positively ferocious – bring insecticide coils or make sure your room is furnished with electric vapour pads. One of the oldest and largest complexes of rooms and apartments, close to the beach and with verdant views, is run by *Vaso Stamataki* (☎0281/51 346; ③). Newer and higher-standard choices include the *Helios Pansion* run by Panayiota and Khryssa Gavriel (☎0281/51 066; ③), just above the road as you arrive at Livadháki, or the *Medusa* further along (☎0281/51 127; ③). Near the end of things, beside one of only two public access tracks to the beach and behind the best patch of sand, the *Coralli Camping Bungalows* (☎0281/51 500; bungalows ④) has a restaurant and landscaped tenting-down area, but no prizes for a warm welcome.

The Livádhi seafront has a makeshift road running along its length, filled with traffic, restaurants, shops, and all the services you might need. At the strategic southerly crossroads, the *Galanos* bakery has exceptionally good cheese pies and – if you ask – whole-grain bread under the counter. A butcher plus a handful of fruit shops and **supermarkets** are scattered along the beach, while there's a **pharmacy** at the foot of the quay.

You'll pay through the nose for **meals** in the obvious places near the quay in Livádhi; walk up the beach, and meals get less expensive and more Greek. The two best traditional tavernas are the busy *Stamatis*, and the welcoming restaurant under the *Hotel Cyclades*. At the extreme far northeast end of the beach, *Sklavenis* (aka *Marietta's*) has its loyal adherents for its down-home feel and courtyard seating, but many find the food overly deep-fried and over-priced. Closer to the yacht harbour, *Meltemi* is a good – if slightly expensive – *ouzeri*, something out of the ordinary for the island. For crepes and ice cream, try *Meli*, in the commercial centre, by the port police.

Nightlife is surprisingly lively, though few establishments stay in business more than two consecutive seasons. Two of the most durable are *Vitamin C* and *Froggie's*, the latter presumably named in honour of the island's many noisy amphibians; on the beachfront itself the sound systems of *Karnayio* and *Agria Menta* currently battle it out from adjacent premises.

Hóra

Quiet and atmospheric **HÓRA**, teetering precariously above the harbour, is one of the most spectacular villages of the Cyclades. The best sights are to be found on the town's borders: tiny churches cling to the cliff edge, and there are breathtaking views across the valleys below. At odd intervals along its alleyways you'll find part of the old castle making up the wall of a house, or a marble statue leaning incongruously in one corner. A pleasant diversion is the hour-or-less walk down to Psilí Ámmos: start from beside Hóra's cemetery; to avoid getting lost, aim for the lower of two visible pigeon towers, and then keep close to the phone wires, which will guide you towards the continuation of the double-walled path descending to a bend in the road just above the beach.

Buses connect Livádhi with Hóra, 2km away, some ten times daily, but only manage one or two daily trips to Megálo Livádhi, Galaní, and Kállitsos. You may well want to walk, if you're travelling light, however; it's a pleasant if steep forty minutes up a cobbled way to Hóra, with the *kalderími* leading off from a bend in the road about 300m out of Livádhi. Out of season (by the beginning of October) you'll have no choice, since the bus – like nearly everything else – ceases operation during the winter.

Among two or three **tavernas**, *Stavros* just east of the bus-stop *platía* is the most consistent and can arrange beds, too. The island's **post office** is found in the lowest quarter, and a few more expensive **rooms** for rent lie about 200m north of town, on the street above the track to the cemetery.

The north

North of Hóra, the island's high water table sometimes breaks the surface to run in delightful rivulets swarming with turtles and frogs, though in recent years many of the open streams seem to have dried up. Reeds, orchards, and even the occasional palm tree still take advantage of the unexpected moisture, even if it's no longer visible. This is especially true at **KÁLLITSOS** (Kéndarhos), reached by a ninety-minute path from Hóra, marked by fading red paint splodges along an initial donkey track above the cemetery. Once at Kállitsos (no facilities), a paved road leads west within 3km to the fifteenth-to-seventeenth-century **monastery of Taxiarhón**, designed for sixty monks but presently home only to Makarios, one of the island's two parish priests. He is one of a dying breed of farmer-fisherman monks; if he's about, he'll show you treasures in the monastic church, such as an ivory-inlaid bishop's throne, silver lamps from Egypt (to where many Serifots emigrated), and the finely carved *témblon*. There are no longer any frescoes of note visible.

As you loop back towards Hóra from Kállitsos on the asphalt, the fine villages of Galaní and Panayiá (named after its tenth-century church) make convenient stops. In **GALANÍ** you can get simple **meals** at the central store, which also sells excellent, tawny-pink, sherry-like wine; its small-scale production in the west of the island is highly uneconomic, so you'll find it at few other places on Sérifos. Below the village, trails lead to the remote and often windswept beach of **Sikamiá**, with no facilities and no camping allowed; a better bet for a local swim is the more sheltered cove of **Platís Yialós** at the extreme northern tip of the island, reached by a rough track (negotiable by moped) that branches off just east of Taxiarhón. The church at **PANAYIÁ** is usually locked, but comes alive on its feast day of Ksilopanayía (16 August); traditionally the first couple to dance around the adjacent olive tree would be the first to marry that year, but this led to unseemly brawls – so the priest always goes first these days.

The southwest

A little way south of Panayiá, you reach a junction in the road. Turn left to return to Hóra, or continue straight towards **Megálo Horió** – the site of ancient Sérifos, but with little else to recommend it. **Megálo Livádhi**, further on, is a remote and quiet beach resort 8km west of Hóra, with two tavernas and some rooms. Iron and copper ore were once exported from here, but cheaper African deposits sent the mines into decline and today most of the idle machinery rusts away, though some gravel-crushing still goes on. An alternate turning just below Megálo Horió leads to the small mining and fishing port of **Koutalás**, a pretty if shadeless sweep of bay with a church-tipped rock, a lone taverna and a tiny beach. There's also a direct but rough mule-path from here back to Livádhi, but this shouldn't be attempted without clear local directions or a good map.

Sífnos

Sífnos is a more immediately appealing island than its northern neighbours: prettier, more cultivated and with some fine architecture. This means that it's also much more popular, and extremely crowded in July or August, when rooms are nearly impossible to find. Take any offered as you land, come armed with a reservation, or, best of all, time your visit for June or early in September, though bear in mind that most of the trendier bars and the souvenir shops will be shut for the winter by the middle of the latter month. In keeping with the island's somewhat upmarket clientele, freelance camping is forbidden (and the two designated sites are substandard), while nudism is tolerated only in isolated coves. The locals tend, if anything, to be even more dour and introverted than on Sérifos.

On the other hand, Sífnos' modest size – no bigger than Kíthnos or Sérifos — makes it eminently explorable. The **bus service** is excellent, most of the roads quite decent and there's a network of paths that are fairly easy to follow. Unhappily, one of the best trails was destroyed in late 1992, and plans are mooted to bulldoze yet another unnecessary road straight through the heart of the island from Kamáres to Platís Yialós. Sífnos also has a strong tradition of pottery and was long esteemed for its distinctive cuisine, although most tourist-orientated cooking is average at best. However, the island's shops and greengrocers are well stocked in season.

Ferry connections have improved in recent years, keeping pace with the island's increasing popularity. The main lines head south, via Kímolos to Mílos, with occasional extensions to Thíra, Crete and select Dodecanese, or north, via Sérifos and Kíthnos to Pireás. The only links with the central Cyclades are provided by the unreliable small excursion boat *Aphrodite Express*, which sails to Páros, Náxos, Síros and Míkonos most days but is not for the seasick-prone; and a bona fide ferry, the *Paros Express*, which calls once weekly (at Sérifos too) – usually Tuesday – to deposit you on Síros at a rather uncivilized hour.

Kamáres

KAMÁRES, the port, is tucked away at the foot of high, bare cliffs in the west which enclose a beach. A busy, fairly downmarket resort with concrete blocks of villas edging up to the base of the cliffs, Kamáres has a seafront crammed with bars, travel agencies, ice-cream shops and fast-food places. You can store luggage at the semi-official **tourist office** while hunting for a room (proprietors tend not to meet boats); they also change money and can advise on bed availability throughout the island.

Accommodation is relatively expensive, though bargaining can be productive outside peak season. Try the **rooms** above the *Katzoulakis Tourist Agency* near the quay, as well as the reasonable *Hotel Stavros* (☎0284/31 641; ③), just beyond the church. If desperate, you might try the unofficial *Vangelis* **youth hostel** (①) further inland. At the other end of the scale, there's the good but expensive *Voulis Hotel* (☎0284/32 122; ⑤) across the bay. An extremely scruffy, semi-official campsite appears to have been closed down. You're probably better off anyway at the rooms to let right at the north end of the sands; these are often the last to fill, perhaps because of noise from the adjacent taverna and disco.

The best **restaurants** are the *Meropi*, ideal for a pre-ferry lunch or a more leisurely meal, and the no-name establishment whose decor seems to consist chiefly of a dozen or so retsina barrels (customer self-service). Kamáres also boasts a fair proportion of the island's **nightlife**: try the *Collage Bar* for your sunset cocktail, and move on to the *Mobilize Dancing Club* or the *Cafe Folie*.

Apollonía and Artemónas

A steep twenty-minute bus ride (hourly service until late at night) takes you up to **APOLLONÍA**, the centre of the *hóra*, an amalgam of three hilltop villages which have merged over the years into one continuous community. With white buildings, flower-draped balconies, belfries and pretty squares, it is eminently scenic, though not yet self-consciously so in the Míkonos manner. On the *platía* itself, the **Folk Museum** (open by request; a sign on the door tells you how to find the guard) is well worth a visit. Most of the exhibits celebrate a certain Kyria Tselemende, who wrote a famous local recipe book (fragments of which are kept here), and there's also an interesting collection of textiles, laces, artwork, costumes and weaponry.

Radiating out from the *platía* is a network of stepped marble footways and the main pedestrian street, flagstoned Odhós Styliánou Prókou – lined with shops, churches and restaurants. The garish, cakebox-cathedral of **Áyios Spíridhon** is nearby, while the eighteenth-century church of **Panayía Ouranoforía** stands in the highest quarter of town, incorporating fragments of a seventh-century BC temple of Apollo and a relief of Saint George over the door. **Áyios Athanásios**, next to Platía Kleánthi Triandafílou, has frescoes and a wooden *témblon*. Some 3km southeast, a short distance from the village of Exámbela, you'll find the active monastery of **Vríssis**, dating from 1612 and home to a good collection of religious artefacts and manuscripts.

ARTEMÓNAS, fifteen minutes south of Apollonía on foot, is worth a morning's look around for its churches and elegant Venetian-era and Neoclassical houses alone. **Panayía Gourniá** (key next door) has vivid frescoes; the clustered-dome church of **Kohí** was built over an ancient temple of Artemis (also the basis of the village's name); and seventeenth-century **Áyios Yióryios** contains fine icons. Artemónas is also the point of departure for **Herónissos**, an isolated hamlet with a few potteries behind a deeply indented, rather bleak bay at the northwestern tip of the island. There's a motorable dirt track there or occasional boat trips from Kamáres, though it's only worth the effort on calm days.

Practicalities

The **bank, post office, OTE** and **tourist police** are all grouped around Apollonía's central plaza. Most of the village's **rooms** establishments are along the road towards Fáros, and thus a bit noisy; the *Margarita* (☎0284/31 701; ③) is comfortable and fairly representative. If you want quieter premises with a better view, be prepared to pay more: your best bet is to head up the stair-street north of the *platía* café, where there's an excellent travel agency, *Aegean Thesaurus* (☎0284/32 190 & 31 145; also in Kamáres at ☎31 804), which can book you into more expensive rooms (③–④). They also sell a worthwhile package consisting of an accurate topographical map, bus/boat schedules and a short text on Sífnos for a few hundred drachmas. Near the central *platía*, there's the popular late-arrival fallback *Sofia* (☎0284/31 238; ③), though most people find somewhere else the next day, as it's a rather cheerless 1970s construction; the *Galini*, 400m south, up in Katavatí (☎0284/31 011; ③), is preferable.

In Hóra there are still a bare handful of quality **tavernas**, the doyen of which is the *Liotrivi* up in Artemónas. Though currently housed in an old olive mill, with orchard seating, and featuring local wine and island specialities, word out is that the owner will shortly move to purpose-built premises and re-open under his own name, *Manganas*. Next to the post office in Apollonía, *Iy Orea Sifnos* is the current incarnation of a taverna which for years has operated on this site, offering chickpea soup on Sundays, local cheese and various vegetarian specialities, all served in a flower-decked garden.

Nightlife in Apollonía tends to be dominated by the thirty-something crowd which, having dined early by Greek-island standards, lingers over its *oúzo* until late. The central *Argo* music bar plays lots of Seventies music and is very popular; try also the *Andromeda* club on the north side of the village, which bills itself as "more than a bar".

The east coast

Most of Sífnos' coastal settlements are along the less precipitous eastern shore, within a modest distance of Hóra and its surrounding cultivated plateau. These all have good bus services, and a certain amount of food and accommodation.

Kástro

An alternative east-coast base which seems the last place on Sífnos to fill up in season, **KÁSTRO** can be reached on foot from Apollonía in 35 minutes, all but the last ten on a clear path beginning at the *Hotel Anthoussa* and threading its way via Káto Petáli hamlet. Built on a rocky outcrop with an almost sheer drop to the sea on three sides, the ancient capital of the island retains much of its medieval character. Parts of its boundary walls survive, along with a full complement of sinuous, narrow streets graced by balconied, two-storey houses and some fine sixteenth- and seventeenth-century churches with ornamental floors. Venetian coats-of-arms and ancient wall-fragments can still be seen on some of the older dwellings; there are remains of the ancient acropolis (including a ram's head sarcophagus by one of the medieval gates), as well as a small **archeological museum** (Tues–Sat 9am–3pm, Sun 10am–2pm; free) installed in a former Catholic church in the higher part of the village.

Besides a fair number of rooms, there are at least two tavernas – the *Star* with the nicest seating, though the food can be dubious. There's nothing approximating a beach in Kástro; for a swim you have to walk to the nearby, rocky coves of **Serália** (to the southeast, and with more rooms) and **Paláti**. You can also hike, from the windmills on the approach road near Káto Petáli, to either the sixteenth-century monastery of **Hrissostómou**, or along a track opposite to the cliff face that overlooks the church of the **Eptá Martíres** (Seven Martyrs); nudists sun themselves and snorkel on and around the flat rocks below.

Platís Yialós

From Apollonía there are almost hourly buses to the resort of **PLATÍS YIALÓS**, some 12km distant, near the southern tip of the island. Despite claims to be the longest beach in the Cyclades, the sand can get very crowded at the end near the watersport facilities rental. Diversions include a pottery workshop, but for many the ugly *Xenia* hotel at the southern end of the beach, and troublesome winds, rule the place out. **Rooms** are expensive, although the comfortable *Pension Angelaki* (☎0284/31 688; ③), near the bus stop, is more reasonably priced. The local **campsite** is rather uninspiring: a stiff hike inland, shadeless, and on sloping, stony ground. Among several fairly pricey **tavernas** are the straightforward *Toh Steki* and *Bus Stop*.

A more rewarding walk uphill from Platís Yialós brings you to the convent of **Panayía tou Vounoú**, though it's easy to get lost on the way without the locally sold map; the caretaker should let you in, if she's about.

Fáros and around

Less crowded beaches are to be found just to the northeast of Platís Yialós (though unfortunately not directly accessible along the coast). **FÁROS**, again with regular bus links to Apollonía, makes an excellent fallback base if you don't strike lucky elsewhere. A small and friendly resort, it has some of the cheapest **accommodation** on the island (☎0284/31 822 & 31 989; both ②) and a few early-evening **tavernas**, the best of which is *Toh Kima*. The closest beaches are not up to much: the town strand itself is muddy, shadeless and crowded, and the one to the northeast past the headland not much better. Head off in the opposite direction, however, through the older part of the village, and things improve at **Glifó**, a longer, wider beach favoured by naturists and snorkellers.

Continuing from Glifó, a fifteen-minute cliffside path – threatened by a proposed road project – leads to the beach of **Apokoftó**, with a good taverna, *Vasilis*, and, up an access road, the *Pension Flora* (☎0284/31 778; ③), with superb views. The shore itself tends to collect seaweed, however, and a rock reef must be negotiated to get into the water. Flanking Apokoftó to the south, marooned on a sea-washed spit and featuring on every EOT poster of the island, is the disestablished, seventeenth-century, **Hrissopiyís monastery**, whose cells are rented out in summer (☎0284/31 255; ②), although you'll need to book well in advance. According to legend, the cleft in the rock appeared when two village girls, fleeing to the spit to escape the attentions of menacing pirates, prayed to the Virgin to defend their virtue.

The interior and Vathí

Apollonía is a good base from which to start your explorations of remoter Sífnos. You can **rent bikes** at *Moto Apollo*, beside the BP station on the road to Fáros, but the island is best explored on foot.

Taking the path out from Katavatí (the district south of Apollonía) you'll pass, after a few minutes, the beautiful empty **monastery of Firáyia** and – fifteen minutes along the ugly new bulldozer track – the path climbing up to **Áyios Andhréas,** where you'll be rewarded with tremendous views over the islands of Síros, Páros, Íos, Folégandhros and Síkinos. Just below the church is an enormous Bronze-Age archeological site.

Even better is the all-trail walk to Vathí, around three hours from Katavatí and reached by bearing right at a signed junction in Katavatí. Part-way along you can detour on a conspicuous side trail to the **monastery of Profítis Ilías**, on the very summit of the island, with a vaulted refectory and extensive views.

Vathí

A fishing village on the shore of a stunning funnel-shaped bay, **VATHÍ** is the most attractive and remote base on the island though, with the recent completion of the road in from Áyios Andhréas, the tranquil days of this little backwater seem numbered. There are a few **rooms** to let – though rarely enough, so freelance camping is tolerated – and one or two tavernas, of which *Okeanis* is best for *mezédhes*, *Manolis* for grills. The two potteries which once functioned here have closed down, but the wonderful, tiny **monastery of the Archangel Gabriel** still watches over the quay.

Well-publicized small boats from Kamáres dock at Vathí (minimum twice daily in season – morning and late afternoon); these are a bit pricey, and most people tend to walk in at least one direction. Rather than retrace your steps to Katavatí, it is theoretically possible to walk back to Platís Yiálos, but be warned that the new road (currently very rough and not yet usable by taxis), has cut the path and caused landslides in several places; even when you reach the pass dividing the two sides of the island, the path's continuation to Platís Yiálos proves steep and hard to find.

Mílos

Mílos has always derived prosperity from its strange geology. Minoan settlers were attracted by obsidian, and other products of its volcanic soil made the island – along with Náxos – the most important of the Cyclades in the ancient world. Today the quarrying of barite, perlite and porcelain brings in a steady revenue, but has left deep and unsightly scars on the landscape. The rocks, however, can be beautiful *in situ*: on the left as your ferry enters Mílos Bay, two outcrops known as the Arkoúdhes (Bears) square off like sumo wrestlers. Off the north coast, accessible only by excursion boat, the Glaroníssia (Seagull Isles) are shaped like massed organ pipes, and there are more weird formations on the southwest coast at Kléftiko. Inland, too, you frequently come across strange, volcanic outcrops, and thermal springs burst forth at surprising spots.

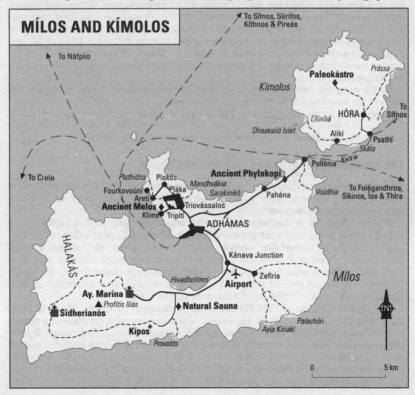

Violated the landscape may be, but as with most weathered volcanic terrain, Mílos is incredibly fertile; away from the summits of **Profítis Ilías** in the southwest and lower hills in the east, a gently undulating countryside is intensively cultivated to produce grain, hay and orchards. The island's domestic architecture, with its lava-built, two-up-and-two-down houses, is reminiscent of Níssiros, while parts of the coast, with their sculpted cliffs and inlets, remind some visitors of Cyprus.

Yet the drab whole is less than the sum of the often interesting parts; Mílos is not and never will become another Santoríni, despite a similar geological history, and is probably the better for it. The locals are reconciled to a very short tourist season lasting from late June to early September, and make most of their money during late July and August; accommodation prices stay uniformly high year-round.

Adhámas

ADHÁMAS is a rather cramped and uninspiring little port, founded by Cretan refugees fleeing a failed rebellion of 1841. Despite sitting on one of the Mediterranean's best natural harbours (created by a volcanic cataclysm similar to, but earlier than, Thira's), it's not a spectacularly inviting place. Most hotel **accommodation** manages to be simultaneously noisy, viewless and relatively expensive. Those that succeed in having only one of these disadvantages include the seafront *Popy* (☎0287/22 393; ④), on the coast road beyond the *Trapatsellis* taverna, and the *Semiramis* (☎0287/22 117; ③), well inland and left off the road to Pláka, with a garden setting. Rooms are concentrated up on the conical hill of the residential district; there is no organized campsite, and you shouldn't attempt to sleep rough. *Trapatsellis* at the start of the tamarisk-lined beach east of the port is easily the best **restaurant** in town, with a full menu of fish and vegetarian specialities, and good local wine from the barrel: dense, unresinated, but not hangover-inducing. *O Kinigos* is a more obvious cheapie near the ferry dock, but the food is greasier.

On the quayside, two travel agencies have information about coastal boat trips, sell maps of the island, and rent out mopeds. Otherwise, Adhámas is the hub of the island's **bus services**, which run hourly to Pláka, four or five times daily in high season to Pollónia, and twice daily to Paleohóri via Zefíria. Incidentally, if you arrive by plane from Athens, the **airport** is 5km southeast of the port, close to Zefíria.

The northwestern villages and ancient Melos

The real appeal of Mílos, however, resides in an area that has been the island's focus of habitation since Classical times, where a cluster of villages huddle in the lee of a crag 4km northwest of the harbour.

PLÁKA (MÍLOS) is the largest of these communities and official capital of the island, a status borne out by the presence of the hospital, **OTE**, **post office**, a part-time **bank** and three **motorbike rental** outfits strewn along the approach road. Unfortunately three or four modern blocks of **rooms** en route overlook this busy boulevard, and so prompt few thoughts of staying. Of three places to **eat**, the *Ouzeri Dhiporto*, a converted general store is the most original, with local specialities such as snails, *pittária* (hollow cheese-laced turnovers) and local wine.

The attractive village of **TRIPITÍ** (meaning "perforated" in Greek), which takes its name from the cliffside tombs of the ancient Melian dead nearby, covers a long ridge a kilometre south of Pláka. Despite semi-desolation (many houses are for sale), it probably makes the best base if you're after a village environment, with its three modest **rooms** establishments, two of which are just down the steep street from the tiny *platía* below the main church. Here also the *Kafenio Iy Hara*, despite a modest appearance, can do simple **meals** to go with its fantastic view of the vale of Klíma (see below); more elaborate and expensive fare is available at the *Ouzeri Methismeni Politea*, at the top of the road to the catacombs. From Tripití, it's possible to walk more or less directly down to Adhámas via Skinópi on the old *kalderími* which begins on the saddle linking Tripití with the hamlet of Klimatovoúni.

TRIOVÁSSALOS and its non-identical twin **PÉRAN TRIOVÁSSALOS** are more workaday, less polished than Pláka or Tripití. There are "rooms to rent" signs out here as well, but they'll inevitably be noisier. Péran can also offer the idosyncratic taverna *O Hamos,* and a naive pebble-mosaic in the courtyard of **Áyios Yióryios church**; dating from 26 January, 1880, it features assorted animal and plant motifs.

Local sites – and the coast

Pláka boasts **two museums** of moderate interest. Behind the lower car park, at the top of the approach boulevard through the newer district, an **archeological collection** (daily except Mon 8.30am–3pm; 400dr) contains numerous obsidian implements plus a whole wing of finds from ancient Phylakopi (see p.434), with highlights including a votive lamp in the form of a bull and a rather Minoan-looking terracotta goddess. Labelling is scant, but isn't really needed for a plaster cast of the most famous statue in the world, the *Venus de Milo*, the original of which was found on the island in 1820 and appropriated by the French; her arms were knocked off in the melée surrounding her abduction. Up in a mansion of the old quarter, the **Folklore Museum** (Tues–Sun 10am–1pm; 100dr) offers in situ room re-creations but is otherwise a Greek-labelled jumble of impedimenta pertaining to milling, brewing, cheese-making, baking and weaving, rounded off by old engravings, photos and mineral samples.

A stairway beginning near the police station leads up to the old Venetian **Kástro**, its slopes clad in stone and cement to channel precious rainwater into cisterns. Near the top looms the enormous chapel of **Panayía Thalassítra**, where the ancient Melians made their last stand against the Athenians before being massacred in 416 BC. Today it offers one of the best views in the Aegean, particularly at sunset in clear conditions.

From the archeological museum, signs point you towards the **early Christian catacombs** (daily except Wed & Sun 8.45am–1pm; free), 1km south of Pláka and just 400m from Tripití village; steps lead down from the road to the inconspicuous entrance. Although some 5000 bodies were buried in tomb-lined corridors which stretch some 200m into the soft volcanic rock, only the first 50m are illuminated and accessible by boardwalk. They're worth a look if you're in the area, but the adjacent ruins of **ancient Melos**, extending down from Pláka almost to the sea, justify the detour. There are huge Dorian walls, the usual column fragments lying around and, best of all, a well-preserved Roman **amphitheatre** (unrestricted access) some 200m west of the catacombs by track, then trail. Only seven rows of seats remain intact, but these evocatively look out over Klíma to the bay. Between the catacombs and the theatre is the signposted spot where the *Venus de Milo* was found; promptly delivered to the French consul for "safekeeping" from the Turks, this was the last the Greeks saw of the statue until the museum's copy was belatedly forwarded from the Louvre in Paris.

At the very bottom of the vale, **KLÍMA** is the most photogenic of several fishing hamlets on the island, with its picturesque boathouses tucked underneath the principal living areas. There's no beach to speak of, and only one place to stay, the impeccably sited *Panorama* (☎0287/21 623; ③), whose restaurant currently seems to be resting on its laurels.

Plathiéna, 45 minutes' walk northwest of Pláka, is the closest proper beach, and thus vastly popular in summer. There are no facilities, but the beach is fairly well protected and partly shaded by tamarisks. Head initially west from near the police station on the marked footpath towards **ARETÍ** and **FOURKOVOÚNI**, two more cliff-dug, boathouse-hamlets very much in the Klíma mould. Although the direct route to Plathiéna is signposted, it's no longer to go via Fourkovoúni; both hamlets are reached by side turnings off the main route, which becomes a jeep track as you approach Fourkovoúni. By moped, access to Plathiéna is only from Plakés, the northernmost and smallest of the five northwestern villages.

The south

The main road to the south of the island splits at **Kánava junction**, an unrelievedly dreary place at first glance owing to the large power plant here. But opposite this, indicated by a rusty sign pointing seaward, is the first of Mílos' **hot springs**, which bubble up in the shallows and are much enjoyed by the locals.

Taking the left or easterly fork leads to **ZEFÍRIA**, hidden among olive groves below the bare hills; it was briefly the medieval capital until an eighteenth-century epidemic drove out the population. Much of the old town is still deserted, though some life has returned, especially to the wonderfully named *Mama Loula* **taverna**, opposite the magnificent seventeenth-century church.

South of here the road progressively deteriorates into yawning ruts capable of swallowing a motorbike tyre whole, such that it's difficult to imagine a bus making it down the final slope of the 19km to the coarse-sand beach of **Paleohóri**. Actually a triple strand totalling about 800m in length and unarguably the island's best, clothing is optional at the westerly cove, where steam vents heat both the shallow water and the rock overhangs onshore. Although the lower, beachfront **taverna** is hard to resist, the *Artemis* (high season only) stands alluringly at the clifftop. There are also a few **rooms** for rent, but the place is really too remote to be a practical base, and most people bike in for the day, since the bus schedule doesn't permit much time here.

The westerly road from Kánava junction leads past the airport gate to **Hivadholímni**, considered to be the best beach on Mílos bay itself. Not that this is saying much: Hivadholímni is north-facing and thus garbage-prone, with shallow sumpy water offshore; better to veer south to **Provatás**, a short but tidy beach, closed off by colourful cliffs on the east. Being so easy to get at, it hasn't escaped some development. There are two-room establishments plus, closer to the shore, a new luxury complex.

Some 2km west of Provatás, you'll see a highway sign for **Kípos** just before the asphalt fizzles out. Below and to the left of the road, a small **medieval chapel** dedicated to the Kímisis (Assumption) sits atop foundations far older – as evidenced by the early Christian reliefs stacked along the west wall and a carved, cruciform baptismal font in the *ierón* behind the altar screen. At one time a spring gushed from the low tunnel-cave beside the font – sufficiently miraculous in itself on arid Mílos.

For the most part **Halakás**, the southwestern peninsula centred on the wilderness of 748-metre Profítis Ilías, is uninhabited and little built upon, with the exception of the much-venerated **monastery of Sidherianós**. Motorbikes if not cars will take a beating on the maze of rough tracks, and the coast is best explored on the round-the-island day trips on offer from travel agents in Adhámas.

The north coast

From either Adhámas or the Pláka area good roads run roughly parallel to the **north coast** which, despite being windswept and largely uninhabited, is not devoid of interest. **Mandhrákia**, reached from Péran Triovássalos, is another boathouse settlement, and **Sarakinikó**, to the east, is a sculpted inlet with a sandy sea-bed. About 8km from Adhámas, the little hamlet of **Pahéna**, not shown on many maps, has a cluster of rooms and a small beach. About a kilometre beyond this, the remains of three superimposed Neolithic settlements crown a small knoll at **Filakopí** (ancient Phylakopi); the site was important archeologically, but hasn't been maintained and is difficult to interpret.

Pollónia

POLLÓNIA, 12km northeast of Adhámas, must be the windiest spot on the island, hence the name of its longest-lived and best **bar**, *Okto Bofor* (meaning "Force 8 gales"), near the church. The second resort on Mílos after Adhámas, it is, not surprisingly, immensely popular with windsurfers. Pollónia is essentially a small harbour protected by a storm-lashed spit of land on the northeast, where self-catering units are multiplying rapidly, fringed by a long but narrow, tamarisk-fringed beach to the rear, and closed off on the south by a smaller promontory on which the tiny original settlement huddles. Besides the town beach, the only other convenient, half-decent beach is at **Voúdhia**, 3km east, where you will find more of the island's hot springs.

On the quay are a row of three **tavernas**, best of these being *Kapetan Nikolaos* (aka *Koula's*; open year-round). Inland and south of here you'll find another concentration of **accommodation**, more simple rooms and less apartments, most with the slight drawback of occasional noise and dust from quarry trucks. Among the newest and highest-quality units here are the *Kapetan Tasos Studios* (☎0287/41 287; June & Sept ③–④, July–Aug ⑥), with good views of the straits between Mílos and Kímolos. Pollónia has no bank or post office, but there is a helpful **travel agency**, *Blue Waters* (☎0287/41 442) which can change money, rent cars, book accommodation and sell *ANEK* ferry tickets (services to Sitía on Crete). A **motorbike rental** place behind the beach, and a well-stocked **supermarket**, completes the list of amenities.

Getting to Kímolos (see below) may be the main reason you're here. Either the *Tria Adhelfia* or one other *kaíki* makes the trip daily year-round at 6.45am and 2pm, returning from Kímolos an hour later; during high season, there may be additional departures and day trips.

Kímolos

Of the three islets off the coast of Mílos, Andímilos is home to a rare species of chamois and Políegos has more ordinary goats, but only **Kímolos** has any human habitation. Volcanic like Mílos, with the same little lava built rural cottages, it profits from its geology and used to export chalk (*kimolía* in Greek) until the supply was exhausted. Still a source of fuller's earth, the fine dust of this clay is a familiar sight on the island, where mining still outstrips fishing and farming as an occupation. Rugged and barren in the interior, there is some fertile land on the southeast coast where low-lying wells provide water, and this is where the population of about eight hundred is concentrated.

Kímolos is sleepy indeed from September to June, and even in August sees hardly any visitors. This is probably just as well, since there are fewer than a hundred beds on the whole island, and little in the way of other amenities; such modest facilities as exist are relatively high-priced for what they are.

Psathí and Hóra

Whether you arrive by ferry, or by *kaíki* from Pollónia, you'll dock at the hamlet of **PSATHÍ**, pretty much a non-event except for one good **taverna** midway along the beach, *Toh Kyma*, with sympathetic proprietors. However, rooms here are worth considering, as they are bound to be quieter than anything in Hóra, where the noise of people, animals and vehicles can defeat sleep. **Ferry tickets** are sold only outside the expensive café on end of the jetty, an hour or so before the anticipated arrival of the boat; the Pollónia *kaíki* comes and goes unremarked from the base of the jetty.

Around the bay there are a few old windmills and the dazzlingly white **HÓRA** perched on the ridge above them. Unsung – and neglected – is the magnificent, two-gated **kastro**, a fortified core of roughly the same design as those at Andíparos and Síkinos; the perimeter houses are intact but its heart is a jumble of ruins. Just outside the *kástro* on the north stands the conspicuously unwhitewashed, late-sixteenth-century church of **Hrissostómos**, oldest surviving and most beautiful on the island.

It takes fifteen minutes to walk up to the surprisingly large town, passing the recommended *Maria's* **rooms** (July–Aug only; ②) on the way; you'll also find a certain amount of accommodation, much of it noisy, managed by *Margaro Petraki* (☎0287/51 314; ②), tucked away in the rather unglamourous maze of backstreets. The aptly named *Panorama*, near the east gate of the *kástro*, is the most elaborate and consistently open **taverna**. Self-catering is an easy proposition – and may be a necessity before June or after August – with a well-stocked supermarket, produce stalls and a butcher. Finally, there's a friendly **OTE** office behind Hrissostómos church, and a **post office**.

Around the island

During summer at least, the hamlet of **ALIKÍ** on the south coast is a better bet for staying than Hóra and Psathí, despite its relative remoteness. You should be able to get there in half an hour by following the track that heads levelly south (between a square relay reflector on the left and some power lines on the right) from the west end of Hóra. Aliki is named after the salt pan which sprawls between a rather mediocre beach with no shade or shelter, and a pair each of **rooms** – try *Passamihalis* (☎0287/51 340; ③) – and simple **tavernas**. You can stroll west one cove to **Bonátsa** for better sand and shallow water, though you won't escape the winds; to the east, between Aliki and Psathí, the smaller, more secluded beach of **Skála** is better for camping.

The 700m coarse-sand beach of **Ellliniká** is 45 minutes' walk west of Aliki: starting on the road, bear left – just before two chapels on a slope – onto a narrower track which runs through the fields in a valley bottom. Divided by a low bluff, the beach is bracketed by two capes and looks out over Dhaskalió islet towards dramatic bits of Mílos, but again tends to catch heavy weather in the afternoon.

Another road leads northeast from Hóra to a beach and radioactive springs at **Prássa**, 7km away. The route takes in impressive views across the straits to Políegos and there are several shady peaceful coves where you could camp out. Innumerable goat tracks invite exploration of the rest of the island; in the far northwest, on Kímolos' summit, the ruins of an imposing Venetian fortress known as **Paleókastro**.

Ándhros

Ándhros, the second largest and northernmost of the Cyclades, has a number of fine features to offer the visitor, although you have to search them out. Thinly populated but prosperous, its fertile, well-watered valleys have attracted scores of Athenian holiday villas whose red-tiled roofs and white walls stand out among the greenery. Some of the more recently built of these have robbed many of the villages of life and atmosphere, turning them into scattered settlements with no nucleus, and have created a weekender mentality manifest in noisy Friday and Sunday evening traffic jams at the ferry dock. The island neither needs, nor welcomes, independent travellers, and it can be almost impossible to get a bed in between the block-bookings during high season. On the positive side, the permanent population is distinctly hospitable; traditionally working on ships, they are only too happy to practise their English on you. Together with some of the more idiosyncratic reminders of the Venetian period, such as the *peristereónes* (pigeon towers) and the *fráktes* (dry-stone walls, here raised to the status of an artform), it is this that lends Ándhros its charm.

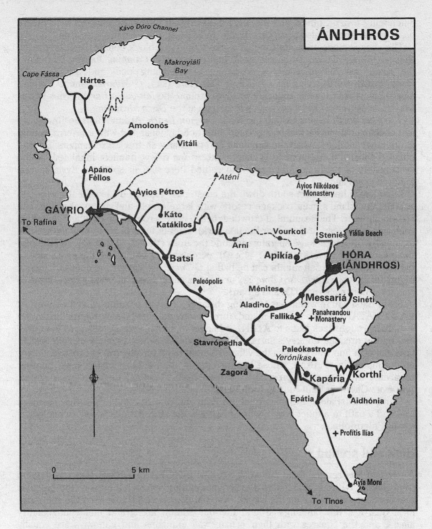

Ferries connect the island with Rafína on the mainland, only an hour from Athens on the bus, and you can loop back onto the central Cycladic routes via Míkonos or Síros. The bus service is poor, and you'd be well advised to consider renting a bike to tour the sights – or face a lot of walking.

Northern and western Ándhros

All ferries arrive at the main port, **GÁVRIO**, a nondescript place whose dirty, windswept beach is usually deserted. The sea in the enclosed harbour is so murky that even the wildfowl aren't interested. A converted dovecote houses a sporadically functioning **tourist office**, and the ferry **ticket agent** only opens half an hour before boats arrive. There's also a part-time **bank**, and a **post office** on the waterfront.

The cheapest **accommodation** is in some rooms in a block behind the hatshop; the *Galaxy* (☎0282/71 228; ③) is also clean and reasonable. *Camping Andros*, 2km down the road, has decent facilities, including a swimming pool and a good café. **Restaurants** worth trying include *Three Star Here* (sic), *O Mourikis* and *O Balmas*, near the port police, while **nightlife** revolves around the *Idhroussa Bar* on Áyios Pétros beach – or you could see if anybody's turned up at the *Disco Marabout*.

The road north begins behind the *Hotel Gavrion Beach*. Around 3km northwest are two beaches named **Féllos**: one, planted with holiday villas but with a taverna behind it; the other hidden beyond the headland and popular with freelance campers. Beyond Ápano Féllos, the countryside is empty except for a few hamlets inhabited by the descendants of medieval Albanians who settled here and in southern Évvia several hundred years ago.

Most traffic heads 8km south down the coast, past *Yiannouli*'s excellent taverna, to **BATSÍ**, the island's main package resort, with large hotels and discos above its fine natural harbour. The beautiful, if crowded, beach curves round the port, and the sea is cold, calm and clean (except near the taxi park). **Hotels** least likely to be inundated by the mostly British package operators include the *Avra* (☎0282/41 216; ②), and the new *Aneroussa Beach Hotel* (☎0282/41 445; ④), perched on a cliff above the south side of the bay. Reasonable fish **meals** can be had at *O Takis*. Except for the open-air cinema, **nightlife**, as typified by *Disco Blue Sky* or *Chaf*, is slick, expensive and geared towards couples. There's also an **OTE** and a **bank**.

From Batsí you're within easy walking distance of some beautiful inland villages. At **KÁTO KATÁKILOS**, one hour inland, three **tavernas** host "Greek nights" organized in Bátsi; a rough track leads to **ATÉNI**, a hamlet in a lush, remote valley, as yet unvisited by the dreaded donkey safaris. **ANO KATÁKILOS** has a couple of undervisited tavernas with fine views across the village. A right-hand turning out of Katákilos heads up the mountain to **ARNÍ**, whose lone taverna is often enshrouded in mist. Another rewarding trip is to a well-preserved, 20-metre-high **Classical tower** at Áyios Pétros, 5km from Gávrio or 9km coming from Batsí.

South of Batsí along the main road are Káto and Áno Apróvato: **Káto** has rooms, a café and a path to a quiet beach, while nearby is the largely unexplored archeological site of **Paleópolis.**

Hóra and around

A minimal bus service links the west coast with **HÓRA** or **ÁNDHROS** town, 35km from Gávrio. With its setting atop a rocky spur cutting across a huge bay, the capital is the most attractive place on the island. Paved in marble and schist from the still-active local quarries, the buildings around the bus station are grand nineteenth-century affairs, and the squares with their ornate wall fountains and gateways are equally elegant. The hill quarters are modern, while the small port acts as a yacht supply station, and below are the sands of Parapórti – a fine beach, if a little exposed to the *meltémi* winds in summer.

The few **hotels** in town are on the expensive side, and tend to be busy with holidaying Greeks: try the *Aigli* (☎0282/22 303, ⑤), opposite the big church on the main walkway. For a less expensive stay, ask around for rooms or check out the seasonal **campsite.** There's a choice of four **tavernas**, the best being the one right by the bus terminus. **Nightlife**, which consists of several bars, together with *Disco Remezzo*, is strongly pitched at a Greek rather than foreign clientele. The **OTE**, **post office** and various shops are just off the seafront road.

From the square right at the end of town you pass through an archway and down to windswept **Platía Ríva**, with its statue of the unknown sailor scanning the sea. Beyond him lies the thirteenth-century Venetian **Kástro**, precariously joined to the mainland by a narrow-arched bridge, which was damaged by German munitions in the last world war. The **Modern Art Museum** (Wed–Sun 10am–2pm, also 6–8pm in summer; 1000dr) has a sculpture garden and a permanent collection that includes works by Picasso and Braque, as well as temporary exhibits. Don't be discouraged by the stark modern architecture of the **Archeological Museum** (Tues–Sun 8.30am–3pm; 400dr); it turns out to be well laid out and labelled with instructive models. The prize items on view are the fourth-century "Hermes of Ándhros", reclaimed from a prominent position in the Athens archeological museum, and the "Matron of Herculaneum".

Hiking inland and west from Ándhros, the obvious destination is **MÉNITES**, a hill village just up a green valley choked with trees and straddled by stone walls. The church of the **Panayía** may have been the location of a Temple of Dionysus, where water was turned into wine; water still flows continuously from the local rocks. Nearby is the medieval village of **MESSARIÁ**, with the deserted twelfth-century Byzantine church of **Taxiárhis** below. The finest monastery on the island, **Panahrándou**, is only an hour's (steep) walk away, via the village of Falliká; reputedly tenth-century, it's still defended by massive walls but occupied these days by just three monks. It clings to an iron-stained cliff southwest of Hóra, to which you can return directly with a healthy two- to three-hour walk down the creek valley, guided by red dots. There is a wonderful taverna, *Pertesis*, at Strapouriés, which boasts a view all the way down to the coast and excellent food.

Hidden by the ridge directly north of Hóra, the prosperous nineteenth-century village of **STENIÉS** was built by the vanguard of today's shipping magnates. Today you can splash out at the good fish tavernas here. Just below, at Yiália, there's a small pebbly beach with a café and watersports. Beyond Steniés is **APIKÍA**, a tidy little village which bottles *Sariza*-brand mineral water for a living; there are a few **tavernas** and a very limited number of **rooms**, as well as the new luxury hotel *Dighi Sarisa* (☎0282/23 799 or 23 899; ③), just below the spring itself. The road is now asphalted up to Vourkotí and even past this point is quite negotiable via Arní to the west coast. There are some stunning views all along this road but bike riders need to take care when the *meltémi* is blowing – it can get dangerously windy.

Southern Ándhros

On your way south, you might stop at **Zagorá**, a fortified Geometric town – unique in having never been built over – that was excavated in the early 1970s. Located on a desolate, flat-topped promontory with cliffs falling away on three sides, it's worth a visit for the view alone.

The village of **KORTHÍ**, the end of the line, is a friendly though nondescript village set on a large sandy bay, cut off from the rest of the island by a high ridge and so relatively unspoilt – and pleasant enough to merit spending the night at *Pension Rainbow* (☎0282/61 344; ③) or at the austere-looking *Hotel Korthion* (☎0282/61218; ③). You could also take in the nearby convent of **Zoödhóhou Piyís** (open to visitors before noon), with illuminated manuscripts and a disused weaving factory.

To the north is **PALEÓKASTRO**, a tumbledown village with a ruined Venetian castle – and a legend about an old woman who betrayed the stronghold to the Turks, then jumped off the walls in remorse, landing on a rock now known as "Old Lady's Leap". In the opposite direction out of Korthí are **AIDHÓNIA** and **KAPÁRIA**, dotted with pigeon towers (*peristereónes*) left by the Venetians.

Tínos

The character of **Tínos** is determined largely by the grandiose shrine of **Panayía Evangelístria**, erected on the spot where a miraculous icon with healing powers was found in 1822. A Tiniote nun, now canonized as Ayía Pelayía, was directed in a dream to unearth the relic just as the War of Independence was getting underway – a timely coincidence which served to underscore the age-old links between the Orthodox Church and Greek nationalism. Today, there are two major annual pilgrimages, on March 25 and August 15, when (around noon) the icon bearing the Virgin's image is carried in state down to the harbour over the prostrate forms of the lame and the ill.

The rest of the island, too, smacks of religion and tradition in varying degrees. The Ottoman tenure here was the most fleeting in the Aegean. **Exóbourgo**, the craggy mount dominating southern Tínos and surrounded by most of the island's sixty-odd villages, is studded with the ruins of a Venetian citadel which defied the Turks until 1715, long after the rest of Greece had fallen. An enduring legacy of the long Latin rule is a persistent Catholic minority, which accounts for almost half the population, and a sectarian rivalry that is responsible for the numerous graceful belfries scattered throughout the island; Orthodox and Catholic parishes vying to build the tallest. The sky is pierced, too, by distinctive pigeon towers, even more in evidence here than on Ándhros. Aside from all this, the inland village architecture is striking and there's a flourishing folk-art tradition which finds expression in the abundant local marble. If there are weak points to Tínos, they are that the religious atmosphere tends to dampen nightlife, and that beaches are few and far between. However, the islanders have remained open and hospitable to the relatively few foreigners who touch down here; and any mercenary inclinations seem to be satisfied by booming sales in religious paraphernalia to the Greek faithful.

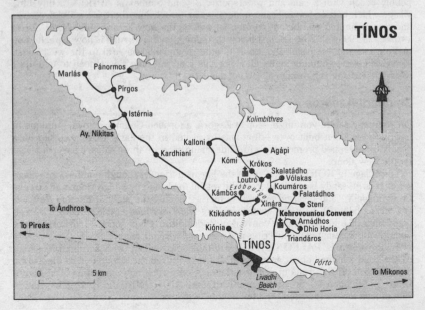

Tínos Town and the southern beaches

Trafficking in devotional articles certainly dominates the busy port town of **TÍNOS**, with the Neoclassical **church** (daily 8.30am–8.30pm) towering above, at the top of Leofóros Megaloháris. Approached via a massive marble staircase, the famous icon inside is all but buried under a dazzling mass of gold and silver *támmata* (votive offerings); below is the crypt (where the icon was discovered) and a mausoleum for the sailors drowned when the Greek warship *Elli*, at anchor off Tínos during a pilgrimage, was torpedoed by an Italian submarine on August 15, 1940. Museums around the courtyard display more objects donated by worshippers, who inundate the island for the two big yearly festivals.

The shrine aside – and all the attendant stalls, shops, and bustle – the port is none too exciting (a beautiful Neoclassical waterfront having been destroyed since the 1960s), with just scattered inland patches of nineteenth-century buildings. You might make time for the **Archeological Museum** (Tues–Sun 8.30am–3pm, closed Mon; 400dr) on the way up to the church, which displays finds, including a fascinating sundial, from the local Roman Sanctuary of Poseidon and Amphitrite (see below).

Practicalities

Most **ferries** now dock at the new jetty, 600m north of the old one. There are at least two boats a day from both Pireás and Rafina, with connections to Andhros and Míkonos. When you're leaving, ask your ticket agent which jetty to head for. **Buses** leave from a small parking area in front of a cubbyhole-office on the quay, and are not terribly frequent. A **moped** is a better strategy for exploring, and *Vidalis*, Zanáki Alavánou 16, is a good rental agency, but watch out for the main road to Pírgos, which is in a state of disrepair in some sections and requires care to avoid the potholes. The **tourist police** have an office right opposite the bus terminal.

To have any chance of securing a reasonably priced **room** around the pilgrimage day of March 25 (August 15 is hopeless), you must arrive several days in advance – and even then, be prepared to do a lot of asking around. At other times there's plenty of choice, though you'll still be competing with out-of-season pilgrims, Athenian tourists and the sick and the disabled seeking a miracle cure. Of the hotels, the *Eleana* (☎0283/22 561; ③), east of the quay about 400m inland at the edge of the bazaar, is the best budget option. The conspicuous waterfront *Yannis Rooms* (☎0283/22 515; ③) is just in front of the *Thalia*, all the way around the bay from the old jetty. Slightly pricier options include the *Avra* (☎0283/22 242; ④), a Neoclassical relic on the waterfront, and the *Favie Souzane* just inland (☎0283/22 693 or 22 176; ④). The *Vyzantio*, Zanáki Alavánou 26 (☎0283/22 454; ④), on the road out towards Pórto and the villages, is not especially memorable but it and the *Meltemi* at Filipóti 7, near Megaloháris (☎0283/22 881; ④), are the only places open off-season. Finally, there is a smart new hotel with swimming pool near the beginning of the beach road east of the promontory – *Peolos Bay Hotel* (☎0283/ 23 410 or 23 411; ⑤). Otherwise, beat the crowds by staying at *Tínos Camping* which has tents and a few nice rooms to let (☎0283/22 502; ②); follow the signs from the port, a ten-minute walk.

As usual, most seafront **restaurants** are rather overpriced and indifferent, with the exception of a friendly *Psitopolio* right opposite the bus terminal and the *Zefyros estiatorio* next to the post office. Further round the quay, the *Milos* taverna has a decent selection and reasonable prices. A cluster of places around the bazaar just to the left of Megaloháris as you face the church include *Ta Fanaria*, an inexpensive local hang-out with a limited selection, and *Palea Pallada* and *Peristereonas*, both of them reasonable. Tucked away in a small alley near the seafront off Evangelistrias, *Pigada* does a fine clay-pot moussaka, as well as some more unusual dishes, while *O Kipos*, further inland on the way to the church, has a pleasant garden setting. Wash down your meals with the island's very good barrelled retsina, which is available just about everywhere.

There are quite a few **bars**, mostly in a huddle near the new quay. *Fevgatos* has a pleasant atmosphere, and *Kala Kathoumena* is pretty lively with a mixture of international hits and Greek music, avidly danced to by some of the locals.

Nearby beaches

Most, though not all, of the island's **beaches** are close to town. **KIÓNIA**, 3km northwest (hourly buses), is functional enough but marred by a luxury holiday complex, though there is a campsite here. More importantly, it's the site of the **Sanctuary of Poseidon and Amphitrite**, discovered in 1902, the excavations yielding principally columns (*kiónia* in Greek), but also a temple, baths, a fountain, and hostels for the ancient pilgrims.

LIVÁDHI, though conveniently close (2km) to the port, is rocky and relatively exposed. **PÓRTO**, 8km east, boasts two good beaches to either side of **Áyios Sostís** headland, with another campsite nearby (and four buses daily), but bring food – development here consists of apartments, villas and rooms, and the nearest tavernas are quite a way back towards town, with the exception of the reasonably priced restaurant belonging to *Akti Aegeou* (☎0283/24248, winter ☎0283/22048; ⑥) on the first beach of Ayíos Pandelímon.

Northern Tínos

A good beginning to a foray into the interior is to take the stone stairway – the continuation of Odhós Ayíou Nikoláou – that passes behind and to the left of Evangelístria. This climbs for an hour and a half through appealing countryside to **KTIKÁDHOS**, a fine village with a good sea-view taverna, *Iy Dhrosia*, although it tends to be overrun with bus tours in summer. You can either flag down a bus on the main road or stay with the trail until Xinára (see "Around Exóbourgo" below).

Heading northwest from the junction flanked by Ktikádhos, Tripótamos and Xinára, there's little to stop for – except the fine dovecotes around Kámbos – until you reach **KARDHIANÍ**, one of the most strikingly set and intrinsically beautiful villages on the island, with its views across to Síros from amid a dense oasis. Nestled in the small sandy bay below is a fine little restaurant by the name of *Anemos*, which serves octopus stew and other dishes at good prices. Kardhianí has recently been discovered by wealthy Athenians and expatriates, and now offers the exotic *Toh Perivoli* taverna. **ISTÉRNIA**, just a little beyond, is not nearly so appealing but it does have a pension at the top of the village and a few cafés, perched above the turning for **Órmos Isterníon**, a comparatively small but overdeveloped beach.

Four daily buses along this route finish up at **PÍRGOS**, a few kilometres further north and smack in the middle of the island's marble-quarrying district. A beautiful village, its local artisans are renowned throughout Greece for their skill in producing marble ornamentation; ornate fanlights and bas-relief plaques crafted here adorn houses throughout Tínos. With an attractive shady *platía*, Pírgos is popular in summer, but you should be able to find a **room** easily enough, and you have a choice of two **tavernas**, *Vinia* being the more elegant by far.

The marble products were once exported from **PÁNORMOS** (Órmos) harbour, 4km northeast, with its tiny and surprisingly commercialized beach, but little reason to linger. If you get stuck, there are rooms, a campsite and some tavernas.

Around Exóbourgo

The ring of villages **around Exóbourgo** mountain is the other focus of interest on Tínos. The fortified pinnacle itself, 570m above sea level, with ancient foundations as well as the ruins of three Venetian churches and a fountain, is reached most quickly by steep steps from **XINÁRA** (near the island's major road junction), the seat of the island's Roman Catholic bishop. Most villages in north central Tínos have mixed populations, but Xinára and its immediate neighbours are purely Catholic; the inland villages also tend to have a more sheltered position, with better farmland nearby – the Venetians' way of rewarding converts and their descendants. Yet **TRIPÓTAMOS**, just south of Xinára, is a completely Orthodox village with possibly the finest architecture in this region – and has accordingly been pounced on by foreigners keen to restore its historic properties.

At **LOUTRÓ**, the next community north of Xinára, there's an Ursuline convent and carpet-making school: to visit, leave the bus at the turning for Skaládho. From Krókos, which has a couple of scenically situated restaurants, it's a forty-minute walk to **VÓLAKAS**, one of the highest and most remote villages on the island, a windswept oasis surrounded by bony rocks. Here, half a dozen elderly Catholic basketweavers fashion some of the best examples of that craft in Greece. If the workshops are not open, you can have a drink and buy baskets, at fair prices, in the ground-floor café run by a German–Greek couple.

At Kómi, 5km beyond Krókos, you can take a detour for **KOLIMBÍTHRES**, a magnificent double beach: one wild, huge and windswept, the other sheltered and with a taverna and rooms, but no camping. Any bus marked "Kalloni" passes through Kómi.

From either Skaládho or Vólakas you can traipse on foot to Koúmaros, where another long stairway leads up to Exóbourgo, or skirt the pinnacle towards Stení and Falatádhos, which appear as white speckles against the fertile plain of Livadhéri. From Stení you can catch the bus back to the harbour (seven daily). On the way down, try and stop off at one of the beautiful settlements just below the important twelfth-century **convent of Kehrovouníou**, where Ayía Pelayía dreamed of the icon, and the nuns still float down lavender-tinted corridors and under Lilliputian arches. In particular, **DHÍO HORIÁ** has a fine main square where cave-fountains burble, and **TRIANDÁROS** has a good, reasonable taverna in *Iy Levka*. If you have your own transport, there are some quite wide and fairly negotiable tracks down to some lovely secluded bays on the east of the island from the area of Steni. One such is Santa Margarita; given the lack of tourist development here, it's a good idea to take at least something to drink with you.

This is hardly an exhaustive list of Tíniote villages; armed with a map and good walking shoes for tackling the many old trails that still exist, you could spend days within sight of Exóbourgo and never pass through the same hamlets twice. Take warm clothing too, especially if you're on a moped, since the forbidding mountains behind Vólakas and the Livadhéri plain keep things noticeably cool almost year-round.

Míkonos (Mykonos)

Originally visited only as a stop on the way to ancient Delos, **Míkonos** has become easily the most popular (and the most expensive) of the Cyclades. Boosted by direct air links with Britain and domestic flights from Athens, an incredible 800,000 tourists pass through in a good year, producing some spectacular overcrowding in high summer on Míkonos' 75 square kilometres. But if you don't mind the crowds, or – and this is a much more attractive proposition – you come out of season, the prosperous capital is still one of the most beautiful of all island towns, its immaculately whitewashed houses concealing hundreds of little churches, shrines and chapels.

The sophisticated nightlife is pretty hectic, amply stimulated by Míkonos' former reputation as *the* gay resort of the Mediterranean – a title lost in recent years to places like Ibiza and Sitges in Spain; whatever, the locals take this comparatively exotic clientele in their stride. Unspoilt it isn't, but the island does offer excellent (if crowded and mainly nude) beaches, picturesque windmills, and a rolling arid interior. An unheralded Míkonian quirk is the legality of scuba diving, a rarity in Greece, and dive centres have sprung up on virtually every beach.

Míkonos Town

Don't let the crowds put you off exploring **MÍKONOS TOWN**, the archetypal postcard image of the Cyclades. Its sugar-cube buildings are stacked around a cluster of seafront fishermen's dwellings with every nook and cranny scrubbed and shown off. Most people head out to the beaches during the day, so early morning or late afternoon are the best times to wander the maze of narrow streets. The labyrinthine design was intended to confuse the pirates who plagued Míkonos in the eighteenth and early nineteenth centuries, and it still has the desired effect.

You don't need any maps or hints to scratch around the convoluted streets and alleys of town; getting lost is half the fun. There are, however, a few places worth seeking out if you require more structure to your strolling. Coming from the ferry quay, you'll pass the **Archeological Museum** (Tues–Sat 9am–3pm, Sun 9.30am–2.30pm; 400dr) on your way into town, home to some good Delos pottery – and a superb *souvláki* bar next door. The town also boasts a **Marine Museum** displaying various nautical artefacts (daily 10.30am–1pm & 6.30–9pm; 200dr). Alternatively, behind the two banks there's the **Library**, with Hellenistic coins and late medieval seals, or, at the base of the Delos jetty, the **Folklore Museum** (Mon–Sat 4–8pm, Sun 5–8pm; free), housed in an eighteenth-century mansion and cramming in a larger-than-usual collection of bric-a-brac, including a vast four-poster bed. The museum shares the same promontory as the old Venetian *kástro*, the entrance to which is marked by Míkonos' oldest and best-known church, **Paraportianí**, which is a fascinating asymmetrical hodge-podge of four chapels amalgamated into one.

The shore leads to the area known as "Little Venice" because of its high, arcaded Venetian houses built right up to the water's edge. Its real name is **Alefkándhra**, a trendy district packed with art galleries, chic bars and discos. Back off the seafront, behind Platía Alefkándhra, are Míkonos' two **cathedrals**: Roman Catholic and Greek Orthodox. Beyond, the famous **windmills** look over the area, a little shabby but ripe with photo opportunities. Instead of retracing your steps along the water's edge, follow Énoplon Dhinaméon (left off Mitropóleos) to **Tría Pigádhia** fountain. The name means "Three Wells" and legend has it that should a maiden drink from all three she is bound to find a husband, though these days she'd be more likely to end up with a water-borne disease.

Arrival and information

There is some accommodation information at the **airport**, but unless you know where you're going it's easier to take a taxi the 3km to town and sort things out at the jetty. The vast majority of visitors arrive by boat at the new northern **jetty**, where a veritable horde of room-owners pounce on the newly arrived. The scene is actually quite intimidating and so, if you can avoid the grasping talons, it is far better to go a hundred metres further where a row of offices deal with official hotels, rented rooms and camping information.

The harbour curves around past the dull, central Polikandhrióti beach; behind it is the **bus station** for Toúrlos, Áyios Stéfanos and Áno Méra. Just beyond, next to the **post office**, is the *Olympic Airways* office. Further around the seafront to the southern jetty you'll find the **tourist police** (☎0289/22 482) and *kaíkia* **to Delos**. A second **bus terminus**, for beaches to the south, is right at the other end of the town, beyond the windmills. Buses to all the most popular beaches and resorts run frequently, and until very late in the evening. It is also here that the largest cluster of **motorbike rental** agencies is to be found; prices vary little.

Accommodation

Accommodation **prices** in Míkonos rocket in the high season to a greater degree than almost anywhere else in Greece: a 5000–6000dr town room in early June can reach 15,000dr by August, and hotel rates at the nearby beaches are even more expensive. If you're after **rooms**, it's worth asking at *O Megas* grocery store on Andhroníkou

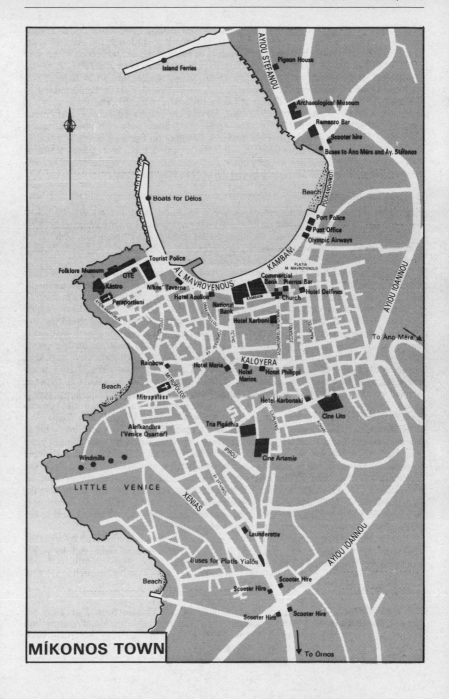

MÍKONOS TOWN

Matoyiánni – they tend to know what's available. One establishment that comes recommended is *Villa Giovani* (☎0289/22 485; ④), near the bus station at the edge of town. Out of season, you could try some of the **hotels in town**, such as *Delfines* on Mavroyéni (☎0289/22 292; ④–⑤), *Karbonis* at Andhroníkou Matoyiánni 53 (☎0289/23 127; ④–⑤), *Apollon* on Mavroyénous (☎0289/22 223; ④–⑤), *Maria* at Kaloyéra 18 (☎0289/22 317; ③–④), *Philippi* at Kaloyéra 32 (☎0289/22 294; ④–⑤), *Karbonaki* at Panahrándou 21 (☎0289/23 127, ③–④), or the *Galini* at Lákka (☎0289/22 626; ③). There are plenty of splurge hotels like *Elysium* (☎0289/23 952; ⑥) on Skholíou Kalón Tehnon and *Petasos* (☎0289/22608; ⑥). As a last resort, the *Apollo 2001* disco may rent out roof space. Otherwise, there are two **campsites**: *Mykonos Camping* on Paranga beach is infinitely superior to the busier *Paradise Camping* – it is less crowded, has a more pleasant setting and is generally a relaxed and friendly place. Both campsites have regular courtesy minibuses to meet the ferries, so getting in and out of town is no problem.

Eating and nightlife

Even **light meals** and **snacks** are expensive in Míkonos, but there are several bakeries – the best is *Andhrea's*, just off Platía Mavroyénous – and plenty of supermarkets and takeaways in the backstreets, including *Spilia* on Énoplon Dhinaméon, which does decent burgers. For **late-night** snacks, try *Margarita's* on Flórou Zouganéli, or after 3am head for the port, where *The Yacht Club* is open until sunrise.

The area around Kaloyéra is a promising place to head for a **full meal**. The *Edem Garden* at the top of Kaloyéra, is a popular gay restaurant with an adventurous menu, and *El Greco* at Tría Pigádhia is expensive but romantic. Alefkándhra can offer *La Cathedral*, by the two cathedrals on the *platía*, the pricey but well-sited *Pelican*, behind the cathedrals, and *Spiro's* for good fish on the seafront. *Kostas*, also behind the two cathedrals has competitive prices, a good selection including barrelled wine (not easily found on Míkonos) and friendly service. Less than fifty metres further along Mitropoleos, the small *Yiavroutas Estiatorio* is probably the least expensive and most authentically Greek place on the island, again with good barrelled wine. There's something for most tastes in the Lákka (bus station) area: a variety of salads at *Orpheas*, French cuisine at *Andromeda*, and Italian at *Dolce Vita*. Just behind the Town Hall is *Nikos' Taverna* – crowded, reasonable and recommended – and 1km north you can dine by a floodlit pool overlooking the cruise ships at the luxury *Hotel Cavo Tagoo*.

Nightlife in town is every bit as good as it's cracked up to be – and every bit as pricey. *Remezzo* (near the OTE) is one of the oldest bars, now a bit over the hill but a nice place to watch the sunset before the onslaught of the hilarious Greek dancing lessons. *Scandinavia Bar* is a cheap and cheerful party spot, as is the nearby *Irish Bar*, and there are more drinking haunts over in the Alefkándhra area. For classical music, try *Kastro's* for an early evening cocktail, moving on later to the fairly swanky *Montparnasse*. *Bolero's* and *Piano Bar* both have live music, while *Le Cinema* is a newish club worth trying. The **gay** striptease and drag-show scene has shifted to the *Factory* by the windmills; *Manto* and adjacent bars are also popular.

Last but not least, the narcissistic beach ethos of Míkonos is well served by an excellent **gym** for weight-trainers and body-builders: *The Bodywork Gym*, run by Ankie Feenstra, lets you show with pride those well-oiled cuts.

The beaches

The closest **beaches** to town are those to the north, at Toúrlos (only 2km away but horrid) and **ÁYIOS STÉFANOS** (4km, much better), both developed resorts and connected by very regular bus service to Míkonos. There are tavernas and rooms to let (as well as package hotels) at Áyios Stéfanos, away from the beach; *Nikos* taverna at the far end of the bay has a pleasant setting and good prices.

Other nearby destinations include southwest peninsula resorts, with undistinguished beaches tucked into pretty bays. The nearest to town, 1km away, is **Megáli Ámmos,** a good beach backed by flat rocks and pricey rooms, but nearby Kórfos bay is disgusting, thanks to the town dump and machine noise. Buses serve **Órnos** – home to the *Lucky Divers Scuba Club* (☎0289/23 220) – with an average beach, though room prices are over-the-top, and **Áyios Ioánnis**, a dramatic bay with a tiny, stony beach and a chapel.

The south coast is the busiest part of the island. *Kaíkia* ply from town to all of its beaches, which are among the straightest on the island, and still regarded to some extent as family strands by the Greeks. You might begin with **PLATÍS YIALÓS**, 4km south of town, though you won't be alone: one of the longest-established resorts on the island, it's not remotely Greek any more, the sand is monopolized by hotels, and you won't get a room to save your life between June and September. **PSAROÚ**, next door, is very pretty – 150m of white sand backed by foliage and calamus reeds, but covered in sunbathers unless it's dawn, dusk, or out of season. Facilities here include a diving club (☎0289/23 579), waterskiing and windsurfer rental, but again you'll need to reserve well in advance to secure a room between mid-June and mid-September.

A dusty footpath beyond Platís Yialós crosses the fields and caves of the headland, leading to **Paránga** beach, where there's an inexpensive and well-appointed **campsite**. There's some good snorkelling to be done around the east of the bay, cluttered with volcanic rocks, starfish, and sea urchins. More footpaths continue across the clifftops and drop down to **Paradise Beach**, well sheltered by its headland, predominantly nudist, and packed full of beautiful people. The crescent of fine white sand makes it a handsome place

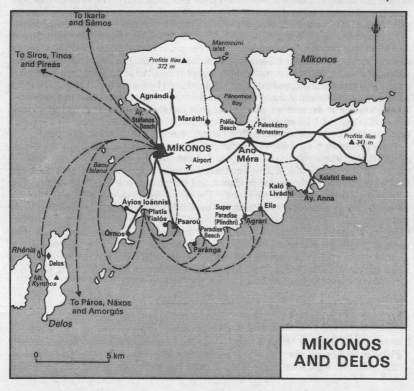

MÍKONOS
AND DELOS

to stay; there's an official campsite (April–Oct) with a diving club and two tavernas. The next bay east contains **Super Paradise** (officially "Plindhrí") beach, again, accessible by footpath or by *kaíki*. Once renowned as an exclusively gay, nudist beach, it's now pretty mixed, and a has a good, friendly atmosphere and a couple of tavernas.

Probably the **best beach** on Míkonos, though, is **Elía**, the last port of call for the *kaíkia*. A broad, sandy stretch with a verdant backdrop, it's the longest beach on the island, though split in two by a rocky area. Almost exclusively nudist, it boasts an excellent restaurant, *Matheos*. If the crowds have followed you this far, one last escape route is to follow the bare rock footpath over the spur (look for the white house) at the end of Elía beach. This cuts upwards for grand views east and west and then winds down to **Kaló Livádhi** (seasonal bus service), a stunning beach adjoining an agricultural valley scattered with little farmhouses; even here there's a restaurant (a good one at that) at the far end of the beach. **Lía,** further on, is smaller but delightful, with bamboo windbreaks and clear water, plus another taverna.

The rest of the island

If time is limited, any of the beaches above will be just fine. There are others, though, away from Míkonos Town, as well as a few other destinations worth making the effort for.

East of Elía, roughly 12km by road from the town, **AYÍA ÁNNA** boasts a shingle beach and taverna, with the cliffs above granting some fine vistas; the place achieved its moment of fame as a location for the film *Shirley Valentine*. **TARSANÁ**, on the other side of the isthmus, has a long, coarse sand beach, with watersports, a taverna and smart bungalows on offer. **KALAFÁTI**, almost adjacent, is more of a tourist community, its white-sand beach supporting a few hotels, restaurants and a disco. There's a local bus service from here to Áno Méra (see below), or you can jump on an excursion boat to **Tragoníssi**, the islet just offshore, for spectacular coastal scenery, seals and wild birds. The rest of the east coast is difficult – often impossible – to reach: there are some small beaches, really only worth the effort if you crave solitude, and the region is dominated by the peak of Profítis Ilías, sadly spoiled by a huge radar dome and military establishment. The **north coast** suffers persistent battering from the *meltémi*, plus tar and litter pollution, and for the most part is bare, brown and exposed. **Pánormos Bay** is the exception to this – a lovely, relatively sheltered beach, and one of the least crowded on the island, with a couple of decent tavernas.

From Pánormos, it's an easy walk to the only other settlement of any size on the island, **ÁNO MÉRA**, where you should be able to find a **room**. The village strives to maintain a traditional way of life: in the main square there's a proper *kafenío* and fresh vegetables are sold, *ouzo* and a local cheese are produced, and there's just one hotel; the taverna *Tou Apostoli toh Koutouki* is popular with locals. The red-roofed church near the square is the sixteenth-century **monastery of Panayía Tourlianí**, where a collection of Cretan icons and the unusual eighteenth-century marble baptismal font are worth seeing. It's not far, either, to the late twelfth-century **Paleokástro monastery** (also known as Dárga), just north of the village, in a magnificent green setting on an otherwise barren slope. To the northwest are more of the same dry and wind-buffeted landscapes, though they do provide some enjoyable, rocky walking with expansive views across to neighbouring islands – stroll down to Áyios Stéfanos for buses back to the harbour.

Delos (Dhílos)

The remains of **ancient Delos**, Pindar's "unmoved marvel of the wide world", though skeletal and swarming now with lizards and tourists, give some idea of the past grandeur of this sacred isle a few sea-miles west of Míkonos. The ancient town lies on the west coast

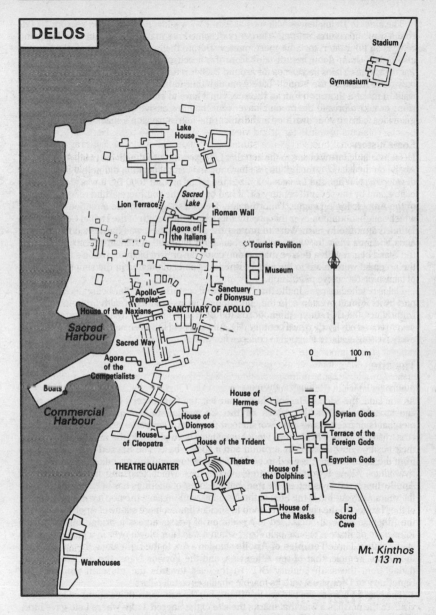

DELOS

Stadium

Gymnasium

Lake
House

Sacred
Lake

Lion Terrace

Roman Wall

Agora of
the Italians

Tourist Pavilion

Museum

Apollo
Temples

Sanctuary
of Dionysus

House of the Naxians

SANCTUARY OF APOLLO

Sacred
Harbour

Sacred Way

Agora
of the
Competialists

Boats

Commercial
Harbour

House of
Dionysos

House
of Cleopatra

House of
Hermes

House of the Trident

Theatre

THEATRE QUARTER

House of
the Dolphins

House of
the Masks

Syrian Gods

Terrace of the
Foreign Gods

Egyptian Gods

Sacred
Cave

Warehouses

Mt. Kinthos
113 m

0   100 m

on flat, sometimes marshy ground which rises in the south to **Mount Kínthos**. From the
summit – an easy walk – there's a magnificent view of almost the entire Cyclades group;
the name of the archipelago means "those [islands] around [Delos]".

The *kaíki* to Delos leaves Míkonos at 9am (2–7 weekly, depending on season; 1500dr round-trip) and returns at 1pm. A larger craft sometimes makes the trip an hour later, and returns an hour later, for a bit more money. During the busier summer months there is also a daily *kaíki* doing return trips from the beaches with pick-up points at Paradise, Paránga, Platís Yialós and Órnes for around 2000dr return. The regular boats will give you only three hours on the island – barely enough time to take in the main attractions. If you want to make a thorough tour of the site, you'll have to come on several morning excursions or take a private afternoon charter tour, both expensive options. In any case, it's a good idea to bring your own food and drink as the tourist pavilion's snack bar is a rip-off.

Some history

Delos' ancient fame was due to the fact that Leto gave birth to the divine twins Artemis and Apollo on the island, although its fine harbour and central position did nothing to hamper development. When the Ionians colonized the island around 1000 BC it was already a cult centre, and by the seventh century BC it had become the commercial and religious centre of the Amphictionic League. Unfortunately Delos also attracted the attention of Athens, which sought dominion over this prestigious island; the wealth of the Delian Confederacy, founded after the Persian Wars to protect the Aegean cities, was harnessed to Athenian ends, and for a while they controlled the Sanctuary of Apollo. Athenian attempts to "purify" the island began with a decree that no one could die or give birth on Delos – the sick and the pregnant were taken to the islet of Rheneia – and culminated in the simple expedient of banishing the native population.

Delos reached its peak in the third and second centuries BC, after being declared a free port by its Roman overlords. In the end, though, its undefended wealth brought ruin: first Mithridates (88 BC), then Athenodorus (69 BC), plundered the treasures and the island never recovered. By the third century AD, Athens could not even sell it, and for centuries, every passing seafarer stopped to collect a few prizes.

The site

Admission 1000dr, including the museum

As you land, the Sacred Harbour is on your left, the Commercial Harbour on your right; and straight ahead is the **Agora of the Competialists**. Competialists were Roman merchants or freed slaves who worshipped the *Lares Competales*, the guardian spirits of crossroads; offerings to Hermes would once have been placed in the middle of the *agora*, their position now marked by a round and a square base. The **Sacred Way** leads north from the far left corner; it used to be lined with statues and the grandiose monuments of rival kings. Along it you reach three marble steps which lead into the **Sanctuary of Apollo**: much was lavished on the god, but the forest of offerings has been plundered over the years. On your left is the Stoa of the Naxians, while against the north wall of the House of the Naxians, to the right, there stood in ancient times a huge statue of Apollo. In 417 BC the Athenian general Nicias led a procession of priests across a bridge of boats from Rheneia to dedicate a bronze palm tree; when it was later blown over in a gale it took the statue with it. Three **Temples of Apollo** stand in a row to the right along the Sacred Way: the Delian Temple, that of the Athenians, and the Porinos Naos, the earliest of them, dating from the sixth century BC. To the east towards the museum you pass the **Sanctuary of Dionysus**, with its marble phalluses on tall pillars.

The best finds from the site are in Athens, but the **museum** (if it's open) still justifies a visit. To the north is a wall that marks the site of the **Sacred Lake** where Leto gave birth, clinging to a palm tree. Guarding it are the superb **Lions**, their lean bodies masterfully executed by Naxians in the seventh century BC; of the original nine, three have disappeared and one adorns the Arsenale at Venice. On the other side of the lake is the City Wall, built in 69 BC – too late to protect the treasures.

Set out in the other direction from the Agora of the Competialists and you enter the residential area, known as the **Theatre Quarter**. Many of the walls and roads remain, but there is none of the domestic detail that brings such sites to life. Some colour is added by the mosaics: one in the **House of the Trident**, and better ones in the **House of the Masks**, most notably a vigorous portrayal of Dionysus riding on a panther's back. The **Theatre** itself seated 5500 spectators, and, though much ravaged, offers some fine views. Behind the theatre, a path leads past the **Sanctuaries of the Foreign Gods** and up **Mount Kínthos** for more panoramic sightseeing.

Síros (Syros)

Don't be put off by first impressions of **Síros**. From the ferry it looks grimly industrial, but away from the Neórion shipyard things improve quickly. Very much a working island with no real history of tourism, it's probably the most Greek of the

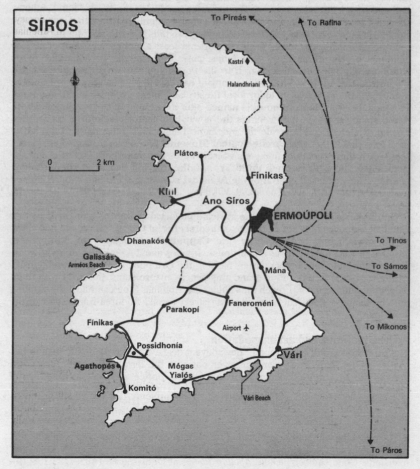

SÍROS

0   2 km

To Pireás
To Rafina

Kastrí
Halandhrianí

Plátos
Fínikas
Klul
Áno Síros
ERMOÚPOLI

Dhanakós
To Tinos

Galissás
Arméos Beach
Mána
To Sámos

Parakopí
Faneroméni

Fínikas
Airport
To Míkonos

Possidhonía
Vári

Agathopés
Mógas
Yialós
Komitó

Vári Beach

To Páros

Cyclades; there are few holiday trappings and what there is exists for the benefit of the locals. You probably won't find, as Herman Melville did when he visited in 1856, shops full of ". . . fez-caps, swords, tobacco, shawls, pistols, and orient finery . . .", but you're still likely to appreciate Síros as a refreshing change from having to compete with the beautiful people. Of course, outsiders do come to the island; in fact there's a thriving permanent foreign community, and the beaches are hardly undeveloped, but everywhere there's the underlying assumption that you're a guest of an inherently private people.

Ermoúpoli

The main town and port of **ERMOÚPOLI** was founded during the War of Independence by refugees from Psará and Híos, becoming Greece's chief port in the nineteenth century. Although Pireás outran it long ago, Ermoúpoli is still the largest town in the Cyclades, and the archipelago's capital. Medieval Síros was largely a Catholic island, but an influx of Orthodox refugees during the War of Independence created two distinct communities; almost equal in numbers, the two groups today still live in their respective quarters, occupying two hills that rise up from the sea.

Ermoúpoli itself, the **lower town**, is worth at least a night's stay, with grandiose buildings a relic of its days as a major port. Between the harbour and **Áyios Nikólaos**, the fine Orthodox church to the north, you can stroll through its faded splendour. The **Apollon Theatre** is a copy of La Scala in Milan and once presented a regular Italian opera season; today local theatre and music groups put it to good use. The long, central **Platía Miaoúli** is named after an admiral of the revolution whose statue stands there; in the evenings the population parades in front of its arcaded *kafenía*, while the children ride the mechanical animals. Up the stairs to the left of the Town Hall is the small **Archeological Museum** (Tues–Sun 8.30am–3pm; closed Mon) with three rooms of finds from Síros, Páros and Amorgós. To the left of the clock tower more stairs climb up to **Vrondádho**, the hill that hosts the Orthodox quarter. The wonderful church of the **Anástasi** stands atop the hill, with its domed roof and great views over Tínos and Míkonos; if it's locked, ask for the key at the priest's house.

On the taller hill to the left is the intricate medieval quarter of **Áno Síros**, with a clutch of Catholic churches below the cathedral of Saint George. There are fine views of the town below, and, close by, the **Cappuchin monastery of Saint Jean**, founded in 1535 to do duty as a poorhouse. It takes about 45 minutes of tough walking up Omírou to reach this quarter, passing the Orthodox and Catholic cemeteries on the way – the former full of grand shipowners' mausoleums, the latter with more modest monuments and French and Italian inscriptions. (You can halve the walking time by taking a short cut on to the stair-street named Andhréa Kárga, part of the way along.)

Arrival, facilities and accommodation

The **quayside** is still busy, though nowadays it deals with more touristic than industrial shipping; Síros is a major crossover point on the ferryboat routes. Also down here is the **bus station**, along with the **tourist police** and several **bike rental** places. Between them shops sell the *loukoúmia* (Turkish delight) and *halvadhópita* (sweetmeat pie) for which the island is famed. **Odhós Híou**, the market street, is especially lively on Saturday when people come in from the surrounding countryside to sell fresh produce.

Keeping step with a growing level of tourism, **rooms** have improved in quality and number in recent years; many are in garishly decorated, if crumbling, Neoclassical mansions. Good choices include *Apollon Rooms* at Odhisséou 8 (☎0281/22 158; ③),

Kástro Rooms, Kalomenopoúlou 12 (☎0281/28 064; ③), or *Rooms Paradise*, Omírou 3 (☎0281/23 204; ③) – follow the little white signposts. Close to the seafront and parallel to the market street is the office of Nick Gavalas, at Ándhrou 14 (☎0281/24451; ②), with rooms and bikes for rent.

A notch up in price and quality is the well-sited *Hotel Hermes* (☎0281/28 011; ④) on Platía Kanári, overlooking the port, or for a slice of good-value opulence, try the *Ksenon Ipatias* (☎0281/23 575; ④), beyond Áyios Nikólaos. At peak times the *Team*

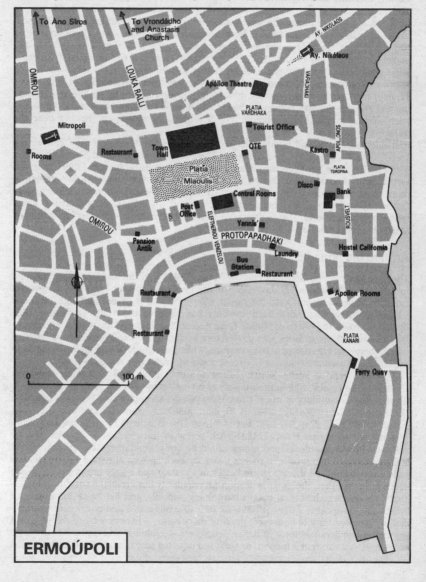

ERMOÚPOLI

Work agency (on the waterfront) may be able to help with accommodation – or place you in their very own *Hotel Europe* (☎0281/28 771; ④), a converted convent. For plusher places around town and hotels of all categories around the island there is a kiosk belonging to the *Syros Hoteliers Association* along the waterfront – turn right after disembarking.

Eating, drinking and nightlife

The most authentic and reasonably priced of the harbour **tavernas** are *Medusa*, at Ándhrou 3, a block in from the water, and *1935*, just inland from the new ferry dock; places actually on the quay tend to be more touristy and expensive. There are one or two exceptions, including the very reasonable *Caro D'Oro* with casseroles and barrelled wine. Highly recommended for an Italian treat is *Il Giardino*, set in a beautifully restored villa opposite the *Apollon*. Just to the left of where the boats dock is an excellent seafront *ouzeri* called *Boubas*. Finally, way up in Vrondádho, at Anastáseos 17, on the corner of Kalavrítou, the cooking at *Tembelis* makes up for the limited seating and grouchy service; *Folia*, at Athanasíou Dhiakoú 6, is more expensive but serves such exotica as rabbit and pigeon. For a musical breakfast, try *Yanni's* near the waterfront.

Incidentally, Síros still honours its contribution to the development of **rembétika** (see "Music" in *Contexts*); *bouzoúki* great Markos Vamvakaris hailed from here and a *platía* in Áno Síros has been named after him. **Taverna-clubs** such as *Lillis* (up in Áno Síros) and *Rahanos*, with music on weekends, now take their place beside a batch of more conventional disco-clubs down near the Apollon Theatre. There are several more (often expensive) *bouzoúki* bars scattered around the island, mostly strung along routes to beach resorts. The seafront has a rash of lively **bars** – *Tramps* has a relaxed atmosphere and the most eclectic music.

Around the island

The main loop road (to Gallissás, Fínikas, Mégas Yialós, Vári and back), and the road west to Kíni, are good: **buses** ply the routes hourly in season, and run until late. Elsewhere, expect potholes – especially to the **north** where the land is barren and high, with few villages. The main route north from Áno Síros has improved and is quite easily negotiable by bike; en route, the village of Mitikas has a decent taverna just off the road. A few kilometres further on the road forks, with the left turn leading to the small settlement of Sirioúga where there's an interesting cave to explore, while the right fork eventually descends to the north-east coast after passing an excellent *kafenío* with views across to Tinos.

The well-trodden route **south** offers more tangible and accessible rewards. Closest to the capital, fifteen minutes away by bus, is the coastal settlement of **KÍNI**. Though the community is more villas than village, there are two separate beaches, the *Sunset Hotel* (☎0281/71 211; ③–④) and, just away from the seafront, the *Hotel Elpida* (☎0281/71 224; ③). Last but not least, the excellent *Iliovasilema* taverna is just below the *Sunset Hotel*. **GALISSÁS**, a few kilometres south, but reached by different buses, has developed along different lines. Fundamentally an agricultural village, it's been taken over in recent years by backpackers attracted by the island's only **campsites** (*Two Hearts* is the better of the two) and a very pretty beach, much more protected than Kíni's. This new-found popularity has created a surplus of unaesthetic **rooms**, which at least makes bargaining possible, and five bona fide hotels, of which the cheapest is *Petros* (☎0281/42 067; ③). Galissás' identity crisis is exemplified by the proximity of bemused, grazing dairy cattle, a heavy-metal music pub, and upmarket handicrafts shops. Still, the people are welcoming, and if you feel the urge to escape, you can rent a moped, or walk ten minutes past the headland to the nudist beach of **Arméos**, where there's fresh springwater and unofficial camping. Note that buses out are erratically routed; to be sure of making your connection you must wait at the high-road stop, not down by the beach. Dhelfíni just to the north is also a fine beach, though it's slowly falling prey to the developers under the translated name of Dolphin Bay.

A pleasant one-hour walk or a ten-minute bus ride south from Galissás brings you to the more mainstream resort of **FÍNIKAS**, purported to have been settled originally by the Phoenicians (although an alternative derivation could be from *fínikas*, meaning "palm tree" in Greek). The beach is narrow and gritty, right next to the road but protected to some extent by a row of tamarisk trees; the pick of the hotels is the *Cyclades* (☎0281/42 255; ③), which also has an acceptable restaurant.

Fínikas is separated by a tiny headland from its neighbour **POSSIDHONÍA** (or Delagrazzia), a nicer spot with some idiosyncratically ornate mansions and a bright blue church right on the edge of the village. It's worth walking ten minutes further south, past the naval yacht club and its patrol boat, to Agathopés, with a sandy beach and a little islet just offshore. Komitó, at the end of the unpaved track leading south from Agathopés, is nothing more than a stony beach fronting an olive grove.

The road swings east to **MÉGAS YIALÓS**, a small resort below a hillside festooned with brightly painted houses. The long, narrow beach is lined with shady trees and there are pedal-boats for hire. **VÁRI** is more – though not much more – of a town, with its own small fishing fleet. Beach-goers are in a goldfish bowl, as it were, with tavernas and **rooms** looming right overhead, but it is the most sheltered of the island's bays, something to remember when the *meltémi* is up. The adjacent cove of **AHLADHI** is far more pleasant and boasts two small good-value hotels, including *Achladi* (☎0281/61400; ②) on the seafront, and one taverna, all under the same management.

Páros and Andíparos

Gently and undramatically furled around the single peak of Profítis Ilías, **Páros** has a little of everything one expects from a "Greek island" – old villages, monasteries, fishing harbours, a labyrinthine capital – and some of the best nightlife and beaches in the Aegean. Parikía, the *hóra*, is the major hub of inter-island ferry services, so that if you wait long enough you can get to just about anywhere else in the Aegean except the Ionian group; making it a favourite starting point for island wanderings. However, the island is almost as heavily touristed and expensive as Míkonos: in peak season, it's touch-and-go when it comes to finding rooms and beach space. At such times, the attractive inland settlements or the satellite island of **Andíparos** handle the overflow. Incidentally, the August 15 festival here is one of the best such observances in Greece, with a parade of flare-lit fishing boats and fireworks delighting as many Greeks as foreigners, but it's a real feat to secure accommodation around this time.

Parikía and around

PARIKÍA sets the tone architecturally for the rest of Páros, with its ranks of typically Cycladic white houses punctuated by the occasional Venetian-style building and church domes. But all is awash in a constant stream of ferry passengers, and the town is relentlessly commercial. The busy waterfront is jam-packed with bars, restaurants, hotels and ticket agencies, while the maze of houses in the older quarter behind,

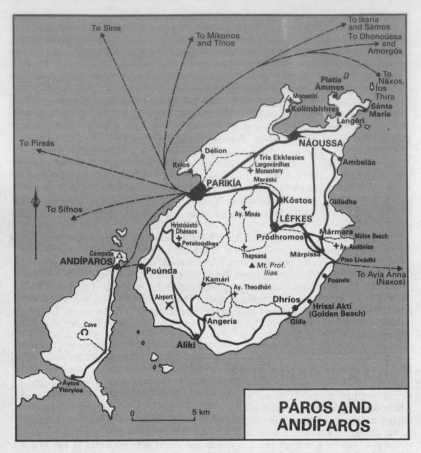

To Síros
To Míkonos
and Tínos
To Ikaría
and Sámos
To Dhonoússa
and
Amorgós

Platía
Ámmos
To
Náxos,
Íos
Thíra
Sánta
María
Monastíri
Kolimbíthres
Langéri

To Pireás
Délion
NÁOUSSA
Tris Ekklesíes
Largovárdhas
Monastery
Maráthi
Ambelás
Kríos
PARIKÍA
Kóstos
Glifádha
To Sífnos
Ay. Minás
LÉFKES
Hristoústó
Dhássos
Mármara
Mólos Beach
Pródhromos
Ay. Andónios
Petaloúdhes
Márpissa
Campsite
Thapsaná
Píso Livádhi
ANDÍPAROS
Poúnda
▲ Mt. Prof.
Ílias
Poúnda
To Ayía Ánna
(Náxos)
Kamári
Airport
Ay. Theodhóri
Dhríos
✕
Hrissí Aktí
(Golden Beach)
Cave
Angeriá
Glifá
Ω
Alikí
Áyios
Ylóryios
0   5 km

**PÁROS AND
ANDÍPAROS**

designed to baffle wind and pirates, has surrendered to an onslaught of chi-chi boutiques.

Just beyond the central clutter, though, the town has one of the most architecturally interesting churches in the Aegean – the **Ekatondapilianí**, or "The One-Hundred-Gated" (daily 9am–1pm & 5–9pm). What's visible today was designed and supervised by Isidore of Miletus in the sixth century, but construction was actually carried out by his pupil Ignatius. It was so beautiful on completion that the master, consumed with jealousy, is said to have grappled with his apprentice on the rooftop, flinging them both to their deaths. They are portrayed kneeling at the column bases across the courtyard: with the old master tugging at his beard in repentance and his rueful pupil clutching a broken head. The church was substantially altered after a severe earthquake in the eighth century, but its essentially Byzantine aspect remains, its shape an imperfect Greek cross. Enclosed by a great wall to protect its icons from pirates, it is in fact three churches interlocking with one another; the oldest, the chapel of Áyios Nikólaos to the left of the apse, is an adaptation of a pagan building dating from the early fourth century

BC. Behind Ekatondapilianí, the **Archeological Museum** (daily except Mon 8.30am–2.30pm; 400dr) has a fair collection of antique bits and pieces, its prize exhibits a fifth-century winged Nike and a piece of the *Parian Chronicle*, a social and cultural history of Greece up to 264 BC engraved in marble.

These two sights apart, the real attraction of Parikía is simply to wander the town itself. Arcaded lanes lead past Venetian-influenced villas, traditional island dwellings and the three ornate wall fountains donated by the Mavroyénnis family in the eighteenth century. The town culminates in a seaward Venetian **Kástro**, whose surviving east wall is constructed of masonry pillaged from ancient temples to Demeter and Apollo. The beautiful, arcaded church of Áyios Konstandínos and Ayía Eléni crowns the highest point, from where the fortified hill drops sharply to the quay in a series of hanging gardens.

If you're staying in town, you'll want to get **out into the surroundings** at some stage, if only to the beach. The most rewarding excursion is the hour's walk along an unsurfaced road starting just past the museum up to **Áyii Anáryiri** monastery. Perched on the bluff above town, this makes a great picnic spot, with cypress groves, a gushing fountain and some splendid views.

There are **beaches** immediately north and south of the harbour, though none are particularly attractive when compared to Páros' best. In fact, you might prefer to avoid the northern stretch altogether; heading **south** along the asphalt road is a better bet. The first unsurfaced side track you come to leads to a small, sheltered beach; fifteen minutes further on is **PARASPÓROS**, with a reasonable **campsite** and beach near the remains of an ancient *asklepeion* ("therapy centre"). Continuing for 45 minutes (or a short hop by bus) brings you to arguably the best of the bunch, **AYÍA IRÍNI**, with good sand and a taverna next to a farm and shady olive grove.

Off in the same direction, but a much longer two-hour haul each way, is **PETALOÚDHES**, the so-called "Valley of the Butterflies", a walled-in oasis where millions of Jersey tiger moths perch on the foliage during early summer (June–Sept 9am–8pm; 200dr). The trip pays more dividends when combined with a visit to the eighteenth-century nunnery of **Hristoú stó Dhássos**, at the crest of a ridge twenty minutes to the north. Only women are allowed in the sanctuary, although men can get as far as the courtyard. The succession of narrow drives and donkey paths linking both places begins just south of Parikía, by the *Ksenon Ery*. Petaloúdhes can be reached from Parikía by bus (in summer), by moped, or on an overpriced excursion by mule.

Arrival, information and accommodation

Ferries **dock** in Parikía by the windmill, which houses a summer tourist information centre. Although there's a bus timetable posted here, the **bus stop** itself is 100m or so to the left; routes extend to Náoussa in the north, Poúnda (for Andíparos) in the west, Alikí in the south, and Dhríos on the island's east coast (with another very useful service between Dhríos and Náoussa). The **airport** is around 12km from town, close to Alikí – from where six daily buses run to Parikía.

Most of the island is flat enough for bicycle rides, but mopeds are more common and are available for rent at several places in town. *Polos Tours* is one of the more together and friendly **travel agencies**, issuing air tickets when *Olympic* is shut, acting as agents for virtually all boats and offering free luggage-storage for customers. *Olympic Airways* itself is at the far end of Odhós Probóne, while the **tourist police** occupy a building at the back of the seafront square.

As for **accommodation**, Parikía is a pleasant and central base, but absolutely mobbed in summer. You'll be met off the ferry by locals offering rooms, even at the most unlikely hours, and late at night it's a good idea to capitulate straightaway. If you arrive on an August day without a reservation, consult the tourist office in the windmill itself which can advise on any (rare) vacancies. Avoid persistent offers of rooms or hotels to the north; they're invariably a long walk away from town, and mosquitos can be a problem. Popular hotels include *Dina* (☎0284/21 325; ④), near Platía Veléntza, and *Kondes* (☎0284/21 246; ④), very close to the windmill by the *ITS Travel Agency*. *Oasis Rooms* (☎0284/21 227; ③–④), near the post office, is fairly reasonable, and there are more rooms to let along the sea front, turning right (south) from the quayside. In the town centre, try *Maria Aliprandi* (☎0284/21 464; ③) or *Mimikos* (☎0284/21 437; ③–④). One of the best deals is to be had at the new branch of *Pension Festos*, managed by young Brits (☎0284/21 635; ③–④).

Eating, drinking and nightlife

Many Parikía **tavernas** are run by outsiders operating under municipal concession, so year-to-year variation in proprietors and quality is marked. However, the following seem to be long-established and/or good-value outfits. Rock-bottom is the *Koutouki Thanasis*, which serves oven food for locals and bold tourists and lurks in a back street behind the (expensive) *Hibiscus*. Also in the picturesque backstreets are *Kyriakos Place* on Lohagou Grivari, which has seats out under a fine tree, and the *Garden of Dionysos* nearby. In the exotic department, *Mey Tey* serves average Chinese food at moderate markup, while Italian dishes can be found at *La Barca Rossa* on the seafront or *Bella Italia* across a waterfront square.

There is a welter of places of varying quality and prices along the seafront towards the bar enclave. Of these, *Asteris Grill House* is very good with some decent specials as well as the usual grilled meats. Further out of town, *Nisiotissa* has a highly entertaining chef-proprietor and is rarely crowded; *Delfini*, on the first paved drive along the road to Poúnda, is long-established and famous for its Sunday barbecue with live music.

Parikía has a wealth of **pubs**, **bars** and low-key **discos**, not as pretentious as those on Míkonos or as raucous as the scene on Íos, but certainly everything in between. The most popular cocktail bars extend along the seafront, all tucked into a series of open squares and offering competing but staggered (no pun intended) "Happy Hours", so that you can drink cheaply for much of the evening. *Kafenio O Flisvos*, about three-quarters of the way south along the front, is the last remaining traditional *oúzo/ mezédhes* outfit among the rash of pizzerias, snack-bars, juice and ice-cream joints. A rowdy crowd favours *Ballos, Apollo's* and the conspicuous *Saloon D'Or*, while the *Pirate Bar* features jazz and blues. *Statue Bar*, *Evinos* and *Pebbles* are more genteel, the latter pricey but with good sunset views and the occasional live gig. The "theme" pubs are a bit rough and ready for some: most outrageous is the *Dubliner Complex*, comprising four bars, a snack section, disco and seating area. Other popular **dance** floors include *Disco 7* and *Hesperides*.

Finally, a thriving cultural centre, *Arhilohos* (near Ekatondapilianí) caters mostly to locals, with occasional **film** screenings; there are also two open-air cinemas, *Neo Rex* and *Paros*, where foreign films are shown in season.

Náoussa and around

The second port of Páros, **NÁOUSSA** was until recently an unspoiled, sparkling labyrinth of winding, narrow alleys and simple Cycladic houses. Alas, a rash of new concrete hotels and attendant trappings have all but swamped its character, though down at the small harbour, fishermen still tenderize octopuses by thrashing them against the walls. The local festivals – an annual Fish and Wine Festival on July 2, and an August 23 shindig celebrating an old naval victory over the Turks – are also still celebrated with enthusiasm; the latter tends to be brought forward to coincide with the August 15 festival of the Panayías. Most people are here for the local beaches (see below) and the relaxed nightlife; there's really only one sight, a **museum** in the church of Áyios Nikólaos Mostrátos, with interesting icons on display.

Despite encroaching development, the town is noted for its nearby beaches and is a good place to head for as soon as you reach Páros. **Rooms** are marginally cheaper here than in Parikía; track them down with the help of Katerini Simitzi's **tourist office** on the main square. Hotels are much more expensive, though out of season you should haggle for reduced prices at the *Madaki* (☎0284/51 475; ④), the *Drossia* (☎0284/51 213; ④), and the *Stella* (☎0284/51 317; ④). There are two campsites in the vicinity: the relaxed and friendly *Naoussa* **campsite** (☎0284/51565), out of town towards Kolimbíthres (see below), and the newer *Surfing Beach* at Alíki, northeast of Náoussa; both run courtesy mini-buses to and from Parikía.

Most of the harbour **tavernas** are surprisingly good, specializing in fresh fish and seafood. *Diamante* is reasonably priced, *Mouragio* and *Psariana* are average, and *Limanakis* is cheap-ish and traditional; avoid the self-service cafés. There are more places to eat along the main road leading inland from just beside the little bridge over the canal. *Zorbas*, with good barrelled unresinated wine, and the friendly *Glaros* next door are both open 24 hours.

Bars cluster around the old harbour: *Linardo* is the big dance spot, *Agosta* plays more rock, while *Remezzo* is quieter; *Camaron* and *Castello* play Greek pop and traditional music respectively. Before the bridge the adjacent *Island* and *Pirate* bars cater to a more laid-back crowd, with classic tracks, and *Pico Pico* plays world music.

Local beaches

Náoussa has no town beach, but there are some good-to-excellent **beaches** within walking distance, and a summer *kaíki* service also connects them. To the west, an hour's tramping brings you to **Kolimbíthres** (Basins), where there are three tavernas and the wind- and sea-sculpted rock formations from which the place draws its name. A few minutes beyond, **Monastíri** beach, below the abandoned Pródhromos monastery, is similarly attractive, and partly nudist. If you go up the hill after Monastíri onto the rocky promontory, the island gradually shelves into the sea via a series of flattish rock ledges, making a fine secluded spot for diving and snorkelling, as long as the sea is calm. Go northeast and the sands are better still, the barren headland spangled with good surfing beaches: **Langéri** is backed by dunes; the best surfing is at **Sánta María**, a trendy beach connected with Náoussa by road which also has a pleasant taverna named *Aristofanes*; and **Platiá Ámmos** perches on the northeasternmost tip of the island.

The northeast coast and inland

AMBELÁS hamlet marks the start of a longer trek down the **east coast**. Ambelás itself has a good beach, a small taverna, some rooms and hotels, of which the *Hotel Christiana* (☎0284/51 573; ④) is excellent value, with great fresh fish and local wine in the restaurant served by extremely friendly proprietors. From here a rough track leads south, passing several undeveloped stretches on the way: after about an hour you reach **Mólos** beach, impressive and not particularly crowded. **MÁRMARA**, twenty minutes further on, has rooms to let and makes an attractive place to stay, though the marble that the village is built from and named after has largely been whitewashed over.

If Mármara doesn't appeal, then serene **MÁRPISSA**, just to the south, might – a maze of winding alleys and aging archways overhung by floral balconies, all clinging precariously to the hillside. There are rooms here too, and you can while away a spare hour climbing up the conical Kéfalos hill, on whose fortified summit the last Venetian lords of Páros were overpowered by the Ottomans in 1537. Today the monastery of **Áyios Andónios** occupies the site, but the grounds are locked; to enjoy the views over eastern Páros and the straits of Naxos fully, pick up the key from the priest in Máripissa before setting out. On the shore nearby, **PÍSO LIVÁDHI** was once a quiet fishing village, but has been ruined by rampant construction in the name of package tourism. The main reason to visit is to catch a (seasonal) *kaíki* to Ayía Ánna on Naxos; if you need to overnight here, try *Pension Márpissa* (☎0284/41 288; ④), *Hotel Leto* (☎0284/41 283 or 41 479; ④) or the *Magia* (☎0284/41 390; ④), which may also let you sleep on the roof; there's a **campsite** as well.

Inland

The road runs west from Píso Livádhi back to the capital, and while there are regular buses back along it you'd do better, if you have time, to return on foot. A medieval flagstoned path once linked both sides of the island, and parts of it survive in the east between Mármara and the villages around Léfkes. **PRÓDHROMOS**, encountered first, is an old fortified farming settlement with defensive walls girding its nearby monastery. **LÉFKES** itself, an hour up the track, is perhaps the most beautiful and unspoilt village on Páros. The town flourished from the seventeenth century on, its population swollen by refugees fleeing from coastal piracy; indeed it was the island's *hóra* during most of the Ottoman period. Léfkes' marbled alleyways and amphitheatrical setting are unparalleled and, despite the presence of an oversized hotel, a very few rooms, a disco and a taverna on the outskirts, the area around the main square has steadfastly resisted change; the central *kafenío* and bakery observe their siestas religiously.

Half an hour further on, through olive groves, is **KÓSTOS**, a simple village and a good place for lunch in a taverna. Any traces of path disappear at **MARÁTHI**, on the site of the ancient marble quarries which once supplied much of Europe. Considered second only to Carrara marble, the last slabs were mined here by the French in the nineteenth century for Napoleon's tomb. From Maráthi, it's easy enough to pick up the bus on to Parikía, but if you want to continue hiking, strike south for the monastery of **Áyios Minás**, twenty minutes away. Various Classical and Byzantine masonry fragments are worked into the walls of this sixteenth-century foundation, and the friendly couple who act as custodians can put you on the right path up to the convent of **Thapsaná**. From here, other paths lead either back to Parikía (two hours altogether from Áyios Minás), or on up to the island's summit for the last word in views over the Cyclades.

The south of the island

There's little to stop for **south of Parikía** until **POÚNDA**, 6km away, and then only to catch the ferry to Andíparos (see below). What used to be a sleepy hamlet is now a concrete jungle – a far cry from the days when you left the Poúnda church door open to summon the boat over from the smaller island. Neighbouring **ALIKÍ** appears to be permanently under construction, and the **airport** is close by, making for lots of unwelcome noise; the sole redeeming feature is an excellent beachside restaurant, by the large tamarisk tree. The end of the southern bus route is at Angería, about 3km inland of which is the **convent of Áyii Theodhóri**. Its nuns specialize in weaving locally commissioned articles and are further distinguished as *paleomeroloyítes*, or old-calendarites, meaning that they follow the medieval Orthodox (Julian) calendar, rather than the Gregorian calendar.

Working your way around the **south coast**, there are two routes east to Dhríos. Either retrace your steps to Angería and follow the (slightly inland) coastal jeep track, which skirts a succession of isolated coves and small beaches; or keep on, across the foothills, from Áyii Theodhóri – a shorter walk. Aside from an abundant water supply (including a duck pond) and surrounding orchards, **DHRÍOS** village is mostly modern and characterless, lacking even a well-defined *platía*. Follow the lane signed "Dhríos Beach", however, and things improve a bit.

Between here and Píso Livádhi to the north are several sandy coves – Hrissí Aktí (Golden Beach), Tzirdhákia, Mezádha, Poúnda and Logarás – prone to pummelling by the *meltémi*, yet all favoured to varying degrees by campers, and windsurfers making a virtue out of necessity. **HRISSÍ AKTÍ** is now thoroughly overrun with tavernas, room complexes and the whole range of watersports; there are also tavernas at Logarás, but other facilities are concentrated in Dhríos, which is still the focal point of this part of the island.

Andíparos

In recent years the islet of **Andíparos** has become something of an open secret among those who consider Páros to be irredeemably sullied. Inevitably, development has pursued the cognoscenti: there are now at least a dozen places to drink, and in July and August there's a steady stream of vehicles around and through the single village. This is not to say that Andíparos is horrendously commercialized; it isn't – yet. Early in the year it's still a good place to rent a small cottage or apartment, but in high season it can be full of the same young, international crowd you were hoping to leave behind on Páros.

Most of the population of 500 live in the surprisingly large northern **village**, with a long, flagstoned pedestrian street forming its backbone and ending at two squares linked by archways. One has a giant eucalyptus and several cafés; the other is a small, exquisite replica of the *kástro* on Síkinos, with the dwellings on the periphery surviving to their original heights and a central cistern instead of a church. Elsewhere there is the usual complement of Cycladic domes and arches – all in all, a pleasant surprise for those expecting the generally unremarkable architecture of other minor islets.

Andíparos' **beaches** begin right outside town: Psaralidháki, where clothing is optional, is just to the east, and better than "Sunset" beach on the opposite side of the island, though the latter often hosts evening soccer matches. Glífa lies about halfway down the eastern coast, with Livadháki its counterpart to the west. For real seclusion, however, head for Áyios Yióryios on the southwest side, where fine, small sandy coves remain uncluttered despite incipient villa development.

The great **cave** (daily 9.45am–4.45pm; 400dr), inland, just before Áyios Yióryios is the chief attraction for day-trippers. In these eerie chambers the eccentric Marquis de Nointel celebrated Christmas Mass in 1673 while 500 bemused but well-paid Parians looked on; at the exact moment of midnight explosives were detonated to emphasize the enormity of the event. Although electric light and cement steps have diminished its mystery and grandeur, the cave remains impressive. Two buses a day run from the port to the cave. Should you miss them it's a stoney ninety-minute hike from the village, or you can jump on one of the morning boats which will transfer you down the coast to within a short, if tiring, walk of it. In the off-season, you'll have to fetch the key for the cave from the village.

Practicalities

To get here, you have a choice of summer-only **kaíkia** from Parikía (4–5 daily; 1hr) or the year-round, **barge-ferry** (hourly; 15min) from Poúnda, which takes vehicles and is also designed to dovetail with the comings and goings of the Páros buses. If you decide to take in Andíparos as a day-trip from Páros, there is no problem taking rental bikes across on the ferry from Poúnda.

There are two inexpensive **hotels**, the *Mandalena* (☎0284/61 206; ③) and the *Anargyros* (☎0284/61 204; ③) and two slightly more expensive ones, *Galini* (☎0284/61 420; ④) and *Akrogiali* (☎0284/61231; ④), as well as plenty of **rooms**, plus a very popular **campsite** ten minutes' walk northwest along a track, next to its own nudist beach. If you yearn for the quiet life, but with a degree of comfort, try the *Delfini* apartments (☎01/80 53 613 – no local telephone yet; ④) out at Áyios Yióryios; a bus and a mobile food wagon make the journey out here twice daily in high summer.

Of the dozen or so **tavernas** in the village, the *Anargyros*, right on the dock below the namesake hotel, and *Klimataria*, 100m inland, stay open at lunchtime, and *Mario's*, just before the square, features local wine; there's an excellent sweetshop in the eucalyptus-filled *platía* itself. A short-schedule **bank**, a tiny **OTE** booth with morning and evening hours, a **post office**, a **cinema** and several travel agents round out the list of amenities, so that you need never go to Parikía for errands if you don't wish to.

Náxos

Náxos is the largest and most fertile of the Cyclades, and with its green and mountainous interior seems immediately distinct from many of its neighbours. The difference is accentuated by the unique architecture of many of the interior villages: the Venetian occupation (from the thirteenth to the sixteenth century) left towers and fortified mansions scattered throughout the island, while late medieval Cretan refugees bestowed a singular character upon Náxos' eastern settlements.

Today Náxos could easily support itself without tourism by relying on its production of potatoes, olives, grapes and lemons, but has thrown its lot in with mass tourism, so that the island is now almost as busy and commercialized as Páros in season. An airport, which generally acts as a catalyst in such matters, finally opened in 1992; the runway, however, cannot accommodate large jets, and was built atop a former salt-marsh.

Few visitors venture away from the harbour and beach area, though more people trickle inland each year, refusing to be scared off by exaggerated tales of the gruffness of the villagers. And the island certainly has plenty to see if you know where to look: intriguing central valleys, a windy but spectacular north coast, and marvellously sandy beaches in the southwest – these last some of the best in Greece.

Náxos Town

A long causeway, built to protect the harbour to the north, connects **NÁXOS TOWN** (or Hóra) with the islet of Palátia – the place where, according to legend, Theseus abandoned Ariadne on his way home from Crete. The huge stone portal of a **Temple of Apollo** still stands there, built on the orders of the tyrant Lygdamis in the sixth century BC but never completed. Most of the town's life goes on down by the crowded port esplanade or just behind it; move into the back streets and there's an almost medieval atmosphere. Claustrophobic, silent alleys behind the harbour lead up past crumbling balconies and through low arches to the fortified **Kástro**, from where Marco Sanudo and his successors ruled over the Cyclades for the Venetians. Only two of the *kástro's* original seven towers – those of the Sanudo and Glezos families – remain, although the north gate (approached from Apóllonos) survives as a splendid example of a medieval fort entrance. The Venetians' Catholic descendants, now dwindling in numbers, still live in the old mansions which encircle the site, many with ancient coats-of-arms above crumbling doorways. Other brooding relics survive in the same area: a seventeenth-century Ursuline convent and the Roman Catholic Cathedral – restored in questionable taste in the 1950s, though still displaying a thirteenth-century crest inside. Nearby is one of Ottoman Greece's first

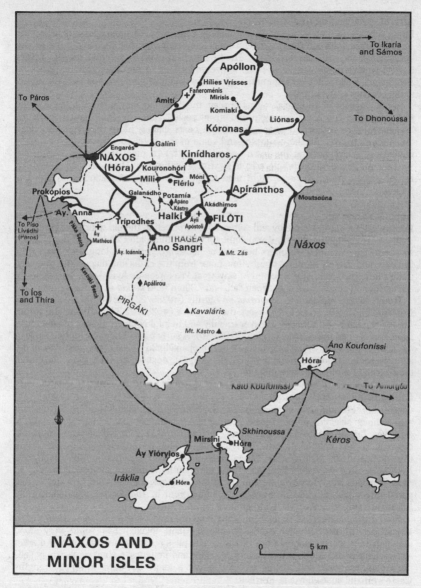

NÁXOS AND MINOR ISLES

0   5 km

schools, the French School; opened in 1627 for Catholic and Orthodox students alike, its pupils included, briefly, Nikos Kazantzakis. The school building now houses an excellent **Archeological Museum** (daily except Mon 8.30am–3pm; 400dr), whose range of finds – mostly pottery – indicates that Náxos was continually occupied throughout antiquity, from Neolithic to Roman times.

Arrival, information and transport

Large ferries dock along the northerly harbour causeway. All small boats, including the *kaíkia* to Ayía Ánna and the very useful small ferry *Skopelitis*, use the jetty in the fishing harbour, *not* the main car ferry dock. The **bus station** (with a useful left-luggage office) is at its landward end: services run up to five times daily to Apóllon in the far north, via Áno Sangrí, Halkí, Filóti and Apíranthos (for all of which see below), and virtually hourly to the beaches at Ayía Ánna.

In the absence of an official tourist bureau, the **"info"** agency just at the base of the ferry jetty has the most complete and disinterested range of information, probably because they're authorized agents for all the boats calling here; they can also book (expensive) **rooms**. All the campsites and some of the hotel complexes send courtesy minibuses (which park at the town end of the jetty) to meet the ferries during the summer months, and the whole area is swarming with touts. There are two good **bike rental** places: *Nikos Katsaras*, right next to the post office, and another by the bus station.

Accommodation

Rooms can be hard to come by and somewhat overpriced in the old quarter of Hóra, and single rooms are non-existent. If you come up with nothing after an hour of hunting, the southern extension of town offers better value, although you are a long walk from most facilities, and there's significant night-time noise from the clubs and discos. Alternatively, there's little inconvenience involved in staying at Prokópios or Ayía Ánna, with buses in each direction almost hourly between 8am and 7.30pm (and *kaíkia* almost as regularly).

Hotel choices include the *Panorama* on Afitrítis (☎0285/22 330; ④), the nearby *Anixis* (☎0285/22 112; ④), or, as a last resort, the *Dionyssos* (☎0285/22 331; ③) near the *kástro*. Around the back of the *kástro*, the ever friendly and helpful Nikos Katsaras, of bike-rental fame, has opened the *Kastelli* (☎0285/23 082; ④). A fairly bland but cheap option close to the quay is the *Proto* (☎0285/22 394; ③) at Protopapadháki 13, or make your way to the attractive ochre-coloured *Hermes* (☎0285/23 208; ⑤), next to the OTE at the far end of the seafront, for plusher surroundings.

Eating, drinking and nightlife

One of the best quayside breakfast bars is the *Bikini*, which also has a fine bar upstairs with a choice selection of rock music. Further along to the south are a string of relatively expensive but simple oven-food **tavernas** – *Iy Kali Kardhia* is typical, serving acceptable casserole dishes washed down with *híma* wine – which nevertheless offer better value than places in the "Old Market Street" area inland. Much better for the money are *Papagalos*, a mostly vegetarian place in the new southern district, almost all the way to Áyios Yióryios bay; *Karnayio*, behind the *National Bank*, for fish; and *O Tsitas* on the paved street just behind the seafront. A hidden gem is *Toh Roupel*, a wonderful old *kafenío* in a tiny square up Old Market Street.

For local fresh fruit and vegetables, something of a rarity in the Cyclades, there's often a morning **market** outside the Agricultural Bank. Náxos has some very good sandal-makers, particularly Markos Skylakis, who plies his trade near the former market square. The island is also renowned for its wines and liqueurs; a shop on the quay sells the *Prombonas* white and vintage red, plus *kítron*, a lemon firewater in three strengths (there's also a banana-flavoured variant).

Much of the evening action goes on at the south end of the waterfront, and slightly inland in the new quarter. **Nightlife** tends more towards tippling than music clubs, though the misnamed *Day Club* belts out jazz to a well-heeled clientele, and *Jam-Jam* pumps out an average mixture of sounds behind the OTE. The *Ocean Club* is more lively, subsisting on pop-chart fodder, and there are other discos towards Áyios Yióryios – some of them with distinctly uninviting bouncers.

The southwestern beaches

The **beaches** around Náxos Town are considered to be the island's best. For some unusual swimming just to the **north** of the port, beyond the causeway, *Grotta* is easiest to reach. Besides the caves for which the place is named, the remains of submerged Cycladic buildings are visible, including some stones said to be the entrance to a tunnel leading to the unfinished Temple of Apollo.

The finest spots, though, are all **south** of town, the entire southwestern coastline boasting a series of excellent **beaches** accessible by regular bus and *kaíki*. ÁYIOS YIÓRYIOS, a long sandy bay fringed by the southern extension of the hotel "colony", is within walking distance. There are several tavernas here and a windsurfing school, plus the first of three **campsites**, with whose touts you will no doubt have become acquainted at the ferry jetty. A word of warning for campers: although this entire coast is relatively sheltered from the *meltémi*, the plains behind are boggy and you should bring along mosquito repellent, as well as plenty of fresh water.

Skipping the bus, a pleasant hour's walk south through the salt marshes brings you to PROKÓPIOS beach, with reasonably priced hotels, rooms and basic tavernas, plus the relaxed *Apollon* campsite nearby. Or follow the track a little further to AYÍA ÁNNA (habitually referred to as "Ayi'Ánna"), a small fishing and potato-shipping port where there are plenty of **rooms** to let and a few modest tavernas (plus summer *kaíkia* to Píso Livádhi on Páros). The sea-view *Hotel Ayia Anna* (☎0285/24 430; ④) and adjacent *Gorgona* taverna, co-managed by the Kapri family, are both highly recommended. Away from the built-up area, the beach here is nudist, and the busy *Maragas* **campsite** thrives.

Beyond the headland stretch the five lovely kilometres of PLÁKA beach, a vegetation-fringed expanse of white sand that comfortably handles the summer crowds of nudists and campers. There are only a couple of buildings right in the middle of Pláka beach, so bring your own provisions. For real isolation, stalk off to the other side of Mikrí Vígla headland, along a narrow footpath across the cliff edge, to KASTRÁKI beach – almost as good, and with a single taverna. Be warned, however, that the sea at the southern end of this beach (at Alikó promontory) catches the sewage swept down from Náxos Town. From Kastráki, it's an hour's walk up to the castle of Apalírou which held out for two months against the besieging Marco Sanudo. The fortifications are relatively intact and the views are magnificent. Even more remote is PIRGÁKI beach, the last stop on the coastal bus route and 21km from Náxos Town; four kilometres further on is Ayiássos beach, where the *Hotel Neraida* (☎0285/75 301; ③) offers decent long-stay terms and has a reasonable but rather slow restaurant.

The rest of the **southern coast** – indeed, virtually the whole of the southeast of the island – is almost completely deserted, and studded by mountains; you'd have to be a very dedicated and well-equipped camper/hiker to get much out of the region.

Central Náxos and the Tragéa

Although buses for Apóllon (in the north) link up the central Naxian villages, the core of the island – between Náxos town and Apíranthos – is best explored by moped or on foot. Much of the region is well off the beaten track, and can be a rewarding excursion if you've had your fill of beaches.

Out of Hóra, you quickly arrive at the neighbouring villages of GLINÁDHO and GALANÁDHO, forking respectively right and left. Both are scruffy market centres: Glinádho is built on a rocky outcrop above the Livádhi plain; Galanádho displays the first of Náxos' fortified mansions and an unusual "double church". A combined Orthodox chapel and Catholic sanctuary separated by a double arch, the church reflects both the tolerance of the Venetians during their rule and of the locals to established Catholics afterwards. Continue beyond Glinádho to TRÍPODHES (ancient Biblos),

9km from Náxos Town. Noted by Homer for its wines, this old-fashioned agricultural village has nothing much to do except enjoy a coffee at the shaded *kafenío*. The start of a long but rewarding walk is a rough road (past the parish church) which leads down the colourful Pláka valley – past an old watchtower and the Byzantine church of Áyios Mathéos (mosaic pavement) – and ends at the glorious Pláka beach (see above).

To the east, the twin villages of **SANGRÍ**, on a vast plateau at the head of a long valley, can be reached by continuing to follow the left-hand fork past Galanádho, a route which allows a look at the domed eighth-century church of **Áyios Mámas** (on the left), once the Byzantine cathedral of the island but neglected during the Venetian occupation and now a sorry sight. Either way, **KÁTO SANGRÍ** boasts the remains of a Venetian castle, while **ÁNO SANGRÍ** is a comely little place, all cobbled streets and fragrant courtyards. A half hour's stroll away, on a path leading south out of the village, is a small Byzantine chapel, **Áyios Ioánnis Yíroulas**, which boasts a breathtaking view down to the sea; the site originally held a Classical temple of Demeter, then a Christian basilica, leaving marble chunks and column fragments scattered around.

The Tragéa

From Sangrí the road twists northeast into the **Tragéa** region, a densely fertile area occupying a vast highland valley. It's a good jumping-off point for all sorts of exploratory rambling, and **HALKÍ** is a fine introduction to what is to come. Set high up, 16km from the port, it's a noble and silent town with some lovely churches. The **Panayía Protóthronis** church, with its eleventh- to thirteenth-century frescoes, and the romantic **Grazia (Frangopoulos) Pírgos**, are open to visitors, but only in the morning. Tourists wanting to stay here are still something of a rarity, although you can usually get a room in someone's house by asking at the store. The olive and citrus plantations surrounding Halkí are crisscrossed by paths and tracks, the groves dotted with numerous Byzantine chapels and the ruins of fortified *pírgi* or Venetian mansions. Between Halkí and Akadhímos, but closer to the latter, sits the peculiar twelfth-century "piggyback" church of **Áyii Apóstoli**, with a tiny chapel (where the ennobled donors worshipped in private) perched above the narthex; there are brilliant thirteenth-century frescoes as well.

A delightful circular path starts from Halkí, heading north to Kalóxilos and, beyond, picking up a track and a road to **MONÍ**. Just before the village, you pass the sixth-century monastery of **Panayía Dhrossianí**, a group of stark grey stone buildings with some excellent frescoes; the monks allow visits at any time, though you may have to contend with coach tours from Náxos Town. Moní itself enjoys an outstanding view of the Tragéa and surrounding mountains, and has three **tavernas**, and some **rooms**, from which you can enjoy both. A dirt road leads on to Kinídharos with its old marble quarry, above the village, and a few kilometres beyond a signpost points you down a rough track to the left, to **FLÉRIO** (also commonly called Melanés). The most interesting of the ancient marble quarries on Náxos, this is home to two famous **koúri**, dating from the sixth century BC, that were left recumbent and unfinished because of flaws in the material. Even so, they're finely detailed figures, over five metres in length: one of the statues lies in a private, irrigated orchard; the other is up a hillside some distance above, and you will need to seek local guidance to find it.

From Flério you could retrace your steps to the road and head back to the *hóra* via Míli and the ruined Venetian castle at Kouronohóri, both pretty hamlets connected by footpaths. If you're feeling more adventurous, ask to be directed south to the footpath which leads over the hill to the Potamía villages. The first of these, **ÁNO POTAMÍA**, has a fine taverna and a rocky track back towards the Tragéa. Once past the valley the landscape becomes craggy and barren, the forbidding Venetian fortress of **Apáno Kástro** perched on a peak just south of the path. This is believed to have been Sanudo's summer home, but the fortified site goes back further if the Mycenean tombs found nearby are any indication. From the fort, paths lead back to Halkí in around an hour.

Alternatively you can continue further southwest down the Potamía valley toward Hóra, passing first the ruined **Cocco pírgos** – said to be haunted by one Constantine Cocco, the victim of a seventeenth-century clan feud – on the way to **MÉSO POTAMÍA**, joined by some isolated dwellings with its twin village **KÁTO POTAMÍA**, nestling almost invisibly among the greenery flanking the creek.

At the far end of the gorgeous Tragéa valley, **FILÓTI**, the largest village in the region, lies on the slopes of Mount Zas (or Zeus) which, at 1000m, is the highest point in the Cyclades. Essentially agricultural, the village's only concession to tourism is a garish fast-food restaurant; otherwise nights out are spent in the very Greek and friendly tavernas and *kafenía*, sampling the region's locally bottled orange and lemonade drinks. Water shortages caused a mass exodus in the 1960s, though Filóti seems to have partly recovered. There are, perhaps as a consequence, plenty of old **houses to rent** and you could do worse than use Filóti as a long-term base; rooms or hotels on the other hand are virtually non-existent. From the village, it's a round-trip walk of two to three hours to the summit of Zás, a climb which rewards you with an astounding panorama of virtually the whole of Náxos and its Cycladic neighbours. From the main Filóti–Apóllon road, take the side road towards Dhánakos until you reach a small chapel on the right, just beside the start of the waymarked final approach trail.

APÍRANTHOS, a hilly, winding 10km beyond, shows the most Cretan influence of all the interior villages. The houses, built mostly of unwhitewashed local stone, present a mottled grey and tan aspect, and the inhabitants are reserved and dignified, though helpful when approached – and reputed to be the best musicians on the island. Among the subdued houses, there are two small **museums** and two Venetian fortified mansions, while the square contains a miniature church with a three-tiered belltower. Ask to be pointed to the start of the spectacular path up over the ridge behind; this ends either in Moní or Kalóxilos, depending on whether you fork right or left respectively at the top.

Apíranthos has a beach annexe of sorts at **MOUTSOÚNA**, 12km east. Emery mined near Apíranthos used to be transported here, by means of an aerial funicular, and then shipped out of the port. The industry collapsed recently and the sandy cove beyond the dock now features a growing colony of vacation villas. The coast south of here is completely isolated, the road petering out into a rutted track – ideal for self-sufficient campers, but take enough water.

Northern Náxos

The route northeast to Apóllon is very scenic and the roads are in good condition all the way. Jagged ranges and hairpin bends confront you before reaching Kóronos, the halfway point, where a road off to the right threads through a wooded valley to **LIÓNAS**, a tiny and very Greek port with a pebbly beach. You'd do better to continue, though, past Skádho, to the high, remote, emery-miners' village of **KOMIAKÍ** – the original home of *kitron* liqueur, and a pleasing, vine-covered settlement which is also the starting-point for perhaps the most extraordinary walk on Náxos. Head up the mountainside path and cross the ridge as far as an improbably long marble *kalderími* or staircase, which descends into the valley. It's overwhelmingly tempting to climb down this Jack-and-the-Beanstalk fixture (though bear in mind that you'll need to come back up at some point): the views are marvellous, the experience exhilarating, and the hamlet at the bottom, **MIRÍSIS**, is enchanting. People from Komiakí migrate downwards in spring and summer to tend and harvest their crops; there are no amenities and all the food is locally produced in this veritable oasis.

Back on the main road, a series of slightly less hairy bends lead down a long valley to **APÓLLON** (Apóllonas), an embryonic and rather tatty resort, with the beach by turns clean and calm, or marred by washed-up tar. There are, however, **rooms** above the shops and tavernas, several **hotels**, and one major attraction – a **koúros**, approached along an unsurfaced road. Lying in situ at a former marble quarry, this largest of Náxos' abandoned stone figures is just over ten metres long, but, compared to those at Flério, disappointingly lacking in detail. Here since 600 BC, it serves as a singular reminder of the Naxians' traditional skill; the famous Delian lions (see p.450) are also made of Apollonian marble. Not surprisingly, bus tours descend upon the village during the day, but by nightfall Apóllon is a peaceful place; the local festival, celebrated on August 29, is one of Náxos's best, though the place is all but shut a month later.

Apóllon is as far as the bus goes, but with your own transport it's possible to loop back to Náxos Town on the northern coastal route: windswept, bleak, and far removed from the verdant centre of the island. Make sure that you're equipped for this trip, since there are few settlements along the way. Ten kilometres past the northern cape sprouts the beautiful Ayía *pírgos*, another foundation (in 1717) of the Cocco family. There's a tiny hamlet nearby, and, 7km further along, a track leads off to ÁVRAM beach, an idyllic spot with a family-run taverna and **rooms** to let. Just beyond Híllies Vrísses, the only real village in this region, is the abandoned **monastery of Faneroménis**, built in 1606. Nearby, there's another deserted beach, **AMITÍ**, and then the track leads inland, up the Engarés valley, to Engarés and **GALÍNI**, only 6km from Hóra. The road at last becomes paved here, and on the final stretch back to the port passes a unique eighteenth-century Turkish fountain-house and the fortified monastery of **Ayíou Ioánnou Hrisostómou**, where a couple of aged nuns are still in residence. A footpath from the monastery and the road below lead straight back to town.

Koufoníssi, Skhinoússa, Iráklia and Dhonoússa

In the patch of the Aegean beween Náxos and Amorgós there is a chain of six small islands neglected by tourists and by the majority of Greeks, few of whom have heard of them. **Kéros** – ancient *Karos* – is an important archeological site but has no permanent population, and **Káto Koufoníssi** is inhabited only by goatherds. However, the other four islands – **Áno Koufoníssi, Skhinoússa, Iráklia** and **Dhonoússa** – are all inhabited, served by ferry, and can be visited. Now just beginning to be discovered by Greeks and foreigners alike, the islets' increasing popularity has hastened the development of better faciltities, but they're still a welcome break from the mass tourism of the rest of the Cyclades, especially during high season. If you want real peace and quiet – what the Greeks call *isikhía* – get there soon.

A few times weekly in summer a Pireás-based **ferry** – usually the *Apollon Express* or the tardy *Ergina* – calls at each of the islands, linking them with Náxos and Amorgós and (usually) *Páros, Síros, Sérifos* and *Sífnos*. A *kaíki*, the *Skopelitis*, is a reliable daily fixture, leaving Náxos in mid-afternoon for relatively civilized arrival times at all the islets. *Ilios* lines hydrofoil calls on demand at all the islands except Dhonoússa on its twice-weekly foray to Amorgós; you must let the steward, if you're on the hydrofoil,or agent, if you're on the island, know if you want to be picked up or put down.

Koufoníssi and Kéros

Ano Koufoníssi is the most populous island of the group; there is a reasonable living to be made from fishing, and an increasing number of Greek holidaymakers and more adventurous foreigners are being attracted here. The smallest and flattest of the minor islands, it can easily be walked round in a day. The single village of **HÓRA** clusters around the harbour: amenities include a post office, an OTE booth and rooms to let, although they can be in short supply in peak season; an official but rather poorly serviced campsite takes up the slack. Hóra has a number of **eating** and **drinking**

establishments: recommended places are the *Mavros* taverna, a *psistariá* belonging to Dimitris Skopelitis, and the café/restaurant *Soroccos*. *Ta Kalamia* café is also a good spot, as is the *Karnayio Ouzeri*, which offers a fine array of seafood. The best beaches are Fínikas, ten minutes walk from Hóra and blessed with a taverna, and Borí.

Káto Koufoníssi, the isolated islet to the southwest of Áno Koufoníssi, has no accommodation but there is a taverna and some more secluded beaches; local *kaíkia* shuttle people across according to demand.

Kéros is uninhabited and communications are less certain, but if there is a willing group of people keen to visit the ancient site, a boat and boatmen can be hired for around 15,000dr for the day.

Skhinoússa

A little to the west, the island of **Skhinoússa** is just beginning to awaken to its touristic potential, largely due to the energetic efforts being made in that direction by one Yiorgos Grispos.

Boats dock at the small port of Mirsíni, which has one pension (☎0285/71 157; ④) and a couple of cafés; a road leads up to **HÓRA**, the walk takes just over ten minutes. As you enter the village, the well-stocked shop of the Grispos family is one of the first buildings on the left and the aforementioned Yiorgos is a mine of information. Indeed, he is personally responsible for the island's map and postcards, as well as being the boat/hydrofoil agent, having the OTE phone and selling the Greek and foreign press.

Accommodation is mostly in fairly simple rooms, such as *Pension Meltemi* (☎0285/71195; ④), *Anesis* (☎0285/71180; ③), *Drossos* and *Nomikos* (no phone; both ③). The main concentration of **restaurants**, cafés and bars is along the main thoroughfare, including a lively *ouzeri* and, further along on the left, the pleasant *Schoinoussa* restaurant – another Grispos family venture.

There are no less than sixteen beaches dotted around the island and accessible by a lacework of trails. Freelance campers congregate on **Tsigoúri beach**, a little over five minutes from Hóra, where there's a large bar and hotel complex under construction by the ubiquitous Grispos. The only other beach with any refreshments is Almirós, which has a simple canteen.

Iráklia

The westernmost of the minor Cyclades, **Iráklia** (pronounced Irakliá by locals) is a real gem, with an atmosphere reminiscent of the Greece of fifteen years ago. There is a small but sprawling settlement at the port with several places to eat, rooms to let and the café/shop *Melissa*, which also acts as a ticket agency for boats and hydrofoils. Hóra, with a few rooms and limited provisions, is the best part of an hour's stroll inland through mountainous terrain; further still, there is a fine cave on the far side of the island. Most visitors stay about fifteen minutes' walk from the port across the hill to the left at Fínikas beach, where there are some **rooms and tavernas** – including one run by the friendly and animated Yiorgos Gavalas, who usually meets ferries at the dock. The beach really is lovely, both deep and wide, with plenty of large bushes and a few trees for shade, and crystal-clear sea – as close as you can get to paradise in modern Greece.

Dhonoússa

Dhonoússa is a little out on a limb in comparison with the others, especially because it is not served by the hydrofoils and the other ferries call far less frequently. Being more northeasterly it is also prone to having its limited connections cut by the winds.

Hóra, where the boat docks, is pleasant enough, and the number of cafés, restaurants and tavernas has now reached double figures; the island has about a hundred rooms for rent, almost all in Hóra. Smaller settlements are dotted around the island and there are several beaches to choose from; including Kéndros and Livádhi to the east, via the hamlets of Haravyí and Mirsíni. The latter has the only springs, orchards and vegetable patches on the island, which may explain the scarcity of fresh produce in these parts.

Amorgós

Amorgós is virtually two islands. Roads through its splendidly rugged terrain are so poor that by far the easiest way of getting between Katápola in the southwest and Egiáli in the northeast is by ferry, *kaíki* or hydrofoil. Hydrofoils in particular dovetail well with the schedules of the main-line ferries, and have greatly lessened the island's isolation; gone are the days when you were sure to get marooned here. Currently all large and most small boats call at both ports, and accept short-hop passengers between one and the other. The bus service between Katápola and Egiáli has also improved, now running five or six times a day.

The island can get extremely crowded in mid-summer, the numbers swollen by Europeans paying their respects to the film location of Luc Besson's *The Big Blue*, although few actually venture out to the wreck of the *Olympia*, at the island's west end, which figured so prominently in the movie. In general it's a low-key, escapist clientele, happy to have found a relatively large, interesting and uncommercialized island with excellent walking.

This may change, however, since the provincial authorities have big plans, including such drastic measures as extensive asphalting of roads, banning ferries from Egiáli altogether and turning its port into a yacht marina. It seems an incongruous fate for an island which, like Folégandhros, has been used as a neglected place of political exile for thousands of years.

The southwest

KATÁPOLA, set at the head of a deep bay, is actually three separate hamlets: Katápola proper on the south flank, Rahídhi on the ridge at the head of the gulf, and Ksilokeratídhi along the north shore. The beach here won't win many awards, unless they're conferred by the two dozen ducks who waddle contentedly across the foreshore, but by virtue of its convenience the place has become a resort of sorts.

There are plenty of small **hotels** and **pensions** and, except in high summer when rooms are almost impossible to find, proprietors tend to meet those boats arriving around sunset – though not necessarily those that show up in the small hours. Among the better places is *Dhimitri's* in Rahídhi (③–④), an enormous compound of interconnecting buildings in an orchard where rooms with bath and use of kitchen vary in price, depending on the season and the number of people. The more obvious *Pension Amorgos* (☎0285/71 013; ③) and fancy *Hotel Minoa* (☎0285/71 480; ④) on the water will be considerably noisier. Best of all is *Tasia Pension* (☎0285/71 313; ②), although it's often booked up by regular guests during the busier months. In Katápola proper, *Mourayio* is the most popular **taverna** with foreigners, though the locals hang out at *O Kamari* mid-quay, whose main attraction seems to be a wide range of sweets. The best bet for a winning combination of food, prices and atmosphere is the *Akrogiali* taverna, while what **nightlife** there is focuses on a handful of cafés and pubs.

Prekas is the one-stop **boat ticket agency**, and a new **OTE** stays open until 11pm. **Moped rental** is available at *Thomas Rentabike* (☎0285/71 007), though the local bus service is more than adequate and walking trails delightful. The **campsite** is well signed between Rahídhi and Ksilokeratídhi; in the latter district are three **tavernas**, of which the middle one – *Vitzentzos* – is by far the best.

Steps, and then a jeep track, lead out of Katápola to the remains of **ancient Minoa**, which are apt to disappoint up close: some Cyclopean wall four or five courses high,

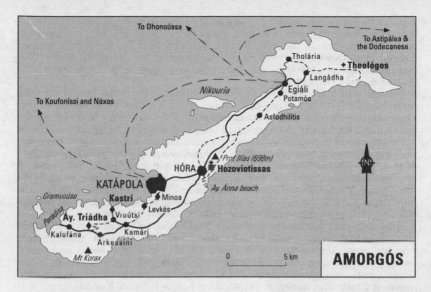

the foundations of an Apollo temple, a crumbled Roman structure and bushels of unsorted pottery shards. It's only the site, with views encompassing Hóra and ancient Arkessíni, that's the least bit memorable. Beyond Minoa the track soon dwindles to a trail, continuing within a few hours to Arkessíni (see below) via several hamlets – a wonderful **excursion** with the possibility of catching the bus back.

The **bus** shuttles almost hourly until 11pm between Katápola and Hóra, the island capital; several times daily the service continues to Ayía Ánna via Hozoviotíssas monastery, and twice a day there's a run out to the "Káto Meriá", made up of the hamlets of Kamári, Arkessíni and Kolofána. **HÓRA**, also accessible by an hour-long path beginning from behind the Rahídhi campsite, is a bleak introverted place, but not without character. Dominated by a rock plug wrapped with a chapel or two, the thirteenth-century Venetian fortifications look down on countless other bulbous churches – including Greece's smallest, **Áyios Fanoúrios**, which holds just three worshippers – and a line of decapitated windmills beyond. Of the half-dozen or so **places to stay**, *Pension Hora* (☎0285/71 110; ④), whose minibus sometimes meets ferries, is the fanciest place, just right of the village entrance, and *Rooms Nomikos* (②), further back by the phone antenna, is the most basic. In addition to the pair of traditional **tavernas**, *Kastanis* and *Klimataria*, there are several noisy bistro-café-pubs, with *Toh Steki* in the upper plaza perennially popular in the late afternoon. On the same square are the island's main **post office** and a **bank**; further up the hill is the main OTE office, with somewhat limited opening hours.

From the top of Hóra, next to the helipad, a wide cobbled *kalderími* drops down to two major attractions, effectively short-cutting the road and taking little longer than the bus to reach them. Bearing left at an inconspicuous fork ten minutes' along takes you towards the spectacular monastery of **Hozoviotíssas** (daily 9am–7pm; donation), which appears suddenly as you round a bend, its vast wall gleaming white at the base of a towering orange cliff. Only three monks occupy the fifty rooms now, but they are quite welcoming, considering the number of visitors who file through; you can see the eleventh-century icon around which the monastery was founded, along with a stack of other treasures. The foundation legend is typical for such institutions in outlandish places: during the Iconoclastic period a precious icon of the Virgin was committed to the sea by beleagured monks at Hózova, somewhere in the Middle East, and it washed up safely at the base of the palisade here. The view from the *katholikón*'s terrace, though, overshadows all for most visitors. To round off the experience, visitors are ushered into a comfy reception room and treated to a sugary lump of *loukoúmi*, a fiery shot of *kítro* and a cool glass of water.

The right-hand trail leads down, within forty minutes, to the pebble **beaches** at **Ayía Ánna**. Skip the first batch of tiny coves in favour of the path to the westernmost bay, where naturists cavort, almost in scandalous sight of the monastery far above. As yet there are no tavernas here, nor a spring, so bring food and water for the day.

For alternatives to Ayía Ánna, take the morning bus out toward modern Arkessíni, alighting at Kamári hamlet (where there's a single taverna) for the twenty-minute path down to the adjacent beaches of **Notiná**, **Moúros** and **Poulopódhi**. Like most of Amorgós' south-facing beaches, they're clean, with calm water, and here, too, a fresh-water spring dribbles most of the year. For those with their own transport, the road is surprisingly good all the way to the southern tip of the island, leading you past an unbroken chain of magnificent views to some lovely deserted beaches.

Archeology buffs will want to head north from Kamári to Vroútsi, start of the overgrown hour-long route to **ancient Arkessini**, a collection of tombs, six-metre-high walls and houses out on the cape of Kastrí. The main path from Minoa also passes through Vroútsi, ending next to the well-preserved Hellenistic fort known locally as the "Pírgos", just outside modern **ARKESSÍNI**. The village boasts a single **taverna** with **rooms**, and, more importantly, an afternoon bus back to Hóra and Katápola.

The northeast

The energetically inclined can walk the four to five hours from Hóra to Egiáli. On the Hóra side you can start by continuing on the faint trail just beyond Hozoviotíssas, but the islanders themselves, in the days before the road existed, preferred the more scenic and sheltered valley route through Terláki and Rikhtí. The two alternatives, and the modern jeep road, more or less meet an hour out of Hóra. Along most of the way, you're treated to amazing views of **Nikouriá islet**, nearly joined to the main island and in former times a leper colony. The only habitations on the way are the summer hamlet of **ASFODILÍDHI**, with well water but little else for the traveller, and **POTAMÓS**, a double village you encounter on the stroll down towards Egiáli bay.

EGIÁLI (Órmos), smaller than Katápola, is a delightful beachside place stuck in a 1970s time-warp. Accommodation tends to be reasonably priced: possible places are *Nikitas* (☎0285/73 237; ③) and *Akrogiali* (☎0285/73 249; ③), both above the harbour, and *Lakki* (☎0285/73 244; ④), which has a fine setting along the beach but a rather fierce management style. A couple of kilometres up on the way to Tholária is a new luxury hotel *Aegialis* (☎0285/73 253; ⑥). Behind the *Lakki* there is a very friendly official **campsite**, one of the cheapest in the Cyclades. For **eating out**, the *Korali* has decent fish and the best sunset view, but ultimately loses out to *Toh Limani* (aka *Katerina's*) on the single inland lane, packed until midnight by virtue of its excellent food and barrel-wine, and superb taste in taped music. A few seasonal music **bars**, such as *Selini*, also attempt to compete with *Katerina's*.

The main Egiáli **beach** is more than serviceable, getting less weedy and reefy as you stroll further north. If it's still not to your taste, a trail here leads over various headlands to an array of clothing-optional bays: the first sandy, the second mixed sand and gravel, the last shingle. There are no facilities anywhere so bring along what you need.

Egiáli has its own **bus service** up to each of the two villages visible above and east, with half a dozen departures daily up and down, but it would be a shame to miss out on the beautiful **loop walk** linking them with the port. **THOLÁRIA**, reached by the path starting at the far end of the main beach, is named after certain vaulted Roman tombs whose exact location nobody seems to know of or care about. A handful of **taverna-cafés**, including a handsome wooden-floored establishment near the church, are more contemporary concerns, and there are now several places to stay, including some fairly fancy **rooms** (reserve through *Pension Lakki* in Egiáli). Or try the *Vigla* (☎0285/73 288; ④), with breakfast included, and the *Thalassino Oneiro* (☎0285/73 345; ③), which has a fine restaurant and an extremely friendly owner. Curling around the head of the vast *kámbos* below is **LANGÁDHA**, home to a sizeable colony of expatriates – something reflected in the German-Greek cooking at *Nikos'* **taverna** at the lower end of the village, which also has some **rooms** (☎0285/73 310; ④), as does *Yiannis'* taverna.

Beyond Langádha, another rocky path leads around the base of the island's highest peak, the 821-metre-high **Kríkelon**, passing on the way the fascinating church of **Theológos**, with lower walls and ground plan dating to the fifth century. Somewhat easier to reach, by a slight detour off the main Tholária–Langádha trail, are the church and festival grounds of **Panayía Epanohóri** – not so architecturally distinguished but a fine spot nonetheless.

Íos

No other island is quite like **Íos**, nor attracts the same vast crowds of young people. The beach is packed with naked bodies by day, and nightlife in the village is loud and long. However, crowded as it is, the island hasn't been commercialized in quite the same way as, say, Míkonos – mainly because few of the visitors have much money. You'll either decide that Íos (short for "Ireland Over Seas", as some would have it) is the island paradise you have always been looking for and stay for weeks, as many people do, or you'll hate it and take the next boat out – an equally common reaction.

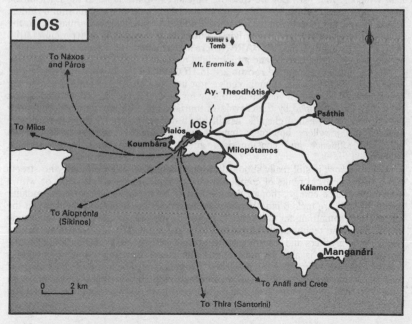

Most visitors stay along the arc delineated by the port – at Yialós, where you'll arrive (there's no airport), in Hóra above it, or at the beach at Milopótas; it's a small area, and you soon get to know your way around. **Buses** constantly shuttle between the three places, with a daily service running roughly from 8am to midnight; you should never have to wait more than fifteen minutes, but at least once try the short walk up (or down) the stepped path between Yialós and the Hóra.

Despite its past popularity, **sleeping on the beach** on Íos is really worth avoiding these days. Violent crime and police raids are becoming more frequent as the island strains under the sheer impact of increasing youth tourism, and the police have been known to turn very nasty. They prefer you to sleep in the official campsites and, given the problem of theft, you should probably take their advice. A further problem is **water shortage**, which occasionally has dire effects, above all, on local toilets. Things can get particularly grim in Yialós, and even in the beachside tavernas only the desperate and foolish dare venture out the back. In the village, you may find a toilet which flushes, although officially water is too scarce to be used for so frivolous a purpose.

Yialós and Hóra

From **YIALÓS** quayside, **buses** turn around just to the left, while Yialós **beach** – surprisingly peaceful and uncrowded – is another five minutes' walk in the same direction. You might be tempted to grab a room in Yialós as you arrive: owners meet the ferries, hustling the town's **accommodation**. There are also a couple of kiosks by the jetty that will book rooms for you, but you won't find anything below the ④ range in high season and, surprisingly, there are no dormitories; if you're after a budget room, you might do better in Hóra (see below). At the far end of the beach are a couple of the plusher options: *Ios Beach Bungalows* (☎0285/91267; ⑤) and *Hotel Leto* (☎0286/91357; ⑥). Beware that the official **campsite** here, to the right of the harbour on a scruffy beach, is the worst of the island's three – and mosquito-ridden. Yialós has all the other essentials: a tourist office, a reasonable supermarket (to the right of the bus stop), and a few fairly authentic **tavernas**. A twenty-minute stroll over the headland at **KOUMBÁRA**, there's a smaller and less crowded beach, largely nudist, with a taverna and a rocky islet to explore.

Most of the less expensive **rooms** are in **HÓRA** (aka Íos Town), a twenty-minute walk up behind the port, though you've got a better chance of getting something reasonable by haggling if you intend to stay for several days. The old white village is becoming overwhelmed by the crowds of tourists, but with any number of arcaded streets and whitewashed chapels, it still has a certain charm. A bevy of expensive fashion and jewellery boutiques have begun to appear recently, reflecting an increased affluence and consumerism among the once avidly anti-materialist clientele.

What the *hóra* is still really about, though, is **nightlife**. Every evening the streets throb to music from ranks of competing discos and clubs – mostly free, or with a nominal entrance charge, though drinks tend to be expensive. Most of the smaller **bars** and pubs are tucked into the thronging narrow streets of the old village on the hill, offering something for everyone – unless you just want a quiet drink. A welcome exception to the techno-pop dancing fodder can be found at the *Taboo* bar, run by two friendly brothers and featuring underground rock, eclectic decor and a clientele to match; *Pegasus* is also recommended. The larger **dancing clubs,** including a branch of Athens' *West Club* and the *Disco Scorpion*, are to be found on the main road to Milopótamos. Finally the *Ios Club*, perched right up on the hill, organizes an annual **festival of live music** for the month of August, showcasing international and Greek acts.

Eating is a secondary consideration but there are plenty of cheap and cheerful *psistariés* and take-away joints: sound choices include *Iy Folia*, near the top of the village, and *Ikoyeniaki Taverna Iy Stani*, at the heart of town.

Around the island

The most popular stop on the island's bus routes is **MILOPÓTAMOS** (universally abbreviated to Milópotas), the site of a magnificent beach and a mini-resort. By day, young people cover every inch of the bus-stop end of the sand; for a bit more space head the other way, where there are dunes behind the beach. There are three busy **campsites**, of which *Far Out*, the furthest away, is probably the best, followed by the nearest, *Stars*, and then *Costas*, but they can all be pretty noisy. There are **rooms** and one good self-service **café**, the *Far Out* – so named for the standard reaction to the view on the ride in. Right at the far end of the bay there is a little quay and a remarkably good and quiet taverna/café called *Drakos*.

From Yialós, daily boats depart at around 10am (returning in the late afternoon) to **MANGANÁRI** on the south coast, where there's a beach and a swanky hotel; you can also get there by moped on the newish road. Predominantly nudist, this is the beach to come to for serious tans, although there's more to see, and a better atmosphere, at **ÁYIOS THEODHÓTIS**, up on the east coast. In high season, a **bus** runs at 10am from Yialós (or ten minutes later from the stop behind the windmills in Hóra), but purists can walk there on a decaying walled track across the heart of the island. This begins just to the north of the windmills; carry water as the hike will take two to three hours. Once there, Áyios Theodhótis boasts a ruined Venetian castle which encompasses the ruins of a marble-finished town and a Byzantine church. In the unlikely event that the beach – a good one and mainly nudist – is too crowded, try the one at **PSÁTHIS**, an hour's stroll to the southeast. Frequented by wealthy Athenians, this small resort has a couple of pricey tavernas, making it better for a day-trip than an extended stay. The other island beach is at **KÁLAMOS**, a three-hour walk along a rough road from Hóra. It's very remote indeed, although at Perivólia – one hour into the walk – there are welcome shady trees and fresh water.

Homer's "tomb", the only cultural diversion on the island, is an expensive one. The story goes that, while on a voyage from Sámos to Athens, Homer's ship was forced to put in at Íos, where the poet subsequently died. Ask at the tourist office in Yialós if you want to visit: you'll need to hire either a donkey or a *kaíki* and, ideally, a guide as it's difficult to find. You can walk, but it's a good three hours' slog to the northeastern tip of the island, passing the Psarápirgos tower on Mount Eremítis, until you reach the site of the ancient town of Plakatos. The town itself has long since slipped down the side of the cliff, but the rocky ruins of the entrance to a tomb remain, as well as some graves – one of which is claimed to be Homer's, but which in reality probably dates only to the Byzantine era.

Síkinos

Síkinos has so small a population that the mule-ride or walk up from the port to the village was only replaced by a bus late in the 1980s and, until the new jetty was completed at roughly the same time, it was the last major Greek island where ferry passengers were still taken ashore in launches. With no dramatic characteristics, nor any nightlife to speak of, few foreigners make the short trip over here from neighbouring Íos and Folégandhros or from sporadically connected Páros, Náxos, or Thíra. In addition to the regular ferries there are unreliable local *kaíkia*, in season only, to and from Íos and Folégandhros. There is no bank on the island, but there is a **post office** up in Kástro-Hóra, near the **OTE**, and you can sometimes change cash at the store in Aloprónia.

SÍKINOS AND FOLÉGANDHROS

Aloprónia and Kástro-Hóra

Such tourist facilities as exist are concentrated in the little harbour of **ALOPRÓNIA**, with its long sandy beach and the recent additions of an extended breakwater and jetty. More and more formal **accommodation** is being built here, and the days of a discreet slumber under the tamarisks at one end of the beach are probably over. For rooms, try *Flora* (☎0286/51 214 or 51 239; ③, en suite ④); alternatively, the comfortable *Hotel Kamares* (☎0286/51 234; ④), in traditional style, is more affordable than the conspicuous *Porto Sikinos* luxury complex (☎0286/51 247, winter ☎01/41 72 043; ⑤). The **taverna** on the quay is the locals' hangout, while the fancier *Ostria* is affiliated with the *Hotel Kamares*.

The double village of **KÁSTRO-HÓRA** is served by the single island bus, which meets the ferries for transport up the hill, but otherwise schedules are subject to the whim of the driver. In theory, they go up on the hour, and return on the half hour from 7am to 10pm. On the ride up, the scenery turns out to be less desolate than initial impressions suggest. Draped across a ridge overlooking the sea, Kástro-Hóra makes for a charming day trip, though rooms tend to be substandard and poor value, and choices for eating out are similarly limited. A partly ruined monastery, **Zoödhóhou Piyís** ("Spring of Life", a frequent name in the Cyclades), crowns the rock above; the architectural highlight of the place, though, is the central quadrangle of **Kástro**, a series of ornate eighteenth-century houses arrayed defensively around a chapel-square, their backs to the exterior of the village.

Around the island

West of Kástro-Hóra, an hour-plus walk (or hired-mule ride) takes you through a landscape lush with olives to **Episkopí**, where elements of an ancient temple-tomb have been ingeniously incorporated into a seventh-century church – the structure is known formally as the **Iroön**. Ninety minutes from Kástro-Hóra, in the opposite direction, lies **Paleokástro**, the patchy remains of an ancient fortress. If you turn down and right (south) from this path you'll come to a pair of beaches, **Áyios Yióryios** and **Áyios Nikólaos**, which face Íos; the former cove has a well. With slightly less effort, the pebble beach at **Áyios Pandelímonas** is just under an hour's trail-walk southwest of Aloprónia, and is considered the most scenic and sheltered on the island. All of these beaches are served by excursion *kaíkia* in season.

Folégandhros

The cliffs of **Folégandhros** rise sheer in places over 300m from the sea – until the early 1980s as effective a deterrent to tourists as they always were to pirates. Used as an island of political exile right up until 1974, life in the high, barren interior has been eased since the junta years by the arrival of electricity and the construction of a lengthwise road from the harbour to Hóra and beyond. Development has been given further impetus by the recent exponential increase in tourism and the mild commercialization this has brought.

A veritable explosion in accommodation for most budgets, and slight improvement in ferry arrival times, means there is no longer much need for – or local tolerance of – sleeping rough on the beaches. The increased wealth and trendiness of the heterogenous clientele is reflected in fancy jewellery shops, an arty postcard gallery and a newly constructed helipad. Yet away from the showcase *hóra* and the beaches, the countryside remains mostly pristine, and is largely devoted to the spring and summer cultivation of barley, the mainstay of many of the Cyclades before the advent of tourism. Donkeys and donkey-paths are also still very much in evidence, since the terrain on much of the island is too steep for vehicle roads.

Karavostássi and around

KARAVOSTÁSSI, the rather unprepossessing port, serves as a last-resort base, offering one **hotel**, the *Poseidon* (☎0286/41 205; ③) just behind the pebble shore. Another, the *Vardia Bay*, is under construction on a site overlooking the harbour from the south and will have the added bonus of a good taverna, *Iy Kali Kardhiá*, just below. The island's first moped-rental place has also made its rather furtive appearance here.

The closest **beach** is the smallish, but attractive enough, sand-and-pebble **Vardhiá**, signposted just north over the headland. Some twenty minutes' walk south lies **Loustriá**, a rather average beach with tamarisk trees and the island's official **campsite** (sporadic water supply).

Easily the most scenic beach on Folégandhros, with an offshore islet and a 300-m stretch of pea-gravel, is at **Katergó**, on the southeastern tip of the island. Most people visit on a boat excursion from Karavostássi or Angáli, but you can also get there on foot from the hamlet of Livádhi, a short walk inland from Loustriá. Be warned, though, that it's a rather arduous trek, with some nasty trail-less slithering in the final moments.

Hóra

The island's real character and appeal are to be found in the spectacular **HÓRA**, perched on a cliff-top plateau some 45 minutes' walk from the dock; an hourly high-season **bus** service (6 daily spring/autumn) runs from morning until late at night. Locals and foreigners – hundreds of them in high season – mingle at the cafés and tavernas under the almond, flowering judas and pepper trees of the two main *platías*, passing the time unmolested by traffic, which is banned from the village centre. Toward the cliff-edge, and entered through two arcades, the defensive core of the medieval **kástro** is marked by ranks of of two-storey houses, whose repetitive, almost identical stairways and slightly recessed doors are very appealing.

From the square where the bus stops, a zig-zag path with views down to both coastlines climbs to the cragtop, wedding-cake church of **Kímisis Theotókou**, nocturnally illuminated to grand effect. Beyond and below it hides the **Hrissospiliá**, a large cave with stalactites, accessible only to proficient climbers; the necessary steps and railings have crumbled away into the sea, although a minor, lower grotto can still be visited.

Practicalities

Hóra **accommodation** seems slightly weighted to favour hotels over rooms, with concentrations around the bus plaza at the east entrance to the village and at the western edge. Recommended rooms places include the purpose-built complex run by *Irini Dekavalla* (☎0286/41 235; ③), east of the bus stop. The nearby *Hotel Polikandia* (☎0286/41 322, winter ☎01/68 25 484; ③) has an engaging proprietress and far lower rates than appearances suggest. The most luxurious facilities are at the cliff-edge *Anemomilos Apartments* (☎ 0286/41 309; winter ☎01/68 23 962; ⑤), whose immaculate appointments and sock-you-in-the-eye views are particularly good value in spring or autumn, when rates drop to the ④ mark. The only hotel within the *hóra* – the *Castro* (☎0286/41 230, winter ☎01/77 81 658; ④) is a bit overpriced, despite recent renovation and undeniable atmosphere, with three rather dramatic rooms looking directly out on an alarming drop to the sea. At the western edge of Hóra near the police station, densely packed rooms outfits tend to block each other's views; the least claustrophobic is the long-established *Odysseas* (☎0286/41 276; ③), which also manages some attractive apartments near the *Anemomilos*. By the roadside on the way to Áno Meriá, the *Fani-Vevis* (☎0286/41 237; ④), in a Neoclassical mansion overlooking the sea, seems to function only in high season.

Hóra's half a dozen **restaurants** are surprisingly varied. The *Ouzeri Folegandhros* in water-cistern plaza, is fun, if a bit eccentrically run, with Greek music in the evenings to balance the New-Age noodlings over breakfast. The latter is probably best taken on the adjacent Platía Kondaríni at *Iy Melissa*, which does good fruit-and-yogurt, omelettes and juices. *Iy Piatsa* has a nightly changing menu of well-executed Greek dishes, while their neighbour and local hangout *O Kritikos* is notable only for its grills. Self-catering is an attractive option, with two well-stocked fruit shops and two supermarkets. Hóra is inevitably beginning to sprawl unattractively at the edges, but this at least means that the burgeoning **nightlife** – two dancing bars and a quantity of musical pubs and *ouzeris* – can be exiled to the south, away from most accommodation. A combination **OTE/ post office** (no bank) completes the list of amenities, though the single **ferry agent** also does money exchange.

The rest of the island

Northwest of Hóra a narrow, cement road threads its way towards **ÁNO MERIÁ**, the other village of the island; after 4km you pass its first houses, clustered around the three churches of Áyios Pandelímonas, Áyios Yióryios and Áyios Andhréas. Two tavernas operate in high season only: *O Mimis*, about halfway along, and *Iy Sinandisi*, at the turning for Áyios Yióryios beach.

Up to six times a day in high season a **bus** trundles out here to drop people off at the footpaths down to the various sheltered beaches on the southwest shore of the island. Busiest of these is **Angáli** (aka Vathí), with five rather basic rooms outfits (no phones; all ②) and three equally simple summer-only tavernas, reached by a fifteen-minute walk along a dirt road from the bus stop.

Nudists are urged to take the paths which lead twenty minutes east or west to **Firá** or **Áyios Nikólaos** beaches respectively; the latter in particular, with its many tamarisks, coarse sand and view back over the island, is Katergó's only serious rival in the best-beach sweepstakes. At Áyios Nikólaos, a lone taverna operates up by the name-sake chapel; Firá has no facilities at all.

Thíra (Santoríni)

As the ferry manoeuvres into the great caldera of **Thíra**, the land seems to rise up and clamp around it. Gaunt, sheer cliffs loom hundreds of feet above, nothing grows or grazes to soften the view, and the only colours are the reddish-brown, black and grey pumice striations layering the cliff face. The landscape tells of a history so dramatic and turbulent that legend hangs as fact upon it.

From as early as 3000 BC the island developed as a sophisticated outpost of Minoan civilization, until around 1550 BC when catastrophe struck: the volcano-island erupted, its heart sank below the sea, and earthquakes reverberated across the Aegean. Thíra was destroyed and the great Minoan civilizations on Crete were dealt a severe blow. At this point the island's history became linked with legends of Atlantis, the "Happy Isles Submerged by Sea". Plato insisted that the legend was true, and Solon dated the cataclysm to 9000 years before his time – if you're willing to accept a mistake and knock off the final zero, a highly plausible date.

These apocalyptic events, though, scarcely concern modern tourists, who are here mostly to stretch out on the island's dark-sand beaches and absorb the peculiar, infernal atmosphere: as recently as a century ago, Thíra was still reckoned to be infested with vampires. Though not nearly so predatory as the undead, current visitors have in fact succeeded in pretty much killing off any genuine island life, creating in its place a rather expensive and stagey playground.

Arrival and departure

Ferries dock at the somewhat grim port of **Órmos Athiniós**; **Skála Firás** and **Ía** in the north are reserved for local ferries, excursion *kaíkia* and cruise ships. **Buses**, astonishingly crammed, connect Athiniós with the island capital Firá, and, less frequently, with the main beaches at Kamári and Périssa – disembark quickly and take whatever's going, if you want to avoid a long walk. You're also likely to be accosted at Athiniós by people offering rooms all over the island; it may be a good idea to pay attention to them, given the scramble for beds in Firá especially. If you alight at Skála Firás, you have the traditional route above you – 580 mule-shit-splattered steps to Firá itself. It's not that difficult to walk but the intrepid can also go up by mule or by cable car (summer only, weather permitting), which runs every fifteen minutes between 7am and 8.30pm. The **airport** is located towards the other side of the island, near Monólithos; the shuttle bus service to the *Olympic Airways* office in Firá has been suspended, so you'll need to take a shared taxi.

When it comes to **leaving** – especially for summer/evening ferry departures – get to Athiniós a couple of hours in advance, since unbelievable crowds gather on the dock-side. Note, too, that although the bus service stops around midnight, a shared taxi isn't outrageously expensive. Incidentally, **ferry information** from any source is notoriously unreliable on Thíra, so departure details should be quadruple-checked. If you do get stranded in Athiniós waiting for a ferry connection, there's no place to stay, and the tavernas are pretty awful. With time on your hands, it's well worth zigzagging the 3500m up to the closest village, **Megalohóri**. Between Megalohóri and Pírgos village, quite near the junction of the main and Athiniós road, is *Hotel Zorbas* (☎0286/31 433; ④), with very personable Greek and American management. At the centre of Megalohóri, the *Yeromanolis* is a surprisingly reasonable and tasty grill which offers the increasingly rare homemade Santorini wine.

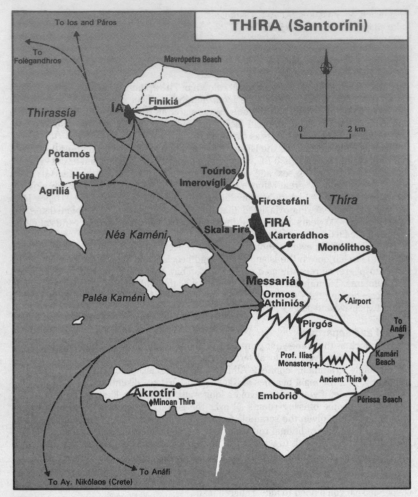

THÍRA (Santoríni)

To Íos and Páros

To Folégandhros

Mavrópetra Beach

Thirassía

ÍA
Finikiá

Potamós

Hóra

Agriliá

Toúrlos
Imerovígli

Néa Kaméni

Skala Firá

Firostefáni

FIRÁ

Karterádhos

Thíra

Monólithos

Paléa Kaméni

Messariá

Ormos
Athiniós

Airport

Pirgós

To
Anáfi

Prof. Ilias
Monastery

Kamári
Beach

Ancient Thira

Akrotíri
Minoan Thira

Embório

Périssa Beach

To Anáfi

To Ay. Nikólaos (Crete)

0   2 km

Firá

Half-rebuilt after a devastating earthquake in 1956, **FIRÁ** (also known as Thíra or Hóra) still lurches dementedly at the cliff's edge. With a stunningly attractive setting, it appears on postcards and tourist brochures and, naturally, you pay the price for its position. Besieged by hordes of day-trippers from the cruise boats, in summer at least, initial impressions of Firá are of gross commercialism; gone are the simple restaurants and bakeries of a decade ago, replaced by supernumerary jewellery and fur boutiques, fast-food places and tourist agencies.

Firá's cliff-top position justifies a visit, but it's not a place to linger. Make time, however, for the **Archeological Museum** (daily except Mon 8.30am–3pm; 400dr), near the cable car to the north of town. An excellent collection, it includes a curious set of erotic Dionysiac figures, and a separate wing to house finds from the Akrotíri site (see below) is due to open soon; there's also the interesting **Museum Megaro** (also known as the Cultural Centre of Gizi Palace; daily 10am–1pm & 5–8pm; 350dr) near the Kamares hostel, displaying old engravings, maps and photos.

Practicalities

If you insist on staying here, you'll have to move quickly on arrival, particularly if you want one of the better (and ruinously expensive) **rooms** with views over the caldera; beds are at a premium in summer and by noon nearly everything is full. You'd be well advised to take any reasonable offer, including places just outside the town. You might try **KARTERÁDHOS**, a small village about twenty minutes' walk south of Firá, where there are rooms and the pleasant Hotel Albatros (☎0286/23 431; ③), or **MESSARIÁ**, another 2km further, with some more expensive hotels. Otherwise there are three **youth hostels** in the northern part of town, cheap, often full, but not too bad if you have your own bedding and sleep on the roof; the unofficial Kamares hostel is cleaner than the official IYHF one. Even the Santorini Camping, a few hundred metres inland from the central square, with a nice swimming pool and decent restaurant, has to turn away late arrivals in peak season. In the same neighbourhood, single women can stay at the Dominican convent. Out of season it's easier to track down rooms, and prices fall acccordingly; officially, the police only allow hotels to stay open, but you should eventually find someone prepared to put you up.

Restaurants worth trying include The Roosters, along 25 Martiou, which is cheap and unpretentious; Barbara's, close by the Loucas Hotel, is quite the opposite but worth it. Any restaurant overlooking the caldera is going to have prices as high as the cliffs it stands on. As for **nightlife**, Bizarre video bar is youth-orientated, with good music and cheap drinks, Dionysus Disco boasts free entry, and Franco's classical music bar is pricey but great for sunset-watching; Enigma, a soul disco, occupies a converted house and garden.

Buses to points further afield leave Firá from the large square straight ahead from the top of the steps, running approximately hourly to Ía, Périssa, Akrotíri, half-hourly to Kamári; timetables are posted in the kiosk at the far end. However, if you want to see the whole island in a couple of days a rented **moped** is useful; Moto Chris (☎0286/23 431) at the top of the road that leads down to Santorini Camping is particularly recommended.

The north

Once outside Firá, the rest of Santoríni comes as a nice surprise. The volcanic soil is highly fertile, with every available space terraced and cultivated: wheat, tomatoes (most made into paste), pistachios and grapes are the main crops, all still harvested and planted by hand. The island's visándo and nikhtéri wines are a little sweet for many tastes but are among the finest produced in the Cyclades.

ÍA, 12km from Firá in the northwest of the island, was once a major fishing port of the Aegean, but it has declined in the wake of economic depression, wars, earthquakes and depleted fish stocks. Partly destroyed in the 1956 earthquake, it presents a curious mix of pristine white reconstruction and tumbledown ruins clinging to the cliff face – by any standards one of the most dramatic towns of the Cyclades. Ía is also much the calmest place on the island, and with a **post office**, part-time **bank** and **bike-rental** office there's no reason to feel stuck in Firá. Regular buses ply between Firá and Ía, but the walk in from Imerovígli is rewarding (see below).

Rooms aren't too easy to come by: the local EOT authorities restored, then privatized, some of the old houses as expensive guest-lodges (all ⑥); less expensive choices include the troglodytic Pension Lauda (☎0286/71 204; ④), the Hotel Anemones (☎0286/71 220; ④), and the Hotel Fregata (☎0286/71 221; ④). Quite near the bus terminal, also reachable by the main road that continues round to the back end of the village, is an excellent new hostel, the Oia (☎0286/71 465; ①), with a terrace and shady courtyard, a good bar, clean dormitories and breakfast included. Recommended **restaurants** include Petros (for fish) and the popular *Neptune*; generally, the further you go along the central ridge towards the new end of Ía, the better value the restaurants. **Nightlife** revolves around sunset-gazing, for which people are bussed in from all over the island, creating traffic chaos; when this pales, there's *Strofi* rock-music bar.

Below the town, 200-odd steps switchback hundreds of metres down to two small harbours: **AMMOÚDHI**, for the fishermen, and **ARMÉNI**, where the ferries dock. Off the cement platform at Ammoúdhi you can swim past floating pumice and snorkel among shoals of giant fish, but beware the currents around the church-islet of Áyios Nikólaos. At Arméni, a single taverna specializes in grilled-octopus lunches.

A satisfying approach to Ía is to walk the stretch from **IMEROVÍGLI**, 3km out of Firá, using a spectacular footpath along the lip of the caldera. Imerovígli has a taverna and one moderate hotel, the *Katerina* (☎0286/22 708; ④); if you carry on to Ía you'll pass Toúrlos, an old Venetian citadel on Cape Skáros, on the way. **FINIKIÁ**, 1km east of Ía, has an excellent unofficial **youth hostel** on the north side of the road, and a couple of recommended restaurants – *Markozanes* and the expensive but varied *Finikias*.

The east and south

Beaches on Santoríni, mostly in the east and south, are bizarre – long black stretches of volcanic sand which get blisteringly hot in the afternoon sun. They're no secret and in the summer the crowds can be a bit overpowering. Closest to Firá, **MONÓLITHOS** has a couple of tavernas but is nothing special. Further south, **KAMÁRI** has surrendered lock, stock and barrel to the package-tour operators and there's not a piece of sand that isn't fronted by concrete villas. Nonetheless it's quieter and cleaner than most, with some beachfront **rooms** available, two inexpensive, co-managed **hotels**, the *Prekamaria* and *Villa Elli* (☎0286/31 266; both ③), and a relatively uncrowded **campsite**.

Things are scruffier at **PÉRISSA**, around the cape. Despite (or perhaps because of) its attractive situation and abundance of cheap rooms, it's noisy and overrun by inconsiderate backpackers. The official **campsite** is very crowded; if you're low on funds, you'd do better to stay in the popular, well-run *Anna* hostel (May–Oct; no phone; ①), at the inland entrance to town; they also have a few double rooms to let. The beach itself extends almost 7km to the west, sheltered by the occasional tamarisk tree, but it tends to be dirty and wind-buffeted.

Kamári and Périssa are separated by the Mésa Vounó headland, on which stood **ancient Thíra** (daily except Mon 9am–3pm), the post-eruption settlement dating from the ninth century BC. Expensive taxis and cheaper buses go up from Kamári, but the best approach is the half-hour walk from Périssa, following a clear **path** up past the hillside chapel. Though impressively large, most of the ruins (dating from between the third and first century BC) are difficult to place, but there are temples and houses with mosaics. The view from the theatre is awesome – beyond the stage there's a sheer drop to the sea. You can continue one hour on the path, soon a cobbled way, down to Kamári, slicing across the switchbacks of the road up. Part way down you pass a huge cave which contains a tiny shrine and a **freshwater spring** – the only one on Thíra and a lifesaver on a hot day.

Inland along the same mountain spine is the monastery of **Profítis Ilías**, now sharing its refuge with Greek radio and TV pylons and antennae of a NATO station. With just one monk remaining to look after the church, the place only really comes to life for the annual Profítis Ilías festival, when the whole island troops up here to celebrate. The views are still rewarding, though, and from near the entrance to the monastery an old footpath heads across the ridge in about an hour to ancient Thíra. The easiest ascent is the half-hour walk from the village of Pírgos.

PÍRGOS itself is one of the oldest settlements on the island, a jumble of old houses and alleys that still bear the scars of the 1956 earthquake. It climbs to another Venetian fortress crowned by several churches and you can clamber around the battlements for sweeping views over the entire island and its Aegean neighbours. By way of contrast **MESSARIÁ**, a thirty-minute stroll north, has a skyline consisting solely of massive church domes that lord it over the houses huddled in a ravine.

Akrotíri

Evidence of the Minoan colony that once thrived here has been uncovered at the other ancient site of **Akrotíri** (Tues–Sat 8.30am–3pm; 1000dr), at the southwestern tip of the island. Tunnels through the volcanic ash uncovered structures, two and three storeys high, first damaged by earthquake then buried by eruption; Professor Marinatos, the excavator and now an island hero, was killed by a collapsing wall and is also buried on the site. Only about three percent of what was the largest Minoan city outside of Crete has been excavated thus far. Lavish frescoes adorned the walls, and Cretan pottery was found stored in a chamber; most of the frescoes are currently exhibited in Athens, but there are plans to bring them back if and when a new museum is built. For now, you'll have to content yourself with the (very good) archeological museum in Firá (see p.480); Akrotíri itself can be reached by bus from Firá or Périssa, and there are rooms and a basic restaurant at the site. The excellent *Glaros* fish taverna on the way to the beach has excellent food and barrelled wine.

Thirassía and Kaméni

From either Firá or Ía, boat excursions and local ferries run to the charred volcanic islets of **Paleá Kaméni** and **Néa Kaméni**, and to the relatively unspoiled islet of **Thirassía**, which was once part of Santoríni until shorn off by an eruption in the third century BC. Néa Kaméni, with its mud-clouded hot springs and shoe-slicing hike to a volcanically active crater, gets mixed reviews, but everybody seems to enjoy Thirassía. There are three small villages on the islet – including the port with its steep stairs – some tavernas and rooms, and you could enjoy the simple life here while waiting for the once-weekly proper ferry or the islanders' *kaíki* to Ammoúdhi.

Anáfi

An two-hour boat ride to the east of Thíra, **Anáfi** is the end of the line for the three weekly ferries which call there, and something of a travellers' dead end now that the occasional link with Crete and the Dodecanese has been discontinued. Not that this is likely to bother most of the visitors, who intentionally come here for weeks in mid-summer, and take over the island's beaches with a vengeance.

At most other times the place seems idyllic, and indeed may prove too sleepy for some: except for the road up to Hóra, there are no paved roads on Anáfi, nor any bona fide hotels, mopeds, discos or organized excursions; donkeys are still the main method of transport in the interior. Anáfi, though initially enchanting, is a harsh place, its mixed granite/limestone core overlaid by volcanic rock spewed out by Thíra's eruptions.

The harbour and Hóra

Virtually all of the approximately three hundred inhabitants live on the south coast, in the port or the *hóra*. In the minuscule harbour hamlet of **ÁYIOS NIKÓLAOS**, *Toh Akroyiali* is the most permanently open taverna and doubles as the main **ferry agent**; in high season a single pub provides a semblance of nightlife. Most **places to stay** are in Hóra; a bus meets all ferries – as do accommodation proprietors, who seem to have a system for dividing clients up among themselves.

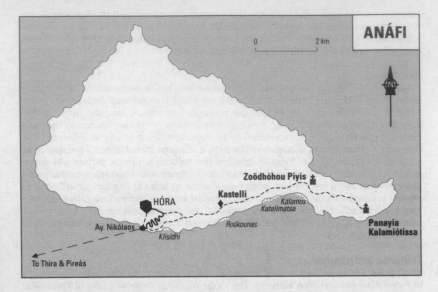

Otherwise **HÓRA**, adorning a conical hill overhead, is a stiff, 25-minute climb up the obvious old mule path which shortcuts the modern road. Exposed and blustery whether or not the *meltémi* is blowing, Hóra can initially seem a rather forbidding ghost town. This impression is slowly dispelled as you discover the hospitable islanders taking their coffee in sheltered, south-facing terraces, or under the anti-earthquake barrel vaulting that features in domestic architecture here.

The modern, purpose-built **rooms** run by *Ioannis Halaris* (☎0286/61 271; ②) or *Manolis Loudharos* (☎0286/61 279; ②), at the extreme east edge of the village, are about the most comfortable – and boast stunning views south over various islets and the distinctive monolith at the southeastern corner of Anáfi. Somewhat simpler are the rooms of the *Gavalas* family (②), looking down over the village from the top of the mule path. Evening **diners** seem to divide their custom between the simple, welcoming *Toh Steki*, with reasonable food and barrel wine served on its terrace, and the more upmarket *Alexandhra's* on the central walkway, which doubles as a bar. Otherwise there are two shops, sporadic fresh produce, a bakery, a **post office** and an OTE station.

East along the coast: beaches and monasteries

The glory of Anáfi is a string of south-facing beaches, currently accessible only by foot or boat, culminating in a pair of intriguing monasteries at the far southeastern tip of the island. The closest to Áyios Nikólaos is **KLISÍDHI**, a short walk along the cliffs to the east of the harbour, where 200m of tan, gently shelving sand gets pounded by a gentle surf; splendidly malapropic signs announce that "Nubbism Is Not Allowed". Above the calamus-and-tamarisk oasis backing the beach, there's a well-patronised **snack bar** (*Toh Kyma*) and adjacent, popular **rooms** (☎0286/61 237; ②).

From a point on the paved road just east of Hóra, the **main path** skirting the south flank of the island is signposted: "Kastélli – Paleá Hóra – Roúkouna – Monastíri". The primary branch of this trail roller-coasters in and out of several agricultural valleys that provide most of Anáfi's produce and fresh water. Just under an hour along, beside a well, you veer down a side trail to **Roúkounas**, easily the island's best beach, with some 500m of broad sand rising to tamarisk-stabilized dunes, which provide welcome shade. A single taverna, *Tou Papa*, operates up by the main trail in season; the suggestively craggy hill of **Kastélli**, an hour's scramble above the taverna, is the site both of ancient Anaphi and a ruined Venetian castle.

Beyond Roúkounas, it's another half hour on foot to the first of the exquisite half-dozen **Katelímatsa** coves, of all shapes and sizes, and 45 minutes to **Kálamos** beach – all without facilities, so come prepared.

The monasteries

Between Katelímatsa and Kálamos, the main route keeps inland, past a rare spring, to arrive at the **monastery of Zoödhóhou Piyís**, some two hours out of Hóra. Masonry from a temple of Apollo which once stood here is plainly visible around the main gate and in a standing structure just behind. According to legend, Apollo caused Anáfi to rise from the waves, pulling off a dramatic rescue of the storm-lashed Argonauts; not surprisingly, he has been venerated on the island ever since.The courtyard, with a welcome cistern, is the venue for the island's major festival, celebrated eleven days after Easter. A family of cheesemakers lives next door and can point you up the start of the spectacular onward path to **Panayía Kalamiótissa**, a little monastery perched atop the abrupt pinnacle at the extreme southeast of the island. It takes another hour to reach, but is eminently worthwhile for the stunning scenery and views over the entire south coast. Kalamiótissa comes alive only during its 7–8 September festival; at other times, you could haul a sleeping bag up here to witness the amazing sunsets and sunrises, with your vantage point often floating in a sea of cloud. There is no water up here, so bring enough with you. It's a full day's outing from Hóra to Kalamiótissa and back; you might wish to take advantage, in at least one direction, of the excursion **kaíki** that runs from Áyios Nikólaos or Klisídhi to Kálamos, on demand, during high season. There is also a slightly larger mail-and-supplies *kaíki* (currently Tuesday and Thursday mornings between 10 and 11am) which takes passengers to and from Thíra (Athinios), supplementing the main-line ferries to Pireás.

travel details

Ferries

Most of the Cyclades are served by main-line ferries from **Pireás**, but there are also boats which depart from **Lávrio** (for Kéa, and less often, Síros and Kíthnos) and **Rafína**, which has become increasingly important of late, as work proceeds on the new international airport at nearby Spáta. At the moment there are regular services from Rafína to Ándhros, Tínos, Míkonos, Síros, Páros, Náxos and Amorgós, with infrequent extensions of the line into the Dodecanese (of late Pireás-based ships have more regularly included select Cyclades en route to the Dodecanese). All three ports are easily reached by bus from Athens.

The frequency of sailings given below is intended to give an idea of services from April to October, when most visitors tour the islands.

During the winter expect departures to be at or below the minimum level listed with some routes cancelled entirely. Conversely, routes tend to be more comprehensive in spring and autumn, when the government obliges shipping companies to make extra stops to compensate for numbers of boats still in drydock.

AMORGÓS 4–6 ferries weekly to Náxos, Páros, and Síros, some of these continuing to Rafína rather than Pireás; 3–4 weekly to Tínos and Míkonos; 2–3 weekly to Dhonoússa; 2 weekly to Astipálea; 1 a week to Kálimnos, Íos, and Thíra.

ANÁFI 3 weekly to Thíra (1hr 30min) and Pireás (12hr 30min), via Íos, Náxos, Páros; 2 weekly to Síros; 2 weekly *kaíkia* to Thíra (2hr).

ÁNDHROS At least 3 daily to Rafína (2hr), Tínos (2hr), and Míkonos; daily to Síros; 1

weekly to Amorgós and the minor islets behind Náxos.

DHONOÚSSA As for the preceding three, plus 2 weekly to Míkonos, Tínos, Síros; 2 extra weekly to Náxos and Páros; 1 weekly to Íos and Thíra.

ÍOS At least daily to Pireás (10hr), Páros (5hr), Náxos (3hr), Síros and Thíra (2hr); 3 weekly to Crete (Iráklion); 2–6 weekly to Síkinos and Folégandhros; 1–3 weekly to Mílos, Kímolos, Sérifos, Sífnos and Kíthnos; 3 weekly to Anáfi. Irregular seasonal *kaíkia* to Síkinos and Folégandhros.

KÉA 1–3 daily to Lávrio (1hr 30min); several weekly to Kíthnos.

KÍMOLOS 2 daily *kaíkia* to Mílos (Pollónia) year-round, more in summer; 2–5 weekly to Mílos (Adhámas), Sífnos, Sérifos, Kíthnos, and Pireás (7hr); 1 weekly to Folégandhros, Síkinos, Thíra, eastern Crete (Áyios Nikólaos or Sitía), Kássos, Kárpathos, Hálki, Sími and Rhodes

KÍTHNOS 2–12 weekly to Pireás (3hr 15min); 2–10 weekly to Sérifos, Sífnos, and Mílos; 2–4 weekly to Kímolos, Folégandhros, Síkinos, Íos and Lávrio.

KOUFONÍSSI, SKHINOÚSSA, IRÁKLIA 1–3 weekly to Pireás or Rafína, Náxos, Páros, Síros, Amorgós, Dhonoússa, and each other; 1 weekly to Astipálea and Kálimnos.

MÍKONOS At least 2 daily to Pireás (5hr), Rafína (3hr 30min), Tínos (1hr), Ándhros (3hr 30min) and Síros (2hr); 2–7 weekly *kaíkia* to Delos; 2 weekly to Iráklion (Crete), Thessaloníki, Skíros, Skíathos, Astipálea; 1–2 weekly to Pátmos, Léros, Kálimnos, Kos, Níssiros, Tílos, Rhodes.

MÍLOS At least daily to Pireás (8hr); 5–8 weekly to Sífnos (2hr), Sérifos and Kíthnos; 2 daily *kaíkia* or 4–6 weekly ferries to Kímolos; 2–3 weekly to Folégandhros, Síkinos, Íos and Thíra; 1–3 weekly to Crete (Iráklion or Sitía); 1 weekly to Náxos, Amorgós, Náfplio (Peloponnese), Kássos, Kárpathos, Hálki, Sími and Rhodes (Ródhos).

NÁXOS At least 3 daily to Pireás (8hr), Páros (1hr), Síros, Íos and Thíra; 2–3 weekly to Iráklion, Skhinóussa, Koufoníssi, Dhonoússa, and Amorgós; 1–3 weekly to Ikaría and Sámos; 1–2 a week to Crete (Iráklion), Foúrni, Rafína (6hr 30min). Seasonal *kaíkia* from Ayía Ánna to Páros (Píso Livádhi).

PÁROS At least 3 daily to Pireás (7hr), Andíparos, Náxos, Íos, Thíra, and Síros; almost daily to Iráklion (Crete); 3–6 weekly to Ikaría and Sámos; 3 weekly to Amorgós and the islets behind Náxos, and Rafína (5 hr), 3 or 4 weekly to Síkinos and Folégandhros; 3 weekly to Rhodes, Kárpathos, Thessaloníki; 2 weekly to Skíathos, Skíros, Anáfi. Seasonal small ferries to Sífnos and Náxos (Ayía Ánna).

SÉRIFOS AND SÍFNOS 5–12 weekly to Pireás (4hr 30min/6hr) and each other; 4–11 weekly to Mílos; 4–6 weekly to Kímolos; 2–3 weekly to Folégandhros, Síkinos, Íos, and Thíra (Santoríni); once weekly to Síros; once weekly to eastern Crete and select Dodecanese; daily (June–Aug) from Sífnos to Páros.

SÍKINOS and FOLÉGANDHROS 2–4 weekly with each other, and to Pireás (10hr), Kíthnos, Sérifos, Sífnos, Mílos; 1–3 weekly to Íos, Thíra, Síros, Páros, Náxos, and Kímolos; 1 weekly to eastern Crete (Áyios Nikólaos or Sitía), Kássos, Kárpathos, Hálki, Sími and Rhodes; unreliable seasonal *kaíkia* to Íos.

SÍROS At least 2 daily to Pireás (4hr), Tínos (1hr), Míkonos (2hr), Náxos, and Páros; 4 weekly to Rafína (3hr 30min), Amorgós and the islets behind Náxos; 2 weekly to Íos, Síkinos, Folégandhros and Thíra; 2 weekly to Ikaría, Sámos, Astipálea; 1–2 weekly to Pátmos, Léros, Kálimnos, Kos, Níssiros, Tílos, Rhodes.

THÍRA At least 2 daily to Pireás (10–12hr), Páros, Íos and Náxos; 3–6 weekly to Iráklion, Crete (5hr); 3–5 weekly to Síkinos and Folégandhros; 3 weekly to Thessaloníki; 2–3 weekly to Siros, Anáfi, Mílos, Kímolos, Sífnos, Sérifos and Kíthnos; 2 weekly to Skíros, Skíathos; Astipálea, Kálimnos, Kos and Rhodes; 1 weekly to Náfplio (Peloponnese), Crete (Áyios Nikólaos or Sitía), Kárpathos, Kássos, Hálki and Rhodes; also weekly to Amorgós and minor islets. Regular shuttle *kaíki* from Ía to Thirassía.

TÍNOS At least 2 daily to Pireás (5hr), Rafína (4hr), Ándhros, Síros and Míkonos; 4 weekly to Páros; 2 weekly to Náxos, Thíra, Iráklion (Crete), Skíros, Skíathos, Thessaloníki; 1–2 weekly to Páros, Náxos, Amorgós and minor islets between last two. Unreliable *kaíkia* to Delos.

Other services

To simplify the lists above, certain strategic **hydrofoil** and **small-boat services** have been omitted. Of these, the *Skopelitis* plies daily in season between Míkonos and Amorgós, spending each night at the latter and threading through all of the minor isles between it and Náxos, as well as Náxos and Páros (Píso Livádhi), in the course of a week. Note that this boat has no café or restaurant on board, so take provisions for what can be quite lengthy journeys. The *Aphrodite Express* follows an intricate route linking Náxos, Míkonos, Síros, Páros, Sífnos and Mílos; the popular *Ios Express* links Thíra (Skála Firás), Íos, Náxos, Páros and Míkonos daily in season. The *Paros Express* is actually a small car ferry, based on Síros despite its name, which does a very useful weekly circle route linking that island with Páros, Náxos, Íos, Thíra, Síkinos, Folégandhros, Sífnos, Sérifos and Kíthnos. The *Katamaran*, a small-capacity (and expensive) jet-boat, operates almost daily during summer out of Rafína and connects Síros, Tínos, Míkonos, Páros and Náxos with either the minor isles and Amorgós or a selection from among Íos, Síkinos, Folégandhros, Thíra and Anáfi (☎0294/22 888 for details). Another jetboat, the *Nearchos*, links Páros, Íos and Thíra with either Iráklion or Réthimnon on Crete on an almost-daily basis. In summer there are *Ilio Line* hydrofoils (*Delfini I, II, III, IV, V*), based in Rafína, which venture out at least once a week as far down as Mílos in the western Cyclic chain, rather more frequently through the central islands. A recent, welcome development is the appearance of *Ceres* "Flying Dolphins" between Zéa (Pireás), Kéa and Kíthnos – twice daily Friday to Monday in high season, once daily mid-week.

International ferries

Between May and October, *Minoan Lines* links Páros with Kuşadası (Turkey) and Ancona (Italy) twice weekly. One domestic stopover – either on Páros or Kefalloniá – may be allowed.

Flights

There are **airports** on **Páros, Míkonos, Thíra, Síros, Mílos** and **Náxos**. In season, or during storms when ferries are idle, you have little chance of getting a seat on less than three days' notice. The Athens–Milos route is probably the best value for money; the other destinations seem deliberately overpriced, in a usually unsuccessful attempt to keep passenger volume manageable. Expect off-season (Oct–April) frequencies to drop by at least eighty percent.

Athens–Páros (6–11 daily; 45min)

Athens–Míkonos (4–8 daily; 50min)

Athens–Thíra (4–5 daily; 1hr)

Athens–Síros (3–4 daily; 35min)

Athens–Mílos (3 daily; 45min)

Athens–Náxos (3–5 daily; 45min)

Mikonos–Thira (4 weekly; 40min)

Míkonos–Iráklion (3 weekly; 1hr 10min)

Míkonos–Rhodes (4 weekly; 1hr 10min)

Thíra–Iráklion (2–3 weekly; 40min)

Thíra–Rhodes (4 weekly; 1hr)

CHAPTER EIGHT

CRETE

Crete (Krīti) is a great deal more than just another Greek island. Often, especially in the cities or along the developed north coast, it doesn't feel like an island at all, but rather a substantial land in its own right: a mountainous, wealthy and surprisingly cosmopolitan one. But when you lose yourself among the mountains, or on the less-known coastal reaches of the south, it has everything you could want of a Greek island and more: great beaches, remote hinterlands and hospitable people.

In **history**, Crete is distinguished above all as the home of Europe's earliest civilization. It was only at the beginning of this century that the legends of King Minos and of a Cretan society that ruled the Greek world in prehistory were confirmed by excavations at Knossós and Festós. Yet the **Minoans** had a remarkably advanced society, the centre of a maritime trading empire as early as 2000 BC. The pre-Classical artworks produced on Crete at this time are unsurpassed anywhere in the ancient world, and it seems clear, that life on Crete in those days was good. This apparently peaceful culture survived at least three major natural disasters. Each time the palaces were destroyed, and each time they were rebuilt on a grander scale. Only after the last destruction, probably the result of a eruption of Thíra (Santoríni) and subsequent tidal waves and earthquakes, do significant numbers of weapons begin to appear in the ruins. This, together with the appearance of

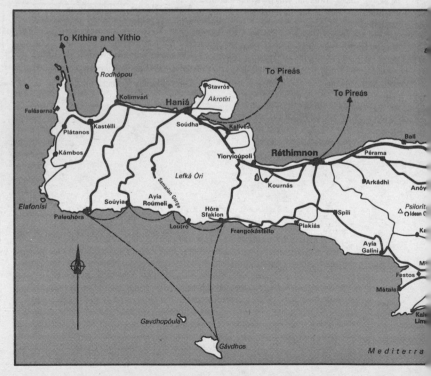

the Greek language, has been interpreted to mean that Mycenaean Greeks had taken control of the island. Nevertheless, for nearly 500 years, by far the longest period of peace the island has seen, Crete was home to a culture well ahead of its time.

The Minoans of Crete came originally from Anatolia; at their height they maintained strong links with Egypt and with the people of Asia Minor, and this position as meeting point and strategic fulcrum between east and west has played a major role in Crete's subsequent history. Control of the island passed from Greeks to Romans to Saracens, through the Byzantine Empire to Venice, and finally to Turkey for more than two centuries. During World War II, the island was occupied by the Germans and attained the dubious distinction of being the first place to be successfully invaded by paratroops.

Today, with a flourishing agricultural economy, Crete is one of the few islands which could probably support itself without **tourists**. Nevertheless, tourism is heavily promoted. The northeast coast in particular is overdeveloped, and though there are parts of the south and west coasts that have not been spoiled, they are getting harder to find. By contrast, the high mountains of the interior are still barely touched, and one of the best things to do on Crete is to **rent a vehicle** and explore the remoter villages.

Where to go

Every part of Crete has its loyal devotees and it's hard to pick out highlights, but generally if you want to get away from it all you should head west, towards **Haniá** and the smaller, less well-connected places along the south and west coasts. It is in this part of the island that the White Mountains rise, while below them yawns the famous **Samarian Gorge**. The far east, around **Sitía**, is also relatively unscathed.

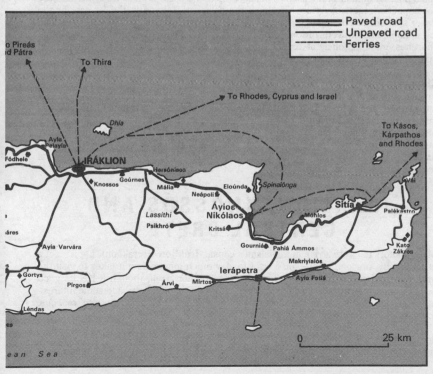

ROOM PRICE SCALES

All establishments listed in this book have been price-graded according to the scale outlined below. The rates quoted represent the cheapest available room in high season; all are prices for a double room, except for category ①, which are per person rates. Out of season, rates can drop by up to fifty percent, especially if you negotiate rates for a stay of three or more nights. Single rooms, where available, cost around seventy percent of the price of a double.

Rented private rooms on the islands usually fall into the ② or ③ categories, depending on their location and facilities, and the season; a few in the ④ category are more like plush self-catering apartments. They are not generally available from late October through the beginning of April, when only hotels tend to remain open.

① 1400–2000dr (£4–5.50/US$6–8.50)   ④ 8000–12000dr (£22–33/US$33–50)
② 4000–6000dr (£11–16.50/US$17–25)   ⑤ 12000–16000dr (£33–44/US$50–66)
③ 6000–8000dr (£16.50–22/US$25–33)   ⑥ 16000dr (£44/US$66) and upwards

For more accommodation details, see pp.34–35.

Whatever you do, the first main priority is to leave **Iráklion** (Heraklion) as quickly as possible, having paid the obligatory, and rewarding, visit to the **archeological museum** and nearby **Knossós**. The other great Minoan sites cluster around the middle of the island: **Festós** and **Ayía Triádha** in the south (with Roman **Górtys** to provide contrast), and **Mália** on the north coast. Almost wherever you go, though, you'll find a reminder of the island's history, whether it's the town of **Gourniá** near the cosmopolitan resort of **Áyios Nikólaos**, the palace of **Zákros** in the far east or the lesser sites scattered around the west. Unexpected highlights include Crete's Venetian forts, dominant at **Réthimnon**, and magnificent at **Frangokástello**; its Byzantine churches, most famously at **Kritsá**; and, at Réthimnon and Haniá, the cluttered old quarters full of Venetian and Turkish relics.

Climate

Crete has by far the longest summers in Greeceand you can get a decent tan here right into October and swim at least from May until November. Several annual harvests, also make it the most promising location for finding **casual work**. The cucumber greenhouses and pickling factories around Ierápetra have proved to be winter lifelines for many long-term Greek travellers. The one seasonal blight is the *meltémi*, which blows harder here and more continuously than anywhere else in Greece – the best of several reasons for avoiding an **August** visit.

IRÁKLION, KNOSSÓS AND CENTRAL CRETE

Many visitors to Crete arrive in the island's capital, **Iráklion** (Heraklion), but it's not a beautiful city, nor one where you'll want to stay much longer than it takes to visit the **archeological museum** and nearby **Knossós**. Iráklion itself, though it has its good points – superb fortifications, a fine market, atmospheric old alleys, and some interesting lesser museums – is for the most part an experience in survival: modern, raucous, traffic-laden, overcrowded and expensive.

The area immediately around the city is less touristy than you might expect, mainly because there are few decent beaches of any size on this central part of the coast. To the west, mountains drop straight into the sea virtually all the way to Réthimnon, with just two significant coastal settlements – **Ayía Pelayía**, a sizeable resort, and **Balí**, which is gradually becoming one. Eastwards, the main resorts are at least 40km away, at **Hersónissos** and beyond, although there is a string of rather unattractive development all the way there. Inland, there's agricultural country, the richest on the island, and a series of wealthy but rather dull villages. Directly behind the capital rises **Mount Ioúktas** with its characteristic profile of Zeus; to the west the Psilorítis massif spreads around the peak of **Mount Ída** (Psilorítis), the island's highest. On the south coast there are few roads and little development of any kind, except at **Ayía Galíni** in the southwest, a nominal fishing village long since swamped with tourists, and **Mátala**, which has thrown out the hippies that made it famous and is now crowded with package-trippers. **Léndas** has to some extent occupied Mátala's old niche.

Despite the lack of resorts, there seem constantly to be thousands of people trekking back and forth across the centre of the island. This is largely because of the superb archeological sites in the south: **Festós**, second of the Minoan palaces, with its attendant villa at **Ayía Triádha**, and **Górtys**, capital of Roman Crete.

Iráklion

The best way to approach **IRÁKLION** is by sea; that way you see the city as it should be seen, with Mount Ioúktas rising behind and the Psilorítis range to the west. As you get closer, it's the city walls that first stand out, still dominating and fully encircling the oldest part of town; finally you sail in past the great fort defending the harbour entrance. Unfortunately, big ships no longer dock in the old port but at great modern concrete wharves alongside, which neatly sums up Iráklion itself. Many of the old parts have been restored from the bottom up, but they're of no relevance to the dust and noise characterizing the city today. These renovations invariably look fake, far too polished and perfect alongside the grime that seems to coat even the newest buildings.

Orientation, arrival and information

Virtually everything you're likely to want to see in Iráklion lies within the walled city, and even here the majority of the interest falls into a relatively small sector, the northeastern corner. The most vital thoroughfare, **25 Avgoústou**, links the harbour with the commercial city centre. At the bottom it is lined with shipping and travel agencies, and rental outlets, but as you climb these give way to banks, restaurants and stores. **Platía Venizélou** (or Fountain Square), off to the right, is crowded with cafés and restaurants; behind Venizélou is **El Greco Park**, with the OTE office and more bars, while on the opposite side of 25 Avgoústou are some of the more interesting of Iráklion's older buildings. Further up 25 Avgoústou, **Kalokerinoú** leads down to Haniá Gate and out of the city westwards; straight ahead, Odhós 1821 goes nowhere very much, but adjacent 1866 is given over to the animated **market**. To the left, Dhikeosínis, a major shopping street, heads for **Platía Eleftherías**, paralleled by the touristy pedestrian alley, Dedhálou, the direct link between the two squares. Eleftherías is very much the traditional centre of the city, both for traffic, which swirls around it constantly, and for life in general: ringed by more expensive tourist cafés and restaurants and in the evening alive with hordes of strolling locals.

Points of arrival

Iráklion **airport** is right on the coast, 4km east of the city. The #1 bus leaves for Platía Eleftherías every few minutes from the car park in front of the terminal; buy your ticket (130dr) at the booth before boarding. There are also plenty of taxis outside, and prices to major destinations are posted; it's about 1000dr to the centre of town.

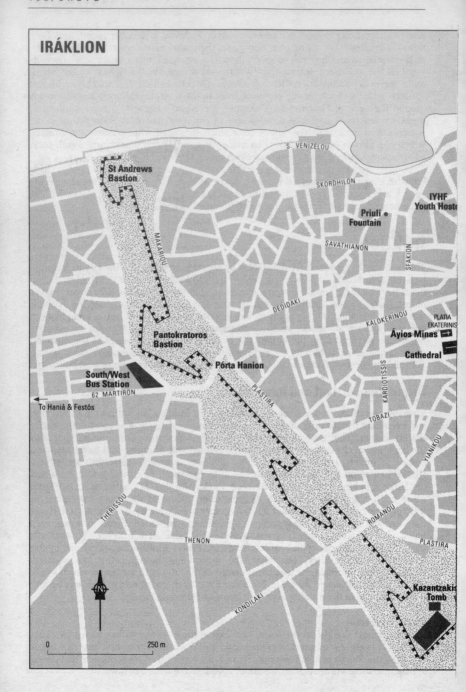

IRÁKLION

St Andrews
Bastion

S. VENIZELOU

SKORDHILON

Priuli
Fountain

IYHF
Youth Hostr

MAKARIOU

SAVATHIANON

SFAKION

OEDIDAKI

KALOKERINOU

PLATIA
EKATERINIS

Áyios Minas

Pantokratoros
Bastion

Cathedral

Pórta Hanion

KARDIOTISSIS

South/West
Bus Station

PLASTIRA

62 MARTIRON

To Haniá & Festós

TOBAZI

YIANNIKOU

ROMANOU

THEBISSOU

PLASTIRA

THENON

Kazantzaki
Tomb

KONDILAKI

0   250 m

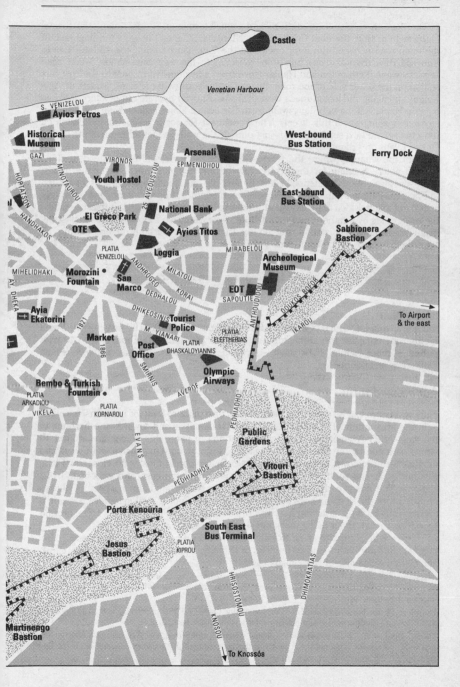

There are three main **bus stations** and a small terminus. Services along the coastal highway to or from the **east** (Mália, Áyios Nikólaos, Sitía, etc) use the terminal just off the main road between the ferry dock and the Venetian harbour; the #2 local bus to Knossós runs from the city bus stop, adjacent to the east bus station. Main road services **west** (Réthimnon and Haniá) leave from a terminal right next to the east bus station on the other side of the road. Buses for the **southwest** (Festós, Mátala or Ayía Galíni) and along the inland roads west (Tílissos, Anóyia) operate out of a terminal just outside Haniá Gate, a very long walk from the centre along Kalokerinoú (or jump on any bus heading down this street). The **southeast** (basically Ierápetra and points en route) is served by a small terminus just outside the walls in Platía Kíprou at the end of Odhós Evans on Trikoúpi.

From the wharves where the **ferries** dock, the city rises directly ahead in steep tiers. If you're heading for the centre, for the archeological museum or the tourist office, cut straight up the stepped alleys behind the bus station onto Doukos Bofor and to Platía Eleftherías. This will take about fifteen minutes. For accommodation, though, and to get a better idea of the layout of Iráklion's main attractions, it's simplest to follow the main roads by a rather more roundabout route. Head west along the coast, past the major east-bound bus station and on by the Venetian harbour before cutting up towards the centre on 25 Avgoústou.

> The telephone code for Iráklion is ☎081

Information

Iráklion's **tourist office** (Mon–Fri 8am–2.30pm; ☎228 825) is just below Platía Eleftherías, opposite the archeological museum at Zanthoudhídhou 1. The **tourist police** – more helpful than most – are on Dhikeosínis, halfway between Platía Eleftherías and the market.

Accommodation

Finding a **room** can be difficult in season. The best place to look for inexpensive rooms is in the area around Platía Venizélou, along Handhákos and towards the harbour to the west of 25 Avgoústou. Other concentrations of affordable places are around El Greco park and by the bottom of the market (slightly more expensive and noisy) and off Kalokerinoú, down towards Haniá Gate. Better hotels mostly lie closer to Platía Eleftherías, to the south of Platía Venizélou and near the east- and west-bound bus stations. The dusty park between the main bus station and the harbour is always crowded with the sleeping bags of those who failed to find, or couldn't afford, a room; if you're really hard up, crashing here has the advantage that local farmers come around recruiting casual labour in the mornings, but a pleasant environment it's not.

There are no **campsites** near to Iráklion now that *Camping Iraklion* has closed. The nearest sites are both found to the east of the city: *Creta Camping* at Gouves(16km), and *Caravan Camping* at Hersonisos (28km).

Atlas, Kandanoleon 11 (☎288 989). Rather run-down old pension in convenient but noisy alley between Platía Venizélou and El Greco park. Pleasant roof garden and freshly squeezed orange juice for breakfast. ②.

Dedalos, Dedhálou 15 (☎244 812). Very centrally placed on the pedestrianized alley between Venizélou and Eleftherías. Decent balcony rooms with private bath. ④.

Marin, Doukos Bofor 12 (☎224 736). A short distance along from the *Kris* and two other more expensive hotels, the *Lato* and the *Alaira*, but the best value of the lot. Very convenient for the bus stations and the archeological museum. ④.

Metropol, Karterou 48 (☎242 330). Quieter area near cathedral. Dated 1960s-style hotel but one of the best of the moderate hotels; rooms with shower are good value, more so as price also includes breakfast. ④.

Mirabello, Theotokopoulou 20 (☎285 052). Good-value, family-run place in a quiet street close to El Greco park. ③.

Olympic, Platía Kornarou (☎288 861). Overlooking busy *platía* and the famous Bembo and Turkish fountains. One of the many hotels built in the 1960s, but one of the few that has been refurbished. ⑤.

Paladion, Handhákos 16 (☎282 563). Very basic and cheap, near Platía Venizélou with stuffy rooms upstairs, but a pleasant garden at the back with rooms off it. No private facilities. ②.

Rea, Kalimeráki 1 (☎223 638). A friendly, comfortable and clean hotel in quiet street. Some rooms with washbasin, others with own shower. One of the best of the cheaper hotels. ②.

Rent Rooms Vergina, Hortatson 32 (☎242 739). Basic but pleasant rooms (with washbasins) in quiet street around a courtyard with an enormous banana tree. ②.

Youth hostel, Vironos 5 (☎286 281). The original youth hostel which has operated since 1963. Family run, very friendly and helpful with plenty of space and up to 50 beds on the roof if you fancy sleeping out under the stars. In addition to dormitories, family and double rooms are also available. Hot showers, breakfast (400dr) and TV. ①.

The Town

From the port, the town rises overhead, and you can cut up the stepped alleys for a direct approach to Platía Eleftherías (Liberty Square) and the archeological museum. The easiest way to the middle of things, though, is to head west along the coast road, past the main bus stations and the *arsenali*, and then up 25 Avgoústou, which leads into **Platía Venizélou**. This is crowded with Iráklion's youth, patronizing outdoor cafés (marginally cheaper than those on Eleftherías) and with travellers who've arranged to meet in "Fountain Square". The **fountain** itself is not particularly spectacular at first glance, but on closer inspection is really a very beautiful work; it was built by Venetian governor Francesco Morosini in the seventeenth century, incorporating four lions which were some 300 years old even then. From the *platía* you can strike up Dedhálou, a pedestrianized street full of tourist shops and restaurants, or continue on 25 Avgoústou to a major traffic junction. To the right, Kalokerinoú leads west out of the city, the **market** lies straight ahead, and Platía Eleftherías is a short walk to the left up Dhikeosínis.

Platía Eleftherías and the archeological museum

Platía Eleftherías is very much the traditional heart of the city: traffic swirls around it constantly, and in the evening strolling hordes jam its expensive cafés and restaurants. Most of Iráklion's more expensive shops are in the streets leading off the *platía*.

The **Archeological Museum** (Mon 12.30–7pm, Tues–Sat 8am–7pm, Sun 8.30am–3pm; 1000dr) is nearby, directly opposite the EOT office. Almost every important prehistoric and Minoan find on Crete is included in this fabulous, if bewilderingly large, collection. The museum tends to be crowded, especially when a guided tour stampedes through, but it's worth taking time over. You can't hope to see everything, nor can we attempt to describe it all (several good museum guides are sold here; best is probably the glossy one by J A Sakellarakis) but highlights include the **town mosaics** in Room 2 (galleries are arranged basically in chronological order), the famous **inscribed disc** from Festós in Room 3 (itself the subject of several books), most of Room 4, especially the magnificent bull's head **rhyton** (drinking vessel), the **jewellery** in Room 6 (and everywhere) and the engraved **black vases** in Room 7. Save some of your time and energy for upstairs, where the **Hall of the Frescoes**, with intricately reconstructed fragments of the wall paintings from Knossós and other sites, is especially wonderful.

Walls and fortifications

The massive **Venetian walls**, in places up to fifteen metres thick, are the most obvious evidence of Iráklion's later history. Though their fabric is incredibly well preserved, access is virtually nonexistent. It is possible, just, to walk on top of them from St Anthony's bastion over the sea in the west as far as the tomb of Nikos Kazantzakis, Cretan author of *Zorba the Greek*. His epitaph reads: "I believe in nothing, I hope for nothing, I am free." At weekends, Iraklians gather here to pay their respects and enjoy a free view of the soccer matches below. If the walls seem altogether too much effort, the **port fortifications** are very much easier to see. Stroll out along the jetty (crowded with courting couples after dark) and you can get inside the sixteenth-century **castle** (Mon–Sat 8am–4pm, Sun 10am–3pm; 400dr) at the harbour entrance, emblazoned with the Venetian Lion of St Mark. Standing atop this, you can begin to understand how Iráklion (or Candia as it was known until the seventeenth century) withstood a 22-year siege before finally falling to the Ottomans. On the landward side of the port, the Venetian **arsenali** can also be seen, their arches rather lost amid the concrete road system all around.

Churches, icons and the Historical Museum

From the harbour, 25 Avgoústou will take you up past most of the rest of what's interesting. The **church of Áyios Títos**, on the left as you approach Platía Venizélou, borders a pleasant little *platía*. It looks magnificent principally because, like most of the churches here, it was adapted by the Turks as a mosque and only reconsecrated in 1925; consequently it has been renovated on numerous occasions. On the top side of this *platía*, abutting 25 Avgoústou, is the Venetian **City Hall** with its famous loggia, again almost entirely rebuilt. Just above this, facing Platía Venizélou, is the **church of San Marco**, its steps usually crowded with the overflow of people milling around in the *platía*. Neither of these last two buildings has found a permanent role in its refurbished state, but both are generally open to house some kind of exhibition or craft show.

Slightly away from the obvious city-centre circuit, but still within the bounds of the walls, there are a couple of lesser museums worth seeing if you have the time. First of these is the collection of **icons** in the **church of Ayía Ekateríni** (daily except Sun 10am–1pm, Tues, Thurs & Fri also at 4–6pm; 400dr), an ancient building just below the undistinguished cathedral, off Kalokerinoú. This excellent display might inspire you to seek out less-known icons in churches around the island. The finest here are six large scenes by Mihalis Damaskinos (a near-contemporary of El Greco) who fused Byzantine and Renaissance influences. Supposedly both Damaskinos and El Greco studied at Ayía Ekateríni in the sixteenth century when it functioned as a sort of monastic art school.

The **Historical Museum** (Mon–Fri 9.30am–4.30pm, Sat 9.30am–2.30pm; 600dr) is some way from here, down near the waterfront opposite the stark *Xenia* hotel. Its display of folk costumes and jumble of local memorabilia includes the reconstructed studies of both Nikos Kazantzakis and Emanuel Tsouderos (Cretan statesman and Greek prime minister). There's enough variety to satisfy just about anyone, including the only El Greco painting on Crete, *View of Mount Sinai and the Monastery of St Catherine*.

The beaches

Iráklion's **beaches** are some way out, whether east or west of town. In either direction they're easily accessible by public bus: #6 west from the stop outside the *Astoria* hotel in Platía Eleftherías; #7 east from the stop opposite this, under the trees in the centre of the *platía*.

Almirós (or Amoudhári) to the west has been subjected to a degree of development, taking in a campsite, several medium-size hotels and one giant one (the *Zeus Beach*, in the shadow of the power station at the far end), which makes the beach hard to get to without walking through or past something built up.

Amnissós, to the east, seems the better choice, with several tavernas and the added amusement of planes swooping in immediately overhead to land. This is where most locals go on their afternoons off; the furthest of the beaches is the best, although new hotels are encroaching here, too. Little remains here to indicate the once-flourishing port of Knossós aside from a rather dull, fenced-in dig. If you're seriously into antiquities, however, you'll find a more rewarding site in the small villa, known as **Nirou Hani** (daily except Mon 8.30am–3pm) at Háni Kokkíni, the first of the full-blown resort developments east of Iráklion.

Eating

Big city as it is, Iráklion disappoints when it comes to eating. The cafés and tavernas of *platías* **Venizélou** and **Eleftherías** are essential places to sit and watch the world pass, but their food is expensive and mediocre. One striking exception is *Bouyatsa Kirkor*, by the fountain in Venizélou, where you can sample authentic *bouyatsa*, alternatively, try a plate of *loukoumades*, available from a number of cafés at the top of Dhikeosinis. The cafés and tavernas on **Dedhálou**, the pedestrian alley linking the two main *platías*, are very run of the mill, enticing you in with persistent waiters and faded photographs of what appears to be food.

A more atmospheric option is to head for the little alley, **Fotíou Theodosáki**, which runs through from the market to Odhós Evans. It is entirely lined with the tables of rival taverna owners, certainly authentic and catering for market traders and their customers as well as tourists. Compared to some, they often look a little grimy, but they are by no means cheap, which can come as a surprise. Nearby, at the corner of Évans and Yiánari, is the long-established taverna *Ionia*, which is the sort of place to come to if you are in need of a substantial, no-nonsense feed, with a good range of Greek dishes.

Other good tavernas are more scattered. Still near the centre, just off Eleftherías at **Platía Dhaskaloyiánnis** (where the post office is), are some inexpensive and unexceptional tavernas; but the *platía* is a pleasant and relaxing venue, if not for a meal then to sit at one of its cafés. Nearer Venizélou, try exploring some of the back streets to the east, off Dedhálou and behind the *loggia*. The *Taverna Giovanni*, on the alley Korai parallel to Dedhálou, is one of the better tavernas in Iráklion: a friendly place with a varied menu that uses fresh, good quality ingredients but with reasonable prices and a good atmosphere both inside and out. It also caters for vegetarians.

The **waterfront** is lined with fish tavernas with little to recommend them. Instead, walk across the road to *Ippokambus*, which specializes in *mezédhes* at moderate prices. It is deservedly popular with locals and is often crowded late into the evening – you may have to wait in line or turn up earlier than the Greeks eat. Even if you see no space it is worth asking as the owner may suddenly disappear inside the taverna and emerge with yet another table to carry further down the pavement.

Should you have a craving for **non-Greek food**, there is Italian at the *Loukoulos* and Chinese at the *New China Restaurant*, both with leafy courtyards and both in the same street as the *Taverna Giovanni*. There is also the *Curry House* just off Dedhálou, which advertises both Indian and Mexican food, but don't expect the real thing. You can eat decent pizza at many tavernas in the centre, or far better at the excellent *Tartuffo* on Dhimokratias (the road towards Knossós) near the *Galaxy* hotel. Go early, as it's usually packed with locals.

For **snacks and takeaways,** there's a whole group of *souvlaki* stalls clustering around 25 Avgoústou at the entrance to El Greco park, which is handy if you need somewhere to sit and eat. For cheese or spinach pies or some other pastry, sweet or savoury, there are no shortage of *zaharoplastía*, such as the *Samaria* next to the Harley Davidson shop across from the park. If you want to buy your own food, the **market** on Odhós 1866 is the place to go; it's an attraction in itself, which you should see even if you don't plan to buy.

Drinking, nightlife and entertainment

Iráklion is a bit of a damp squib as far as **nightlife** goes, certainly when compared to many other towns on the island. If you're determined, however, there are a few city-centre possibilities, and plenty of options if all you want to do is sit and **drink**. In addition, there are a number of **cinemas** scattered about, for which check the posters on the boards by the tourist police office. Most enjoyable is the open-air cinema on the beach to the west of the city.

Bars

Bars tend to fan out into the streets around Handhákos, and while you will stumble on many places by following the crowds, *Odysseia* (Handhákos 63), *Jasmin* (tucked in an alley mid-way down Handhákos) and *El Azteca* (Psavomilingou 32, west of Handhákos), a Mexican bar serving *tacos*, are all good places for which to aim.

The most animated place is a *platía* behind Dedhálou (up from the *Giovanni*), where there are several trendy bars (including *Flash* and *Notos*) with outdoor tables and popular with students in term time. Enjoy a game of backgammon here during the day or early evening; later it can get get extremely lively with many distractions. In and around Platía Venizélou, there are many bars, again some are very fashionable, with *De Facto* being one of the most popular. This is one of the new breed of *kafenío* emerging in Iráklion, attracting younger people; the drinks are cocktails rather than *raki*, the music is western or modern Greek and there are prices to match. Another is the *Idaean Andron*, on Pardhikari around the corner from the *Selena* hotel, which has a nice atmosphere, and there are more along Kandanoléon, off El Greco park.

Iráklion looks a great deal better than you'd expect from above, and there are fancier **roof-top places** above most of the restaurants in Platía Eleftherías, the *Cafe-Bar Dore* for example. This serves food as well, and while it's not exactly the sort of place to wear cut-offs and T-shirt, it's no more expensive than the restaurants in the *platía* below. Many hotels around the city have roof-top bars which welcome non-residents; those just above the bus stations and harbour, such as the *Alaira* have particularly stunning views.

Less elevated romance is to be had at the *Onar* café (Handhákos 36b, north of Venizélou); there's a small terrace and they serve a wide variety of teas as well as great ices, just the thing when you're winding down around around midnight. *Tasso's* is a popular hang-out for young hostellers, lively at night and with good breakfasts to help you recover in the morning; similar bars in the area include the *Utopia*, further down Handhákos, and the *Bonsai*, next to *Christakos Rooms*.

Clubs and discos

For **discos** proper, there is a greater selection even if they are all playing "techno" at the moment, interspersed with Greek music (and not the Greek music you get for tourists). *Trapeza* is still the most popular, down towards the harbour at the bottom of Doukos Bofor, below the archeological museum. *Makao* also has a following and is on the opposite side of the street to *Trapeza*; or try *Genesis* next door. Another cluster of nightclubs can be found on Ikarou, about a twenty-minute walk away. Retrace your steps towards the archeological museum, but before emerging onto Platía Eleftherías turn left downhill and follow the main road, Ikarou. Here you'll find the *Minoica*, the *Korus Club* and the *Athina*, again playing similar music and popular with the young Iraklions.

Listings

Airlines *Olympic*, on Platía Eleftherías (☎229 191), is the only airline with a permanent office in Iráklion. Charter airlines flying in to Iráklion mostly use local travel agents as their representatives.

Airport For airport information call ☎282 025. Bus #1 runs from Platía Eleftherías to the airport every few minutes.

Banks The main branches are on 25 Avgoústou, many of which have 24hr cash machines (not always working); there's also a *VISA* machine at *Ergo Bank* on Dhikeosínis.

Car and bike rental 25 Avgoústou is lined with rental companies, but you'll find cheaper rates on the backstreets and it is always worth asking for discounts. Good places to start – out of dozens – include *Eurocreta* (Sapotie 2; ☎226 700) for cars and *Motor Speed* (Ariadnis; ☎224 812) for bikes, both near the archeological museum; *Blue Sea* (Kosma Zotou 7, near the bottom of 25 Avgoústou; ☎241 097); *Ritz* in the *Hotel Rea* for cars (Kalimeráki 1; ☎223 638); and *Sun Rise* (25 Avgoústou 46; ☎221 609) for cars and bikes.

Ferry tickets Available from *Minoan Lines* (25 Avgoústou 78; ☎224 303), *Kavi Club* near the tourist office (☎221 166), or any of the travel agents listed below.

Hospital Most central is the hospital on Apollónion, southwest of Platía Kornarou, between Alber and Moussoúrou.

Laundry There's a launderette in the backstreets below the archeological museum (Mon–Fri 9am–2pm & 5–7pm, Sat 9am–2pm).

Left luggage Offices in the east-bound and southwest bus stations (daily 6am–8pm; 200dr per bag per day), as well as a commercial agency at 25 Avgoústou (daily 7am–11pm; 450dr per bag per day); you can also leave bags at the youth hostel (even if you don't stay there) for 200–300dr per bag per day. If you want to leave your bag while you go off on a bike for a day or two, the rental company should be prepared to store it.

Newspapers and books For English-language newspapers, novels as well as local guides and maps, Dedhálou is the best bet. *Planet International Bookstore* at the corner of Handhákos and Kidoninio, behind Platía Venizélou, has a huge stock of English-language titles.

Pharmacies Plentiful on the main shopping streets – at least one is open 24hr on a rota basis, check the list on the door of any.

Post office Main office in Platía Dhaskaloyiánnis, off Eleftherías (Mon–Fri 7.30am–8pm). There's also a temporary office (a van) at the entrance to El Greco Park (daily 7.30am–7pm), handy for changing money.

Taxis Major taxi ranks in Platía Eleftherías and El Greco Park or call ☎210 102 or 210 168. Prices displayed on boards at ranks.

Telephones The OTE head office is in El Greco Park – often long waits, though an efficient 24hr service.

Travel agencies Budget operators and student specialists include the extremely helpful *Blavakis Travel* (Platía Kallergon 8, just off 25 Avgoústou by the entrance to El Greco Park; ☎282 541) and *Prince Travel* (25 Avgoústou 30, ☎282 706). For excursions around the island, villa rentals etc, the bigger operators are probably easier: *Irman Travel* (Dedhálou 26; ☎242 527) or *Creta Travel Bureau* (20–22 Epiménidhou; ☎243 811). The latter is also the local *American Express* agent.

Knossós

KNOSSÓS, the largest of the Minoan palaces, reached its cultural peak more than 3000 years ago, though a town of some importance persisted here well into the Roman era. It lies on a low, largely man-made hill some 5km southeast of Iráklion; the surrounding hillsides are rich in lesser remains spanning 25 centuries, starting at the beginning of the second millennium BC.

Barely a hundred years ago the palace existed only in mythology. Knossós was the court of the legendary King Minos, whose wife Pasiphae bore the Minotaur, half-bull, half-man. Here the labyrinth was constructed by Daedalus to contain the monster, and youths were brought from Athens as human sacrifice until Theseus arrived to slay the beast, and with Ariadne's help, escape its lair. The discovery of the palace, and the interplay of these legends with fact, is among the most amazing tales of modern archeology. Heinrich Schliemann, the excavator of Troy, suspected that a major Minoan palace lay under the various tumuli here, but was denied the necessary permission to dig by the local Ottoman authorities at the end of the last century. It was left for Sir Arthur Evans, whose name is indelibly associated with Knossós, to excavate the site, from 1900 onwards.

The Site

April–Sept Mon–Fri 8am–7pm, Sat & Sun 8.30am–3pm; Oct–March daily 8.30am–3pm; 1000dr, students 500dr.

As soon as you enter the **palace of Knossós** through the West Court, the ancient ceremonial entrance, it is clear how the legends of the labyrinth grew up around it. Even with a detailed plan, it's almost impossible to find your way around the site with any success. The best advice is not to try; wander around for long enough and you'll even-

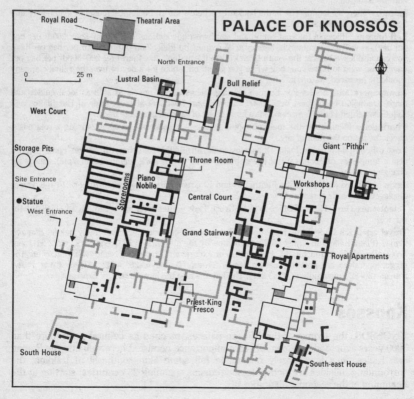

PALACE OF KNOSSÓS

Royal Road · Theatral Area · North Entrance · Lustral Basin · Bull Relief · West Court · Storage Pits · Site Entrance · Statue · West Entrance · Storerooms · Piano Nobile · Throne Room · Central Court · Grand Stairway · Giant "Pithoi" · Workshops · Royal Apartments · Priest-King Fresco · South House · South-east House

0   25 m

tually stumble upon everything. If you're worried about missing the highlights, you can always tag along with one of the constant guided tours for a while, catching the patter and then backtracking to absorb the detail when that particular crowd has moved on. You won't get the place to yourself, whenever you come, but exploring on your own does give you the opportunity to appreciate individual parts of the palace in the brief lulls between groups.

Knossós was liberally "restored" by Evans, and these restorations have been the source of furious controversy among archeologists ever since. It has become clear that much of Evans's upper level – the so-called *piano nobile* – is pure conjecture. Even so, his guess as to what the palace might have looked like is certainly as good as anyone else's, and it makes the other sites infinitely more meaningful if you have seen Knossós first. Without the restorations, it would be almost impossible to imagine the grandeur of the multistorey palace or to see the ceremonial stairways, strange, top-heavy pillars and gaily painted walls that distinguish the site. For some idea of the size and complexity of the palace in its original state, take a look at the cutaway drawings (wholly imaginary but probably not too far off) on sale outside.

Royal Apartments

The superb **Royal Apartments** around the central staircase are not guesswork, and they are plainly the finest of the rooms at Knossós. Unfortunately, extensive renovations are currently taking place and these mean that the apartments are likely to be closed for some time, although glimpses can be had through the wooden railings. The **Grand Stairway** itself is a masterpiece of design: not only a fitting approach to these sumptuously appointed chambers but also an integral part of the whole plan, its large well bringing light into the lower storeys. Light wells such as these, usually with a courtyard at the bottom, are a constant feature of Knossós and a reminder of just how important creature comforts were to the Minoans, and of how skilled they were at providing them.

For evidence of this luxurious lifestyle you need look no further than the **Queen's Suite**, off the grand **Hall of the Colonnades** at the bottom of the staircase. Here, the main living room is decorated with the celebrated **dolphin fresco** (a reproduction; the original is now in the Iráklion archeological museum) and with running friezes of flowers and abstract spirals. On two sides, it opens out onto courtyards that let in light and air; the smaller one would probably have been planted with flowers. In use, the room would have been scattered with cushions and hung with plush curtains, while doors and further curtains between the pillars would have allowed for privacy, and for cool shade in the heat of the day. This, at least, is what they'd have you believe, and it's a very plausible scenario. Remember, though, that all this is speculation and some of it is pure hype; the dolphin fresco, for example, was found in the courtyard, not the room itself, and would have been viewed from inside as a sort of *trompe l'oeil*, like looking through a glass-bottomed boat. Whatever the truth, this is an impressive example of Minoan architecture, the more so when you follow the dark passage around to the queen's **bathroom**. Here is a clay tub, protected behind a low wall (and again probably screened by curtains when in use), and the famous "flushing" toilet (a hole in the ground with drains to take the waste away – one flushed it by throwing a bucket of water down).

The much pored over **drainage system** was a series of interconnecting terracotta pipes running underneath most of the palace. Guides to the site never fail to point these out as evidence of the advanced state of Minoan civilization, and they are indeed quite an achievement, in particular the system of baffles and overflows to slow down the runoff and avoid any danger of flooding. Just how much running water there would have been, however, is another matter; the water supply was, and is, at the *bottom* of the hill, and even the combined efforts of rainwater catchment and hauling water up to the palace can hardly have been sufficient to supply the needs of more than a small elite.

Going up the Grand Stairway to the floor above the queen's domain, you come to a set of rooms generally regarded as the **King's Quarters**. These are chambers in a considerably sterner vein; the staircase opens into a grandiose reception chamber known as the **Hall of the Royal Guard**, its walls decorated in repeated shield patterns. Immediately off here is the **Hall of the Double Axes**, believed to be have been the ruler's personal chamber, a double room that would allow for privacy in one portion while audiences were held in the more public section. Its name comes from the double-axe symbol carved into every block of masonry.

The Throne Room and the rest of the palace

Continuing to the top of the Grand Stairway, you emerge onto the broad **Central Court**. Open now, this would once have been enclosed by the walls of the buildings all around. On the far side, in the northwestern corner of the courtyard, is the entrance to another of Knossós's most atmospheric survivals, the **Throne Room**. Here, a worn stone throne sits against the wall of a surprisingly small chamber; along the walls around it are ranged stone benches, and behind there's a reconstructed fresco of two griffins. In all probability this was the seat of a priestess rather than a ruler (there's nothing like it in any other Minoan palace), but it may just have been an innovation wrought by the Mycenaeans, since it seems that this room dates only from the final period of Knossós's occupation. The Throne Room is now closed off with a wooden gate, but you can lean over this for a good view, and in the antechamber there's a wooden copy of the throne on which everyone perches to have their picture taken.

The rest you'll see as you wander, contemplating the legends of the place which blur with reality. Try not to miss the giant *pithoi* in the northeast quadrant of the site, an area known as the palace workshops; the storage chambers which you see from behind the Throne Room and the reproduction frescoes in the reconstructed room above it; the fresco of the Priest-King looking down on the south side of the central court, and the relief of a charging bull on its north side. This last would have greeted you if you entered the palace through its north door; you can see evidence here of some kind of gate house and a lustral bath, a sunken area perhaps used for ceremonial bathing and purification. Just outside this gate is the **theatral area**, an open space a little like a stepped amphitheatre, which may have been used for ritual performances or dances. From here the **Royal Road**, claimed as the oldest road in Europe, sets out. At one time, this probably ran right across the island; nowadays it ends after about a hundred yards in a brick wall beneath the modern road. Circling back around the outside of the palace, you get more idea of its scale by looking up at it; on the south side are a couple of small reconstructed Minoan houses worth exploring.

Practicalities

The #2 local **bus** sets off every ten minutes from the Iráklion's city bus stop (adjacent to the east bus station), runs up 25 Avgoústou (with a stop by Platía Venizélou) and out of town on Odhós 1821 and Évans.

At Knossós, outside the fenced site, is the *caravanserai* where ancient wayfarers would rest and water their animals. Head out onto the road and you'll find no lack of watering holes for modern travellers either – a string of rather pricey tavernas and tacky souvenir stands. There are several **rooms** for rent here, and if you're really into Minoan culture, there's a lot to be said for staying out this way to get an early start. Be warned that it's expensive and unashamedly commercial.

Beyond Knossós

If you have transport, the drive beyond Knossós can be an attractive and enjoyable one, taking minor roads through much greener country, with vineyards draped across low hills and flourishing agricultural communities. If you want specific things to seek out, head first for **MIRTIÁ**, an attractive village with a small **Kazantzakis Museum** (daily except Sun 9am–4pm; 400dr) in a house where the writer's parents once lived. **ARHÁNES**, at the foot of Mount Ioúktas, is a much larger place that was also quite heavily populated in Minoan times. None of the three sites here is open to the public, but one of them, **Anemospília**, has caused huge controversy since its excavation in the 1980s. Many traditional views of the Minoans, particularly that of Minoan life as peaceful and idyllic, have had to be rethought in the light of the discovery of an apparent human sacrifice. From Arhánes you can also drive to the top of Mount Ioúktas to enjoy the panoramic views. At **VATHÍPETRO**, south of the mountain, is a Minoan villa (with wine press in situ) which can be explored (daily 8.30am–3pm).

Southwest from Iráklion: sites and beaches

If you take a **tour** from Iráklion (or one of the resorts) and you'll probably visit the Górtys, Festós and Ayía Triádha sites in a day, with a lunchtime swim at Mátala thrown in. Doing it by public transport, you'll be forced into a rather more leisurely pace, but there's still no reason why you shouldn't get to all three and reach Mátala within the day; if necessary, it is easy enough to hitch the final stretch. **Bus services** to the Festós site are excellent, with some nine a day to and from Iráklion (fewer run on Sunday), five of which continue to or come from Mátala; there are also services direct to Ayía Galíni. If you're arriving in the afternoon, plan to visit Ayía Triádha first, as it closes early.

The route to Áyii Dhéka

The road from Iráklion towards Festós is a pretty good one by the standards of Cretan mountain roads, albeit a dull one, too. The country you're heading towards is the richest agricultural land on the island, and right from the start the villages en route are large and business-like. In the largest of them, Ayía Varvára, there's a great rock outcrop known as the *Omphalos* (Navel) of Crete, supposedly the very centre of the island.

Past here, you descend rapidly to the fertile fields of the Messará plain, where the road joins the main route across the south near the village of **ÁYII DHÉKA**. For religious Cretans Áyii Dhéka is something of a place of pilgrimage; its name, "The Ten Saints", refers to ten early Christians martyred here under the Romans. In a crypt below the modern church you can see the martyrs' tombs. It's an attractive village to wander around, with several places to eat and even some **rooms** along the main road.

Górtys

Daily 8.30am–3pm; 400dr

Within easy walking distance of Áyii Dhéka, either through the fields or along the main road, sprawls the site of **Górtys**, ruined capital of the Roman province that included not only Crete but also much of North Africa. Cutting across the fields will give you some idea of the scale of this city at its zenith in approximately the third century AD; an enormous variety of other remains, including an impressive **theatre**, are strewn across your route. Even in Áyii Dhéka you'll see Roman pillars and statues lying around in people's yards or propping up their walls.

There had been a settlement here from the earliest times, but the extant ruins date almost entirely from the Roman era. Only now is the site being systematically excavated, by the Italian School. At the main entrance to the fenced site, alongside the road, are the ruins of the still impressive **basilica of Áyios Títos**; the eponymous saint converted the island to Christianity and was its first bishop. Beyond this is the **Odeion** which houses the most important discovery on the site, the **Law Code**. These great inscribed blocks of stone were incorporated by the Romans from a much earlier stage of the city's development; they're written in an obscure early Greek-Cretan dialect, and in a style known as *boustrophedon* (ox-ploughed), with the lines reading alternately in opposite directions like the furrows of a ploughed field. At ten metres by three metres, this is reputedly the largest Greek inscription ever found. The laws set forth reflect a strictly hierarchical society: five witnesses were needed to convict a free man of a crime, only one for a slave; raping a free man or woman carried a fine of a hundred staters, violating a serf only five. A small **museum** in a loggia (also within the fenced area) holds a number of large sculptures found at Górtys.

Míres

Some 20km west of Górtys, **MÍRES** is an important market and focal point of transport for the Messará plain: if you're switching buses to get from the beaches on the south coast to the archeological sites or the west, this is where you'll do it. There are good facilities including a **bank**, lots of **restaurants** and plenty of **rooms**, though there's no particular reason to stay unless you are waiting for a bus or looking for work (it's one of the better places for agricultural jobs). Heading straight for Festós, there's usually no need to stop.

Festós

Mon–Fri 8am–7pm, Sat & Sun 8.30am–7pm; 800dr, Sun free.

The **Palace of Festós** was excavated by the Italian, Federico Halbherr (also responsible for the early work at Górtys), at almost exactly the same time as Evans was working at Knossós. The style of the excavations, however, could hardly have been more different. Here, to the approval of most traditional archeologists, reconstruction was kept to an absolute minimum – it's all bare foundations, and walls which rise at most a metre above ground level. This means that despite a magnificent setting overlooking the plain of Messará, the palace at Festós is not as immediately arresting as those at Knossós or Mália. Much of the site is fenced off and, except in the huge central court, it's almost impossible to get any sense of the place as it was; the plan is almost as complex as at Knossós, with none of the reconstruction to bolster the imagination.

It's interesting to speculate why the palace was built halfway up a hill rather than on the plain below; certainly not for defence, for this is in no way a good defensive position. Psychological superiority over the peasants or reasons of health are both possible, but it seems quite likely that it was simply the magnificent view that finally swayed the decision. The site looks over Psilorítis to the north and the huge plain, with the Lasíthi mountains beyond it, to the east. Towards the top of Psilorítis you should be able to make out a small black smudge: the entrance to the Kamáres cave (see p.513).

On the ground closer at hand, you can hardly fail to notice the strong similarities between Festós and the other palaces: the same huge rows of storage jars, the great courtyard with its monumental stairway, and the theatral area. Unique to Festós, however, is the third courtyard, in the middle of which are the remains of a **furnace** used for metalworking. Indeed, this eastern corner of the palace seems to have been home to a number of craftsmen, including potters and carpenters. Oddly enough, Festós was much less ornately decorated than Knossós; there is no evidence, for example, of any of the dramatic Minoan wall paintings.

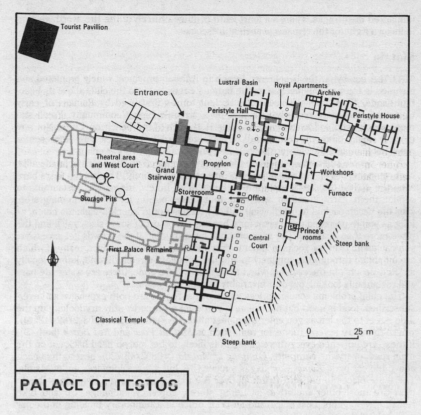

Tourist Pavilion

Lustral Basin
Royal Apartments
Archive
Entrance
Peristyle House
Peristyle Hall
Theatral area
and West Court
Propylon
Grand
Stairway
Workshops
Storage Pits
Storerooms
Office
Furnace
Prince's
rooms
Steep bank
Central
Court
First Palace Remains
Classical Temple
Steep bank

0   25 m

PALACE OF FESTÓS

The **Tourist Pavilion** at Festós serves drinks and food and also has a few beds, though these are very rarely available (thanks to advance bookings) and expensive when they are. The nearby village of **ÁYIOS IOÁNNIS**, along the road towards Mátala, has a few more **rooms**, including some at *Taverna Ayios Ioannis*, which is also a good place to eat.

Ayía Triádha

Daily 8.30am–3pm; 400dr.

Some of the finest artworks in the museum at Iráklion came from **Ayía Triádha**, about a 45-minute walk (or a short drive) from Festós. No one is quite sure what this site is, but the most common theory has it as some kind of royal summer villa. It's smaller than the palaces, but if anything even more lavishly appointed and beautifully situated. In any event, it's an attractive place to visit, far less crowded than Festós, with a wealth of interesting little details. Look out in particular for the **row of stores** in front of what was apparently a marketplace, and for the remains of the **paved road** that once led down to the Gulf of Messará. The sea itself looks invitingly close, separated from the base of the hill only by Timbáki airfield (mainly used for motor racing these days), but if you try to drive down there, it's almost impossible to find your way around the unmarked dust tracks. There's a fourteenth-century **church** at the site, worth visiting in its own right for the remains of ancient frescoes.

Mátala

MÁTALA has by far the best-known **beach** in Iráklion province, widely promoted and included in tours mainly because of the famous **caves** cut into the cliffs above its beautiful sands. These are believed to be ancient tombs first used by Romans or early Christians, but more recently inhabited by a sizeable hippie community. You'll still meet people who will assure you that this is *the* travellers' beach on Crete. Not any more it isn't. Today, the town is full of package tourists and tries hard to present a respectable image; the cliffs are now cleared and locked up every evening.

A few people still manage to evade the security, or sleep on the beach or in the adjacent campsite, but on the whole the place has changed entirely. The last ten years have seen the arrival of crowds and the development of hotels, discos and restaurants to service them; early afternoon, when the tour buses pull in for their swimming stop, sees the beach packed to overflowing. All of which is not to knock Mátala too much; as long as you're prepared to accept it for what it is – a resort of some size– you'll find the place more than bearable. The town beach *is* beautiful, but if the crowds get excessive, you can climb over the rocks in about twenty minutes (past more caves, many of which are inhabited through the summer) to another excellent stretch of sand, known locally as "Red Beach". In the evening, when the trippers have gone, there are waterside bars and restaurants looking out over invariably spectacular sunsets.

The chief problems concern prices and crowds: rooms are both expensive and over-subscribed, food is good but not cheap. If you want a **place to stay**, try looking up the little street to the left as you enter town, just after the *Zafiria* hotel (☎0892/42 112; ④), where there are several rooms for rent, such as *Matala View* and *Red Beach* (both ③). If these are full, then everywhere closer in is likely to be, too, so head back out on the main road, or try the **campsite**, *Camping of Matala* (☎0892/42 720), next to the beach above the car park; *Komos Camping* is a nicer site, but a few kilometres out of Mátala. There are places to **eat and drink** all over the main part of town. Also impossible to miss are most other **facilities**, including stores, currency exchange, car and bike rental, travel agents, post office, and an OTE office in a temporary building in the car park behind the beach.

Around Mátala: Pitsídhia and Kalamáki

One way to enjoy a bit more peace is to stay at PITSÍDHIA, about 5km inland. This is already a well-used option, so it's not quite as cheap as you might expect, but there are plenty of rooms, lively places to eat and even music bars. If you decide to stay here, the beach at KALAMÁKI is an alternative to Mátala. Both beaches are approximately the same distance to walk, though there is a much better chance of a bus or a lift to Mátala. Kalamáki itself is beginning to develop somewhat, with a number of rooms and a couple of tavernas, but so far it's a messy and unattractive little place. The beach stretches for miles, surprisingly wild and windswept, lashed by sometimes dangerously rough surf. At the southern end (more easily reached by a path off the Pitsídhia–Mátala road) lies **Kómmos**, once a Minoan port serving Festós and now the site of a major archeological excavation. As yet there's not a great deal to see, but this is another good beach.

Iráklion's south coast

South of the Messará plain are two more beach resorts, Kalí Liménes and Léndas, with numerous other little beaches along the coast in between, but nothing spectacular. **Public transport** is very limited indeed; you'll almost always have to travel via Míres (see above). If you have your own transport, the roads in these parts are all passable, but most are very slow going; the Kófinas Hills, which divide the plain from the coast, are surprisingly precipitous.

Kalí Liménes

While Mátala itself was an important port under the Romans, the chief harbour for Górtys lay on the other side of Cape Líthinon at **KALÍ LIMÉNES**. Nowadays, this is once again a major port – for oil tankers. This has rather spoiled its chances of becoming a major resort, especially when aggravated by the lack of a paved road and proper facilities. Some people like Kalí Liménes: the constant procession of tankers gives you something to look at, there are a number of places offering **rooms** – the best is the *Kanavourissia Beach* (③), a kilometre or so east of the village – the coastline is broken up by spectacular cliffs and, as long as there hasn't been a recent oil spill, the beaches are reasonably clean and totally empty. But (fortunately) not too many share this enthusiasm.

Léndas

LÉNDAS, further east along the coast, is far more popular, with a couple of buses daily from Iráklion and a partly justified reputation for being peaceful (sullied by considerable summer crowds). Many people who arrive think they've come to the wrong place: at first sight, the village looks filthy; the beach is small, rocky and dirty; and the rooms are frequently all booked. A number of visitors leave without ever correcting that initial impression, but the attraction of Léndas is not the village at all but on the other (west) side of the headland. Here, there's an enormous, excellent sandy beach, part of it usually taken over by nudists, and a number of taverna/bars overlooking it from the roadside. It's a couple of kilometres by car from Léndas, along a rough track; if you're walking, you can save time by cutting across the headland. Camping on the beach, or with luck getting one of the few **rooms** (②–③) at the tavernas, is a considerably more attractive prospect than staying in the village. After you've discovered the beach, even Léndas begins to look more welcoming, and at least it has most of the **facilities** you'll need, including a shop which will change money and numerous places to eat.

Once you've come to terms with the place, you can also explore some less good but quite deserted beaches eastwards, and the scrappy remains of **ancient Lebena** on a hilltop overlooking them. There was an important *Asclepieion* (temple of the god Asclepios) here around some now-diverted warm springs, but only the odd broken column and fragments of mosaic survive.

East of Iráklion: the package-tour coast

East of Iráklion the startling pace of tourist development in Crete is all too plain to see. The merest hint of a beach is an excuse to build at least one hotel, and these are outnumbered by the concrete shells of resorts-to-be. It's hard to find a room in this monument to the package-tour industry, and expensive if you do.

Goúrnes and Goúves

As a general rule, the further you go, the better things get: when the road detours all too briefly inland, the real Crete of olive groves and stark mountains asserts itself. You certainly won't see much of it at **GOÚRNES**, where there used to be a US Air Force base, or at nearby Kato Goúves, where there's a **campsite**, *Camping Creta* (☎0897/41 400), which will be quiet until the Greek air force move in next door. From here, however, you can head inland to the old village of **GOÚVES**, a refreshing contrast, and just beyond to the **Skotinó Cave**, one of the largest and most spectacular on the island (about an hour's walk from the coast).

Not far beyond Goúrnes is the turning for the direct route up to the Lasíthi plateau, and shortly after that you roll into the first of the big resorts, Hersónisos (or, more correctly, Límin Hersonísou; Hersónisos is the village in the hills just behind, also overrun by tourists).

Hersónisos (Límin Hersonísou)

HERSÓNISOS was once the port that served the Minoan city of Knossós, and more recently just a small fishing village; today it's the most popular of Crete's package resorts. If all you want is plenty of bars, tavernas, restaurants and Eurodisco nightlife then come here. The resort has numerous small patches of sand beach between rocky outcrops, but a shortage of places to stay in peak season.

Along the modern seafront, a solid line of restaurants and bars is broken only by the occasional souvenir shop: in their midst you'll find a small pyramidal **fountain** with broken mosaics of fishing scenes. This is Roman and the only real relic of the ancient town of Chersonesos. Around the headland above the harbour and in odd places along the seafront, you can see remains of Roman harbour installations, mostly submerged.

Beach and clubs excepted, the only distraction is **Lychnostatis** (daily 9.30am–2pm; 1000dr), an open-air "museum" of traditional Crete, on the coast on the eastern edge of the town next to the *Caravan* campsite.

A short distance inland are the three **hill villages** of Koutoulafari, Piskopiano and "old" Hersónisos, which all have a good selection of tavernas, and are worth searching out for accommodation.

Practicalities

Hersónisos is well provided with all the back-up **services** you need to make the holiday go smoothly. Banks, bike and car rental, post office and OTE are all on or just off the main drag, as are the taxi ranks. **Buses** in either direction leave every half-hour.

Finding somewhere to stay can be difficult in July and August. Much of the **accommodation** here is allocated to package-tour operators and what remains is not that cheap. To check for availability of accommodation generally, the quickest and best option is to visit the very helpful **tourist office** on Giaboudaki, just off the main street towards the harbour. Reasonably priced central options include the *Crystal* on Giaboudaki (☎0897/22 546; ③) and the *Nancy* on Ayía Paraskevis (☎0897/22 212; ③), but be prepared for a fair amount of noise. At the eastern end of town, is a good **campsite**, *Caravan Camping* (☎0897/22 025), and almost opposite, on the inland side of the main road, is a **youth hostel** (☎0897/23 674; ①). The hostel is well run by the very helpful and friendly American-born Greek Kostas Zikos, who is a mine of information on the general area, including bus and ferry schedules.

Despite the vast number of **places to eat**, there are few in Hersónisos worth recommending, and the tavernas down on the harbour front should be avoided. One of the few Greek tavernas that stands out is *Kavouri* along Arheou Theátrou, but it is more expensive. Better to head out of town on the Piskopiano road where, near the junction to Koutoulafari, the friendly *Fengari Taverna* serves good Greek food at a reasonable price. Sitting at your table overlooking the street below you can marvel at the steady trek of clubbers heading down the hill to the bars and nightclubs of Hersónisos. The hill villages have the greatest selection of tavernas, particularly Koutoulafari, where a more relaxed evening is had in its narrow streets and small *platías*.

Hersónisos is reknowned for its **nightlife** and there is no shortage of it. Most of the better bars and clubs are along the main road. Especially popular are *La Luna*, with up-to-date music, and the *Hard Rock Cafe*, which also has live music on a Sunday. *Aria*, a large glass-fronted disco, is the biggest on Crete and always attracts. *Club 99* is also worth a visit. If you fancy a quiet drink then you have come to the wrong resort. There is an open-air **cinema** at the *Creta Manis* hotel.

Stalídha

STALÍDHA is a Cinderella town, sandwiched in between its two louder, brasher and some would say uglier sisters of Mália and Hersónisos, but it is not quiet or undeveloped. This rapidly expanding beach resort, with more than sixty tavernas and bars and a few discos, can offer the best of both worlds with a friendlier and more relaxed setting, a better beach (and usual array of water sports) and very easy access to its two livelier neighbours. If you're content soaking up the sun, then make sure you find somewhere to stay at the English end of the resort where two sunbeds and an umbrella only set you back 1000dr. At the German end it can be twice the price.

Finding a **place to stay** can be difficult as most rooms are already booked by the package companies. Try the travel agencies in the village first, as they will know what is available, but expect to pay 5000–8000dr for a room or studio. Finding **somewhere to eat** is less difficult as there are plenty of rather ordinary tavernas. One of the better and most popular is *Maria's Taverna*, in the centre of resort.

Stalídha is completely overshadowed by its neighbours when it comes to **nightlife**, though you can dance at *Bells* disco, on the main coast road, or at *Rhythym*, on the beach; the *Sea Wolf Cocktail Bar* and *Akti Bar* are near each other along the beach.

Mália

Much of **MÁLIA** is taken up by the package industry, so in the peak season finding a place to stay is not always easy. You're best off, especially if you want any sleep during the night, trying one of the numerous **rooms** (③) signposted in the old town. Tracking back from here, along the main Iráklion road, there are a number of reasonably priced **pensions** on the left including the *Argo* (☎0897/31 636; ③). Further along this road, on the right opposite the *Mobil* station, lies the **youth hostel** (☎0897/31 555; ①), which is rundown, unwelcoming and not especially clean – strictly a desperation option. To save time, it would be sensible in the first instance to call in at one of the travel companies in Mália, for example, *Foreign Office* (☎0897/31 217) on the main road.

Eating in Malia is unlikely to be a problem as **restaurants** jostle for your custom at every step, especially along the beach road. None of these are particularly good, but that's the price of mass production. The best places are around Platía Ayíou Dhimitríou, a pleasant square beside the church in the centre of the old town. Try a meal at *Totto-Lotto*, or even better at *Taverna Minos Knossos*, after an aperitif at the *Ouzeri Kapilla*, where they serve excellent local wine from the wood. There are a number of other welcoming tavernas off the *platía*.

The beach road comes into its own when the profusion of **bars**, **discos** and **clubs** erupt into a pulsating cacophony during the hours either side of midnight. *Zoo* is a new club, and once past midnight, one of the internal walls parts to reveal an even larger dance area. *Zig Zag* and *Cloud 9* are the other really popular clubs in Mália. *Desire*, along the beach road, concentrates on rock and has good-quality live music some nights. Unfortunately, a good night's clubbing and dancing is frequently spoilt by drunken groups of youths pouring out of the bars. The situation has got so bad that tour operators have threatened to pull out of the resort if action isn't taken to deal with the hooligans.

The Palace of Mália

Tues–Sun 8.30am–3pm; 400dr, Sun free.

The archeological site lies forty minutes' walk east of Mália town on the main road. Any passing bus should stop, or you could even rent a bike for a couple of hours as it's a pleasant, flat ride. Much less imposing than either Knossós or Festós, the **Palace of Mália** in some ways surpasses both. For a start, it's a great deal emptier and you can wander among the remains in relative peace. While no reconstruction has been attempted, the palace was never reoccupied after its second destruction, so the ground plan is virtually intact. It's a great deal easier to comprehend than Knossós and, if you've seen the reconstructions there, it's easy to envisage this seaside palace in its days of glory. There's a real feeling of an ancient civilization with a taste for the good life, basking on the rich agricultural plain between the Lasíthi mountains and the sea.

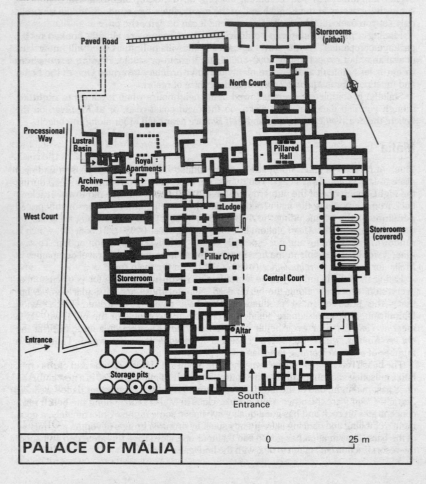

From this site came the famous gold pendant of two bees (which can be seen in the Iráklion museum or on any postcard stand), allegedly part of a horde that was plundered and whose other treasures can now be found in the British Museum in London. The beautiful leopard's-head axe, also in the museum at Iráklion, was another of the treasures found here. At the site, look out for the strange indented stone in the central court, which probably held ritual offerings; for the remains of ceremonial stairways; and for the giant *pithoi* which stand like sentinels around the palace. To the south and east, digs are still going on as a large town comes slowly to light.

Moving on

Leaving the archeological zone, you can follow the dirt track that runs around it to a lovely stretch of near-deserted sand. Considering its position this is an amazingly little-visited patch of beach. You can walk back along the shore to Mália from here, or take a bus (every half-hour in either direction) from the stop on the main road.

Head **east**, and it's not long before the road leaves the coast, climbing across the hills towards Áyios Nikólaos. If you want to escape the frenetic pace of all that has gone before, try continuing to **SÍSI** or **MÍLATOS**. These little shore villages are bypassed by the main road as it cuts inland, and so far have seen only the beginnings of a tourist industry; each has a few villa/apartments and a few tavernas, and there's a **campsite** at Sísi (☎0841/71 247), the more developed of the two. The beaches aren't great, but they make for a refreshing change of pace.

West of Iráklion: around Psilorítis

Most people heading **west from Iráklion**, speed straight out on the new coastal highway, non-stop to Réthimnon. If you're in a hurry this is not such a bad plan; the road is fast and spectacular, hacked into the sides of mountains which for the most part drop straight to the sea. On the other hand, there are no more than a couple of places where you might consider stopping. By contrast, the old roads inland are agonizingly slow, but they do pass through a whole string of attractive villages beneath the heights of the Psilorítis range. From here you can set out to explore the mountains and even walk across them to emerge in villages with views of the south coast.

The coastal route towards Réthimnon

Leaving the city, the **new highway** runs behind a stretch of highly developed coast, where the hotels compete for shore space with a cement works and power station. As soon as you reach the mountains, though, all this is left behind and there's only the clash of rock and sea to contemplate. As you start to climb, look out for **Paleókastro**, beside a bridge which carries the road over a small cove; the castle is so weathered as to be almost invisible against the brownish face of the cliff.

Ayía Pelayía and Fódhele

Some 3km below the highway, as it rounds the first point, lies the resort of **AYÍA PELAYÍA**. It looks extremely attractive from above (less so close up), but it is also very commercial: not somewhere to roll up without a reserved room, though out of season you might find a real bargain at an apartment.

Not far beyond Ayía Pelayía, there's a turning inland to the village of **FÓDHELE**, allegedly El Greco's birthplace. A plaque from the University of Toledo acknowledges the claim and, true or not, the community has built a small tourist industry on that basis. There are a number of craft shops and some pleasant tavernas where you can sit outside along the river: there's also "El Greco's house" and a picturesque Byzantine church. None of this amounts to very much but it is a pleasant, relatively unspoiled village if you simply want to sit in peace for a while. A couple of **buses** a day run here from Iráklion, and there's the odd tour; if you arrive on a direct bus, the walk back down to the highway (about 3km), where you can flag down a passing service, is not too strenuous.

Balí and Pánormos

BALÍ, on the coast approximately halfway between Iráklion and Réthimnon, also used to be tranquil and undeveloped, and by the standards of the north coast it still is in many ways. The village is built around a couple of small coves, some 2km from the highway (a hot walk from the bus), and is similar to Ayía Pelayía except that the beaches are not quite as good and there are no big hotels. There are, however, lots of **rooms** (more every month it seems) and a number of "modest hotels" (brochure-speak). You'll have plenty of company. The last and best beach, known as "Paradise", no longer really deserves the name; it's a beautiful place to splash about, surrounded by mountains rising straight from the sea, but there's rarely a spare inch on the sand.

Continuing along the coast, the last stop before you emerge on the flat stretch leading to Réthimnon is at **PÁNORMOS**. This, too, is an attractive village with a small sandy beach and a few rooms, but again there are crowds, mostly arriving by boat on day trips from Réthimnon.

Inland towards Mount Psilorítis

Of the **inland routes** the old main road (via Márathos and Dhamásta) is not the most interesting. This, too, was something of a bypass in its day and there are few places of any size or appeal, though it's a very scenic drive. If you want to dawdle, you're better off on the road which cuts up to Tílissos and then goes via Anóyia. It's a pleasant ride through fertile valleys filled with olive groves and vineyards, a district (the Malevísi) renowned from Venetian times for the strong, sweet Malmsey wine.

Tílissos and Anóyia

TÍLISSOS has a significant archeological site (daily 8.30am–3pm; 400dr) where three Minoan houses were excavated; unfortunately, its reputation is based more on what was found here (many pieces in the Iráklion museum) and on its significance for archeologists than on anything which remains to be seen. Still, it's worth a look, if you're passing, for a glimpse of Minoan life away from the big palaces, and for the tranquillity of the pine-shaded remains.

ANÓYIA is a much more tempting place to stay, especially if the summer heat is becoming oppressive. Spilling prettily down a hillside close below the highest peaks of the mountains, it looks traditional, but closer inspection shows that most of the buildings are actually concrete; the village was destroyed during the war and the local men rounded up and shot – one of the German reprisals for the abduction of General Kreipe. The town has a reputation as a handicrafts centre (especially for woven and woollen goods), skills acquired both through bitter necessity after most of the men had been killed, and in a conscious attempt to revive the town. At any rate it worked, for the place is thriving today – thanks, it seems, to the number of elderly widows keen to subject any visitor to their terrifyingly aggressive sales techniques.

Quite a few people pass through Anóyia during the day, but not many of them stay; it shouldn't be hard to find a **room** in the upper half of town. On the other hand, there's almost nowhere to eat: one **taverna** on the main road where it loops out of the lower village, and a *souvláki* place near the top of the town, both of which serve barbecued lamb, the local speciality. Vegetarians are advised to buy their own bread and cheese (local cheese is also excellent).

Mount Psilorítis and its caves

Heading for the mountains, a rough track leads 13km from Anóyia to the **Nídha plateau** at the base of Mount Psilorítis. Here there's a taverna that used to let rooms but seems now to have closed to the public altogether, though it's still used by groups of climbers. A short path leads from the taverna to the celebrated **Idhéon Ándron** (Idean Cave), a rival of that on Mount Dhíkti (see next page) for the title of Zeus's birthplace and certainly associated from the earliest of times with the cult of Zeus. Unfortunately, there's a major archeological dig going on inside, which means the whole cave is fenced off, with a miniature railway running into it to carry all the rubble out. In short, you can see nothing.

The taverna also marks the start of the way to the top of **Mount Psilorítis** (2456m), Crete's highest mountain, a climb that's not for the unwary, but for experienced, properly shod hikers is not at all arduous. The route is well marked with the usual red dots and it should be a six- to seven-hour return journey to the chapel at the summit; in spring, thick snow may slow you down.

If you're prepared to camp on the plateau (it's very cold, but there's plenty of available water) or can prevail on the taverna to let you in, you could continue on foot next day down to the southern slopes of the range. It's a beautiful hike, at least while the road they're attempting to blast through is out of sight, and also relatively easy, four hours or so down a fairly clear path to **VORÍZIA**. If you're still interested in caves, there's a more rewarding one above the nearby village of **KAMÁRES**, a climb of some three hours on a good path. Both Vorízia and Kamáres have a few **rooms** and some tavernas, at least one daily **bus** down to Míres, and alternate (more difficult) routes to the peak of Psilorítis if you want to approach from this direction.

EASTERN CRETE

Eastern Crete is dominated by **Áyios Nikólaos**, and while it is a highly developed resort, by no means all of the east is like this. Far fewer people venture beyond the road south to **Ierápetra** and into the eastern isthmus, where only **Sitía** and the famous beach at **Vái** ever see anything approaching a crowd. Inland, too, there's interest, especially on the extraordinary **Lasíthi** plateau, which is worth a night's stay if only to catch its abidingly rural life.

Inland to the Lasíthi plateau

Leaving the palace at Mália, the highway cuts inland towards Neápoli, soon beginning a spectacular climb into the mountains. Set in a high valley, **NEÁPOLI** is a market town little touched by tourism. There is one hotel, some rooms, a modern church and a couple of museums. Beyond the town, it's about twenty minutes before the bus suddenly emerges high above the Gulf of Mirabéllo and Áyios Nikólaos, the island's biggest resort. If you're stopping, Neápoli also marks the second point of access to the **Lasíthi Plateau**.

Scores of bus tours drive up here daily to view the "thousands of white-cloth-sailed windmills" which irrigate the high plain, and most groups will be disappointed. There are very few working windmills left, and these operate only for limited periods (mainly in June). This is not to say the trip is not justified, as it would be for the drive alone, and there are many other compensations. The plain is a fine example of rural Crete at work, every inch devoted to the cultivation of potatoes, apples, pears, figs, olives and a host of other crops; stay in one of the villages for a night or two and you'll see real life return as the tourists leave. There are plenty of easy rambles around the villages as well, through orchards and past the rusting remains of derelict windmills. You'll find rooms in the main town of **TZERMIÁDHO**, and at Áyios Konstandínos, Áyios Yióryios (where there's a folk museum and the friendly *Hotel Dias*; ☎0844/31 207; ③) and Psihró.

Psihró and the Dhiktean cave

PSIHRÓ is much the most visited, as it's the base for visiting Lasíthi's other chief attraction, the **Dhiktean Cave**, birthplace of Zeus (daily 10.30am–5pm; 400dr; watch out for slippery stones inside). In legend, Zeus's father, the Titan Kronos, was warned that he would be overthrown by a son and accordingly ate all his offspring; however, when Rhea gave birth to Zeus in the cave, she fed Kronos a stone and left the child concealed, protected by the Kouretes, who beat their shields outside to disguise his cries. The rest, as they say, is history (or at least myth). There's an obvious path running up to the cave from Psihró and, whatever you're told, you don't have to have a guide if you don't want one, though you will need some form of illumination. On the other hand, it is hard to resist the guides, who do make the visit much more interesting, and they're not expensive if you can get a small group together (about 500–600dr each). It takes a Cretan imagination to pick out Rhea and the baby Zeus from the lesser stalactites and stalagmites.

Buses run around the plateau to Psihró direct from Iráklion and from Áyios Nikólaos via Neápoli. Both roads offer spectacular views, coiling through a succession of passes guarded by lines of ruined windmills.

Áyios Nikólaos and around

ÁYIOS NIKÓLAOS ("Ag Nik" to the majority of its British visitors) is set around a supposedly bottomless salt lake, now connected to the sea to form an inner harbour. It is supremely picturesque, has some style, exudes confidence and exploits this to the full. The lake and port are surrounded by restaurants and bars, which charge above the odds, and whilst still very popular, some tourists are distinctly surprised to find themselves in a place with no decent beach at all.

Practicalities

The greatest concentration of **stores** and **travel agents** are on the hill between the bridge and Platía Venizélou. The main **ferry agent** is *Massaros Travel* (☎0841/22 267), on Koundoúrou near the **post office**. The **tourist office** (daily 8.30am–9.30pm; ☎0841/22 357), situated between the lake and the port, is one of the best on the island for information about accommodation.

Accommodation

The town is no longer packed solid with tourists, so it is much easier to find a place to stay, though in the peak season you will not have so much choice. One thing in your favour is that there are literally thousands of **rooms**, scattered all about town. The tourist office normally has a couple of boards with cards and brochures about hotels and rooms, including their prices. If the prices seem very reasonable it is because they are for the low season. There is no longer a youth hostel, and the nearest **campsite** is 17km away at *Gournia Moon* (see p.517).

Atlantis, (☎0841/28 964) Nothing special but handy hotel next to the bus station; it has a snack bar below for breakfast. ②.

Dias, Latous 6 (☎0841/28 263). If you can afford the extra then this is one of the best-value hotels around. ③.

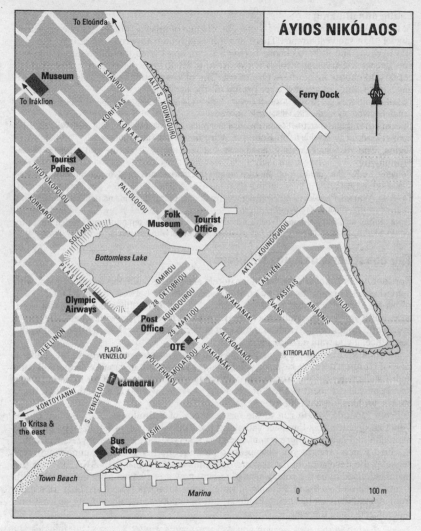

ÁYIOS NIKÓLAOS

To Eloúnda

Museum
To Iráklion

E. STAVROU
KORITSAS
KORAKA
AKTI S. KOUNDOUROU

Ferry Dock

Tourist
Police

THEOTOKOPOLOU
KORNAROU
PALEOLOGOU

Folk
Museum
Tourist
Office

SOLOMOU
PLASTIRA

Bottomless Lake

OMIROU
28 OKTOBRIOU
KOUNDOUROU

AKTI I. KOUNDOUROU
LASTHENI
M. SFAKIANAKI
EVANS
PASIFAIS
ARIADNIS
MILOU

Olympic
Airways

Post
Office

25 MARTIOU

FILELLINON

PLATÍA
VENIZELOU

OTE

K. SFAKIANAKI
MODATSOU
POLITEHNIOU

ALEXOMANOLI

KITROPLATÍA

KONTOYIANNI

Cathedral

S. VENIZELOU

To Kritsa &
the east

Bus
Station

KOSIRI

Town Beach

Marina

0   100 m

Green House, Modatsou 15 (☎0841/22 025). Probably the best cheap place to stay in town; clean with shared facilities. ②.

Katerina, Stratigou Koraka 30 (☎0841/22 766). A pension close to the *Marilena* and another good choice in the same price bracket. ②.

Lida, Salaminos 3a (☎0841/22 130). All rooms in this friendly hotel have a shower, balcony and a partial sea-view. ④.

Loukas, Platía Venizélou 13 (☎0841/23 169). A very central location in the heart of the shopping area of Áyios Nikólaos. ③.

Marilena, Erithrou Stavrou 14 (☎0841/22 681). One of the cheaper pensions and excellent value. ②.

Eating and drinking

At least when it comes to eating there's no chance of missing out, even if the prices are fancier than the restaurants. There are tourist-oriented **tavernas** all around the lake and harbour and little to choose between them, apart from the different perspectives you get on the passing fashion show. Have a drink here perhaps or a mid-morning coffee and choose somewhere else to eat. The places around the Kiroplatía are generally fairer value, but again you are paying for the location.

Ellinikon, on Kapetan Kozyri. A small *kafenío* with loads of character that serves traditional mountain dishes, freshly made with village raki or wine.

Ikaros and **Loukakis**, on the Elounda road, a few minutes' walk away from the port. Very competitively priced and good value tavernas, next to each other on the waterfront.

Itanos, Kyprou 1. Serves Cretan food and wine, and has a terrace across the road opposite; popular with the locals.

Pelagos, on Koraka, just back off the lake behind the tourist office. A stylish fish taverna, serving good food but at a price.

Taverna Alouasi, Paleologou 40. Serves good, traditional Cretan food in and under a plant-covered trellised courtyard, and is reasonably cheap.

Trata, corner of Sfakianaki and Tselepi. Good restaurant, with a tempting roof garden for sultry nights. Slightly more expensive than *Itanos*, but also popular with the locals.

The coast north of Áyios Nikólaos

North of Áyios Nikólaos, the swankier hotels are strung out along the coast road, with upmarket restaurants, discos and cocktail bars scattered between them. **ELOÚNDA**, a resort on a more acceptable scale, is about 8km out along this road. Buses run regularly, but if you feel like renting a moped it's a spectacular ride, with impeccable views over a gulf dotted with islands and moored supertankers. Try *Olous Travel*, next to the post office, if you want a **room** here.

Just before the village a track (signposted) leads across a causeway to the "sunken city" of **Oloús**. There are restored windmills, a short length of canal, Venetian salt pans and a well-preserved dolphin mosaic, but of the sunken city itself no trace beyond a couple of walls in about two feet of water. At any rate swimming is good, though there are sea urchins to watch out for.

From Eloúnda, *kaíkia* run to the fortress-rock of **Spinalónga**. As a bastion of the Venetian defence, this tiny islet withstood the Turkish invaders for 45 years after the mainland had fallen; in more recent decades, it served as a leper colony. As you watch the boat which brought you disappear to pick up another group, an unnervingly real sense of the desolation of those years descends over the place. **PLÁKA**, back on the mainland, used to be the colony's supply point; now it is a haven from the crowds, with a small pebble beach and a couple of ramshackle tavernas. There are boat trips daily from Áyios Nikólaos to Oloús, Eloúnda and Spinalónga, usually visiting at least one other island along the way.

Inland to Kritsá and Lató

The other excursion everyone from Áyios Nikólaos takes is to **KRITSÁ**, a "traditional" village about 10km inland. Buses run at least every hour from the bus station, and despite the commercialization it's still a good trip: the local crafts (weaving, ceramics and embroidery basically, though they sell almost everything here) are fair value and it's also a welcome break from living in the fast lane at "Ag Nik". In fact, if you're looking for somewhere to stay around here, Kritsá has a number of advantages: chiefly availability of **rooms**, better prices, and something at least approaching a genuinely Greek atmosphere; try *Argyro* (☎0841/51 174; ②) on your way to the village. There are a number of decent places to eat, too, or just to have a coffee and a cake under one of the plane trees.

On the approach road, some 2km before Kritsá, is the lovely Byzantine **church of Panayía Kirá** (Mon–Sat 9am–3pm, Sun 9am–2pm; 400dr), inside which are preserved perhaps the most complete set of Byzantine frescoes in Crete. The fourteenth- and fifteenth-century works have been much retouched, but they're still worth the visit. Excellent (and expensive) reproductions are sold from a shop alongside. Just beyond the church, a metalled road leads off towards the archeological site of **Lató** (daily except Mon 8.30am–3pm), a Doric city with a grand hilltop setting. The city itself is extensive, but neglected, presumably because visitors and archeologists on Crete are concerned only with the Minoan era. Ruins aside, you could come here just for the views: west over Áyios Nikólaos and beyond to the bay and Oloús (which was Lató's port), and inland to the Lasíthi mountains.

The eastern isthmus

The main road south and then east from Áyios Nikólaos is not a wildly exciting one, essentially a drive through barren hills sprinkled with villas and above the occasional sandy cove. Five kilometres beyond a cluster of development at Kaló Hório, a track is signed on the right for the **Moní Faroméni**. The track is a rough one and climbs dizzily skywards for 6km, giving spectacular views over the Gulf of Mirabélo along the way. The view from the monastery itself must be the among the finest in Crete. To get in to the rather bleak-looking monastery buildings, knock loudly. You will be shown up to the chapel, built into a cave sanctuary, and the frescoes are quite brilliant.

Gourniá, Pahiá Ámmos and Móhlos

Back on the coast road, another 2km brings you to the site of **Gourniá** (daily except Mon 8.30am–3pm; 400dr), slumped in the saddle between two low peaks. The most completely preserved Minoan town, its narrow alleys and stairways intersect a throng of one-roomed houses centred on a main square and the house of the local ruler. Although less impressive than the great palaces, the site is strong on revelations about the lives of the ordinary people ruled from Knossós. Its desolation today (you are likely to be alone save for a dozing guard) only serves to heighten the contrast with what must have been a cramped and raucous community 3500 years ago.

It is tempting to cross the road here and take one of the paths through the wild thyme to the sea for a swim. Don't bother – the bay and others along this part of the coastline act as a magnet for every piece of floating detritus dumped off Crete's north coast. There is a larger beach, and rooms to rent, in the next bay along at **PAHIÁ ÁMMOS**, about twenty minutes' walk, where there is also an excellent fish taverna, *Aiolus*; or in the other direction, there's the campsite of *Gournia Moon*, with its own small cove and its own swimming pool.

This is the narrowest part of the island, and from here a fast new road cuts across the isthmus to Ierápetra in the south. In the north, though, the route on towards Sitía is one of the most exhilarating in Crete. Carved into cliffs and mountainsides, the road teeters above the coast before plunging inland at Kavoúsi. Of the beaches you see below, only **MÓHLOS** is at all accessible, some 5km below the main road. This sleepy village has a few rooms, a hotel or two and a number of tavernas; if you find yourself staying the night, try the rooms at *Limenaria* (☎0841/94 206; ②). Nearer Sitía the familiar olive groves are interspersed with vineyards, and in late summer the grapes, spread to dry in the fields and on rooftops, make an extraordinary sight in the varying stages of their slow change from green to gold to brown.

Sitía

SITÍA is the port and main town of the relatively unexploited eastern edge of Crete. It's a pleasant if unremarkable place, offering a plethora of waterside restaurants, a long sandy beach and a lazy lifestyle little affected even by the thousands of visitors in peak season. There's an almost Latin feel to the town, reflected in (or perhaps caused by) the number of French and Italian tourists, and it's one of those places you may end up

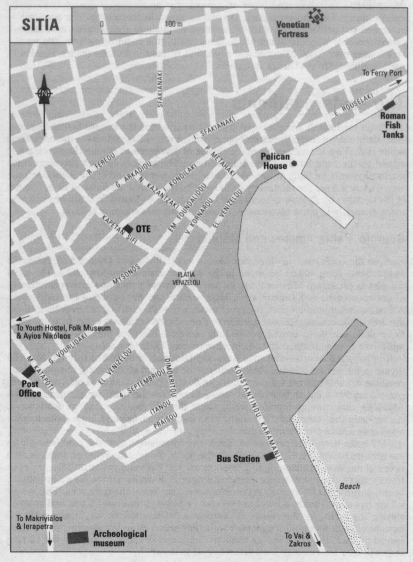

staying longer than you intended. For entertainment, there's the **beach**, providing good swimming and windsurfing; or in town a mildly entertaining **folklore museum** (Tues, Thurs & Fri 9am–1pm & 5–8pm, Wed 9am–1pm, Sat 5–8pm; closed Mon & Sun), a Venetian fort and Roman fish tanks to explore, and an interesting **archeological museum** (Tues–Sat 8.45am–3pm, Sun 9.30am–2pm; 400dr). Look out, too, for the town's resident pelicans, Níkos and Alítis.

Practicalities

There are plenty of cheap pensions and **rooms**, especially in the streets around the OTE, a good **youth hostel** (☎0843/22 693; ①) on the main road as it enters town, and rarely any problem about sleeping on the beach (though it is worth going a little way out of town to avoid any danger of being rousted by police). For rooms, try *Pension Venus*, Kondhiláki 60 (☎0843/24 307; ②), *Hotel Arhontiko*, Kondhiláki 16 (☎0843/28 172; ②), and *Hotel Nora*, Rouselaki 31 (☎0843/23 017; ②), near the ferry port; if you have problems finding somewhere to stay, the **tourist police** at Mysonos 24 in the centre of town may be able to help.

For **food**, the waterside places are expensive enough to make you careful about what you eat; best value here is *Remegio*, or there are cheaper options in the streets behind, including a couple of excellent ice-cream parlours. **Nightlife** centres on a few bars and discos near the ferry dock and out along the beach. The one major excitement of the year is the August **Sultana Festival** – a celebration of the big local export, with traditional dancing and all the locally produced wine you can consume included in the entrance to the fairground.

Onward to Vái beach and Palékastro

Leaving Sitía along the beach, the Vái road climbs above a rocky, unexceptional coastline before reaching a fork to the **Monastery of Toploú**. The monastery's forbidding exterior reflects a history of resistance to invaders, but doesn't prepare you for the gorgeous flower-decked cloister within. The blue-robed monks keep out of the way as far as possible, but their cells and refectory are left discreetly on view. In the church is one of the masterpieces of Cretan art, the eighteenth-century icon *Lord Thou Art Great*. Outside you can buy enormously expensive reproductions.

Vái beach itself features alongside Knossós or the Lasíthi plateau on almost every Cretan travel agent's list of excursions. Not surprisingly, it is now covered in sunbeds and umbrellas, though it is still a superb beach. Above all, it is famous for its palm trees, and the sudden appearance of the grove is indeed an exotic shock. Lying on the fine sand in the early morning, the illusion of a Caribbean island is hard to dismiss. As everywhere, notices warn that "Camping is forbidden by law"; for once the authorities seem to mean it and most campers climb over the headlands to the south or north. If you do sleep out, watch your belongings since this seems to be the one place on Crete with crime on any scale. There's a café and an expensive taverna at the beach, plus toilets and showers. By day you can find a bit more solitude by climbing the rocks or swimming to one of the smaller beaches which surround Vái. **Ítanos**, twenty minutes' walk north by an obvious trail, has a couple of tiny beaches and some modest ruins of the Classical era.

PALÉKASTRO, some 9km south, is in many ways a better place to stay. Although its beaches can't begin to compare, you'll find several modest places with rooms, a number of reasonable restaurants (good rooms and food at the *Hotel Hellas*; ☎0843/61 240; ②), and plenty of space to camp out without the crowds; the sea is a couple of kilometres down a dirt track. Palékastro is also the crossroads for the road south to Zákros.

Zákros

ZÁKROS town is a little under 20km from Palékastro, at the end of the paved road. There are several tavernas and a hotel, the *Zakros* (☎0843/61 284; ③), in the village that seems to have seen better days, but the Minoan palace is actually at Káto Zákros, 8km further down a newly paved road to the sea. Most buses run only to the upper village, but in summer, a couple every day do run all the way to the site. Part way along you can, if on foot, take a short cut through an impressive **gorge** (the "Valley of the Dead", named for ancient tombs in its sides) but it's usually not difficult to hitch if your bus does leave you in the village.

The **palace of Zákros** (daily except Mon 8.30am–3pm; 400dr) was an important find for archeologists; it had been occupied only once, and abandoned hurriedly and completely. Later, it was forgotten almost entirely and as a result was never plundered or even discovered by archeologists until very recently. The first major excavation began only in 1960; all sorts of everyday objects (tools, raw materials, food, pottery) were thus discovered intact among the ruins, and a great deal was learned from being able to apply modern techniques (and knowledge of the Minoans) to a major dig from the very beginning. None of this is especially evident when you're at the palace, except perhaps in a particularly simple ground plan, so it's as well that it is also a rewarding visit in terms of the setting. Although the site is some way from the sea, parts of it are often marshy and waterlogged: partly the result of eastern Crete's slow subsidence, partly the fault of a spring which once supplied fresh water to a cistern beside the royal apartments, and whose outflow is now silted up. Among the remains of narrow streets and small houses higher up, you can keep your feet dry and get an excellent view down over the central court and royal apartments. If you want a more detailed overview of the remains, buy the guide to the site on sale at the entrance.

The village of **KÁTO ZÁKROS** is little more than a collection of tavernas, some of which rent out rooms around a peaceful beach and minuscule fishing anchorage. It's a wonderfully restful place, but it is often unable to cope with the volume of visitors seeking rooms in high season. The *Poseidon* (☎0843/93 316; ③) has good views.

Ierápetra and the southeast coast

From Sitía, the route south is a cross-country roller-coaster ride until it hits the south coast at **MAKRIYIALÓS**. This little fishing village has one of the best beaches at this end of Crete, with fine sand which shelves so gently you feel you could walk the 340km to Africa. Unfortunately, in the last few years it has been heavily developed, so while still a very pleasant place to stop for a swim or a bite, it's not somewhere you're likely to find a cheap room.

From here to Ierápetra, there's little reason to stop; the few beaches are rocky and the coastal plain submerged under ranks of polythene-covered greenhouses. One exception, however, is **Dasaki Butterfly Gorge**, which although affected by forest fires in recent years is certainly worth a visit. Beyond here, beside the road leading in to Ierápetra, are long but exposed stretches of sand, including the appropriately named "Long Beach", where you'll find a campsite, *Camping Koutsounar* (☎0842/61 213), which has plenty of shade.

Ierápetra

IERÁPETRA itself is a cheerless modern supply centre for the region's farmers. It also attracts an amazing number of package tourists and not a few backpackers looking for work, especially out of season. The tavernas along the tree-lined front are scenic enough and the beach, its remotest extremities rarely visited, stretches for a couple of miles to the east. But as a town, most people find it pretty uninspiring. Although there has been a port here since Roman times, only the **Venetian fort** guarding the harbour and a crumbling minaret remain as reminders of better days. What little else has been salvaged is in the one-room **museum** (Tues–Sat 8.30am–2.30pm; 400dr) near the post office.

If you want to stay, head up Kazantzakís from the chaotic bus station, and you'll find **rooms** at the *Four Seasons* (☎0842/24 390; ③); nearby is the *Cretan Villa*, Lakerda 16 (☎0842/26 522; ③), a beautiful 180-year-old house. More central, and also g⁊od value, is the *Hotel Ersi*, Platía Eleftherías 20 (☎0842/23 208; ②). You'll find places to eat and drink all along the waterfront (the better places being towards the Venetian fort); there is a clutch of bars and fast-food places along the central Kyrba, behind the promenade.

West from Ierápetra

Heading west from Ierápetra, the first stretch of coast is grey and dusty, the road jammed with trucks and lined with drab ribbon development. There are a number of small resorts along the beach, though little in the way of public transport. If travelling under your own steam, there is a scenic detour worth taking at Gra Ligiá. the road, on the right, is signed for Anatolí and climbs to Máles, a village clinging to the lower slopes of the **Dhíkti range**. Here would be a good starting point if you wanted to take a walk through some stunning mountain terrain. Otherwise, the dirt road back down towards the coast (signed Míthi) has spectacular views over the Libyan Sea, and eventually follows the Mírtos river valley down to Mírtos itself.

Mírtos and Árvi

MÍRTOS is the first resort that might actually tempt you to stop, and it's certainly the most accessible, just off the main road with numerous **buses** to Ierápetra daily and a couple direct to Iráklion. Although developed to a degree, it nonetheless remains tranquil and inexpensive, with lots of young travellers (many of them sleeping on the beach, to the irritation of locals). If you want a **room**, try *Rooms Angelos* (☎0842/51 106; ②) or *Rooms Mertini* (☎0842/51 386; ②), though there are plenty of others. Just off the road from Ierápetra are a couple of excavated **Minoan villas** you might want to explore: Néa Mírtos and Pírgos.

After Mírtos the main road turns inland towards Áno Viánnos, then continues across the island towards Iráklion; several places on the coast are reached by a series of rough side tracks. That hasn't prevented one of them, **ÁRVI**, from becoming a larger resort than Mírtos. The beach hardly justifies it, but it's an interesting little excursion (with at least one bus a day) if only to see the bananas and pineapples grown here and to experience the microclimate (noticeably warmer than neighbouring zones, especially in spring or autumn) that encourages them.

Beyond Árvi

Two more villages, **KERATÓKAMBOS** and **TSOÚTSOUROS**, look tempting on the map. The first has a rather stony beach and only the most basic of rooms available, but it's popular with Cretan day-trippers and great if you want to escape from the tourist grind for a spell. The second is developed and not really worth the tortuous thirteen-kilometre dirt road in.

If you hope to continue across the south of the island, be warned that there are no buses, despite completion of the road towards Míres after years of work. It's an enjoyable, rural drive, but progress can be slow; there's very little traffic if you're trying to hitch.

RÉTHIMNON AND AROUND

The relatively low, narrow section of Crete which separates the Psilorítis range from the White Mountains in the west seems at first a nondescript, even dull part of the island. Certainly in scenic terms it has few of the excitements that the west can offer, there are no major archeological sites as in the east and many of the villages seem modern and ugly. On the other hand, **Réthimnon** itself is an attractive and lively city, with some excellent beaches nearby. And on the south coast, in particular around **Plakiás**, are beaches as fine as any Crete can offer, and as you drive towards them the scenery and villages improve by the minute.

Réthimnon

In the past ten years or so, **RÉTHIMNON** has seen a greater influx of tourists than perhaps anywhere else on Crete, with the development of a whole series of large hotels extending almost 10km along the beach to the east. For once, though, the middle of town has been spared, so that at its heart Réthimnon remains one of the most beautiful of Crete's major cities (with only Haniá as a serious rival), with an enduringly provincial air. A wide sandy beach and palm-lined promenade border a labyrinthine tangle of Venetian and Turkish houses lining streets where ancient minarets lend an exotic air to the skyline. Dominating everything from the west, is the superbly preserved outline of the fortress built by the Venetians after a series of pirate raids had devastated the town.

The Town

With a beach right in the heart of town, it's tempting not to stir at all from the sands, but Réthimnon repays at least some gentle exploration. For a start, you could try checking out the further reaches of the **beach** itself. The waters protected by the breakwaters in front of town have their disadvantages, notably crowds and dubious hygiene, but less sheltered sands stretch for miles to the east, crowded at first but progressively less so if you're prepared to walk a bit.

Away from the beach, you don't have far to go for the most atmospheric part of town, immediately behind the **inner harbour**. Almost anywhere here, you'll find unexpected old buildings, wall fountains, overhanging wooden balconies, heavy, carved doors and rickety shops, many still with local craftsmen sitting out front, gossiping as they ply their trades. Look out especially for the **Venetian loggia**, now being converted into a library (it used to house the town museum); the **Rimóndi fountain**, another of the more elegant Venetian survivals; and the **Nerandzes mosque**, best preserved of several in Réthimnon, whose minaret you can climb (daily 11am–7pm; closed Aug) for excellent free views over the town and surrounding countryside. Simply by walking past these three, you'll have seen many of the liveliest parts of Réthimnon. Ethníkis Andistásis, the street leading straight up from the fountain, is also the town's **market** area.

The old city ends at the Porta Guora at the top of Andistásis, the only surviving remnant of the city walls. Almost opposite are the quiet and shady **Public Gardens**. These are always a soothing place to stroll, but most visitors only bother in the latter half of July, when the **Réthimnon Wine Festival** is staged here. Though touristy, it's a thoroughly enjoyable event, with spectacular local dancing as the evening progresses and the barrels empty. The entrance fee includes all the wine you can drink, though you'll need to bring your own cup or else buy one of the souvenir glasses and carafes on sale outside the gardens.

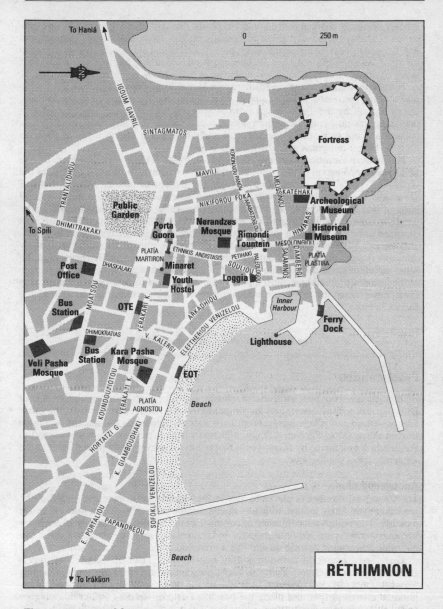

The museums and fortress

Heading in the other direction from the fountain, you can approach the mighty fortress via two interesting museums. The **Historical and Folk Art Museum** (daily except Mon 9am–1pm), on Mesolongíou, is small but tremendously enjoyable. Gathered within its two modest rooms are musical instruments, old photos, basketry, farm implements, an explanation of traditional bread-making techniques, smiths' tools, traditional costumes and jewellery, lace, weaving and embroidery, pottery, knives and old wooden chests. It makes for a fascinating insight into a fast disappearing rural (and urban) lifestyle, which had often survived virtually unchanged from Venetian times to the 1960s, and is well worth a look.

The **archeological museum** (daily except Mon 8.30am–3pm; 400dr, Sun free) occupies a newly converted building almost directly opposite the entrance to the fortress. This was built by the Turks as an extra defence for the entry, and later served as a prison, but it's now entirely modern inside: cool, spacious and airy. Unfortunately, the collection is not particularly exciting, and really only worth seeing if you're going to miss the bigger museums elsewhere on the island.

The massive **Venetian Fortress** (daily 9am–4pm; 200dr) is a must, however. Said to be the largest Venetian castle ever built, this was a response, in the last quarter of the sixteenth century, to a series of pirate raids (by Barbarossa among others) that had devastated the town. Inside now is a vast open space dotted with the remains of all sorts of barracks, arsenals, officers' houses, earthworks and deep shafts, and at the centre a large domed building that was once a church and later a mosque. It was designed to be large enough for the entire population to take shelter within the walls, and you can see that it probably was. Although much is ruined, it remains thoroughly atmospheric, and you can look out from the walls over the town and harbour, or in the other direction along the coast to the west. It's also worth walking around the outside of the fortress, preferably at sunset, to get an impression of its fearsome defences, plus great views along the coast and a pleasant resting point around the far side at the *Sunset Taverna*.

The telephone code for Réthimnon is ☎0831

Practicalities

Réthimnon has two **bus stations** diagonally opposite each other at the corner of Dhimokratías and Moátsou, one for long-distance and north-coast services, the other for trans-island and village buses. From here walk north towards the sea; the waterside **tourist office** (Mon–Fri 8am–3.30pm; ☎29 148) will be in front of you when you get to the beach. If you arrive by **ferry**, you'll be even more conveniently placed, over at the western edge of the harbour.

Accommodation

There's a great number of places to stay in Réthimnon, and only at the height of the season are you likely to have difficulty finding somewhere; though you may get weary looking. The greatest concentration of **rooms** is in the tangled streets west of the inner harbour, between the Rimóndi fountain and the museums; there are also quite a few places on and around Arkadhíou and Platía Frakidaki.

There are a couple of **campsites** 4km east of town. Take the bus for the hotels (marked *Scaleta/El Greco*) from the long-distance bus station to get there. *Camping Elizabeth* (☎28 694) is a pleasant, large site on the beach, with all facilities. Only a few hundred metres further east along the beach is *Camping Arkadia* (☎28 825), a bigger and slightly less friendly site.

Anna, Katehaki (☎25 586). Comfortable pension in a quiet position on the street that runs straight down from the entrance to the fortress to Melissinou. ④.

Atelier, Himáras 32 (☎24 440). Pleasant rooms close to *Rooms George*, run by a talented potter, who has her studio in the basement and sells her wares in a shop on the other side of the building. ③.

Barbara Dokimaki, Plastíra 14 (☎22 319). Strange warren of a rooms place, with one entrance at the above address, just off the seafront behind the *Ideon*, and another on Dambergi, opposite *Corina*; some excellent rooms. ③.

Byzantine, Vosporou 26 (☎55 609). Excellent-value rooms in a renovated old Byzantine palace. The tranquil patio bar is open to all. ④.

Corina, Dambergi 9 (☎26 911). Very friendly pension with a couple of good balcony rooms at the front, several darker ones behind. ③.

Ideon, Platía Plastíra 10 (☎28 667). Hotel with a brilliant position just north of the ferry dock; little chance of space in season, though. ⑥.

Leo, Vafiou 2 (☎29 851). Good hotel with lots of wood and traditional feel. Price includes breakfast, and there's a good bar. ④.

Réthimnon Haus, V. Kornarou 1 (☎23 923). Very pleasant, upmarket rooms place in an old building just off Arkadhíou. Bar downstairs. ③.

Rooms George, Makedonias 32 (☎27 540). Decent rooms (some with fridge), near the archeological museum. ③.

Vrisinas, Heréti 10 (☎26 092). Pension in a narrow street parallel to Kalérgi, worth checking as you walk from the bus station, but often full. Lovely rooms, though some are noisy. ③.

Youth hostel, Tombázi 41 (☎22 848). Cheapest beds in town are in the youth hostel dormitories (or on the roof). It's large, clean, very friendly and popular, and there's food, showers, clothes-washing facilities and even a library of books in an assortment of languages. ①.

Zania, 3 Pavlou Vlastou (☎28 169). Pension right on the corner of Arkadhíou by the old youth hostel building; a well-adapted old house, but only a few rooms. ③.

Eating and drinking

Immediately behind the town **beach** are arrayed the most touristy restaurants. One that maintains its integrity (and reasonable prices) is *Taverna Samaria*, almost opposite the tourist office. Around the **inner harbour**, there's a second, rather more expensive group of tavernas, specializing in fish, though as often as not the intimate atmosphere in these places is spoilt by the stench from the harbour itself: *O Zefyros* and *Seven Brothers* are two of the less outrageously pricey of these.

The cluster of *kafenía* and tavernas **by the Rimóndi fountain** and the newer places spreading into the surrounding streets generally offer considerably better value. A couple of the old-fashioned *kafenía* serve magnificent yoghurt and honey. Places to try include *Kyria María* at Moshovitou 20, tucked down an alley behind the fountain (after the meal, everyone gets a couple of Maria's delicious *tiropitákia* with honey on the house); *Agrimi*, a reliable standard on Platía Petiháki; and the *Zanfoti kafenío* overlooking the fountain, relatively expensive, but a great place to people-watch over a coffee, and with good yoghurt and honey, too. Slightly cheaper places in the surrounding backstreets include *Stelios Soumbasakis*, a simple, friendly taverna at Nikiforou Foka 98, corner of Koronaíou; and *Taverna Haroulas Kargaki*, Melissinou by Mesolongíou, for big, cheap breakfasts plus standard taverna fare at reasonable prices. A good lunchtime stop close to the archeological museum is *O Pontios*, Melissinou 34, a simple place with tables outside and an enthusiastic female proprietor. A noisier evening alternative is *Taverna O Gounos* at Koroneou 6 in the old town, where the family running it perform live *lyra* every night. When things get really lively the dancing starts.

If you want takeaway food, there are numerous **souvláki** stalls, including a couple on Arkadhíou and Paleológou and *O Platanos* at Petiháki 44, or you can buy your own ingredients at the **market** stalls set up daily on Andistásis below the Porta Guora. There are small general stores scattered everywhere, particularly on Paleológou and Arkadhíou; east along the beach road you'll even find a couple of mini supermarkets. The **bakery** *I Gaspari*, on Mesolongíou just behind the Rimóndi fountain, sells the usual cheese pies, cakes and the like, and it also bakes excellent brown, black and rye bread. There's a good *zaharoplasteío* on Petiháki.

Nightlife

Nightlife is concentrated in the same general areas as the tavernas. At the west end of Venizélou, approaching the inner harbour, a small cluster of noisy **music bars** rock the beach – *Rouli's* is one of the liveliest. Several glitzier bar/discos, including *Fortezza* and *Metropolis*, gather on an alley between the inner harbour and Arkadhíou. Larger **discos** are mostly out to the east, among the big hotels, but there are one or two in town. *Odysseas*, on Venizélou right by the inner harbour, is a touristy Cretan music and dancing place, with live performances every evening from 9.30pm.

Around Réthimnon

While some of Crete's most drastic resort development spreads ever eastwards out of Réthimnon, to the west a sandy coastline, not yet greatly exploited, runs all the way to the borders of Haniá. But of all the short trips that can be made out of Réthimnon, the best known and still the most worthwhile is to the **monastery of Arkádhi**.

Southeast to Arkádhi

The **monastery of Arkádhi** (daily 6am–8pm), some 25km southeast of the city and immaculately situated in the foothills of the Psilorítis range, is also something of a national Cretan shrine. During the 1866 rebellion against the Turks, the monastery became a rebel strongpoint in which, as the Turks gained the upper hand, hundreds of Cretan guerrillas and their families took refuge. Surrounded and, after two days of fighting, on the point of defeat, the defenders ignited a powder magazine just as the Turks entered. Hundreds (some sources claim thousands) were killed, Cretan and Turk alike, and the tragedy did much to promote international sympathy for the cause of Cretan independence. Nowadays, you can peer into the roofless vault where the explosion occurred and wander about the rest of the well-restored grounds. The sixteenth-century Rococo church survived, and is one of the finest Venetian structures left on Crete; other buildings house a small museum devoted to the exploits of the defenders of the (Orthodox) faith. The monastery is easy to visit by public bus or on a tour.

West to Yioryoúpoli and beyond

Leaving Réthimnon to the west, the main road climbs for a while above a rocky coastline before descending (after some 5km) to the sea, where it runs alongside sandy **beaches** for perhaps another 7km. An occasional hotel and a campsite (*George*) offer accommodation, but on the whole there's nothing but a line of straggly bushes between the road and the windswept sands. If you have your own vehicle, there are plenty of places to stop here for a swim, and rarely anyone else around – but beware of some very strong currents.

If you want to stay for any time, virtually the only base is **YIORYOÚPOLI** at the far end, where the beach is cleaner, wider and further from the road. It's not exactly unknown, but neither is it heavily developed. If you're after a base for a few days that's peaceful but not too quiet, there are a lot of **rooms** for rent and several **hotels**, well used in mid-season. Most of the better rooms are found by heading for the main *platía* and then looking along the road down towards the beach. More central possibilities include *Rooms Voula* (☎0825/61 359; ③), above a gift shop to the east of the *platía*, or the *Paradise Taverna* (☎0825/61 313; ③), which has rooms and is a good place to eat, off the southeast corner of the *platía*.

Within walking distance inland is **Kournás**, Crete's only lake, set deep in a bowl of hills and almost constantly changing colour. There's a taverna on the shore with a few rooms for rent, or you could try for a bed in the nearby village of Moúri.

Beyond Yioryoúpoli, the main road heads inland, away from a cluster of coastal villages beyond Vámos. It thus misses the Dhrápano peninsula, with some spectacular views over the sapphire Bay of Soudha, several quiet beaches and the setting for the film of *Zorba the Greek*. **KÓKKINO HORIÓ**, the movie location, and nearby **PLÁKA** are indeed postcard-picturesque (more so from a distance), but **KEFALÁS**, inland, outdoes both of them. On the exposed north coast there are beaches at **ALMIRÍDHA** and **KALÍVES**, and off the road between them. Both have quite a few apartments but not many rooms available; Almirídha, though, makes an enjoyable lunch stop.

South from Réthimnon

There are a couple of alternative routes south from Réthimnon, but the main one heads straight out from the centre of town, an initially featureless road due south across the middle of the island towards Ayía Galíni. About 23km out, a turning cuts off to the right for Plakiás and Mírthios, following the course of the spectacular Kourtaliótiko ravine.

Plakiás and the south coast

PLAKIÁS has undergone a major boom and is no longer the pristine village all too many people arriving here expect. That said, it's still quite low key, there's a satisfactory beach and a string of good tavernas around the dock. There are hundreds of **rooms**, but at the height of summer you'll need to arrive early if you hope to find one; the last to fill are generally those on the road leading inland, away from the waterside. Try *Rooms Nefeli* (③) at the end of the road inland behind *Candia Tours*. If needed, there's a **youth hostel** (☎0832/31 306; ①) on the edge of town. The beach is long and nobody is likely to mind if you sleep out on the middle section – but Damnóni (see below) is far better if that's your plan.

Once you've found a room there's not a lot else to discover here. You'll find every facility strung out around the waterfront, including a temporary post office, bike rental, money exchange, supermarket and even launderette. Places to eat are plentiful, too. The attractive **tavernas** on the waterfront in the centre are a little expensive; you'll eat cheaper further inland, or around the corner at one of the tavernas facing west (*Julia's Place*, here, has good vegetarian food).

Mírthios

For a stay of more than a day or two, **MÍRTHIOS**, in the hills behind Plakiás, also deserves consideration. It's no longer a great deal cheaper, but at least you'll find locals still outnumbering the tourists and something of a travellers' scene based around another popular **youth hostel** (☎0832/31 202; ①), with a friendly taverna and several rooms for rent. The Plakiás bus will usually loop back through Mírthios, but check; otherwise, it's less than five minutes' walk from the junction. It takes twenty minutes to walk down to the beach at Plakiás, a little longer to Damnóni, and if you're prepared to walk for an hour or more, there are some entirely isolated coves to the west – ask directions at the hostel.

Damnóni

Some of the most tempting beaches in central Crete hide just to the east of Plakiás, though unfortunately they're now a very poorly kept secret. These three splashes of yellow sand, divided by rocky promontories, are within easy walking distance and together go by the name **DAMNÓNI**. At the first, Damnóni proper, there's a taverna with showers and a wonderfully long strip of sand, but there's also a lot of new development including a number of nearby rooms for rent and a huge new German hotel, which has colonized half of the main beach. At the far end, you'll generally find a few people who've dispensed with their clothes, while the little cove which shelters the middle of the three beaches (barely accessible except on foot) is entirely nudist. Beyond this, Ammoúdhi beach has another taverna (with good rooms for rent) and a slightly more family atmosphere. All these are considerably more attractive than Plakiás's own beach, though you'd have less far to walk, and probably spend less, staying in the village of **LEFKÓYIA**, 2km away. The disadvantages are that Lefkóyia is not itself on the coast, and besides a couple of tavernas and four or five places renting **rooms**, it has no facilities at all.

Préveli and "Palm Beach"

Next in line comes **PRÉVELI**, some 6km southeast of Lefkóyia. It takes its name from a **monastery** (daily 8am–1pm & 3–7pm) high above the sea which, like every other in Crete, has a proud history of resistance, in this case, accentuated by its role in the last war as a shelter for marooned Allied soldiers awaiting evacuation off the south coast. There are fine views and a monument commemorating the rescue operations, but little else to see. The evacuations took place from **"Palm Beach"**, a sandy cove with a small date-palm grove and solitary drink stand where a stream feeds a little oasis. The beach usually attracts a summer camping community and is now also the target of day-trip boats from Plakiás. Sadly, these two groups between them have left this lovely place filthy, and despite a belated clean-up campaign it seems barely worth the effort. The climb down from the monastery is steep, rocky and surprisingly arduous; if you do come, it's a great deal easier on the boat.

Spíli and Ayía Galíni

Back on the main road south, **SPÍLI** lies about 30km from Réthimnon. A popular coffee break for tours passing this way, Spíli warrants time if you can spare it. Sheltered under a cliff are narrow alleys of ancient houses, all leading up from a *platía* with a famous 24-spouted fountain. If you have your own transport, it's a worthwhile place to stay, peacefully rural at night but with several good **rooms** for rent. Try the *Green Hotel* (☎0832/22 056; ③) or the pleasant and cheaper *Rooms Herakles* (☎0832/22 411; ②) just behind.

The ultimate destination of most people on this road is **AYÍA GALÍNI**. If heading here was your plan, maybe you should think again since this picturesque "fishing village" is so busy that you can't see it for the tour buses, hotel billboards and British package tourists. It also has a beach much too small for the crowds that congregate here. Even so, there are some saving graces – mainly some excellent restaurants and bars, plenty of rooms and a friendly atmosphere that survives and even thrives on all the visitors. Out of season, it can be quite enjoyable, and from November to April the mild climate makes it an ideal spot to spend the winter. A lot of long-term travellers do just that, so it's a good place to find work packing tomatoes or polishing cucumbers. If you want somewhere to stay, start looking at the top end of town, around the main road: the good-value *Hotel Minos* (☎0832/91 292; ②) with superb views is a good place to start, but there are dozens of possibilities, and usually something to be found even at the height of summer.

The coastal plain east of Ayía Galíni, hidden under acres of polythene greenhouses and burgeoning concrete sprawl, must be among the ugliest regions in Crete, and Timbáki the dreariest town. Since this is the way to Festós and back to Iráklion, however, you may have no choice but to grin and bear it.

The Amári Valley

An alternative route south from Réthimnon, and a far less travelled one, is the road which turns off on the eastern fringe of town to run via the **Amári Valley**. Very few buses go this way, but if you're driving it's well worth the extra time. There's little specifically to see or do (though hidden away are a number of frescoed Byzantine churches), but it's an impressive drive under the flanks of the mountains and a reminder of how, in places, rural Crete continues to exist regardless of visitors. The countryside here is delightfully green even in summer, with rich groves of olive and assorted fruit trees, and if you **stay** (there are rooms in Thrónos and Yerákari) the nights are cool and quiet. It may seem odd that many of the villages along the way are modern; they were systematically destroyed by the Germans in reprisal for the 1944 kidnapping of General Kreipe.

HANIÁ AND THE WEST

The substantial attractions of Crete's westernmost quarter are all the more enhanced by its relative lack of visitors; and despite the now-rapid spread of tourist development, the west is likely to remain one of the emptier parts of the island. This is partly because there are no big sandy beaches to accommodate resort hotels, and partly because it's so far from the great archeological sites. But for mountains and empty (if often pebbly) beaches, it's unrivalled.

Haniá itself is one of the best reasons to come here, perhaps the only Cretan city which could be described as enjoyable in itself. The immediately adjacent coast is relatively developed and not overly exciting; if you want beaches head for the **south coast**. **Paleohóra** is the only place which could really be described as a resort, and even this is on a thoroughly human scale; others are emptier still. **Ayía Rouméli** and **Loutró** can be reached only on foot or by boat; **Hóra Sfakíon** sees hordes passing through but few who stay; **Frangokástello**, nearby, has a beautiful castle and the first stirrings of development. Behind these lie the **Lefká Óri** (White Mountains) and, above all, the famed walk through the **Gorge of Samariá**.

Haniá

HANIÁ, as any of its residents will tell you, is the spiritual capital of Crete, even if the nominal title has passed (in 1971) to Iráklion. For many, it is also by far the island's most attractive city, especially if you can catch it in spring, when the Lefká Óri's snow-capped peaks seem to hover above the roofs. Although it is for the most part a modern city, you might never know it as a tourist. Surrounding the small outer harbour is a wonderful jumble of half-derelict Venetian streets that survived the wartime bombardments, and it is here that life for the visitor is concentrated. Restoration and gentrification, consequences of the tourist boom, have made inroads of late, but it remains an atmospheric place.

Arrival and orientation

Large as it is, Haniá is easy to handle once you've reached the centre; you may get lost wandering among the narrow alleys of the old city but that's a relatively small area, and you're never far from the sea or from some other obvious landmark. The **bus station** is on Kidhonías, within easy walking distance from the action – turn right out of the

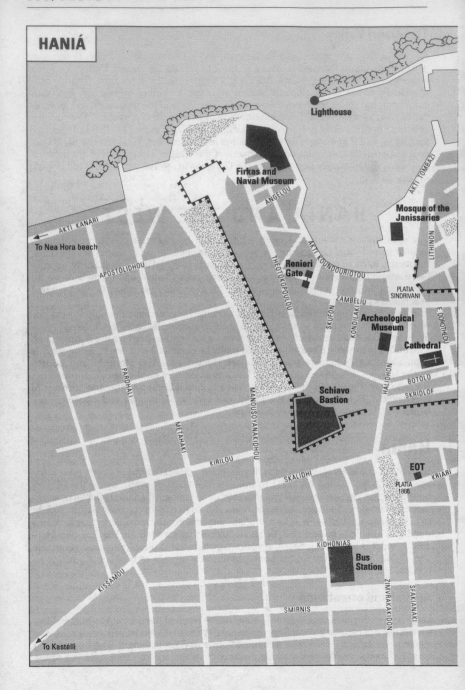

HANIÁ

Lighthouse

Firkas and
Naval Museum

ANGELOU

Mosque of the
Janissaries

AKTI TOMBAZI

NONIHILI

LITHINON

AKTI KANARI

← To Nea Hora beach

AKTI KOUNDOURIOTOU

APOSTOLIDHOU

THEOTOKOPOULOU

Renieri
Gate

ZAMBELIU

PLATIA
SINDRIVANI

PLATIA
SINDRIVANI

E. DOROTHEOU

SKUFON

KONDILAKI

Archeological
Museum

Cathedral

PARDHALI

MANOUSOYANAKIDHOU

HALIDHON

BOTOLO

SKRIDLOF

METAHAKI

Schiavo
Bastion

KIRILOU

SKALIDHI

EOT

KRIARI

PLATIA
1866

KISSAMOU

KIDHONIAS

Bus
Station

ZIMVRAKAKIDON

SFAKIANAK

SMIRNIS

← To Kastélli

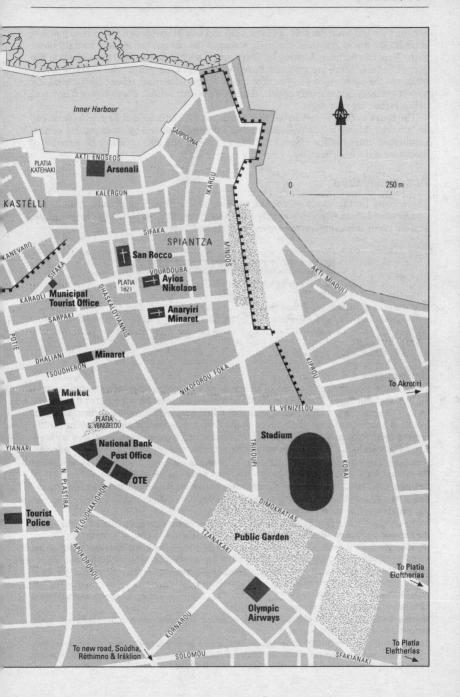

Inner Harbour

SARPIDONA

AKTI ENOSEOS

PLATIA
KATEHAKI

Arsenali

KALERGHON

KASTELLI

SIFAKA

SPIANTZA

KANEVARO

SIFAKA

San Rocco

VOURDOUBA

Ayios
Nikolaos

KARAOLI

PLATIA
1821

Municipal
Tourist Office

MINOOS

IKAROU

AKTI MIAOULI

0   250 m

SARPAKI

DHASKALOYIANNIS

Anaryiri
Minaret

POTIE

DHALIANI

Minaret

KIPROU

TSOUDHERON

NIKOFOROU FOKA

Market

EL VENIZELOU

PLATIA
S. VENIZELOU

YIANARI

National Bank

Stadium

Post Office

TRIKOUPI

KORAI

OTE

N. PLASTIRA

VELOUDHAKIDHON

DIMOKRATIAS

To Akrotiri

Tourist
Police

TZANAKAKI

Public Garden

APOKORONOU

To Platía
Eleftherías

Olympic
Airways

KORNAROU

To new road, Soúdha,
Réthimno & Iráklion

SOLOMOU

SFAKIANAKI

To Platía
Eleftherías

station, then left down the side of Platía 1866 and you'll emerge at a major road junction opposite the top of Hálidhon, the main street of the old quarter leading straight down to the Venetian harbour. Arriving by **ferry**, you'll anchor about 10km from Haniá at the port of Soúdha: there are frequent buses which will drop you by the **market** on the fringes of the old town, or you can take a taxi. From the **airport** (about 15km) taxis will almost certainly be your only option, though it's worth a quick check to see if any sort of bus is meeting your flight.

The **tourist office** is now in the new town, just off Platía 1866 at Kriári 40 (suite 14/ 15, 4th floor; Mon–Fri 7.30am–2.30pm). This is complemented by an extremely helpful **municipal tourist office** (Mon–Fri 8.30am–1.30pm; ☎59 990) at Sifaka 22, a couple of blocks from the inner harbour.

Accommodation

There must be thousands of **rooms to rent** in Haniá and, unusually, quite a few comfortable **hotels**. Though you may face a long search for a bed at the height of the season, eventually everyone does seem to find something.

HANIÁ AND THE TELEPHONE

The telephone code for Haniá is ☎0821

At the time of writing, the Haniá phone system is being modernized and some numbers listed may have changed. Many starting with a "2" digit, for example, now begin with "9". Other innovations are far too complex and brain-taxing to list here; if in doubt, contact the tourist office.

Harbour area

Perhaps the most desirable rooms of all are those overlooking the harbour, and, surprisingly, such rooms are sometimes available at reasonable rates: be warned that this is often as they're very noisy at night. Most are approached not direct from the harbourside itself but from Zambelíu, the alley behind, or from other streets leading off the harbour further around (where you may get more peace). The nicest of the more expensive places are here, too, usually set back a little, so they're quieter, but often with views from the upper storeys.

Amphora, Theotokopóulou 20 (☎43 132). Large, traditional hotel, and beautifully renovated; worth the expense if you get a view, but probably not for the cheaper rooms with no view. ⑥.

Artemis, Kondiláki 13 (☎91 196). One of many in this touristy street running inland from Zambelíu. ③

Lucia, Akti Koundouriótou (☎90 302). Harbour-front hotel with balcony rooms; less expensive than you might expect for one of the best views in town. ③.

Meltemi, Angelou 2 (☎40 192). First of a little row of pensions in a great situation on the far side of the harbour; perhaps noisier than its neighbours, but ace views and a good café downstairs. ③

Piraeus, Zambelíu 10 (☎94 665). One of the oldest hotels in Haniá; basic and somewhat run-down but friendly, English-speaking and excellent value even for a room with a balcony over the harbour. ③

Rooms George, Zambelíu 30 (☎43 542). Old building with steep stairs and eccentric antique furniture; rooms vary in price according to position and size. ③.

Rooms Eleonora, Theotokopóulou 13 (☎50 011). One of several in the backstreets around the top of Angelou: prices are lower at nearby *Eugenia*. ③.

Rooms Stella, Angelou 10 (☎73 756). Creaky, eccentric old house, close to the Lucia, with plain, clean rooms above a ceramics shop. ③.

Thereza, Angelou 8 (☎40 118). Beautiful old house in a great position with stunning views from roof terrace and some rooms; classy decorations, too. A more expensive pension than its neighbours but deservedly so; unlikely to have room in season unless you book. ④.

The old town: east of Hálidhon

In the eastern half of the old town, rooms are far more scattered, and in the height of the season your chances are much better over here. **Kastélli**, immediately east of the harbour, has some lovely places with views from the height. Take one of the alleys leading left off Kaneváro if you want to try these, but don't be too hopeful since they are popular and often booked up.

Fidias, Sarpáki 8 (☎52 494). Signposted from the cathedral. Favourite backpackers' meeting place: rather bizarrely run, but extremely friendly pension and has the real advantage of offering single rooms or fixing shares. ③.

Kastelli, Kaneváro 39 (☎57 057). Not the prettiest location, but comfortable, modern, reasonably priced pension and very quiet at the back. Alex, who runs the place, is exceptionally helpful and also has a few apartments and a beautiful house (for up to 5 people) to rent. ③.

Kydonia, Isódhion 15 (☎57 179). Between the cathedral *platía* and Platía Sindrívani, in the first street parallel to Hálidhon. Rather dark, but good value for so central a position. ③.

Lito, Episkópou Dorothéou 15 (☎53 150). Pension very near the cathedral; another street with several options. ③.

Marina Ventikou, Sarpáki 40 (☎57 601). Small, personally run rooms place in quiet corner of old town. Others nearby. ③.

Monastíri, Áyíou Markou 18, off Kaneváro (☎54 776) Pleasant rooms, some with a sea view in the restored ruins of a Venetian monastery. ③.

Nikos, Dhaskaloyiánnis 58 (☎54 783). One of a few down here near the inner harbour; relatively modern rooms all with shower. ③.

Youth hostel and campsites

Youth hostel, Dhrakoniánou 33 (☎53 565). The youth hostel is a long way from anywhere you might otherwise visit and is not much of a place: four or five rooms with about eight metal bunks in each, but it is at least cheap and friendly, with a good view inland. You get here on the *Ay. Iouánnis* bus (every 15min; last one at midnight) from the *platía* opposite the market – ask for Platía Dhexameni. Organizes cheap guided tours to the Samarian Gorge and other places. ①.

Camping Ayía Marína (☎48 555). About 8km or so west of Haniá, on an excellent beach at the far end of Ayía Marína village. This is beyond the range of Haniá city buses, so to get here by public transport you have to go from the main bus station. Check before turning up, because the site is earmarked for redevelopment.

Camping Hania (☎31 686). A smaller, cheaper site behind the beach some 4km west of Haniá, just about in walking distance if you follow the coast around, but much easier reached by taking the local bus (see "Beaches" below). There's a large sign to warn you where to get off. The site is lovely, if rather basic in terms of facilities; small, shady and just a short walk from some of the better beaches.

The City

Haniá has been occupied almost continuously since Neolithic times, so it comes as a surprise that a city of such antiquity should offer little specifically to see or do. It is, however, a place which is fascinating simply to wander around, stumbling upon surviving fragments of city wall, holes in which ancient Kydonia is being excavated and odd segments of Venetian or Turkish masonry.

Kastélli and the harbour

The port area is as ever the place to start, the oldest and the most interesting part of town. It's at its busiest and most attractive at night, when the lights from bars and restaurants reflect in the water and crowds of visitors and locals turn out to promenade. By day, things are quieter. Straight ahead from Platía Sindrivani (also known as Harbour Square) lies the curious domed shape of the **Mosque of the Janissaries**, until recently the tourist office, but currently without a function. The little hill that rises behind the mosque is **Kastélli**, site of the earliest habitation and core of the Venetian and Turkish towns. There's not a great deal left, but it's here that you'll find traces of the oldest walls (there were two rings, one defending Kastélli alone, a later set encompassing the whole of the medieval city) and the sites of various excavations. Beneath the hill, on the **inner (eastern) harbour**, the arches of sixteenth-century Venetian arsenals survive alongside remains of the outer walls; both are currently undergoing restoration.

Following the esplanade around in the other direction leads to a hefty bastion which now houses Crete's **Naval Museum** (Tues, Thurs & Sat 10am–2pm & 4–6pm). The collection is not exactly riveting, but wander in anyway for a look at the seaward fortifications and the platform where the modern Greek flag was first flown on Crete (in 1913). Walk around the back of these restored bulwarks to a street heading inland and you'll find the best-preserved stretch of the outer walls.

The old city

Behind the harbour, lie the less picturesque but more lively sections of the old city. First, a short way up Hálidhon on the right, is Haniá's **Archeological Museum** (daily except Mon 8.30am–3pm; 400dr, Sun free), housed in the Venetian-built church of San Francesco. Damaged as it is, especially from the outside, this remains a beautiful building and a fine little display, covering the local area from Minoan through to Roman times. In the garden, a huge fountain and the base of a minaret survive from the period when the Turks converted the church into a mosque; around them are scattered various other sculptures and architectural remnants.

The **Cathedral**, ordinary and relatively modern, is just a few steps further up Hálidhon on the left. Around it are some of the more animated shopping areas, particularly **Odhós Skrídlof** (Leather Street), with streets leading up to the back of the market beyond. In the direction of the Spiántza quarter are ancient alleys with tumbledown Venetian stonework and overhanging wooden balconies; though gentrification is spreading apace, much of the quarter has yet to feel the effect of the city's modern popularity. There are a couple more **minarets**, too, one on Dhaliáni, and the other in Platía 1821, which is a fine traditional *platía* to stop for a coffee.

The new town

Once out of the narrow confines of the maritime district, the broad, traffic-choked streets of the **modern city** have a great deal less to offer. Up Tzanakáki, not far from the market, you'll find the **Public Gardens**, a park with strolling couples, a few caged animals (including a few *kri-kri* or Cretan ibex) and a café under the trees; there's also an open-air auditorium which occasionally hosts live music or local festivities. Beyond here, you could continue to the **Historical Museum** (Mon–Fri 9am–1pm), but the effort would be wasted unless you're a Greek-speaking expert on the subject; the place is essentially a very dusty archive with a few photographs on the wall. Perhaps more interesting is the fact that the museum lies on the fringes of Haniá's desirable residential districts. If you continue to the end of Sfakianáki and then go down Iróön Politehníou towards the sea, you'll get an insight into how Crete's other half lives. There are several (expensive) garden restaurants down here and a number of fashionable café-bars where you can sit outside.

The beaches

Haniá's beaches all lie to the west of the city. For the packed **city beach**, this means no more than a ten-minute walk following the shoreline from the naval museum, but for good sand you're better off taking the local bus out along the coast road. This leaves from the east side of Platía 1866 and runs along the coast road as far as **Kalamáki beach**. Kalamáki and the previous stop, **Oasis beach**, are again pretty crowded but they're a considerable improvement over the beach in Haniá itself. In between, you'll find emptier stretches if you're prepared to walk: about an hour in all (on sandy beach virtually all the way) from Haniá to Kalamáki, and then perhaps ten minutes from the road to the beach if you get off the bus at the signs to *Aptera Beach* or *Camping Hania*. Further afield there are even finer beaches at **Ayía Marín**: to the west, or **Stavrós** (see p.537) out on the Akrotíri peninsula (reached by *KTEL* buses from the main station).

Eating

You're never far from something **to eat** in Haniá: in a circle around the harbour is one restaurant, taverna or café after another. All have their own character, but there seems little variation in price or what's on offer. Away from the water, there are plenty of slightly cheaper possibilities on Kondiláki, Kanévaro and most of the streets off Hálidhon. For snacks or lighter meals, the cafés around the harbour on the whole serve cocktails and fresh juices at exorbitant prices, though breakfast (especially "English") can be good value. For more traditional places, try around the market and along Dhaskaloyiánnis (*Singanaki* here is a good traditional bakery serving *tiropitta* and the like, with a cake shop next door). Fast food is also increasingly widespread, with numerous *souvláki* places on Karaolí; at the end of the outer harbour, near the naval museum; and around the corner of Plastíra and Yianári, across from the **market** (see "Listings", below, for details of the market and supermarkets)

Boúyatsa, Sífaka 4. Tiny place serving little except the traditional creamy *boúyatsa*: eat in or take away.

Dino's, inner harbour by bottom of Sarpidóna. One of the best choices for a pricey seafood meal with a harbour view; *Apostolis*, almost next door, is also good.

Karnáyio, Platía Kateháki 8. Set back from the inner harbour near the port police. Not right on the water, but one of the best harbour restaurants nonetheless.

Kings, Kondiláki. The first of numerous good places as you head up Kondiláki from Zambelíu. Again, some vegetarian food.

Le Saladier, Kanévaro just off Platía Sindriváni. French-run joint offering salads of every kind.

Lito, Episkópou Dorothéou 15. Café/taverna with live music (usually Greek-style guitar), one of several in this street.

Meltomi, Angelou ?. Slow, relaxed place for breakfast, and where locals (especially expats) sit whiling the day away or playing *tavli*.

Neorion, Sarpidóna. Café to sit and be seen in the evening; some tables overlook the harbour. Try an expensive but sublime lemon *granita*.

Pafsilipon, Sífaka 19. Good, standard taverna. Tables on the street and also on the raised pavement opposite. House speciality is *toúrta*.

Tamam, Zambelíu just before Renieri Gate. Young, fashionable place with adventurous Greek menu including much vegetarian food. Unfortunately only a few cramped tables outside, and inside it's very hot. Slow service.

Tasty Souvlaki, Hálidhon 80. Always packed despite being cramped and none-too-clean, which is a testimonial to the quality and value of the *souvláki*. Better to take away.

Taverna Ela, top of Kondiláki. Live Greek music to enliven your meal.

Toh Dhiporto, Skridhlóf 40. Long-established, very basic taverna amid all the leather shops. Multilingual menu offers such delights as "Pigs' Balls", or, more delicately, *Testicules de Porc*.

Vasilis, Platía Sindriváni. Perhaps the least changed of the harbourside cafés. Reasonably priced breakfasts.

Bars and nightlife

There are NATO air force and navy bases out on Akrotíri, which means there are some **bars** in Haniá that are a lot heavier than you'd expect, full of servicemen. Over the last couple of years, some of these places have been closed and others tamed, however, and the troops have been on their best behaviour in the face of local opposition to their presence: tourists and young locals predominate in most places.

The smartest and newest places are on and around **Sarpidóna**, in the far corner of the inner harbour: bars like *Fraise*, on Sarpidóna; and late night disco-bars such as *Berlin Rock Café*, on Radimánthus, just around the corner at the top of Sarpidóna. Heading from here around towards the outer harbour, you'll pass others including the *Four Seasons*, a very popular bar by the port police, and then reach a couple of the older places including *Remember* and *Scorpio* behind the *Plaza*. *Fagotto*, Angelou 16, is a pleasant, laid-back jazz bar, often with live performers. **Discos** proper include *Ariadni*, on the inner harbour (opens 11.30pm, but busy later), and *Agora Club*, a big, bright place on Tsoudherón behind the market, which doesn't really get going until 2am. Tucked down a passage near the Schiaro Bastion (Skalidhi and Hálidhon) *Anayennisi Club* is a new place that becomes frenetic after midnight.

A couple of places that offer more traditional entertainment are the *Café Kriti*, Kalergón 22, at the corner of Androgéo, basically an old-fashioned *kafenío* where there's **Greek music and dancing** virtually every night, and the *Firkas* (the bastion by the naval museum), with Greek dancing at 9pm every Tuesday; pricey but authentic entertainment. It's also worth checking for events at the open-air auditorium in the public gardens, and for performances in restaurants outside the city, which are the ones the locals will go to. Look for posters, especially in front of the market and in the little *platía* across the road from there.

For **films**, you should also check the hoardings in front of the market. There are open-air screenings at *Attikon*, on Venizélou out towards Akrotíri, about 1km from the centre, and occasionally in the public gardens.

Listings

Airlines *Olympic*, Tzanakáki 88 (☎57 701; Mon–Fri 9am–4pm). There's a bus from here connecting with their flights. For airport information phone ☎63 245.

Banks The main branch of the *National Bank* is directly opposite the market. Convenient smaller banks for exchange are next to the bus station, at the bottom of Kaneváro just off Platía Sindrivani, or at the top of Hálidhon. There are also a couple of exchange places on Hálidhon, open long hours, and a post office van parked through the summer in the cathedral *platía*.

Bike and car rental Possibilities everywhere, especially on Hálidhon, though these are rarely the best value. For cars try *Hermes*, Tzanakáki 52 (☎54 418), friendly and efficient; for bikes and cars *Duke of Crete*, Sífaka 3, (☎21 651), Skalídhi 16 (☎57 821) and branches in Ayía Marína and Plataniás (discount for cash).

Boat trips Various boat trips are offered by travel agents around town, mostly round Soúdha Bay or out to beaches on the Rodhópou peninsula. *Domenico's* on Kaneváro offers some of the best of these.

Ferry tickets The agent for *Minoan* is *Nanadakis Travel*, Hálidhon 8 (☎23 939); for *ANEK* on Venizélou, right opposite the market (☎23 636).

Launderette There are three, at Kaneváro 38 (9am–10pm), Episkópou Dorothéou 7 and Áyii Dhéka 18. All do service washes.

Left luggage The bus station has a left luggage office.

Market and supermarkets If you want to buy food or get stuff together for a picnic, the market is the place to head. There are vast quantities of fresh fruit and vegetables as well as meat and fish, bakers, dairy stalls and general stores for cooked meats, tins and other standard provisions. There are also several small stores down by the harbour *platía* which sell cold drinks and a certain amount of food, but these are expensive (though they do open late). A couple of large supermarkets can be found on the main roads running out of town, for instance *Inka* on the way to Akrotíri.

Post office The main post office is on Tzanakáki (Mon–Fri 7am–8pm, plus Sat for exchange 8am–2pm). In summer, there's a handy Portakabin branch set up in the cathedral *platía*.

Taxis The main taxi ranks are in the cathedral *platía* and, especially, Platía 1866. For radio taxis try ☎29 405 or ☎58 700.

Telephones OTE headquarters (daily 6am–midnight) is on Tzanakáki just past the post office. It's generally packed during the day, but often blissfully empty late at night.

Tourist police Kareskáki 44 (☎94 477). Town and harbour police are on the inner harbour.
Travel agencies For cheap tickets home (*Magic Bus* and student/charter flights) *Bassias Travel*, Skridhlóf 46 (☎44 295), is the place, very helpful for regular tickets, too. They also deal in standard excursions. Other travel agents for tours and day trips are everywhere.

Around Haniá: the Akrotíri and Rodhopoú peninsulas

Just north of Haniá, the **Akrotíri peninsula** loops around to protect the Bay of Soúdha and a NATO military base and missile-testing area. In an ironic twist, the peninsula's northwestern coastline is fast developing into a luxury suburb; the beach of Horafákia, long popular with jaded Haniotes, is surrounded by villas and apartments. STAVRÓS, further out, has not yet suffered this fate, and its **beach** is absolutely superb if you like the calm, shallow water of an almost completely enclosed lagoon. It's not very large, so it does get crowded, but rarely overpoweringly so. You can rent rooms here, and there are two tavernas.

Inland are the **monasteries of Ayía Triádha** and **Gouvernétou** (both daily 9am–2pm & 5–7pm). The former is much more accessible and has a beautiful seventeenth-century church inside its pink-and-ochre cloister; it's also one of the few Cretan monasteries in which genuine monastic life continues. Beyond the latter, you can clamber down a craggy path to the abandoned ruins of the monastery of Katholikó and the remains of its narrow (swimmable) harbour.

West to Rodhopoú

The coast to the west of Haniá was the scene of most of the fighting during the German invasion in 1941. As you leave town, an aggressive diving eagle commemorates the German parachutists, and at Máleme there's a big German cemetery; the Allied cemetery is in the other direction, on the coast just outside Soúdha. There are also beaches and considerable tourist development along much of this shore. At AYÍA MARÍNA there's a fine sandy beach, and an island offshore said to be a sea monster petrified by Zeus before it could swallow Crete. Seen from the west, its "mouth" still gapes open.

Between PLATANIÁS and KOLIMBÁRI an almost unbroken strand unfurls, by no means all sandy, but deserted for long stretches between villages. The road here runs through mixed groves of calamus reed (Crete's bamboo) and oranges; the windbreaks fashioned from the reeds protect the ripening oranges from the *meltémi*. At Kolimbári, the road to Kastélli cuts across the base of another mountainous peninsula, **Rodhopoú**. Just off the main road here is a monastery, **Goniá** (daily 9am–2pm & 5–7pm; respectable dress), with a view most luxury hotels would envy. Every monk in Crete can tell tales of his proud ancestry of resistance to invaders, but here the Turkish cannon balls are still lodged in the walls to prove it, a relic of which the good fathers are far more proud than of any of the icons.

South to the Samarian Gorge

From Haniá the **Gorge of Samariá** (May to mid-Oct; 1000dr for entry to the national park) can be visited as a day trip or as part of a longer excursion to the south. At over 16km, it's Europe's longest gorge and is startlingly beautiful. **Buses** leave Haniá for the top at 6.15am, 7.30am and 8.30am, plus 1.30pm, and you'll normally be sold a return ticket (valid from Hóra Sfakíon at any time). It's well worth catching the early bus to avoid the full heat of the day while walking through the gorge, though be warned that

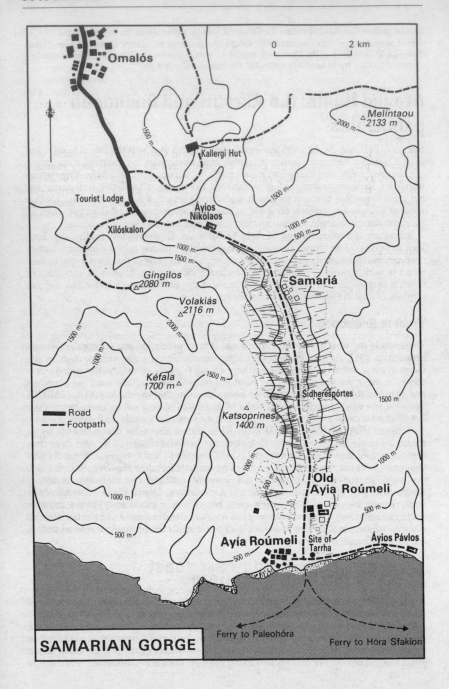

Omalós

0   2 km

Melíntaou
2133 m
2000 m

1500 m

Kallergi Hut

1500 m

Tourist Lodge

Áyios
Nikólaos

1000 m

Xilóskalon

500 m

1000 m

Samariá

1500 m

Gíngilos
2080 m

Volakiás
2116 m

2000 m

1500 m

1000 m

Kéfala
1700 m

1500 m

Sidherespórtes

1500 m

Road
Footpath

Katsoprínes
1400 m

1000 m

1000 m

Old
Ayia Roúmeli

1000 m

500 m

500 m

1000 m

Ayía Roúmeli

Site of
Tarrha

Áyios Pávlos

500 m

500 m

SAMARIAN GORGE

Ferry to Paleohóra

Ferry to Hóra Sfakíon

you will not be alone – there are often as many as five coachloads setting off before dawn for the nail-biting climb into the White Mountains. There are also direct early-morning buses from Iráklion and Réthimnon, and bus tours from virtually everywhere on the island. Despite all the crowds, the walk is hard work, especially in spring when the stream is a roaring torrent. Early and late in the season, there is a danger of flash floods, which are not to be taken lightly. In 1993, a number of walkers perished when they were washed out to sea. If in doubt, phone the Haniá Forest Service (☎0821/67 140) for information.

Omalós

One way to avoid the early start would be to stay at **OMALÓS**, in the middle of the mountain plain from which the gorge descends. There are some ordinary **rooms** for rent and a couple of surprisingly fancy **hotels**; try the *Neos Omalos* (☎0821/67 269; ③). But since the village is some way from the start of the track, and the buses arrive as the sun rises, it's almost impossible to get a head start on the crowds. Some people sleep out at the top (where there's a bar-restaurant and kiosks serving drinks and sand-wiches), but a night under the stars here can be a bitterly cold experience. The one significant advantage to staying up here would be if you wanted to undertake some other climbs in the White Mountains, in which case there's a **mountain hut** (☎0821/24 647; ①) about ninety minutes' walk from Omalós or from the top of the gorge.

Through the gorge

The **Gorge** itself begins at the *Xilóskala*, or "wooden staircase", a stepped path plunging steeply down from the southern lip of the Omalós plain. Here, at the head of the track, opposite the sheer rock face of Mount Gíngilos, the crowds pouring out of the buses disperse rapidly as keen walkers march purposefully down while others dally over breakfast, contemplating the sunrise for hours. You descend at first through almost alpine scenery: pine forest, wild flowers and very un-Cretan greenery – a verdant shock in the spring, when the stream is also at its liveliest (and can at times be positively dangerous). Small churches and viewpoints dot the route, and about halfway down you pass the abandoned village of **Samariá**, now home to a wardens' station, with picnic facilities and filthy toilets. Further down, the path levels out and the gorge walls close in until at the narrowest point (the *Sidherespórtes* or "Iron Gates") one can practically touch both tortured rock faces at once, and, looking up, see them rising sheer for almost a thousand feet.

At an average pace, with regular stops, the walk down takes five or six hours, and the upward trek considerably longer. It's hard work (you'll know all about it next day), the path is rough, and solid shoes vital. On the way down, there is plenty of water from springs and streams (except some years in September and October), but nothing to eat. The park that surrounds the gorge is the only mainland refuge of the Cretan wild ibex, the *kri-kri*, but don't expect to see one; there are usually far too many people around.

Villages of the southwest coast

When you finally emerge from the gorge, it's not long before you reach the village of **AYÍA ROUMÉLI**, which is all but abandoned until you reach the beach, a mirage of iced drinks and a cluster of tavernas with **rooms** for rent. If you want to get back to Haniá, buy your boat tickets now, especially if you want an afternoon on the beach; the last boat (connecting with the final 6.30pm bus from Hóra Sfakíon) tends to sell out first. If you plan to stay on the south coast, you should get going as soon as possible for the best chance of finding a room somewhere nicer than Ayía Rouméli.

Loutró

For tranquillity, it's hard to beat **LOUTRÓ**, two-thirds of the way to Hóra Sfakíon, and accessible only by boat or on foot. The chief disadvantage of Loutró is its lack of a real beach; most people swim from the rocks around its small bay. If you're prepared to walk, however, there are deserted beaches along the coast to the east. Indeed, if you're really into walking there's a coastal trail through Loutró which covers the entire distance between Ayía Rouméli and Hóra Sfakíon, or you could take the daunting zigzag path up the cliff behind to the mountain village of Anópoli. Loutró itself has a number of tavernas and rooms, though not always enough of the latter. Call the *Blue House* (☎0825/91 127) if you want to book ahead; this is also the best place to eat. There is also space to camp out on the cape by a ruined fort, but due to a long history of problems, you should be aware that campers are not very popular in the village.

Hóra Sfakíon and beyond

HÓRA SFAKÍON is the more usual terminus for walkers traversing the gorge, with a regular boat service along the coast to and from Ayía Rouméli. Consequently, it's quite an expensive and not an especially welcoming place; there are plenty of rooms and some excellent tavernas, but for a real beach you should jump straight on the evening bus going toward Plakiás. Plenty of opportunities present themselves en route, one of the most memorable at **Frangokástello**, a crumbling Venetian attempt to bring law and order to a district that went on to defy both Turks and Germans. Its square, crenellated fort, isolated a few kilometres below a chiselled wall of mountains, looks like it's been spirited out of the High Atlas or Tibet. The place is said to be haunted by ghosts of Greek rebels massacred here in 1829; every May, these *dhrossoulítes* (dewy ones) march at dawn across the coastal plain and disappear into the sea near the fort. The rest of the time Frangokástello is peaceful enough, with a superb beach and numbers of tavernas and rooms, but it's on its way to development. Slightly further east, and less influenced by tourism or modern life, are the attractive villages of **SKALOTÍ** and **RODHÁKINO**, each with basic lodging and food.

Soúyia

In quite the other direction from Ayía Rouméli, less regular boats also head to **SOÚYIA** and on to Paleohóra. Soúyia, until World War II merely the anchorage for Koustoyérako inland, is low key with a long, grey pebble beach and mostly modern buildings (except for a church with a sixth-century Byzantine mosaic as the foundation). Since the completion of the new road to Haniá, the village has started to expand; even so, except in the very middle of summer, it continues to make a good fallback for finding a room or a place to camp, eating cheaply and enjoying the beach when the rest of the island is seething with tourists.

Kastélli and the western tip

Apart from being Crete's most westerly town, and the end of the main road, **KASTÉLLI** (Kíssamos, or Kastélli Kissámou as it's variously known) has little obvious attraction. It's a busy town with a rocky beach visited mainly by people using the boat that runs twice weekly to the island of Kíthira and the Peloponnese. The very ordinariness of Kastélli, however, can be attractive: life goes on pretty much regardless of outsiders, but there's every facility you might need. The **ferry agent's office** in Kastélli is right on the main *platía* (*Ksirouksakis*; ☎0822/22 655), and nothing else is far away apart from the dock, a wearying two-kilometre walk (or inexpensive taxi ride) from town.

Falásarna to Elafonísi

To the west of Kastélli lies some of Crete's loneliest, and, for many visitors, finest coastline. The first place of note is ancient **Falásarna**, city ruins which mean little to the non-specialist, but they do overlook some of the best beaches on Crete, wide and sandy with clean water. There's a handful of tavernas and an increasing number of rooms for rent; otherwise, you have to sleep out, as many people do. This can mean that the main beaches are dirty, but they remain beautiful, and there are plenty of others within walking distance. The nearest real town is **PLÁTANOS**, 5km up the recently paved road, along which there are a couple of daily buses.

Further south, the western coastline is still less discovered and the road is surfaced only as far as Kámbos; there is little in the way of official accommodation. **SFINÁRI** has several houses which rent rooms, and a quiet pebble beach a little way below the village. **KÁMBOS** is similar, but even less visited, its beach a considerable walk down a hill. Beyond them both is the **monastery of Hrissoskalítissa**, hard to get to down a rough dirt road (though increasingly visited by tours from Haniá or Paleohóra), but well worth the effort for its isolation and nearby beaches; the bus gets as far as Váthi, from where the monastery is another two hours' walk away.

Five kilometres beyond Hrissoskalítissa, the road bumps down to the coast opposite the tiny uninhabited islet of **Elafonísi**. You can easily wade out to the island with its sandy beaches and rock pools, and the shallow lagoon is warm and crystal-clear. It looks magnificent, but daily boat trips from Paleohóra and coach tours from elsewhere on the island ensure that, in the middle of the day at least, it's far from deserted. Even bigger changes are now on the horizon here as Greek and German companies have bought up large tracts of land to create a monster tourist complex. If you want to stay, and really appreciate the place, there are a couple of seasonal tavernas, but bring some supplies unless you want to be wholly dependent on them.

A round trip

If you have transport, a circular drive from Kastélli, taking the coast road in one direction and the inland route through Élos and Topólia, makes for a stunningly scenic circuit. Near the ocean, villages cling desperately to the high mountainsides, apparently halted by some miracle in the midst of calamitous seaward slides. Around them, olives ripen on the terraced slopes, the sea glittering far below. Inland, especially at **ÉLOS**, the main crop is the chestnut, whose huge old trees shade the village streets.

In **TOPÓLIA**, the chapel of Ayía Sofía is sheltered inside a cave which has been known since Neolithic times. Cutting south from Élos, a partly paved road continues through the high mountains towards Paleohóra; on a motorbike, with a sense of adventure and plenty of fuel, it's great: the bus doesn't come this way, villagers still stare at the sight of a tourist, and a host of small, seasonal streams cascade beside or under the track.

Kándhanos and Paleohóra

Getting down to Paleohóra by the main road, which is paved the whole way, is a lot easier, and several daily buses from Haniá make the trip. But although this route also has to wind through the western outriders of the White Mountains, it lacks the excitement of the routes to either side. **KÁNDHANOS**, at the 58-kilometre mark, has been entirely rebuilt since it was destroyed by the Germans for its fierce resistance to their occupation. The original sign erected when the deed was done is preserved on the war memorial: "Here stood Kándanos, destroyed in retribution for the murder of 25 German soldiers".

When the beach at **PALEOHÓRA** finally appears below it is a welcome sight. The little town is built across the base of a peninsula, its harbour on one side, the sand on the other. Above, on the outcrop, Venetian ramparts stand sentinel. These days Paleohóra has become heavily developed, but it's still thoroughly enjoyable, with a main street filling, in the evening, with tables as diners spill out of the restaurants, and with a pleasantly chaotic social life. A good place to eat with some good imaginative vegetarian specials is *The Third Eye*, just out of the centre towards the sandy beach. There are scores of places to stay (though not always many vacancies) and there's also a fair-sized **campsite**; in extremis, the beach is one of the best to sleep out on, with showers, trees and acres of sand. Nearby discos and a rock'n'roll bar, or the sound-track from the open-air cinema, combine to lull you to sleep. When you tire of Paleohóra and the excellent windsurfing in the bay, there are excursions up the hill to Prodhrómi, for example, or along a five-hour coastal path to Soúyia.

You'll find a helpful **tourist office** (daily 9.30am–1pm & 5.30–9pm) in the town hall on Venizélos, in the centre of town; they have full accommodation lists and a map (though you'll hardly need this). The **OTE**, **banks** and **travel agents** are all nearby; the **post office** is on the road behind the sandy beach. **Boats** run from here to Elafonísi, the island of Gávdhos, and along the coast to Soúyia and Ayía Rouméli.

Gávdhos

The island of **Gávdhos**, some fifty kilometres of rough sea south of Paleohóra, is the most southerly landmass in Europe. Gávdhos is small (about 10km by 7km at the most) and barren, but it has one major attraction: the enduring isolation which its inaccessible position has helped preserve. There are now a few package tours (travel agents in Paleohóra can arrange a room if you want one), and there's a semi-permanent community of campers through the summer, but if all you want is a beach to yourself and a taverna to grill your fish, this remains the place for you.

travel details

Ferries

Áyios Nikólaos and Sitía 1–3 ferries a week to Kássos, Kárpathos, Hálki, Rhodes and the Dodecanese; 1-2 weekly to Thíra, Folégandhros, Mílos, Sífnos and Pireás.

Haniá 1 or 2 ferries daily to Pireás (12hr).

Hóra Stakíon 5 ferries daily to Loutró/Ayía Rouméli; 3 weekly to Gávdhos in season.

Iráklion 2 ferries daily to Pireás (12hr); 3 ferries weekly to Thessaloníki; at least one daily ferry to Thíra (4hr), also fast boats and hydrofoils (2hr 30min); daily ferries to Páros in season; most days to Míkonos and Íos; at least twice weekly to Náxos, Tínos, Skíros, Skíathos, Kárpathos and Rhodes. Ferries to Ancona (Italy) twice weekly and Çeşme (Turkey) weekly and weekly to Limassol (Cyprus) and Haifa (Israel).

Kastélli (Kíssamos) 1–3 ferries weekly to Kíthira, Yíthio (8hr), Monemvassía and Pireás.

Paleohóra 3 boats a week in season to Gávdhos. Also daily sailings to Elafonísi and Soúyia.

Réthimnon 3 ferries a week to Pireás (12hr); weekly service and seasonal day trips to Thíra.

Buses

Áyios Nikólaos–Sitía (7 daily 6.30am–8pm; 2hr).

Haniá–Réthimnon–Iráklion (30 daily 5.30am–9.30pm; 3hr total).

Haniá–Hóra Sfakíon (4 daily 8.30am–3.30pm; 2hr).

Haniá–Paleohóra (5 daily 8.30am–5pm; 2hr).

Iráklion–Áyios Nikólaos (27 daily 6.30am–7.30pm; 1hr 30min).

Iráklion–Ierápetra (7 daily 7.30am–6.30pm; 2hr 30min).

Iráklion–Ayía Galíni (7 daily 6.30am–4.15pm; 2hr 15min).

Iráklion–Festós (9 daily 7.30am–5.30pm; 1hr 30min).

Kastélli–Haniá (15 daily 5am–7.30pm; 1hr 30min).

Réthimnon–Spíli–Ayía Galíni (7 daily 6.30am–5pm; 45min/1hr 30min).

Flights

Haniá Several flights a day to Athens, one weekly to Thessaloníki.

Iráklion Many daily flights to Athens; 4 weekly to Rhodes, 2 weekly to Míkonos, and 3 weekly to Thessaloníki.

CHAPTER NINE

DODECANESE

The most distant of the Greek islands, the **Dodecanese** (*Dhodhekánisos*) lie close to the Turkish coast – some, like Kós and Kastellórizo, almost within hailing distance of the shore. Because of this position, and their remoteness from Athens, the islands have had a turbulent history: they were the scene of ferocious battles between German and British forces in 1943–44, and were only finally included in the modern Greek state in 1948 after centuries of occupation by Crusaders, Turks and Italians. Even now the threat (real or imagined) of invasion from Turkey is very much in evidence. When you ask about the heavy military presence, locals talk in terms of "*when* the Turks come", rarely "*if* . . .".

Whatever the rigours of the occupations, their legacy includes a wonderful blend of architectural styles and of eastern and western cultures. Medieval Rhodes is the most famous, but almost every island has its Classical remains, its Crusaders' castle, its traditional villages, and abundant grandiose public buildings. For these last the Italians, who occupied the islands from 1912 to 1943, are mainly responsible. In their determination to beautify the islands and turn them into a showplace for fascism they undertook public works, excavations and reconstruction on a massive scale; and if historical accuracy was sometimes sacrificed in the interests of style, only the expert is likely to complain. A more sinister aspect of the Italian administration was the attempted forcible Latinization of the populace: spoken Greek and Orthodox observance were banned in public from 1920 to 1943. The most tangible reminder of this policy is the great number of older people whose preferred language is Italian rather than Greek.

Aside from this frequently encountered bilingualism, the Dodecanese themselves display a marked topographic and economic schizophrenia. The dry limestone outcrops of **Kastellórizo**, **Sími**, **Hálki**, **Kássos** and **Kálimnos** have always been forced to rely on the sea for their livelihoods, and the wealth generated by the maritime culture – especially in the nineteenth century – fostered the growth of attractive port towns. The sprawling, relatively fertile giants, **Rhodes** (Ródhos) and **Kós**, have recently seen their traditional agricultural economies almost totally displaced by a tourist industry attracted by good beaches and nightlife, as well as the Aegean's most exciting ensembles of historical monuments. **Kárpathos** lies somewhere in between, with a (formerly) forested north grafted on to a rocky limestone south; **Tílos**, despite its lack of trees, has ample water, though the green volcano-island of **Níssiros** does not. **Léros** shelters softer contours and more amenable terrain than its map outline would suggest, while **Pátmos** and **Astipálea** at the fringes of the archipelago boast architecture and landscapes more appropriate to the Cyclades.

The largest islands in the group are connected almost daily with each other, and none (except for Astipálea) is hard to reach. Rhodes is the main transport hub, with services to Turkey, Israel, Cyprus and (very sporadically) Egypt, as well as connections with Crete, the northeastern islands, the Cyclades and mainland. Kálimnos is an important secondary terminus, with useful ferry and hydrofoil services.

Kássos

Barren and depopulated since an 1824 Ottoman massacre and subsequent emigration, **Kássos** attracts few visitors despite being a regular port of call for the ferries. What is

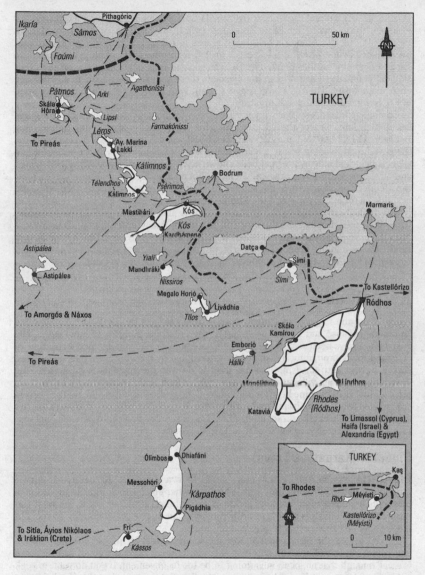

left of the population is grouped together in five villages in the north, under the shadow of Kárpathos, leaving most of the island accessible only to those on foot. There's little sign here of the wealth brought into other islands by emigrant workers, nor, since the island has little to offer them, by tourists; the crumbling houses which line the village streets and the disused terraces covering the land poignantly recall better days.

It's just ten minutes' walk from the port at Emborió to **FRÍ**, the capital; indeed the furthest village, **PÓLIO**, is only 3km away. There are two **hotels** in Frí, the *Anagenissis*

(☎0245/41 323; ④) and the *Anessis* (☎0245/41 201; ③) and in summer a few rooms, for example, those owned by Elias Koutlakis (☎0245/41 303; ②) or Katerina Markou (☎0245/41 613; ②). Among a half-dozen places to **eat** in Frí, *Kassos* is good for basic oven dishes, while *Milos* specializes in grilled fish; otherwise, fresh produce can be hard to come by on the island. The **beach**, such as it is, is at Ammoúa, on the other side of the underused airstrip; in high season, there are excursion boats to a better one on Armathiá islet. There's a large **cave** (Seláï), with impressive stalactites, southwest of Frí, beyond the hamlet of Kathístres.

Continuing inland, especially if you're seeking isolation, is more rewarding; the single **bus** which links five of the villages will give you a head start in your wanderings. Between **AYÍA MARÍNA** and **ARVANITOHÓRI**, the dirt track across the island leaves the paved road heading south. Civilization is soon left behind as you are wrapped in a silence disturbed only by the goat bells and an occasional wheeling hawk; smallholdings and olive groves are still sporadically tended, but no one stays long. After about an hour the Mediterranean appears to the south of the island, an expanse of water ruffled by the odd ship en route to Cyprus and the Middle East.

The higher fork leads to the mountain chapel and monastery of **Áyios Yióryios**, while the other drops gradually down to the coast, finally emerging at **Helathrós**, a beautiful cove at the end of a cultivated but uninhabited valley. The beach is small and sandy, the swimming great after the rigours of the walk, and seabirds of every kind circle the cliffs. With plenty of supplies, it could be a great place to camp.

Kárpathos

Alone of the the major Dodecanese, **Kárpathos** was held by the Venetians after the Byzantine collapse and so has no castle of the crusading Knights of Saint John. The island has always been something of a backwater and, despite a magnificent coastline of cliffs and rocky promontories constantly interrupted by little beaches, has succumbed surprisingly little to tourism. This has a lot to do with the appalling road system, the dearth of interesting villages and the high cost of food, which offsets reasonable room prices. Most visitors come here for a glimpse of the traditional village life that prevails in the isolated north of the island and for the superb, secluded beaches. Although there's an airport which can take direct international flights, only a few charters use it, and visitors are concentrated in a couple of resorts in the south.

Pigádhia (Kárpathos Town)

PIGÁDHIA, the capital, is now more often known simply as Kárpathos. It curves around one side of Vróndis Bay, with a harbour where boats dock right in the heart of town, while a three-kilometre-long sickle of sandy beach stretches out to the west and north. The place itself is almost entirely modern, and there's really nothing to see, but it does offer just about every facility you might need.

As you get off the ferry you'll almost inevitably be met by people offering **rooms**, and you might as well take up an offer – standards seem generally good, and the town is small enough that no location is going to be too inconvenient. If you do want to seek out somewhere yourself, walk into town and follow the signs up past the *Hotel Coral* to *Anna's Rooms* (☎0245/22 313; ②) or the *Artemis Pension* (②), both good value and very well positioned. Nearby *Vittoroulis Furnished Apartments* (☎0245/22 639; ③) are available only on a weekly basis, but worth it if you are staying that long. Other, simpler rooms establishments include *Sofia's* (☎0245/22 154; ②), *Konaki* (☎0245/22 908; ②), on the upper through-road west of the town hall, and the *Filoxenia* (☎0245/22 623; ②). Hotels include the *Avra* (☎0245/22 388; ②) and the more comfortable *Karpathos*

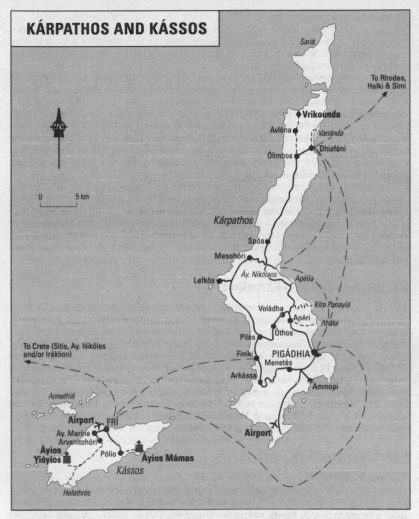

KÁRPATHOS AND KÁSSOS

Sariá

To Rhodes,
Halki & Simi

◆ **Vrikoúnda**

Avlóna ● Vanánda

Ólimbos ● Dhiafáni

0   5 km

Kárpathos

Spóa

Mesohóri

Lefkós   *Áy. Nikólaos*   Apélla

Kíra Panayiá

Voládha   Apéri

Ahata

Píles   Óthos

Finíki   **PIGÁDHIA**

To Crete (Sitía, Ay. Nikólas   Menetés
and/or Iráklion)

Arkássa

Ammopi

Armathiá

Airport FRÍ

Ay. Marina
Arvanitohóri

Áyios   Pólio   **Áyios Mámas**
Yióyios

Kássos   **Airport**

Helathrós

(☎0245/22 347; ③). More expensive places are generally further out and tend to be occupied by package groups as far as the ruined fifth-century basilica of **Ayía Fotiní** – though development is gradually spreading beyond here; *Toh Limanaki* taverna, at the southern end, is good but opens only at lunchtime.

Most of the waterfront **tavernas** are much of an expensive muchness, with some notable exceptions: the *Psistaria Olympia* is good for meat-lovers, while fish aficionados should head for *Iy Kali Kardhia*, at the north end on the way to the beach. Places inland tend to work out less expensive: try *Mike's*, inland up a pedestrian way from the stylish *Kafenio Cafe*, for friendly service. Live **music** can be heard nightly at *Kafenio Halkia*, in one of the few surviving old buildings next to the church on Apodhímon Karpathíon; the limited menu of supper dishes seems to be a secondary consideration.

Services and transport

There's an **OTE** office (Mon–Sat 7.30am–3.10pm, Sun 9am–2pm) on Platía Pémptis Oktovríou at the west end of Apodhímon Karpathíon; the *Olympic* office is right by this; and the **post office** is directly south, on Ikosiogdhóïs Oktovríou, the main inland street running parallel to Apodhímon Kapathíon.

If you want to get out and explore the island there are four **buses** a day to Pilés, via Apéri, Voládha and Óthos, four to Ammopí, and one or two to Arkássa and Fíniki. **Taxis** aren't too expensive to get to these villages on the paved roads, but can charge a fortune to go anywhere further afield. Places up by the post office like *Holiday* (☎0245/22 813) or *Circle* (☎0245/22 690) rent **cars**, while *Hermes* (☎0245/22 090) does **bike rental** and repairs. Be warned that the only fuel on the island is to be found just to the north and south of town, and the tanks on the small bikes are barely big enough to complete a circuit of the south, let alone head up north; the latter is expressly forbidden by most outfits, in any case.

The north is better explored by boat or on a **tour**: *Olympos Travel* (☎0245/22 993), on the front near the port, offers very good deals on all-in trips (from around 4500dr to Ólimbos), though the rival boat (*Chrisovalandou Lines*; pay on board for best deals) is much more attractive. *Olympos* and other agents can also offer trips to Kássos and to isolated east coast beaches. Less well-publicized is the fact that you can use these boats to travel one-way between the north and the south, paying about one-third of the going rate for day trips.

Southern and central Kárpathos

The flat southern extremity of Kárpathos, towards the airport, is extraordinarily desolate – its natural barenness has been exacerbated by fires. There are a couple of empty, sandy beaches, but they're not at all attractive and are exposed to any wind that may be blowing. The nicest beach here is the tiny cove by the *Hotel Poseidon*, which has some shelter. You're better off in this direction going no further than **AMMOPÍ**, just 7km from Pigádhia. This, together with the recent development at Arkássa (see below), is the closest thing on Kárpathos to a developed beach resort: two sandy coves serviced by a couple of tavernas and a few rooms places. It's scattered and not exactly pretty, but as yet is far from overwhelming. Heading across the island, there's a steep climb up to **MENETÉS**, a lovely village on the ridge of the hills with handsome old hilltop houses, a tiny folklore museum and a spectacularly sited church. There's a good taverna here, *Manolis*, and a memorial with views back to the east.

The west coast

Beyond Menetés, you immediately start to descend to **ARKÁSSA** on the west coast, with excellent views across to Kássos as you come down. Arkássa has recently been heavily developed, with hotels and restaurants dotted along a rocky coast and beaches both south past the headland and north at Fíniki, neither a very long walk; most places are aimed squarely at the package market, but you could try *Rooms Irini* (☎0245/61 263; ②). Signs point along a cement road to Ayía Sofía, just five minutes' walk, where you can see a whitewashed chapel. Around this are various remains of **ancient and Byzantine Arkessia**, above all several mosaic floors with geometric patterns. Some are part-buried, including one running diagonally under the floor of a half-buried chapel, emerging from the walls on either side. Various bits of marble, broken statuary and columns are propped up in and around this chapel.

The tiny fishing port of **FINÍKI**, just a couple of kilometres away, boasts a small beach, three or four tavernas, and several rooms establishments lining the road to the jetty; *Fay's Paradise* (☎0245/61 308; ②) is noted for the squid and stuffed cabbage in the attached taverna. The continuation of the road up the west coast isn't too bad, and it's gradually being improved as the tarmac encroaches round the southern half of the island, currently running out halfway to the attractive resort of **LEFKÓS** (Paraliá Lefkoú). Although this is a delightful place for flopping on the beach, it necessitates some advance planning: there are only three buses weekly, no vehicle rental, and Lefkós marks the furthest point you can reach from Pighádhia on a small motorbike and return safely before running out of gas. Your efforts will be rewarded by striking topography of cliffs, hills, islets and sandspits surrounding a triple bay. The *Sunlight Restaurant* has garnered an enviable tamarisk-shaded position on the southern cove, and several **rooms** places (no phones; ③) dot the promontory overlooking the two more northerly and progressively wilder bays.

Back on the main road, you climb higher to **MESOHÓRI** through one of the few sections of pine forest not scarred by fire. The village tumbles down towards the sea around narrow, stepped alleys; the road ends at the top of town, where a snack bar represents the only tourist facility of any sort. Alternatively, you can carry on to Spóa, overlooking the east coast.

The centre and the east coast

The centre of Kárpathos supports a quartet of villages – **APÉRI, VOLÁDHA, ÓTHOS** and **PILÉS** – blessed with superb hillside settings and ample running water. In these settlements nearly everyone has "done time" in North America, then returned home with their nest eggs: New Jersey, New York and Canadian car plates tell you exactly where repatriated islanders struck it rich. From Apéri, the largest and wealthiest of them, you can bike 7km along a very rough road to the dramatic and isolated pebble beach of **Aháta**, with a spring but no other facilities. Óthos is almost at the highest point of the island and is dwarfed by a huge wind generator up above it, while Pilés is perhaps the prettiest of these villages, with great views to the west.

Beyond Apéri, the road up the **east coast** is extremely rough in places, but a beautiful drive, passing above beaches most easily accessible by boat trips from Pigádhia. **Kíra Panayiá** is the first encountered, via a rutted side road; there's a surprising number of villas, rooms and tavernas in the ravine behind the 150m of fine gravel and turquoise water. **Apélla** is the best of the beaches you can – just about – reach by road, but has no amenities. The end of this route is **SPÓA**, high above the shore, where the road stops by a snack bar at the edge of the village; there's also a good traditional *kafenío* a short way down. **Áyios Nikólaos**, 5km below, is an excellent beach with tavernas, and an ancient basilica to explore.

Northern Kárpathos

Although connected by road with Spóa, much the easiest way to get to northern Kárpathos is by boat – inter-island ferries call at Dhiafáni once a week or there are smaller tour boats from Pigádhia daily. These take a couple of hours, and are met at Dhiafáni by buses to take you up to Ólimbos, the traditional village that is the main attraction of this part of the island.

High in the mountains, **ÓLIMBOS** straddles two small peaks, the ridges above studded by windmills, a couple of them still operational though most are now ruined. Although the road and electricity, together with a growing number of tourists, are dragging the place into the twentieth century, it hasn't fully arrived yet. The women here are immediately striking in their magnificent **traditional dress** and after a while you notice that they also dominate the village: working in the gardens, carrying goods on their shoulders, or tending the mountain sheep. Nearly all Ólimbos men emigrate or work outside the village, sending money home and returning only on holidays. The long-isolated villagers also speak a unique dialect, said to maintain traces of its Doric and Phrygian origins. Traditional music is still heard regularly and draws crowds of visitors at festival times.

The number of day trippers is increasingly changing the atmosphere here; it's still a very picturesque place, full of photo oportunities, but the traditions are dying fast (or at least they're hard to find in season). On the whole, it's only the older women and those who work in tourist shops who wear traditional dress nowadays and during the day you'll almost certainly see more visitors than locals. This might be a good reason to stay, either as an organized excursion or in one of an increasing number of **rooms** places: the *Ólimbos* (☎0245/51 252; ②), near the village entrance, is a good bare-bones option, while *Hotel Aphrodite* (☎0245/51 307; ②) offers both en suite facilities and a southerly ocean view. There are also plenty of places to **eat** – *Parthenonas*, on the square by the church, is excellent; try their *makaroúnes*, a local dish of homemade pasta with onions and cheese.

From the village, the west coast and tiny port and beach at **Frísses** are a dizzy drop below, or there are various walks up into the mountains. It's also possible to walk between Ólimbos and Spóa or Messohóri in the south, a six-to-seven hour trek made less scenic by the aftermath of fires. Perhaps the most attractive option, however, and certainly the easiest, is to walk back down a ravine through extensive unburnt forest to Dhiafáni. A small stream trickles alongside most of the way, and there is a spring; at your approach, snakes slither into hiding and partridges break cover. The hike takes around 90 minutes downhill – too long to accomplish in the standard three or four hours allowed on day trips if you want to explore Ólimbos as well. By staying overnight in Ólimbos, you could also tackle the trail north to the Byzantine ruins at **Vrikoúnda**, via Avlóna hamlet; Ólimbos was originally founded as a refuge from pirates that plagued the coast here.

Dhiafáni

Although its popularity is growing – and will do so exponentially on completion of the new dock – rooms in **DHIAFÁNI** are still inexpensive, and life slow. There's plenty of places at which to stay and eat, shops that will change money and even a small travel agency. Try the garrulously friendly *Pansion Delfini* (0245/51 391; ②) or *Pansion Glaros* (0245/51 259; ②; high season only), up on the southern hillside. Back on the front, the favourite taverna is *Anatoli*, easily recognizable by the folk reliefs that sprout from its roof.

There are boat trips to various nearby beaches – as well as to the uninhabited islet of **Sariá** or through the narrow strait to Trístomo anchorage and the ruins of Vrikoúnda (see above) – or there are several in walking distance. Closest is **Vanánda**, a stoney beach with an eccentric campsite snack bar in the spring-fed oasis behind. To get there, follow the pleasant signposted path north through the pines, but don't believe the signs that say ten minutes – it's over half an hour away.

Rhodes (Ródhos)

It's no accident that **Rhodes** is among the most-visited Greek islands. Not only is its east coast lined with numerous sandy beaches, but the kernel of the capital is a beautiful and remarkably preserved medieval city, the legacy of the crusading Knights of Saint John who used the island as their main base from 1309 until 1522. Unfortunately this showpiece is jammed to capacity with up to 50,000 tourists a day, ten months of the year. The island revels in cheap drink (extended duty-free status was one of the conditions of Dodecanese incorporation into Greece in 1948), and can seem swamped, particularly in August as *smörgåsbord*, fish fingers and pizza jostle alongside *moussaká* on menus.

Blessed with an equable climate and strategic position, Rhodes was important from earliest times despite a lack of many good harbours. The best natural port spawned the ancient town of Lindos which, together with the other city states, Kameiros and Ialyssos, united in 408 BC to found the new capital of Rhodes at the northern tip of the island. The cities had always allied themselves promiscuously with Alexander, Persians, Athenians or Spartans as prevailing conditions suited them, generally escaping retribution for backing the wrong side by a combination of seafaring, audacity, sycophancy and its burgeoning wealth as a trade centre. Following the failed siege of Demetrius Polyorkites in 305 BC, Rhodes prospered even more, displacing Athens as the major venue for rhetoric and the arts in the east Mediterranean. The town, underneath virtually all of the modern city, was laid out by one Hippodamus in the grid layout much in vogue at the time, with planned residential and commercial quarters.

Decline set in when Rhodes became involved in the Roman civil wars, and Cassius sacked the town; by late imperial times, it was a backwater, a status confirmed by numerous Barbarian raids during the Byzantine period. The Byzantines were compelled to cede the island to the Genoese, who in turn handed it over to the Knights of St John. The second great siege of Rhodes, during 1522-23, saw Ottoman sultan Süleyman the Magnificent oust the stubborn knights, who departed for Malta; the town once again lapsed into relative obscurity, though heavily colonized and garrisoned, until the Italian seizure of 1912.

Ródhos Town

RÓDHOS TOWN divides into two unequal parts: the compact old walled city, and the amorphous new town which sprawls around it in three directions. Throughout, the tourist is king. In the **modern district**, especially the part west of Mandhráki yacht harbour, the few buildings which aren't hotels are souvenir shops, car rental or travel agencies and bars – easily a hundred in every category. Around this to the north and west stretches the **town beach** (standing room only for latecomers), complete with deckchairs, parasols and showers. At the northernmost point of the island an art deco combined **aquarium** and **museum** (daily 9am–9pm; 400dr) with apparently rotting stuffed fish and an extraordinary collection of grotesque freaks of nature (a Cyclopean goat, an eight-legged calf, etc) offer some distraction.

Simply to catalogue the principal monuments and attractions cannot do full justice to the infinitely more rewarding **medieval city**. There's an enormous amount of pleasure to be had merely in slipping through the nine surviving gates and strolling the streets, under flying archways built for earthquake resistance, past the warm-toned sandstone and lava walls splashed with ochre and blue paint, and over the *hokhláki* (pebble) pavement, the little stones arranged into mosaics in certain courtyards.

First thing to meet the eye, and dominating the northeast sector of the city's originally fourteenth-century fortifications, is the **Palace of the Grand Masters** (Tues–Sat 8am–6pm, Sun 8.30am–3pm; 800dr, includes medieval exhibit). Destroyed by an ammunition depot explosion in 1856, it was reconstructed by the Italians as a summer home for Mussolini and Victor Emmanuel III ("King of Italy and Albania, Emperor of Ethiopia"), neither of whom used it much. The exterior is as authentic as possible, but inside things are on an altogether grander scale: a marble staircase leads up to rooms paved with Hellenistic mosaics from Kós, and the movable furnishings rival many a northern European palace. The ground floor is home to the splendid **Medieval Exhibit** (Tues–Sat 8am–2.30pm), whose collection highlights the importance of Christian Rhodes as a trade centre. The Knights are represented with a display on their sugar-refining industry and a gravestone of a Grand Master; precious manuscripts and books precede a wing of post-Byzantine icons, moved here permanently from Panayía Kástrou (see below). On Tuesday and Saturday afternoons, there's a supplementary tour of the

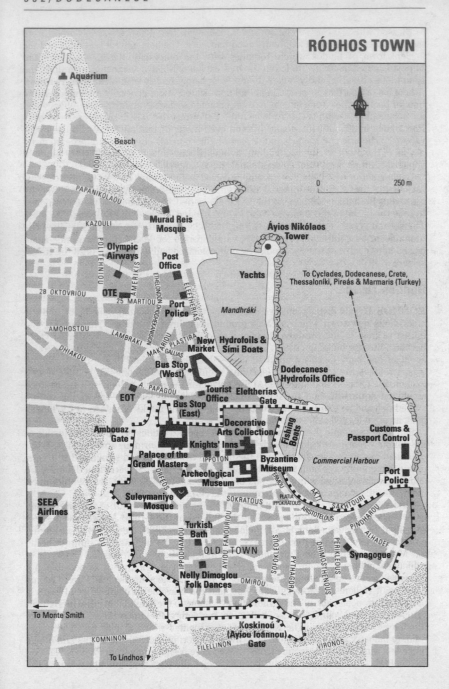

RÓDHOS TOWN

Aquarium

Beach

PAPANIKOLAOU

KAZOULI

Murad Reis Mosque

Áyios Nikólaos Tower

Olympic Airways

POLITEHNIOU

AMERIKIS

ETHELONDON DHODHEKANISIOU

Post Office

Yachts

To Cyclades, Dodecanese, Crete, Thessaloníki, Pireás & Marmaris (Turkey)

28 OKTOVRIOU

OTE

25 MARTIOU

Port Police

ELEFTHERIAS

Mandhráki

AMOHOSTOU

LAMBRAKI

DHIAKOU

MAKARIOU

PLASTIRA

GALLIAS

New Market

Hydrofoils & Sími Boats

Bus Stop (West)

A. PAPAGOU

Dodecanese Hydrofoils Office

EOT

Tourist Office

Eleftherías Gate

Bus Stop (East)

Decorative Arts Collection

Ambouaz Gate

Knights' Inns

Fishing Boats

Customs & Passport Control

Palace of the Grand Masters

IPPOTON

Byzantine Museum

Commercial Harbour

OREOS

Archeological Museum

ERMOU

PLATIA IPPOKRATOUS

AKTI

Port Police

SEEA Airlines

RIGA FEREOU

Suleymaniye Mosque

SOKRATOUS

ARISTOTELOUS

SAKHTOURI

PINOHAROU

IPPODHAMOU

Turkish Bath

AYIOU FANOURIOU

OLD TOWN

SOFOKLEOUS

PYTHAGORA

PYTHAGORA

DHIMOSTHENOUS

PERIKLEOUS

ALHADEF

Synagogue

Nelly Dimoglou Folk Dances

OMIROU

To Monte Smith

KOMNINON

Koskinoú (Ayíou Ioánnou) Gate

FILELLINON

VIRONOS

To Líndhos

0   250 m

city walls (one hour, starting 2.45–3pm), beginning from a gate next to the palace – the only permitted access, incidentally.

The heavily restored **Street of the Knights** (Odhós Ippotón) leads due east from the Platía Kleovoúlou in front of the Palace; the "Inns" lining it housed the Knights of St John, according to linguistic and ethnic affiliation, until the Ottoman Turks compelled them to leave for Malta after a six-month siege in which the defenders were outnumbered thirty to one. Today the Inns house various government offices and cultural institutions vaguely appropriate to their past, but the whole effect of the renovation is predictably sterile and stagey (indeed, nearby streets were used in the filming of *Pascali's Island*).

At the bottom of the grade, the Knights' Hospital has been refurbished as the **Archeological Museum** (Tues–Sat 8.30am–6pm, Sun 8.30am–3pm; 600dr), though the arches and echoing halls of the building somewhat overshadow the contents – largely painted pottery dating from the sixth and seventh centuries. Behind the secondstorey sculpture garden, the Hellenistic statue gallery is more accessible: in a rear corner stands the so-called "Marine Venus", beloved of Lawrence Durrell, but lent a rather sinister aspect by her sea-dissolved face – in contrast to the friendlier *Aphrodite Bathing*. Virtually next door is the **Decorative Arts Collection** (Tues–Sun 8.30am–3pm; 400dr), gleaned from old houses across the Dodecanese; the most compelling artefacts are carved cupboard doors and chest lids painted with mythological or historical episodes in naïve style.

Across the way stands the **Byzantine Museum** (Tues–Sun 8.30am–3pm; 400dr), housed in the old cathedral of the Knights, who adapted the Byzantine shrine of Panayía Kástrou for their own needs. Medieval icons and frescoes lifted from crumbling chapels on Rhodes and Hálki, as well as photos of art still in situ, constitute the exhibits; it's worth a visit since most of the Byzantine churches in the old town and outlying villages are locked, although the collection has been severely depleted by transfers of the best items to the Palace of the Grand Masters.

If you leave the Palace of the Grand Masters going straight south, it's hard to miss the most conspicuous Turkish monument in Rhodes, the candy-striped **Süleymaniye mosque**, rebuilt in the nineteenth century on foundations 300 years older. The old town is in fact well sown with mosques and *mescids* (the Islamic equivalent of a chapel), many of them converted from Byzantine shrines after the 1522 conquest, when the Christians were expelled from the medieval precinct and founded new quarters outside. A couple of these mosques are still used by the sizeable **Turkish-speaking minority** here, some of them descended from Muslims who fled Crete between 1913 and 1923. Their most enduring civic contribution is the imposing **hamam** or Turkish bath on Platía Ariónos up in the southwest corner of the medieval city, although sadly this is shut indefinitely.

Heading downhill and east from the Süleymaniye mosque, **Odhós Sokrátous**, once the heart of the Ottoman bazaar, is now the "Via Turista", packed with fur and jewellery stores and milling tourists. Beyond the fountain in Platía Ippokrátous, Odhós Aristotélous leads into the Platía ton Evreón Martirón (Square of the Jewish Martyrs), renamed in memory of the large local community that was almost totally annihilated in early 1944. You can visit the ornate **synagogue** on Odhós Simíou just to the south, maintained essentially as a memorial to the 2000 Jews of Rhodes and Kos sent from here to the deathcamps.

About a kilometre southwest of the new town, overlooking the west-coast road, the sparse remains of **Hellenistic Rhodes** – a restored theatre and stadium, plus a few columns of an Apollo temple – perch atop Monte Smith, the hill of Áyios Stéfanos renamed after a British admiral who used it as a watchpoint during the Napoleonic wars. The wooded site is popular with joggers and strollers, but for summer shade and greenery the best spot is the **Rodini park**, nearly two kilometres south of town on the road to Lindos. On August evenings a wine tasting festival is held here by the municipal authorities.

Arrival, orientation and information

All international and inter-island **ferries** dock at the middle of Rhodes' three ports, the commercial harbour; the only exceptions are local **boats** to and from Sími, and the **hydrofoils**, which use the yacht harbour of Mandhráki. Its entrance was supposedly once straddled by the Colossus, an ancient statue of Apollo built to celebrate the end of the 305 BC siege; today two columns surmounted by bronze deer are less overpowering replacements.

The **airport** is 17km southwest of town, near the village of Paradhíssi; public urban buses make the trip just six times daily. Those arriving at an unsociable time of day on a charter may find that the night taxi fare into town is barely any less than the cost of hiring a car for a day at the airport counter.

Orange-and-white *KTEL* **buses** for both the west and east coasts of Rhodes leave from two almost adjacent terminals on Odhós Papágou, within sight of the so-called New Market (a tourist trap). Between the lower eastern station and the **taxi** rank at Platía Rimínis there's a helpful **municipal tourist office** (Mon–Fri 8am–7pm, Sat 8am–6pm), while some way up Papágou on the corner of Makaríou is the **EOT office** (Mon–Fri 7.30am–3pm); both dispense bus and ferry schedules plus information sheets on archeological site times and admissions.

Accommodation

Inexpensive pensions abound in the old town, contained almost entirely in the quad bounded by Odhós Omírou to the south, Sokrátous to the north, Perikléous to the east and Ippodhámou to the west. Even in peak season, lodging is the one thing in Rhodes that's still reasonably priced. At crowded times, or late at night, it's prudent to accept the offers of proprietors meeting the ferries and change base next day if necessary.

Andreas, Omírou 28D (☎0241/34 156). Perennially popular, this hotel is the best, most imaginative of the old-house restorations. All rooms have sinks, and there is a terrace bar with a view, and French and English is spoken. ③.

Apollo, Omírou 28C (☎0241/35 064). Basic but clean and friendly rooms place. Self-catering kitchen makes this good for longer stays. ②.

Casa de la Sera, Thisséos 38 (☎0241/75 154). Another Jewish-quarter renovation, with wonderful floor tiles in the en suite rooms and a breakfast bar. ④.

Kastro, Platía Ariónos (☎0241/20 446). Vassilis the proprietor is a famous eccentric artist renowned for his royalist leanings, but the hotel is fine for budget rooms; expect some noise from nearby restaurants. ②.

Iliana, Gavála 1 (☎0241/30 251). This former Jewish mansion exudes a Victorian boarding-house atmosphere, but is clean and quiet enough with private facilities. ③.

Minos, Omírou 5 (☎0241/31 813). Modern and hence a bit sterile, but with great views, this pension is managed by an English-speaking family. ③.

S. Nikolis, Ippodhámou 61 (☎0241/34 561). A range of establishments at the top of the old town. Hotel rates (⑤) include a huge breakfast, or there's the option of self-catering apartments, a simple pension (③) or a youth hostel (①). Booking essential for hotel and apartments, but accepted only with credit-card number.

Eating and drinking

Eating well for a reasonable price is a challenge, but not an insurmountable one. As a general rule, the further back from Sokrátous you go, the better value you'll find.

Aigaion, corner Eskhílou and Aristofánous. Run by a welcoming Kalymniot family, this *ouzeri* features brown bread and curiosities such as *foúski* (soft-shell oyster).

Le Bistrot, Omírou 22–24. Open for lunch and supper daily except Sun, this is a genuine French-run bistro with excellent if pricey food. Always full, with a loyal expatriate clientele.

Mikis, in alley behind Sokrátous 17. Very inexpensive hole-in-the-wall place, serving only fish, salads and wine.

Nireas, Platía Sofkléous 22. Another good, family-run Greek *ouzeri*; reservations advised in the evenings.

O Meraklis, Aristotélous 32. This *pátsas* (tripe-and-trotter soup) kitchen is only open 3–7am for a clientele of post-club lads, Turkish stallholders, night-club singers and travellers just stumbled off an overnight ferry. Great free entertainment, and the soup's good, too.

O Yiannis, in Koskinoú village. *Mézedhes* and wine here works out very reasonably for a group; you can get the last bus out here, but will have to take a taxi back.

Palia Istoria, Mitropóleos 108, corner of Dhendhrínou, in south extension of new town, Álmoss district. Reckoned to be the best *ouzeri* on Rhodes, but very expensive.

Sea Star, Platía Sofokléous. The Nireas' rival, with seafood offered by a colourful proprietor.

Yiannis, Apéllou 41, below *Hotel Sydney*. Fair portions of Greek oven food, dished out by a family long resident in New York.

Nightlife

Except for some low-key pubs around Platía Dhorléus, such as *Mungo Dar*, Rhodes old town is tomb-silent at night. Most of the action is in the new town, particularly along Dhiákou. Theme night and various drinks-with-cover gimmicks predominate; for sheer tackiness none can match *Tropical Oasis* near the EOT, where loud music videos, a "Dancing Waters" show and several bars with exorbitant prices surround a pool to which admission is allegedly free. More sedate are the **folk dances** (Mon–Fri at 9.20pm, April–Oct; 2500dr, students 1250dr) presented by the *Nelly Dimoglou Company*, performed in the gardens of Andhroníkou, near Platía Ariónos. There are also three cinemas: the *Rodou* in Makaríou 45, the *Dhimotikou* in Efstathiádhi and the *Esperia* on Ikostipémptis Martíou, all in the new town.

Listings

Airlines *British Airways*, Platía Kíprou 1 (☎0241/27 756); *KLM*, Ammohóstou 3 (☎0241/21 010); *Olympic*, Iérou Lóhou 9 (☎0241/24 571); *SEEA*, Pávlou Melá 17 (☎0241/21 998). Scheduled flights are exorbitant; there's a very faint chance of picking up an unclaimed return charter seat to northern Europe – ask at the various group tour offices.

Bike rental Mopeds will make little impact on Rhodes' huge area, and gain you scant respect from motorists. Sturdier Yamaha 125s, suitable for two persons, go for as little as 3500dr a day. There are plenty of outlets, especially around Odhós Dhiákou.

Bookstores *Academy*, Iónos Dhragoúmi 7, *Moses Cohen*, Thevréli 83D, both in the new town.

Car rental Prices are the island standard of £33/US$50 per day, but can be bargained down to about £27/US$40 a day, all-in, out of season. Among the more flexible local outfits are *Holiday Autos*, Yioryíou Leónidos 38 (☎0241/74 532), *Orion*, next door at no. 36 (☎0241/22 137); *MBC*, Ikostipémptis Martíou 29 (☎0241/28 617) and *Kosmos*, Papaloúka 31 (☎0241/74 374).

Exchange Most bank branches are in the new town, keeping weekday evening and Saturday morning hours; at other times use the ATMs of the *Commercial Bank*, *Credit Bank*, *Ionian Bank* (with a useful branch in the old town), or *National Bank*.

Ferries Tourist office handouts list the bewildering array of representatives for the seven boat and two hydrofoil companies which operate here. A recommended general travel agency in the old town is *Castellania*, Evripídhou 1–3, corner Platía Ippokrátous; schedule information is available at the *limenarheio*, on Mandhráki esplanade near the post office.

Phones At the corner of Amerikís and Ikostipémptis Martíou in the new town, open daily 6am–11pm. Many of the booths offer long-distance phone service, but beware of possible surcharges on the basic OTE rates.

Post office Main branch with ougoing mail, poste restante and exchange windows on Mandhráki harbour, open Mon–Fri 7.30am–8pm; mobile office on Órfeos in the old town, open shorter hours.

The east coast

Heading down the coast from the capital you have to go some way before you escape the crowds from local beach hotels, their numbers swelled by visitors using the regular buses from town or on boat tours out of Mandhráki. Nostalgia buffs might look in at the decayed, all-but-abandoned spa of **Thérmes Kallithéas**, dating from the Italian period. Located 3km south of Kallithéa resort proper, down an unsigned road through pines, the spa is set in a palm grove and is illuminated at night to create a hugely enjoyable spectacle of mock-orientalia. The former fishing village of **FALIRÁKI**, which draws a youngish package clientele, is all too much in the mode of a Spanish *costa* resort, while the scenery just inland – arid, scrubby sand-hills at the best of times – has been made that much more dreary by fire damage that stretches way beyond Líndhos. **TSAMBÍKAS**, 26km south of town, is the first place at which most will seriously consider stopping. Actually the very eroded flank of a much larger extinct volcano, the hill has a monastery at the summit offering unrivalled views along some 50km of coastline. A steep, 1500-metre-long cement drive leads to a small car park and a snack bar, from which concrete steps lead to the summit. The monastery here is unremarkable except for the happier consequences of the September 8 festival: childless women climb up – sometimes on their knees – to be relieved of their barrenness, and any children born afterwards are dedicated to the Virgin with the names Tsambikos or Tsambika, names particular to the Dodecanese.

From the top you can survey **KOLÍMBIA** just to the north, once an unspoiled beach stretching south from a tiny cove ringed with volcanic rocks but now backed by a dozen, scattered low-rise hotels. Shallow **Tsambíkas bay** on the south side of the headland warms up early in the spring, and the excellent beach, though protected by the forest service from development other than a couple of tavernas, teems with people all summer. If it's too much, you can walk further south over another cape to the relatively deserted bay of **Stégna**. This, however, gets a fair bit of traffic from the many tourists staying in **ARHÁNGELOS**, a large village just inland overlooked by a crumbling castle and home to a dwindling leather crafts industry. Though you can disappear into the warren of alleys between the main road and the citadel, the place is now firmly caught up in package tourism, with a full complement of banks, tavernas, mini-marts and jewellery stores. A more peaceful overnight base on this stretch of coast would be **HARÁKI**, a pleasant if undistinguished, two-street fishing port with mostly self-catering accommodation (generally ③) overlooked by the stubby ruins of **Feraklós castle**. You can swim off the town beach if you don't mind an audience from the handful of waterfront cafés and tavernas, but most people head north a kilometre beyond the castle – the last stronghold of the Knights to fall to the Turks – to the secluded **Agáthi beach**. At Haráki, on the right as you face the sea, past the military outpost, is *Efterpi*, the best restaurant on this coast; the Turkish chef used to cook at the Istanbul Hilton.

Líndhos

LÍNDHOS, the island's number-two tourist attraction, erupts 12km south of Haráki. Like Ródhos Town itself, its charm is heavily undermined by commercialism and crowds, and there are only two places to stay that are not booked semi-permanently by tour companies. These are *Pension Electra* and *Pension Katholiki*, next door to each other on the way to the north beach, but both are of a low standard and overpriced at ③. Recommendable eating places are similarly thin on the ground, although *Agostino's*, by the southerly beach car park, is notable for bulk wine, real country sausages and the fact that it counts some locals among its customers. Otherwise, the village is now a mess of bars, crêperies, package villas, bad restaurants and travel agents – the last redeemed by car rental rates 25–30 percent less than in Ródhos Town.

At midday dozens of coaches park nose-to-tail on the access road, with even more on the drive down to the beach. Back in the village itself, traditional houses not snapped up by the package outfits have been bought and refurbished by wealthy British and Italians and, although high-rise hotels have been prohibited, the result is not much better – a curiously lifeless, fake resort.

Nevertheless, if you arrive before or after the tours, when the pebble streets between the immaculately whitewashed houses are relatively empty, you can still appreciate the beautiful, atmospheric setting of Líndhos. The **Byzantine church** is covered with eighteenth-century frescoes, and several of the older fifteenth-to-eighteenth-century mansions are open to the public; entrance is free but you may come under pressure to buy something, especially the lace for which the village is noted.

On the bluff above the town, the ancient acropolis with its scaffolding-swaddled Doric **Temple of Athena** is found inside the Knights' **castle** (daily 8.30am–5pm; 800dr) – a surprisingly felicitous blend of two cultures. Though the ancient city of Líndhos and its original temple date from at least 1100 BC, the present structure was begun by the tyrant Kleovoulos in the sixth century BC and completed over the next two centuries.

Líndhos' sandy coves, though numerous, are overrated, overcrowded and can be polluted; if you do base yourself here, better, quieter beaches are to be found south of Lárdhos (see p.561). At the southern flank of the acropolis huddles the small, sheltered **Saint Paul's harbour**, where the apostle is said to have landed on a mission to evangelize the island, though he would doubtless turn in his grave faced with today's ranks of topless sun-worshipppers.

The west coast

Rhodes' west coast is the windward flank of the island, so it's damper, more fertile and more forested; most beaches, however, are exposed and decidedly on the rocky side. None of this has deterred development and as in the east the first few kilometres of the busy shore road down from the capital have been surrendered entirely to industrial tourism. From the aquarium down to the airport the asphalt is fringed by an uninterrupted line of Miami-beach-style mega-hotels, though such places as Triánda, Kremastí and Paradhísi are still nominally villages, and appear so in their centres. This was the first part of the island to be favoured by the package operators, and tends to be frequented by a decidedly middle-aged, sedate clientele that often can't be bothered to stir much out of sight of the runways.

Neither the planes buzzing over Paradhísi or the giant power plant at Soroní are much inducement to pause, and you probably won't want to until reaching the important archeological site of **KAMEIROS**, which with Líndhos and Ialyssos was one of the three Dorian powers that united in the fifth century BC to found the powerful city-state of Rhodes. Soon eclipsed by the new capital, Kameiros was abandoned and only rediscovered in the last century. As a result it is a particularly well-preserved Doric townscape, doubly worth visiting for its beautiful hillside site (Tues–Sun 8.30am–3pm;

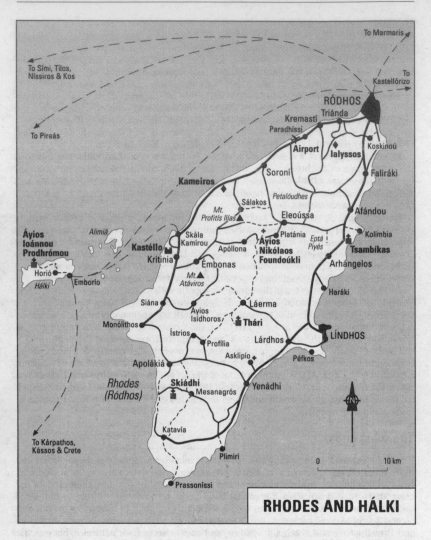

To Marmaris

To Sími, Tílos,
Níssiros & Kos

To
Kastellórizo

To Pireás

RÓDHOS

Kremastí Triánda
Paradhíssi

Airport **Ialyssos** Koskinoú

Soroní Faliráki

Kameiros

Petalóudhes

Sálakos

Eleoússa

Mt.
Profítis Ilías

Afándou

Skála Platánia Eptá Kolimbía
Kamírou Piyés

Kastéllo Apóllona **Áyios** **Tsambíkas**
Nikólaos

Kritínia **Émbonas** **Foundoúkli** Arhángelos

Alimiá

**Áyios
Ioánnou
Prodhrómou**

Horió
Hálki Emborió

Mt.
Atáviros Haráki

Siána Láerma

Áyios
Isídhoros

Monólithos **Thári** **LÍNDHOS**

Ístrios Lárdhos

Profilía Asklipío Péfkos

Apolákiá

*Rhodes
(Ródhos)* **Skiádhi** Yenádhi
Mesanagrós

Katavía

0   10 km

Plimíri

Prassoníssi

RHODES AND HÁLKI

400dr). While none of the individual remains are spectacular, you can make out the foundations of a few small temples, the *stoa* of the *agora*, and a water catchment basin. Because of the gentle slope of the site, there were no fortifications, nor was there an acropolis.

On the beach below Kameiros there are several tavernas, ideal while waiting for one of the two daily buses back to town (if you're willing to walk 4km back to Kalavárda you'll have a better choice of service). There are more tavernas clustered at **SKÁLA KAMÍROU** 15km south, a tiny anchorage which somewhat inexplicably is the hapless target of coach tours come to see Ye Olde Authentic Fishing Village (decals on the windows of several restaurants attest to the fact). Less heralded is the daily *kaíki* that leaves for the island of **Hálki** at 2.30pm, weather permitting, returning early the next morning; on Wednesdays and Sundays, there are day trips departing at 9am and returning at 4pm.

A couple of kilometres south of Skála, the "Kastello", signposted as **Kástro Kritinías**, is from afar the most impressive of the Knights' rural strongholds, and the access road is too rough for tour buses to pass. Close up it proves to be no more than a shell, with only a chapel and a rubbish-filled cistern more or less intact inside – a glorious shell, though, with fine views west to assorted islets and Hálki. You make a "donation" to the formidable woman at the car park in exchange for fizzy drinks, seasonal fruit or flowers.

Mountain villages

Beyond Kritiniá itself, a quiet hillside village with a few rooms and tavernas, the main road winds south through the forest to **SIÁNA**, the most attractive mountain settlement on the island, famous for its aromatic pine-sage honey and *soúma*, the local firewater. Bus tours also stop in at the church on the square, with heavily restored eighteenth-century frescoes. The tiered, flat-roofed farmhouses of **MONÓLITHOS**, 4km southwest at the end of the public bus line, are scant justification for the long trip out here, and food at the two **tavernas** is indifferent owing to the tour-group trade, but the view over the bay is striking, and you could use the village as a base by staying in rooms or at the pricier *Hotel Thomas* (☎0246/61 291; ③). Diversions in the area include yet another **Knights' castle** 2km west of town, photogenically perched on its own pinnacle and enclosing a couple of chapels, and the fine gravel beach of **Foúrni**, five bumpy, curvy kilometres below the castle, its 800-metre extent unsullied except for a seasonal drinks stand. Beyond the headland, to the left as you face the water, are some caves that were hollowed out by early Christians fleeing persecution.

The interior

Inland Rhodes is hilly, and still mostly wooded, despite the depredations of arsonists. You'll need a vehicle to see much here, especially as the main enjoyment is in getting away from it all: no one oito justifies the tremendous expense of a taxi or the inconvenience of trying to make the best of the sparse bus schedules.

In retrospect it will probably be the scenery which stands out, along with the last vestiges of the old agrarian life in the slowly depopulating villages. Young Rhodians that do remain in the interior stay largely to help with the grape harvest in late summer (when there's some chance of work for foreigners too). If you have time to spare, and a bit of Greek at your command, traditional hospitality in the form of a drink at the *kafenío*, or perhaps more, is still very much alive.

Ialyssos and the Valley of the Butterflies

Starting from the west coast, turn inland at Triánda for the five-kilometre uphill ride to ancient **Ialyssos** on Filérimos hill. Important as this city was, its visible remains are few; most conspicuous are a subterranean chapel covered with faded frescoes and a Doric fountain. The pine-covered slopes here also shelter the grounds of Filérimos monastery (which you can visit) and a Byzantine-cum-Turkish castle, but the whole ensemble won't take more than an hour of your time.

Beyond Paradhísi, another side turning leads within 7km to **Petaloúdhes**, the "Valley of the Butterflies" (daily June–Sept 9am–6pm; 200dr). Actually a rest stop for Jersey tiger moths, it might more accurately be christened the "Valley of the Tour Buses", but is an appealing place, with liquidambar trees shading and wooden bridges crossing a small stream. Do not imitate the practice of clapping or shouting to launch the tree-roosting moths into flight – this stresses them and interferes with their reproduction.

Eptá Piyés to Profítis Ilías

From the Kolímbia bus stop on the east coast road, it's a three-kilometre walk or drive inland to **Eptá Piyés** (daily April–Nov 9am–6pm; 200dr), a superb oasis with a tiny reservoir for swimming and an unusual streamside taverna. Continuing inland, you reach **ELEOÚSSA** after another 9km, in the shade of the dense forest at the east end of Profítis Ilías ridge. Two other undisturbed villages, Platánia and Apóllona, nestle on the south slopes of the mountain overlooking the start of the burned area, but most people keep straight on 3km further to the late Byzantine church of **Áyios Nikólaos Foundoúkli** (St Nicholas of the Hazelnuts). The partly shaded site has a fine view north over cultivated valleys, and locals descend in force for picnics on weekends; the frescoes inside, dating from the thirteenth to the fifteenth centuries, could use a good cleaning but various scenes from the life of Christ are recognizable.

Negotiating an unsignposted but fairly obvious welter of dirt tracks gets you finally to **Profítis Ilías**, where the Italian-vintage chalet-hotel *Elafos/Elafina* (☎0246/22 225; ⑤) hides in deep woods just north of the 798-metre marker, Rhodes' third-highest point. There's good, gentle strolling around the summit and the namesake monastery, and the lodge's snack bar is generally open in season.

Atáviros villages

All tracks and roads west across Profítis Ilías more or less converge upon the main road from Kalavárda bound for **ÉMBONAS**, a large and architecturally nondescript village backed up against the north slope of 1215-metre Mount Atáviros, roof of the island. Émbonas, with its two pensions and rather carnivores-oriented tavernas (of which *Skevos* is the best), is more geared to handling tourists than you might expect, since it's the venue for summer "folk-dance tours" from Ródhos Town. The village also lies at the heart of the island's most important wine-producing districts, and CAIR – the vintners' cooperative – produce a range of generally excellent varieties: the white *Ilios*, the red *Chevaliers*, and the premium label *Emery*. To see what Émbonas would be like without tourists, carry on clockwise around the peak past the Artámiti monastery, to less-celebrated **ÁYIOS ISÍDHOROS**, with as many vines and tavernas (try *Snag* (sic) *Bar Ataviros*), a more open feel, and the **trailhead** for the five-hour return ascent of Atáviros.

Thári Monastery

There's a mediocre road from Áyios Isídhoros to Siána, and an even worse one that runs the 12km east to Láerma, but the latter is worth enduring if you've any interest at all in Byzantine monuments. In **LÁERMA** proper, the church of Áyios Yióryios, just above the plane-shaded fountain, looks modern but actually contains fourteenth-century frescoes; get the keys from the adjacent *kafenío*. This is just an appetiser for the **monastery of Thári**, lost in pine forests five well-marked kilometres south. The oldest religious foundation on the island, the monastery was re-established as a living community of half a dozen monks in 1990 by a charismatic abbot from Pátmos. The striking *kathólikon* consists of a long nave and short transept surmounted by barrel vaulting. Despite two recent cleanings, the damp of centuries has smudged the frescoes, dating from 1300 to 1450, but they are still exquisite: the most distinct, in the transept, depict the Evangelist Mark and the Archangel Gabriel, while the nave boasts various acts of Christ, including such rarely illustrated scenes as the storm on the Sea of Galilee, meeting Mary Magdalene, and healing the cripple.

The monastery, dedicated to the Archangel Michael, takes its name from the legend of its foundation. A princess, kidnapped by pirates, was abandoned here by her captors; she saw the Archangel in a dream, and he promised her eventual deliverance. In gratitude, she vowed to build as many monasteries in his honour as the gold ring cast from her hand travelled in cubits. Upon being reunited with her parents the deed was done, but the ring was lost in some bushes, and never found. Thus "Thári" comes from *tharévo*, "I hazard, guess, venture", after the family's futile search for the heirloom. In their pique, apparently only one cloister was founded.

The far south

South of a line connecting Monólithos and Lárdhos, you could easily begin to think you had strayed onto another island – at least until the still-inflated prices brought you back to reality. Gone are the five-star hotels and roads to match, and with them most of the crowds. Gone too are most tourist facilities and public transport. Only one daily bus runs to Kataviá, along the east coast, where deserted beaches are backed by sheltering dunes that offer scope for private camping. Tavernas grace the more popular stretches of sand but there are still relatively few places to stay.

A new auxiliary airport is planned for the area, however, so this state of affairs won't persist indefinitely. Already massive construction is beginning behind the sandier patches south of **LÁRDHOS**, solidly on the tourist circuit despite an inland position between Láerma and the peninsula culminating in Líndhos. The beach 2km south is gravelly and the water can be dirty, but is well served by the best of the island's three campsites and the outriders of the small *Lárdhos Bay* complex. Four kilometres east, **PÉFKOS** (*Péfki* on some maps) is a low-key package resort on the beach road to Líndhos; the sea is cleaner than at Lárdhos but beaches are minimal.

Asklipío

Nine kilometres beyond Lárdhos, a paved side road heads 4km inland to **ASKLIPÍO**, a sleepy village guarded by a crumbling castle and graced by the Byzantine church of **Kímisis Theotókou**, whose frescoes are in far better condition than Thári's owing to the drier local climate. To gain admission, call at the priest's house behind the apse, or if that doesn't work, haul on the belfry rope. The building dates from 1060, with a ground plan nearly identical to that of Thári, except that two subsidiary apses were added during the eighteenth century, partly to conceal a secret school in a subterranean crypt. The frescoes themselves are somewhat later than Thári's, though the priest claims that the final work at Thári and the earliest here were executed by the same hand, a master from Híos.

The format and subject matter of the frescoes is rare in Greece: didactic "cartoon strips" which extend completely around the church in some cases, and extensive Old Testament stories in addition to the more usual lives of Christ and the Virgin. There's a complete sequence from Genesis, from the Creation to the Expulsion from Eden; note the comically menacing octopus among the fishes on the Fifth Day. A seldom-encountered *Revelation of John the Divine* takes up most of the east transept, and pebble mosaic flooring decorates both the interior and the vast courtyard.

To the southern tip

Returning to the coast road, there are ample facilities at **YENÁDHI**, though tour operators have yet to arrive. The shore is empty again until **PLIMÍRI**, which consists of a single **taverna** on a sheltered, sandy bay; just off the crumbling jetty, a ten-year-old wreck attracts expert scuba divers. Beyond Plimíri the road curves inland to **KATAVIÁ**, nearly 100km from the capital. There are several tavernas at the junction that doubles as the *platía*, and a few rooms to rent; the village, like so many in the south, is three-quarters deserted, the owners of the closed-up houses off working in Australia or North America.

From Kataviá a rough, marked track leads on to **Prassoníssi**, Rhodes' southern-most extremity and site of a lighthouse automated only in 1989. From May to October you can stroll across the wide, low sandspit to visit, but winter storms swamp this tenuous link and render Prássonissi a true island. Even in summer the prevailing northwesterly winds drive swimmers to the lee side of the spit, leaving the exposed shore to the world-class windsurfers who come to train here. In season the scrubby junipers rustle with tents and caravans; water comes from two **tavernas** flanking the access road. The outfit next to the old windmill is more characterful, but beware of their fish grills, which are tasty but among the most expensive in Greece.

The southwest coast

West of Kataviá, the island loop road emerges onto the deserted, sandy southwest coast, and soon deteriorates in a long, yet-to-be-improved stretch. If freelance camping and nudism are your thing, this is the place to indulge, though you'll need your own transport, or lots of supplies and a stout pair of shoes. Just before the road shapes up again, there's a turning for the fourteenth-century hilltop monastery of **Skiádhi**, which houses a miraculous icon of the Virgin and Child; in the fifteenth century a heretic stabbed the painting, and blood was said to have flowed from the wound in the Mother of God's cheek. The offending hand was, needless to say, instantly paralysed; the fissure, and suspicious brown stains around it, are still visible. You can stay the night upon arrangement with the caretaker, but as with the beaches below you'll have to bring your own kit and on weekends you'll have plenty of (local) company.

The nearest town is modern and unexciting **APOLAKIÁ**, a few kilometres inland but equipped with a couple of **rooms** and **tavernas** plus a general store, ideal for those beachcombers undaunted by the logistics of staying in southern Rhodes. At the central, badly marked roundabout, there always seem to be a few visiting motorists scratching their heads over maps: northwest leads to Monólithos, due south goes back to Kataviá, and the northeast option is a paved scenic road cutting quickly back to Yennádhi. Just a bit further on is the proudly featured side track to an irrigation dam just north, oddly scenic as these things go and plainly visible from Siána overhead.

Hálki

Hálki, a tiny (20 square kilometres) limestone speck west of Rhodes, is a member of the Dodecanese in its own right, though all but three hundred of the population have decamped (mostly to Rhodes or to Tarpon Springs, Florida) in the wake of a devastating sponge blight early in this century. Despite a renaissance of tourism in recent years, the island is tranquil compared to Rhodes, with a slightly weird, hushed atmosphere; the big event of the day is when someone catches a fish.

The first hint of development came in 1983, when UNESCO designated Hálki as the "isle of peace and friendship", and made it the seat of an annual summer international youth conference. (Tílos was approached first but declined the honour.) As part of the deal, 150 crumbling houses in the harbour town of Emborió were to be restored as guest lodges for the delegates and other interested parties, with UNESCO footing the bill. In the event, only one hotel was actually finished, after the critical lack of fresh water which had hampered all previous attempts at tourist development was supposedly remedied by the discovery of undersea aquifers by a French geological team. By 1988 the rest of the grandiose plans had still not been seriously acted on. The only tangible sign of "peace and friendship" was an unending stream of UNESCO and Athenian bureaucrats and their dependents occupying every available bed at unpredictable intervals and staging drunken, musical binges under the guise of "ecological conferences". The islanders, fed up with what had obviously turned out to be a scam, sent the freeloaders packing at the end of that year.

Emborió

Since then, in conjunction with specialist tour operators, most of the designated houses in **EMBORIÓ** have been restored, but all are pretty much block-booked by the companies themselves and occupied by a rather staid, well-mannered clientele; independent travellers will be lucky to find anything at all. Places to start hunting include *The Captain's House* (☎0241/45 201; ③), where the English co-manager, Christine Sakelaridhes, can point you in likely directions, *Pension Kleanthi* (☎0241/37 648 or 57 334; ③), and *Hotel Manos* (☎0241/45 295; ②). Of the several **tavernas** on Emborío waterfront, *Maria's* and *Yiannis* are about the most reliable, while *Omonia* offers more authenticity.

There's a **post office** (the best place to change money), three stores, a bakery, and two **beaches** nearby. Póndamos is sandy and minute, with *Nick's Taverna*, which serves good lunches to beach-goers and also has rooms (☎0241/57 295; ②); Yialí, north of Emborío, is larger and pebbly.

The rest of the island

Three kilometres inland lies the old pirate-safe village of **HORIÓ**, abandoned in the 1950s but still crowned by the Knights' castle. Across the way, the little church of **Stavrós** is a venue for one of the two big island festivals on September 14. There's little else to see or do here, though you can spend a few enjoyable hours **walking** across the island. A newly bulldozed dirt road picks up where the cement "Tarpon Springs Boulevard" mercifully ends; the latter was donated by the expatriate community in Florida to ensure easy Cadillac access to the Stavrós *paniyíri* grounds, though what Hálki really needed (and still needs) is a proper sewage system and salt-free water supply. At the end of the walk you'll come to the monastery of **Ayíou Ioánniou Prodhrómou**. The caretaking family there can put you up in a cell (except around August 29, the other big festival date), but you'll need to bring supplies. The terrain en route is monotonous, but compensated by views over half the Dodecanese and Turkey.

Kastellórizo (Méyisti)

Kastellórizo's official name, Méyisti (biggest), seems more an act of defiance than a statement of fact. While the largest of a tiny group of islands, it is in fact the smallest of the Dodecanese, barely more than three nautical miles off the Turkish coast but over seventy from its nearest Greek neighbour (Rhodes). At night you find its lights quite outnumbered by those of the Turkish town of Kaş, across the bay.

Less than a century ago there were 16,000 people here, supported by a fleet of schooners which made fortunes transporting goods, mostly timber, from the Greek towns of Kalamaki (now Kalkan) and Andifelos (Kaş) on the Anatolian mainland. But the advent of steam power and the Italian seizure of the Dodecanese in 1912 sent the island into decline. Shipowners failed to modernize their fleets, preferring to sell their ships to the British for the Dardanelles campaign, and the new frontier between the island and republican Turkey, combined with the expulsion of all Anatolian Greeks in 1923, deprived any remaining vessels of their trade. During the 1930s the island enjoyed a brief renaissance when it became a major stopover point for French and Italian seaplanes, but events at the close of World War II put an end to any hopes of the island's continued viability.

When Italy capitulated to the Allies in the autumn of 1943, a few hundred British commandos occupied Kastellórizo until displaced by a stronger German force in the spring of 1944. At some stage during the hasty departure of Commonwealth forces, the fuel dump caught fire and an adjacent arsenal exploded, taking with it more than half of the 2000 houses on Kastellórizo. Enquiries have concluded that the retreating Allies did some looting, though it was probably Greek pirates engaging in some pillaging of their own who accidentally or deliberately caused the conflagration. In any event the British are not especially popular here; islanders were further angered by the fact that an Anglo-Greek committee delayed for many years the payment of reparations to 850 surviving applicants in Athens; furthermore, those who had emigrated to Australia, and the few who chose to stay on the island after 1945, were strangely ineligible for such benefits. Even before these events most of the population had left for Rhodes, Athens, Australia and North America. Today there are less than 200 people living permanently on Kastellórizo, and they are largely maintained by remittances from emigrants and by subsidies from the Greek government, which fears that the island will revert to Turkey should their numbers diminish any further.

Kastellórizo Town

The remaining population is concentrated in the northern harbour, KASTELLÓRIZO – the finest, so it is said, between Beirut and Pireás – and its little "suburb" of Mandhráki, just over the fire-blasted hill with its half-ruined castle of the Knights. The castle now houses the local museum (Tues–Sun 7.30am–2.30pm; free), with displays including plates from a Byzantine shipwreck, frescoes rescued from decaying churches, and a reconstruction of an ancient basilica. The surviving quayside mansions, with their tiled roofs, wooden balconies and long, narrow windows, have obvious counterparts in Anatolian villages across the water. One street behind the waterfront, though, all is desolation – abandonment having succeeded where the 1944 fire failed.

Despite its apparently terminal plight, Kastellórizo may have a future of sorts. During the 1980s the government dredged the harbour to accommodate cruise ships, completed an airport for flights to and from Rhodes, and briefly contemplated making the island an official port of entry, a measure calculated to appeal to the many yachties who call here. Each summer, too, the population is swelled by returnees of "Kassie" ancestry, some of whom celebrate traditional weddings in the Áyios Konstandínos cathedral, betwen the port and Mandhráki, with its ancient columns pilfered from Patara in Asia Minor. Perhaps the biggest boost for the island's tourism industry in recent years has come from its use as the location for the film Mediterraneo, which has resulted in a tidal wave of Italian visitors.

Practicalities

Despite its recent strut in front of the cameras, Kastellórizo is not prepared for more than a few dozen visitors; water and fresh produce, apart from fish, can be in short supply. Pensions tend to be fairly basic, with long climbs up and down stairs to a single bathroom. If you're not met off the boat, the best budget option is the restored mansion-pension of the Mavrothalassitis family (☎0241/49 202; ②), or try Paradhísos (☎0241/49 074; ②) at the west end of the seafront, Barbara (☎0241/49 295; ②), at the opposite end of things, or the more modern Kristallo (☎0241/41 209; ②). More luxury is available, at a price, at the Hotel Meyisti (☎0241/49 272; ⑥).

Waterfront tavernas have had a long and detrimental acquaintance with the yacht market; much better restaurants are to be found inland. Especially recommended are Iy Orea Meyisti, run by the Mavrothalassitis family (they of the pension), and Ouzeri O Meyisteas, behind the disused municipal market building, which specializes in reasonably priced and generous helpings of goat chops.

The post office is at the far end of things, behind Hotel Meyisti; there's no OTE or bank. Most ferry companies are represented by one of several grocery stores, while the only travel agency, DiZi Travel, has a monopoly on flights back to Rhodes.

Kastellórizo has traditionally depended heavily on produce smuggled across from Kaş and lately it has been possible to arrange a ride over to Turkey on the supply boat

Varvara, run by the *Taverna Apolavsi*. It's a bit of a racket, however: since Kastellórizo is not an official port of entry/exit, non-"Kassies" must pay a hefty "special visa fee" to customs; the ride itself, though, may be free – if the *Varvara*'s crew were going shopping anyway.

The rest of the island

Swimming is complicated by the total absence of beaches and the abundance of sea urchins and razor-sharp limestone reefs everywhere; the easiest access is beyond the graveyard at Mandhráki. Perseverance is rewarded by clear waters graced by a rich variety of marine life. Over on the east coast, accessible only by boat, is the grotto of **Perastá**, famed for its stalactites and the strange blue light effects inside; rubber-raft trips give you just two hours there or, for more money, you can take it in as part of a day tour that includes Rho islet (see below).

Heat (infernal in summer) permitting, you can hike forty minutes west of the port on a track, then a path, passing country chapels along the way to **Paleokástro**, site of the Doric city. From the heights you've tremendous views over the elephant's-foot-shaped harbour and surrounding Greek islets across to Turkey. Until her death in 1982, "The Lady of **Rhó**", on the **islet** of that name, resolutely hoisted the Greek flag each day in defiance of the Turks on the mainland. Should you take a *kaíki* day trip out here, her grave is the first things you see when you dock; from the tomb a path heads southeast for 25 minutes to the islet's southerly port. The islet has no facilities – just one caretaker, four dogs and hundreds of goats – so bring your own food and water.

Sími

Sími's most pressing problem, lack of water, is in many ways also its greatest asset. If the rain cisterns don't fill in winter, brackish water must be imported at great expense from Rhodes. So, however much it might want to, the island can't hope to support more than two or three large hotels. Instead hundreds of people are shipped in daily during the season from Rhodes, relieved of their money and sent back. This arrangement suits both the islanders and those visitors lucky enough to stay longer. Many foreigners return regularly, or even own houses here – indeed since the mid-1980s the more desirable dwellings, ruined or otherwise, have been sold off in such numbers that the island has essentially become the Ídhra of the Dodecanese.

Sími Town

The island's capital – and only proper town – consists of **Yialós**, the port, and **Horió**, on the hillside above, collectively known as **SÍMI**. Incredibly, less than a hundred years ago the town was richer and more populous (30,000) than Ródhos Town. Wealth came from expertise in shipbuilding and sponge-diving nurtured since pre-Classical times. Under the Ottomans, Sími, like many of the Dodecanese, enjoyed considerable autonomy in exchange for a yearly tribute in sponges to the sultan; but the 1919–22 war, the advent of synthetic sponges, and the gradual replacement of the crews by Kalymniotes spelt doom for the local economy. Vestiges of both activities remain, but the souvenir-shop sponges are mostly of North American origin today, and now many of the magnificent nineteenth-century mansions are roofless and deserted, their windows gaping blankly across the fine natural harbour. The 3000 remaining Simiotes are scattered fairly evenly throughout the mixture of Neoclassical and more typical island dwellings, though despite the surplus of properties many outsiders have preferred to build anew, rather than restore shells accessible only by donkey or on

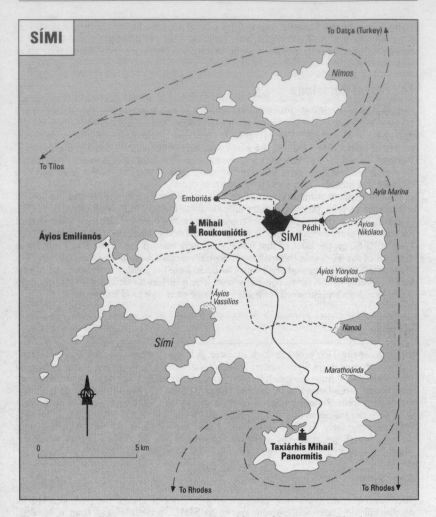

foot. As on Kastellórizo, a wartime ammunition blast – this time set off by the retreating Germans – levelled hundreds of houses up in Horió. Shortly afterwards, the official surrender of the Dodecanese to the Allies was signed here on May 8, 1945: a plaque marks the spot at the present-day *Restaurant Les Katerinettes* (not otherwise recommended), and each year on that date there's a fine festival with music and dance.

The **port**, a protected historical area since the early 1970s, is deceptively lively, especially between noon and 4pm when the Rhodes-based excursion boats are in, but one street back from the water, the more peaceful pace of village life takes over. Two massive stair-paths, the Kalí Stráta and Katarráktes, effectively deter many of the daytrippers and are most dramatically climbed towards sunset; the massive ruins along the lower reaches of the Kalí Stráta are lonely and sinister after dark, home only to wild figs and nightjars.

Follow blue arrows through Horió to the excellent local **museum** (Tues–Sun 10am–2pm; 400dr). Housed in a fine old mansion at the back of the village, the museum concentrates on Byzantine and medieval Sími, with exhibits on frescoes in isolated churches and a gallery of medieval icons. On the way back to central Horió, the nineteenth-century pharmacy, with its apothecary jars and wooden drawers full of exotic remedies, is worth a look.

At the very pinnacle of things a **castle of the Knights** occupies the site of Sími's ancient acropolis, and you can glimpse a stretch of Cyclopean wall on one side. A dozen churches grace Horió; that of the Ascension, inside the fortifications, is a replacement of the one blown to bits when the Germans torched the munitions cached there. One of the bells in the new belfry is the nose-cone of a thousand-pound bomb, hung as a memorial.

Arrival and services

There are daily **excursion boats** from Mandhráki in Ródhos Town, but you'll come under considerable pressure at the quay to buy an expensive return ticket – not what you want if you're off island-hopping and don't plan to return to Rhodes. Either insist on a one-way ticket, or better still, buy tickets through travel agents on Rhodes or take the islanders' own unpublicized and significantly cheaper boat, the *Symi I*, which sails to Rhodes in the morning, returning between 2pm and 6pm after shopping hours are done. Twice a week there are mainline ferries as well.

The **OTE** and **post office** are open the standard Monday to Friday hours; there are full-service **banks** and designated exchange agents for odd hours. In summer an unmarked green-and-white van shuttles between Yialós and Pédhi via Horió at regular intervals until 11pm; in winter, it is replaced by a blue van. There are also three taxis, though this is a perfect island for boat and walking excursions. *ANES*, the outlet for *Symi I* tickets, and *Psihas*, the agent for all big inter-island **ferries**, are one alley apart in the market place.

Accommodation

The accommodation situation for independent travellers is tough, though not nearly so bad as on Hálki. Studios, rather than simple rooms, predominate, and package operators control most of these; if there are any vacancies, proprietors meet arriving boats. Best value are rooms with kitchen facilities let by the English-speaking *Katerina Tsakiris* (☎0241/71 813; ③), with a grandstand view over the harbour; reservations usually essential. Rather more basic are two standbys down by the market area, the *Glafkos* (☎0241/71 358; rooms ②, studios ③) on the square, and the fairly cramped, last-resort *Egli* (☎0241/71 392; ②). With a bit more to spend, there are rooms, studios and houses managed by the *Jean & Tonic* bar (☎0241/71 819; ③–④), or the *Hotel Horio* (☎0241/71 800; ④) and the adjacent *Hotel Fiona* (☎0241/72 088; ④) are good, traditional-style outfits at the top of the Kalí Stráta up in Horió. If money's no object, the *Aliki* (☎0241/71 665; ⑤), a few paces right from the clocktower, is also a famous monument. Failing all of these, the best strategy is to appeal for help from *Sunny Land* (☎0241/71 320), the first agency you encounter after disembarking: their weekly rates for villas, houses and apartments are highly competitive even if you don't stay a full seven days.

Eating and drinking

You're best off avoiding entirely the north and west side of the port, where menus, prices and attitudes tend to have been terminally warped by the day-trade. Exceptions are *Tholos*, an excellent female-run *ouzeri* out beyond the Haráni boatyard, and two places with unbeatable views – *Elpidha*, an *ouzeri*-café near *Sunny Land*, which looks straight across the water at *Tembeloskala*, another good *ouzeri*-bar. Matters improve perceptibly as you press further inland or up the hill. At the very rear of what remains of Sími's bazaar, *O Meraklis* has polite service and well-cooked dishes; *Neraïdha*, well back from the water near the OTE, is delicious and still reasonably priced despite its discovery by tours. Up in Horió, *Georgios* is a decades-old institution, serving what can only be described as large portions of Greek *nouvelle cuisine* in a pebble-mosaic courtyard – excellent value, but open for dinner only.

Nearly half a dozen **bars** satisfy the urge for a drink in Yialós. With a large ex-pat community, a few bars are run by foreigners: in Horió, *Jean & Tonic* caters to a mixed clientele; down at Yialós, *Vapori* is the oldest bar on the island, welcoming customers with desserts, breakfast and free newspapers.

Around the island

Sími has no big sandy beaches, but there are plenty of pebbly stretches at the heads of the deep narrow bays which indent the coastline. **PÉDHI**, 45 minutes' walk from Yialós, still has much of the character of a fishing hamlet, with enough water in the plain behind – the island's largest – to support a few vegetable gardens. The beach is average-to-poor, though, and the giant *Pedhi Beach* hotel (packages only) has considerably bumped up prices at the three local tavernas, of which the most reasonable and authentic is *Iy Kamares*. Many will opt for another twenty minutes of walking via goat track along the south shore of the almost landlocked bay to **Áyios Nikólaos**, the only all-sand beach on Sími, with sheltered swimming and a mediocre taverna. Alternatively, a marked path on the north side of the inlet leads within an hour to **Ayía Marína**, where you can swim out to a monastery-capped islet.

Around Yialós, you'll find tiny **Nós** "beach" ten minutes past the boat yards at Haráni, but there's sun here only until lunchtime and it's packed with day-trippers. You can continue along the coastal track here past tiny gravel coves and rock slabs where nudists disport themselves, or cut inland from the Yialós *platía* past the abandoned desalination plant, to the appealing **Emborió** bay, with two tavernas – *Maria's* is the best. Inland from this are a Byzantine mosaic fragment and, nearby, a catacomb complex known locally as *Dhodheka Spilia*.

Plenty of other, more secluded coves are accessible by energetic walkers with sturdy footwear, or those prepared to pay a modest sum for the taxi-boats that leave daily in season from 10am, with the last trip out around noon or 1pm. These are the best way to reach the southern bays of **Marathoúnda** and **Nanoú**, and the only method of getting to the spectacular, cliff-girt fjord of **Áyios Yióryios Dhissálona**. Dhissálona lies in shade after 1pm, and Marathoúnda lacks a taverna, making Nanoú the most popular destination for day-trips. The beach at Nanoú consists of 200m of gravel sand and pebbles, with a scenic backdrop and a taverna behind – the latter probably the most reasonable of Sími's far-flung eateries.

On foot, you can cross the island – which has retained patches of its natural juniper forest – in two hours to **Áyios Vassílios**, the most scenic of the gulfs, or in a little more time to **Áyios Emilianós**, where you can stay the night (bring supplies) in a wave-lashed cloister at the island's extreme west end. On the way to the latter you might look in at the monastery of **Mihaíl Roukouniótis**, Sími's oldest, with lurid eighteenth-century frescoes and a peculiar ground plan: the *kathólikon* is actually two stacked churches, the currently used one built atop an earlier structure abandoned to the damp. The less intrepid can explore on guided walks to several beaches led by Hugo Tyler (☎0241/71 670), which are generally met by a boat for the ride home.

The Archangel is also honoured at the huge monastery of **Taxiárhis Mihaíl Panormítis**, Sími's biggest rural attraction and generally the first port of call for the excursion boats from Rhodes. You get a quick half-hour tour with them; if you want more time, you'll have to come on a "jeep safari" from Yialós, or arrange to stay the night (for a donation), in the *ksenónas* set aside for pilgrims. There are numbers of these in summer, as Miháíl has been adopted as the patron of sailors in the Dodecanese.

Like many of Sími's monasteries, it was thoroughly pillaged during the last war, so don't expect too much of the building or its treasures. An appealing pebble court surrounds the central *kathólikon*, tended by the single remaining monk, lit by an improbable number of oil lamps and graced by a fine *témblon*, though the frescoes are recent and mediocre. The small museum (100dr) contains a strange mix of precious antiques, junk (stuffed crocodiles and koalas), votive offerings, models of ships named *Taxiarhis* or *Panormitis*, and a chair piled with messages-in-bottles brought here by Aegean currents – the idea being that if the bottle or toy boat arrived, the sender got his or her wish. A tiny beach, a shop/*kafenío* and a taverna round out the list of amenities; near the latter stands a memorial commemorating three Greeks, including the monastery's abbot, executed in February 1944 by the Germans for aiding British commandos.

Tílos

The small, blissfully quiet island of **Tílos**, with a population of only 350 (shrinking to 80 in winter), is one of the least visited of the Dodecanese, although it can be visited as a day trip by hydrofoil once or twice a week. Why anyone should want to come for just a few hours is unclear: while it's a wonderful place to rest on the beach or go walking, there is nothing very striking at first glance. After a few days, however, you may have stumbled on several of the seven small castles of the Knights of Saint John which stud the crags, or gained access to some of the inconspicuous medieval chapels, some fres-

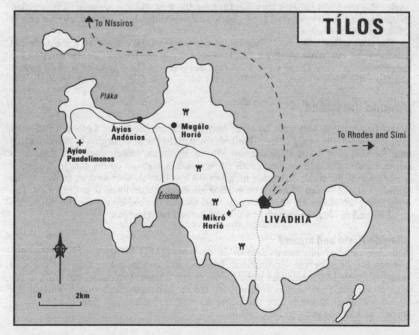

coed or pebble-mosaiced, clinging to hillsides. Though rugged and scrubby on the heights, the island has ample water – mostly pumped up from the agricultural plains – and groves of oak and terebinth near the cultivated areas. The volcano on neighbouring Níssiros has contributed pumice beds and red-lava-sand beaches to the landscape as well. From many points on the island you've fine views across to Sími, Turkey and Níssiros.

The single paved road runs the seven kilometres from Livádhia, the port village, to Megálo Horió, the capital and only other significant habitation. When boats arrive a rust-coloured **minibus** links the two, and accommodation proprietors from Éristos lay on their own vehicles, but at other times you can walk, charter said minibus or rent a motorbike.

Livádhia

Of the two settlements, **LIVÁDHIA** is more equipped to deal with tourists and is closer to the best hikes. The port town retains an overall feel of traditional Greece – though a rash of building sites behind Livádhia's long pebble beach is an ominous sign. If there are vacancies, **room** and **hotel** owners meet the ferries, but in high season it may be worth phoning ahead. Budget options include *Stamatia's* (☎0241/44 334; ②), on the waterfront but rather pokey, or the recently refurbished and good-value *Hotel Livadhia* (☎0241/44 266; ②), which also runs *Studios Sofia* just behind (③). Nearby is the *Pension Periyali* (☎0241/44 398; ②), and east down the beach, then inland, is *Kastello* (☎0241/44 292; ③).

Of the seafront **tavernas**, *Sofia's* is a convivial meeting place, but you'll probably get a better meal at *Irina* (aka *Yiorgos*); the best place for fish grills is *Blue Sky*, an unmissable place perched above the ferry dock. For breakfast or pre-dinner drinks, *Omonia* – under the trees strung with fairy lights, near the post office – is enduringly popular. **Nightlife** on Tílos is restricted to two bars: *La Luna* at the ferry pier and a music pub in Mikró Horió (see below).

The **post office** is the only place to change money; **OTE** consists of a phone box in the larger of two grocery stores; and two agencies at the jetty divide the **ferry-ticket** trade between them. There's also a bakery, and plenty of other produce sold off pickup trucks.

Around the island

From Livádhia you can walk an hour north to the pebble bay of **Lethrá**, or slightly longer south to the sandy cove of **Thólou**; the path to the latter begins by the cemetery and the chapel of **Áyios Pandelímon** with its Byzantine mosaic court and then curls around under the hard-to-climb castle of **Agriosikiá**; once up on the saddle, a cairned route leads to the citadel in twenty minutes. It's less than an hour west by trail up to the ghost village of **Mikró Horió**, whose 1500 inhabitants abandoned it in the 1950s. The only intact structures are the castle-guarded church (locked except for the August 15 festival) and an old house which has been restored as a music pub.

Megálo Horió and around

The rest of Tílos' inhabitants live in or near **MEGÁLO HORIÓ**, with an enviable perspective over its vast agricultural *kámbos*, and overlooked in turn by the vast Knights' castle which encloses a sixteenth-century chapel. The castle was built on the site of ancient Tílos, and is reached by a stiff, half-hour climb that begins at the *Ikonomou* supermarket before threading its way through a vast jumble of cisterns, house foundations and derelict chapels.

Your choices for **accommodation** are the *Pension Sevasti* (☎0241/44 237; ③), *Milio Apartments* (☎0241/44 204; ③), or *Studios Ta Elefandakia* (☎0241/44 213; ③). The restaurant attached to the *Pension Sevasti* is the most reliably open at lunchtime and has the best view. Two more fortresses stare out across the plain: the easterly one of **Massariá** helpfully marks the location of a cave where Pleiocene midget-elephant bones were discovered in 1971. A trail goes there from the road, ending just beyond the spring-fed cypress below the cave-mouth, which was hidden for centuries until a World War II artillery barrage exposed it. The bones themselves have been transferred to a small museum in Megálo Horió, which isn't currently open to the public.

Below Megálo Horió, a sign points left for the 75-minute walk to the one-kilometre-long **Éristos** beach, behind which are two **tavernas** with **rooms** (②), the *Tropikana* and *Navsika*. Both are set well back from the sand, hidden among orchards, but the food is nothing exceptional.

The far northwest

The main road beyond Megálo Horió hits the coast again at **Áyios Andónios**, with a single hotel/taverna (the *Australia*, ☎0241/44 296; ③) and an exposed, average beach. At low tide you can find more lava-trapped skeletons strung out in a row – human this time, presumably tide-washed victims of a Nissirian eruption in 600 BC, and discovered by the same archeologists who found the miniature pachyderms.

There's better swimming at isolated **Pláka** beach, 2km west of Áyios Andónios, and the road finally ends 8km west of Megálo Hório at the fortified fifteenth-century monastery of **Ayíou Pandelímonas**, deserted except from July 25 to 27, when it hosts the island's biggest festival. The tower-gate and oasis setting, over 200 forbidding metres above the west coast, are more memorable than the damaged frescoes within; to guarantee access, you need to visit with the regular Sunday morning tour, as there's no caretaker.

Níssiros

Volcanic **Níssiros** is noticeably greener than its southern neighbours Tílos, Hálki, and Sími, and unlike them has proved attractive and wealthy enough to retain more of its population, staying lively even in winter. While remittances from abroad (particularly Astoria, New York) are inevitably important, much of the island's income is derived from quarrying; offshore towards Kós the islet of Yialí is a vast lump of gypsum and pumice on which the miners live as they slowly chip it away.

The main island's peculiar geology is potentially a source of even more benefits: DEI, the Greek power company, spent much of the years between 1988 and 1992 sinking exploratory **geothermal wells** and attempting to convince the islanders of the benefits of cheap electricity. Mindful of the DEI's poor behaviour in similar circumstances on Mílos, however, the locals rallied against the project, fearing noxious fumes, industrial debris and land expropriation as in the Cyclades. In 1991 DEI bulldozed a new road of dubious necessity around the southwest flank of the island, damaging farmland and destroying a beautiful 500-year-old *kalderími* in the process; metal litter from unsuccessful test bores also did little to endear them to the local populace.

In 1993, a local referendum went massively against the projects, and DEI, together with its Italian contractor, took the hint and packed up. The desalination plant, reliant on expensive power from the fuel-oil generator, scarcely provides enough fresh water to spur a massive growth in package tourism. The relatively few tourists who stay the night, as opposed to the day-trippers from Kós, still find peaceful villages with a minimum of concrete eyesores, and a friendly population.

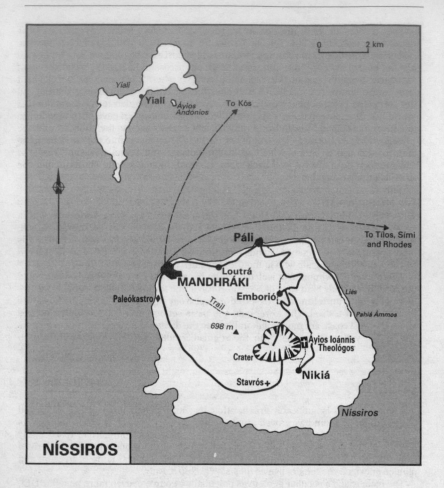

NÍSSIROS

Mandhráki

MANDHRÁKI is the port and capital, the wood balconies and windows on its tightly packed white houses splashed in bright colours, with blue swatches of sea visible at the ends of the narrow streets. Except for the drearier fringes near the ferry dock, the bulk of the place looks cheerful, arrayed around the community orchard or *kámbos* and overlooked by two ancient fortresses which also protect it somewhat from the wind.

Into a corner of the first of these, the predictable Knights' castle, is wedged the little monastery of **Panayía Spilianí**, built on this spot in accordance with the instructions of the Virgin herself, given in a vision to one of the first Christian islanders. Its prestige grew after raiding Saracens failed to discover the vast quantities of silver secreted here, in the form of a rich collection of Byzantine icons. On the way up to the monastery, you might stop in at the house restored for the **Historical and Popular Museum** (no set hours).

As a defensive bastion, the 2600-year-old Doric **Paleókastro**, twenty minutes' well-signposted walk out of the Langadháki district, is infinitely more impressive than the Knights' castle, and one of the more underrated ancient sites in Greece.

Practicalities

You'll see a handful of hotels and tavernas on your left as you disembark; best of the mid-range options, helpful and friendly, are the *Hotel/Restaurant Three Brothers* (☎0242/31 344; ③) and the *Romantzo* (☎0242/31 340; ③). In all honesty, though, these are best passed up in favour of establishments in the town proper. Just beyond the public toilets is the simple pension *Maria Intze* (②), across from *Enetikon Travel*, the main **travel agency**. A more popular budget option is the basic but clean *Pension Iy Dhrosia* (☎0242/31 328; ②), tucked right under the castle on the shore; enquire at Mihalis Orsaris's butcher shop on the main street. If it's full, the same management has slightly more expensive rooms inland. Also set back from the sea, but overlooking the *kámbos*, is Mandhráki's luxury accommodation, the *Porfíris* (☎0242/31 376; ③), with gardens and a pool.

Eating options include *Kleanthis*, a popular local hangout at lunchtime, and adjacent *Mike's* which looks tacky, but isn't particularly. The inland *Taverna Nissiros* is inexpensive and always packed after dark, whereas the *Karava*, next to *Enetikon*, is pricey and empty – a sea view and good menu compensate; the excellent *Taverna Irini* on the old *platía* does a fine *souvlaki* and fresh seafood dishes. Island **specialities** include pickled caper greens, *pittiá* (chickpea croquettes), and *soumádha*, an almond-extract drink nowadays only available from one family or two tavernas (*Romantzo* and *Karava*). The focus of **nightlife**, oddly enough, is not the shore but various bars and cafés near the lively inland Platía Ilikioménis such as *Cactus Bar*.

There's a short-hours **OTE** near the same *platía*, a **bank agent** and a **post office** at the harbour. Also by the jetty is a small **bus station**, with (theoretically) early morning and early afternoon departures into the interior and another four or so as far as Páli. In practice these are subject to cancellation, so you might consider renting a **moped**: the half-day or overnight rates offered by an inland tourist shop are better than the *Hotel Romantzo's* somewhat expensive full day rates.

Beaches – and Páli

Beaches on Níssiros are in even shorter supply than water – the tour agency here can successfully market excursions to a beach on **Áyios Andónios** islet, just next to the mining apparatus on Yialí. Closer at hand, the black-rock beach of **Hokhláki**, behind the Knights' castle, is impossible if the wind is up, and the town beach at the east edge of the harbour would be a last resort in any weather. Better to head out along the main road, passing the half-abandoned spa of **Loutrá** (hot mineral-water soaks by prior arrangement) and the smallish **White Beach**, 2km along and dwarfed by an ugly new namesake hotel (☎0242/31 498; generally fully booked by tour groups), whose guests crowd onto the beach.

A kilometre further, 45 minutes' walk in all from Mandhráki, the fishing village of **PÁLI** makes a more attractive proposition as a base. Here you'll find the *Hotel Hellenis* (☎0242/31 453; ③), two **rooms** places (fanciest at the west end of the quay) and arguably the best and cheapest **taverna** on the island, *Afroditi*, featuring white Cretan wine and homemade desserts. Another dark-sand beach extends east of Páli to an apparently abandoned new spa, but to reach Níssiros' best beaches, continue in that direction for an hour on foot (or twenty minutes by moped along the road), past an initially discouraging seaweed- and cowpat-littered shoreline, to the delightful cove of **Líes**, where the track ends. A ten-minute scramble past a headland to the idyllic expanse of **Pahiá Ámmos**, as broad and sand-red as the name implies, is well worth it.

The interior

It is the **volcano** which gives Níssiros its special character and fosters the growth of the abundant vegetation – and no stay would be complete without a visit. When excursion boats arrive from Kós or Rhodes, the *Polyvotis Tours* coach and usually one of the public buses are pressed into service to take customers up the hill, but if you want to get up there without the crowds it's best to use either the morning and afternoon scheduled buses, a moped or your own feet to get up and back. Tours tend to set off at about 10.30am and 2.30pm, so time yourself accordingly for relative solitude.

Winding up from Páli, you'll first pass the virtually abandoned village of **EMBORIÓ**, where pigs and cows far outnumber people, though the place is slowly being bought up and restored by Athenians and foreigners. New owners are surprised to discover natural **saunas**, heated by volcano steam, in the basements of the crumbling houses; at the outskirts of the village there's a public one in a cave, whose entrance is outlined in white paint. If you're descending to Páli from here, an old cobbled way offers an attractive shortcut.

NIKIÁ, the large village on the east side of the volcano's caldera, is a more lively place, and its spectacular situation offers views out to Tílos as well as across the volcanic crater. Of the three **kafenía** here, the one on the engaging, round *platía* is rarely open, while the one in the middle of town usually has food. There is also **accommodation**, but it tends to be substandard and expensive. By the bus turnaround area, signs point to the 45-minute **trail** descending to the crater floor; a few minutes downhill, you can detour briefly to the eyrie-like **monastery of Áyios Ioánnis Theológos**, with a shady tree and yet another perspective on the volcano. The picnic benches and utility buildings come to life at the annual festival, the evening of September 25. To **drive** directly to the volcanic area you have to take the unsignposted road which veers off just past Emborió.

Approaching from any direction a sulphurous stench drifts out to meet you as the fields and scrub gradually give way to lifeless, caked powder. The sunken main **crater** is extraordinary, a Hollywood moonscape of grey, brown and sickly yellow; there is another, less visited double-crater to the west, equally dramatic visually, with a clear trail leading up to it. The perimeters of both are pocked with tiny blow-holes from which jets of steam puff constantly and around which little pincushions of pure sulphur crystals form. The whole floor of the larger crater seems to hiss, and standing in the middle you can hear something akin to a huge cauldron bubbling away below you. In legend this is the groaning of Polyvotis, a titan crushed here by Poseidon under a huge rock torn from Kós. When there are tourists around a small café functions in the centre of the wasteland.

Since the destruction of the old trail between the volcano and Mandhráki, pleasant options for walking back to town are limited. If you want to try, backtrack along the main crater access road for about 1km to find the start of a clear but unmarked path which passes the volcanic gulch of **Káto Lákki** and the monastery of **Evangelistrías** on its two-hour course back to the port.

Kós

After Rhodes, **Kós** is easily the most popular island in the Dodecanese, and there are superficial similarities between the two. On Kós as on Rhodes, the harbour is guarded by an imposing castle of the Knights of Saint John, the waterside is lined with grandiose Italian public buildings, and minarets and palm trees punctuate extensive Hellenistic and Roman remains.

Though sandy and fertile, the hinterland of Kós lacks the wild beauty of Rhodes' interior, and it must also be said that the main town has little charm aside from its antiquities, and is overrun by high-rise hotels. Rhodes-scale tourist development imposed on an essentially sleepy, small-scale island economy, with a population of only 22,000, has resulted most obviously in even higher food and transport prices than on Rhodes. While Rhodes is a provincial capital in its own right, Kós is purely and simply a holiday resort, although there's also a strong military presence here – which itself exacerbates pressure on scarce food and housing resources and effectively puts large tracts of the island off-limits. Except for its far west end, this is not an island that attracts many independent travellers, and in high season you'll be lucky to find any sort of room at all.

Kós Town

The town of **KÓS** spreads in all directions from the harbour; apart from the **castle** (Tues–Sun 8.30am–3pm; 400dr), its sole compelling attraction lies in the wealth of Hellenistic and Roman remains, many of which were only revealed by an earthquake in 1933, and restored afterwards by the Italians. The largest single section is the ancient **agora**, linked to the castle by a bridge or reached by a signposted walkway from Platía Eleftherías next to the **Archeological Museum** (same hours as the castle; 400dr). The **Casa Romana** (same hours; admission free), a palatial Roman house at the rear of town, and the sections of the ancient town bracketed by the **odeion** and the **stadium** are more impressive up close. Both have well-preserved fragments of mosaic floors, although the best have been carted off to the Palace of the Grand Masters in Rhodes – and what remains tends to be under several inches of protective gravel.

There are, in fact, so many broken pillars, smashed statues and fragments of bas-relief lying around among the ruins here that nobody knows quite what to do with them. The best pieces have been taken for safekeeping into the castle, where most of them are piled up, unmarked and unnoticed. A couple of pillars, now replaced by scaffolding, were once even used to prop up the branches of **Hippocrates' plane tree**. This venerable tree has guarded the entrance to the castle for generations, and although not really elderly enough to have seen the great healer, it has a fair claim to being one of the oldest trees in Europe. Just next door is the imposing eighteenth-century **mosque of Hatzi Hassan**, its ground floor – like that of the **Defterdar mosque** on Platía Eleftherías – taken up by rows of shops.

Kós also boasts a rather bogus "**old bazaar**": a lone pedestrianized street, today crammed with tatty tourist boutiques, running from behind the overpriced produce market on Eleftherías as far as Platía Dhiagóras and the isolated minaret overlooking the inland archeological zone. About the only genuinely old thing here is a capped **Turkish fountain** with an inscription, found where the walkway cobbles cross Odhós Venizélou.

Arrival, transport and services

Large **ferries** anchor just outside the harbour at a special jetty by one corner of the castle; **excursion boats** to neighbouring islands sail right in and dock all along Aktí Koundouriótou. **Hydrofoils** dock beyond the main archeological zone, on Aktí Miaoúli. Virtually all ferry and excursion boat agents sit within 50m of each other at the intersection of Vassiléos Pávlou and the waterfront. Important exceptions include the head office of *Stefamar*, out on Avérof, for boats to Kálimnos, Psérimos and Níssiros, and the booking office for *Nearhos Mamidhakis (Dodecanese Hydrofoils)*, on Platía Iróön Politehníou (the round plaza at the back of the harbour).

The **airport** is 26km west of Kós Town in the centre of the island; an *Olympic Airways* shuttle bus meets *Olympic* flights, but if you arrive on any other flight you'll have to either take a taxi or head towards the giant roundabout outside the airport gate and find a *KTEL* bus – they run from here to Mastihári, Kardhámena and Kéfalos as

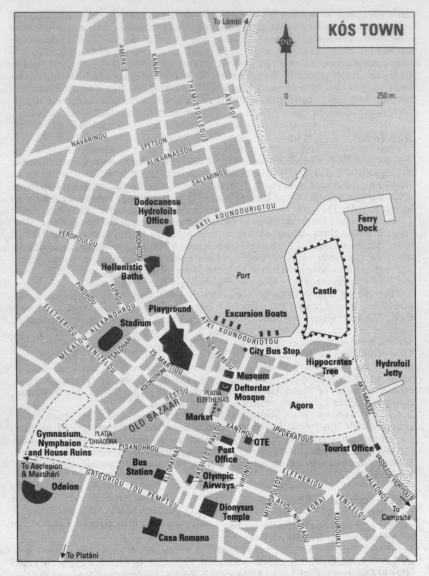

KÓS TOWN

To Lámbi

0   250 m.

To Lámbi

Dodecanese
Hydrofoils
Office

Ferry
Dock

AMERKIS

KANARI

THEMISTOKLEOUS

AVEROF

NAVARINOU

SPETSON

ALIKARNASSOU

SALAMINOS

AKTÍ KOUNDOURIOTOU

VEROPOULOU

RODHOTOU

Port

Castle

Hellenistic
Baths

PINDHOU

KIPROU

ELEFTHERIOU

MEGALOU VENIZELOU

ALEXANDHROU

TSALDHARI

Playground

Stadium

Excursion Boats

AKTÍ KOUNDOURIOTOU

City Bus Stop

Hydrofoil
Jetty

25 MARTIOU

KOLOKOTRONI

RIGA FEREOU

Hippocrates'
Tree

AKTÍ MIAOULI

IFESTOU

OLD BAZAAR

PLATÍA
ELEFTHERÍAS

Museum

Defterdar
Mosque

Agora

IPPOKRATOUS

Gymnasium,
Nymphaion
and House Ruins

PLATÍA
DHIÁGORA

PISANDHROU

Market

XANTHOU

OTE

Tourist Office

VASSILEOS YIORYIOU B

To Asclepion
& Mastihári

GRIGORIOU TOU PEMPTOU

KLEOPATRAS

VASSILEOS PAVLOU

Post
Office

VIRONOS

ELEFTHERIOU

HALKONOS

To
Campsite

Odeion

Bus
Station

Olympic
Airways

MITROPOLEOS

AYIOU NIKOLAOU

KORAI

VENIZELOU

KOUROUKLI

Dionysus
Temple

Casa Romana

To Platáni

well as Kós Town. The **KTEL terminal** in town is a series of stops around a triangular park 500m back from the water; the municipality also runs a **local bus** service through the beach suburbs and up to the Asclepion, with a ticket and information office on Aktí Koundouriótou.

The *Trapeza Pisteos/Credit Bank* on the waterfront opens on Saturday morning for **exchange**; some other banks open in the evenings, and there are various ATMs. The

post office is at Venizélou 14, and may open Saturday and Sunday mornings in season, while the **OTE** at Víronos on the corner of Xánthou, is open until 11pm daily. *Happy Wash* laundry is at Mitropóleos 14.

Accommodation

If you're just in transit, then it makes sense to **stay** in Kós Town. Good budget alternatives in the centre include the *Dodekanissos* (☎0242/28 460; ③), around the corner at Ipsilándou 2; the *Elena* (☎0242/22 740; ③), at Megálou Alexándhrou 5; or the deservedly popular *Pension Alexis* (☎0242/28 798; ③), Irodhótou 9 at the corner of Omírou, across from the Roman *agora;* the same management has the *Hotel Afendoulis* (☎0242/25 321; ④), about 600m south at Evripílou 1. For longer stays, the rooms let by *Moustafa Tselepi* (☎0242/28 896; ③) at Venizélou 29, on the corner of Metsóvou, are a good choice, and some have cooking facilities. Across the port, along Avérof, are some other reasonable, if noisier, options: try the *Pension Popi* (☎0242/23 475; ③) at no. 37, or the *Nitsa* (☎0242/25 810; ③) at no. 41. The well-appointed **campsite** is 2500m out towards Cape Psalídhi, and can be reached by the city bus service, but is open only during the warmer months.

Eating, drinking and nightlife

Eating out well and cheaply is likely to pose more problems. You can pretty much write off most of the waterfront tavernas, though the *Romantica*, one of the first as you come from the ferry jetty, and its neighbour the *Limnos*, are within the bounds of reason. Inland, the least expensive and most authentic establishments are the *Australia Sydney* at Vassiléos Pávlou 29, with an amazingly well-stocked bar and an ample menu, and the *Olimpiadha* at Kleopátras 2, both near *Olympic Airways*. You might also try the *Ambavris*, 800m south out of town, and the atmospheric *Anatolia Hamam*, housed partly in an old Turkish bath off Platía Dhiagóras. If you're craving an English – or even American – **breakfast**, various cafés serve that or just coffee under giant trees on Platía Ayías Paraskevís, behind the produce market: expensive but worth it.

In terms of **nightlife**, you need look no further than the inland pedestrian way joining Platía Eleftherías and the castle; every address is a bar, just choose according to the crowd and the noise level. Otherwise there is one active **cinema**, the *Orfevs* with summer and winter premises.

The Asclepion and Platáni

Hippocrates is justly celebrated on Kós; not only does he have a tree named after him, but the star exhibit in the town museum is his statue, and the Asclepion (city bus via Platáni 8.30am–2.30pm, to Platáni only 2.30–11pm; or a 45-minute walk) is a major tourist attraction. Treatments described by Hippocrates and his followers were still used as recently as a hundred years ago, and his ideas on medical methods and ethics remain influential.

The **Asclepion** whose ruins can be seen (Tues–Sun 8.30am–3pm; 600dr) was actually built after the death of Hippocrates, but it's safe to assume that the methods used and taught here were still his. Both a temple to Asclepius (son of Apollo, god of medicine) and a renowned centre of healing, its magnificent setting on terraces levelled from a hillside overlooking the Anatolian mainland reflects early doctors' recognition of the importance of the therapeutic environment: springs still provide the site with a constant supply of clean fresh water. There used to be a rival medical school in the ancient town of Knidos, on the Asia Minor coast southeast of Kós, at a time when there was far more traffic across the straits than today. Incidentally, there are no facilities at the Asclepion.

A mild social segregation still prevails close at hand in the bi-ethnic village of **PLATÁNI** (*Kermete* in Turkish), on the road to the Asclepion; the Greek Orthodox stay in their *kafenía* while the Muslim minority still manage the three establishments dominating the crossroads. All of the latter – particularly *Arap* – serve excellent, relatively cheap, Turkish-style food, far better than anything you generally get in Kós Town. There's a working Ottoman fountain nearby, and the older domestic architecture of Platáni is strongly reminiscent of rural styles in provincial Crete, from where many of Platáni's Turks came early this century.

Just outside Platáni on the road back to the harbour, the Jewish cemetery stands in a dark pine grove, 300m from the Muslim graveyard. Dates on the headstones stop ominously after 1940, after which none were allowed the luxury of a natural death. The old synagogue, locked and crumbling since the 1944 deportations to the concentration camps, is back in Kós Town between the ancient *agora* and the waterfront.

Eastern Kós

If you're looking for anything resembling a deserted **beach** near the capital, you'll need to make use of the city bus line connecting the various resorts to either side of town, or else rent a vehicle. Closest is **Lámbi**, 3km north towards Cape Skandhári with its military watchpoint, the last vestige of a vast army camp which has deferred to the demands of tourism. On the same coast, 12km west of the harbour, **TIGÁKI** is still just about a village, easily accessible by *KTEL* bus or rented push-bike (a popular option in the flat east end of Kós). As a result it's crowded until evening, when everyone except those lucky enough to have rented a room has disappeared.

The far end of the city bus line beginning at Lámbi is Áyios Fokás, 8km out, with the unusual and remote **Brós Thermá** 5km further on, easiest reached by moped. Here **hot springs** trickle over black sand into the sea, warming it up for early or late-season swims. There's a small seasonal café but no other facilities.

Inland, the main interest of eastern Kós resides in the villages of **Mount Dhíkeos**, a handful of settlements collectively referred to as Asfendhíou, nestling among the slopes of the island's only forest. They are accessible either via the curvy side-road from Zipári, or a more straightforward turning signed as "Píli".

Modern **PÍLI** is sprawling and unattractive, and the lack of tourist amenities seems an admission that no-one will stop here. **Old Píli**, signposted inconspicuously as such on a house corner in Amaníou, the next hamlet east, gets more attention; a paved road leads up a wooded canyon, stopping by a spring at the base of a crag with a Byzantine castle and the ruined houses of the abandoned village tumbling away from it. The frescoes in the handful of medieval churches are in bad condition, however, and all told the place is more impressive from a distance.

From Amaníou the main dirt track leads northeast via the untouristed hamlet of Lagoúdhi to **EVANGELÍSTRIA**, where there's a taverna and an interesting "suburb", **ASÓMATI**, with fine whitewashed houses. **ZIÁ**, further up the now paved road, is the hapless target of up to six tour buses per night; several rather commercialized tavernas take advantage of the spectacular sunsets, but it's a good idea to clear out immediately afterwards.

Beyond Ziá the way deteriorates to dirt once more, continuing to **ÁYIOS YIÓRYIOS**, where only around thirty villagers and a handful of foreigners and Athenians renovating houses dwell; there is one tiny store where you can get a drink. **ÁYIOS DHIMÍTRIOS**, 2km beyond, on an exceedingly rough track, was abandoned entirely during the junta years, when the inhabitants went to Zipári or further afield. Indeed, the best reason for coming up this way is to get some idea of what Kós looked like before tourism and ready-mix concrete took root.

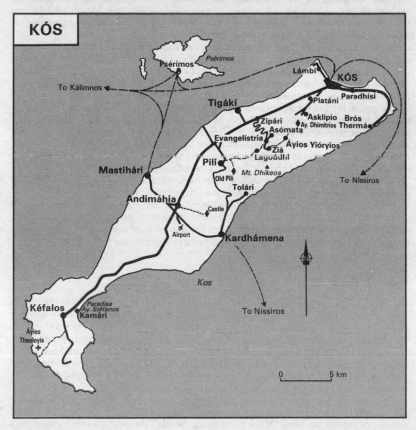

Western Kós

Near the centre of the island, a pair of giant roundabouts by the airport funnels traffic northwest towards Mastihári, northeast back towards town, southwest towards Kéfalos, and southeast to Kardhámena.

The beach at **MASTIHÁRI** is smaller than those at Tigáki or Kardhámena, and the small town is increasingly built up, but it is the port for the least expensive *kaíkia* to Kálimnos and the tiny Greek islet of Psérimos (see below), so you may want to come here; there are plenty of rooms to rent if you need to stay. In season there are daily morning and mid-afternoon sailings, with an extra late-night departure when charter landings warrant it – though be warned that boats can be fully occupied by package clients.

KARDHÁMENA, on the southeast-facing coast, is the island's second-largest package resort, packed in season; runaway local development has banished whatever redeeming qualities it may once have had. A beach stretches to either side of the town, backed on the east with ill-concealed military bunkers and a road as far as Tolári, where there is a massive hotel complex. Halfway back towards Andimáhia an enormous **castle** (the Knights' again) sprawls atop a ridge. Like Mastihári, Kardhámena is most worth knowing about as a place to catch inter-island *kaíkia*, in this case to Níssiros. There are supposedly two daily sailings in season, at approximately 9am and 5pm, but in practice the afternoon departure takes place any time between 1.30 and 6.30pm, depending on when the Nissirians have finished their shopping.

Outside high season, there are generally a few **rooms** not taken by tour companies and prices, at ②–③ depending on the facilities and number of people, are not outrageous. The one reasonable **taverna**, *Andreas*, is right on the harbour; inland, a **bakery** (signed with red arrows) does homemade ice cream, yoghurt and sticky cakes, and *Peter's* **rent a bike** across the street is one of the more flexible outfits.

The end of the line for buses is the inland village of Kéfalos, which squats on a mesa-like hill looking back down the length of Kós. Most visitors will have alighted long before, either at **KAMÁRI** or **ÁYIOS STÉFANOS**, where the exquisite remains of a fifth-century basilica overlook tiny Kastrí islet; both places have plenty of accommodation. The beach begins at Kamári and runs five kilometres east, virtually without interruption, to the cliff-framed and aptly-named **Paradise beach**. Unfortunately the entire area between Kamári and Áyios Stéfanos has been overshadowed by a huge Club Med complex of bungalows surrounding the main luxury hotel.

Kéfalos itself is rather dull but is the staging point for expeditions into the rugged southwest peninsula. To the west, around the monastery of **Áyios Theológos**, you can still find deserted stretches of coastline, but the nearest cove is about 6km distant over rough tracks – and none are as sheltered as the bays on the island's southeast flank.

Psérimos

If it weren't for its proximity to Kós and Kálimnos, which results in day-trippers by the boatload every day of the season, **Psérimos** could be an idyllic little island. Even in April and October, however, you can be guaranteed at least 100 outsiders a day (which doubles the population), so imagine the scene in high season as visitors spread themselves along the main sandy beach, which stretches around the bay in front of the twenty or thirty houses that constitute **PSÉRIMOS VILLAGE**. There are a couple of other, less attractive pebbly beaches, no more than thirty walking minutes distant – in fact nowhere on Psérimos is much more than half an hour's walk away.

When the day-trippers have gone you can, out of season, have the place to yourself and even in season there won't be too many other overnighters, since there's a limited number of **rooms** available. Of the three small "hotels", the best for value, cleanliness and friendliness is the one run by Katerina Fyloura above her taverna on the eastern side of the harbour. She has a total of thirteen beds apportioned over five rooms (③) and the food's good too. Katerina also acts as postmistress if you want to write home, since the island can't support a post office. There's just one small **store**, not very well-stocked, and most of the island's supplies are brought in daily from Kálimnos. **Eating out**, however, won't break the bank and there's plenty of fresh fish in the handful of tavernas.

The island is easily reached from either Kálimnos or Kós: most Kós Town–Kálimnos and Mastihári–Kálimnos excursion *kaíkia* make a stop at Psérimos in each direction.

Astipálea

Both geographically and architecturally, Astipálea would be more at home among the Cyclades – on a clear day the island can be seen quite clearly from Anáfi or Amorgós, and it looks and feels more like them than its neighbours to the east. Despite its butter-fly shape, it's not the most beautiful of islands: the barren coastline gives way in parts to fields, citrus groves and decent, mountainous walking country, but the beaches are often stony and litter-strewn.

In antiquity the island's most famous citizen was Kleomedes, a boxer disqualified from an early Olympic Games for killing his opponent. He came home so enraged that he demolished the local school, killing all its pupils. Things have calmed down a bit in the intervening 2500 years and today the capital is a quiet fishing port – the catch is locally consumed, as the island is too remote for it to be shipped to the mainland. This is also a reflection of the notoriously poor ferry links; things have improved recently with the introduction of two new services to the Cyclades, but you still risk being marooned here for an extra day or three. Despite the relative isolation, plenty of people find their way to Astipálea in summer, though relatively few are English-speaking – it seems more popular with French, Italian and Athenian second-home owners.

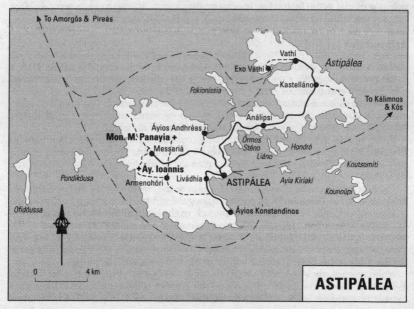

Yialós and Hóra

The main harbour of **YIALÓS** dates from the Italian era (Astipálea was the first island the Italians occupied in the Dodecanese) and most of the settlement between the quay and the line of nine windmills is even more recent. As you climb up beyond the port towards **HÓRA**, though, the neighbourhoods get progressively older and their steep streets are enlivened by the *poúndia* or colourful wooden balconies of the whitewashed houses. The whole culminates in the fourteenth-century *kástro*, one of the finest in the Aegean. Until well into this century over 3000 souls dwelt within, but depopulation and wartime damage have combined to leave only a desolate shell today; the fine groin vaulting over the entrance and a couple of maintained churches remain an attraction, though restoration is now beginning.

There are several inexpensive **hotels** down in the port – the *Astynea* (☎0243/61 209; ③), the *Paradisos* (☎0243/61 224; ③), the *Vangelis* (☎0243/61 281; ③) and the *Egeon* (☎0243/61 236; ③) – but if you can get them, **rooms** in the upper town near the windmills that mark the *platía* in Hóra are better. Further up the scale, *Viva Mare* (☎0243/61 292; ⑤) are well-appointed studio units a bit inland from Yialós. Finally, there's a **campsite** halfway along the 5km to Analípsi, easily reached by bus.

Toh Akroyiali, *Babis* and *Karlos* **tavernas** are the local haunts, *Astynea*, on the wharf, *Australia* and *Iy Monaxia*, behind the ferry dock, are also good. The stepped hill of Maltezána constitutes the business district; here you'll find more places to eat, several discos, shops, the **OTE** and a **travel agency** arranging boat excursions to remote beaches. The **post office** is well up in the Hóra, as are some subdued clubs like *Kastro Bar* and *Artemis*. You can change money at the post office or a bank agent (there's no actual bank).

A **bus** runs regularly between Hóra, Skala, Livádhia and Analípsi in July and August, less frequently out of season – the posted timetables are far from reliable. There are only two official **taxis**, far too few in season when lots of Athenians visit; several places rent out mopeds. The island **map** sold locally is grossly inaccurate.

Around the island

Half an hour's walk (or a short, frequent bus journey) from the capital is **LIVÁDHIA**, a fertile green valley with a popular, good beach and shaded restaurants by the waterside. You can **camp** here or **rent a room** or bungalow in the beach hamlet – for example from the Nikos Kondaratos family (☎0243/61 269; ②), which has been known to offer a mattress in the local citrus and banana orchards when they're full inside. Among the **tavernas**, *Yiesenia*, *Thomas* and *Kalamia* are all decent.

If the beach here is not to your liking, continue southwest on a footpath to **Tzanáki**, with nude bathing and fewer people. Continuing to **Áyios Konstandínos** cove is well worthwhile, where a taverna plus the shade from the fringing orchards are a plus.

The best outing on the island, however, has to be the two-hour walk from Astipálea to the oasis of **Áyios Ioánnis**. Walk one hour along the dirt track beginning from the sixth or seventh windmill, then bear left at the fork (right leads to the anchorage of **Áyios Andhréas**: one ramshackle taverna, good swimming and snorkelling). After a while, you pass another path going right towards the uninspiring monastery of Panayía Flevariotíssas; carry on above **Arménohori** (a pillaged ancient site) and the farming hamlet of Messariá, before turning left, at the top of a pass, on to a footpath heading for some bony-white rock outcrops. Soon the walled orchards of the farm-monastery of Áyios Ioánnis (not to be confused with a seaside cloister of the same name to the north) come into view. Just below, a ten-metre waterfall plunges into deep pools fine for bathing. A rather arduous trek down the valley ends at a fine pebbly bay, and proper paths lead back towards Armenohóriif you don't fancy a reprise of the jeep tracks you arrived on.

Northeast of the harbour, a series of bays nestle in the "body" of the "butterfly". Of the two coves known as **Marmári**, one is home to the power plant, and the next one hosts the island's only organized **campsite**. Beyond, at **Stenó**, the middle beach, with clean sand and fresh-water wells, is the best.

ANÁLIPSI, universally known as Maltezána after Maltese pirates, is about a five-kilometre taxi-ride or walk beyond the campsite. Although the second-largest settlement on Astipálea, there's little for outsiders save a narrow, sea-urchin-speckled beach and two small **tavernas** (*Obelix* is excellent), plus quite a few **rooms**. At the edge of the surrounding olive groves are the well-preserved remains of **Roman baths**, with floor mosaics of zodiacal signs and the seasons personified. In high season, Análipsi can be a welcome escape – once you find your way around, there are other beaches accessible around the bay. The road ends at **VATHÍ**, an even sleepier fishing village with a single taverna and a superb harbour, which is where the ferry docks in winter when Astipálea Town is battered by the prevailing southerly winds. At such times, and only then, there is a bus between Vathí and Astipálea. Occasional *kaíkia* shuttle back and forth in season between Vathí and either Áyios Andhréas or Yialós.

Kálimnos

Most of the population of **Kálimnos** lives in or around the large port of Pothiá, a wealthy but not conventionally beautiful town famed for its sponge divers. Sadly almost all the Mediterranean's sponges, with the exception of a few deep-water beds off Italy, have been devastated by disease, and only three or four of the fleet of thirty or more boats can currently be usefully occupied. In response to this economic disaster, the island is attempting to establish a tourist industry – so far confined to several tiny beach resorts – and has customized its sponge boats for deep-sea fishing. The warehouses behind the harbour, however, still process and sell sponges (imported from Asia and America) to tourists all year round. During the Italian occupation houses here were painted blue and white to keep alive the Greek colours and irritate the invaders. The custom is beginning to die out, but is still evident; even some of the churches are painted blue.

Since Kálimnos is the home port of two hydrofoil lines, and of the very useful local ferry of that name (see "Travel Details"), and is also where the long-distance ferry lines from the outer Cyclades and Astipálea join up with the main Dodecanesian ones, many travellers unwittingly find themselves here, and are initially most concerned with how to move on quickly. The islanders have so far remained welcoming, and indulgent of short stays, perhaps realizing that the place won't hold most people's interest for more than a day or two.

Pothiá

POTHIÁ, without being particularly picturesque, is colourful and authentically Greek, the overwhelming impression being of the phenomenal amount of noise engendered by the cranked-up sound systems of the dozen waterfront cafés, and the exhibitionist motorbike traffic. **Accommodation** is rarely a problem, since pension proprietors usually meet the ferries; otherwise the *Hotel Patmos* (☎0243/22 750; ③), in a relatively quiet sidestreet at the west end of the front near the **EOT** booth, or the *Pension Greek House* (☎0243/29 559; ②), 200m to the north in Amoudhára district, are dependable fall backs. Slightly to the south, the well-signposted *Hotel Panorama* (☎0243/23 138; ③) perches above *Greek House*.

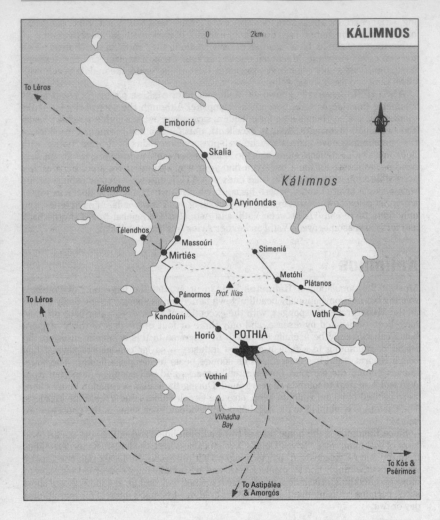

For **eating out**, the best strategy is to follow the waterfront west past the Italian-built municipal "palace" to a line of **fish tavernas and ouzerís**. The first, nameless joint under the tamarisks is okay, *Barba Petros* at the far end is a bit glitzy, while *Psarouzeri O Kambourakis* in between represents fair value. Sticky-cake fans will want to take three paces west to *Zaharoplastiki O Mihalaras*, while still further in the same direction, *Apothiki* is currently the coolest waterfront bar/café. The local speciality is octopus croquettes.

The **OTE** and the **post office** are virtually opposite each other inland on Venizélou; all **boat and hydrofoil agents** line the waterfront as you bear right out of the pier-area gate, and there's an *Olympic Airways* office at Patriárhou Maxímou 17. Finally, waterfront branches of the *National* and *Ionian* **banks** both have autotellers.

Around the island

Buses run as far as Aryinóndas in the northwest and Vathí in the east, while for more freedom there are plenty of places to rent a **moped**. Chances are you'll want to escape, at least during the day, to one of the smaller coastal settlements.

Heading northwest across the island, the first place you come to is the old capital, **HORIÓ**, sandwiched between an eroded **castle** of the Knights of Saint John and the miniature Byzantine precinct of **Péra Kástro**. The crumbling ruins of the latter are peppered with conspicuously white churches, but it's the Knights' castle (known locally as *Kástro Hrissoherías*) that especially merits a visit, with its stupendous views over the entire west coast of the island.

From the ridge at Horió the road dips into a cultivated ravine, heading for the consecutive beach resorts of Kandoúni, Pánormos, Mirtiés and Massoúri. All of them are far more developed than is warranted by the scanty shelves of grey sand or pebbles in the vicinity; at **MIRTIÉS** and **MASSOÚRI** there is scant possibility of finding a room amid the package-holiday paraphernalia. The trip across the strait to the striking, volcanic-plug island of **TÉLENDHOS** is arguably the best reason to come to Mirtiés; little boats shuttle to and fro constantly throughout the day. On the islet you'll find a ruined monastery, a castle, a couple of tiny beaches and several tavernas and pensions, all in or near the single village; if you want to book ahead, try *Pension Uncle George* (☎0243/47 502; ②), *Dhimitris Harinos* (☎0243/47 916; ②), or *Foukena Galanomati* (☎0243/47 401; ②). It's also possible to go from Mirtiés directly to Léros aboard the daily *kaíki*.

Beyond Mirtiés, **ARYINÓNDAS** and **EMBORIÓ** both have relatively empty, decent beaches, the latter alongside a couple of good tavernas which have rooms (*Harry's*, ☎0243/47 434 and *Themis*, ☎0243/47 277). If the bus fails you, there is sometimes a shuttle boat back to Mirtiés.

East from Póthia, an initially unpromising, forty-minute ride ends dramatically at **VATHÍ**, whose colour provides a startling contrast to the lifeless greys elsewhere on Kálimnos. A long, fertile valley, verdant with orange and tangerine groves, it seems a continuation of the cobalt-blue fjord which penetrates finger-like into the landscape. In the simple port, known as Rína, there are a handful of *kafenía* and tavernas to choose from, as well as a the *Galini* **hotel** (☎0243/31 241; ③) and a few **rooms**. For **walkers** the lush valley behind, criss-crossed with rough tractor-tracks and paths, may prove an irresistible lure, but be warned that it will take you the better part of three hours, most of it shadeless once you're out of the orchards, to reach points on the opposite coast. The only facilities en route lie in the hamlets of Plátanos and Metóhi at the head of the valley; once past these, the route divides, with one option going to Massoúri, the other to Aryinóndas via the third hamlet of Stiménia.

Southwest of Pothiá, the attractive little sandy bay of **Vlihádha**, with the village of **VOTHINÍ** perched above, is plainly visible from most ferries coming or going, and considerably less crowded than the northwestern beaches. Local *kaíkia* make well-publicized excursions to the southerly caves of **Kéfalos**, **Skaliá** and **Ayía Varvára**, all nearly as impressive as the photographs they use to tempt you to go there.

Léros

Léros is so indented with deep, sheltered anchorages that during the last world war it harboured, in turn, the entire Italian, German, and British Mediterranean fleets. Unfortunately, these magnificent fjords and bays seem to absorb rather than reflect light, and the island's relative fertility can seem unruly when compared to the crisp lines of its more barren neighbours. These characteristics, coupled with the island's absence until recently from the lists of most major tour operators, mean that barely

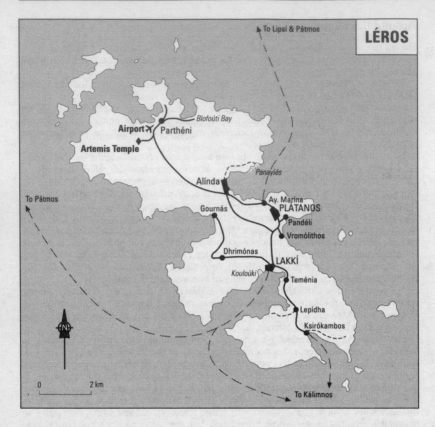

10,000 foreigners a year (many of them Italians who grew up on the island), and not many more Greeks, come to stay. Although lacking spectacularly good beaches, Léros is on the verge of being "discovered" by those in search of more understated pleasures, such as gentle walks, botanizing and the company of islanders unjaded by mass tourism. Things should stay that way until or unless the extension to the airport runway that will enable it to accommodate jets, mooted for years, takes place.

Not that the island needs, nor particularly encourages, tourism; various prisons and sanitariums have long dominated the Lerian economy. Under the junta the island was the site of an infamous detention centre, and today mental hospitals on Léros are still the repository for many of Greece's more intractable psychiatric cases; another asylum is home to hundreds of mentally handicapped children. The island's domestic image problem is compounded by its name, the butt of jokes by mainlanders who pounce on its similarity to the word *léra*, connoting rascality and unsavouriness. Islanders are in fact extremely friendly to those who visit, but their island's role and image seem unlikely to change. In 1989 a major scandal burst forth concerning the administration of the various asylums, with EC maintenance and development funds found to have been embezzled by administrators and staff, and the inmates kept in degrading and inhumane conditions. By 1991 EC inspectors pronounced themselves satisfied that the abuses had stopped, and there have been drastic improvements in the treatment of patients, including the establishment of halfway houses across the island. Although Léros will be a long time overcoming this additional stigma, the institutional identity is not as pervasive as you might expect.

More obvious is the legacy of the Battle of Léros late in 1943, when overwhelming German forces displaced a British division: unexploded bombs and shells turn up as gaily painted garden ornaments in the courtyards of churches and tavernas, or have been pressed into service as gateposts.

Unusually for a small island, Léros has abundant groundwater. This, combined with the avenues of eucalyptus trees planted by the Italians, makes for a horrendously active mosquito contingent, so come prepared. The island is small enough to walk around, but there is a bus service and several bike-rental outfits.

Lakkí and Ksirókambos

All large **ferries**, and *Ilio Line* hydrofoils arrive at the main port of **LAKKÍ**, once the headquarters of a bustling Italian naval base, which accounts for the extraordinary look of the place. Wide boulevards, laid out around little parks and statues, are lined with some marvellous Art Deco edifices – most notably the round-fronted cinema (closed since 1985), the school and the defunct *Leros Palace Hotel*.

Buses don't meet the ferries; instead, there are taxis that charge set fares to standard destinations. Accordingly, few people stay in Lakkí, preferring to head straight for the resorts of Pandéli or Vromólithos (see below), though you can **eat** very well at *Sotos*, a Swedish co-run place with plenty of choice for vegetarians. The nearest **beach** is at Kouloúki, 600m west, where there's a seasonal snack-bar.

KSIRÓKAMBOS, nearly 5km from Lakkí at the extreme south of the island, is the point of arrival for *kaikía* from Mirtiés on Kálimnos. Billed as a resort, it's essentially a fishing port where people also happen to swim – the beach here is poor to mediocre, improving as you head west. **Accommodation** is available at *Villa Maria* (☎0247/22 827; ③) or, a bit inland, at *Yianoukas Rooms* (☎0247/23 148; ②); the island's **campsite** is in an olive grove at the village of Lepídha, 750m back up the road to Lakkí. **Meals** can be had at *Taverna Tzitzifies*, just by the jujube trees at the east end of things, where the road hits the shore.

Pandéli and Vromólithos

Just under 3km north of Lakkí, Pandéli and Vromólithos together form the fastest-growing resort on the island – and are certainly the most attractive and scenic places to stay.

PANDÉLI is still very much a working port, with a negligible beach, but is a good bet for non-package **accommodation**, such as *Pension Roza* (☎0247/22 798; ②) or *Pension Kavos* (☎0247/23 247; ③), further east, with a pleasant breakfast terrace. Up on the ridge dividing Pandéli from Vromólithos, the peace at the *Hotel Rodon* (☎0247/23 524; ③) is disturbed only by wafts of R&B or soul from the *Beach Bar*, perched on a rock terrace some distance below. The other, long-lived bar is the civilized *Savana*, at the opposite end of Pandéli, but the soul of the place is its waterfront **tavernas**, which come alive after dark. These get less expensive and less pretentious as you head east, culminating in *Maria's*, a local institution, decked out in coloured lights and whimsically painted gourds – try the grilled octopus. *Zorba's* offers large portions of well-prepared food, with vegetarians well catered for.

VROMÓLITHOS boasts the best easily accessible beach on the island, hemmed in by hills studded with massive oaks. The **beach** is gravel and coarse sand, and the water's fine, but a nasty reef must be crossed before you reach a sharp dropoff to deeper water. Two tavernas behind the beach trade more on their location than their cuisine, but the standard of **accommodation** here is higher than at Pandéli, with the result that it tends to be monopolized by package companies; *Tony's Beach Rooms & Studios* (☎0247/27 742; ④) is worth a try.

Plátanos and Ayía Marína

The Neoclassical and vernacular houses of **PLÁTANOS**, the island capital 1km west of Pandéli, are draped gracefully along a saddle between two hills, one of them crowned by the inevitable Knights' castle. Locally known as the **Kástro**, this is reached either by a rough road peeling off the Pandéli road, or a more scenic stair-path from the central square; the battlements, and the views from them, are dramatic, especially at sunrise or sunset. Except for the *Hotel Eleftheria* (☎0247/23 550; ③), elevated and quiet enough to be desirable, it's not really a place to stay or eat, although it's admirably provided with **shops and services** – including seven hairdressers. *Leros Travel* acts as a ferry-ticket agent and is conveniently located next door to *Olympic Airways* (☎0247/24 144), while the **post office** and short-hours **OTE** are down the road towards Ayía Marína. **Buses** ply four to six times daily between Parthéni in the north and Ksirókambos in the south.

Plátanos merges seamlessly with **AYÍA MARÍNA**, 1km north on the shore of a fine bay. Although there's no accommodation here, *DRM* and *Kastis* travel agencies can book rooms elsewhere, as well as arranging tickets for ferries and hydrofoils. On the water, *Taverna Ayia Marina* has the broadest menu, while *Garbo's* (evenings only in summer), on the road to Plátanos, seems to have hit upon a winning formula of English food (including curries) and movie-poster decor.

The north

ALÍNDA, 3km northwest of Ayía Marína, ranks as the longest-established resort on Léros, with development focused around a narrow strip of pea-gravel and hotels block-booked by package companies. Seven kilometres further along the main route north is the marked side track for the **Temple of Artemis**. In ancient times, Léros was sacred to the goddess, and the temple here was supposedly inhabited by guinea fowl – the grief-stricken sisters of Meleager, metamorphosed by Artemis following their brother's death. All that remains now are some jumbled walls, but the view is superb. The onward road skims the shores of sumpy and reed-fringed Parthéni Bay, until the paved road runs out at **Blefoúti**, a rather more inspiring sight with its huge, virtually land-locked bay with greenery-flecked hills behind. The beach is fairly ordinary, but there are tamarisks to shelter under and a decent taverna, *Iy Thea Artemi*, for lunch.

Pátmos

Arguably the most beautiful, certainly the best known of the smaller islands in the Dodecanese, **Pátmos** is unique. It was in a cave here that Saint John the Divine (in Greek, *O Theologos*), had his revelation (the Bible's Book of Revelation) and unwittingly shaped the island's destiny. The monastery which commemorates him, founded here in 1088, dominates the island both physically – its fortified bulk towering high above anything else – and, to a considerable extent, politically. While the monks no longer run the island as they did for more than 700 years, their influence has nevertheless stopped Pátmos going the way of Rhodes or Kós. Despite vast numbers of visitors, and the island's firm presence on the cruise, hydrofoil and yacht circuits, tourism has not been allowed to take the island over. There are a number of clubs and even one disco around Skála, the port and main town, but everywhere else development of any kind is appealingly subdued.

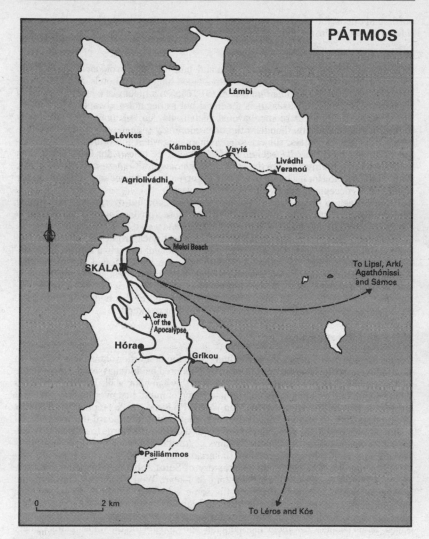

Skála and around

SKÁLA seems initially to contradict this image of Pátmos. The waterside, with its ritzy-looking cafés and clientele, is a little too sophisticated for its own small-town good, and it must be said that some of the world-weary service personnel are none too civil at times. In season it's crowded by day with excursionists from Kós and Rhodes; by night with well-dressed cliques of visitors. In winter the shops and restaurants close and most of their owners and staff leave for Rhodes; the town itself taking on a somewhat depressed air, with no place for the kids to roar their motorbikes towards. If you feel like moving straight out, the most obvious possibility is **Méloï Beach**, 1500m to the north, and one of the most convenient and popular on the island; Hóra, a bus or taxi-ride up the mountain, is a more attractive base but has few rooms.

Practicalities

Accommodation in Skála itself is in demand but, for noise-avoidance reasons, you might be better off away from the centre. Good mid-range hotels are the *Galini* (☎0247/31 740; ④) or the *Blue Bay* (☎0247/31 165; ④), a quiet place just to the east of town; the *Rex* (☎0247/31 242; ②) is a central but rather noisy cheapie. More likely, however, you'll end up in rooms, hawked vociferously on the quay; they are mostly higher than usual quality, though with correspondingly higher prices, too. There are plenty of places for **meals**, subject to sudden rushes when the cruise boats arrive – among the best are *Pandelis*, behind the *Café Arion* (see below), for fish, *Grigori's*, on your left as you disembark from the ferry, and the *Skorpios Creperie* and *Platanos* grill, both on the way to Hóra. The trendiest **bar** is currently the barn-like *Café Arion* on the waterside, its deceptively small entrance easily missed.

If you're keen to stay nearer to a beach, there's a good but overpriced **campsite** at Méloï, together with some **rooms** – best are those run by *Loula Koumendhourou* (☎0247/32 281; ③), on the slope south of the bay – and a couple of tavernas.

Everything else is near the police station: the boat docks right opposite; **bus and boat timetables** are posted outside; and the fairly helpful municipal **tourist information** (daily except Sun, 9am–1pm & 5–8pm) is at the back. Moped and **motorbike rental** outfits are common, with lowish rates owing to the modest size of the island; at the south end of the front, *DRM* is about the most useful **ferry-ticket agent**, representing the *Nissos Kalimnos*, *Miniotis Lines*, *G&A*, and one of the hydrofoil companies. There are **banks**, a **post office** and an **OTE** (closed at weekends).

Hóra and the monasteries

For cruise-ship passengers and overnighters alike the first order of business is likely to be heading up to the Monastery of Saint John, sheltered behind massive defences in the hilltop capital of Hóra. There is a bus up, but the half-hour walk by a beautiful old cobbled path puts you in a more appropriate frame of mind. Just over halfway, pause at the **Monastery of the Apocalypse** (Mon Wed & Fri 8am–2pm & 4–6pm, Tues Thur Sat & Sun 8am–2pm; free) built around the cave where Saint John heard the voice of God issuing from a cleft in the rock, and where he sat dictating His words to a disciple. A leaflet left for visitors points out that the "fissure . . . (divides) the rock into three parts, thus serving as a continual reminder of the Trinitarian nature of God".

This is merely a foretaste of the **Monastery of Saint John** (erratic hours, but theoretically Mon Tues Thur & Sun 8am–2pm & 4–6pm, Wed Fri & Sat 8am–2pm; the cloister of the Apocalypse adheres to the same schedule; "modest" dress essential; 500dr admission to treasury). Behind its imposing fortifications have been preserved a fantastic array of religious treasures dating back to the earliest days of Christianity: relics, icons, books, ceremonial ornaments and apparel of the most extraordinary richness.

Outside Saint John's stout walls, **HÓRA** is a beautiful little town whose antiquated alleys shelter over forty churches and monasteries. The churches, many of them containing beautiful icons and examples of the local skill in wood carving, are almost all locked, but someone living nearby will have the key. Among the best are the church of **Dhiassozoússas** and the monastery of **Zoödhóhou Piyís**.

You can **eat** well at *Vangelis* on the inner square, which has the edge over nearby *Olympia* in terms of freshness and variety. There are, however, very few **places to stay**; foreigners here are mostly long-term occupants, and almost a third of the crumbling mansions have been bought up and restored in the past two decades. Getting a short-term room can be a pretty thankless task, even in spring or autumn; the best strategy is to contact *Vangelis* taverna early in the day, or phone ahead for reservations at *Yioryia Triandafyllou* (☎0247/31 963; ④) or *Marouso Kouva* (☎0247/31 026; ④).

Finally, don't miss the **view** from Platía Lótzas, particularly at dawn or dusk: the land-masses to the north, going clockwise, include Ikaría, Thímena, Foúrni, Sámos with the brooding mass of Mount Kérkis, Arkí, and the double-humped Samsun Dag (ancient Mount Mikale) in Turkey.

The rest of the island

Pátmos, as a locally published guide memorably proclaimed, "is immense for those who know how to wander in space and time". The more conventionally propelled may find it easier to get around on foot, or by bus. This is a rewarding island for **walking** with a network of paths, while the overworked **bus** which connects Skála with Hóra, Kámbos and Gríkou is still fairly reliable – the terminal, with a posted-up timetable, is right in front of the main ferry dock.

After the extraordinary atmosphere and magnificent scenery, it's the **beaches** that are Patmos' principal attraction. From Hóra a good trail heads southeast to the sandiest part of generally overdeveloped and cheerless **Gríkou** within forty minutes. From either Gríkou or Hóra, you can ride a moped over dirt roads as far as Stavrós Church on the Dhiakoftí isthmus, beyond which a thirty-minute walk leads to **Psilí Ámmos** beach, the only all-sand cove on the island, with shade lent by tamarisks and a good taverna. There's also a summer *kaíki* service here from Skála. More good beaches are to be found in the north of the island, most of them accessible on foot by following the old paths which (with the exception of some paved or cross-country stretches) parallel the startling, indented eastern shore.

The first beach beyond Méloï, **Agriolivádhi**, has a strip of sand at its centre and a taverna; the next, **Kámbos**, is popular with Greeks, and the most developed strand on the island, with seasonal watersports facilities and tavernas, though the shore is rocky underfoot. If you head east from Kámbos, **Vayiá** and **Livádhi Yeranoú** are less-visited, although the latter can be subject to drifting rubbish. From Kámbos you can also head north to the bay of **Lámbi**, best for swimming when the prevailing wind is from the south, and renowned for an abundance of multicoloured stones. A hamlet of sorts here has rooms and two adjacent tavernas which are among the best on the island. This is also the most northerly port of call for the daily excursion *kaíkia* which shuttle constantly around the coast in season.

As is so often the case, you'll find the island at its best in spring or autumn. It can get cold in winter, but there is a hard core of foreigners who live here year-round, so things never entirely close down. Many of the long-term residents rent houses in **Léfkes**, a fertile valley just west of Kámbos with a lonely and sometimes wild beach at its end.

Lipsí

Of the various islets to the north and east of Pátmos, **Lipsí** is the largest and most populated, and the one that is beginning to get a significant summer tourist trade; now also a port of call for main-line ferries between the Cyclades and the larger Dodecanese, Lipsí can be crowded out in August. Deep wells water many small, well-tended farms, but there is only one spring, and pastoral appearances are deceptive – four times the relatively impoverished full-time population of 450 is overseas (many in Tasmania, for some reason). Most of those who stayed cluster around the fine harbour, as does most of the food and lodging.

Accommodation choices include *Rooms Panorama* (☎0247/41 279; ③), *Angeliki Petrandi* (③), and *Studios Barbarosa* (☎0247/41 312; ③), just up the stairway into the town centre. The best **tavernas** are the *Mongos Brothers'* premises affiliated to the *Kalypso*, and *Toh Dhelfini*, next to the police station. A Lipsian quirk are the bizarre local **kafenía**: some seem to have a double life as bars and the front rooms of private dwellings; others have garish posters or juke boxes, and there are fishermen's joints with nonexistent decor where you'll be served grilled seafood *mezédhes*. There is a **post office** and an **OTE**, and the combination **tourist office** and **Ecclesiastical Museum** is hilariously indiscriminate, featuring such "relics" as oil from the sanctuary on Mount Tabor and water from the Jordan River.

The island's **beaches** are rather scattered: closest is Liendoú, just west of town, but the most attractive is **Katsadhiá**, a collection of small, sandy coves south of the port, with a very good taverna, *Andonis* (May–Sept only), just inland from an eyesore of a music bar, *Dilaila*. **Kohlakoúras**, on the east coast, is by contrast rather grubby shingle with no facilities. An hour's walk along the road leading west from town brings you to **Platís Yialós**, a small, shallow, sandy bay with no development but sheltered from winds. In high season enterprising individuals run pick-up trucks, with bench seats, to the various coves.

A number of paths provide opportunities for a variety of **walks** through the undulating countryside, dotted with blue-domed churches – you can walk from one end of Lipsí to the other in less than two hours. A **carpet-weaving school** for girls operates sporadically on the quay, and some evenings a *santoúri* (Levantine hammer-dulcimer) player performs. Other than that there's absolutely nothing to do or see, but you won't find many better places to do nothing.

Arkí, Maráthi and Agathónissi

Arkí is considerably more primitive, lacking both electricity and a ferry dock, with no discernible village centre. About half the size of Lipsí, just thirty inhabitants cling to life here; most are engaged in fishing. It's an elective stop on the route of the **Nissos Kalimnos**: if you want to stay here, you must warn the captain well in advance, so he can radio for the shuttle service from the island. A desperately poor place, its complete depopulation seems conceivable within the next decade. While there is a seasonal taverna with rooms, there's not even a proper beach; the nearest one just offshore is on the islet of **Maráthi**, where a taverna caters to the day-trippers who come a couple of times a week from Pátmos – links with Arkí are unreliable. The pair of tavernas here both rent some fairly comfortable **rooms**, making Maráthi a better option than Arkí for acting out Robinson Crusoe fantasies.

Agathoníssi is sufficiently remote – much closer to Turkey than Pátmos, in fact – to be out of reach even of these excursions; just 150 people live here, fishing and raising goats. Pebble beaches can be found west of the harbour settlement of Áyios Yióryios, and at **Katholikó** and **Hokhliá**, reached by walking to opposite ends of the island. There's a bona fide inland village, **MEGÁLO HORIÓ**, a hundred or so people, two stores, and one pension run by the Katsouleri family (☎0247/24 385; ②); the *Kafenio Dhekatria Adhelfia* does generous home-style lunches. There are three **places to stay** in Áyios Yioryios, in descending order of preference: *Theoloyia Yiameou* (☎0247/23 692; ②), *Maria Kamitsa* (☎0247/23 690; ②), and some rooms above *George's Taverna* (☎0247/24 385; ②). For **meals** out, *George's* and *Yiannnis* are both good bets; George does meat and game dishes, while Yiannis offers fish and meat grills. Of late, Agathoníssi has begun to attract some intrepid backpackers, and with hydrofoil connections dovetailing fairly well with the appearances of the *Nissos Kalimnos*, you needn't be marooned here for more than two or three days during the tourist season.

travel details

To simplify the lists below, the *Nissos Kalimnos* has been left off. Since 1989, this car ferry has been the most regular lifeline of the smaller islands – it visits them all at least once a week between March and December. Its schedule is currently as follows: Monday and Friday morning, leaves Kálimnos for Kós, Níssiros, Tílos, Sími, Rhodes and Kastellórizo. Tuesday and Saturday morning, departs Rhodes for Sími, Tílos, Níssiros, Kós, with an evening out-and-back trip to Kálimnos; Wednesday and Sunday departs Kálimnos for Léros, Lipsí, Pátmos, Agathónissi, Pithagório (Sámos), and back to Kálimnos via the same islands; Thursday morning from Kálimnos to Kós and back, then to Astipálea and back, then to Kós and back once more to Kálimnos;. This ship is often poorly publicized on islands other than its home port; for current, disinterested information you're strongly advised to phone the central agency on Kálimnos (☎0243/29 612).

Ferries

AGATHONÍSSI 1 weekly to Lipsí, Pátmos, Sámos.

ASTIPÁLEA 2–3 weekly to Amórgos, Náxos, Páros, Síros, Pireás; 1–2 weekly to Kós, Kálimnos, Rhodes, Níssiros, Tílos, Míkonos, Tínos.

HÁLKI Twice weekly to Kárpathos and Rhodes Town; once weekly to Crete and select western Cyclades, subject to cancellation in bad weather. Once-daily **kaíki** to Rhodes (Skála Kamírou).

KÁLIMNOS Similar **ferry** service to Kós, but with fewer to Páros and Pireás and no services to Thessaloníki. Morning **kaiki**, afternoon **speed-boat** to Kós Town; 2 or 3 daily **kaikía** to Mastihári, usually via Psérimos. Daily **kaíki** from Mirtiés to Ksirókambos on Léros.

KÁRPATHOS (PIGÁDHIA) AND KÁSSOS Twice-weekly connections between the islands, and to Rhodes, Hálki, Crete (Iráklion and Sitía), Mílos and Pireás; once to Crete (Áyios Nikólaos), Sími, Thíra, Páros, Náxos, Folégandhros, Síkinos and Sífnos.

Note: Dhiafáni is served by only one weekly mainline ferry to Crete, select western Cyclades and Rhodes, subject to cancellation in bad weather until the new pier is completed.

KASTELLÓRIZO (Méyisti) 3 weekly to Rhodes; 1 weekly to Pireás indirectly, via select Dodecanese and Cyclades.

KÓS 10–17 weekly to Rhodes and Pireás; 7–10 weekly to Kálimnos; daily to Léros and Pátmos; 2 weekly to Tílos and Níssiros; 1 weekly to Thessaloníki; 1 weekly to Astipálea, Sími, Lipsí, Náxos, Páros, Síros. **Excursion boats** 3 daily in season from Mastihári to Psérimos and Kálimnos, daily from Kós Town to Kálimnos via Psérimos, and Rhodes; 1 or 2 daily from Kardhámena to Níssiros, 4–5 weekly from Kós Town to Níssiros; 3 weekly to Pátmos.

LÉROS Daily to Pireás, Pátmos, Kálimnos, Kós and Rhodes; 1 weekly to Lipsí, Náxos, Páros, Míkonos, Síros. Seasonal daily **excursion boats** from Ayía Marína to Lipsí and Pátmos, and from Ksirókambos to Mirtiés on Kálimnos.

LIPSÍ 1–2 weekly to Síros, Páros, Náxos, Pireás, Pátmos, Sími, Tílos, Níssiros, Kós, Kálimnos, Léros.

NÍSSIROS AND TÍLOS Same as for Sími, plus 1 weekly between each other, Rhodes, Kós, Kálimnos, Astipálea, Páros, Síros. **Excursion boats** between Níssiros and Kós as follows: to Kardhámena 2 weekly at 4pm and the islanders' "shopping special" at 0am; 4–5 weekly to Kós town (seasonal and expensive).

PÁTMOS Similar **ferry** service to Léros, with the addition of 2 weekly to Foúrni, Ikaría, Sámos; seasonal **tourist boats** to Sámos, Lipsí, and Maráthi on a daily basis; less often to Arkí.

RHODES 10–12 weekly to Kós and Pireás; 7–10 weekly to Kálimnos; daily to Léros and Pátmos; 4 weekly to Crete (Áyios Nikólaos/Sitía or Iráklion); 1–2 weekly to Sími, Lipsí, Tílos, Níssiros, Astipálea, Hálki, Kárpathos, Kássos; once weekly to Folégandhros, Mílos, Sífnos, Síros, Thessaloníki. **Excursion boats** twice daily to Sími.

SÍMI 1 weekly to Rhodes, Tílos, Níssiros, Kós, Kálimnos, Léros, Lipsí, Pátmos, Náxos, Páros and Pireás. **Excursion boats** twice daily to Rhodes.

Hydrofoils

Two hydrofoil companies, *Ilio Lines* and *Nearhos Mamidhakis* (aka Dodecanese Hydrofoils) serve the Dodecanese between May and mid-October, operating out of Rhodes and Kálimnos. For current schedule information, phone ☎0241/24 000 or 0242/25 920 for *Nearhos Mamidhakis*, and ☎0273/27 337 or 0273/61 914 for the agent for *Ilio Lines*.

Flights

KÁRPATHOS 2–7 daily to Rhodes; 2–4 weekly to Kássos; 2 weekly to Athens; 1 weekly to Crete (Sitía).

KÁSSOS 2–4 weekly to Kárpathos; 3–7 weekly to Rhodes; 1 weekly to Crete (Sitía).

KASTELLÓRIZO (Méyisti) 2/3 weekly to Rhodes.

KÓS 2–3 daily to Athens; 2–3 daily to Rhodes.

LÉROS 3 –7 weekly to Athens.

RHODES 4–5 daily to Athens; 4 weekly to Iráklion; 2 weekly to Thessaloníki.

International ferries

KÓS 1–14 weekly to Bodrum, Turkey (45min).

RHODES Daily to Marmaris, Turkey (1–2hr) by Greek hydrofoil or more expensive Turkish car ferry; 2–3 weekly to Limassol, Cyprus (18hr) and Haifa, Israel (39hr). Services to Egypt are currently suspended.

CHAPTER TEN

THE EAST AND NORTH AEGEAN

T he seven substantial islands and four minor islets scattered off the coast of Asia Minor and northeast Greece form a rather arbitrary archipelago. Although there is some similarity in architecture and landscape, virtually the only common denominator is the strong individual character of each island. Despite their proximity to modern Turkey, members of the group bear few signs of an Ottoman heritage, especially when compared to Rhodes and Kós. There's the odd minaret or two, and some of the domestic architecture betrays obvious influences from Constantinople, Thrace and further north in the Balkans, but by and large the enduring Greekness of these islands is testimony to the 4000-year Hellenic presence in Asia Minor, which only ended in 1923.

This heritage is regularly referred to by the Greek government in its propaganda war with the Turks over the sovereignty of these far-flung outposts. The tensions here are, if anything, worse than in the Dodecanese, aggravated by potential undersea oil deposits in the straits between the islands and Turkey. The Turks have also persistently demanded that Límnos, astride the sea lanes to and from the Dardenelles, is demilitarized, but so far Greece has shown no signs of cooperating.

The heavy military presence can be disconcerting, especially for lone woman travellers, and large tracts of land are off-limits as military reserves. But, as in the Dodecanese, local tour operators do a thriving business shuttling passengers for absurdly high tariffs (caused partly by the need for payoffs at both ends) between the easternmost islands and the Turkish coast with its amazing archeological sites and watering holes. Bear in mind, if you're thinking of making the journey, that, if you have travelled to Greece on a charter flight, your ticket will be invalidated by an overnight stay in Turkey. Many of the islands' main ports and towns are not the quaint picturesque places you may have become used to in other parts of Greece; indeed a number are relatively large and uninteresting university, military and commercial centres. In most cases you should suppress your initial impulse to take the next boat out and press on into the worthwhile interiors.

Sámos is the most visited of the group and, if you can leave the crowds behind, is perhaps also the most verdant and beautiful. **Ikaría** to the west is relatively unspoiled, and nearby **Foúrni** is a haven for determined solitaries. **Híos** is culturally interesting, but its natural beauty has been ravaged and the development of tourism has until recently been deliberately retarded. **Lésvos** is an acquired taste, though once you get a feel for the island you may find it hard to leave – the number of repeat visitors grows yearly. By contrast virtually no foreigners and few Greeks visit **Áyios Efstrátios**, and with good reason. **Límnos** is considerably better, but its appeal is confined mostly to the area around the pretty port town. To the north, Samothráki and Thássos are totally isolated from the others, except via the mainland port Kavála, and it's easiest to visit them en route to or from Istanbul. **Samothráki** has one of the most dramatic seaward

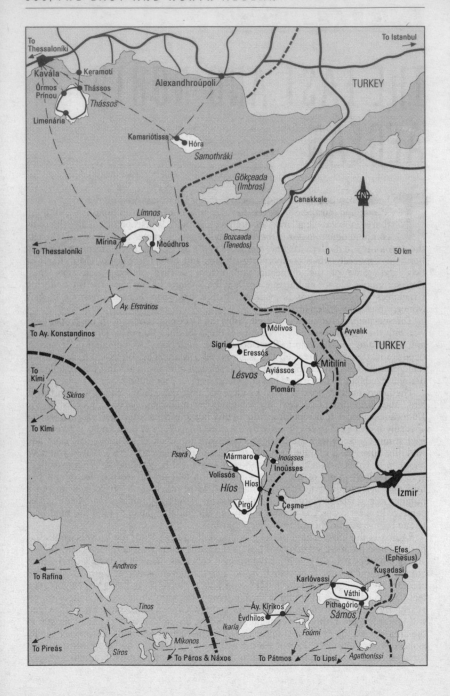

ROOM PRICE SCALES

All establishments in this book have been price-graded according to the scale outlined below. The rates quoted represent the cheapest available room in high season; all are prices for a double room, except for category ①, which are per person rates. Out of season, rates can drop by up to fifty percent, especially if you negotiate rates for a stay of three or more nights. Single rooms, where available, cost around seventy percent of the price of a double.

Rented private rooms on the islands usually fall into the ② or ③ categories, depending on their location and facilities, and the season; a few in the ④ category are more like plush self-catering apartments. They are not generally available from late October through to the beginning of April, when only hotels tend to remain open.

① 1400–2000dr (£4–5.50/US$6–8.50)   ④ 8000–12000dr (£22–33/US$33–50)
② 4000–6000dr (£11–16.50/US$17–25)   ⑤ 12000–16000dr (£33–44/US$50–66)
③ 6000–8000dr (£16.50–22/US$25–33)   ⑥ 16000dr (£44/US$66) and upwards

For more accommodation details, see pp.34–35.

approaches of any Greek island, and one of the more important ancient sites. The appeal of **Thássos** is rather broader, with a varied offering of sandy beaches, forested mountains and minor archeological sites. Easily accessible from the mainland, however, it can be overrun in high season.

Sámos

The lush and seductive island of **Sámos** was formerly joined to the Asia Minor until sundered from Mount Mycale opposite by Ice Age cataclysms. The resulting 2500-metre strait is now the narrowest distance between Greece and Turkey, and, accordingly, military watchpoints bristle on both sides.

There's little physical evidence of it today, but Sámos was once the wealthiest island in the Aegean and, under the patronage of the tyrant Polycrates, home to a thriving intellectual community; Epicurus, Pythagora, Aristarchus and Aesop were among the residents. Decline set in when the star of Classical Athens was in the ascendant, though its status was improved somewhat in early Byzantine times when Sámos constituted its own *theme* (imperial administrative district). Later, towards the end of the fifteenth century, Turkish pirates pillaged the island, which then remained empty for more than a hundred years until an Ottoman admiral received permission from the sultan to repopulate it with Greek Orthodox settlers, a role which goes far to explaining the local identity crisis and a rather thin topsoil of indigenous culture. Most of the village names are either clan surnames, or adjectives indicating origins elsewhere – constant reminders of refugee descent. There is no genuine Samiote music, dance or dress, and little that's original in the way of cuisine and architecture (the latter, in particular, is a blend of styles from northern Greece and Asia Minor).

The Samiotes compensated somewhat for their deracination by fighting fiercely for independence during the 1820s, but, despite their accomplishments in decimating a Turkish fleet in the narrow strait and annihilating a landing army, the Great Powers handed the island back to the Ottomans in 1830, with the consoling proviso that it be semi-autonomous, ruled by an appointed Christian prince. This period, referred to as the *Iyimonía* (Hegemony), was marked by a mild renaissance in fortunes, courtesy of the shipping and tobacco trades. However, union with Greece, the ravages of a bitter World War II occupation and mass emigration effectively reversed the recovery until tourism appeared on the horizon during the 1980s.

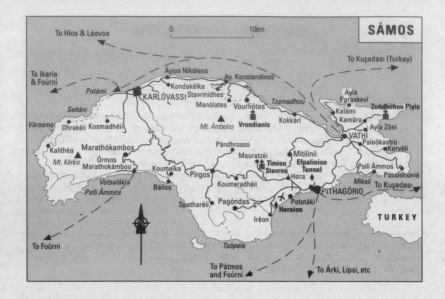

Today, the Samian economy is increasingly dependent on package **tourism**, far too much of it in places; the eastern half of the island has pretty much been surrendered to the onslaught of holidaymakers, although the more rugged western part has retained much of its undeveloped grandeur. The rather sedate clientele is overwhelmingly Scandinavian, Dutch and German, and a far cry from the singles scene of the Cyclades. The absence of an official campsite on such a large island, and phalanxes of self-catering villas, tell you exactly what sort of custom is expected.

Getting there and getting around

Sámos has no less than three **ferry ports** – Karlóvassi in the west, Vathí and Pithagório in the east – as well as an **airport**, which is 14km southwest of Vathí and just 3km west of Pithagório. All ferries between Pireás, the Cyclades and Sámos call at both Karlóvassi and Vathí, as do the smaller *Miniotis Line* ferries linking the island with Híos, Foúrni, Ikaría and Pátmos, and the *Gianmar* and *Ilio Line* hydrofoils to the Dodecanese and north Aegean. In addition, Vathí receives the once-weekly *NEL* sailing between northern Greece and the northern Dodecanese, via all intervening islands, as well as the lion's share of hydrofoils and small ferries from Kuşadası; Pithagório siphons off a bit of the Turkey shipping in high season, and additionally sees two regular weekly ferry connections from as far south as Kós in the Dodecanese.

The **bus terminals** in Pithagório and Vathí lie within walking distance of the ferry dock; at Karlóvassi, a bus is occasionally on hand to take you the 3km into town from the port. There is no *Olympic* shuttle bus to and from the airport; you are at the mercy of the numerous taxi drivers, who shouldn't charge you more than 2000dr for the trip to Vathí. In high season, **taxis** to the airport or docks must be booked several hours in advance (☎0273/28 404 in Vathí) – have your hotel do it for you.

The bus service itself is excellent along the Pithagório–Vathí and Vathí–Karlóvassi via Kokkári routes, but poor otherwise. However, you're almost certain to have to **rent a motorbike** or **car**, and with literally dozens of outlets – at least for bikes – there's little problem in finding good deals.

Vathí

Lining the steep northeast shore of a deep bay, **VATHÍ** is the provincial capital, founded after 1830 to replace Hóra as the island's main town. It's of minimal interest for the most part – although the pedestrianized bazaar and tiers of Neoclassical houses have some attraction – and the only real highlight is the excellent **Archeological Museum** (daily except Mon 8.30am–3pm; 500dr), set behind the small central park beside the derelict old town hall. One of the best provincial collections in Greece is housed in both the old *Paskallion* building and a modern wing across the way, specially constructed to house the star exhibit: a majestic, five-metre-tall *kouros*, discovered out at the Heraion sanctuary (see p.603). The *kouros*, the largest free-standing effigy to survive from ancient Greece, was dedicated to Apollo but found together with a devotional mirror to Hera from a Nile workshop, only one of two discovered in Greece.

In the *Paskallion*, more votive offerings of Egyptian design – a hippo, a dancer in Nilotic dress, Horus-as-Falcon, an Osiris figurine – prove trade and pilgrimage links between Sámos and the Nile valley going back to the eighth century BC. Visible Mesopotamian and Anatolian influences in other artwork confirm the exotic trend, most tellingly in a case full of ivory miniatures: Perseus and Medusa in relief, a kneeling, perfectly formed mini-*kouros*, a pouncing lion, and a drinking horn terminating in a bull's head. The most famous artefacts are the dozen or so bronze **griffin-heads**, for which Sámos was the major centre of production in the seventh century BC; mounted on the edge of bronze cauldrons, they were believed to ward off evil spirits.

The provincial authority's plans for the **waterfront** have been stalled for lack of funds. However, near the much-needed car park and new fishing harbour you can see the fishermen peddle their catch on the flagstone quay mornings before 10am. The dumping of raw sewage in the bay has ceased, but still nobody in their right mind goes swimming at Vathí; the closest appealing beaches are some way distant. One waterfront curiosity is the old French Catholic church, labelled "ECCLESIA CATOLICA" in Latin, which has stood disused except for monthly masses since 1974, when the last nuns departed Sámos after having schooled several elite generations for nearly a century.

Strolls inland can be more rewarding. You might visit the museum-like **antique store** of Mihalis Stavrinos, just off the central Platía Pithagóra (the so-called "Lion Square"), where you can invest in assorted precious baubles or rescue rare engravings from the silverfish. Even better is **ÁNO VATHÍ**, 150m above sea level, an officially preserved community of tottering, tile-roofed houses that's the goal of many a day-stroller. The village's late medieval churches are neglected, but still worth a look: the tiny chapel of **Áyios Athanásios**, near the main cathedral, boasts a fine *temblon* and naive frescoes.

Arrival, information and facilities

From the **ferry dock** the shore boulevard, Themistokléous Sofoúli, describes a 1300-metre arc around the bay. About 400m along is Platía Pithagóra, distinguished by its lion statue; while 800m along is the major turning inland to the **bus terminal**, merely a chaos of vehicles at a perennially cluttered intersection, next to a booking office. The two most comprehensive **ferry/travel agents** are *By Ship* on the front (☎0273/27 337) and *Samina Tours* at Themistokléous Sofoúli 67 (☎0273/28 841); between them they sell tickets for just about every boat or hydrofoil, domestic or international (except *NEL* lines to the North Aegean and mainland, and the *Agapitos Lines* ferry towards Pireás); they also have money-exchange facilities.

The municipal **tourist information office** is on Ikostipémptis Martíou (summer Mon–Fri 8am–8pm, Sat–Sun 9am–1pm; winter variable hours), not especially cheerful but worth a stop for leaflets, comprehensive bus and ferry schedules and accommodation listings – staff do not make reservations for you.

Vathí is chock-a-block with **bike-and-car-rental** franchises, which keeps rates reasonable. Try *Europe Rent a Car* (two outlets, near the bus station, and near *Number Nine* pub), *Louis* (just behind the waterfront, 400m south of the dock), or for cars only, *Budget* at Themistokléous Sofoúli 31 (☎0273/28 856) or *Autoplan* at no. 67 (☎0273/23 555). Other amenities include the **post office** (Mon–Fri only) on Smírnis, 150m inland from the *Olympic* offices; OTE across the way from the cathedral and street produce market; three waterfront **banks**; and two automatic **laundries** – *Alex* at Yimnasiárhou Katevéni 17 is the friendlier, providing service washes.

Accommodation

Most **accommodation** establishments catering for independent travellers cluster in the hillside district of Katsoúni, more or less directly above the ferry dock. Their proprietors tend not to meet arriving ferries, since even these rooms are partly block-booked by tour groups. However, hunting for yourself, affordable options are surprisingly numerous, except in August. They include the waterfront *Hotel Parthenon*, oldest in town but clean and acceptable other than bar noise from below (☎0273/27 234; ②; open all year); the somewhat more comfortable *Hotel Artemis*, just off "Lion Square" (☎0273/27 792; ③); *Pension Ionia*, inland at Manoli Kalomíri 5 (☎0273/28 782; ②; open all year); the *Pension Trova* around the corner at Kalomíri 26 (☎0273/27 759; ②); or the *Pension Avli*, a wonderful period piece up a nearby stair-street at Aréos 2 (☎0273/22 939; ②). This is the former convent school of the French nuns, so the rooms, arrayed around a courtyard (*avlí* in Greek) are appropriately institutional.

None of these outfits are palaces by any means; for more luxury you'll have to spread your net a bit wider. Start at the surprisingly affordable *Hotel Galaxy*, at Angéou 1, near the top of Katsoúni (☎0273/22 665; ③), set in garden surroundings, with a small pool. *Samos Hotel* (☎0273/28 377; ④), right by the ferry dock, frequently drops its rates in winter, and is open all year. Only the front rooms of the *Hotel Paradise* at Kanári 21 (☎0273/23 911; ④–⑤) look out over the bus stop – side and rear rooms have views of local orchards and the pool.

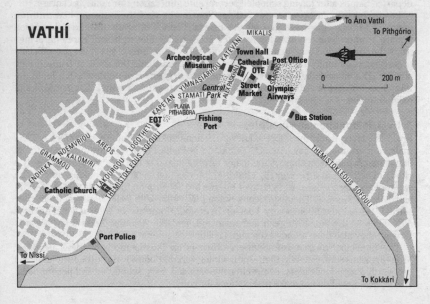

Eating and drinking

The only waterfront **tavernas** worth a second glance are *Ta Dhiodhia*, 1km south along Sofoúli, next to the military headquarters, serving pricey but well-prepared seafood and *mezédhes* (evening only); *Stelios*, 150m north of the dock on the right, ideal for a no-nonsense, pre-ferry meal; and finally *Ouzeri Apanemia*, at the far west end of the shore boulevard, where slightly above-average prices are justified by the appetizing fare from the Athenian chef. Up in Áno Vathí, the only place to eat is the popular *Agrambeli*, whose menu varies nightly.

Vathí nightlife revolves around a half-dozen **bars**, longest lived of these being *Number Nine*, on a sea-view terrace at Kefalopoúlou 9 (north of the jetty). Another standby is the inconspicuously marked *Cleary's Pub*, just behind Platía Pithagóra, run by Desireé, aka "Spooky", who played one of the naked witches in Polanski's *Macbeth*. *Metropolis*, in the orchards behind the *Hotel Paradise*, is Vathí's recently built **disco**.

Around Vathí

The immediate environs of Vathí offer some modest beaches and small hamlets with tavernas, ideal targets for day trips.

Two kilometres **east** of (and above) Vathí spreads the vast inland plateau of Vlamarí, devoted to vineyards and supporting the hamlets of **AYÍA ZÓNI** and **KAMÁRA**. Of the two simple tavernas in Kamára, *O Kriton* is recommended. From Kamára you can climb up a partly cobbled path to the cliff-top **monastery of Zoödhóhou Piyís**, for views across the end of the island to Turkey.

Heading **north** out of Vathí, the narrow, street threads through beachless **KALÁMI** – formerly the summer retreat of rich Vathiots and now home to resort hotels – before ending after 7km at the pebbly bay and fishing port of **AYÍA PARASKEVÍ** (or Nissí), with two tavernas and good (if rather unsecluded) swimming.

As you head southeast from Vathí along the main island loop road, the triple chapel at **Treis Ekklisíes** marks an important junction, with another fork 100m along the left-hand turning. Bearing left twice takes you through the hilltop village of **PALEOKÁSTRO**, remarkable only for its evening-only taverna *Ta Dhilina*, for which Vathiots regularly undertake the special six-kilometre trip out here. After another 6km you reach the quiet, striking bay of **Kervéli**, with a small gravel beach, a pair of expensive tavernas and two new luxury hotels. It's not worth continuing to the road's end at **POSSIDHÓNIO**, whose tavernas are mediocre and beach negligible.

Turning right at the second junction leads to the beaches of Mikáli and Psilí Ámmos. **Mikáli**, a kilometre of windswept sand and gravel, has been recently developed. **Psilí Ámmos**, further east around the headland, is a crowded, sandy cove, whose best and longest-established namesake taverna is on the right as you arrive. If you swim to the islet, a tempting target, beware of strong west-to-east currents which sweep through the narrow straits even in the shallows. There's a bus service out here up to five times daily in season.

Pithagório and around

Most traffic south of Vathí heads for **PITHAGÓRIO**, the island's premier resort, renamed in 1955 to honour its native ancient mathematician, philosopher and mystic. Prior to that it was known as Tigáni (Frying Pan) – in mid-summer you'll learn why. The sixth-century BC tyrant Polycrates had his capital here, and beyond the village core of cobbled lanes overshadowed by thick-walled mansions lie acres of currently suspended archeological excavations – which have had the effect of forcing modern Pithagório to expand northeastward and uphill. The small **harbour**, fitting more or less perfectly into the confines of Polycrates's ancient port, and still using his jetty, is today devoted almost entirely to pleasure craft and overpriced cocktail bars.

Sámos's principal surviving attempt at a **castle**, the nineteenth-century *pírgos* (tower-house) of Lykourgos Logothetis, overlooks both the town and the shoreline where this local chieftain oversaw decisive victories by "Kapetan Stamatis" and Admiral Kanaris over the Turks in the summer of 1824. The final battle was won on Transfiguration Day (6 August), and accordingly the church beside the tower bears a huge sign in Greek announcing that "Christ Saved Sámos 6 August 1824".

More ancient antiquities include the fairly dull **Roman baths** west of town (Tues, Wed, Fri 9am–2.30pm; Thurs & Sun 11.30am–2.30pm; Sat 10.30am–2.30pm; free) and a miniscule **archeological collection** in the town hall (Tues, Thur & Fri 9.30am–12.45pm; Wed 11am–12.45pm; Sun 9am–12.45pm; free). Rather more interesting is the **Efpalínion tunnel** (Tues & Fri 11am–12.45pm; Wed, Thur & Sun 9.30am–12.45pm; Sat 10.30am–12.45pm; free), an aqueduct bored through the mountain just north of Pithagório at the behest of Polycrates. Its mid-section has collapsed but you should be able to explore the intial portion of its one-kilometre length with a flashlight. To get there, take the signposted path from the shore boulevard at the west end of town.

If you're keen, you can also climb to the five remaining chunks of the Polycratian **perimeter wall** enclosing his citadel. There's a choice of routes: one leading up from the Glífa lagoon west of Pithagório, past an **ancient watchtower** now isolated from any other fortifications, and the other – which is easier – leading from the monastery of **Panayía Spilianí** and the adjacent ancient **amphitheatre**.

Practicalities

If there are any **accommodation** vacancies – and it's best not to count on it in mid-season – proprietors meet incoming ferries. Otherwise it's a matter of phoning ahead or chancing on a spot as you tramp the streets. The **tourist information booth** (☎0273/61 389), on the main thoroughfare, Likoúrgou Logothéti, can help in finding rooms.

Quietly located at the seaward end of Odhos Pithagóra, south of Likoúrgou Logothéti, the modest *Tsambika* and *Sydney* (②) pensions are worth considering as nocturnal noise can be a problem elsewhere. Another peaceful area is the hillside north of Platí Irínis, where the *Hotel Galini* is one of the better small outfits here (☎0273/61 167; winter ☎01/98 42 248; ④–⑤). Further uphill, on the road to Vathí, the rear units of *Studios Anthea* (☎0273/62 086; ④) are fairly noise-free and allow you to self-cater.

Eating out can be frustrating in Pithagório, with value for money often a completely alien concept here. Away from the water, *Taverna Platania*, under two eucalypts opposite the town hall, is a good choice for a simple meal; *Maritsa*, on the first side street above the quay, south of Likoúrgou Logothéti, does fish for about as reasonably as you can expect in a tourist resort. For waterside dining, you're best off at the extreme east end of the quay, near what passes for a town beach, at either of two *ouzerís*, *Remataki* or *Odysseas*.

If none of this appeals, the **bus stop** to get you away is just west of the intersection of Likoúrgou Logothéti and the road to Vathí. Two **banks** and the **post office** also line Likoúrgou Logothéti, while the **OTE** is on the quay below the *Hotel Damo*. The flattish country to the west is ideal for pedal-bike touring, a popular activity, though if you want to rent a **moped**, *Evelin's* – 1500m out of town by the airport junction and namesake hotel – is reasonable and helpful.

Around Pithagório

The main local beach stretches for several kilometres west of the Logothetis castle, punctuated about halfway along by the end of the airport runway, and the cluster of hotels known as **POTOKÁKI**. Just before the turnoff to the heart of the beach sprawls the ultra-luxurious *Doryssa Bay* complex, which includes a meticulously concocted fake village, guaranteed to confound archeologists of future eras. No two of the units, joined by named lanes, are alike, and there's even a *platía* with an expensive café. If you actually intend to stay in the area, however, the *Fito Bungalows Hotel* (☎0273/61 58; ⑤–⑥) is more affordable, with breakfast included in the price. If you don't mind the crowds generated by these two hotels, the sand-and-pebble **beach** here is well groomed and the water clean; misanthropes will have to head out to the end of the road for more seclusion.

The Potokáki access road is a dead end, with the main island loop road pressing on from the turnoff for the airport and Iréon hamlet. Under layers of alluvial mud, plus today's runway, lies the Sacred Way joining the ancient city with the **Heraion**, the massive shrine of the Mother Goddess (daily except Mon 8.30am–3pm; 500dr). Much touted in tourist literature, this assumes humbler dimensions – one re-erected column and assorted foundations – upon approach. Yet once inside the precinct you sense the former grandeur of the temple, never completed owing to Polycrates's untimely death at the hands of the Persians. The site chosen was the legendary birthplace of the goddess, near the mouth of the still-active Imvrassós stream; in the far corner of the fenced-in zone you glimpse a large, exposed patch of the paved processional Sacred Way.

The modern resort of **IRÉON** nearby is a nondescript grid of dusty streets, unobjectionable enough except in midsummer. The clientele seems a bit younger, more active and less packaged than in Pithagório, with more independent rooms in evidence. The most locally patronized **taverna** is the westernmost on the shore, and there are a series of bars behind the coarse-shingle beach.

The island loop road continues from the Iréon/airport turnoff to another junction in long, narrow **HÓRA**, the medieval capital and still a large, noisy village packed with military personnel and employees in the local tourist industry. It's worth knowing about principally for a handful of tavernas, such as *Iy Sintrofia*, on the road in from Pithagório; a grill on Platía Ayías Paraskevís; and *O Andonis* on the square with the running fountain. None are especially cheap but they are at least more down-to-earth than anything in Pithagório.

Heading north from the crossroads takes you through a ravine to **MITILINIÍ** which initially seems an amorphous sprawl; a brief exploration, however, turns up a fine main square with some atmospheric *kafenía*, the unmarked *Dionyssos* taverna opposite them – by itself worth the trip up from the coast – and the island's last remaining indoor cinema, down a side street. A **Paleontological Museum** on the top floor of the community offices (Mon–Fri 8.30am–2pm; 200dr) is essentially a room of barely sorted bones from an Ice-Age animal dying-place nearby, and not worth the bother.

Southern Sámos

Since the circum-island bus only passes through or near the places below once or twice daily, you really need your own vehicle to explore them.

Some 4km west of Hóra an inconspicuous turning leads uphill to the monastery of **Timíou Stavroú**, currently the island's most important monastery, although the annual festival (14 September) is more an excuse for a tatty bazaar in the courtyards than any for music or feasting. A similarly poorly marked detour takes off a kilometre further ahead to **MAVRATZÉII**, one of the two Samian "pottery villages"; this one specializes in the *Koúpa tou Pithagóra* or "Pythagorean cup", supposedly designed by the sage to leak over the user's lap if he over-indulged beyond the "fill" line. More practical wares can be found in **KOUMARADHÉII**, back on the main road, another 2km along.

From here you can descend a dirt track through burnt forest to the sixteenth-century monastery of **Megális Panayías** (daily 10am–1pm or at the whim of the caretaker), re-opened after a lengthy restoration and containing the finest frescoes on the island. The track, accessible to the average car, continues to the village of **MÍLI**, submerged in lemon groves – you can also get here from the Iréon road. Four kilometres above sprawls **PAGÓNDAS**, a large hillside community with a splendid main square and an unusual communal laundry house. From here, a wild but scenic dirt road curls 9km around the hill to **SPATHARÉII**, set on a natural balcony offering the best sea views this side of the island. From Spatharéii a paved road leads back 6km to **PÍRGOS** on the main road, lost in pine forests at the head of a ravine, and the centre of Samian honey production. A short distance down the gorge, **KOÚTSI** is a small oasis of plane trees – seventeen of them, according to a sign – shading a gushing spring and a taverna that's an excellent lunch stop if the tour buses haven't beaten you to it.

The rugged and beautiful coast south of the Pagóndas–Pírgos route is largely inaccessible, glimpsed by most visitors for the first and last time from the descending plane bringing them to Sámos; **Tsópela** is the only beach here with marked road access. The western reaches of this shoreline are approached via the small village of **KOUMÉÏKA**, with a massive inscribed marble fountain and a pair of *kafenía* on its square. Below extends the long, pebbly bay at **Bállos**, with sand, a cave and naturists at the far east end. Bállos itself is merely a sleepy collection of summer houses, several **rooms** to rent and a few **tavernas**, best of which is the *Cypriot*. Much of the food here is oven-cooked in limited portions; the garrulous couple running it prefer advance notice (☎0273/36 394).

Returning to Kouméïka, the apparently dodgy side road just before the village marked "Velanidhiá" is in fact quite passable to any vehicle, and a very useful short cut if you're travelling towards the beaches beyond Órmos Marathókambos (see "Western Sámos", below).

Kokkári and around

Leaving Vathí on the north coastal section of the island loop road, there's little to stop for until you reach **KOKKÁRI**, the third major Samian tourist centre after Pithagório and the capital. It's also the prime prompter of nostalgia among Sámos regulars; while lower Vathí and Pithagório had little beauty to sacrifice, much has been irrevocably lost here. The town's profile, covering two knolls behind twin headlands, is still recognizable, and even today several families doggedly untangle their fishing nets on the quay, lending some credence to brochure-touting of the place as a "fishing village". But in general the identity of what is now merely a stage set has been altered beyond recognition, with constant inland expansion over vineyards and the abandoned baby-onion fields that gave the place its name. With exposed, uncomfortably rocky beaches adjacent buffeted by near constant winds, Kokkári seems an unlikely candidate for further gentrification, although its Germanic promoters seem to have made a virtue of necessity by developing it as a highly successful windsurfing resort.

Practicalities

As in Vathí and Pithagório, a fair proportion of Kokkári's **accommodation** is block-booked by tour companies; one establishment not completely devoted to such trade is the pleasant *Hotel Olympia Beach* (☎0273/92 353; ④), on the western beach road, co-managed with the *Olympia Village* (☎0273/92 420; ⑤ for apartments). Otherwise *Yiorgos Mihelios* (☎0273/92 456; ③–④) has a wide range of rooms and apartments to rent. If you get stuck, seek assistance from the seasonal **EOT post** (☎0273/92 217), directly seaward from the main church.

Most **tavernas** line the waterfront, and most charge above the norm – even *Toh Kyma*, oldest and westernmost, still with a considerable local clientele. At the eastern end of things, *Ta Adhelfia* is as close as you'll get to a simple, unpretentious *psistariá* (although even it has credit-card stickers on display), while for a blow-out, the Athenian-run *Kariatidha*, a few doors down, is worth the extra cost. Inland, *Farmer's* – on the village through-road, a few steps east of the summer **cinema** – is highly regarded for its locally grown food, and in autumn may offer *moustalevriá* (grape must dessert).

Other amenities include a short-hours **bank** on the through road, a **post office** in a Portakabin on a lane to seaward, and a **laundrette** next to that.

West of Kokkári: the coast

The closest half-decent beaches are thirty to forty minutes' walk away to the west. The first, **Lemonákia**, is a bit too close to the road, with an obtrusive café; the graceful crescent of **Tzamadhoú** (as in Coleridge's Xanadu) figures in virtually every EOT poster of the island. It's a bit more natural, with path-only access and the west end of the saucer-shaped pebble beach by tacit consensus a nudist zone. Unfortunately a spring just inland has been fenced off to discourage the colonies of freelance campers who used to congregate here, and to encourage everyone to patronize the fairly pricey **taverna** signposted up in the vineyards. There's one more pebbly bay west of Avlákia (a mostly Greek resort 6km from Kokkári) called **Tzábou**, but unless you're passing by and want a quick dip it's not worth a special detour.

The next spot of any interest along the coast road is **Platanákia**, essentially a handful of tavernas and rooms for rent at a plane-shaded bridge and turn-off for Manolátes (see below). Platanákia is actually the eastern suburb of **ÁYIOS KONSTANDÍNOS**, whose surf-pounded esplanade has at long last been repaved. However, there are no usable beaches within walking distance, so the collection of warm-toned stone buildings (increasingly adulterated by concrete structures) serves as a more peaceful alternative to Kokkári. In addition to modest **hotels** such as the *Ariadne* (☎0273/94 206; ④), the *Four Seasons* (③) or the *Atlantis* (☎0273/94 329; ③), along the highway, there's a new generation of luxury bungalows and rooms in the new buildings; the **tavernas** of Platanákia are 1500m distant if the two here don't appeal.

Once past "Áyios" (as the bus conductors habitually bellow it out), the mountains hem the road in against the sea, and the terrain doesn't relent until near **KONDAKEÏKA**, whose *platía*-with-*kafenío* is worth a visit at dusk for its fabulous sunsets, after which you can descend to its diminutive shore annexe of **ÁYIOS NIKÓLAOS** for excellent fish suppers, particularly at the westernmost of the two **tavernas** here. There's also a reasonable beach here, not visible from the upper road – walk east, ten minutes past the last studios.

Hill villages

Inland between Kokkári and Kondakéïka, an idyllic landscape of pine, cypress and orchards is overawed by dramatic, often cloud-shrouded mountains, so far *little* burned. Excursions into this quintessentially Romantic countryside are *as you* *making* popular. Despite destructive nibblings by bulldozers, some of *most of the* the various **hill villages** is still intact, and you can *place only really comes a popular desti-* like, returning to the main highway *trished* *from its typical tile-roofed houses, a special cereal-and-meat* communities can provide *with* *that you'll want to make a spritzer of several tavernas is Snack Bar* *bakestédhes (chickpea patties), and home-* The monaster *select butchers between September and May).* *trying if you've access to a kitchen are the* nation

MANOLÁTES, further uphill and an hour-plus walk away via a deep river canyon, also has a pair of simple snack bars, and is the most popular trailhead for the five-hour round-trip up **Mount Ámbelos** (Karvoúnis), the island's second highest summit. From Manolátes you can no longer easily continue on foot to Stavrinídhes, the next village, but should plunge straight down, partly on a cobbled path, through the shade-drenched valley known as **Aïdhónia** (Nightingales) to Platanákia. Aïdhónia has a couple of mock-rustic tavernas under its trees, popular targets of "Greek Nights Out".

Karlóvassi

KARLÓVASSI, 37km west of Vathí and the second town of Sámos, divides into no less than four, occasionally unattractive, neighbourhoods: Néo well inland, whose untidy growth was spurred by the influx of post-1923 refugees; Meséo, across the usually dry river bed, draped appealingly on a knoll: and postcard-worthy Paleó (or Áno), above Limáni, the small harbour district. Undistinguished as it generally is, Karlóvassi makes an excellent base from which to explore the west of the island (see below). The name, incidentally, despite a vehement lack of Ottoman legacy elsewhere on Sámos, appears to be a corruption of the Turkish for "snowy plain" – the plain in question being the conspicuous saddle of Mount Kérkis overhead, which is indeed snow-covered in a harsh winter.

Limáni

Most tourists stay at or near **LIMÁNI**, which has a handful of rooms and several expensive hotels. The **rooms**, all in the inland pedestrian lane behind the through road, are quieter – try those of *Vangelis Feloukatzis* (☎0273/33 293; ③) or *Ioannis Moskhoyiannis* (③). The port itself, its quay pedestrianized at night, is an appealing place with a boat-building industry at the west end and all the **ferry-ticket agencies** grouped at the middle; often a shuttle bus service operates from Néo Karlóvassi, timed to boat arrivals and departures. Tavernas and bars are abundant, but by far the best and most reasonable place to **eat** is *Steve's*, run by a genial South-African Greek and easily worth a special trip for lunch or dinner.

Paleó and Meséo

Immediately overhead, the partly hidden hamlet of **PALEÓ** is deceptively large, its hundred or so houses draped on either side of a leafy ravine. The only facilities are the sporadically functioning café *Toh Mikro Parisi*, and a seasonal taverna on the path down towards **MESÉO**. The latter is a conceivable alternative base to Limáni, with one pension just behind the playground, and other **rooms** scattered through the intervening half-kilometre between here and the sea. Lost in the residential streets near the top of Meséo's hill is a simple but satisfying **taverna**, *O Kotronis*, while down on the small and the there's a small year-round bar-*ouzerí*, *Para Pende*, which attracts a mix of locals the blue-and-yellowing the street linking the square to the waterfront, you pass one of coast road. , turn-of-the-century churches, topped with twin belfries and a place in town , h dot the coastal plain here. Just at the intersection with the good-value *Ouzeri Toh Kima* (April–Oct), the best a selection of *mezédhes*.

Néo
NÉO has little to re houses and mansions which flo leather industry which you're staying at Limáni, banks, the **post office**, the though not all, of the buses com

ss of derelict stone-built ware-
lers of the long-vanished
sentury. However, if
ne of the two
Some,

While waiting for a bus, one of two traditional *kafenía* might interest you: *O Kleanthis*, on the lower *platía*, or *O Kerketevs*, by the upper square. Any enforced halt in Néo, or Karlóvassi in general, is mitigated somewhat by the fact that the people here are appreciably friendlier than in the east of the island.

Western Sámos

Visitors put up with the dullness of Karlóvassi partly for the sake of western Sámos' excellent **beaches**. The closest of these is **Potámi**, forty minutes' walk away via the coast road from Limáni or an hour by a more scenic, high trail from Paleó. This broad arc of sand and pebbles, flecked at one end with tide-lashed rocks, gets crowded at summer weekends, when seemingly the entire population of Karlóvassi descends on the place. Near the end of the trail from Paleó stands *Toh Iliovasilima*, a friendly fish taverna; there are also a very few **rooms** signposted locally, but most individuals stay ing camp rough along the lower reaches of the river which gives the beach its name.

A path leads twenty minutes inland, past the eleventh-century church of **Metamórfosis** – the oldest on Sámos – and the campers' tents, to an apparent dead end. From here on you must swim and wade in heart-stoppingly cold water through a fern-tufted rock gallery to a series of **pools and waterfalls**; bring shoes with good tread and perhaps even rope if you want to explore above the first cascade. You probably won't be alone until the trail's end, since the canyon is well known to locals and even included in certain "Jeep Safaris".

Just above the Metamórfosis church, a clear path leads up to a small, contemporaneous **Byzantine fortress**. There's little to see inside other than a subterranean cistern and badly crumbled lower curtain wall, but the views out to sea and up the canyon are terrific, while in October the place is carpeted with pink autumn crocus.

The coast beyond Potámi is the most beautiful and unspoiled on Sámos. The dirt track at the west end of Potámi bay ends after twenty minutes of walking, from which you backtrack a hundred metres or so to find the well-cairned side trail running parallel to the water. Within twenty minutes' walking along this you'll arrive at **Mikró Seïtáni**, a small pebble cove guarded by sculpted rock walls. A full hour's walk from the trailhead, through partly fire-damaged olive terraces, brings you to **Megálo Seïtáni**, the island's finest beach, at the mouth of the intimidating Kakopérato gorge. You'll have to bring food and water along, though not necessarily a swimsuit – there's no dress code at either of the Seïtáni beaches.

Beach resorts

Heading south out of Karlóvassi on the island loop road, the first place you'd be tempted to stop off is **MARATHÓKAMBOS**, a pretty, amphitheatrical village overlooking the eponymous gulf; there's a taverna or two, but no short-term accommodation.

Its port, **ÓRMOS MARATHOKÁMBOU**, 18km from Karlóvassi, has recently been pressed into service as a tourist resort, though some character still peeks through in its backstreets. The port has been improved, with *kaïkia* offering day trips to Foúrni and the nearby islet of Samiopoúla, while the pedestrianized quay has become the centre of attention. A curiosity at its western end is the island's only stop light, installed to control entry to a one-lane alley. Three or four tavernas seem pretty indistinguishable, although *Trata* at least offers bulk wine, a Sámos rarity.

The beach extending immediately east from Órmos is hardly the best; for better ones you'll need to continue 2km west to **VOTSALÁKIA**, Sámos' fastest-growing resort, straggling for 2km more behind the island's longest – if not its most beautiful beach. Its appeal as an overwhelmingly family resort has been diminished in recent years by the solid carpet of rooms, apartments and often rather poor tavernas behind. But Votsalákia is still a vast improvement on the Pithagório area, and the hulking mass of 1437-metre Mount Kérkis overhead rarely fails to impress (see below). As far as **accommodation** goes, *Emmanuil Dhespotakis* (☎0273/31 258; ③) seems to control a good quarter of the beds available, with most of his premises towards the quieter, more scenic western end of things. Also in this vicinity is *Akroyialia*, the most traditional **taverna**, with courtyard seating and fish and meat grills; *Loukoullos*, on the ocean side of the road near the last of the Dhespotakis rooms, is a fancier, enjoyable bistro-bar. Other facilities include branches of nearly all the main Vathí travel agencies, offering **vehicle rental** (necessary, as only two daily buses call here) and money exchange.

If Votsalákia (officially signposted as Kámbos) is not to your taste, you can continue 3km past to **Psilí Ámmos**, more aesthetic and not to be confused with its namesake beach in the southeast corner of Sámos. The sea shelves gently here – ridiculously so, as you're still only knee-deep a hundred paces out – and cliffs shelter clusters of naturists at the east end of 600m of sand. Surprisingly there are only a few **taverna/room** outfits: one fair-sized apartment complex in the pines at mid-beach, the other two back up on the road as you approach, both of these fine for a simple lunch.

German interests have more or less completely taken over **Limniónas**, a smaller cove 2km further west, by constructing a large villa complex rather grandiosely labelled as "Samos Yacht Club". Yachts do occasionally call at the protected bay, which offeres decent swimming away from a rock shelf at mid-strand, two **tavernas** at the east end and a few short-term accommodation facilities.

Mount Kérkis

Gazing up from a supine seaside position, some people are inspired to go and climb **Mount Kérkis** (Kerketévs). The classic route begins at the west end of the Votsalákia strip, along the bumpy jeep track leading inland towards the Evangelistrías convent. After 30 minutes on the track system, through fire-damaged olive groves and past charcoal pits (a major industry hereabouts), the path begins, more or less following power lines steeply up to the convent. A friendly nun will proffer an *oúzo* in welcome and point you up the paint-marked trail, continuing even more steeply up to the peak.

The views are tremendous, though the climb itself is humdrum once you're out of the trees. About an hour before the top, there's a chapel with an attached cottage for sheltering in emergencies and, just beyond, after a wet winter, a welcome spring. Elation at attaining the **summit** may be tempered somewhat by the knowledge that on August 3, 1989, one of the worst Greek aviation disasters ever occurred here, when an aircraft flying out of Thessaloníki slammed into the mist-cloaked peak with the loss of all 34 aboard. All told, it's a seven-hour outing from Votsalákia and back, not counting rest stops.

Less ambitious walkers might want to circle the flanks of the mountain, first by vehicle and then by foot. The road beyond Limniónas to Kallithéa and Dhrakéii, truly back-of-beyond villages with views across to Ikaría, has recently been paved as far as Kallithéa, making it possible to venture out here on an ordinary motorbike. The bus service is better during the school year, when a vehicle leaves Vathí daily at 11.30am bound for these remote spots; during summer it only operates two days a week (currently Mon & Fri).

From **DHRAKÉII**, the end of the line with just a pair of very simple *kafenía* to its credit, a ninety-minute trail descends through partly burned forest to Megálo Seïtáni, from where it's easy enough to continue on to Karlóvassi within another two-and-a-half hours. People attempting to reverse this itinerary often discover to their cost that the bus (if any) returns from Dhrakéii early in the day, at 2pm, compelling them to stay overnight at two rather expensive **rooms** establishments (summer only) in **KALITHÉA**, and dine there at either the simple *psistariá* on the square or a newer taverna on the western edge of the village.

From Kallithéa, a newer track (from beside the cemetery) and an older trail lead up within 45 minutes to a spring, rural chapel and plane tree on the west flank of Kérkis, with path-only continuation for another half-hour to a pair of cave-churches. **Panayía Makriní** is free-standing, at the mouth of a high, wide but shallow grotto, whose balcony affords terrific views of Sámos' west end. **Ayía Triádha**, a ten-minute scramble overhead, has by contrast most of its structure made up of cave wall; just adjacent, another long, narrow, volcanic cavern can be explored by flashlight some hundred metres into the mountain, and perhaps further with proper equipment and a willingness to crab along on hands and knees.

After these subterranean exertions, the closest spot for a swim is **Vársamo** (Válsamo) cove, 4km below Kallithéa and reached via a well-signposted dirt road. The beach here consists of wonderful multicoloured volcanic pebbles, and there's a single rooms/snack bar place and two caves to shelter in.

Ikaría

Ikaría, a narrow, windswept landmass between Sámos and Míkonos, is little visited and invariably underestimated. Its name is supposed to derive from the unexpected appearance of Icarus, who fell into the sea just offshore after the wax bindings on his wings melted; and (as some locals are quick to point out) the island is clearly wing-shaped. For years the only substantial tourism was generated by a few radioactive hot springs on the south coast, some reputed to cure rheumatism and arthritis, some to make women fertile, though others are so potent that they've been closed for some time. The unnerving dockside sign which once read "Welcome to the Island of Radiation" has now been replaced by one proclaiming "Welcome to Icarus' Island".

Ikaría, along with Thessaly on the mainland, western Sámos and Lésvos, has traditionally been one of the Greek Left's strongholds. This tendency was accentuated during the long decades of right-wing domination in Greece, when the island was used as a place of exile for political dissidents. Apparently the strategy backfired, with the transportees outnumbering, and proseletyzing, their hosts; at the same time, many

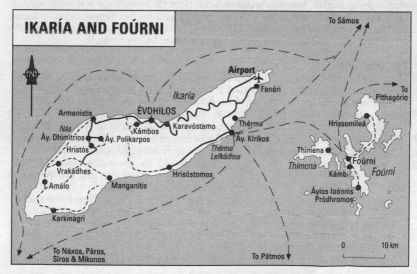

IKARÍA AND FOÚRNI

Ikarians emigrated to North America, and ironically their regular capitalist remittances help keep the island going. It can be a bizarre experience to be treated to a monologue on the evils of US imperialism, delivered by a retiree in perfect Alabaman English.

These are not the only Ikarian quirks, and for many the place is an acquired taste. It is not a strikingly beautiful island except for the forested portions of the northwest; the north face is less sheer than the south shore, but nonetheless furrowed by deep canyons which deflect the road system into sinuosities extreme even by Greek standards. The southern coastline drops steeply in cliffs and most of the landscape is scrub-coated schist, though there is ample ground water. Neither are there many picturesque villages, since the rural schist-roofed houses are generally scattered so as to be next to their famous apricot orchards, vineyards and fields, while the community store or taverna is equally hidden. Finally, the people, while not unfriendly – quite the contrary in fact – have resisted most attempts to develop Ikaría for conventional tourism, which splutters along principally between July and September. An airport in the northeast, its runway graded right across the tip of the island into the sea to permit approaches in any wind, is due to begin operation in the near future. Long periods of seemingly punitive neglect by Athens have made the locals profoundly self-sufficient and idiosyncratic, and tolerant of the same characteristics in others.

Áyios Kírikos

Most, though not all, ferries call at the south-coast port and capital of **ÁYIOS KÍRIKOS**, about 1km southeast of the island's main thermal resort. Because of the spa trade, beds are at a premium in town; arriving in the evening, as is often the case, accept any reasonable offers of rooms at the jetty, or – if in a group – proposals of a taxi ride to the north coast, which won't be much more than 6000dr *per vehicle* to the end of the line. A cream-and-green-coloured **bus** sets out across the island from the main square, daily at 10am (to Armenistís; in practice, any time from 9–11am), weekdays at noon (to Évdhilos only), and additionally at 1.30pm Monday and Friday to Armenistís.

The baths in **Thérma** are rather slimey, open 8am–1pm only. A far better bet if you're after a soak are the more natural hot springs at **Thérma Lefkádhos**, 3km southwest of Áyios Kírikos, below a cluster of villas. Here the seaside spa is derelict, leaving the water to boil up right in the shallows, mixing with the sea between giant volcanic boulders to a pleasant temperature. The only drawback is the landward setting; a 1993 fire devastated all the trees hereabouts, besides killing fourteen people.

Practicalities

There are several **hotels**, like the *Isabella* (☎0275/22 238; ④), or the friendly, basic but spotless *Akti* (☎0275/22 694; ②–③), on a knoll east of the fishing quay, with views of Foúrni from the garden. Otherwise, **rented rooms** fill fast and are not especially inexpensive: *Adam's Pension* (☎0275/22 418; ③) is about the fanciest, while those of *Ioannis Proestos* (☎0275/23496; ③), above the sweet shop next to *Iy Sinandisis* (see below), are squeaky clean and excellent value; there are two more quiet, well-placed establishments directly behind the base of the ferry jetty and a little to the west. In desperation, you might try one of the three unmarked, spartan outfits grouped around the **post office** on Dhioníso, the inland high street. There are also two **banks**, a limited-hours **OTE**, and assorted ferry **agents**, such as *Ikariadha* and *Dolihi Tours* – though all are coy about the daily noontime *kaíki* to Foúrni, whose tickets are sold on board. You can **rent** motorbikes and cars here, too, but both are cheaper in Armenistís.

Eating out, you've slightly more choice than in lodging. On the way from the ferry to the main square you'll pass the barn-like *Ta Adhelfia* and *Ta Votsalsa*, open only in the evenings; *Ouzeri Psistaria*, inland towards the post office, is a very good and reasonable combination *ouzerí* and *loukoumádhiko*. Just around the corner from the latter, *Iy*

Klimataria is no culinary marvel but worth noting because, unlike most, it operates year-round. Finally, the giant *Iy Sinandisis* on the tree-shaded esplanade is utterly unlike any other *kafenío* in the Greek islands: in a reversal of the norm, young adults play *távli* and cards inside, while outside their elders and assorted foreigners suck on sweets or watch each other – better entertainment by far than anything dished up at the summer cinema.

Évdhilos and around

The twisty, 41-kilometre road from Áyios Kírikos to Évdhilos is one of the most hair-raising on any Greek island, and the long ridge which extends the length of Ikaría often wears a streamer of cloud, even when the rest of the Aegean sky is clear. **KARAVÓSTAMO**, with its tiny, scruffy port, is the first substantial north coast place, and has a series of three beaches leading up to **ÉVDHILOS**. Although this is the island's second town and a ferry stop at least three times weekly in summer, it's considerably less equipped to deal with visitors than Áyios Kírikos. There are two **hotels**, the *Evdoxia* on the slope west of the harbour (☎0275/31 502; ③) and the *Georgios* (☎0275/31 218; ③), plus a few **rooms**. Of the trio of waterfront **restaurants**, *O Kokkos* has the largest menu but is expensive; try *O Flisvos* next door instead. A **post office** and **OTE**, and a surprisingly good town **beach** to the east, are also worth knowing about.

KÁMBOS, 2km west, sports a small museum in the village centre with finds from nearby ancient **Oinoe**, the twelfth-century church of Ayía Iríni next to the museum, the sparse ruins of a Byzantine palace (just above the road) used to house exiled nobles, as well as a large beach. **Rooms** are available from the store run by *Vassilis Dhionysos* (☎0275/31 300; ②), which also acts as the unofficial tourist office for this part of Ikaría, and meals from a **taverna** (dinner only).

Kámbos is also the start and end point of a road loop up through the hamlet-speckled valley inland: **MARATHÓ** isn't up to much but **FRANDÁTO** has a summer-time taverna; **STÉLI** and **DHÁFNI** are good, attractive examples of the little oases which sprout on Ikaría.

Armenistís and around

Most people don't stop until reaching **ARMENISTÍS**, 57km from Áyios Kírikos, and with good reason: this little resort lies in the heart of Ikaría's finest wooded scenery, with two enormous, sandy beaches – **Livádhi** and **Messakhtí** – five and fifteen minutes' walk to the east respectively. Campers in the marshes behind each stretch set the tone for the place, but the islanders' tolerance doesn't yet extend to nude bathing, as signs warn you; a semi-official campsite is in the process of being set up.

A dwindling number of older buildings lends Armenistís the air of a Cornish fishing village; it's a tiny place, reminiscent of similar youth-oriented spots on the south coast of Crete, though lately gentrification has definitely set in. A "music bar" operates seasonally behind the nearer beach, but nightlife is mostly about extended sessions in the tavernas and cafés overlooking the anchorage. The *Paskhalia* taverna/**rooms** (☎0275/71 302; winter ☎01/24 71 411; ③) is the cleanest in both categories, with doubles with bath; the food, including full breakfasts, is good, too, and not exorbitant. Should you require more luxury, there's the *Armena Inn* (④) well up the hillside or the luxury *Cavos Bay Hotel* (☎0275/71 381; winter ☎01/76 40 235 ④–⑤), 1km west. A giant bakery/cake shop caters to sweet teeth for the entire west end of the island, and the *Marabou Travel Agency* changes money and rents clapped-out **mopeds** and somewhat sturdier jeeps, although you don't really need either, since the best of Ikaría lies within an hour's walk of the port.

The sole drawback to staying in Armenistís is **getting away**, since both taxis and buses are elusive. Theoretically, **buses** head at least as far as Évdhilos – all the way up to Áyios Kírikos on Mondays and Fridays – at 7am, and to Évdhilos daily at 3pm, but school kids have priority on the early departure, and the second one is unreliable even by Ikarian standards.

Beyond Armenistís: the southwest

Armenistís is actually the shore annexe of three inland hamlets – Áyios Dhimítrios, Áyios Políkarpos and Hristós – collectively known as **RÁHES**. Despite the modern dirt roads in through the pines, they still retain a certain Shangri-La quality, with the older residents speaking a positively Homeric dialect. On an island not short of foibles, Hristós is particularly strange, inasmuch as the locals sleep much of the day, but shop, eat and even send their children to school at night; in fact most of the villages west of Évdhilos adhere to this schedule, defying central-government efforts to bring them in line with the rest of Greece. Near the small main square there's a **post office** and a **hotel/restaurant**, but for lunch you'll have to scrounge something at one of two unusual *kafenía*. The slightly spaced-out demeanours of those serving may be attributable to over-indulgence in the excellent home-brewed **wine** which everyone west of Évdhilos makes – strong but hangover-free, and stored in rather disgusting goat-skins which are also used as shoulder bags, sold in some shops.

By tacit consent, Greek or foreign hippies, naturists and dope-fiends have been allowed to shift 4km west of Armenistís to **Nás**, a tree-clogged river canyon ending in a small but sheltered pebble beach. This little bay is almost completely enclosed by weirdly sculpted rock formations, and it's unwise to swim outside the cove's natural limits – there are drownings nearly every year in the open sea here, as well as at Messakhtí closer to Armenistís. The crumbling foundations of the fifth-century temple of **Artemis Tavropoleio** (Patroness of Bulls) overlook the permanent deep pool at the mouth of the river; people who used to camp rough just upstream are now encouraged to use the semi-official site at *Snack Bar River*. If you continue inland along this, Ikaría's only year-round watercourse, you'll find secluded rock pools for freshwater dips. Back at the top of the path leading down to the beach from the road are two or three tavernas and as many **rooms** – try the *Pension Nas* (☎0275/41 255; ②).

Should you be persuaded to rent a vehicle from *Marabou* in Armenistís, or join one of their jeep safaris, you can run through half a dozen villages at the southwest tip of the island. **VRAKÁDHES**, with two *kafenía* and a natural-balcony setting, makes a good first or last stop on a tour. A sharp drop below it, the impact of the empty convent of **Evangelistrías** lies mostly in its setting amidst gardens overlooking the sea. Nearby **AMÁLO** has two summer tavernas; just inland, **Langádha** is not a village but a hidden valley containing an enormous and seasonally popular *exohikó kéndro* (rural taverna).

The puny mopeds will go down *from* Langádha *to* Kálamos, not the other way around; in any case it's a tough bike that gets all the way to **KARKINÁGRI**, built at the base of cliffs near the southern extremity of Ikaría and a dismal anticlimax to a journey out here. The only thing likely to bring a smile to your lips is the marked intersection of Leofóros Bakunin and Odhós Lenin – surely the only two such streets in Greece – at the edge of town, which boasts a couple of sleepy, seasonal tavernas and a rooms establishment near the jetty. Before the road was opened (the continuation to Manganítis and Áyios Kírikos is stalled at an unblastable rock-face), Karkinágri's only easy link with the outside world was by **ferry** or *kaíki*, both of which still call once or twice a week in mid-summer.

Satellite islands: Foúrni and Thímena

The straits between Sámos or Ikaría are speckled with a number of spidery-looking islets. The only ones permanently inhabited are Thímena and Foúrni, the latter home to a huge fishing fleet and one of the more thriving boatyards in the Aegean. As a result of these, and the improvement of the jetty to receive car ferries, Foúrni's population is stable, unlike so many small Greek islands. The islets were once the lair of Maltese pirates, and indeed many of the islanders have a distinctly North African appearance.

Foúrni

Apart from the remote hamlet of Hrissomiliá in the north, where the island's main motorable road goes, most of the inhabitants of **Foúrni** are concentrated in the **port** and Kámbi hamlet just south. The harbour community is larger than it looks from the sea, and there are several **rooms** establishments, the most desirable being those run by *Manolis and Patra Markakis* (☎0275/51 268; ②–③), immediately to your left as you disembark – they have both cold-water rooms in front and all-mod-cons units in the rear. If they're full (usually the case in August), you can head inland to the modern blocks of *Evtihia Amoryianou* (☎0275/51 364; ③) or *Maouni* (☎0275/51 367; ③).

Of the three waterfront **tavernas**, the local favourite is *Rementzo*, better known as *Nikos'*; if you're lucky the local *astakós* or Aegean lobster, actually an oversized saltwater crayfish, may be on the menu. The central "high street", fieldstoned and mulberry-shaded, ends well inland at a little *platía* with a handful of more conventional *kafenía,* a modern snack bar, and a **post office** where you can change money.

A fifteen-minute walk south from the port, skirting the cemetery and then slipping over the windmill ridge, brings you to **KÁMBI**, a scattered community overlooking a pair of sandy, tamarisk-shaded coves which you'll share with chickens and hauled-up fishing boats. There are two cafés, the upper one providing filling snacks, the lower one controlling seven **rooms** that are admittedly spartan but have arguably the best views on the island; another family also has some cottages to let. A path continues to the next bay south, which like Kámbi cove, is a preferred anchorage for wandering yachts.

Continuing further south along the coast is problematic on foot; best to arrange boat trips in the harbour to **Marmári** cove, so named for its role as a quarry for ancient Ephesus in Asia Minor; you can still see some unshipped marble blocks lying about. From Marmári, a faint trail climbs up to the spine of the island, emerging onto the dirt road just south of Theológos chapel. Most of the old ridge path can still be followed south of the chapel, shortcutting the road as it drops to the hamlet and monastery of **ÁYIOS IOÁNNIS PRÓDHROMOS**. There are no facilities whatsover here – sometimes not even reliable fresh water – but you'll find two tiny, secluded beaches below the hamlet to either side of the jetty.

Heading north from the harbour via steps, then a trail, there are more **beaches**: an average one by the fish-processing plant, and two better ones further on, following the path. At the extreme north of the island, idyllic **HRISSOMILEÁ** is again usually approached by boat as the dirt road in is so bad. The village, split into a shore district and a hill settlement at the top of a canyon, has a decent beach; even better, less accessible, ones flank it to either side. Near the dock are very rough-and-ready combination *kafenía*/tavernas; equally simple **rooms** can be arranged.

Thímena

Thímena has one tiny hillside settlement, at which the regular *kaíki* calls on its way between Ikaría and Foúrni, but no tourist facilities, and casual visits are explicitly discouraged. The **kaíki**, incidentally, leaves Ikaría at about 1pm (five days a week), stays overnight at Foúrni and returns the next morning. The twice-weekly *kaíki* from

Karlóvassi and the larger car ferries which appear at odd intervals are likewise not tourist excursion boats but exist for the benefit of the islanders. The only practical way to visit the island on a day trip is by using one of the summer morning hydrofoils out of Sámos (Vathí or Pithagório).

Híos

"Craggy Híos", as Homer aptly described his (probable) birthplace, has an eventful history and a strong sense of place. It has always been relatively prosperous, in medieval times through the export of gum mastic, a trade controlled by Genoese overlords, and later by virtue of several shipping dynasties. The maritime families and the military authorities did not encourage tourism unitl the late 1980s, but with the worldwide shipping crisis, and the saturation of other, more obviously "marketable" islands, resistance has dwindled. Increasing numbers of foreigners are discovering a Híos beyond its large port capital: fascinating villages, important Byzantine monuments and a respectable complement of beaches. While unlikely ever to be dominated by tourism, the local scene has a definitely modernized flavour – courtesy of numerous returned Greek-Americans – and English is widely spoken.

Unfortunately, the island has suffered more than its fair share of catastrophes during the past two centuries. The Turks perpetrated their most infamous, if not their worst, anti-revolutionary atrocity here in 1822, massacring 30,000 Hiots and enslaving or exiling even more. In 1881, much of Híos was destroyed by a violent earthquake, and throughout the 1980s the natural beauty of the island was markedly diminished by several devastating forest fires, compounding the effect of generations of tree-felling by boat-builders. Nearly two-thirds of the majestic pines are now gone, with patches of woods persisting only in the far northeast and at the exact centre of Híos.

In 1988 the first charters from northern Europe were instituted, an event that signalled equally momentous changes for the island. There are now perhaps 10,000 guest beds on Híos, the vast majority of them in the capital or the nearby beach resort of Karfás. Tourist numbers are evenly divided between a babel of nationalities – Austrian, Belgian, Norwegian, Swiss, Dutch, German, plus a small British contingent brought in by specialist operators. Further expansion, however, is hampered by the lack of direct air links between Britain and Híos, and the refusal of property owners to part with land for the extension of the airport runway.

Híos Town

HÍOS, the harbour and main town, will come as a shock after modest island capitals elsewhere; it's a bustling, concrete-laced commercial centre, with little predating the 1881 quake. Yet in many ways it is the most satisfactory of North Aegean ports; time spent exploring is amply rewarded with a large and fascinating bazaar, a museum or two, some authentic tavernas and, on the waterfront, Greece's best-attended evening *vólta* (promenade). Because of its central location on the island's east shore, and preponderance of tourist facilities, Híos is the obvious base for explorations, especially if you're without a vehicle. Although it's a sprawling town of about 30,000, most things of interest to visitors lie within a hundred or so metres of the water.

South and east of the main *platía*, officially Plastíra but known universally as Vounakíou, extends the marvellously lively tradesmen's **bazaar**, where you can find everything from live monkeys to cast-iron woodstoves. Híos must feature more varieties of bread than any other town in Greece – corn, whole wheat, multi-grain, so-called "dark" and "village" – and most bakers in the marketplace were will offer at least two or three from this list.

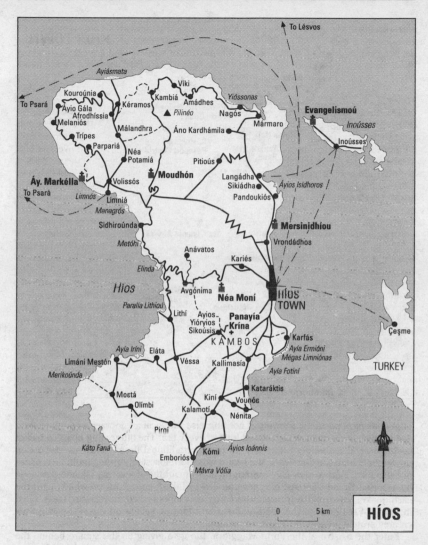

To Lésvos

To Psará

Ayiásmata

Kouroúnia   Víki

Áyio Gála   Kambiá   Amádhes   Yióssonas

Afrodhíssia   Kéramos   Nagós

Melaniós   ▲ Pilinéo   Mármaro

Trípes   Málandhra   Áno Kardhámila

Parpariá   **Evangelismoú**

Néa   *Inoússes*

Potamiá   Pitioús   Inoússes

Áy. Markélla   Volissós   **Moudhón**

To Psará   Langádha

Limnós   Sikiádha   *Áyios Isídhoros*

Limniá   Pandoukiós

Managrós

Sidhiroúnda   **Mersinidhíou**

Metóhi   Vrondádhos

Anávatos

Elínda   Kariés

Híos

Avgónima   **Néa Moní**   **HÍOS TOWN**

Paralía Lithíou   Lithí   Ayios.   **Panayía**

Yióryios   **Krína**   Çeşme

Sikoúsis

K A M B O S   Karfás

Ayía Iríni   Eláta   *Ayía Ermióni*   TURKEY

Límáni Mestón   Véssa   Kallimasía   *Mégas Limniónas*

Merikoúnda   *Ayía Fotiní*

Mestá   Kataráktis

Olímbi   Kiní   Vounós

Kalamotí   Nénita

Pirní

Káto Faná   Kómi   *Áyios Ioánnis*

Emboriós

Mávra Vólia

0   5 km

HÍOS

The grandiosely titled "Byzantine Museum", occupying the old **Mecidiye Mosque** (daily except Mon 10am–1pm; free), opposite the Vounakíou taxi rank, is little more than an archeological warehouse and workshop, awash in marble fragments such as Turkish, Jewish and Armenian gravestones. The official Archeological Museum located on Mihálon is currently closed, and its collection was never very compelling anyway.

More worthwhile is the **Argenti Museum** (Mon–Fri 8am–2pm, also Fri 5–7.30pm, Sat 8am–12.30pm; free), housed on the top floor of the Koraï Library building at Koraï 2 and endowed by a leading Hiot family. Accordingly there's a rather ponderous gallery

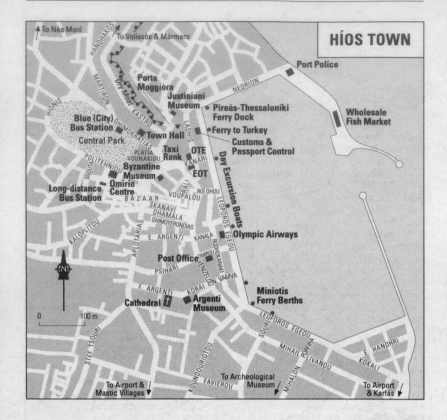

HÍOS TOWN

To Néa Moní
To Volissós & Mármaro
Port Police
HANDHAKOS
Porta Moggiora
NEORION
Justiniani Museum
Pireás-Thessaloníki Ferry Dock
Wholesale Fish Market
MARTIRON
Blue (City) Bus Station
KASTRO
DIMOKRATIAS
Town Hall
Ferry to Turkey
HIONIS
Central Park
LADHIS
Customs & Passport Control
Taxi Rank
OTE
PLATÍA VOUNAKÍOU
KANARI
Byzantine Museum
EOT
POLITEHNÍOU
SGOUTA
Long-distance Bus Station
Omirio Centre
RÓI DHOU
Day Excursion Boats
BALI
VOUPALOU
BAZAAR
SKANAVI
KALOPLITOU
OHAMALA
DHIMOYERONDIAS
LEOFOROS EGEOU
E. ARGENTI
KANALA
Olympic Airways
APLOTARIAS
RODHOKANAKI
Post Office
OMIROU
VENIZELOU
PSIHARI
VAMVA
F. ARGENTI
KORAÍ
Cathedral
Argenti Museum
Miniotis Ferry Berths
LEOFOROS EGEOU
SOURI
STEF TSOURI
0   100 m
KOUNDOURIOTOU
FAVIEROU
To Archeological Museum
MIHALON
MIHAIL LIVANOU
PORERA
E. HANDHRI
KOKALI
To Airport & Mastic Villages
To Airport & Karfás

of genealogical portraits, showing if nothing else the local aristocracy's compulsion to ape English dress and artistic conventions in every era. The other wing boasts a hall of costumes and embroidery, kitsch figurines in traditional dress, and carved wooden implements from the time when the island was more forested. Among multiple replicas of Delacroix's *Massacre at Hios* are engravings of eighteenth-century islanders as seen by assorted Grand Tourists, plus several views of the Genoese *kástro* which, until the earthquake, was completely intact; thereafter developers razed the seaward walls, filled in much of the moat to the south and made a fortune selling off the real estate thus created around present-day Platía Vounakíou.

Enter the **Kástro** at the Porta Maggiora, the gate giving on the square behind the town hall. A small tower just inside is home these days to the Justiniani Museum (closed for repairs; theoretically daily except Mon 9am–8pm; free), up some stairs and housing a satisfying collection of unusual icons and mosaics rescued from local churches. The small dungeon adjacent briefly held 75 Hiot notables before their execution as hostages by the Turks in 1822. The old residential quarter inside what remains of the castle walls, formerly the Muslim and Jewish neighbourhoods, is well worth a wander; among the wood-and-plaster houses you'll find assorted Ottoman monuments in various states of decay, including a cemetery, a small mosque, several inscribed fountains and a former dervish convent converted into a church after 1923.

Arrival, information and services

The **airport** lies 4km south along the coast at Kondári; any of the blue urban buses labelled "Kondári Karfás", departing from the station on the north side of the park, passes the airport gate. The green-and-cream long-distance **buses** leave from a parking area on the opposite side of the park, behind the Omirio Cultural Centre. **Ferry** agents cluster to either side of the customs building, towards the north end of the waterfront Egéou and its continuation Neoríon. *Miniotis Lines*, at Neoríon 21–23 (☎0271/24 670 or 41 073), operates a regular morning service to Çeşme, small ferries to many neighbouring islands, and excursions to Inoússes. The Turkish evening ferry to Çeşme is currently handled by *Faros Travel* (☎0271/27 240), while the *Gianmar* **hydrofoil** agent is *Omiros Tours*, on Egéou at the corner of Kanári (☎0271/41 319).

The helpful municipal **tourist office** (May–Sept Mon–Fri 7am–2.30pm & 6–9.30pm; Sat 10am–1.30pm; Sun 10am–noon; Oct–April Mon–Fri 7am–2.30pm) is at Kanári 18, near the *Ionian Bank*. The conspicuous "Hadzelenis Tourist Information Office" (☎0271/26 743) on the quay is a private entity geared to accommodation placement.

While **bus services** to the south of Híos are adequate, those to the centre and northwest of the island are almost non-existent. For such excursions it's well worth renting a powerful **motorbike** (not a moped) or a car, or **sharing a taxi** (a common practice) – uniquely in Greece, they're bright red. **Car rental agencies** sit in a row along Evyenías Handhrí, behind the *Chandris Hotel*; of these, *George Sotirakis/European Rent a Car* at no. 3 (☎0271/29 754) can be recommended.

The **OTE** (daily 7am–midnight) is directly opposite the tourist office, while the **post office** is on Omírou. **Banks** are numerous, as you'd expect for such a well-off island. A Hiot idiosyncrasy is the complete lack of afternoon **shopping hours** during summer – if you want to buy anything, make sure you do so before 2pm.

Accommodation

Híos Town has a relative abundance of affordable accommodation, rarely – if ever – completely full. Most of it lines the water or the perpendicular alleys and parallel streets behind, and almost all of it is plagued by traffic noise to some degree – we've listed some of the more peaceful establishments.

Anesis, corner of Vasilikári and Aplotariás, in the bazaar (☎0271/44 801). Rooms with bath, fridges and air conditioning; quiet after dark. ③

Apollonio, Roídhou 5 (☎0271/24 842). Fairly quiet hotel tucked onto a tiny plaza just inland from the water. A seaward annexe, the *Acropolis*, has simpler rooms in the next category down. ③.

Faidra, Mihaíl Livanoú 13 (☎0271/41 130). Well-appointed pension, in an old mansion complete with stone arches in the downstairs winter bar; in summer the bar operates outside, so ask for a rear room to avoid nocturnal noise. Prices vary according to season and length of stay. ④–⑤.

Hios Rooms, Kokáli 1, corner Egéou (☎0271/27 295 or 26 743). Clean, antique rooms above a ships' chandler's; relatively quiet for a seafront locale. ②

Kyma, east end of Evyenías Handhrí (☎0271/44 500). A Neoclassical mansion with a modern extension, splendid service and big breakfasts. The old wing saw a critical moment in modern Greek history in September 1922, when Colonel Nikolaos Plastiras commandeered it as his HQ after the Greek defeat in Asia Minor, and announced the deposition of King Constantine I. ⑤.

Pelineon Rooms, Omírou 9, corner of Egéou (☎0271/28 030). Many rooms have sea view (though not the singles), and the owner also does bike and car rental. ②–③.

Rodhon, Zaharíou 17 (☎0271/24 335). The owners can be crotchety, and the more basic rooms are a bit steeply priced, but this is virtually the only place inside the *kástro*, and very quiet. ③

Rooms Alex, Mihaíl Livanoú 29 (☎0271/26 054). The friendly proprietor often meets late-arriving ferries; otherwise ring the bell. There's a roof garden above the well-furnished rooms, which come with and without bath. ②–③.

Eating

Eating out in Híos Town can be more pleasurable than the rash of obvious, mostly bogus, *ouzerís* on the waterfront would suggest; it is also usually a fair bit cheaper than on the neighbouring islands of Sámos and Lésvos.

Estiatorio Dhimitrakopoulos, corner of Sgoúta and Vlatariás, near KTEL station. Simple, inexpensive oven-cooked lunches in a tiny hole-in-the-wall, which attracts an interesting mixed clientele of locals and foreign residents. Lunch only.

Iakovos Pavtas, beside the wholesale fish market at far northeast end of harbour jetty. Go early for the best quality at this *ouzerí*; mostly seafood, pricier than *Theodhosiou*, but blissfully free of exhaust fumes. Dinner only.

No-name, corner of Roídhou and Venizélou, immediately behind the *Apollonio* lodgings. Small milkshop, which serves sheep's-milk yogurt from Lésvos, *loukoumádhes* and rice pudding.

O Hotzas, Yioryíou Kondhíli 3, near Stefánou Tsoúri. Long the premier taverna in Híos Town, this has now moved to new premises featuring an arcaded interior and summer garden. The cooking has deteriorated of late, but you might still catch them on a good night. Dinner only; closed Sun.

Ouzeri Theodhosiou, junction of Egéou and Neoríon. The genuine article, with a good, inexpensive, huge menu, though it's best to wait until the ferries which dock immediately opposite have departed. Dinner only.

Drinking, nightlife and entertainment

Iviskos, on the quay. The most tasteful café on the quay, with a range of juices, coffees and alcoholic drinks.

O Kavos, south end of the quay, near the "kink" in Egéou. The best (and oldest) bar in terms of music, decor and crowd.

Omírio, south side of the central park. Cultural centre and events hall well worth stopping in at: frequently changing exhibitions, and foreign musicians often come here after Athens concerts to perform in the large auditorium.

Beaches around Híos Town

Híos Town itself has no beaches worth mentioning and the closest one of interest is at **KARFÁS**, 7km south past the airport and served by frequent blue buses. Most of the recent growth in the Hiot tourist industry has occurred here, to the considerable detriment of the 500-metre-long beach itself, but the one bright spot is a unique **pension**, *Markos' Place* (☎0271/31 990; ②–③), installed in the former pilgrims' cells at the **monastery of Áyios Yióryios and Áyios Pandelímon**, on the hillside south of the bay. The church still functions as such, separate from the activities of the many groups who book the place; individuals (there are several single "cells") are more than welcome, though advance reservations are strongly suggested. At the south end of the beach, *O Karfas* (locally known as *Yiamos'* after the proprietor) is a fair bet for cheap and abundant **food**. Service and atmosphere are better at the more expensive *Karatzas* at mid-beach, whose seaview **hotel** upstairs (☎0271/31 180; ③) is one of the few establishments here that still is geared to non-package-tour custom. However, the best food of all is to be had at *Toh Dholoma*, 3km back towards town at Kondári, on a side road between the swimming pool and the *Morning Star Hotel*.

Some 2km further along the coast from Karfás, **AYÍA ERMIÓNI** is less of a beach than a fishing anchorage surrounded by a handful of tavernas and rooms to rent. The actual beach is at **Mégas Limniónas**, a few hundred metres further, even smaller than Kárfas but rather more scenic, especially at its south end where low cliffs provide a backdrop. Both Ayía Ermióni and Mégas Limniónas are served by extensions of the blue bus route to either Karfás or Thimianá, the nearest inland village.

The coast road loops up to Thimianá, from where you can (with your own transport only) continue 3km south towards Kalimassiá to the turning for **Ayía Fotiní**, a 700-metre pebble beach with exceptionally clean water. There's no shade, however, unless you count shadows from the numerous blocks of rooms under construction behind the main road; there is a small cluster of **tavernas** around the parking area where the side road meets the sea.

The last settlement on this coast, 5km beyond Kalimassiá and served by long-distance bus, is **KATARÁKTIS**, remarkable mainly for its pleasant waterfront of balconied houses, its fishing port and a few tavernas. There are no appreciable beaches nearby, and inland explorations of the nearby narrow-alleyed hill villages of **NÉNITA** (same bus service) and **VOUNÓS** may be more rewarding.

Southern Híos

The olive-covered, gently rolling countryside in the **south of the island** is also home to the mastic bush, *Pistacia lentisca* to be precise, which here alone in Greece produces an aromatic gum of marketable quantity and quality. The resin scraped from Híos branches was for centuries the base of paints, cosmetics and chewable jelly beans which became a somewhat addictive staple in the Ottoman harems. Indeed the interruption of the flow of mastic from Híos to Istanbul by the revolt of spring 1822 was one of the root causes of the brutal Ottoman reaction. The wealth engendered by the mastic trade supported a half-dozen *mastikhohoriá* (mastic villages) from the time the Genoese set up a monopoly in the substance during the fourteenth and fifteenth centuries, but the end of imperial Turkey, and the industrial revolution with its petroleum-based products, knocked the bottom out of the mastic market. Now it's just a curiosity, to be chewed – try the sweetened *Elma* brand gum – or drunk as a liqueur called *mastíha*, though it has had medicinal applications since ancient times. These days, the *mastihohoriá* live mainly off their tangerines, apricots and olives. The towns themselves, the only settlements on Híos spared by the Turks in 1822, are architecturally unique, laid out by the Genoese but distinctly Middle-Eastern-looking.

The mastic villages

ARMÓLIA, 20km from town, is the first, smallest and least imposing of the mastic villages. Its main virtue is its pottery industry – the best shops are the last two on the right, driving southwest – and there are three snack bars: two on the road, and another in the centre, all open year-round. Out of season it can be difficult to find open places to eat in the south of the island.

PIRGÍ, 25km from the port, is perhaps the liveliest and certainly the most colourful of the communities, its houses elaborately embossed with *hristá*, geometric patterns cut into the plaster and then outlined with paint. On the northeast corner of the central square the twelfth-century Byzantine church of **Áyii Apóstoli** (Tues–Thurs & Sat 10am–1pm), embellished with much later frescoes, is tucked under an arcade. The giant **Cathedral of the Assumption** on the square itself boasts a *témblon* in an odd folk style dating from 1642, and an equally bizarre carved figure peeking out from the base of the pulpit. Pirgí has a handful of **rooms**, many of them bookable through the *Women's Agricultural and Tourist Cooperative* (☎0271/72 496; ③). Otherwise, there's *Rita's Rooms*, on the main bypass road (☎0271/72 479; ②), with a noisy pub nearby. In the medieval core you'll find a bank, a post office, a miniscule OTE stall on the *platía* and a couple of **tavernas**, best of these *Iy Manoula*, right next to OTE.

OLÍMBI, 7km further along the same bus route serving Armólia and Pirgí, is the least visited of the villages but not devoid of interest. The characteristic tower-keep, which at Pirgí stands virtually abandoned away from the modernized main square, here looms bang in the middle of the *platía*, its ground floor occupied by two *kafenía*. By now you will have grasped the basic layout of a mastic village: an originally rectangular warren of stone houses, the outer row doubling as the town's perimeter fortification, and pierced by just a few gates. More recent additions, although in traditional architectural style, straggle outside the original defences.

MESTÁ, 11km west of Pirgí, has a more sombre feel and is considered the finest example of the genre. From the main square, dominated by the **church of Taxiárhis** (the largest on the island), a bewildering maze of cool, shady lanes, provided with anti-earthquake buttresses and tunnels between the usually unpainted houses, leads off in all directions. But most streets end in blind alleys, except the critical half-dozen leading to as many gates; the northeast one still has an iron grate installed. If you'd like to stay, there are half a dozen **rooms** in restored traditional dwellings managed by *Dhimitris Pipidhis* (☎0271/76 319; ③); those run by the *Zervoudhi* (☎0271/76 240; ②) and *Yialouri* (☎0271/76 137; ②) households are somewhat less costly. Of the two **tavernas** on the main *platía*, *O Morias sta Mesta* is renowned for its tasty rural specialities, including edible mountain weeds and the locally produced raisin wine: heavy, semi-sweet and sherry-like.

The south coast

One drawback to staying in Mestá is the dearth of good beaches nearby. Its harbour **LIMÁNI MESTÓN** (or Passá Limáni), 3km north, has come down considerably in the world since the ferry service here ceased some years ago. With no beach of any sort in sight, you wonder who stays in the handful of rooms; it's only worth a trip for the two **fish tavernas**. The closest beach worthy of the name is at **Merikoúnda**, 4km west of Mestá.

Reached by a rough seven-kilometre side road just east of Olímbi, the little beach of **Káto Faná** is popular with Greek summer campers, who blithely disregard signs forbidding the practice; there are no facilities. A vaunted Apollo temple in the vicinity amounts to scattered masonry around a medieval chapel built atop it, by the roadside some 400m above the shore.

Pirgí is actually closest to the two major beach resorts in this corner of the island. The nearest of these, 6km distant, is by **EMBORIÓS**, an almost landlocked harbour with a few mediocre tavernas (most passable of these *Ifestio*); there's a scanty, British-excavated archeological zone nearby, the ancient Hiots not having been slow to realize the advantages of the site as a trading-post. For swimming, follow the road to its end at an oversubscribed car park and the beach of **Mávra Vólia**, then continue by clear trail over the headland to two more dramatic pebble strands of red and black volcanic stones, twice the length and backed by impressive cliffs.

If you want sand you'll have to go to **KOMÍ**, 3km northeast, also accessible from Armólia via Kalamotí. It's bidding to become a sort of Greek-pitched Karfás, though so far there are just a few fairly undistinguished tavernas and summer apartments behind the brown sand. The bus service, at least, is fairly good in season, often following a loop route through Pirgí and Emboriós.

Central Híos

The **central** portion of Híos, extending west from Híos Town, matches the south in terms of monumental interest, and a recently improved road network makes touring under your own power an easy matter. There are beaches as well, on the far shore of the island, still not the best on Híos (see "Northern Híos" below) but serviceable for a dip at the end of the day.

The Kámbos

The **Kámbos**, a vast, fertile plain carpeted with citrus groves, extends southwest from Híos Town almost as far as the village of Halkío. The district was originally settled by the Genoese during the fourteenth century and remained a preserve of the local aris-tocracy until 1822. Exploring it with a bicycle or motorbike is apt to be less frustrating than going by car, since the poorly marked roads form a web of lanes sandwiched between high walls, guaranteeing disorientation and frequent backtracking. Behind these walls you catch fleeting glimpses of ornate old mansions built from a tawny, peanut-brittle-pattern masonry. Courtyards are paved in pebbles or alternating light-and-dark tiles, and most still contain a *mánganos*, or water-wheel, onced used to draw water up from thirty-metre-deep wells.

Many of the sumptuous three-storey dwellings, constructed in a hybrid Italo-Turco-Greek style, have languished in ruins since 1881, but a few have been converted for use as unique accommodation. Most famous of these is the *Villa Argenti* (☎0271/31 599; fax 31 465; or in Milan, ☎02/49 88 254), ancestral home of the Italo-Greek counts Argenti de Scio. Initially restored early this century, it has become the most exclusive accommodation in Greece, consisting of four self-contained apartments installed in outbuildings in the orange orchards, plus a few luxury double rooms in the main mansion. If you have to ask how much, you can't afford it.

Lesser mortals can stay at the contrastingly well-marked and publicized *Hotel Perivoli* (☎0271/31 513 ⑤), just 100m north of *Villa Argenti*, whose orchard is also home to a popular **restaurant** (dinner only). The rooms, no two alike, are equipped with fireplaces and (in most cases) en-suite baths and sofas. Blue urban buses bound for Thimianá pass just 200m to the east.

Not strictly speaking in Kámbos, but most easily reached from it en route to the *mastikhohoriá*, the thirteenth-century Byzantine **church of Panayía Krína** is well worth the effort required to find it. Starting from Vavíli village, 9km from town, follow a maze of vaguely marked dirt tracks to the church, isolated amidst orchards and woods. It is usually closed for snail's-pace restoration, but you get a fair idea of the finely frescoed interior, sufficiently lit by a twelve-windowed drum, through the apse window. The alternating brick-and-stonework of the exterior alone justifies the trip out, though harmony is marred by a clumsy lantern over the narthex, added later.

Néa Moní

Almost exactly in the physical centre of the island, the **monastery of Néa Moní**, founded by the Byzantine Emperor Constantine Monomakhos (The Dueller) IX in 1042 where a wonder-working icon had been discovered, is among the most beautiful and important monuments on any of the Greek islands. Its mosaics rank with those of Dháfni and Óssios Loukás as being among the finest art of their age, and its setting – high in still partly forested mountains west of the port – is no less memorable. **Bus excursions** are provided by the KTEL on Tuesday and Friday mornings; otherwise come by motorbike, or walk from Kariés, 7km northeast, to which there is a regular blue-bus service. Taxis from town, however, are not prohibitive at about 5000dr round-trip per carload, and a suitable wait while you look around is included in the price.

Once a powerful and independent community of 600 monks, Néa Moní was pillaged during the events of 1822 and most of its residents put to the sword. The 1881 tremor caused comprehensive damage (skilfully repaired), while a century later a forest fire threatened to engulf the place until the resident icon was paraded along the perimeter wall, miraculously repelling the flames. Today the monastery, with its giant refectory and vaulted water cisterns, is inhabited by just two elderly nuns and a similar number of lay workers; when the last nun dies, Néa Moní will be taken over by monks.

Just inside the **main gate** (daily 8am–1pm & 4–8pm) stands a chapel/charnel house containing the bones of those who met their death here in 1822; axe-clefts in children's skulls attest to the savagery of the attackers. The *katholikón*, with the cupola resting on an octagonal drum, is of a design seen elsewhere only in Cyprus; the frescoes in the exonarthex are badly damaged by holes allegedly from Turkish bullets, but the **mosaics** are another matter. The narthex contains portrayals of the *Saints of Hios* sandwiched between *Christ Washing the Disciples' Feet* and *Judas' Betrayal*; in the dome of the sanctuary, which once contained a complete life-cycle of Christ, only the *Baptism*, part of the *Crucifixion*, the *Descent from the Cross*, the *Resurrection* and the *Evangelists Mark and John* survived the earthquake.

The west coast

With your own transport, you can proceed 5km west of Néa Moníto **AVGÓNIMA**, a jumble of houses on a knoll perched above the coast; the name means "Clutch of Eggs", an apt description of the clustered houses as seen from the ridge above. Since the 1980s, the place has been almost totally restored as a summer haven by descendants of the original villagers, though the permanent population is just seven. A returned Greek-American family runs an excellent, reasonable **taverna**/*kafenío* on the main square, *O Pyrgos*, but as yet there's no place to stay. A paved side road continues another 4km north to **ANÁVATOS**, whose empty, dun-coloured dwellings, soaring above pistachio orchards, are almost indistinguishable from the 300-metre-high bluff on which they're built. During the 1822 insurrection the 400 inhabitants threw themselves over this cliff rather than surrender to the besieging Ottomans, and it's still a preferred suicide leap. Anávatos itself is two persons less populous than Avgónima, and, given a lack of reliable facilities plus an eerie, traumatized atmosphere, it's no place to be stranded at dusk.

West of Avgónima, the main road descends 6km to the coast in well-graded loops; in the wake of recent surfacing this also makes a good alternative approach to the northwest of Híos (see below). Turning right (north) at the junction leads first to the much-advertised beach at **Elínda**, alluring from afar but rocky-shored and murky-watered up close; better to continue towards more secluded coves to either side of Metóhi, or below **SIDHIROÚNDA** (snack bar), the only village hereabouts, which enjoys a spectacular hilltop setting overlooking the coast.

All along this coast, as far southwest as Limáni Mestón, loom round **watchtowers** erected by the Genoese to look out for pirates; one of these has furnished the name of **Kastélla**, the first swimmable cove you reach by turning left from the junction. The weekday-only bus service resumes 7km south of the junction at **LITHÍ**, a friendly village of whitewashed buildings perched on a wooded ledge overlooking the sea. There are tavernas and *kafenía* near where the bus turns around, but the only places to stay are down at windswept, dreary **Paralía Lithioú** 2km below, a weekend target of Hiot townies for the sake of its large but garbage-fringed beach.

Some 5km south of Lithí, the valley-bottom village of **VÉSSA** is an unsung gem, more open than Mestá or Pirgí but still homogeneous. Its honey-coloured buildings are arrayed in a vast grid punctuated by numerous belfries; there's a simple taverna, and you can stay at an old inn, *Toh Petrino* (☎0271/25 016 or 41 097; ④). The ridgetop village of **ÁYIOS YIÓRYIOS SIKOÚSSIS**, nearly 8km east and above on the way back to Híos Town, has had its architectural profile spoilt by new construction, but a popular and well-marked taverna near the church offers sweeping views. Your last chance for a swim near Véssa is provided by a series of secluded sandy bays along the 16-kilometre road west to Limáni Mestón; only that of **Ayía Iríni** has a taverna, and all suffer from periodic wind and rubbish attacks owing to the northerly exposure.

Northern Híos

Northern Híos never really recovered from the Turkish massacre, and the desolation left by the fires of 1981 and 1987 will further dampen the spirits of inquisitive travellers. Since early this century the villages have languished all but deserted much of the year, which means that bus services are correspondingly sparse. About one-third of the former population now lives in Híos Town, venturing out here only on the dates of major festivals or to tend grapes and olives, time which barely adds up to four months of the year. The balance of the northerners or their descendants, based in Athens or the US, visit their ancestral homes for just a few weeks at mid-summer, this brief but intense season being used to arrange marriages between local families.

The road to Kardhámila

Blue city buses run north from Híos Town only as far as **VRONDÁDHOS**, an elongated coastal suburb which is the favourite residence of the island's many seafarers. Homer is reputed to have lived and taught here, and just above the little fishing port and pebble beach you can visit his purported lectern, more probably an ancient altar of Cybele and surrounded by terraced parkland. Accordingly many of the buses out here are labelled *Dhaskalópetra* (Teacher's Rock).

If you have transport, by all means make a stop at the **monastery of Panayía Mirsinidhíou** (Mirtidhiótissis) – of little intrinsic interest but most photogenically set overlooking the sea. Some 5km along, the route swoops down to the tiny hamlet at **Pandoukiós** bay, bereft of amenities but economically important by virtue of several offshore fish nurseries raising bass and gilt-head bream. A side road just north leads to stony **Áyios Isídhoros** cove, home to the rather inconveniently located island **campsite**, though the site itself is shaded and faces Inoússes islet across the water.

Travelling by bus, **LANGÁDHA** is probably the first point on the eastern coast road where you might be tempted to alight. Set at the mouth of a deep valley, this attractive little harbour settlement looks across its bay to a pine grove, and beyond to Turkey. There are three **rooms** establishments (try *Eleni Sidheri*, ✆0271/74 637; ③), but most night-time visitors come for the sake of the excellent seafood at the two surviving **tavernas** at the start of the quay; the remainder of the esplanade has been taken over by patisseries, bars and cafés. There is no proper beach anywhere nearby; **Dhelfíni** bay just to the north is an off-limits naval base.

Just beyond Langádha an important side road leads 5km up and inland to **PITIOÚS**, an oasis in a mountain pass presided over by a tower-keep; continuing 4km more brings you to a junction allowing quick access to the west of the island and the Volissós area (see below).

Kardhámila and around

Most traffic proceeds to **ÁNO** and **KÁTO KARDHÁMILA**, the latter 37km out of the main town. Positioned at opposite edges of a fertile plain rimmed by mountains, they initially come as welcome, green relief from Homer's crags. Káto, better known as **MÁRMARO**, is the larger, its waterside streets flanked by the hillside neighbourhood diotricts of Ráhi and Perivoláki, and indeed it's the second largest town on the island, with a bank, post office, OTE branch and filling station (the only one in the entire north). However, there is little to attract a casual visitor: the port, mercilessly exposed to the *meltémi*, is strictly businesslike, and there are few tourist facilities. One exception is the *Hotel Kardamyla* (✆0272/23 353; ⑤–⑥), co-managed with Híos Town's *Hotel Kyma* by Theodhore Spordhilis. The hotel sits behind the bay's only pebble beach, and its **restaurant** is a reliable source of meals for non-guests as well.

For better swimming head west – by car from the signposted junction by the church, on foot past the harbour-mouth windmill for an hour along a cemented coastal driveway – to **Nagós**, a gravel-shore bay at the foot of an oasis. The lush greenery is nourished by active springs up at a bend in the road, enclosed in a sort of grotto and flanked by a *psistariá*, all overawed by tall cliffs. The place name is a corruption of *naós*, after a large Poseidon temple that once stood near the springs, but centuries of orchard-tending, antiquities-pilfering and organized excavations after 1912 mean that nothing remains visible. Down at the shore the swimming is good, if a bit chilly, and there are two tavernas, one renting **rooms** (✆0272/23 540; ③). Several more are under construction, and your only chance of relative solitude in July or August lies fifteen minutes' walk west at **Yióssonas**. This is a much longer beach, but less sheltered, rockier and with no facilities.

Northwestern villages

Few outsiders venture beyond Yióssonas; an afternoon bus occasionally covers the distance between Mármaro and Kambiá village, 20km west. Along the way, **AMÁDHES** and **VÍKI** are attractive enough villages at the base of 1297-metre **Pilinéo**, the island's summit, easiest climbed from Amádhes. **KAMBIÁ**, overlooking a chapel-strewn ravine, has very much an end-of-the-line feel, despite the recent paving of the onward road south through Spartoúnda and Kipouriés to its union with the trans-island road to Volissós.

Around 4km north of this junction, you can detour to visit the sixteenth-century **monastery of Moudhón**, once ranked second on the island after Néa Moní before its partial destruction in 1822. Among its naive frescoes is one of the *Ouranódhromos Klímax* (Stairway to Heaven), a trial-by-ascent in which ungodly priests are beset by demons who hurl them into the mouth of Leviathan, while the righteous clergy are assisted upwards by angels. In an era when illiteracy was the norm, such panels were intended quite literally to scare the hell out of simple parishioners.

If without transport, go to one of the *kafenía* by the main church in Kambiá to be pointed along the one-hour path across the canyon to the abandoned hamlet of Agrelopó; from the church there a system of jeep tracks leads in another ninety minutes to the tumbledown pier and seaweed-strewn beach at **AYIÁSMATA**. This is one of the strangest spots on Híos, consisting of perhaps twenty buildings (four of them churches), including the miraculous hot springs after which the place is named. The spa is currently in the throes of restoration, so it's best not to count on staying or eating here.

Roads **south of Ayiásmata**, paved once more, pass through strikingly beautiful countryside up to the villages of Kéramos and Afrodhíssia. Here the surfaced road system splits: the southerly turning continues south through Hálandhra and Néa Potamiá – the latter an ugly prefab village built to replace an older one destroyed by landslide – for 20km towards Volissós.

A northwesterly turning from Afrodhíssia is more worthwhile, approximating a coastal road for this part of the island. **KOUROÚNIA**, 6km along, is beautifully arranged in two separate neighbourhoods, looking out from thick forest cover. After 10km more, you reach **ÁYIO GÁLA**, where a disproportionate number of old ladies in headscarves hobble about; there's a single telephone in the *kafenío*, whose proprietor summons those called over a loud hailer. The place's claim to fame is a grotto-church complex, built into a palisade at the bottom of the village. Except on the 23 August festival date, you'll need to find Petros the key-keeper, who lives beside a eucalyptus tree at the top of the stairs leading down to it. The larger of the two churches occupies the mouth of the cave system; it's originally fifteenth century but has had an unfortunate pink exterior paint job that makes it look like a recent villa. Inside, however, a fantastically intricate *témblon* vies for your attention with a tinier, older chapel, built entirely within the rear of the cavern. Its frescoes are badly smudged, except for a wonderfully mysterious and mournful Virgin holding a knowing Child in the apse.

Volissós and around

VOLISSÓS, 42km from Híos Town by the most direct route, was once the most important of the northwestern villages, and its old stone houses still curl appealingly beneath the crumbling hilltop Byzantine fort. The Genoese improved the towers, and near the top of the village you may be shown an utterly spurious "House of Homer". Today Volissós can seem depressing at first, with the bulk of its 250 remaining, mostly elderly, permanent inhabitants living in newer constructions around the main square – impressions improve with longer acquaintance.

Grouped around the *platía* you'll find a post office (but no bank), two shops and three evening-only **tavernas**, none especially noteworthy. Since the **bus** only comes out here on Sundays on a day-trip basis, and on Monday and Thursday in the afternoon, you should plan on **staying overnight**. This should cause no dismay, since the area has the best beaches on Híos, unspoiled because most inland property owners have thus far refused to sell land to developers. Houses in the village itself are, however, for sale, and eleven have been meticulously restored by *Stella Tsakiri* (☎0274/21 421; ③–④) and accommodate from two to four persons – all have terraces, fully equipped kitchens and original features such as tree trunks upholding sleeping lofts.

Otherwise, there are four conventional rooms 2km south at **LIMNIÁ**, the port of Volissós, above the single permanent **taverna** on the jetty (☎0274/21 315; ③). Limniá itself is a lively working fishing anchorage, with *kaíki* skippers coming and going from Psará (Mon, Wed & Fri at mid-morning) and very occasionally to Plomári on Lésvos.

At Limniá you're not far from the fabled beaches either. A kilometre's walk southeast over the headland brings you to **Managrós**, a seemingly endless sand-and-pebble beach where nudism is tolerated; the nearest **lodgings** are the bungalows of *Marvina Alvertou* (☎0274/21 335; ③). The more intimate **Lefkáthia** lies just a ten-minute stroll along the jeep track threading over the headland north of the harbour; amenities are limited to a seasonal snack bar on the sand, and *Ioannis Zorbas* apartments (☎0274/21 436; ④), sited just where the jeep track joins a paved road down from Volissós. This is headed for **Límnos** (not to be confused with Limniá), the next protected cove 400m east of Lefkáthia, with a seasonal *psistariá* operating behind the sand.

Ayía Markélla, 5km further west of Límnos, stars in many local postcards: a long, stunning beach fronting the monastery of the same name, the latter not especially interesting, or useful, to outsiders. Its cells are reserved for Greek pilgrims, while in an interesting variation on the expulsion of the money changers from the temple, only religious souvenirs are allowed to be sold in the holy precincts, while all manner of plastic junk is on offer just outside. There's a single snack bar as well, and around July 22 – the local saint's festival and biggest island celebration – the "No Camping" signs doubtless go unenforced. Some old maps show **hot springs** at one end of the beach; these, actually twenty minutes' walk away around the headland, turn out to be tepid seeps into pot-sized cavities at the tidal zone, not worth the bother. A handier bit of intelligence is that the dirt road past the monastery grounds is passable to any vehicle, emerging up on the paved road between Melaniós and Volissós.

Satellite islands: Psará and Inoússes

There's a single settlement, with beaches and a lone rural monastery, on both of Híos's satellite isles, but each is surprisingly different from the other, and the main island, too. **Inoússes**, the closer one, has daily *kaíkia* from the main harbour in season; **Psará** is served six days a week, with ferries or *kaíkia* on alternate days from Híos Town and Limniá.

Psará

The birthplace of revolutionary war hero Admiral Kanaris, **Psará** devoted her merchant fleets – the third largest in 1820s Greece after Ídhra and Spétses – to the cause of independence, and paid dearly for it. Vexed beyond endurance, the Turks landed overwhelming forces in 1824, to stamp out this nest of resistance. Perhaps 3000 of the 30,000 inhabitants escaped in small boats which were rescued by a French fleet, but the majority retreated to a hilltop powder magazine and blew it, and themselves, up rather than surrender. The nationalist poet Solomos immortalized the incident in famous stanzas:

> *On the Black Ridge of Psará,*
> *Glory walks alone.*
> *She meditates on her heroes,*
> *And wears in her hair a wreath*
> *Made from a few dry weeds*
> *Left on the barren ground.*

Today the year-round population barely exceeds four hundred, and it's a sad, stark place, never having really recovered from the holocaust; the Turks burned whatever houses and vegetation the blast had missed. The only positive recent development was a decade-long revitalization project instigated by a French-Greek descendant of Kanaris and a Greek team. The port was improved, mains electricity and pure water provided, a secondary school opened, and cultural links between France and the island established, though so far this has not been reflected in increased tourism or tourist facilities.

Arriving can be something of an ordeal: the regular ferry from Híos Town takes four hours to cover the 35 nautical miles of habitually rough sea. Use the port of Limniá to cross in at least one direction if you can; this route takes half the time at half the price.

Since few buildings in the east-facing harbour community predate this century, it's a strange hotchpotch of ecclesiastical and domestic architecture that greets the eye on disembarking. There's a distinctly southern feel, more like the Dodecanese or the Cyclades, and some strange churches, no two alike in style, in and out of town.

If you **stay overnight**, your choices are limited to a single studio behind the dockside string of *kafenía* and tavernas; some rooms let by the priest's wife; the municipal (and overpriced) inn (②), and the EOT *ksenónas* in a restored prison (☎0274/61 293; ③). For **eating**, the best and cheapest place by far is the EOT-run *Spitalia*, housed in a restored medieval hospital at the edge of town. A **post office**, bakery and shop complete the tally of amenities; there's no bank.

Psará's **beaches** are decent, getting better the further northeast you walk from the port. You quickly pass Káto Yialós, Katsoúni and Lazoréta with its off-putting power station; **Lákka**, fifteen minutes along, seems to be named after its grooved rock formations in which you may have to shelter, as much of this coast is windswept, with a heavy swell offshore. **Límnos**, 25 minutes out along the coastal path, is big and pretty, but there's no reliable taverna here, or indeed at any of the other beaches. The only other thing to do on Psará, really, is to walk north across the island to the **monastery of the Assumption**; this – uninhabited since the 1970s – comes to life only during the first week of August when its revered icon is taken in procession to town, and then back again on 6 August, with great ceremony.

Inoússes

Inoússes has a permanent population of about three hundred – down from more than twice that number since World War II – and a very different history from Psará. For generations, this medium-sized islet has provided the Aegean with many of her wealthiest shipping families: the richest Greek shipowner in the world, Kostas Lemos, was born here, and virtually every street or square here is named for one member or other of the numerous Pateras clan. This helps explain the large villas and visiting summer yachts in an otherwise sleepy Greek backwater – as well as a sporadically open **Maritime Museum** near the quay, endowed by various shipping magnates and devoted to nautical exhibits and souvenirs. The bigwigs have also funded a large nautical academy to train future seamen, at the west end of the quay.

Only on Saturdays and Sundays can you make an inexpensive **day-trip** to Inoússes from Híos with the locals' ferry *Inousses*; on other days of the week this arrives at 3pm, returning early the next morning. On weekdays during the tourist season you must participate in the pricey excursions offered from Híos, with return tickets running up to three times the cost of the regular ferry.

Two church-tipped islets, each privately owned, guard the unusually well-protected harbour; the **town** of Inoússes is surprisingly large, draped over hillsides enclosing a ravine. Despite the wealthy reputation, it's of unpretentious appearance, with the houses displaying a mix of vernacular and modest Neoclassical style. There is just one, fairly comfortable **hotel**, the *Thalassoporos* (☎0272/51 475; ④), on the main easterly hillside lane. **Eating out** is similarly limited to *O Glaros*, a simple *ouzerí* just below the nautical academy. It's best to come equipped with picnic materials, or be prepared to patronize one of the three shops (one on the waterfront, two up the hill). Beside the museum is a **post office** and a **bank**, with the OTE a few paces further west.

The rest of this tranquil island, at least the southern slope, is surprisingly green and well tended; there are no springs, so water comes from a mix of fresh and brackish wells, though there are mutterings of a reservoir in the offing. The sea is extremely clean and calm on this lee shore; among the sheltered southerly beaches, choose from **Zepága, Biláli** or **Kástro**, five, twenty and thirty minutes' walk west of the port respectively, or the more secluded **Farkeró**, 25 minutes east: first along a cement drive ending at a seaside chapel, then by path past pine groves and over a ridge. As on Psará, there are no reliable facilities at any of the beaches.

At the end of the westerly road, beyond Kástro, stands the somewhat macabre convent of **Evangelismoú**, endowed by the Pateras family. Inside reposes the mummified body of the lately canonized daughter, Irini, whose prayers to die of cancer in place of her terminally ill father Panagos were answered early in the 1960s on account of her virtue and piety; he's entombed here, also, having outlived Irini by some years. The abbess, presiding over some twenty nuns, is Mrs Pateras. Only women are allowed admission, and even then casual visits are not encouraged.

Lésvos (Mitilíni)

Lésvos, the third largest Greek island after Crete and Évia, is not only the birthplace of Sappho, but also of Aesop, Arion and, more recently, the Greek primitive artist Theophilos, the poet Odysseus Elytis and the novelist Stratis Myrivilis. Despite these artistic associations, it may not at first strike the visitor as particularly beautiful or interesting; much of the landscape is rocky, volcanic terrain, dotted with thermal springs and alternating with vast grain fields, salt pans or even near-desert. But there are also oak and pine forests as well as vast olive groves, some of these over five hundred years old. With its balmy climate and suggestive contours, the island tends to grow on you with prolonged acquaintance.

Lovers of medieval and Ottoman **architecture** certainly won't be disappointed. Genoese castles survive at the main town of Mitilíni, at Mólivos and near Ándissa: these date from the late fourteenth century, when Lésvos was given as a dowry to a Genoese prince of the Gatelouzi clan following his marriage to the niece of one of the last Byzantine emperors. Along with Crete, Lésvos was the only Greek island where Turks settled significantly in rural villages (they usually stuck to the safety of towns), so driving along you frequently encounter the odd Ottoman bridge or crumbling minaret in the middle of nowhere. Again, unusually for the Aegean islands, there was an approximation of a post-Byzantine Greek Orthodox urban aristocracy here, who built rambling mansions and tower-houses, some of which have survived the destruction which claimed the rest in this century.

Social and economic idiosyncrasies persist: anyone who has attended one of the lengthy village *paniyíria*, with music for hours on end and tables in the streets groaning with food and drink, will not be surprised to learn that Lésvos has the highest alcoholism rate in Greece. Breeding livestock, especially horses, is disproportionately important, and traffic jams caused by mounts instead of parked cars are not unheard of – signs reading "Forbidden to Tether Animals Here" are still part of the picture.

Historically, the olive plantations, *oúzo* distilleries, animal husbandry and a fishing industry supported the inhabitants, but with these enterprises relatively depressed, mass-market **tourism** has made considerable inroads. However, there are few large hotels outside the capital or Mólivos, rooms still just outnumber villa-type accommodation, and the first official campsites opened only in 1990. While Lésvos is far more developed than Híos, it is far less so than Sámos, a happy medium that will accord with many people's tastes. Public buses tend to radiate out from the harbour for the benefit of working locals, not tourists who may want to do an out-and-back day trip. Carrying out such excursions is next to impossible anyway, owing to the size of the island – about 70km by 45km at its widest points – and the occasionally appalling roads (at long last being improved, along with their signposting). Furthermore, the topography is complicated by the two deeply indented gulfs of Kalloní and Yéra, which means that going from A to B usually involves an obligatory change of bus at either the port capital, on the east shore, or the town of Kalloní, in the middle of the island. In short, it's best to decide on a base and stay there for at least a few days, exploring its immediate surroundings on foot or by vehicle, rather than constantly trying to move on.

Mitilíni Town

MITILÍNI is the port and capital, and in Greek fashion sometimes doubles as the name of the island, something to watch out for when travelling by ferry or plane. The town sprawls between and around two broad bays divided by a promontory where the **Genoese fortress** sits – open much of the day but not to be photographed since it's a military area. Further inland, the town skyline is dominated in turn by the Germanic spire of **Áyios Theodhóros** and the mammary dome of **Áyios Therápon**, together expressions of the post-Baroque taste of the nineteenth-century Ottoman Greek bourgeoisie. They stand more or less at opposite ends of the **bazaar**, whose main street, Ermoú, links the town centre with the little-used north harbour. On its way there Ermoú passes half a dozen antique shops near the roofless **Yeni Tzami**, now a venue for art exhibits. Between Ermoú and the castle lies a maze of atmospheric lanes lined with grandiose Belle Epoque mansions and elderly houses.

More formal stimulation is provided by the excellent **Archeological Museum** (daily except Mon 8.30am–3pm; 400dr), currently housed partly in the mansion of a large estate just behind the ferry dock (although a large modern installation is under construction). Among the more interesting of the well-labelled and well-lit exhibits are a complete set of mosaics from a Hellenistic dwelling, rather droll terracotta figurines, votive offerings from a sanctuary of Demeter and Kore excavated in the castle, and Neolithic finds from present-day Thermí. A specially built annexe at the rear contains stone-cut inscriptions of various edicts and treaties, and – more interesting than you'd think – *stelae* featuring *nekródhipna* or portrayals of funerary meals.

There's also a **Byzantine Art Museum** behind Áyios Therápon, containing various icons (Mon–Sat 9am–1pm; 100dr), and a small **Folk Art Museum** (sporadic hours; 150dr) on the quay next to the blue city-bus stop.

All of the foregoing may sound like a lot but in fact the town's pleasures are easily exhausted in half a day. Most visitors, repulsed by the general urban bustle, get out as soon as possible; Mitilíni returns the compliment by being in fact a very impractical and expensive place to base yourself.

Arrival, transport and information

You should pause long enough to stop at the jointly housed **tourist police/EOT post** (daily 8.30am–5.30pm), behind the customs building, in order to get hold of their excellent town and island maps, plus other brochures.

There are two **bus stations** in town. The *astikó* (blue bus) service departs from the middle of the quay, while *iperastikó* (standard *KTEL*) buses leave from a small station near Platía Konstandinopóleos at the southern end of the harbour, all the way around from where ferries dock. There is no bus link with the **airport**, and a shared taxi (they're expensive) for the 8km into Mitilíni is the usual method. If you're intent on getting over to Ayvalık in Turkey, book **ferry tickets** through either *Aeolic Cruises*

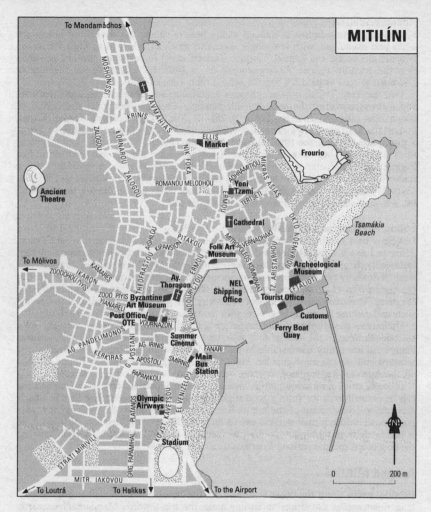

(☎0251/23 960) or *Mytilana Travel* nearby at Koundouriótou 69 (☎0251/41 318). Agencies for standard *NEL* and *Nomicos* ferries, and *Ilio Line* hydrofoils, are bunched together on the easterly reach of Koundouriótou, the quay street; *Olympic Airways* is southwest of the bay and central park, at Kavétsou 44.

Car rental is best arranged through reputable chain franchises like *Payless* or *Europcar* – though it's generally cheaper to rent at the resort of your choice. Mopeds or even proper motorbikes will make little impact on this huge island, and will certainly go for a spill on some of the rougher dirt roads.

Other amenities include the **OTE** and **post office**, next to each other on Vournázon, a block behind the central park, and three **banks** with autotellers: the *Ethniki* (*National*), *Pisteos* (*Credit*) – both on Koundouriótou – and the *Emboriki* (*Commercial*) on Ermoú.

Accommodation

Finding **accommodation** is difficult at the best of times: the waterfront hotels are noisy and exorbitant, with few single rooms to speak of. It's best to hunt for rooms between the castle and Ermoú. Yioryíou Tertséti street in particular has two possibilities: the friendly *Pelayia Koumniotou* at no. 6 (☎0251/20 643; ②), or the fancier *Dhiethnes* at no. 1 (☎0251/24 968; ③), whose rooms are en-suite.

Past the Yeni Tzami, quieter, cheaper establishments between the north harbour and fortress advertise themselves – for example *Cuckoo's Nest*, near the corner of Navmahías Ellís and Nikifóro Foká (☎0251/23 901; ②), or *Salina's Garden Rooms*, behind the Yeni Tzami at Fokéas 7 (☎0251/42 073; ③). The Neoclassical *Hotel Rex* at Katsakoúli 3, behind the Archeological Museum (☎0251/28 523; ③), looks inviting from the outside, but the en-suite rooms (no singles) are gloomy and overpriced. For Belle Epoque character you're better off in the far south of town, at the *Villa 1900*, a restored mansion with period furnishings and ceiling murals, at P. Vostáni 24 (0251/43 437; ④), where you may be able to bargain the price down a little. There's another similar, if less preserved, outfit nearby at E. Vostáni 24 (③).

Eating, drinking and nightlife

Lunch is best had at the *Iy Lesvos* on Ermoú. Further down, beside the Yeni Tzami, *Albatross* has a bizarre interior, with a human clientele to match, and the food – pickled *krítama* herb and grilled sardines, served up by the wild-eyed owner himself, and washed down by peculiar wine – seems incidental. Another example of a dying breed is the *Ouzeri Krystal*, on the seafront Koudourióti betwen the *Ionian Bank* and the *Bank of Greece*. The cavernous, wood-floored interior has walls lined by mirrors and bench seats and gaming tables at the centre, with more contemporary seating outside.

Options for more conventional dining are somewhat limited; the obvious venue for a seafood blowout is the line of four **fish tavernas** on the southerly quay known as Fanári. All are pretty comparable in price and food, though *Stratos* and *Strofi* at the seaward end are the most popular. Right around the port from here at Koundouriótou 56, the *Asteria* is a safe option for more involved, meat-and-veg oven casseroles.

If you're stuck here involuntarily, awaiting a dawn-departing ferry, some consolation can be derived from the town's good **nightlife** and **entertainment**. *Hot Spot* is a fairly accurate self-description of the bar at Koundouriótou 63, near the *NEL* agency, with good music. More formal musical events form the heart of the *Lesviakó Kalokéri*, held in the castle from mid-July to mid-September. The summer **cinema** *Pallas* is between the post office and the park on Vournázon.

Around Mitilíni

Heading north along the coast from Mitilíni, the beaches are negligible but the startling views across the straits to Turkey make the trip towards Mandamádhos worthwhile. On the way you can detour to see a Roman aqueduct at **MÓRIA**, and various *pírgi* (tower-mansions), relics of the nineteenth-century gentry, at **PÁMFILLA** and **PÍRGI THERMÍS**. However, the most compelling attraction is the **baths** at **LOUTRÓPOLI THERMÍS**, sunken indoor hot-spring pools overarched by great vaults. There's a half-hourly blue bus service to them, but enquire first before boarding since the spa is periodically closed for repairs.

Just south of the town, on the road to the airport, you can visit more tower-mansions at **HRISSOMALOÚSSA** and **AKLIDHÍOU**. Beyond the airport, but reached easiest by taking a blue city bus as far as the village of Loutrá (and then a taxi), the remote double-cove beach of **Áyios Ermoyénis** is attractive, but it's crowded on weekends and for pleasant immersions near Mitilíni (the fee-entry town "beach" at Tsamákia is mediocre) you're best advised to make for **Loutrá Yéras**, 8km along the main road to

Kalloní. These public baths (summer daily 8am–7pm, winter daily 10am–6pm; 150dr) are just the thing if you've spent a sleepless night on a malodorous ferry, with three ornate spouts that feed just-above-body-temperature water into a marble-lined pool in a vaulted chamber; there are separate facilities for each sex. A snack-bar/café operates seasonally on the roof of the bath house, overlooking the gulf, and there is even an old **inn** nearby (☎0251/21 643; ②).

The Variá museums

Perhaps the most rewarding single targets near Mitilíni are a pair of museums at **VARIÁ**. 3km south of town (regular half-hourly buses). The **Theophilos Museum** (daily except Mon 9am–1pm & 4.30–8pm; 250dr) honours the naive painter born here in 1868, and presents four rooms of wonderful, little-known compositions specifically commissioned by his patron Thériade (see below) in the several years leading up to his death in 1934; virtually the only familiar piece is likely to be *Erotokritos and Arethousa* in Room 3. Theophilos brought a wealth of accurate sartorial detail to bear on the pastoral Lésvos which he obviously knew best, in such elegiac scenes as fishing, reaping, olive-picking and baking; there are droll touches also, such as a cat slinking off with a fish in *The Fishmongers*. In classical scenes – such as *Sappho and Alkaeos* in Room 4, a landscape series of Egypt, Asia Minor and the Holy Land, and historical episodes from wars historical and contemporary – Theophilos was clearly on shakier ground. *Abyssinians Hunting an Italian Horseman*, for instance, is clearly fantastic, being nothing more than Native Americans chasing down a Conquistador.

The adjacent **Thériade Museum** (daily except Mon 9am–2pm & 5–8pm; 500dr) is the brainchild of another native son, Stratis Eleftheriades. Leaving the island at an early age for Paris, he Gallicized his name to Thériade and went on to become a renowned art publisher, convincing some of the leading artists of the twentieth century to participate in his ventures. The displays consist of lithographs, engravings, woodblock prints and watercolours by the likes of Miró, Chagall, Picasso, Léger, Rouault and Villon, either annotated by the painters themselves or illustrations for the works of prominent poets and authors – an astonishing collection for a relatively remote Aegean island. Near the two museums is an enterprising snack bar.

Southern Lésvos

The southernmost portion of the Island is indented by two great inlets, the gulfs of **Kalloní** and **Yéra** – the first curving in a northeasterly direction, the other northwesterly, thus creating a fan-shaped peninsula at the heart of which is the 968-metre Mount Ólimbos. Both shallow gulfs are in turn almost landlocked by virtue of very narrow outlets to the open sea.

Plomári and around

PLOMÁRI is the only sizeable coastal settlement in the south, the second largest on Lésvos, and presents an odd mix of beauty and its famous *oúzo* distilling industry. Despite a lack of sandy beaches nearby, it's besieged in summer by hordes of Scandinavian tourists, but you can usually find a **room** – they are signposted literally everywhere – at the edge of the old, charmingly dilapidated town. Unfortunately, rustling up a decent meal is considerably harder, with the dinner-only *Platanos* taverna at the central plane tree often unbearably busy, and nothing special at that. Best of a very mediocre bunch on the waterfront is *D'Annelise*, within sight of the bus stop.

You'll probably do no worse at **ÁYIOS ISÍDHOROS**, 3km east, which is where most tourists actually stay; try *Iy Mouria*, where the road turns inland to cross the creek draining to the long, popular pebble beach. The closest sandy beach is ninety minutes' walk west of Plomári, past isolated coves in the direction of **Melínda**. Back in

LÉSVOS

town the *Okeanis Hotel* (☎0252/32 469; ③) is one of several local outlets for car rental and runs boat trips to the still-better beaches of **Tárti** (24km east; food and lodging) and Vaterá (see below). The local *paniyíri* season kicks off in mid-July with the **Oúzo Festival**, culminating on the 27–28 of the month with celebrations in honour of Áyios Harálambos, featuring such rurally focused activities as horse races and a bull sacrifice.

The bus line into Plomári runs via the pretty villages of Paleókipos and Skópelos (as well as Áyios Isídhoros), but if you're hitching or have your own two-wheeler (no cars carried) you can take a slight shortcut by using the daytime-only ferry at **PÉRAMA**, across the neck of the Yéra Gulf. The road north from Plomári to Ayiássos has paving and public transport only up to Megalohóri – rough dirt and your own conveyance thereafter, though the surface should improve in future years.

Ayiássos
AYIÁSSOS, nestled in a remote, wooded valley under the crest of Mount Ólimbos, is the most beautiful hill town on Lésvos – the ranks of traditional houses lining the narrow, cobbled streets are all protected by law. On the usual, northerly approach, there's no clue of the enormous village until you see huge ranks of parked cars at the southern edge of town (where the bus also leaves you).

Don't be put off by the huge phalanxes of wooden and ceramic kitsch souvenirs, aimed mostly at Greeks, but continue past the central **church of the Panayía Vrefokratoússa** to the old bazaar, with its *kafenía*, yogurt shops and unusually graphic butcher's stalls. Video-game arcades have made certain inroads, but in some cafés bands of *santoúri*, clarinet, lap-drum and violin play on weekend afternoons, accompanying inebriated dancers on the cobbles outside. Rather more packaged are the products of *santoúri* player Ioannis Kakourgos, who plays and sells cassettes from his little studio underneath the church, built in the twelfth century to house an icon supposedly painted by the Evangelist Luke. With such a pedigree, the local 15 August festival is one of the liveliest in Greece, let alone Lésvos, and makes clear the country-fair element in a traditional *paniyíri*, where pilgrims came to buy and sell as well as perform devotions.

There are a very few **rooms** available for the increasing number of visitors. The best **restaurants** are *Dhouladhelli*, on your left as you enter the village from the extreme south (bus stop) end, or *Dhayielles*, further along. At either of these spots you can eat for a fraction of the prices asked at the coastal resorts.

Vaterá – and its approaches

A different bus route from Mitilíni leads to Vaterá beach via the inland villages of Polihnítos, whose spa has long been closed for repairs, and more attractive Vríssa. If you're after a bath, try the working **hot springs of Áyios Ioánnis** (100dr), fairly well signposted 2km below the village of Lisvóri. Flanking the chapel are two vaulted-chamber pools, though the water is odiferous, iron-stained and best enjoyed on a cool evening.

VATERÁ itself is a huge, seven-kilometre-long sand beach, backed by vegetated hills; the swimming is delightfully calm, clean and warm. The west end of this strip has several accommodation options, the nicest of the **hotels** clustered here the Greek- and American-run *Vatera Beach* (☎0252/61 212; open winter by arrangement; ④–⑤). It also has a good attached restaurant with shoreline tables from where you can gaze on the cape of Áyios Fokás, whose **temple of Dionysus** and early Christian basilica are finally being properly excavated. The **campsite** here lies slightly inland from the portion of the beach east of the T-junction, where studio/villa units predominate. Here several more **tavernas** line the shore road, and because the clientele are mostly local weekenders, they're reasonably priced and good – for example, *Ta Kalamakia*. **Nightlife** – thus far a pub or two, and the *Arena Disco* – is rather low-key, reflecting Vaterá's status as a family resort. If you intend to stay here you'll probably want your own transport, as the closest shops are 4km away at Vríssa, and the bus appears only three times daily.

To the east, a fair-to-poor dirt road leads via Stavrós and hidden Ambelikó to either Ayiássos or Plomári within an hour and a half. A direct coastal road to Melínda is on the cards, though Plomári is opposing this, fearful of losing tourist trade to the infinitely superior beach at Vaterá. Leaving the area going north towards Kallóni, the short cut via the coast guard base at **Ahladherí** is well worth using and passable in its present state to all but the more underpowered mopeds – moreover, it should be paved shortly.

Western Lésvos

The main road west of Loutrá Yéra is surprisingly devoid of settlement, with little to stop for before Kallóni other than the traces of an ancient **Aphrodite temple** at Mési (Messon), signposted just east of the Ahladherí cutoff and about 1km north of the main road. At the site (daily except Mon 8.30am–3pm; free) just the eleventh-century BC foundations and a few column stumps remain, plus the ruins of a fourteenth-century Genoese-built basilica; it was once virtually on the sea but a nearby stream has silted things up in the intervening millennia. All told, it's not worth a special trip, but certainly make the short detour if passing by – and brace yourself for the manically voluble caretaker.

Some 7km beyond lies the turning for the **AYÍA PARASKEVÍ**, where a famous bull-sacrifice rite is observed at the end of June or beginning of July; at other times the village presents an intriguing tableau of nineteenth-century bourgeois architecture.

KALLONÍ itself is an unembellished agricultural and market town more or less in the middle of the island, but you may spend some time here since it's the intersection of most bus routes. If you have a lot of time to spare, you might make the three-kilometre walk to **SKÁLA KALLONÍS**, a principally Dutch and English package resort with a long, if coarse, beach on the lake-like gulf. None of the handful of restaurants merits a mention, and **push-bike rental** – ideal for the flat terrain hereabouts – is the resort's only distinction.

Inland monasteries and villages

West of Kallóni the road winds 4km uphill to the **monastery of Limónos**, founded in 1527 by one Ignatios. It is a huge complex, with just a handful of monks and lay workers to maintain three storeys of cells ringing the giant courtyard, adorned with strutting peacocks and huge urns sporting potted plants. Beside, behind and above are respectively an old-age home, a lunatic asylum, and a hostel for pilgrims; the *katholikón*, with its carved-wood ceiling and archways, is built in Asia-Minor style and traditionally off-limits to women. A former abbot established a **museum** (daily 9am–1pm & 5–7.30pm; 100dr) on two floors of the rear wing; the ground-floor ecclesiastical collection is fine enough, but you should prevail upon the warden (easier done in large groups) to open the upper, ethnographic hall. The first room is a re-created Lesvian salon, while the next is crammed with an indiscriminate mix of kitsch and priceless objects – Ottoman copper trays to badly stuffed, rotting egrets by way of brightly painted trunks – donated since 1980 by surrounding villages. An overflow of farm implements is stashed in a corner storeroom below, next to a chamber where giant *pithária* (urns) for grain and olive oil are embedded in the floor.

Beyond, the road west passes through Fília, where you can turn off for a time-saving short cut to Skoutáros and the north of Lésvos; the dirt surface has recently been regraded and should be passable to any car. Most traffic continues through to the unusually neat village of **SKALOHÓRI**, its houses in tiers at the head of a valley facing the sea and the sunset, and **VATOÚSSA**, the most landlocked but also the most beautiful of the western settlements.

Eight kilometres beyond Vatoússa, a short track leads down to the sixteenth-century **monastery of Perivolís** (daily 8am–7pm; pull on the bell rope for admission), built as the name suggests in the midst of a riverside orchard. You should appear well before sunset, as only natural light is available to view the fine if faded frescoes in the narthex. In an apocalyptic panel worthy of Bosch, *The Earth and Sea Yield Up Their Dead*, the *Whore of Babylon* rides her chimaera and assorted sea-monsters disgorge their victims. On the north side you see a highly unusual iconography of *Abraham, the Virgin, and the Good Thief of Calvary in Paradise*. Further interest is lent by a humanized icon of Christ, under glass at the *témblon*.

ÁNDISSA nestles under the west's only pine grove; at the edge of the village a sign implores you to "Visit our Central Square", and that's not a bad idea, for the sake of its three enormous plane trees, shading several cafés and tavernas. Directly below Ándissa, a paved road leads 6km north toward the fishing hamlet of **GAVATHÁS**, with a narrow, partly protected beach and a few places to eat and stay – such as the *Hotel Restaurant Paradise* (☎0253/56 376; ③) – among its 25 or so buildings. A dirt side track leads to the huge, duned but wave-battered beach of **Kámbos**, one headland east; you can keep going in the same direction, following signs pointing to "Ancient Andissa". Where they actually lead you to is **Ovriókastro**, the most derelict of the island's Genoese castles, evocatively placed on a promontory within sight of Mólivos and a goodly swathe of coast to either side. Dirty exposed beaches adjacent are unlikely to appeal, though there is a small snackbar. The locals mistakenly identify the castle with the ancient town, but the latter is actually a fair way inland, and difficult to find.

Just beyond modern Ándissa there's an important junction. Keeping straight ahead leads you past the still-functioning **monastery of Ipsiloú**, founded in 1101 atop an extinct volcano and still home to four monks. The *katholikón*, tucked in one corner of a large, irregular courtyard, has a fine wood-lattice ceiling but had its frescoes repainted to worsening effect in 1992 and no longer ranks as meritorious art; more intriguing are bits of Iznik tiles stuck in the facade. Upstairs you can visit a fairly rich museum of ecclesiastical treasure (donation in exchange for a postcard). Ipsiloú's patron saint is John the Theologian, a frequent dedication for monasteries overlooking apocalyptic landscapes like the surrounding parched, boulder-strewn hills.

Near here is one of the main concentrations of specimens from Lésvos' rather over-rated **petrified forest**, indicated by forest service placards which also warn of severe penalties for pilfering souvenir chunks. For once contemporary Greek arsonists cannot be blamed for the state of the trees, created by the combined action of volcanic ash and hot springs some 15 million years ago. The other main cluster is south of Sígri (see below), but locals seem amazed that anyone would want to trudge though the barren countryside in search of them; upon arrival you may agree, since the mostly horizontal, three-metre-long chunks aren't exactly one of the world's wonders. If you're curious, there are a fair number of petrified logs strewn about the courtyard of Ipsiloú.

Sígri

SÍGRI, near the western tip of Lésvos, has an appropriately end-of-the-line feel. The bay here is guarded both by a Turkish **castle** and the long island of Nissopí athwart its mouth, which protects the place somewhat from prevailing winds; very occasionally, in what seems an experimental programme, a *NEL* ferry plying the line between Skíros and Límnos is diverted to call here. The castle sports the sultan's monogram over the entrance, something rarely seen outside Istanbul and a token of the high regard in which this productive island was held. A vaguely Turkish-looking church is in fact a converted **mosque**, while the town itself is an uneasy mix of old and cement dwellings. The town **beach**, south of the castle headland, is narrow and scrappy; there's a better one – glimpsed on the way in – 3km north at a river mouth, as well as an even better one 2km south at another creek mouth, just off the one-lane track to Eressós.

If you want to **stay**, there's a mid-range hotel and a handful of **rooms**, including *Nelly's Room and Apartments* (☎0253/54 230; ③), looking right at the castle. Among several **tavernas**, *Remezzo* may have the best view of the town beach and the fanciest menu, but *Galazio Kyma* – the unmarked white building with blue trim, opposite the jetty – gets first pick of the fishermen's catch and can offer unbeatably fresh seafood.

Skála Eressoú and Eressós

Most visitors to western Lésvos park themselves at **SKÁLA ERESSOÚ**, a growing resort accessible via the southerly turning between Ándissa and Ipsiloú. The beach here, given additional character by an islet that's within easy swimming distance, runs a close second to the one at Vaterá, and consequently the place is beginning to rival Plomári and Mólivos in numbers of visitors – who form an odd mix of Brits, Scandinavians, Greek families, neo-hippies and lesbians (of whom more below). Behind stretches the largest and most attractive agricultural plain on Lésvos, a welcome green contrast to the volcanic ridges above. Coming south the 15km from the junction there's no hint of the approaching oasis, something that adds to its idyllic quality as it erupts suddenly just beyond the inland town of **ERESSÓS**. This supports a contented colony of expatriates who have bought or rented property, and a stroll along lanes flanked by the vernacular houses is well worthwhile, but only during the cooler hours of the day. During summer half of the population is down at Skála, in the older cottages on the slope leading up to Vígla hill.

There's not much to Skála – just a roughly rectangular grid of perhaps five streets by eight, including the waterfront pedestrian zone (officially Papanikolí). A café-lined square at mid-waterfront is dominated by a bust of Theoprastus – a renowned botanist who originally hailed from **ancient Eressos**. This was not, as you might suppose, on the site of the modern village, but atop Vígla hill at the east end of the beach; you can still see some remaining crumbled bits of citadel wall from a distance. Once on top the ruins prove even scantier, but it's worth the scramble up for the comprehensive views – you can discern the ancient jetty, submerged out beyond the modern fishing anchorage.

Another famous reputed native of ancient Eressos was **Sappho**, and there are usually appreciable numbers of gay women here paying homage, particularly at the campsite and in the clothing-optional zone of the beach west of the river mouth. In the river itself live about a hundred terrapins who have learned to come ashore for bread-feedings.

Skála has countless **rooms**, most of the sea-view ones block-booked in advance by tour companies; in high season, often the best and quietest you can hope for is something inland overlooking a garden or fields. At such times it's wise to entrust the search to an agency, such as *Snapi Travel* on the east waterfront (☎0253/53 855;); you pay a small commission but it saves trudging about for vacancies. There are few bona fide **hotels**; longest established of these, well placed on the front if a bit noisy, is *Sappho the Eressia* (☎0253/53 233; ③), open all year. Otherwise, there's a free **campsite** at the west edge of town, under some trees behind the sand, with toilets, a shower and sinks.

Most **tavernas**, with elevated wooden dining platforms, crowd the beach; the best, both on the eastern walkway, are *Iy Gorgona*, with friendly service and a large menu of Greek standards, and the British-run *Bennett's*, at the extreme east end of things opposite the islet. Inland, on the way to the museum, the *Aphrodite Home Cooking* taverna is as described. Canadian-run *Yamas* is the place for pancake breakfasts; they also rent out mountain bikes and function as an Anglophone bar at night. *Sympathy*, a few doors down, has an arty-Greek clientele and an uncanny double for Charles Manson serving behind the bar. The gay women's contingent favours *Marianna's*, near the bust of Theophrastos; a summer **cinema** rounds out the nightlife.

Skála has an adjacent **post office** and **OTE**, a coin-op **laundrette** near the church, but no bank; exchange rates offered at the various travel agencies are disadvantageous, so come prepared.

Moving on

If you're returning to the main island crossroads at Kalloní, you can complete a loop from Eressós along the western shore of the Gulf of Kalloní via the hill villages of Mesótopos and Ágra; this route is currently all paved except for the first 11km out of Eressós, with that stretch scheduled for completion soon.

A marked track leads down from **MESÓTOPOS** to beaches at **Tavári** and **Kroússos**, both popular with Greeks and offered as destinations of boat-trips from Skála Eressoú. The only settlement of any consequence on the gulf's west shore is **PARÁKILA**, which boasts a ruined mosque, an Ottoman bridge and a fair proportion of Lesvos' citrus groves; nearby beaches are unlikely to prompt a halt.

Northern Lésvos

The main road north of Kalloní winds up a pine-flecked ridge and then down the other side into increasingly attractive country, stippled with poplars and blanketed by olive groves. Long before you can discern any other architectural detail, the silhouette of Mólivos castle indicates your approach to the oldest established tourist spot on Lésvos.

Mólivos (Míthimna)

MÓLIVOS (officially Míthimna), 61km from Mitilíni, is arguably the most aesthetically pleasing spot on Lésvos. Tiers of sturdy, red-tiled houses, some standing defensively with their rear walls to the sea, mount the slopes between the picturesque harbour and the **Genoese castle** (daily except Mon 7.30am–sunset; free), which provides interesting rambles around its perimeter walls, and views of Turkey across the straits. Closer examination reveals a dozen weathered Turkish fountains along flower-fragrant, cobbled alleyways, a reflection of the fact that before 1923 Turks constituted 35 percent of the local population, and owned most of the finest mansions. You can try to gain admission to the Greek-built **Krallis** and **Yiannakos mansions**; a small municipal **library**, in the rather vaguely signposted town hall, is usually open during weekday working hours. Until proper excavations begin, **ancient Mithymna** to the northwest is of essentially specialist interest, though a necropolis has been unearthed next to the bus stop; it's mainly the use of the Classical name that has been revived. The motivation for this, as so often in the Balkans, is political; *Mólivos* ("Graphite", of which there is none locally) is a futile Hellenization of the Turkish name *Molova*.

Modern dwellings and hotels have been sensibly banned from the preserved municipal core – a powerful Athenian watchdog group, "Friends of Molyvos", has seen to that – but this has inevitably sapped all the authentic life from the upper bazaar; just one lonely tailor still plies his trade amongst the redundant souvenir shops, and the last locals' *ouzerí* shut down in 1990. Having been cast as upmarket, there are no phallic postcards or other tacky accoutrements in Mólivos, but there are still constant reminders that you are strolling through a stage-set for mass tourism. Yet, except in August, the town's vine-canopied streets seem readily to absorb all who make their way here.

The **town beach** is mediocre – rocky and riddled with sea-urchins in the shallows – though it improves somewhat as you head towards the southern end and a clothing-optional zone. Advertised **boat excursions** to bays as remote as Ánaxos and Tsónia (see below for descriptions) seem a frank admission of this failing; there are also eight daily **minibus shuttles** in season, not appearing on any printed bus schedules, linking all points between Ánaxos and Eftaloú.

There are plenty of **rooms** (② & ③) available in town, most easily reserved through the municipal **tourist office** by the bus stop (daily 9am–1pm, 2.30–4pm & 6–8pm), which operates a no-fee telephone booking service. The main sea-level thoroughfare, straight past the tourist office, heads towards the harbour, where a couple of small **hotels** overlook the water; of these, the *Sea Horse* (☎0253/71 320; ④) is fine if you're not interested in making an early night of it. At some hotels in town, you may come upon an insistence that you take mandatory half-board. Otherwise, take the street heading upwards from just beyond the tourist office, past houses with shaded courtyards and – if you're lucky – you'll find room vacancies here; look for placards with the blue-on-white official EOT logo of a face in profile. One of the nicest and quietest (but highest up) are the three kept by *Varvara Kelesi* (☎0253/71 460; ②); few such houses, incidentally, have more rooms than that. There is now also an official **campsite**, *Camping Methymna*, 2km northeast of town.

Around the tourist office you'll find an automatic foreign-money-changing machine, and several **moped and car rental** places. The **post office** is near the top of the upper commercial street, Kástrou, while the **OTE** and a **bank** stand opposite each other on the lower market lane, Dhekátou Évdhomou Noemvríou, at the intersection with the shore road.

Choose carefully when **eating out**. You're usually better off forsaking the sea-view panoramas for Australian-run *Melinda's* at no. 52 of the lower market lane, where the partially vegetarian food is good; it's also the only place open between October and May. On the harbour itself, *Toh Khtapodhi* is the oldest outfit, while *The Captain's Table* at the far end, offers seafood, *mezédhes* and meat. *Medusa*, an *ouzerí* behind *Toh Khtapodh*i, has some highly unusual dishes such as seafood turnovers and cream-stuffed peppers. For dessert, try the pudding-and-cake shop *El Greco*, across the street and downhill from *Melinda's*, where Panayiotis the proprietor is a wonderful ranconteur (in several languages) and acts as a sort of mother hen to aspiring foreign artists, as the numerous paintings on the wall testify.

Midsummer sees a short **festival** of musical and theatrical events up in the castle. As fas as **nightlife** goes, the dancing bar *Q*, one of several down near the old port, and the state-of-the-art outdoor disco *Gatelouzi* near Pétra – the place to be seen on Saturday night – easily outstrip the attractions offered by the perennially empty disco on the water directly below *El Greco*. There's also a summer cinema next to the tourist office; the old mosque spanning the bazaar street supposedly functions as a movie house in winter.

Pétra and Ánaxos

Since there are limits to the expansion of Mólivos, many package companies are now shifting their emphasis towards **PÉTRA**, 5km due south and marginally less busy. The town is beginning to sprawl untidily behind its broad sand beach and seafront square, and diners on the square regularly get sprayed by the exhaust fumes from buses, but the core of old stone houses, many with Levantine-style balconies overhanging the street, remains. Pétra takes its name from the giant rock monolith located some distance inland and enhanced by the eighteenth-century church of the **Panayía Glikofiloússa**. Other local attractions include the sixteenth-century church of **Áyios Nikólaos** and the intricately decorated **Vareltzidhena** mansion (daily except Mon 8.30am–3pm; 200dr).

There are plenty of **rooms** plus a few small hotels, and as at Pirgí on Híos a *Women's Agricultural Tourism Cooperative*, formed by Pétra's women in 1984 to offer something more unusual for visitors. In addition to operating a lunchtime-only **restaurant** on the square (which also serves as a **tourist office**, crafts shop and general information centre; Mon–Sat 9am–3.30pm), they arrange accommodation where it's possible to participate in the proprietors' daily routine and learn a bit about village life. Advance reservations are usually needed (✿0253/41 238 or 41 340; ③). Aside from the cooperative's eatery, **tavernas** (like those behind the north beach) are generally a bit tatty, and you're better off either at the *Ouzeri Pittakos* (dinner only) 100m south of the square, or the *Grill Bar* right on the *platía*, ideal for a quick *souvláki* or tentacle of octopus.

ÁNAXOS, 3km south of Pétra, is a bit overdeveloped but still by far the cleanest beach in the area. Half-a-dozen or so restaurants sit behind a kilometre of sand dotted with pedaloes and sunloungers; the **rooms** here seem unaffiliated with any tour company, making Ánaxos a good bet for short-notice accommodation in high season, though you may be plagued by mosquitoes from the river mouth. From anywhere along here you enjoy beautiful sunsets between and beyond three offshore islets.

Around Mount Lepétimnos

East of Mólivos, the villages of **Mount Lepétimnos**, marked by tufts of poplars, offer a day or two of rewarding exploration. The first stop, though not exactly up the hill, might be **Loutrá Eftaloú**, some rustic (and painfully hot) **thermal baths** 5km along the road passing the campsite. These are housed in an attractive old domed structure, which has remained open while much-need renovation proceeds on the adjacent inn; there's a 200-drachma fee if the caretaker is about. Nearby, there are a considerable number of luxury hotels and bungalow complexes, some surprisingly reasonable – try the *Aeolis* (☎0253/71 772; ⑤). In the opposite direction, behind the baths, is a pebble beach for taking a cooling-off dip (clothing optional).

The main road around the mountain first heads 6km east to **VAFIÓS**, with one of two well-advertised **tavernas** featuring live music some nights, before curling north around the base of the peaks. This stretch is in the process of being surfaced, but currently the asphalt, and twice-daily bus service back toward Mitilíni, does not resume until Áryennos, 6km before the exquisite hill village of **SIKAMINIÁ** (Sikamiá), the birthplace of the novelist Stratis Myrivilis. Below the "Plaza of the Workers' First of May", with its two traditional *kafenía* and views north to Turkey, one of the imposing basalt-built houses is marked as his childhood home. A trail shortcuts the twisty road down to **SKÁLA SIKAMINIÁS**, easily the most picturesque fishing port on Lésvos. Myrivilis used it as the setting for his best-known book, *The Mermaid Madonna*, and the tiny rock-top chapel at the end of the jetty will be instantly recognizable to anyone who has read the novel.

On a practical level, Skála has a few **pensions** (such as the sea-view *Gorgona*), and three or four **tavernas**, best and longest-lived of these *Iy Mouria* (aka *Iy Skamnia*), with seating under the mulberry tree in which Myrivilis used to sleep on hot summer nights. In addition to good seafood courtesy of the active local fleet, you can try the late-summer speciality of *kolokitholoúloudha yemistá* (stuffed squash blossoms). The only half-decent local beach, however, is the rather average one of **Káyia** just to the east, so Skála is perhaps better as a lunch stop rather than a base. A fairly rough, roller-coaster track follows the coast west back to Mólivos.

Continuing east from upper Sikaminiá, you soon come to **KLIÓ**, whose single main street leads down to a *platía* with a plane tree, fountain, *kafenía* and views across to Turkey. The village is set attractively on a slope down which six kilometres of dirt road, better than maps suggest, descend to **Tsónia** beach. This proves to be 600 metres of beautiful pink volcanic sand, with just a single taverna and another café at the fishing-anchorage end. Tsónia is essentially the summer annexe of Klió, with the entire population down here at weekends in season.

South of Klió, the route forks at **KÁPI**, from where you can complete a loop of the mountain by bearing west along a partly paved road. **PELÓPI**, where the asphalt currently runs out, is the ancestral village of the unsuccessful 1988 US presidential candidate Michael Dukakis, and sports a former mosque now used as a warehouse on the main square. Garden-hidden **IPSILOMÉTOPO**, the next village along, is punctuated by a minaret (but no mosque) and hosts revels on July 17, the feast of Ayía Marína.

By the time you reach sprawling **STÍPSI**, you're almost back to the main Kalloní–Mólivos road; consequently there's a sporadic bus service out again, as well as a large **taverna** at the edge of town where busloads of tourists descend in season for "Greek Nights". There are also **rooms** to let, so Stípsi makes a good base for rambles along Lepétimnos' steadily dwindling network of trails; in recent years donkey-trekking has become more popular than walking, and you'll see outfitters advertising throughout the north of the island.

The main highway south from Klió and Kápi leads back to the capital through **MANDAMÁDHOS**. This attractive inland village is famous for its pottery, including the Ali-Baba style *pithária* (olive-oil urns) seen throughout Lésvos, but more so for the "black" icon of the Archangel Michael, whose enormous **monastery** (daily summer 6am–10pm, winter 6.30am–7pm), just to the north, is the powerful focus of a thriving cult and a popular venue for baptisms. The image – legendarily made from a mixture of mud and the blood of monks slaughtered in a massacre – is really more idol than icon, both in its lumpy three-dimensionality and in the manner of veneration which seems a holdover from pagan times. First there was the custom of the coin-wish, whereby you pressed a coin to the Archangel's forehead; if it stuck, then your wish would be granted. Owing to wear and tear on the image, the practice is now forbidden, with supplicants referred to an alternative icon by the main entrance.

It's further believed that in carrying out his various errands to bring about the desires of the faithful, the Archangel wears through enough footwear to stock a small shoeshop. Accordingly the icon was until recently surrounded not by the usual *támmata* (votive medallions) but by piles of miniature gold and silver shoes left by those he had helped. The ecclesiastical authorities, perhaps embarrassed by these "primitive" practices, had all of the little shoes removed in 1986. Of late, a token substitute has re-appeared, taking the form of several pairs of tin slippers which can be dedicated (ie filled with money) and left in front of the icon. Exactly why his devotees should want to encourage these perpetual peripatetics is uncertain, since in Greek folklore the Archangel Michael is also the one who comes for the souls of the dying.

Límnos

Límnos is a prosperous agricultural island which has only recently awoken to tourism; its remoteness and inconvenient ferry schedules have until now protected it from the worst excesses of the holiday trade. Most summer visitors are Greek, and as a foreign traveller, you're still likely to find yourself an object of curiosity and hospitality, though the islanders are becoming increasingly used to numbers of German and British visitors. Accommodation tends to be comfortable and pricey (④–⑤ is the norm), with a strong bias towards self-catering units.

Among Greeks, Límnos has a reputation for being dull, largely due to its unpopularity as an army posting, and there is a conspicuous **military** presence. In recent years, the island has been the focus of disputes between the Greek and Turkish governments; Turkey has a long-standing demand that Límnos should be demilitarized and Turkish aircraft regularly overfly the island, serving to worsen already tense Greek–Turkish relations.

The bays of Pourniá and Moúdhros, the latter one of the largest natural harbours in the Aegean, almost divide Límnos in two. The west of the island is dramatically bare and hilly, with the abundant volcanic rock put to good use as street cobbles and the walls of the village houses and rural cottages. Like most volcanic islands, Límnos produces excellent **wine**: a dry white of denomination quality, and some of the best retsina in Greece, neither exported unfortunately. The east is low-lying and speckled with ponds or marshes popular with duck-hunters, where it's not occupied by cattle, combine harvesters and vast cornfields.

Despite popular slander to that effect, Límnos is not flat, barren or treeless; much of the countryside consists of rolling hills, well vegetated except on their heights, and with substantial clumps of almond, jujube, poplar and mulberry trees. The island is, however, extremely dry, with irrigation water pumped from deep wells, and a limited number of potable springs. Yet somehow various terrapin-haunted creeks bring sand to the many long, sandy **beaches** around the coast, where it's easy to find a stretch to yourself – though there's no escaping the stingless jellyfish which periodically pour out of the Dardanelles and die here in the shallows. On the plus side, the beaches shelve gently, making them ideal for children, and thus warm up early in summer, with no cool currents except near the river mouths.

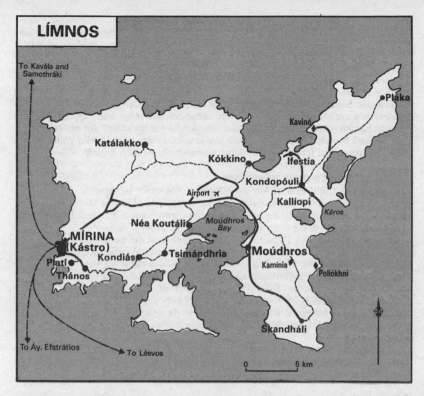

LÍMNOS

To Kaválla and Samothráki

Pláka

Kavinó

Katálakko

Kókkino

Ifestía

Kondopóuli

Airport ✈

Kallíopi

Kéros

Néa Koutáli

Moúdhros Bay

MÍRINA (Kástro)

Kondiás

Tsimándhria

Moúdhros

Platí

Kamínia

Thános

Poliókhni

To Áy. Efstrátios

To Lésvos

Skandháli

0   5 km

Mírina

MÍRINA (also called Kástro), the capital and port on the west coast, with its five thousand inhabitants, has the atmosphere of a provincial market town rather than of a resort. It's pleasant enough, if not especially picturesque apart from a core neighbourhood of old stone houses dating from the Ottoman occupation. Few explicitly Turkish monuments have survived – there's no mosque, for example – though a fountain at the harbour end of Kídha retains its inscription and is still highly prized for its drinking water. Mírina is fairly large for an island town, but most things of interest are on the main shopping street, Kídha – stretching from the harbour to **Romeïkós Yialós**, the beach and esplanade to the north of the castle – or its perpendicular offshoot, roughly halfway along, Garoufalídhou.

The originally Byzantine **castle** (access unrestricted), located on a headland between the ferry dock and Romeïkós Yialós, is quite ruinous despite later additions by the Genoese and Ottomans, but warrants a climb at sunset for views over the town, the entire west coast and – in exceptional conditions – over to Mount Áthos, 35 nautical miles west.

The **Archeological Museum** (daily except Mon 8.30am–3pm; 400dr) occupies an old mansion behind Romeïkós Yialós, not far from the site of Bronze-Age Myrina in the suburb of Ríha Nerá. Finds are assiduously labelled in Greek, Italian and English, and the entire premises are exemplary in terms of presentation – the obvious drawback being that the best exhibits have been spirited away to Athens, leaving a collection that's often of scholarly interest and no more. The south ground-floor gallery is mainly devoted to pottery from Polióhni (Polychni); the north wing contains more of the same, plus items from ancient Myrina; while upstairs are galleries of post-Bronze-Age artefacts from Kavírio (Kabireio) and Ifestía (Hephaestia). The star upper-storey exhibits are votive lamps in the shape of **sirens**, found in an Archaic sanctuary at Hephaestia. Seeming rather less vicious than the harpie-like creatures described in Homer, they are identified more invitingly as the "muses of the underworld, creatures of superhuman wisdom, incarnations of a nostalgia for paradise". An entire room is also devoted to metal objects, of which the standouts are gold jewellery and bronze items, both practical (cheese graters) and whimsical (a vulture, a snail).

Arrival, transport and other facilities

The **airport** is 22km east of Mírina, almost at the exact geographic centre of the island, sharing space with an enormous air force base. Límnos is one of the few remaining destinations with a shuttle bus to the *Olympic* town terminal. **Ferries** dock at the southern end of the town, in the shadow of the castle.

The **bus station** is on Platía Eleftheríou Venizélou, at the north end of Kídha. One look at the sparse schedules (only a single daily afternoon departure to most points except more frequently to Kondiás and Moúdhros) will convince you of the need to **rent a vehicle**. Cars, motorbikes and bicycles can be had from either *Myrina Car* (☎0254/24 476), *Petridou Tours* (☎0254/24 787) or the hopefully named *Rent a Reliable Car* (☎0254/24 587); rates for bikes are only slightly above the island norm, but cars are expensive. A motorized two-wheeler is generally enough to explore the coast and the interior, as there are few steep grades but many perilously narrow village streets.

Among three **banks**, the *Ethniki Trapeza*, just off Kídha next to the **OTE**, has an autoteller; the **post office** and *Olympic* airlines terminal are adjacent to each other on Garoufalídhou.

Accommodation

You may be met off the boat with offers of a **room**. Otherwise, try the simple but friendly *Hotel Aktaion* (☎0254/22 258; ③), somewhat noisily located by the harbour, or the secluded *Apollo Pavillion* on Frínis (☎0254/23 712), a cul-de-sac about halfway along Garoufalídhou, with options ranging from pricey hostel-type facilities in the basement (②–③) to large studios on the upper floors (③–④), whose balconies have views of either the castle or the mountains. Romeïkós Yialós has several rooms-only **pensions** installed in its restored houses, though all are plagued to some extent by evening noise from the bars below; best value of the bunch is *Kosmos*, above the namesake pizzeria (☎0254/22 050; ④). One block inland at Sakhtoúri 7, the *Pension Romeïkós Yialos* (☎0254; 23 787; ④) is quieter and a bit less expensive. Just north of Romaïkós Yialós, the areas of Ríha Nerá and Áyios Pandelímonas are likely bets for **self-catering units**; *Poseidon Apartments* (☎0254/23 982 or 51 304; ④) is one possibility, set a little behind the beach, though the best positioned are the hilltop *Afroditi Apartments* at Áyios Pandelímonas (☎0254/23 489; ⑤). Finally, the *Akti Myrina* (☎0254/22 310; winter ☎01/41 37 907) is a self-contained, luxury complex of 110 wood-and-stone bungalows at the north end of Romeïkós Yialós, with all conceivable diversions and comforts at hand. It's horribly expensive, but costs considerably less if booked through a British tour operator.

There's **no official campsite** on Límnos, though Greek caravanners and campers tend to congregate at the north end of Platí and Avlónas beaches (see below for accounts).

Eating and drinking

About halfway along Kídha, *O Platanos* serves traditional oven food on an atmospheric little square hemmed in by old houses; while *Avra*, on the quay next to the port police, makes a good choice for a pre-ferry meal or an evening grill. This close to the Dardanelles and its seasonal migrations of fish, **seafood** is excellent on Límnos; accordingly there are no less than five tavernas arrayed around the little fishing port. There's little between them, and in any case all the proprietors (and proprietresses) are related by blood or marriage, though *O Glaros* at the far end is considered the best – and works out slightly more expensive.

Not too surprisingly given the twee setting, the restaurants and bars along Romeïkós Yialós are pretty poor value for a drink in sight of the nocturnally illuminated castle. For **beachside eating**, it's better to walk further north to *Iy Tzitzifies* with its tree-shaded tables. Finally, worth a mention – though not a taverna – is an unusual **shop** next to *O Platanos* in the bazaar, devoted to top-grade Cretan products such as wine, honey, oil and spices.

Western Límnos

As town beaches go, Romeïkós Yialós is not at all bad, but if you're looking for more pristine conditions strike out further north, past *Akti Myrina*, to the beach at **Avlónas**, unspoiled except for a new luxury complex flanking it on the south. Some 6km from town you work your way through **KÁSPAKAS**, its north-facing houses in pretty, tiled tiers, before plunging down to **Áyios Ioánnis**. Here, the island's most unusual taverna features seating in the shade of a volcanic outcrop, with a sandy beach stretching beyond.

PLATÍ, 2km southeast of Mírina, is a village of some character – athough since it becomes very busy at night, rooms here are a bad proposition. However, you'll find an excellent and popular *ouzerí* on the smaller *platía*, the *Zimbabwe*, where the quality of the food (and the prices) belie its humble appearance. The long and sandy **beach**, 700m below, proves popular and usually jellyfish-free; except for the luxury compound at the south end, the area is still resolutely rural, with sheep parading to and fro at dawn and dusk. In the middle of the beach, the low-rise *Plati Beach Hotel* (☎0254/23 583; ④) has an enviable position; there are also scattered rooms available, like those behind *Tzimis Taverna* (☎0254/24 142; ③). More expensively, both for rooms and food, there's the poolside bar/restaurant attached to the tastefully landscaped *Villa Afroditi* (☎0254/23 141 or 24 795; winter ☎01/96 41 910; ⑤), which offers what could be the best buffet breakfast in Greece.

THÁNOS, roughly 2km to the southeast, is little more than a bigger version of Platí village, with only a few tavernas and rooms in evidence; **Paralía Thánous**, a rough track ride below the village, is perhaps the most scenic of the southwestern beaches, with two tavernas, one (*O Nikos*) renting studio-apartments (☎0254/22 787; ③). Beyond Thános, the road curls over to the enormous beach at **Áyios Pávlos** (Nevgátis), flanked by weird volcanic crags on the west and reckoned to be the island's best.

The closest amenities – such as they are – lie 3km further along (11km from Mírina) at **KONDIÁS**, the island's third largest settlement, cradled between two hills tufted with Limnos' only pine forest. Stone-built, red-tiled houses combine with the setting to make Kondiás the most attractive inland village, though facilities are limited to a few noisy **rooms** above one of two *kafenía*. **Eating** is better at the two simple tavernas of **Dhiapóri**, 2km east, the shore annexe of Kondiás; the beach is unappealing, with the main interest lent by the narrow isthmus dividing the bays of Kondiás and Moúdhros.

Eastern Límnos

The shores of **Moúdhros bay**, glimpsed south of the trans-island road, are muddy and best avoided; the bay itself enjoyed considerable importance during World War I, including Allied acceptance of the Ottoman surrender aboard the British warship *HMS Agamemnon* on October 30 1918. The port of **MOÚDHROS**, the second largest town on Límnos, is a dreary place, with only a once-weekly ferry to Samothráki and a wonderful kitsch church to recommend it. Yet there are three **hotels** here, including *Toh Kyma* (✆0254/71 333; ⑤) and *Blue Bay* (✆0254/71 041; ④), both with **tavernas**, at the harbour; and some **rooms** just outside the town on the main paved road to Roussopoúli (✆0254/71 470 or 71 422; ③), all of use as bases for visiting the archeological sites and beaches of eastern Límnos.

A little further along the Roussopoúli road, you unexpectedly pass an **Allied military cemetery** (unlocked) maintained by the Commonwealth War Graves Commission, its neat lawns and rows of white headstones incongruous in such parched surroundings. In 1915, Moúdhros Bay was the principal base for the disastrous Gallipoli campaign. Of the 36,000 Allied dead, 887 are buried here, with 348 more at another graveyard near Portianós – mainly battle casualties who died after having been evacuated to the base hospital at Moúdhros.

Indications of the most advanced Neolithic civilization in the Aegean have been unearthed at **Polióhni (Polyochni)**, 3km by dirt track from the gully-hidden village of **KAMÍNIA** (7km east of Moúdhros; two simple grill-tavernas). Since the 1930s, Italian excavations have uncovered four layers of settlement, the oldest from late in the fourth millennium BC, pre-dating Troy on the Turkish coast opposite; the town met a sudden, violent end from war or earthquake in about 2100 BC. The actual **ruins** (9.30am–5.30pm daily; free) are of essentially specialist interest, though a *bouleuterion* (assembly hall) with bench seating, a mansion and the landward fortifications are labelled. During August and September the Italian excavators are about, and if they are free to show you around the place may become that much more interesting. The site occupies a bluff overlooking a long, narrow rock-and-sand beach flanked by stream valleys, the mouth of one of these comprising the old port.

Ifestía and Kavírio, the other significant ancient sites on Límnos, are most easily reached via the village of Kondopoúli, 7km northeast of Moúdhros. Both sites are rather remote, and only feasible to visit if you have your own transport.

Ifestía (Hephaestia), in Classical times the most important city on the island, took its name from Hephaistos, god of fire and metal-working. According to legend, Hephaistos landed on Límnos after being hurled from Mount Olympus by Zeus, the fall leaving him lame forever. Much of the site (daily 9.30am–3.30pm; free) remains unexcavated, but there are scant remains of a theatre and a temple dedicated to the god.

Kavírio (Kabireio), on the opposite shore of Tigáni Bay from Ifestía, is a little more evocative. The **ruins** (daily 9.30am–3.30pm; free) are those of a sanctuary connected with the cult of the Kabiroi on Samothraki (see p.647), although the site on Límnos is probably older. Little survives other than the groundplan, but the setting is undeniably impressive. Eleven column stumps stake out a stoa, behind eight spots marked as column bases in the main *telestirio* or shrine where the cult mysteries took place. More engaging, perhaps, is a nearby sea grotto identified as the Homeric **Spiliá tou Filoktíti**, where the Trojan war hero Philoctetes was abandoned by his comrades-in-arms until his stinking, gangrenous leg had healed. The cave has landward access as well, via the steps leading down from the caretaker's sunshade.

The east-coast beach at **Kéros**, 4km by dirt road below **KALLIÓPI** (two snack bar/tavernas), in turn 2km from Kondopoúli, is one of the best on the island. A long stretch of sand with dunes and shallow water, it attracts a number of Greek tourists and Germans with camper vans and windsurfers, but is large enough to remain uncrowded. By contrast, mediocre beaches near the village of **PLÁKA** at the north-eastern tip of the island, are not worth the extra effort, and the adjacent hot springs appearing on some maps are actually warm mud baths.

Áyios Efstrátios (Aï Strátis)

Áyios Efstrátios is without doubt one of the most isolated islands in the Aegean. Historically, the only outsiders to stay here have been those who were compelled to do so – it served as a place of exile for political prisoners under both the Metaxas regime of the 1930s and the various right-wing governments that followed the civil war. It's still unusual for travellers to show up on the island, and, if you do, you're sure to be asked why you came.

You may well ask yourself the same question, for **ÁYIOS EFSTRÁTIOS** village – the only habitation on the island – is one of the ugliest in Greece. Devastated by an earthquake in 1967, it was grimly rebuilt as rows of concrete prefabs, attended by a concrete church and an underused shopping centre. The remains of the old village – some two dozen houses which escaped damage – overlook the modern village from a neighbouring hillside. Sadly, most of the destruction was caused by army bulldozers rather than the earthquake: the re-building contract went to a company with junta connections, and the islanders were prevented from returning to their homes, although many could have been repaired. All in all, the village constitutes a sad monument to the corruption of the junta years. If you're curious, there's an old photograph of the village, taken before the earthquake, in the *kafenío* by the port.

Architecture apart, Áyios Efstrátios still functions as a very traditional fishing and farming community, with the prefabs set at the mouth of a wooded stream valley draining to the harbour beach. Tourist amenities consist of just two very basic **tavernas** and a single **pension** in one of the surviving old houses, which is likely to be full in the summer, so call in advance (☎0254/93 202; ②). Nobody will object, however, if you **camp** at the far end of the town beach.

As you walk away from the village – there are hardly any cars and no real roads – things improve rapidly. The landscape, dry hills and valleys scattered with a surprising number of oak trees, is deserted apart from wild rabbits, sheep, an occasional shepherd, and some good beaches where you can camp in desert-island isolation perhaps the only reason you're likely to visit Áyios Evstrátios. **Alonítsi**, on the north coast, a ninety-minute walk from the village following a track up the north side of the valley, is a two-kilometre stretch of sand with rolling breakers and views across to Límnos.

A little to the south of the village, there's a series of greyish sand beaches, most with wells and drinkable water, although with few proper paths in this part of the island, getting to them can be something of a scramble. **Lidharío**, at the end of an attractive wooded valley, is the first worthwhile beach, but again, it's a ninety-minute walk, unless you can persuade a fisherman to take you by boat. Some of the caves around the coast are home to the rare Mediterranean monk seal, but you're unlikely to see one.

Ferries between Límnos and Kavála to either Rafína, Kími or Áyios Konstandínos call at Áyios Efstrátios every two or three days throughout the year; in summer, there's also a *kaíki* from Límnos twice a week. Despite harbour improvements, it is still a very exposed anchorage, and in bad weather you could end up stranded here far longer than you bargained for.

Samothráki (Samothrace)

After Thíra, **Samothráki** has the most dramatic profile of all the Greek islands. Originally colonized by immigrants from Sámos (hence the name), it rises abruptly from the sea in a dark mass of granite, culminating in 1600-metre Mount Fengári. Seafarers have always been guided by its imposing outline, and in legend its summit provided a vantage point for Poseidon to watch over the siege of Troy. The forbidding coastline provides no natural anchorage, and landing is still very much subject to the vagaries of the wind. Yet despite these difficulties, for over a millennium pilgrims journeyed to the island to visit the **Sanctuary of the Great Gods** and to be initiated into its mysteries. The Sanctuary is still the outstanding attraction of the island, which, home to under 3000 people and too remote for most tourists (although July and August can be busy), combines an earthy simplicity with its natural grandeur.

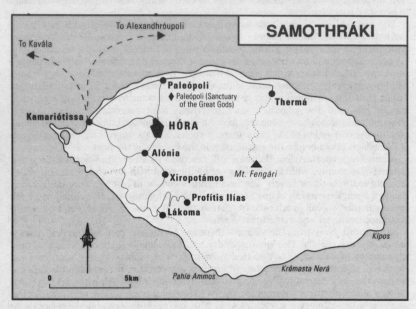

Kamariótissa and Hóra

Ferries and the new hydrofoils dock at the little port of **KAMARIÓTISSA**, where there are three hotels on the seafront and numerous **rooms** for rent in the maze of streets behind. Turning left as you step ashore, the first – and cheapest – hotel is the homely *Kyma* (☎0551/41 263; ②–③), which also has a good, family-run restaurant. The seafront is lined with **tavernas**, the best of which are the *Klimataria* and *Horizon*, which, with a couple of nearby bars and discos, constitute the island's only real nightlife. There's a **bank** and *Niki Tours* (☎0551/41 465), which rents out **motorbikes and mopeds**, and can also help with accommodation. Otherwise, Kamariótissa isn't a picturesque or particularly interesting village, and you're unlikely to want to stay too long.

Buses run hourly in season (but only twice weekly in winter) along the north coast to Thermá via Palaeópoli (the site of the Sanctuary) and Kariotes, or inland to **HÓRA**, the only other village of any size, an attractive community of whitewashed Thracian-style houses overshadowed by the western flanks of Mount Fengári and the ruins of a Byzantine fort. Hóra has no accommodation, but there are two popular **tavernas** with fine views down the valley and out to sea. There's also another bank, the **post office**, the **OTE** branch and **tourist police** (☎0551/41 203).

The Sanctuary of the Great Gods

A track leads north from Hóra to the hamlet of Paleópoli (see below), and, in a stony ravine between it and the plunging, northeasternmost ridgeline of Mount Fengári, lie the remains of the **Sanctuary of the Great Gods**. From the late Bronze Age to the last years of the Roman occupation, the mysteries and sacrifices of the cult of the Great Gods were performed on Samothráki. The island was the spiritual focus of the northern Aegean, and its importance in the ancient world was comparable (although certainly secondary) to that of the Mysteries of Eleusis.

The religion of the Great Gods revolved around a hierarchy of ancient Thracian fertility figures: the Great Mother, a subordinate male deity known as Kadmilos, and the potent and ominous twin demons, the *Kabiroi*. When the Samian colonists arrived (traditionally c700 BC) they simply syncretized the resident deities with their own – the Great Mother became Demeter, her consort Hermes, and the *Kabiroi* were fused interchangeably with the *Dioskouroi*. Around the nucleus of a sacred precinct the newcomers made the beginnings of what is now the Sanctuary.

The mysteries of the cult were never explicitly recorded, since ancient writers feared incurring the wrath of the *Kabiroi*, but it has been established that two levels of initiation were involved. Incredibly, both ceremonies, in direct opposition to the elitism of Eleusis, were open to all comers, including women and slaves. The lower level of initiation may, as is speculated at Eleusis, have involved a ritual simulation of the life, death and rebirth cycle; in any case, it's known that it ended with joyous feasting and it can be conjectured, since so many clay torches have been found, that it took place at night by their light. The higher level of initiation carried the unusual requirement of a moral standard (the connection of theology with morality – so strong in the later Judeo-Christian tradition – was rarely made at all by the early Greeks). This second level involved a full confession followed by absolution and baptism in bull's blood.

The site

The **site** (daily except Mon 8.30am–3pm; 400dr) is well labelled, simple to grasp and strongly evokes its proud past. It's a good idea to visit the **museum** (open same hours as the site, admission with the same ticket) first, where sections of the buildings have been reconstructed and arranged with friezes and statues to give you an idea of their original scale. An excellent guide by Karl Lehmann – the American site excavator – is on sale.

The first structure you come to is the **Anaktoron**, the hall of initiation for the first level of the mysteries, dating in its present form from Roman times. Its inner sanctum was marked by a warning *stele* (now in the museum) and at the southeast corner you can make out the libation pit. Next to it is the **Arsinoeion**, the largest circular ancient building known in Greece. Within its rotunda are the walls of a double precinct (fourth century BC) where a rock altar, the earliest preserved ruin on the site, has been uncovered. A little further on, on the same side of the path, you come to the **Temenos**, a rectangular area open to the sky where the feasting probably took place, and, edging its rear corner, the conspicuous **Hieron**. Five columns and an architrave of the facade of this large Doric edifice which hosted the higher level of initiation have been erected; dating in part from the fourth century BC, it was heavily restored in Roman times. Its stone steps have been replaced by modern blocks but the Roman benches for spectators remain in situ, along with the sacred stones where confession was heard.

To the west of the path you can just discern the outline of the **theatre**, and above it on a ridge is the **Nike fountain**, famous for the exquisitely sculpted marble centrepiece – the *Winged Victory of Samothrace* – which once stood breasting the wind at the prow of a marble ship. It was discovered in 1863 by the French and carried off to the Louvre, with a copy belatedly forwarded to the local museum. Higher up along the ridge, opposite the rotunda, is an elaborate medieval fortification made entirely of antique material. Finally, on the hill across the river stands a monumental **gateway** dedicated to the Great Gods by Ptolemy II; many of its blocks lie scattered across the ravine.

The rest of the island

The only accommodation near the site itself is in the hamlet of **PALEÓPOLI**, where the old and basic *Xenia Hotel* (☎0551/41 166; ③–④) tries hard to compete with the *Kastro Hotel* (☎0551/41 001; ⑥), which comes with pool and restaurant. Four kilometres east, near Kariotes, is the much smaller *Elektra* (☎0551/98 243; ④–⑤), though despite the family feel here, the lack of a restaurant means you may prefer to be nearer the action – such as it is – in **THÉRMA** (Loutrá), a further 2km east.

With its running streams, plane trees and namesake hot springs, Thérma is one of the better places to stay on Samothráki, although it's packed in July and August (mainly with an odd mixture of German hippies and elderly Greeks here to take the waters). It's a rather dispersed place, with a small harbour under construction to accommodate the ferries and recently introduced hydrofoils – up in the woods, are the well-established *Kaviros Hotel* (☎0551/98 277; ⑤), open May to October, and – 700m from the beach – the bungalows of the *Mariva Hotel* (☎0551/98 258; ④). The nearby *Restaurant Iphestos* is lively and popular; try the spit-roast goat or chicken. The *Shelter* café-pub, in the old schoolhouse, attracts a younger crowd.

Beyond Thérma, on the wooded coastline, are two municipal **campsites**, open June to September. The first, 1500m from the village, although large, has no facilities except toilets; the second, 2km from the village, is more expensive but has hot water, electricity, a small shop, restaurant and bar. The bus from Kamariótissa passes both sites.

The lush countryside beyond Thérma is fine for walking, and the more ambitious can climb the highest mountain in the Aegean, **Mount Fengári** (the Mountain of the Moon, also known as *Sáos*), in a six-to-eight hour round trip. (You could also start from Horá but the route is more difficult.) From the top, a clear day permits views from the Trojan plain in the east to Mount Áthos in the west.

Beaches on Samothráki's north shore are uniformly pebbly and exposed; for better ones head for the warmer south flank of the island. A couple of daily buses go as far as **PROFÍTIS ILÍAS**, an attractive hill village with good tavernas but no place to stay, via Lákoma, where you alight for the beautiful two-hour walk to **Pahiá Ámmos**, an 800-metre sandy beach with a hidden freshwater spring at its eastern end. The nearest supplies are at **LÁKOMA**, but this doesn't deter big summer crowds who also arrive by excursion *kaíki*. These also continue past the Krémasta Nerá coastal waterfalls to **Kípos**, another good sandy beach with fresh water nearby, at the extreme southeast tip of the island.

Thássos

Just twelve kilometres from the mainland, **Thássos** has long been a popular resort for northern Greeks, and in recent years has been attracting considerable numbers of foreign tourists. Without being spectacular, it's a very beautiful island, its almost circular area covered in gentle slopes of pine, olive and chestnut that rise to a mountainous backbone and plunge to a line of good sandy beaches. It's by no means unspoiled, but visitors tend to be spread over six or seven fair-sized villages as well as the two main

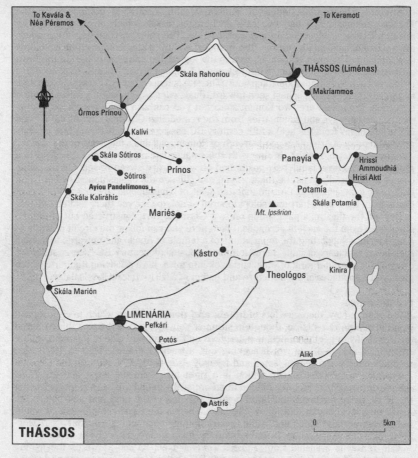

To Kavála &
Néa Péramos

To Keramotí

Skála Rahoníou

THÁSSOS (Liménas)

Makríammos

Órmos Prínou

Kalívi

Skála Sótiros

Panayía

Hrissí
Ammoudhiá
Hrisí Aktí

Sótiros

Prínos

Ayíou Pandelímonos

Potamiá

Skála Kaliráhis

Mt. Ipsárion

Skála Potamiá

Mariés

Kástro

Theológos

Kínira

Skála Marión

LIMENÁRIA

Pefkári

Potós

Alikí

Astrís

0   5km

THÁSSOS

towns, so enclaves of bars and discos haven't swamped the ordinary Greek life of marble-quarrying, beekeeping and harvesting nuts, olives or fruit. Beehives often line the roadsides, and local honey can be bought all over the island, as can thick, treacle-like walnut jam. Among the less pleasant wildlife is the ubiquitous mosquito, so come prepared. Also, most of the inland forests were ravaged by fire in 1985, so do heed the many forest-fire prevention warnings and be extra careful if camping.

Thássos Town

THÁSSOS TOWN, or Liménas/Limín as it's also known, is the island capital and nexus of life, though not the main port. Kavála-based ferries usually stop down the coast at Órmos Prínou, but a few each day continue on here – a trip worth making for the pine-clad mountain views. The town, though largely modern, is partly redeemed by its pretty fishing harbour, a popular sand beach just to the east, and the substantial remains of the ancient city which pop up between and above the streets.

Ancient **Thássos** abounded in mineral wealth, controlled goldmines on the Thracian mainland and had two safe anchorages, assets which ensured prosperity through Classical, Macedonian and Roman rule. The ruins surrounding the modern town – Limín, incidentally, means "the harbour" – show traces from each phase of this development. The main excavated area is the **agora**, the entrance is beside the town **museum** (Tues–Fri 8am–7pm, winter closes at 5pm, Sat & Sun 8.30am–3pm; 400dr), a little way back from the modern harbour. The site is fenced but not always locked and, taking advantage of this, is best seen towards dusk when a calm, slightly misty air often descends. Prominent are two Roman *stoas* but you can also make out shops, monuments, passageways and sanctuaries from the remodelled Classical city. At the far end of the site (away from the sea) a fifth-century BC passageway leads through to an elaborate sanctuary of Artemis, a good stretch of Roman road and a few seats of the *odeion*.

Above the town, roughly in line with the smaller fishing port, steps spiral up to a **Hellenistic theatre**, fabulously positioned above a broad sweep of sea. On the same corner of the headland as the theatre, you can still see the old-fashioned *kaíkia* being built, and gaze across to the uninhabited islet of Thassopoúla. It's possible to **rent boats** from the fishing harbour, self-skippered or not, to take you there and elsewhere.

Beyond the theatre, a path winds on to a **Genoese fort**, constructed out of numerous stones from the ancient acropolis. From here you can follow the circuit of **walls** to a high terrace supporting the foundations of a temple of Apollo and onwards to a small rock-hewn sanctuary of Pan. Below it a precarious, sixth-century BC "secret stairway" descends to the outer rank of walls and back into town. It's a satisfying itinerary, which gives you a good idea of the structure and extent of a fairly typical Classical city.

Practicalities

If you want to stay, there are lots of **hotels and pensions** from which to choose, and plentiful **rooms** to rent, too, though in summer you should take the first thing offered on arrival. If you get the choice, the *Acropolis* on the landward side of the main square (☎0593/22 488; ③–④), is worth seeking out, a traditional house built in 1900. Also recommended is the central, small and friendly *Astir* (☎0593/22 160; ③); the pleasant *Diamanto* (☎0593/22 622; ②), which is a right turn from the ferry; and the *Hotel Athanaria* (☎0593/22 545; ②), hidden in an orchard – to find this, turn right on leaving the ferry, make for the *Xenia* hotel beyond the end of the quay and just before the *Xenia* turn left (inland) and follow the lane. There's the usual complement of waterfront **tavernas and cafés** and while there's nothing outstanding, you can eat reasonably well if you shop around. In and around the main square, try *Iy Piyi* or *Zorba's*.

Car rental is available from *Thassos Tours* (☎0593/23 250), towards the fishing harbour, or *Thassos Rent-a-Car* (☎0593/22 535) on the main square; **mopeds and motorbikes** from *Thassos Tours* or the widely advertised *Billy's Bikes*. **Bicycles** are also available, though be aware that there's little flat terrain. The **bus station** is on the front, near the ferry mooring. The service is good, with about five buses per day doing the full island circuit in season, and several more to and from different villages, with a bias towards the west coast. The **tourist police** (May–Sept daily 9am–10pm; ☎0593/23 111) are in the police station on the front, near the bus station.

Around the coast

The first beach clockwise from Liménas, **Makriámmos**, is an expensive, limited-access playground for package tourists, and it's best to carry on to **PANAYÍA** or **POTAMIÁ**, two attractive villages situated on a mountainous ledge overlooking Potamiá Bay. Panayía is a bustling and pretty mountain village where life revolves around the central square with its large plane tree and fountain. There are a few souvenir shops, two small **hotels** – the *Helvetia* (☎0593/61 231; ③) and the *Chrysalis* (☎0593/61 979; ④) – and

rooms for rent, but you'll also see sheep and goats being herded through the middle of the village. This is an ideal place for a drink and a meal in the lively evenings, and food tends to be less expensive than elsewhere – try the *Kostas* or *Ethitrio* restaurants. Potamiá has one of the best marked paths up to the 1204-metre summit of **Mount Ipsárion**; and by the lovely church there is a small **art museum** (Tues–Sat 9am–1pm, summer also 6–9pm, Sun 10am–2pm; free).

There are more tavernas, two more hotels and a campsite at the excellent, sandy **Hrissí Ammoudhiá** beach, 4km downhill from Panayía at the north end of the bay. No buses go here but it's easy enough to walk from Panayía (though not with heavy luggage) or cheap enough to get a taxi. Once you get there you can choose between the *Villa Chrysalis* (☎0593/61 979; ③), the hugely expensive *Hotel Dionysus* (☎0593/61 822; ⑥) or the *Golden Beach* **campsite** (☎0593/61 472), the only one on this side of the island. **SKÁLA POTAMIÁS**, at the southern end of the bay, is less attractive with its rocky beach; every building seems to be a souvenir shop, hotel, cafeteria or "rooms to let". Skála's main virtue is the local fishing fleet and the corresponding quality of the seafood restaurants.

KÍNIRA is a tiny hamlet further south with a moderate beach, a couple of grocery stores and hotels – cheapest is the *Villa Athina* (☎0593/41 214; ②–③) – a few rooms and a lot of beehives. **Paradise Beach**, nicely situated, sandy, and mainly nudist, lies 1km south, and there are more beautiful and deserted coves beyond in the same direction if you're willing to explore.

The south-facing coast of Thássos has most of the island's best beaches. **Alikí** (32km from Thássos Town) faces a double bay which almost pinches off a headland. The mixed sand-and-pebble spit gets too popular for its own good in high season, but the water is crystal-clear and the four beachside tavernas offer good food. The roadside hamlet here is at least worth a stopover and there are several **rooms** to rent; *Suzanna's*, above the road, are clean, basic and cheap. Nearby, on the headland, were ancient marble quarries which supplied the Greek city-states and later the Romans, and on the western cove the pillars of a Doric sanctuary are still visible. It is possible to walk away from the crowds and find some excellent spots for snorkelling, sunbathing and picnics, using the slabs of marble that are scattered around the headland, both above and below the waterline; these have occasionally been eroded into convenient bathtub shapes.

At the extreme south tip of Thássos, **ASTRÍS** is a quiet village with some rooms, a sandy beach, and a couple of restaurants, but the best-appointed local resort is **Potós**, where there are two modest **hotels**, the *Io* (☎0593/51 216; ②) and *Katerina* (☎0593/51 345; ②), and a fine one-kilometre sandy beach facing the sunset. **Pofkári**, 1km west, is essentially an annexe of Potós but the manicured sand has been overwhelmed by the touristic development behind.

As an alternative to Thássos Town you can base yourself in the marginally quieter and quainter **LIMENÁRIA**, the island's second town, built to house German mining executives brought in by the Turks at the turn of the century. Their remaining mansions lend some distinctive character, but this apart it's a rather ordinary tourist resort, handy mainly for its **banks**, **post office** and **OTE** station. There are a few **hotels**, the best of which is the *Menel* (☎0593/51 396; ③), and numerous **rooms**, so you'll eventually find something affordable and vacant. There's also a **campsite** between Limenária and Pefkári: the *Pefkari* (☎0593/51 190; April–Sept).

Continuing clockwise from Limenária to Thássos town, the bus service is more frequent, but there's progressively less to stop off for. The various *skáles* (coastal annexes of villages built inland during piratic ages) such as Skála Marión, Skála Kaliráhis and Skála Sotíros, are bleak, straggly and windy, uninviting even on the rare occasions when the shore is sandy.

ÓRMOS PRÍNOU has little to recommend it, other than the ferry connections to Kavála. Buses are usually timed to coincide with the ferries, but if you want to stay, there are numerous **rooms**, quayside **tavernas** and an EOT **campsite** (☎0593/71 171; May–Sept). There's a better **campsite** near **SKÁLA RAHONÍOU**, between here and Thássos Town (though the beach is mediocre), as well as rooms, hotels and fish restaurants.

The interior

Few people get around to exploring inland Thássos, but there are several worthwhile rambles around the hill villages besides the aforementioned walk up Mount Ipsárion from Potamiá. From Potós you can hitch or take a bus up to **THEOLÓGOS**, a linear community of old houses founded by refugees from Constantinople, which was the island's capital under the Turks (the last of whom only departed after 1923). It has a small square with a couple of cafés under a tree, and a few **rooms** are available (though none are advertised) – there are some above one of the cafés and the baker on the square has rooms near the *Restaurant Lambiris*.

From Theológos you can walk down to Kínira on the east coast on a gravel jeep track, or take your chances with narrower trails leading north through whatever remains of the forest. The most interesting return to Potós involves a westward trek, on a variety of surfaces, to **KÁSTRO**, the most naturally fortified of the anti-pirate redoubts. Thirty houses and a church surround a rocky pinnacle which is a sheer drop on three sides; summer occupation is becoming the rule after total abandonment in the last century. You could perhaps be put up for the night – there's one taverna, one phone, no power – but without transport you will have to walk or hitch 15km down a dirt road to Limenária.

From Kalívi on the west coast a minor road leads 4km up to **PRÍNOS**, start of the signposted, one-hour walk up to Ayíou Pandelímonos nunnery. From there you can press on to **SOTÍROS**, an untouched old village to the west, or take the much more confusing way (on lumber roads) to **MARIÉS** in the direction of the Kástro. You can often hitch down from the inland villages with people who've been tending their beehives, but take food along for the day – there are often no facilities at all.

travel details

To simplify the lists that follow we've excluded a regular sailing of the *NEL* company, which once a week runs a ferry in each direction, usually the *Alcaeos*, linking Thessaloníki or Kavála with Límnos, Áyios Efstrátios, Lésvos, Híos, Sámos and Pátmos. Each one-way trip takes about 24 hours – exact days subject to change according to season.

SÁMOS (Vathí) 3–7 weekly to Ikaría, Páros, Pireás (14hr); 2–3 weekly to Híos and Náxos; 1–2 weekly to Foúrni, Míkonos, Tínos, Síros.

SÁMOS (Karlóvassi) As for Vathí, plus 2 weekly *kaíki* departures, usually early Mon and Thurs afternoon, to Foúrni.

SÁMOS (Pithagório) 1–2 weekly to Foúrni, Ikaría, Pátmos; 1–2 weekly (usually Wed and Sun afternoon) to Agathónissi, Lipsí, Pátmos, Léros, Kálimnos, with onward connections to all other

Dodecanese (see the *Nissos Kalimnos* summary in *The Dodecanese*). Also expensive excursion *kaíkia* daily in season to Pátmos.

IKARÍA 3–7 weekly to Sámos (both northern ports), Páros and Pireás (at least 2 weekly services via Évdhilos year-round); 2–3 weekly to Náxos; 1–2 weekly to Híos, Foúrni, Pátmos, Míkonos, Tínos, Síros; 4–5 weekly, from Áyios Kírikos, to Foúrni.

FOÚRNI 1–2 weekly ferries, usually Wed or Sun, to Sámos (northern ports), Páros and Pireás; smaller ferries twice weekly (often Tues and Fri) to Sámos (Pithagório), Ikaría, Pátmos, Híos; morning *kaíki* to Ikaría, Mon, Wed, Fri, Sun, and on Sat only by demand; twice weekly (usually Mon and Thur) morning *kaíki* to Karlóvassi (Sámos).

HÍOS 4–7 weekly to Pireás (10hr) and Lésvos (3hr 30min); 3 weekly to Límnos and Thessaloníki; 2–3

weekly to Sámos (5hr); 1–2 weekly to Foúrni and Pátmos; 1 weekly to Rafína, Psará, Áyios Efstrátios, Kavála. Daily *kaíki* to Inoússes; 3 weekly to Psará (4hr), 2 weekly on different days from Limniá to Psará (2hr).

LÉSVOS 4–13 weekly to Pireás (12hr direct, 14hr via Híos); 4–9 weekly to Híos (3hr 30min); 4 weekly to Límnos (7hr); 3 weekly to Thessaloníki (17hr); 2 weekly to Áyios Efstrátios (4hr 30min); 1 weekly to Kavála (15hr) and Rafína.

LÍMNOS 5 weekly to Kavála, Lésvos, Híos, Pireás; 3 weekly to Thessaloníki, Áyios Efstrátios and Rafína; 1 weekly to most of the Sporades, Rafína, and either Kími (Évvia) or Áyios Konstandínos (Thessaly). Also a summer-only *kaíki* to Áyios Efstrátios twice weekly.

ÁYIOS EFSTRÁTIOS 3 weekly to Límnos, Rafína; 2 weekly to Kavála, Mitilíni, Híos; 1 weekly to Skíros.

SAMOTHRÁKI 2–5 daily ferries to/from Alexandhroúpoli (2hr) in season, dropping to 5–6 weekly out of season. Also a connection with Moúdhros on Límnos once a week throughout the year (originating in Alexandhroúpoli), and with Kavála (and therefore other North Aegean islands) once a week, currently on Fri, returning on Sat.

THÁSSOS 7–15 ferries daily (depending on season) between Kavála and Órmos Prínou (1hr), with a few of these services extending to Liménas. Similar frequencies between Liménas and Keramotí (45min). No direct connections with any other island; usually you must travel via Kavála.

Hydrofoils

Two companies – *Ilio Lines* and *Gianmar* – divide the **hydrofoil** trade between them in the east Aegean. *Gianmar* craft are based on Híos, operating almost-daily morning runs to Sámos, Ikaría and Pátmos to the south, Lésvos (Plomári) and Límnos to the north, with occasional trips to Psará. *Ilio Lines* link Sámos (Vathí and/or Pithagório) with Pátmos, Lipsí, Léros, Kálimnos and Kós (in the Dodecanese) daily in season; Lésvos and Híos five times weekly; and Ikaría, Foúrni, Agathónissi (Dodecanese) and Alexandroúpoli (Thrace) twice weekly. Many of the craft are actually based on Lésvos, from where there are services 6 weekly (indirectly) to

Alexandhroúpoli, 5 weekly to Híos and Sámos (Vathí), 2 weekly to Kavála and 1 weekly to Límnos. All routes reverse themselves exactly on the return leg, so frequencies between all points are the same in each direction.

In addition to the domestic lines, there is also an **international hydrofoil** service twice daily (in theory), June–Sept between Vathí (Sámos) and Kusadaşı (Turkey), and several times weekly between Híos and Çeşme (Turkey). Fares are currently much the same as for a conventional ferry (see section below) if you bargain.

International ferries

Vathí (Sámos)–Kusadaşı (Turkey) At least 1 daily, late April to late October; otherwise a Turkish boat only by demand in winter, usually on Fri or Sat. Morning Greek boat (passengers only), afternoon Turkish boats (usually 2 in season – they take 2 cars apiece). Rates are £32/US$48 one way including taxes on both the Greek and Turkish sides, £41/$61 return all-in; no day return rate. Small cars £30/$45 one way. Journey time 1hr 30min. Also regular (3–4 weekly) services in season from **Pithagório**.

Híos–Çeşme (Turkey) 2–12 boats weekly, depending on season. Thurs night and Sat morning services tend to run year-round. Rates are £31/$47 one-way, £40/$60 return, including Greek taxes; no Turkish taxes. Small cars £36/$54 each way. Journey time 45min.

Mitilíni (Lésvos)–Ayvalık (Turkey) 5–9 weekly in season; winter link unreliable. The current rates are about £25/$38 one way, £33/$49 return including Greek taxes; no Turkish tax on this crossing. Small cars cost £30/$45 each way. Journey time 1hr 30min. Once weekly in high season there is also a link with **Dikili**, a few kilometres south of Ayvalık (same prices and crossing time).

Flights

Sámos–Athens (3–4 daily; 1hr)

Híos–Athens (4–5 daily; 50min)

Lésvos–Athens (3–4 daily; 45min)

Lésvos–Thessaloníki (10 weekly; 1hr 10min)

Límnos–Athens (2–3 daily; 1hr)

Límnos–Lésvos (1 daily; 40min)

Límnos–Thessaloníki (1 daily; 50min)

CHAPTER ELEVEN

THE SPORADES AND ÉVVIA

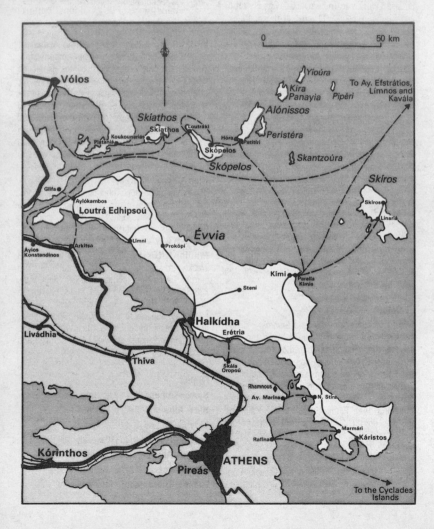

T he three northern **Sporades**, Skíathos, Skópelos and Alónissos, are scattered (as their Greek name suggests) head-to-tail, just off the mainland, their mountainous terrain betraying their origin as extensions of Mount Pelion in Thessaly. They're archetypal holiday islands, with a wide selection of good beaches, transparent waters and thick, pine forests. They are all very busy in season, and both Skíathos and Skópelos have sacrificed their entire character to tourism. None has any prominent historical sites, nor much history until the Middle Ages – Skíathos Town is nineteenth century, while the oldest area of Skópelos sits within its thirteenth-century *kástro*. There is, therefore, no pressure to do much sightseeing.

Skíathos has the best beaches, and is still the busiest island in the group, though these days **Skópelos** gets very crowded, too. **Alónissos** is the quietest of the three, and has the wildest scenery, but it's only really worth a visit if you stay outside the ugly, post-earthquake main town. **Skíros**, further southeast, retains more of its traditional culture than the other three islands, though development is now well under way. The main town doesn't yet feel like a resort, but is not uncommercialized either. Unlike the other three islands, the only good beaches are those close to the main town. To the south, the huge island of **Évvia** (or Euboea) runs for 150km alongside the mainland. It is one of the more attractive Greek islands, with a forested mountain spine and a rugged, largely undeveloped coast. Perhaps because it lacks any real island feel or identity due to its proximity to the mainland, Évvia is explored by few foreign tourists. Athenians, in contrast, visit in force, unbothered by such scruples and attracted to half a dozen or so major resorts.

The Sporades are well connected by bus and ferry both with Athens (via Áyios Konstantínos or Kími) and with Vólos, and it's easy to island-hop in the northern group. The only ferry connection to Skíros is from Kími, plus a *Flying Dolphin* service in summer from Vólos via the other Sporades. Évvia is linked to the mainland by a bridge at its capital Halkídha, and by a series of shuttle-ferries.

Skíathos

The commercialization of **Skíathos** is legendary among foreigners and Greeks – it's a close fourth to that of Corfu, Míkonos and Rhodes. But if you've some time to spare, or a gregarious nature, you might still break your journey here in order to sample the best, if most overcrowded, **beaches** in the Sporades. Along the south and southeast coasts, the road serves an almost unbroken line of concrete villas, hotels and restaurants, and although this isn't enough to take away the island's natural beauty, it makes it difficult to

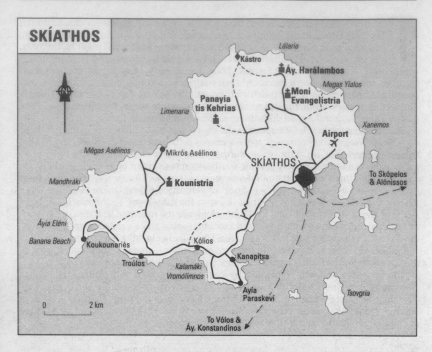

find anything unspoilt or particularly Greek about it all. As almost the entire population lives in Skíathos Town, a little walking soon pays off. However, camping outside official sites is strongly discouraged, since summer turns the dry pine-needles to tinder, and you should be aware of the risk of fire on each of the Sporades islands.

Skíathos Town

SKÍATHOS Town, where the ferries dock, looks great from a distance, but as you approach, the tourist development becomes all too apparent. Even the little offshore **Boúrtzi fortress**, surrounded by crumbling segments of Venetian wall, houses a taverna, and the old quarters (on the slopes away from Alexándhrou Papadhiamándi street) are in danger of being overwhelmed by ranks of hotels, restaurants and "English" pubs. Skíathos is very like Corfu – a tourist sprawl around the coast, and a very busy *hóra*.

As for sights, there aren't many, apart from the excellent **Galerie Varsakis** (open usual shop hours), near the fishing port on Platía Tríon Ierarhón. This is one of the best folklore displays in Greece, and many of the older items on display would do the Benaki Museum proud; Mr Varsakis neither expects, nor wants, to sell the more expensive of these, which include antique textiles, handicrafts and jewellery.

Arrival, transport and other facilities

Buses and **taxis** ply from near the **ferry harbour**. To Koukounariés, the bus is the cheapest option; it runs roughly every thirty minutes in summer and the last one returns at 12.30am. Also in summer, *Aselinos Tours* run a private bus to Asélinos beach once a day, leaving at 11am from outside their office, close to the official bus stop and returning at 4.30pm (300dr). If shared among a few people, taxis should work out to be only a little more expensive – though ask the fare first.

A large number of competing **rental outlets** in town, most on the front behind the ferry harbour, offer bicycles, mopeds, motorbikes, cars and motorboats. The lowest priced, beach buggy-type cars go for around 12,000dr a day, motorboats for 15,000dr a day; fuel and insurance are extra. At a slower pace, several travel agents organize "round the island" **mule trips** (5200dr a day), or there's horse riding at the *Pinewood Riding Club* on the road to Tróulos to Mégas Asélinos, 1km north of the junction.

Most other facilities are on Alexándhrou Papadhiamándi, including the **OTE, post office, banks** and *Olympic Airways* office.

Accommodation

Most of the island's accommodation is in Skíathos Town. The few reasonably priced **hotels** or **pensions** will be full in season, though you can usually find a room, albeit slightly more expensively than on most islands. At other times, supply exceeds demand and you can find very cheap **rooms** with a little bargaining. There is no official accommodation bureau but there are several tourist agencies. For an honest and helpful approach, try Dimitris Mathinos, a former sea captain with an office at the bottom of Alexándhrou Papadhiamándi, though avoid lodgings in the flatlands to the north as they tend to be noisy. Also ask at the *Art Café* (opposite the ferry gates), which serves a good breakfast and runs a network of good **pensions**, including *Dina Rooms* (☎0427/21 508; ③), *Adonis Stamelos Rooms* (☎0427/22 962; ④) and the *Pension Kvouli* (☎0427/21 082; rooms ④, maisonettes ⑥). The best location for accommodation is beyond the *Stamatis* taverna, overlooking the fishing harbour. There's another concentration of good rooms on Kapodhistríou 14. If you're looking for more **upmarket accommodation** in high season – say the *Alkyon Hotel*, on the seafront at the commercial port end (☎0427/37 002; ⑤), or the *Meltemi Hotel*, on the front near the taxi rank (☎0427/21 593; ⑥) – try and book a season ahead, or a month ahead for April, May and October.

The island now has four official **campsites** – at Koliós, Koukounariés, Asélinos and Xanémos beach. Koliós is okay, but Koukounarlés and Asélinos are probably the best choices. Xanémos beach is 3km northeast of Skíathos Town, right next to the airport runway, and, apart from being within walking distance of the town, has little to recommend it.

Eating, drinking and nightlife

You're spoilt for choice for **eating places**, but nothing's particularly cheap apart from the few burger/*gyros* bars. One of the best and cheapest tavernas is *Zorba's*, opposite the taxi rank, while *Toh Trigono*, on Alexándhrou Papadhiamándi, does good pasta. If you fancy a change, there's an Italian restaurant, *La Piazza*, up the steps at the end of the harbour. The English-run *Lemon Tree Restaurant*, with its vegetarian food and *tapas*, now has a nearby rival, the *Daskalio Cafe Bar*, whose laid-back Brits serve excellent curries. For more elegant dining, head for the area above and to the west of Plátia Tríon Ierarhón, where you'll find *Le Bistrot* and *Alexanders'* (for excellent moussaka and chicken dishes). Further along, above the flat rocks where people sunbathe, *Tarsanas* is a converted boatbuilders' yard with a picturesque veranda – the best place in town for an evening drink as the harbour lights come on.

Nightlife centres on the clubs on or near Politechníou – the new *West* and *Borzoi* are the latest favourites, the *Apothiki Music Hall* has live music and a good atmo-sphere, while *BBCE* on the seafront rocks till dawn. Bars show more musical variety – places like the *Banana* are pop-oriented and popular, the pricey *Kirki* and *Kentavros* play jazz and blues, *Adagio* has classical music in the evenings, and stalwart *Admiral Benbow* belts out classic Sixties soul.

Around the island

Other than using the buses or the various rental outlets in town (for which see above), you could also get your bearings on a **boat trip** around the island. These cost around 2500dr per person and leave around 10am. Or try a boat trip to the islet of Tsougriá (opposite Skíathos Town), where there's a good beach and a taverna. Boats leave from the fishing harbour beyond the Boúrtzi, and not the yacht anchorage to the north of the ferry harbour; east coast *kaíki* leave from the quay area in front of the bus station.

If you're interested in seeing more of Skíathos **on foot**, the locally produced Skíathos guide by Rita and Dietrich Harkort (available in larger tourist shops) has detailed instructions and maps for walks all over the island. It's a good way to escape the crowds, although you're never going to get away from it all completely.

Monasteries and Kástro

The **Evangelístria monastery** (daily 8am–noon & 4–8pm), more than an hour on foot out of Skíathos Town, is also accessible by rented moped, car or mule. The Greek flag was raised here in 1807, and, among other heroes of the War of Independence, Kolokotronis pledged his oath to fight for freedom here. It is exceptionally beautiful, even beyond the grandeur of isolation you find in all Greek monasteries. To reach it, walk 500m out of the centre of town on the road towards the airport until, at the point where the asphalt veers to the right, you take a prominently signposted tarmac track that veers left; be careful to stick to the tarmac and not to wander off onto the dirt roads.

Beyond Evangelístria, a mule track continues to the abandoned **monastery of Áyios Harálambos**, from where it's possible to walk across the island to the old ruined capital of Kástro (see below) along another dirt road, taking about two hours. To reach Kástro from Skíathos Town, it's quicker to take the direct road, though in all it's still a hard five- to six-kilometre uphill slog; the turning is signposted on the road behind town, some distance beyond the turning for Evangelístria.

Just over halfway between Evangelístria and Kástro, a well-used dirt track (signposted) turns left and heads towards the abandoned fifteenth-century monastery of **Panayía tis Kehrias**, three hours' walk from town. It's said to be the oldest on the island and has a colony of bats inside. It's a beautiful walk (or organized donkey-ride), and there are two pebbly beaches below, one with a welcoming stream that powers a cool shower. Ignoring this excursion, the paved road continues to within a thirty-minute walk of **Kástro** – a spectacular spot, built on a windswept headland. In the past, the entrance was only accessible by a drawbridge (now ruined), which has been replaced by a flight of steps. The village was built in the sixteenth century, when the people of the island moved here for security from pirate raids. It was abandoned 300 years later in 1830, following independence from Turkey, when the population moved back to build the modern town on the site of ancient Skíathos. The ruins are largely overgrown, and only three churches survive intact, the largest still retaining some original frescoes. From outside the gates, a path leads down the rocks to a good pebble **beach**. With a stream running down from the hills and a daytime café (with slightly overpriced food and drinks), it wouldn't make a bad place to camp. However, for an apparently inaccessible spot, it does attract a surprising number of people. All the island excursion boats call here, and even when they've gone, there's little chance of having the ruins or beach to yourself.

Finally, the seventeenth-century **Kou*n*ístria monastery**, can be reached by turning right off the road that runs from Tróulas to Asélinos. It's a very pretty spot, with a beautiful carved temple, spendid icons, a grape arbour and a taverna.

The beaches

The real business of Skíathos is **beaches**. There are reputed to be more than sixty of them on the island, even so hardly enough to soak up the numbers of summer visitors:

at the height of season, the local population of 4000 can be eclipsed by up to 50,000 outsiders. The beaches on the northeast coast aren't easily accessible unless you pay for an excursion *kaíki*. Reaching them on foot requires treks more arduous than those described above. The bus, though, runs along the entire south coast, and from strategic points along the way you can easily reach a good number of beaches. The prevailing summer *meltémi* wind blows from the north, so the beaches on the south coast are usually better protected. Most of the popular beaches have at least a drinks/snacks stall; those at Vromólimnos, Asélinos and Troúlos have proper tavernas.

The beaches before the **Kalamáki peninsula** are unexciting, but on the promontory itself, flanked by the campsite and Kanapítsa hamlet, **Rígas**, **Ayía Paraskeví** and **Vromólimnos** are highly rated, the last offering windsurfing and waterskiing. The water along this stretch, however, is cloudy and appears contaminated, though it improves after Troúlos. For scuba enthusiasts, there is the new *Dolphin Diving Centre* (☎0427/22 520) at the *Nostos* hotel, on the eastern side of the Kalamáki peninsula.

Just before Troúlos you can turn right up a paved road, which runs 4km north to **Mégas Asélinos**, a very good beach with a campsite and a reasonable taverna. A daily bus and excursion boats stop here, so it's crowded in season. A fork in the paved road leads to Kounístria monastery (see above) and continues to **Mikrós Asélinos**, just east of its larger neighbour and somewhat quieter.

The bus only goes as far as **KOUKOUNARIÉS**, a busy resort, though the three beaches are excellent if you don't mind the crowds. There's a majestic sandy bay of clear, gradually deepening water, backed by acres of pines, and despite its popularity it merits at least one visit if only to assess the dubious claim that it's the best beach in Greece. The road runs behind a small lake at the back of the pine trees, and features a string of hotels, **rooms and restaurants**, as well as a good campsite. The *Strofilia* apartments here (☎0427/49 251; ⑤) are particularly nicely furnished. If you feel like entering into the spirit of things, jet-skis, motorboats, windsurfing and waterskiing are all available off the beach.

Banana Beach (also known as Krássa), the third cove on the far side of Poúnda headland, is the trendiest of the island's nudist beaches. For the less adventurous, the turning for **Ayía Eléni** (the penultimate bus stop), leads one kilometre to the pleasant beach (with a drinks kiosk). Or ask the driver to set you down before here, at the start of the thirty-minute path to **Mandhráki** and **Elia** beaches, which have similar facilities.

The famed **Lalaria beach**, on the northern stretch of coast, can be reached by "taxi-boats" from the town. It's beautiful, with steep cliffs rising behind it and excellent swimming, but beware of the undertow. The island's three natural grottos – Skotini, Glazia and Halkini – are nearby and are included in many of the "round-the-island" trips. Southwest of Kástro are the greyish sands of **Megas Yialos**, one of the less crowded beaches, and **Xanemos**, another nudist beach, though both suffer from airport noise.

The only real way to get away from the crowds is to persuade a boat owner to take you out to one of Skiáthos' **islets**. Tsougriá, in particular, has three beaches, with a snack bar on the main one.

Skópelos

Bigger, more rugged and better cultivated than Skiáthos, **Skópelos** is, in its way, just as busy. As you approach the island from the sea, it appears a peaceful place, but once on land, little has remained immune to tourism. Most of the beaches have sunbeds, umbrellas and some watersports, despite the island-wide jellyfish problem. Inland, it is a well-watered place, harvesting olives, plums, pears and almonds. Glóssa and Skópelos, its two main towns, are also among the prettiest in the Sporades, clambering uphill along paved steps, their houses distinguished by attractive wooden balconies and grey slate roofs.

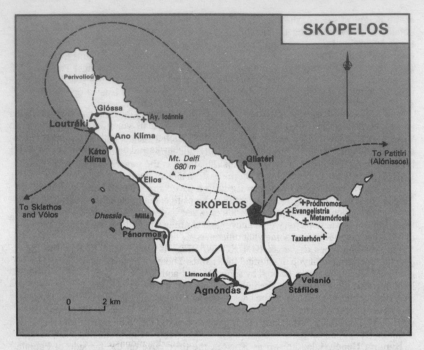

A number of nationalities have occupied the island at various stages of its history, among them the Romans, Persians, Venetians, French and, of course, the Turks. Indeed the Turkish admiral, Barbarossa (Redbeard), had the entire population of the island slaughtered in the sixteenth century.

Loutráki, Glóssa and the west

Most boats call at both ends of Skópelos, stopping first at the small port of **LOUTRÁKI** with its thin pebble beach, filthy water, couple of hotels and few rooms for rent. The town has been spoilt a little by developments at either end, but it's still not a bad place to stay if you're after peace and quiet; try *O Stelios* (②), a simple pension above the taverna *Flisvos*, or the *Avra* (☎0424/33 550; ④), a fancier hotel. Unfortunately most of the quayside tavernas are a rip-off, although the café/shop in the *platía* by the harbour is shaded by beautiful chestnut trees and sells a highly recommended, home-made retsina; the *Flisvos* isn't bad either, a friendly place with decent pasta dishes.

High above Loutráki, **GLÓSSA** is perhaps a preferable base, a sizeable and quite beautiful, totally Greek town, with several *kafenía*, a taverna and rooms to let – some of which are hot and musty, with erratic water pressure. *Kostas and Nina's* place (☎0424/33 686; ②) has simple, clean rooms, some with a view; they also rent out studios longer term. You could also try *H. Tsoukala* (☎0424/33 223 or 33 767; ③), near the bus stop for rooms, or the *Pension Valentina* (☎0424/33 694; ③). There's one taverna, *Toh Agnandi*, which is a lively and authentic place to eat, and full most evenings. Incidentally, it's a good idea to accept offers of a taxi ride up to Glóssa from Loutráki; it's a stiff walk up even if you know the path short cuts, and taxi drivers will know which pensions have vacancies. If it's really high season, though, and even Glóssa is packed, three nearby villages, Athéato, Káto Klíma and Paleo Klíma all have rooms, while Neo Klíma has two hotels and *O Xenos,* a decent *ouzerí.*

Ninety minutes' walk from Glóssa, up to the north coast, will bring you to a **beach** the locals call Perivolioú. The walk itself is worthwhile, passing a **monastery** next to a hollow stone cairn containing masses of human bones and skulls. There's also a huge hollow oak tree here, in the heart of which is a small tank of drinking water. The beach, when you get there, is nothing out of the ordinary, but there's spring water for drinking and a cave for shade.

East of Glóssa, a new dirt road leads to the splendidly sited monastery of **Áyios Ioánnis**, perched on the top of a rock high above a small sandy cove where you can swim. The buildings themselves are modern and rather ugly, but the walk from Glóssa (again, about 90min) is beautiful and peaceful, with hawks and nightingales for company.

Skópelos Town

If you stay on the ferry beyond Loutráki – and this is probably the best plan – you reach **SKÓPELOS** town, sloping down one corner of a huge, almost circular bay. The best way to arrive is by sea, with the town revealed slowly as the boat rounds the final headland. Be prepared for the crowds though, since Skópelos Town has seen enormous commercialization over recent years, with a huge increase in visitors and prices. The centre is a mass of boutiques and pricey tavernas, with an untidy sprawl of new hotels to the southeast. Spread below the oddly whitewashed ruins of a Venetian **Kástro**, are an enormous number of churches – 123 reputedly, though some are small enough to be mistaken for houses and most are locked except for their annual festival day.

Outside town, perched on the slopes opposite the quay, are two convents, **Evangelístria** (daily 8am–1pm & 4–7pm), which is within view of the town, and **Pródhromos** (daily 8am–1pm & 5–8pm). The nearby monastery of **Metamórfosis** was abandoned in 1980 but is now being restored by the monks and is open to visitors. You should dress respectfully, although the hospitable nuns at the two convents will lend you leg-covering if necessary. Access is simplest by following an old road behind the line of hotels in town to Evangelístria (an hour's walk). From there it's an extra half hour's scramble over mule tracks to Pródhromos, the remotest and most beautiful of the three. Ignore the new road that goes part way – it's longer and takes away most of the beauty of the walk.

Practicalities

The **ferry quay** is at the western end of a long promenade, lined with an array of boutiques, bars, stores and restaurants. Where the quay meets the main road, turn left and follow the sea until you pass the children's swings and the second *períptero*; at the point where the road divides around a car park, you'll find the **bus station**. Opposite the bus station entrance, a short road leads into a maze of lanes, though signposts lead you to the **post office**. There is a branch of the *Commercial Bank* about 50m from the quay.

In the main body of the town there are dozens of **rooms** for rent; take up one of the offers when you land, since most are otherwise unadvertised. Alternatively, try the *Lina Guest House* on the front (☎0424/22 637; ④) or, among the allotments, the very pleasant *Hotel Captain* (☎0424/22 110 or 22 980; ③) – both have clean, if basic, rooms with private bathrooms; some rooms have balconies. For more **expensive hotels**, you're unlikely to find a space without having booked through a tour operator, but if you fancy the likes of the *Elli* (☎0424/22 549; ⑤), *Aperiton* (☎0424/22 322; ⑥) or *Dionysos* (☎0424/23 210; ⑥) – each with a pool – ask about vacancies at *Madro Travel* on the quay (☎0424/22 145); they're also the local *Flying Dolphin* agents.

There's a wide variety of **places to eat**, ranging from the good to the truly terrible. Those at either end of the harbour are a rip-off, while the clutch along the main prom, near the park, are in stiff competition in terms of price and variety of dishes offered. Best of these is definitely *Toh Aktaion*, with exceptionally pleasant staff and big, delicious, reasonably priced portions. Otherwise, *La Costa* is average but friendlier than most, *Pirate's* (follow the signposts) does curries and vegetarian food. There's a creperie, the *Greca*, and the best *yíros* are from *O Platanos*, near the post office. It's also worth heading a couple of kilometres towards Stáfilos to the *Terpsis* taverna for their stuffed-chicken speciality – book twelve hours in advance.

Nightlife in Skópelos is on the increase, but is more the late-night bar than nightclub variety. That said, the *Disco 52*, neighbouring *Labikos* and *Kounos* are popular in season, and the *Skopelitissa* plays Greek pop music till the early hours.

Around the rest of the island

Buses cover the island's one paved road between Skópelos Town and Loutráki (via Glóssa) about six times daily between 7am and 10.30pm, stopping at the paths to all the main beaches and villages. **Stáfilos**, 4km south of town, is the closest beach, if small and rocky. It is getting increasingly crowded, but the *Terpsis* taverna, which rents **rooms**, is a very pleasant spot shaded by a vast pine tree.

There's a very prominent "No Camping" sign at Stáfilos, but if you walk five minutes around the coast north to **Velanió**, there is spring water and a campsite near the beach. Here the pines and surf always draw a small, summer (often nudist) community.

Further around the coast to the west, the very touristy, beachless, fishing anchorage of **AGNÓNDAS** (with a combination restaurant/rooms) is the start of a fifteen-minute path (2km by road) or half-hourly *kaíki* to **LIMNONÁRI**, 100m of fine sand set in a rather grim and shadeless rock-girt bay. There are a couple of places to stay and eat, but camping would be a bit cramped, and it's all a bit commercial and rather tatty. However, the *Takonis* taverna here isn't bad, serving good, fresh fish.

PÁNORMOS is very much a full-blown resort, with rooms, tavernas, a campsite (where people of all income levels may find themselves at times when Skópelos is choc-full) and watersports. The beach here is gravelly and steeply shelving, but there are small secluded bays close by. The enormous *Panormos Beach Hotel*, a stalwart of package holidays, has a beautiful garden and fine views – it's worth trying for space at *Madro Travel* in Skópelos Town (see "Practicalities" above). Slightly further on at **MILIÁ**, there is a tremendous, 1500m sweep of tiny pebbles beneath a bank of pines, facing the islet of Dhassía. There's one taverna and just a couple of houses with rooms (π0424/22 735 for both; ③) in this languid setting; nudist swimming is possible at a lovely 500-metre-long beach a little way north, though the sea both here and at Miliá teems with jellyfish.

Further north, **ELIOS**, 9km short of Glóssa, is a medium-sized resort in its own right, and not a particularly pleasant one either, although its usually crowded beach is nice and there's a reasonable taverna, *Theophilos*, with good, if pricey fish. Beyond here, the virtually abandoned village of Paleo Klíma marks the start of a beautiful fortyminute **trail** to Glóssa, via the earthquake-ruined settlement of Áyii Anaryiri and the oldest village on the island, Athéato.

West of Skópelos town various jeep tracks and old paths wind through olive and plum groves toward **Mount Dhélfi** and the Vathiá forest, or skirt the base of the mountain northeast to Revíthi hill with its fountains and churches, and the site of **Karyá**, with its *sendoúkia* or ancient tombs. Tracks on the north flank of Dhélfi, beyond Karyá, might just conceivably lead all the way to the Klíma villages, but the main, old trans-island donkey track ends disappointingly in the vicinity of Élios.

To the northwest of Skópelos Town, **Glistéri** is a small pebble beach with no shade but a taverna much frequented by locals on Sundays. **Sáres**, reached by half-hourly *kaíkia* from town, is also a popular beach. A fork off the Glistéri and Mount Dhélfi tracks can – in theory – be followed across the island to Pánormos within ninety minutes; it's a pleasant walk though the route isn't always obvious. As usual, local maps of the island are mostly very inaccurate, a situation aggravated by the many new tracks bulldozed across the island since the maps were printed, making exploration interesting but sometimes frustrating.

Alónissos and some minor islets

The most remote of the Sporades, **Alónissos** is also, on initial appearance, the least attractive. It has an unfortunate recent history. The vineyards were wiped out by disease in 1950 and the *hóra* was damaged by an earthquake in 1965. Although its houses were mostly repairable, corruption and the social control policies of the new junta were instrumental in the forcible transfer of virtually the entire population down

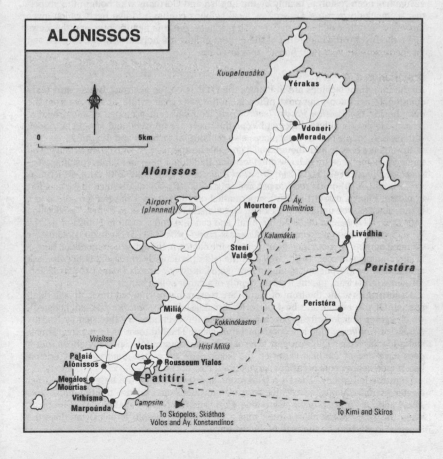

to the previously unimportant anchorage of Patitíri. The result is a little soulless, but on closer acquaintance the island turns out to be one of the most traditional in Greece, though this can leave single, female travellers open to hassle. That said, if you're polite and dress respectably, the people are charming. Take time and explore.

Patitíri and the old town

PATITÍRI is not a good introduction to the island. The flat-roofed concrete buildings are relieved only by a row of bars and near-identical restaurants along the seafront. Although Alónissos attracts fewer visitors than Skíathos or Skópelos, most of those who do come stay in Patitíri, and from mid-July to the end of August it can get very crowded. Travelling independently, there seems little reason to stay longer than you have to, though it's the easiest place for picking up connections for beaches and the old town.

PALAIÁ ALÓNISSOS is a fine but steep fifty-minute walk via a donkey track – signposted on the left just outside Patitíri. Alternatively, there's a bus (theoretically 4 daily, though it actually runs every 15min from late morning until lunch and 7–9pm if there are enough passengers). Although many houses are still derelict, much of the village has been restored, mainly by the English and Germans who bought the properties at knock-down rates. Only a few local families continue to live here, which gives the village a rather odd and un-Greek atmosphere, but it is picturesque, and the views make the trip worthwhile. Most of the owners only come here in July and August, and for the rest of the year their houses are closed up.

Practicalities

All the important facilities are in Patitíri; the OTE is on the seafront, buses and taxis congregate next door, the post office is on the *hóra* road, while *kaíki* leave from the quay beside the *Pension Flisvos* (see below). You can rent a moped or motorbike at reasonable prices, although beyond Vótsi the roads are unpaved and should be ridden with care. A couple of the rental places also rent out motorboats and dinghies.

Rooms are easy to find, though you'll probably be approached with offers as you get off the ferry, sometimes by older women wearing traditional blue and white costumes. Try *Nikolaos Dimakis* (☎0424/65 244; ③), *Elini Athanasiou* (☎0424/65 240; ②), *O M Kyriazis* (☎0424/65 229; ③) or the *Ioulieta* pension (☎0424/65 463; ③), all of which make an effort to please. Finally, ask at the third supermarket on the left on Pelasgon for access to a brand new, as yet unnamed, building of rooms. The local room-owners' association (☎0424/65 577) has an office on the front, and can find you a room in Patitíri or nearby Vótsi, but you'll end up paying more. *Alonissos Travel* (☎0424/65 511) can do bookings for a limited number of rooms and apartments in the old town, though accommodation here is in short supply so expect to pay well over the odds, particularly in season. Otherwise, ask around; few people put up "room for rent" signs, but try *Fadasia House* (☎0424/65 186; ④), simple and clean, and the least unfriendly of a rather sullen bunch.

Restaurants along the front of Patitíri are reasonably priced, but the food is nothing special. Of the bunch, the best place for breakfast is the *Balcony Bar* (signposted), which serves delicious fresh peach juice; and in the evenings, try the friendly *Pension Flisvos*, or *Naffilos*, which has occasional musicians. The old town has a bar, two shops, and a few tavernas. The *Paraport* taverna is good, though not especially cheap, but it does have one of the best views on the island. The *Aloni* has good views of Vrisítsa beach (see below) plus occasional art exhibitions.

Nightlife is low key. There's a pool room, and several bars; the best of the seafront cluster is *Pub Dennis,* whose ice-cream concoctions are divine, though both *Nine Muses* and *La Vie* are popular. Club-wise, *Borio* and the *Disco 4 x 4* are fairly European, while the *Disco Rocks* plays Greek music (and is not for solo females), as does the superior *Rembetika*, on the road to the old town.

The island's beaches

Alónnisos has some of the cleanest water in the Aegean, but it's sadly lacking in good beaches. There's only one really sandy beach on the island (Vithísma), the rest varying from rough to fine pebbles. There's no bus, but *kaíki* run half-hourly from Patitíri north to Hrisí Miliá, Kokkinókastro, Stení Vála, Kalamákia and Áyios Dhímitrios, and south around the coast to Marpoúnda, Vithísma and Megálos Moúrtias. *Kaíki* also sail occasionally to Livádhia and the Peristéra islets.

Patitíri itself has a grimy stretch of shingle, but decent swimming can be had from the rocks around the corner to the north, past the cranes; pick your way along a hewn-out path and you're there (ladder provided). To the north, above the headlands, Patitíri merges into two adjoining settlements. **Roussoúm Yialós** holds nothing of interest, but fancies itself as a budding resort. There's an attractive harbour, tavernas and a few rooms – try the unnamed building on the front (☎ 0424/65 334; ③). **Vótsi** is still being built. The best beaches, however, are well to Patitíri's north, mostly on the eastern side.

Hrisí Miliá, the first good beach, has pine trees down to the sand and a taverna; there are a couple of new hotels on the hillside above, and it can get crowded in summer. At **Kokkinókastro**, over the hill to the north, excavations have revealed the

---

THE MEDITERRANEAN MONK SEAL

The Mediterranean Monk Seal has the dubious distinction of being the European mammal most in danger of extinction. Perhaps 800 survive in total worldwide, the majority around the Portuguese Atlantic island of Madeira and the coast of the West African state of Mauritania, and in small numbers in the Ionian and Aegean seas, having disappeared entirely from the Mediterranean. The largest population, an estimated 25–30 seals, lives around the deserted islands north of Alónissos.

Monk seals can travel up to 200km a day in search of food, but they usually return to the same places to rear their pups. They have one pup every two years, and the small population is very vulnerable to disturbance and the possibility of mother seals being separated from and losing their pups. Originally, the pups would have been reared on sandy beaches, but with increasing disturbance by man, they have retreated to isolated sea caves, particularly around the coast of the remote islet of Pipéri.

Unfortunately, the seals compete with fishermen for limited stocks of fish, and, in the overfished Aegean, often destroy nets full of fish. Until recently it was common for seals to be killed by fishermen. This occasionally still happens, but in an attempt to protect the seals, the seas around the northern Sporades have been declared a marine wildlife reserve: fishing is restricted in the area north of Alónissos and prohibited within 5km of Pipéri. On Alónissos, the conservation effort and reserve have won a great deal of local support, mainly through the efforts of the Hellenic Society for the Protection of the Monk Seal (HSPMS), based at Stení Vála. The measures have won particular support from local fishermen, as tighter restrictions on larger, industrial-scale fishing boats from other parts of Greece should help preserve fish stocks and benefit them financially.

Despite this, the government has made no serious efforts to enforce the restrictions, and boats from outside the area continue to fish around Pipéri. There are also government plans to reduce the prohibited area around Pipéri to 500m. On a more positive note, the HSPMS, in collaboration with the Pieterburen Seal Creche in Holland, has reared three abandoned seal pups, all of which have been successfully released in the seas north of Alónissos.

For the moment, your chances of actually seeing a seal are remote, unless you plan to spend a few weeks on a boat in the area. It's recommended that you shouldn't visit Pipéri or approach sea caves on other islands which might be used by seals, or encourage boat owners to do so. Spear fishing, by tourists or professional fishermen, is a particular threat near caves used by seals and is strongly discouraged.

site of ancient Ikos and evidence of the oldest known prehistoric habitation in the Aegean. There's nothing much to see, but it's a beautiful spot with a good pebble beach, and, in July and August, a daytime taverna.

STENÍ VÁLA, opposite the island of Peristéra, is perhaps the most obvious place to stay. It's almost a proper village, with a shop, a few houses, a bar, rooms and three tavernas, one of which stays open more or less throughout the year. There's a campsite (☎0424/65 258) in an olive grove by the harbour, a long pebble beach and other beaches within reasonable walking distance in either direction. **KALAMÁKIA**, to the north, also has a couple of tavernas, and a few rooms.

If you want real solitude, **Áyios Dhímitrios**, nearby **Megaliamos** (where fossils have been found), **Yérakas** (an old shepherds' village much further north) and **Koupelousáko** are recommended, but be aware that currents along this stretch can be treacherous. However, before committing yourself, take one of the round-the-island trips available, and return the next day with enough food for your stay – there are no stores outside the port.

In the opposite direction from Patitíri, **Marpoúnda** features a large hotel and bunga-low complex and a rather grim beach. Better to turn left after the campsite towards **Megálos Moúrtias**, a pebble beach with several tavernas linked by dirt track with Palaiá Alónnisos, 200m above. Just before Megálos Moúrtias, a path heads down through the pine trees to **Vithísma**, a much better sand and shingle beach that's hardly visible from above. A windsurfing school operates from here in summer.

Further north, visible from Palaiá Alónnisos, **Vrisítsa** is tucked into its own finger-like inlet. There's sand and a sometime taverna, but little else.

Beyond Alónissos: some minor islets

Northeast of Alónissos half a dozen tiny islets speckle the Aegean. Virtually none of these has any permanent population, nor any ferry service, and the only way you can reach them – at least Peristéra, Kirá Panayía and Yioúra – is by excursion *kaíki*, and even then only in high season (the excursion boats serve primarily as fishing boats from September to May) and as weather permits. Considerable powers of persuasion will be required to get the fishermen to take you to the other, more remote islets. It is possible to be left for a night or more on any of the islands, but when acting out your desert-island fantasies, be sure to bring more supplies than you need: if the weather worsens you'll be marooned until such time as small craft can make it out to you.

Peristéra is the closest islet to Alónissos, to which it was once actually joined, but subsidence (a common phenomenon in the area) created the narrow straits beween the two. It is graced with some sandy beaches and there is rarely anyone around, though some Alónissans do come over for short periods to tend the olive groves, and in season there are regular evening "barbecue boats" from the main island. As on Alónissos, a few unofficial campers are tolerated, but there is only one spot, known locally as "Barbecue Bay", where campfires are allowed.

Kirá Panayía (also known as Pelagós) is the next islet out and is equally fertile. It's owned by the Orthodox Church and there are two monasteries here, one inhabited as recently as 1984. Boats call at a beach and anchorage on the south shore, one of many such sandy stretches and coves around the island, which is popular with yachtsmen. There's no permanent population other than the wild goats. The island boasts a stalactite cave reputed to be that of Homer's Polyphemus (the Cyclops that imprisoned Odysseus).

Nearby **Yioúra** has a similar, larger cave with perhaps better credentials as the lair of Polyphemus. The main feature, though, is a herd of rare wild goats, distinctive enough to have earned the island the status of a reserve. Two middle-aged couples live here as wardens; part of their job is to unlock the cave for visiting parties and provide a hurri-cane lamp. You'll need more than a single source of illumination to see much, however, and getting down into the cavern is fairly strenuous. Apart from the tourist boats, the wardens' only contact with the outside world is a twice-monthly mail-and-provisions boat, which, like all other craft, cannot land at the primitive jetty in rough seas.

Pipéri, near Yioúra, is a sea-bird and monk seal refuge, and permission from the EOT (in Athens) is required for visits by non-specialists. Tiny, northernmost **Psathoúra** is dominated by its powerful modern lighthouse, although here, as around many of these islands, there's a submerged ancient town, brought low by the endemic subsidence. Roughly halfway between Alónissos and Skíros, green **Skantzoúra**, with a single monastery (still inhabited by one monk) and a few seasonal shepherds, seems a lesser version of Kirá Panayía.

Skíros (Skyros)

Despite its closeness to Athens, **Skíros** had until recently remained a very traditional and idiosyncratic island. Any impetus for change had been neutralized by the lack of economic opportunity (and even secondary schooling), forcing the younger Skyrians to live in Athens and leaving behind a conservative gerontocracy. A high school has at last been provided, and the island has been "discovered" in the past decade. It's now the haunt of continental Europeans, chic Athenians and British, many of whom check in to the "New Age" Skyros Centre, catering to those who feel Skíros by itself isn't enough to "rethink the form and direction of their lives".

Meanwhile, Skíros still ranks as one of the most interesting places in the Aegean. It has a long tradition of ornate woodcarving, and a *Salonáki Skiriani* (handmade set of chairs) is still considered an appropriate partial dowry for any young Greek woman. A very few old men still wear the vaguely Cretan traditional costume of cap, vest, baggy trousers, leggings and *trohádhia* (Skyrian clogs), but this is dying out. Likewise, old women still wear the favoured yellow scarves and long embroidered skirts.

The theory that Skíros was originally two islands seems doubtful, but certainly the character of the two parts of the island is very different. The north has a greener and more gentle landscape, and away from the port and town it retains much of its original pine forest. The sparsely inhabited south is mountainous, rocky and barren; there are few trees and the landscape is more reminiscent of the Cyclades than the Sporades. Compared to Skíathos, Skópelos and Alónissos, Skíros isn't a great place for out-of-the-way beaches. Most **beaches** along the west coast attract more than their fair share of sea-borne rubbish, and, although the scenery is sometimes spectacular, the swimming isn't that good. The beaches on the east coast are all close to Skíros Town, and the best option is probably to stay here rather than heading for somewhere more isolated.

GOAT DANCES AND WILD PONIES

Skíros has some particularly lively, even outrageous festivals. The *Apokriatiká* (pre-Lenten) carnival here is structured around the famous "Goat Dance" performed by masked revellers in the village streets. The foremost character in this is the Yéros, a menacing figure concealed by a goatskin mask and weighed down by garlands of sheep bells. Accompanying him are Korélles and Kyriés (transvestites – only the men participate) and Frangi (maskers in "Western" garb). For further details, read Joy Koulentianou's *The Goat Dance of Skyros*, available in Athens and occasionally on the island.

The other big annual event takes place near Magaziá beach on August 15, when children race domesticated members of the wild pony herd native to Skíros and said to be related to the Shetland pony (if so, it must be very distantly). They are thought, perhaps, to be the diminutive horses depicted in the Parthenon frieze, and at any time of the year you might find some of the tame individuals tethered and grazing near Skíros Town.

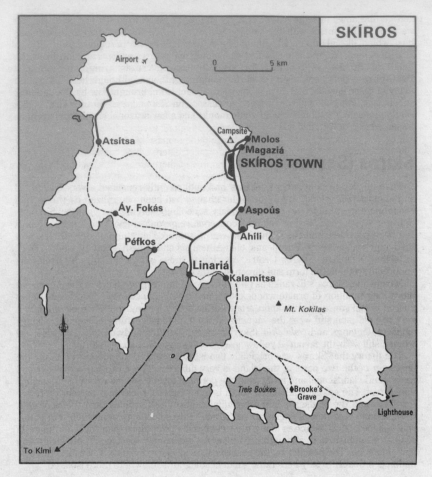

Linariá

After crossing a seemingly endless expanse of sea, the boat docks at the tiny port of **LINARIÁ**, a functional place on the island's west coast. Most buildings are in the modern Greek-concrete-box style, and while it's a pleasant place to while away time waiting for the ferry, there's little else to keep you. If you do stay the night, there are two tavernas (one with rooms) and a bar around the harbour. In high season, *kaíki* ply from Linariá to the Pentekali and Yerania **grottos**, and to the **islet of Skiropoúla**, which has a cave and some of the Skyrian wild ponies. There's a reasonable sandy **beach** called Kalóyeros a few minutes' walk along the main road from Linariá, and there should be no problem if you want to camp here.

A road connects Linariá to Skíros town, 10km away, and then continues round, past the airport, to Atsítsa; the **bus to Skíros** leaves from the quay. Midway up the Linariá to Skíros-town route, a side road links Ahíli with Kalamítsa. Most other roads are passable on a rented moped, apart from the direct track between Skíros town and Atsítsa.

Skíros Town

SKÍROS Town (also known as Hóra), with its decidedly Cycladic architecture, sits on the landward side of a high rock rising precipitously from the coast. According to legend, King Lycomedes pushed Theseus to his death from its summit. It has a workaday atmosphere without feeling like a resort or being especially picturesque. The older and more intriguing parts of town are higher up, climbing towards the **Kástro**, a mainly Byzantine rather than Venetian building, built on the site of the ancient acropolis. There are few traces of this, although remains of the Classical city walls survive below on the seaward side of the rock. The *kástro* is open to visitors; to reach its upper parts you pass through a rather private-looking gateway into the monastery, then through an attractive shaded courtyard and up a whitewashed tunnel. There's little to see at the top, apart from a few churches in various states of ruin, but there are great views over the town and this part of the island, and the climb up takes you through the quieter and more picturesque part of town, with glimpses into traditionally decorated houses.

Perhaps equally striking, and splendidly incongruous, is the **Memorial to Rupert Brooke** at the northern end of town. It takes the form of a bronze statue of "Immortal Poetry" and its nakedness caused a scandal among the townspeople when it was first set up. Brooke, who visited the south of the island very briefly in April 1915, died shortly after of blood poisoning on a French hospital ship anchored offshore and was buried in an olive grove above the bay of Treis Boukés. (The site can be reached on foot from Kalamítsa, by *kaíki*, or, less romantically, by taxi.) Brooke has become something of a local hero, despite his limited acquaintance with Skíros, and ironically was adopted by Kitchener and later Churchill as the paragon of patriotic youth, despite his forthrightly expressed socialist and internationalist views.

Just below the Brooke statue are two museums. The **Archeological Museum** (Tues–Sat 9am–3.30pm, Sun 9.30am–2.30pm; 400dr) has a modest collection of pottery and statues from excavations on the island, and a reconstruction of a traditional Skíros house interior. The privately run **Faltaitz Museum** (daily 10am–1pm & 5.30pm–8pm; free), in a nineteenth-century house built over one of the bastions of the ancient walls, is more interesting with a collection of domestic items.

Practicalities

Arriving in Skíros Town, the **bus** from Linariá leaves you by the school, just below the main *platía*; the OTE, **post office** and **bank** are all nearby. *Skiros Travel* (☎0222/91 123 or 91 600), on the main street above the *platía*, can provide **information** and advice and can find a room or hotel; in high season, it's a good idea to telephone them in advance. There are a few **moped and motorbike** rental places in the area around the *platía*.

You'll probably be met off the bus with offers of **rooms**, which it's as well to accept. *Anna Stergiou* (☎0222/91 657; ③–④) on Ayía Mena has clean, homely rooms, some in her house and some with kitchens nearby. Or call *Vangeliou Mavrikos* (☎0222/91 115; ②–④) for dormitory-type rooms with shared bathroom or more private ones. There's a **campsite** at the bottom of the steps below the archeological museum, with basic amenities but a good bar.

The *platía* and the main street running by it are the centre of village life, with a couple of noisy pubs and a wide choice of *kafenía*, tavernas and fast-food places. There are few outstanding **places to eat;** most are overpriced, or serve rather average food. *O Glaros*, just below the *platía*, is an exception, and many of the local people eat here. It's a very basic taverna with a limited menu, but the owners are friendly and the food is good and reasonably priced. Also the *psistariá, O Skyros,* is worth a try for its hefty portions, *Moraiti* on Agoras is cheap and cheerful, *Sisyphos* has vegetarian specialities and the *Sweets Workshop* does some wonderful cakes.

The town's **nightlife** is mostly bar-based until very late, when the few clubs get going. The *Pub Bar* is the most popular meeting place, while *Kalypso* is mellow and uncrowded. Best clubs include the *Skyropoula, On The Rocks* and *Apocalypsis*. At high-season weekends though, it can be more fun to join in the dancing at the Magaziá campsite.

Magaziá and Mólos and some beaches

A path leads down past the archeological museum towards the small coastal village of **MAGAZIÁ**, coming out by the official campsite (see above). From Magaziá, an 800-metre-long sandy beach stretches to the adjacent village of **MÓLOS**. In recent years, a sprawl of new development between the road and the beach has more or less joined the two villages together. Despite this, the beach is good, and if you don't feel like walking down from Skíros Town to go swimming, it would be a good place to stay. There are lots of **rooms** down here, reflecting the young crowd that uses the beach's watersports and volleyball facilities. *Stamatis Marmaris* (☎0222/91 672; ④) and *Manolis Balotis* (☎0222/91 386; ③), near the campsite, are both popular. The beach-front **tavernas** compare favourably with those in town: a small taverna in a converted windmill at the Mólos end of the beach has good food and the best view, and the taverna *Akti*, also in Mólos, does a cheap and filling moussaká.

For quieter beaches, take the road past Mólos, or better, try the excellent and undeveloped beach directly below the *kástro*. The path down to it is 150m beyond the disco *Skyropoula* – it isn't obvious from above. However, following the road beyond here, the beaches are disappointing until **Méalos beach** (known more commonly as **Aspoús**), which has a couple of tavernas and rooms to rent. To the south, **Ahíli**, had one of the best beaches on the island until it was effectively destroyed by the construction of a new marina. South of Ahíli, the coast is rocky and inaccessible, although you can take a *kaíki* trip down to the bay of **Treis Boukés**, passing some picturesque sea caves on the way.

Kalamítsa, on the west coast across from Ahíli, lacks character and the beach and sea aren't that clean. There's a better and more remote beach halfway along the road to Treis Boukés, though it has absolutely no facilities.

Around the rest of the island

In summer, the whimsical bus service visits the more popular beaches if that's all you want to do. Otherwise, from Skíros Town it's best to direct your footsteps (or moped) due west, following Kifissós Creek into the pine-filled heart of this half of Skíros, which contrasts sharply with the barren rockiness of the south.

Just north of town, turn right off the airport road onto a track leading to **Ayía Ekaterína**, a pretty, small beach with its own chapel. There are also two nice beaches near the airport, and **Kalogrias**, further on, is quiet but pleasant. You can reach them via a track beyond Áyios Dhimítrios.

The dirt track from Skíros Town across to **Atsítsa** is well worth the effort (3–4hr walk), but isn't practical with a moped. Atsítsa is an attractive bay with pine trees down to the sea (tapped by the Skyrian retsina industry), and an increasing number of rooms. The beach is rocky and isn't great for swimming; there's a small sandy beach fifteen minutes' walk to the north at **Kirá Panayiá**, but it's nothing special.

Elsewhere in the coniferous north, **Áyios Fokás** and **Péfkos** bays are easiest reached by a turning from the paved road near Linariá, though there is (more difficult) access from Atsítsa. Both are in the process of being discovered by villa companies, but each has a few rooms. Áyios Fokás is quite primitive, but Péfkos boasts a taverna (it's only open in season, as are all other tavernas away from Linariá, Skíros Town, Magaziá and Mólos). The bay is beautiful and the beach reasonable but not that clean – the beaches around Skíros Town are much better for swimming.

Évvia (Euboea)

Évvia is the second-largest Greek island (after Crete), and seems more like an extension of the mainland to which it was in fact once joined. At **Halkídha**, the gateway to the island, the connecting bridge has only a forty-metre channel to span, the island reputedly having been split from Attica and Thessaly by a blow from Poseidon's trident (earthquakes and subsidence being the more pedestrian explanations). There are ferry crossings at no fewer than seven points along its length, and the south of the island is closer to Athens than it is to northern Évvia.

Nevertheless, Évvia *is* an island, in places a very beautiful one. But it has an idiosyncratic history and demography, and an enduringly strange feel that is not to most foreigners' tastes. A marked Albanian influence in the south, and scattered Lombard and Venetian watchtowers can make it seem "un-Greek". Indeed, the island was the longest-surviving southerly outpost of the Ottoman Turks, who had a keen appreciation of the island's wealth, as did the Venetians and Lombards before them. The last Ottoman garrison was not evicted until 1833, hanging on in defiance of the peace settlement that awarded Évvia to the new Greek state. Substantial Turkish communities, renowned for their alleged brutality, remained until 1923.

Economically, Évvia has always been prized. By Greek standards, it's exceptionally fertile, producing everything from grain, corn and cotton to kitchen vegetables and livestock (the Classical name "Euboea" means "rich in cattle"). High-quality meat is far easier to come by than fish, reinforcing the continental feel; retsina from the many vineyards is held in similar high regard, flavoured by lately fire-ravaged pine trees. Despite the collapse of much of its mining industry, the island remains relatively prosperous, so there has been no need or inclination to encourage mass foreign tourism. Accordingly, Greeks predominate, especially in the north around the spa of **Loutrá Edhipsoú**. In high season, Évvia can seem merely a beach annexe for much of Thessaly and Athens.

In the rolling countryside of the **north**, grain-combines whirl even on the sloping hay-meadows between olive groves and pine forest. This is the most conventionally scenic part of the island, echoing the beauty of the smaller Sporades. The **northeast coast** is rugged and largely inaccessible, its few sandy beaches surf-pounded and often dirty; the **southwest** is gentler and more sheltered, though much disfigured by industrial operations. The **centre** of the island, between Halkídha and the easterly port of Kími, is mountainous and dramatic, while the far **southeast** is mostly denuded and poor.

Public **transport** consists of seasonal hydrofoils along the protected southwest coast from Halkídha upwards, and passable bus services along the main roads to Káristos in the southeast and Loutrá Edhipsoú in the northwest. Otherwise, explorations are best conducted by rented car; any two-wheeler will make little impact on the enormous distances involved.

Halkídha

The heavily industrialized island-capital of **HALKÍDHA** (the ancient Halkís, an appellation still used) is the largest town on Évvia, with a population of 50,000. A shipyard, rail sidings and cement works make it a dire place apart from the old Ottoman quarter of **Kástro**, still home to gypsies, some Turks from Thrace and, at most, a hundred Jews – all that remains of the oldest Jewish community in Greece.

The entrance to the *kástro* – on the right as you head inland from the old *Euripos* bridge – is marked by the handsome fifteenth-century **mosque**, nominally a museum of Byzantine artefacts, but permanently locked. Beyond lie the remains of the old fortress, an arcaded aqueduct and the unique basilican **church of Ayía Paraskeví**

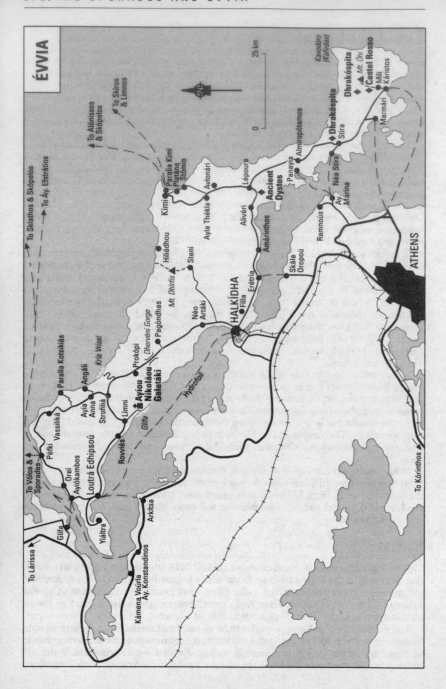

(also generally shut). The church is an odd structure, converted by the Crusaders during the fourteenth century into a Gothic cathedral. In the opposite direction, in the new town, an **archeological museum**, Venizélou 13 (daily except Mon 8.30am–3pm; 400dr), contains finds principally from nearby ancient Erétria.

The waterside overlooks the **Evripós**, the narrow channel dividing Évvia from the mainland, whose strange currents have baffled scientists for centuries. You can stand on the bridge that spans the narrowest point and watch the water swirling by like a river. Every few hours the current changes and the "tide" reverses. Aristotle is said to have thrown himself into the waters in despair at his inability to understand what was happening, so if you're puzzled you're in good company; there is still no entirely satisfactory explanation.

Practicalities

For most visitors, though, such activities are strictly time-fillers, with much the best view of the place to be had from the bus, train or hydrofoil on the way out. **Trains** arrive on the mainland-side of the channel, beneath the seventeenth-century Ottoman fortress of Kara Baba; given numerous, quick rail links with Athens, there's no conceivable reason to stay overnight. Most other services of interest lie within sight of the old Evripós bridge. The **hydrofoil** terminal sits just northeast, on the mainland side of the channel. The **bus station** is 400m from the bridge along Kótsou, then 50m right; no schedules are posted, but you should get a connection for any corner of the island as long as you show up by 2pm. The OTE is on Venizélou, near the museum.

Options for **eating out** are not brilliant, least of all at the obvious quayside tourist-traps; the immediate vicinity of the bus station has a handful of acceptable grills serving adequate lunches.

East from Halkídha

The coast road heading east out of Halkídha is an exceptionally misleading introduction to the interior of Évvia. Just what British and German package-tour companies see in the disappointing scenery around Erétria and Amárinthos is hard to imagine. There are some intriguing **Frankish towers** at Fílla, worth a detour inland from Vasilikó if you have a car, and some easy connections to Athens, but little else.

Modern **ERÉTRIA** is a rather dreary resort laid out on a grid plan; for non-packaged travellers its main asset is a well-advertised ferry service across to Skála Oropoú in Attica. The **site of ancient Erétria** is more distinguished, though much of it lies under the town. A few scanty remains are dotted around the town centre, most conspicuously an **agora** and a **Temple of Apollo**, but marginally more interesting are the excavations in the northwest corner, behind the small museum (rarely open). Here a **theatre** has been uncovered; steps from the orchestra descend to an underground vault used for sudden entrances and exits. Beyond the theatre are the ruins of a **gymnasium** and a **sanctuary**. While most of the "highlights" are diligently signposted, all appear to be suffering from years of neglect and are currently fenced off.

Just before Alivéri, an enormous modern power plant and a virtually intact medieval castle seem incongruously juxtaposed, and more Fílla-type towers look down from nearby hills; thereafter, the route mercifully heads inland. Beyond Lépoura, where the road branches north and south, the scenery improves drastically. Take the north fork towards Kími, and cross some of the most peaceful countryside in Greece.

Twelve kilometres north of Lépoura, at Háni Avlonaríou, stands the Romanesque thirteenth- or fourteenth-century **basilica of Áyios Dhimítrios**, Évvia's largest and finest, though unhappily locked. **AVLONÁRI** proper, 2km east, is dominated by a hill that commands most of the island's centre. At its crown is a huge Lombard or Venetian tower, rearing above the Neoclassical and vernacular houses that tier the lower slopes. This is the first place you'd probably choose to break a journey from Halkídha, if you have your own vehicle; there's a single taverna below the *platía*, though no accommodation.

This part of Évvia is particularly well endowed with Byzantine chapels, since Avlonári was an archiepiscopal see from the sixth century onwards. Back on the road to Kími, a left fork just north of Háni Avlonaríou (the bus goes this way) leads past the hamlet of Ayía Thékla, where a small, shed-like **chapel** of that saint, probably slightly later than Áyios Dhimítrios, hides in a lush vale below the modern church. Inside, enough fresco fragments remain with their large-eyed faces to suggest that some fine art has been lost over time. The right fork leads towards the coast and takes you past Oxílithos, with its somewhat more elaborate **chapels of Áyios Nikólaos** and **Ayía Ánna**, both at least a century older than Áyios Dhimítrios.

The road hits the coast at the fine beach of **Stómio** (known also, and confusingly, as Paralía or "Beach"), some 1500m of sand closing off the mouth of a river, which is deep, swimmable and often cleaner than the sea. To the north and east you glimpse the capes enclosing the broad bay of Kími. Up on the road, there are a couple of cafés and a small pension; most facilities, however, are further round the coast at **PLATÁNA**, where another river is flanked by a line of older houses, many with rooms or flats to rent.

Despite its name, the extremely functional port of **PARALÍA KÍMIS** has no real beach, and does not make a particularly congenial place to be stuck overnight waiting for a ferry or hydrofoil to the Sporades or Límnos. The most substantial and traditional **taverna** is *Spanos/Toh Egeo*, at the south end of the front; the two **hotels**, *Coralli* (☎0222/22 212; ④) and *Beis* (☎0222/22 604; ④), will work out more expensive than anything in Platána or Kími proper.

Most travellers get to **KÍMI** (the main ferry port to Skíros) by bus, which takes the inland route via Ayía Thékla. The upper part of town is built on a green ridge overlooking both the sea and Paralía Kími, 4km below. At the bottom of town, on the harbour-bound road, you can visit the **Folklore Museum**, which has an improbably large collection of costumes, household and agricultural implements and old photos recording the doings of Kimians both locally and in the USA, where there's a huge community. Among the emigrants was Dr George Papanikolaou, deviser of the "Pap" cervical smear test, and there's a statue honouring him up in the upper-town *platía*. Nearby are a couple of cheapish **hotels**, the *Kími* (☎0222/22 408; ③) and the *Krineion* (☎0222/22 287; ③), plus some unadvertised **rooms**, and good **tavernas** where you can sample the products of the local vineyards.

To get up into the rugged country west of Kími, you must negotiate jeep tracks through the forest, or return to Halkídha for the bus service up to **STENÍ**, a large and beautiful village at the foot of Mount Dhírfis. The village has a few cheap *psistariés* and two **hotels**, the *Dirfys* (☎0228/51 217; ③) and the *Steni* (☎0228/51 221; ④). It's a good area for hiking, most notably up the peaks of Dhírfis and Ksirovoúni, and beyond to the isolated beach hamlets of Hiliádhou and Ayía Iríni, though you'll need a specialist hiking guide to do this (see "Books" in *Contexts*).

South from Halkídha

The extension of Évvia southeast of Lépoura, usually so narrow that you can sometimes glimpse the sea on both sides simultaneously, has a flavour very distinct from the rest of the island. Often bleak and windwept, it forms a geological unit with neighbouring Ándhros, with shared slates and marble. Ethnically, the south has much in common with that northernmost Cyclade: both were heavily settled by Albanian immigrants from the early fifteenth century onwards, and *Arvanítika* (a medieval dialect of

Albanian) was until recently the first language of the remoter villages here. Even non-*Arvanítika* speakers often betray their ancestry by their startlingly fair colouring and aquiline features. For a place so close to Athens, the south is often surprisingly rural; some of the houses have yet to lose their original slate roofs, and the few fields on the steep slopes are far more often worked by donkeys and horses than by farm machinery.

Immediately southeast of Lépoura, most foreign maps persist in showing the lake of Dhístos in bright blue. In fact, the lake area has been almost totally drained and reclaimed as rich farmland, much to the detriment of the migratory birds who used to stop off here, and to the annoyance of Greek and foreign environmentalists who would prefer that they still did so. Atop the almost perfectly conical hill in the centre of the flat basin are the sparse fifth-century-BC ruins of **ancient Dystos**, and a subsequent medieval citadel.

Beyond the Dhístos plain, the main road continues along the mountainous spine of the island to Káristos at the southern end of the paved road system and bus line. If you have your own transport, it's worth stopping off at **STÍRA**, above which are a cluster of **Dhrakóspita** (Dragon Houses), signposted at the north edge of the village and reached by track, then trail. They are so named after the only semi-mythological beings thought capable of shifting into place their enormous masonry blocks, and the structures' origins and uses have yet to be definitively established. The most convincing theory holds that they are sixth-century-BC temples built by immigrants or slaves from Asia Minor working in the nearby marble and slate quarries.

The shore annexe of **NÉA STÍRA**, 5km downhill from the hill village, is a fairly standard package resort, worth knowing about only for its handy ferry connection to Ayía Marína (which gives access to ancient Rhamnous) on the Attic peninsula. Much the same can be said for **MARMÁRI**, 19km south, except in this case the ferry link is with Rafína.

Káristos and around

At first sight **KÁRISTOS** is a bleak grid, courtesy of nineteenth-century Bavarian town-planners, which ends abruptly to east and west and is studded with modern buildings. Your opinion will improve with prolonged acquaintance, though this is still unlikely to be for more than a few days. What Káristos can offer to a handful of independent travellers is its superb (if often windy) beach of **Psilí Ámmos** to the west, and a lively, genuine working-port atmosphere. Only one plot of fenced in foundations, in the central bazaar, bears out the town' ancient provenance, and the oldest obvious structure is the fourteenth-century Venetian **Bourtzi** (permanently locked) on the waterfront. This small tower is all that remains of once-extensive fortifications. Every evening the shore road is blocked with a gate at this point to permit an undisturbed *vólta* or promenade by the locals.

Practicalities

Rafína-based **ferries** and **hydrofoils** also serve Káristos, docking rather obviously at mid-quay; **buses** arrive inland, above the central *platía* and below the *National Bank*, near a tiny combination grill/ticket office labelled *KTEL*. This has information on the extremely infrequent (once daily at best) departures to the remote villages of the Kavodoro (Kafiréas) cape to the east.

Affordable **accommodation** can prove to be a headache. Very close to the Bourtzi on the shore road, the *Hironia* (☎0224/22 238; ④) is in need of maintenance but undeniably well placed, with quiet rear rooms. The *Als*, just inland at mid-esplanade (☎0224/22 202; ④), will be pretty noisy; perhaps the best strategy is to follow up signs in restaurant windows advertising **rooms** inland.

By contrast, you're spoilt for choice when **eating out**, as Káristos must have more restaurants than the rest of Évvia put together. One of the best choices is the *Kavo Doros*, a friendly and reasonable taverna on Párodos Sachtoúri just behind the front, which serves oven food; another is the cheap, filling and popular lunchtime option, *Ta Kalamia*, at the west end of the esplanade by the start of Psilí Ámmos beach.

Around Káristos

The obvious excursion from Káristos is inland towards **Mount Óhi** (1399m) Évvia's highest peak after Dhírfis and Ksirovoúni. **MÍLI**, a fair-sized village around a spring-fed oasis, 3km straight inland, makes a good first stop, with its few tavernas. Otherwise, the medieval castle of **Castel Rosso** beckons above, a 20-minute climb up from the main church (longer in the frequent, howling gales). Inside the castle is a total ruin, except for an Orthodox **chapel of Profítis Ilías** built over the Venetians' water cistern, but the sweeping views over the sea and the town make the trip worthwhile.

Behind, the ridges of Óhi are as lunar and inhospitable as the broad plain around Káristos is fertile. From Míli, it's a three-hour-plus hike up the largely bare slopes, mostly by a path cutting across the new road, past a little-used alpine-club shelter (fed by spring water) to the summit and yet another *dhrakóspito*, even more impressive than the three smaller ones at Stíra. Built of enormous schist slabs, seemingly sprouting from the mountain, this one is popularly supposed to be haunted.

North from Halkídha

The main road due north from Halkídha crosses a few kilometres of flat farmland and salt marsh on either side of ugly Néa Artáki, after which it climbs steeply through forested hills and the **Dhervéni gorge**, gateway to the north of Évvia.

The village of **PROKÓPI** lies beyond the narrows, in a valley defined by the rich and beautiful woods that make it famous. A counterpoint, in the village itself, is the eyesore pilgrimage church of **Saint John the Russian**, which holds the saint's relics. The "Russian" was actually a Ukranian soldier, captured by the Turks in the early eighteenth century and taken to Turkey where he died. According to locals, his mummified body began to sponsor miracles, and the saint's relics were brought here by Orthodox Turks from Cappadocian Prokópi (today Ürgüp) in the 1923 population exchange – Evvian Prokópi is still occasionally referred to by its old name of Ahmetága.

Following a shady, stream-fed glen for the 8km north of Prokópi, you suddenly emerge at Mandoúdhi, much the biggest village in the north of the island, though now squarely in the doldrums following the collapse of the local magnesite industry; ignore signs or depictions on certain maps of a beach at Paralía Mandoúdhi, which is nothing more than abandoned quarries and crushing plants. The closest serviceable beach is at **Paralía Kírinthos**, better known as **Kría Vrissí** (take a right-hand turning off the main road, 3km beyond Mandoúdhi). At the coast, two rivers – one salt-water, one fresh – bracket a small beach, with the headland south of the sweet river supporting the extremely sparse remains of **ancient Kirinthos**. The hamlet of Kirinthos, just inland, is edged by cornfields and consists merely of a cluster of summer houses, with one sporadically functioning taverna and no short-term accommodation.

Back on the main road, a fork at Strofiliá, 8km north of Mandoúdhi, offers a choice of routes: continue north to the coastal resorts that curl round the end of the island (see below), or head west for Límni.

Límni

If you're hunting for a place to stay, **LÍMNI**, on the west coast 19km from Strofiliá, is by far the most practical and attractive base north of Halkídha. The largely Neoclassical, tile-roofed town, built from the wealth engendered by nineteenth-century shipping prowess, is the most appealing on the island, with serviceable beaches and a famous convent nearby.

There is a regular **hydrofoil** service to Halkídha and the Sporades, and buses from Halkídha stop at the north side of the quay. Límni has an **OTE**, a **post office** and two **banks**, all inland just off the main through-road into town from Strofiliá.

As yet, Límni gets few package tours, and vacancies at the two **hotels** are usually available except during August. At the extreme south end of the waterfront, and thus quieter, the *Limni* (☎0227/31 316; ③) is good value, with singles and doubles; the *Plaza* beside the bus stop, (☎0227/31 235; ②), is even more reasonable, but has no singles and gets some noise from nocturnal revels outside. The *Pirofanis* (☎0227/31 640; ③), an *ouzerí* beyond the *Plaza,* rents some **rooms** upstairs and apartments north of town. The best **place to eat** in terms of setting, menu and popularity is *O Platanos* (under the enormous quayside plane tree). *Toh Astron*, 3km south of town on the coast road past the *Limni*, is a well-regarded taverna, specializing in meat dishes.

Around Límni

The outstanding excursion from Límni is 7km south (under your own steam) to the **convent of Ayíou Nikoláou Galatáki**, superbly set on the wooded slopes of Mount Kandhíli, overlooking the north Evvian Gulf. To get there, veer up and left at the unsigned fork off the coast road; there's no formal scheme for visiting, but don't bother showing up between 3pm and 5pm when all of Greece – secular and monastic – sleeps. Though much rebuilt since its original Byzantine foundation atop a Poseidon temple, the convent retains a thirteenth century tower built to guard against pirates. One of a dozen or so shy but friendly nuns will show you frescoes in the *katholikón* dating from the principal sixteenth-century renovation. Especially vivid, on the right of the narthex, is the *Entry of the Righteous into Paradise*; they ascend a perilous ladder, being crowned by angels and received by Christ – the wicked miss the rungs and fall directly into the maw of Leviathian.

Below Ayíou Nikoláou Galatáki, and easily combined with it to make a full half-day outing, are the pebble-and-sand **beaches of Glífa**, arguably the best on Évvia's south-west-facing coast. There are several in succession, leading up to the very base of Mount Kandhíli, with path-only access to the last few. The shore is remarkably clean, considering the number of summer campers who pitch tents here for weeks on end; a single roadside spring, 2km before, is the only facility in the whole zone.

There are no recommendable beaches in Límni itself, though if you continue 2500m northwest from the town you reach the gravel strand of **Kohíli**, with a basic but leafy **campsite** out on the cape, 500m beyond mid-beach.

ROVVIÉS, some 10km further in the same direction, doesn't stand out, but with its medieval tower, grid of weekenders' apartments and services is the last place of any sort before Loutrá Edhipsoú.

Northern coastal resorts

Returning to the junction at Strofiliá, take the main road north for 8km to **AYÍA ÁNNA** (locally and universally elided to Ayiánna), which has long enjoyed the unofficial status of Évvia's most folkloric village by virtue of some lingering traditional costumes on the older women, and an assiduous local ethnographer, Dimitris Settas, who died in 1989. The place itself is nothing extrordinary, and most passers-by are interested in the prominently marked turnoff for **Angáli beach**, 5km east. This is billed as the area's best, and it's sandy enough, but like this entire coast it's exposed and garbage-strewn, the low hills behind lending little drama. A frontage road, set back 200m or so, is lined by a few kilometres of anonymous villas and apartments, with the "village" at the north end.

Ten kilometres beyond Ayía Ánna, a side road heads downhill for 6km, past the village of Kotsikiá, to **Paralía Kotsikiás**. The small cove with its taverna and rooms serves primarily as a fishing-boat anchorage, and its tiny, seaweed-strewn beach will interest few. **Psaropoúli beach**, 2km below Vassiliká village (13km north of the Kotsikiá turnoff), is more usable in its three-kilometre length, but like Ayía Ánna it seems flotsam-scruffy and shadeless, with a smattering of rooms, self-catering units and tavernas not imparting much sense of community. **Elliniká**, the next signposted beach, lies only 800m below its namesake village inland; it's far smaller than Angáli or Psaropoúli, but cleaner and certainly the most picturesque spot on this coast, with a church-capped islet offshore as a target to swim to. The approach driveway has a very limited number of facilities comprising a minimarket, one taverna and a few studios.

Beyond Elliniká the road (and bus line) skirts the northern tip of Évvia to curl southwest towards **PÉFKI**, a seaside resort, mobbed with Greeks in summer, which straggles for some two kilometres along a mediocre beach. The best **restaurants**, near the north end of this strip, include *Ouzeri Ta Thalassina* and *Psitopolio O Thomas*, while *Zaharoplastio O Peristeras* proffers every decadent sweet known to Greek man. **Accommodation** is the usual Évvian mix of self-catering units and a few fancy hotels, all resolutely pitched at mainlanders; the **campsite**, *Camping Pefki*, is 2km north of town behind the beach, rather pricey and of most interest to those in caravans.

The next resort (14km southwest), **OREÍ**, is so poorly signposted from the bypass road that one suspects that they don't especially want any casual trade. A detour yields a grid-planned, not especially attractive place, with only its role as the last **hydrofoil stop** en route to Vólos and the Sporades to recommend it. Some 7km further along the coast, **AYIÓKAMBOS** has a frequent ferry connection to Glífa on the mainland opposite, whence there are buses to Vólos. Ayiókambos itself proves suprisingly pleasant considering its port function, with a patch of beach, two or three tavernas and a few rooms for rent.

The trans-island bus route ends 14km south of Ayiókambos at **LOUTRÁ EDHIPSOÚ**, which attracts older Greeks (filling more than a hundred creaky hotels and pensions) who come to bathe at the **spas** renowned since antiquity for curing everything from gallstones to depression. There are less regimented **hot springs** at Yiáltra, 15km west around the head of Edhipsós bay, where the water boils up on the rocky beach, warming the shallows to comfortable bath temperature. From Loutrá Edhipsoú, the coast road heads southeast to Límni, permitting a loop of northern Évvia while based there.

travel details

Alkyon Tours (in cooperation with Nomicos ferry lines), and the competing Goutos Lines, provide expensive **conventional ferry** services out of Vólos, Áyios Konstandínos and Kími, with fares almost double those on Cyclades or Dodecanese lines. On the plus side, Alkyon maintain an Athens office (Akadhimías 97) for purchase of ferry, Flying Icarus and combined bus-and-ferry tickets.

Between April and October, Flying Dolphin and Flying Icarus **hydrofoils** operate between various mainland ports and the Sporades. These are pricier than the ferries but cut journey times virtually in half.

SKÍATHOS, SKÓPELOS AND ALÓNISSOS

Ferries

Áyios Konstandínos: to Skíathos (9 weekly; 3hr); Skópelos (7 weekly; 5hr, 3 continuing to Alónissos, 6hr).

Kími: to Alónissos (4 weekly; 3hr) and Skópelos (4 weekly; 3hr 30min), 2 continuing to Skíathos (5hr 30min).

Vólos: to Skíathos (3–4 daily; 3hr) and Skópelos (3–4 daily; 4hr); Alónissos (at least daily; 5hr; this is the most consistent service out of season, and is always the cheapest).

Ceres *Flying Dolphins* (April–Oct only)

Áyios Konstandínos: to Skíathos, Glóssa, Skópelos and Alónissos (April, May & early Oct 1–3 daily; June–Sept 3–5 daily).

Néos Marmarás (Halkidhikí): to Skíathos, Skópelos, Alónissos and Skíros (June–Aug daily).

Plataniás (Pílion): to Skíathos, Skópelos and Alónissos (June–Aug 2 daily).

Thessaloníki: to Skíathos, Glóssa, Skópelos and Alónissos (June–Aug daily).

Tríkeri (Pílion): to Vólos (June–mid-Oct daily); Skíathos (June–mid-Sept 2 daily); Skíathos, Skópelos and Alónissos (April–Oct daily).

Vólos: to Skíathos, Glóssa and Skópelos (April, May & Oct 2 daily; June–Sept 4 daily); at least 2 daily (April–Oct) continue from Skópelos to Alónissos.

Flights

Athens: to Skíathos (3 daily; 40min).

SKÍROS
Ferries

Skíros is served by conventional ferry, the *Lykomides*, from **Kími** ((2hr 20min). Services are at least twice daily mid-June to mid-Sept (usually at around noon & 5pm), once daily (5pm) the rest of the year; ☎0222/22 020 for current information. There is a connecting bus service for the afternoon boat, from the Liossíon 260 terminal in Athens (departs 12.30pm).

Flying Dolphins

A daily **hydrofoil** (June–Aug) links Skíros with Skíathos, Skópelos and Alónissos, as well as Néos Marmarás on Halkidhikí.

Flights

Athens: to Skíros (June–Oct; 5 weekly; Nov–May 2 weekly).

ÉVVIA
Buses

Athens (Liossíon 260 terminal): to Halkídha (every 30min 7.15am–9pm; 1hr 40min); Kími (4–5 daily; 3hr 40min).

Halkídha to: Káristos (1–2 daily; 3hr); Límni (4 daily; 1hr 30min); Loutrá Edhipsoú (4 daily; 3hr); Kími (4 daily; 1 hr 45 min)

Trains

Athens (Laríssis station): to Halkídha (18 daily; 1hr 25min).

Ferries

Arkítsa: to Loutrá Edhipsoú (12 daily 6.45am–11pm; 50min).

Ayía Marína: to Néa Stíra (summer 12–20 daily; 50min); Panayía (summer 3–4 daily; 50min).

Glífa: to Ayiókambos (8 daily; 30min).

Rafína: to Káristos (Mon–Thurs & Sat 3 daily, Fri & Sun 4 daily; 2hr); Marmári (2 daily; 1hr).

Skála Oropoú: to Erétria (hourly 5am–10pm; 25min).

Ceres *Flying Dolphins*

Halkídha: to Límni, Loutrá Edhipsoú, Oreí, Skíathos and Skópelos (May to mid-Oct 5 weekly; usually late afternoon).

Oreí: to Vólos, Skópelos and Alónissos (June to mid-Sept daily); Skíathos (June to mid-Oct 2 daily).

Ilio Line Hydrofoils

Rafína: to Káristos (mid-June to late Sept 4 weekly).

Tínos/Míkonos (Cyclades): to Káristos (mid-June to late Sept 3 weekly).

*Connecting buses **from Athens** run to Rafína (every 30min; 1hr 30min), Ayía Marína (5 daily; 1hr 15min) and Skála Oropoú (hourly; duration) all from the Mavromatéon terminal, and to Arkítsa and Glífa from the Liossíon 260 terminal.*

CHAPTER TWELVE

THE IONIAN

The six **Ionian** islands, shepherding their satellites down the west coast of the mainland, float on the haze of the Adriatic, their green, even lush, silhouettes coming as a shock to those more used to the stark outlines of the Aegean. The fertility is a direct result of the heavy rains which sweep over the archipelago – and especially Corfu – from October to March, so if you visit in the off-season, come prepared.

The islands were the Homeric realm of Odysseus, centred on Ithaca (modern Itháki) and here alone of all modern Greek territory the Ottomans never held sway. After the fall of Byzantium, possession passed to the **Venetians** and the islands became a keystone in that city state's maritime empire from 1386 until its collapse in 1797. Most of the population must have remained immune to the establishment of Italian as the official language and the arrival of Roman Catholicism, but Venetian influence remains evident in the architecture of the island capitals, despite damage from a series of earthquakes.

On Corfu, the Venetian legacy is mixed with that of the **British**, who imposed a military "protectorate" over the Ionian at the close of the Napoleonic Wars, before ceding the archipelago to Greece in 1864. There is, however, no question of the islanders' essential Greekness: the poet Dionissios Solomos, author of the National Anthem, hailed from the Ionians, as did Nikos Mantzelos, who provided the music, and the first Greek president, Ioannis Kapodistrias.

Today, **tourism** is the dominating influence, especially on **Corfu** (Kérkira), which was one of the first Greek islands established on the package-holiday circuit. Its east coast is one of the few stretches in Greece with development to match the Spanish *costas*, and in summer even its distinguished old capital, Kérkira Town, wilts beneath the onslaught. However, the island is large enough to retain some of its charms and is perhaps the most scenically beautiful of the group. Parts of **Zákinthos** (Zante) – which with Corfu has the Ionians' best beaches – seem to be going along the same tourist path, following the introduction of charter flights from northern Europe, but elsewhere the pace and scale of development is a lot less intense. Little **Páxi** is a bit too tricky to reach and lacks the water to support a large-scale hotel, while **Lefkádha** – which is connected to the mainland by a causeway and "boat bridge" – has, so far at least, a quite low-key straggle of resorts. Perhaps the most rewarding duo for island-hopping are **Kefalloniá** and **Itháki**, the former with a series of "real towns" and a life in large part independent of tourism, the latter, Odysseus's rugged capital, protected by an absence of sand. The Ionian islands' claims to Homeric significance are manifested in the countless bars, restaurants and streets named after characters in the Odyssey including the "nimble-witted" hero himself, Penelope, Navsicaa, Calypso and Cyclops.

Corfu (Kérkira)

The seductive beauty of **Corfu** (Kérkira in Greek) has been a source of inspiration for generations. It is thought that Shakespeare took tales of the island as his setting for *The Tempest*; Lawrence Durrell echoed this tribute by naming his book about the island *Prospero's Cell*; and Edward Lear enthused that it made him "grow younger every hour". Henry Miller, totally in his element, became euphoric, lying for hours in

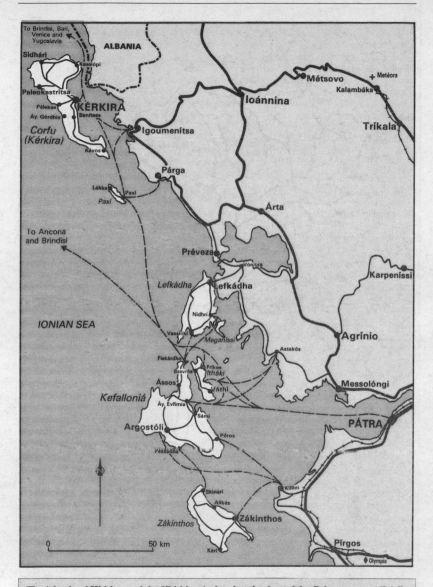

The islands of **Kíthira** and **Andíkithira**, isolated at the foot of the Peloponnese, officially belong to the Ionian group. However, as they have no ferry connections with other Ionian islands, and are most easily reached from Yíthio or Neápoli, they are covered in the **Peloponnese** chapter.

Likewise, the islet of **Kálamos**, the most distant of Lefkádha's "satellites" is covered in the **Thessaly and Central Greece** chapter, as it is reached only from the port of Mitíkas.

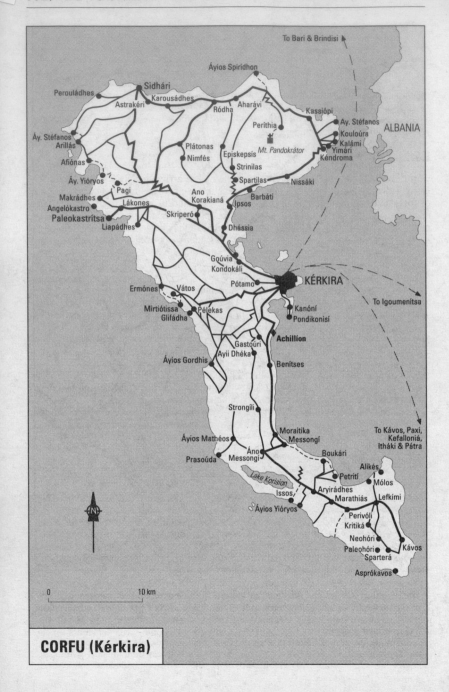

To Bari & Brindisi

Áyios Spiridhon

Perouládhes
Sidhári
Karousádhes
Astrakéri
Ródha
Aharávi
Kassiópi

Áy. Stéfanos
Arillás
Perithia
Áy. Stéfanos
Kouloúra
Kalámi
Yimári
Kéndroma

Plátonas
Episkepsis
Mt. Pandokrátor

Afiónas
Nimfés

Áy. Yióryos
Strinilas
Spartilas
Nissáki

Makrádhes
Pagi
Ano
Korakianá
Barbáti
Ipsos

Angelókastro
Lákones
Skriperó
Paleokastrítsa
Liapádhes
Dhássia

ALBANIA

Goúvia
Kondokáli

Ermónes
Vátos
Pótamo
KÉRKIRA

Mirtiótissa
Glifádha
Pélekas
Kanóni
Pondikonísi

To Igoumenítsa

Gastoúri
Achíllion
Áyios Gordhis
Ayii Dhéka
Benítses

Strongíli

Moraítika
Messongí
Áyios Mathéos
Áno
Messongí
Boukári

Prasoúda
Alikés
Petrití
Mólos

Lake Korision
Issos
Aryirádhes
Lefkími
Marathiás

Áyios Yióryos
Perivóli
Kritiká

Neohóri
Paleohóri
Kávos
Sparterá

Asprókavos

To Kávos, Paxí,
Kefalloniá,
Itháki & Pátra

N

0   10 km

CORFU (Kérkira)

the sun "doing nothing, thinking of nothing". Some claim Corfu to be Homer's kingdom of Phaeacia where Odysseus was washed ashore and met the beautiful Nausicaa.

With a reputation as the "greenest Greek island", its natural appeal, the shapes and scents of its lemon and orange trees, its figs, cypresses and, above all, its three million olive trees, all remain an experience – if sometimes a beleaguered one, for Corfu has more package hotels and holiday villas than any other Greek island. Yet for all the commercialism – and the wholesale spoiling of its northeast coast – it remains an island where you can still leave the crowds behind, and where almost everyone seems to end up having a good time.

Kérkira Town

Corfu's scale of tourism is apparent the moment you arrive in **KÉRKIRA TOWN** (or Corfu Town). It is a graceful, elegant town – almost a city – sandwiched between a pair of **forts** and with a gorgeous esplanade, the **Spianádha**, where the Corfiotes play cricket most Sundays – one of the town's more obvious British legacies. The town even reminded Evelyn Waugh of Brighton, as he noted in his diary. However, the crowds in summer are overpowering and in season, at least, you'll probably find a night or two here at the beginning or end of your stay is time enough.

Arrival, information and services

Ferries from Italy dock at the New Port to the west of the Néo Froúrio (New Fort); those to and from the mainland (Igoumenitsa, Párga, etc) arriving slightly further west. The Paleó Froúrio (Old Fort) dock is now only used for excursions and by some ferries to Paxos. If in doubt, check with the ticket agent or the **port police** (☎0661/32 655). Coming from the **airport**, 2km south of the centre, you can walk (about 40min), get a taxi (1200dr, but agree the fare in advance; ☎0661/33 811 for radio taxis), or catch local bus #5 or #6 blue bus, which leave from 500m north of the terminal gates.

The **tourist office** is 800m east of the New Port, at Zavitsianou 17 (☎0661/37 520). Here you can pick up free maps of the town and island, bus timetables, a list of hotels and campsites and information on rooms for rent (see below).

The *Corfu News* (published by and available from the tourist office) is useful for details of **services** (launderettes, doctors and dentists, etc); branches of most of the major **banks** are dotted throughout the town. *Greek Skies Travel* (☎0661/30 883) are the agents for *American Express* at Kapodhistríou 20. The central **post office** is at Alexandros 19; while OTE is at Montzarou 9 (daily 6am–midnight).

Transport

All the island's **buses** start and finish in town. There are two terminals: one on Platía San Rócco for numbered **blue bus** routes to the suburbs and across the island; the other at 9 Paradhos, I Theotóki, second left up this street from the New Port, for **green buses** to more remote destinations. For schedules, consult the tourist office or check the terminal boards. If you are heading for Athens, you can buy combination bus and ferry tickets for the trip (at least daily in season) from the KTEL bus terminal just off I Theotóki.

Mopeds, bicycles and cars are available for rent in the town, with most of the agencies found around the Old and New Ports and along Xenofondos Stratigou. Try *Top Cars* (☎0661/35 237) for reasonable rates. Motorbikes are more reliable than mopeds and less likely to have been pushed beyond their capacity but only take them if you're an experienced rider. An incredible number of people have accidents on the gravelly, potholed tracks. Note that almost all of the garages on the island are closed on Sundays.

In season there are also a few excursion **kaíkia** boats to certain beaches on the southern coast of the island – providing easier and more pleasant access than the buses.

Accommodation

There are usually **accommodation** touts meeting the boats – and taxi drivers, too, will often know of places to stay. Alternatively, pick up a list of rooms from the tourist office (see above), which can point you in the right direction; rooms are mainly located near the New Port.

Things fill so quickly in high season, that it's barely worth offering recommendations. If space is available, the best option by far is the *Hotel Kypros*, Áyion Patéron 13 (☎0661/40 675; ③). If you strike out here, other **hotels** worth phoning ahead for include: *Pension Anthis*, Kefalomandoúkou (☎0661/25 804; ④); *Hotel Arcadian*, Kapodistríou 44 (☎0661/37670; ④); *Hotel Bretagne*, Georgáki 27 (☎0661/31 129; ⑤); *Hotel Dalia*, 7 Ethnikou Stadiou (☎0661/36 048; ⑤); *Hotel Europa*, Yitsiali 10, New Port (☎0661/39 304; ③); *Hotel Hermes*, Markóra 14 (☎0661/39 268; ④); *Hotel Ionian*, 46 Xen. Stratigou (☎0661/39915; ④); and *Hotel Phoenix*, H. Smírnis 2 (☎0661/42 290; ④).

At Kondokáli village, 4.5km north of town, there is a **youth hostel** (☎0661/9 1292) and **campsite** (☎0661/91 202), neither in an ideal location for the town but certainly inexpensive enough.

ROOM PRICE SCALES

All establishments in this book have been price-graded according to the scale outlined below. The rates quoted represent the cheapest available room in high season; all are prices for a double room, except for category ①, which are per person rates. Out of season, rates can drop by up to fifty percent, especially if you negotiate rates for a stay of three or more nights. Single rooms, where available, cost around seventy percent of the price of a double.

Rented private rooms on the islands usually fall into the ② or ③ categories, depending on their location and facilities, and the season; a few in the ④ category are more like plush self-catering apartments. They are not generally available from late October through the beginning of April, when only hotels tend to remain open.

① 1400–2000dr (£4–5.50/US$6–8.50)   ④ 8000–12000dr (£22–33/US$33–50)
②4000–6000dr(£11–16.50/US$17–25)   ⑤ 12000–16000dr (£33–44/US$50–66)
③6000–8000dr(£16.50–22/US$25–33)   ⑥ 16000dr (£44/US$66) and upwards
For more accommodation details, see pp.34–35.

The Town

A stroll around the old parts of town offers a fascinating blend of Venetian, French, British and occasional Greek architecture. The most obvious sights are the forts, the **Paleó Froúrio** and **Néo Froúrio**, whose designations (*paleó* – "old", *néo* – "new") are a little misleading since what you see of the older structure was begun by the Byzantines in the mid-twelfth century, a mere hundred years before the Venetians began work on the newer citadel. They have both been modified and damaged by various occupiers and besiegers since, the last contribution being the Neoclassical shrine of **St George**, built by the British in the middle of Paleó Froúrio during the 1840s. The Paleó Froúrio is open daily from 8am to 7pm (free) and hosts a sound-and-light show most evenings; the Néo Froúrio is home to the Greek navy and off-limits to the public.

The **Spianádha** (Esplanade) has a leisured and graceful air, and many are ensnared by one of the cafés facing the **Listón**, an arcaded legacy of the brief French occupation, built by the architect of the Rue de Rivoli in Paris. If paying high prices for your *tsíntsi* *bírra* (ginger beer – another British influence) puts you off, stroll along the far side of the promenade close to the fort, where in the splendid flower gardens you can join groups of women chatting and lace-making in the evening sun.

Fronting the north end of the Spianádha is the **Palace of St Michael and St George** (Tues–Sat 8.30am–3pm, Sun 9.30am–2.30pm; 500dr, students 200dr), a solidly British edifice built as the residence of their High Commissioner, one of the last of whom was the future Prime Minister William Gladstone, and later used as a palace by the Greek monarchy. Its former staterooms house a large collection of Asiatic art, together with Byzantine relics from the island. Outside is a row of Doric columns book-

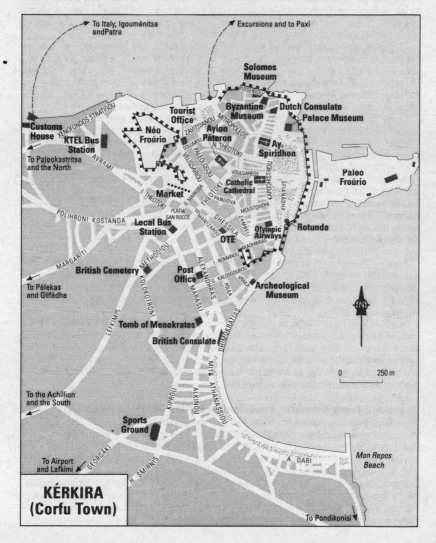

KÉRKIRA (Corfu Town)

ended by monumental arches, with reliefs of the Ionian islands and Odysseus's rudderless ship. Through the archway is the loggia of the *Corfu Reading Society*, which has exhibitions of manuscripts, maps and art (daily 9am–1pm, plus 5–8pm Thurs & Fri), and close by is a Venetian landing stage and city gate, framing the Vido islet.

Towards the south of the Spianádha is the **Maitland Rotunda**, a graffiti-covered bandstand commemorating the first British High Commissioner, and, just beyond it a **statue of Ioannis Kapodistrias** (1776–1831), first president of modern Greece and an agitator for the union of Greece with the Ionian islands. Following the coast south, turn right on Vrála St just after the *Corfu Palace Hotel* and you come to the **Archeological Museum** (Tues–Sun 9am–3pm; 400dr, students 200dr, free Sun), which houses a modest collection whose prize exhibit is a 2500-year-old gorgon's-head pediment. Keep heading south from here and you reach **Mon Repos**, the town's public beach, a sand and shingle strip with a little jetty and a snack bar.

The most atmospheric part of town is the area known as **Campiello** – a maze of Venetian-era alleyways between the Palace of St Michael and St George and the old port. At the edge of the quarter, on the waterfront at Arseníou 41, is the **Solomos Museum** (Mon–Fri 5–8pm), former home of the Greek national poet and housing his archives and memorabilia. Nearby is the sixteenth-century Antivouniótissa church, which houses a little **Byzantine Museum** (Tues–Sun 9am–3pm) of icons.

To the southwest of the quarter is Corfu's **Cathedral**, packed with icons, including a fine sixteenth-century painting of *St George Slaying The Dragon* by the Cretan artist Michael Damaskinos. The building shares religious precedence with the church of **Áyios Spirídhon**, a few blocks to the east on Vouthrótou, where you will find the silver-encrusted coffin of the island's patron saint, Spirídhon – Spiros in the diminutive – after whom about half the male population is named. Four times a year (Palm Sunday and the following Saturday; August 11; and first Sunday in November), to the accompaniment of much celebration and feasting, the relics are paraded through the streets of Kérkira. Each of the days commemorates a miraculous deliverance of the island credited to the saint – twice from plague during the seventeenth century, from a famine of the sixteenth century and (a more blessed release than either of those for any Greek) from the Turks in the eighteenth century.

Another twisted grid of streets, south from the cathedral and backing onto the new fort, was the town's **Jewish quarter**, home to a community of some five thousand from the sixteenth century until 1940, when they were rounded up by the Germans and sent off to the death camp at Auschwitz. A **synagogue** survives on Velissáriou, at the southern edge of the ghetto.

South of Platía San Rócco, at the start of Kolokotroni, is the **British Cemetery**. It's a tranquil place and a botanist's heaven, well known for its numerous species of orchids which flower in April and May. The graves and gardens are lovingly tended to by George Psáilascoho who has lived and worked here for over fifty years. He will show you the memorial to the 44 British soldiers who died in 1946 when an Albanian mine destroyed their ship in the Corfu channel.

Near Corfu Town: Vlahérna, Pondikoníssi and the Achillion Palace

The most popular excursion from Corfu Town is to the islets of Vlahérna and Pondikoníssi, just offshore from the plush suburb of **Kanóni**, 4km south of town (take blue bus #2 from end of G.Theotóki, next to Platía San Rócco, every 30min). The closer is **Vlahérna**, capped by a small monastery and joined to the mainland by a short causeway. Just beyond, a boat trip, swim or pedalo-push will bring you to **Pondikoníssi** (Mouse Island). Tufted with greenery and a small chapel, this is legendarily identified with a ship from Odysseus's fleet, petrified by Poseidon in revenge for the blinding of his son Polyphemus. The Homeric echoes are somewhat marred by the thronging masses and low flying aircraft from the nearby runway.

Three kilometres further to the south, past the resort sprawl of Peramá, is a rather more bizarre attraction: the **Achillion**, a palace built in a (fortunately) unique blend of Teutonic and Neoclassical styles in 1890 by Elizabeth, Empress of Austria. Henry Miller considered it "the worst piece of gimcrackery" that he'd ever laid eyes on and thought it "would make an excellent museum for surrealistic art". It is today a casino by night, though you can just visit the gardens in the daytime. If you are driving, you might combine a visit with a **meal** at the *Taverna Tripas* – one of the island's most imaginative, and not overpriced for the quality of its food– at the village of Kinopiástes, 3km inland.

Eating and drinking

Eating out, you need to pick your way through the tourist joints if you want to find anywhere vaguely Greek in style and price; for picnics, the best place is the produce **market** on G.Markóra.

Good **restaurant** choices include the *Averof*, at the Old Port, for traditional Greek dishes – it's a bit pricey but the food is well-prepared and presented. For a fine open-air setting next to Old Port, try the *Restaurant Skouna*, on Plateía Mitropóleos. *Yisdhakis*, Solomoú 20, off N. Theotóki, is as authentic as they come; while *Naftikon*, N.Theotóki 150, is unpretentious, with typical Greek and Corfu specialities. There's excellent seafood at *Orestes*, Stratigoú 78, by the New Port; and consider *Psistaria Ninos*, Sevastianoú 44, just off Kapodhistríou, a pleasant backstreet restaurant, or *Psistaria Poulis*, Arvanitáki 11, off G.Theotóki, for those of carnivorous taste.

For **drinks** and snacks, Platia San Rocco retains a local flavour – the *Café Espresso* here is good. *Café Plakádha*, in Platia Ayíou Spiridhóna, is enclosed by elegant architecture; while *The Cubby Hole*, Cotardou 42, just off N. Theotóki, is a cosy, friendly bar.

Nightlife and entertainment

Corfu Town has no shortage of **bars and clubs**, and during the summer there's a fair number of **open-air concerts** and **cultural events**. Indeed brass bands can sometimes be heard practising around the old town. For details of events, check the *Corfu News*, or tune into *Radio Rama* (96.3 FM; Mon–Sat 3–5pm), with news and chat in Greek and English and spirited DJ-ing. Best of the town's **cinemas** – all of which show undubbed English/American films – is the one on G. Theotóki.

The most popular **clubs** are to the west of the New Port. *Coco Flash* and *Apokalypsis* are two of the best, the latter with wildly over-the-top decor of pyramids and Olympic torches. The *Hippodrome* has a pool and giant video screen but a reputation for attracting *kamákia* (lecherous locals on the hunt for women tourists).

The northeast coast

The coastline **north of Kérkira** has been remorselessly developed and the initial stretches are probably best written off. The concentration of hotels, villas and campsites give little sense of being in Greece, the beaches vary between pebbly and rocky and are often sullied with rubbish washed up from the mainland, and the sea looks murky and polluted, too. Things improve considerably, however, as you progress north and especially once you round the coast beyond Kassiópi.

Kérkira Town to Píryi

The first resort past Kérkira's suburbs is **KONDOKÁLI**, where the island's youth hostel and the town's nearest campsite are located (see "Accommodation", p.684). Their siting is uninspired, to say the least– a built-up area, with the stench of a sewage plant blowing in on the wind. Tourists are shuttled through en route to the **Danilia Village** (daily 9am–1pm & 6pm–dawn), five minutes up the main road, a slick operation supposed to look like nineteenth-century Corfu, with workshops and museum, and evening entertainment.

Next stop around the bay is GOÚVIA, off the main road but on the routes of most green buses (plus blue bus *Dhassia #7*) and with lots of rooms for rent. The resort hugs the edge of the huge bay, once used by the French fleet to hide from Nelson, though the downflow from Kondokáli means that the sea here is absolutely filthy. Still, it's a friendly place and has an attractively low-key nightlife compared with the next resorts along the coast.

Continuing north, it's best to bypass **Cape Komméno**, which looks lovely from the distance, with thick foliage on the promontory, but up close turns out to be just a trio of dirty beaches, fronted by *Dionysos Camping* and a cluster of large hotels. There are more campsites at the next resort, **DHÁSSIA**, a touristic sprawl with little to recommend it. For a bit more life, you'd do better at **ÍPSOS**, every inch the package resort, with an esplanade, fish and chips, water-slides, and bars named *Irish Shamrock*, *Wurzeis* and *Pig and Whistle*. There are quite a few **rooms** for rent and two **campsites**; *Corfu Camping* (☎0661/93 246) and *Ipsos Ideal* (☎0661/93 583). To swim, wander over to **PÍRYI**, a village which has more or less merged with Ípsos, fronted by a better and sandy beach. From Píryi, too, a road trails up Mount Pandokrátor (see below).

North to Áyios Stéfanos
North of Píryi, a rather different island emerges, as you move from hotel to villa country. The resorts are smaller, and the sea is cleaner, too – indeed, away from the main road, there's still a hint of the Corfu of Gerald Durrell's books, some of which were set on this coast.

BARBÁTI is the first place of note – a former fishing hamlet, surrounded by hills and woods, and still identifiably Greek, despite a sizeable hotel and taxi-boats to and from Ípsos. The few rooms for rent here are mainly located in the new hamlet area, a hundred steep metres above the sea. A kilometre to the north is **Glífa**, a pebble beach with a taverna.

The next focal point is **NISSÁKI**, a rather spread-out village with a number of coves, the first and last accessible by road, the rest only by track. There's a vast hotel, a *Club Med* complex and a tiny, stony beach, plus good watersports. Rooms in summer are like gold dust, but if you can find a bed, it's a good base. If you're prepared to walk, you can pick your way along the coast to find a number of quiet bays. **Kéndroma**, a kilometre out, has a few rooms for rent. Beyond here, there are more rooms at the villages of **YIMÁRI** – though this has poor swimming and a pebble beach – and **KAMINÁKI**, where there's a limestone cave full of bats.

KALÁMI, set on a curved bay, was the site of Lawrence Durrell's *Prospero's Cell* – which he wrote at the *White House*, where there is now an excellent taverna. A once-pretty hamlet, it's being developed fast, with a rash of garish, pink villas stamping out the charm of the grand old houses. There are a number of expensive rooms – including, if you're organised and reasonably affluent, the *White House* itself (bookable by the week through *CV Travel* in London, ☎0171/581 0851).

There are more little coves around the headland between Kalámi and **KOULOÚRA**, a tiny harbour that has retained its charm, set beside a deep, U-shaped bay enclosed by tall cypresses, palm and eucalyptus trees. It's postcard-pretty and has a small, shingle beach, a lovely taverna, but no rooms for rent. Another good taverna, *Nikos's*, is to be found at the tiny nearby hamlet of Agnistíni, and there are lovely beaches down some of the tracks around; **Kerásia**, down a very grotty track, is a large shady cove with a beach café.

The deep bay of **ÁYIOS STÉFANOS** looks better from the distance. It's a pretty cove with clear water but flanked by a well-heeled resort, marred by some insensitive hotels.

Since 1991, and the collapse of Communist rule in Albania, it has been possible to take day trips from Corfu to the Albanian coast – little more than a nautical mile from northern Corfu. These can be arranged at the resorts of Áyios Stéfanos, Kalámi and Kassiópi and involve a bus transfer to Corfu Town where it is necessary to clear customs. Based next to the New Port the main operators are *Petrakis Shipping Company*, Elefthériou Venizélou 9 (☎0661/31 649). The boats dock at the Albanian seaside town of Sarandë, a predominantly Greek-speaking settlement. The trip costs around 7000dr, plus US$30 which covers the entry permit to Albania and port taxes. The excursion includes a visit to the Roman archeological site at Vouthrota. *Petrakis* may also be running longer tours, depending on Albanian political conditions – which at present are extremely volatile.

Kassiópi and around the coast to Ródha

Set in a sheltered bay, **KASSIÓPI** has a resort history dating back to Tiberius, who had a villa here. Recently it has become very developed and anglicised, but retains pockets of old village life and has an ancient plane tree dominating its main square. Accommodation is often block-booked, but there are a few rooms for rent and some excellent **restaurants** – try the *Kassiopi Star* or the harbourside *Three Brothers*. Nightlife includes some decent **bars**; the *Wave Bar* is by a small jetty and *Bar Tropicana* has pop quizzes and bingo. There are also two **discos**, *Unicorn* and *Axis*, and, fifteen minutes' walk out of town, a *bouzoukia* joint, the *Kan Kan*.

People bathe from the promontory below Kassiópi's fortress, around the promontory to the west, but all the beaches are out of town. The closest, around ten minutes' walk, is known as **Imerólia**; beyond it is **Avlídhi**, stony, more secluded and reached from a rough track off the main road. Footpaths and boat excursions give access to other rocky coves and sand.

West of Kassiópi, the coast is initially barren, and forms one of the quietest stretches in Corfu. **Avláki**, a long stretch of mixed sand and shingle, has a taverna and attracts a few windsurfers; **Kalamáki** has a pebbled beach but little accommodation. Just beyond here a road (near the garage) turns off up **Mount Pandokrátor**, past the tumbledown and overgrown village of **PERITHÍA**, with its beehives, nut trees and a taverna, the *Capricorn Grill*; from the village a footpath leads to the summit.

Back on the coast, the first settlement of any size is **ÁYIOS SPIRÍDHON**, where there are a few rooms, a small, sandy beach and an ugly hotel. If you continue on a little way you'll see a sign to **Almirós** beach, the start of a continuous strand that sweeps around to Ródha. At this end it's very quiet, with just one taverna and the occasional camper van ignoring conspicuous "No Camping" signs. Nearby, a small channel leads through to the Antinióti lagoon, an oasis-like cove with tepid water and wild birds.

Halfway to Sidhári is **AHARÁVI**, a staid tourist community that straggles along a huge, sandy beach. It's purpose-built and a bit soulless, the hotels and beach packed to the brim with young families. There are two decent bars, *Skandros* and *The Barn*, but little in the way of rooms for rent, and camping is not encouraged. **South from Aharávi** a road heads back to Píryi, skirting the western foothills of Mount Pandokrátor. It runs past **EPISKEPSÍS**, a farming community strung out along a ridge, with a couple of cafés and a three-storey Venetian manor, and on to **SPARTÍLAS**, whose square and bar (with superb local wine) is shaded by a vast elm tree. Off the main route a side road leads up to Pandokrátor's 906-metre summit, via **STRINÍLAS**, which is served by a twice daily bus from Corfu Town. This unspoilt village sits in an exposed position and the stone buildings have a very weatherbeaten look about them.

Ródha and around

RÓDHA was once a small village but has been taken over by tour operators, whose clients revel in the watersports on the narrow, shelving beach, and snap up the opportunity to go horse-riding and play tennis. Motorboats can be rented for fishing trips from *Sam's* (☎0663/93258). Hotels are generally block-booked but there's a fair **campsite**, *Roda Camping* (☎0663/63 120).

A pleasant road heads inland from here, passing nearby traditional villages like NIMFÉS (with a nice taverna, and a nearby cave-chapel and spring) and VALANIÓN (with an abandoned monastery and lovely pool). Between Nimpés and Plátonas a small factory produces bottles and sells ouzo, wine and the local liquor, *Kum Kuat*.

Just down the coast from Ródha, ASTRAKÉRI has the first "Rooms for Rent" signs for miles, a trio of **hotels** – best value are the *Sandra* (☎0663/31 120; ④) and *Astrakeri Beach* (☎0663/31 238; ④) – and a campsite. It's a little windswept but has some nice coves nearby as well as a fishing harbour. The west end of the bay merges into the beginning of Sidhári's resort development (see below).

Paleokastrítsa and the northwest

The topography of PALEOKASTRÍTSA – a perfect, sand-fringed natural harbour between cliff-headlands – has led it to be identified with Homer's *Scheria*, where Odysseus was washed ashore and escorted by Nausica to the palace of her father Alcinous, King of the Phaeacians. It's a stunning site, though as you would expect, one that's long been engulfed by tourism. The hotels spread ever further up the hill around the bay, and have been boosted by the construction of a marina, invaded during the day by hordes of day trippers. On the plus side, there are excellent watersports: the bay is superb for snorkelling and there's one of the few Greek opportunities for scuba diving (equipment and lessons from the *Baracuda Club*; ☎0663/41 211).

For **accommodation**, there's the *Green House* (☎0663/41 311; ③), with less expensive places up the hill or hidden in the olive groves on either side of the main road. The best **campsite** is *Paleokastritsa Camping* (☎0663/41 204) but it's a long walk down to the sea. Paleokastrítsa also boasts excellent fish restaurants, mopeds for rent, and an impressive range of boat trips.

If you're staying in town, boat rides provide the easiest access to **beaches to the south** – such as cliff-backed Áyia Triádha, Yérifa and Stiliári; by road, these can be reached via Liapádhes (which has rooms for rent). Attached to the small promontory is the impressive **Theotokos Monastery** (daily 7am–1pm & 3–8pm), inhabited by four monks who still produce olive oil from a working press. More enjoyable is a walk up to the Byzantine fortress of **Angelókastro**, reached by following a narrow road (making it off limits to tourist buses) from Kríni and up a cobbled path. Perched on a rocky outcrop it has a tremendous setting and dramatic views of the coast.

North of Paleokastrítsa

To the north of Paleokastrítsa are the inland villages of LÁKONES, increasingly a suburb of Paleokastrítsa, and MAKRÁDHES, with its fading whitewashed alleys; both have rooms for rent. Six kilometres of winding, often unsurfaced, road brings you to the superb bay of **Áyios Yióryios**, a long sweep of sand set beneath towering limestone cliffs. There's no village as such at Áyios Yióryios, but a fair bit of package accommodation, a line of tavernas (best are the *Marina* and *Nafsika*), two discos, a relaxed atmosphere and lots of watersports.

Around Áyios Yióryios bay to the north is AFIÓNAS, a tiny village up on the cape. *Taverna Bardhis* has rooms with views of Ionian sunsets and Gránia islet, said to be the Phaeacian boat that was turned to stone by Poseidon. Up the coast from here, ARILÁS, is a fairly low-key resort backing another wide bay, with a narrow beach and friendly atmosphere. Nearby **MAGOULÁDHES** is a small village with an old convent, **Móni Ithamíni**, and a monk's hermitage, **Móni Ipsí**, which has some valuable icons.

At windswept **ÁYIOS STÉFANOS** (not to be confused with the east coast resort), there are enjoyable breakers – making this an up-and-coming watersports centre. At present the resort boasts a handful of hotels and a fair scattering of **rooms** for rent. Day-trippers descend most mornings, but leave the village almost empty at night. Stroll north for seclusion, or into the hills for coastal views.

PEROULÁDHES, around the corner, is quite a surprise. For a start it's a genuine, if somewhat run-down, village. Then there's the beach, reached by a steep path to the brick-red sand below spectacular, wind-eroded cliffs. *Sunset Taverna* and *Panorama Restaurant* have views across to some of the islets off Corfu's northwest coast. The lack of a bus service, plus afternoon shade over the beach, keeps the place distinctly underfrequented.

All of which is in dramatic contrast to **SIDHÁRI**, whose long beach, shallow water and picturesque rock forms have made it a favourite family resort. It's not, in fact, very attractive: there are lots of mosquitoes, tacky gift shops and fast food joints; murk seeps from the river onto the beach, and crowds fill the two main roads. The best restaurants are *Oasis* (a little way out of town) and *Sophocles*, the best bar *Legends*, and the best disco *Remezzos*. As it's a flat part of the island, there are bicycles for rent. You can also escape by excursion boat to the offshore islets of Othóni, Erikoússa and Mathráki (see p.693).

Central and southern Corfu

Two natural features divide the centre and south of Corfu. The first is the **Plain of Rópa**, whose bleak landscape harbours an inaccessible coast. Settlements and development stop a little to the south of Paleokastrítsa and only resume around **Ermónes** and **Pélekas** – a quick bus ride across the island from Corfu Town. Down to the south, a second dividing point is the **Korissíon lagoon**. The sandy plains and dunes that skirt this natural feature are great places for botanists and ornithologists. Beyond, a single road trails the interior, with sporadic side roads to resorts on either coast. The landscape here is flat, with salt pans forming an undistinguished backdrop for a series of relatively undefiled beaches – and, in the far south, **Kávos**, Corfu's big youth resort.

Ermónes to Koríssion lagoon: the west coast

ERMÓNES has one feature that must be unique in Greece: a lift down to the beach, linked to the *Corfu Golf Club* and a large hotel complex. The beach, below heavily wooded cliffs, has pebbly sand and freshwater streams; another strand at nearby **Kóndo Yiálo** is small, sheltered and beautiful.

Just inland is **VÁTOS**, an unspoilt village with **rooms** for rent and a **campsite**, *Vatos Camping* (☎0661/94 393); both tavernas are called *Spiro's*. Opposite a small church near these tavernas, a tiny path leads to a steep track cut into the cliffs down to **Mirtiótissa** beach, one of the best on the island. It has a nudist section at one end, a monastery at the other, and rooms halfway down the path. Take snacks and water as there are no facilities. It's greatly preferable to the next resort, **GLIFÁDHA**, dominated by a huge hotel, scores of identical apartments, and seemingly under permanent construction.

PÉLEKAS is also busy, since it's the main crossroads in the west-centre of the island, and its beach is usually packed solid. *Spirós Taverna* has a travel agency and a few rooms. The village above the beach, however, has remained quite pleasant, with unpretentious tavernas such as *Acropolis* and *Panorama*. Cheapish **rooms** can be found at *Pension Alexandros* (☎0661/94215; ③) and *Jimmys* next door. During the evenings, tourists arrive to watch the sunsets; if you're not the tour-bus type, take the #11 bus from Platía San Rócco in Corfu Town. Signs point to the place where the Kaiser used to watch the sunset (*iliovasílema*) on a small hill above the town. The predictably named *Sunset Restaurant* charges predictably higher prices, but its position merits a drink at least.

Heading south, the next real resort is **ÁYIOS GÓRDHIS** and it's arguably the nicest on the island. Vines spread down from pine-clad cliffs to a mile-long, sandy coastal strip, with Plitíri point behind, and jagged rocks thrusting skyward below the one big hotel. The resort is dominated by the bizarre *Pink Palace* (③), an American-run holiday complex that claims to cater for backpackers – the price includes room, break-fast, dinner as well as volleyball, watersports and cliff diving.

Mount Áyii Dhika – Corfu's second peak – casts its shadow over this central part of the island, and the roads on its west side are a bit erratic. Edging through a landscape of cypresses, citrus and olive groves, you eventually reach a long swathe of beaches beside a calm sea leading down to the Korissíon lagoon. On its north side is **PARAMÓNAS**, with rooms for rent and a sand and pebble beach. A little further on is **Prasoúda**, an amphitheatre-shaped beach with a single taverna. The road south of here becomes a track, leading to a more isolated beach with another taverna, and to the thirteenth-century **Gardiki castle**, an octagonal structure on a low knoll, still partly intact.

Benítses to Boukári: the east coast

The **east coast** of the island, from Corfu Town's suburb-resorts of Kanóni and Pérama south to Messónghi is almost as developed as the stretch north of the capital. South of the suburbs is **BENÍTSES**, which used to be *the* Corfu package resort. Only slightly more bearable for having engulfed a genuine village, it has a very mediocre beach adja-cent to the busy main road, and an olive grove with a fish-and-chip shop and a go-kart track. The clientele is mainly British families with teenagers; bars advertise British beers and discos have names like *Summer Lovers* and *G-Spot*. The only redeeming feature – and not much of one at that – is a small **shell museum**.

Things don't improve much until you reach **MESSÓNGÍ**, set beneath Hlomós mountain, which is fast merging with **MORAÍTIKA**, along a sandy stretch of beach, separated from the road by a line of low-rise hotels, restaurants and discos. There are, at least, a lot of **rooms** for rent – some of the best value at the *Hotel Three Stars* (☎0661/92 457; ③) – and a **campsite**, *Sea Horse Camping* (☎0661/75 364).

The road immediately south of Messónghi is due to be surfaced to Boukári, though at present it's a bit rough. If you make it, **BOUKÁRI** rewards with a small hotel, some rooms and Spiro's friendly **taverna**, and fishermen who still fish. For swimming, walk some way around the coast towards the north, as there are various crude sewage outlets near the village.

Alternatively, head for **PETRITÍ**, a working fishing port – reached on an unsurfaced road from Boukári or by a side road off the Boukári–Aryirádhes road – where you can share a rather modest strand with a few villa dwellers. Fishermen here still spread their nets under the olive trees. *Pension Egripos* (☎0661/51 949; ③) is worth trying and **rooms** are quite easy to find.

Southern Corfu

The roads from west and east coasts join at **ARYIRÁDHES**, a small town that could make a nice inland base if you have transport to visit the local beaches. It has a few rooms for rent advertised, as does **KOUSPÁDHES**, on the Boukári road.

At **ÁYIOS YIÓRYIOS**, on the west coast, 3500m from Aryirádhes, a short walk north will take you to a beautiful undeveloped stretch of surf-pounded sand known as **Issos Beach**. The village proper is an expanding straggle of hotels, apartments and restaurants, with a few rooms for rent. Its drawback is daily excursion-boat invasions from Paleokastrítsa. The island is only about 5km wide at this point and it would be feasible to spend the morning on the east coast and walk to the west for the afternoon.

Further south down the central main road is **MARATHIÁS** whose beach merges with Santa Barbara and Maltas Beach, a long trek down a dirt road from the delapidated village of Perivóli. The strand is a continuation of the one at Áyios Yióryios, but made somewhat unenticing by a couple of open sewers. It's better to stay at one of the rooms places a little inland, and walk to the far end of the beach to swim; there are several tavernas.

There isn't much to see at **LEFKÍMI**, the main town and administrative centre of the south, which has a dirty beach to the east. In season there is a daily ferry service to Igoumenitsa (75min) from the port, 2km to the south. **ALIKÉS** is to the north – still small-time, with a sandy beach; **MÓLOS**, is plain, simple and dominated by a German-run hotel.

At **KÁVOS**, near the southern tip of the island, young British package tourists have made the place the nightlife capital of Corfu: most of the "rave" crowd that come here don't leave until it's time to go home. The resort is huge, stretching for several kilometres and encompassing eighty bars and clubs. Good **restaurants** include *O Naftis* and *Mandella's* (which offers Greek dishes and roast dinners); among **bars** catering for the young party animal are the *Ship Inn, JC's* and numerous video bars; while for **discos** there's *The Venue, Limelight* and – perhaps the country's best – the *Future Pace*. The beach is fair, with lots of watersports on offer.

An hour's walk from Kávos, following the path just before *Spiros Bar*, at the south end of the village, brings you to **Cape Asprókavos** and the ruined **monastery of Arkoudhílas**. This path also offers a view of Arkoudhílas beach, which can be reached on foot via quiet **SPARTÉRA**, a hamlet which rents rooms to the respectable. If you take this road, and loop around to the west coast, you reach the village of **DRAGOTÍNA**, which has a handful of rooms for rent and a couple of tavernas. A half hour's walk along a track (impossible for mopeds) leads to one of Corfu's best beaches – secluded, isolated and reasonably empty, with just a single summer beach-taverna.

Corfu's satellite islands: Eríkousa, Mathráki and Othoní

Northwest of Corfu there are three small and little-known satellite isles – **Eríkousa**, **Mathráki** and **Othoní**. They get few visitors and, if you go, you'll probably have to stay a couple of days between ferries. There'll be little to do besides swim, lie on the beach and relax; choices of accommodation and places to eat are very limited, and there's nowhere to change money. These are islands for those in search of peace and solitude – *isikhía*, as the Greeks put it. Each is connected to Corfu Town by **car ferry** and to Sidhári by **kaíki** (see "Travel Details" at the end of this chapter for schedules).

Development of the islands has been restricted largely by their scarcity of water rather than anything lacking in the way of scenery and beaches. Without much land or tourism, job prospects on the islands are few and, since the 1950s, most of the island populations have left – usually for New York. Many of those still living here have spent part of their lives in America, and almost everybody speaks a few words of English.

Eríkousa (Merlera)

Of the three islands, **Eríkousa** attracts most visitors. **Kaíkia** from Sidhári bring daytrippers several times a week, while the *Hotel Erikousa* (☎0663/71 555; ④) and a few cheaper rooms cater for those staying longer. There's a good, long sandy beach in front of the island port and village, and even when the excursion boats have arrived, you can walk further on and have the end of the beach to yourself. If this isn't isolated enough for you, there's a longer and totally empty beach beyond the headland to the east.

The small village is pleasant enough, without being particularly picturesque. There's a shop, a couple of *kafenía* and a single **taverna** on the beach which takes advantage of its monopoly by charging over the odds. Inland, a couple of smaller, more traditional settlements stand amid hills covered by cypress and olive trees.

Mathráki (Samothráki)

Mathráki is smaller than Eríkousa, and apart from returning Greek-Americans, who swell the population in summer, very few people come here. This is quite fortunate, for its sandy beach, stretching from the harbour for the length of the eastern side of the island, is a nesting site for the endangered **loggerhead turtle** (see p.705). It's important not to camp anywhere near the beach – and not to make any noise there at night.

From the harbour, a road climbs the hillside up to the tiny village of **KÁTO MATHRÁKI**, where brightly painted houses are scattered amongst the olive groves. There are very few rooms to rent – don't count on finding one – and a combination shop-*kafenío*-taverna at the top of the hill overlooking the sea; the food is good, but the choice is limited to say the least, and you'd do well to bring some supplies with you. The scenic island road takes you to the slightly larger village of **ÁNO MATHRÁKI** at the other end of the island, with a single, old-fashioned *kafenío* next to the church. From here, a path leads down to the far end of the beach.

Othoní (Fano)

Othoní is the largest, and, at first sight, the least inviting of Corfu's satellite isles. Around the harbour, the landscape is dry and barren, and the village has a definite end-of-the-line feel. There are no great sandy beaches, and most people swim from the shingle in front of the village. Inland, however, there's some fine scenery, and on closer acquaintance you'll find that the village has an enjoyable atmosphere. A small foreign community usually gathers during the summer, and there are always a few yachts moored in the bay. Among a handful of *kafenía* and **tavernas**, try *O Mikros* for Greek standards, and the Italian-run *La Locanda dei Sogni* for pricier meals – and nice **rooms** (☎0663/71 640; ③). In addition, there are a few cheaper private rooms in the village.

To explore the island, follow the donkey track up the valley left of the harbour, which leads to the main inland village, **HORIÓ**. This route takes you through rocky peaks and valleys with hillsides cloaked by cypress trees. Horió, like other inland villages, is heavily depopulated – only about sixty people still live on the island through the winter – but it's very attractive, and the architecture is completely traditional. From the road, a track leads down to the far side of the island and some more rocky and isolated beaches.

Paxí (Paxos) and Andípaxi (Antipaxos)

Paxí is just 12km by 4km in extent and devoted almost completely to olive cultivation. Like Corfu's northern satellite isles, a dire water shortage has prevented construction of all but one luxury hotel, though the island is not exactly remote – or unvisited. There are **ferries** almost every day in season from Corfu and from Igoumenitsa, Sívota and Párga on the mainland, and seats on the latter crossing must be reserved a day ahead in summer. The island's population of just over two thousand is often matched in season by visitors. Paxos is popular with the yachting fraternity and villa crowd so has quite an exclusive air. Late July and August are best avoided when the island swarms with designer-clad tourists, prices are bumped up and rooms are scarce. However, there are plenty of places to escape to, and by evening most of the calm has returned.

Gáïos

Most people stay in or around the main harbour and village of **GÁÏOS**, whose three- and four-storey, pastel-tinted houses front a channel of water, giving the impression of being built on a river. Opposite is the islet of **Áyios Níkoláos**, endowed with an inevitable ruined Venetian fort; it can be reached by boat and offers the best view of the town – one not much changed since it was sketched by Edward Lear last century.

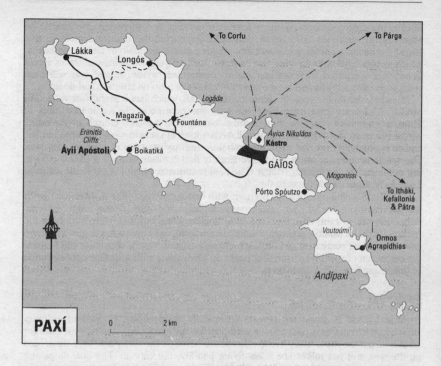

To Corfu

To Párga

Lákka

Longós

Logáda

Magaziá

Fountána

Erimitis
Cliffs

Áyii Apóstoli

Boikatiká

Áyios Nikoláos

Kástro

GÁIOS

Mogoníssi

Pórto Spóutzo

To Itháki,
Kefalloniá
& Pátra

Voutoúmi

Ormos
Agrapídhias

Andípaxi

PAXÍ

0   2 km

Unless it's the height of the season, you should be able find a **room** in or around Gáïos. If you're not met on arrival with offers, go through the square away from the waterside and take the road that leads out of the town. When you get to the edge of the built-up area, turn left at the crossroads/bus stop up a steep concrete road and keep an eye out for the signs. Don't be afraid to haggle.

Food is slightly overpriced, but no more than you would expect on a small island with a short tourist season. Some of the best-value meals are to be had at *Spiro's* (also called *Beautiful Paxi*), *Volcano* and *Andreas'* fish taverna, all in or around the square. For **drinks**, try the *Akteion Kafeniou* on the corner of the main square, where you'll pay about one-fifth of the price charged at the trendier bars used by the foreign yachting crowds.

The island's only sandy beach is **Mogoníssi**, 45 minutes' walk to the south, set in a pleasant bay and flanked by the *Kingfisher* bar and taverna. En route to the beach you pass numerous rocky covelets with fun-sized shingle beaches. Above one of these is *Taverna Klis* which advertises Greek dancing and "crayfish". A free bus/boat service leaves Gáïos for the beach every evening at 7.30pm, and there's unofficial camping behind the beach.

Around the island

Paxí's single main road splits halfway up the island, with one branch leading from Gáïos to Lákka and the other to Longós. A **bus** travels between these three main communities about six times a day, though they're also within easy enough walking distance – as is everywhere on the island. Plentiful olive trees provide shade; the island homes are scattered, forming many tiny communities; and there are also said to be over seventy churches. The *Greek Islands Club* – one of the main operators to this island – puts out a useful wildflower and walking guide, available in Gáïos and Lákka, which details hard-to-find paths. Get an early start on your ramblings, as all of Paxí's beaches are exposed to prevailing summer afternoon winds. Inland you will pass redundant olive presses and beautiful white houses with green shutters and doors.

Midway point on the road to Lákka is **MAGAZÍA**, which has a friendly taverna with rooms. A pleasant trail from here leads to the enormous chalk-coloured cliffs of **Erimítis**, which can also be viewed from behind Ayii Apóstoli church in Boikatiká which is a good viewpoint for sunsets. **LÁKKA** itself is set in a small, almost circular, bay with a pebbly cove for swimming, though the bay in general is rather stagnant. Short-term **accommodation** is quite difficult to find but there are a few rooms to rent; ask at *Planos Travel* (☎0622/31 103). The best **restaurant** is the *Rose of Paxos* and best **bar** *The Harbour Light*.

LONGÓS facing northeast, is prettier, with better tavernas – like *Kakarántzas* (with vegetarian dishes such as mushroom *stifádo*) and the *Nassos* fish taverna. Accommodation in the village is limited to holiday villas, but this doesn't concern the multitudes at the island's premier unofficial **campsite**, one cove to the south. That, and two more coves southwest of Longós, including Logáda beach, constitute the highest concentration of (pebbly) swimming spots on Paxí, along with a similar concentration of Italian and Greek holidaymakers.

Andípaxi

Andípaxi island is connected several times daily by speedboat (15min) or ordinary *kaíki* service from Gáïos. The trip – a very popular day excursion – seems expensive for what it is, but the route takes in the spectacular caves on the rocky southern tip of Paxí on the way, and you might see a few flying fish into the bargain. The boat stops at a couple of superb beaches (sandy and better than any on Paxí) before going on to the main anchorage and village – such as it is – known as Órmos Agrapídhias.

There are two tavernas at the first beach (one has a **campsite**), while the second has a bar with food and a panoramic view. The beaches are connected by a dirt road and there are paths all over the island. There are no rooms to be rented and, if you camp, the tavernas are not likely to stay open just for you in the evening, so bring provisions. Small vineyards abound on Andípaxi and the sweet red *krasí* is sold in Gáïos (behind the square) and packs a powerful punch.

Lefkádha (Lefkas)

Lefkádha is an oddity. Connected to the mainland by a long causeway through salt marshes, it barely feels like an island – and in fact, historically it isn't. It is separated from the mainland by a canal cut by Corinthian colonists in the seventh century BC, This has been redredged (after silting up) on various occasions since and today is connected by a thirty-metre boat-drawbridge built in 1986.

Lefkádha was long an important strategic base, and approaching the causeway you pass a series of fortresses, climaxing in the fourteenth-century castle of **Santa Maura** – the Venetian name for the island. These defences were too close to the mainland to avoid an Ottoman tenure, which began in 1479, but the Venetians wrested back control a couple of centuries later. They were in turn overthrown by Napoleon in 1797 and then the British took over as Ionian protectors in 1810. It wasn't until 1864 that Lefkádha, like the rest of the Ionian archipelago, was reunited with Greece.

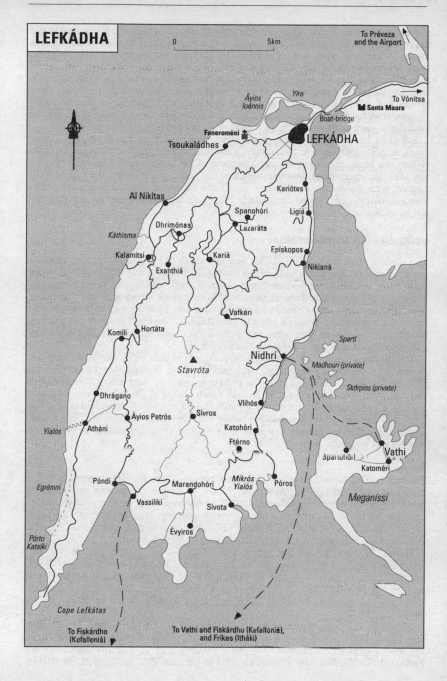

LEFKÁDHA

0   5km

To Préveza
and the Airport

To Vónitsa

Santa Maura

Áyios
Ioánnis

Yíra

Boat-bridge

Faneroméni

LEFKÁDHA

Tsoukaládhes

Kariótes

Aï Nikítas

Spanohóri

Ligiá

Dhrimónas

Lazaráta

Káthisma

Kalamítsi

Kariá

Epískopos

Exanthiá

Nikianá

Vafkèri

Komíli

Hortáta

Spartí

Madhouri (private)

Stavróta

Nidhrí

Skórpios (private)

Dhrágano

Sívros

Vlihós

Yíalós

Áyios Petrós

Katohóri

Atháni

Ftérno

Spartohóri

Vathi

Katoméri

Póndi

Marandohóri

*Mikrós
Yíalós*

Póros

Egrémni

Vassilikí

Sívota

Meganíssi

*Pórto
Katsíki*

Évyiros

Cape Lefkátas

To Fiskárdho
(Kefalloniá)

To Vathi and Fiskárdho (Kefalloniá),
and Fríkes (Itháki)

At first glance Lefkádha is not overwhelmingly attractive, although it is a substantial improvement on the mainland just opposite. The whiteness of its rock strata – *Lefkás* means "white" – is often brutally exposed by roadcuts and quarries, and the highest ridge is bare except for ugly military and telecom installations. With the marshes and sumpy inlets all around, both mosquitoes and foul smells can be a midsummer problem. On the other hand, the island is a verdant place, supporting cypresses, olive groves and vineyards, particularly on the western slopes, and life in the mountain villages remains relatively untouched, with the older women still wearing traditional local dress – two skirts (one forming a bustle), a dark headscarf and a rigid bodice.

Lefkádha has been the home of various literati, including two prominent Greek poets, Angelos Sikelianos and Aristotelis Valaoritis, and the short-story writer Lefcadio Hearn, son of American missionaries. Support of the arts continues in the form of a well-attended international **festival** of theatre and folk-dancing lasting the bulk of each August, with most events staged in the Santa Maura castle. On a smaller scale, frequent village celebrations accompanied by *bouzouki* and clarinet ensure that the strong local wine flows well into the early hours.

Lefkádha Town and around

The island's main town, **LEFKÁDHA**, lies just south of the shallow lagoon, opposite the mainland fortress. It was badly hit by earthquakes in 1948 and 1953, and its **houses** have been rebuilt in an extraordinary fashion, with the upper storeys typically constructed of plywood and corrugated metal to lay as little stress as possible upon the foundations; indeed the erection of anything over two floors in height is supposedly forbidden, although a few hotels seem to flout this law. The tilted shutters and porches on stilts, the numerous **fish traps** out in the lagoon, and summer flotillas of yachts, complete a portscape that could almost be Caribbean.

The business district, festive at night with strings of light bulbs overhead, lines the town's long, narrow thoroughfare, with narrow alleys disappearing to either side. Scattered about are a score of Italianate **churches**, most of them dating from just after the start of the Venetian occupation, though much altered in the wake of various earthquakes. If you manage to gain entrance you'll find, as elsewhere in the Ionian, that the icons and frescoes show Renaissance rather than Byzantine influences. Take a look also at the self-styled *Mousio Fonografou*, an antique shop specialising in old 78rpm records and wonderful horn-machines.

Practicalities

The **bus station** faces the southern yacht anchorage. There are regular services to the main resorts of Nidhrí, Vassilikí and Aï Nikítas, as well as the interior settlement of Kariá. To get anywhere else efficiently you'll need to **rent** a car or a very tough motorbike. For hardy cyclists mountain bikes are also available. Most of the rental agencies are on Aristotélous Valaóriti. Incidentally, Lefkádhan road-signing is atrocious, so get a good, detailed map and don't be shy about asking for directions.

Hotels in town are on the pricey side. Two decent, budget choices are the *Vyzantion*, near the entry to town on the main street at Dorpfeld 4 (☎0645/22 692; ③), and the *Patras* on the main square (☎0645/22 539; ③). More upmarket is *Santa Maura* on Dorpfeld (☎0645/22342; ⑤). There are also a few signs pointing towards **rooms** on the lagoon shore-road, including those run by a friendly family at SteFaníssi 14 (☎0645/23118; ③).

Among town centre **restaurants**, try *Regantos* at Dhimárhou Verióti 17 (a minor street going north from the main square), or the cosy *Eftikia Taverna* on Kerfákis near the town's entrance. *Romantica Taverna* at Mitropoleos 11 and *The Lighthouse* (*O Faros*) on Filarmónikis have reasonable food in pleasant little gardens. At the start of the road to Aï Nikítas is the *Adriatica*, one of the more elegant restaurants on the island; it's not cheap but it features unusual vegetarian dishes, an excellent fish pie and various seafood dishes. Swanky cafés predominate in the main square – *kafenío* culture becomes more evident closer to the junction at the top of the street. *Barbarosa* is one of the best **bars**.

Around Lefkádha Town

The closest decent beach to the capital is at **Áyios Ioánnis**, the spit bordering the Yíra lagoon on its west – about 45 minutes away if you choose to walk. It's sandy but also has pebbles that the wind-churned surf can hurl with bruising force. Continuing clockwise past a couple of stone windmills around the Yíra from here would bring you to a calmer, north-facing bay and the inexpensive *Estiatorio/Psitopolio Yira*, serving good food to a mainly local clientele. From there it's easy enough to complete a loop back to town, past the bridge.

West of the harbour, you can follow the Aï Nikítas road up to **Faneroméni monastery** (closed 2–4pm). It's no longer inhabited but has beautiful views and retains its old *símandro* (oxen's yoke and hammer), which was used to call the monks to prayer when first the Turkish, and later German, occupying forces forbade the use of bells.

Inland, a confusion of roads lead from the port to a welter of tiny villages in the north-centre of the island, overlooking a broad agricultural upland whose existence you hardly suspect gazing up from sea level. Possible targets here include the rickety hilltop hamlet of **SPANOHÓRI**, near the thriving crossroads town of **LAZARÁTA** with its *platía* tavernas, or the embroidery centre of **KARIÁ**, with expensive lace for sale and a few rooms for rent. It also has a fine *platía* enclosed by plane trees and *kafenios*, making it an excellent lunchtime or evening excursion.

The east coast to Vassilikí

Heading south from Lefkádha town along the eastern shore, there's little initially to demand a halt except for **campsites** at Kariótes (☎0645/23 594) and Epískopos (☎0645/71 388), where there's a rocky beach. Only **LIGIÁ**, with its fishing port, has retained any village feel, and most of this coast is dotted with small, nondescript resorts patronised mostly by Greeks. Hotels charge well over the odds; if you choose to stop, there is a veritable plethora of rooms on offer, while the village also has the superbly named taverna, *The Breath of Zorba*.

Few foreigners, in fact, stop before **NIDHIRÍ**, built on the site of a drained swamp. Useful as a ferry port to other islands and in a marvellous setting, the town itself has little character. The swimming off the tiny beach here is very average, and the only redeeming feature is the view out over various islets. **Rooms** are generally reserved in advance, but the tourist agencies on the front might turn up something for you. There is no shortage of cocktail bars, discos or **restaurants**, though the last present few gastronomic surprises.

The German archeologist **Wilhelm Dörpfeld** believed Nidhrí, rather than Itháki, to be the site of Odysseus's capital, and did indeed find Bronze Age tombs on the plain nearby. His theory identifying ancient Ithaca with Lefkádha fell into disfavour after his death in 1940, although his obsessive attempts to give the island some status over its neighbour are honoured by a statue on Nidhrí's quay. His tomb is tucked away at Ayía Kiriakí on the opposite side of the bay, near the house in which he once lived, visible just above the chapel and lighthouse on the far side of the water.

VLIHÓS, 3km south of Nidhrí at the head of an all-but-landlocked bay, is essentially an annexe of the bigger resort, though the presence of more old buildings, a quieter setting away from the road, and summer *bouzouki* events count in its favour. The bay is unsuitable for swimming; there is a **campsite** on the far side at Desími.

Beyond Vlihós, the main island road twists through or past the attractive hill villages of Katohóri, Ftérnos and Póros, all of which have at least one evening taverna apiece. The main resort in this corner of the island is the deep bay of **Mikrós Yialós** below **PÓROS**, which has **rooms** and a rather luxurious **campsite**. It's a scenic spot but the pebble beach gets both busy and dirty in July and August. Heading inland from here **SÍVROS** is neither the picturesque mountain village one had hoped for nor does it have a decent taverna or *kafenio*.

The next inlet to the west, **SÍVOTA**, has no beach to speak of and is really just a yacht harbour – albeit a fairly scenic one. A brief evening visit is perhaps best, when the five fish tavernas get going. A more functional swimming beach and a semi-official **campsite** can be found at **Kastrí**, 4km down a very rough side road between Marandohóri and Kondaréna. Looking down on the valley is the quiet village of **ÉVYI-ROS** with the odd room and one taverna.

The southeastern bus route ends around 40km from Lefkádha Town at **VASSILIKÍ**, which enjoys a fine setting with the island's largest agricultural strip just behind the broad bay. However, the beach is drab and the town tacky, dominated by a role as one of Europe's premier windsurfing centres. If you've not come on an instructional package, you can usually find a stray board to rent, but beginners may be forced to confine their efforts to the morning hours, since afternoon gusts off the plain behind sweep all except experts from the water.

In the end, Vassilikí is probably of most interest for its **ferry connections** south to Kefalloniá. The **campsite** behind the beach is well appointed but relatively expensive; alternatively there are various rooms, a **post office** (with an exchange), and an **OTE** station with handy evening and Sunday afternoon hours. **Eating out**, you're advised to try **Póndi**, a quieter district a kilometre distant on the far side of the bay, where the *Kamares Restaurant* is recommended.

ÁYIOS PÉTROS, 4km inland and to the north, has some unusual half-timbered houses and a lively main square, on and around which are several tavernas. *Ta Batsanakia* is a good, characterful grill with palatable local wine.

The west coast

Starting out from Lefkádha Town, the west coast begins with rather more promise. Past the Móni Faneroméni (see above) and village of Tsoukaládhes, you arrive at **AÏ NIKÍTAS**, a fine, little-developed hamlet, with a single, flagstoned main street flanked by a half-dozen **tavernas**, about as many **rooms**, a campsite (just inland) and a few bars leading down to a tiny beach. It's not exactly traditional but makes a superb base and a ten-minute boat ride around the headland, or an hour's hike through scrub and bushes, will bring you to **Mílos beach** – a mile-long sweep of sand and shingle.

The next stop south is **Káthisma beach**. This attracts large numbers of freelance campers, though thus far there is just one proper taverna-rooms establishment, plus a trio of mobile canteens with showers and toilets. More substantial facilities are to be found (well up the hill) at **KALAMÍTSI**, host to dozens of **rooms** and a few **tavernas**. The tiled roofs, pleasant setting – facing a terraced hillside – and friendly locals make it an agreeable spot. This has its own large beach, too, 3km away, connected by a particularly steep track. There is no road directly between Káthisma and Kalamítsi beaches; between the two main bays, however, you can walk through several inviting coves frequented by nudists, and past a freshwater spring.

Visible just inland from Kalamítsi are two unspoilt communities reachable by meandering roads: **DHRIMÓNAS**, something of an architectural showcase with its uniform, old stone houses, and **EXANTHIÁ**, as good or better in its amphitheatrical arrangement. Neither has any tourist facilities.

Heading south again on the main route, a right turn at Komíli leads to **ATHÁNI**, another popular village, with plenty of **rooms** and **tavernas**. The choice of nearby beaches consists of **Yialós**, 4km south and marked after a fashion; **Egrémni**, 6km distant; and, most picturesque (but also most crowded), **Pórto Katsíki**, 10km along an increasingly bumpy road, at the base of high cliffs and with a single taverna. It's not as isolated as it first appears – *kaíkia* ferry in sun-worshippers from Vassiliki, just around the headland.

If the west wind is up, none of these coves will be inviting, and you might make the best of things and drive past the monastery of Áyios Nikólaos to the Lefkadhan "Land's End" at **Cape Lefkátas** (Doukato), which drops 75 abrupt metres into the sea. Byron's Childe Harold sailed past this point, and "saw the evening star above, Leucadia's far projecting rock of woe: And hail'd the last resort of fruitless love". The fruitless love is a reference to Sappho, who in accordance with the ancient legend that you could cure yourself of unrequited love by leaping into these waters, leaped – and died. In her honour the locals termed the place *Kávos tis Kirás* (Lady's Cape), and her act was imitated by the lovelorn youths of Lefkádha for centuries afterwards. And not just by the lovelorn, for the act (known as *katapontismós*) was performed annually by scapegoats – always a criminal or a lunatic – selected by priests from the Apollo temple whose sparse ruins lie close by. Feathers and even live birds were attached to the victim to slow his descent and boats waiting below took the chosen one, dead or alive, away to some place where the evil banished with him could do no further harm.

The rite continued into the Roman era, when it degenerated into little more than a fashionable stunt of decadent youth. These days, Greek hang-gliders hold a tournament from the cliffs every July. Weather permitting, there are *kaíki* trips out of Vassiliki for the more sedentary or those without vehicles capable of reaching the cape overland.

Lefkádha's satellites

Lefkádha has a string of satellite islets – Spartí, Madhourí, Skórpios and Meganíssi – over to the east of the island. **Meganíssi** is the only one with a village population and public access, from the port of Nidhrí. Of the other Lefkádha satellites, **Skórpios** is the retreat of the (now almost extinct) Onassis family and its staff, with landing still strictly forbidden. It was here that Aristotle married Jackie Kennedy. Landing is also forbidden on **Madhourí**, the property of the poet Nanos Valaoritis and his family. **Spartí** is uninhabited and covered in scrub.

Meganíssi

Meganíssi, a twenty-minute ferry or excursion-boat crossing from Nidhrí, has been for some time a closely guarded secret among island aficionados, without a postcard or souvenir shop in sight. A severe water shortage, and little scope for more ambitious building, is likely to thwart any of the major operators from moving in and for the present, rented rooms are readily available and cheap.

The main ferry stop is **VATHÍ**, a fishing port, whose harbour entrance is flanked by chapels to bless all boats and grant safe passage. That aside, it's a rather scruffy place, moving at its own slow pace. A road leads up from here to the more attractive village of **KATOMÉRI**, where visitors are likely to be greeted with a free *oúzo* at the taverna and an invitation to join in a game of cards. Here also is the island's first **hotel**, the *Meganisi* (☎0645/51240; ④) – small, simple and very pleasant.

The road continues in a westerly loop to **SPARTOHÓRI**, an immaculate village with whitewashed buildings and an abundance of bougainvillea. The locals – many returned emigrés from Australia – live from farming and fishing and are genuinely welcoming. There are a few tavernas, with limited choice, but excellent cooking and decent prices; the best is *Taverna Lakis*. Through the village and at the end of the island road is Pórto

Spílio, a stop for some of the Nidhrí excursion boats. A minibus service meets the ferry at Vathí to connect the three villages but the distances are easily walkable.

Several tracks lead over the hills of the island and down through the olive-grove terracing to secluded bays. The most popular of these is **Ambelákia**, which attracts visiting yacht flotillas. You might also persuade a boat to take you to the caves on the southwest coast which reputedly sheltered submarines during World War II.

Kefalloniá (Cephallonia, Kefallinía)

Kefalloniá is the largest of the Ionian islands – a place that has real towns as well as resorts and which, until the late 1980s, paid scant regard to tourism. Perhaps this was in part a feeling that the island could not easily be marketed. Virtually all of its towns and villages were levelled in the 1953 earthquake, and these masterpieces of Venetian architecture had been the one touch of elegance in a severe, mountainous landscape. A more likely explanation, however, for the island's late emergence on the Greek tourist scene is the Kefallonians' legendary reputation for insular pride and stubbornness.

Having decided on the advantages of an easily exploitable industry, however, Kefalloniá is at present in the midst of a tourism boom. Long favoured by Italians, it has begun attracting British package companies, for whom a new airport terminal has been constructed, while virtually every decent beach has been endowed with a sprinkling of restaurants. There are definite attractions here, too, with some beaches as good as any in the Ionian, and a fine, if pricey, local wine, the dry white *Rombola*. Moreover, the island seems able to soak up a lot of people without feeling at all crowded, and the magnificent scenery can speak for itself, the escarpments culminating in the 1632-metre bulk of **Mount Énos**, declared a national park to protect the fir trees (*Abies cephalonica*) named after the island.

The size of Kefalloniá, a poor bus service and a distinct shortage of summer rooms makes **moped or car rental** almost essential. Fortunately, most of the towns, beaches and larger resorts have a rental outlet. If you are depending on the buses, be warned that there's only a basic grid of services: Sámi, the main port, to Argostóli, the island capital, and Fiskárdho (in the north); and Argostóli to the resorts of Skála and Póros in the southeast. Using a moped, take care as the terrain is very rough in places – almost half the roads are unsurfaced – and the gradients can sometimes be a bit challenging for underpowered machines.

Sámi and around

Most boats dock at the large, and not very characterful, port and town of **SÁMI**, built and later rebuilt near the south end of the Itháki straits, more or less on the site of ancient Sámi. This was the capital of the island in Homeric times, when Kefalloniá was part of Ithaca's maritime kingdom: today the administrative hierarchy is reversed, Itháki being considered the backwater. With ferries to most points of the Ionian, and several companies introducing direct links to Italy – and one even to Piraeus, Samos and Turkey – the town is clearly preparing itself for a burgeoning future.

For the moment, though, most arriving passengers tend to get out as fast as possible. In addition to **moped rentals** (available on the waterfront), there are three daily **buses** to Argostóli, plus one bus (change at Dhivaráta) and a ferry to Fiskárdho. If you need or decide to stay, the town has a few **rooms** for rent and the four cheapest hotels are the waterfront *Hotel Kyma* (☎0674/22 064; ③), *Hotel Melissani* (☎0674/22 464; ③), *Hotel Ionion* (☎0674/22 035; ④) and *Hotel Krinos* (☎0674/32 002; ③). Best of the rather mediocre **restaurants** are *Faros* and *Dolphin* on the Paralia.

Four kilometres to the east of Sami, along a track that climbs and descends a steep hill is the excellent **Andisámos** beach, renowned for its clear water.

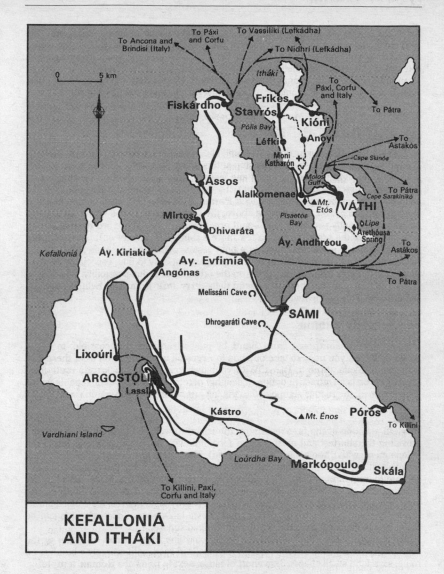

**KEFALLONIÁ
AND ITHÁKI**

Karavómilos beach and the Melissáni and Dhrogaráti caves

More rooms and a **campsite**, *Karavomilos Beach* (☎0674/21 680), are to be found at **Karavómilos beach**, 2km to the north of Sámi. The beach itself is not very exciting but there is the opportunity of a boat ride to the **Spíli Melissáni** (daily 9am–8pm; 700dr), a blue-tinged sea-cave partly submerged in brackish water. You're taken into an inner lake-grotto, whose waters, amazingly, emerge from an underground fault which leads the whole way under the island to a point near Argostóli. At this point, known as

Katavóthres, the sea gushes endlessly into a subterranean channel – and, until the 1953 earthquake disrupted it, the current was used to drive seamills. That the water, now as then, still ends up in the cave has been shown with fluorescent tracer dye. The lake grotto can also be reached from the village itself.

Another, more conventional, cavern, the **Spíli Dhrogaráti** (daily, dawn to dusk; 600dr), is to be found 4km inland of Sámi, just off the main road to Argostóli. A very impressive stalagmite-bedecked chamber, it was previously used for concerts thanks to its marvellous acoustics – Maria Callas once sang here.

Áyia Evfimía

At **ÁYIA EVFIMÍA**, 10km north of Sámi, the road (and bus) turns inland towards Fiskárdho. You could do worse than stop at this pretty port town, which seems to have just about the right mixture of locals and visitors, and boasts the best **restaurant** on the island, *Stavros Dendrinos's Taverna*. To find it, walk round the harbour past the main dock and 500m on to the so-called **Paradise beach**. The small pebble beach is fine for swimming, and, on a terrace above, the multilingual Stavros serves an unusual range of excellently prepared food – and great house wine. There are **rooms** (②–③) available above the premises (and a few more a short walk further on), but they suffer from the heat and noise generated by a busy restaurant. This is a shame, because the view is superb, and rooms back in Áyia Evfimía are not easy to find, especially for short stays. *Hotel Pilaros* (☎0674/612 10; ④) on the promenade is one possibility.

Note that in summer there is a useful daily **ferry link** from Áyia Evfimía to Itháki and on to Astakós on the mainland.

Southeast Kefalloniá

Heading directly **southeast from Sámi** by public transport is impossible; to get to **Skála** or **Póros** you need to take one bus to Argostóli and another on from there; five daily run to Skála, three to Póros. With your own vehicle, the backroads route from Sámi to Póros is an attractive option. It's eighty percent dirt track but negotiable with a decent moped; the road is signposted to the left just before the Dhrogaráti cave.

Póros

PÓROS was one of the first resorts on the island to wake up to the idea of tourism, providing the shortest and most popular ferry link with the mainland (to Killíni in the Peloponnese, with three boats a day in season). The port is just over the headland from the main village. Several foreign tour operators maintain offices in the village, and a few **rooms** to rent are available for independent tourists but the place hasn't really changed that much. With its houses encroaching onto the dark green hillsides, the long beach, a small separate bay for boats, and nearby shady coves, it's a more attractive entry point than Sámi. To **eat**, a good choice is *Dionysos Taverna* which can be found by heading west from the small, palm-fringed square.

A dirt road twists 12km around the rocky coastline from **Póros to Skála** at the southern extremity of the island. It's a lovely, isolated road, with scarcely a building en route, save for a small chapel, 3km short of Skála, next to ruins of a **Roman temple**.

Skála

The village of **SKÁLA** has well and truly arrived as a thriving, albeit not unpleasant, beach resort. Alongside the standard bars and restaurants, a fair proportion of the decent stretch of sand is covered by sunbeds and parasols. At the north end of town, opposite the *Hotel Skala*, the remains of a **Roman villa** are on show, featuring finely detailed mosaics. **Rooms** aren't easy to find in summer, as tour operators have cleaned up on accommodation in both hotels and village houses. If you're stuck, ask at the

LOGGERHEAD TURTLES

The Ionian islands harbour the Mediterranean's main concentration of loggerhead sea turtles (*Caretta caretta*). These creatures, which lay their eggs at night on sandy coves, are under direct threat from the tourist industry in Greece.

Each year, many turtles are injured by motorboats, their nests are destroyed by bikes ridden on the beaches, and the newly hatched young die entangled in deckchairs and umbrellas thoughtlessly left out at night on the sand. The turtles are easily frightened by noise and lights, too, which makes them uneasy cohabitants with freelance campers and late-night discos.

The Greek government has passed laws designed to protect the loggerheads, including restrictions on camping at some beaches but, in addition to the thoughtlessness of visitors, local economic interests tend to prefer a beach full of bodies to a sea full of turtles.

On Kefalloniá, the turtles' principal nesting ground is Potomákia beach, 5km to the west of Skála. Other important locations for the loggerhead turtles include Zákinthos, although numbers have dwindled to half their former strength in recent years, and now only about 800 remain. Nesting grounds are concentrated around the fourteen-kilometre bay of Laganás, but Greek marine zoologists striving to protect and study the turtles are in dispute with locals and the burgeoning tourist industry.

Ultimately, the turtles' main hope of survival may rest in their being appreciated as a unique tourist attraction in their own right.

---

small *Kinotikó Grafío* (Council Office) on the main street, or try at Ratzíkli, 3km from Skála on the Argostóli road – a little inland from the sea.

Skála to Argostóli

Skála is edged by a fine stretch of sand, which continues around the headland and on to the south coast of the island. For the first few kilometres, the road runs a little inland and there is little development. At **Potomákia Beach**, 5km along the coast from Skála and reached by a turning at Ratzíkli, there are breeding grounds of loggerhead turtles (see feature above). The sands and dunes are popular with locals at weekends and development looks set, with large clearings of land in preparation for tavernas and hotels. If you visit, or stay, leave the beach to the turtles at night.

The Argostóli road meets the sea midway around Loúrdha Bay at **KÁTO KATELIÓN**, where an absurd number of restaurants compete for the seasonal occupants of unsightly, purpose-built apartments and a few freelance campers. One possible attraction is that the local **moped rental** agency arranges **scuba dives**.

Continuing west, the road heads inland again, past **MARKÓPOULO**, where the **Assumption of the Virgin festival** (Aug 15) is celebrated in unique style at the local church with small, harmless snakes with cross-like markings on their heads. Each year, so everyone hopes, they converge on the site to be grasped to the bosoms of the faithful; a few, in fact, are kept by the priests for years when they don't naturally arrive. The celebrants are an interesting mix of locals and gypsies – some of whom come over from the mainland for the occasion. It's quite a spectacle.

Further on, rooms are available at Vlaháta and Moussáta, and from the former a track winds its way up to the 5000-foot summit of Mount Énos. On a clear day, you might not quite see forever, but should at least get a glimpse of neighbouring Zákinthos. Note that the main access route is from the Argostóli–Sámi road.

There are more rooms and unofficial summer camping at **LOURDHÁTA**, a little village just inland from its one-kilometre-long beach – which is flanked by a trio of tavernas. It's an attractive base, and just beyond the beach, across some rocks, a tall overhanging tree directs a trickling freshwater-fall into the sea. Further west, there's another good beach and a taverna at ÁYIOS THOMÁS. At PESSÁDHA a ferry plies in the summer months to Ayios Nikoláos on Zákinthos; the tiny, uninhabited harbour is some way below the village.

Argostóli and around

ARGOSTÓLI, Kefalloniá's capital, is a large and thriving town, virtually a city, with a marvellous site on a bay within a bay. The stone bridge, connecting the two sides of the bay, was initially constructed by the British in 1813. A small obelisk remains, but the plaque commemorating "the glory of the British Empire" has disappeared. The town was totally rebuilt after the earthquake but has an enjoyable streetlife that remains defiantly Greek, especially during the evening *volta* around Platía Metaxá – nerve centre of the town.

A couple of museums near each other on Rokou Veryoti are worth a little time. The **Historical and Cultural Museum** (Mon–Sat 8.30am–2.30pm; 500dr) is strong on photographic documentation of Argostóli, including the British and French occupations and the 1953 earthquake and its aftermath. A bit less imaginative is the **Archeological Museum**, a block down on G. Veryóti (Tues–Sun 8.30am–3pm; 400dr); it consists mainly of pottery, including pieces from a number of Mycenaean tombs discovered in the village to the south.

Practicalities

The **EOT**, on the waterfront Metaxá street, keeps a list of rooms for rent and will phone to book for you – assuming there are vacancies. If you'd rather look around yourself, try *Spiros Rouhatas* at Metaxá 44 (☎0671/23 941 or 24 936; ③), who has rooms above his café opposite the Lixoúri ferry quay, or the *Adherfi Tzivras* (②) restaurant, on the side street V. Vandaroú, opposite the petrol pumps by the bus station. Two budget **hotels** exist, *Hotel Pantheon*, Zakínthou 4 (☎0671/22246; ②), next to the post office, and *Hotel Chava* (☎0671/22427; ③), up from the bridge. Close to the bus station, *Hotel Allegro* (☎0671/22268; ④) is also reasonably priced.

More mundane and harder work is the **campsite**, a two-kilometre walk (no bus) to the end of the promontory at Fanári. The site is just after the **Katavóthres**, the point at which the sea drains into the ground to re-emerge at Karavómilos (see "Sámi and around", above).

For **meals**, the *Adherfi Tzivras* (see above) is very good value, though *Kalafitis* and *Taverna Anonymous* have better locations facing the bay. *Patsoura's* has a good reputation, too, while for a highly recommended splurge, go for the *mezédhes* at the *Cyprus Taverna*. The liveliest **bars** are *Phoenix* and *Allodi* in Platia Metáxa.

Buses run from Argostóli to most points of the island and *KTEL* tries to make up for (or exploit) the shortcomings of its network by offering tours, and trips to nearby islands and Olympia. There is one daily **boat** to Killíni and a daily **hydrofoil** to Zákinthos, then Patras. The walk-on **ferry to Lixoúri** (see below) leaves every hour. Numerous agencies rent out **cars and mopeds**: *Express Cars* in the main square is one of the most reliable.

South of Argostóli: beaches and Kástro

For a swim, locals and visitors alike take a bus to **LÁSSI**, across the headland from Argostóli. Flanking the village, on either side of a hill, are two excellent but crowded beaches: **Platís** (wide) and **Makrís Yiálos** (long). Both are lined with hotels and tavernas, with Lássi itself developing rapidly whilst trying to absorb the increase in volume of tourists, generated by improvements to the airport a few kilometres south.

With a moped, the best inland excursion is to **KASTRO** (also known as Áyios Yióryos or San Giorgio), the medieval Venetian capital of the island. The old town here supported a population of 15,000 until its destruction by an earthquake in the seventeenth century: substantial ruins of its castle (daily except Mon 8.30am–3pm), churches and houses can be visited on the hill above the modern village of Travliatata. Byron was impressed by the view from the summit in 1823, when he lived for a few months in the village of Metaxáta, some kilometres below; sadly, as at Messolónghi, the dwelling where he stayed no longer exists. Two kilometres south of Kastro is a fine collection of religious icons and frescoes kept in a restored church that was part of the nunnery of Ayios Andréas.

Lixoúri

A quick ferry hop across the bay will bring you to LIXOÚRI, the only sizeable centre on Kefalloniá's rugged western peninsula. The town itself is a bit downbeat, but would be a quiet and inexpensive base if you could get one of the rooms at the *Estiatorio Maria* on Kósti Palamá (②), near the main square. The restaurant is basic to the point of scruffy, and won't suit all tastes. For a bit more class try *Antony's* opposite the quay, or the *Ocean Breeze* at the end of the promenade. On the road south, the *Bella Vista Pension* (☎0671/91911; ③) has a few rooms.

Walking south of Lixoúri, Lepídha beach is the first of a series of sand-and-seaweed beaches, reached after about thirty minutes. Proceed along these (and along tracks where necessary), and eventually you'll reach **Cape Áyios Yióryios**. Around the cape, ninety minutes' walk from Lixoúri, are the red sands of Mégas Lákos, facing Vardhiani island. Largely undeveloped, save for a small cluster of apartments, it's advisable to bring provisions as there is no café for miles around. The same strand continues to the more publicised **Xi Beach**, now dominated by a modern hotel complex.

The west coast and the road north

From Argostóli, most people board a bus bound for Fiskárdho (see below) in the north – a highly scenic journey that passes side roads to several excellent beaches. The first of these is **Áyia Kiriakí**, reached by a 2km track from Angón. The next, **Mírtos**, is signposted just past Dhivaratá and reached along a steep track. Seen from the cliff road above, it is one of the most spectacular and most photographed beaches in Greece – a splendid strip of pure white sand and pebbles – and in summer it attracts a fair number of day-trippers and campers. It's not an ideal place to stay, however, as it has no shade (apart from the cave at one end), and no toilet facilities. A seasonal bar rustles up sandwiches and drinks – overpriced, of course, but the alternative is a 4km slog up to Dhivaratá's two grills and a shop.

The main road, hacked out of the palisades on this road, continues north to **ÁSSOS**, a fishing village built on a narrow isthmus that links it with a castle-crowned headland. It's a placid place with a few cafés and tavernas, and plenty of daytime visitors, but it is far from spoilt and would make a fine base if you could get one of the few rooms for rent.

Fiskárdho

Kefalloniá's picture-postcard village, **FISKÁRDHO**, is notable mainly for having escaped damage in the earthquake, preserving intact its eighteenth-century Venetian houses. It is pretty, but also totally dominated by tourism, with a yacht club, lots of boutiques, and restaurants serving expensive fish and bottled wine. If you're going to eat anywhere, try *Nikolas's Taverna*; at least service here is with good grace and a twinkle in his eye. **Rooms** in season are like gold dust, with only the odd cancellation from a package company on offer. Particularly nice ones are offered by *Anna Barzouka* (☎0674/51 572; ④); to find her, ask, as the streets are not named. *Hotel Panorama* (☎0674/51 340; ④) is likely to be full, but worth a try.

Close to the town, there's reasonable swimming off a mixture of rock and pebble beaches, One of the most popular, **Emblísi**, one kilometre away, has slanted slabs of rock, good to sunbathe on and snorkel from. On the hill above, the *Herodotus Taverna* is a decent place to eat and, apart from one unsightly pylon, has a panoramic view of Lefkáda, Itháki and the mainland. Daily **ferries** run to Vassilikí and Nidhrí on Lefkádha, as well as to Itháki and down the coast to Sámi. There are also **kaíkia** to Itháki in season.

Itháki (Ithaca)

Rugged **Itháki**, Odysseus's legendary homeland, has had no substantial archeological discoveries but it fits Homer's description to perfection: "There are no tracks, nor grasslands . . . it is a rocky severe island, unsuited for horses, but not so wretched, despite its small size. It is good for goats." In C Cavafy's splendid poem *Ithaca*, the island is symbolised as one's journey and destination to life:

> *When you set out on the voyage to Ithaca*
> *Pray that your journey may be long*
> *full of adventures, full of knowledge.*

Despite the romance of its name, and its proximity to Corfu, very little tourist development has arrived to spoil the place. This is doubtless in part accounted for by a dearth of beaches, though the island is good walking country, with a handful of small fishing villages and various pebbly coves to swim from. In the north, apart from the ubiquitous drone of mopeds the most common sounds are sheep bells jangling and cocks (a symbol of Odysseus) crowing.

Váthi

Ferries from Pátra, Kefalloniá, Astakós, Corfu or Italy land at the main port and capital of **VÁTHI** (Itháki Town), sited at the mouth of a bay so deep it seems to close completely around. The small capital features old tiled houses, either undamaged or faithfully rebuilt after the terrible 1953 earthquake, and a small archeological museum on Odhos Kalliniko (daily 9am–3pm; free). Dozens of yachts and cruise ships stop here for a couple of hours but not many people actually stay – tourist development is for once at a virtual standstill.

Rooms for rent are, however, inconspicuous and in very short supply. If nobody meets you off the ferry, try looking around the backstreets south of the ferry quay. Alternatively, head for one of the two hotels, the *Odysseus* (☎0674/32 381; ④) and the *Mentor* (☎0674/32 433; ⑤), at opposite ends of the long quay. There's a little more choice for meals, with seven or eight **tavernas**, though all seem remarkably similar in price and fare. Among the more reliable are the *Psistaria Athinaiki Gonia*, *Toh Trehandiri* (authentic food in the bazaar) and *Toh Kantouni* (next to the water, near the ferry dock). Further around the bay, *Gregorys* and *Tsiribis* face the town and are popular with foreign nautical types. The island speciality, is *ravaní*, a syrupy sponge cake.

In season the usual small boats shuttle tourists from the harbour to a series of tiny coves along the peninsula northeast of Váthi – a service that's particularly useful, as road links around the island are very poor. The pebble-and-sand **beaches** between Cape Skinós and Sarakinikó Bay, such as Filiátro and Gidháki, are excellent, many people learning of them too late as the ferry they're departing on steams past. Most of those closer to town are little more than concrete diving platforms, though you might reflect that Byron enjoyed daily swims off the Lazzaretto islet in mid-harbour during his visit of 1823.

With some determination, you can walk out to the better beaches when the *kaíkia* aren't running. However, as long as you have good footwear you may prefer to spend your time hiking out to a handful of nearby sites tentatively identified with Homeric locations, or to head further north on Itháki for swimming or more sedentary pastimes.

Odysseus sites

Two paths to "Odysseus sites" are signposted from Váthi and either of them makes for an easy morning's walk across beautiful country of cypress, olives and vineyards. Both walks lack shade, so take a hat and plenty of water.

The Arethoúsa spring and Perahóra

The **Arethoúsa spring**, ninety minutes' walk south from the port, is down to a trickle in summer but interestingly positioned. Immediately above towers a crag known locally as *Korax* (the raven), exactly as described by Homer in the meeting between Odysseus and his swineherd Eumaeus, on his return to the island to fight the suitors. To reach it, take the signposted track south out of Váthi, and turn down and left on to a narrower path after an hour; the final approach is signalled by occasional green markings on the stones.

If you miss the turning, the main thoroughfare continues on to the **Maráthia plateau** (today called Perapigádhi after its capped well), where Eumaeus had his pigsties, but fails to reach remote **Ayíou Andhréou Bay** (accessible only by sea), where Telemachus disembarked to avoid Penelope's suitors who were lying in ambush for him on Asteris Island (the modern Dhaskalío). Below Arethoúsa, more tiny paths drop down to a pair of good swimming coves in the lee of Lípa islet.

Perapigádhi shouldn't be confused with **PERAHÓRA**, an old pirate-proof inland village some 2km above Váthi. The upper settlement – with one *kafenío*/taverna and a rooms place – makes a good return option from Arethoúsa or a trip in itself; obvious paths lead up to it from the olive-swathed plain or there's a direct track, signposted from Váthi's Odhós Penelópis.

The Grotto of the Nymphs and ancient Alaikomenae

Of equally questionable authenticity but fun to visit in any case is the **Grotto of the Nymphs** (known locally as *Marmarospíli*), a large cavern about 2500m southwest of Váthi, where local lore suggests Odysseus, on the advice of Athena, hid the treasure he had with him on his return to Ithaca. It was certainly known in ancient times and seems to have once been used as a place of worship. If its attribution is correct then the **Bay of Dhexiá** (west of Váthi and below the cave) would be where the Phaeacians put in to deposit the sleeping Odysseus and which he failed to recognise as his homeland.

Further to the north, **Mount Etós** looms over the head of the Molos gulf. On its summit are the ruins of **ancient Alaikomenae**, excavated by Schliemann (of Mycenae fame) and mistakenly declared to be the "Castle of Odysseus"; in fact it dates from at least five centuries after Homer. The site is almost impossible to find, and the search for others is complicated by the studiously inaccurate "Odysseus maps" sold on Itháki.

A side road skirts the base of the mountain and crosses the narrowest point on the island to get to pebbly **Pisaetos Bay**, nearly 7km in all from Váthi but with some of the best swimming near town. From the tiny quay, there are three or four daily ferries to Sami on Kefalloniá. Buses don't go to Pisaetos but the short half-hour crossing justifies a taxi ride from Váthi (1500dr).

Northern Itháki

The main road out of Váthi continues across the isthmus and takes a spectacular route to the northern half of Itháki, serving the villages of **Léfki**, **Stavrós**, **Fríkes** and **Kióni**. There are three evenly spaced daily **buses**, though the north of Itháki is excellent moped country. Likewise the close proximity of the settlements, small coves and Homeric interest make it suitable rambling country. Once a day a *kaíki* also visits the last two of those communities – a cheap and scenic ride used by locals and tourists alike to meet the main-line ferries in Váthi. As with the rest of Itháki there is only a limited amount of accommodation.

Stavrós

STAVRÓS, near the base of arid Mount Korífi (or officially Mount Nisíti – a re-adoption of its old Homeric name), is a fair-sized village with a couple of rather pricey tavernas (the best is *Fatouro*) and some rooms. **Pólis Bay**, fifteen minutes' walk below it, has rocky swimming; people camp here, though there are no facilities whatsoever. Supported by a few nearby Mycenaean remains, the bay is the archeologists' current candidate for the main port of ancient Ithaca.

One kilometre north of Stavrós, more Mycenaean remains have been found amid the ruins of a Venetian fort, on a hill known as **Pelikáta**. This could perhaps have been the site of Odysseus's palace and capital: speculation that is supported by the fact that it enjoys a marvellous simultaneous view over Pólis Bay and Fríkes Bay. The tiny Stavrós **museum** (daily except Mon 9am–3pm) has a modest collection of terracotta jugs, bronze figurines and a fragment of a clay face mask claimed to be a votive offering to Odysseus.

Make your way up the four-kilometre track to the all-but-abandoned village of **EXOYÍ** in the northwest corner of the island and climb the belltower next to the blue-domed church for even more stunning views of this part of Itháki.

Fríkes, Kióni and Anoyí

FRÍKES is a half-hour walk downhill beyond Stavrós, smaller but with a handful of tavernas, a hotel (*Nostos*, ☎0674/31 644; ⑤), a few rooms and a pebbly strip of beach. Seasonal ferries to and from Lefkádha and Fiskárdho on northern Kefalloniá dock here. The port is linked by bus to Váthi. The very helpful *Kiki Travel* (☎0674/31 726) rents mopeds, boats and can help finding accommodation. From Fríkes a lovely coastal path leads to a couple of reasonable beaches; Mamakás beach, over the hill, is even better. Try and get to them early as a strong wind blows from mid-afternoon onwards.

Around three kilometres east, at the end of the road, is the village of **KIÓNI**, one of the more attractive bases on the island, though its few rooms (including the luxurious *Kioni Apartments*, ☎0674/31 362; ⑥) seem to be permanently occupied during summer. There's good swimming nearby, free of sea urchins, at the end of the path to Áyios Ilías chapel to the southeast.

With Kióni as your starting point, you can also walk or go by moped due south to the still inhabited **monastery of Katharón**, via the inland village of **ANOYÍ**, where the proprietress of the one taverna will lend you the keys to the fourteenth-century village church and its excellent frescoes. From the monastery, the vista of Vathí in its horse-shoe bay must rank as one of the most magnificent in all the Ionian.

Zákinthos (Zante)

Zákinthos, which once exceeded Corfu itself in architectural distinction, was hit hard-est by the 1953 Ionian earthquake, and the island's grand old capital was completely destroyed. Rebuilt, it feels a rather sad, soulless town and the island's attractions lie more in the thick vineyards, orchards and olive groves of the interior, and some excellent beaches scattered about the coast. Although the forests are inevitably depleted one can still feel the sense of Homer's description of "wooded Zákinthos".

However, in contrast to Itháki, the island is one of the fastest-growing tourist resorts in Greece. Pessimists mutter darkly of Zákinthos being turned into another Corfu, and with upwards of 300,000 visitors a year that's understandable. Most tourists, though, are conveniently housed in one place – Laganás, on the south coast. As well as the foreign visitors, July and August also sees an influx of Greek holidaymakers, particularly Athenians, attracted by the island's proximity to the mainland. If you avoid those months, and steer clear of Laganás and the developing resort villages of Argási and Tsilívi, there is still a peaceful Zákinthos to be found.

Spring's the time to see the **flowers**, and autumn if you want to eat the produce. Any time's a good time for the local **wines**, such as the white *Popolaro*, which is among the best in the Ionians. For dessert or a snack, try *mandoláto*, the ubiquitous and delicious honey/egg/almond nougat, or the very strong and pungent *grapéria* **cheese**. You may see temporary stalls by the roadside selling *fitouri* and *pasteli*, sweet, fried local delicacies. From late August to mid-March, beware the local **hunting season** – everywhere in the island you'll see what look like little playhouses on stilts; these are the hunters' blinds.

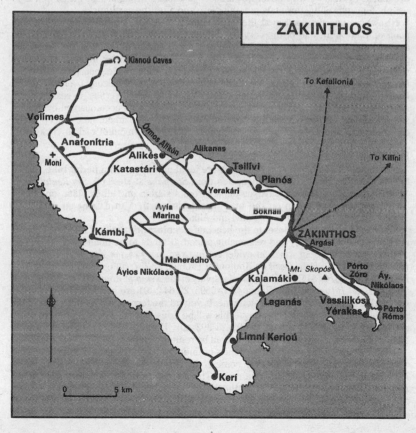

Zákinthos Town

The town, like the island, is known as both **ZÁKINTHOS** and Zante. This former "Venice of the East" (*Zante, Fior di Levante*, "Flower of the Levant", in an Italian jingle), rebuilt on the old plan, has bravely tried to recreate some of its style, though reinforced concrete can only do so much.

The most tangible hints of former glory are to be found in **Platía Solómou**, the grand and spacious main square. At its north (waterside) corner stands the beautiful fifteenth-century sandstone church of **Áyios Nikólaos**, while paintings and icons salvaged from here and other island churches are displayed in the imposing **Neo-Byzantine Museum** (Tues–Sun 8.30am–3pm; 400dr, students 200dr) by the town hall. This collection is exceptional for during the seventeenth and eighteenth centuries Zante became the centre of an Ionian School of painting, given impetus by Cretan refugees unable to practise under Turkish rule.

The square itself is named after the island's great poet **Dionissios Solomos**, who was responsible for introducing demotic Greek (the spoken language of the people) as a literary idiom and who also wrote the words to the Greek national anthem. A small museum (daily 9am–2pm; free) is dedicated to him in the nearby Platía Ayíou Márkou, two blocks up; it is worthwhile for its glimpses of Zante's strong artistic life as well as to see photographs of the town taken both before and after the earthquake.

Elsewhere in town, look in at the large church of **Áyios Dhioníssios** (daily 7am–noon & 4.30–9pm), one of the very few buildings left standing after the earthquake, and with impressive frescoes. And, if you've a few hours to fill, walk up an old cobble path to the town's massive **Venetian fortress** (daily 8am–8pm; 400dr), which has views south to Pílos and north to Messolóngi and is a great picnic spot. En route to the fortress lies the suburb village of **Boháli**, occupying a natural balcony overlooking the harbour, and with a number of popular if slightly expensive tavernas. In season these are the venues for *kantádhes*, an Italianate style of trio-singing accompanied by guitars and mandolins. At the edge of the town, on the road to Kalamáki, take a peep at the charming blue and white church Áyios Elípios, virtually hewn out of a small, rocky hill.

Practicalities

The flatlands of south and east Zákinthos are ideal places to rent a **pedal bike**, available along with **mopeds** and **motorcycles** from *Stainatis* at Desila 9, *Sky Rentals* at A. Makri 7, and other agencies. **Buses** depart from a station on Odhós Filitá (one block back from the *Fina* pump on the main waterside road), with a frequent service to Laganás, and reasonable ones to Tsilívi and Alikés.

Since most people stay closer to the beaches, **accommodation** in Zákinthos Town is relatively easy to come by and reasonably priced. It tends to be hotel-based, however, with rooms for rent not much in evidence. In town, try *Pension Zenith* at Tertséti 44 (☎0695/22 134; ③), *Hotel Oasis* on Koutoulist (☎0695/22 287; ③) or *Hotel Ionian* at Alex Roma 18 (☎0695/42 511; ③). For a bit of a splurge, the *Xenia* at Róma 60 (☎0695/42 666; ④) and *Hotel Bitzaro* at Dion Roma 46 (☎0695/23 644; ⑤) are worth trying. If a short man with a Mexican bandit moustache meets you off the ferry and offers you a lift in his red Opel Manta it is worth accepting – this will be Fotis Giatvas whose rooms are some of the best value on Zákinthos (☎0695/23 392; ②). They lie 2km out of town towards Planos but the mobility issue is easily solved by renting a moped.

The one time you'll stand little chance of finding a room is around August 24, the feast of Áyios Dioníssios, when even some of the Greek visitors have to resort to sleeping outside the church for lack of a room. The **tourist police** have information about accommodation (and bus services); they're to be found in the police station on the front, sandwiched between Tzouláti and Merkáti streets, next to the helpful travel agency *Spring Tours*, which offers round the island boat tours.

There's an adequate selection of **restaurants and tavernas**. One of these, *Taverna Arekia*, east of Platía Solómou at Kryeneniou 80, is a must – great food, barrelled wine and an earthy atmosphere make it popular with Greeks and tourists alike. Just before it is *Alivizos*, another good choice. You can also work up an appetite by walking a good way in the opposite direction to Ayíou Dhionissíou (an approach road to the church) – here, *Malvetis* and the *Grill House*, two almost identical *psistaries*, have limited menus but offer good, cheap food. More central is *Bukios* restaurant, the best value of the places on the main square.

The south and west

The road heading southeast from Zákinthos harbour passes under Mount Skopós on its way to some of the finest scenery and best beaches on the island. If you're just after a quick swim, head for the beach at **Pórto Zóro**, just to the northeast of the road with two seafront bars.

Vassilikó and around to Laganás

Further south, **VASSILIKÓ** lies within easy striking distance of a series of good-to-excellent beaches and has a few modest hotels and a scattering of rooms for rent. There is a long stretch of sand known as the Ionian beach and the *Ionian Taverna* offers rooms (☎0695/35211; ④). Nearby is the *Costas Brothers Taverna*, set in a beautiful gardens and featuring quality food and folk songs. Through a wood the next turning takes you to **St Nicholas beach** with watersports and reasonable snorkelling.

Campers congregate under the trees at the popular **Pórto Róma** beach, just to the east – a pleasant enough strand, but nothing more. There are rooms here, too, but the seasonal tavernas are oversubscribed and overpriced.

Yérakas – signposted straight ahead – is a good beach and the impressive rock strata and formations of the peninsula make a fine backdrop. There are **rooms** for rent on the way down to Yérakas, though camping is strictly illegal both here and on the beaches to the west – Dephní and Kalamáki – as they are the nesting grounds of **loggerhead turtles** (see feature on p.705). Zákinthos is the most important Ionian location for the turtles, though local numbers today are down to about 800, roughly half of what they were as recently as the mid-1970s.

West of tourist-dominated **Kalamáki**, the beach becomes progressively muddier and more commercialized until new heights (or depths) are demonstrated at the resort of **LAGANÁS** proper. Around the bay, there are further nesting grounds for the **loggerhead turtles**, though the majority now lay their eggs on two small beaches, whereas until recently they used the whole of the fourteen-kilometre bay. In recent years, Greek marine zoologists, attempting to protect and document the turtles, have come into violent dispute with locals, uneasy at restrictions on developing their land for tourism. All things considered, one can't help feeling pessimistic about the turtles' future. As for Laganás itself – there's little to be said, save that if you're not already booked into a hotel here, you probably won't find a room.

Kerí

KERÍ, in the southwest corner of the island, retains some of its pre-earthquake houses and, more curiously, natural **tar pools** commented on by both Pliny and Herodotus and still used for caulking boats. You can also visit the lighthouse by following a dusty track, which leads to spectacular views at the tip of the peninsula where limestone cliffs plunge into turquoise waters. There is a passable beach at **Limní Kerioú**, a few kilometres east, where as at Kerí you can stay, eat and drink inexpensively and in generally local company. Small *kaïkia* take people to Keri Cave and Marothonissi island.

Maherádho, Kilioméno and Kámbi

If you have transport, an enjoyable route away from Laganás or Kerí is the mountain road, which leads ultimately to Alikés in the north. Around 15km from either is the village of **MAHERÁDHO**, which shelters the spectacularly ornate church of Ayía Mávra. It is certainly the place to be if you're on the island for her feast day, which usually falls on the first weekend in July.

The road from here to the rural mountain village of **KILIOMÉNO** (sometimes known as Ayios Nikólaos after its grand old church) has recently been improved and is just about passable for a 50cc scooter. However, a sturdier, more powerful bike – not a moped – is more suitable for traversing some of the mountain roads west, over to Kámbi. As well as the state of the roads, you also have the local maps to contend with – roads rated as major on these are often little more than goat tracks, or even non-existent; some of the newer and better roads are not shown, while others are placed inaccurately.

The effort of such safaris can be worth it, though, as the sunsets to be viewed from the clifftops on the rocky western coast are spectacular. **KÁMBI** is the favoured place for organised "Sunset Trips", when the busloads turn up at the taverna, teetering 300m above the sea on the cliff's edge; there's no denying that the performance here is stunning. Even higher than the taverna is an enormous cross, erected to commemorate the deaths of islanders who were thrown off the cliffs during the 1940s, some say by the Nazis, others by nationalist troops in the civil war.

The north

North and west from Zákinthos Town, the roads thread their way through luxuriantly fertile farmland, punctuated with tumulus-like hills. **TSILÍVI**, 4km out, is the closest beach to town worthy of the name, shallow and sandy with warm water, though the evening breeze whips up the surf. It's another settlement riding on the wave of the tourist boom, and there are plenty of rooms, eateries and cocktail bars. Slightly further north is *Camping Zante* (☎0695/24 754).

A pleasant cycle ride from Tsilívi takes inland back roads through lemon groves to Alíkanas. En route you pass the quiet, hilltop village of **ÁNO YERAKÁRI**, one of three settlements within a few hundred metres of each other and offering a couple of rooms. From the church there are fine 360-degree vistas. Ammoúdhi beach is an unspoilt place for a quick dip.

Alikón bay

Ormós Alikón, 13km further north of Tsilívi, is a huge, gently sloping expanse of sand washed by good breakers. At its eastern end is the village of **ALÍKANAS**. Villas are block-booked here by a couple of tour companies, and there's an alarming amount of building going on. Nearby, however, are two excellent **restaurants**. *Ta Neraidha*, with a great setting on Alíkanas harbour, always has fresh, well-cooked fish; while a friendly family runs *Mantalena*, on the road to Alikés, which serves a variety of delicious traditional dishes from the kitchen, a genuine house wine from the proprietors' own grapes, and water from a well on the premises.

Towards the northwest end of the bay, **ALIKÉS** is an increasingly busy package resort with rooms, restaurants and mopeds for rent. There are half a dozen hotels, but as yet nothing on the scale of Laganás, possibly because of the presence of rats and mosquitoes, aggravated by the stagnant water from the river.

A pleasant excursion by moped – or even on foot – from Alikés is to the small cove of **Koróni**, where sulphur springs discharge into the sea. Swimming is quite an experience, if you don't mind the smell, with a few inches of cool, fresh seawater on the surface and warm tracts below. Butterflies abound here in summer.

Further north, **Ayíos Nikólaos** functions as a port for the short, twice-daily crossing to Pessada on Kefallonía. From here another good trip is a ride by **kaíki** (1000dr) to the extreme northern tip of the island, where the **Kianoú (Blue) Caves** are some of the more realistically named of the many contenders in Greece. They're terrific for snorkelling, and when you go for a dip here your skin will appear bright blue. The road snakes onwards through a landscape of gorse bushes and dry stone walls until it ends at the lighthouse of **Cape Skinani**. With one cafeteria, and a view of the mountainous expanse of Kefallonia, it's a good spot for unofficial camping.

Volímes, Katastári and Ayía Marina

The large village of **VOLÍMES** is renowned for its embroidered handicrafts and you know when you've arrived – mats, rugs and linen hang by the roadside and local women holler "oriste!" at passing tourists. This aside, the place remains very rural. **KATASTÁRI**, the island's largest community after the capital, lies just inland from Alikés. It's a workaday place, of interest for a chance to witness ordinary island life; stop here and you're likely to be waved over to the *kafenío* to have an *oúzo* plonked in front of you.

With a moped, you might be tempted to head 18km northwest to **Anafonítria monastery**. This withstood the earthquake remarkably well and is today tenanted by a few nuns who will show you the frescoed *katholikón*, a medieval tower, and the purported cell of Saint Dhionissios, the patron of Zákinthos whose festivals are on August 24 and December 17. Well represented on postcards, there's a shipwreck (*Toh Navágio*) 3500m from the village down a very rough track. The rusty remains lie embedded on a fantastic beach which isn't accessible by foot, but can be viewed from above. The cliff top vantage point is assuredly not recommended for those with vertigo.

AYÍA MARÍNA, a few kilometres south of Katastári, has a church with an impressive Baroque altar screen, and a belfry that's being rebuilt from the remnants left after the 1953 earthquake. Like most Zákinthos churches, the belltower is detached, in Venetian fashion. Just above Ayía Marína is the *Parthenonas Taverna* rightly boasting one of the best views on the island. From it you can see the whole of the central plain from beyond Alikés in the north to Laganás Bay in the south.

travel details

Corfu (Kérkira)

Roughly hourly (5am–10pm) **ferries** from Igoumenítsa to Corfu and vice versa (1hr). Additionally, most of the ferries between Italy and Greece (especially those from Brindisi) call at Corfu; stopover is free if specified in advance. In season a catamaran service connects Brindisi, Corfu, Paxos and Igoumenítsa. Contact *Charitos Shipping* for details (☎0661/44 611)

Several **flights** daily between Corfu and Athens (45min). Seasonal flights (twice weekly) to/from Kefalloniá and Zákinthos.

Eríkousa, Mathráki and Othoní

A **car ferry**, the *Alexandros II*, runs from Corfu Town to all the islands twice weekly, currently leaving Corfu on Tues and Sat at 6.30am. The route is Corfu–Eríkousa–Mathráki–Othoní–Mathráki–Eríkousa–Corfu. The ferry leaves Corfu Town from opposite the *BP* station on Eleftherioú Venizeloú street, midway between the Igoumenítsa and Italy ferries. Tickets and information from *Star Travel Agency* (☎0661/36 355), Eleftherioú Venizeloú 4, Corfu Town. *Star Travel* also run an excursion boat to Eríkousa and Othoní on Sundays in season.

Kaíkia leave Eríkousa and Othoní for Sidhári early on Mon and Thurs morning, returning to Eríkousa at about 11am, and to Othoní, via Mathráki, at about 1pm. These are primarily supply boats for the local people. To check days and times, ask at Sidhári's jetty, or call Stamatis Zoupanos (☎0663/95 141) at *Budget Travel* in Sidhári, who can also give you information on excursion boats from Sidhári to Eríkousa.

Lefkádha

4 **buses** daily to and from Athens (6hr) and regular services from Áktio (near Préveza). At least daily **boats**, in season, from Nidhrí to Meganíssi, Kefalloniá (Fiskárdho) and Itháki (Fríkes or Pisaetós); 30min from Vassilikí to Kefalloniá (Fiskárdho and Sámi). From June to September *Ilio Line* **hydrofoils** link Lefkádha with Préveza, Paxí, Corfu, Itháki and Kefalloniá.

Itháki (Ithaca) and Kefalloniá

Daily **ferry** connection between Pátra, Itháki (Váthi – 5hr 30min), and Kefalloniá (Sámi). Year-round daily ferries between Astakós on the mainland and Váthi on Itháki, usually continuing to/from Ayía Evfimía on Kefalloniá. Three or four quick (half-hour) daily hops from Pisaetós on Itháki to Sámi on Kefallonia. Also 4 ferries daily in season (once daily out) between Póros (southeast tip of Kefalloniá) and Killíni (Peloponnese); 2 daily in season (1 out) between Lixoúri on Kefalloniá and Killíni; 2 daily in season between Pessádha (Kefalloniá) and Áyios Nikoláos (Zákinthos); daily in season ferries from Fiskárdho (Kefalloniá) to Fríkes and Váthi on Itháki and Nidhrí and Vassilikí on Lefkádha.

From June to September *Europe II* hydrofoils link Argostóli (Kefalloniá) with Pátras and Katakolo (mainland) and Zákinthos Town. *Almer* hydrofoils connect Póros with Lefkhádha and Itháki.

Kefalloniá is also on an international *Minoan Lines* route, whose *Ariadne* ferry runs weekly (mid-May to early October) from **Ancona** to the island, then on to Pátra and Iráklion.

Daily **flights** between Argostóli (Kefalloniá) and Athens (45min); useful seasonal link to/from Zákinthos and Corfu.

Paxí

Year-round there is a twice-weekly car and passenger **ferry**, the *Kamelia*, from Corfu (3hr), which in season usually calls at Sívota (also known as Moúrtos) on the mainland en route; information from *Sivota Travel* (☎0665/93 222). From June to September, there are also daily **ferries** from Corfu (3hr) and Párga (2hr), and **hydrofoils** from Igoumenítsa, Préveza and Lefkádha.

Zákinthos (Zante)

Up to 5 **ferries** a day in summer (2 out of season; 1hr 30min) between Zákinthos and Killíni (Peloponnese). At least four daily bus/ferry services to Athens. Unreliable, twice-daily connection in summer from Áyíos Nikoláos to Pessádha (Kefalloniá), as described above.

From June to September *Europe II* hydrofoils link Zákinthos with Kefalloniá and Pátras (see above).

Daily **flights** between Athens and Zákinthos (45min). Twice weekly **flights** to/from Kefalloniá and Corfu.

PART FOUR

THE

CONTEXTS

THE HISTORICAL FRAMEWORK

This Historical Framework is intended just to lend some perspective to travels in Greece, and is heavily weighted towards the era of the modern, post-Independent nation – especially the twentieth century. More detailed accounts of particular periods (Mycenae, Minoan Crete, Classical Athens, Byzantine Mystra, etc) are to be found in relevant sections of the guide.

NEOLITHIC, MINOAN AND MYCENAEAN AGES

Other than the solitary discovery of a fossilised Neanderthal skull near Thessaloníki, the earliest **evidence of human settlement** in Greece is to be found at Néa Nikomedhía, near Véria. Here, traces of large, rectangular houses dated to around 6000 BC have been excavated.

It seems that people originally came to this land in the eastern Mediterranean in fits and starts, predominantly from Anatolia. These **proto-Greeks** settled in essentially peaceful farming communities, made pottery and worshipped Earth/Fertility goddesses – clay statuettes of whom are still found on the sites of old settlements. This simple way of life eventually disappeared, as people started to tap the land's resources for profit and to compete and exchange in trade.

MINOANS AND MYCENAEANS

The years between around **2000 and 1100 BC** were a period of fluctuating regional dominance, based at first upon sea power, with vast **royal palaces** serving as centres of administration. Particularly important were those at **Knossos** in Crete, and **Mycenae**, **Tiryns** and **Argos** in the Peloponnese.

Crete monopolised the eastern Mediterranean trade routes for an era subsequently called the **Minoan Age**, with the palace at Knossos surviving two earthquakes and a massive volcanic eruption on the island of Thíra (Santoríni), at some undefinable point between 1500 and 1450 BC. The most obvious examples of Minoan culture can be seen in frescoes, in jewellery, and in pottery, the distinctive red-and-white design on a dark background marking the peak period of Minoan achievement. When Knossos finally succumbed to disaster, natural or otherwise, around 1400 BC, it was the flourishing centre of **Mycenae** that assumed the leading role (and gives its name to the civilisation of this period), until it in turn collapsed around 1200 BC.

This is a period whose history and remains are bound up with its **legends**, recounted most famously by Homer. Knossos was the home of King Minos, while the palaces of Mycenae and Pylos were the respective bases of Agamemnon and Nestor; Menelaus and Odysseus hailed from Sparta and Ithaca. The Homeric and other legends relating to them almost certainly reflect the prevalence of violence, revenge and **war** as increasing facts of life; instigated and aggravated by trade rivalry. The increasing scale of conflict and militarisation is exemplified in the massive fortifications – dubbed Cyclopean by later ages – that were built around many of the palaces.

The Greece of these years, certainly, was by no means a united nation – as the Homeric legend reflects – and its people were divided into what were in effect a series of splinter groups, defined in large part by sea and mountain barriers and by access to **pasture**. Settlements flourished according to their proximity to and prowess on the sea and the fertility of their land; most were self-sufficient, specialising in the production of particular items for **trade**. Olives, for example, were associated with the region of Attica, and minerals with the island of Mílos.

THE DORIAN AND CLASSICAL ERAS

The Mycenaean-era Greek states had also to cope with and assimilate periodic influxes of new peoples and trade. The traditional view of the collapse of the Mycenaean civilisation has it that a northern "barbarian" people, the **Dorians**, "invaded" fom the north, devastating the existing palace culture and opening a "dark age" era. These days, archeologists see the influx more in terms of shifting trade patterns, though undoubtedly there was major disruption of the palace cultures and their sea powers during the eleventh century.

Two other trends are salient to the period: the almost total supplanting of the mother goddesses by **male deities** (a process begun under the Mycenaeans), and the appearance of an **alphabet** still recognisable by modern Greeks, which replaced the so-called "Linear A" and "Linear B" Minoan/Mycenaean scripts.

CITY-STATES: SPARTA AND ATHENS

The ninth century BC ushered in the beginnings of the Greek **city-state** (*polis*). Citizens – rather than just kings or aristocrats – became involved in government and took part in community activities and organised industry and leisure. Colonial ventures increased, as did commercial dealings, and the consequent rise in the import trade was gradually to give rise to a new class of manufacturers.

The city-state was the life of the people who dwelt within it and each state retained both its independence and a distinctive style, with the result that the sporadic attempts to unite in a league against an enemy without were always pragmatic and temporary. The two most powerful states to emerge were Athens and Sparta, and these were to exercise a rivalry over the next five centuries.

Sparta was associated with the Dorians, who had settled in large numbers on the fertile Eurotas (Évrotas) river plain. The society of Sparta and its environs was based on a highly militaristic ethos, accentuated by the need to defend the exposed and fertile land on which it stood. Rather than build intricate fortifications, the people of Sparta relied upon military prowess and a system of laws decreed by the (semi-legendary) **Lycurgus**. Males were subjected to military instruction between the ages of seven

and thirty. Weak babies were known periodically to "disappear". Girls too had to perform athletic feats of sprinting and wrestling, and even dwellings were more like barracks than houses.

Athens, the fulcrum of the state of Attica, was dynamic and exciting by contrast. Home of the administrations of **Solon** and **Pericles**, the dramatic talents of Sophocles and Aristophanes, the oratory of Thucydides and Demosthenes, and the philosophical power of Socrates and Plato, it made up in cultural achievement what it lacked in Spartan virtue. Yet Sparta did not deserve all the military glory. The Athens of the sixth and fifth centuries BC, the so-called **Classical period** in Greek history, is the Athens which played the major part in repelling the armies of the Persian king Darius at Marathon (490 BC) and Salamis (480 BC), campaigns depicted later by Aeschylus in *The Persians*.

It was also Athens which gave rise to a tradition of **democracy** (*demokratia*), literally "control by the people" – although at this stage "the people" did not include either women or slaves. In Athens there were three organs of government. The *Areopagus*, composed of the city elders, had a steadily decreasing authority and ended up dealing solely with murder cases. Then there was the Council of Five Hundred (men), elected annually by ballot to prepare the business of the Assembly and to attend to matters of urgency. The Assembly gave every free man a political voice; it had sole responsibility for law-making and provided an arena for the discussion of important issues. It was a genuinely enfranchised council of citizens.

This was a period of intense creativity, particularly in Athens, whose actions and pretensions were fast becoming imperial in all but name. Each city-state had its **acropolis**, or high town, where religious activity was focused. In Athens, Pericles endowed the acropolis with a complex of buildings, whose climax was the temple of the Parthenon. Meanwhile, the era saw the tragedies of Sophocles performed, and the philosophies of Socrates and Plato expounded.

Religion at this stage was polytheistic, ordering all under the aegis of Zeus. In the countryside the proliferation of names and of sanctuary finds suggests a preference for the slightly more mundane Demeter and Dionysus.

THE PELOPONNESIAN WARS

The power struggles between Athens and Sparta, allied with various networks of city-states, eventually culminated in the **Peloponnesian Wars** of 431–404 BC. After thiese conflicts, superbly recorded by Thucydides and nominally won by Sparta, the city-state ceased to function so effectively.

This was in part due to drained resources and political apathy, but to a greater degree a consequence of the increasingly commercial and complex pressures on everyday life. Trade, originally spurred by the invention of **coinage** in the sixth century BC, continued to expand; a revitalised Athens, for example, was exporting wine, oil and manufactured goods, getting corn in return from the Black Sea and from Egypt.

The amount of time each man had to devote to the affairs of government decreased and a position in political life became a professional job rather than a natural assumption. Democracy had changed, while in philosophy there was a shift from the idealists and mystics of the sixth and fifth centuries BC to the Cynics, Stoics and Epicureans – followers, respectively, of Diogenes, Zeno and Epicurus.

HELLENISTIC AND ROMAN GREECE

The most important factor in the decline of the city-states was meanwhile developing outside their sphere, in the kingdom of Macedonia.

MACEDONIAN EMPIRE

Based at the Macedonian capital of Pella, **Philip II** (359–336 BC) was forging a strong military and unitary force, extending his territories into Thrace and finally establishing control over Athens and southern Greece. His son, **Alexander the Great**, in an extraordinarily brief but glorious thirteen-year reign, extended these gains into Persia and Egypt and parts of modern India and Afghanistan.

This unwieldy empire splintered almost immediately upon Alexander's death in 323 BC, to be divided into the three Macedonian dynasties of **Hellenistic Greece**: the Antigonids in Macedonia, the Seleucids in Syria and Persia, and the Ptolemies in Egypt. Each were in turn conquered and absorbed by the new Roman Empire, the Ptolemies – under their queen Cleopatra – last of all.

ROMAN GREECE

Mainland Greece was subdued by the Romans over some seventy years of campaigns, from 215 to 146. Once in control, however, **Rome** allowed considerable autonomy to the old territories of the city-states. Greek remained the official language of the eastern Mediterranean and its traditions and culture coexisted fairly peacefully with that of the overlords during the next three centuries.

In central Greece both **Athens** and **Corinth** remained important cities but the emphasis was shifting north – particularly to towns, such as **Salonica** (Thessaloníki), along the new *Via Egnatia*, a military and civil road engineered between Rome and Byzantium via the port of Brundisium (modern Brindisi).

THE BYZANTINE EMPIRE AND MEDIEVAL GREECE

The shift of emphasis to the north was given even greater impetus by the decline of the Roman Empire and its apportioning into eastern and western empires. In the year 330 AD the Emperor Constantine moved his capital to the Greek city of Byzantium and here emerged Constantinople (modern Istanbul), the "new Rome" and spiritual and political capital of the **Byzantine Empire**.

While the last western Roman emperor was deposed by barbarian Goths in 476, this oriental portion was to be the dominant Mediterranean power for some 700 years, and only in 1453 did it collapse completely.

CHRISTIANITY

Christianity had been introduced under Constantine and by the end of the fourth century was the official state religion, its liturgies (still in use in the Greek Orthodox church), creed and New Testament all written in Greek. A distinction must be drawn, though, between perceptions of Greek as a language and culture and as a concept. The Byzantine Empire styled itself Roman, or *Romios*, rather than Hellenic, and moved to eradicate all remaining symbols of pagan Greece. The Delphic Oracle was forcibly closed, and the Olympic Games discontinued, at the end of the fourth century.

The seventh century saw **Constantinople** besieged by Persians, and later Arabs, but the Byzantine Empire survived, losing only Egypt, the least "Greek" of its territories. From the ninth to the early eleventh centuries it enjoyed an archetypal "golden age", in culture, confidence and security. Tied up in the Orthodox Byzantine faith was a sense of spiritual superiority, and the emperors saw Constantinople as a "new Jerusalem" for their "chosen people". It was the beginning of a diplomatic and ecclesiastical conflict with the Catholic west that was to have disastrous consequences over the next five centuries. In the meantime the eastern and western patriarchs mutually excommunicated each other.

From the seventh through to the eleventh centuries **Byzantine Greece**, certainly in the south and centre, became something of a provincial backwater. Administration was absurdly top-heavy and imperial taxation led to semi-autonomous provinces ruled by military generals, whose lands were usually acquired from bankrupted peasants. This alienation of the poor provided a force for change, with a floating populace ready to turn towards or cooperate with the empire's enemies if terms were an improvement.

Waves of **Slavic raiders** needed no encouragement to sweep down from the north Balkans throughout this period. At the same time other tribal groups moved down more peaceably from **central Europe** and were absorbed with little difficulty. According to one theory, the nomadic **Vlachs** from Romania eventually settled in the Píndhos Mountains, and later, from the thirteenth century on, immigrants from **Albania** repopulated the islands of Spétses, Ídhra, Ándhros and Évvia, as well as parts of Attica and the Peloponnese.

THE CRUSADES: FRANKISH AND VENETIAN RULE

From the early years of the eleventh century, less welcome and less assimilable western forces began to appear. The **Normans** landed first at Corfu in 1085, and returned again to the mainland, with papal sanction, a decade later on their way to liberate Jerusalem.

These were only a precursor, though, for the forces that were to descend en route for the **Fourth Crusade** of 1204, when Venetians, Franks and Germans turned their armies directly on Byzantium and sacked and occupied Constantinople. These Latin princes and their followers, intent on new lands and kingdoms,

settled in to divide up the best part of the Empire. All that remained of Byzantium were four small peripheral kingdoms or **despotates**: the most powerful in Nicaea in Asia Minor, less significant ones at Trebizond on the Black Sea, and (in present-day Greece) in Epirus and around Mystra in the Peloponnese (known in these times as the Morea).

There followed two extraordinarily involved centuries of manipulation and struggle between Franks, Venetians, Genoese, Catalans and Turks. The Paleologos dynasty at Nicaea recovered the city of Constantinople in 1261 but little of its former territory and power. Instead, the focus of Byzantium shifted to the Peloponnese, where the autonomous **Despotate of Mystra**, ruled by members of the imperial family, eventually succeeded in wresting most of the peninsula from Frankish hands. At the same time this despotate underwent an intense cultural renaissance, strongly evoked in the churches and the shells of cities remaining today at Mystra and Monemvassía.

TURKISH OCCUPATION

Within a generation of driving out the Franks, the Byzantine Greeks faced a much stronger threat in the expanding empire of the **Ottoman Turks**. Torn apart by internal struggles between their own ruling dynasties, the **Palaeologi** and **Cantacuzenes**, and unaided by the Catholic west, they were to prove no match. On Tuesday, May 29, 1453, a date still solemnly commemorated by the Orthodox church, Constantinople fell to besieging Muslim Turks.

Mystra was to follow within seven years, and Trebizond within nine, by which time virtually all of the old Byzantine Empire lay under Ottoman domination. Only the **Ionian islands** and the **Cyclades**, which remained Venetian, and a few scattered and remote enclaves – like the Máni in the Peloponnese, Sfákia in Crete and Soúli in Epirus – were able to resist the Turkish advance.

OTTOMAN RULE

Under what Greeks refer to as the "Dark Ages" of **Ottoman rule**, the lands of present-day Greece passed into rural provincialism, taking refuge in a self-protective mode of village life that has only recently been disrupted. Taxes and discipline, sporadically backed up by the genocide of dissenting communities, were inflicted from the Turkish Porte but estates passed into the hands of local chieftains who often had considerable independence.

Greek identity, meanwhile, was preserved through the offices of the **Orthodox church** which, despite instances of enforced conversion, the Sultans allowed to continue. The **monasteries**, often secretly, organised schools and became the trustees of Byzantine culture, though this had gone into stagnation after the fall of Constantinople and Mystra, whose scholars and artists emigrated west, adding impetus to the Renaissance.

As Ottoman administration became more and more decentralised and inefficient, individual Greeks rose to local positions of considerable influence and a number of communities achieved a degree of autonomy. Ambelákia village in Thessaly, for example, established an industrial cooperative system to export dyed cloth to Europe, paying only direct taxes to the Sultan. And on the Albanian repopulated islands of the Argo-Saronic, a **Greek merchant fleet** came into being in the eighteenth century, permitted to trade throughout the Mediterranean. Greeks, too, were becoming organised overseas in the sizeable expatriate colonies of central Europe, which often had affiliations with the semi-autonomous village clusters of Zagória (in Epirus) and Mount Pílion.

THE STRUGGLE FOR INDEPENDENCE

Opposition to Turkish rule was becoming widespread, exemplified most obviously by the **Klephts** (brigands) of the mountains. It was not until the nineteenth century, however, that a resistance movement could muster sufficient support and firepower to prove a real challenge to the Turks. In 1770 a Russian-backed uprising had been easily and brutally suppressed but fifty years later the position was different.

In Epirus the Turks were over-extended, subduing the expansionist campaigns of local ruler **Ali Pasha**; the French revolution had given impetus to the confidence of "freedom movements"; and the Greek fighters were given financial and ideological underpinnings by the *Filikí Etería*, or "Friendly Society", a secret group recruited among the exiled merchants and intellectuals of central Europe.

This somewhat motley coalition of *Klephts* and theorists launched their insurrection at the monastery of **Ayia Lávra** near Kalávrita in the Peloponnese, where on March 25, 1821, the Greek banner was openly raised by the local bishop, Yermanos.

THE WAR OF INDEPENDENCE

To describe in detail the course of the **War of Independence** is to provoke unnecessary confusion, since much of the rebellion consisted of local and fragmentary guerilla campaigns. What is important to understand is that Greeks, though fighting for liberation from the Turks, were not fighting as and for a nation. Motives differed enormously: landowners assumed their role was to lead and sought to retain and reinforce their traditional privileges, while the peasantry saw the struggle as a means towards land redistribution.

Outside Greece, prestige and publicity for the insurrection was promoted by the arrival of a thousand or so European **Philhellenes**, almost half of them German, though the most important was the English poet, **Lord Byron**, who died while training Greek forces at Messolóngi in April 1824.

Though it was the Greek guerilla leaders, above all **Theodhoros Kolokotronis**, "the old man of the Morea", who brought about the most significant military victories of the war, the death of Byron had an immensely important effect on public opinion in the west. Aid for the Greek struggle had come neither from Orthodox Russia, nor from the western powers of France and Britain, ravaged by the Napoleonic Wars. But by 1827, when Messolóngi fell again to the Turks, these three powers finally agreed to seek autonomy for certain parts of Greece and sent a combined fleet to put pressure on the Sultan's Egyptian army, then ransacking and massacring in the Peloponnese. Events took over, and an accidental naval battle in **Navarino Bay** resulted in the destruction of almost the entire Turkish-Egyptian fleet. The following spring Russia itself declared war on the Turks and the Sultan was forced to accept the existence of an autonomous Greece.

In 1830 Greek independence was confirmed by the western powers and **borders** were drawn. These included just 800,000 of the 6 million Greeks living within the Ottoman empire, and the Greek territories were for the most part the poorest of the Classical and Byzantine lands, comprising Attica, the Peloponnese and the islands of the Argo-Saronic and Cyclades. The rich agricultural belt of Thessaly, Epirus in the west, and Macedonia in the north, remained in Turkish hands. Meanwhile, the Ionian islands were controlled by a British Protectorate and the Dodecanese by the Ottomans (and subsequently by the new Italian nation).

THE EMERGING STATE

Modern Greece began as a republic and **Ioannis Capodistrias**, its first president, concentrated his efforts on building a viable central authority and govenment in the face of diverse protagonists from the independence struggle. Almost inevitably he was assassinated – in 1831, by two chieftains from the ever-disruptive Máni – and perhaps equally inevitably the great western powers stepped in. They created a monarchy, gave limited aid, and set on the throne a Bavarian prince, **Otho**.

The new king proved an autocratic and insensitive ruler, bringing in fellow Germans to fill official posts and ignoring all claims by the landless peasantry for redistribution of the old estates. In 1862 he was eventually forced from the country by a popular revolt, and the Europeans produced a new prince, this time from Denmark, with Britain ceding the Ionian islands to bolster support. **George I**, in fact, proved more capable: he built the first railways and roads, introduced limited land reforms in the Peloponnese, and oversaw the first expansion of the Greek borders.

THE MEGÁLI IDHÉA AND WAR

From the very beginning, the unquestioned motive force of Greek foreign policy was the **Megáli Idhéa** (Great Idea) of liberating Greek populations outside the country and incorporating the old territories of Byzantium into the kingdom. In 1878 **Thessaly**, along with southern Epirus, was ceded to Greece by the Turks.

Less illustriously, the Greeks failed in 1897 to achieve *énosis* (union) with **Crete** by attacking Turkish forces on the mainland, and in the process virtually bankrupted the state. The island was, however, placed under a High Commissioner, appointed by the Great Powers, and in 1913 became a part of Greece.

It was from Crete, also, that the most distinguished Greek statesman emerged. **Eleftherios Venizelos**, having led a civilian campaign for his island's liberation, was in 1910 elected as Greek Prime Minister. Two years later he organised an alliance of Balkan powers to fight the **Balkan Wars** (1912–13), campaigns that saw the Turks virtually driven from Europe. With Greek borders extended to include the northeast Aegean, nothern Thessaly, central Epirus and parts of Macedonia, the *Megáli Idhéa* was approaching reality. At the same time Venizelos proved himself a shrewd manipulator of domestic public opinion by revising the constitution and introducing a series of liberal social reforms.

Division, however, was to appear with the outbreak of **World War I**. Venizelos urged Greek entry on the British side, seeing in the conflict possibilities for the "liberation" of Greeks in Thrace and Asia Minor, but the new king, Konstantinos I, married to a sister of the German Kaiser, imposed a policy of neutrality. Eventually Venizelos set up a revolutionary government in Thessaloníki, and in 1917 Greek troops entered the war to join the French, British and Serbians in the **Macedonian campaign**. On the capitulation of Bulgaria and Ottoman Turkey, the Greeks occupied **Thrace**, and Venizelos presented at Versailles demands for the predominantly Greek region of Smyrna on the Asia Minor coast.

It was the beginning of one of the most disastrous episodes in modern Greek history. Venizelos was authorised to move forces into Smyrna in 1919, but by then Allied support had evaporated and in Turkey itself a new nationalist movement was taking power under Mustafa Kemal, or **Atatürk** as he came to be known. In 1920 Venizelos lost the elections and monarchist factions took over, their aspirations unmitigated by the Cretan's skill in foreign diplomacy. Greek forces were ordered to advance upon Ankara in an attempt to bring Atatürk to terms.

This so-called **Anatolian campaign** ignominiously collapsed in summer 1922 when Turkish troops forced the Greeks back to the coast and a hurried evacuation from **Smyrna**. As they left Smyrna, the Turks moved in and systematically massacred whatever remained of the Armenian and Greek populations before burning most of the city to the ground.

THE EXCHANGE OF POPULATIONS

There was now no alternative but for Greece to accept Atatürk's own terms, formalised by the Treaty of Lausanne in 1923, which ordered the **exchange of religious minorities** in each country. Turkey was to accept 390,000 Muslims resident on Greek soil. Greece, mobilised almost continuously for the last decade and with a population of under five million, was faced with the resettlement of over 1,300,000 Christian refugees. The *Megáli Idhéa* had ceased to be a viable blueprint.

Changes, inevitably, were intense and far-reaching. The great agricultural estates of Thessaly were finally redistributed, both to Greek tenants and refugee farmers, and huge shantytowns grew into new quarters around Athens, Pireás and other cities, a spur to the country's then almost nonexistent industry.

Politically, too, reaction was swift. A group of army officers assembled after the retreat from Smyrna, "invited" King Konstantinos to abdicate and executed five of his ministers. Democracy was nominally restored by the proclamation of a republic, but for much of the next decade changes in government were brought about by factions within the armed forces. Meanwhile, among the urban refugee population, unions were being formed and the Greek Communist Party (KKE) was established.

By 1936 the Communist Party had enough democratic support to hold the balance of power in parliament, and would have done so had not the army and the by then restored king decided otherwise. King Yiorgos (George) II had been returned by a plebiscite held – and almost certainly manipulated – the previous year, and so presided over an increasingly factionalised parliament.

THE METAXAS DICTATORSHIP

In April 1936 George II appointed as prime minister **General John Metaxas**, despite the latter's support from only six elected deputies. Immediately a series of KKE-organised strikes broke out and the king, ignoring attempts to form a broad liberal coalition, dissolved parliament without setting a date for new elections. It was a blatantly unconstitutional move and opened the way for five years of ruthless and at times absurd dictatorship.

Metaxas averted a general strike with military force and proceeded to set up a state based on **fascist** models of the age. Left-wing and trade union opponents were imprisoned or forced into exile, a state youth movement and secret police set up, and rigid censorship, extending even to passages of Thucydides, imposed. It was, however, at least a Greek dictatorship, and though Metaxas was sympathetic to Nazi organisation he completely opposed German or Italian domination.

WORLD WAR II AND THE GREEK CIVIL WAR

The Italians tried to provoke the Greeks into **World War II** by surreptitiously torpedoing the Greek cruiser *Elli* in Tínos harbour on August 15, 1940. To this, they met with no response. However, when Mussolini occupied Albania and sent, on October 28, 1940, an ultimatum demanding passage for his troops through Greece, Metaxas responded to the Italian foreign minister with the apocryphal one-word answer *"óhi"* (no). (In fact, his response, in the mutually understood French, was *"C'est la guerre"*). The date marked the entry of Greece into the war, and the gesture is still celebrated as a national holiday.

OCCUPATION AND RESISTANCE

Fighting as a nation in a sudden unity of crisis, the Greeks drove Italian forces from the country and in the operation took control of the long-coveted and predominantly Greek-populated northern Epirus (the south of Albania). However, the Greek army frittered away their strength in the snowy mountains of northern Epirus rather than consolidate their gains or defend the Macedonian frontier, and coordination with the British never materialised.

In April of the following year Nazi mechanised columns swept through Yugoslavia and across the Greek mainland, effectively reversing the only Axis defeat to date, and by the end of May 1941 airborne and seaborne **German invasion** forces had completed the occupation of Crete and the other islands. Metaxas had died before their arrival, while King George and his new self-appointed ministers fled into exile in Cairo; few Greeks, of any political persuasion, were sad to see them go.

The joint **Italian–German–Bulgarian Axis occupation** of Greece was among the bitterest experiences of the European war.

Nearly half a million Greek civilians starved to death as all available food was requisitioned to feed occupying armies, and entire villages throughout the mainland and especially on Crete were burned and slaughtered at the least hint of resistance activity. In the north the Bulgarians desecrated ancient sites and churches in a bid to annex "Slavic" Macedonia.

Primarily in the north, too, the Nazis supervised the deportation to concentration camps of virtually the entire **Greek-Jewish population**. This was at the time a sizeable community. Thessaloníki – where the former UN and Austrian president Kurt Waldheim worked for Nazi intelligence – contained the largest Jewish population of any Balkan city, and there were significant populations in all the Greek mainland towns and on many of the islands.

With a quisling government in Athens – and an unpopular, discredited Royalist group in Cairo – the focus of Greek political and military action over the next four years passed largely to the **EAM**, or National Liberation Front. By 1943 it was in virtual control of most areas of the country, working with the British on tactical operations, with its own army (**ELAS**), navy, and both civil and secret police forces. On the whole it commanded popular support, and it offered an obvious framework for the resumption of postwar government.

However, most of its membership was communist, and the British Prime Minister, **Churchill**, was determined to reinstate the monarchy. Even with two years of the war to run it became obvious that there could be no peaceable post-liberation regime other than an EAM-dominated republic. Accordingly, in August 1943 representatives from each of the main resistance movements – including two non-communist groups – flew from a makeshift airstrip in Thessaly to ask for guarantees from the "government" in Cairo that the king would not return unless a plebiscite had first voted in his favour. Neither the Greek nor British authorities would consider the proposal and the one possibility of averting civil war was lost.

The EAM contingent returned divided, as perhaps the British had intended, and a conflict broke out between those who favoured taking peaceful control of any government imposed after liberation, and the hard-line Stalinist ideologues, who believed such a situation should not be allowed to develop.

In October 1943, with fears of an imminent British landing force and takeover, ELAS launched a full-scale attack upon its Greek rivals; by the following February, when a cease-fire was arranged, they had wiped out all but the EDES, a right-wing grouping suspected of collaboration with the Germans. At the same time other forces were at work, with both the British and Americans infiltrating units into Greece in order to prevent the establishment of communist government when the Germans began withdrawing their forces.

CIVIL WAR

In fact, as the Germans began to leave in October 1944, most of the EAM leadership agreed to join a British-sponsored "official" **interim government**. It quickly proved a tactical error, however, for with ninety percent of the countryside under their control the communists were given only one-third representation, the king showed no sign of renouncing his claims, and, in November, Allied forces ordered ELAS to disarm. On December 3 all pretences of civility or neutrality were dropped; the police fired on a communist demonstration in Athens and fighting broke out between ELAS and **British troops**, in the so-called **Dhekemvrianá** battle of Athens.

A truce of sorts was negotiated at Várkiza the following spring but the agreement was never implemented. The army, police and civil service remained in right-wing hands and while collaborationists were often allowed to retain their positions, left-wing sympathisers, many of whom were not communists, were systematically excluded. The elections of 1946 were won by the right-wing parties, followed by a plebiscite in favour of the king's return. By 1947 guerilla activity had again reached the scale of a full **civil war**.

In the interim, King George had died and been succeeded by his brother Paul (with his consort Frederika), while the **Americans** had taken over the British role, and begun putting into action the cold war **Truman doctrine**. In 1947 they took virtual control of Greece, their first significant postwar experiment in anti-communist intervention. Massive economic and military aid was given to a client Greek government, with a prime minister whose documents had to be countersigned by the American Mission in order to become valid.

In the mountains US "military advisers" supervised **campaigns against ELAS**, and there were mass arrests, court-martials, and imprisonments – a kind of "White Terror" – lasting until 1951. Over three thousand executions were recorded, including a number of Jehovah's Witnesses, "a sect proved to be under communist domination", according to US Ambassador Grady.

In the autumn of 1949, with the Yugoslav–Greek border closed after Tito's rift with Stalin, the last ELAS guerillas finally admitted defeat, retreating into Albania from their strongholds on Mount Grámmos. Atrocities had been committed on both sides, including, from the left, widescale destruction of monasteries, and the dubious evacuation of children from "combat areas" (as told in Nicholas Gage's virulently anti-communist book *Eleni*). Such errors, as well as the hopelessness of fighting an American-backed army, undoubtedly lost ELAS much support.

RECONSTRUCTION AMERICAN-STYLE 1950–67

It was a demoralised, shattered Greece that emerged into the Western political orbit of the 1950s. It was also perforce American-dominated, enlisted into the Korean War in 1950 and NATO the following year. In domestic politics, the US Embassy – still giving the orders – foisted a winner-take-all electoral system, which was to ensure victory for the right over the next twelve years. All leftist activity was banned; those individuals who were not herded into political "re-education" camps or dispatched by firing squads, legal or vigilante, went into exile throughout Eastern Europe, to return only after 1974.

The American-backed, highly conservative **"Greek Rally"** party, led by General Papagos, won the first decisive post-civil war elections in 1952. After the general's death, the party's leadership was taken over – and to an extent liberalised – by **Konstantinos Karamanlis**. Under his rule, stability of a kind was established and some economic advances registered, particularly after the revival of Greece's traditional German markets. However, the 1950s was also a decade that saw wholesale **depopulation of the villages** as migrants sought work in Australia, America and western Europe, or the larger Greek cities.

The main crisis in foreign policy throughout this period was **Cyprus**, where a long terrorist campaign was waged by Greeks opposing British rule, and there was sporadic threat of a new Greek–Turkish war. A temporary and unworkable solution was forced on the island by Britain in 1960, granting independence without the possibility of self-determination or union with Greece. Much of the traditional Greek–British goodwill was destroyed by the issue, with Britain seen to be acting with regard only for its two military bases (over which, incidentally, it still retains sovereignty).

By 1961, unemployment, the Cyprus issue and the imposition of US nuclear bases on Greek soil were changing the political climate, and when Karamanlis was again elected there was strong suspicion of a fraud arranged by the king and army. Strikes became frequent in industry and even agriculture, and King Paul and autocratic, fascist-inclined Queen Frederika were openly attacked in parliament and at protest demonstrations. The far right grew uneasy about **"communist resurgence"** and, losing confidence in their own electoral influence, arranged the assassination of left-wing deputy **Grigoris Lambrakis** in Thessaloníki in May 1963. (The assassination, and its subsequent cover-up, is the subject of Vassilis Vassilikos's thriller *Z*, filmed by Costa-Gavras.) It was against this volatile background that Karamanlis resigned, lost the subsequent elections and left the country.

The new government – the first controlled from outside the Greek right since 1935 – was formed by **Yiorgos Papandreou's** Centre Union Party, and had a decisive majority of nearly fifty seats. It was to last, however, for under two years as conservative forces rallied to thwart its progress. In this the chief protagonists were the army officers and their constitutional Commander-in-Chief, the new king, 23-year-old **Konstantinos (Constantine) II**.

Since power in Greece depended on a pliant military as well as a network of political appointees, Papandreou's most urgent task in order to govern securely and effectively was to reform the armed forces. His first Minister of Defence proved incapable of the task and, while he was investigating the right-wing plot that was thought to have rigged the 1961 election, "evidence" was produced of a leftist conspiracy connected with Papandreou's son

Andreas (himself a minister in the government). The allegations grew to a crisis and Yiorgos Papandreou decided to assume the defence portfolio himself, a move for which the king refused to give the necessary sanction. He then resigned in order to gain approval at the polls but the king would not order fresh elections, instead persuading members of the Centre Union – chief among them **Konstantinos Mitsotakis**, the current premier – to defect and organise a coalition government. Punctuated by strikes, resignations and mass demonstrations, this lasted for a year and a half until new elections were eventually set for May 28, 1967. They failed to take place.

THE COLONELS' JUNTA 1967–74

It was a foregone conclusion that Papandreou's party would win popular support in the polls against the discredited coalition partners. And it was equally certain that there would be some sort of anti-democratic action to try and prevent them from taking power. Disturbed by the party's leftward shift, King Konstantinos was said to have briefed senior generals for a *coup d'état*, to take place ten days before the elections. However, he was caught by surprise, as was nearly everyone else, by the **coup of April 21, 1967**, staged by a group of "unknown" colonels. It was, in the words of Andreas Papandreou, "the first successful CIA military putsch on the European continent".

The **Colonels' Junta**, having taken control of the means of power, was sworn in by the king and survived the half-hearted counter-coup which he subsequently attempted to organise. It was an overtly fascist regime, absurdly styling itself as the true "Revival of Greek Orthodoxy" against western "corrupting influences", though in reality its ideology was nothing more than warmed-up dogma from the Metaxas era.

All political activity was banned, trade unions were forbidden to recruit or meet, the press was so heavily censored that many papers stopped printing, and thousands of "communists" were arrested, imprisoned, and often tortured. Among them were both Papandreous, the composer Mikis Theodorakis (deemed "unfit to stand trial" after three months in custody) and Amalia Fleming (widow of Alexander). The best-known Greek actress,

Melina Mercouri, was stripped of her citizenship in absentia and thousands of prominent Greeks joined her in exile. Culturally, the colonels put an end to popular music (closing down most of the Pláka *rembétika* clubs) and inflicted ludicrous censorship on literature and the theatre, including (as under Metaxas) a ban on production of the Classical tragedies.

The colonels lasted for seven years, opposed (especially after the first year) by the majority of the Greek people, excluded from the European community, but propped up and given massive aid by US presidents **Lyndon Johnson** and **Richard Nixon**. To them and the CIA the junta's Greece was not an unsuitable client state; human rights considerations were considered unimportant, orders were placed for sophisticated military technology, and foreign investment on terms highly unfavourable to Greece was open to multinational corporations. It was a fairly routine scenario for the exploitation of an underdeveloped nation.

Opposition was from the beginning voiced by exiled Greeks in London, the United States and western Europe, but only in 1973 did demonstrations break out openly in Greece. On November 17 the students of Athens **Polytechnic** began an occupation of their buildings. The ruling clique lost its nerve; armoured vehicles stormed the Polytechnic gates and a still-undetermined number of students were killed. Martial law was tightened and junta chief **Colonel Papadopoulos** was replaced by the even more noxious and reactionary **General Ioannides**, head of the secret police.

THE RETURN TO CIVILIAN RULE 1975–81

The end of the ordeal, however, came within a year as the dictatorship embarked on a disastrous political adventure in **Cyprus**. By attempting to topple the Makarios government and impose *énosis* (union) on the island, they provoked a Turkish invasion and occupation of forty percent of the Cypriot territory. The army finally mutinied and **Konstantinos Karamanlis** was invited to return from Paris to again take office. He swiftly negotiated a ceasefire (but no solution) in Cyprus, withdrew temporarily from NATO, and warned that US bases would have to be removed except where they specifically served Greek interest.

In November 1974 Karamanlis and his *Néa Dhimokratía* (New Democracy) party was rewarded by a sizeable majority in **elections**, with a centrist and socialist opposition. The latter was comprised by PASOK, a new party led by Andreas Papandreou.

The election of *Néa Dhimokratía* was in every sense a safe conservative option but to Karamanlis's enduring credit it oversaw an effective and firm return to democratic stability, even legitimising the KKE (Communist Party) for the first time in its history. Karamanlis also held a **referendum on the monarchy** – in which 59 percent of Greeks rejected the return of Constantine – and instituted in its place a French-style presidency, which post he himself occupied from 1980 to 1985 (and has done so again from 1990). Economically there were limited advances although these were more than offset by inflationary defence spending (the result of renewed tension with Turkey), hastily negotiated entrance into the EC, and the decision to let the drachma float after decades of its being artificially fixed at 30 to the US dollar.

Crucially, though, Karamanlis failed to deliver on vital reforms in bureaucracy, social welfare and education; and though the worst figures of the junta were brought to trial the ordinary faces of Greek political life and administration were little changed. By 1981 inflation was hovering around 25 percent, and it was estimated that tax evasion was depriving the state of one-third of its annual budget. In foreign policy the US bases had remained and it was felt that Greece, back in NATO, was still acting as little more than an American satellite. The traditional right was demonstrably inadequate to the task at hand.

PASOK: 1981–89

Change – *allayí* – was the watchword of the election campaign which swept Andreas Papandreou's Panhellenic Socialist Movement, better known by the acronym **PASOK**, to power on October 18, 1981.

The victory meant a chance for Papandreou to form the first socialist government in Greek history and break a near fifty-year monopoly of authoritarian right-wing rule. With so much at stake the campaign had been passionate even by Greek standards, and PASOK's victory was greeted with euphoria both by the generation

whose political voice had been silenced by defeat in the civil war and by a large proportion of the young. They were hopes which perhaps ran naively and dangerously high.

The victory, at least, was conclusive. PASOK won 174 of the 300 parliamentary seats and the Communist KKE returned another thirteen deputies, one of whom was the composer Mikis Theodorakis. *Néa Dhimokratía* moved into unaccustomed opposition. There appeared to be no obstacle to the implementation of a radical **socialist programme**: devolution of power to local authorities, the socialisation of industry (though it was never clear how this was to be different from nationalisation), improvement of the social services, a purge of bureaucratic inefficiency and malpractice, the end of bribery and corruption as a way of life, an independent and dignified foreign policy following expulsion of US bases, and withdrawal from NATO and the European Community.

A change of style was promised, too, replacing the country's long traditions of authoritarianism and bureacracy with openness and dialogue. Even more radically, where Greek political parties had long been the personal followings of charismatic leaders, PASOK was to be a party of ideology and principle, dependent on no single individual member. Or so, at least, thought some of the youthful PASOK political enthusiasts.

The new era started with a bang. The wartime resistance was officially recognised; hitherto they hadn't been allowed to take part in any celebrations, wreath-layings or other ceremonies. Peasant women were granted pensions for the first time – 3000 drachmas a month, the same as their outraged husbands – and wages were indexed to the cost of living. In addition, civil marriage was introduced, family law reformed in favour of wives and mothers, and equal rights legislation was put on the statute book.

These popular **reformist moves** seemed to mark a break with the past, and the atmosphere had indeed changed. Greeks no longer lowered their voices to discuss politics in public places or wrapped their opposition newspaper in the respectably conservative *Kathimeriní*. At first there were real fears that the climate would be too much for the military and they would once again intervene to choke a dangerous experiment in democracy, especially when Andreas Papandreou assumed the defence portfolio himself in a move strongly reminiscent of his father's attempt to remove the king's appointee in 1965. But he went out of his way to soothe **military susceptibilities**, increasing their salaries, buying new weaponry, and being super-fastidious in his attendance at military functions.

THE END OF THE HONEYMOON

Nothing if not a populist, **Papandreou** promised a bonanza he must have known, as a skilled and experienced economist, he could not deliver. As a result he pleased nobody on the **economic** front.

He could not fairly be blamed for the inherited lack of investment, low productivity, deficiency in managerial and labour skills and other chronic problems besetting the Greek economy. On the other hand, he certainly aggravated the situation in the early days of his first government by allowing his supporters to indulge in violently anti-capitalist rhetoric, and by the prosecution and humiliation of the Tsatsos family, owners of one of Greece's few modern and profitable businesses – cement, in this case – for the illegal export of capital, something of which every Greek with any savings is guilty. These were cheap victories and were not backed by any programme of public investment, while the only "socialisations" were of hopelessly lame-duck companies.

Faced with this sluggish economy, and burdened with the additional charges of (marginally) improved social benefits and wage indexing, Papandreou's government had also to cope with the effects of **world recession**, which always hit Greece with a delayed effect compared with its more advanced European partners. **Shipping**, the country's main foreign-currency earner, was devastated. Remittances from emigré workers fell off as they joined the lines of the unemployed in their host countries, and tourism receipts diminished under the dual impact of recession and Reagan's warning to Americans to stay away from insecure and terrorist-prone Athens airport.

With huge quantities of imported goods continuing to be sucked into the country in the absence of domestic production, the **foreign debt** topped £10 billion in 1986, with inflation at 25 percent and the balance of payments deficit approaching £1 billion. Greece also began to experience the social strains of **unemployment** for the first time. Not that it didn't exist before, but it had always been concealed as under-employment by the family and the rural structure of the economy – as well as by the absence of statistics.

The result of all this was that Papandreou had to eat his words. A modest spending spree, joy at the defeat of the right, the popularity of his Greece-for-the-Greeks foreign policy, and some much needed reforms saw him through into a **second term**, with an electoral victory in June 1985 scarcely less triumphant than the first. But the complacent and, frankly, dishonest slogan was "Vote PASOK for Even Better Days". By October they had imposed a two-year wage freeze and import restrictions, abolished the wage-indexing scheme and devalued the drachma by 15 percent. Papandreou's fat was pulled out of the fire by none other than that former bogeyman, the **European Community**, which offered a huge two-part loan on condition that an IMF-style **austerity programme** was maintained.

The political fallout of such a classic right-wing deflation, accompanied by shameless soliciting for foreign investment, was the alienation of the Communists and most of PASOK's own political constituency. Increasingly autocratic – ironic given the early ideals of PASOK as a new kind of party – Papandreou's response to **dissent** was to fire recalcitrant trade union leaders and expel some 300 members of his own party. Assailed by strikes, the government appeared to have lost direction completely. In local elections in October 1986 it lost a lot of ground to *Néa Dhimokratía*, including the mayoralties of the three major cities. Athens, Thessaloníki and Pátra.

Papandreou assured the nation that he had taken the message to heart but all that followed was a minor government reshuffle and a panicky attempt to undo the ill-feeling caused by an incredible freeing of **rent controls** at a time when all wage-earners were feeling the pinch badly. Early in 1987 he went further and sacked all the remaining PASOK veterans in his cabinet, including his son, though it is said, probably correctly, that this was a palliative to public opinion. The new cabinet was so un-Socialist that even the right-wing press called it **"centrist"**.

WOMEN'S RIGHTS IN GREECE

Women's right to vote wasn't universally achieved in Greece until 1956, and less than a decade ago adultery was still a punishable offence, with cases regularly brought to court. The socialist party, PASOK, was elected for terms of government in 1981 and 1985 with a strong theoretical progamme for **women's rights**, and their women's council review committees, set up in the early, heady days, effected a landmark reform with the 1983 **Family Law**. This prohibited dowry and stipulated equal legal status and shared property rights between husband and wife.

Subsequently, however, the PASOK governments did little to follow through on **practical issues**, like improved child care, health and family planning. Contraception is not available as part of the skeletal Greek public health service, leaving many women to fall back on abortions – only recently made legal under certain conditions, but running (as for many years past) to an estimated 70–80,000 a year.

The **Greek Women's Movement** has in recent years conspicuously emerged. By far the largest organization is the *Union of Greek Women*. Founded in 1976, this espouses an independent feminist line and is responsible for numerous consciousness-raising activities across the country, though it remains too closely linked to the scandal-ridden opposition party, PASOK, for comfort. As a perfect metaphor for this, Margaret Papandreou felt compelled to resign from the Union following her well-publicized divorce from ex-Premier Andreas, leaving it without her effective and vocal leadership. Other, more autonomous groups, have been responsible for setting up advice and support networks, highlighting women's issues within trade unions, and campaigning for changes in media representation.

None of this is easy in a country as polarized as Greece. In many rural areas women rely heavily on traditional extended families for security, and are unlikely to be much affected by legislative reforms or city politics. Yet Greek men of all classes and backgrounds are slowly becoming used to the notion of women in positions of power and responsibility, and taking a substantial share in child-rearing – both postures utterly unthinkable two decades ago, and arguably one of the few positive legacies with which PASOK can at least in part be credited.

Similar about-faces took place in **foreign policy**. The initial anti-US, anti-NATO and anti-EC rhetoric was immensely popular, and understandable for a people shamelessly bullied by bigger powers for the past 150 years. There was some high-profile nose-thumbing, like refusing to join EC partners in condemning Jaruzelski's Polish regime, or the Soviet downing of a Korean airliner, or Syrian involvement in terrorist bomb-planting. There were some forgettable embarrassments, too, like suggesting Gaddafi's Libya provided a suitable model for alternative Socialist development, and the Mitterrand-Gaddafi-Papandreou "summit" in Crete, which an infuriated Mitterrand felt he had been inveigled into on false pretences.

Much was made of a strategic opening to the Arab world. Yasser Arafat, for example, was the first "head of state" to be received in Athens under the PASOK government. Given Greece's geographical position and historical ties, it was an imaginative and appropriate policy. But if Arab investment was hoped for, it never materialised.

In stark contrast to his early promises and rhetoric, the "realistic" policies that Papandreou pursued were far more conciliatory towards his big Western brothers. This was best exemplified by the fact that **US bases** remained in Greece, largely due to the fear that snubbing NATO would lead to Greece being exposed to Turkish aggression, still the only issue that unites the main parties to any degree. As for the once-reviled **European Community**, Greece had become an established beneficiary and its leader was hardly about to bite the hand that feeds.

SCANDAL

Even as late as mid-1988, despite the many betrayals of Papandreou, despite his failure to clean up the public services and do away with the system of patronage and corruption, and despite a level of popular displeasure that brought a million striking, demonstrating workers into the streets (February 1987), it seemed unlikely that PASOK would be toppled in the following year's **elections**.

This was due mainly to the lack of a credible alternative. Konstantinos Mitsotakis, a bitter personal enemy of Papandreou's since 1965, when his defection had brought down his father's government and set in train the events that culminated in the junta, was an unconvincing and unlikeable character at the helm of *Néa Dhimokratía*. Meanwhile, the liberal centre had disappeared and the main communist party, KKE, appeared trapped in a Stalinist timewarp under the leadership of Harilaos Florakis. Only the *Ellenikí Aristerá* (Greek Left), formerly the European wing of the KKE, seemed to offer any sensible alternative programme, and they had a precariously small following.

So PASOK could have been in a position to win a third term by default, as it were, when a combination of spectacular **own goals**, plus perhaps a general shift to the Right, influenced by the cataclysmic events in Eastern Europe, conspired against them.

First came the extraordinary cavortings of the Prime Minister himself. Towards the end of 1988, the seventy-year-old Papandreou was flown to Britain for open-heart surgery. He took the occasion, with fear of death presumably rocking his judgement, to make public a year-long liaison with a 34-year-old *Olympic Airways* hostess, **Dimitra "Mimi" Liani**. The international news pictures of an old man shuffling about after a young blonde, to the public humiliation of Margaret, his American-born wife, and his family, were not popular (Papandreou has since divorced Margaret and married Mimi). His integrity was further questioned when he missed several important public engagements – including a ceremony commemorating the victims of the 1987 Kalamáta earthquake – and was pictured out with Mimi, reliving his youth in nightspots.

The real damage, however, was done by **economic scandals**. It came to light that a PASOK minister had passed off Yugoslav corn as Greek in a sale to the EC. Then, far more seriously, it emerged that a self-made con-man, **Yiorgos Koskotas**, director of the **Bank of Crete**, had embezzled £120m (US$190m) of deposits and, worse still, slipped though the authorities' fingers and sought asylum in the US. Certain PASOK ministers and even Papandreou himself were implicated in the scandal. Further damage was done by allegations of illegal **arms dealings** by still more government ministers.

United in disgust at this corruption, the other Left parties – KKE and *Ellinikí Aristerá* –

formed a coalition, the **Synaspismós**, taking support still further from PASOK.

THREE BITES AT THE CHERRY

In this climate of disaffection, an inconclusive result to the **June 1989 election** was no real surprise. What was less predictable, however, was the formation of a bizarre **"katharsis" coalition** of conservatives and communists, united in the avowed intent of cleansing PASOK's increasingly Augean stables.

That this coalition emerged was basically down to Papandreou. The *Synaspismós* would have formed a government with PASOK but set one condition for doing so – that Papandreou stepped down as Prime Minister – and the old man would have none of it. In the deal finally cobbled together between the left and *Néa Dhimokratía*, Mitsotakis was denied the premiership, too, having to make way for his compromise party colleague, **Tzanetakis**.

During the three months that the coalition lasted, the *katharsis* turned out to be largely a question of burying the knife as deeply as possible into the ailing body of PASOK. Andreas Papandreou and three other ministers were officially accused of involvement in the Koskotas affair – though there was no time to set up their **trial** before the Greek people returned once again to the polls. In any case, the chief witness and protagonist in the affair, Koskotas himself, was still imprisoned in America, awaiting extradition proceedings.

Contrary to the Right's hope that publicly accusing Papandreou and his cohorts of criminal behaviour would pave the way for a *Néa Dhimokratía* victory, PASOK actually made a slight recovery in **November 1989 elections**, though the result was still inconclusive. This time the Left resolutely refused to do deals with anyone and the result was a consensus caretaker government under the neutral aegis of an academic called Zolotas, who was pushed into the Prime Minister's office, somewhat unwillingly it seemed, from Athens University. His only mandate was to see that the country didn't go off the rails completely while preparations were made for yet more elections.

These took place in **April 1990** with the same captains at the command of their ships and with the *Synaspismós* having completed its about-turn to the extent that in the five single-seat constituencies (the other 295 seats are drawn from multiple-seat constituencies in a complicated system of reinforced proportional representation), they supported independent candidates jointly with PASOK. Greek communists are good at about-turns, though; after all, composer Mikis Theodorakis, musical torch-bearer of the Left during the dark years of the junta, and formely a KKE MP, was by now standing for *Néa Dhimokratía*.

On the night, *Néa Dhimokratía* scraped home with a majority of one, later doubled with the defection of a centrist, and **Mitsotakis** finally got to achieve his dream of becoming Prime Minister. The only other memorable feature of the election was the first parliamentary representation for a party of the Turkish minority in Thrace, and for the ecologists – a focus for many disaffected PASOK voters.

A RETURN TO THE RIGHT: MITSOTAKIS

On assuming power, Mitsotakis followed a course of **austerity measures** to try and revive the chronically ill economy. Little headway was made, though given the world recession, it was hardly surprising. Greece still has **inflation** up towards 20 percent and a growing **unemployment** problem.

The latter has been exacerbated, since 1990, by the arrival of thousands of impoverished **Albanians**. They have formed something of an underclass, especially those who aren't ethnically Greek, and are prey to vilification for all manner of ills. They have also led to the first real immigration measures in a country whose population is more used to being on the other side of such laws.

Other conservative measures introduced by Mitsotakis included laws to combat strikes and **terrorism**. The terrorist issue had been a perennial source of worry for Greeks since the appearance in the mid-1980s of a group called **17 Novemvriou** (the date of the Colonels' attack on the Polytechnic in 1973). They have killed a number of industrialists and attacked buildings of military attachés and airlines in Athens, so far without any police arrests. It hardly seemed likely that Mitsotakis's laws, however, were the solution. They stipulated that statements by the group could no longer

be published and led to one or two newspaper editors being jailed for a few days for defiance – much to everyone's embarrassment.

The **anti-strike laws** threatened severe penalties but were equally ineffectual, as breakdowns in public transport, electricity and rubbish collection all too frequently illustrated.

As for the **Koskotas scandal**, the villain of the piece was eventually extradited and gave evidence for the prosecution against Papandreou and various of his ministers. The trial was televised and proved as popular as any soap opera, as indeed it should have been, given the twists of high drama – which included one of the defendants, Koutsoyiorgas, dying in court of a heart attack in front of the cameras. The case against Papandreou gradually petered out and he was officially acquitted in early 1992. The two other surviving ministers, Tsovolas and Petsos, were convicted and given short prison sentences.

The great showpiece trial thus went with a whimper rather than a bang, and did nothing to enhance Mitsotakis's position. If anything, it served to increase sympathy for Papandreou, who was felt to have been unfairly victimized. The real villain of the piece, Koskotas, was eventually convicted of major **fraud** and is now serving a lengthy sentence.

THE MACEDONIAN QUESTION

Increasingly unpopular because of the desperate austerity measures, and perceived as ineffective and out of his depth on the international scene, the last thing Mitsotakis needed was a major **foreign policy** headache. That is exactly what he got when, in 1991, one of the breakaway republics of the former Yugoslavia named itself Macedonia, thereby injuring Greek national pride and sparking off vehement protests at home and abroad. Diplomatically, the Greeks fought tooth and nail against the use of the name, but their position became increasingly isolated and by 1993 the new country had gained official recognition, from both the EC and the UN – albeit under the convoluted title of the Former Yugoslav Republic of Macedonia (FYROM).

Salt was rubbed into Greek wounds when the FYROM started using the Star of Veryína as a national symbol on their new flag. Greece still refuses to call its northerly neighbour

Macedonia, instead referring to it as Ta Skópia after the capital – and you can't go far in Greece these days without coming across officially placed protestations that "Macedonia was, is, and always will be Greek and only Greek!" Strong words.

THE PENDULUM SWINGS BACK

In effect, the Macedonian problem more or less directly led to Mitsotakis's **political demise**. In the early summer of 1993 his ambitious young Foreign Minister, **Andonis Samaras**, disaffected with his leader, jumped on the bandwagon of resurgent Greek nationalism to set up his own party, **Politikí Ánixi** (Political Spring), after leaving *Néa Dhímokratía*. His platform, still right-wing, was largely based on action over Macedonia and during the summer of 1993 more ND MPs broke ranks, making *Politikí Ánixi* a force to be reckoned with. When parliament was called upon to approve severe new budget proposals, it became clear that the government lacked support, and early elections were called for October 1993. Mitsotakis had also been plagued for nearly a year by accusations of phone-tapping, and had been linked with a nasty and complicated contracts scandal centred around a national company, AGET.

Many of ND's disillusioned supporters reverted directly to PASOK, and **Papandreou** romped to election victory.

THE MORNING AFTER

And so, a frail-looking Papandreou, now well into his 70s, became Prime Minister for the third time. He soon realized that the honeymoon was going to be neither as sweet nor as long as it had been in the 80s.

PASOK immediately fulfilled two of its pre-election promises by removing restrictions on the reporting of statements by terrorist groups and renationalizing the Athens city bus company. The new government also set about improving the health system, and began to set the wheels in motion for Mitsotakis to be tried for his alleged misdemeanours.

The thrust of popular dissatisfaction, of course, remains **the economy**, which is still in dire straits, and PASOK can hardly claim to have won any diplomatic battles over Macedonia, despite a lot of tough posturing. The only concrete move has been the imposition of a trade embargo by the Greeks, which has landed them in trouble with the European Court of Justice. There is also increased **tension with Albania**, where five ethnic Greek activists are on trial for terrorism, in retaliation for which droves of illegal Albanian workers are periodically rounded up and bussed back across the border.

At home, the Minister of Public Order, Papathemelis, has made the government extremely unpopular with the youth and bar/restaurant owners by re-introducing licensing laws and imposing, for the first time, minimum age requirements.

THE CURRENT SITUATION

Both the major parties received a good slap in the face at the **Euroelections** of June 1994, losing ground to the smaller parties. The major winner was Samaras, whose *Politikí Ánixi* almost doubled its share of the vote, while the two left-wing parties both fared quite well.

The country is currently in the run-up to the spring 1995 presidential elections: Papandreou would like to assume the presidency when the aged Karamanlis finally retires, but lacks the necessary majority. If he fails to consolidate his position, it is most likely that new general elections would be called, the outcome of which is highly unpredictable.

THE GREEK MINORITIES

The Greek minorities – Vlachs, Sarakatsáni, Albanians, Turks, Jews and other relict communities – are little known, even within Greece. Indeed to meet Vlachs or Sarakatsáni who remain true to their roots you'll have to get to some fairly remote parts of Epirus. Greco-Turks are another matter, a sizeable (and recently problematic) community living, as they have done for centuries, in Thrace. The Jews of Greece, as ever, have the saddest history, having been annihilated by the Nazi occupiers during the latter stages of World War II.

THE VLACHS

The **Vlachs'** homeland is in the remote fastness of the **Píndhos Mountains** in northwestern Greece near the Albanian frontier. Traditionally they were transhumant shepherds, although some have long led a more settled existence in villages around Métsovo. As the town grew in prosperity, the Vlachs traded their sheep products further and further afield. Local merchants established themselves in Constantinople, Vienna, Venice and elsewhere, expanding into other lines of business: Vlachs played a major role in Balkan mule-back haulage and the hotel trade –specifically *caravanserais* where mule convoys halted.

They are an ancient, close-knit community with a strong sense of identity, like their rival shepherd clan, the *Sarakatsáni*, whom they despise as "tent-dwellers" and who, in turn, just as passionately despise them for living in houses. Unlike the Sarakatsans, however, their mother tongue is not Greek, but Vlach, a Romance language, which even today is full of words that anyone with a little Latin can easily recognize: *loop* for wolf, *mulier* for women, *pene* for bread. When the Italians invaded Greece in World War II, Vlach soldiers were often used as interpreters.

It used to be thought that the Vlachs were Slavs, descendants of Roman legionaries stationed in the provinces of Illyria and Dacia, who over the centuries had wandered down through the Balkans in search of grazing for their sheep and finally settled in northern Greece, where they had been trapped by the creation of modern frontiers on the disintegration of the Austro-Hungarian and Ottoman empires. Because of these supposed Slav connections and the old Greek anxieties about the Slavophile, separatist tendencies of the peoples of northern Greece, the Vlachs have been objects of suspicion to the modern state. To their chagrin many villages with Slav-sounding names were officially renamed during the Metaxas dictatorship of the 1930s, and Vlach schoolchildren forbidden to use their mother tongue.

There is, however, a new theory about their origins, which argues that the Greek Vlachs are of Greek descent and have always inhabited these same regions of the Píndhos Mountains; that during Roman times the Romans found it convenient to train local people as highway guards for the high passes on the old Roman road, the Via Egnatia, which connected Constantinople with the Adriatic. Thus the Vlachs learned their Latin through their association with the Romans and preserved it because of the isolation of their homeland and the exclusive nature of their pastoral way of life.

Sadly, though probably inevitably, the Vlachs' unique traditions are in danger of extinction. Only fifty or so years back, a prosperous Vlach family might have 10,000 sheep, and when they set off on the annual migration from their lowland winter pastures to the mountains it was like a small army on the march, with two or three complete generations together with all their animals and belongings. Nowadays few flocks number more than 250 ewes, and the annual migration takes place in lorries – though a few veterans still do it on foot. Hundreds of Vlachs have sold their flocks and moved to the town or emigrated; many a sheepfold boasts a former Volkswagen-factory hand. There are depressingly few young men among the remaining shepherds. The hardships of their life are too many and the economic returns too small.

JEWS AND TURKS

Jews and Turks in Greece are, for historical reasons, conveniently considered together. Since the decline of the Ottoman empire, these two Greek minorities have often suffered similar fates as isolated groups in a non-assimilating culture. Yet it seems that enclaves of each will endure for the forseeable future.

ORIGINS AND SETTLEMENTS

The **Greek Jewish community** is one of the oldest established in Europe, dating back to the late Classical period. During the Roman and Byzantine eras, the Jews were termed *Romaniot* and colonies flourished throughout the Balkans. In Greece these included Corfu, Zákinthos, Pátra, Kórinthos, Athens, Halkídha, Véria, Crete and, most importantly, Ioánnina.

The most numerically significant Jewish communities in Greece, however, date back to shortly after the taking of Constantinople by the **Ottomans**. In 1493 Sultan Beyazit II invited Spanish and Portuguese Jews expelled from those countries to settle in the Ottoman empire. The great influx of *Sephardim* (Ladino-speaking Jews) soon swamped the original Romaniot centres, and within two centuries, Ladino, a mix of medieval Spanish and Portuguese with Turkish, Hebrew and Arabic augments, had largely supplanted Greek as the lingua franca of Balkan Jewry. However, *Ladinismo* (the medieval Iberian Jewish culture) never penetrated the Romaniot enclaves of Ioánnina and Halkídha, which remain Greek-speaking to this day.

Turkish officials and their families fanned out across the Balkans to consolidate imperial administration, thus sowing the seeds of the numerous **Muslim communities** in present-day Bulgaria, Albania, Yugoslavia and Greece. The Ottoman authorities often appointed Jews as civil servants and tax collectors; one, Joseph Nassi, became governor of the Cyclades.

As a result Jews became identified with the ruling hierarchy in the eyes of the Orthodox Christian population, and at the outset of the 1821 **War of Independence** the Jewish quarters of Pátra, Kórinthos, Athens and virtually all others within the confines of the nascent Greek state, were put to the sword along with Turkish villages. Survivors of the various massacres fled north, to the territories that remained under Ottoman control. Within the new Greek kingdom, a small community of Ashkenazi Jews arrived in Athens, along with the Bavarian king Otho, in the 1830s.

UNDER THE GREEK STATE

The **expansion of the Greek nation** thereafter resulted in the decline of both the Greek-Jewish and Greek-Turkish populations. New annexations or conquests (Thessaly in 1878, Epirus, Macedonia, the northeast Aegean and Crete in 1913) provoked a wave of forced or nervous Judaeo-Turkish migration to the other side of the receding Ottoman frontier. While Jews were never forbidden to stay in newly occupied territory, rarely were they explicitly welcomed. The Turks – or more correctly, Muslims, since "Turk" was a generic term for any Muslim, including ethnic Greeks who had converted to Islam for economic advantage – were subject to various expulsion orders.

Between 1913 and 1923 the **Muslims of Crete**, mostly converted islanders, were forced to choose between apostasy to Christianity or exile. (The newly Orthodox can today often be distinguished by their ostentatiously Christian surnames, such as Stavroulakis, Hristakis, etc.) Those who opted to stand by their faith were summarily deposited in the closest Turkish-Muslim settlements on Greek islands just over the Ottoman border; Kós Town, the nearby village of Platáni, and Rhodes Town were three of the more convenient ones.

When the Italians formally annexed the **Dodecanese** after World War I, the **Muslims** were allowed to remain and they were thus rendered exempt from any of the provisions of the Treaty of Lausanne (which stipulated the wholescale exchange of "Turk" and "Greek" populations in the wake of the Asia Minor war). It is not certain exactly how or when the Dodecanese Muslims learned Greek, which they today mix unconcernedly in conversation with Turkish. Education in Greek, which has been compulsory since 1948, when the Dodecanese were reunited with Greece, must have played a part. But it's likely that the Muslim refugees from Crete, when they were not actually converted to Greek Orthodoxy, knew enough Greek both to communicate with neighbouring Christians and to teach any purely Turkish villagers the new tongue.

In **Rhodes** there is a long tradition of co-operation between the Muslim and the Jewish communities. In Ottoman days Jews were the only *milet* (subject ethnic group) allowed out after the city gates were closed at dusk, and more recently Muslim and Jewish leaders have consulted on how best to counter government strategies to deprive each of their rights and property. The dilapidated refugee village of Kritiká ("the Cretans") still huddles by the seaside on the way to the airport, and walking through Rhodes' old town it's easy to spot Turkish names on the marquees of various sandalmakers, *kafenía*, and kebab stands. Those Turks who live in the old town itself, however, have in some cases been there since the sixteenth century and will proudly tell you that they have every right to be considered native Rhodians.

In **Kós**, Cretan Muslims settled both in the port town – where they seem to have gravitated to the antique and shoe-making trade – and at Platáni, which still has a mixed Greek Orthodox and "Turkish" population.

During the early 1900s, the same era as the Cretan deportations, the status of mainland Jews and Turks in the path of Greek nationalism was more ambivalent. Even after the respective 1878 and 1913 acquisitions of **Thessaly**, **Epirus** and **Macedonia**, Muslim villages continued to exist in these regions. The Tsamidhes, an Albanian Muslim tribe localised in Epirus and Thesprotía, were left alone until World War II, when they made the grievous error of siding with the invading Axis armies; they were hunted down and expelled forthwith by first the National Army and later guerrilla bands.

Thessaloníki in the late nineteenth century was one of the largest Jewish towns in the world. Jews made up 75 percent of the population, and dominated the sailing, shipping and chandlery trades. In addition there were numerous *Dönmeh*, descendants of the false seventeenth-century messiah Sabbatai Zvi, who were outwardly Muslims but practised Judaism in secret. When the city passed to Greek control, the authorities allowed the "pure" Jews to stay but insisted on the departure of the *Dönmeh*, along with other Turkic Muslims. The *Dönmeh* (Turkish for "turncoats", after Zvi's conversion to Islam at swordpoint) insisted that they were "really" Jews, but to no avail. After 1913 the city began rapidly to lose its Hebraic character; the fire of 1917, emigration to Palestine and the arrival of the Nazis effectively brought an era to a close.

The same period, around the time of World War I, also saw the end of Muslim enclaves on the islands of **Thássos**, **Samothráki**, **Límnos**, **Lésvos** and **Híos**, where the Turks themselves, in a dog-in-the-manger mood, destroyed their fine Turkish bath before leaving. On **Sámos** there is a special, tiny Jewish cemetery with the graves of two brothers – apparently Ashkenazi merchants who died between the world wars; otherwise there had not been a significant Jewish community here since Byzantine times, and Muslim Turks were uniquely forbidden to settle here after the seventeenth century.

Western Thrace, the area from the Néstos River to the Évros, was always home to large numbers of Greek Muslims, and it remained their last bastion after the 1919–1922 Asia Minor War. The **Treaty of Lausanne** (1923) confirmed the right of this minority to remain in situ, in return for a continued Greek Orthodox presence in Istanbul (still known to Greeks as Konstantinoúpoli), the Prince's Islands, and Tenedos/Imvros Islands.

Over the years the Turks have repeatedly abrogated the terms of the pact and reduced the Turkish Greek Orthodox population to five percent of pre-1923 levels. The Greeks have acted comparatively leniently, and today Muslims still make up a third of the population of Greek Thrace, being highly visible in the main towns of **Alexandhroúpoli**, **Komotiní** and **Xánthi**. Muslims control much of the tobacco culture hereabouts and the baggy-trousered women can be glimpsed from the trains which pass through their fields.

The loyalty of these Thracian "Turks" to the Greek state was amply demonstrated during **World War II**, when they resisted the invading Bulgarians and Nazis side-by-side with their Christian compatriots. In return the two occupying forces harassed and deported to death camps many local Muslims. During the 1946–49 civil war Thracian Muslims suffered again at the hands of ELAS, who found the deep-seated conservatism of these villagers exasperating and laboured under the misconception that all local Muslims were traitors.

Only the **Pomaks**, a non-Turkic Muslim group of abouty 40,000 centred around Ehinós, north of Xánthi, collaborated to any extent with the Bulgarians, probably on the basis of ethnic affinity. The Pomaks as a group were probably Christian Slavs forcibly converted to Islam in the sixteenth century; they speak a degenerate dialect of Bulgarian with generous mixtures of Greek and Turkish. The authorities still keep them on a tight rein; they require a travel permit to leave their immediate area of residence around Ehínos, and visitors require a permit for their villages, too.

As if the foregoing were not complex enough, there is also a small (several thousand strong) population of **Gagauz**, Christian Turks, around Alexandhroúpoli.

Until recently, the Orthodox and "Turkish" Thracian communities lived in a fairly easy (if distant) relationship with each other, but in early 1990 a series of ugly intercommunal incidents, and official prosecution of Turkish political leaders cast doubt on the carefully cultivated international image of Greece's toleration of its minorities. It has, in fact, always been true that treatment of these Muslims functions as a barometer of relations at a more general level between Greece and Turkey, and as a quid pro quo for perceived maltreatment of the remaining Greek Orthodox in Turkey.

But it is the **Jews** rather than the Muslims who have suffered greater catastrophes during and since **World War II**. Eighty-five percent of a Jewish population of around 80,000 was rounded up by the Nazis in the spring of 1944, never to return. Greek Christians often went to extraordinary lengths to protect their persecuted countrymen, overshadowing the few instances of sordid betrayal. The city council of Zákinthos and the bishops of Athens and Halkídha, for example, put themselves at risk to save many who would otherwise have been killed.

Those Jews who remained in the country either went into hiding or joined the guerrillas in the hills. **Athens Jewry**, indistinguishable from their Orthodox neighbours in appearance and tongue, fared best, but the Ladino-speaking Jews of northern Greece, with their distinctive surnames and customs, were easy targets for the Nazis. It must also be said that certain portions of the Greek business community in **Thessaloníki** benefited greatly from the expulsion of the Jews, and needed little encouragement to help themselves to the contents of the abandoned Jewish shops. Jewish sensibilities were further offended in the post-war era when the German desecration of the huge Jewish cemetery was completed by the construction of the University of Thessaloníki on the site.

The paltry number of survivors returning from the death camps to Greece was insufficient to form the nucleus of a revival, and emigration to Israel was often a preferable alternative to living with ghosts. **Currently** barely 6000 Jews remain in Greece. In Thessaloníki there are around 1100 Sephardim, while small Ladino communities continue in Kavála, Sérres, Dhidhimótiho, Tríkala and Véria. Lárissa has a modest number who are still disproportionately important in the clothing trade. However young Jewish women outnumber their male counterparts, with the result that they tend to marry into the Orthodox faith. In Ioánnina, once a major centre of Jewry, less than 100 Romaniot Jews remain. Only 75 or so of the original community of Rhodes survived the war (that at Kós was completely wiped out), and these are almost outnumbered by recent Egyptian Jewish refugees.

The *Platía ton Evreón Martirón* (Square of the Jewish Martyrs) is a memorial to the 2000 Jews of Kós and Rhodes slaughtered by the Germans; it occupies the site of the (mostly demolished) old Jewish quarter. Three thousand of today's Greek Jews live in Athens, which is also the home of the **National Jewish Museum** (see p.89).

250 YEARS OF ARCHEOLOGY

Archeology until the second half of the nineteenth century was a very hit-and-miss affair. The early students of antiquity went to Greece to draw and make plaster casts of the great masterpieces of Classical sculpture. Unfortunately, a number soon found it more convenient or more profitable to remove objects wholesale, and might be better described as looters than scholars or archeologists.

EARLY EXCAVATIONS

The British **Society of Dilettanti** was one of the earliest promoters of Greek culture, financing expeditions to draw and publish antiquities. Founded in the 1730s as a club for young aristocrats who had completed the Grand Tour and fancied themselves arbiters of taste, the Society's main qualification for membership (according to most critics) was habitual drunkenness. Its leading spirit was Sir Francis Dashwood, a notorious rake who founded the infamous Hellfire Club. Nevertheless, the Society was the first body organized to sponsor systematic research into Greek antiquities, though it was initially most interested in Italy. Greece, then a backwater of the Ottoman Empire, was not a regular part of the Grand Tour and only the most intrepid adventurers undertook so hazardous a trip.

In the 1740s, two young artists, **James Stuart and Nicholas Revett**, formed a plan to produce a scholarly record of the ancient Greek buildings. With the support of the society they spent three years in Greece, principally Athens, drawing and measuring the surviving antiquities. The first volume of *The Antiquities of Athens* appeared in 1762, becoming an instant success. The publication of their exquisite illustrations gave an enormous fillip to the study of Greek sculpture and architecture, which became the fashionable craze among the educated classes; many European Neoclassical town and country houses date from this period.

The Society financed a number of further expeditions to study Greek antiquities, including one to Asia Minor in 1812. The expedition was to be based in Smyrna, but while waiting in Athens for a ship to Turkey, the party employed themselves in excavations at **Eleusis**, where they uncovered the Temple of Demeter. It was the first archeological excavation made on behalf of the Society, and one of the first in Greece. After extensive explorations in Asia Minor, the participants returned via Attica, where they excavated the Temple of Nemesis at **Rhamnous** and examined the Temple of Apollo at **Sounion**.

Several other antiquarians of the age were less interested in discoveries for their own sake. A French count, **Choiseul-Gouffier**, removed part of the **Parthenon frieze** in 1787 and his example prompted **Lord Elgin** to detach much of the rest in 1801. These were essentially acts of looting – "Bonaparte has not got such things from all his thefts in Italy", boasted Elgin – and their legality was suspect even at the time.

Other discoveries of the period were more ambiguous. In 1811, a party of English and German travellers, including the architect CR Cockerell, uncovered the **Temple of Aphaia** on **Aegina** (Áyina) and shipped away the pediments. They auctioned off the marbles for £6000 to Prince Ludwig of Bavaria and, inspired by this success, returned to Greece for further finds. This time they struck lucky with 23 slabs from the **Temple of Apollo Epicurius** at **Bassae**, for which the British Museum laid out a further £15,000. These were huge sums for the time and highly profitable exercises, but they were also pioneering archeology for the period. Besides removing the finds was hardly surprising: Greece, after all, was not yet a state and had no public museum; antiquities discovered were sold by their finders – if they recognized their value.

THE NEW NATION

The **Greek War of Independence** (1821–28) and the establishment of a modern Greek nation changed all of this – and provided a major impetus to archeology. Nationhood brought an increased pride in Greece's Classical heritage, nowhere more so than in **Athens**, which succeeded Náfplio as the nation's capital in 1834 largely on the basis of its ancient monuments and past.

As a result of the selection of Prince Otho of Bavaria as the first king of modern Greece in

1832, the **Germans**, whose education system laid great stress on Classical learning, were in the forefront of archeological activity.

One of the dominant Teutonic figures during the early years of the new state was **Ludwig Ross**. Arriving in Greece as a student in 1832, he was on hand to show the new king around the antiquities of Athens when Otho was considering making the town his capital. Ross was appointed deputy keeper of antiquities to the court, and in 1834 began supervising the **excavation and restoration of the Acropolis**. The work of dismantling the accretion of Byzantine, Frankish and Turkish fortifications began the following year. The graceful Temple of Athena Nike, which had furnished many of the blocks for the fortifications, was rebuilt, and Ross's architect, Leo von Klenze, began the reconstruction of the Parthenon.

The Greeks themselves had begun to focus on their ancient past when the first stirrings of the independence movement were felt. In 1813 the **Philomuse Society** was formed, which aimed to uncover and collect antiquities, publish books and assist students and foreign philhellenes. In 1829 an orphanage on the island of Éyina, built by Kapodistrias, the first President of Greece, became the first Greek **archeological museum**.

In 1837 the **Greek Archeological Society** was founded "for the discovery, recovery and restoration of antiquities in Greece". Its moving spirit was **Kyriakos Pittakis**, a remarkable figure who during the War of Independence had used his knowledge of ancient literature to discover the Clepsydra spring on the Acropolis – solving the problem of lack of water during the Turkish siege. In the first four years of its existence, the Archeological Society sponsored excavations in Athens at the **Theatre of Dionysus**, the **Tower of the Winds**, the **Propylaia** and the **Erechtheion**. Pittakis also played a major role in the attempt to convince Greeks of the importance of their heritage; antiquities were still being looted or burnt for lime.

THE GREAT GERMANS: CURTIUS AND SCHLIEMANN

Although King Otho was deposed in 1862 in favour of a Danish princeling, Germans remained in the forefront of Greek archeology in the 1870s. Two men dominated the scene, Heinrich Schliemann and Ernst Curtius.

Ernst Curtius was a traditionally Classical scholar. He had come to Athens originally as tutor to King Otho's family and in 1874 returned to Greece to negotiate the **excavations of Olympia**, one of the richest of Greek sanctuaries and site of the most famous of the ancient panhellenic games. The reigning German Kaiser Wilhelm I intended that the excavation would proclaim to the world the cultural and intellectual pre-eminence of his empire. Curtius took steps to set up a **German Archeological Institute** in Athens and negotiated the **Olympia Convention**, under the terms of which the Germans were to pay for and have total control of the dig; all finds were to remain in Greece, though the excavators could make copies and casts; and all finds were to be published simultaneously in Greek and German.

This was an enormously important agreement, which almost certainly prevented the treasure of Olympia and Mycenae following that of Troy to a German museum. The Europeans were still in very acquisitive mode. French consuls, for example, had been instructed to purchase any "available" local antiquities in Greece and Asia Minor, and had picked up the Louvre's great treasures, the *Venus de Milo* and *Winged Victory of Samothrace*, in 1820 and 1863 respectively.

At **Olympia**, digging began in 1875 on a site buried beneath many feet of river mud, silt and sand. Only one corner of the Temple of Zeus was initially visible, but within months the excavators had turned up statues from the east pediment. Over forty magnificent sculptures, as well as terra cottas, statue bases, and a rich collection of bronzes were uncovered, together with more than 400 inscriptions. The laying bare of this huge complex was a triumph for official German archeology.

While Curtius was digging at Olympia, a man who represented everything that was anathaema to orthodox Classical scholarship was standing archeology on its head. **Heinrich Schliemann's** beginnings were not auspicious for one who aspired to dig for ancient cities. The son of a drunken German pastor, he left school at fourteen and spent the next five years as a grocer's assistant. En route to seeking his fortune in Venezuela, he was left for dead on the Dutch coast after a shipwreck. Later, working as a bookkeeper in Amsterdam, he began to study languages. His phenomenal memory enabled him to master four by the age of 21. Following a six-week study of Russian, Schliemann was sent to Saint Petersburg as a trading agent and had amassed a fortune by the time he was 30. In 1851 he visited California, opened a bank during the Gold Rush and made another fortune.

His financial position secure for life, Schliemann was almost ready to tackle his life's ambition – **the search for Troy** and the vindication of his lifelong belief in the truth of Homer's tales of prehistoric cities and heroes. By this time he spoke no less than seventeen languages; and had excavated on the island of **Ithaca**, writing a book which earned him a doctorate from the University of Rostock.

Although most of the archeological establishment, led by Curtius, was unremittingly hostile to the millionaire amateur, Schliemann sunk his first trench at the hill called Hisarlik, in northwest Turkey, in 1870; excavation proper began in 1871. In his haste to find the city of Priam and Hector and to convince the world of his success, Schliemann dug a huge trench straight through the mound, destroying a mass of important evidence, but he was able nevertheless to identify nine cities, one atop the next. In May of 1873 he discovered the so-called **Treasure of Priam**, a stash of gold and precious jewellery and vessels. It convinced many that the German had indeed found Troy, although others contended that Schliemann, desperate for academic recognition, assembled it from other sources. The finds disappeared from Berlin at the end of World War II, but in 1994 archeologists discovered that artefacts held by some museums in Russia originated in Troy and announced plans to put the Treasure of Priam on display – probably in Saint Petersburg – in 1996.

Three years later Schliemann turned his attentions to **Mycenae**, again inspired by Homer, again following a hunch. Alone among contemporary scholars, he sought and found the legendary graves of Mycenean kings *inside* the existing Cyclopean wall of the citadel rather than outside, unearthing in the process the magnificent treasures that today form the basis of the prehistoric collection in the National Archeological Museum in Athens.

He dug again at Troy in 1882, assisted by a young architect, Willhelm Dörpfeld, who was destined to become one of the great archeologists of the next century (though his claim for Lefkádha as ancient Ithaca never found popular acceptance). In 1884 Schliemann returned to Greece to excavate another famous prehistoric citadel, this time at **Tiryns**.

Almost single-handedly, and in the face of continuing academic hostility, Schliemann had revolutionized archeology and pushed back the knowledge of Greek history and civilization a thousand years. Although some of his results have been shown to have been deliberately falsified in the sacrifice of truth to beauty, his achievement remains enormous.

The last two decades of the nineteenth century saw the discovery of other important Classical sites. Excavation began at **Epidaurus** in 1881 under the Greek archeologist **Panayotis Kavvadias**, who made it his life's work. Meanwhile at **Delphi**, the French, after gaining the permission to transfer the inhabitants of the village to a new town and demolishing the now-vacant village, began digging at the sanctuary of Apollo. Their excavations began in 1892, proved fruitful and continued non-stop for the next eleven years; they have gone on sporadically ever since.

EVANS AND KNOSSOS

The beginning of the twentieth century saw the domination of Greek archeology by an Englishman, **Sir Arthur Evans**. An egotistical maverick like Schliemann, he too was independently wealthy, with a brilliantly successful career behind him when he started his great work and recovered for Greek history another millennium. Evans excavated the **Palace of Minos** at **Knossos** on Crete, discovering one of the oldest and most sophisticated of Mediterranean societies.

The son of a distinguished antiquarian and collector, Evans read history at Oxford, failed to get a fellowship and began to travel. His chief interest was in the Balkans, where he was special correspondent for the *Manchester Guardian* in the uprising in Bosnia. He took enormous risks in the war-torn country, filing brilliant dispatches and still finding time for exploration and excavation.

In 1884, at the age of 33, Evans was appointed curator of the Ashmolean Museum in Oxford. He travelled whenever he could, and it was in 1893, while in Athens, that his attention was drawn to **Crete**. Evans, though very short-sighted, had almost microscopic close vision. In a vendor's stall he came upon some small drilled stones with tiny engravings in a hitherto unknown language; he was told they came from Crete. He had seen Schliemann's finds from Mycenae, and had been fascinated by this prehistoric culture. Crete, the cross-roads of the Mediterranean, seemed a good place to look for more.

Evans visited Crete in 1894 and headed for the legendary site of **Knossos**, where a Cretan had already done some impromptu digging, revealing massive walls and a storeroom filled with jars. Evans bought a share of the site and five years later, after the Turks had been forced off the island, returned to purchase the rest of the land. Excavations began in March 1899 and within a few days evidence of a great complex building was revealed, along with artifacts which indicated an astonishing cultural sophis-tication. The huge team of excavation workers unearthed elegant courtyards and verandahs, colourful wall paintings, pottery and jewellery and sealstones – the wealth of a 'civilization which dominated the eastern Mediterranean 3500 years ago.

Evans continued to excavate at Knossos for the next thirty years, during which time he established, on the basis of changes in the pottery styles, the system of dating that remains in use today for classifying Greek prehistory: Early, Middle and Late Minoan (Mycenean on the mainland). He published his account of the excavation in a massive six-volume work, *The Palace of Minos*, which appeared intermittently from 1921 to 1936. Like Schliemann, Evans attracted criticism and controversy for his methods – most notably his decision to reconstruct parts of the palace – and many of his interpretations of what he found. Nevertheless, his discoveries and his dedication put him near to the pinnacle of Greek archeology.

INTO THE 20TH CENTURY: THE FOREIGN INSTITUTES

In 1924 Evans gave to the **British School of Archeology** the site of Knossos, along with the Villa Ariadne (his residence there) and all other lands within his possession on Crete. At the time the British school was one of several foreign archeological institutes in Greece; founded in 1886, it had been preceded by the **French School**, the **German Institute** and the **American School**.

Greek archeology owes much to the work and relative wealth of these foreign schools and others that would follow. They have been responsible for the excavation of many of the most famous sites in Greece: the **Heraion on Sámos** (German), the sacred island of **Delos** (French), sites on **Kós** and in **southern Crete** (Italian), **Corinth** and the **Athenian Agora** (American). Life as a resi-dent foreigner in Greece at the beginning of the century was not for the weak-spirited (one unfortunate member of the American school was shot and killed by bandits while on a trip to visit sites in the Peloponnese); but there were compensations in unlimited access to antiquities in a countryside as yet unscarred.

The years **between the two world wars** saw an expansion of excavation and scholar-ship, most markedly concerning the **prehis-toric civilisations**. Having been shown by Schliemann and Evans what to look for, a new generation of archeologists was uncovering numerous **prehistoric sites** on the mainland and Crete, and its members were spending proportionately more time studying and inter-preting their finds. Digs in the 1920s and 1930s had much smaller labour forces (there were just 55 workmen under Wace at Mycenae, as compared to hundreds in the early days of Schliemann's or Evans' excavations) and they were supervised by higher numbers of trained archeologists. Though perhaps not as spectacu-lar as their predecessors, these scholars would prove just as pioneering as they established the history and clarified the chronology of the newly discovered civilisations.

One of the giants of this generation was **Alan Wace**, who while Director of the British School of Archeology from 1913–23 conducted excavations at Mycenae and established a chronological sequence from the nine great **tholos** tombs on the site. This led Wace to propose a new chronology for prehistoric Greece, and put him in direct conflict with Arthur Evans. Evans believed that the mainland citadels had been ruled by Cretan overlords, whereas Wace was convinced of an indepen-dent Mycenaean cultural and political develop-ment. Evans was by this time a powerful member of the British School Managing Committee, and his published attacks on Wace's claims, combined with the younger archeologist's less than tactful reactions to

Evans' dominating personality, resulted in the abrupt halt of the British excavations at Mycenae in 1923 and the no less sudden termination of Wace's job. Wace was pressured to leave Greece, and it was not until 1939 that he returned. In the interval his theories gained growing support from the archeological community, and are today universally accepted.

Classical archeology was not forgotten in the flush of excitement over the Mycenaeans and Minoans. The period between the wars saw the continuation of excavation at most established sites, and many new discoveries, among them the sanctuary of Asclepius and its elegant Roman buildings on **Kós**, excavated by the Italians from 1935 to 1943, and the Classical Greek city of **Olynthos**, in northern Greece, which was dug by the American school from 1928 to 1934. After the wholesale removal of houses and apartment blocks that had occupied the site, the American school also began excavations in the **Athenian Agora**, the ancient marketplace, in 1931, culminating in the complete restoration of the Stoa of Attalos.

The advent of **World War II** and the invasion of Greece first by the Italians and then the Germans called a halt to most archeological work, although the Germans set to work again at **Olympia**, supposedly due to the personal interest in the site of Hitler.

A few Allied nation archeologists also remained in Greece, principal among them **Gorham Stevens** and **Eugene Vanderpool**, of the American School, both of whom did charitable work. Back in America and Britain, meanwhile, archeologists were in demand for the intelligence arm of the war effort, both for their intimate knowledge of the Greek terrain and their linguistic abilities, which proved invaluable in decoding enemy messages.

POSTWAR EXCAVATIONS

Archeological work was greatly restricted in the years after World War II, and in the shadow of the Greek civil war. A few monuments and museums were restored and reopened but it was not until 1948 that excavations were resumed with a Greek clearance of the Sanctuary of Artemis at **Brauron** in Attica. In 1952 the American School resumed its activities with a dig at **Lerna** in the Peloponnese. Greek archeologists began work at the

Macedonian site of **Pella**, the **Necromanteion of Ephyra**, and, in a joint venture with the French, at the Minoan site of **Kato Zakros** on Crete.

These and many other excavations – including renewed work on the major sites – were, by comparison with earlier digs, relatively minor operations. This reflected a modified approach to archeology, which laid less stress on discoveries than on documentation. Instead of digging large tracts of a site, archeologists concentrated on small sections, establishing chronologies through meticulous **analysis** of data. Which is not to say that there were no **finds**. At Mycenae, in 1951, a second circle of graves was unearthed; at Pireás (Piraeus), a burst sewer in 1959 revealed four superb Classical bronzes; and a dig at the Kerameikos (cemetery) site in Athens in 1966 found 4000 potsherds used as ballots for ostracism. Important work has also been undertaken on **restorations** – in particular the **theatres** of the Athens Acropolis, Dodona and Epidaurus, which are used in summer festivals.

The two great postwar excavations, however, have been as exciting as any in the past. At **Akrotiri** on the island of **Thíra** (Santorini), **Spiros Marinatos** revealed, in 1967, a Minoan-era site that had been buried by volcanic explosion around 1550 BC. The buildings were two and three storeys high and superbly frescoed.

A decade later came an even more dramatic find at **Veryína**, in northern Greece. Here, **Manolis Andronikos** found a series of royal tombs dating from the fourth century BC. Unusually, these had escaped plundering by ancient grave robbers and contained an astonishing hoard of exquisite gold treasures. Piecing together clues – the hurriedness of the tomb's construction, an ivory head, gilded leg armour – Andronikos showed this to have been the tomb of Philip II of Macedon, father of Alexander the great. Subsequent forensic examination of the body supported historical accounts of Philip's limp and blindness.

It was an astonishing and highly emotive find, as the artifacts and frescoed walls showed the sophistication and Hellenism of ancient Macedonian culture. With the background of an emerging Macedonian state on Greece's northern border, archeology had come head to head with politics.

WILDLIFE

Greek wildlife – and in particular flora – may well prove an unexpected source of fascination. In spring, the colour, scent and sheer variety of wild flowers, and the resulting wealth of insect life, are breathtaking. Isolated areas, whether they are true islands or remote mountains such as Olympus, have had many thousands of undisturbed years to develop their own individual species. Overall, there are some 6000 species of flowering plants (three times that of Britain, for example), many of them unique to Greece.

SOME BACKGROUND

Around 8000 years ago, Greece was thickly forested. Aleppo and maritime (Calabrian) pines grew in coastal regions, giving way to Cephallonian and silver fir or black pine up in the hills and low mountains. But early civilisations changed all that, and most of Greece, like most of Europe, is an artificial mosaic of habitats created by forest clearance followed by agriculture, either row crops or stock-grazing. As long ago as the fourth century BC, Plato was lamenting the felling of native forests on the hills around Athens. This wasn't all bad for wildlife, though: the scrubby hillsides created by forest clearing and subsequent grazing are one of the richest habitats of all.

In this century, Greece has on the whole escaped the intensification of agriculture so obvious in Northern Europe. For the most part,

crops are still grown in small fields and without excessive use of pesticides and herbicides, while flocks of goats graze the hillsides in much the same way as they have done for the last few thousand years. On the minus side is damage from rapid development of industry, logging and tourism, all carried out with little sympathy for the environment. The pollution around Athens and Pireás, in particular, is appalling, while new hotels and resorts have often destroyed rich wildlife areas. In the Ionian, for example, the breeding grounds of the loggerhead turtle have been put under threat by tourist development of beaches.

One peculiarly Greek bonus to the naturalist is that wildlife here probably has the longest recorded history of anywhere in the world. Aristotle was a keen naturalist, Theophrastus in the fourth century BC was one of the earliest botanists, and Dioscorides, a physician in the first century AD, wrote a comprehensive book on the herbal uses of plants.

FLOWERS

What you will see of the Greek **flora** depends on where and when you go. Plants cease flowering (or even living, in the case of annuals) when it is too hot and dry for them – the high summer in Greece does the same to plants as does the winter in northern Europe. So, if you want to see flowers in high summer, head for the mountains.

The best time to go is **spring** – which comes to the south coast of Crete in early March, to the northern Píndhos mountains as late as the end of June. In early **summer**, the spring anemones, orchids and rockroses are replaced by plants like brooms and chrysanthemums. The onset of summer ranges from late April in southern Crete to late August or even early September in the high northern mountains.

Once the worst heat is over, there is a burst of activity on the part of **autumn** flowering species such as cyclamens and autumn crocus, flowering from October in the north into December in the south. And the first of the spring bulbs flower in January!

SEASHORE

You might find the spectacular yellow horned poppy growing on shingled banks, and sea stocks and Virginia stocks among the rocks behind the beach. A small pink campion, *Silene colourata*, is often colourfully present.

Sand dunes are rare in Greece, but sometimes there is a flat grazed area behind the beach; these can be fertile ground for orchids. Tamarisk trees often grow down to the shore, and there are frequent groves of Europe's largest grass, the giant calamus reed, which can reach 4m high.

In the autumn, look for the very large white flowers of the sea daffodil, as well as autumn crocuses on the banks behind the shore. The sea squill also flowers in early autumn, with tall spikes of white flowers rising from huge bulbs.

CULTIVATED LAND

Avoid large fields and plantations, but look for small hay meadows. These are often brilliant with annual "**weeds**" in late spring – various chrysanthemum species, wild gladiolus, perhaps wild tulips (especially in Crete and the central Peloponnese), and in general a mass of colour such as you rarely see in northern Europe. (Hot summers force plants into flowering simultaneously.) Fallow farmland is also good for flowers; you can often find deserted terraces full of cyclamens, anemones and orchids.

LOW HILLSIDES

This is a versatile habitat. The trees and shrubs are varied and beautiful, with colourful brooms flowering in early summer, preceded by bushy rockroses – *Cistaceae* – which are a mass of pink or white flowers in spring. Scattered among the shrubs is the occasional tree, such as the Judas tree, which flowers on bare wood in spring, making a blaze of pink against the green hillsides, and stands out for miles.

Lower than the shrubs are the **aromatic herbs** – sage, rosemary, thyme and lavender – with perhaps some spiny species of *Euphorbia*. These occur principally on the *frígana*, limestone slopes scattered with scrubby bushes. (The other hillside type, *maquis*, with its dense prickly scrub, is better for birds.)

Below the herbs is the ground layer; peer around the edges and between the shrubs and you will find a wealth of orchids, anemones, grape hyacinths, irises and perhaps fritillaries if you are lucky. The **orchids** are extraordinary; some kinds – the *Ophrys* species – imitate insect colouration in order to attract them for pollination, and have delicate and unusual flowers. They're much smaller and altogether more dignified than the big blowsy tropical orchids that you see in florists' shops. The **irises** are beauties, too; of them, a small, blue species called *Iris sisyrinchium* only flowers in the afternoon, and you can actually sit and watch them open around midday.

Once the heat of the summer is over, the **autumn bulbs** come into their own, with species of crocus and their relatives, the colchicums and the sternbergias, more squills and finally the autumn cyclamens flowering through into early December. Heather (genus *Erica*) provides a blaze of pink on acidic slopes around the New Year.

MOUNTAINS

These are good to visit later in the season, with flowers until June in water-scarce Crete, and well into August on Olympus and in the Píndhos. The rocky mountain gorges are the home of many familiar garden rock plants, such as the aubretias, saxifrages and alyssums, as well as dwarf bellflowers and anemones.

The mountains are also the place to see the remaining Greek native coniferous and deciduous forests, and in the woodland glades you will find gentians, cyclamens, violets and perhaps some of the rare and dramatic lilies, such as the crimson *Lilium heldrecheii*. Above 1700m or so the forests begin to thin out, with treeline at about 1900m, and in some of these upland meadows you will find the loveliest crocuses, flowering almost before the snow has melted in spring. As in the lowlands, autumn-flowering species of crocus make a visit worthwhile later in the year.

BIRDS

Greece has a large range of the resident **Mediterranean species**, plus one or two very rare ones such as the Ruppells warbler and the lammergeier vulture, which have most of their European breeding strongholds in Greece.

The great thing about birdwatching here is that, if you pick your time right, you can see both resident and **migratory species**. Greece is on the main flyway for species that have wintered in East Africa, but breed in northern Europe; they migrate every spring up the Nile valley, and then move across the eastern Mediterranean, often in huge numbers. This happens from mid-March to mid-May, depending on the species and the weather. The return migration in autumn is less spectacular because less concentrated, but still worth watching out for.

On the outskirts of towns and in the fields there are some colourful residents. Small **predatory birds** such as woodchat shrikes, kestrels and red-footed falcons can be seen perched on telegraph wires, and lesser kestrels nest communally and noisily in many small towns and villages. The dramatic pink, black and white hoopoe and the striking yellow and black golden oriole are sparsely represented in woodland and olive groves, and Scops owls (Europe's smallest owl) can often be heard calling around towns at night. They repeat a monotonous single "poo" sound, sometimes in mournful vocal duets.

Look closely at the **swifts and swallows**, and you will notice a few species not found in northern Europe; some of the swallows will be red-rumped, for example, and you may see the large alpine swift, which has a white belly. The Sardinian warbler dominates the rough scrubby hillsides, the male with a glossy black cap and an obvious red eye.

Wetlands and coastal lagoons are excellent bird territories, especially at spring and autumn migration. Both European species of pelican breed in Greece, and there is a wide variety of herons and egrets, as well as smaller waders such as the avocet and the black-winged stilt, which has ridiculously long, pink legs. The coast is often the best place to see migration, too. Most birds migrate up the coast, navigating by the stars; a thick mist or heavy cloud will force them to land, and you can sometimes see spectacular "falls" of migrators.

The most exciting birds, however, are to be seen in **the mountains**. Smaller birds like blue rock thrush, alpine chough and rock nuthatch are pretty common, and there is a good chance of seeing large and dramatic birds of prey. The buzzards and smaller eagles are confusingly similar, but there are also golden eagles. The Greek mountains contain all four European species of **vulture**. The small black and white Egyptian vulture, with a one-metre wingspan, is the commonest, but you might also see the **black** or the **griffon vulture**, which have three-metre wingspans and look like flying tables. The final vulture is the **lammergeier**, also with a three-metre wingspan but narrower wings, once almost extinct in Europe but now recovering slowly.

MAMMALS

Greek mammals include the usual range of rats, mice and voles, and some interesting medium-sized creatures, like the beech marten. There is also a fairly typical range of European species such as fox, badger, red squirrel, hare and so on, though the Greek hedgehog is distinctive in having a white breast.

Again it's the **mountains** that host the really exciting species. In the north, the ranges are home to some of the last remnants of big mammals that used to be widespread in the European forests and mountains. **Wolves, brown bears, lynx, chamois** and **wild boar** are all present, though the chance of the average traveller seeing one are slim to say the least. The Rhodhópi hills, north of Xánthi on the Bulgarian border, and the Elatía (Kara Dere) valleys north of Dhráma, are good places to go to try to see these rare mammals, as are the Píndhos around mounts Gamíla and Smólikas, between Ioánnina and Kónitsa. A rare **ibex**, known locally as the *kri-kri*, is found around the Samaria gorge in Crete, as well as on some of the islets offshore.

The extremely rare Mediterranean **monk seal** (see p.665) also breeds on some stretches of remote coast; if spotted, it should be treated with deference – it's endangered and easily scared away from its habitat.

REPTILES AND AMPHIBIANS

A hot, rocky country like Greece suits reptiles well and there are over forty indigenous species, half of the European total. Many of these are **wall lizards**. Most of the islands have their own species, all confusingly similar: small lizards with a brownish striped back, often with an orange or yellow belly. Sit and watch a dry, sunny wall almost anywhere in Greece and you're bound to see them.

On a few islands, notably the Dodecanese and the northern Cyclades, you may see the **agama** or **Rhodes dragon**. Growing up to 30cm, though usually smaller, they really do look like miniature, spiny-backed dragons with a series of pale diamonds on a brown or grey background.

In the bushes of the maquis and *frígana* you may see the **Balkan green lizard**, a truly splendid, brightly tinted animal up to half a metre long, most of which is tail; you can often spot it running on its hind legs, as if possessed, from one bush to another.

At night, **geckos** replace the lizards. Geckos are small (less than 10cm long), have big eyes, and round adhesive pads on their toes which enable them to walk upside down on the ceiling. Sometimes they come into houses, in which case welcome them, since they will keep down the mosquitoes and other biting insects. The **chameleon** is found infrequently in eastern Crete and some of the northern Aegean islands such as Sámos. It lives in bushes and low trees, and hunts by day, its colour is greenish but (obviously) variable.

All three European **tortoises** occur in Greece. They have suffered to varying extents from collection for the pet trade but you can still find them easily enough, on sunny hillsides. The best time is mid-morning, when they'll be basking between the shrubs and rocks. They come in all sizes depending on age – from 5cm to 30cm long. A good way to find them is by ear; they make a constant rustle as they lumber around, and if you find one, look for more, since they often seem to stick together.

A closely related reptile is the **terrapin**, which is basically an aquatic tortoise. Again, both European species occur in Greece, and they're worth looking for in any freshwater lakes or ponds, including on the islands. There are also **sea turtles** in the Ionian; you might be lucky and see one while you're swimming or on a boat, since they sometimes bask on the surface of the water. The one you're most likely to see is the **loggerhead turtle** (*Caretta caretta*), which can grow up to a metre long. It is endangered, and protected (see p.705).

The final group of reptiles are the **snakes**. Greece has plenty of them, but (as in most habitats) they're shy and easily frightened. Although most snakes are non-poisonous, Greece does have a number of viper species, which are front-fanged venomous snakes, including the nose-horned viper, as poisonous as they come in Europe.

Snakes actually cause only a handful of deaths a year in Europe but they should nonetheless be treated with with respect. If you get bitten, sit and wait to see if a swelling develops. If it doesn't, then the snake was harmless or didn't inject venom. If it does, move the area bitten as little as possible, and get medical attention. Don't try anything fancy like cutting or sucking the wound, but bind the limb firmly so as to slow down the blood circulation (but not so tightly as to stop the blood flow).

Greek **amphibians** either have tails (newts and salamanders) or they don't (frogs and toads). Newts can be seen in a few alpine tarns; search for salamanders in ponds at breeding time, and under stones and in moist crevices outside the breeding season.

You can't miss the frogs and toads, especially in spring. Greece has the **green toad**, which has an obvious marbled green and grey back, as well as the common toad. **Tree frogs** are small, live in trees, and call very noisily at night. They have a stripe down the flank and vary in colour from bright green to golden brown, depending on where they are sitting – they can change colour like a chameleon.

INSECTS

About a third of all insect species are **beetles**, and these are very obvious in Greece. You might see one of the dung beetles rolling a ball of dung along a path like the mythological Sisyphus, or a rhinoceros-horned beetle digging a hole in a sand dune.

The **grasshopper** and **cricket** family are well represented, and most patches of grass will hold a few. Grasshoppers produce their chirping noise by rubbing a wing against a leg, but crickets do it by rubbing both wings together. **Cicadas**, which most people think of as a type of grasshopper or locust, aren't actually related at all – they're more of a large leafhopper. Their continuous whirring call is one of the characteristic sounds of the Mediterranean noontime, and is produced by the rapid vibration of two cavities called tymbals on either side of the body. If you have time to look closely at bushes and small trees, you might be rewarded with a stick insect or a **praying mantis**, insects that are rarely seen because of their excellent camouflage.

The most obvious Greek insects are the **butterflies**. Any time from spring through most of the summer is good for butterfly-spotting, and there's usually a second flight of adults of many species in the autumn.

Dramatic species include three species of **swallowtail**, easily distinguished by their large size, yellow and black shading, and long spurs at the back of the hind wings. **Cleopatras** are large, brilliant yellow butterflies, related to the brimstone of northern Europe, but larger and more colourful. Look out for **green hairstreaks** – a small green jewel of a butterfly that is particularly attracted to the flowers of the asphodel, a widespread plant of overgrazed pastures and hillsides.

One final species typical of southern Greece and the islands are the **festoons**, unusual butterflies with tropical colours, covered in yellow, red and black zigzags.

FLORA AND FAUNA FIELD GUIDES

MEDITERRANEAN WILDLIFE

Pete Raine *The Rough Guide to Mediterranean Wildlife* (Rough Guides, UK/US). A good overview, written by the author of the preceding essay, which it expands upon, along with a site-by-site guide to the best Greek wildlife habitats.

FLOWERS

Marjorie Blainey and Christopher Grey-Wilson *Mediterranean Wild Flowers* (HarperCollins, UK). Comprehensive field guide.

Paul and Jenne Davies *The Wild Orchids of Britain and Europe* (Chatto & Windus, UK). A splendid book for orchid freaks, with details on where to look for them – including sites in Greece.

Anthony Huxley and William Taylor *Flowers of Greece and the Aegean* (Hogarth Press, UK). Best book for flower identification. It doesn't describe all the Greek flowers – no book does – but it's an excellent general guide with quality photographic illustrations.

Oleg Polunin *Flowers of Greece and the Balkans* (Oxford University Press, UK/US). Good on the mountain biomes.

BIRDS

Petersen, Mountfort and Hollom *Field Guide to the Birds of Britain and Europe* (Collins, UK/ Stephen Green Press, US); **Heinzel, Fitter and Parslow** *Collins Guide to the Birds of Britain and Europe* (Collins, UK/Stephen Green Press, US).

There are no specific reference books on Greek birds. These two European field guides have the best coverage, with the former, ageing but excellent, retaining an edge.

Michael Shepherd *Let's Look at North-East Greece* (Ornitholidays). Useful short guide.

MAMMALS

Corbet and Ovenden *Collins Guide to the Mammals of Europe* (Collins, UK/Stephen Green Press, US). As good a guide as they come.

INSECTS

Michael Chinery *Collins Guide to the Insects of Britain and Western Europe* (Collins, UK/Stephen Green Press, US). Although this doesn't include Greece, it gives good general information about the main insects you may see.

Higgins and Riley *A Field Guide to the Butterflies of Britain and Europe* (Collins, UK/Stephen Green Press, US). A field guide that will sort out all the butterflies for you, though it's a bit detailed for the casual naturalist.

REPTILES

Arnold and Burton *Collins Guide to the Reptiles and Amphibians of Britain and Europe* (Collins, UK/ Stephen Green Press, US). A useful guide which, infuriatingly for Greek travellers, excludes the Dodecanese and eastern Aegean islands.

MUSIC

Music, like most Greek cultural traditions, is a mix of East and West. The older songs, invariably in Eastern-flavoured minor keys, have direct precedents in the forms and styles of both the religious chants of the Byzantines and of medieval Turkey and Iran, and almost all native Greek instruments are descendants, or near-duplicates, of ones used throughout the Islamic world. To this Middle Eastern base both Slavs and Italians have added their share, and as a result the repertoire of traditional and more modern Greek pieces is extraordinarily varied.

REGIONAL FOLK MUSIC

The most promising times to hear regional folk music are at the numerous **summer festivals** – local saints' day ones, as well as larger cultural programmes – when musicians (who are often based in Athens or city clubs in winter) tour the islands and villages.

CRETE, KÁSSOS, HÁLKI AND KÁRPATHOS

This arc of southern islands is the most promising area in Greece for hearing live music at any season of the year. The main instrument here is the **lyra**, a three-stringed fiddle directly related to the Turkish *kemençe*. This is played not on the shoulder but balanced on the thigh, often with tiny bells attached to the bow, which the musician can jiggle for rhythmical accent. The strings are metal, and since the centre one is just a drone the player improvises only on the outer two – a distinctive, intriguing sound.

Usually the *lyra* is backed up by one or more **laoúta**, similar to the Turkish/Arab *oud* and not unlike the medieval lute. These are rarely used to their full potential but a good player will find the harmonics and overtones of a virtuoso *lyra* piece, at the same time coaxing a pleasing, chime-like tone from his instrument. A *laoúto* solo is an uncommon treat.

In several places in the southern Aegean, notably traditional Kárpathos, a primitive bagpipe, the **askómandra** or **tsamboúna**, joins the *lyra* and *laoúto*. During the colonels' dictatorship the playing of the bagpipe in the Cyclades further north was banned lest anyone think the Greeks too primitive – though hopefully, all concerned have recovered from any sense of cultural inferiority. If you remember Kazantzakis's classic novel (or the movie), Zorba himself played a **sandoúri**, or hammer dulcimer, for recreation. Today, accomplished players are few and in *Kritikí* (Cretan music), *nisiótiká* (island songs) and *rombétika* (see below), it's been relegated to a supporting role.

On older recordings you may hear solos on the *voúlgari*, a stringed instrument, essentially a small *saz* (Turkish long-necked, fretted lute), which has all but died out today.

OTHER AEGEAN ISLANDS

On most of the Aegean islands, and particularly the Cyclades, you'll find the *lyra* replaced by a more familiar-looking **violí**, essentially a western violin. The music is lyrical and usually up-tempo. Backing is again often provided by *laoúto* or *sandoúri*, though these days you're more likely to be confronted with a rock-'n'-roll-type, bass-guitar-and-drum rhythm section. Hilltop shepherds used to pass the time fashioning a reed-wailer known as the *karamoúza*, made from two goat horns.

Unlike on Crete, where you can often catch the best music in special clubs or *kéndra*, Aegean island performances tend to be spontaneous and less specialized. Festivals and saints' days in a village square are as usual the most promising times and venues.

IONIAN ISLANDS

Alone of all modern Greek territory, the Ionian islands – except for Lefkádha – never saw Turkish occupation and have a predominantly western musical tradition. The indigenous song-form is Italian both in name, (**kantádhes**) and instrumentation (guitar, mandolin); it's most often heard these days on **Lefkádha** and **Zákinthos**.

THE PELOPONNESE, CENTRAL GREECE AND EPIRUS

The folk lyrics of the the Peloponnese, central and western Greece generally hark back to the years of Turkish occupation and to the War of Independence. The main type of music is **paleá dhimotiká**, traditional folk ballads with very basic accompaniment on the klaríno (clarinet). Kithára (guitar), laoúto, violí, and toumberléki (lap drum) or défi (tambourine) can also add to the backing.

The music of **Epirus** (Ípiros) still exhibits strong connections with that of neighbouring Albania and the Former Yugoslav Republic of Macedonia, particularly in the polyphonic pieces sung by both men and women. They tend to fall into three basic categories, which are also found further south: **mirolóyia** or laments (the instrumental counterpart is called skáros); drinking songs or **tis távlas**; and various danceable melodies. As throughout the mainland, the clarinet tradition is almost wholly the domain of gypsies.

Most pieces are danceable, and they are divided by rhythm into such categories as kalamatianó, tsámiko, hasaposérviko or syrtó. Those that are not include the slow, stately kleftikó, similar to the rizítiko of Crete, both of which relate, baldly or in metaphor, incidents or attitudes from the years of the Ottomans and the rebellions for freedom.

Since the paleá dhimotiká are strongly associated with national identity, it's not surprising that they were for many years pressed into political service. During election campaigns each party's local storefront-headquarters or soundtrucks blasted out continuous paleá dhimotiká interspersed with political harangues. Since 1989, however, this practice has been (officially) banned.

THRACE AND THE NORTH

Thrace and **Macedonia** were in the hands of the Ottomans until the beginning of this century, with a bewilderingly mixed population, so music here – louder and less lyrical than in the south – has an unremitting Oriental feel.

The Thracian **kaváli**, or end-blown flute, is identical to the Turkish article (and to the disappearing floyéra of the south mainland); so, too, is the northern bagpipe, or **gaída**.

In Macedonia you'll find the **zournás**, a screechy, double-reed oboe similar to the Islamic world's shenai. It's much in evidence at local festivals, as is the **daoúli**, or deep-toned drum. The klaríno and toumberléki are not unknown, either, but even in their presence dances are fast and hard-stamping.

REMBETIKA

Rembétika began as the music of the Greek urban dispossessed – criminals, refugees, drug-users, defiers of social norms. It has existed in some form in Greece since at least the turn of the century. But it is as difficult to define or get to the origins of as jazz or blues, with which it shares marked similarities in spirit and circumstance.

The themes of the songs – illicit love, drug addiction, police oppression, disease and death – and the tone of the delivery – resignation to the singer's lot, coupled with defiance of authority – will certainly be familiar. But even the word "rembétika" is of uncertain derivation, the most likely one being rembet, an old Turkish word meaning "of the gutter", and searches for the birth of rembétika must be conducted in the Asia Minor of the last years of the Ottoman empire as well as in Greece proper.

Most outsiders equate Greek music with the **bouzoúki**, a long-necked, fretted lute derived from the Turkish saz and baglamás, though early in this century only a small proportion of Greek musicians used it. At the same time, across the Aegean in Smyrna and Constantinople, musical cafés had become popular. Groups usually featured a violinist, a sandoúri (hammer dulcimer) player and a female vocalist, who usually jingled castanets and danced on stage. The style was known as café-amanés or just **amanédhes**, after both the setting and the frequent repetition of the exclamation aman aman (alas, alas), used both for its sense and to fill time while the performers searched their imaginations for more explicit lyrics.

Despite a sparse instrumentation, this was an elegant, riveting music, and a style of singing requiring considerable skill, harking back to similar vocalization in Central Asia. Some of its greatest practitioners included **Andonis**

"**Dalgas**" (Wave), so nicknamed for the undulations in his voice; **Rosa Eskenazi**, a Greek Jew who grew up in Istanbul; her contemporary **Rita Abatzi**, from Smyrna; and **Dhimitris "Salonikiyeh" Semsis**, a master fiddler from Macedonia.

The 1923 **exchange of populations** was a key event in the history of *rembétika*, resulting in the influx to Greece of over a million Asia Minor Greeks, many of whom settled in shantytowns around Athens and Pireás. The musicians, like most of the other refugees, were, in comparison to the Greeks of the host country, extremely sophisticated; many were highly educated, could read and compose music, and had even been unionized in the towns of Asia Minor. It was galling for them to live on the periphery of the new society in poverty and degradation; most had lost all they had in the hasty evacuation, and many, from inland Anatolia, could speak only Turkish. In their misery they sought relief in another Ottoman institution, the *tekés* or hashish den.

In the **tekédhes** of Pireás, Athens and Thessaloníki, a few men would sit on the floor around a charcoal brazier, passing around a *nargilés* (hookah) filled with hashish. One of them might begin to improvise a tune on the *baglamá* or the *bouzoúki* and begin to sing. The words, either his own or those of the other *dervíses* ("dervishes" – many rombetic terms were a burlesque of those of mystical Islamic tradition), would be heavily laced with slang, in the manner of the Harlem jive of the same era – a way of keeping outsiders at bay. As the *taksími* (long, studied introduction) was completed, one of the smokers might rise and begin to dance a **zeïbékiko**, named after a warrior caste of western Anatolia. It would be a slow, intense, introverted performance following an unusual metre (9/8), not for the benefit of others but for himself.

Markos Vamvakaris was one of the greatest performers to emerge from the *tekés* culture. His proficiency on the *bouzoúki* was indisputable, though he protested to his friends that his voice, ruined perhaps from too much hash-smoking, was no good for singing. But he bowed to their encouragement and his gravelly, unmistakeable sound set the standard for male vocals over the next decade.

This "Golden Age" of *rembétika* – as indeed it was, despite the unhappy lives of many

performers – was short-lived. The association of the music with this underworld would prove its undoing. The harder-core musicians, with their uncompromising lyrics and lifestyles, were blackballed by the recording industry; anti-hashish laws were finally enforced, and police harassment of the *tekédhes* was stepped up after the Metaxas dictatorship took power in 1936. Even possession of a *bouzoúkii* or *baglamás* became a criminal offence. Most of the big names served time in jail.

For a while, the persecution failed to dim the enthusiasm of the **mánges** (roughly translatable as "wide boys" or "hep cats"). They were notoriously generous and impulsive, if occasionally violent and unscrupulous, and appeared to enjoy life to the fullest. Beatings or prison terms were taken in their stride; time behind bars could be used, as it always had been around the Aegean, to make *skaptó* (dugout) instruments. A *baglamás* could easily be fashioned from a gourd cut in half (the sound box), a piece of wood (the neck), catgut (frets), and wire for strings.

Jail songs were composed and became popular in the underworld. The excerpt below, which is very freely translated from the 1930s argot, is typical:

Iy Lahanádhes (The Pickpockets)
Down in Lemonádhika there was a ruckus
They caught two pickpockets who acted innocent
They took 'em to the slammer in handcuffs
They'll get a beating if they don't cough up the loot.
Don't beat us, coppers, you know very well
This is our job, and don't ask for bribes.
We lift purses and wallets so we can
Have a regular rest in jail.

Vangelis Papazoglou

Not too surprisingly, the *rembétes* suffered from the disapproval of the puritanical left as well as the puritanical right; the growing Communist Party of the 1930s considered the music and its habitués hopelessly decadent and counter-revolutionary. There was some overlap, however, in the 1940s, as the singers of *andártika* (resistance songs) learned the lesson of referring in code to issues that were not publicly discussable. Another exception from the later decade was **Sotiria Bellou**, a *rembétissa* (female rembetic musician) and active Communist.

In general, however, the Metaxas era and World War II signalled the decline of the authentic rembetic tradition. Worthwhile material was certainly composed and recorded between 1936 and 1955 – notably the work of **Ioanna Yiorgakopoulou**, **Vassilis Tsitsanis** and **Marika Ninou** – but by the 1950s the music was most often characterized by maudlin lyrics and over-orchestration. The addition of an extra string to the *bouzoúki*, and its subsequent electrification, turned a delicate, lightly strung instrument into an overamplified monster. The presentation, in huge, barnlike clubs, became debased and vulgarized. Virtuoso *bouzoúki* players, assisted by kewpie-doll-type female vocalists, became immensely rich. The clubs themselves, also called *bouzoúkia*, were clip-joints where Athenians paid large sums to break plates and to watch dancing whose flashy steps and gyrations were a travesty of the simple dignity and precise, synchronized footwork of the old style.

Ironically, the original *rembétika* material was rescued from oblivion by the colonels. Along with dozens of other highpoints of Greek culture, *rembétika* verses were banned. The younger generation coming of age under the dictatorship took a closer look at the forbidden fruit and derived solace, and deeper meanings, from the nominally apolitical lyrics. When the junta fell in 1974 – and even a little before – there was an outpouring of reissued recordings of the old masters.

Over the next decade live *rembétika* also enjoyed a revival, beginning with a clandestine 1979 club whose street credentials were validated when it was raided and closed by the police. Today, however, the fashion has long since peaked, and only a handful of clubs and bands remain from the dozens which made their appearance between 1978 and 1986.

NEO KIMA AND CONTEMPORARY MUSIC

Néo Kíma (New Wave) music emerged in small Athenian clubs, or *boîtes*, during the early 1960s. It was in part a rediscovery and adaptation of the forms of *rembétika*, in part a politicized folk movement with connections to such trends as the Latin American *Nueva Canción*. Like them, its young, improvisatory composers strongly identified with the Communists, whose revolutionary songs from the 1940s they revived and adapted. Like

rembétika bars, too, most of the *Néo Kíma* boites were closed down during the 1967–74 military junta, and failed to revive thereafter.

Although not directly associated with the *Néo Kíma* movement, Mikis Theodorakis and the late Manos Hadzidhakis, the two best-known modern Greek composers – had much in common with its spirit.

Theodhorakis's international reputation is perhaps a bit overblown, due to his overplayed soundtrack for *Zorba the Greek*. However, he is an interesting character – a long-time Communist dissident and MP who in 1989 suddenly shifted right to become a *Néa Dhimokratía* (conservative) Minister Without Portfolio – and he deserves a listening for his astonishing settings of poetry by **Odysseas Elytis**, and his work with the *Horodhia Trikalon* (The Trikala Choir) and vocalist **Maria Farandouri**.

Hadzidhakis, who died in June 1994, mostly steered clear of political statements; instead he launched, during the 1980s, his own record label, *Sirios*, to provide a forum for various non-mainstream musicians. Like Theodorakis, his own compositional weakness was a tendency towards quasi-symphonic, highly arranged instrumentation.

Less well known, but perhaps more interesting, are the more vernacular Greek sounds of the third big composer to emerge in the 1960s, the Cretan **Ioannis Markopoulos**. His material – labelled *éntehno* or "art" composition – mixes authentic folk material and instruments in juxtapositions never heard in their natural environment.

Perhaps the first musician to break out of the *bouzoúki* mould was **Dhionisios Savvopoulos**, who appeared on the scene in the mid-1960s with his maniacal, rasping voice and elliptical, angst-ridden lyrics, his persona rounded out by shoulder-length hair and outsized glasses. Because his material was not overtly political, Savvopoulos was one of the few "protest" artists able to perform under the junta, and was something of a consolation and password to the generation coming of age under it; Thessaloníki born, he paid due homage to the gypsy tradition in Greek music. Early in the 1990s, however, he did a bit of a Cliff Richard, with a much-publicized return to the Orthodox Church – and an apparent loss of musical inspiration.

A more explicit tip of the hat to the gypsies was made by **Nikos Ksidhakis and Nikos Papazoglou** in their landmark 1978 pressing, *Ekdhikisi tis Yiftias* (The Revenge of Gypsydom). The spirited, defiant lyrics and highly rhythmic melodies were both homage to and send-up the sort of music beloved by the itinerant truck-drivers who peddle cheap bedding and potted plants in rural Greece. The pair later edged more explicitly into the territory of urban folk and even *rembétika* without completely forsaking gypsydom. More recently, Ksidhakis collaborated with Ross Daly (see below) and vocalist Eleftheria Arvanitaki on *Konda sti Dhoxa mia Stigmi* and *Tenedhos* – simply some of the best Greek discs ever.

A Thessalonikian, **Nikos Papazoglou** is perhaps a better songwriter than Ksidhakis, effortlessly filling stadiums on his tours. His material, based on rock, folk and *rembétika*, is at its most accessible on *Haratsi* and the more recent *Synerga*.

Also from northern Greece came *Himerini Kolimvites*, a group of architects led by Aryiris Bakirtzis, whose eponymous first album has acquired enduring cult status in the decade since its 1981 release. Rembetic mainland pop and island influences meld with rich, drunken harmonies drawn out on both bowed and plucked strings.

A listen to any of the preceding names will make it clear that Greece has an enormous tradition of guitar-playing, much but by no means all of it attributable to Latin American influences. **Notis Mavroudhis**, who still occasionally appears in the rarefied confines of Athens concert halls, is something of a godfather to the movement; his discs are worth searching out. More down-to-earth is **Kostas Hadzis**, an elderly gypsy guitarist, whose work can veer towards banal pop but whose recent collaboration with stalwart vocalist **Haris Alexiou** featured two tracks of them singing in Romany.

The round-up of guitarist-writers would be incomplete without a mention of **Yiorgos (George) Dalaras**, a musical phenomenon in Greece for the last twenty years – and often dubbed the "Greek Springsteen". Born in 1950, the son of a Pireás *rembétika* player, Dalaras has spanned the gamut of Greek music, recording over forty LPs, ranging through Asia Minor and *dhimotiká* songs, the works of

Theodhorakis, Hadzidhakis and Markopoulos, and, more recently, collaborations with the flamenco guitarist Paco de Lucia and American blues star, Al Di Meola.

Although something of a national institution, Dalaras remained through the junta years a fierce supporter of popular struggles and has scrupulously avoided the banalities of the *bouzoúki* pop scene. In Greece, his concerts pack 80,000 at a time into football stadiums – rather more than the football teams themselves – and they produce rivers of tears.

Other less easily classifiable composers include **Thanos Mikroutsikos**, Minister of Culture since the death of Melina Mercouri, and **Lina Nikolakopoulou**. Nikolakopoulou burst on the scene in 1985 with *Kykloforo keh Oploforo*, a thoughtful, if somewhat slick, exploration of the boundary between rock, jazz-cabaret and *éntehno*; she also co-composed, with Mikroutsikos, the bestselling *Krataiei Hronia Ayti iy Kolonia*, and its huge hit single *Mia Pista apo Fosforo*. Both composers work often with Haris Alexiou (see above). A third, younger name to look out for is **Kostas Malamas**, whose orchestrated style recalls the early Himerini Kolimvites.

Another Greek approach in the 1970s and early 80s was to combine **folk and Byzantine traditions**. Instrument maker and arranger **Hristodhoulos Halaris** followed up a version of the Cretan epic *Erotokritos* with *Dhrossoulites* that introduced **Hrisanthos**, a male singer with a distinctive high-register voice together with star female vocalist **Dhimitri Galani**. Halaris has gone on to concentrate exclusively on Byzantine chants, reworking the hymns of Constantinople composer Petros Peloponnisios. More authentic renditions of these have been recorded by **Lykourgos Angelopoulos** and his choir, and are featured on a recent CD, *Liturgie Byzantine*.

Medieval – rather than Byzantine – Constantinopole was the inspiration of **Vosforos**, a group coordinated in Istanbul from 1986 to 1992 by **Nikiforos Metaxas** to preserve and play Ottoman classical, devotional and popular music. Their specific appeal and pertinence to Grecophiles was demonstrated by their first album, subtitled "Greek Composers of The City" (ie Constantinople) and concentrating on the contribution of Greek and other non-Turkish musicians to the Ottoman courtly tradition. In more recent concerts and recordings the group has varied the programme with Anatolian dance pieces and even Istanbul taverna songs from the turn of the century.

Ross Daly, whose interests and style frequently overlap those of Vosforos, is also worth looking out for on disc or live – in Athens clubs or on tour. English-born but Irish by background, Daly plays a dozen traditional instruments and has absorbed influences not only from Crete, where he was long resident, but from throughout the Near East. Alone or with his group, he has recorded strikingly contempo-

rary interpretations of folk tunes, as well as original "Greek" compositions.

There are a handful of other groups reviving folk music, from the islands and Smyrna. They include the accessible and popular **Dhinameis tou Egeou**, who add in bells, sitar and Egyptian *ney*, and the more rigorously authentic **Domna Samiou**, a musical equivalent to the Dora Stratou dance group. Still robust in her 70s, Domna sings, collects material from obscure corners of the country and has directed a school of like-minded musicians dedicated to the preservation of traditional music.

A SELECTIVE DISCOGRAPHY

*For suggestions on **record hunting** in Greece, see the Athens "Markets and shops" listings (p.118). In the UK the best source is **Trehantiri**, 367 Green Lanes, London N4; (☎0 181/802 6530), which also operates a worldwide mail-order service. In the USA, try **Moundanos** on Eddy St in San Francisco, CA, or **Down Home Music** on San Pablo Avenue in El Cerrito, CA.*

*The * symbol designates a disc is available on CD.*

EARLY REMBÉTIKA

*Various Greek Oriental Rembétika 1911–37 (Arhoolie, US). An essential compilation, with great names like Rosa Eskenazi, Anonis Dalgas, and many more. Includes Rosa's "Why I Smoke Cocaine". A must.

*Various Iy Megali tou Rembetikou (Margo, Greece). A collection of over twenty albums, arranged by artist. Highlights include #1 (Early Performers), #2 (Apostolos Hadzikhristos), #4 (Ioannis Papaioannou), #6 (Markos Vamvakaris) and #8 (Kostas Roukounas).

*Various The Greek Archives, Vols 1–12 (FM Records, Greece). This looks set to become the classic selection of rembétika; the series covers every aspect of the music – and other Greek styles and traditions, too. Particular rembétika gems, so far, include #7 "Unknown Smyrna" and #9 "Constantinople in song".

*Various Greek Orientale (Polylyric, Greece). A superb collection of smymeïka-style songs form the 1920s and 1930s, including songs by Rosa Eskenazi, Rita Abatsi, Marika Papagika and Semsis. Good sleeve notes in English and translations of many lyrics.

*Various Historic urban folk songs from Greece (Rounder, US). A collection of archive recordings of top rembétes. Really terrific stuff, mostly from the 1930s.

*Andonis Dalgas Periorismena Atitypa yai Syllektes (Lyra, Greece). A varied, well-edited collection of the gifted Constantinopolitan singer.

*Anestos Delias *1912–1944* (Adherfi Falirea, Greece). Collection by one of the best songwriters of the 1930s, better known as Artemis. Performed by the famous quartet of Stratos, Markos Vamvakaris, Batis and Artemis.

*Vangelis Papazoglou *1897–1943* (Adherfi Falirea, Greece). A double album of classic songs from the 1920s and 1930s written by Papazoglou and sung by most of the top stars of the era, including Stellakis, Rosa Eskenazi, Kostas Roukounas and Rita Abatsi.

LATER AND CONTEMPORARY REMBÉTIKA

*Sotiriou Bellou *1946–1956* (Margo, Greece). Early work by the Greek "Billie Holliday", without the electric backing of later years.

Marika Ninou…at Jimmy the Fat's (Venus/ Tzina, Greece). Poor sound quality since it was a clandestine wire recording, but still a classic. Ninou sings live with Tsitsanis in the early 1950s, including two cuts in Turkish.

*Vasilis Tsitsanis Yia Panta 1937–1940 vols 1 and **2** (EMI, Greece). A CD-release of two early Tsitsanis albums, mostly with Stratos on vocals.

* Vasilis Tsitsanis 1938–1955 (EMI, Greece) is a good collection with Sotiriou Bellou, Marika Nainou and Stratos singing.

*Stratis Xarhakos and Nikos Gatsos Rembetiko (CBS, US). Soundtracks to the namesake film, available as a double LP or, in slightly edited form, on one CD. Virtually the only "original" rembétika to be composed in the last 30 years.

*Mihalis Yennitsaris **Saltadoros** (Trikort, Germany). One of the last surviving composer/performers from the early days appears live on this German collection with singer Maria Nalbandi and the group Prosekhos.

Various **Iy Rembetiki Istoria, 1922-55**. (EMI, Greece, 6 vols). Vols 1&4 are especially worthwhile: old Smyrna & Anatolian pieces.

FOLK MUSIC

*Various **Grèce – Chants polyphoniques et musique d'Epiré** (Ocora, France). One of the best recordings from Epirus. Klaríno, frame drums and bells for the dances, polyphonic vocals on the ballads and laments.

Various **Greek Music from the Island of Crete** (Lyrichord, Greece). A good mixture of ballads and dance tunes, played on lyra, laoúto and bagpipes.

Various **Songs of...** (Society for the Dissemination of National Music, Greece). A thirty-strong series of LPs, each covering the traditional music of one region or type. All contain lyrics in English and are easily available in Athens at the Musicological Museum.

*Various **Takoutsia, Musiciens de Zagori: Inédit – Grêce - Epiré** (Inédit/Auvidis, France). Drinking songs, dance tunes and dirges performed by one of the last working clans of Epirot gypsy musicians. Wonderful.

*Hronis Aïdhonidhis **Songs of Thrace and Asia Minor** (Minos Matsas, Greece). The best and most accessible collection available, featuring Thrace's top folk singer, plus accompaniment by Ross Daly and solos by pop stalwart George Dalaras.

*Ross Daly **Selected Works** (RCA, Greece). The best place to start for budding Daly fans, with good notes. His latest album, *Anki* (RCA, Greece), was released in late 1994. Daly's local cassettes, *Anadhysi* (Sirios, Greece), *Okto tragoudhia keh ena Semai*, *O Kyklos sto Stavrodhromi* and *Hori* (all three on BMG Ariola, Greece) are all worthy of investigation.

*Yiorgis Mangas **Yiorgis Mangas** (GlobeStyle, UK). Studio-recorded gypsy-derived klaríno music from one of the less well known clarinettists. A fairly good introduction and widely available.

*Yannis Parios *Ta Nisiotika* Vols 1 and 2 (Minos Matsas, Greece). Parios sparked a renewal of interest in *nisiotikó* (traditional, island) music –

maybe not the most authentic renditions, but easy on the ear.

NEA KIMA AND NEW GREEK MUSIC

*Kostas Hadzis and Haris Alexiou **Alexiou Tragoudhaei Hadzis** (Minos Matsas, Greece). Hadzis by himself is disappointing; but with Alexiou, singing in Greek or Romany, it's Greek flamenco.

Notis Mavroudhis and Nikos Houliaras **Ekdhromi** (Zodiac, Greece). Rare, guitar-voice duo: one side contains haunting versions of Epirot folk songs, the other original pieces.

*Dhinameis tou Egeou **Anatoliko Parathiro** (Sirios, Greece). Last recording from five folk revivalists now working independently.

* *Himerini Kolimvites* (self-produced, 1981). First, cult-status recording by a group of architects from Thessaloníki and Kavála, milking rembétika, pop and island traditions for surreal lyrics and rich melodies.

*Stamatis Kraounakis and Lina Nikolakopoulou **Kykloforo keh Oploforo** (Polydor, Greece). Perhaps most representative of the "pop" wing of New Music trends.

*Nikos Ksidhakis and Nikos Papazoglou **Iy Ekdhikisi tis Yiftias** (Lyra, Greece). Groundbreaking recording of the late 1970s, still much loved in Greece.

*Nikos Ksidhakis and Eleftheria Arvanitaki **Konda sti Dhoxa mia Stigmi** (Lyra, Greece). One of the best Greek discs of the last twenty years, featuring superb Ksidhakis arrangements and compositions.

*Nikos Papazoglou **Synerga** (Lyra, Greece). Recent offering from the composer-performer, returning to his introspective earlier style.

*Domna Samiou **Seryiani** (Sirios, Greece). "New" traditional music by a folk-music collector, interpreter and revivalist.

*Dhionisios Savvopoulos **Dheka Hronia Kommatia** (Lyra, Greece). Retrospective anthology of the singer's best decade.

*Mikis Theodhorakis and Maria Farandouri (Minos Matsas). A good album, representative of their long collaboration.

*Vosforos **Greek Composers of Constantinople** (EMI, Greece). First and best exploration of the Anatolian dimension of Greek music.

The preceding account and this discography is a slightly modified version of those that appear in the **Rough Guide to World Music** (Penguin, UK £14.99, Can$25.99, US$19.95).

BOOKS

Where separate editions exist in the UK and USA, publishers are detailed below in the form "British Publisher/American Publisher", unless the publisher is the same in both countries. Where books are published in one country only, this follows the publisher's name.

O/p signifies an out-of-print – but still highly recommended – book. University Press is abbreviated as UP.

TRAVEL AND GENERAL ACCOUNTS

MODERN ACCOUNTS

Kevin Andrews *The Flight of Ikaros* (Penguin, o/p). Intense and compelling account of an educated, sensitive archeologist loose in the back-country during the aftermath of the civil war.

Gerald Durrell *My Family and Other Animals* (Penguin). Sparkling, very funny anecdotes of Durrell's childhood on Corfu – and his passion for the island's fauna: toads, tortoises, bats, scorpions, the lot.

Lawrence Durrell *Prospero's Cell* (Faber & Faber/Penguin, the latter o/p); *Reflections on a Marine Venus* (Faber & Faber/Penguin); *The Greek Islands* (Faber & Faber/Penguin, the former o/p). The elder Durrell lived before the second world war with Gerald and the family on Corfu, the subject of *Prospero's Cell*. *Marine Venus* recounts Lawrence's wartime experiences and impressions of Rhodes and other Dodecanese Isands. *Greek Islands* is a dated, lyrical and occasionally bilious guide to the archipelagos.

Sheelagh Kanneli *Earth and Water: A Marriage in Kalamata* (Efstathiadhis, Athens).

A classic account of that rare thing – a foreign woman integrating successfully into provinvcial Greek society. Rich in period detail of pre-tourism and pre-earthquake Kalamata.

Patrick Leigh Fermor *Roumeli* (Penguin); *Mani* (Penguin/Peter Smith, o/p). Leigh Fermor is an aficionado of the vanishing minorities, relict communities and disappearing customs of rural Greece. These two books, written in the 1950s, are not so much travelogues as scholarship interspersed with strange and hilarious yarns. They are among the best books written on any aspect of modern Greece.

Peter Levi *The Hill of Kronos* (Harvill/Dutton, both o/p). Beautifully observed landscape, monuments and eventually politics as Levi describes how he is drawn into resistance to the colonels' junta.

Henry Miller *The Colossus of Maroussi* (Minerva/New Directions). Corfu and the soul of Greece in 1939, with Miller, completely in his element, at his most inspired.

James Pettifer *The Greeks: the Land and People since the War* (Viking). A hugely recommended introduction to contemporary Greece – and its recent past. Pettifer roams across the country and charts the state of the nation's politics, food, family life, religion, tourism, and all points in between.

Jackson Webb *The Last Lemon Grove* (Weidenfeld, UK, o/p). Published in 1977, this is the account of an American living in the then-remote village of Paleohóra on Crete. It is as good a choice of book as you could make for a stay on the island today.

Sarah Wheeler *An Island Apart* (Abacus, UK). Entertaining chronicle of a five-month ramble through one of the least-visited islands. Wheeler has a sure touch with Greek culture and an open approach to the people she meets, whether nuns, goatherds or academics.

OLDER ACCOUNTS

James Theodore Bent *The Cyclades, or Life Among Insular Greeks* (o/p). Originally published in 1881, this remains the best account of island customs and folklore; it's also a highly readable, droll account of a year's Aegean travel, including a particularly violent Cycladic winter.

Robert Byron *The Station* (Century, o/p). Travels on Mount Áthos in the 1930s, by one of the pioneering scholars of Byzantine art and architecture.

Martin Garrett *Greece: A Literary Companion* (John Murray, UK). Brief nuggets of travel writing and the classics, arranged by region. Enjoyable and frustrating in equal measure.

Nikos Kazantzakis *Journey to the Morea* (o/p). Slightly stilted translation of the Cretan novelist's journey around the Peloponnese and his increasing alienation from 1930s Greece.

Edward Lear *Journals of a Landscape Painter in Greece and Albania* (Century, o/p). Highly entertaining journals of two journeys through Greece and Albania in autumn 1848 and spring 1849, by the famous landscape painter and author of *The Book of Nonsense*. Further doses of Lear, *The Corfu Years* and *The Cretan Journal*, are published by Denise Harvey in Athens, but may be o/p now.

Sidney Loch *Athos, The Holy Mountain* (reprinted by Molho, Thessaloniki, Greece). A resident of Ouranópoli, on the periphery of Mount Áthos, from 1924 to 1954, Loch recounts the legends surrounding the various monasteries, as gleaned from his years of walking through the monastic republic.

Terence Spencer *Fair Greece, Sad Relic: Literary Philhellenism from Shakespeare to Byron* (Denise Harvey, Athens, but available in UK/published by Scholarly Press in the US). Greece from the Fall of Constantinople to the War of Independence, through the eyes of English poets, essayists and travellers.

CLASSICS, HISTORY AND ETHNOGRAPHY

THE CLASSICS

Many of the classics make good companion reading for a trip around Greece – especially the historians **Thucydides** and **Herodotus**. It is also hard to beat **Homer**'s *Odyssey*, for reading when you're battling with or resigning yourself to the vagaries of island ferries. One slightly less well-known Roman source, which you might consider taking on travels, especially to the Peloponnese, is **Pausanias**'s fourth-century AD Guide to Greece, annotated by Peter Levi in its Penguin edition with notes on modern identifications of sites mentioned.

The following are all available in Penguin Classic paperback editions:

Homer *The Odyssey, The Iliad.*

Herodotus *The Histories.*

Pausanias *The Guide to Greece* (2 vols).

Plutarch *The Age of Alexander; Plutarch on Sparta; The Rise and Fall of Athens.*

Thucydides *History of the Peloponnesian War.*

Xenophon *The History of My Times.*

ANCIENT HISTORY

A R Burn *History of Greece* (Penguin). Probably the best general introduction to ancient Greece, though for fuller and more interesting analysis you'll do better with one or other of the following.

M I Finley *The World of Odysseus* (Penguin). Good on the interrelation of Mycenaean myth and fact.

Robin Lane Fox *Alexander the Great* (Penguin). An absorbing study, which mixes historical scholarship with imaginative psychological detail.

John Kenyon Davies *Democracy and Classical Greece* (Fontana/Harvard UP). Established and accessible account of the period and its political developments.

Oswyn Murray *Early Greece* (Fontana/Harvard UP). The Greek story from the Mycenaeans and Minoans through to the beginning of the Classical period.

F W Walbank *The Hellenistic World* (Fontana/Harvard UP). Greece under the sway of the Macedonian and Roman empires.

R Gordon Wasson, Albert Hoffmann, Carl Ruck *The Road to Eleusis: Unveiling the Secret of the Mysteries* (Harcourt, Brace, o/p). Well-argued monograph extolling the theory that the Eleusinian mysteries were at least in part a psychedelic trip, courtesy of grain-ergot fungus. Guaranteed to outrage conventional classicists.

BYZANTINE, MEDIEVAL AND OTTOMAN

Timothy Callistos Ware *The Orthodox Church* (Penguin). Good introduction to what is effectively the established religion of Greece.

Nicholas Cheetham *Medieval Greece* (Yale UP, o/p in US). General survey of the period and its infinite convolutions in Greece, with Frankish, Catalan, Venetian, Byzantine and Ottoman struggles for power.

Molly Mackenzie *Turkish Athens* (Ithaca Press). Readable monograph, drawing on primary sources, that's the best single introductory volume to a neglected topic.

John Julius Norwich *Byzantium: the Early Centuries* and *Byzantium: the Apogee* (both Penguin/Knopf). Perhaps the main surprise for first-time travellers to Greece is the fascination of Byzantine monuments, above all at Mystra; these first two volumes of Norwich's history of the empire are terrific narrative accounts.

Michael Psellus *Fourteen Byzantine Rulers* (Penguin). A fascinating contemporary source, detailing the stormy but brilliant period from 976 to 1078.

Steven Runciman *The Fall of Constantinople, 1453*, *The Great Church in Captivity* (both Cambridge UP) *Byzantine Style and Civilisations* (Penguin, o/p in US), *Mistra* (Thames & Hudson, o/p in US). Good narrative histories, with more of a slant towards art, culture and monuments.

MODERN GREECE

Timothy Boatswain and Colin Nicolson *A Traveller's History of Greece* (Windrush Press/ Interlink). Slightly dated but well-written overview of all periods Greek.

Richard Clogg *A Concise History of Greece* (Cambridge UP). A remarkably clear and well-illustrated account of Greece from the decline of Byzantium to 1991, stressing recent decades.

Douglas Dakin *The Unification of Greece, 1770–1923* (Ernest Benn/St Martin's Press, both o/p). Account of the foundation of the Greek state and the struggle to extend its boundaries.

John S Koliopoulos *Brigands with a Cause* (Oxford UP). History of the brigandage in newly independent Greece and its significance in the struggle for the recovery of territory from Turkey in the nineteenth century.

Michael Llewellyn Smith *Ionian Vision, Greece in Asia Minor, 1919–22* (Allen Lane/St Martin's Press, both o/p). Standard work on the Anatolian campaign and the confrontation between Greece and Turkey leading to the exchange of populations.

Mark Mazower *Inside Hitler's Greece: The Experience of Occupation 1941–44* (Yale UP). Somewhat choppily organized, but the standard of scholarship is high and the photos alone justify the price. Demonstrates how the complete demoralization of the country and incompetence of conventional politicians led to the rise of ELAS and the onset of civil war.

Yiannis Roubatis *Tangled Webs: The US in Greece 1947–67* (Pella Publishing, US). Chronicles growing American involvement in Greece during the lead-up to the miltary coup.

C M Woodhouse *Modern Greece, A Short History* (Faber & Faber). Woodhouse was active in the Greek Resistance during World War II. Writing from a right-wing perspective, his history (spanning from the foundation of Constantinople in 324 to the present), is briefer and a bit drier than Clogg's, but he is scrupulous with facts. *The Rise and Fall of the Greek Colonels* (Granada, o/p/Watts), recounts the (horror) story of the dictatorship, while *The Struggle for Greece, 1941–49* (Hart-Davis, o/p/ Beekman), is a masterly and by no means uncritical account of this crucial decade, explaining how Greece emerged without a Communist government.

ETHNOGRAPHY

J K Campbell *Honour, Family and Patronage* (Oxford UP). A classic study of the Sarakatsáni communities in the mountains of northern Greece.

Rae Dalven *The Jews of Ioannina* (Lycabettus Press, Greece, but available in the US). History and culture of the thriving pre-Holocaust community, related by a poet and translator of Cavafy (see "Modern Greek Poetry", below), herself an Epirot Jew.

Juliet du Boulay *Portrait of a Greek Mountain Village* (Oxford UP, o/p in UK). An account of the village of Ambli, on Évvia, in the 1960s. Boulay observes and evokes the habits and customs of a fast disappearing life in an absorbing narrative.

Gail Holst *Road to Rembétika: Songs of Love, Sorrow and Hashish* (Denise Harvey, Greece, but available in the UK). The predominant Greek urban musical style of this century, evocatively traced by a Cornell University musicologist. Be sure to get the most recent edition, as the discography is regularly updated.

Clay Perry *Vanishing Greece* (Conran Octopus Abbeville Press). Well-captioned photos depict the threatened landscapes and way of life in rural Greece.

Nikos Stavroulakis *Salonika: Jews and Dervishes* (Talos Press, Athens, but available in the US). Monograph, lavishly illustrated with old photos, of two of Thessaloníki's most distinctive communities – which have vanished only this century.

T J Winnifrith *The Vlachs: The History of a Balkan People* (Duckworth/St Martin's Press). Rather heavy-going hotchpotch on the existing Vlach communities in Greece and the rest of the Balkans, but the only study easily available.

BIOGRAPHY

Oriana Falacci *A Man* (Arrow/Pocket Books). Account of the junta years, relating the author's involvement with Alekos Panagoulis, the anarchist who attempted to assassinate Colonel Papadopoulos in 1968. Issued as a "novel" in response to threats by those who were named.

Nicholas Gage *Eleni* (Collins Harvill/ Ballantine). Controversial account by a Greek-born *New York Times* correspondent who returns to Epirus to avenge the death of his mother, condemned to death by an ELAS tribunal in 1948. Superb descriptions of village life, but very blinkered political "history" – and the basis of a truly forgettable movie. The book inspired a response by a left-wing writer, Vassilis Kavathas, whose family had been decimated by the right, entitled *Iy Alli Eleni* (The Other Eleni), not as yet translated into English.

Edmund Keeley *The Salonika Bay Murder* (Princeton UP, US). Wartime murders of journalists are now commonplace, but the dispatch in 1948 of a CBS correspondent, apparently by minions of the Royalist government, was a major incident. This analysis fingers the colluding Greek and US intelligence services.

Kati Marton *The Polk Conspiracy* (Times Books, US). Another treatment of the Polk case, written as a gripping early Cold War whodunnit, and reaching a similar conclusion.

George Psychoundakis *The Cretan Runner* (John Murray/Transatlantic Arts, the latter o/p). Narrative of the invasion of Crete and subsequent resistance, by a participant, who was a guide and message-runner for all the British protagonists, including Patrick Leigh Fermor, translator of the book.

Vassilis Vassilikos *Z* (Four Walls Eight Windows). Another "novel" based very closely on events – the 1963 political assassination of Gregoris Lambrakis in Thessaloníki – and brilliantly filmed by Costa-Gavras in 1968.

ARCHEOLOGY AND ART

John Beckwith *Early Christian and Byzantine Art* (Penguin/Yale UP). Illustrated study placing Byzantine art within a wider context.

John Boardman *Greek Art* (Thames & Hudson, UK). A very good concise introduction in the "World of Art" series.

Reynold Higgins *Minoan and Mycenaean Art* (Thames & Hudson). A clear, well-illustrated round-up.

Sinclair Hood *The Arts in Prehistoric Greece* (Penguin/Yale UP). Sound introduction to the subject.

Roger Ling *Classical Greece* (Phaidon, UK). Another useful and illustrated introduction.

Colin Renfrew *The Cycladic Spirit* (Thames & Hudson/Abrams). A fine, illustrated study of the meaning and purpose of Cycladic artefacts.

Gisela Richter *A Handbook of Greek Art* (Phaidon/Da Capo). Exhaustive survey of the visual arts of ancient Greece.

Suzanne Slesin et al *Greek Style* (Thames & Hudson/Crown). Stunning and stylish interiors from Corfu, Rhodes and Serifos, among other spots.

R R R Smith *Hellenistic Sculpture* (Thames & Hudson, UK). Modern reappraisal of the art of Greece under Alexander and his successors.

David Talbot Rice *Art of the Byzantine Era* (Thames & Hudson). Talbot Rice was, with Robert Byron, one of the pioneering scholars in the "rediscovery" of Byzantine art; this is an accessible, illustrated study.

Peter Warren *The Aegean Civilizations* (Phaidon/P Bedrick Books, the latter o/p). Illustrated account of the Minoan and Mycenaean cultures.

MODERN GREEK FICTION

Maro Douka *Fool's Gold* (Kedros, Greece*). Describes an upper-class young woman's involvement, and subsequent disillusionment, with the clandestine resistance to the junta and her pompous male colleagues.

Eugenia Fakinou *The Seventh Garment* (Serpent's Tail). The modern history of Greece – from the War of Independence to the colonels' junta – is told through the life stories (interspersed in counterpoint) of three generations of women. It is a rather more succesful experiment than Fakinou's *Astradeni* (Kedros, Greece*), in which a young girl – whose slightly irritating narrative voice is adopted throughout – leaves the island of Sími, with all its traditional values, for Athens.

Stratis Haviaras *When the Tree Sings* (Picador/Simon & Shuster, both o/p) and *The Heroic Age* (Penguin, o/p). Two-part, faintly disguised autobiography about coming of age in Greece in the 1940s, by the poetry curator at Harvard library. Written in English because Haviaris felt his experiences too keenly to set them down in Greek.

Nikos Kazantzakis *Zorba the Greek; Christ Recrucified* (published in the US as *The Greek Passion*); *Report to Greco; Freedom or Death* (*Captain Mihalis* in the US); *The Fratricides* (all Faber & Faber/Touchstone). The most accessible (and Greece-related) of the numerous novels by the Cretan master. Even with inadequate translation, their strength – especially that of *Report to Greco* – shines through.

Stratis Myrivilis *Life in the Tomb* (Quartet/New England UP). A harrowing and unorthodox war memoir, based on the author's experience on the Macedonian front during 1917–18, well translated by Peter Bien. Completing a kind of trilogy are two later novels, set on the north coast of Lésvos, Myrivilis's homeland: *The Mermaid Madonna* and *The Schoolmistress with the Golden Eyes* (Efstathiadis, Athens, Greece). Translations of these are not so good, and tend to be heavily abridged.

Alexandros Papadiamantis *The Murderess* (Writers & Readers, US). Turn-of-the-century novel set on the island of Skíathos. Also available is a collecton of Papadiamantis short stories, *Tales from a Greek Island* (Johns Hopkins UP).

Dido Sotiriou *Farewell Anatolia* (Kedros, Greece*). A classic since its initial appearance in Greece three decades ago (it is now in its 52nd printing), this is an epic chronicle of the traumatic end of Greek life in Asia Minor, from the 1912 Balkan War to the catastrophe of 1922. The narrator is a fictionalized version of the author's father.

Irini Spanidhou *God's Snake* (Picador/Penguin, the former o/p). The story of a daughter trying to break free of the all-pervasive legacy of her father, a Greek army general.

Demetrios Vikelas *Loukas Laras* (Doric Publications, UK, o/p). Classic nineteenth-century novel set mainly on Híos.

Yiorgos Yatromanolakis *The History of a Vendetta* (Dedalus). Greek magic realism as the tales of two families unravel from a murder in a small Cretan village.

Alki Zei *Achilles' Fiancée* (Kedros, Greece*). A recent bestseller, exploring identity and values amid a maze of timeshifts, from the German occupation to the civil war, exile in Tashkent and Paris, and a return to Greece.

*These books are part of a highly recommended "Modern Greek Writers" series, currently numbering ten titles, issued by the Athenian company Kedros Publishers.

MODERN GREEK POETRY

With two Nobel laureates in recent years – George Seferis and Odysseus Elytis – modern Greece has an extraordinarily intense and dynamic poetic tradition. Translations of all of the following are excellent.

C P Cavafy *Collected Poems* (Chatto and Windus/Princeton UP). The complete works of perhaps the most accessible modern Greek poet, resident for most of his life in Alexandria.

Odysseus Elytis *The Axion Esti* (Anvil Press/Pittsburgh UP); *Selected Poems* (Anvil Press/Viking Penguin, the latter o/p); *The Sovereign Sun* (Bloodaxe Books). The major works in good English versions.

George Pavlopoulos *The Cellar* (Anvil Press, UK). Less well-known poet from Pírgos in the Peloponnese. English translation by Peter Levi.

Yannis Ritsos *Exile and Return, Selected Poems 1967–1974* (Anvil Press/Ecco Press). A fine volume of Greece's foremost leftist poet.

Modern Greek Poetry (Efstathiadis, Athens, Greece). Decent anthology of translations, predominantly of Seferis and Elytis.

George Seferis *Collected Poems, 1924–1955* (Anvil Press/Princeton UP, the latter o/p). Virtually the complete works of the Nobel laureate, with Greek and English verses on facing pages.

GREECE IN FOREIGN FICTION

Louis de Bernières *Captain Corelli's Mandolin* (Secker & Warburg, UK). Set on Kef0loniá during the World War II occupation, this is a brilliant tragicomedy by an author best known for his South American extravaganzas.

Lawrence Durrell *Tunc* (Faber & Faber/Penguin). An inventor's adventures – in London, Istanbul and Athens.

John Fowles *The Magus* (Picador/Dell). Fowles's biggest and best novel: a tale of mystery and manipulation, and Greek island life, inspired by his stay on Spetses, as a teacher, in the 1950s.

Mary Renault *The King Must Die*, *The Last of the Wine*, *The Mask of Apollo*, and others (Sceptre/Random). Mary Renault's imaginative reconstructions are more than the children's reading they're often taken for. The research is impeccable and the writing tight. The trio above retell, respectively, the myth of Theseus, the life of a pupil of Socrates, and that of a fourth-century BC actor.

Evelyn Waugh *Officers and Gentleman* (Penguin). This volume of the wartime trilogy includes an account of the Battle for Crete and subsequent evacuation.

SPECIFIC GUIDES

ARCHEOLOGY

Robin Barber (ed) *The Blue Guide Greece* (A & C Black/Norton). Definitive reference guide for the ancient sites.

A R and Mary Burn *The Living Past of Greece: A Time Traveller's Tour of Historic and Prehistoric Places* (Herbert Press/HarperCollins). Unusual in extent, this covers sites from Minoan through to Byzantine and Frankish, with good clear plans and lively text.

Paul Hetherington *Byzantine and Medieval Greece: Churches, Castles and Art* (John Murray). Gazetteer of all major mainland sites. Readable, authoritative and with useful plans.

Evi Melas (ed) *Temples and Sanctuaries of Ancient Greece: A Companion Guide* (Thames & Hudson, o/p). Excellent collection of essays on the main sites, written by archeologists who have worked at them.

REGIONAL GUIDES

Marc Dubin *The Rough Guide to Rhodes and the East Aegean* (Penguin). Forthcoming title – due to hit the shelves in 1996 – from longtime resident of Sámos.

John Fisher *The Rough Guide to Crete* (Penguin). An expanded and practical guide to the island by the affable and eccentric contributor of the Crete chapter in this book.

Peter Greenhalgh and Edward Eliopoulos *Deep Into Mani* (Faber & Faber, o/p). A former member of the wartime Resistance revisits the Máni 40 years after first hiding there, and 25 years after Patrick Leigh Fermor's work, in the company of a British scholar. The result is a superb guide to the region and excellent armchair reading.

Lycabettus Press Guides (Athens, Greece). This series takes in many of the more popular islands and certain mainland highlights; most pay their way both in interest and usefulness – in particular those on Páros, Pátmos, Náfplio, and the travels of Saint Paul.

HIKING

Marc Dubin *Trekking in Greece* (Lonely Planet). An excellent walkers' guide, expanding on the hikes covered in this book and adding others, both around the mainland and on the islands. Includes day-hikes and longer treks, plus extensive preparatory and background information.

Tim Salmon *The Mountains of Greece: A Walker's Guide* (Cicerone Press/Hunter). The emphasis in this highly practical walkers' handbook (by another contributor to this guide) is more specifically on the mountains, with only

BOOKSHOPS

Athens has a number of excellent bookshops, at which many of the recommendations above should be available: see p.119 for addresses. In **London**, the *Hellenic Bookservice*, 91 Fortess Rd, Kentish Town, London NW5 1AG (☎0171/267 9499), and *Zeno's Greek Bookshop*, 6 Denmark St, WC2H 8LP (☎0171/836 2522), are knowledgeable and well-stocked specialist dealers in new, secondhand and out-of-print books on all aspects of Greece.

Sámos covered among the islands. The highlight is a superb walk from Delphi to Albania.

Landscapes of . . . (Sunflower Books/Hunter). A series of walking and car-tour titles devoted most usefully to Crete, Rhodes, Sámos, and Corfu. Strong on maps but a little pedestrian and timid in the choice of routes.

FERRIES

Frewin Poffley *Greek Island Hopping* (Thomas Cook, UK). Absolutely superb, user-friendly guide to the complex networks of Greek ferries, featuring full timetables and highly imaginative maps. If only the ferries lived up to it all!

LANGUAGE

So many Greeks have lived or worked abroad in America, Australia and, to a much lesser extent, Britain, that you will find someone who speaks English in the tiniest island village. Add to that the thousands attending language schools or working in the tourist industry – English is the lingua franca of most resorts, with German second – and it is easy to see how so many visitors come back having learnt only half a dozen restaurant words between them.

You can certainly get by this way, but it isn't very satisfying, and the willingness and ability to say even a few words will transform your status

from that of dumb *tourístas* to the honourable one of *ksénos*, a word which can mean foreigner, traveller and guest all rolled into one.

Greek is not an easy language for English speakers but it is a very beautiful one and even a brief acquaintance will give you some idea of the debt owed to it by western European languages.

On top of the usual difficulties of learning a new language, Greek presents the additional problem of an entirely separate **alphabet**. Despite initial appearances, this is in practice fairly easily mastered – a skill that will help enormously if you are going to get around independently (see the alphabet box following). In addition, certain combinations of letters have unexpected results. This book's transliteration system should help you make intelligible noises but you have to remember that the correct **stress** (marked throughout the book with an acute accent) is crucial. With the right sounds but the wrong stress people will either fail to understand you, or else understand something quite different from what you intended.

Greek **grammar** is more complicated still: nouns are divided into three genders, all with different case endings in the singular and in the plural, and all adjectives and articles have to agree with these in gender, number and case. (All adjectives are arbitrarily cited in the

---

LANGUAGE-LEARNING MATERIALS

TEACH-YOURSELF GREEK COURSES

Breakthrough Greece (Pan Macmillan; book and two cassettes). Excellent, basic teach-yourself course – completely outclasses the competition.

Greek Language and People (BBC Publications, UK; book and cassette available). More limited in scope but good for acquiring the essentials, and the confidence to try them.

Anne Farmakides *A Manual of Modern Greek* (Yale/McGill; 3 vols). If you have the discipline and motivation, this is one of the best for learning proper, grammatical Greek; indeed, mastery of just the first volume will get you a long way.

PHRASEBOOKS

The Rough Guide to Greek (Penguin, UK/US). Practical and easy-to-use, the *Rough Guide*

phrasebooks allow you to speak the way you would in your own language. Feature boxes fill you in on do's and don'ts and cultural know-how.

DICTIONARIES

The Oxford Dictionary of Modern Greek (Oxford University Press, UK/US). A bit bulky but generally considered the best Greek-English, English-Greek dictionary.

Collins Pocket Greek Dictionary (Harper Collins, UK/US). Very nearly as complete as the Oxford and probably better value for the money.

Oxford Learner's Dictionary (Oxford University Press, UK/US). If you're planning a prolonged stay, this pricey two volume set is unbeatable for usage and vocabulary. There's also a more portable one-volume *Learner's Pocket Dictionary*.

neuter form in the following lists.) Verbs are even worse. To begin with at least, the best thing is simply to say what you know the way you know it, and never mind the niceties. "Eat meat hungry" should get a result, however grammatically incorrect. If you worry about your mistakes, you'll never say anything.

KATHAREVOUSSA, DHIMOTIKI AND DIALECTS

Greek may seem complicated enough in itself, but its impossibilities are multiplied when you consider that for the last century there has been an ongoing dispute between two versions of the language: **katharévoussa** and **dhimotikí**.

When Greece first achieved independence in the nineteenth century, its people were almost universally illiterate, and the language they spoke – **dhimotikí**, "demotic" or "popular" Greek – had undergone enormous change since the days of the Byzantine Empire and Classical times. The vocabulary had assimilated countless borrowings from the languages of the various invaders and conquerors, from the Turks, Venetians, Albanians and Slavs.

The finance and inspiration for the new Greek state, and its early leaders, came largely from the diaspora – Greek families who had been living in the sophisticated cities of central and eastern Europe, or in Russia. With their European notions about the grandeur of Greece's past, and lofty conception of Hellenism, they set about obliterating the memory of subjugation to foreigners in every possible field. And what better way to start than by purging the language of its foreign accretions and reviving its Classical purity.

They accordingly set about creating what was in effect a new form of the language, **katharévoussa** (literally "cleansed" Greek). The complexities of Classical grammar and syntax were reinstated, and Classical words, long out of use, were re-introduced. To the country's great detriment, *katharévoussa* became the language of the schools and the prestigious professions, government, business, the law, newspapers and academia. Everyone aspiring to membership of the elite strove to master it, and to speak it – even though there was no absolute and defined idea of how many of the words should be pronounced.

. The *katharévoussa/dhimotikí* debate has been a highly contentious issue through most of this century. Writers – from Sikelianos and Seferis to Kazantzakis and Ritsos – have all championed the demotic in their literature. Meanwhile, crackpot right-wing governments forcibly (re-)instated *katharévoussa* at every opportunity. Most recently, the **colonels' junta** of 1967–1974 reversed a decision of the previous government to teach in *dhimotikí* in the schools, bringing back *katharévoussa*, even on sweet wrappers, as part of their ragbag of notions about racial purity and heroic ages.

Dhimotikí returned once more after the fall of the colonels and now seems here to stay. It is used in schools, on radio and TV, in newspapers (with the exception of the extreme right-wing *Estia*) and in most official business. The only institutions which refuse to bring themselves up to date are the church and the legal professions – so beware rental contracts.

This is not to suggest that there is any less confusion. The Metaxas dictatorship of the 1930s changed scores of village names from Slavic to Classical forms and these official **place names** still hold sway on most road-signs and maps – even though the local people may use the *dhimotikí* form. Thus you will see "Leonídhion" or "Spétsai" written, while everyone actually says Leonídhi or Spétses.

DIALECTS AND MINORITY LANGUAGES

If the lack of any standard Greek were not enough, Greece still offers a rich field of linguistic diversity, both in its dialects and minority languages. Ancient **dialects** are alive and well in many a remote area, and some of them are quite incomprehensible to outsiders. The dialect of Sfákia in Crete is one such. *Tsakónika* (spoken in the east-central Peloponnese) is another, while the dialect of the Sarakatsáni shepherds is said to be the oldest, a direct descendant of the language of the Dorian settlers.

The language of the Sarakatsáni's traditional rivals, the **Vlachs**, on the other hand, is not Greek at all, but a derivative of early Latin, with strong affinities to Romanian. In the Yugoslav and Bulgarian frontier regions you can still hear Slavic **Macedonian** spoken, while small numbers of Sephardic Jews in the north speak **Ladino**, a medieval form of Spanish. Until a few decades ago **Arvanitika** – a dialect of medieval Albanian – was the first language of many villages of inland Attica, southern Évvia, northern Ándhros, and much of the Argo-Saronic area; it is still widely spoken among the older generation. Lately the clock has been turned back as throngs of Albanian refugees circulate in Athens and other parts of the country. In Thrace there is also a substantial **Turkish**-speaking population, as well as some speakers of **Pomak** (a relative of Bulgarian with a large Greco-Turk vocabulary).

THE GREEK ALPHABET: TRANSLITERATION

Set out below is the Greek alphabet, the system of transliteration used in this book, and a brief aid to pronunciation.

Greek	Transliteration	Pronounced
Α, α	a	a as in father
Β, β	v	v as in vet
Γ, γ	y/g	y as in yes when before an e or i; when before consonants or a, o or ou when its a breathy, throaty d, g as in gap.
Δ, δ	dh	th as in then
Ε, ε	e	e as in get
Ζ, ζ	z	z sound
Η, η	i	ee sound as in feet
Θ, θ	th	th as in theme
Ι, ι	i	i as in bit
Κ, κ	k	k sound
Λ, λ	l	l sound
Μ, μ	m	m sound
Ν, ν	n	n sound
Ξ, ξ	ks	ks sound
Ο, ο	o	o as in toad
Π, π	p	p sound
Ρ, ρ	r	rolled r sound
Σ, σ, ς	s	s sound
Τ, τ	t	t sound
Χ, υ	i	ee, indistinguishable from η
Φ, φ	f	f sound
Χ, χ	h	harsh h sound, like ch in loch
Ψ, ψ	ps	ps as in lips
Ω, ω	o	o as in toad, indistinguishable from ο

Combinations and dipthongs

ΑΙ, αι	e	e as in get
ΑΥ, αυ	av/af	av or af depending on following consonant
ΕΙ, ει	i	ee, exactly like η
ΟΙ, οι	i	ee, identical again
ΕΥ, ευ	ev/ef	ev or ef, depending on following consonant
ΟΥ, ου	ou	ou as in tourist
ΓΓ, γγ	ng	ng as in angie
ΓΚ, γκ	g/ng	g as in goat at the beginning of a word; ng in the middle
ΜΠ, μπ	b	b at the beginning of a word; mb in the middle
ΝΤ, ντ	d/nd	d at the beginning of a word, nd in the middle
ΤΣ, τσ	ts	ts as in hits
ΣΙ, σι	sh	sh as in shame
ΤΖ, τζ	ts	j as in jam

Note. An umlaut on a letter indicates that the two vowels are pronounced separately, eg Αόös is Ah-oh-s, rather than A-ooos

GREEK WORDS AND PHRASES

Essentials

Yes	*Néh*	Yesterday	*Khthés*	Big	*Megálo*
Certainly	*Málista*	Now	*Tóra*	Small	*Mikró*
No	*Óhi*	Later	*Argótera*	More	*Perisótero*
Please	*Parakaló*	Open	*Aniktó*	Less	*Ligótero*
Okay, agreed	*Endáksi*	Closed	*Klistó*	A little	*Lígo*
Thank you	*Efharistó (polí)*	Day	*Méra*	A lot	*Polí*
(very much)		Night	*Níkhta*	Cheap	*Ftinó*
I (don't)	*(Dhen) Katalavéno*	In the morning	*To proí*	Expensive	*Akrivó*
understand		In the afternoon	*To apóyevma*	Hot	*Zestó*
Excuse me, do	*Parakaló, mípos*	In the evening	*To vrádhi*	Cold	*Krío*
you speak	*miláteh angliká?*	Here	*Edhó*	With	*Mazí*
English?		There	*Ekí*	Without	*Horís*
Sorry/excuse	*Signómi*	This one	*Aftó*	Quickly	*Grígora*
me		That one	*Ekíno*	Slowly	*Sigá*
Today	*Símera*	Good	*Kaló*	Mr/Mrs	*Kírios/Kiría*
Tomorrow	*Ávrio*	Bad	*Kakó*	Miss	*Dhespinís*

Other Needs

To eat/drink	*Trógo/Píno*	Stamps	*Gramatósima*	Toilet	*Toualéta*
Bakery	*Foúrnos, psomádhiko*	Petrol station	*Venzinádhiko*	Police	*Astinomía*
Pharmacy	*Farmakío*	Bank	*Trápeza*	Doctor	*Iatrós*
Post office	*Tahidhromío*	Money	*Leftá/Hrímata*	Hospital	*Nosokomío*

Requests and Questions

To ask a question, it's simplest to start with *parakaló*, then name the thing you want in an interrogative tone.

Where is the bakery?	*Parakaló, o foúrnos?*	How many?	*Póssi or pósses?*
Can you show me the	*Parakaló, o dhrómos*	How much?	*Póso?*
road to . . . ?	*ya . . ?*	When?	*Póteh?*
We'd like a room for two	*Parakaló, éna dhomátio*	Why?	*Yatí?*
	ya dhío átoma?	At what time . . . ?	*Ti óra . . . ?*
May I have a kilo of	*Parakaló, éna kiló*	What is/Which is . . . ?	*Ti íneh/pió íneh..?*
oranges?	*portokália?*	How much (does it cost)?	*Póso káni?*
Where?	*Pou?*	What time does it open?	*Tí óra aníyi?*
How?	*Pos?*	What time does it close?	*Tí óra klíni?*

Talking to People

Greek makes the distinction between the informal (*esí*) and formal (*esís*) second person, as French does with *tu* and *vous*. Young people, older people and country people nearly always use *esí* even with total strangers. In any event, no one will be too bothered if you get it wrong. By far the most common greeting, on meeting and parting, is *yá sou/yá sas* – literally "health to you".

Hello	*Hérete*	My name is . . .	*Meh léneh . . .*
Good morning	*Kalí méra*	Speak slower, please	*Parakaló, miláte pió sigá*
Good evening	*Kalí spéra*	How do you say it in	*Pos léyeteh sta Eliniká?*
Good night	*Kalí níkhta*	Greek?	
Goodbye	*Adhío*	I don't know	*Dhen kséro*
How are you?	*Ti kánis/Ti káneteh?*	See you tomorrow	*Tha se dho ávrio*
I'm fine	*Kalá ímeh*	See you soon	*Kalí andhámosi*
And you?	*Keh esís?*	Let's go	*Pámeh*
What's your name?	*Pos se léneh?*	Please help me	*Parakaló, na me voithísteh*

Greek's Greek

There are numerous words and phrases which you will hear constantly, even if you rarely have the chance to use them. These are a few of the most common.

Éla!	Come (literally) but also Speak to me! You don't say! etc.	*Po-po-po!*	Expression of dismay or concern, like French "O la la!"
Orísteh?	What can I do for you?	*Pedhí mou*	My boy/girl, sonny, friend, etc.
Bros!	Standard phone response	*Maláka(s)*	Literally "wanker", but often used (don't try it!) as an infor-
Ti néa?	What's new?		
Ti yíneteh?	What's going on (here)?		mal address.
Étsi k'étsi	So-so	*Sigá sigá*	Take your time, slow down
Ópa!	Whoops! Watch it!	*Kaló taxídhi*	Bon voyage

Accommodation

Hotel	*Ksenodhohío*	Cold water	*krío neró*
A room . . .	*Éna dhomátio . . .*	Can I see it?	*Boró na to dho?*
for one/two/three people	*ya éna/dhío/tría átoma*	Can we camp here?	*Boróume na váloumeh ti*
for one/two/three nights	*ya mía/dhío/trís vradhiés*		*skiní edhó?*
with a double bed	*moh megálo kreváti*	Campsite	*Kamping/Kataskínosi*
with a shower	*meh doús*	Tent	*Skiní*
hot water	*zestó neró*	Youth hostel	*Ksenodhohío neótitos*

On the Move

Aeroplane	*Aeropláno*	Where are you going?	*Pou pas?*
Bus	*Leoforío*	I'm going to . . .	*Páo sto . . .*
Car	*Aftokínito*	I want to get off at . . .	*Thélo na katévo sto . . .*
Motorbike, moped	*Mihanáki, papáki*	The road to . . .	*O dhrómos ya . . .*
Taxi	*Taksí*	Near	*Kondá*
Ship	*Plío/Vapóri/Karávi*	Far	*Makriá*
Bicycle	*Podhílato*	Left	*Aristerá*
Hitching	*Otostóp*	Right	*Dheksiá*
On foot	*Meh ta pódhia*	Straight ahead	*Katefthía*
Trail	*Monopáti*	A ticket to . . .	*Éna isistírio ya . . .*
Bus station	*Praktorío leoforíon*	A return ticket	*Éna isistírio me epistrofí*
Bus stop	*Stási*	Beach	*Paralía*
Harbour	*Limáni*	Cave	*Spiliá*
What time does it leave?	*Ti óra févyi?*	Centre (of town)	*Kéndro*
What time does it arrive?	*Ti óra ftháni?*	Church	*Eklissía*
How many kilometres?	*Pósa hiliómetra?*	Sea	*Thálassa*
How many hours?	*Pósses óres?*	Village	*Horió*

Numbers

1	*énos éna/mía*	12	*dhódheka*	90	*enenínda*
2	*dhío*	13	*dhekatrís*	100	*ekató*
3	*trís/tría*	14	*dhekatésseres*	150	*ekatón penínda*
4	*tésseres/téssera*	20	*íkosi*	200	*dhiakóssies/ia*
5	*pénde*	21	*íkosi éna*	500	*pendakóssies/ia*
6	*éksi*	30	*triánda*	1000	*hílies/ia*
7	*eftá*	40	*saránda*	2000	*dhío hiliádhes*
8	*okhtó*	50	*penínda*	1,000,000	*éna ekatomírio*
9	*enyá*	60	*eksínda*	first	*próto*
10	*dhéka*	70	*evdhomínda*	second	*dhéftero*
11	*éndheka*	80	*ogdhónda*	third	*tríto*

The time and days of the week

Sunday	*Kiriakí*	Saturday	*Sávato*	Five minutes past	*Eftá keh pénde*
Monday	*Dheftéra*	What time is it?	*Ti óra íneh?*	seven	
Tuesday	*Tríti*	One/two/three	*Mía/dhío/trís*	Half past eleven	*Éndheka keh misí*
Wednesday	*Tetárti*	o'clock	*óra/óres*	Half-hour	*Misí óra*
Thursday	*Pémpti*	Twenty minutes	*Tésseres pará*	Quarter-hour	*Éna tétarto*
Friday	*Paraskeví*	to four	*íkosi*		

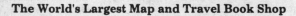

A GLOSSARY
OF WORDS
AND TERMS

ACROPOLIS Ancient, fortified hilltop.

AGORA Market and meeting place of an ancient Greek city.

AMPHORA Tall, narrow-necked jar for oil or wine.

ÁNO Upper; as in upper town or village.

APSE Polygonal or curved recess at the altar end of a church.

ARCHAIC PERIOD Late Iron Age period, from around 750 BC to the start of the Classical period in the fifth century BC.

ARHONDIKHÓ A stone mansion in the villages of the Zagóri.

ASTIKÓ (Intra) city, municipal, local; adjective applied to phone calls and bus services.

ATRIUM Open, inner courtyard of a house.

ÁYIOS/AYÍA/ÁYII Saint or holy (m/f/plural). Common place name prefix (abbreviated Ag. or Ay.), often spelt AGIOS or AGHIOS.

BASILICA Colonnaded, "hall-" or "barn-" type church, most common in northern Greece.

BEMA Rostrum for oratory (and later the chancel) of a church.

BOULEUTERION Auditorium for meetings of an ancient town's deliberative council.

BYZANTINE EMPIRE Created by the division of the Roman Empire in 395 AD, this, the eastern half, was ruled from Constantinople (modern Istanbul). In Greece, Byzantine culture peaked twice: in the eleventh century, and again at Mystra in the early fifteenth century.

CAPITAL The top, often ornamented, of a column.

CELLA Sacred room of a temple, housing the cult image.

CLASSICAL PERIOD Essentially from the end of the Persian Wars in the fifth century BC until the unification of Greece under Phillip II of Macedon (338 BC).

CORINTHIAN Decorative columns, festooned with acanthus florettes.

DHIMARHÍO Town hall.

DHOMÁTIA Rooms for rent in private houses.

DORIAN Northern civilization that displaced and succeeded the Mycenaeans and Minoans through most of Greece around 1100 BC.

DORIC Primitive columns, dating from the Dorian period.

ENTABLATURE The horizontal linking structure atop the columns of an ancient temple.

EPARHÍA Greek Orthodox diocese, also the smallest subdivision of a modern province.

EXONARTHEX The outer vestibule or entrance hall of a church.

FORUM Market and meeting place of a Roman-era city.

FRAKTES Dry-stone walls.

FRIEZE Band of sculptures around a temple. Doric friezes consist of various tableau of figures (METOPES) interspersed with grooved panels (TRIGLYPHS); Ionic ones have continuous bands of figures.

FROÚRIO Medieval castle.

GARSONIÉRA/ES Studio self-catering apartment/s.

GEOMETRIC PERIOD Post-Mycenaean Iron Age era named for the style of its pottery; begins in the early eleventh century BC with the arrival of Dorian peoples. By the eighth century BC, with the development of representational styles, it becomes known as the ARCHAIC period.

HELLENISTIC PERIOD The last and most unified "Greek empire", created in the wake of Alexander the Great's Macedonian empire and finally collapsing with the fall of Corinth to the Romans in 146 BC.

HEROÖN Shrine or sanctuary, usually of a demigod or mortal; war memorials.

HÓRA Main town of an island or region; literally it means "the place". An island *hóra* may also be known by the same name as the island.

IERÓN Literally, "sacred" – the space between the altar screen and the apse of a church, reserved for a priest.

IKONOSTÁSI Screen between the nave of a church and the altar, supporting at least three icons.

IONIC Elaborate, decorative development of the older DORIC order; Ionic temple columns are slimmer with deeper "fluted" edges, spiral-shaped capitals, and ornamental bases. CORINTHIAN capitals are a still more decorative development, with acanthus florettes.

IPERASTIKÓ Inter-city, long-distance – as in phone calls and bus services.

JANISSARY Member of the Turkish Imperial Guard, often forcibly recruited in childhood from the local population.

KAFENÍO Coffee house or café; in a small village the centre of communal life and probably serving as the bus stop, too.

KAÍKI (plural KAÍKIA) Caique, or medium-sized boat, traditionally wooden and used for transporting cargo and passengers; now refers mainly to island excursion boats.

KALDERÍMI Cobbled mule- and footpaths.

KÁMBOS Fertile agricultural plateau, usually near a river mouth.

KÁSTRO Any fortified hill (or a castle), but most usually the oldest, highest, walled-in part of an island HÓRA.

KATHOLIKÓN Central chapel of a monastery.

KÁTO Lower; as in lower town or village.

KENTRIKÍ PLATÍA Central square.

KOUROS Nude statue of an idealized young man, usually portrayed with one foot slightly forward of the other.

MACEDONIAN EMPIRE Empire created by Philip II in the mid-fourth century BC.

MEGARON Principal hall or throne room of a Mycenaean palace.

MELTÉMI North wind that blows across the Aegean in summer, starting softly from near the mainland and hitting the Cyclades, the Dodecanese and Crete full on.

METOPE see FRIEZE

MINOAN Crete's great Bronze Age Civilisation, which dominated the Aegean from about 2500 to 1400 BC.

MONÍ Formal term for a monastery or convent.

MOREA Medieval term for the Peloponnese; the outline of the peninsula was likened to the leaf of a mulberry tree, *moreá* in Greek

MYCENAEAN Mainland civilization centred on Mycenae and the Argolid from about 1700 to 1100 BC.

NAOS The inner sanctum of an ancient temple; also, any Orthodox Christian shrine.

NARTHEX Vestibule or church entrance hall.

NEOLITHIC Earliest era of settlement in Greece, characterised by the use of stone tools and weapons together with basic agriculture. Divided arbitrarily into Early (c 6000 BC), Middle (c 5000 BC), and Late (c 3000 BC).

NÉOS, NÉA, NÉO "New" – a common part of a town or village name.

NOMÓS Modern Greek province – there are more than fifty of them. Village bus services are organized according to their borders.

ODEION Small amphitheatre, used for musical performances, minor dramatic productions, or councils.

ORCHESTRA Circular area in a theatre where the chorus would sing and dance.

PALAESTRA Gymnasium for athletics and wrestling practice.

PALEÓS, PALEÁ, PALEÓ "Old" – again common in town and village names.

PANAYÍA Virgin Mary.

PANIYÍRI Festival or feast – the local celebration of a holy day.

PANDOKRÁTOR Literally "The Almighty"; generally refers to the stern portrayal of Christ in Majesty frescoed or in mosaic in the dome of many Byzantine churches.

PARALÍA Beach or seafront promenade.

PEDIMENT Triangular, sculpted gable below the roof of a temple.

PENDENTIVE Any of four triangular sections of vaulting with concave sides, positioned at a corner of a rectangular space to support a circular or polygonal dome; often adorned with frescoes of the four evangelists.

PERÍPTERO Street kiosk.

PERISTEREÓNES Pigeon towers.

PERISTYLE Gallery of columns around a temple or other building.

PIRGOS Tower or bastion.

PITHOS (plural PITHOI) Large ceramic jar for storing oil, grain etc. Very common in Minoan palaces and used in almost identical form in modern Greek homes.

PLATÍA Square, plaza.

PROPYLAION Portico or entrance to an ancient building; often used in the plural, *propylaia*.

SQUINCH Small concavity across a corner of a columnless interior space, which supports a superstructure such as a dome.

SKÁLA The port of an inland island settlement, nowadays often larger and more important than its namesake, but always younger since built after the disappearance of piracy.

STELE Upright stone slab or column, usually inscribed; an ancient tombstone.

STOA Colonnaded walkway in Classical-era marketplace.

TAVERNA Restaurant; see "Eating and Drinking" in *Basics*, p.37, for details of the different types of specialist eating places.

TÉMBLON Wooden altar screen of an Orthodox church, usually ornately carved and painted and studded with icons.

TEMENOS Sacred precinct, often used to refer to the sanctuary itself.

THEATRAL AREA Open area found in most of the Minoan palaces with seat-like steps around. Probably a type of theatre or ritual area, though this is not conclusively proven.

THOLOS Conical or beehive-shaped building, especially a Mycenaean tomb.

TRIGLYPH see FRIEZE

TYMPANUM The recessed space, flat or carved in relief, inside a pediment.

ACRONYMS

ANEK *Anonimí Navtikí Etería Krítis* (Shipping Co of Crete, Ltd), which runs most ferries between Pireás and Crete, plus many to Italy.

EA Greek Left (*Ellenikí Aristerá*), formerly the Greek Euro-communist Party (*KKE-Esoterikoú*).

EAM National Liberation Front, the political force behind ELAS.

ELAS Popular Liberation Army, the main resistance group during World War II and the basis of the communist army in the civil war.

EK Fascist party (*Ethnikó Kómma*), consisting mostly of adherents to the imprisoned junta colonel, Papadopoulos.

ELTA The postal service.

EOS Greek Mountaineering Federation, based in Athens.

EOT *Ellinikós Organismós Tourismoú*, the National Tourist Organisation.

FYROM Former Yugoslav Republic of Macedonia.

KKE Communist Party, unreconstructed.

KTEL National syndicate of bus companies. The term is also used to refer to bus stations.

ND Conservative (*Néa Dhimokratía*) party.

NEL *Navtikí Etería Lésvou* (Lesvian Shipping Co), which runs most of the northeast Aegean ferries.

OSE Railway corporation.

OTE Telephone company.

PASOK Socialist party (Pan-Hellenic Socialist Movement).

SEO Greek Mountaineering Club, based in Thessaloníki.

INDEX

PLACE NAME SPELLINGS

Throughout the guide, we've used a largely phonetic transliteration system, with *Y* rather than *G* for the Greek gamma, and *DH* rather than *D* for delta, in the spelling of all modern Greek place names. Thus, if you're looking for Aegina, Gytheion/Githion or Geraki, for example, you'll find them under Éyina, Yithio and Yeraki respectively. We have, however, retained the accepted "English" spellings for the ancient sites such as Sparta and Mycenae, and for more familiar places like Athens.

HELP US UPDATE

We've gone to a lot of effort to ensure that this edition of The *Rough Guide to Greece* is up-to-date and accurate. However, prices, addresses and opening hours are all liable to change, while hotels, restaurants and bars, and above all ferry routes and schedules, are notoriously fickle. Any suggestions, comments, corrections or updates towards the next edition would be much appreciated.

We'll credit all contributions, and send a copy of the next edition (or any other Rough Guide, if you prefer) for the best letters. Please mark letters "Rough Guide Greece update", and send to:

Rough Guides, 1 Mercer Street, London WC2H 9QJ

or

Rough Guides, 375 Hudson Street, 4th Floor, New York NY10014.

THANKS

We'd like to thank all those **readers of previous editions** of the guide who took time to annotate our errors, omissions and lapses of taste. On this edition, we were helped enormously by letters from:

Neilson Abeel, Graham Anderson, Dominique Aspey, Costas Azariadis, Sarah Bailey, Becky Baynham, Andrew Bell, Stephen Bell, S J Biddle, Rebecca Blair, J Blake, Simon and Ruth Blake, Richard Blakeway-Phillips, Ian Broad, Peter Broadbridge, Garry Brooks, S H Brough, Mike Burton and Daryl, Pascall, Angus Carpenter and Jessica Folkes, Miette Carstensen and Jeus Christophensen, Simon D Carter, Tim and Jane Carter, Gill Casey and Ian Woodhouse, Peter Ceulemans, Sally Chater, Sinikismos Christou, Nicholas Clawson, Sarah Clifford, Richard Clogg, Sandy Coles, Elizabeth Colley and Douglas Pether, Marco Daane and Carla Mastbroek, John Dallimore, Michael Davies, Chris De Voecht and Jan Tielemans, Steve and Debbie Donne, P J Driver, Gareth H Edwards, James Foote and Jenny Child, Rosie Fulton, Sarah Gellner, Mike Gerrard, Jan Goldsmith, Amanda Gunn, Guy Hansford, R J Hartley, Jan Hewson and Alfy Lucas, Christopher Hill and Helena Bridge, Chris Himsworth, Richard Hogg, P D Howley, John Hults, Nick Humphries, Seema Jayachandran, Mark Jones, Jeanne M Julian and Brian Turner, G H P Karney, Helen Kelliner, Sue Kennedy, A Kinniment, Adela Kwan, Michelle Kwintner, Mark Larkin and Felicity Fallon, Pete Lawrence, G Llewelyn, Martin Lunnon, Kevin McCarthy, Louise McKevett, Denis McTurk, Pamela Marriott, Simon Martin, Nick Meagher, Claire Morgan, Howard Morgan, Pat Morgan, Geoff Morrow, Perry Munn, Jill Nash, Mark Nicholls, Keith Nuthall, Mark Ontkush, Kate Owens, Kim Paley, Zena L Polin, Penny and Sandy Pontac, Neil Poulter, Sarah Rodman, James S Ryan, Paula Slack and Sarah Mouse, Damian Slee, Coleman South, Katy Spink, Simon Stravosconfis, Ted Sumner, Judi Sutherland, Marion Temple, Rosemary Trouton and Hilary Barendson, Andrew Turner, Stavros Ventouris, Christine Vernon, Nigel Warrington, John Watson, Ros Watson, Anthony Weir, Les Whitehouse, Brian Williams, Bryan Williams, Michael Williams, Christine Winter, Dave Wright and Carolyn Smith, Pat Yale, David Young, Alex Zambellis, and an anonymous correspondent from *The Loders Arms* in Bridport, Dorset. . . plus a few indecipherables.

SLEEP EASY
BOOK AHEAD

AUSTRALIA
02 261 1111

CANADA
FREEPHONE 0800 663 5777

DUBLIN
01 301766

LONDON
071 836 1036

BELFAST
0232 324733

GLASGOW
041 332 3004

WASHINGTON
0202 783 6161

NEW ZEALAND
09 379 4224

IBN INTERNATIONAL BOOKING NETWORK

Call any of these numbers and your credit card secures a good nights sleep ...

in more than 26 countries

up to six months ahead

with immediate confirmation

HOSTELLING INTERNATIONAL

Budget accommodation you can **Trust**

You are
A STUDENT

You travel
THE WORLD

You want
TO SAVE MONEY

Here's how

The International Student Identity Card

Entitles you to discounts and special services worldwide.